MEANINGFUL HELP AND FEEDBACK

- Personalized interactive learning aids are available for point-of-use help and immediate feedback. These learning aids include:

  - Help Me Solve This walks students through solving an algorithmic version of the questions they are working, with additional detailed tutorial reminders. These informational cues assist the students and help them understand concepts and mechanics.

  - Demo Docs are entire problems worked through step by step from start to finish, replicating the in-class experience for students anytime, anywhere.

  - eText links students directly to the concept covered in the problem they are completing.

  - Homework and practice exercises with additional algorithmically generated problems are available for further practice and mastery.

  - NEW! Worked Out Solutions—now available to students when they are reviewing their submitted and graded homework. The Worked Out Solutions provide step-by-step explanations on how to solve select problems using the exact numbers and data that were presented to the student in the problem.

- NEW! Dynamic Study Modules—Using a highly personalized, algorithmically driven process, Dynamic Study Modules continuously assess students' performance and provide additional practice in the areas where they struggle the most.

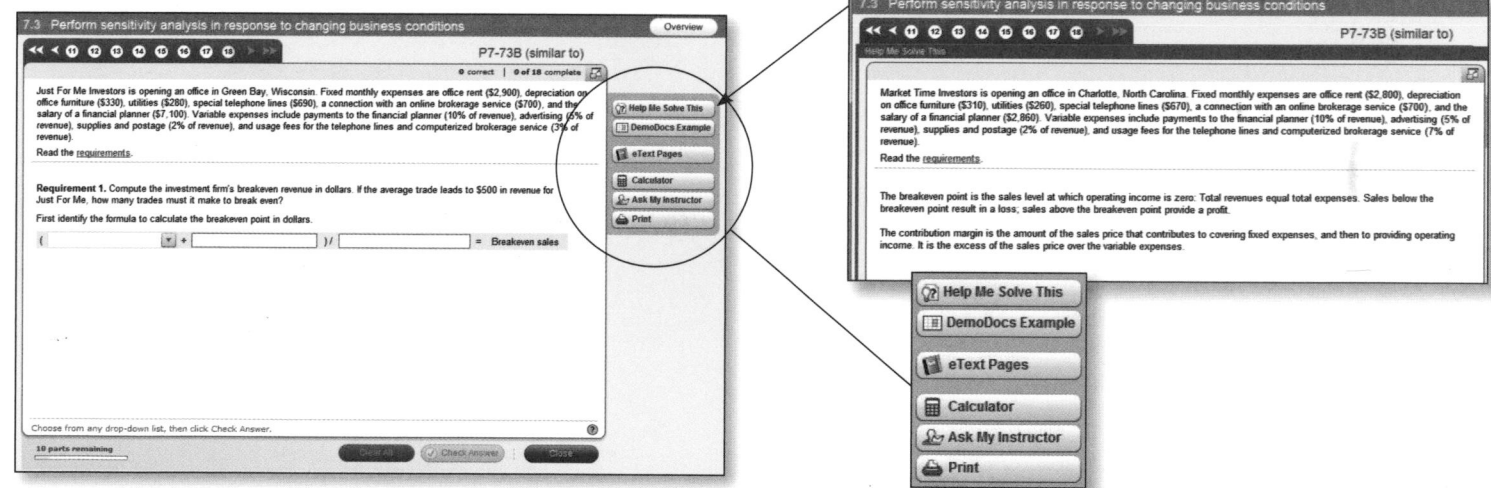

PERSONALIZED AND ADAPTIVE STUDY PATH

- Assist students in monitoring their own progress by offering them a customized study plan powered by Knewton, based on Homework, Quiz, and Test results.

- Regenerated exercises offer unlimited practice and the opportunity to prove mastery through Quizzes on recommended learning objectives.

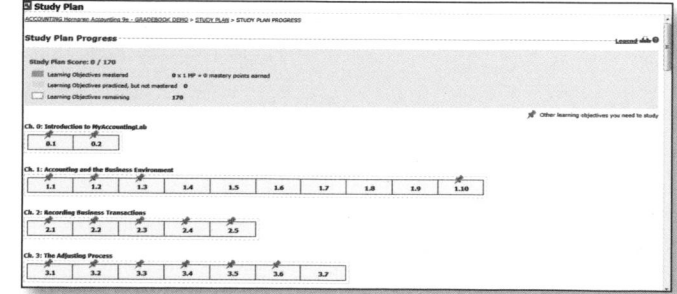

Managerial Accounting

Fourth Edition

Karen Wilken Braun, PhD, CPA, CGMA
Case Western Reserve University

Wendy M. Tietz, PhD, CPA, CGMA, CMA
Kent State University

Boston   Columbus   Indianapolis   New York   San Francisco   Upper Saddle River
Amsterdam   Cape Town   Dubai   London   Madrid   Milan   Munich   Paris   Montréal   Toronto
Delhi   Mexico City   São Paulo   Sydney   Hong Kong   Seoul   Singapore   Taipei   Tokyo

Editor in Chief: Donna Battista
Acquisitions Editor: Ellen Geary
Editorial Assistant: Christine Donovan
Marketing Manager: Alison Haskins
Marketing Assistant: Chris D'Amato
Managing Editor: Jeff Holcomb
Production Project Manager: Karen Carter
Operations Specialist: Carol Melville

Cover Designer: Liz Harasymczuk
Cover Art: iStockphoto/Thinkstock
Media Producer: James Bateman
Full-Service Project Management: S4Carlisle
Composition: S4Carlisle
Printer/Binder: Courier/Kendallville
Cover Printer: Lehigh-Phoenix Color/Hagerstown
Text Font: Sabon Roman 10/12

Credits and acknowledgments borrowed from other sources and reproduced, with permission, in this textbook appear on the appropriate page within text.

Many of the designations by manufacturers and sellers to distinguish their products are claimed as trademarks. Where those designations appear in this book, and the publisher was aware of a trademark claim, the designations have been printed in initial caps or all caps.

Library of Congress Cataloging-in-Publication Data
Braun, Karen Wilken.
  Managerial accounting/Karen Wilken Braun, Case Western Reserve University, Wendy M. Tietz, Kent State University.—Fourth edition.
    pages cm
Includes index.
ISBN-13: 978-0-13-342837-7
ISBN-10: 0-13-342837-0
  1. Managerial accounting.   I. Tietz, Wendy M.   II. Title.
HF5657.4.B36 2015
658.15'11—dc23   2013035886

10 9 8 7 6 5 4 3 2 1

ISBN-13: 978-0-13-342837-7
ISBN-10:   0-13-342837-0

BRIEF CONTENTS

CONTENTS

11   Standard Costs and Variances   642

12   Capital Investment Decisions and the Time Value of Money   698

Visual Walk-Through

 **Try It! Interactive Questions**
Found throughout the chapter, Try It! interactive questions give students the opportunity to apply the concept they just learned. Linking in the eText will allow students to practice in MyAccountingLab® without interrupting their interaction with the eText. Students' performance on the questions creates a precise adaptive study plan for additional practice.

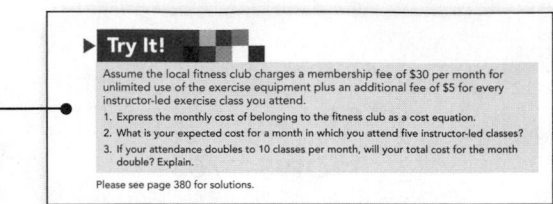

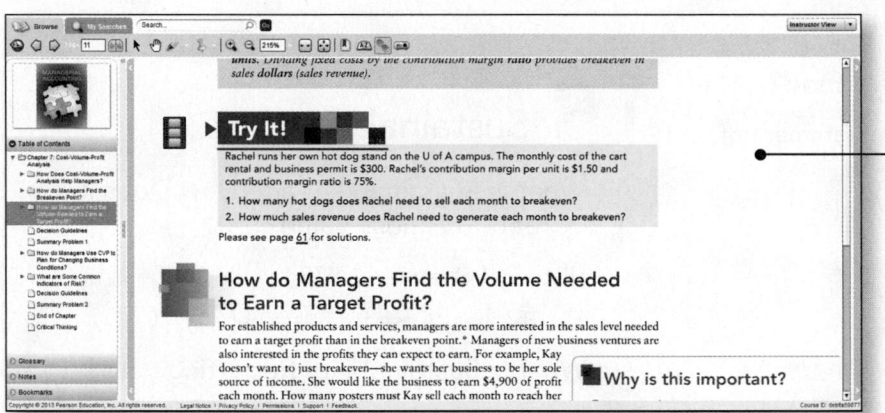

Video Solutions
Found in the eText and MyAccountingLab, the video solutions feature the author walking through the Try It! problems on a white board. Designed to give students detailed help when they need it.

Excel Exhibits
To give students a glimpse into the real world presentation of managerial accounting topics, all financial statements and schedules are presented in Excel. In the eText, a video link on selected exhibits will teach students how to create the same schedule using Excel.

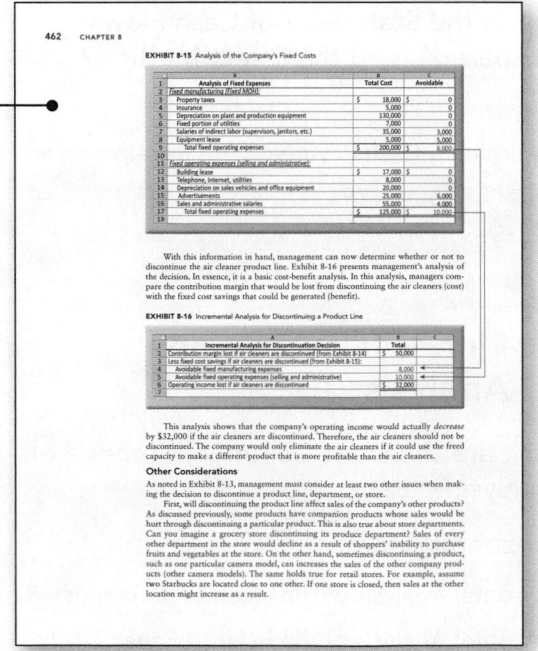

Sustainability

Within every chapter is a section on how sustainability relates to the main chapter topic.

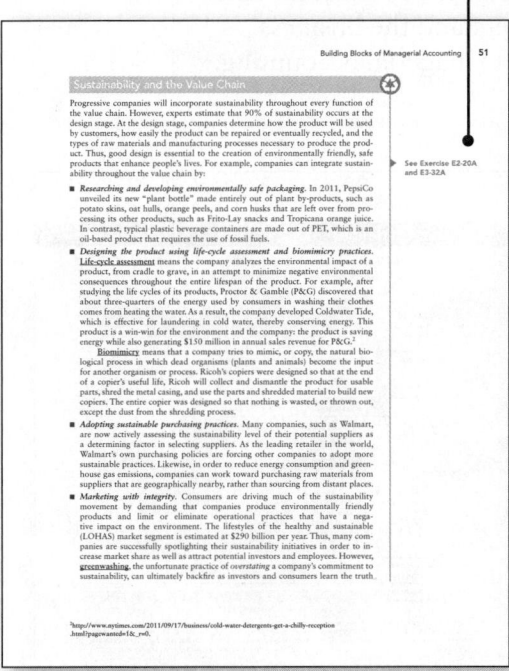

Also included is a quick reference on which end-of-chapter problems correspond to this concept.

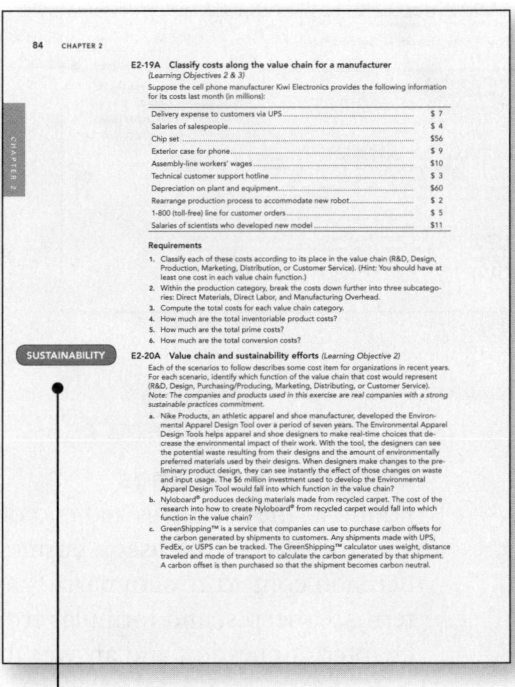

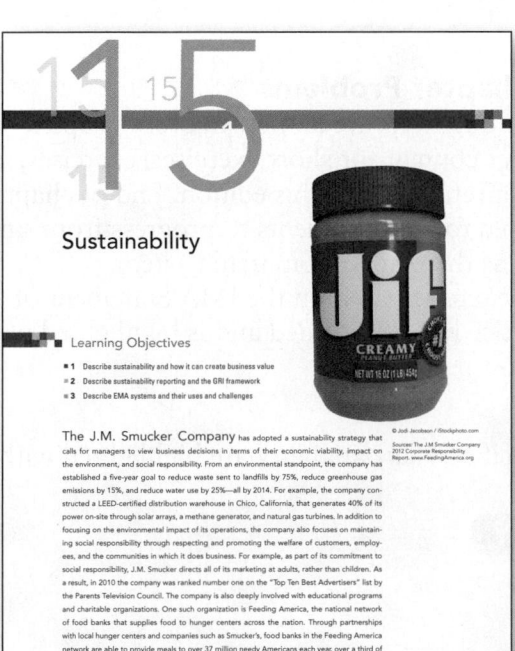

Sustainability Chapter

This chapter provides a deeper dive into how sustainability can generate business value. It also includes sections on sustainability reporting and environmental management accounting systems.

Why is this important?

Found throughout the chapter, this feature connects accounting with the business environment so that students can better understand the business significance of managerial accounting.

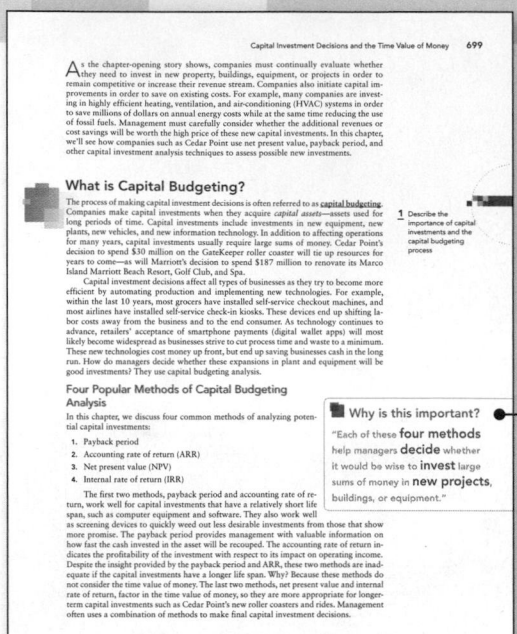

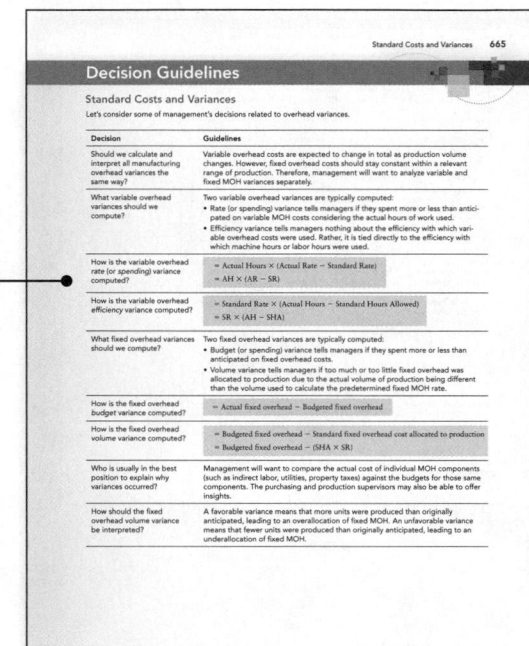

Decision Guidelines

Found at the midpoint and end of each chapter, this feature uses a business decision context to summarize key terms, concepts, and formulas from the chapter in question and answer format.

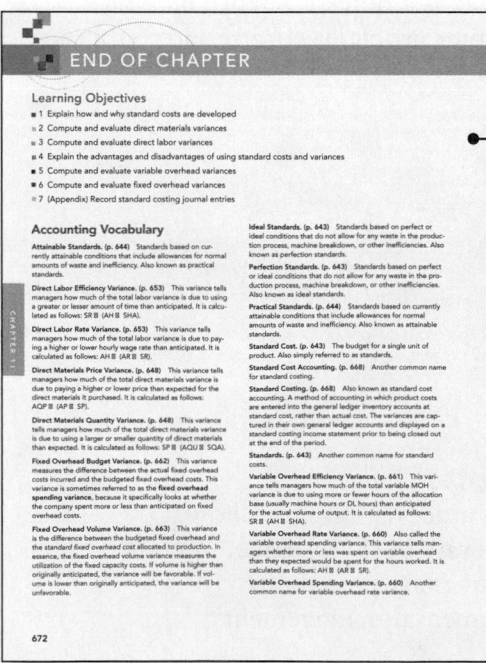

New!

New End-of-Chapter Problems

The Quick Check questions are all new in every chapter. The end-of-chapter content for short exercises, exercises, and problems has been refreshed for this edition. End of chapter items are structured to allow students to progress from simple to more rigorous as they move from item to item.

A new ethics exercise based on the IMA Statement of Professional Practice has been added and is highlighted with an icon.

ETHICS

Problems specific to sustainability are highlighted with an icon.

SUSTAINABILITY

Critical Thinking End-of-Chapter Problems

Additional problems were developed to provide students with the opportunity for applied critical thinking. These problems include ethical topics, mini cases, and decision-making cases in real companies.

- New Ethics Mini Cases based on the IMA Statement of Professional Practice are highlighted with an icon.

  ETHICS

- New Real Life Mini Case focusing on a real company and the decisions presented in business are highlighted with an icon.

  REAL LIFE

Stop & Think

Found at various points within each chapter, this feature includes a question-and-answer snapshot asking students to critically examine a concept they just learned.

Excel in MyAccountingLab

- Now students can get real-world Excel practice in their classes.
- Instructors have the option to assign students end-of-chapter questions that can be completed in an Excel-simulated environment.
- Questions will be auto-graded, reported, and visible in the grade book.
- Excel remediation will be available to students.

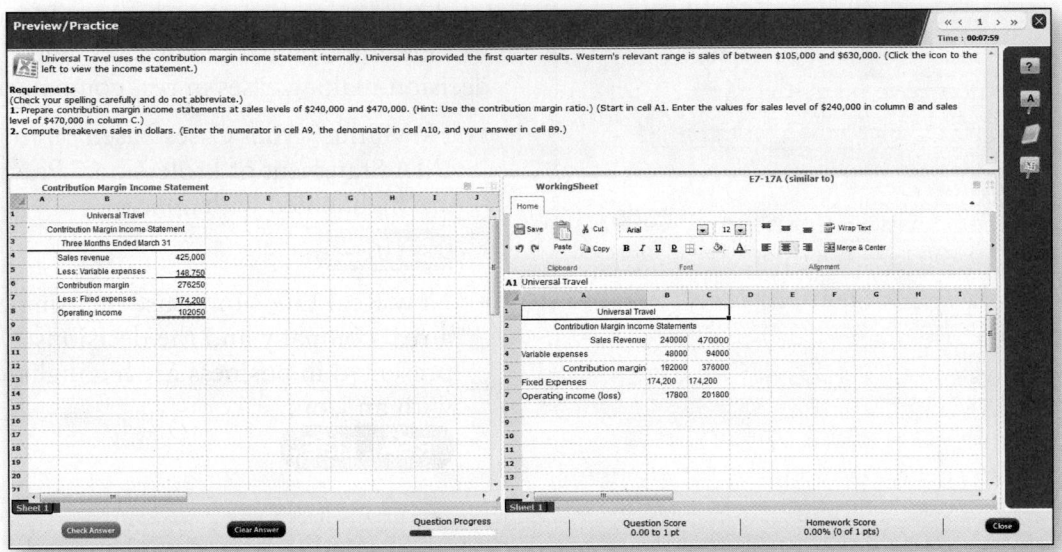

Test Bank and PowerPoints

Test bank now includes algorithmic questions and 30% new material. PowerPoints have been updated and refreshed for the new edition. Worked-out problems now contain the entire problem statement.

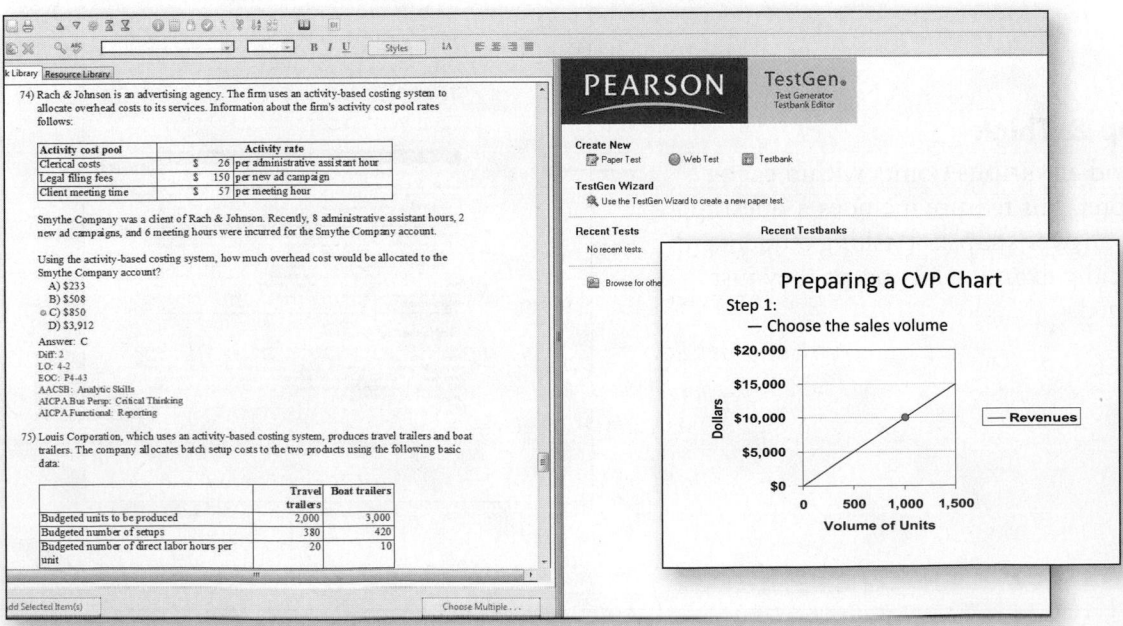

CONTENT CHANGES TO THE FOURTH EDITION

Both students and instructors will benefit from a variety of new content in the fourth edition.

New and updated content within the text:

- New focus on Excel. Chapter exhibits are now illustrated as Excel spreadsheets to get students used to looking at and working with Excel. "Technology Makes it Simple" features teach students how to use Excel applications. Select Excel exhibits are video-demonstrated in the eText.

- New Try It! features in each chapter allow students to self-assess whether they understand the concept just discussed. Author-produced video demonstrations of the solutions are provided in the eText and MyAccountingLab.

- Updated and expanded sections in each chapter show how sustainability relates to the chapter content.

- Refreshed chapter opening stories attract student attention and lay the groundwork for the chapter using recognizable, real-world companies.

- Select modifications and enhancements were made to each chapter to make it easier for students to grasp difficult concepts including:

Chapter 1	Updated coverage of current topics, such as integrated reporting and the CGMA designation.
Chapter 2	New exhibits help students differentiate between period costs and inventoriable product costs.
Chapter 3	New exhibits help students link job cost records to job costing journal entries.
Chapter 7	New "sales basket" approach to teaching CVP analysis in a multiproduct firm.
Chapter 10	New company (PepsiCo) used to illustrate responsibility accounting. New learning objective, example, and end-of-chapter problems on transfer pricing.
Chapter 11	Updated coverage of fixed overhead volume variance.
Chapter 12	Revised section on Payback and ARR; inclusion of "Technology Makes it Simple" features in the main text illustrates using Excel to calculate NPV and IRR.
Chapter 14	Updated with the latest financial information from Target, JC Penney, Kohl's and Walmart.
Chapter 15	All new content including an expanded section on why sustainability makes good business sense and expanded coverage of the GRI sustainability reporting framework.

New and updated content within the end-of-chapter material:

Quick Checks   All new quick checks in each chapter. These questions are conceptual in nature.

Short Exercises   All short exercises have been updated. In addition a new Ethics short exercise based on the IMA Statement of Professional Practice is included in every chapter.

ETHICS

Exercises   All exercises have been updated.

Problems   All problems have been updated.

Ethics Mini Cases All new case at the end of each chapter based on the IMA Statement of Professional Practice.

ETHICS

Real Life Mini Cases All new case at the end of each chapter focusing on a real company situation.

REAL LIFE

ABOUT THE AUTHORS

Karen Wilken Braun is an associate professor for the Weatherhead School of Management at Case Western Reserve University. Professor Braun was on the faculty of the J.M. Tull School of Accounting at the University of Georgia before her appointment at Case Western. She has received several student-nominated Outstanding Teacher of the Year awards at both business schools.

Professor Braun has been a Certified Public Accountant since 1985 and holds membership in the American Accounting Association (AAA), the Institute of Management Accountants, and the American Institute of Certified Public Accountants. She also holds the Chartered Global Management Accountant designation, and is a member of the AAA's Management Accounting Section as well as the Teaching, Learning and Curriculum Section. Her research and teaching interests revolve around lean operations, sustainability, corporate responsibility, and accounting education. Dr. Braun's work has been published in *Contemporary Accounting Research, Issues in Accounting Education*, and *Journal of Accounting Education*.

Dr. Braun received her Ph.D. from the University of Connecticut, where she was an AICPA Doctoral Fellow, a Deloitte & Touche Doctoral Fellow, and an AAA Doctoral Consortium Fellow. She received her B.A., summa cum laude, from Luther College, where she was a member of Phi Beta Kappa. Dr. Braun gained public accounting experience while working at Arthur Andersen & Co. and accumulated additional business and management accounting experience as a corporate controller.

Professor Braun has two daughters who are both in college. In her free time she enjoys biking, gardening, hiking, skiing, and spending time with family and friends.

To my children, Rachel and Hannah, who are the joy of my life, and to my father,
David, who taught me to cherish nature.

Karen W. Braun

Wendy M. Tietz is an associate professor for the Department of Accounting in the College of Business Administration at Kent State University, where she has taught since 2000. Prior to Kent State University, she was on the faculty at the University of Akron. She teaches in a variety of formats, including large sections, small sections, and web-based sections. She has received numerous college and university teaching awards while at Kent State University. Most recently she was named the Beta Gamma Sigma Professor of the Year for the College of Business Administration at Kent State University.

Dr. Tietz is a Certified Public Accountant, a Certified Management Accountant, and a Chartered Global Management Accountant. She is a member of the American Accounting Association (AAA), the Institute of Management Accountants and the American Institute of Certified Public Accountants. She has published in *Issues in Accounting Education, Accounting Education: An International Journal*, and *Journal of Accounting & Public Policy*. She regularly presents at AAA regional and national meetings. She also leads a short-term Study Abroad trip for accounting majors to Paris and London each year.

David Maxwell/DavidMaxwellPhotography.com

Dr. Tietz received her Ph.D. from Kent State University. She received both her M.B.A. and B.S.A. from the University of Akron. She worked in industry for several years, both as a controller for a financial institution and as the operations manager and controller for a recycled plastics manufacturer.

Dr. Tietz and her husband, Russ, have two grown sons. In her spare time, she enjoys bike riding, walking, and reading. She is also very interested in using technology in education.

To Russ, Jonathan, and Nicholas, who enrich my life through laughter and love.

Wendy M. Tietz

ACKNOWLEDGMENTS

We'd like to extend a special thank you to our reviewers who took the time to help us develop teaching and learning tools for Managerial Accounting courses to come. We value and appreciate their commitment, dedication, and passion for their students and the classroom:

Managerial Accounting, 4e

Arinola Adebayo, *University of South Carolina Aiken*
Nasrollah Ahadiat, *California State Polytechnic University*
Markus Ahrens, *St. Louis Community College*

Previous Editions

Dave Alldredge, *Salt Lake Community College*; Natalie Allen, *Texas A&M University*; Vern Allen, *Central Florida Community College*; Lynn Almond, *Virginia Tech*; Felix E. Amenkhienan, *Radford University*; Arnold I. Barkman, *Texas Christian University*; Gary Barnett, *Salt Lake Community College*; Scott Berube, *University of New Hampshire*; Michael T. Blackwell, *West Liberty State College*; Phillip A. Blanchard, *The University of Arizona*; Charles Blumer, *St. Charles Community College*; Kevin Bosner, *SUNY Genesco*; Anna Boulware, *St. Charles Community College*; Ann K. Brooks, *University of New Mexico*; Molly Brown, *James Madison University*; Molly Brown, *James Madison University*; Nina E. Brown, *Tarrant County College*; Helen Brubeck, *San Jose State University*; Janet B. Butler, *Texas State University–San Marcos*; Jennifer Cainas, *University of South Florida*; David Centers, *Grand Valley State University*; Sandra Cereola, *James Madison University*; Mike Chatham, *Radford University*; Julie Chenier, *Louisiana State University*; Robert Clarke, *Brigham Young University–Idaho*; Thomas Clevenger, *Washburn University*; Jay Cohen, *Oakton Community College*; Cheryl Copeland, *California State University Fresno*; Robert Cornell, *Oklahoma State University*; Deb Cosgrove, *University of Nebraska at Lincoln*; Patrick Cunningham, *Dawson Community College*; Alan B. Czyzewski, *Indiana State University*; Kreag Danvers, *Clarion University*; David L. Davis, *Tallahassee Community College*; Mike Deschamps, *MiraCosta College*; Patricia A. Doherty, *Boston University School of Management*; Jimmy Dong, *Sacramento City College*; Kevin Dooley, *Kapiolani Community College*; Jan Duffy, *Iowa State University*; Barbara Durham, *University of Central Florida*; Lisa Dutchik, *Kirkwood Community College*; Darlene K. Edwards, *Bellingham Technical College*; Robert S. Ellison, *Texas State University–San Marcos*; Anita Ellzey, *Harford Community College*; Gene B. Elrod, *The University of North Texas*; Jame M. Emig, *Villanova University*; Martin Epstei, *Central New Mexico Community College*; Diane Eure, *Texas State University*; Robert Everett, *Lewis & Clark Community College*; Dr. Kurt Fanning, *Grand Valley State University*; Amanda Farmer, *University of Georgia*; Janice Fergusson, *University of South Carolina*; Richard Filler, *Franklin University*; Jean Fornasieri, *Bergen Community College*; Ben Foster, *University of Louisville*; Faith Fugate, *University of Nevada, Reno*; Mary Anne Gaffney, *Temple University*; Karen Geiger, *Arizona State University*; Lisa Gillespie, *Loyola University–Chicago*; Shirley Glass, *Macomb Community College*; Marina Grau, *Houston Community College*; Timothy Griffin, *Hillsborough Community College*; Michael R. Hammond, *Missouri State University*; Michael R. Hammond, *Missouri State University*; Fei Han, *Robert Morris University*; Sheila Handy, *East Stroudsburg University*; Christopher Harper, *Grand Valley State University*; Sueann Hely, *West Kentucky Community & Technical College*; Pamela Hopcroft, *Florida State College at Jacksonville*; Audrey S. Hunter, *Broward College*; Frank Ilett, *Boise State University*; Ron Jastrzebski, *Penn State University–Berks*; Catherine Jeppson, *California State University, Northridge*; Nancy Jones, *California State University-Chico*; Mark T. Judd, *University of San Diego*; Mark Judd, *University of San Diego*; David Juriga, *St. Louis Community College*; Thomas Kam, *Hawaii Pacific University*; Ken Koerber, *Bucks County Community College*; Emil Koren, *Saint Leo University*; Ron Lazer, *University of Houston–Bauer College*; Pamela Legner, *College of DuPage*; Elliott Levy, *Bentley University*; Harold T. Little, *Western Kentucky University*; William Lloyd, *Lock Haven University* D. Jordan Lowe, *Arizona State University, West Campus*; Lois S. Mahoney, *Eastern Michigan University*; Diane Marker, *University of Toledo*; Linda Marquis, *Northern Kentucky University*; Lizbeth Matz, *University of Pittsburgh at Bradford*; David Mautz, *University of North Carolina–Wilmington*; Florence McGovern, *Bergen Community College*; Noel McKeon, *Florida State College at Jacksonville*; Mallory McWilliams, *San Jose State University*; Robert Meyer, *Parkland College*; Michael Newman, *University of Houston*; Kitty O'Donnell, *Onondaga Community College*; Mehmet Ozbilgin, *Baruch College, City University of New York*; Abbie Gail Parham, *Georgia Southern University*; Glenn Pate, *Palm Beach Community College*; Paige Paulsen, *Salt Lake Community College*; Deborah Pavelka, *Roosevelt University*; Sheldon Peng, *Washburn University*; Tamara Phelan, *Northern Illinois University*; Letitia Pleis, *Metropolitan State College of Denver*; Cindy Powell, *Southern Nazarene University*; Will Quilliam, *Florida Southern College*; Paulette A. Ratliff-Miller, *Grand Valley State University*; Donald Reynolds, *Calvin College*; Christina M. Ritsema, *University of Northern Colorado*; Doug Roberts, *Appalachian State University*; Amal Said, *University of Toledo*; Anwar Salimi, *California State Polytechnic University*; Kathryn Savage, *Northern Arizona University*; Christine Schalow, *California State University–San Bernadino*; Tony Scott, *Norwalk Community College*; Lloyd Seaton, *University of Northern Colorado*; David Skougstad, *Metropolitan State College of Denver*; John Stancil, *Florida Southern College*; Jenny Staskey, *Northern Arizona University*; Dennis Stovall, *Grand Valley State University*; Olin Scott Stovall, *Abilene Christian University*; Gloria Stuart, *Georgia Southern University*; Iris Stuart, *California State University, Fullerton*; Gracelyn V. Stuart-Tuggle, *Palm Beach State College, Boca Raton*; Gracelyn Stuart-Tuggle, *Palm Beach State College*; Jan Sweeney, *Baruch College, City University of New York*; Pavani Tallapally, *Slippery Rock University*; Lloyd Tanlu, *University of Washington*; Diane Tanner, *University of North Florida*; Linda Hayden Tarrago, *Hillsborough Community College*; Linda Tarrago, *Hillsborough Community College*; Steven Thoede, *Texas State University*; Geoffrey Tickell, *Indiana University of Pennsylvania*; Don Trippeer, *SUNY Oneonta*; Igor Vaysman, *Baruch College*; John Virchick, *Chapman University*; Terri Walsh, *Seminole State*; Andy Williams, *Edmonds Community College*; Jeff Wong, *University of Nevada Reno*; Michael Yampuler, *University of Houston (Main Campus)*; Jeff Jiewei Yu, *Southern Methodist University*; Judith Zander, *Grossmont College*; James Zeigler, *Bowling Green State University*

Kristoffer Tripplaar/SIPA/Newscom

Source: Chipotle.com

Introduction to Managerial Accounting

Learning Objectives

- **1** Identify managers' three primary responsibilities

- **2** Distinguish financial accounting from managerial accounting

- **3** Describe organizational structure and the roles and skills required of management accountants within the organization

- **4** Describe the role of the Institute of Management Accountants (IMA) and use its ethical standards to make reasonable ethical judgments

- **5** Discuss and analyze the implications of regulatory and business trends

Steve Ells opened the first Chipotle Mexican Grill in 1993 near the University of Denver campus. Although he had never taken a business class, he was fascinated by the simple economic model he saw in place at small burrito shops in San Francisco. By putting his own spin on that simple, cost-effective business model, Steve launched what has now become a tremendously successful company with over 1,400 restaurants in 38 states. Although Steve was first drawn to the business model by its limited costs—few workers, sparse furnishing, food served in foil wrappers—his resulting business was not solely driven by profits. Rather, Steve sought to run his business in a manner that included the ethical treatment of the people, animals, and the planet. Chipotle's motto, "Food with Integrity," has become the driving force for every aspect of the company's operations. Chipotle uses management accounting to help make operating decisions that focus on sustainability, while also keeping the company financially strong.

As the Chipotle story shows, managers use accounting information for much more than preparing annual financial statements. They use managerial accounting information to guide their actions and decisions. For Chipotle, these decisions might include opening new restaurants, adding new items to the menu, or sourcing ingredients from different suppliers. Management accounting information helps management decide whether any or all of these actions will help accomplish the company's ultimate goals. In this chapter, we'll introduce managerial accounting and discuss how managers use it to fulfill their duties. We will also explore how managerial accounting differs from financial accounting, and discuss the role of management accountants within the organization. Finally, we will discuss the regulatory and business environment in which today's managers and management accountants operate.

What is Managerial Accounting?

As you will see throughout the book, managerial accounting is very different from financial accounting. Financial accounting focuses on providing stockholders and creditors with the information they need to make investment and lending decisions. This information takes the form of financial statements: the balance sheet, income statement, statement of shareholders' equity, and statement of cash flows. On the other hand, managerial accounting focuses on providing internal management with the information it needs to run the company efficiently and effectively. This information takes many forms depending on management's needs.

To understand the kind of information managers need, let's first look at their primary responsibilities.

Managers' Three Primary Responsibilities

1 Identify managers' three primary responsibilities

Managerial accounting helps managers fulfill their three primary responsibilities, as shown in Exhibit 1-1: planning, directing, and controlling. Integrated throughout these responsibilities is **decision making** (identifying alternative courses of action and choosing among them).

EXHIBIT 1-1 Managers' Three Primary Responsibilities

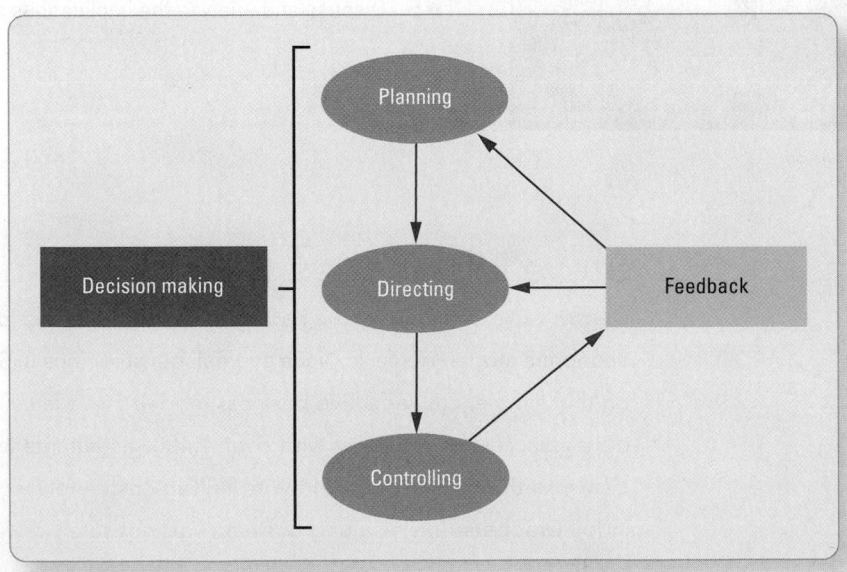

- **Planning** involves setting goals and objectives for the company and determining how to achieve them. For example, one of Chipotle's goals may be to generate more sales. One strategy to achieve this goal is to open more restaurants. For example, the company opened 183 new restaurants in 2012.[1] Managerial accounting translates these plans into **budgets**—the quantitative expression of a plan. Management analyzes the budgets before proceeding to determine whether its expansion plans make financial sense.

- **Directing** means overseeing the company's day-to-day operations. Management uses product cost reports, product sales information, and other managerial accounting reports to run daily business operations. Chipotle would use product sales data to determine which items on the menu are generating the most sales and then uses that information to adjust menus and marketing strategies.

- **Controlling** means evaluating the results of business operations against the plan and making adjustments to keep the company pressing toward its goals. Chipotle would use performance reports to compare each restaurant's actual performance against the budget and then would use that *feedback* to take corrective actions if needed. If actual costs are higher than planned, or actual sales are lower than planned, then management may revise its plans or adjust operations. Perhaps the newly opened restaurants are not generating as much income as budgeted. As a result, management may decide to increase local advertising to increase sales.

Management is continually making decisions while it plans, directs, and controls operations. Chipotle must decide where to open new restaurants, which restaurants to refurnish, what prices to set for meals, what items to offer on its menu, and so forth. Managerial accounting gathers, summarizes, and reports on the financial impact of each of these decisions.

A Road Map: How Managerial Accounting Fits In

This book will show you how managerial accounting information helps managers fulfill their responsibilities. The rest of the text is organized around the following themes:

1. **Managerial Accounting Building Blocks**　Chapter 1 helps you understand more about the management accounting profession and today's business environment. Chapter 2 teaches you some of the language that is commonly used in managerial accounting. Just as musicians must know the notes to the musical scale, management accountants *and* managers must have a common understanding of these terms in order to communicate effectively with one another.

2. **Determining Unit Cost (Product Costing)**　In order to run a business profitably, managers must be able to identify the costs associated with manufacturing its products or delivering its service. For example, Chipotle's managers need to know the cost of producing each item on the menu as well as the cost of operating each restaurant location. Managers must have this information so that they can set prices high enough to cover costs and generate an adequate profit. Chapters 3, 4, and 5 show you how businesses determine these costs. These chapters also show how managers can effectively control costs by understanding the activities that drive costs.

3. **Making Decisions**　Before Steve Ells opened the first Chipotle restaurant, he must have thought about the volume of sales needed just to break even—that is, just to cover costs. In order to do so, he had to first identify and estimate the types of costs the restaurant would incur, as well as the profit that would be generated on each meal served. These topics are covered in Chapters 6 and 7. Chapter 6 shows how managers identify different types of cost behavior, while Chapter 7 shows how managers determine the profitability of each unit sold as well as the company's breakeven point. Chapter 8 continues to use cost behavior information to walk through common

[1]http://ir.chipotle.com

business decisions, such as outsourcing and pricing decisions. Finally, Chapter 12 shows how managers decide whether to invest in new equipment, new projects, or new locations, such as when Chipotle decides to open a new restaurant.

4. **Planning**   Budgets are management's primary tool for expressing its plans. Chapter 9 discusses all of the components of the master budget and the way companies like Chipotle uses the budgeting process to implement their business goals and strategies.

5. **Controlling and Evaluating**   Management uses many different performance evaluation tools to determine whether individual segments of the business are reaching company goals. Chapters 10 and 11 describe these tools in detail. Chapters 13 and 14 describe how the statement of cash flows and financial statement analysis can be used to evaluate the performance of the company as a whole. Finally, Chapter 15 discusses how companies are beginning to address the sustainability of their operations, by measuring, reporting, and minimizing the negative impact of their operations on people and the environment. As you saw in the opening story, one of Chipotle's primary business concerns is to operate in a fashion that has minimal negative consequences for people, animals, and the planet.

Differences Between Managerial Accounting and Financial Accounting

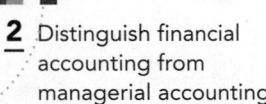

2 Distinguish financial accounting from managerial accounting

Managerial accounting information differs from financial accounting information in many respects. Exhibit 1-2 summarizes these differences. Take a few minutes to study the exhibit (on page 5) and then we'll apply it to Chipotle.

Chipotle's *financial accounting* system is geared toward producing annual and quarterly consolidated financial statements that will be used by investors and creditors to make investment and lending decisions. The financial statements, which must be prepared in accordance with Generally Accepted Accounting Principles (GAAP), objectively summarize the transactions that occurred between Chipotle and external parties during the previous period. The Securities and Exchange Commission (SEC) requires that the annual financial statements of publicly traded companies, such as Chipotle, be audited by independent certified public accountants (CPAs). Chipotle's financial statements are useful to its investors and creditors, but they do not provide management with enough information to run the company effectively.

Chipotle's *managerial accounting* system is designed to provide its managers with the accounting information they need to plan, direct, and control operations. There are no GAAP-type standards or audits required for managerial accounting. Chipotle's managerial accounting system is tailored to provide the information managers need to help them make better decisions. Chipotle must weigh the benefits of the system (useful information) against the costs to develop and run the system. The costs and benefits of any particular managerial accounting system differ from one company to another. Different companies create different systems, so Chipotle's managerial accounting system will differ from Toyota's system.

In contrast to financial statements, most managerial accounting reports focus on the *future,* providing *relevant* information that helps managers make profitable business decisions. For example, before putting their plans into action, Chipotle's managers determine if their plans make sense by quantitatively expressing them in the form of budgets. Chipotle's managerial accounting reports may also plan for and reflect *internal* transactions, such as any movement of beverages and dry ingredients from central warehouses to individual restaurant locations.

To make good decisions, Chipotle's managers need information about smaller units of the company, not just the company as a whole. For example, management uses revenue and cost data on individual restaurants, geographical regions, and individual menu items to increase the company's profitability. Regional data helps Chipotle's management decide where to open more restaurants. Sales and profit reports on individual menu items help management choose menu items and decide what items to offer on a seasonal basis. Rather than preparing these reports just once a year, companies prepare and revise managerial accounting reports as often as needed.

EXHIBIT 1-2 Managerial Accounting Versus Financial Accounting

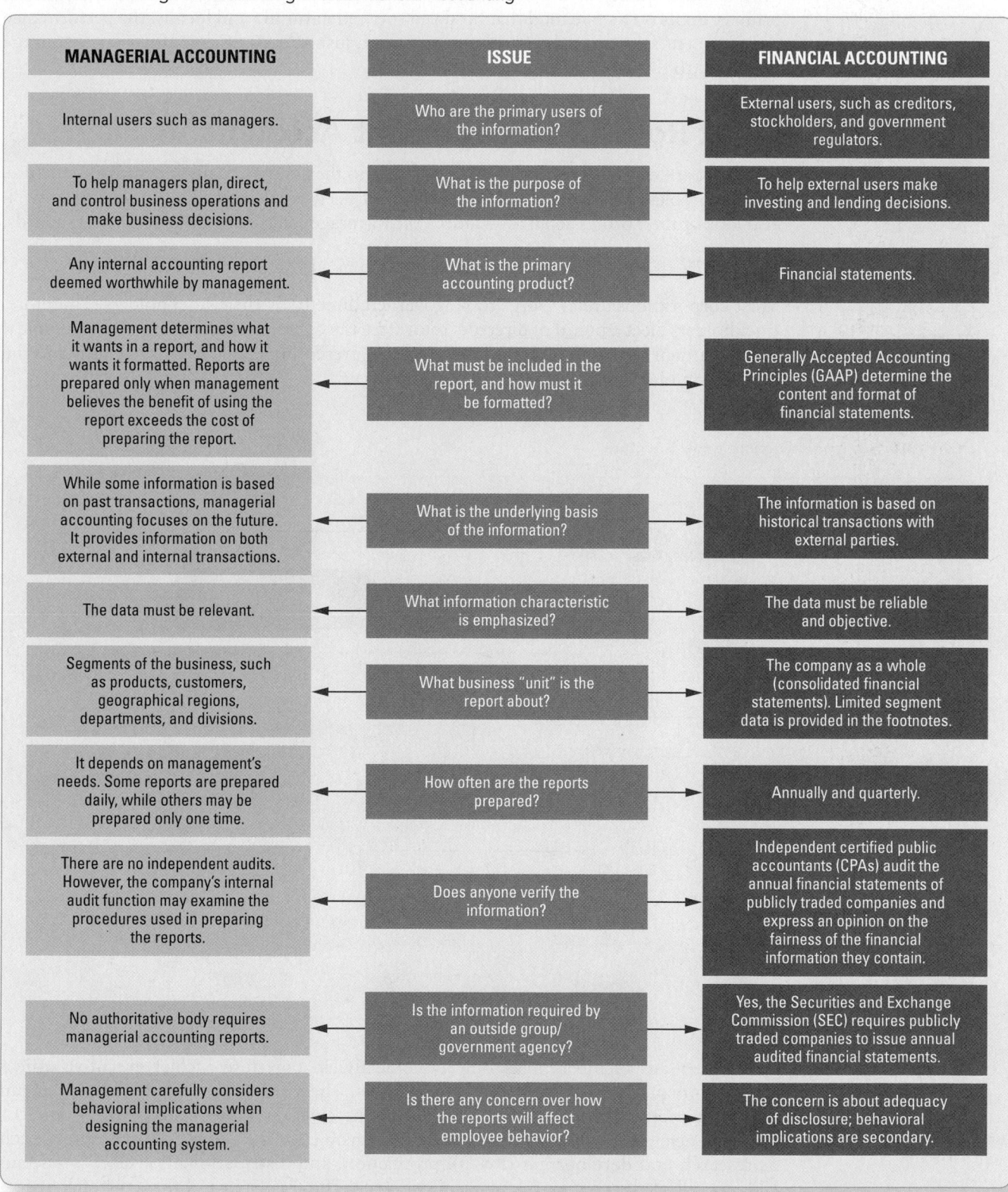

MANAGERIAL ACCOUNTING	ISSUE	FINANCIAL ACCOUNTING
Internal users such as managers.	Who are the primary users of the information?	External users, such as creditors, stockholders, and government regulators.
To help managers plan, direct, and control business operations and make business decisions.	What is the purpose of the information?	To help external users make investing and lending decisions.
Any internal accounting report deemed worthwhile by management.	What is the primary accounting product?	Financial statements.
Management determines what it wants in a report, and how it wants it formatted. Reports are prepared only when management believes the benefit of using the report exceeds the cost of preparing the report.	What must be included in the report, and how must it be formatted?	Generally Accepted Accounting Principles (GAAP) determine the content and format of financial statements.
While some information is based on past transactions, managerial accounting focuses on the future. It provides information on both external and internal transactions.	What is the underlying basis of the information?	The information is based on historical transactions with external parties.
The data must be relevant.	What information characteristic is emphasized?	The data must be reliable and objective.
Segments of the business, such as products, customers, geographical regions, departments, and divisions.	What business "unit" is the report about?	The company as a whole (consolidated financial statements). Limited segment data is provided in the footnotes.
It depends on management's needs. Some reports are prepared daily, while others may be prepared only one time.	How often are the reports prepared?	Annually and quarterly.
There are no independent audits. However, the company's internal audit function may examine the procedures used in preparing the reports.	Does anyone verify the information?	Independent certified public accountants (CPAs) audit the annual financial statements of publicly traded companies and express an opinion on the fairness of the financial information they contain.
No authoritative body requires managerial accounting reports.	Is the information required by an outside group/government agency?	Yes, the Securities and Exchange Commission (SEC) requires publicly traded companies to issue annual audited financial statements.
Management carefully considers behavioral implications when designing the managerial accounting system.	Is there any concern over how the reports will affect employee behavior?	The concern is about adequacy of disclosure; behavioral implications are secondary.

When designing the managerial accounting system, management must carefully consider how the system will affect employees' behavior. Employees try to perform well on the parts of their jobs that the accounting system measures. If Chipotle's restaurant managers were evaluated only on their ability to control costs, they may use cheaper ingredients or hire less experienced help. Although these actions cut costs in the short run, they can hurt

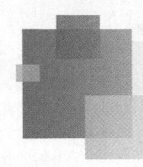

profits if the quality of the meals or service declines as a result. Since one of Chipotle's primary goals is to serve food that has been sourced naturally and locally, the performance measurement system needs to include more than just a focus on cost if it is to encourage managers to think beyond cost.

What Role do Management Accountants Play?

Let's look at how management accountants fit into the company's organizational structure, how their roles are changing, and the skills they need to successfully fill their roles. We'll also look at their professional association, their average salaries, and their ethical standards.

3 Describe organizational structure and the roles and skills required of management accountants within the organization

Organizational Structure

Most corporations are too large to be governed directly by their stockholders. Therefore, stockholders elect a **board of directors** to oversee the company. Exhibit 1-3 shows a typical organizational structure with the green boxes representing employees of the firm and the orange and blue boxes representing nonemployees.

EXHIBIT 1-3 Typical Organizational Structure

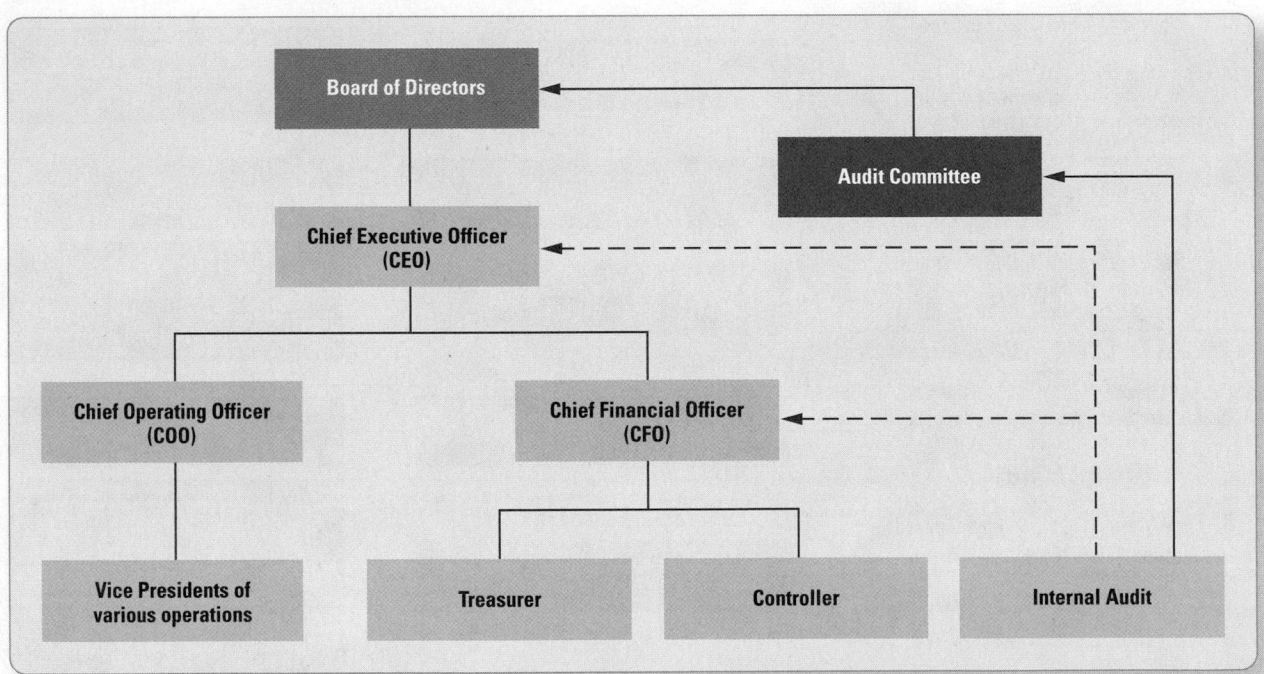

The board members meet only periodically, so they hire a **chief executive officer (CEO)** to manage the company on a daily basis. The CEO hires other executives to run various aspects of the organization, including the **chief operating officer (COO)** and the **chief financial officer (CFO)**. The COO is responsible for the company's operations, such as research and development (R&D), production, and distribution. The CFO is responsible for all of the company's financial concerns. The **treasurer** and the **controller** report directly to the CFO. The treasurer is primarily responsible for raising capital (through issuing stocks and bonds) and investing funds. The controller is usually responsible for general financial accounting, managerial accounting, and tax reporting.

The New York Stock Exchange requires that listed companies have an **internal audit function**. The role of the internal audit function is to ensure that the company's internal controls and risk management policies are functioning properly. The Internal Audit

Department reports directly to a subcommittee of the board of directors called the **audit committee**. The audit committee oversees the internal audit function as well as the annual audit of the financial statements by independent CPAs. Both the Internal Audit Department and the independent CPAs report directly to the audit committee for one very important reason: to ensure that management will not intimidate them or bias their work. However, since the audit committee meets only periodically, it is not practical for the audit committee to manage the internal audit function on a day-to-day basis. Therefore, the internal audit function also reports to a senior executive, such as the CFO or CEO, for administrative matters.

When you look at the organizational chart pictured in Exhibit 1-3, where do you think management accountants work? It depends on the company. Management accountants used to work in accounting departments and reported directly to the controller. Now, over half of management accountants are located throughout the company and work on cross-functional teams. **Cross-functional teams** consist of employees representing various functions of the company, such as R&D, design, production, marketing, distribution, and customer service. Cross-functional teams are effective because each member can address business decisions from a different viewpoint. These teams often report to various vice presidents of operations. Management accountants often take the leadership role in the teams. Here is what two managers had to say in a study about management accountants:[2]

> *Finance (the management accountant) has a unique ability and responsibility to see across all the functions and try and make sense of them. They have the neat ability to be a member of all of the different groups (functions) and yet not be a member of any of them at the same time. (U.S. West)*
>
> *Basically the role of the financial person on the team is analyzing the financial impact of the business decision and providing advice. Does this make sense financially or not? (Abbott Laboratories)*

The Changing Roles of Management Accountants

Technology has changed the roles of management accountants. Management accountants no longer perform routine mechanical accounting tasks. Computer programs perform those tasks. Yet, management accountants are in more demand than ever before. Company managers used to view management accountants as "scorekeepers" or "bean counters" because they spent most of their time recording historical transactions. Now, they view management accountants as internal consultants or business advisors.

Does this mean that management accountants are no longer involved with the traditional task of recording transactions? No. Management accountants must still ensure that the company's financial records adequately capture economic events. They help design the information systems that capture and record transactions and make sure that the information system generates accurate data. They use professional judgment to record nonroutine transactions and make adjustments to the financial records as needed. Management accountants still need to know what transactions to record and how to record them, but they let technology do most of the routine work.

Freed from the routine mechanical work, management accountants spend more of their time planning, analyzing, and interpreting accounting data and providing decision support. Because their role is changing, management accountants rarely bear the job title "management accountant" anymore; managers often refer to them as business management support, financial advisors,

Why is this important?

"Management **accountants** act as internal business advisors. They provide the **financial** information and in-depth **analysis** that managers need to make good business **decisions**."

[2]*Counting More, Counting Less: The 1999 Practice Analysis of Management Accounting,* Institute of Management Accountants, Montvale, NJ, 1999.

business partners, or analysts. Here is what two management accountants have said about their jobs:[3]

> *We are looked upon as more business advisors than just accountants, which has a lot to do with the additional analysis and forward-looking goals that we are setting. We spend more of our time analyzing and understanding our margins, our prices, and the markets in which we do business. People have a sense of purpose; they have a real sense of "I'm adding value to the company." (Caterpillar, Inc.)*
>
> *Accounting is changing. You're no longer sitting behind a desk just working on a computer, just crunching the numbers. You're actually getting to be a part of the day-to-day functions of the business. (Abbott Laboratories)*

The Skills Required of Management Accountants

Because computers now do the routine "number crunching," do management accountants need to know as much as they did 20 years ago? The fact is, management accountants now need to know *more*! They have to understand what information management needs and how to generate that information accurately. Therefore, management accountants must be able to communicate with the computer/information technology (IT) system programmers to create an effective information system. Once the information system generates the data, management accountants interpret and analyze the raw data and turn it into *useful* information management can use.[4]

> *Twenty years ago we would say, "Here are the costs and you guys need to figure out what you want to do with them." Now we are expected to say, "Here are the costs and this is why the costs are what they are, and this is how they compare to other things, and here are some suggestions where we could possibly improve." (Caterpillar, Inc.)*

Today's management accountants need the following skills:

- Solid knowledge of both financial and managerial accounting
- Analytical skills
- Knowledge of how a business functions
- Ability to work on a team
- Oral *and* written communication skills

In order to perform financial analysis in the most efficient manner possible, businesses also expect management accountants to have

- Strong Microsoft Excel skills

Because Excel is so frequently used in business, you will see many of the exhibits in this book featured in Excel. Next to selected exhibits you will be able to click on the icon and watch a short video to see how the analysis is performed in Excel. Your instructor may also assign Excel-based homework problems. Regardless of your future career path, becoming as proficient as you can with Excel during this course will help you become more marketable and more valuable to your future employer.

The skills shown in Exhibit 1-4 are critical to these management accountants:[5]

> *We're making more presentations that are seen across the division. So you have to summarize the numbers . . . you have to have people in sales understand what those numbers mean. If you can't communicate information to the individuals, then the information is never out there; it's lost. So, your communication skills are very important. (Abbott Laboratories)*

---

[3]*Counting More, Counting Less: The 1999 Practice Analysis of Management Accounting,* Institute of Management Accountants, Montvale, NJ, 1999.

[4]Ibid.

[5]Ibid.

Usually when a nonfinancial person comes to you with financial questions, they don't really ask the right things so that you can give them the correct answer. If they ask you for cost, well, you have to work with them and say, "Well, do you want total plant cost, a variable cost, or an accountable cost?" Then, "What is the reason for those costs?" Whatever they're using this cost for determines what type of cost you will provide them with. (Caterpillar, Inc.)

Chapter 2 explains these cost terms. The point here is that management accountants need to have a solid understanding of managerial accounting, including how different types of costs are relevant to different situations. Additionally, they must be able to communicate that information to employees from different business functions.

EXHIBIT 1-4 The Skills Required of Management Accountants

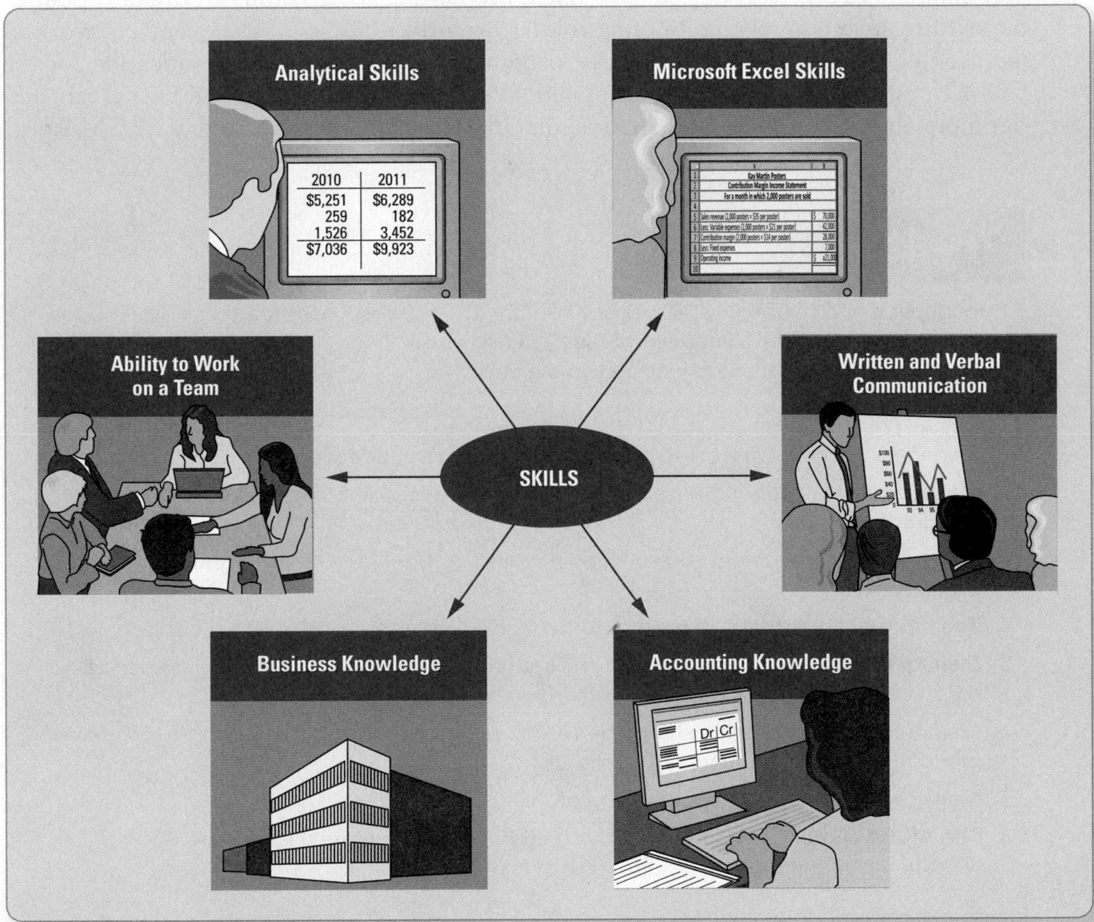

Professional Associations

The <u>Institute of Management Accountants (IMA)</u> is the professional association for management accountants in the United States. The mission of the IMA is to provide a forum for research, practice development, education, knowledge sharing, and advocacy of the highest ethical and best practices in management accounting and finance. The IMA also educates society about the role management accountants play in organizations. According to the IMA, about 85% of accountants work in organizations, performing the roles discussed earlier. The IMA publishes a monthly journal called *Strategic Finance* that addresses current topics of interest to management accountants and helps them keep abreast of recent techniques and trends.

The IMA also issues the <u>Certified Management Accountant (CMA)</u> certification. To become a CMA you must pass a rigorous examination and maintain continuing professional education. The CMA exam focuses on managerial accounting topics similar to

4 Describe the role of the Institute of Management Accountants (IMA) and use its ethical standards to make reasonable ethical judgments

those discussed in this book, as well as economics and business finance. While most employers do not require the CMA certification, management accountants bearing the CMA designation tend to command higher salaries and obtain higher-level positions within the company. You can find out more about the IMA and the CMA certification it offers at its website: www.imanet.org.

In 2012, the **American Institute of Certified Public Accountants (AICPA)**, the world's largest association representing the accounting profession, joined forces with England's Chartered Institute of Management Accountants (CIMA) to launch a separate specialized credential geared toward members who work, or have worked, in accounting roles in business, industry, or government. The **Chartered Global Management Accountant (CGMA)** designation, which is available to qualifying AICPA and CIMA members, is meant to recognize the unique business and accounting skill set possessed by those certified public accountants (CPAs) who fill, or have filled, accounting roles within an organization, as opposed to strictly public accounting roles. Currently, 40% of AICPA members work in industry, government, or education rather than public accounting.[6] Qualification for the CGMA designation is based on examination and professional experience. You can find out more about the CGMA designation, qualifications, and benefits at www.CGMA.org.

▶ Try It!

Throughout each chapter you will see several "Try It!" features. These features will allow you to see if you understand something you just learned about in the reading. Click the Try It! Icon to practice and get immediate feedback in the etext.

Determine whether each of the following statements is true or false:

1. Managers' three primary responsibilities are planning, directing, and controlling.
2. Management accounting is geared toward external stakeholders, such as investors and creditors.
3. Management accountants often work in cross-functional teams throughout the organization.
4. The internal audit function reports to the audit committee of the board of directors.
5. Management accountants are now more often looked upon as internal business advisors, rather than "bean counters" recording historical transactions.
6. Management accountants should be technically proficient, but they don't need strong oral and written communication skills.
7. Management accountants should be proficient in Excel.
8. The AICPA (American Institute of Certified Public Accountants) issues the CMA (Certified Management Accountant) certification.

Please see page 45 for solutions.

Average Salaries of Management Accountants

The average salaries of management accountants reflect their large skill set. Naturally, salaries will vary with the accountant's level of experience, his or her specific job responsibilities, and the size and geographical location of the company. However, to give you a general idea, in 2012, the average salary of IMA members with one to five years of experience was $70,356. The average salary of all IMA members was $112,625 and the median salary was $100,000. In general, those professionals with the CMA certification earned salaries that were about 24% higher than members with no certification. You can obtain more specific salary information in the IMA's 2012 Salary Survey.[7]

[6]www.aicpa.org/About/Pages/About.aspx
[7]Lee Schiffel, D. Schroeder, and K. Smith "2012 Salary Survey: Leaning into the Wind." *Strategic Finance,* June 2013, pp. 27–44.

Robert Half International, Inc., is another good source for salary information. Robert Half publishes a free yearly guide to average salaries for all types of finance professionals. The guide also provides information on current hiring trends. To download a free copy of the *Salary Guide*, go to www.roberthalf.com/SalaryGuide. Robert Half also offers a free online interactive salary calculator, which allows you to drill down to salary information by zip code, years of experience, job title, and company size. To explore salaries in the fields of accounting and finance, go to www.roberthalffinance.com/salary-calculator.

Ethics

Management accountants continually face ethical challenges. The IMA has developed principles and standards to help management accountants deal with these challenges. The principles and standards remind us that society expects professional accountants to exhibit the highest level of ethical behavior. The IMA's *Statement of Ethical Professional Practice* requires management accountants to do the following:

- Maintain their professional competence
- Preserve the confidentiality of the information they handle
- Uphold their integrity
- Perform their duties with credibility

These ethical standards are summarized in Exhibit 1-5, while the full *Statement of Ethical Professional Practice* appears in Exhibit 1-6.

> ### ■ Why is this important?
>
> "At the **root** of all business relationships is **trust**. Would you put your **money** in a bank that you didn't trust, invest in a company you knew was '**cooking the books**,' or loan money to someone you thought would never pay you back? As a **manager**, your trust in the other party's **ethical** behavior, and vice versa, will be a vital component of the business **decisions** you make."

EXHIBIT 1-5 Summary of Ethical Standards

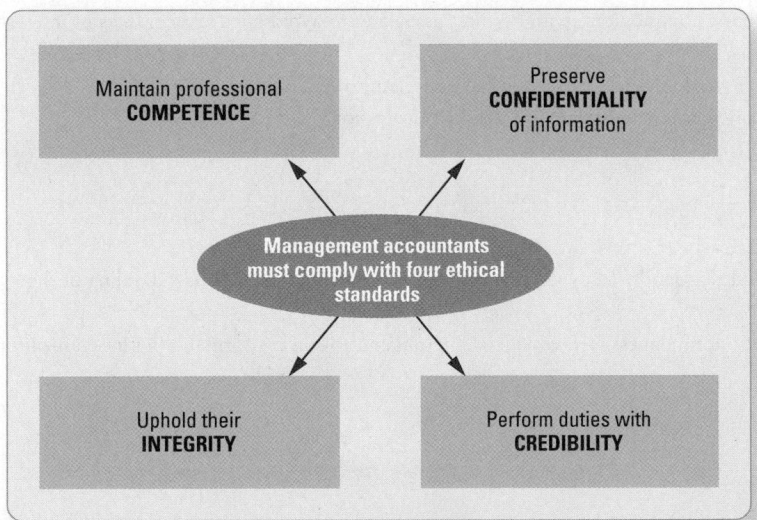

To resolve ethical dilemmas, the IMA suggests that management accountants first follow their company's established policies for reporting unethical behavior. If the conflict is not resolved through the company's procedures, the management accountant should consider the following steps:

- Discuss the unethical situation with the immediate supervisor unless the supervisor is involved in the unethical situation. If so, notify the supervisor at the next higher managerial level. If the immediate supervisor involved is the CEO, notify the audit committee or board of directors.

EXHIBIT 1-6 IMA Statement of Ethical Professional Practice

Members of IMA shall behave ethically. A commitment to ethical professional practice includes: overarching principles that express our values, and standards that guide our conduct.

Principles

IMA's overarching ethical principles include: Honesty, Fairness, Objectivity, and Responsibility. Members shall act in accordance with these principles and shall encourage others within their organizations to adhere to them.

Standards

A member's failure to comply with the following standards may result in disciplinary action.

I. Competence

Each member has a responsibility to:

1. Maintain an appropriate level of professional expertise by continually developing knowledge and skills.
2. Perform professional duties in accordance with relevant laws, regulations, and technical standards.
3. Provide decision support information and recommendations that are accurate, clear, concise, and timely.
4. Recognize and communicate professional limitations or other constraints that would preclude responsible judgment or successful performance of an activity.

II. Confidentiality

Each member has a responsibility to:

1. Keep information confidential except when disclosure is authorized or legally required.
2. Inform all relevant parties regarding appropriate use of confidential information. Monitor subordinates' activities to ensure compliance.
3. Refrain from using confidential information for unethical or illegal advantage.

III. Integrity

Each member has a responsibility to:

1. Mitigate actual conflicts of interest. Regularly communicate with business associates to avoid apparent conflicts of interest. Advise all parties of any potential conflicts.
2. Refrain from engaging in any conduct that would prejudice carrying out duties ethically.
3. Abstain from engaging in or supporting any activity that might discredit the profession.

IV. Credibility

Each member has a responsibility to:

1. Communicate information fairly and objectively.
2. Disclose all relevant information that could reasonably be expected to influence an intended user's understanding of the reports, analyses, or recommendations.
3. Disclose delays or deficiencies in information, timeliness, processing, or internal controls in conformance with organization policy and/or applicable law.

Institute of Management Accountants. Adapted with permission (2006).

- Discuss the unethical situation with an objective advisor, such as an IMA ethics counselor. The IMA offers a confidential "Ethics Hotline" to its members. Members may call the hotline and discuss their ethical dilemma. The ethics counselor will not provide a specific resolution but will clarify how the dilemma relates to the IMA's *Statement of Ethical Professional Practice* shown in Exhibit 1-6.
- Consult an attorney regarding legal obligations and rights.

Examples of Ethical Dilemmas

ETHICS

Because professional ethical behavior is so critical, we have included short exercises and cases related to ethical behavior in each chapter of the book. An ethics icon will mark each of these exercises so that they are readily identifiable to you and your instructor.

Unfortunately, the ethical path is not always clear. You may want to act ethically and do the right thing, but the consequences can make it difficult to decide what to do. Let's consider several ethical dilemmas in light of the *Statement of Ethical Professional Practice*.

Dilemma #1

Sarah Baker is examining the expense reports of her staff, who counted inventory at Top-Flight's warehouses in Arizona. She discovers that Mike Flinders has claimed but not included hotel receipts for over $1,000 of accommodation expenses. Other staff, who also claimed $1,000, did attach hotel receipts. When asked about the receipts, Mike admits that he stayed with an old friend, not in the hotel, but he believes that he deserves the money he saved. After all, the company would have paid his hotel bill.

By asking to be reimbursed for hotel expenses he did not incur, Flinders violated the IMA's integrity standards (conflict of interest in which he tried to enrich himself at the company's expense). Because Baker discovered the inflated expense report, she would not be fulfilling her ethical responsibilities of integrity and credibility if she allowed the reimbursement.

Dilemma #2

As the accountant of Entreé Computer, you are aware of your company's weak financial condition. Entreé is close to signing a lucrative contract that should ensure its future success. To do so, the controller states that the company must report a profit this year (ending December 31). He suggests, "Two customers have placed orders that are really not supposed to be shipped until early January. Ask production to fill and ship those orders on December 31 so we can record them in this year's sales."

The resolution of this dilemma is less clear-cut. Many people believe that following the controller's suggestion to manipulate the company's income would violate the standards of competence, integrity, and credibility. Others would argue that because Entreé Computer already has the customer orders, shipping the goods and recording the sale in December is still ethical behavior. In this situation, you might discuss the available alternatives with the next managerial level or the IMA ethics hotline counselor.

Dilemma #3

As a new accounting staff member at Central City Hospital, your supervisor has asked you to prepare the yearly Medicare Cost Report, which the government uses to determine its reimbursement to the hospital for serving Medicare patients. The report requires specialized knowledge that you don't believe you possess. The supervisor is busy planning for the coming year and cannot offer much guidance while you prepare the report.

This situation is not as rare as you might think. You may be asked to perform tasks that you don't feel qualified to perform. The competence standard requires you to perform professional duties in accordance with laws, regulations, and technical standards; but laws and regulations are always changing. For this reason, the competence standard also requires you to continually develop knowledge and skills. CPAs and CMAs are required to complete annual continuing professional education (about 40 hours per year) to fulfill this responsibility. However, even continuing professional education courses will not cover every situation you may encounter.

In the Medicare cost report situation, advise your supervisor that you currently lack the knowledge required to complete the Medicare report. By doing so, you are complying with the competence standard that requires you to recognize and communicate any limitations that would preclude you from fulfilling an activity. You should ask for training on the report preparation and supervision by someone experienced in preparing the report. If the supervisor denies your requests, you should ask him or her to reassign the Medicare report to a qualified staff member.

Dilemma #4

Your company is negotiating a large multiyear sales contract that, if won, would substantially increase the company's future earnings. At a dinner party over the weekend, your friends ask you how you like your job and the company you work for. In your enthusiasm, you tell them not only about your responsibilities at work, but also about the contract negotiations. As soon as the words pop out of your mouth, you worry that you've said too much.

This situation is difficult to avoid. You may be so excited about your job and the company you work for that information unintentionally "slips out" during casual conversation with friends and family. The confidentiality standard requires you to refrain from disclosing information or using confidential information for unethical or illegal advantage. Was the contract negotiation confidential? If so, would your friends invest in company stock in hopes that the negotiations increase stock prices? Or were the negotiations public knowledge in the financial community? If so, your friends would gain no illegal advantage from the information. Recent cases in the news remind us that insider trading (use of inside knowledge for illegal gain) has serious consequences. Even seemingly mundane information about company operations could give competitors an advantage. Therefore, it's best to disclose only information that is meant for public consumption.

Unethical Versus Illegal Behavior

Finally, is there a difference between unethical and illegal behavior? Not all unethical behavior is illegal, but all illegal behavior is unethical. For example, consider the competence standard. The competence standard states that management accountants have a responsibility to provide decision support information that is accurate, clear, concise, and timely. Failure to follow this standard is unethical but in most cases not illegal. Now, consider the integrity standard. It states that management accountants must abstain from any activity that might discredit the profession. A management accountant who commits an illegal act is violating this ethical standard. In other words, ethical behavior encompasses more than simply following the law. The IMA's ethical principles include honesty, fairness, objectivity, and responsibility—principles that are much broader than what is codified in the law.

Decision Guidelines

Managerial Accounting and Management Accountants

Chipotle made the following considerations in designing its managerial accounting system to provide managers with the information they need to run operations efficiently and effectively.

Decision	Guidelines
What is the primary purpose and focus of managerial accounting?	Managerial accounting provides information that helps managers plan, direct, and control operations and make better decisions; it has a • *future* orientation. • *focus* on *relevance* to business decisions.
How do managers design a company's managerial accounting system that is not regulated by GAAP?	Managers design the managerial accounting system so that the benefits (from helping managers make better decisions) outweigh the costs of the system.
Where should management accountants be placed within the organizational structure?	In the past, most management accountants worked in isolated departments. Now, over 50% of management accountants are deployed throughout the company and work on cross-functional teams. Management must decide which structure best suits its needs.
What skills should management accountants possess?	Because of their expanding role within the organization, most management accountants need financial and managerial accounting knowledge, analytical skills, knowledge of how a business functions, ability to work on teams, and written and oral communication skills. They should also possess strong Excel skills.
What professional associations advocate for management accountants in the United States?	The Institute of Management Accountants (IMA) is the premier organization advocating strictly for the advancement of the management accounting profession. The IMA also issues the CMA certification. In addition, the American Institute of Certified Public Accountants (AICPA) has recently launched a specialized credential (the CGMA) for its CPA members who have experience in industry, business, and government as opposed to strictly public accounting experience.
By what ethical principles and standards should management accountants abide?	The IMA's overarching ethical *principles* include the following: • Honesty • Objectivity • Fairness • Responsibility The IMA's ethical *standards* include the following: • Competence • Integrity • Confidentiality • Credibility

SUMMARY PROBLEM 1

Requirements

1. Each of the following statements describes a responsibility of management. Match each statement to the management responsibility being fulfilled.

Statement	Management Responsibility
1. Identifying alternative courses of action and choosing among them	a. Planning
2. Running the company on a day-to-day basis	b. Decision making
3. Determining whether the company's units are operating according to plan	c. Directing
4. Setting goals and objectives for the company and determining strategies to achieve them	d. Controlling

2. Are the following statements more descriptive of managerial accounting or financial accounting information?

   a. Describes historical transactions with external parties

   b. Is not required by any authoritative body, such as the SEC

   c. Reports on the company's subunits, such as products, geographical areas, and departments

   d. Is intended to be used by creditors and investors

   e. Is formatted in accordance with GAAP

3. Each of the following statements paraphrases an ethical responsibility. Match each statement to the standard of ethical professional practice being fulfilled. Each standard may be used more than once or not at all.

Responsibility	Standard of Ethical Professional Practice
1. Do not disclose company information unless authorized to do so.	a. Competence
2. Continue to develop skills and knowledge.	b. Confidentiality
3. Don't bias the information and reports presented to management.	c. Integrity
4. If you do not have the skills to complete a task correctly, do not pretend that you do.	d. Credibility
5. Avoid actual *and* apparent conflicts of interest.	

▪ SOLUTIONS

Requirement 1

1. (b) Decision making
2. (c) Directing
3. (d) Controlling
4. (a) Planning

Requirement 2

a. Financial accounting
b. Managerial accounting
c. Managerial accounting
d. Financial accounting
e. Financial accounting

Requirement 3

1. (b) Confidentiality
2. (a) Competence
3. (d) Credibility
4. (a) Competence
5. (c) Integrity

What Regulatory Issues Affect Management Accounting?

The regulatory landscape is continually changing. In this section, we'll look at some of regulations that affect managers and the managerial accounting systems that support them.

5 Discuss and analyze the implications of regulatory and business trends

Sarbanes-Oxley Act of 2002

As a result of corporate accounting scandals, such as those at Enron and WorldCom, the U.S. Congress enacted the **Sarbanes-Oxley Act of 2002 (SOX)**. The purpose of SOX is to restore trust in publicly traded corporations, their management, their financial statements, and their auditors. SOX enhances internal control and financial reporting requirements and establishes new regulatory requirements for publicly traded companies and their independent auditors. Publicly traded companies have spent millions of dollars upgrading their internal controls and accounting systems to comply with SOX regulations.

As shown in Exhibit 1-7, SOX requires the company's CEO and CFO to assume responsibility for the financial statements and disclosures. The CEO and CFO must certify that the financial statements and disclosures fairly present, in all material respects, the operations and financial condition of the company. Additionally, they must accept responsibility for establishing and maintaining an adequate internal control structure and procedures for financial reporting. The company must have its internal controls and financial reporting procedures assessed annually.

EXHIBIT 1-7 Some Important Results of SOX

CEO and CFO assume responsibility for the company's financial statements, internal control system, and procedures for financial reporting.	Audit committee must be independent and should include a financial expert.
Sarbanes-Oxley Act of 2002	
New requirements for CPA firms, including limited non-audit services for audit clients and periodic quality review.	Stiffer imprisonment and monetary fines for white-collar crimes. Previously paid CEO and CFO bonuses can be recovered if financial statements were improperly stated due to misconduct.

Source: Based on information from http://fmcenter.aicpa.org/Resources/Sarbanes-Oxley+Act/Summary+of+the+Provisions+of+the+Sarbanes-Oxley+Act+of+2002.htm

SOX also requires audit committee members to be independent, meaning that they may not receive any consulting or advisory fees from the company other than for their service on the board of directors. In addition, at least one of the members should be a financial expert. The audit committee oversees not only the internal audit function but also the company's audit by independent CPAs.

To ensure that CPA firms maintain independence from their client company, SOX does not allow CPA firms to provide certain non-audit services (such as bookkeeping and financial information systems design) to companies during the same period of time in which they are providing audit services. If a company wants to obtain such services

■ **Why is this important?**

"**SOX** puts more pressure on companies, their **managers**, and their auditors to ensure that **investors** get financial information that **fairly reflects** the company's **operations**."

from a CPA firm, it must hire a different firm to do the non-audit work. Tax services may be provided by the same CPA firm if pre-approved by the audit committee. The audit partner must rotate off the audit engagement every five years, and the audit firm must undergo quality reviews every one to three years.

SOX also increases the penalties for white-collar crimes such as corporate fraud. These penalties include both monetary fines and substantial imprisonment. For example, knowingly destroying or creating documents to "impede, obstruct, or influence" any federal investigation can result in up to 20 years of imprisonment.[8]

SOX also contains a "clawback" provision in which previously paid CEO and CFO incentive-based compensation can be recovered if the financial statements were misstated due to misconduct. The Frank-Dodd Act of 2010 further strengthens the clawback rules, such that firms *must* recover all incentive compensation paid to *any* current or former executive, in the three years preceding the restatement, if that compensation would not have been paid under the restated financial statements. In other words, executives will not be allowed to profit from misstated financial statements, even if the misstatement was not due to misconduct.[9]

Since its enactment in 2002, SOX has significantly affected the internal operations of publicly traded corporations and their auditors. SOX will continue to play a major role in corporate management and the auditing profession.

International Financial Reporting Standards (IFRS)

As a result of globalization, the need for consistent reporting standards for all companies in the world has grown. As a result, the SEC is considering whether to require all publicly traded companies to adopt **International Financial Reporting Standards (IFRS)**. Currently, all publicly traded U.S. companies must adhere to U.S. GAAP, as promulgated by the Financial Accounting Standards Board (FASB). In many instances, IFRS vary from GAAP. However, the FASB is working on a convergence project with the International Accounting Standards Board (IASB) to converge U.S. GAAP with IFRS so that companies would have a single set of accounting standards to use both domestically and overseas. In the long run, having a single set of standards should save companies money and make the markets more efficient. Currently, a company operating in several different countries often must prepare several sets of financial statements using different accounting standards. As a result of IFRS, these companies will only need to prepare one set of financial statements that will be acceptable to all countries that have adopted IFRS. You can keep abreast of current IFRS developments and implications for accounting information at www.IFRS.org or www.IASB.org and the GAAP convergence project at FASB.org.

Extensible Business Reporting Language (XBRL)

Wouldn't it be nice if managers, analysts, investors, and regulators could easily access public company information over the Internet without having to *manually* read pdf documents and extract the data they need for decision making? The **Extensible Business Reporting Language (XBRL)** enables companies to release financial and business information in a format that can be quickly, efficiently, and cost-effectively accessed, sorted, and analyzed over the Internet. XBRL uses a standardized coding system to "tag" each piece of reported financial and business data so that it can be read by computer programs, rather than human eyes.

For example, *Sales Revenue* would be tagged with the same code by all companies so that a computer program could extract *Sales Revenue* information from an individual company or a selected group of companies. This standardized tagging system allows

---

[8]Go to www.AICPA.org to learn more about SOX.
[9]www.pepperlaw.com/publications_update.aspx?ArticleKey=1868

computers, rather than humans, to sift through financial reports and extract only the information that is needed. XBRL has several advantages:

- It decreases the need for laborious, manual searches though corporate reports for specific pieces of information.

- It decreases the time companies will spend converting their financial information into various government-prescribed formats.

- It will allow managers to easily compare their results to other companies and to industry averages.

- Investors and managers can "slice and dice" financial information however they want, to suit their decision-making needs.

- It should promote the more consistent use of financial terminology since all data must be tagged using a preset, yet extensible, classification system.

Because of these benefits, the SEC requires that all publicly traded companies use XBRL for filing their financial reports for all periods after June 15, 2011. The United States joins Australia, Canada, China, Japan, the United Kingdom, and other countries in mandating the use of XBRL for publicly traded companies. You can keep abreast of XBRL developments at www.XBRL.org and www.sec.gov.

What Business Trends Affect Management Accounting?

In this section, we'll consider some of the business trends that are currently impacting companies and the managerial accounting systems that support them.

Sustainability, Social Responsibility, and the Triple Bottom Line

In recent years, there has been an increasing awareness and growing interest in sustainability and social responsibility by both consumers and corporations. The dictionary definition of **sustainability** refers to the ability of a system to maintain its own viability, endure without giving way, or use resources so they are not depleted or permanently damaged.[10] In other words, it's the ability of a system to operate in such a manner that it is able to continue indefinitely. The United Nations has defined sustainability as "the ability to meet the needs of the present without compromising the ability of future generations to meet their own needs."[11] Others have defined sustainability as an expansion of the golden rule: "Do unto others, including future generations, as you would have done unto you."[12]

As pictured in Exhibit 1-8, sustainability has three pillars: environmental, social, and economic. A company will only be viable in the long run if all three of these three factors are considered when making business decisions. For example, a company will not be able to survive in the long run if the natural resources (e.g., air, water, soil, minerals, plants, fuel supplies, etc.) or people (e.g., suppliers, customers, employees, communities) it relies on are put in jeopardy. Thus, sustainability is also viewed as the intersection of all three factors, as pictured in Exhibit 1-9. As a result, many companies are beginning to adhere to the notion of a triple bottom line. The **triple bottom line** recognizes that a company's performance should be viewed not only in terms of its ability to generate economic profits for its owners, as has traditionally been the case, but also by its impact on people and the planet.

[10]www.merriam-webster.com; http://dictionary.reference.com
[11]1987 World Commission on Environment and Development, www.un.org/documents/ga/res/42/ares42-187.htm
[12]Gary Langenwalter, Business Sustainability: Keeping Lean but with More Green for the Company's Long Haul, 2010, AICPA, Lewisville, Texas.

EXHIBIT 1-8 The Three Pillars of Sustainability

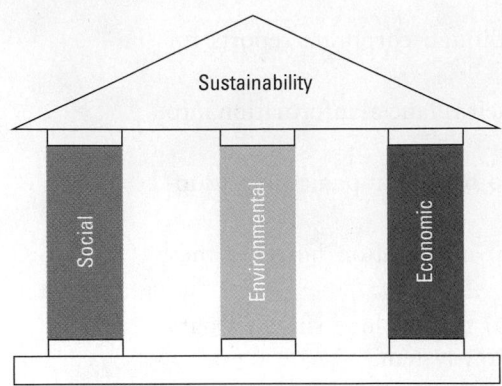

EXHIBIT 1-9 Sustainability as the Intersection of Three Factors

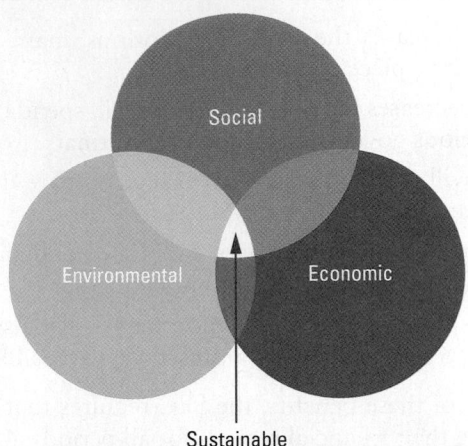

To move toward sustainability, companies are introducing "green initiatives"—ways of doing business that have fewer negative consequences on the earth's resources. They are innovating new products and manufacturing processes that use recycled materials to reduce the amount of waste going to landfills. They've also recognized the need to be socially responsible—carefully considering how their business affects employees, consumers, citizens, and entire communities. Many companies have introduced means of giving back to their local communities, by monetarily supporting local schools, employee volunteerism, and charities. Most of the leading companies in the world are now issuing corporate social responsibility (CSR) reports through which they communicate their social and environmental impact. Businesses are now viewing sustainability and social responsibility as opportunities for innovation and business development. These initiatives not only allow a company to "do the right thing," but they also can lead to economic profits by increasing demand for a company's products and services and reducing costs.

In every chapter of this text, you will see a special section illustrating how management accounting can help companies pursue sustainable, socially responsible business practices. These sections will be marked with a green recycle symbol, and will also point you to corresponding homework problems. In addition, Chapter 15 is devoted to sustainability. Chapter 15 examine the reasons sustainability makes good business sense and the framework and methods companies use to measure and report on their social and environmental impact.

Integrated Reporting

The corporate reporting landscape is constantly changing. One of the most notable recent global movements is toward integrated reporting. According to the International Integrated Reporting Committee (IIRC), **integrated reporting** (symbolized as <IR>) "is a process that results in communication, most visibly a periodic 'integrated report,' about value creation over time. An integrated report is a concise communication about how an organization's strategy, governance, performance and prospects lead to the creation of value over the short, medium and long term."[13] As such, it is a broader, more holistic, balanced, and future-looking report as compared to traditional financial statements, which tend to focus on short-term financial measures of past performance. An integrated report essentially describes and measures all material elements of value creation, not just those relating to financial capital. In addition to financial capital, the report takes into consideration manufactured, intellectual, human, social, and natural (environmental) capital, which are often more difficult for investors to access through traditional financial reporting.

Integrated reporting, which is still in its infancy, is being driven by businesses and institutional investors who want more information for better decision making than that

[13]www.theiirc.org

offered by traditional financial statements. Several well-known companies, including Microsoft, Prudential, and Coca-Cola, as well as the Big Four accounting firms, the CFA Institute, and Goldman Sachs, are working closely with the IIRC to help develop the <IR> reporting framework, which is scheduled to be released in 2014. You may keep abreast of current developments in <IR> by visiting www.theiirc.org.

Shifting Economy

In the last several decades, North American economies have shifted away from manufacturing and toward service. Service companies provide health care, communication, transportation, banking, and other important benefits to society. Service companies now make up the largest sector of the U.S. economy. Technology and healthcare are expected to be among the fastest-growing industries over the next decade. Even companies that traditionally carried out manufacturing, such as General Electric (GE), are shifting toward selling more services.

Managerial accounting has its roots in the industrial age of manufacturing. Most traditional managerial accounting practices were developed to fill the needs of manufacturing firms. However, since the U.S. economy has shifted away from manufacturing, managerial accounting has shifted, too. The field of managerial accounting has *expanded* to meet the needs of service and merchandising firms as well as manufacturers. For example, consider the following:

1. Manufacturers still need to know how much each unit of their product costs to manufacture. In addition to using this information for inventory valuation and pricing decisions, manufacturers now use cost information to determine whether they should outsource production to another company or to an overseas location, or even relocate it back in the United States.

2. Service companies also need cost information to make decisions. They need to know the cost of providing a service rather than manufacturing a product. For example, banks must include the cost of servicing checking and savings accounts in the fees they charge customers. And hospitals need to know the cost of performing appendectomies to justify reimbursement from insurance companies and from Medicare.

3. Retailers need to consider importing costs when determining the cost of their merchandise. Because many goods are now produced overseas rather than domestically, determining the cost of a product is often more difficult than it was in the past. Management accountants need to consider foreign currency translation, shipping costs, and import tariffs when determining the cost of imported products.

Management accounting has expanded to meet decision-making needs for all types of businesses, including those that wish to compete globally.

Global Marketplace

The barriers to international trade have fallen over the past decades, allowing foreign companies to compete with domestic firms. Firms that are not highly efficient, innovative, and responsive to business trends will vanish from the global market. However, global markets also provide highly competitive domestic companies with great opportunities for growth.

Globalization has several implications for managerial accounting:

- Stiffer competition means managers need more accurate and timely information to make wise business decisions. Companies can no longer afford to make decisions by the "seat of their pants." Detailed, accurate, and real-time cost information has become a necessity for survival.

- Companies must decide whether to expand sales and/or production into foreign countries. To do so, managers need comprehensive estimates of the costs of running international operations and the benefits that can be reaped. They also need to be aware of regulations and laws in other countries that could impact their operations. For example, England and Europe tend to have much stricter environmental protection laws than the United States.

- Companies can learn new management techniques by observing their international competitors. For example, the management philosophy of lean production, developed in Japan by Toyota, is now being used by many U.S. companies to cut costs, improve quality, and speed production.

Advanced Information Systems

Many small businesses utilize ready-to-use accounting software packages, such as Quick-Books or Sage Peachtree, to track their costs and to develop the information that owners and managers need to run the business. But large companies use <u>enterprise resource planning (ERP)</u> systems that can integrate all of a company's worldwide functions, departments, and data. ERP systems such as SAP and Oracle gather company data into a centralized data warehouse. The system feeds the data into software for all of the company's business activities, from budgeting and purchasing to production and customer service.

Advantages of ERP systems include the following:

- Companies streamline their operations before mapping them into ERP software. Streamlining operations saves money.
- ERP helps companies respond quickly to changes. A change in sales instantly ripples through the ERP's purchases, production, shipping, and accounting systems.
- An ERP system can replace hundreds of separate software systems, such as different software in different regions, or different payroll, shipping, and production software.

Although ERP systems are initially expensive, they are almost a necessity for running large companies as efficiently as possible over the long run. How do managers arrive at this conclusion? They use <u>cost-benefit analysis</u>, which weighs the expected costs of taking an action against the expected benefits of the action. The following Stop & Think illustrates a cost-benefit analysis.

STOP & THINK

Advances in technology have made electronic billing (e-billing) popular. Analysts estimate the following:

1. Companies save $7 per invoice by billing customers electronically.
2. The average large company issues 800,000 invoices a year.
3. The average cost of installing an e-billing system is $500,000.

Should companies that issue 800,000 invoices a year consider e-billing?

Answer: The following one-year analysis reveals significant monetary benefit from e-billing:

	A	B	C	D
1	**Cost-Benefit Analysis**	**Total**		
2	*Expected Benefits:*			
3	800,000 invoices × $7 savings per invoice	$ 5,600,000		
4	*Expected Costs:*			
5	Installation of e-billing system	500,000		
6	**Net expected benefit in first year**	$ 5,100,000		
7				

Not only does e-billing save the company money, but also it is more environmentally friendly than traditional paper-based billing. Thus, the company should strongly consider using e-billing for as many customers as possible.

Lean Operations

Lean thinking is both a philosophy and a business strategy of operating without waste. The more waste that is eliminated, the lower the company's costs will be. Why is this important? With lower costs, companies are better able to compete. One primary goal of a lean production system is to eliminate the waste of *time and money* that accompanies large inventories. Inventory takes time to store and unstore. The costs of holding inventory can add up to 25% or more of the inventory's value. Also, inventory that is held too long quickly becomes obsolete because of changing technology and consumer tastes.

Companies that advocate lean operations usually adopt the **just-in-time (JIT)** inventory philosophy that was first pioneered by Toyota. By manufacturing products *just in time* to fill customer orders, and no sooner, companies are able to substantially reduce the quantity of raw materials and finished products kept on hand. This, in turn, reduces storage costs (warehousing and associated security, utilities, and shrinkage costs) and handling costs (labor costs associated with storing and unstoring inventory). Since companies are making inventory *just in time* to fill customer orders, they must be able to produce a quality product very quickly. Therefore, lean companies focus on reducing **throughput time**, the time between buying raw materials and selling finished products, while still maintaining high quality. In Chapter 4, we'll look at some of the unique features of lean operations.

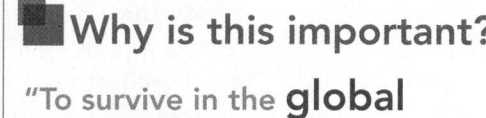

Why is this important?

"To survive in the **global marketplace**, businesses must quickly respond to customer **demand**, providing high-quality products and **services** at a reasonable price."

Total Quality Management

All companies, not just lean producers, must deliver high-quality goods and services to remain competitive. **Total quality management (TQM)** is one key to succeeding in the global economy. The goal of TQM is to delight customers by providing them with superior products and services. As part of TQM, each business function examines its own activities and works to improve performance by *continually* setting higher goals. In Chapter 4, we'll discuss how companies analyze the costs associated with their current level of quality as well as the costs of quality improvement initiatives.

ISO 9001:2008

Many firms want to demonstrate their commitment to continuous quality improvement. The International Organization for Standardization (ISO), made up of 163 member countries, has developed international quality management standards and guidelines. Firms may become **ISO 9001:2008** certified by complying with the quality management standards set forth by the ISO and undergoing extensive audits of their quality management processes. The prestigious certification gives firms a competitive advantage in the global marketplace. Many companies will purchase supplies only from firms bearing the ISO 9001 certification. To better understand the ISO's global impact, consider the following: in 2006, almost 897,000 certificates had been issued to firms in 170 countries. By 2011, the number of certifications exceeded 1,111,000.[14] The certification applies to service firms as well as manufacturers. The American Institute of Certified Public Accountants was the first professional membership organization in the United States to earn the ISO 9001 certification.

---

[14]www.iso.org/iso/home/standards/certification/iso-survey.htm

▶ Try It!

Determine whether each of the following statements is true or false:

1. The Sarbanes-Oxley Act of 2002 (SOX) imposes stricter requirements over financial reporting and internal controls and stricter consequences for those who engage in financial statement misconduct and other white-collar crimes.

2. U.S. companies that have operations overseas must use the International Financial Reporting Standards (IFRS) to issue their financial statements.

3. Extensible Business Reporting Language (XBRL) is a standardized coding system that allows financial information to be "tagged" so that it can be read by computer programs.

4. The triple bottom line assesses company performance on three factors: people (social impact), planet (environmental impact), and profit (economic impact).

5. Manufacturing makes up the largest sector of the U.S. economy.

6. The globalization of business has little bearing on management accounting.

7. Computer systems that integrate all of a company's worldwide functions into one database are known as Integrated Worldwide Systems (IWSs).

8. Lean thinking focuses on eliminating waste from operations in an effort to reduce costs.

9. The ISO 9001:2008 certification focuses on environmental management.

Please see page 45 for solutions.

Decision Guidelines

The Changing Regulatory and Business Environment

Successful companies have to respond to changes in the regulatory and business environment. Here are some of the decisions managers need to consider.

Decision	Guidelines
Which companies need to comply with SOX?	Publicly traded companies must comply with SOX. Many of the law's specific requirements focus on implementing adequate internal controls and financial reporting procedures and maintaining independence from the company's auditors.
How will IFRS benefit international companies?	Companies that operate in more than one country will no longer be required to prepare multiple financial statements using different standards for each country in which they operate. Rather, they will prepare one set of financial statements in accordance with International Financial Reporting Standards (IFRS).
How will XBRL help managers?	XBRL will allow managers to more easily obtain and analyze publicly available financial data from their competitors, from companies they may wish to purchase, or from companies in which they may want to invest.
How do companies compete in a global economy?	They advocate sustainable and socially responsible business practices, use advanced information systems, lean operations, and TQM to compete more effectively.
How does the concept of sustainability affect business?	Businesses will only be viable in the long run if they take a sustainable approach to operations: carefully considering the impact of the company's operations on people and the planet as well as on profit. Thus, company performance is often evaluated using a triple-bottom-line approach. Businesses are viewing sustainability as an opportunity to "do the right thing" while simultaneously increasing the company's value through innovation, risk minimization, and cost reduction.
How do companies decide whether to undertake new initiatives such as international expansion, ERP, lean operations, and TQM?	They use cost-benefit analysis: comparing the estimated benefits of the initiative with the estimated costs. They consider the impact of the decision not only on profits, but also on people and on the planet.

SUMMARY PROBLEM **2**

EZ-Rider Motorcycles is considering whether to expand into Germany. If gas prices increase, the company expects more interest in fuel-efficient transportation such as motorcycles. As a result, the company is considering setting up a motorcycle assembly plant on the outskirts of Berlin.

EZ-Rider Motorcycles estimates it will cost $850,000 to convert an existing building to motorcycle production. Workers will need training, at a total cost of $65,000. The additional costs to organize the business and to establish relationships is estimated to be $150,000.

The CEO believes the company can earn sales profits from this expansion (before considering the costs in the preceding paragraph) of $1,624,000.

Requirement

Use cost-benefit analysis to determine whether EZ-Rider should expand into Germany.

▪ SOLUTION

The following cost-benefit analysis indicates that the company should expand into Germany:

	A	B	C	D
1	**Cost-Benefit Analysis**		**Total**	
2	***Expected Benefits:***			
3	Expected profits from increase in sales		$ 1,624,000	
4	***Expected Costs:***			
5	Conversion of building	$ 850,000		
6	Workforce training	65,000		
7	Organizing and establishing relationships	150,000		
8	Total expected costs		1,065,000	
9	**Net expected benefit**		$ 559,000	
10				

END OF CHAPTER

Learning Objectives

- 1 Identify managers' three primary responsibilities
- 2 Distinguish financial accounting from managerial accounting
- 3 Describe organizational structure and the roles and skills required of management accountants within the organization
- 4 Describe the role of the Institute of Management Accountants (IMA) and use its ethical standards to make reasonable ethical judgments
- 5 Discuss and analyze the implications of regulatory and business trends

Accounting Vocabulary

American Institute of Certified Public Accountants (AICPA). (p. 10) The world's largest association representing the accounting profession; together with the Chartered Institute of Management Accountants (CIMA) offers the Chartered Global Management Accountant (CGMA) designation.

Audit Committee. (p. 7) A subcommittee of the board of directors that is responsible for overseeing both the internal audit function and the annual financial statement audit by independent CPAs.

Board of Directors. (p. 6) The body elected by shareholders to oversee the company.

Budget. (p. 3) Quantitative expression of a plan that helps managers coordinate and implement the plan.

Certified Management Accountant (CMA). (p. 9) A professional certification issued by the IMA to designate expertise in the areas of managerial accounting, economics, and business finance.

Chartered Global Management Accountant (CGMA). (p. 10) A designation available to qualifying American Institute of Certified Public Accountants (AICPA) members that is meant to recognize the unique business and accounting skill set possessed by those CPAs who work, or have worked, in business, industry or government.

Chief Executive Officer (CEO). (p. 6) The position hired by the board of directors to oversee the company on a daily basis.

Chief Financial Officer (CFO). (p. 6) The position responsible for all of the company's financial concerns.

Chief Operating Officer (COO). (p. 6) The position responsible for overseeing the company's operations.

Controller. (p. 6) The position responsible for general financial accounting, managerial accounting, and tax reporting.

Controlling. (p. 3) One of management's primary responsibilities; evaluating the results of business operations against the plan and making adjustments to keep the company pressing toward its goals.

Cost-Benefit Analysis. (p. 22) Weighing costs against benefits to help make decisions.

Cross-Functional Teams. (p. 7) Corporate teams whose members represent various functions of the organization, such as R&D, design, production, marketing, distribution, and customer service.

Decision Making. (p. 2) Identifying possible courses of action and choosing among them.

Directing. (p. 3) One of management's primary responsibilities; running the company on a day-to-day basis.

Enterprise Resource Planning (ERP). (p. 22) Software systems that can integrate all of a company's worldwide functions, departments, and data into a single system.

Extensible Business Reporting Language (XBRL). (p. 18) A data tagging system that enables companies to release financial and business information in a format that can be quickly, efficiently, and cost-effectively accessed, sorted, and analyzed over the Internet.

Institute of Management Accountants (IMA). (p. 9) The professional organization that promotes the advancement of the management accounting profession.

Integrated Reporting. (p. 20) A process resulting in a report that describes how a company is creating value over time using financial, manufactured, intellectual, human, social, and natural capital.

Internal Audit Function. (p. 6) The corporate function charged with assessing the effectiveness of the company's internal controls and risk management policies.

International Financial Reporting Standards (IFRS). (p. 18) The SEC is considering whether to require all publicly traded companies to adopt IFRS. In many instances, IFRS vary from GAAP.

ISO 9001:2008. (p. 23) A quality-related certification issued by the International Organization for Standardization (ISO). Firms may become ISO 9001:2008 certified by complying with the quality management standards set forth by the ISO and undergoing extensive audits of their quality management processes.

Just-in-time (JIT). (p. 23) An inventory philosophy first pioneered by Toyota in which a product is manufactured *just in time* to fill customer orders. Companies adopting JIT are able to substantially reduce the quantity of raw materials and finished products kept on hand.

Lean Thinking. (p. 23) A philosophy and business strategy of operating without waste.

Planning. (p. 3) One of management's primary responsibilities; setting goals and objectives for the company and deciding how to achieve them.

Sarbanes-Oxley Act of 2002 (SOX). (p. 17) A congressional act that enhances internal control and financial reporting requirements and establishes new regulatory requirements for publicly traded companies and their independent auditors.

Sustainability. (p. 19) The ability to meet the needs of the present without compromising the ability of future generations to meet their own needs.

Throughput Time. (p. 23) The time between buying raw materials and selling finished products.

Total Quality Management (TQM). (p. 23) A management philosophy of delighting customers with superior products and services by continually setting higher goals and improving the performance of every business function.

Treasurer. (p. 6) The position responsible for raising the firm's capital and investing funds.

Triple Bottom Line. (p. 19) Evaluating a company's performance not only by its ability to generate economic profits, but also by its impact on people and on the planet.

MyAccountingLab Go to http://myaccountinglab.com/ **for the following Quick Check, Short Exercises, Exercises, and Problems. They are available with immediate grading, explanations of correct and incorrect answers, and interactive media that acts as your own online tutor.**

Quick Check

1. *(Learning Objective 1)* Which of the following management responsibilities often involves the use of budgets?
   a. Planning
   b. Directing
   c. Controlling
   d. None of the above

2. *(Learning Objective 2)* Managerial accounting differs from financial accounting in that managerial accounting
   a. is used primarily by external decision makers.
   b. is required by Generally Accepted Accounting Principles (GAAP).
   c. tends to report on the company as a whole rather than segments of the company.
   d. emphasizes data relevance over data objectivity.

3. *(Learning Objective 3)* Which of the following corporate positions is responsible for raising capital and investing funds?
   a. Controller
   b. Treasurer
   c. Internal audit
   d. Chief operating officer (COO)

4. *(Learning Objective 3)* Of the following skills, which are needed by today's management accountants?
   a. Knowledge of both financial and managerial accounting
   b. Knowledge of how a business functions
   c. Oral and written communication skills
   d. All of the above

5. *(Learning Objective 4)* Which of the following organizations is the professional association for management accountants?
   a. AICPA
   b. IMA
   c. IFRS
   d. FASB

6. *(Learning Objective 4)* Which of the following professional standards requires management accountants to mitigate conflicts of interest?
   a. Competence
   b. Confidentiality
   c. Integrity
   d. Credibility

7. *(Learning Objective 4)* Which of the following professional standards requires management accountants to communicate information fairly and objectively?
   a. Competence
   b. Confidentiality
   c. Integrity
   d. Credibility

8. *(Learning Objective 5)* Which of the following requires the company's CEO and CFO to assume responsibility for the company's financial statements and disclosures?
   a. Sarbanes-Oxley Act of 2002 (SOX)
   b. International Financial Accounting Standards (IFRS)
   c. Extensible Business Reporting Language (XBRL)
   d. Lean operations

9. *(Learning Objective 5)* Which of the following is *false*?

a. Lean operations is a philosophy and business strategy of operating without waste.

b. Globalization has increased the necessity for more detailed and accurate cost information.

c. TQM is a standardized coding system used to tag financial and business data so that it can be read by computer programs.

d. ERP systems integrate information from all company functions into a centralized data warehouse

10. *(Learning Objective 5)* The triple bottom line focuses on

a. profit.

b. people.

c. the planet.

d. all of the above.

Quick Check Answers

1.a 2.d 3.b 4.d 5.b 6.c 7.d 8.a 9.c 10.d

Short Exercises

S1-1   Managers' responsibilities *(Learning Objective 1)*

Categorize each of the following activities as to which management responsibility it fulfills: planning, directing, or controlling. Some activities may fulfill more than one responsibility.

a. Management conducts variance analysis by comparing budget to actual.

b. Management uses information on product costs to determine sales prices.

c. Management decides to increase sales growth by 10% next year.

d. To lower product costs, management moves production to Mexico.

e. Management reviews hourly sales reports to determine the level of staffing needed to service customers.

S1-2   Contrast managerial and financial accounting *(Learning Objective 2)*

Managerial accounting differs from financial accounting in several areas. Specify whether each of the following characteristics relates to managerial accounting or financial accounting.

a. Main characteristic of data is that it must be reliable and objective

b. Reports are prepared as needed

c. Not governed by legal requirements

d. Primary users are external (i.e., creditors, investors)

e. Focused on the future

f. Reporting is based mainly on the company as a whole

g. Reports are usually prepared quarterly and annually

h. Information is verified by external auditors

i. Focused on the past

j. Main characteristic of data is that it must be relevant

k. Reports tend to be prepared for the parts of the organization rather than the whole organization

l. Primary users are internal (i.e., company managers)

m. Governed by Generally Accepted Accounting Principles (GAAP) or International Financial Reporting Standards (IFRS)

S1-3   Accounting roles in the organization *(Learning Objective 3)*

The following is a list of job duties or descriptions. For each item, specify whether it would be most likely to describe the duties or responsibilities of someone working for the treasurer, the controller, or in the Internal Auditing Department.

a. Invest company funds

b. Report to the audit committee of the board of directors *and* to a senior executive, such as the CFO or CEO

c. Prepares company tax returns

d. Perform cash counts at branch offices

e. Prepare journal entries for month-end closing

f. Issue company stock

g. Ensure that the company's internal controls are functioning properly

h. Create an analysis about whether to lease or buy a delivery truck

i. Calculate the cost of a product

j. Issue company bonds

k. Check to make sure that company risk management procedures are being followed

l. Work with various departments in preparing operating budgets for the upcoming year

m. Oversee accounts payable activities

S1-4 Role of internal audit function (Learning Objective 3)

The following table lists several characteristics. Place a check mark next to those items that pertain directly to the internal audit function and its role within the organization.

Characteristic	Check (✓) if related to internal auditing
a. Ensures that the company achieves its profit goals	
b. Is part of the Accounting Department	
c. Usually reports to a senior executive (CFO or CEO) for administrative matters	
d. Performs the same function as independent certified public accountants	
e. External audits can be performed by the Internal Auditing Department	
f. Helps to ensure that company's internal controls are functioning properly	
g. Reports to treasurer or controller	
h. Required by the New York Stock Exchange (NYSE) if company stock is publicly traded on the NYSE	
i. Reports directly to the audit committee	

S1-5 Classify roles within the organization (Learning Objective 3)

Complete the following statements with one of the terms listed here. You may use a term more than once, and some terms may not be used at all.

Audit committee	Board of directors	CEO	CFO
Treasurer	Controller	Cross-functional teams	COO

a. Raising capital and investing funds are the direct responsibilities of the _____.

b. Financial accounting, managerial accounting, and tax reporting are the direct responsibilities of the _____.

c. The internal audit function reports to the CFO or the _____ and the _____.

d. The CEO is hired by the _____.

e. The company's operations are the direct responsibility of the _____.

f. Management accountants often work with _____.

g. The _____ and the _____ report to the CEO.

h. A subcommittee of the board of directors is called the _____.

S1-6 Professional organizations and certifications (Learning Objective 4)

Complete the following sentences:

1. The Institute of Management Accountants says that more accountants work in organizations rather than at _____.

2. The certification offered by the Institute of Management Accountants is called the _____ and focuses on managerial accounting, economics, and finance topics.

3. The monthly professional magazine published by the Institute of Management Accountants is called _____.

4. The certification launched in 2012 jointly by the American Institute of Certified Public Accountants and the Chartered Institute of Management Accountants is called the _____.

5. The certification for accounting professionals in public accounting roles is the _____.

S1-7 Importance of ethical standards *(Learning Objective 4)*

ETHICS

Explain why each of the four broad ethical standards in the IMA's *Statement of Ethical Professional Practice* is necessary.

S1-8 Violations of ethical standards *(Learning Objective 4)*

ETHICS

The IMA's *Statement of Ethical Professional Practice* (Exhibit 1-6) requires management accountants to meet standards regarding the following:

- Competence
- Confidentiality
- Integrity
- Credibility

Consider the following situations. Which guidelines are violated in each situation?

a. You tell your brother that your company will report earnings significantly above financial analysts' estimates.

b. You see that other employees take office supplies for personal use. As an intern, you do the same thing, assuming that this is a "perk."

c. At a conference on sustainability, you skip the afternoon session and go sightseeing. Your company paid for the registration fee, and you are getting paid for the day.

d. You failed to read the detailed specifications of a new software package that you asked your company to purchase. After it is installed, you are surprised that it is incompatible with some of your company's older accounting software.

e. You do not provide top managers with the detailed job descriptions they requested because you fear they may use this information to cut a position from your department.

S1-9 Identify current competitive tools *(Learning Objective 5)*

Companies are facing a great amount of change in every facet of their operations today. To remain competitive, companies must keep abreast of current developments in several areas. You recently got together with a group of friends who work for different companies. Your friends share information about their current challenges in adopting new tools or complying with new regulations. Excerpts from the conversation are presented in the following section. Tell whether each excerpt describes XBRL, ISO 9001:2008, sustainability, the Sarbanes-Oxley Act (SOX), or enterprise resource planning (ERP) systems.

a. Ethan: We have just installed a system at our company that integrates all of our company's data across all systems. We have one central data warehouse that contains information about our suppliers, our customers, our employees, and our financial information. The software retrieves information from this single data warehouse and all systems are integrated. The process of implementing this system has been very expensive and time consuming, but we are reaping the benefits of being more streamlined, of being able to respond more quickly to changes in the market, and of not having several different software systems operating independently.

b. Kelsey: We have been working on a system to tag all of the financial information in our quarterly and annual reports so that our financial information can be shared easily. We will be able to attach a tag to each piece of financial information. For example, we can tag our "net profits" wherever it appears in the financial reports. Any user accessing the financial reports would then be able to download the numbers for "net profits." Our stockholders and the analysts will be able to retrieve the information they need quickly, efficiently, and cost-effectively.

c. John: I just started a new job in the Auditing Department. My new duties include assisting in the development of testing procedures and methods for determining internal controls effectiveness. I also oversee the testing for assurance of compliance with corporate policies. I am coordinating the review of SEC filings with our external auditors. I also am responsible for preparing periodic compliance status reports for management, the audit committee, and the external auditors.

d. Sam: My company has a new initiative at work. All employees are encouraged to recycle paper and other materials. Employees are also given one work day a year to volunteer to help local nonprofit organizations. Employees are also urged to think outside the box to find ways to reduce the company's carbon footprint. The company has also begun an internal reporting system that reports on its triple bottom line.

e. Lipang: My company is working to demonstrate its commitment to continuous quality improvement. We are currently undergoing an extensive audit of our quality management processes. We hope to gain a competitive advantage through this process.

ETHICS

S1-10 Identify ethical standards violated *(Learning Objective 4)*

For each of the situations listed, identify the primary standard from the IMA *Statement of Ethical Professional Practice* that is violated (competence, confidentiality, integrity, or credibility.) Refer to Exhibit 1-6 for the complete standard.

a. Even though Kayla's company is adopting International Financial Accounting Standards (IFRS) this year, Kayla (a management accountant) has not completed the required IFRS training.

b. David, a purchasing agent for his company, received two tickets from a supplier to the upcoming Ohio State vs. University of Michigan football game. These tickets sell for over $500 each.

c. The CFO directed that certain expenses be reclassified as assets, so that target profit could be achieved. The CFO rationalized that jobs would be saved by reaching the targeted income figures.

d. Tara, an accountant for a smartphone manufacturer, told her friends about a new model of smartphone being released by the company in the following quarter. For competitive reasons, the company keeps its models shrouded in secrecy until the release date.

e. Daniel provides an analysis of the profitability of a company-owned store that is managed by Daniel's best friend, Stuart. Daniel neglects to include allocated fixed costs in Stuart's report. If Daniel includes those allocated fixed costs, the store will show a loss and Stuart's job could be in danger.

S1-11 Define key terms *(Learning Objective 5)*

Complete the following statements with one of the terms listed here. You may use a term more than once, and some terms may not be used at all.

CEO	Environmental	ISO 9001:2008	Social
CFO	ERP	Lean thinking	Sustainability
Controlling	IFRS	Planning	Throughput time
Directing	Integrated report	Sarbanes-Oxley Act	Triple bottom line
Economic	Internal audit	of 2002	XBRL

a. _____ is a broad holistic report that describes all material elements of value creation, not just the financial elements.

b. _____ is the management process of overseeing the company's day-to-day operations.

c. The _____ manages the company on a daily basis.

d. The _____ was enacted to restore trust in publicly traded corporations, their management, their financial statements, and their auditors.

e. Firms acquire the _____ certification to demonstrate their commitment to quality.

f. The three pillars of sustainability are: _____, _____, and _____.

g. The _____ focuses on people, planet, and profit.

h. _____ is the management process of setting goals and objectives for the company and determining how to achieve them.

i. The role of the _____ function is to ensure that the company's internal controls and risk management policies are functioning properly.

j. _____ serves the information needs of people in accounting as well as people in marketing and in the warehouse.

k. _____ is a language that utilizes a standardized coding system companies use to tag each piece of financial and business information in a format that can be quickly and efficiently accessed over the Internet.

l. _____ is both a philosophy and a business strategy of operating without waste.

m. Typically, the treasurer and the controller report directly to the _____.

n. _____ is the time between buying raw materials and selling the finished products.

o. _____ is the management process of evaluating the results of business operations against the plan and making adjustments to keep the company pressing toward its goals.

p. _____ is the ability to meet the needs of the present without compromising the ability of future generations to meet their own needs.

EXERCISES Group A

E1-12A Define key terms (*Learning Objectives 1 & 2*)

Complete the following statements with one of the terms listed here. You may use a term more than once, and some terms may not be used at all.

Budget	Creditors	Managerial accounting	Planning
Controlling	Financial accounting	Managers	Shareholders

a. _____ systems report on various segments or business units of the company.

b. When managers evaluate the company's performance compared to the plan, they are performing the _____ role of management.

c. Information on a company's past performance is provided to external parties by _____.

d. _____ systems are chosen by comparing the costs versus the benefits of the system and are not restricted by GAAP or IFRS.

e. CPAs audit the _____ statements of public companies.

f. Financial accounting develops reports for external parties such as _____ and _____.

g. Companies must follow GAAP or IFRS in their _____ systems.

h. Decision makers inside a company are the _____.

i. Choosing goals and the means to achieve them is the _____ function of management.

E1-13A Identify users of accounting information (*Learning Objective 3*)

For each of the following users of financial accounting information and managerial accounting information, specify whether the user would primarily use financial accounting information or managerial accounting information or both.

1. SEC examiner
2. Bookkeeping Department
3. Division controller
4. External auditor (public accounting firm)
5. Loan officer at the company's bank
6. State tax agency auditor
7. Board of directors
8. Manager of the Service Department
9. Wall Street analyst
10. Internal auditor
11. Potential investors
12. Current stockholders
13. Reporter from *The Wall Street Journal*
14. Regional division managers

E1-14A Classify ethical responsibilities (*Learning Objective 4*)   ETHICS

According to the IMA's *Statement of Ethical Professional Practice* (Exhibit 1-6), management accountants should follow four standards: competence, confidentiality, integrity, and credibility. Each of these standards contains specific responsibilities. Classify each of the following responsibilities according to the standard it addresses.

Responsibility:

1. Maintain an appropriate level of professional expertise by continually developing knowledge and skills.
2. Recognize and communicate professional limitations that would preclude responsible judgment or successful performance of an activity.
3. Disclose all relevant information that could reasonably be expected to influence an intended user's understanding of the reports, analyses, or recommendations.
4. Disclose delays or deficiencies in information, timeliness, processing, or internal controls in conformance with organization policy and/or applicable law.
5. Perform professional duties in accordance with relevant laws, regulations, and technical standards.
6. Abstain from engaging in or supporting any activity that might discredit the profession.
7. Refrain from engaging in any conduct that would prejudice carrying out duties ethically.
8. Provide decision support information and recommendations that are accurate, clear, concise, and timely.
9. Keep information confidential except when disclosure is authorized or legally required.
10. Communicate information fairly and objectively.
11. Refrain from using confidential information for unethical or illegal advantage.
12. Inform all relevant parties regarding the appropriate use of confidential information. Monitor subordinates' activities to ensure compliance.
13. Mitigate actual conflicts of interest. Regularly communicate with business associates to avoid apparent conflicts of interest. Advise all parties of any potential conflicts.

E1-15A   Lean production cost-benefit analysis *(Learning Objective 5)*

Shark Rides manufactures snowboards. Roy Bettano, the CEO, is trying to decide whether to adopt a lean thinking model. He expects that adopting lean production would save $67,000 in warehousing expenses and $38,200 in spoilage costs. Adopting lean production will require several one-time up-front expenditures: $26,000 for an employee training program, $68,000 to streamline the plant's production process, and $7,500 to identify suppliers that will guarantee zero defects and on-time delivery.

Requirements

1. What are the total costs of adopting lean production?
2. What are the total benefits of adopting lean production?
3. Should Shark Rides adopt lean production? Why or why not?

SUSTAINABILITY

E1-16A   Identify sustainability efforts as impacting people, planet, or profit *(Learning Objective 5)*

Sustainability involves more than just the impact of actions on the environment. The triple bottom line recognizes that a company has to measure its impact on its triple bottom line for its long-term viability. To follow are examples of green initiatives recently undertaken at The Coca-Cola Company. For each example, indicate whether this initiative would primarily impact environmental, social, or economic factors.

Initiative at The Coca-Cola Company	Environmental, Social, or Economic?
a. Provided on-site wellness coaching for employees in the Baltimore sales facility to help to improve employee health.	
b. Diverted more than 2.5 million beverage containers from landfills by placing more than 3,000 recycling bins at NASCAR racetracks across the United States.	
c. Generated a positive economic benefit in every community in which Coca-Cola has facilities in the United States.	

Initiative at The Coca-Cola Company	Environmental, Social, or Economic?

d. Reduced beverage calories in U.S. schools by 88% since 2006.

e. Prohibited marketing to children under the age of 12 in its global marketing policy.

f. Deployed hybrid electric trucks, which generate approximately one-third fewer CO_2 emissions than a regular truck, in several major U.S. cities.

g. Minimized the amount of water used in the manufacturing and cleaning processes, resulting in a water use savings of over 2 billion liters since 2008.

h. Recruited from a wide cross section of the communities that it services so that the representation of women and minority groups in management can be improved.

i. Displayed total calorie counts on the selection buttons on company-controlled vending machines so that consumers can make informed choices.

j. Generated a profit for the company's shareholders.

k. Removed the side walls on the corrugated trays that carry products, which resulted in savings of almost 2,400 metric tons of corrugated packaging.

l. Provided training and career planning for employees to help to provide a rewarding work life.

m. Reduced the bottle cap size by .5 millimeters and shortened the bottle neck, which resulted in a total plastics savings of more than 11,000 metric tons since 2007.

EXERCISES Group B

E1-17B Define key terms (Learning Objectives 1 & 2)

Complete the following statements with one of the terms listed here. You may use a term more than once, and some terms may not be used at all.

Budget	Creditors	Managerial accounting	Planning
Controlling	Financial accounting	Managers	Shareholders

a. U.S. companies must follow GAAP or IFRS in their _____ systems.

b. Financial accounting develops reports for external parties such as _____ and _____.

c. When managers evaluate the company's performance compared to the plan, they are performing the _____ role of management.

d. _____ are decision makers inside a company.

e. _____ provides information on a company's past performance to external parties.

f. _____ systems are not restricted by GAAP or IFRS but are chosen by comparing the costs versus the benefits of the system.

g. Choosing goals and the means to achieve them is the _____ function of management.

h. _____ systems report on various segments or business units of the company.

i. _____ statements of public companies are audited annually by CPAs.

E1-18B Identify users of accounting information (Learning Objective 3)

For each of the following users of financial accounting information and managerial accounting information, specify whether the user would primarily use financial accounting information or managerial accounting information or both.

1. Internal auditor

2. Potential shareholders

3. Loan officer at the company's bank

4. Manager of the Sales Department

5. Bookkeeping Department
6. Managers at regional offices
7. IRS agent
8. Current shareholders
9. Wall Street analyst
10. News reporter
11. Company controller
12. Board of directors
13. SEC employee
14. External auditor (public accounting firm)

ETHICS

E1-19B   Classify ethical responsibilities (*Learning Objective 4*)

According to the IMA's *Statement of Ethical Professional Practice* (reproduced in the chapter), management accountants should follow four standards: competence, confidentiality, integrity, and credibility. Each of these standards contains specific responsibilities. Classify each of the following responsibilities according to the standard it addresses.

1. Communicate information fairly and objectively.
2. Recognize and communicate professional limitations that would preclude responsible judgment or successful performance of an activity.
3. Mitigate actual conflicts of interest. Regularly communicate with business associates to avoid apparent conflicts of interest. Advise all parties of any potential conflicts.
4. Provide decision support information and recommendations that are accurate, clear, concise, and timely.
5. Abstain from engaging in or supporting any activity that might discredit the profession.
6. Disclose all relevant information that could reasonably be expected to influence an intended user's understanding of the reports, analyses, or recommendations.
7. Inform all relevant parties regarding the appropriate use of confidential information. Monitor subordinates' activities to ensure compliance.
8. Perform professional duties in accordance with relevant laws, regulations, and technical standards.
9. Refrain from engaging in any conduct that would prejudice carrying out duties ethically.
10. Keep information confidential except when disclosure is authorized or legally required.
11. Disclose delays or deficiencies in information, timeliness, processing, or internal controls in conformance with organization policy and/or applicable law.
12. Refrain from using confidential information for unethical or illegal advantage.
13. Maintain an appropriate level of professional expertise by continually developing knowledge and skills.

E1-20B   Lean production cost-benefit analysis (*Learning Objective 5*)

Paradise Rides manufactures snowboards. Tom Posney, the CEO, is trying to decide whether to adopt a lean thinking model. He expects that adopting lean production would save $87,000 in warehousing expenses and $35,200 in spoilage costs. Adopting lean production will require several one-time up-front expenditures: $45,100 for an employee training program, $35,000 to streamline the plant's production process, and $7,750 to identify suppliers that will guarantee zero defects and on-time delivery.

Requirements

1. What are the total costs of adopting lean production?
2. What are the total benefits of adopting lean production?
3. Should Paradise Rides adopt lean production? Why or why not?

E1-21B Identify sustainability efforts as impacting people, planet, or profit
(Learning Objective 5)

Sustainability involves more than just the impact of actions on the environment. The triple bottom line recognizes that a company has to measure its impact on its triple bottom line for its long-term viability. To follow are examples of green initiatives recently undertaken at The J.M. Smucker Company. For each example, indicate whether this initiative would *primarily* impact environmental, social, or economic factors.

Initiative at The J.M. Smucker Company	Environmental, Social, or Economic?
a. Constructed a solar-powered warehouse	
b. Provided time off for employees to volunteer at organizations such as Boys and Girls Clubs of America and United Way	
c. Added a sustainability leader to every manufacturing facility to help to achieve established environmental goals	
d. Achieved Gold LEED Certification on its company store renovations	
e. Generated a profit for the company's shareholders	
f. Helped to establish the Heartland Education Initiative based in Orrville, Ohio, which is focused on improving education through a partnership between community organizations, parents, school, and businesses	
g. Achieved Silver LEED Certification on its new office building	
h. Reduced the amount of plastic used in Jif peanut butter jars by 2.2 million pounds	
i. Provided financial support to American Red Cross	
j. Submitted a report to the Carbon Disclosure Project, which is an effort to have organizations from around the world measure and disclose their greenhouse gas emissions and other sustainability efforts	
k. Generated a positive economic benefit in every community in which Smuckers has facilities	
l. Reduced delivery truck traffic and energy consumption by producing plastic bottles for *Crisco* products at its own manufacturing facility in Cincinnati rather than having the bottles shipped to them by a third party	
m. Received the Waste Reduction Awards Program Award from the State of California Waste Management Board	

PROBLEMS Group A

P1-22A Management processes and accounting information
(Learning Objectives 1 & 2)

Bryan Haas has his own electronics retail chain, TechnoGeek. His stores sell computer parts, audio visual equipment, consumer electronics, and related items. Custom computer building and electronics repair are also offered. In addition, TechnoGeek has a website to sell its merchandise. The store has a staff of 90 people working in six departments: Sales, Customization, Repairs, Web Development, Accounting, and Human Resources. Each department has its own manager.

Requirements

1. For each of the six departments, describe at least one decision/action for each of the three stages of management (planning, directing, and controlling). Prepare a table similar to the following for your answer:

	Planning	Directing	Controlling
Sales			
Repairs			
Customization			
Web Development			
Accounting			
Human Resources			

2. For each of the decisions/actions you described in Part 1, identify what information is needed for that decision/action. Specify whether that information would be generated by the financial accounting system or the managerial accounting system at TechnoGeek.

P1-23A   Ethical dilemmas *(Learning Objective 4)*

Eve Dalton is the new controller for Smashing Hits, a designer and manufacturer of tennis attire. Shortly before the December 31 fiscal year-end, Liz Sinclair (the company president) asks Dalton how things look for the year-end numbers. Sinclair is not happy to learn that earnings growth may be below 10% for the first time in the company's five-year history. Sinclair explains that financial analysts have again predicted a 12% earnings growth for the company and that she does not intend to disappoint them. She suggests that Dalton talk to the assistant controller, who can explain how the previous controller dealt with this situation. The assistant controller suggests the following strategies:

a. Postpone planned advertising expenditures from December to January.

b. Do not record sales returns and allowances on the basis that they are individually immaterial.

c. Persuade retail customers to accelerate January orders to December.

d. Reduce the allowance for bad debts (and bad debts expense).

e. Smashing Hits ships finished goods to public warehouses across the country for temporary storage until it receives firm orders from customers. As Smashing Hits receives orders, it directs the warehouse to ship the goods to nearby customers. The assistant controller suggests recording goods sent to the public warehouses as sales.

Requirement

Which of these suggested strategies are inconsistent with IMA standards? What should Dalton do if Sinclair insists that she follow all of these suggestions?

P1-24A   ERP cost-benefit analysis *(Learning Objective 5)*

As CEO of OceanSide Marine, Rebecca Thornberg knows it is important to control costs and to respond quickly to changes in the highly competitive boat-building industry. When BG Consulting proposes that OceanSide Marine invest in an ERP system, she forms a team to evaluate the proposal: the plant engineer, the plant foreman, the systems specialist, the human resources director, the marketing director, and the management accountant. A month later, management accountant Mark Cole reports that the team and BG estimate that if OceanSide Marine implements the ERP system, it will incur the following costs:

a. $360,000 in software costs

b. $95,000 to customize the ERP software and load Oceanside's data into the new ERP system

c. $112,000 for employee training

The team estimates that the ERP system should provide several benefits:

a. More efficient order processing should lead to savings of $189,000.

b. Streamlining the manufacturing process so that it maps into the ERP system will create savings of $270,000.

c. Integrating purchasing, production, marketing, and distribution into a single system will allow OceanSide Marine to reduce inventories, saving $210,000.

d. Higher customer satisfaction should increase sales, which, in turn, should increase the present value of profits by $150,000.

Requirements

1. If the ERP installation succeeds, what is the dollar amount of the benefits?

2. Should OceanSide Marine install the ERP system? Why or why not? Show your calculations.

3. Why did Thornberg create a team to evaluate BG's proposal? Consider each piece of cost-benefit information that management accountant Cole reported. Which person on the team is most likely to have contributed each item? (*Hint:* Which team member is likely to have the most information about each cost or benefit?)

P1-25A   E-commerce cost-benefit analysis *(Learning Objective 5)*

Northern Gas wants to move its sales order system to the Internet. Under the proposed system, gas stations and other merchants will use a secure site to check the availability and current price of various products and place an order. Currently, customer service representatives take dealers' orders over the phone; they record the information on a paper form, then manually enter it into the firm's computer system.

CFO Karen Jensen believes that dealers will not adopt the new Internet system unless Northern Gas provides financial assistance to help them purchase or upgrade their computer systems. Jensen estimates this one-time cost at $740,000. Northern Gas will also have to invest $145,000 in upgrading its own computer hardware. The cost of the software and the consulting fee for installing the system will be $215,000. The Web system will enable Northern Gas to eliminate 25 clerical positions. Jensen estimates that the benefits of the new system's lower labor costs will have saved the company $1,430,000.

Requirement

Use a cost-benefit analysis to recommend to Jensen whether Northern Gas should proceed with the Internet-based ordering system. Give your reasons, showing supporting calculations.

P1-26A   Continuation of P1-25A: revised estimates *(Learning Objective 5)*

Jensen revises her estimates of the benefits from the new system's lower labor costs as calculated in P1-25A. She now thinks the savings will be only $928,000.

Requirements

1. Compute the expected benefits of the Internet-based ordering system.
2. Would you recommend that Northern Gas accept the proposal?
3. Before Jensen makes a final decision, what other factors should she consider?

PROBLEMS Group B

P1-27B   Management processes and accounting information
(Learning Objectives 1 & 2)

Sarah Miracle has her own chain of music stores, Miracle Music. Her stores sell musical instruments, sheet music, and other related items. Music lessons and instrument repair are also offered through the stores. Miracle Music also has a website that sells music merchandise. The store has a staff of 80 people working in six departments: Sales, Repairs, Lessons, Web Development, Accounting, and Human Resources. Each department has its own manager.

Requirements

1. For each of the six departments, describe at least one decision/action for each of the three stages of management (planning, directing, and controlling). Prepare a table similar to the following for your answer:

	Planning	Directing	Controlling
Sales			
Repairs			
Lessons			
Web Development			
Accounting			
Human Resources			

2. For each of the decisions/actions you described in Part 1, identify what information is needed for that decision/action. Specify whether that information would be generated by the financial accounting system or the managerial accounting system at Miracle Music.

ETHICS

P1-28B Ethical dilemmas *(Learning Objective 4)*

Vicki Thornton is the new controller for EduTechno Software, which develops and sells educational software. Shortly before the December 31 fiscal year-end, Phil Nelson, the company president, asks Thornton how things look for the year-end numbers. He is not happy to learn that earnings growth may be below 15% for the first time in the company's five-year history. Nelson explains that financial analysts have again predicted a 15% earnings growth for the company and that he does not intend to disappoint them. He suggests that Thornton talk to the assistant controller, who can explain how the previous controller dealt with this situation. The assistant controller suggests the following strategies:

a. Persuade suppliers to postpone billing until January 1.

b. Record as sales certain software awaiting sale that is held in a public warehouse.

c. Delay the year-end closing a few days into January of the next year so that some of next year's sales are included as this year's sales.

d. Reduce the allowance for bad debts (and bad debts expense).

e. Postpone routine monthly maintenance expenditures from December to January.

Requirement

Which of these suggested strategies are inconsistent with IMA standards? What should Thornton do if Nelson insists that she follow all of these suggestions?

P1-29B ERP cost-benefit analysis *(Learning Objective 5)*

As CEO of SeaSpray Marine, Ramona Raney knows it is important to control costs and to respond quickly to changes in the highly competitive boat-building industry. When JT Consulting proposes that SeaSpray invest in an ERP system, she forms a team to evaluate the proposal: the plant engineer, the plant foreman, the systems specialist, the human resources director, the marketing director, and the management accountant.

A month later, management accountant Miles Cobalt reports that the team and JT estimate that if SeaSpray implements the ERP system, it will incur the following costs:

a. $390,000 in software costs

b. $73,000 to customize the ERP software and load SeaSpray's data into the new ERP system

c. $110,000 for employee training

The team estimates that the ERP system should provide several benefits:

a. More efficient order processing should lead to savings of $185,000.

b. Streamlining the manufacturing process so that it maps into the ERP system will create savings of $255,000.

c. Integrating purchasing, production, marketing, and distribution into a single system will allow SeaSpray to reduce inventories, saving $215,000.

d. Higher customer satisfaction should increase sales, which, in turn, should increase profits by $165,000.

Requirements

1. If the ERP installation succeeds, what is the dollar amount of the benefits?

2. Should SeaSpray install the ERP system? Why or why not? Show your calculations.

3. Why did Raney create a team to evaluate JT's proposal? Consider each piece of cost-benefit information that management accountant Cobalt reported. Which person on the team is most likely to have contributed each item? (*Hint:* Which team member is likely to have the most information about each cost or benefit?)

P1-30B   E-commerce cost-benefit analysis *(Learning Objective 5)*

Star Gas wants to move its sales order system to the Internet. Under the proposed system, gas stations and other merchants will use a secure site to check the availability and current price of various products and place an order. Currently, customer service representatives take dealers' orders over the phone; they record the information on a paper form, then manually enter it into the firm's computer system.

CFO Carrie Smith believes that dealers will not adopt the new Internet system unless Star Gas provides financial assistance to help them purchase or upgrade their computer network. Smith estimates this one-time cost at $735,000. Star Gas will also have to invest $165,000 in upgrading its own computer hardware. The cost of the software and the consulting fee for installing the system will be $235,000. The Internet system will enable Star Gas to eliminate 25 clerical positions. Smith estimates that the new system's lower labor costs will have saved the company $1,210,000.

Requirement

Use a cost-benefit analysis to recommend to Smith whether Star Gas should proceed with the Internet-based ordering system. Give your reasons, showing supporting calculations.

P1-31B   Continuation of P1-30B: revised estimates *(Learning Objective 5)*

Consider the Star Gas proposed entry into the Internet-based ordering system in P1-30B. Smith revises her estimates of the benefits from the new system's lower labor costs. She now thinks the savings will be only $934,000.

Requirements

1. Compute the expected benefits of the Internet-based ordering system.
2. Would you recommend that Star Gas accept the proposal?
3. Before Smith makes a final decision, what other factors should she consider?

CRITICAL THINKING

Discussion & Analysis

A1-32 Discussion Questions

1. What are the three main areas of management's responsibility? How are these three areas interrelated? How does managerial accounting support each of the responsibility areas of managers?

2. What is the Sarbanes-Oxley Act of 2002 (SOX)? How does SOX affect financial accounting? How does SOX impact managerial accounting? Is there any overlap between financial and managerial accounting in terms of the SOX impact? If so, what are the areas of overlap?

3. Why is managerial accounting more suitable for internal reporting than financial accounting?

4. A company currently has all of its managerial accountants reporting to the controller. What might be inefficient about this organizational structure? How might the company restructure? What benefits would be offered by the restructuring?

5. What skills are required of a management accountant? In what college courses are these skills taught or developed? What skills would be further developed in the workplace?

6. What is the Institute of Management Accountants (IMA)? How could being a member of a professional organization help a person's career?

7. How might a Certified Management Accountant (CMA) certification benefit a person in his or her career? How does the CMA certification differ from the Certified Public Accountant (CPA) certification? What skills are assessed on the CMA exam?

8. What are the four ethical standards in the Institute of Management Accountants' *Statement of Ethical Professional Practice*? Describe the meaning of each of the four standards. How does each of these standards impact planning, directing, and controlling?

9. How has technology changed the work of management accountants? What other business trends are influencing managerial accounting today? How do these other trends impact management accountants' roles in the organization?

10. What significant regulatory trends are impacting accounting in general today? How do these regulatory trends affect the field of managerial accounting?

11. The effect of sustainability on the planet (environment) is probably the most visible component of the triple bottom line. For a company with which you are familiar, list two examples of its sustainability efforts related to the planet.

12. One controversial area regarding sustainability is whether organizations should use their sustainability progress and activities in their advertising. Do you think a company should publicize its sustainability efforts? Why or why not?

Application & Analysis

Mini Cases

A1-33 Accountants and Their Jobs

Basic Discussion Questions

1. When you think of an accountant, whom do you picture? Do you personally know anyone (family member, friend, relative) whose chosen career is accounting? If so, does the person "fit" your description of an accountant or not?

2. Before reading this chapter, what did you picture accountants doing, day-in and day-out, at their jobs? From where did this mental picture come (e.g., movies, first accounting class, speaking with accountants, etc.)?

3. What skills are highly valued by employers? What does that tell you about "what accountants do" at their companies?

4. This chapter includes several quotes from accountants at Abbott Laboratories, Caterpillar, and U.S. West. After reading these quotes and from what you know about accountants, how would you describe the role/job responsibilities of accountants?

5. Many accounting majors start their careers in public accounting. Do you think most of them stay in public accounting? Discuss what you consider to be a typical career track for accounting majors.

6. If you are not an accounting major, how do the salaries of accountants compare with those of your chosen field? How do the opportunities compare (i.e., demand for accountants)?

A1-34 Ethics at Enron

Watch the movie *Enron: The Smartest Guys in the Room* (Magnolia Home Entertainment, 2005, Los Angeles, California).

Basic Discussion Questions

1. Do you think such behavior is common at other companies or do you think this was a fairly isolated event?

2. How important is the "tone at the top" (the tone set by company leadership)?

3. Do you think you could be tempted to follow along if the leadership at your company had the same mentality as the leadership at Enron, or do you think you would have the courage to "just say no" or even be a "whistle-blower"?

4. Why do you think some people can so easily justify (at least to themselves) their unethical behavior?

5. In general, do you think people stop to think about how their actions will affect other people (e.g., the elderly in California who suffered due to electricity blackouts) or do they just "do their job"?

6. What was your reaction to the psychology experiment shown in the DVD? Studies have shown that unlike the traders at Enron (who received large bonuses), most employees really have very little to gain from following a superior's directive to act unethically. Why then do some people do it?

7. Do you think people weigh the potential costs of acting unethically with the potential benefits?

8. You are a business student and will someday work for company or own a business. How will watching this movie impact the way you intend to conduct yourself as an employee or owner?

9. The reporter from *Fortune* magazine asked the question, "How does Enron make its money?" Why should every employee and manager (at every company) know the answer to this question?

10. In light of the "mark-to-market" accounting that enabled Enron to basically record any profit it wished to record, can you understand why some of the cornerstones of financial accounting are "conservatism" and "recording transactions at historical cost"?

11. How did employees of Enron (and employees of the utilities company in Oregon) end up losing billions in retirement funds?

A1-35 Interviewing a local company about sustainability *(Learning Objective 5)*

In this project, you will be conducting an interview about sustainability efforts at a local organization. Find a local company or organization with which you are familiar. Arrange an interview with a manager from that organization. Before the interview, do a search on the Internet about sustainability efforts of companies in that same industry so that you can ask related questions. Use the following questions to start your interview; add relevant questions related to what you discover through your Internet search about sustainability efforts at similar companies. After the interview, write up a report of what you found during the interview. Conclude your report with your overall assessment of that organization's sustainability efforts.

1. What is the company's primary product or service? (*Note:* You should be able to answer this question BEFORE your interview.)

2. Does your company have a stated policy on sustainability? (Note: The company might refer to "green" practices or use some other similar term rather than using the exact term of "sustainability.") What is the policy?

3. How would this manager define "sustainability"? Is the manager's definition similar to the definition of "sustainability" in this chapter?

4. Regardless of whether the company has a sustainability policy or not, what sustainability efforts does the company make with respect to the environment? For example, does the company recycle its waste? What specific types of waste are recycled? Does the company purchase recycled-content products?

5. Is the amount (or percentage) of waste that is recycled tracked in a reporting system? Who gets reports on the organization's recycling efforts?

6. How does the company measure its impact on the environment (if it does)? (For example, does it measure its carbon footprint in total? Does it measure the carbon footprint of individual projects?)

7. Does the company do any external reporting of sustainability? If so, how long has the company been reporting on its sustainability efforts? If the company does not do any sustainability reporting at the current time, does it anticipate starting to report on its sustainability efforts in the near future?

8. In the manger's opinion, is sustainability important within that organization's industry? Why or why not?

ETHICS

A1-36 Ethics and casual conversations *(Learning Objective 4)*

Jane is an accountant at Merelix, a large international firm where she works on potential acquisitions. When Merelix is preparing to acquire a company, Jane is involved in filing the necessary paperwork with the Securities and Exchange Commission (SEC).

Jane has been dating Tom for two years; they are now discussing marriage. Tom works as a salesperson for a golf equipment distributor.

Over the past two years, Jane has talked with Tom about what she's doing at work. She does not go into great detail, but does occasionally mention company names. Jane has given her phone passcode to Tom so he can answer calls for her or look things up for her when she's the one driving. Tom has read some of her emails by using the phone passcode. He has also eavesdropped on a few phone conversations she has had when a colleague calls her from work with a question.

Unbeknownst to Jane, Tom has been sharing the information he has gotten from her with his stockbroker friend, Allen. Tom will call Allen to give him a "heads up" that Jane's company is going to be acquiring another company soon. Allen will then place an order to buy the stock of the company and will later split the profits with Tom.

Jane has not shared any information intentionally, nor has she directly profited from it.

Requirements

Using the IMA Statement of Ethical Professional Practice as an ethical framework, answer the following questions:

1. What is (are) the ethical issue(s) in this situation?

2. What are Jane's responsibilities as a management accountant?

3. Has Jane violated any part of the IMA Statement of Ethical Professional Practice? Support your answer.

A1-37 Using managerial accounting information to manage a Broadway production *(Learning Objectives 1 and 2)*

The Shubert Organization operates 20 theatres, including 17 on Broadway. It has brought hundreds of shows to Broadway over the decades, including *The Phantom of the Opera*, *Cats*, and *Les Miserables*. Several of its shows have been in the news in recent years including:

Mamma Mia!

In 2013, the Broadway musical *Mamma Mia!* moved from the Winter Garden Theatre to the Broadhurst Theatre, both of which are on Broadway in New York City. *Mamma Mia!* will save up to $100,000 per week[1] in operating costs due to the Broadhurst's smaller size; the Broadhurst seats 1,160, while the Winter Garden seats 1,530. Theatre experts estimate the show's weekly costs to be approximately $600,000 to $700,000, and its weekly ticket sales are usually in the mid- to high-six-figure range.

Once

Once is a Tony Award–winning show on Broadway also produced by the Shubert Organization. *Once* is a musical about the story of an Irish musician and a Czech immigrant who are drawn together by their shared love of music. *Once* opened on Broadway in March 2012. The show earned back the amount that the Shubert Organization had invested in it after just 21 weeks (169 performances).[2] The show continues its run on Broadway.

---

[1] "'Mamma Mia!' to Move," *The New York Times*, April 18, 2013, retrieved from http://artsbeat.blogs.nytimes.com/2013/04/18/mamma-mia-to-move/?_r=0 on July 1, 2013.

[2] "'Once' is a Hit!," August 13, 2013, retrieved from http://www.shubertorganization.com/organization/news/article.asp?id=48 on July 1, 2013.

Memphis

Another Shubert-produced musical, *Memphis*, is loosely based on the story of a Memphis disc jockey (DJ) who was one of the first white DJs to play black music in the 1950s. *Memphis* was composed by David Bryan, the keyboard player of the band Bon Jovi. The show opened on Broadway in the Shubert Theatre in October 2009 and won several awards, including four Tony Awards. The Shubert Organization had planned to run M*emphis* through November 2012, but closed the show in August 2012 because ticket revenues could not support the longer run. Instead of finding another show to use the Shubert Theatre between August 2012 and April 2013, when the show M*atilda* was scheduled to open, the Shubert Organization decided to use the time to renovate the theatre.

Questions

1. For each show that the Shubert Organization produces, what type of financial accounting information would be generated or recorded?

2. What information would producers of *Mamma Mia!* have needed to make the decision to move the show to a different theatre? What information would be provided by the financial accounting system? What information would be provided by the management accounting system?

3. What information would the producers of O*nce* have needed to calculate that the original investment of the show had been earned? What information would producers need to decide to keep the show open? What information would be provided by the financial accounting system? What information would be provided by the management accounting system?

4. What information would the producers of M*emphis* have needed to decide to close the show early? What information would the Shubert Organization management have needed to decide to renovate the theatre rather than produce another show after *Memphis* closed its run? What information would be provided by the financial accounting system? What information would be provided by the management accounting system?

Try It Solutions

page 10:

1. True
2. False. Management accounting is geared toward helping internal managers run the company efficiently and effectively.
3. True
4. True
5. True
6. False. Management accountants must be able to effectively communicate with people throughout the organization. As a result, they need to have strong oral and written communication skills.
7. True
8. False. The IMA (Institute of Management Accountants) issues the CMA certification. However, the AICPA has recently instituted the CGMA designation for qualified CPAs who have experience in business and industry.

page 24:

1. True
2. False. Currently, publicly traded U.S. companies must adhere to U.S. GAAP, not IFRS.
3. True
4. True
5. False. Service makes up the largest sector of the U.S. economy, although manufacturing is currently experiencing a U.S. renaissance.
6. False. Globalization has several significant implications for management accounting.
7. False. These types of systems are known as enterprise resource planning (ERP) systems.
8. True
9. False. The ISO 9001:2008 certification focuses on quality management.

Building Blocks of Managerial Accounting

Learning Objectives

Dreamstime

Sources: Toyota.com, 2012 and 2008
Annual Reports.

■ **1** Distinguish among service, merchandising, and manufacturing companies

■ **2** Describe the value chain and its elements

■ **3** Distinguish between direct and indirect costs

■ **4** Identify the inventoriable product costs and period costs of merchandising and manufacturing firms

■ **5** Prepare the financial statements for service, merchandising, and manufacturing companies

■ **6** Describe costs that are relevant and irrelevant for decision making

■ **7** Classify costs as fixed or variable and calculate total and average costs at different volumes

Building on the success of the iconic Prius, Toyota continues to

develop new vehicles that "redefine what it means to be environmentally considerate." Toyota's use of solar energy and waste-water recycling at its plants has not only decreased the harmful environmental consequences related to manufacturing but also reduced energy costs and improved productivity. To understand whether these "green" investments are worth it, Toyota's managers need to understand costs across all business functions. They also need to consider which costs should be *increased* and which costs should be *reduced*. For example, by spending *more* money on green technologies, product quality, production efficiency and safety improvements, Toyota has increased its market share, decreased warranty and liability costs, and saved over $1.19 billion in one year. In this chapter, we discuss costs incurred by many different internal business functions: costs that both managers and management accountants must understand to successfully run a business.

So far, we have seen how managerial accounting provides information that managers use to run their businesses more efficiently. Managers must understand basic managerial accounting terms and concepts before they can use the information to make good decisions. This terminology provides the "common ground" through which managers and accountants communicate. Without a common understanding of these concepts, managers may ask for (and accountants may provide) the wrong information for making decisions. As you will see, different types of costs are useful for different purposes. Both managers and accountants must have a clear understanding of the types of costs that are relevant to the decision at hand.

What are the Most Common Business Sectors and Their Activities?

Before we talk about specific types of costs, let's consider the three most common types of companies and the business activities they perform.

Service, Merchandising, and Manufacturing Companies

Recall from Chapter 1 that many companies are beginning to adhere to the notion of a **triple bottom line**, in which the company's performance is evaluated not only in terms of profitability, but also in terms of its impact on people and the planet. Even so, for a business to flourish and grow in the long run, it will need to generate economic profits that are sufficiently large enough to attract and retain investors, as well as fuel future expansion of operations. Companies typically generate profit through one of three basic business models: they provide a service, they sell merchandise, or they manufacture products.

1 Distinguish among service, merchandising, and manufacturing companies

Service Companies

Service companies are in business to sell intangible services—such as health care, insurance, banking, and consulting—rather than tangible products. Recall from the last chapter that service firms now make up the largest sector of the U.S. economy. Because these types of companies sell services, they generally don't have inventory. Some service providers carry a minimal amount of supplies inventory; however, this inventory is generally used for internal operations—not sold for profit. Service companies incur costs to provide services, develop new services, advertise, and provide customer service. For many service providers, salaries and benefits make up over 70% of their costs.

Merchandising Companies

Merchandising companies such as Walmart and Best Buy resell tangible products they buy from suppliers. For example, Walmart buys clothing, toys, and electronics and resells them to customers at higher prices than what it pays its own suppliers for these goods. Merchandising companies include retailers (such as Walmart) and wholesalers. **Retailers** sell to consumers like you and me. **Wholesalers**, often referred to as "middlemen," buy products in bulk from manufacturers, mark up the prices, and then sell those products to retailers.

Because merchandising companies sell tangible products, they have inventory. The cost of inventory includes the cost merchandisers pay for the goods *plus* all costs necessary to get the merchandise in place and ready to sell, such as freight-in costs and any import duties or tariffs. A merchandiser's balance sheet has just one inventory account called "Inventory" or "Merchandise Inventory." Besides incurring inventory-related costs, merchandisers also incur costs to operate their retail stores and websites, advertise, research new products and new store locations, and provide customer service.

Manufacturing Companies

Manufacturing companies use labor, plant, and equipment to convert raw materials into new finished products. For example, Toyota converts steel, tires, and fabric into high-performance vehicles using production labor and advanced manufacturing equipment. The vehicles are then sold to car dealerships at a price that is high enough to cover costs and generate a profit.

As shown in Exhibit 2-1, manufacturers carry three types of inventory:

1. <u>Raw materials inventory</u>: *All raw materials used in manufacturing.* Toyota's raw materials include steel, glass, tires, upholstery fabric, engines, and other automobile components. They also include other physical materials used in the plant, such as machine lubricants and janitorial supplies.

2. <u>Work in process inventory</u>: *Goods that are partway through the manufacturing process but not yet complete.* At Toyota, the work in process inventory consists of partially completed vehicles.

3. <u>Finished goods inventory</u>: *Completed goods that have not yet been sold.* Toyota is in business to sell completed cars, not work in process. Once the vehicles are completed, they are no longer considered work in process, but rather they become part of finished goods inventory.

EXHIBIT 2-1 Manufacturers' Three Types of Inventory

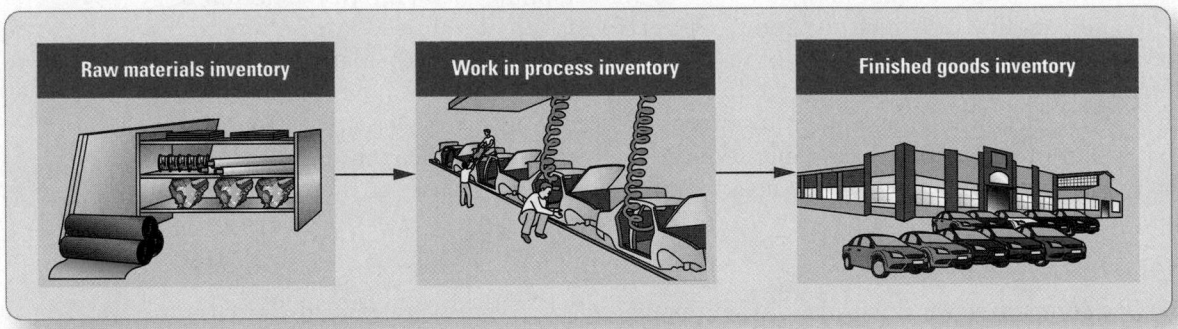

Exhibit 2-2 summarizes the differences among service, merchandising, and manufacturing companies.

EXHIBIT 2-2 Service, Merchandising, and Manufacturing Companies

	Service Companies	Merchandising Companies	Manufacturing Companies
Examples	Advertising agencies	Amazon.com	Procter & Gamble
	Banks	Best Buy	General Mills
	Law firms	Walmart	Dell Computer
	Insurance companies	Wholesalers	Toyota
Primary Output	Intangible services	Tangible products purchased from suppliers	New tangible products made using raw materials, labor, and production equipment
Type(s) of Inventory	None	Inventory (or Merchandise Inventory)	Raw materials inventory Work in process inventory Finished goods inventory

STOP & THINK

What type of company is Outback Steakhouse, Inc.?

Answer: Some companies don't fit nicely into one of the three categories discussed previously. Restaurants are usually considered to be in the service sector. However, Outback has some elements of a service company (it serves hungry patrons), some elements of a manufacturing company (its chefs convert raw ingredients into finished meals), and some elements of a merchandising company (it sells ready-to-serve bottles of wine and beer).

As the "Stop & Think" shows, not all companies are strictly service, merchandising, or manufacturing firms. Recall from Chapter 1 that the U.S. economy is shifting more toward service. Many traditional manufacturers, such as General Electric (GE), have developed profitable service segments that provide much of their company's profits. Even merchandising firms are getting into the "service game" by selling extended-warranty contracts on merchandise sold. Retailers offer extended warranties on products ranging from furniture and major appliances to sporting equipment and consumer electronics. While the merchandiser recognizes a liability for these warranties, the price charged to customers for the warranties greatly exceeds the company's cost of fulfilling its warranty obligations, thus providing additional profit to the merchandiser.

Which Business Activities Make up the Value Chain?

Many people describe Toyota, General Mills, and Dell as manufacturing companies. But it would be more accurate to say that these are companies that *do* manufacturing. Why? Because companies that do manufacturing also do many other things. Toyota also conducts research to determine what type of new technology to integrate into next year's models. Toyota designs the new models based on its research and then produces, markets, distributes, and services the cars. These activities form Toyota's **value chain**—the activities that add value to the company's products and services. The value chain is pictured in Exhibit 2-3.

> ### Why is this important?
>
> "All employees should have an **understanding** of their company's basic business model. The **Enron scandal** was finally brought to light as a **result** of someone seriously asking, "How does this company actually **make money**?" If the business model does not make **logical sense**, something fishy may be going on."

EXHIBIT 2-3 The Value Chain

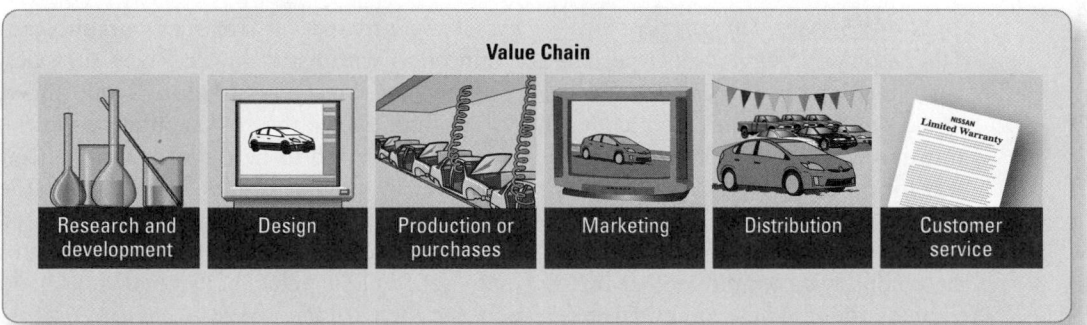

The value chain activities also cost money. To set competitive, yet profitable selling prices, Toyota must consider all of the costs incurred along the value chain, not just the costs incurred in manufacturing vehicles. Let's briefly consider some of the costs incurred in each element of the value chain.[1]

2 Describe the value chain and its elements

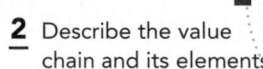

[1] Toyota Motor Corp. 2012 Annual Report.

<u>Research and Development (R&D)</u>: *Researching and developing new or improved products or services and the processes for producing them.* Toyota continually engages in researching and developing new technologies to incorporate in its vehicles (such as fuel cells and pre-crash safety systems) and in its manufacturing plants (such as environmentally friendly and efficient manufacturing robotics). In 2012, Toyota spent 779 million yen (approximately $8.1 million) on R&D.

<u>Design</u>: *Detailed engineering of products and services and the processes for producing them.* Toyota's goal is to design vehicles that create total customer satisfaction, including satisfaction with vehicle style, features, safety, and quality. As a result, Toyota updates the design of older models (such as the Corolla) and designs new prototypes (such as the new ultra-energy-efficient, zero-emission "iQ" model) on a regular basis. Part of the design process also includes determining how to mass-produce the vehicles. Because Toyota produces over 7 million vehicles per year, engineers must design production plants that are efficient, yet flexible enough to allow for new features and models.

<u>Production or Purchases</u>: *Resources used to produce a product or service or to purchase finished merchandise intended for resale.* For Toyota, the production activity includes all costs incurred to *make* the vehicles. These costs include raw materials (such as steel), plant labor (such as machine operators' wages), and manufacturing overhead (such as factory utilities and depreciation). As you can imagine, factories are very expensive to build and operate.

For a merchandiser such as Best Buy, this value chain activity includes the cost of purchasing the inventory that the company plans to sell to customers. It also includes all costs associated with getting the inventory to the store, including freight-in costs and any import duties and tariffs that might be incurred if the merchandise was purchased from overseas.

<u>Marketing</u>: *Promotion and advertising of products or services.* The goal of marketing is to create consumer demand for products and services. Toyota uses print advertisements in magazines and newspapers, billboards, television commercials, and the internet to market its vehicles. Some companies use star athletes and sporting events to market their products. Each method of advertising costs money, but adds value by reaching different target customers.

<u>Distribution</u>: *Delivery of products or services to customers.* Toyota sells most of its vehicles through traditional dealerships. However, more customers are ordering "build-your-own" vehicles through Toyota's website. Toyota's distribution costs include the costs of shipping the vehicles to retailers and the costs of administering Web-based sales portals. Other industries use different distribution mechanisms, such as catalog sales, brick-and-mortar retail locations, and home-based parties.

<u>Customer Service</u>: *Support provided for customers after the sale.* Toyota incurs substantial customer service costs, especially in connection with warranties on new car sales. Toyota generally warranties its vehicles for the first three years and/or 36,000 miles, whichever comes first. Historically, Toyota has had one of the best reputations in the auto industry for excellent quality. However, 2010 proved to be a costly and difficult year for the company, as recalls were made on over 14 million vehicles. In addition to the cost of repairing the vehicles, the company incurred millions of dollars in costs related to government fines, lawsuits, and public relations campaigns. However, as a result of the company's commitment to building safe and reliable vehicles, Toyota once again regained the title of the number-one carmaker in the world in 2012.

Coordinating Activities Across the Value Chain

Many of the value chain activities occur in the order discussed here. However, managers cannot simply work on R&D and not think about customer service until after selling the car. Rather, cross-functional teams work on R&D, design, production, marketing, distribution, and customer service simultaneously. As the teams develop new model features, they also plan how to produce, market, and distribute the redesigned vehicles. They also consider how the new design will affect warranty costs. Recall from the last chapter that management accountants typically participate in these cross-functional teams. Even at the highest level of global operations, Toyota uses cross-functional teams to implement its business goals and strategy.

The value chain pictured in Exhibit 2-3 also reminds managers to control costs over the value chain as a whole. For example, Toyota spends more in R&D and product design to increase the quality of its vehicles, which in turn reduces customer service costs. Even though R&D and design costs are higher, the total cost of the vehicle—as measured throughout the entire value chain—is lower as a result of this trade-off. Enhancing its reputation for high-quality products has also enabled Toyota to increase its market share and charge a slightly higher selling price than some of its competitors.

 Why is this important?

"All activities in the **value chain** are important, yet each costs **money** to perform. Managers must understand how **decisions** made in one area of the value chain will **affect the costs** incurred in other areas of the value chain."

Sustainability and the Value Chain

Progressive companies will incorporate sustainability throughout every function of the value chain. However, experts estimate that 90% of sustainability occurs at the design stage. At the design stage, companies determine how the product will be used by customers, how easily the product can be repaired or eventually recycled, and the types of raw materials and manufacturing processes necessary to produce the product. Thus, good design is essential to the creation of environmentally friendly, safe products that enhance people's lives. For example, companies can integrate sustainability throughout the value chain by:

See Exercises E2-20A and E2-32B

- *Researching and developing environmentally safe packaging.* In 2011, PepsiCo unveiled its new "plant bottle" made entirely out of plant by-products, such as potato skins, oat hulls, orange peels, and corn husks that are left over from processing its other products, such as Frito-Lay snacks and Tropicana orange juice. In contrast, typical plastic beverage containers are made out of PET, which is an oil-based product that requires the use of fossil fuels.

- *Designing the product using life-cycle assessment and biomimicry practices.* <u>Life-cycle assessment</u> means the company analyzes the environmental impact of a product, from cradle to grave, in an attempt to minimize negative environmental consequences throughout the entire lifespan of the product. For example, after studying the life cycles of its products, Proctor & Gamble (P&G) discovered that about three-quarters of the energy used by consumers in washing their clothes comes from heating the water. As a result, the company developed Coldwater Tide, which is effective for laundering in cold water, thereby conserving energy. This product is a win-win for the environment and the company: the product is saving energy while also generating $150 million in annual sales revenue for P&G.[2]

  <u>Biomimicry</u> means that a company tries to mimic, or copy, the natural biological process in which dead organisms (plants and animals) become the input for another organism or process. Ricoh's copiers were designed so that at the end of a copier's useful life, Ricoh will collect and dismantle the product for usable parts, shred the metal casing, and use the parts and shredded material to build new copiers. The entire copier was designed so that nothing is wasted, or thrown out, except the dust from the shredding process.

- *Adopting sustainable purchasing practices.* Many companies, such as Walmart, are now actively assessing the sustainability level of their potential suppliers as a

---

[2]http://www.nytimes.com/2011/09/17/business/cold-water-detergents-get-a-chilly-reception
.html?pagewanted=1&_r=0

determining factor in selecting suppliers. As the leading retailer in the world, Walmart's own purchasing policies are forcing other companies to adopt more sustainable practices. Likewise, in order to reduce energy consumption and greenhouse gas emissions, companies can work toward purchasing raw materials from suppliers that are geographically nearby, rather than sourcing from distant places.

■ *Marketing with integrity.* Consumers are driving much of the sustainability movement by demanding that companies produce environmentally friendly products and limit or eliminate operational practices that have a negative impact on the environment. The lifestyles of the healthy and sustainable (LOHAS) market segment is estimated at $290 billion per year. Thus, many companies are successfully spotlighting their sustainability initiatives in order to increase market share as well as attract potential investors and employees. However, **greenwashing**, the unfortunate practice of *overstating* a company's commitment to sustainability, can ultimately backfire as investors and consumers learn the truth about company operations. Hence, honesty and integrity in marketing are imperative.

■ *Distributing using fossil-fuel alternatives and carbon offsets.* While the biofuel industry is still in its infancy, the production and use of biofuels, especially those generated from non-food waste, are expected to grow exponentially in the near future. Companies whose business is heavily reliant upon fossil fuels, such as oil companies (Valero), airlines (United), and distribution companies (UPS), are especially interested in the development of fuel sources, as limited oil reserves coupled with global demand put a squeeze on fuel prices. In fact, many companies, such as UPS and Walmart, are investing in hybrid fleets in order to reduce energy consumption, which thereby reduces their costs. In addition, United Airlines offers a carbon-offset program that allows companies and consumers to calculate the carbon emissions resulting from their air travel and air-freighting activities. The customer has an option of purchasing carbon offsets (reforestation projects, renewable energy projects, etc.) to mitigate the emissions resulting from shipping and travel.

■ *Providing customer service past the warranty date.* Currently, the average life of many home appliances such as dishwashers and refrigerators is less than 10 years. However, the original manufacturer could provide valuable customer service, prevent appliances from ending up in landfills, while at the same time creating a new revenue stream by offering reasonably priced repair services for products that have exceeded the warranty date. For those products that are not repairable, the company could institute a policy such as Ricoh's, in which the company takes back the old product and recycles it into new products.

How do Companies Define Cost?

Now that you understand the most common types of companies and the activities they perform, let's consider some of the specialized language that accountants use when referring to costs.

3 Distinguish between direct and indirect costs

Cost Objects, Direct Costs, and Indirect Costs

A **cost object** is anything for which managers want a separate measurement of cost. Toyota's cost objects may include the following:

■ Individual units (a specific, custom-ordered Prius)

■ Different models (the Prius, Rav4, and Corolla)

■ Alternative marketing strategies (sales through dealers versus built-to-order Web sales)

- Geographic segments of the business (United States, Europe, Japan)
- Departments (human resources, R&D, legal)
- A "green" initiative (developing fuel cells)

Costs are classified as either direct or indirect with respect to the cost object. A <u>direct cost</u> is a cost that can be traced to the cost object. For example, say the cost object is one Prius. Toyota can trace the cost of tires to a specific Prius; therefore, the tires are a direct cost of the vehicle. An <u>indirect cost</u> is a cost that relates to the cost object but cannot be traced to it. For example, Toyota incurs substantial cost to run a manufacturing plant, including utilities, property taxes, and depreciation. Toyota cannot build a Prius without incurring these costs, so the costs are related to the Prius. However, it's impossible to trace a specific amount of these costs to one Prius. Therefore, these costs are considered indirect costs of a single Prius.

As shown in Exhibit 2-4, the same costs can be indirect with respect to one cost object yet direct with respect to another cost object. For example, plant depreciation, property taxes, and utilities are indirect costs of a single Prius. However, if management wants to know how much it costs to operate the Prius manufacturing plant, the plant becomes the cost object; so the same depreciation, tax, and utility costs are direct costs of the manufacturing facility. Whether a cost is direct or indirect depends on the specified cost object. In this chapter, we'll be talking about a unit of product (such as one Prius) as the cost object.

If a company wants to know the *total* cost attributable to a cost object, it must <u>assign</u> all direct *and* indirect costs to the cost object. Assigning a cost simply means that you are "attaching" a cost to the cost object. For example, if Toyota wants to know the entire cost of manufacturing a Prius, it will need to assign both direct costs (such as the tires on the car) and indirect costs (such as factory utilities) to the vehicle.

Toyota assigns direct costs to each Prius by <u>tracing</u> those costs to specific vehicles. This results in a very precise cost figure, giving managers great confidence in the cost's accuracy. However, Toyota cannot trace indirect cost, such as utilities, to specific vehicles. Therefore, Toyota must <u>allocate</u> these indirect costs among all of the vehicles produced at the plant. The allocation process results in a less precise

■ Why is this important?

"As a manager **making decisions**, you'll need different types of **cost information** for different types of decisions. To get the **information** you really want, you'll have to **communicate** with the accountants using precise **definitions** of cost."

EXHIBIT 2-4 The Same Cost Can Be Direct or Indirect, Depending on the Cost Object

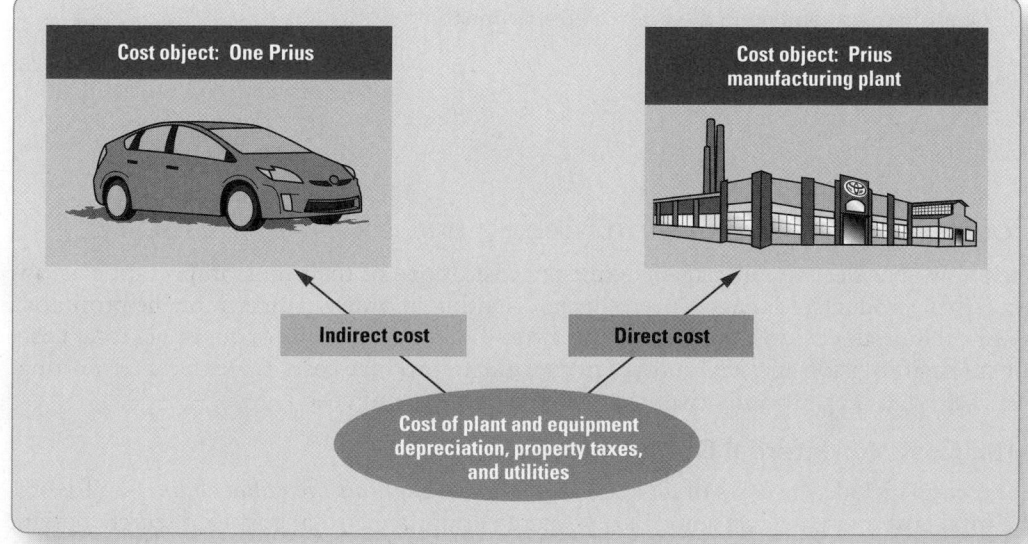

cost figure being assigned to each vehicle. We will discuss the allocation process in more detail in the following two chapters; but for now, think of allocation as dividing up the total indirect costs over all of the units produced, just as you might divide a pizza among friends. Exhibit 2-5 illustrates these concepts.

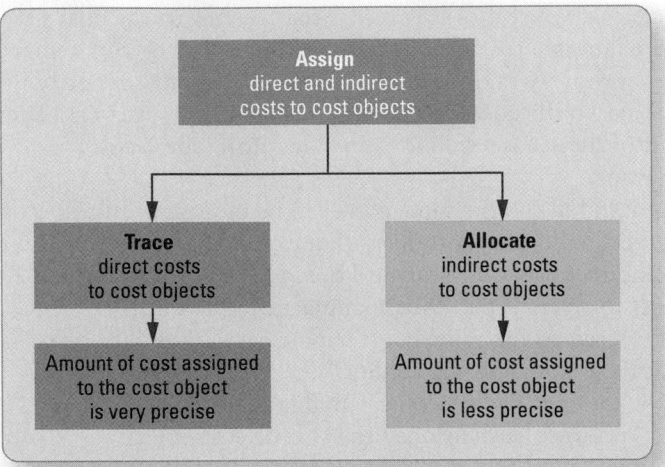

EXHIBIT 2-5 Assigning Direct and Indirect Costs to Cost Objects

Try It!

Assume a grocery store manager wants to know the cost of running the Produce Department. Thus, the Produce Department is the cost object. Which of the following would be considered direct costs of the Produce Department?

1. Wages of checkout clerks
2. Wages for workers in the Produce Department
3. Depreciation on refrigerated produce display cases
4. Cost of weekly advertisements in local newspaper
5. Cost of bananas, lettuce, and other produce
6. Baggies and twist ties available for shoppers in the Produce Department
7. Monthly lease payment for grocery store retail location
8. Cost of scales hanging in the Produce Department

Please see page 101 for solutions.

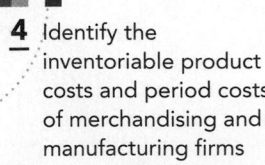

4 Identify the inventoriable product costs and period costs of merchandising and manufacturing firms

Costs for Internal Decision Making and External Reporting

Let's now consider how managers define the cost of one of their most important cost objects: their products. Managers need this information in order to determine the profitability of each product. Most companies use two different definitions of costs: (1) total costs for internal decision making and (2) inventoriable product costs for external reporting. Let's see what they are and how managers use each type of cost.

Total Costs for Internal Decision Making

<u>Total costs</u> include the costs of *all resources used throughout the value chain*. For Toyota, the total cost of a particular model, such as the Prius, is the total cost to research, design,

manufacture, market, distribute, and service that model. Before launching a new model, managers predict the total costs of the model to set a selling price that will cover *all costs* plus return a profit. Toyota also compares each model's sale revenue to its total cost to determine which models are most profitable. Perhaps Rav4s are more profitable than Corollas. Marketing can then focus on advertising and promoting the most profitable models. We'll talk more about total costs in Chapter 8, where we discuss many common business decisions. For the next few chapters, we'll concentrate primarily on inventoriable product costs.

Inventoriable Product Costs for External Reporting

Generally Accepted Accounting Principles (GAAP) does not allow companies to use total costs to report inventory balances or cost of goods sold in the financial statements. For external reporting, GAAP allows only a *portion* of the total cost to be treated as an inventoriable product cost. GAAP specifies which costs are inventoriable product costs and which costs are not. **Inventoriable product costs** include *only* the costs incurred during the "production or purchases" stage of the value chain. Inventoriable product costs are treated as an asset (inventory) until the product is sold. Hence the name "inventoriable" product cost. When the product is sold, these costs are removed from inventory and expensed as cost of goods sold. Since inventoriable product costs include only costs incurred during the production stage of the value chain for manufacturers, and the purchases stage of the value chain for merchandising companies, all costs incurred in the *other* stages of the value chain must be expensed in the period in which they are incurred. Therefore, we refer to R&D, design, marketing, distribution, and customer service costs as **period costs**. Keep the following important rule of thumb in mind:

Period costs are often called "operating expenses" or "selling, general, and administrative expenses" (SG&A) on the company's income statement. Period costs are *always* expensed in the period in which they are incurred and *never* become part of an inventory account.

Exhibit 2-6 shows that a company's total cost has two components: inventoriable product costs (those costs treated as part of inventory until the product is sold) and period

EXHIBIT 2-6 Total Costs, Inventoriable Product Costs, and Period Costs

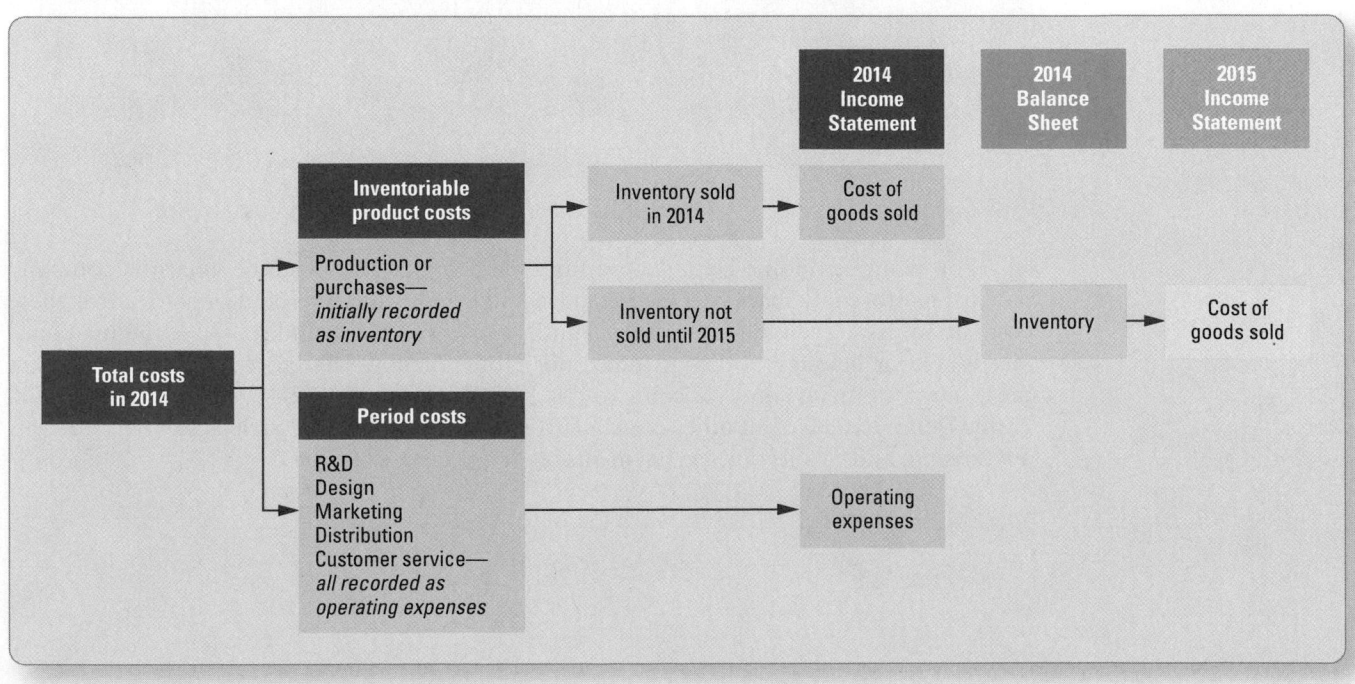

costs (those costs expensed in the current period regardless of when inventory is sold). GAAP requires this distinction for external financial reporting. Study the exhibit carefully to make sure you understand how the two cost components affect the income statement and balance sheet.

Now that you understand the difference between inventoriable product costs and period costs, let's take a closer look at the specific costs that are inventoriable in merchandising and manufacturing companies.

Merchandising Companies' Inventoriable Product Costs

Merchandising companies' inventoriable product costs include *only* the cost of purchasing the inventory from suppliers plus any costs incurred to get the merchandise to the merchandiser's place of business and ready for sale. Typically, these additional costs include freight-in costs and import duties or tariffs, if the products were purchased from overseas. Why does the cost of the inventory include freight-in charges? Think of the last time you made a purchase from an online website, such as Amazon.com. The website may have shown the product's price as $15, but by the time you paid the shipping and handling charges, the product really cost you around $20. Likewise, merchandising companies pay freight-in charges to get the goods to their place of business. If they purchased the goods from overseas, there is a good chance they also had to pay import duties to bring the goods into the United States. As shown in Exhibit 2-7, these charges become part of the cost of their inventory.

EXHIBIT 2-7 Summary of Merchandising Companies' Costs

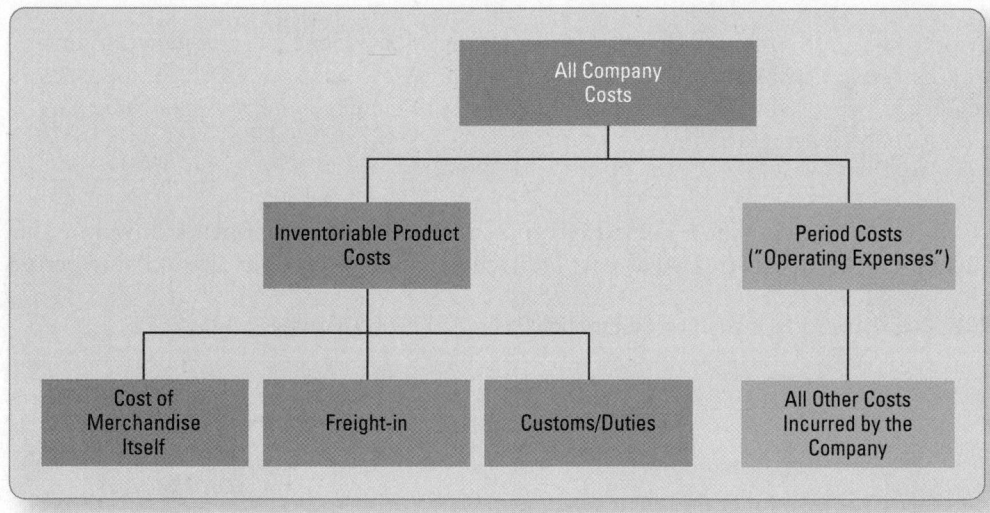

For example, Home Depot's inventoriable product costs include what the company paid for its store merchandise plus freight-in and import duties. Home Depot records these costs in an asset account—Inventory—until it *sells* the merchandise. Once the merchandise is sold, it belongs to the customer, not Home Depot. Therefore, Home Depot takes the cost out of its inventory account and records it as an expense—the *cost of goods sold*. Home Depot expenses all other costs incurred during the period, such as salaries, utilities, advertising, and property lease payments, as "operating expenses."

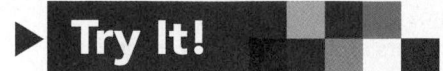

▶ Try It!

Which of the following costs are treated as inventoriable product costs by a *merchandising company*, such as Walmart? Which costs are treated as period costs?

1. Cost of leasing the retail locations
2. Cost of manager's and sales associates' salaries
3. Cost of merchandise purchased for resale
4. Cost of designing and operating the company's website
5. Cost of shipping merchandise to the store
6. Cost of providing free shipping to customers who buy product online
7. Cost of utilities used in running the retail locations
8. Cost of import duties paid on merchandise purchased from overseas suppliers
9. Depreciation on store shelving and shopping carts

Please see page 101 for solutions.

Manufacturing Companies' Inventoriable Product Costs

Manufacturing companies' inventoriable product costs include *only* those costs incurred in the production of the product. As shown in Exhibit 2-8, manufacturers such as Toyota incur three types of manufacturing costs when making a vehicle: direct materials, direct labor, and manufacturing overhead.

EXHIBIT 2-8 Summary of the Three Types of Manufacturing Costs

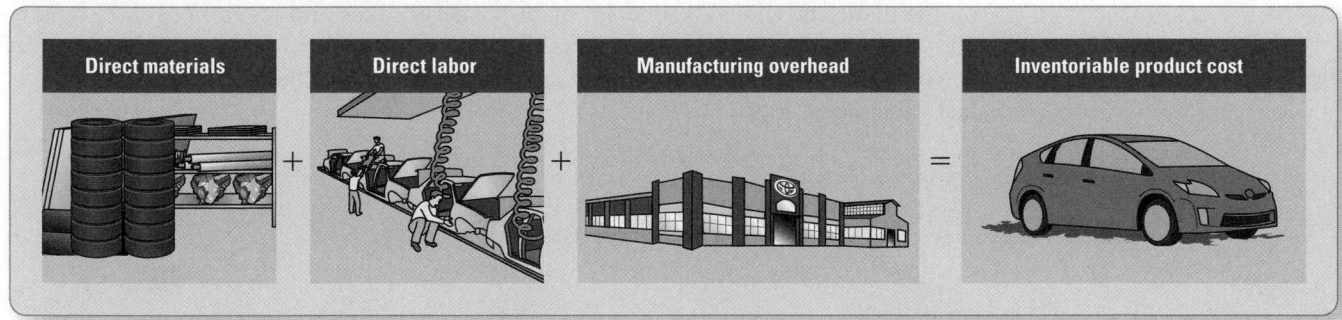

Direct Materials (DM)

Manufacturers convert raw materials into finished products. **Direct materials** are the *primary* materials that become a physical part of the finished product. The Prius's direct materials include steel, tires, engines, upholstery, carpet, dashboard instruments, and so forth. Toyota can trace the cost of these materials (including freight-in and import duties) to specific units or batches of vehicles; thus, they are considered direct costs of the vehicles.

Direct Labor (DL)

Although many manufacturing facilities are highly automated, most still require some direct labor to convert raw materials into a finished product. **Direct labor** is the cost of compensating employees who physically convert raw materials into the company's products.

At Toyota, direct labor includes the wages and benefits of machine operators and technicians who build and assemble completed vehicles. These costs are *direct* with respect to the cost object (the vehicle) because Toyota can *trace* the time each of these employees spends working on specific units or batches of vehicles.

Manufacturing Overhead (MOH)

The third production cost is manufacturing overhead. <u>**Manufacturing overhead**</u> *includes all manufacturing costs other than direct materials and direct labor.* In other words, manufacturing overhead includes *all indirect manufacturing costs.* Manufacturing overhead is also referred to as factory overhead because all of these costs relate to the factory. Manufacturing overhead has three components: indirect materials, indirect labor, and other indirect manufacturing costs.

- <u>**Indirect materials**</u> include materials used in the plant that are not easily traced to individual units. For example, indirect materials often include janitorial supplies, oil and lubricants for the machines, and any physical components of the finished product that are very inexpensive. For example, Toyota might treat the invoice sticker placed on each vehicle's window as an indirect material rather than a direct material. Even though the cost of the sticker (roughly 10 cents) *could* be traced to the vehicle, it wouldn't make much sense to do so. Why? Because the cost of tracing the sticker to the vehicle outweighs the benefit management receives from the increased accuracy of the information.

- <u>**Indirect labor**</u> includes the cost of all employees *in the plant* other than those employees directly converting the raw materials into the finished product. For example, at Toyota, indirect labor includes the salaries, wages, and benefits of plant forklift operators, plant security officers, plant janitors, and plant supervisors.

- <u>**Other indirect manufacturing costs**</u> include such *plant-related* costs as depreciation on the plant and plant equipment, plant property taxes and insurance, plant repairs and maintenance, and plant utilities. Indirect manufacturing costs have grown in recent years as manufacturers automate their plants with the latest advanced manufacturing technology.

Exhibit 2-9 summarizes how manufacturers classify their costs.

EXHIBIT 2-9 Summary of Manufacturing Companies' Costs

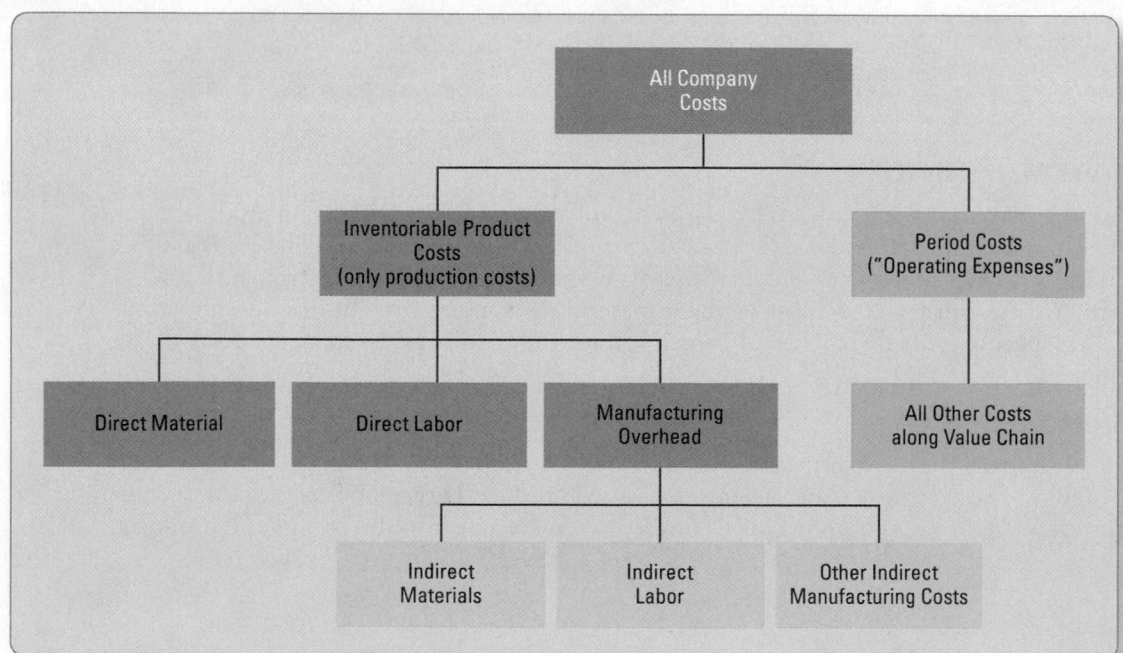

Prime and Conversion Costs

Managers and accountants sometimes talk about certain combinations of manufacturing costs. As shown in Exhibit 2-10, <u>prime costs</u> refer to the combination of direct materials and direct labor. Prime costs used to be the primary costs of production. However, as companies have automated production with expensive machinery, manufacturing overhead has become a greater cost of production. <u>Conversion costs</u> refer to the combination of direct labor and manufacturing overhead. These are the costs of *converting* raw materials into finished goods.

EXHIBIT 2-10 Prime and Conversion Costs

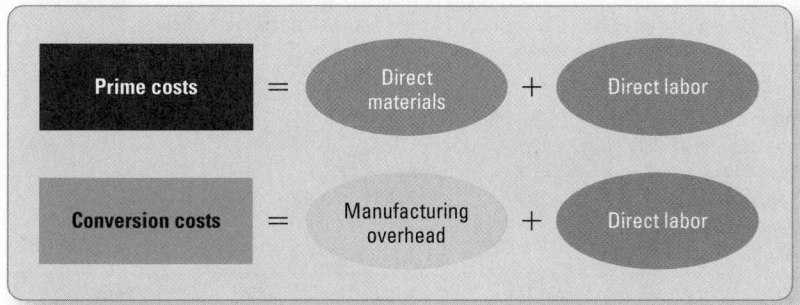

What is the difference between raw materials, direct materials, and indirect materials?

Raw materials are materials that have not yet been used. Once used, materials can be classified as direct or indirect. Direct materials are the primary physical components of a product. Indirect materials are materials used in the production plant that don't become part of the product (such as machine lubricants) or materials that do become part of the product, but are insignificant in cost (such as the price sticker on a car).

Additional Labor Compensation Costs

The cost of labor, in all areas of the value chain, includes more than the salaries and wages paid to employees. The cost also includes company-paid fringe benefits such as health insurance, retirement plan contributions, payroll taxes, and paid vacations. These costs are very expensive. Health insurance premiums, which have seen double-digit increases for many years, often amount to $500–$1,500 per month for each employee electing coverage. Many companies also contribute an amount equal to 3% to 6% of their employees' salaries to company-sponsored retirement 401(k) plans. Employers must pay Federal Insurance Contributions Act (FICA) payroll taxes to the federal government for Social Security and Medicare, amounting to 7.65% of each employee's gross pay. In addition, most companies offer paid vacation and other benefits. Together, these fringe benefits usually cost the company an *additional* 35% beyond gross salaries and wages. Thus, an employee making a $40,000 salary actually costs the company about $54,000 to employ ($40,000 × 1.35). These fringe-benefit costs are expensed as period costs for all non-manufacturing employees. However, they become part of the inventoriable product cost if they relate to employees working in the manufacturing plant. In Chapter 3 we'll discuss how these additional labor costs get assigned to products.

Recap: Inventoriable Product Costs Versus Period Costs

In this half of the chapter you have learned about the activities and costs incurred by three different types of companies. You have also learned the difference between direct and indirect costs. Finally, you have learned the difference between inventoriable product costs and period costs. Exhibit 2-11 summarizes some of these concepts for you.

EXHIBIT 2-11 Summary of Inventoriable Product Costs Versus Period Costs

	---------------------------------All Costs Across the Value Chain---------------------------------	
	Inventoriable Product Costs	**Period costs**
Service Companies	None	All costs across value chain
Merchandising Companies	Cost of merchandise itself Freight-in Import duties and customs, if any	All other costs across value chain
Manufacturing Companies	Direct materials Direct labor Manufacturing overhead	All other costs across value chain
Accounting Treatment	Treat as inventory until product is sold. When sold, expense as "Cost of Goods Sold."	Expense in period incurred as "Operating Expenses" or "Selling, General, and Administrative expenses."

Decision Guidelines

Building Blocks of Managerial Accounting

Dell engages in *manufacturing* when it assembles its computers, *merchandising* when it sells them on its website, and support *services* such as start-up and implementation services. Dell had to make the following types of decisions as it developed its accounting systems.

Decision	Guidelines

How do you distinguish among service, merchandising, and manufacturing companies? How do their balance sheets differ?	*Service companies:*
	• Provide customers with intangible services
	• Have no inventories on the balance sheet
	Merchandising companies:
	• Resell tangible products purchased ready-made from suppliers
	• Have only one category of inventory
	Manufacturing companies:
	• Use labor, plant, and equipment to transform raw materials into new finished products
	• Have three categories of inventory:
	  1. Raw materials inventory
	  2. Work in process inventory
	  3. Finished goods inventory

What business activities add value to companies?	All of the elements of the value chain, including the following: • R&D • Design • Production or purchases • Marketing • Distribution • Customer service
What costs should be assigned to cost objects such as products, departments, and geographic segments?	Both direct and indirect costs are assigned to cost objects. Direct costs are traced to cost objects, whereas indirect costs are allocated to cost objects.
Which product costs are useful for internal decision making, and which product costs are used for external reporting?	Managers use *total costs* for internal decision making. However, GAAP requires companies to use only *inventoriable product costs* for external financial reporting.
What costs are treated as inventoriable product costs under GAAP?	• *Service companies:* No inventoriable product costs • *Merchandising companies:* The cost of merchandise purchased for resale plus all of the costs of getting the merchandise to the company's place of business (for example, freight-in and import duties) • *Manufacturing companies:* Direct materials, direct labor, and manufacturing overhead
How are inventoriable product costs treated on the financial statements?	Inventoriable product costs are initially treated as assets (inventory) on the balance sheet. These costs are expensed (as cost of goods sold) on the income statements when the products are sold.

SUMMARY PROBLEM 1

Requirements

1. Classify each of the following business costs into one of the six value chain elements:

    a. Costs associated with warranties and recalls

    b. Cost of shipping finished goods to overseas customers

    c. Costs a pharmaceutical company incurs to develop new drugs

    d. Cost of a 30-second commercial during the SuperBowl™

    e. Cost of making a new product prototype

    f. Cost of assembly labor used in the plant

2. For a manufacturing company, identify the following as either an inventoriable product cost or a period cost. If it is an inventoriable product cost, classify it as direct materials, direct labor, or manufacturing overhead.

    a. Depreciation on plant equipment

    b. Depreciation on salespeoples' automobiles

    c. Insurance on plant building

    d. Marketing manager's salary

    e. Cost of major components of the finished product

    f. Assembly-line workers' wages

    g. Costs of shipping finished products to customers

    h. Forklift operator's salary

▪ SOLUTIONS

Requirement 1

a. Customer service

b. Distribution

c. Research and development

d. Marketing

e. Design

f. Production

Requirement 2

a. Inventoriable product cost; manufacturing overhead

b. Period cost

c. Inventoriable product cost; manufacturing overhead

d. Period cost

e. Inventoriable product cost; direct materials

f. Inventoriable product cost; direct labor

g. Period cost

h. Inventoriable product cost; manufacturing overhead

How are Inventoriable Product Costs and Period Costs Shown in the Financial Statements?

The difference between inventoriable product costs and period costs is important because these costs are treated differently in the financial statements. All inventoriable product costs remain in inventory accounts until the merchandise is sold—then, these costs become the cost of goods sold. On the other hand, all period costs are expensed as "operating expenses" in the period in which they are incurred. Keep these differences in mind as we review the income statements of service firms (which have no inventory), merchandising companies (which purchase their inventory), and manufacturers (which make their inventory). We'll finish the section by comparing the balance sheets of these three different types of companies.

5 Prepare the financial statements for service, merchandising, and manufacturing companies

Service Companies

Service companies have the simplest income statement. Exhibit 2-12 shows the income statement of eNow!, a group of e-commerce consultants. The firm has no inventory and thus, no inventoriable product costs. Therefore, eNow!'s income statement has no Cost of Goods Sold. Rather, all of the company's costs are period costs, so they are expensed in the current period as "operating expenses."

EXHIBIT 2-12 Service Company Income Statement

	A	B	C	D
1	eNOW!			
2	Income Statement			
3	Year Ended December 31			
4				
5	Revenues		$ 160,000	
6	Less operating expenses:			
7	Salary expense	$ 106,000		
8	Office rent expense	18,000		
9	Depreciation expense	3,500		
10	Marketing expense	2,500		
11	Total operating expenses		130,000	
12	Operating income		$ 30,000	
13				

In this textbook, we will always be evaluating the company's "operating income" rather than its "net income." Why? Because internal managers are particularly concerned with the income generated through the company's ongoing, primary operations. To arrive at net income, we would need to add or subtract non-operating income and expenses, such as interest, and subtract income taxes. In general, **operating income** is simply the company's earnings before interest and income taxes.

Merchandising Companies

In contrast with service companies, a merchandiser's income statement features Cost of Goods Sold as the major expense. Exhibit 2-13 illustrates the income statement for Wholesome Foods, a regional grocery store chain. Notice how Cost of Goods Sold is deducted from Sales Revenue to yield the company's gross profit. Next, all operating expenses (*all period costs*) are deducted to arrive at the company's operating income.

EXHIBIT 2-13 Merchandiser's Income Statement

	A	B	C	D
1	Wholesome Foods			
2	Income Statement			
3	For the Year Ended December 31			
4	(all figures shown in thousands of dollars)			
5				
6	Sales revenues		$ 150,000	
7	Less: Cost of goods sold		106,500	
8	Gross profit		$ 43,500	
9	Less operating expenses:			
10	Salaries and wages	$ 5,000		
11	Rent and utilities	3,000		
12	Marketing	1,000		
13	Total operating expenses		9,000	
14	Operating income		$ 34,500	
15				

But how does a merchandising company calculate the Cost of Goods Sold?

- Most likely, the company uses bar coding to implement a **perpetual inventory** system during the year. If so, all inventory is labeled with a unique bar code that reflects (1) the sales price that will be charged to the customer, and (2) the inventoriable cost of the merchandise to the store. Every time a bar-coded product is "scanned" at the checkout counter, the company's accounting records are automatically updated to reflect (1) the sales revenue earned, (2) the cost of goods sold, and (3) the removal of the product from merchandise inventory.

- However, at the end of the period, merchandisers must also calculate Cost of Goods Sold using the **periodic inventory** method. Why? Because the company's accounting records only reflect those products that were scanned during checkout. Thus, the records would not reflect any breakage, theft, input errors, or obsolescence that occurred during the year. Exhibit 2-14 shows how to calculate Cost of Goods Sold using the periodic method.

EXHIBIT 2-14 Calculation of Cost of Goods Sold for a Merchandising Firm

	A	B	C	D
1	Calculation of Cost of Goods Sold			
2	Beginning inventory	$ 9,500		
3	Plus: Purchases, freight-in, and any import duties	110,000		
4	Cost of goods available for sale	$ 119,500		
5	Less: Ending inventory	13,000		
6	Cost of goods sold	$ 106,500		
7				

In this calculation, we start with the beginning inventory and add to it all of the companies' *inventoriable product costs* for the period: the cost of the merchandise purchased from manufacturers or distributors, freight-in, and any import duties. The resulting total reflects the cost of all goods that were available for sale during the period. Then we subtract the cost of the products still in ending inventory to arrive at the Cost of Goods Sold.

▶ Try It!

Compute Cost of Goods Sold for Ralph's Sporting Goods, a merchandising company, given the following information:

Advertising expense	$ 25,000
Purchases of merchandise	400,000
Salaries expense	80,000
Freight-in and import duties	20,000
Lease of store	75,000
Beginning inventory	35,000
Ending inventory	38,000

Please see page 101 for solutions.

Manufacturing Companies

Exhibit 2-15 shows the income statement for Proquest, a manufacturer of tennis balls. As you can see, the income statement for a manufacturer is essentially identical to that of a merchandising company. The only *real* difference is that the company is selling product that it has *made*, rather than merchandise that it has *purchased*. As a result, the calculation of Cost of Goods Sold is different than that shown in Exhibit 2-14.

EXHIBIT 2-15 Manufacturer's Income Statement

	A	B	C	D
1	Proquest			
2	Income Statement			
3	For the Year Ended December 31			
4	(all figures shown in thousands of dollars)			
5				
6	Sales revenues		$ 65,000	
7	Less: Cost of goods sold		40,000	
8	Gross profit		$ 25,000	
9	Less operating expenses:			
10	Selling and marketing expenses	$ 8,000		
11	General and administrative expenses	2,000		
12	Total operating expenses		10,000	
13	Operating income		$ 15,000	
14				

Calculating Cost of Goods Manufactured and Cost of Goods Sold

Exhibit 2-16 illustrates how the manufacturer's *inventoriable product costs* (direct material used, direct labor, and manufacturing overhead) flow through the three inventory accounts before they become part of Cost of Goods Sold. In order to calculate Cost of Goods Sold, a manufacturer must first figure out the amount of direct materials used and the Cost of Goods Manufactured.

EXHIBIT 2-16 Flow of Costs Through a Manufacturer's Financial Statements

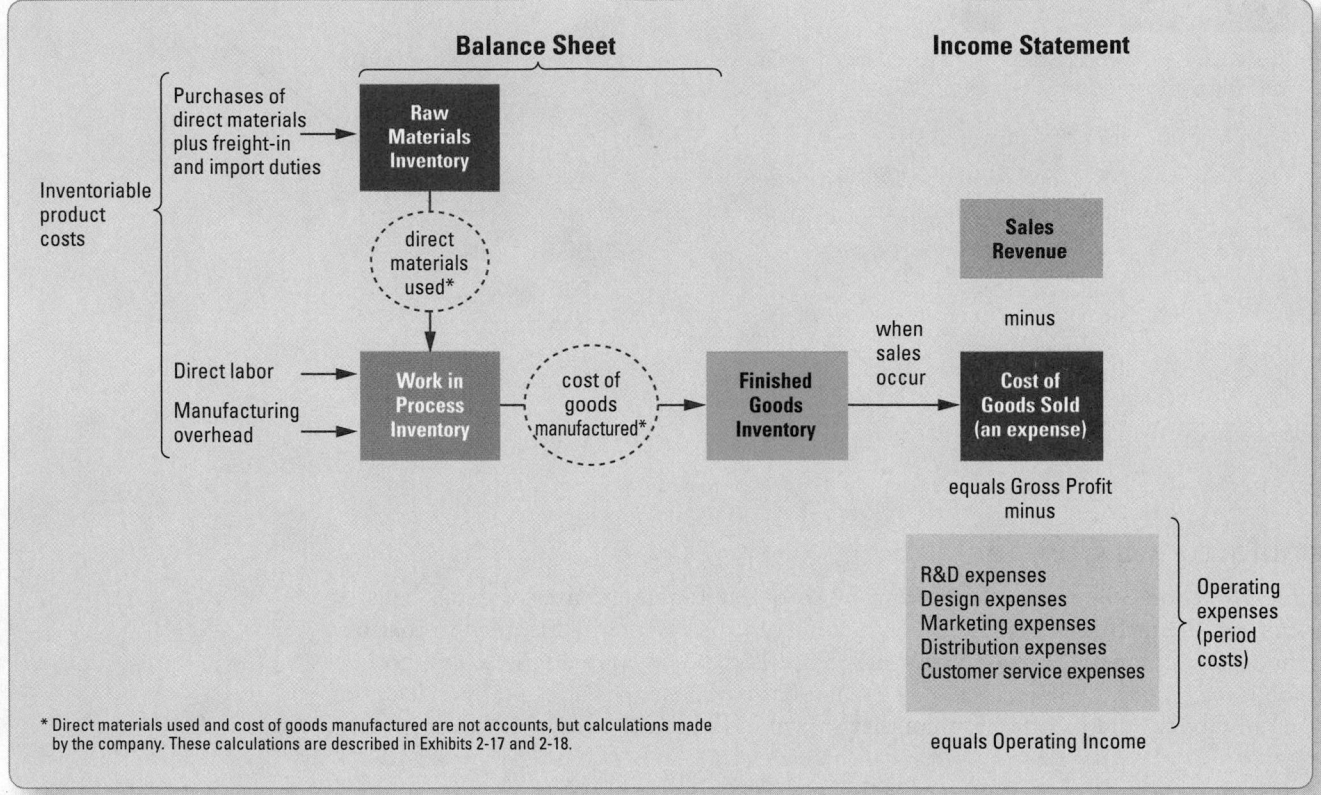

As you see in Exhibit 2-16, the **Cost of Goods Manufactured** represents the cost of those goods that were completed and moved to Finished Goods Inventory during the period.

Using Exhibit 2-16 as a guide, let's walk through the calculation of Cost of Goods Sold. We'll use three steps. Each step focuses on a different inventory account: Raw Materials, Work in Process, and Finished Goods.

STEP 1. Calculate the cost of the direct materials used during the year

Step 1 simply analyzes what happened in the *Raw Materials Inventory* account during the year. As shown in Exhibit 2-17, we start with the beginning balance in the Raw Materials Inventory account and add to it all of the direct materials purchased during the year, including any freight-in and import duties. This tells us the amount of materials that were available for use during the year. Finally, by subtracting out the ending balance of Raw Materials, we are able to back into the cost of the direct materials that were used.[3]

EXHIBIT 2-17 Calculation of Direct Materials Used

	A	B	C
1	**Calculation of Direct Materials Used**		
2	**(Analyze Raw Materials Inventory account)**		
3			
4	Beginning Raw Materials Inventory	$ 9,000	
5	Plus: Purchases of direct materials, freight-in, and import duties	27,000	
6	Materials available for use	$ 36,000	
7	Less: Ending Raw Material Inventory	22,000	
8	Direct materials used	$ 14,000	
9			

[3]In this chapter we'll assume that the Raw Materials account only contains direct materials because the company uses indirect materials as soon as they are purchased. In Chapter 3, we expand the discussion to include manufacturers who store both direct and indirect materials in the Raw Materials Inventory account.

STEP 2. Calculate the cost of goods manufactured

Step 2 simply analyzes what happened in the *Work in Process* account during the year. As shown in Exhibit 2-18, we start with the beginning balance in Work in Process and then add to it all three manufacturing costs that were incurred during the year (direct materials used, direct labor, and materials overhead). Finally, by subtracting out the goods still being worked on at year-end (ending Work in Process Inventory), we are able to back into the Cost of Goods Manufactured. This figure represents the cost of manufacturing the units that were *completed* and sent to Finished Goods Inventory during the year.

EXHIBIT 2-18 Calculation of Cost of Goods Manufactured

	A	B	C
1	**Calculation of Cost of Goods Manufactured**		
2	**(Analyze Work in Process Inventory account)**		
3			
4	Beginning Work in Process Inventory	$ 2,000	
5	Plus manufacturing costs incurred:		
6	Direct materials used	14,000	
7	Direct labor	19,000	
8	Manufacturing overhead	12,000	
9	Total manufacturing costs to account for	$ 47,000	
10	Less: Ending Work in Process Inventory	5,000	
11	Cost of goods manufactured (CGM)	$ 42,000	
12			

STEP 3. Calculate the cost of goods sold

Step 3 simply analyzes what happened in the *Finished Goods Inventory* account during the year. As shown in Exhibit 2-19, we start with the beginning balance of Finished Goods Inventory and add to it the product that was manufactured during the year (CGM) to arrive at the total goods available for sale. Finally, just like with a merchandiser, we subtract what was left in Finished Goods Inventory to back into the Cost of Goods Sold.

EXHIBIT 2-19 Calculation of Cost of Goods Sold

	A	B	C
1	**Calculation of Cost of Goods Sold**		
2	**(Analyze Finished Goods Inventory account)**		
3			
4	Beginning Finished Goods Inventory	$ 6,000	
5	Plus: Cost of goods manufactured (CGM)	42,000	
6	Cost of goods available for sale	$ 48,000	
7	Less: Ending Finished Goods Inventory	8,000	
8	Cost of goods sold	$ 40,000	
9			

By analyzing, step by step, what occurred in each of the three inventory accounts, we were able to calculate the Cost of Goods Sold shown on the company's Income Statement (see Exhibit 2-15). Some companies combine Steps 1 and 2 into one schedule called the Schedule of Cost of Goods Manufactured. Others combine all three steps into a Schedule of Cost of Goods Sold.

You may be wondering where all of the data come from. The beginning inventory balances were simply last year's ending balances. The purchases of direct materials and the incurrence of direct labor and manufacturing overhead would have been captured in the company's accounting records when those costs were incurred. Finally, the ending inventory balances come from doing a physical count of inventory at the end of the year.

In the coming chapters, we'll show you different systems manufacturers use to keep track of the *cost* associated with those units still in the three inventory accounts.

Comparing Balance Sheets

Now that we've looked at the income statement for each type of company, let's consider their balance sheets. The only difference relates to how inventory is shown in the current asset section:

- Service companies show no Inventory.
- Merchandising companies show Inventory or Merchandise Inventory.
- Manufacturing companies show Raw Materials, Work in Process, and Finished Goods Inventory.

Sometimes manufacturers just show "Inventories" on the face of the balance sheet, but disclose the breakdown of the inventory accounts (Raw Materials, Work in Process, and Finished Goods) in the footnotes to the financial statements.

 Sustainability and Corporate Reporting

In addition to generating a full set of financial statements for external users, many companies are now preparing and issuing Corporate Social Responsibility, or CSR, reports. These reports provide sustainability-related information to a variety of stakeholders, including investors and creditors, customers, government regulators, nongovernmental organizations (NGOs), and the general public. Although these reports are still voluntary in the United States, the move toward providing stakeholders with more sustainability-related data is growing. For example, in 2011, the following issued CSR reports:

- 95% of the world's 250 largest companies[4]
- 53% of the U.S. Fortune 500 companies[5]

Although sustainability reporting is still in its infancy, the Global Reporting Initiative, or GRI, has become the dominant framework for sustainability reporting. The GRI report[6] follows the triple-bottom-line approach (people, planet, profit) by specifying metrics that companies should report on related to each of the three pillars of sustainability:

- Social performance metrics—for example, fair labor and human rights practices
- Environmental performance metrics—for example, greenhouse gas emissions and total water use
- Economic performance metrics—for example, revenues, operating costs, and so forth

GRI reporting is not just for external reporting; companies also use it as a tool for internal change management. The GRI reporting process helps an organization illuminate areas of social and environmental impact that need improvement and gives management baseline measurements from which to measure change as the organization progresses on its sustainability journey. The old adage proves just as true for nonfinancial data as it does for financial data: "You can't manage what you don't measure."

In addition to standalone CSR reports, the International Integrated Reporting Committee (IIRC) is currently developing an integrated report that would, combine into one report much of the information currently provided in the separate financial and CSR reports. Currently, over 80 multinational companies, including Microsoft, Coca-Cola, and Prudential, are involved in an integrated

---

[4]KPMG, 2011 International Survey of Corporate Responsibility Reporting.
[5]Governance and Accountability Institute, "An Analysis of S&P 500 Companies' ESG Reporting Trends and Capital Markets Response."
[6]The GRI reporting framework has undergone several revisions, using the input from a multitude of stakeholders. The latest version, G4, issued in May 2013, supersedes the 3.1 framework that was in effect from X to X.

reporting pilot program. The "Big Four" accounting firms (Deloitte, Ernst & Young, KPMG, and PriceWaterhouseCoopers), as well as the Chartered Financial Analysts (CFA) Institute, are also involved in the pilot program. To keep abreast of developments in integrated reporting, visit the website of the IIRC at www.theiirc.org.

Finally, in a 2013 survey, Verdantix found that the Big Four accounting firms dominate both the sustainability consulting and sustainability assurance services (similar to auditing) markets.[7] Thus, students who wish to enter the accounting profession should be aware of these reporting developments.

What Other Cost Terms are Used by Managers?

So far in this chapter, we have discussed direct versus indirect costs and inventoriable product costs versus period costs. Now let's turn our attention to other cost terms that managers and accountants use when planning and making decisions.

6 Describe costs that are relevant and irrelevant for decision making

Controllable Versus Uncontrollable Costs

When deciding to make business changes, management needs to distinguish controllable costs from uncontrollable costs. In the long run, most costs are **controllable**, meaning management is able to influence or change them. However, in the short run, companies are often "locked in" to certain costs arising from previous decisions. These are called **uncontrollable costs**. For example, Toyota has little or no control over the property tax and insurance costs of its existing plants. These costs were "locked in" when Toyota built its plants. Toyota could replace existing production facilities with different-sized plants in different areas of the world that might cost less to operate, but that would take time. To see *immediate* benefits, management must change those costs that are controllable at the present. For example, management can control costs of research and development, design, and advertising. Sometimes Toyota's management chose to *increase* rather than decrease these costs in order to successfully gain market share. However, Toyota was also able to *decrease* other controllable costs, such as the price paid for raw materials, by working with its suppliers.

Relevant and Irrelevant Costs

Decision making involves identifying various courses of action and then choosing among them. When managers make decisions, they focus on those costs and revenues that are relevant to the decision. For example, Toyota plans to build a new state-of-the-art Corolla production facility in the United States. After considering alternative locations, management decided to build the facility in Blue Springs, Mississippi. The decision was based on relevant information such as the **differential cost** of building and operating the facility in Mississippi versus building and operating the facility in other potential locations. Differential cost refers to the difference in cost between two alternatives.

Say you want to buy a new car. You narrow your decision to two choices: the Nissan Sentra or the Toyota Corolla. As shown in Exhibit 2-20, the Sentra you like

EXHIBIT 2-20 Comparison of Relevant Information

	A	B	C	D
1	**Relevant Costs**	**Sentra**	**Corolla**	**Differential Cost**
2	Car's price	$ 18,480	$ 19,385	$ (905)
3	Sales tax (8%) (rounded)	1,478	1,551	(73)
4	Insurance*	11,700	8,940	2,760
5	Total relevant costs	31,658	$ 29,876	$ 1,782
6				

*Over the five years (60 months) you plan to keep the car.

[7]http://www.verdantix.com/index.cfm/papers/Press.Details/press_id/81/verdantix-survey-names-global-brand-leaders-for-sustainability-consulting-assurance-software-and-not-for-profit-services/-

costs $18,480, whereas the Corolla costs $19,385. Because sales tax is based on the sales price, the Corolla's sales tax is higher. However, your insurance agent quotes you a higher price to insure the Sentra ($195 per month versus $149 per month for the Corolla). All of these costs are relevant to your decision because they differ between the two cars.

Other costs are not relevant to your decision. For example, both cars run on regular unleaded gasoline and have the same fuel economy ratings, so the cost of operating the vehicles is about the same. Likewise, you don't expect cost differences in servicing the vehicles because they both carry the same warranty and have received excellent quality ratings in *Consumer Reports*. Because you project operating and maintenance costs to be the same for both cars, these costs are irrelevant to your decision. In other words, they won't influence your decision either way. Based on your analysis, the differential cost is $1,782 in favor of the Corolla. Does this mean that you will choose the Corolla? Not necessarily. The Sentra may have some characteristics you like better, such as a particular paint color, more comfortable seating, or more trunk space. When making decisions, management must also consider qualitative factors, such as effect on employee morale, in addition to differential costs.

Another cost that is irrelevant to your decision is the cost you paid for the vehicle you currently own. Say you just bought a Ford F-150 pickup truck two months ago, but you've decided you need a small sedan rather than a pickup truck. The cost of the truck is a **sunk cost**. Sunk costs are costs that have already been incurred. Nothing you do now can change the fact that you already bought the truck. Thus, the cost of the truck is not relevant to your decision of whether to buy the Sentra versus the Corolla. The only thing you can do now is (1) keep your truck or (2) sell it for the best price you can get.

Managers often have trouble ignoring sunk costs when making decisions, even though they should. Perhaps they invested in a factory or a computer system that no longer serves the company's needs. Many times, new technology makes managers' past investments in older technology look like bad decisions, even though they weren't at the time. Managers should ignore sunk costs because their decisions about the future cannot alter decisions made in the past.

Fixed and Variable Costs

7 Classify costs as fixed or variable and calculate total and average costs at different volumes

Managers cannot make good plans and decisions without first knowing how their costs behave. Costs generally behave as fixed costs or variable costs. We will spend all of Chapter 6 discussing cost behavior. For now, let's look just at the basics. **Fixed costs** stay constant in total over a wide range of activity levels. For example, let's say you decide to buy the Corolla, so your insurance cost for the year is $1,788 ($149 per month × 12 months). As shown in Exhibit 2-21, your total insurance cost stays fixed whether you drive your car 0 miles, 1,000 miles, or 10,000 miles during the year.

EXHIBIT 2-21 Fixed Cost Behavior

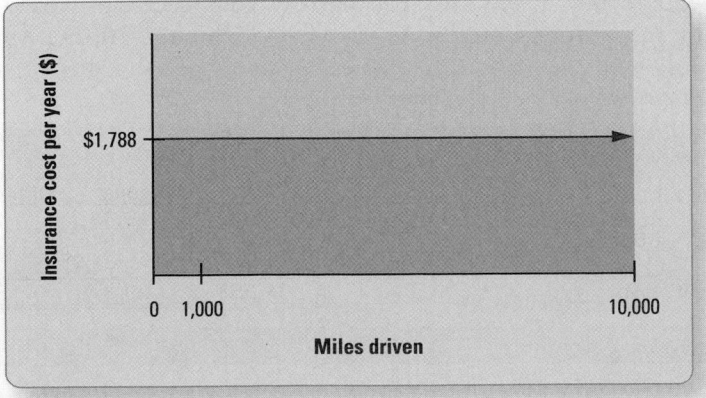

However, the total cost of gasoline to operate your car varies depending on whether you drive 0 miles, 1,000 miles, or 10,000 miles. The more miles you drive, the higher your total gasoline cost for the year. If you don't drive your car at all, you won't incur any costs for gasoline. Your gasoline costs are <u>variable costs</u>, as shown in Exhibit 2-22. Variable costs change in total in direct proportion to changes in volume. To accurately forecast the total cost of operating your Corolla during the year, you need to know which operating costs are fixed and which are variable.

EXHIBIT 2-22 Variable Cost Behavior

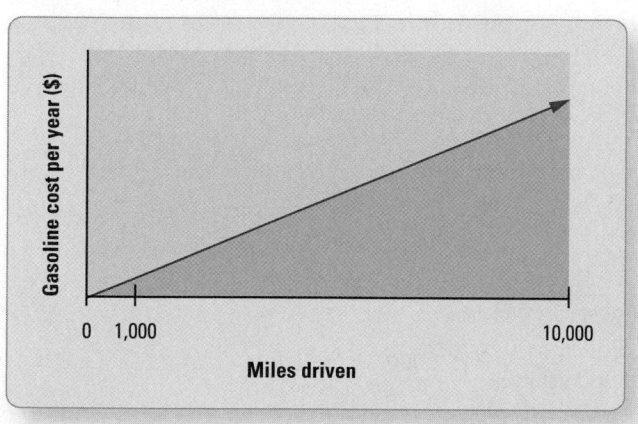

Why is this important?

"Most **business decisions** depend on how costs are **expected** to change at different volumes of **activity**. Managers can't make good decisions without first **understanding** how their costs **behave**."

How Manufacturing Costs Behave

Most companies have both fixed and variable costs. Manufacturing companies know that their direct materials are variable costs. The more cars Toyota makes, the higher its total cost for tires, steel, and parts. The behavior of direct labor is harder to characterize. Salaried employees are paid a fixed amount per year. Hourly wage earners are paid only when they work. The more hours they work, the more they are paid. Nonetheless, direct labor is generally treated as a variable cost because the more cars Toyota produces, the more assembly-line workers and machine operators it must employ. Manufacturing overhead includes both variable and fixed costs. For example, the cost of indirect materials is variable, while the cost of property tax, insurance, and straight-line depreciation on the plant and equipment is fixed. The cost of utilities is partially fixed and partially variable. Factories incur a certain level of utility costs just to keep the lights on. However, when more cars are produced, more electricity is used to run the production equipment. Exhibit 2-23 summarizes the behavior of manufacturing costs.

EXHIBIT 2-23 The Behavior of Manufacturing Costs

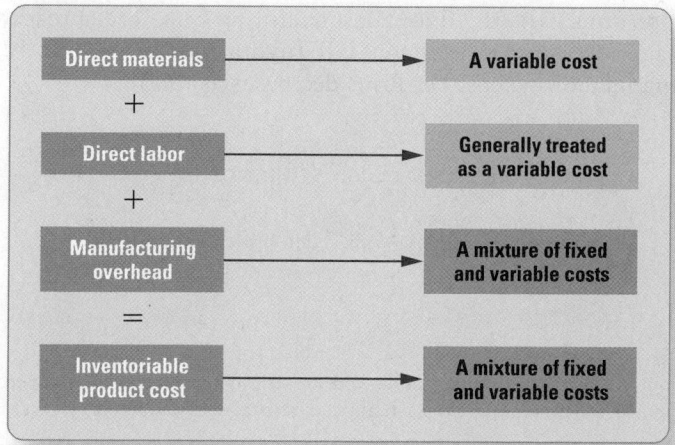

Calculating Total and Average Costs

Why is cost behavior important? Managers need to understand how costs behave to predict total costs and calculate average costs. In our example, we'll look at Toyota's total and average *manufacturing* costs; but, the same principles apply to nonmanufacturing costs.

Let's say Toyota wants to estimate the total cost of manufacturing 10,000 Prius cars next year. To do so, Toyota must know (1) its total fixed manufacturing costs, and (2) the variable cost of manufacturing each vehicle. Let's assume total fixed manufacturing costs for the year at the Prius plant are $20,000,000 and the variable cost of manufacturing each Prius is $5,000.[8] How much total manufacturing cost should Toyota budget for the year? Toyota calculates it as follows:

Total fixed cost + (Variable cost per unit × Number of units) = Total cost
$20,000,000 + ($5,000 per vehicle   ×   10,000 vehicles) = $70,000,000

What is the **average cost** of manufacturing each Prius next year? It's the total cost divided by the number of units:

$$\frac{\text{Total cost}}{\text{Number of units}} = \text{Average cost per unit}$$

$$\frac{\$70,000,000}{10,000 \text{ vehicles}} = \$7,000 \text{ per vehicle}$$

If Toyota's managers decide they need to produce 12,000 Prius cars instead, can they simply predict total costs as follows?

Average cost per unit × Number of units = Total cost???
$7,000   ×   12,000   = $84,000,000???

No! They cannot! Why? *Because the average cost per unit is NOT appropriate for predicting total costs at different levels of output.* Toyota's managers should forecast total cost based on cost behavior:

Total fixed cost + (Variable cost per unit × Number of units) = Total cost
$20,000,000 + ($5,000 per vehicle   ×   12,000 vehicles) = $80,000,000

Why is the *correct* forecasted cost of $80 million less than the *faulty* prediction of $84 million? The difference stems from fixed costs. Remember, Toyota incurs $20 million of fixed manufacturing costs whether it makes 10,000 vehicles or 12,000 vehicles. As Toyota makes more Prius cars, the fixed manufacturing costs are spread over more vehicles, so the average cost per vehicle declines. If Toyota ends up making 12,000 vehicles, the new average manufacturing cost per Prius decreases as follows:

$$\frac{\text{Total cost}}{\text{Number of units}} = \text{Average cost per unit}$$

$$\frac{\$80,000,000}{12,000 \text{ vehicles}} = \$6,667 \text{ per vehicle (rounded)}$$

[8]All references to Toyota in this hypothetical example were created by the author solely for academic purposes and are not intended in any way to represent the actual business practices of, or costs incurred by, Toyota Motor Corporation.

The average cost per unit is lower when Toyota produces more vehicles because it is using the fixed manufacturing costs more efficiently—taking the same $20 million of resources and making more vehicles with it.

Keep the following important rule of thumb in mind:

> *The average cost per unit is valid only at ONE level of output—the level used to compute the average cost per unit. NEVER use average costs to forecast costs at different output levels; if you do, you will miss the mark!*

Finally, a **marginal cost** is the cost of making *one more unit*. Fixed costs will not change when Toyota makes one more Prius unless the plant is operating at 100% capacity and simply cannot make one more unit. If that's the case, Toyota will need to incur additional costs to expand the plant. So, the marginal cost of a unit is simply its variable cost.

As you have seen, management accountants and managers use specialized terms for discussing costs. They use different costs for different purposes. Without a solid understanding of these terms, managers are likely to make serious judgment errors.

Decision Guidelines

Building Blocks of Managerial Accounting

As a manufacturer, Toyota needs to know how to calculate its inventoriable product costs for external reporting. Toyota also needs to know many characteristics about its costs in order to plan and make decisions. The following guidelines helps managers with these types of decisions.

Decision	Guidelines
How do you compute cost of goods sold?	*Service companies:* No cost of goods sold because they don't sell tangible goods • *Merchandising companies:* Beginning inventory + Purchases plus freight-in and import duties, if any = Cost of goods available for sale − Ending inventory = Cost of goods sold • *Manufacturing companies:* Beginning finished goods inventory + Cost of goods manufactured = Cost of goods available for sale − Ending finished goods inventory = Cost of goods sold
How do you compute the cost of goods manufactured?	Beginning work in process inventory + Total manufacturing costs incurred during year (direct materials used + direct labor + manufacturing overhead) = Total manufacturing costs to account for − Ending work in process inventory = Cost of goods manufactured
How do managers decide which costs are relevant to their decisions?	Costs are relevant to a decision when they differ between alternatives and affect the future. Thus, *differential costs* are relevant, whereas *sunk costs* and costs that don't differ are not relevant.
How should managers forecast total costs for different production volumes?	Total cost = Total fixed costs + (Variable cost per unit × Number of units) Managers should *not* use a product's *average cost* to forecast total costs because it will change as production volume changes. As production increases, the average cost per unit declines (because fixed costs are spread over more units).

SUMMARY PROBLEM **2**

Requirements

1. Show how to compute cost of goods manufactured. Use the following amounts: direct materials used ($24,000), direct labor ($9,000), manufacturing overhead ($17,000), beginning work in process inventory ($5,000), and ending work in process inventory ($4,000).

2. Auto-USA spent $300 million in total to produce 50,000 cars this year. The $300 million breaks down as follows: The company spent $50 million on fixed costs to run its manufacturing plants and $5,000 of variable costs to produce each car. Next year, it plans to produce 60,000 cars using the existing production facilities.

   a. What is the current *average cost* per car this year?

   b. Assuming there is no change in fixed costs or variable costs per unit, what is the *total forecasted cost* to produce 60,000 cars next year?

   c. What is the *forecasted average cost* per car next year?

   d. Why does the average cost per car vary between years?

▪ SOLUTIONS

Requirement 1

Cost of goods manufactured:

	A	B	C	D
1	**Calculation of Cost of Good Manufactured**			
2	Beginning Work in Process Inventory	$ 5,000		
3	Plus manufacturing costs incurred:			
4	Direct materials used	24,000		
5	Direct labor	9,000		
6	Manufacturing overhead	17,000		
7	Total manufacturing costs to account for	$ 55,000		
8	Less: Ending Work in Process Inventory	4,000		
9	Cost of goods manufactured (CGM)	$ 51,000		
10				

Requirement 2

a.

Total cost ÷ Number of units = Current average cost

$300 million ÷ 50,000 cars = $6,000 per car

b.

Total fixed costs + Total variable costs = Total projected costs

$50 million + (60,000 cars × $5,000 per car) = $350 million

c.

Total cost ÷ Number of units = Projected average cost

$350 million ÷ 60,000 cars = $5,833 per car

d. The average cost per car decreases because Auto-USA will use the same fixed costs ($50 million) to produce more cars next year. Auto-USA will be using its resources more efficiently, so the average cost per unit will decrease.

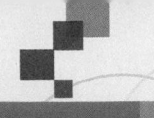

END OF CHAPTER

Learning Objectives

- 1 Distinguish among service, merchandising, and manufacturing companies
- 2 Describe the value chain and its elements
- 3 Distinguish between direct and indirect costs
- 4 Identify the inventoriable product costs and period costs of merchandising and manufacturing firms
- 5 Prepare the financial statements for service, merchandising, and manufacturing companies
- 6 Describe costs that are relevant and irrelevant for decision making
- 7 Classify costs as fixed or variable and calculate total and average costs at different volumes

Accounting Vocabulary

Allocate. (p. 53) To assign an *indirect* cost to a cost object.

Assign. (p. 53) To attach a cost to a cost object.

Average Cost. (p. 72) The total cost divided by the number of units.

Biomimicry. (p. 51) A means of product design in which a company tries to mimic, or copy, the natural biological process in which dead organisms (plants and animals) become the input for another organism or process.

Controllable Costs. (p. 69) Costs that can be influenced or changed by management.

Conversion Costs. (p. 59) The combination of direct labor and manufacturing overhead costs.

Cost Object. (p. 52) Anything for which managers want a separate measurement of costs.

Cost of Goods Manufactured. (p. 66) The cost of manufacturing the goods that were *finished* during the period.

Customer Service. (p. 50) Support provided for customers after the sale.

Design. (p. 50) Detailed engineering of products and services and the processes for producing them.

Differential Cost. (p. 69) The difference in cost between two alternative courses of action.

Direct Cost. (p. 53) A cost that can be traced to a cost object.

Direct Labor. (p. 57) The cost of compensating employees who physically convert raw materials into the company's products; labor costs that are directly traceable to the finished product.

Direct Materials. (p. 57) Primary raw materials that become a physical part of a finished product and whose costs are traceable to the finished product.

Distribution. (p. 50) Delivery of products or services to customers.

Finished Goods Inventory. (p. 48) Completed goods that have not yet been sold.

Fixed Costs. (p. 70) Costs that stay constant in total despite wide changes in volume.

Greenwashing. (p. 52) The unfortunate practice of *overstating* a company's commitment to sustainability.

Indirect Cost. (p. 53) A cost that relates to the cost object but cannot be traced to it.

Indirect Labor. (p. 58) Labor costs that are difficult to trace to specific products.

Indirect Materials. (p. 58) Materials whose costs are difficult to trace to specific products.

Inventoriable Product Costs. (p. 55) All costs of a product that GAAP requires companies to treat as an asset (inventory) for external financial reporting. These costs are not expensed until the product is sold.

Life-cycle Assessment. (p. 51) A method of product design in which the company analyzes the environmental impact of a product, from cradle to grave, in an attempt to minimize negative environmental consequences throughout the entire lifespan of the product.

Manufacturing Company. (p. 47) A company that uses labor, plant, and equipment to convert raw materials into new finished products.

Manufacturing Overhead. (p. 58) All manufacturing costs other than direct materials and direct labor; also called factory overhead and indirect manufacturing cost.

Marginal Cost. (p. 73) The cost of producing one more unit.

Marketing. (p. 50) Promotion and advertising of products or services.

Merchandising Company. (p. 47) A company that resells tangible products previously bought from suppliers.

Operating Income. (p. 63) Earnings generated from the company's primary ongoing operations; the company's earnings before interest and taxes.

Other Indirect Manufacturing Costs. (p. 58)   All manufacturing overhead costs aside from indirect materials and indirect labor.

Period Costs. (p. 55)   Costs that are expensed in the period in which they are incurred; often called operating expenses or selling, general, and administrative expenses.

Perpetual Inventory. (p. 64)   An inventory system in which both Cost of Goods Sold and Inventory are updated every time a sale is made.

Periodic Inventory. (p. 64)   An inventory system in which Cost of Goods Sold is calculated at the end of the period, rather than every time a sale is made.

Prime Costs. (p. 59)   The combination of direct material and direct labor costs.

Production or Purchases. (p. 50)   Resources used to produce a product or service, or to purchase finished merchandise intended for resale.

Raw Materials Inventory. (p. 48)   All raw materials (direct materials and indirect materials) not yet used in manufacturing.

Research and Development (R&D). (p. 50)   Researching and developing new or improved products or services or the processes for producing them.

Retailer. (p. 47)   Merchandising company that sells to consumers.

Service Company. (p. 47)   A company that sells intangible services rather than tangible products.

Sunk Cost. (p. 70)   A cost that has already been incurred.

Total Cost. (p. 54)   The cost of all resources used throughout the value chain.

Trace. (p. 53)   To assign a *direct* cost to a cost object.

Triple Bottom Line. (p. 47)   Evaluating a company's performance not only by its ability to generate economic profits, but also by its impact on people and the planet.

Uncontrollable Costs. (p. 69)   Costs that cannot be changed or influenced in the short run by management.

Value Chain. (p. 49)   The activities that add value to a firm's products and services; includes R&D, design, production or purchases, marketing, distribution, and customer service.

Variable Costs. (p. 71)   Costs that change in total in direct proportion to changes in volume.

Wholesaler. (p. 47)   Merchandising companies that buy in bulk from manufacturers, mark up the prices, and then sell those products to retailers.

Work in Process Inventory. (p. 48)   Goods that are partway through the manufacturing process but not yet complete.

MyAccountingLab   Go to http://myaccountinglab.com/ **for the following Quick Check, Short Exercises, Exercises, and Problems. They are available with immediate grading, explanations of correct and incorrect answers, and interactive media that acts as your own online tutor.**

Quick Check

1. (*Learning Objective 1*) Which of the following types of companies would carry raw materials, work in process, and finished goods inventory?
   a. Service
   b. Merchandising
   c. Manufacturing
   d. All of the above

2. (*Learning Objective 2*) Which of the following is *not* an activity in the value chain?
   a. Design
   b. Administration
   c. Marketing
   d. Customer Service

3. (*Learning Objective 3*) A cost that can be traced to a cost object is known as a
   a. direct cost.
   b. indirect cost.
   c. period cost.
   d. inventoriable product cost.

4. (*Learning Objective 4*) Period costs are often referred to as
   a. Selling, general, and administrative expenses.
   b. Operating expenses.
   c. both Selling, general, and administrative expenses and Operating expenses.
   d. neither Selling, general, and administrative expenses nor Operating expenses.

5. (*Learning Objective 4*) Prime costs consist of
   a. direct materials and manufacturing overhead.
   b. direct labor and manufacturing overhead.
   c. direct materials and direct labor.
   d. direct materials, direct labor, and manufacturing overhead.

6. (*Learning Objective 4*) Which of the following is *not* part of manufacturing overhead?
   a. Indirect materials, such as machine lubricants
   b. Indirect labor, such as forklift operators' wages
   c. Other indirect manufacturing costs, such as plant utilities
   d. Period costs, such as depreciation on office computers

7. (*Learning Objective 5*) Which of the following types of companies will always have the Cost of Goods Sold account on their income statements?

a. Service and merchandising companies

b. Merchandising and manufacturing companies

c. Service and manufacturing companies

d. Service, merchandising, and manufacturing companies

8. (*Learning Objective 5*) Which of the following is a calculated amount, rather than a general ledger account?

a. Cost of goods sold

b. Finished goods inventory

c. Cost of goods manufactured

d. Sales revenue

9. (*Learning Objective 6*) Which of the following is *false*?

a. Sunk costs are generally relevant to decisions.

b. The difference in cost between two alternatives is known as a differential cost.

c. Uncontrollable costs are costs over which the company has little or no control in the short run.

d. Sunk costs are costs that have already been incurred.

10. (*Learning Objective 7*) Which of the following is *false*?

a. Fixed costs stay constant in total over a wide range of activity levels.

b. Direct materials are considered to be variable costs.

c. The average cost per unit is valid for predicting total costs at many different output levels.

d. Manufacturing overhead is a mixture of fixed and variable costs.

Quick Check Answers

1. c 2. b 3. a 4. c 5. d 6. d 7. b 8. c 9. a 10. c

Short Exercises

S2-1   Identify type of company from balance sheets (*Learning Objective 1*)

The current asset sections of the balance sheets of three companies follow. Which company is a service company? Which is a merchandiser? Which is a manufacturer? How can you tell?

Flash Company		Zippy Company		Woody Company	
Cash	$ 2,000	Cash	$ 2,500	Cash	$3,000
Accounts receivable	5,000	Accounts receivable	5,500	Accounts receivable	6,000
Raw materials inventory	1,000	Inventory	8,000	Prepaid expenses	500
Work in process inventory	800	Prepaid expenses	300	Total	$9,500
Finished goods inventory	4,000	Total	$16,300		
Total	$12,800				

S2-2   Identify types of companies and their inventories (*Learning Objective 1*)

Complete the following statements with one of the terms listed here. You may use a term more than once, and some terms may not be used at all.

Finished goods inventory	Inventory (merchandise)	Service companies
Manufacturing companies	Merchandising companies	Work in process inventory
Raw materials inventory	Wholesalers	

a. _____ typically do not have an inventory account.

b. Honda Motors converts _____ into finished products.

c. An insurance company, a health-care provider, and a bank are all examples of _____.

d. _____ buy products in bulk from producers, mark them up, and resell to retailers.

e. _____ report three types of inventory on the balance sheet.

f. _____ for a company such as Staples (office supplies) includes all of the costs necessary to purchase products and get them onto the store shelves.

g. Most for-profit organizations can be described as being in one (or more) of three categories: _____, _____, and _____.

h. _____ is composed of goods partially through the manufacturing process (not finished yet).

i. Lands' End, Sears Roebuck & Co., and L.L. Bean are all examples of _____.

S2-3 Classify costs by value chain function (Learning Objective 2)

Classify each of Hewlett-Packard's costs as one of the six business functions in the value chain.

a. Cost of a prime-time TV ad featuring the new HP logo

b. Salary of engineers who are redesigning the printer's on-off switch

c. Depreciation on Roseville, California, plant

d. Depreciation on delivery vehicles

e. Transportation costs to deliver laser printers to retailers such as Best Buy

f. Costs of a customer support center website

g. Plant manager's salary

h. Purchase of plastic used in printer casings

i. Depreciation on research lab

S2-4 Classify costs as direct or indirect (Learning Objective 3)

Classify each of the following costs as a direct cost or an indirect cost, assuming that the cost object is the Juniors Department (clothing and accessories for teenage and young women) in the Medina Kohl's department store. (Kohl's is a chain of department stores and has stores located across the U.S.)

a. Depreciation of the building

b. Cost of costume jewelry on the mannequins in the Juniors Department

c. Cost of bags used to package customer purchases at the main registers for the store

d. The Medina Kohl's store manager's salary

e. Cost of the security staff at the Medina store

f. Manager of Juniors Department

g. Juniors Department sales clerks

h. Cost of Juniors clothing

i. Cost of hangers used to display the clothing in the store

j. Electricity for the building

k. Cost of radio advertising for the store

l. Juniors clothing buyers' salaries (these buyers buy for all the Juniors Departments of Kohl's stores)

S2-5 Define cost terms (Learning Objectives 3 & 4)

Complete the following statements with one of the terms listed here. You may use a term more than once, and some terms may not be used at all.

Prime costs	Cost objects	Inventoriable product costs
Assigned	Direct costs	Fringe benefits
Period costs	Assets	Cost of goods sold
Indirect costs	Conversion costs	Total costs

a. _____ cannot be directly traced to a(n) _____.

b. _____ include the costs of all resources used throughout the value chain.

c. GAAP requires companies to use only _____ for inventory reported on external financial statements.

d. Company-paid _____ may include health insurance, retirement plan contributions, payroll taxes, and paid vacations.

e. When manufacturing companies sell their finished products, the costs of those finished products are removed from inventory and expensed as _____.

f. _____ are the costs of transforming direct materials into finished goods.

g. _____ include R&D, marketing, distribution, and customer service costs.

h. Direct material plus direct labor equals _____.

i. Steel, tires, engines, upholstery, carpet, and dashboard instruments are used in the assembly of a car. Since the manufacturer can trace the cost of these materials (including freight-in and import duties) to specific units or batches of vehicles, they are considered _____ of the vehicles.

j. Costs that can be traced directly to a(n) _____ are called _____.

k. _____ are initially treated as _____ on the balance sheet.

l. The allocation process results in a less precise cost figure being _____ to the _____.

S2-6 Classify inventoriable product costs and period costs
(Learning Objective 4)

Classify each of Georgia-Pacific's costs as either inventoriable product costs or period costs. Georgia-Pacific is a manufacturer of paper, lumber, and building material products.

a. Cost of TV ads promoting environmental awareness

b. Purchase of lumber to be cut into boards

c. Salaries of scientists studying ways to speed forest growth

d. Cost of new software to track inventory during production

e. Salaries of Georgia-Pacific's top executives

f. Cost of chemical applied to lumber to inhibit mold from developing

g. Life insurance for the CEO

h. Cost of electricity at one of Georgia-Pacific's paper mills

i. Depreciation on the gypsum board plant

S2-7 Classify a manufacturer's costs (Learning Objective 4)

Classify each of the following costs as a period cost or an inventoriable product cost. If you classify the cost as an inventoriable product cost, further classify it as direct material (DM), direct labor (DL), or manufacturing overhead (MOH).

a. Standard packaging materials used to package individual units of product for sale (for example, cereal boxes in which cereal is packaged)

b. Lease payment on administrative headquarters

c. Telephone bills relating to customer service call center

d. Property insurance—40% of building is used for sales and administration; 60% of building is used for manufacturing

e. Wages and benefits paid to assembly-line workers in the manufacturing plant

f. Depreciation on automated production equipment

g. Salaries paid to quality control inspectors in the plant

h. Repairs and maintenance on factory equipment

S2-8 Classify costs incurred by a dairy processing company
(Learning Objective 4)

Each of the following costs pertains to DairyPlains, a dairy processing company. Classify each of the company's costs as a period cost or an inventoriable product cost. Further classify inventoriable product costs as direct material (DM), direct labor (DL), or manufacturing overhead (MOH).

Cost	Period Cost or Inventoriable Product Cost?	DM, DL, or MOH?
1. Cost of milk purchased from local dairy farmers		
2. Depreciation on Marketing Department's computers		
3. Property tax on dairy processing plant		
4. Gasoline used to operate refrigerated trucks delivering finished dairy products to grocery stores		
5. Company president's annual bonus		
6. Depreciation on refrigerated trucks used to collect raw milk from local dairy farmers		

Cost	Period Cost or Inventoriable Product Cost?	DM, DL, or MOH?
7. Plastic gallon containers in which milk is packaged		
8. Research and development on improving milk pasteurization process		
9. Television advertisements for DairyPlains' products		
10. Lubricants used in running bottling machines		
11. Wages and salaries paid to machine operators at dairy processing plant		

S2-9   Determine total manufacturing overhead *(Learning Objective 4)*

Frame Place manufactures picture frames. Suppose the company's May records include the items described below. What is Frame Place's total manufacturing overhead cost in May?

Oil for manufacturing equipment	$ 35
Wood for frames	$50,000
Company president's salary	$28,500
Interest expense	$ 2,100
Plant supervisor's salary	$ 4,500
Depreciation expense on company cars used by sales force	$ 2,500
Plant janitor's salary	$ 1,200
Plant depreciation expense	$10,000
Glue for picture frames	$ 200

S2-10   Compute Cost of Goods Sold for a merchandiser *(Learning Objective 5)*

Given the following information for a retailer, compute the cost of goods sold.

Ending inventory	$ 5,500
Website maintenance	$ 7,300
Revenues	$63,000
Freight-in	$ 3,300
Import duties	$ 700
Marketing expenses	$12,000
Delivery expenses	$ 1,600
Purchases	$45,000
Beginning inventory	$ 3,600

S2-11   Prepare a retailer's income statement *(Learning Objective 5)*

Simply Hair is a retail chain specializing in salon-quality hair-care products. During the year, Simply Hair had sales of $39,225,000. The company began the year with $2,500,000 of merchandise inventory and ended the year with $3,245,000 of inventory. During the year, Simply Hair purchased $21,400,000 of merchandise inventory. The company's selling, general, and administrative expenses totaled $6,850,000 for the year. Prepare Simply Hair's income statement for the year.

S2-12 Calculate direct materials used (Learning Objective 5)

You are a new accounting intern at Thomas Bikes. Your boss gives you the following information and asks you to compute the cost of direct materials used (assume that the company's raw materials inventory contains only direct materials).

Import duties	$ 1,300
Beginning raw materials inventory	$ 4,100
Ending raw materials inventory	$ 1,900
Freight-in	$ 200
Freight-out	$ 800
Purchases of direct materials	$16,400

S2-13 Compute Cost of Goods Manufactured (Learning Objective 5)

Hansen Manufacturing found the following information in its accounting records: $515,500 of direct materials used, $226,700 of direct labor, and $774,800 of manufacturing overhead. The Work in Process Inventory account had a beginning balance of $79,500 and an ending balance of $86,500. Compute the company's Cost of Goods Manufactured.

S2-14 Consider relevant information (Learning Objective 6)

You have been offered an entry-level marketing position at two highly respectable firms: one in Los Angeles, California, and one in Sioux Falls, South Dakota. What quantitative and qualitative information might be relevant to your decision? What characteristics about this information make it relevant?

S2-15 Describe other cost terms (Learning Objectives 6 & 7)

Complete the following statements with one of the terms listed here. You may use a term more than once, and some terms may not be used at all.

Differential costs	Variable costs	Controllable costs
Marginal cost	Fixed costs	Average cost
Uncontrollable costs	Sunk costs	

a. Costs that differ between alternatives are called _____.

b. In the long run, most costs are _____, meaning that management is able to influence or change the amount of the cost.

c. _____ are costs that have already been incurred.

d. A(n) _____ is the cost of making one more unit.

e. Gasoline is one of many _____ in the operation of a motor vehicle.

f. A product's _____ and _____, not the product's _____, should be used to forecast total costs at different production volumes.

g. Within the relevant range, _____ do not change in total with changes in production volume.

h. The _____ per unit declines as a production facility produces more units.

S2-16 Classify costs as fixed or variable (Learning Objective 7)

Classify each of the following costs as fixed or variable:

a. Cost of coffee used at a Starbucks store

b. Hourly wages paid to sales clerks at Best Buy

c. Monthly flower costs for a florist

d. Cost of fuel used for a national trucking company

e. Shipping costs for Amazon.com

f. Monthly rent for a nail salon

g. Sales commissions at a car dealership

h. Monthly insurance costs for the home office of a company

i. Monthly depreciation of equipment for a customer service office

j. Cost of fabric used at a clothing manufacturer

k. Cost of fruit sold at a grocery store

l. Monthly office lease costs for a CPA firm

m. Monthly cost of French fries at a McDonald's restaurant

n. Property taxes for a restaurant

o. Depreciation of exercise equipment at the YMCA

S2-17 Identify ethical standards violated (Learning Objectives 1, 2, 3, 4, 5, 6, & 7)   ETHICS

For each of the situations listed, identify the primary standard from the IMA *Statement of Ethical Professional Practice* that is violated (competence, confidentiality, integrity, or credibility). Refer to Exhibit 1-6 for the complete standard.

1. Chris overhears a subordinate at a mutual friend's party tell others about a confidential deal with a supplier to get raw materials for a price lower than market price. Chris does not do anything about the subordinate's indiscrete conversation.

2. Maxwell pays a Mexican official a bribe of $50,000 to allow the company to locate a factory in that jurisdiction so that the company can take advantage of the cheaper labor costs. Without the bribe, the factory cannot be located in that location.

3. There is a failure in the company's backup system after a system crash. Month-end reports will be delayed. Mark, the manager of the division experiencing the system failure, does not report this upcoming delay to anyone since he does not want to be the bearer of bad news.

4. To reduce the company's tax bill, Jillian uses total cost to value inventory instead of using product cost as required by law.

5. Since Michael works in the accounting department, he is aware that profits are going to fall short of analysts' projections. He tells his father to sell stock in the company before the earnings release date.

EXERCISES Group A

E2-18A Classify costs along the value chain for a retailer (Learning Objective 2)

Suppose Radio Shack incurred the following costs at its Atlanta, Georgia, store:

Newspaper advertisements	$ 5,100
Payment to consultant for advice on location of new store	$ 2,900
Purchases of merchandise	$38,000
Freight-in	$ 3,100
Salespeople's salaries	$ 4,800
Depreciation expense on delivery trucks	$ 1,000
Research on whether store should sell satellite radio service	$ 300
Customer Complaint Department	$ 500
Rearranging store layout	$ 850

Requirements

1. Classify each cost as to which category of the value chain it belongs (R&D, Design, Purchases, Marketing, Distribution, or Customer Service).

2. Compute the total costs for each value chain category.

3. How much are the total inventoriable product costs?

E2-19A   Classify costs along the value chain for a manufacturer
(Learning Objectives 2 & 3)

Suppose the cell phone manufacturer Kiwi Electronics provides the following information for its costs last month (in millions):

Delivery expense to customers via UPS..	$ 7
Salaries of salespeople...	$ 4
Chip set	$56
Exterior case for phone..	$ 9
Assembly-line workers' wages	$10
Technical customer support hotline	$ 3
Depreciation on plant and equipment..	$60
Rearrange production process to accommodate new robot...................	$ 2
1-800 (toll-free) line for customer orders	$ 5
Salaries of scientists who developed new model	$11

Requirements

1. Classify each of these costs according to its place in the value chain (R&D, Design, Production, Marketing, Distribution, or Customer Service). (*Hint:* You should have at least one cost in each value chain function.)
2. Within the production category, break the costs down further into three subcategories: Direct Materials, Direct Labor, and Manufacturing Overhead.
3. Compute the total costs for each value chain category.
4. How much are the total inventoriable product costs?
5. How much are the total prime costs?
6. How much are the total conversion costs?

SUSTAINABILITY

E2-20A   Value chain and sustainability efforts *(Learning Objective 2)*

Each of the scenarios to follow describes some cost item for organizations in recent years. For each scenario, identify which function of the value chain that cost would represent (R&D, Design, Purchasing/Producing, Marketing, Distributing, or Customer Service). *Note: The companies and products used in this exercise are real companies with a strong sustainable practices commitment.*

a. Nike Products, an athletic apparel and shoe manufacturer, developed the Environmental Apparel Design Tool over a period of seven years. The Environmental Apparel Design Tools helps apparel and shoe designers to make real-time choices that decrease the environmental impact of their work. With the tool, the designers can see the potential waste resulting from their designs and the amount of environmentally preferred materials used by their designs. When designers make changes to the preliminary product design, they can see instantly the effect of those changes on waste and input usage. The $6 million investment used to develop the Environmental Apparel Design Tool would fall into which function in the value chain?

b. Nyloboard® produces decking materials made from recycled carpet. The cost of the research into how to create Nyloboard® from recycled carpet would fall into which function in the value chain?

c. GreenShipping™ is a service that companies can use to purchase carbon offsets for the carbon generated by shipments to customers. Any shipments made with UPS, FedEx, or USPS can be tracked. The GreenShipping™ calculator uses weight, distance traveled and mode of transport to calculate the carbon generated by that shipment. A carbon offset is then purchased so that the shipment becomes carbon neutral.

The carbon offset helps to fund the development of renewable energy sources. The cost of these carbon offsets to the company making the shipment to the customer would fall into which function in the value chain?

d. Late in 2010, the U.S. National Park Service approved the use of an erosion control system from GeoHay® for a roadway construction project in the Great Smoky Mountains National Park. GeoHay® erosion and sediment control products are produced from recycled carpet fibers. The cost of these erosion and sediment control products would fall into which function in the value chain?

e. Ford Motor Company's Rouge Center in Dearborn Michigan has a "living roof" on the Dearborn Truck Plant final assembly building. It is the largest living roof in the world, encompassing 10.4 acres. The living roof is made from living grass and its primary purpose is to collect and filter rainfall as part of a natural stormwater management system. It also provides cooler surroundings and offers a longer roof life than a traditional roof. The cost of promoting the company's products and its sustainability efforts would fall into which function in the value chain?

f. The Red Wing Shoe Company manufactures work boots. The company has a philosophy that products should be repaired, not thrown away. After the 12-month warranty has expired on Red Wing boots, the company offers free oiling, free laces, low-cost replacement insoles, and low-cost hardware repairs. The cost of operating this shoe repair service would fall into which function in the value chain?

E2-21A Classify and calculate a manufacturer's costs (Learning Objectives 3 & 4)

An airline manufacturer incurred the following costs last month (in thousands of dollars):

a.	Airplane seats	$ 260
b.	Production supervisors' salaries	$ 140
c.	Depreciation on forklifts	$ 80
d.	Machine lubricants	$ 45
e.	Factory janitors' wages	$ 20
f.	Assembly workers' wages	$ 660
g.	Property tax on corporate marketing office	$ 30
h.	Plant utilities	$ 130
i.	Cost of warranty repairs	$ 225
j.	Machine operators' health insurance	$ 40
k.	Depreciation on administrative offices	$ 70
l.	Cost of designing new plant layout	$ 195
m.	Jet engines	$1,400

Requirements

1. Assuming the cost object is an airplane, classify each cost as one of the following: direct material (DM), direct labor (DL), indirect labor (IL), indirect materials (IM), other manufacturing overhead (other MOH), or period cost. (Hint: Set up a column for each type of cost.) What is the total for each type of cost?
2. Calculate total manufacturing overhead costs.
3. Calculate total inventoriable product costs.
4. Calculate total prime costs.
5. Calculate total conversion costs.
6. Calculate total period costs.

E2-22A Prepare the current assets section of the balance sheet
(Learning Objective 5)

Consider the following selected amounts and account balances of Crater, Inc.:

Manufacturing overhead	$ 22,000
Accounts receivable	$ 75,000
Direct materials used	$ 15,100
Cost of goods sold	$100,000
Raw materials inventory	$ 9,700
Cost of goods manufactured	$ 99,000
Cash	$ 15,200
Direct labor	$ 42,000
Marketing expense	$ 32,000
Work in process inventory	$ 35,000
Finished goods inventory	$ 59,000
Prepaid expenses	$ 5,500

Requirement

Show how this company reports current assets on the balance sheet. Not all data are used. Is this company a service company, a merchandiser, or a manufacturer? How do you know?

E2-23A Prepare a retailer's income statement *(Learning Objective 5)*

Tom Reynolds is the sole proprietor of Pampered Pets, a business specializing in the sale of high-end pet gifts and accessories. Pampered Pets' sales totaled $986,000 during the most recent year. During the year, the company spent $58,500 on expenses relating to website maintenance, $30,700 on marketing, and $28,500 on wrapping, boxing, and shipping the goods to customers. Pampered Pets also spent $640,000 on inventory purchases and an additional $19,500 on freight-in charges. The company started the year with $18,000 of inventory on hand and ended the year with $12,800 of inventory. Prepare Pampered Pets' income statement for the most recent year.

E2-24A Compute direct materials used and Cost of Goods Manufactured
(Learning Objective 5)

Ivanhoe Industries is calculating its Cost of Goods Manufactured at year-end. Ivanhoe's accounting records show the following: The Raw Materials Inventory account had a beginning balance of $17,000 and an ending balance of $15,000. During the year, Ivanhoe purchased $63,000 of direct materials. Direct labor for the year totaled $123,000, while manufacturing overhead amounted to $148,000. The Work Process Inventory account had a beginning balance of $26,000 and an ending balance of $19,000. Compute the Cost of Goods Manufactured for the year. *(Hint: The first step is to calculate the direct materials used during the year.)*

E2-25A Compute Cost of Goods Manufactured and Cost of Goods Sold
(Learning Objective 5)

Compute the Cost of Goods Manufactured and Cost of Goods Sold for Blue Sea Company for the most recent year using the amounts described next. Assume that Raw Materials Inventory contains only direct materials.

	Beginning of Year	End of Year		End of Year
Raw materials inventory	$27,000	$31,000	Insurance on plant	$ 8,000
Work process inventory	$43,000	$28,000	Depreciation—plant building and equipment	$12,700
Finished goods inventory	$16,000	$29,000	Repairs and maintenance—plant	$ 4,100
Purchases of direct materials		$79,000	Marketing expenses	$76,000
Direct labor		$83,000	General and administrative expenses	$27,500
Indirect labor		$46,000		

E2-26A Continues E2-25A: Prepare income statement (*Learning Objective 5*)

Prepare the income statement for Blue Sea Company in E2-25A for the most recent year. Assume that the company sold 39,000 units of its product at a price of $10 each during the year.

E2-27A Work backward to find missing amounts (*Learning Objective 5*)

Rapid Electronics manufactures and sells a line of smartphones. Unfortunately, Rapid Electronics suffered serious fire damage at its home office. As a result, the accounting records for October were partially destroyed—and completely jumbled. Rapid Electronics has hired you to help figure out the missing pieces of the accounting puzzle. Assume that the Raw Materials Inventory contains only direct materials.

Revenues in October	$27,700
Work in process inventory, October 31	$ 1,100
Raw materials inventory, October 31	$ 3,600
Direct labor in October	$ 3,400
Manufacturing overhead in October	$ 6,100
Work in process inventory, October 1	0
Finished goods inventory, October 1	$ 4,500
Direct materials used in October	$ 8,600
Gross profit in October	$12,100
Purchases of direct materials in October	$ 9,500

Requirement

Find the following amounts:

a. Cost of Goods Sold in October

b. Beginning Raw Materials Inventory

c. Ending Finished Goods Inventory

E2-28A Determine whether information is relevant (*Learning Objective 6*)

Classify each of the following costs as relevant or irrelevant to the decision at hand and briefly explain your reason.

a. The interest rate paid on invested funds when deciding how much inventory to keep on hand

b. Cost of computers purchased six months ago when deciding whether to upgrade to computers with a faster processing speed

c. The property tax rates in different locales when deciding where to locate the company's headquarters

d. The type of fuel (gas or diesel) used by delivery vans when deciding which make and model of van to purchase for the company's delivery van fleet

e. Cost of operating automated production machinery versus the cost of direct labor when deciding whether to automate production

f. The fair market value of old manufacturing equipment when deciding whether to replace it with new equipment

g. Cost of purchasing packaging materials from an outside vendor when deciding whether to continue manufacturing the packaging materials in-house

h. Depreciation expense on old manufacturing equipment when deciding whether to replace it with newer equipment

i. The total amount of the restaurant's fixed costs when deciding whether to add additional items to the menu

j. The cost of land purchased three years ago when deciding whether to build on the land now or wait two more years

E2-29A   Compute total and average costs (Learning Objective 7)

Smith Soda spends $1 on direct materials, direct labor, and variable manufacturing overhead for every unit (12-pack of soda) it produces. Fixed manufacturing overhead costs $6 million per year. The plant, which is currently operating at only 75% of capacity, produced 25 million units this year. Management plans to operate closer to full capacity next year, producing 30 million units. Management doesn't anticipate any changes in the prices it pays for materials, labor, and manufacturing overhead.

Requirements

1. What is the current total product cost (for the 25 million units), including fixed and variable costs?
2. What is the current average product cost per unit?
3. What is the current fixed cost per unit?
4. What is the forecasted total product cost next year (for the 30 million units)?
5. What is the forecasted average product cost next year?
6. What is the forecasted fixed cost per unit?
7. Why does the average product cost decrease as production increases?

EXERCISES Group B

E2-30B   Classify costs along the value chain for a retailer (Learning Objective 2)

Suppose Radio Shack incurred the following costs at its Charlotte, North Carolina, store.

Newspaper advertisements	$ 5,700
Payment to consultant for advice on location of new store	$ 2,200
Purchases of merchandise	$32,000
Freight-in	$ 3,700
Salespeople's salaries	$ 4,900
Depreciation expense on delivery trucks	$ 1,800
Research on whether store should sell satellite radio service	$ 500
Customer Complaint Department	$ 600
Rearranging store layout	$ 750

Requirements

1. Classify each cost as to which category of the value chain it belongs (R&D, Design, Purchases, Marketing, Distribution, Customer Service).
2. Compute the total costs for each value chain category.
3. How much are the total inventoriable product costs?

E2-31B   Classify costs along the value chain for a manufacturer
(Learning Objectives 2 & 3)

Suppose the cell phone manufacturer Nokia provides the following information for its costs last month (in millions):

Delivery expense to customers via UPS	$ 6
Salaries of salespeople	$ 4
Chip set	$62
Exterior case for phone	$ 7
Assembly-line workers' wages	$ 8
Technical customer-support hotline	$ 9
Depreciation on plant and equipment	$75
Rearrange production process to accommodate new robot	$ 5
1-800 (toll-free) line for customer orders	$ 2
Salaries of scientists who developed new model	$12

Requirements

1. Classify each of these costs according to its place in the value chain (R&D, Design, Production, Marketing, Distribution, or Customer Service).
2. Within the production category, break the costs down further into three sub-categories: Direct Materials, Direct Labor, and Manufacturing Overhead.
3. Compute the total costs for each value chain category.
4. How much are the total inventoriable product costs?
5. How much are the total prime costs?
6. How much are the total conversion costs?

E2-32B Value chain and sustainability efforts *(Learning Objective 2)*

SUSTAINABILITY

Each of the scenarios to follow describes some cost item for organizations in the recycled carpet industry. For each scenario, identify which function of the value chain that cost would represent (R&D, Design, Purchasing/Producing, Marketing, Distributing, or Customer Service.) *Note:* The companies and products used in this exercise are real companies with a strong sustainable practices commitment.

a. Axminster Carpets offsets the carbon emissions from its carpet distribution process by investing in renewable energy projects such as wind, power, and hydropower plants. This carbon offset is verified independently by the Voluntary Carbon Standard. The cost of these carbon offsets would fall into which function in the value chain?

b. Shaw Industries is a flooring manufacturer. It has created Cradle to Cradle Silver Certified carpet, which is carpet that can be recycled back into new carpet again and again at the end of its useful life or it can go back into the soil. The costs to develop the production process for the Cradle to Cradle Silver Certified carpet would fall into which function in the value chain?

c. Fibre(B)lock® Flooring is manufactured using the waste generated from the manufacture of commercial nylon carpet. The cost of the research into how to create Fibre(B)lock® Flooring would fall into which function in the value chain?

d. Flor®, a company that produces residential carpet tiles made from recycled carpet, has an R&R (return and recycle) Program. Homeowners can arrange to have old tiles picked up and shipped back to the plant for recycling. The cost of operating this R&R program would fall into which function in the value chain?

e. Los Angeles Fiber Company (LAFC) received the EPA/CARE award to recognize Los Angeles Fiber Company's sustainability efforts. Since 2000, LAFC has recycled more than 464 million pounds of post-consumer carpet. Its carpet brand, Reliance Carpet, is made entirely from post-consumer carpet fiber. The cost of promoting the company's products and its sustainability efforts would fall into which function in the value chain?

f. Ford Motor Company purchases cylinder head covers made from a nylon resin containing 100% recycled carpet in its 2011 Mustangs. The cost of the cylinder head covers would fall into which function in the value chain?

E2-33B Classify and calculate a manufacturer's costs *(Learning Objectives 3 & 4)*

An airline manufacturer incurred the following costs last month (in thousands of dollars).

a. Airplane seats	$ 260
b. Production supervisors' salaries	$ 190
c. Depreciation on forklifts	$ 90
d. Machine lubricants	$ 20
e. Factory janitors' wages	$ 10
f. Assembly workers' wages	$ 610
g. Property tax on corporate marketing offices	$ 15
h. Plant utilities	$ 120
i. Cost of warranty repairs	$ 215
j. Machine operators' health insurance	$ 80
k. Depreciation on administrative offices	$ 70
l. Cost of designing new plant layout	$ 170
m. Jet engines	$1,000

Requirements

1. Assuming the cost object is an airplane, classify each cost as one of the following: direct material (DM), direct labor (DL), indirect labor (IL), indirect materials (IM), other manufacturing overhead (other MOH), or period cost. What is the total for each type of cost?
2. Calculate total manufacturing overhead costs.
3. Calculate total inventoriable product costs.
4. Calculate total prime costs.
5. Calculate total conversion costs.
6. Calculate total period costs.

E2-34B   Prepare the current assets section of the balance sheet
(Learning Objective 5)

Consider the following selected amounts and account balances of Domer, Inc.:

Manufacturing overhead	$ 24,000
Accounts receivable	$ 84,000
Direct materials used	$ 22,100
Cost of goods sold	$103,000
Raw materials inventory	$ 10,200
Cost of goods manufactured	$ 96,000
Cash	$ 15,200
Direct labor	$ 49,000
Marketing expense	$ 30,000
Work in process inventory	$ 37,000
Finished goods inventory	$ 66,000
Prepaid expenses	$ 5,800

Requirement

Show how Domer reports current assets on the balance sheet. Not all data are used. Is this company a service company, a merchandiser, or a manufacturer? How do you know?

E2-35B   Prepare a retailer's income statement *(Learning Objective 5)*

Jared Tustin is the sole proprietor of Pretty Pets, a business specializing in the sale of high-end pet gifts and accessories. Pretty Pets' sales totaled $1,125,000 during the most recent year. During the year, the company spent $58,000 on expenses relating to website maintenance, $32,500 on marketing, and $28,500 on wrapping, boxing, and shipping the goods to customers. Pretty Pets also spent $636,000 on inventory purchases and an additional $22,000 on freight-in charges. The company started the year with $18,000 of inventory on hand, and ended the year with $16,000 of inventory. Prepare Pretty Pets' income statement for the most recent year.

E2-36B   Compute direct materials used and Cost of Goods Manufactured
(Learning Objective 5)

Kelvin Industries is calculating its Cost of Goods Manufactured at year-end. The company's accounting records show the following: The Raw Materials Inventory account had a beginning balance of $18,000 and an ending balance of $20,000. During the year, the company purchased $62,000 of direct materials. Direct labor for the year totaled $129,000 while manufacturing overhead amounted to $145,000. The Work in Process Inventory account had a beginning balance of $30,000 and an ending balance of $16,000. Compute the Cost of Goods Manufactured for the year. (*Hint:* The first step is to calculate the direct materials used during the year.)

E2-37B   Compute Cost of Goods Manufactured and Cost of Goods Sold
(Learning Objective 5)

Compute the Cost of Goods Manufactured and Cost of Goods Sold for Striker Company for the most recent year using the amounts described next. Assume that Raw Materials Inventory contains only direct materials.

	Beginning of Year	End of Year		End of Year
Raw materials inventory	$21,000	$30,000	Insurance on plant..	$ 8,500
Work process inventory................	$41,000	$34,000	Depreciation—plant building and equipment	$13,300
Finished goods inventory.............	$15,000	$28,000	Repairs and maintenance—plant............................	$ 3,700
Purchases of direct materials		$70,000	Marketing expenses...	$77,000
Direct labor		$87,000	General and administrative expenses......................	$30,500
Indirect labor..............................		$43,000		

E2-38B   Continues E2-37B: Prepare income statement *(Learning Objective 5)*

Prepare the income statement for Striker Company using the data in E2-37B for the most recent year. Assume that the company sold 35,000 units of its product at a price of $13 each during the year.

E2-39B   Work backward to find missing amounts *(Learning Objective 5)*

Lindy Electronics manufactures and sells smartphones. Unfortunately, the company recently suffered serious fire damage at its home office. As a result, the accounting records for October were partially destroyed and completely jumbled. Lindy has hired you to help figure out the missing pieces of the accounting puzzle. Assume that Lindy Electronics' Raw Materials Inventory contains only direct materials.

Work process inventory, October 31	$ 1,600
Finished goods inventory, October 1..	$ 4,900
Direct labor in October...	$ 3,500
Purchases of direct materials in October...	$ 9,700
Work process inventory, October 1	0
Revenues in October..	$27,200
Gross profit in October..	$12,300
Direct materials used in October...	$ 8,200
Raw materials inventory, October 31..	$ 3,600
Manufacturing overhead in October	$ 6,300

Requirement

Find the following amounts:

a. Cost of Goods Sold in October

b. Beginning Raw Materials Inventory

c. Ending Finished Goods Inventory

E2-40B   Determine whether information is relevant *(Learning Objective 6)*

Classify each of the following costs as relevant or irrelevant to the decision at hand and briefly explain your reason.

a. The purchase price of the old computer when replacing it with a new computer with improved features

b. The cost of renovations when deciding whether to build a new office building or to renovate the existing office building

c. The original cost of the current stove when selecting a new, more efficient stove for a restaurant

d. Local tax incentives when selecting the location of a new office complex for a company's headquarters

e. The fair market value (trade-in value) of the existing forklift when deciding whether to replace it with a new, more efficient model

f. Fuel economy when purchasing new trucks for the delivery fleet

g. The cost of production when determining whether to continue to manufacture the screen for a smartphone or to purchase it from an outside supplier

h. The cost of land when determining where to build a new call center

i. The average cost of vehicle operation when purchasing a new delivery van

j. Real estate property tax rates when selecting the location for a new order processing center

E2-41B Compute total and average costs *(Learning Objective 7)*

Sparkle Soda spends $1 on direct materials, direct labor, and variable manufacturing overhead for every unit (12-pack of soda) it produces. Fixed manufacturing overhead costs $3 million per year. The plant, which is currently operating at only 65% of capacity, produced 20 million units this year. Management plans to operate closer to full capacity next year, producing 30 million units. Management doesn't anticipate any changes in the prices it pays for materials, labor, or manufacturing overhead.

Requirements

1. What is the current total product cost (for the 20 million units), including fixed and variable costs?

2. What is the current average product cost per unit?

3. What is the current fixed cost per unit?

4. What is the forecasted total product cost next year (for the 30 million units)?

5. What is the forecasted average product cost next year?

6. What is the forecasted fixed cost per unit?

7. Why does the average product cost decrease as production increases?

PROBLEMS Group A

P2-42A Classify costs along the value chain *(Learning Objectives 2 & 4)*

Rootstown Cola produces a lemon-lime soda. The production process starts with workers mixing the lemon syrup and lime flavors in a secret recipe. The company enhances the combined syrup with caffeine. Finally, the company dilutes the mixture with carbonated water. Rootstown Cola incurs the following costs (in thousands):

Plant janitors' wages	$ 950
Delivery truck drivers' wages	$ 285
Payment for new recipe	$ 1,090
Depreciation on delivery trucks	$ 300
Plant utilities	$ 850
Lime flavoring	$ 1,080
Rearranging plant layout	$ 1,300
Bottles	$ 1,390
Salt	$ 30
Sales commissions	$ 400
Production costs of "cents-off" store coupons for customers	$ 670
Lemon syrup	$17,000
Replace products with expired dates upon customer complaint	$ 35
Depreciation on plant and equipment	$ 3,200
Wages of workers who mix syrup	$ 8,200
Customer hotline	$ 200
Freight-in on materials	$ 1,600

Requirements

1. Classify each of the listed costs according to its category in the value chain (R&D, Design, Production, Marketing, Distribution, or Customer Service).

2. Further break down production costs into three subcategories: Direct Materials (DM), Direct Labor (DL), or Manufacturing Overhead (MOH).

3. Compute the total costs for each value chain category.

4. How much are the total inventoriable product costs?

5. Suppose the managers of the R&D and design functions receive year-end bonuses based on meeting their unit's target cost reductions. What are they likely to do? How might this affect costs incurred in other elements of the value chain?

P2-43A   Determine ending inventory balances (Learning Objective 5)

Flex Displays designs and manufactures displays used in mobile devices. Serious flooding throughout North Carolina affected Flex Displays' facilities. Inventory was completely ruined, and the company's computer system, including all accounting records, was destroyed.

Before the disaster recovery specialists clean the buildings, Maureen Kennedy, the company controller, is anxious to salvage whatever records she can to support an insurance claim for the destroyed inventory. She is standing in what is left of the Accounting Department with Tom Mitton, the cost accountant.

"I didn't know mud could smell so bad," Tom says. "What should I be looking for?"

"Don't worry about beginning inventory numbers," responds Maureen. "We'll get them from last year's annual report. We need first-quarter cost data."

"I was working on the first-quarter results just before the storm hit," Tom says. "Look, my report's still in my desk drawer. But all I can make out is that for the first quarter, material purchases were $541,000 and that direct labor, manufacturing overhead (other than indirect materials), and total manufacturing costs to account for were $523,000; $213,000; and $1,515,000, respectively. Wait, and cost of goods available for sale was $1,415,000."

"Great," says Maureen. "I remember that sales for the period were approximately $1.8 million. Given our gross profit of 25%, that's all you should need."

Tom is not sure about that, but decides to see what he can do with this information. The beginning inventory numbers are as follows:

- Raw materials, $85,000
- Work in process, $206,000
- Finished goods, $187,000

He remembers several schedules he learned in college that may help him get started.

Requirement

Use exhibits in the chapter to determine the ending inventories of raw materials, work in process, and finished goods.

P2-44A   Prepare income statements (Learning Objective 5)

Part One: In 2012, Penny Henderson opened Penny's Posies, a small retail shop selling floral arrangements. On December 31, 2013, her accounting records show the following:

Sales revenue	$53,000
Utilities for shop	$ 1,400
Inventory on December 31, 2013	$ 9,600
Inventory on January 1, 2013	$12,700
Rent for shop	$ 4,600
Sales commissions	$ 4,900
Purchases of merchandise	$37,000

Requirement

Prepare an income statement for Penny's Posies, a merchandiser, for the year ended December 31, 2013.

Part Two: Penny's Posies was so successful that Penny decided to manufacture her own brand of floral supplies: Floral Manufacturing. At the end of December 2014, her accounting records show the following:

Utilities for plant	$ 4,300
Delivery expense	$ 2,500
Sales salaries expense	$ 4,400
Plant janitorial services	$ 1,550
Work in process inventory, December 31, 2014	$ 3,500
Finished goods inventory, December 31, 2013	0
Finished goods inventory, December 31, 2014	$ 4,000
Sales revenue	$109,000
Customer service hotline expense	$ 1,700
Direct labor	$ 20,000
Direct material purchases	$ 34,000
Rent on manufacturing plant	$ 9,600
Raw materials inventory, December 31, 2013	$ 11,000
Raw materials inventory, December 31, 2014	$ 6,500
Work in process inventory, December 31, 2013	0

Requirements

1. Calculate the Cost of Goods Manufactured for Floral Manufacturing for the year ended December 31, 2014.
2. Prepare an income statement for Floral Manufacturing for the year ended December 31, 2014.
3. How does the format of the income statement for Floral Manufacturing differ from the income statement of Penny's Posies?

Part Three: Show the ending inventories that would appear on these balance sheets:

1. Penny's Posies at December 31, 2013
2. Floral Manufacturing at December 31, 2014

P2-45A   Identify relevant information (Learning Objective 6)

You receive two job offers in the same big city. The first job is close to your parents' house, and they have offered to let you live at home for a year so you won't have to incur expenses for housing, food, or cable and Internet. This job pays $45,000 per year. The second job is far from your parents' house, so you'll have to rent an apartment with parking ($9,000 per year), buy your own food ($2,000 per year), and pay for your own cable and Internet ($800 per year). This job pays $50,000 per year. You still plan to do laundry at your parents' house once a week if you live in the city, and you plan to go into the city once a week to visit with friends if you live at home. Thus, the cost of operating your car will be about the same either way. In addition, your parents refuse to pay for your cell phone service ($680 per year).

Requirements

1. Based on this information alone, what is the net difference between the two alternatives (salary, net of relevant costs)?
2. What information is irrelevant? Why?
3. What qualitative information is relevant to your decision?
4. Assume that you really want to take Job #2, but you also want to live at home to cut costs. What new quantitative and qualitative information will you need to incorporate into your decision?

P2-46A   Calculate the total and average costs *(Learning Objective 7)*

The owner of Bronx Restaurant is disappointed because the restaurant has been averaging 8,000 pizza sales per month, but the restaurant and wait staff can make and serve 10,000 pizzas per month. The variable cost (for example, ingredients) of each pizza is $1.45. Monthly fixed costs (for example, depreciation, property taxes, business license, and manager's salary) are $10,000 per month. The owner wants cost information about different volumes so that some operating decisions can be made.

Requirements

1. Fill in the following chart to provide the owner with the cost information. Then use the completed chart to help you answer the remaining questions.

Monthly pizza volume	5,000	8,000	10,000
Total fixed costs	$	$	$
Total variable costs	___	___	___
Total costs	___	___	___
Fixed cost per pizza	$	$	$
Variable cost per pizza	___	___	___
Average cost per pizza	___	___	___
Selling price per pizza	$ 6.25	$ 6.25	$ 6.25
Average profit per pizza	___	___	___

2. From a cost standpoint, why do companies such as Bronx Restaurant want to operate near or at full capacity?

3. The owner has been considering ways to increase the sales volume. The owner thinks that 10,000 pizzas could be sold per month by cutting the selling price per pizza from $6.25 to $5.75. How much extra profit (above the current level) would be generated if the selling price were to be decreased? *(Hint:* Find the restaurant's current monthly profit and compare it to the restaurant's projected monthly profit at the new sales price and volume.)

PROBLEMS Group B

P2-47B   Classify costs along the value chain *(Learning Objectives 2 & 4)*

Jazzy Cola produces a lemon-lime soda. The production process starts with workers mixing the lemon syrup and lime flavors in a secret recipe. The company enhances the combined syrup with caffeine. Finally, the company dilutes the mixture with carbonated water. Jazzy Cola incurs the following costs (in thousands):

Delivery truck drivers' wages	$ 265
Lemon syrup	$20,000
Depreciation on delivery trucks	$ 100
Lime flavoring	$ 920
Payment for new recipe	$ 1,190
Customer hotline	$ 190
Sales commissions	$ 400
Production costs of "cents-off" store coupons for customers	$ 470
Rearranging plant layout	$ 1,500
Freight-in on materials	$ 1,700
Depreciation on plant and equipment	$ 2,900
Bottles	$ 1,210

Salt		$ 30
Plant utilities		$ 850
Wages of workers who mix syrup		$ 7,900
Plant janitors' wages		$ 1,050
Replace products with expired dates upon customer complaint		$ 60

Requirements

1. Classify each of the listed costs according to its category in the value chain, (R&D, Design, Production, Marketing, Distribution, or Customer Service).
2. Further break down production costs into three subcategories: Direct Materials (DM), Direct Labor (DL), or Manufacturing Overhead (MOH).
3. Compute the total costs for each value chain category.
4. How much are the total inventoriable product costs?
5. Suppose the managers of the R&D and design functions receive year-end bonuses based on meeting their unit's target cost reductions. What are they likely to do? How might this affect costs incurred in other elements of the value chain?

P2-48B Determine ending inventory balances (Learning Objective 5)

Bendt Displays designs and manufactures displays used in mobile devices. Serious flooding throughout North Carolina affected Bendt Displays' facilities. Inventory was completely ruined, and the company's computer system, including all accounting records, was destroyed.

Before the disaster recovery specialists clean the buildings, Annette Plum, the company controller, is anxious to salvage whatever records she can to support an insurance claim for the destroyed inventory. She is standing in what is left of the Accounting Department with Paul Lopez, the cost accountant.

"I didn't know mud could smell so bad," Paul says. "What should I be looking for?"

"Don't worry about beginning inventory numbers," responds Annette. "We'll get them from last year's annual report. We need first-quarter cost data."

"I was working on the first-quarter results just before the storm hit," Paul says. "Look, my report's still in my desk drawer. But all I can make out is that for the first quarter, material purchases were $476,000 and that direct labor, manufacturing overhead (other than indirect materials), and total manufacturing costs to account for were $505,000; $245,000; and $1,425,000, respectively. Wait, and cost of goods available for sale was $1,340,000."

"Great," says Annette. "I remember that sales for the period were approximately $1.7 million. Given our gross profit of 30%, that's all you should need."

Paul is not sure about that, but decides to see what he can do with this information. The beginning inventory numbers are as follows:

- Raw materials, $113,000
- Work in process, $229,000
- Finished goods, $154,000

He remembers several schedules he learned in college that may help him get started.

Requirement

Use exhibits in the chapter to determine the ending inventories of raw materials, work in process, and finished goods.

P2-49B   Prepare income statements (Learning Objective 5)

Part One: In 2012, Robin Prough opened Robin's Roses, a small shop selling floral arrangements. On December 31, 2013, her accounting records show the following:

Sales revenue	$59,000
Utilities for shop	$ 1,200
Inventory on December 31, 2013	$ 9,900
Inventory on January 1, 2013	$12,000
Rent for shop	$ 3,600
Sales commissions	$ 4,600
Purchases of merchandise	$34,000

Requirement

Prepare an income statement for Robin's Roses, a merchandiser, for the year ended December 31, 2013.

Part Two: Robin's Roses succeeded so well that Robin decided to manufacture her own brand of floral supplies: Floral Manufacturing. At the end of December 2014, her accounting records show the following:

Utilities for plant	$ 4,400
Delivery expense	$ 2,000
Sales salaries expense	$ 4,700
Plant janitorial services	$ 1,050
Work in process inventory, December 31, 2014	$ 3,500
Finished goods inventory, December 31, 2013	0
Finished goods inventory, December 31, 2014	$ 6,500
Sales revenue	$102,000
Customer service hotline expense	$ 1,100
Direct labor	$ 21,000
Direct material purchases	$ 35,000
Rent on manufacturing plant	$ 8,600
Raw materials inventory, December 31, 2013	$ 14,000
Raw materials inventory, December 31, 2014	$ 10,500
Work in process inventory, December 31, 2013	0

Requirements

1. Calculate the cost of goods manufactured for Floral Manufacturing for the year ended December 31, 2014.
2. Prepare an income statement for Floral Manufacturing for the year ended December 31, 2014.
3. How does the format of the income statement for Floral Manufacturing differ from the income statement of Robin's Roses?

Part Three: Show the ending inventories that would appear on these balance sheets:

1. Robin's Roses at December 31, 2013.
2. Floral Manufacturing at December 31, 2014.

P2-50B   Identify relevant information (Learning Objective 6)

You receive two job offers in the same big city. The first job is close to your parents' house, and they have offered to let you live at home for a year so you won't have to incur expenses for housing, food, or cable and Internet. This job pays $50,000 per year.

The second job is far away from your parents' house, so you'll have to rent an apartment with parking ($12,000 per year), buy your own food ($2,000 per year), and pay for your own cable and Internet ($700 per year). This job pays $55,000 per year. You still plan to do laundry at your parents' house once a week if you live in the city and plan to go into the city once a week to visit with friends if you live at home. Thus, the cost of operating your car will be about the same either way. Additionally, your parents refuse to pay for your cell phone service ($770 per year).

Requirements

1. Based on this information alone, what is the net difference between the two alternatives (salary, net of relevant costs)?
2. What information is irrelevant? Why?
3. What qualitative information is relevant to your decision?
4. Assume you really want to take Job #2, but you also want to live at home to cut costs. What new quantitative and qualitative information will you need to incorporate in your decision?

P2-51B   Calculate the total and average costs (*Learning Objective 7*)

The owner of Brooklyn Restaurant is disappointed because the restaurant has been averaging 4,000 pizza sales per month but the restaurant and wait staff can make and serve 6,000 pizzas per month. The variable cost (for example, ingredients) of each pizza is $1.25. Monthly fixed costs (for example, depreciation, property taxes, business license, manager's salary) are $6,000 per month. The owner wants cost information about different volumes so that some operating decisions can be made.

Requirements

1. Fill in the chart to provide the owner with the cost information. Then use the completed chart to help you answer the remaining questions.

	3,000	4,000	6,000
Monthly pizza volume			
Total fixed costs			
Total variable costs	___	___	___
Total costs	═══	═══	═══
Fixed cost per pizza			
Variable cost per pizza	___	___	___
Average cost per pizza	═══	═══	═══
Selling price per pizza	$ 6.00	$ 6.00	$ 6.00
Average profit per pizza	___	___	___

2. From a cost standpoint, why do companies such as Brooklyn Restaurant want to operate near or at full capacity?
3. The owner has been considering ways to increase the sales volume. The owner thinks that 6,000 pizzas could be sold per month by cutting the selling price from $6.00 per pizza to $5.50. How much extra profit (above the current level) would be generated if the selling price were to be decreased? (*Hint*: Find the restaurant's current monthly profit and compare it to the restaurant's projected monthly profit at the new sales price and volume.)

CRITICAL THINKING

Discussion & Analysis

A2-52 Discussion Questions

1. Briefly describe a service company, a merchandising company, and a manufacturing company. Give an example of each type of company, but do not use the same examples as given in the chapter.

2. How do service, merchandising, and manufacturing companies differ from each other? How are service, merchandising, and manufacturing companies similar to each other? List as many similarities and differences as you can identify.

3. What is the value chain? What are the six types of business activities found in the value chain? Which type(s) of business activities in the value chain generate costs that go directly to the income statement once incurred? What type(s) of business activities in the value chain generate costs that flow into inventory on the balance sheet?

4. Compare direct costs to indirect costs. Give an example of a cost at a company that could be a direct cost at one level of the organization but would be considered an indirect cost at a different level of that organization. Explain why this same cost could be both direct and indirect (at different levels).

5. What is meant by the term "inventoriable product costs"? What is meant by the term "period costs"? Why does it matter whether a cost is an inventoriable product cost or a period cost?

6. Compare inventoriable product costs to period costs. Using a product of your choice, give examples of inventoriable product costs and period costs. Explain why you categorized your costs as you did.

7. Describe how the income statement of a merchandising company differs from the income statement of a manufacturing company. Also comment on how the income statement from a merchandising company is similar to the income statement of a manufacturing company.

8. How are the cost of goods manufactured, the cost of goods sold, the income statement, and the balance sheet related for a manufacturing company? What specific items flow from one statement or schedule to the next? Describe the flow of costs between the cost of goods manufactured, the cost of goods sold, the income statement, and the balance sheet for a manufacturing company.

9. What makes a cost relevant or irrelevant when making a decision? Suppose a company is evaluating whether to use its warehouse for storage of its own inventory or whether to rent it out to a local theater group for housing props. Describe what information might be relevant when making that decision.

10. Explain why "differential cost" and "variable cost" do *not* have the same meaning. Give an example of a situation in which there is a cost that is a differential cost but *not* a variable cost.

11. Greenwashing, the practice of overstating a company's commitment to sustainability, has been in the news over the past few years. Perform an internet search of the term "greenwashing." What examples of greenwashing can you find?

12. Ricoh is a company that has designed its copiers so that at the end of the copier's life, Ricoh will collect and dismantle the product for usable parts, shred the metal casing, and use the parts and shredded material to build new copiers. This product design can be called "cradle-to-cradle" design. Are there any other products you are aware of that have a "cradle-to-cradle" design? Perform an Internet search for "cradle-to-cradle design" or a related term if you need ideas.

Application & Analysis

Mini Cases

A2-53 Costs in the value chain at a real company and cost objects

Choose a company with which you are familiar that manufactures a product. In this activity, you will be making reasonable assumptions about the activities involved in the value chain for this product; companies do not typically publish information about their value chains.

Basic Discussion Questions

1. Describe the product that is being produced and the company that produces it.
2. Describe the six value chain business activities that this product would pass through from its inception to its ultimate delivery to the customer.
3. List at least three costs that would be incurred in each of the six business activities in the value chain.
4. Classify each cost you identified in the value chain as either being an inventoriable product cost or a period cost. Explain your justification.
5. A cost object can be anything for which managers want a separate measurement of cost. List three different potential cost objects *other* than the product itself for the company you have selected.
6. List a direct cost and an indirect cost for each of the three different cost objects in question 5. Explain why each cost would be direct or indirect.

ETHICS

A2-54 Ethics involved with assigning costs to inventory
(Learning Objectives 4 & 5)

Mike is the production manager of a large manufacturing firm. He is worried about the prospect of bonuses for the upcoming year. The company has paid out bonuses for the past ten years, so Mike has been counting on the bonus to help pay some debts he has accumulated over the year. In addition, Mike and his wife are expecting their first baby in two months. Due to the unexpected downturn in sales, bonuses appear to be unlikely this year.

Joe is the accounting manager for the company. He and Mike are good friends. Over lunch one day, Mike confides in Joe about his financial difficulties. He is stressed out over the bills and the baby on the way. He really needs that bonus.

Joe wants to help Mike. Joe has been with the company for many years and knows that fundamentally the company is strong. This year is just an unusual year. He thinks about ways that he can help Mike. Mike is a good employee and the company does not want to lose him if he were to go to work for a competitor.

Joe thinks about how he can best help Mike. He thinks about a few different options, including the following:

Option #1: Joe could increase income for the year by adding sales commission costs and advertising costs to the products. If he does this, the product cost will be higher. However, there is still a large inventory of units on hand. The units that are still in ending inventory will shield these costs from decreasing net income until the units are sold in a future year.

Option #2: Joe could quietly make Mike a loan from the company to help him get back on his feet. The company does not have a policy prohibiting loans to employees, but neither does it have a policy of allowing such loans to employees.

Joe does not know what to do.

Requirements
Using the IMA Statement of Ethical Professional Practice as an ethical framework, answer the following questions:

a. If Joe were to increase income by adding sales commission costs and advertising costs to product costs as described in Option #1, what ethical principles would be violated?
b. If Joe were to make a company loan to Mike (Option #2), what, if any, ethical principles would be violated?
c. What do you think Joe should do in this situation?

REAL LIFE

A2-55 Cost definitions *(Learning Objectives 1, 2, 3, & 4)*

In 2012, the price that Starbucks paid suppliers for its coffee increased. As a result, Starbucks raised the prices of its brewed coffee in some U.S. areas, including the Northeast and Sunbelt regions.[1]

When making the announcement about the upcoming price increase in 2012, management at Starbucks said that the coffee chain absorbed prior price increases in the cost of coffee by being efficient and cutting costs, and through sales growth. Starbucks has a high-end customer base, so it is less sensitive to price increases than many of its coffee

[1]Source: "Starbucks to Raise Prices," *The Wall Street Journal*, January 4, 2012 (retrieved from http://online .wsj.com/article/SB10001424052970203550304577138922045363052.html on March 5, 2013).

competitors. Management said it did not think that its price increase would impact customer purchases.

Starbucks did not raise prices for its packaged coffee sold at grocery stores and at Starbucks stores, because sales of the packaged coffee have a greater effect on profit margins. The coffee purchased from suppliers represents a bigger portion of the cost of packaged coffee than of brewed coffee. Starbucks says that its retail stores have more tools to absorb the increase because of the other costs included in the cost of a cup of coffee.

Requirements

1. Would you consider Starbucks to be a service company, a merchandiser, a manufacturer, or some combination thereof? Support your answer with specific examples.

2. Describe the value chain for a cup of coffee at Starbucks. Use your imagination and brainstorm possible costs at each phase of the value chain.

3. Think about a Starbucks café in Fairlawn, Ohio, and a cup of coffee served and consumed in that café.

   a. What costs would be included in the cost of a cup of coffee served in the café? Separate these costs into direct materials, direct labor, and overhead costs.

   b. What are the direct costs of a cup of coffee, assuming that the cost object is the Fairlawn location? What are the indirect costs of that same cup of coffee for the Fairlawn location?

   c. Assume now that the cost object is the Starbucks corporation itself. What costs of that cup of coffee will now be reclassified as direct (as compared to using the Fairlawn location as the cost object)?

4. Now think about a Starbucks café in Fairlawn, Ohio, and a pound of packaged ground coffee sold in that café (assume that the beans are ground in the store at the time of sale).

   a. What costs are included in the cost of a pound of packaged ground coffee sold at the Fairlawn location? Separate these costs into direct materials, direct labor, and overhead costs.

   b. What are the direct costs of a pound of packaged ground coffee (to be sold to consumers), assuming that the cost object is the Fairlawn location? What are the indirect costs of that same pound of packaged ground coffee for the Fairlawn location?

   c. Assume now that the cost object is the Starbucks corporation itself. What costs of that packaged ground coffee will now be reclassified as direct (as compared to using the Fairlawn location as the cost object)?

5. Consider the costs of a cup of coffee versus the costs of packaged ground coffee. Why does Starbucks management state that its retail stores "have more tools to absorb the increase because of other costs included in the cost of a cup of coffee"? What are these costs?

Try It Solutions

page 54:

Only those costs that can be traced directly to the Produce Department would be considered direct costs: 2, 3, 5, 6 and 8. All other costs (1, 4, and 7) would be considered indirect costs because they are part of the cost of selling produce at the store, yet cannot be traced directly to the Produce Department.

page 57:

The only costs that become inventoriable costs of the product are numbers 3, 5, and 8. All other costs are classified as period costs, which are shown as "operating expenses" on the income statement.

page 65:

Beginning inventory	$ 35,000
Plus: Purchases of merchandise	400,000
Freight-in and import duties	20,000
Cost of goods available for sale	455,000
Less: Ending inventory	38,000
Cost of goods sold	$417,000

Job Costing

Learning Objectives

- **1** Distinguish between job costing and process costing

- **2** Understand the flow of production and how direct materials and direct labor are traced to jobs

- **3** Compute a predetermined manufacturing overhead rate and use it to allocate MOH to jobs

- **4** Determine the cost of a job and use it to make business decisions

- **5** Compute and dispose of overallocated or under-allocated manufacturing overhead

- **6** Prepare journal entries for a manufacturer's job costing system

- **7** (Appendix) Use job costing at a service firm as a basis for billing clients

Ali Ender Birer/Fotolia

Sources: Brunswick Corp. 2012 10(k) filing, http://lifefitness.com

Life Fitness, a division of the Brunswick Corporation, is the global leader in fitness equipment. The company began in the 1970s by introducing the world's first-ever computerized exercise bike. Since then, the company has grown to design and manufacture over 400 different products, including treadmills, elliptical cross-trainers, stair climbers, and, of course, exercise bikes. While the company's growth has been propelled in part by consumers' ever-increasing zeal for personal fitness, the company has also grown through carefully analyzing the profit margins on each of its products and adjusting its operations accordingly.

How does the company determine the profit margins on each of its 400 different models? Life Fitness first determines how much it costs to manufacture each type of exercise machine. Each batch of units produced is called a "job." The company's job costing system traces the cost of direct materials and direct labor used to each job. It also allocates some manufacturing overhead to each job. By adding up the direct materials, direct labor, and manufacturing overhead assigned to each job, the company can determine how much each machine costs to make. The company then uses this information to prepare the company's financial reports and make vital business decisions.

Whether you plan a career in marketing, engineering, production, general management, or accounting, you'll need to understand how much it costs to produce the company's products. This chapter will show you one way companies determine the costs of their products.

What Methods are Used to Determine the Cost of Manufacturing a Product?

Most manufacturers use one of two product costing systems in order to find the cost of producing their products:

1 Distinguish between job costing and process costing

- Process costing
- Job costing

The end goal of both product costing systems is the same: to find the cost of manufacturing one unit of the product. However, the manner in which this goal is achieved differs. Management chooses the product costing system that works best for its particular manufacturing environment. Let's go over the basics of each system and identify the types of companies that would be most likely to use them.

Process Costing

<u>Process costing</u> is used by companies that produce extremely large numbers of identical units through a series of uniform production steps or processes. Because each unit is identical, in theory, each unit should cost the same to make. In essence, process costing averages manufacturing costs across all units produced so that each identical unit bears the same cost.

For example, let's assume Pace Foods uses two processes to make picante sauce: (1) cleaning and chopping vegetables and (2) mixing and bottling the sauce. First, Pace accumulates all manufacturing costs incurred in the cleaning and chopping process over a period of time, such as a month. The costs incurred in this process include the cost of the vegetables themselves, as well as the cost of cleaning and chopping the vegetables. Next, the company averages the total costs of this process over all units passing through the process during the same period of time.

For example, let's say Pace spends $500,000 on purchasing, cleaning, and chopping the vegetables to make 1 million jars of picante sauce during the month. The average cost per jar of the cleaning and chopping process is as follows:

$$\text{Cleaning and chopping process} = \frac{\$500,000}{1,000,000 \text{ jars}} = \$0.50 \text{ per jar}$$

Now the cleaned and chopped vegetables go through the second production process, mixing and bottling, where a similar calculation is performed to find the average cost of that process. The cost of the second process would include any raw materials used, such as the cost of the glass jars, as well as the cost of mixing the sauce and filling the jars with the sauce. Let's say the average cost to mix and bottle each jar of sauce is $0.25.

Now Pace can determine the total cost to manufacture each jar of picante sauce:

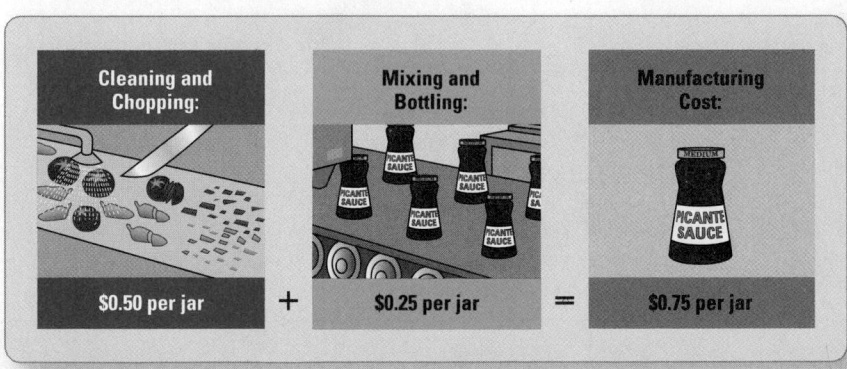

Each jar of picante sauce is identical to every other jar, so each bears the same average cost: $0.75. Once managers know the cost of manufacturing each jar, they can use that information to help set sales prices and make other business decisions. To generate a profit, the sales price will have to be high enough to cover the $0.75 per jar manufacturing cost as well as the company's operating costs incurred in other areas of the value chain, including research and development (R&D), marketing, distribution, customer service, and so forth.

We'll delve more deeply into process costing in Chapter 5. For now, just remember that any company that mass-produces identical units of product will most likely use process costing to determine the cost of making each unit.

Why is this important?

"**Managers** need the most accurate **cost information** they can get in order to make good **business decisions**. They will choose a costing system (usually **job costing** or **process costing**) based on which system best fits their operations."

Job Costing

Whereas process costing is used by companies that mass-manufacture identical units, **job costing** is used by companies that produce unique, custom-ordered products, or relatively small batches of different products. Each unique product or batch of units is considered a separate "job." Different jobs can vary considerably in direct materials, direct labor, and manufacturing overhead costs, so job costing tracks these costs separately for each individual job. For example, Dell custom-builds each personal computer based on the exact components the customer orders. Because each PC is unique, Dell treats each order as a unique job. Life Fitness produces each of its 400 different models of exercise machines in relatively small, separate batches. Each batch of exercise machines produced is considered a separate job. Job costing would also be used by Boeing (airplanes), custom-home builders (unique houses), high-end jewelers (unique jewelry), furniture manufacturers (sofas and chairs with different fabrics), and any other manufacturers that build custom-ordered products.

However, job costing is not limited to manufacturers. Professional service providers such as law firms, accounting firms, consulting firms, and marketing firms use job costing to determine the cost of serving each client. People working in trades, such as mechanics, plumbers, and electricians, also use job costing to determine the cost of performing separate jobs for clients. In both cases, the job cost is used as a basis for billing the client. The appendix to this chapter illustrates a complete example of how a law firm would use job costing to bill its clients.

In summary, companies use job costing when their products or services vary in terms of materials needed, time required to complete the job, and/or the complexity of the production process. Because the jobs are so different, it would not be reasonable to assign them equal costs. Therefore, the cost of each job is compiled separately. We'll spend the rest of this chapter looking at how companies compile, record, and use job costs to make important business decisions. Before moving on, take a look at Exhibit 3-1, which summarizes the key differences between job and process costing.

EXHIBIT 3-1 Differences Between Job and Process Costing

	Job Costing	Process Costing
Cost object:	Job	Process
Outputs:	Single units or small batches with large difference between jobs	Large quantities of identical units
Extent of averaging:	Less averaging—costs are averaged over the small number of units in a job (often one unit in a job)	More averaging—costs are averaged over the hundreds or thousands of identical units that pass through each process

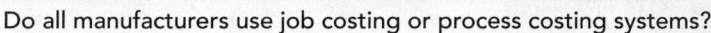

STOP & THINK

Do all manufacturers use job costing or process costing systems?

Answer: Some manufacturers use a hybrid of these two costing systems if neither "pure" system reflects their production environment very well. For example, clothing manufacturers often mass-produce the same product over and over (dress shirts) but use different materials on different batches (cotton fabric on one batch and silk fabric on another). A hybrid costing system would have some elements of a process costing system (averaging labor and manufacturing overhead costs across all units) and some elements of a job costing system (tracing different fabric costs to different batches).

How do Manufacturers Determine a Job's Cost?

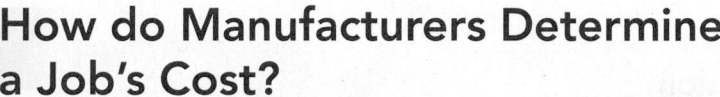

2 Understand the flow of production and how direct materials and direct labor are traced to jobs

As we've just seen, manufacturers use job costing if they produce unique products or relatively small batches of different products. Life Fitness produces each of its 400 different models in relatively small batches, so it considers each batch a separate job. In this section, we will show you how Life Fitness would determine the cost of producing Job 603, a batch of 50 identical X4 Elliptical Cross-Trainers.[1] The company's market for these cross-trainers includes health and fitness clubs, student fitness centers on college campuses, professional athletic teams, hotels, city recreation departments, and direct sales to customers for home fitness gyms. As we walk through the process, keep in mind that most companies maintain the illustrated documents in electronic, rather than hard copy, form. Even so, the basic information stored in the documents and the purpose for the documents remain the same.

Overview: Flow of Inventory Through a Manufacturing System

Before we delve into Life Fitness's job costing system, let's take a quick look at how the physical products, as well as costs, flow through the company. As you learned in Chapter 2, manufacturers such as Life Fitness maintain three separate types of inventory: raw materials, work in process, and finished goods. The cost of each of these inventories is reflected on the company's balance sheet.

As shown in Exhibit 3-2, the raw materials (RM) inventory is maintained in a storeroom, near the factory, until the materials are needed in production. As soon as these materials are transferred to the factory floor, they are no longer considered raw materials because they have become part of the work in process in the factory. The work in process (WIP) inventory consists of all products that are part way through the production process. As soon as the manufacturing process is complete, the products are moved out of the factory and into a finished goods (FG) inventory storage area, or warehouse, where they will await sale and shipment to a customer. Finally, when the products are shipped to customers, the cost of manufacturing those products becomes the Cost of Goods Sold (CGS) shown on the company's income statement.

[1]All references to Life Fitness in this hypothetical example were created by the author solely for academic purposes and are not intended, in any way, to represent the actual business practices of, or costs incurred by, Life Fitness, Inc.

EXHIBIT 3-2 Flow of Inventory Through a Manufacturing System

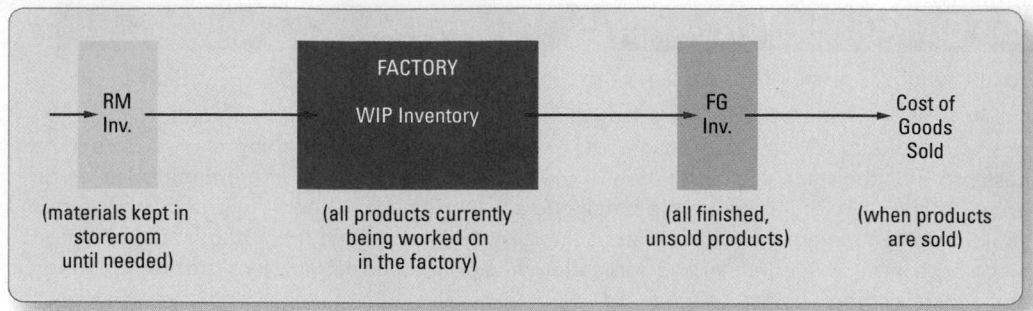

Keep this basic flow of inventory in mind as we delve into Life Fitness's job costing system.

Scheduling Production

Job costing begins with management's decision to produce a batch of units. Sometimes companies produce a batch of units just to meet a particular customer order. For example, the Chicago Bears may custom order treadmills that have characteristics not found on other models. This batch of unique treadmills would become its own job. On the other hand, most companies also produce **stock inventory** for products they sell on a regular basis. They want to have stock available to quickly fill customer orders. By forecasting demand for the product, the manufacturer is able to estimate the number of units that should be produced during a given time period. As shown in Exhibit 3-3, the **production schedule** indicates the quantity and types of inventory that are scheduled to be manufactured during the period. Depending on the company, the types of products it offers, and the production time required, production schedules may cover periods of time as short as one day (Dell, producing customized laptops) or as long as one year or more (Boeing, manufacturing 737 airplanes).

EXHIBIT 3-3 Monthly Production Schedule

Production Schedule For the Month of December					
Job	**Model Number**	**Stock or Customer**	**Quantity**	**Scheduled Start Date**	**Scheduled End Date**
603	X4 Cross-Trainer	For stock	50	12/2	12/6
604	T5-0 Treadmill	For stock	60	12/7	12/17
605	Custom T6-C Treadmill	Chicago Bears	15	12/18	12/21
606	Custom S3-C Stair-Climber	Chicago Bears	12	12/22	12/24
	FACTORY CLOSED FOR HOLIDAYS and ANNUAL MAINTENANCE			12/25	12/31

The production schedule is very important in helping management determine the direct labor and direct materials needed during the period. To complete production on time, management must ensure that an appropriate number of a factory workers with the specific skill-sets required for each job will be available. Management also needs to make sure it will have all of the raw materials needed for each job. The next section shows how this is accomplished.

Purchasing Raw Materials

Production engineers prepare a **bill of materials** for each job. The bill of materials is like a recipe card: It simply lists all of the raw materials needed to manufacture the job. Exhibit 3-4 illustrates a partial bill of materials for Job 603:

EXHIBIT 3-4 Bill of Materials (Partial Listing)

Bill of Materials

Job: 603

Model: X4 Elliptical Cross-Trainer   **Quantity:** 50 units

Part Number	Description	Quantity Needed
HRM50812	Heart rate monitor	50
LCD620	LCD entertainment screen	50
B4906	Front and rear rolling base	100
HG2567	Hand grips	100
FP689	Foot platform	100
	Etc.	

After the bill of materials has been prepared, the purchasing department checks the raw materials inventory to determine which raw materials needed for the job are currently in stock, and which raw materials must be purchased. As shown in Exhibit 3-5, a **raw materials record** shows detailed information about each item in stock, including the number of units received, the number of units used, and the balance of units currently in stock. Additionally, the raw materials record shows the cost of each unit purchased, the cost of each unit used, and the cost of the units still in the raw materials inventory.

EXHIBIT 3-5 Raw Materials Record

Raw Materials Record

Item No.: HRM50812   **Description:** Heart rate monitor

	Received			Used				Balance		
Date	Units	Cost	Total	Requisition Number	Units	Cost	Total	Units	Cost	Total
11-25	100	$60	$6,000					100	$60	$6,000
11-30				#7235	70	$60	$4,200	30	$60	$1,800

According to the raw materials record pictured in Exhibit 3-5, only 30 heart rate monitors are currently in stock. However, the bill of materials shown in Exhibit 3-4 indicates that 50 heart rate monitors are needed for Job 603. Therefore, the purchasing department will need to buy 20 more monitors. The purchasing department must also consider other jobs that will be using heart rate monitors in the near future, as well as the time it takes to obtain the monitors from the company's suppliers. According to the production schedule,

Job 603 is scheduled to begin production on December 2; therefore, the purchasing department must make sure all necessary raw materials are on hand by that date.

Life Fitness's purchasing department will issue a purchase order to its suppliers for any needed parts. Incoming shipments of raw materials are counted and recorded on a receiving report, as well as on the individual raw materials records. The receiving report is typically a duplicate of the purchase order, except it does not pre-list the quantity of parts ordered. The quantity ordered is intentionally left blank to ensure the receiving dock personnel will actually count and record the quantity of materials received. Progressive companies use bar-coding systems to electronically update the raw materials records as soon as incoming shipments are received.

Life Fitness's accounting department will not pay the invoice (bill from the supplier) unless the amount billed agrees with the quantity of parts both ordered *and* received. By matching the purchase order, receiving report, and invoice, Life Fitness ensures that it pays for only those parts that were ordered and received, *and nothing more*. This is an important control that helps companies avoid scams in which businesses are sent and billed for inventory that was not ordered.

In addition to tracking the current level of individual inventory items, the raw materials records also form the basis for valuing the Raw Materials Inventory account found on the balance sheet. On a given date, by adding together the balances in the individual raw materials records, the company is able to substantiate the total Raw Materials Inventory shown on the balance sheet. For example, as shown in Exhibit 3-6, on November 30, Life Fitness had $1,800 of heart rate monitors in stock, $24,000 of LCD entertainment screens, $1,200 of roller bases, and so forth. When combined, these individual balances sum to the Raw Materials Inventory balance shown on Life Fitness's November 30 balance sheet.

EXHIBIT 3-6 Individual Raw Materials Records Sum to the Raw Materials Inventory Balance

Heart Rate Monitors

Date	Received	Used	Balance
11-30			$1,800

LCD Entertainment Screen

Date	Received	Used	Balance
11-30			$24,000

Roller Base

Date	Received	Used	Balance
11-30			$1,200

Hand Grips

Date	Received	Used	Balance
11-30			$500

Wheels

Date	Received	Used	Balance
11-30			$3,000

Foot Platform

Date	Received	Used	Balance
11-30			$1,000

Life Fitness
Balance Sheet
November 30

Assets:	Liabilities and Owners' Equity:
Cash	Accounts Payable
Accounts Receivable	Wages and Salaries Payable
→ Raw Materials Inventory	Other Liabilities
Work in Process Inventory	Total Liabilities
Finished Goods Inventory	Common Stock
Total Current Assets	Retained Earnings
Property and Equipment	Total Owners' Equity
Total Assets	Total Liabilities and Owners' Equity

Using a Job Cost Record to Accumulate Job Costs

Job 603 will be started when the scheduled production date arrives. A job cost record, as pictured in Exhibit 3-7, will be used to accumulate all of the direct materials and direct labor used on the job, as well as the manufacturing overhead allocated to the job.

▶ Try It!

Match the following concepts to their descriptions:

1. Document specifying when jobs will be manufactured
2. Product costing system used by mass manufacturers
3. Bill from supplier
4. Document specifying parts needed to produce a job
5. Product costing system used by manufacturers of unique products
6. Document containing the details and balance of each part in stock
7. Document for recording incoming shipments
8. Products normally kept on hand in order to fill orders quickly

    a. Process costing
    b. Stock inventory
    c. Raw materials records
    d. Production schedule
    e. Receiving report
    f. Invoice
    g. Bill of materials
    h. Job costing

Please see page 175 for solutions.

EXHIBIT 3-7 Job Cost Record

Job Cost Record

Job Number: 603

Customer: For stock

Job Description: 50 units of X4 Elliptical Cross-Trainers

Date Started: Dec. 2   **Date Completed:**

Manufacturing Cost Information:	Cost Summary
Direct Materials	
	$
Direct Labor	
	$
Manufacturing Overhead	
	$
Total Job Cost	$
Number of Units	÷ 50 units
Cost per Unit	$

Shipping Information:			
Date	Quantity Shipped	Units Remaining	Cost Balance

> ### Why is this important?
>
> "**Job cost records** keep track of **all manufacturing costs** assigned to **individual jobs** so that **managers** know the **cost** of making each product."

Each job will have its own job cost record. Note that the job cost record is merely a form (electronic or hard copy) for keeping track of the three manufacturing costs associated with each job:

- direct materials,
- direct labor, and
- manufacturing overhead.

The job cost records also show the number of units produced on the job, as well as the cost per unit.

As we saw in the last section, the individual raw materials records substantiate the total Raw Materials Inventory shown on the balance sheet. Likewise, as shown in Exhibit 3-8, the job cost records on *incomplete* jobs provide the substantiating detail for the total Work in Process Inventory account shown on the balance sheet.

EXHIBIT 3-8 Job Cost Records on Incomplete Jobs Sum to the WIP Inventory Balance

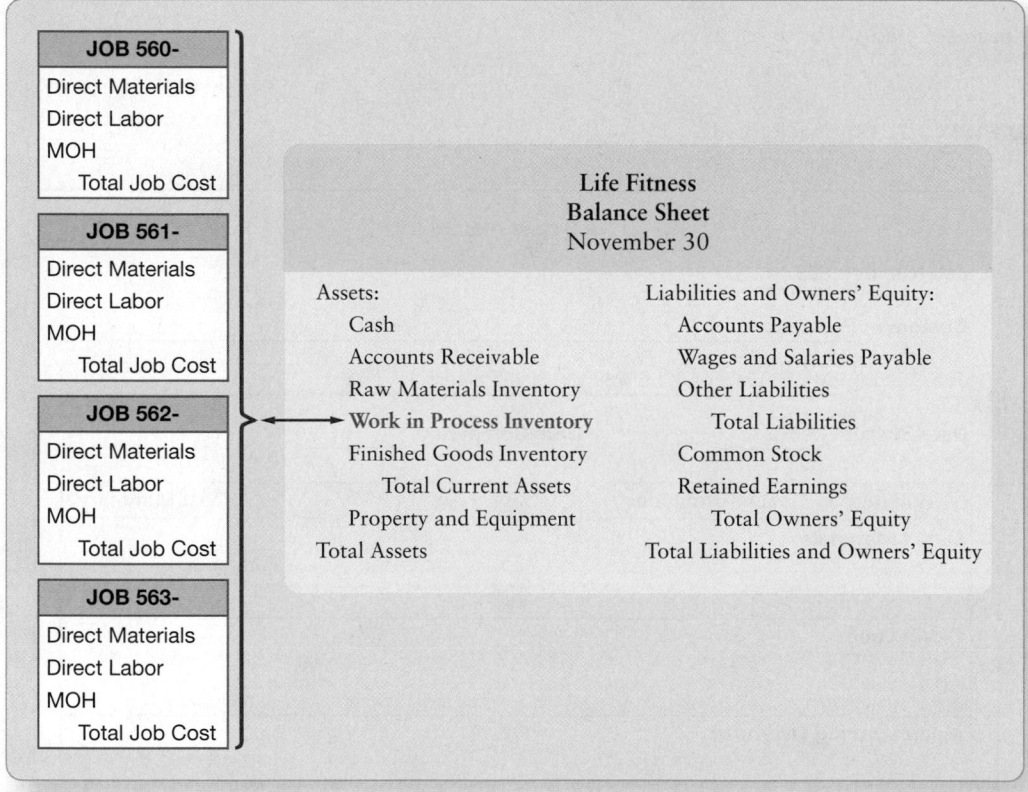

Once jobs are completed, the job cost records serve as a basis for valuing the Finished Goods Inventory account. As shown near the bottom of Exhibit 3-7, job cost records typically list the date and quantity of units shipped to customers, the number of units remaining in finished goods inventory, and the cost of those units. The balance of *unsold* units from *completed* job cost records substantiates the total Finished Goods Inventory account shown on the balance sheet.

As you can see, the job cost records serve a vital role in a job costing system. Now let's take a look at how Life Fitness accumulates manufacturing costs on the job cost record. We'll begin by looking at how direct materials costs are traced to individual jobs.

Tracing Direct Materials Cost to a Job

Production will eventually need all of the parts shown on the bill of materials for Job 603 (Exhibit 3-4). However, according to the production schedule (Exhibit 3-3), this job is scheduled to take five days to complete, so the production crew may not want all of the raw materials at once. Each time materials are needed, production personnel will fill out a **materials requisition**. As shown in Exhibit 3-9, the materials requisition is a document itemizing the materials currently needed from the storeroom. Notice that the root word of *requisition* is *request*. In essence, production personnel use this document to request that the itemized materials be sent from the storeroom into the factory. Most progressive companies use electronic forms, but we show a hard copy here.

EXHIBIT 3-9 Materials Requisition

Materials Requisition

Date: 12/2   Number: #7568

Job: 603

Part Number	Description	Quantity	Unit Cost	Amount
HRM50812	Heart rate monitor	50	$60	$3,000
LCD620	LCD entertainment screen	50	$100	5,000
B4906	Front and rear rolling base	100	$5	500
	Total			$8,500

As soon as the materials requisition is received by the raw materials storeroom, workers **pick** the appropriate materials and send them to the factory floor. Picking is just what it sounds like: storeroom workers pick the needed materials off of the storeroom shelves. The unit cost and total cost of all materials picked are posted to the materials requisition based on the cost information found in the individual raw materials records. The individual raw materials records are also updated as soon as the materials are picked, often using bar-coding systems to simplify the process and provide real-time information. For example, in Exhibit 3-10, we show how the raw material record for heart rate monitors is updated after requisition #7568 (Exhibit 3-9) has been picked.

EXHIBIT 3-10 Raw Materials Record Updated for Materials Received and Used

Raw Materials Record

Item No.: HRM50812   Description: Heart rate monitor

Date	Units	Cost	Total	Requisition Number	Units	Cost	Total	Units	Cost	Total
11-25	100	$60	$6,000					100	$60	$6,000
11-30				#7235	70	$60	$4,200	30	$60	$1,800
12-1	75	$60	$4,500					105	$60	$6,300
12-2				#7568	50	$60	$3,000	55	$60	$3,300

Finally, the raw materials requisitioned for the job are posted to the job cost record. As shown in Exhibit 3-11, each time raw materials are requisitioned for Job 603, they are posted to the direct materials section of the job cost record. Again, bar-coding systems allow this process to be completed with more efficiency. These materials are considered direct materials (rather than indirect materials), because they can be traced specifically to Job 603. By using this system to trace direct materials to specific jobs, managers know *exactly* how much direct materials cost is incurred by each job.

EXHIBIT 3-11 Posting Direct Materials Used to the Job Cost Record

Job Cost Record

Job Number: 603

Customer: For stock

Job Description: 50 units of X4 Elliptical Cross-Trainers

Date Started: Dec. 2   **Date Completed:** _____

Manufacturing Cost Information:	Cost Summary
Direct Materials	
Req. #7568: $ 8,500 (shown in Exhibit 3-9)	
Req. #7580: $14,000	
Req. #7595: $13,500	
Req. #7601: $ 4,000	$ 40,000
Direct Labor	
	$
Manufacturing Overhead	
	$
Total Job Cost	$
Number of Units	÷ 50 units
Cost per Unit	$

Tracing Direct Labor Cost to a Job

Now let's look at how direct labor costs are traced to individual jobs. All direct laborers in the factory fill out <u>labor time records</u>. As shown in Exhibit 3-12, a labor time record simply records the time spent by each employee on each job he or she worked on throughout the day. Oftentimes, these records are kept electronically. Rather than using old-fashioned time tickets and punch clocks, factory workers now "swipe" their bar-coded employee identification cards on a computer terminal and enter the appropriate job number. Based on each employee's unique hourly wage rate, the computer calculates the direct labor cost to be charged to the job. Companies that are even more progressive use biometric scanning devices to quickly capture information about how long individual employees work on each job.

For example, in Exhibit 3-12, we see that Hannah Smith, who is paid a wage rate of $20 per hour, worked on both Jobs 602 and 603 during the week. Hannah spent five hours working on Job 603 on December 2. Therefore, $100 of direct labor cost ($20 × 5) will be charged to Job 603 for Hannah's work on that date. On December 3, Hannah's eight hours of work on Job 603 resulted in another $160 ($20 × 8) of direct labor being charged to the job. The cost of each direct laborer's time will be computed using each employee's unique wage rate, just as was done with Hannah Smith's time. Then, as shown in Exhibit 3-13, the information from the individual labor time records is posted to the direct labor section of the job cost record. Again, this posting is normally done automatically by the company's computer system.

As you can see, by tracing direct labor cost in this fashion, individual jobs are charged only for the exact amount of direct labor actually used in their production.

EXHIBIT 3-12 Labor Time Record

<table>
<tr>
<td colspan="6" align="center">**Labor Time Record**</td>
</tr>
<tr>
<td colspan="3">**Employee:** Hannah Smith</td>
<td colspan="3">**Week:** 12/2 – 12/9</td>
</tr>
<tr>
<td colspan="3">**Hourly Wage Rate:** $20</td>
<td colspan="3">**Record #:** 324</td>
</tr>
<tr>
<td>**Date**</td>
<td>**Job Number**</td>
<td>**Start Time**</td>
<td>**End Time**</td>
<td>**Hours**</td>
<td>**Cost**</td>
</tr>
<tr>
<td>12/2</td>
<td>602</td>
<td>8:00</td>
<td>11:00</td>
<td>3</td>
<td>$60</td>
</tr>
<tr>
<td>12/2</td>
<td>603</td>
<td>12:00</td>
<td>5:00</td>
<td>5</td>
<td>$100</td>
</tr>
<tr>
<td>12/3</td>
<td>603</td>
<td>8:00</td>
<td>4:00</td>
<td>8</td>
<td>$160</td>
</tr>
<tr>
<td>12/4 etc.</td>
<td></td>
<td></td>
<td></td>
<td></td>
<td></td>
</tr>
</table>

EXHIBIT 3-13 Posting Direct Labor Used to the Job Cost Record

Job Cost Record

Job Number: 603

Customer: For stock

Job Description: 50 units of X4 Elliptical Cross-Trainers

Date Started: Dec. 2   **Date Completed:** _____

Manufacturing Cost Information:	Cost Summary	
Direct Materials		
Req. #7568: $ 8,500		
Req. #7580: $14,000		
Req. #7595: $13,500		
Req. #7601: $ 4,000	$	40,000
Direct Labor		
No. #324 (30 DL hours): $100, $160, etc. (shown in Exhibit 3-12)		
No. #327 (40 DL hours): $240, $210, etc.		
No. #333 (36 DL hours): $80, $120, etc.		
Etc.		
(a total of 500 DL hours)	$	10,000
Manufacturing Overhead		
	$	
Total Job Cost	$	
Number of Units	÷	50 units
Cost per Unit	$	

What about employee benefits, such as employee-sponsored retirement plans, health insurance, payroll taxes, and other benefits? As discussed in Chapter 2, these payroll-related benefits often add another 30% or more to the cost of gross wages and salaries. Some companies factor, or load, these costs into the hourly wage rate charged to the jobs. For example, if a factory worker earns a wage rate of $10 per hour, the job cost records would show a loaded hourly rate of about $13 per hour, which would include all benefits associated with employing the worker. However, because coming up with an *accurate* loaded hourly rate such as this is difficult, many companies treat these extra payroll-related costs as part of manufacturing overhead, rather than loading these costs into the direct labor wage rates. Either method is acceptable. We'll next discuss how manufacturing overhead costs are handled.

Allocating Manufacturing Overhead to a Job

3 Compute a predetermined manufacturing overhead rate and use it to allocate MOH to jobs

So far we have traced the direct materials and direct labor costs to Job 603. Recall, however, that Life Fitness incurs many other manufacturing costs that cannot be directly traced to specific jobs. These indirect manufacturing costs, otherwise known as manufacturing overhead (MOH), include depreciation on the factory plant and equipment, utilities to run the plant, property taxes and insurance on plant, equipment maintenance, the salaries of plant janitors and supervisors, machine lubricants, and so forth. Because of the nature of these costs, we cannot tell exactly how much of these costs are attributable to producing a specific job. Therefore, we cannot trace these costs to specific jobs, as we did with direct materials and direct labor. Rather, we will have to allocate some reasonable amount of these costs to each job. Why bother? Generally accepted accounting principles (GAAP) mandate that manufacturing overhead *must* be treated as an inventoriable product cost for financial reporting purposes. The rationale is that these costs are a *necessary* part of the production process: Jobs could not be produced without incurring these costs, so they must become part of each job's stated cost. Let's now look at how companies allocate manufacturing overhead costs to jobs.

What Does Allocating Mean?

Allocating manufacturing overhead[2] to jobs simply means that we will be "splitting up" or "dividing" the total manufacturing overhead costs among the jobs we produced during the year. There are many different ways we could "split up" the total manufacturing overhead costs among jobs. For example, there are a number of different ways you could split up a pizza pie among friends: You could give equal portions to each friend, you could give larger portions to the largest friends, or you could give larger portions to the hungriest friends. All in all, you have a set amount of pizza, but you could come up with several different reasonable bases for splitting it among your friends (based on number of friends, size of friends, or hunger level of friends).

> ■ **Why is this important?**
>
> "Managers use the **predetermined MOH rate** as a way to **'spread'** (allocate) **indirect** manufacturing costs, such as factory utilities, **among all jobs** produced in the factory during the year."

Likewise, a manufacturer has a total amount of manufacturing overhead that must be split among all of the jobs produced during the year. Because each job is unique in size and resource requirements, it wouldn't be fair to allocate an equal amount of manufacturing overhead to each job. Rather, management needs some other reasonable basis for splitting up the total manufacturing overhead costs among jobs. In this chapter, we'll discuss the most basic method of allocating manufacturing overhead to jobs. This method has traditionally been used by most manufacturers, but more progressive companies are learning to use better, more accurate allocation systems, which we will discuss in Chapter 4. However, for now, we'll start with a basic allocation system.

Steps to Allocating Manufacturing Overhead

Manufacturers follow four steps to implement this basic allocation system. The first three steps are taken *before the year begins*:

STEP 1: The company estimates its total manufacturing overhead costs for the coming year.

This is the total "pie" to be allocated. For Life Fitness, let's assume management estimates total manufacturing overhead costs for the year to be $1 million.

---

[2]The term "applying" manufacturing overhead is often used synonymously with "allocating" manufacturing overhead.

STEP 2: The company selects an allocation base and estimates the total amount that will be used during the year.

This is the *basis* management has chosen for "dividing up the pie." For Life Fitness, let's assume management has selected direct labor hours as the allocation base. Furthermore, management estimates that 62,500 of direct labor hours will be used during the year.

Ideally, the allocation base should be the <u>cost driver</u> of the manufacturing overhead costs. As the term implies, a cost driver is the primary factor that causes, or drives, a cost. For example, in many companies, manufacturing overhead costs rise and fall with the amount of work performed in the factory. Because of this, most companies traditionally use either direct labor hours or direct labor cost as their allocation base. This information is also easy to gather from the labor time records or job cost records. However, for manufacturers that have automated much of their production process, machine hours is a more appropriate allocation base because the amount of time spent running the machines drives the utility, maintenance, and equipment depreciation costs in the factory. As you'll learn in Chapter 4, some companies use multiple allocation bases to more accurately allocate manufacturing overhead costs to individual jobs. The important point is that the allocation base selected should bear a strong, positive relationship to the manufacturing overhead costs.

STEP 3: The company calculates its *predetermined* <u>manufacturing overhead (MOH) rate</u> using the information estimated in Steps 1 and 2:

$$\text{Predetermined MOH rate} = \frac{\text{Total estimated manufacturing overhead costs}}{\text{Total estimated amount of the allocation base}}$$

For example, Life Fitness calculates its predetermined MOH rate as follows:

$$\text{Predetermined MOH rate} = \frac{\$1,000,000}{62,500 \text{ DL hours}} = \$16 \text{ per direct labor hour}$$

This rate will be used throughout the coming year. It is not revised, unless the company finds that either the manufacturing overhead costs or the total amount of the allocation base being used in the factory (direct labor hours for Life Fitness) have substantially shifted away from the estimated amounts. If this is the case, management might find it necessary to revise the rate part way through the year.

Why does the company use a *predetermined* MOH rate, based on *estimated or budgeted data*, rather than an actual MOH rate based on actual data for the year? In order to get actual data, the company would have to wait until the *end of the year* to set its MOH rate. By then, the information is too late to be useful for making pricing and other decisions related to individual jobs. Managers are willing to sacrifice some accuracy in order to get timely information on how much each job costs to produce.

Once the company has established its predetermined MOH rate, it uses that rate throughout the year to calculate the amount of manufacturing overhead to allocate to each job produced, as shown in Step 4.

STEP 4: The company allocates some manufacturing overhead to each individual job as follows:

MOH allocated to a job = Predetermined MOH rate × Actual amount of allocation base used by the job

Let's see how this works for Life Fitness's Job 603. Because the predetermined MOH rate is based on direct labor hours (\$16 per DL hour), we'll need to know how many direct labor hours were used on Job 603. From Exhibit 3-13, we see that Job 603 required a total of 500 DL hours. This information was collected from the individual labor time records and summarized on the job cost record. Therefore, we calculate the amount of manufacturing overhead to be allocated to Job 603 as follows:

$$\text{MOH to be allocated to Job 603} = \$16 \text{ per direct labor hour} \times 500 \text{ direct labor hours}$$
$$= \$8,000$$

The $8,000 of manufacturing overhead allocated to Job 603 is now posted to the job cost record, as shown in Exhibit 3-14.

EXHIBIT 3-14 Posting Manufacturing Overhead and Completing the Job Cost Record

Job Cost Record

Job Number: 603

Customer: For stock

Job Description: 50 units of X4 Elliptical Cross-Trainers

Date Started: Dec. 2   **Date Completed:** Dec. 6

Manufacturing Cost Information:	Cost Summary
Direct Materials	
Req. #7568: $ 8,500	
Req. #7580: $14,000	
Req. #7595: $13,500	
Req. #7601: $ 4,000	$ 40,000
Direct Labor	
No. #324 (30 DL hours): $100, $160, etc.	
No. #327 (40 DL hours): $240, $210, etc.	
No. #333 (36 DL hours): $80, $120, etc.	
Etc.	
(a total of 500 DL hours)	$ 10,000
Manufacturing Overhead	
$16/DL hour × 500 DL hours = $8,000	$ 8,000
Total Job Cost	$ 58,000
Number of Units	÷ 50 units
Cost per Unit	$ 1,160

When is Manufacturing Overhead Allocated to Jobs?

The point in time at which manufacturing overhead is allocated to a job depends on the sophistication of the company's computer system. In most sophisticated systems, some manufacturing overhead is allocated to a job each time some of the allocation base is posted to the job cost record. In our Life Fitness example, every time an hour of direct labor is posted to a job, $16 of manufacturing overhead would also be posted to the same job. In less sophisticated systems, manufacturing overhead is allocated only once: as soon as the job is complete and the total amount of allocation base used by the job is known (as shown in Exhibit 3-14). However, if the balance sheet date (for example, December 31) arrives before the job is complete, Life Fitness would need to allocate some manufacturing overhead to the job based on the number of direct labor hours used on the job thus far. Only by updating the job cost records will the company have the most accurate Work in Process Inventory on its balance sheet.

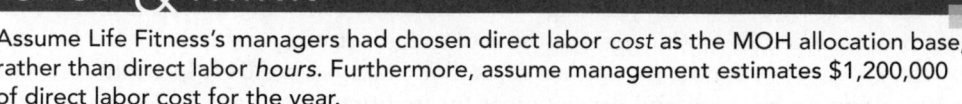

STOP & THINK

Completing the Job Cost Record and Using it to Make Business Decisions

As shown in Exhibit 3-14, now that all three manufacturing costs have been posted to the job cost record, Life Fitness can determine the total cost of manufacturing Job 603 ($58,000) as well as the cost of producing each of the 50 identical units in the job ($1,160 each). Let's look at a few ways this information is used by management.

4 Determine the cost of a job and use it to make business decisions

REDUCING FUTURE JOB COSTS Management will use the job cost information to control costs. By examining the exact costs traced to the job, management might be able to determine ways of reducing the cost of similar jobs produced in the future. For example, are the heart rate monitors costing more than they did on previous jobs? Perhaps management can renegotiate the contracts with its primary suppliers, or identify different suppliers that are willing to sell the parts more cheaply, without sacrificing quality.

What about direct labor costs? By examining the time spent by various workers on the job, management may be able to improve the efficiency of the process so that less production time is required. Management will also examine the hourly wage rates paid to the individuals who worked on the job to determine if less skilled and therefore less costly workers could accomplish the same production tasks, freeing up the more highly skilled employees for more challenging work.

ASSESSING AND COMPARING THE PROFITABILITY OF EACH MODEL Management will also use job cost information to determine the profitability of the various models. Assume the X4 Elliptical Cross-Trainer is listed on the company's website at a sales price of $1,900. That means the company can expect the following gross profit on each unit sold:

Unit sales price...	$1,900
Unit cost (computed on job cost record in Exhibit 3-14)........................	1,160
Gross profit..	$ 740

This profit analysis shows that the company would generate a gross profit of $740 on each unit sold from this job. Although this may seem fairly high, keep in mind that companies incur many operating costs, outside of manufacturing costs, that must be covered by the gross profit earned by product sales. For example, in 2011, Life Fitness spent over $17 million on research and development for its fitness equipment![3] Managers will compare the gross profit on this model to the gross profit of other models to determine which products should be emphasized in sales effort. Obviously, management will want to concentrate on marketing those models that yield the higher profit margins.

DEALING WITH PRICING PRESSURE FROM COMPETITORS Management can also use job cost information to determine how it will deal with pricing pressure. Say a competitor drops the price of its similar elliptical cross-trainer to $1,500. The profit analysis shows that Life Fitness could drop its sales price to $1,500 and still generate $340 of gross profit on the sale ($1,500 − $1,160). In fact, Life Fitness could *undercut* the competitors by charging less than $1,500 to generate additional sales and perhaps increase its market share.

ALLOWING DISCOUNTS ON HIGH-VOLUME SALES Customers will often expect discounts for high-volume sales. For example, say the City of Westlake wants to order 40 of these cross-trainers for the city's recreation center and has asked for a 25% volume discount off of the regular sales price. If Life Fitness won't agree to the discount, the city will take its business to the competitor. Can Life Fitness agree to this discount and still earn a profit on the sale? Let's see:

Discounted sales price (75% of $1,900)	$1,425
Unit cost (computed on job cost record in Exhibit 3-14)	1,160
Gross profit	$ 265

These calculations show that the discounted sales price will still be profitable. We'll talk more about special orders like this in Chapter 8.

BIDDING FOR CUSTOM ORDERS Management also uses product cost information to bid for custom orders. Let's say that the Atlanta Falcons training facility would like to order 15 custom treadmills and is accepting bids from various fitness equipment companies. Management can use the job cost records from past treadmill jobs to get a good idea of how much it will cost to complete the custom order. For example, the custom treadmills may require additional components not found on the standard models. Life Fitness will factor in these additional costs to get an estimate of the total job cost before it is produced. Life Fitness will most likely use <u>cost-plus pricing</u> to determine a bid price for the custom job. When companies use cost-plus pricing, they take the cost of the job (from the estimated or actual job cost record) and add a markup to help cover operating expenses and generate a profit:

$$\text{Cost plus price} = \text{Cost} + \text{Markup on cost}$$

Usually, the markup percentage or final bid price is agreed upon in a written contract before the company goes ahead with production. For example, let's say that Life Fitness typically adds a 40% markup on cost to help cover operating costs and generate a

---

■ **Why is this important?**

"Once managers know how much it **costs** to complete a **job**, they use that **information** to do the following:

- Find **cheaper** ways of completing similar jobs in the future,
- Determine which products are **most profitable**, and
- Establish prices for **custom-ordered** jobs."

---

[3]Brunswick Corp. 2012 10-K filing. Life Fitness is a division of Brunswick Corporation.

reasonable profit. If the estimated total job cost for the 15 treadmills is $25,000, then the bid price would be calculated as follows:

$$\text{Cost-plus price} = \$25,000 + (40\% \times \$25,000)$$
$$= \$35,000$$

Once the management team of the Atlanta Falcons has received Life Fitness's bid as well as bids from other companies, the team will decide which bid to accept based on price, quality, reputation for service, and so forth.

PREPARING THE FINANCIAL STATEMENTS   Finally, the job cost information is critical to preparing the company's financial statements. Why? Because the information is used to determine the total Cost of Goods Sold shown on the income statement, as well as the Work in Process and Finished Goods Inventory accounts shown on the balance sheet. Every time a cross-trainer from Job 603 is sold, its cost ($1,160) becomes part of the Cost of Goods Sold during the period. Likewise, every time a cross-trainer from the job is sold, the balance in Finished Goods Inventory is reduced by $1,160. As shown earlier (Exhibit 3-8), the cost-to-date of unfinished jobs remains in the company's Work in Process Inventory.

How Can Job Costing Information be Enhanced for Decision Making?

We have just finished developing a traditional job cost record and have seen how managers use the information to make vital business decisions. With the help of today's advanced information systems, the job cost information can be further enhanced to help managers make even more informed decisions. This section describes just a few of these enhancements.

Sustainability and Job Costing

Job cost records serve a vital role for manufacturers who embrace sustainability. Because job cost records contain information about the direct materials, direct labor, and manufacturing overhead assigned to each job, they capture the essential resources required to manufacture a product. The summary information on the job cost records can be enhanced to provide management with further information about how the product or production process may affect the environment, employees involved in the manufacturing process, future consumers of the product, and future disposal of the packaging materials and product itself.

For example, the direct materials section of the job cost record can be broken down into subcategories that provide management with useful environmental information. Categories might include:

- material inputs that are post-consumer-use or recycled materials,
- toxic versus non-toxic materials,
- packaging materials that can be recycled or composted versus those that will end up in a landfill,
- materials sourced from local suppliers versus those sourced from geographically distant suppliers (thereby increasing the company's carbon footprint),
- materials that will become waste as a result of the production process,
- materials sourced from companies that embrace fair-labor practices and environmental sustainability,
- materials with heavy fossil-fuel footprints, and
- the percentage of the end product that can be recycled by the consumer.

See Exercises E3-21A and E3-35B

Likewise, the job cost record can help management track the extent of the company's fair-labor practices related to each job, such as:

- the percentage of labor paid at a rate greater than minimum wage as defined by law,
- the percentage of labor force receiving health-care benefits, and
- the diversity of labor force used on the job.

Finally, although MOH resources cannot be traced to specific jobs, the company can provide its potential customers with general information such as:

- percentage of factory utilities generated from renewable sources (wind, solar) versus fossil-fuels, and
- percentage reclaimed and recycled water, versus potable water, used in factory.

We'll discuss MOH and sustainability more in Chapter 4, but this should give you a basic idea of the types of sustainability related data that can be measured and reported.

Once the company has tracked this information on job cost records, how is it used? First, it can be used by management to identify areas of weakness so that the company can move towards a more sustainable business model. Second, it can be used to provide information to potential customers, as part of their supply chain assessment.

Sustainability-related information is becoming increasingly important in supply chain management. Many large companies, such as Walmart and Costco, are now assessing the environmental and social impact of the suppliers they choose to buy products from. In fact, supply chain pressure has become a major driving force in corporate adoption of greener and more socially responsible practices.

Third, this information is useful for marketing and labeling. The Sustainability Consortium, a multi-stakeholder group of companies and organizations, is working on developing a standardized system for measuring and reporting the environmental and social impact of consumer products across their entire life cycles. The Consortium is in the process of developing a "sustainability profile" that would be shown on consumer products, somewhat akin to the nutrition labels currently found on food products. By accurately labeling consumer products with environmental and social impact information, consumers will be in a better position to make informed purchasing decisions.

Fourth, this information can be used to assess the risk of future environmental costs associated with each job. For example, **Extended Producer Responsibility (EPR)** laws, more commonly known as "take-back" laws, create future costs associated with the production of electronic devices and other problem waste, such as mattresses, paint, and batteries. EPR laws, which have been passed in over 25 states as well as several European countries, require manufacturers of electronic devices and other problem waste to take back a large percentage of their products at the end of the products' useful lives. For example, the Wisconsin E-waste Law requires electronics manufacturers to take back 80% of the products they have produced (by weight) in the previous three years; manufacturers that violate this law are subject to a fine.

The goal of EPR laws is to reduce the amount of potentially dangerous waste in landfills by shifting the end-of-life disposal cost back to the manufacturer. By bearing the disposal cost, manufacturers should be motivated to design greener products that are repairable, more easily recyclable, and have a longer life cycle.

How do e-waste EPR laws work? Major electronics retailers, such as Best Buy and Staples, collect unused electronics from consumers free of charge, and then partner with responsible recyclers to ensure that the e-waste is dismantled and recycled rather than dumped in landfills or exported to developing nations. Electronics manufacturers partner with these retailers and recyclers by subsidizing their costs.

To put the size of e-waste into perspective, consider the following: In the first quarter of 2013, Apple sold over 47 million iPhones, 22 million iPads, 4 million Macs, and 12 million iPods.[4] And that's just for three months of sales! When you consider

---

[4]http://www.apple.com/pr/library/2013/01/23Apple-Reports-Record-Results.html
http://electronicstakeback.com/promote-good-laws/state-legislation/

all of the other computer, TV, and smartphone producers, you begin to understand the size of the potential e-waste issue. As a result, many electronics producers, such as Apple, HP, and Dell, are supporting take-back policies and providing recycling options for their old products.

In addition to state EPR laws, the federal government is also considering a bill that will restrict the export of toxic e-waste to developing nations. This bill, if passed, will not only help with environmental and public health issues caused by e-waste, but will also create even more incentive for manufacturers and recyclers to find alternative uses for outdated electronic equipment.

Non-Manufacturing Costs

Job costing in manufacturing companies has traditionally focused on assigning only production-related costs (direct materials, direct labor, and manufacturing overhead) to jobs. The focus on manufacturing costs arises because GAAP requires that *only* inventoriable product costs be treated as assets for external financial reporting purposes. Costs incurred in other elements of the value chain (period costs) are not assigned to products for external financial reporting, but instead are treated as operating expenses.

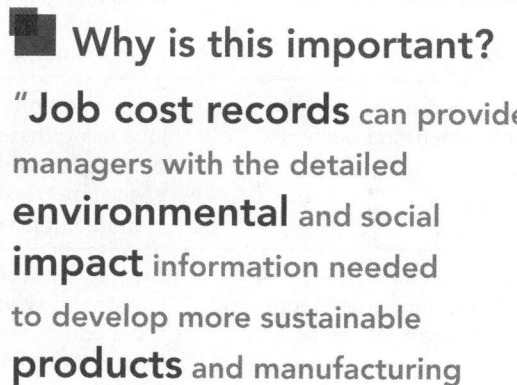

Why is this important?

"**Job cost records** can provide managers with the detailed **environmental** and social **impact** information needed to develop more sustainable **products** and manufacturing processes."

However, for setting long-term average sales prices and making other critical decisions, manufacturers must take into account the total costs of researching and developing, designing, producing, marketing, distributing, and providing customer service for new or existing products. In other words, *they want to know the total cost of the product across the entire value chain.* But how do managers figure this out?

The same principles of tracing direct costs and allocating indirect costs apply to all costs incurred in other elements of the value chain. Managers add these non-manufacturing costs to the inventoriable job costs to build the *total cost of the product across the entire value chain.* For example, say Life Fitness spent $2 million dollars designing and marketing the X4 Elliptical Cross-Trainer. These costs are direct costs of the X4 Elliptical product line. On the other hand, the company may have spent $3 million researching basic technology for the video screen that is used on all of its products, making it an indirect cost of the X4 Elliptical, shared with other products that use the same video screen. Life Fitness may choose to add an additional cost section to the job cost record, indicating specific operating expenses associated with each job. By adding this information to the job cost record, managers have a more complete understanding of the total job costs, not just the job's manufacturing costs.

Keep in mind that these non-manufacturing costs are assigned to products *only* for internal decision making, never for external financial reporting, because GAAP does not allow it. For financial reporting, non-manufacturing costs must *always* be expensed on the income statement as operating expenses in the period in which they are incurred.

Direct or Variable Costing

Even though the job cost records contain information about all three manufacturing costs, managers base certain decisions on just the direct costs (direct materials and labor) or variable costs found on a job cost record. Why? For two reasons: (1) The simple allocation of MOH that we have described in this chapter results in a fairly arbitrary amount of MOH being allocated to jobs, and (2) because many MOH costs are fixed in nature, and will not be affected as a result of producing a job. Later in the book, we'll see how management accountants have addressed these issues. In Chapter 4, we'll show how managers can improve the allocation system so that the amount of manufacturing overhead assigned to the job is much more accurate. In Chapters 6 and 8, we'll discuss how direct costing or variable costing can be used to address the role of fixed MOH costs in the decision-making process.

Decision Guidelines

Job Costing

Life Fitness uses a job costing system that assigns manufacturing costs to each batch of exercise machines that it makes. These guidelines explain some of the decisions Life Fitness made in designing its costing system.

Decision	Guidelines
Should we use job costing or process costing?	Managers use the costing system that best fits their production environment. Job costing is best suited to manufacturers that produce unique, custom-built products or relatively small batches of different products, like Life Fitness. Process costing is best suited to manufacturers that mass-produce identical units in a series of uniform production processes.
How do we determine the cost of manufacturing each job?	The exact amount of direct materials and direct labor can be traced to individual jobs using materials requisitions and labor time records. However, the exact amount of manufacturing overhead attributable to each job is unknown, and therefore *cannot* be traced to individual jobs. To deal with this issue, companies *allocate* some manufacturing overhead to each job.
Should we use a predetermined manufacturing overhead rate or the actual manufacturing overhead rate?	Although it would be more accurate to use the actual manufacturing overhead rate, companies would have to wait until the end of the year to have that information. Most companies are willing to sacrifice some accuracy for the sake of having timely information that will help them make decisions throughout the year. Therefore, most companies use a predetermined overhead rate to allocate manufacturing overhead to jobs as they are produced throughout the year.
How do we calculate the predetermined MOH rate?	$$\text{Predetermined MOH rate} = \frac{\text{Total estimated manufacturing overhead cost}}{\text{Total estimated amount of the allocation base}}$$
What allocation base should we use for allocating manufacturing overhead?	If possible, companies should use the cost driver of manufacturing overhead as the allocation base. The most common allocation bases are direct labor hours, direct labor cost, and machine hours. Some companies use multiple bases in order to more accurately allocate MOH. This topic will be covered in Chapter 4.
How should we allocate manufacturing overhead to individual jobs?	The MOH allocated to a job is calculated as follows: = Predetermined MOH rate × Actual amount of allocation base used by the job
Can job cost records help companies in their journey toward sustainability?	Job cost records can be enhanced to provide more detail about the environmental and social impact of the resources used on the job. In addition to satisfying supply chain assessment, managers can use this information to determine how a product, or production process, can become more sustainable.
Can manufacturers also allocate operating expenses to jobs?	Operating expenses can also be assigned to jobs, but *only* for *internal decision-making* purposes. Operating expenses are *never* assigned to jobs for external financial reporting purposes. Direct operating costs would be traced to jobs (such as the sales commission on a particular job or the design costs related to a particular job, whereas indirect operating costs (such as the R&D costs associated with several product lines) would be allocated to jobs.

SUMMARY PROBLEM 1

E-Z-Boy Furniture makes sofas, loveseats, and recliners. The company allocates manufacturing overhead based on direct labor hours. E-Z-Boy estimated a total of $2 million of manufacturing overhead and 40,000 direct labor hours for the year.

Job 310 consists of a batch of 10 recliners. The company's records show that the following direct materials were requisitioned for Job 310:

Lumber: 10 units at $30 per unit

Padding: 20 yards at $20 per yard

Upholstery fabric: 60 yards at $25 per yard, sourced from a local manufacturer

Labor time records show the following employees (direct labor) worked on Job 310:

Jesse Slothower: 10 hours at $12 per hour

Becky Wilken: 15 hours at $18 per hour

Chip Lathrop: 12 hours at $15 per hour

Requirements

1. Compute the company's predetermined manufacturing overhead rate.

2. Compute the total amount of direct materials, direct labor, and manufacturing overhead that should be shown on Job 310's job cost record.

3. Compute the total cost of Job 310, as well as the cost of each recliner produced in Job 310.

4. The company's customers are concerned about environmental responsibility and social justice and require additional sustainability-related information prior to making their purchasing decisions. To meet customer concerns, determine (a) which materials used for the product are sourced locally, and (b) the percentage of labor paid at a rate greater than minimum wage.

▪ SOLUTIONS

1. The predetermined MOH rate is calculated as follows:

$$\text{Predetermined MOH rate} = \frac{\text{Total estimated manufacturing overhead cost}}{\text{Total estimated amount of the allocation base}}$$

For E-Z-Boy:

$$\text{Predetermined MOH rate} = \frac{\$2,000,000}{40,000 \text{ direct labor hours}} = \$50 \text{ per direct labor hour}$$

2. The total amount of direct materials ($2,200) and direct labor ($570) incurred on Job 310 is determined from the materials requisitions and labor time records, as shown on the following job cost record. Because the job required 37 direct labor hours, we determine the amount of manufacturing overhead to allocate to the job is as follows:

$$= \text{Predetermined MOH rate} \times \text{Actual amount of allocation base used by the job}$$
$$= \$50 \text{ per direct labor hour } \times 37 \text{ direct labor hours used on Job 310}$$
$$= \$1,850$$

These costs are summarized on the following job cost record:

Job Cost Record

Job Number: 310

Job Description: 10 recliners

Manufacturing Cost Information:	Cost Summary	
Direct Materials		
Lumber: 10 units × $30 = $300		
Padding: 20 yards × $20 = $400		
Fabric: 60 yards × $25 = $1,500	$	2,200
Direct Labor		
Slothower: 10 hours × $12 = $120		
Wilken: 15 hours × $18 = $270		
Lathrop: 12 hours × $15 = $180		
Total hours: 37 hours	$	570
Manufacturing Overhead		
37 direct labor hours × $50 = $1,850	$	1,850
Total Job Cost	$	4,620
Number of Units	÷	10 units
Cost per Unit	$	462

3. The direct materials ($2,200), direct labor ($570), and manufacturing overhead ($1,850) sum to a total job cost of $4,620. When the total job cost is averaged over the 10 recliners in the job, the cost per recliner is $462.

4. Supplemental sustainability information for Job 310:
   a. All fabric contained in the product was sourced locally.
   b. All labor used in the manufacturing was paid at a rate higher than minimum wage.

How do Managers Deal with Underallocated or Overallocated Manufacturing Overhead?

5 Compute and dispose of overallocated or underallocated manufacturing overhead

In the first half of the chapter, we showed how managers find the cost of completing a job. Direct materials and direct labor are traced to each job using materials requisitions and labor time records, and manufacturing overhead is allocated to each job using a pre-determined overhead rate. At the end of the period, all manufacturers will have a problem to deal with: Invariably, they will have either <u>underallocated manufacturing overhead</u> or <u>overallocated manufacturing overhead</u> to the jobs worked on during the period.

Recall that manufacturing overhead is allocated to jobs using a *predetermined rate* that is calculated using *estimates* of the company's total annual manufacturing costs and *estimates* of the total annual allocation base (such as direct labor hours). By the end of the period, the *actual* manufacturing overhead costs incurred by the company will be known, and they will likely differ from the total amount allocated to jobs during the period.

For example, suppose Life Fitness incurred the following *actual* manufacturing over-head costs during the month of December:

Manufacturing Overhead Incurred	Actual MOH Costs
Indirect materials used (janitorial supplies, machine lubricants, etc.).........	$ 2,000
Indirect labor (janitors' and supervisors' wages, etc.)	13,000
Other indirect manufacturing costs	
(Plant utilities, depreciation, property taxes, insurance, etc.)...........	10,000
Total actual manufacturing overhead costs incurred	$25,000

Now let's look at the total amount of manufacturing overhead that was *allocated* to individual jobs during the month using the predetermined manufacturing overhead rate of $16 per direct labor hour. For simplicity, we'll assume only two jobs were worked on during December.

Jobs	Amount of MOH Allocated to Job
603 (from Exhibit 3-14) ($16 per DL hour × 500 DL hours)	$ 8,000
604 (not shown) ($16 per DL hour × 1,000 DL hours)......................	16,000
Total MOH allocated to jobs ($16 per DL hour × 1,500 DL hours)........	$24,000

Notice that we don't need to have the individual job cost records available to figure out the total amount of MOH allocated to jobs during the period. Rather, we could do the following calculation to arrive at the same $24,000 figure:

Total MOH allocated = Predetermined MOH rate × Actual *total* amount of allocation base used on all jobs

= $16 per DL hour × 1,500 direct labor hours

= $24,000 total MOH allocated to jobs during the period

To determine whether manufacturing overhead had been overallocated or underallocated, we simply compare the amount of MOH actually incurred during the period with the amount of MOH that was allocated to jobs during the same period.

The difference between the *actual manufacturing overhead costs incurred* and the amount of manufacturing overhead *allocated to jobs* shows that Life Fitness *underallocated* manufacturing overhead by $1,000 during December:

Actual manufacturing overhead costs **incurred**	$25,000
Manufacturing overhead **allocated** to jobs	24,000
Underallocated manufacturing overhead	$ 1,000

By underallocating manufacturing overhead, Life Fitness *did not allocate enough* manufacturing overhead cost to the jobs worked on during the period. In other words, the jobs worked on during the period should have had a total of $1,000 more manufacturing overhead cost allocated to them than the job cost records indicated. These jobs have been undercosted, as shown in Exhibit 3-15. If, on the other hand, a manufacturer finds that the amount of manufacturing overhead allocated to jobs is *greater* than the actual amount of manufacturing overhead incurred, we would say that manufacturing overhead had been overallocated, resulting in overcosting these jobs.

EXHIBIT 3-15 Underallocated Versus Overallocated Manufacturing Overhead

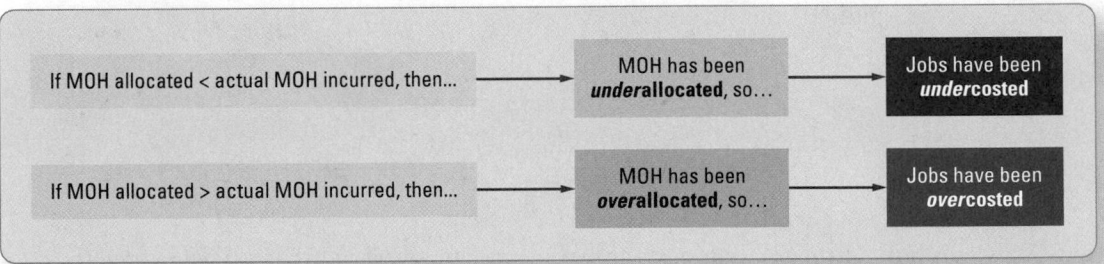

What do manufacturers do about this problem? *Assuming that the amount of underallocation or overallocation is immaterial, or that most of the inventory produced during the period has been sold,* manufacturers typically adjust the Cost of Goods Sold shown on the income statement for the total amount of the under- or overallocation. Why? Because the actual cost of producing these goods differed from what was initially reported on the job cost records. Because the job cost records were used as a basis for recording Cost of Goods Sold at the time the units were sold, the Cost of Goods Sold will be wrong unless it is adjusted. As shown in Exhibit 3-16, by increasing Cost of Goods Sold when manufacturing overhead has been underallocated, or by decreasing Cost of Goods Sold when manufacturing overhead has been overallocated, the company actually corrects the error that exists in Cost of Goods Sold.

EXHIBIT 3-16 Correcting Cost of Goods Sold for Underallocated or Overallocated MOH

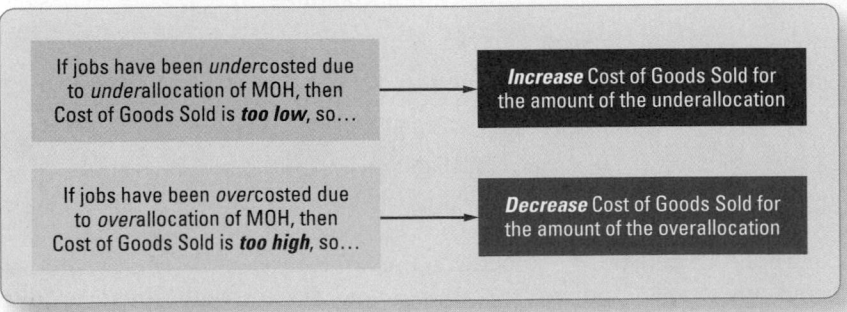

What if the amount of under- or overallocation is large, and the company has *not* sold almost all of the units produced during the period? Then the company will prorate the total amount of under- or overallocation among Work in Process Inventory, Finished Goods Inventory, and Cost of Goods Sold based on the current status of the jobs worked on during the period. For example, if 30% of the jobs are still in Work in Process, 20% are still in Finished Goods, and 50% were sold, then the total amount of underallocation ($1,000 in the case of Life Fitness) would be roughly allocated as follows: 30% ($300) to Work in Process Inventory, 20% ($200) to Finished Goods Inventory, and 50% ($500) to Cost of Goods Sold. The exact procedure for prorating is covered in more advanced accounting textbooks.

▶ **Try It!**

> Recall that Life Fitness had estimated $1,000,000 of MOH for the year and 62,500 DL hours, resulting in a predetermined MOH rate of $16/DL hour. By the end of the year the company had actually incurred $975,000 of MOH costs and used a total of 60,000 DL hours on jobs. By how much had Life Fitness overallocated or underallocated MOH for the year?

Please see page 175 for solutions.

What Journal Entries are Needed in a Manufacturer's Job Costing System?

Now that you know how manufacturers determine job costs and how those costs are used to make business decisions, let's look at how these costs are entered into the company's general ledger accounting system. We'll consider the journal entries needed to record the flow of costs through Life Fitness's accounts during the month of December. We'll use the same examples used earlier in the chapter. For the sake of simplicity, we'll continue to assume that Life Fitness only worked on two jobs during the month:

6 Prepare journal entries for a manufacturer's job costing system

> Job 603: 50 units of the X4 Elliptical Cross-Trainers
> Job 604: 60 units of the T5 Treadmill

You may wish to review the basic mechanics of journal entries, shown in Exhibit 3-17, before we begin our discussion.

EXHIBIT 3-17 Review of Journal Entry and T-account Mechanics

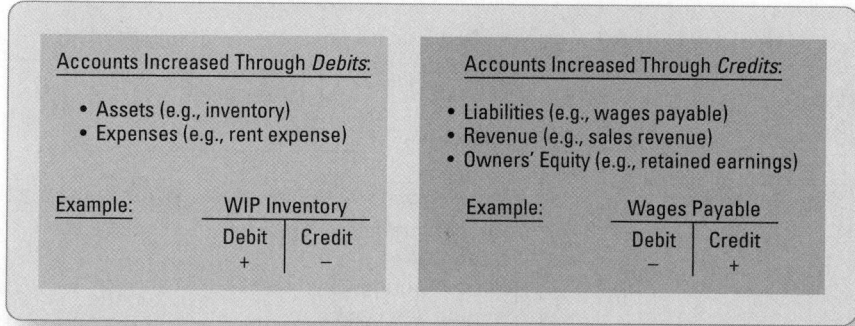

Accounts Increased Through *Debits*:	Accounts Increased Through *Credits*:
• Assets (e.g., inventory) • Expenses (e.g., rent expense)	• Liabilities (e.g., wages payable) • Revenue (e.g., sales revenue) • Owners' Equity (e.g., retained earnings)

Example: WIP Inventory — Debit + / Credit −

Example: Wages Payable — Debit − / Credit +

Additionally, keep in mind the flow of inventory that was first described in Exhibit 3-2. You may find this visual reminder helpful as we describe how the journal entries reflect the flow of inventory through the manufacturing system. Each arrow represents a journal entry that must be made to reflect activities that occur along the process: purchasing raw materials, using direct materials, using direct labor, recording actual MOH costs, allocating MOH to jobs, moving the jobs out of the factory after completion, and, finally, selling the units from a job.

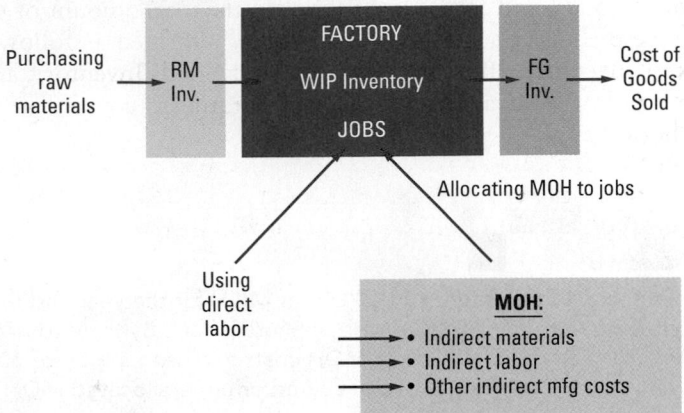

Purchase of Raw Materials

Assume that Life Fitness ordered and received $90,000 of raw materials during December. Once the materials are received and verified against the purchase order and the invoice received from the supplier, the purchase is recorded as follows:

(1)	Raw Materials Inventory	90,000	
	Accounts Payable		90,000
	(to record purchases of raw materials)		

These materials will remain in the raw materials storeroom until they are needed for production. The liability in Accounts Payable will be removed when the supplier is paid.

Use of Direct Materials

Recall that direct materials are the primary physical components of the product. Each time production managers need particular direct materials for Jobs 603 and 604, they fill out a materials requisition informing the storeroom to pick the materials and send them into the manufacturing facility. Once these materials are sent into production, they become part of the work in process on Jobs 603 and 604, so their cost is added to the job cost records, as follows:

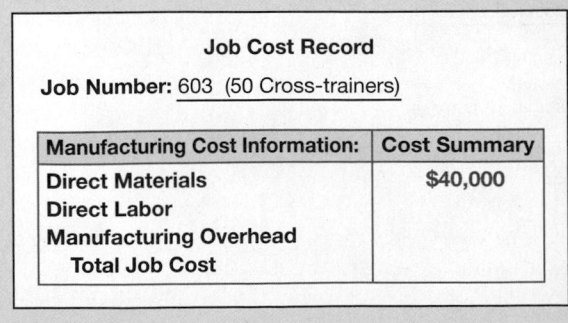

Job Cost Record

Job Number: 603 (50 Cross-trainers)

Manufacturing Cost Information:	Cost Summary
Direct Materials	$40,000
Direct Labor	
Manufacturing Overhead	
Total Job Cost	

Job Cost Record

Job Number: 604 (60 Treadmills)

Manufacturing Cost Information:	Cost Summary
Direct Materials	$72,000
Direct Labor	
Manufacturing Overhead	
Total Job Cost	

From an accounting perspective, the cost of these materials must also be moved into Work in Process Inventory (through a debit) and out of Raw Materials Inventory (through a credit). The following journal entry is made:

(2)	Work in Process Inventory ($40,000 + $72,000)	112,000	
	Raw Materials Inventory		112,000
	(*to record the use of direct materials on jobs*)		

Recall from the first half of the chapter that the individual job cost records form the underlying support for the Work in Process Inventory account shown on the balance sheet.[5] Therefore, the amount posted to the general ledger account ($112,000) must be identical to the sum of the amounts posted to the individual job cost records ($40,000 + $72,000 = $112,000). Keep this rule of thumb in mind:

Whenever a cost is added to a job cost record, a corresponding journal entry is made to increase WIP Inventory.

Use of Indirect Materials

Indirect materials are materials used in the manufacturing plant that *cannot* be traced to individual jobs, and therefore are *not* recorded on any job cost record. Examples include janitorial supplies used in the factory and machine lubricants for the factory machines. Once again, materials requisitions inform the raw materials storeroom to release these materials. However, instead of becoming part of the Work in Process account for a particular job, the indirect materials used in the factory (let's say $2,000) become part of the Manufacturing Overhead account. Therefore, the Manufacturing Overhead account is debited (to increase the account) and Raw Materials Inventory is credited (to decrease the account) as follows:

(3)	Manufacturing Overhead	2,000	
	Raw Materials Inventory		2,000
	(*to record the use of indirect materials in the factory*)		

All indirect manufacturing costs, including indirect materials, indirect labor, and other indirect manufacturing costs (such as plant insurance and depreciation), are accumulated in the Manufacturing Overhead account. The Manufacturing Overhead account is a *temporary* account used to "pool" indirect manufacturing costs until those costs can be allocated to individual jobs. In fact, the MOH account is sometimes referred to as the "MOH pool."

---

[5]The job cost records of unfinished jobs form the subsidiary ledger for the Work in Process Inventory account. Recall that a **subsidiary ledger** is simply the supporting detail for a general ledger account. Many other general ledger accounts (such as Accounts Receivable, Accounts Payable, and Plant & Equipment) also have subsidiary ledgers. The raw material inventory records form the subsidiary ledger for the Raw Materials Inventory account, whereas the job cost records on completed, unsold jobs form the subsidiary ledger for the Finished Goods Inventory account.

We can summarize the flow of materials costs through the T-accounts as follows:

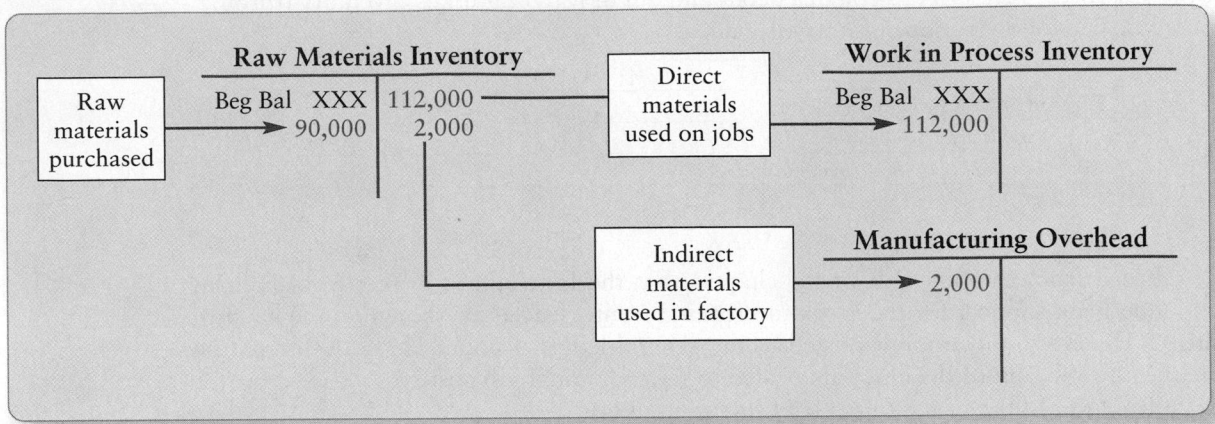

Use of Direct Labor

The labor time records of individual factory workers are used to determine exactly how much time was spent directly working on Jobs 603 and 604. The cost of this direct labor is entered on the job cost records, as shown:

Job Cost Record	
Job Number: 603 (50 Cross-trainers)	
Manufacturing Cost Information:	**Cost Summary**
Direct Materials	$40,000
Direct Labor	$10,000
Manufacturing Overhead	
Total Job Cost	

Job Cost Record	
Job Number: 604 (60 Treadmills)	
Manufacturing Cost Information:	**Cost Summary**
Direct Materials	$72,000
Direct Labor	$20,000
Manufacturing Overhead	
Total Job Cost	

Again, because the job cost records form the underlying support for Work in Process Inventory, an identical amount ($10,000 + $20,000 = $30,000) must be debited to the Work in Process Inventory account. Wages Payable is credited to show that the company has a liability to pay its factory workers:

(4)	Work in Process Inventory ($10,000 + $20,000)	30,000	
	Wages Payable		30,000
	(to record the use of direct labor on jobs)		

The Wages Payable liability will be removed on payday when the workers receive their paychecks.

Use of Indirect Labor

Recall that indirect labor consists of the salary, wages, and benefits of all factory workers who are *not* directly working on individual jobs. Examples include factory janitors, supervisors, and forklift operators. Because their time cannot be traced to particular jobs, the cost of employing these factory workers during the month (let's say $13,000) cannot be posted to individual job cost records. Thus, we record the cost of indirect labor as part of Manufacturing Overhead, *not* Work in Process Inventory:

(5)	Manufacturing Overhead	13,000	
	Wages Payable		13,000
	(to record the use of indirect labor in the factory)		

Again, the Wages Payable liability will be removed on payday when the workers receive their paychecks.

We can summarize the flow of manufacturing labor costs through the T-accounts as follows:

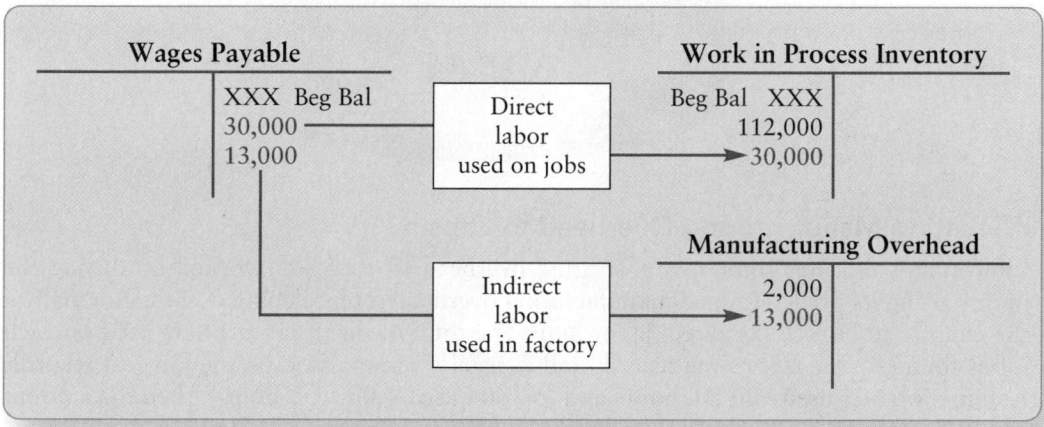

Incurring Other Manufacturing Overhead Costs

We have already recorded the indirect materials and indirect labor used in the factory during December by debiting the Manufacturing Overhead account. However, Life Fitness incurs other indirect manufacturing costs, such as plant utilities ($3,000), plant depreciation ($4,000), plant insurance ($1,000), and plant property taxes ($2,000), during the period. All of these other indirect costs of operating the manufacturing plant during the month are also added to the Manufacturing Overhead account until they can be allocated to specific jobs:

(6)	Manufacturing Overhead	10,000	
	Accounts Payable *(for electric bill)*		3,000
	Accumulated Depreciation—Plant and Equipment		4,000
	Prepaid Plant Insurance *(for expiration of prepaid insurance)*		1,000
	Plant Property Taxes Payable *(for taxes to be paid)*		2,000
	(to record other indirect manufacturing costs incurred		
	during the month)		

After recording all other indirect manufacturing costs, the Manufacturing Overhead account appears as follows:

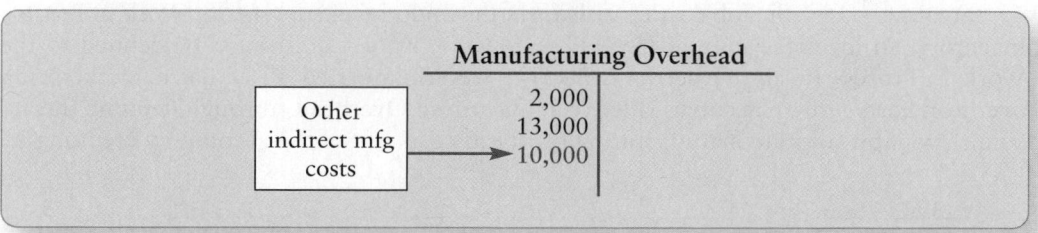

As mentioned earlier, sometimes the MOH account is referred to as a "pool." It might be helpful for you to visualize a pool being filled with MOH costs during the year. In the next section, we'll see how the costs are removed from the pool and assigned to specific jobs.

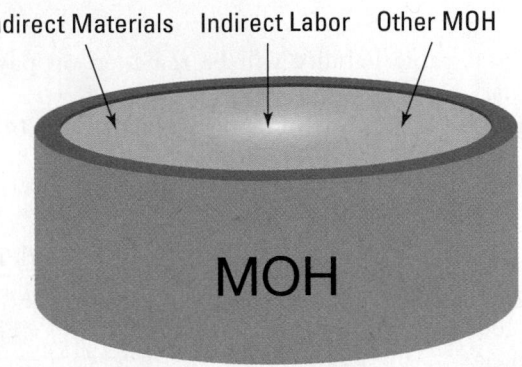

Indirect Materials   Indirect Labor   Other MOH

MOH

Allocating Manufacturing Overhead to Jobs

Life Fitness allocates some manufacturing overhead to each job worked on during the month using its predetermined manufacturing overhead rate, calculated in the first half of the chapter to be $16 per direct labor hour. The total of direct labor hours used on each job is found on the labor time records and is usually summarized on the job cost records. Assume Job 603 used 500 DL hours and Job 604 used 1,000 DL hours. Then the amount of manufacturing overhead allocated to each job is determined as follows:

Job 603: $16 per DL hour × 500 DL hours = $8,000

Job 604: $16 per DL hour × 1,000 DL hours = $16,000

Job Cost Record	
Job Number: 603 (50 Cross-trainers)	
Manufacturing Cost Information:	**Cost Summary**
Direct Materials	$40,000
Direct Labor (500 DL hrs)	$10,000
Manufacturing Overhead	$ 8,000
Total Job Cost	

Job Cost Record	
Job Number: 604 (60 Treadmills)	
Manufacturing Cost Information:	**Cost Summary**
Direct Materials	$72,000
Direct Labor (1,000 DL hrs)	$20,000
Manufacturing Overhead	$16,000
Total Job Cost	

Again, because the job cost records form the underlying support for Work in Process Inventory, an identical amount ($8,000 + $16,000 = $24,000) must be debited to the Work in Process Inventory account. Because we accumulated all actual manufacturing overhead costs *into* an account called Manufacturing Overhead (through debiting the account), we now allocate manufacturing overhead costs *out* of the account by crediting it.

(7)	Work in Process Inventory ($8,000 + $16,000)	24,000	
	Manufacturing Overhead		24,000
	(to allocate manufacturing overhead to specific jobs)		

If it helps, visualize the allocation process as removing, or ladling out, some of the MOH in the pool and allocating it to each job that is worked on in the factory. To recap, the MOH pool is increased through the addition of actual MOH costs as they are incurred, and decreased through the allocation of MOH to individual jobs. In the general ledger, the MOH pool is represented by the MOH account. Thus, the account is increased (debited) whenever an actual MOH cost is incurred, and credited whenever MOH costs are allocated to jobs.

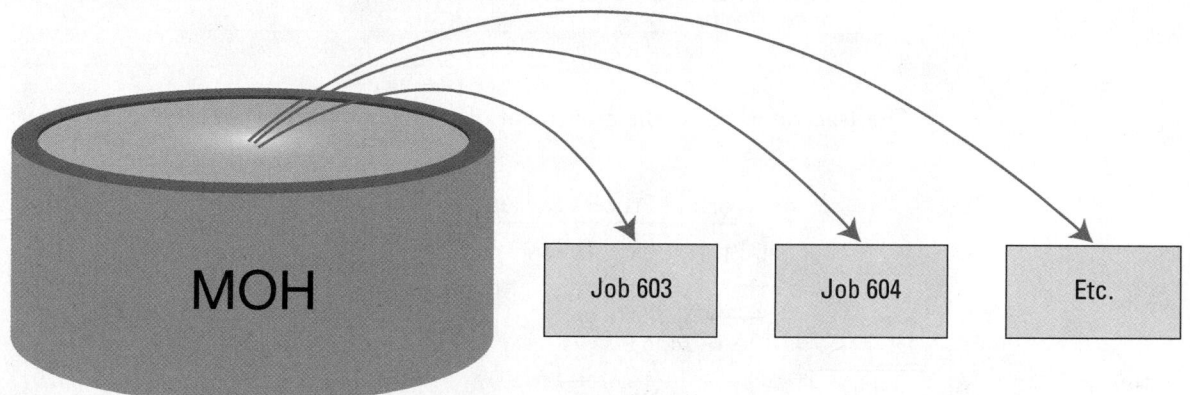

By looking at the Manufacturing Overhead T-account, you can see how actual manufacturing overhead costs are accumulated in the account through debits, and the amount of manufacturing overhead allocated to specific jobs is credited to the account:

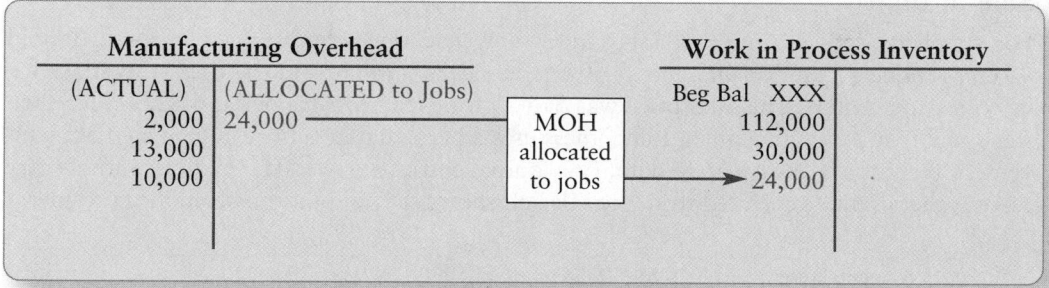

Completion of Jobs

Once the job has been completed, the three manufacturing costs shown on the job cost record are summed to find the total job cost. If the job consists of more than one unit, the total job cost is divided by the number of units to find the cost of each unit:

Job Cost Record

Job Number: 603 (50 Cross-trainers)

Manufacturing Cost Information:	Cost Summary
Direct Materials	$40,000
Direct Labor	$10,000
Manufacturing Overhead	$ 8,000
Total Job Cost	$58,000
Number of Units	÷50
Cost per Unit	$ 1,160

Job Cost Record

Job Number: 604 (60 Treadmills)

Manufacturing Cost Information:	Cost Summary
Direct Materials	$ 72,000
Direct Labor	$ 20,000
Manufacturing Overhead	$ 16,000
Total Job Cost	$108,000
Number of Units	÷60
Cost per Unit	$ 1,800

The units produced in the jobs are physically moved off of the plant floor and into the finished goods warehouse. Likewise, in the accounting records, the jobs are moved out of Work in Process Inventory (through a credit) and into Finished Goods Inventory (through a debit):

(8)	Finished Goods Inventory ($58,000 + $108,000)	166,000	
	Work in Process Inventory		166,000
	(to move the completed jobs out of the factory and into		
	Finished Goods)		

The T-accounts show the movement of completed jobs off of the factory floor:

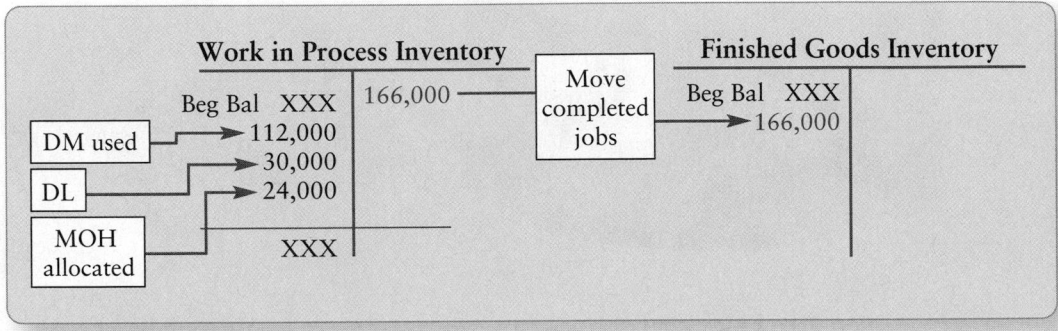

Sale of Units

For simplicity, let's assume that Life Fitness only had one sale during the month: It sold 40 cross-trainers from Job 603 and all 60 treadmills from Job 604 to the City of Westlake for its recreation centers. The sales price was $1,425 for each cross-trainer and $2,500 for each treadmill. Like most companies, Life Fitness uses a perpetual inventory system so that its inventory records are always up to date. Two journal entries are needed. The first journal entry records the revenue generated from the sale and shows the amount due from the customer:

(9)	Accounts Receivable (40 × $1,425) + (60 × $2,500)	207,000	
	Sales Revenue		207,000
	(to record the sale of 40 cross-trainers and 60 treadmills)		

The second journal entry reduces the company's Finished Goods Inventory, and records the Cost of Goods Sold. From the job cost record, we know that each cross-trainer produced in Job 603 cost $1,160 to make, and each treadmill from Job 604 cost $1,800 to make. Therefore, the following entry is recorded:

(10)	Cost of Goods Sold (40 × $1,160) + (60 × $1,800)	154,400	
	Finished Goods Inventory		154,400
	(to reduce Finished Goods Inventory and record Cost of Goods Sold)		

The following T-accounts show the movement of the units out of Finished Goods Inventory and into Cost of Goods Sold:

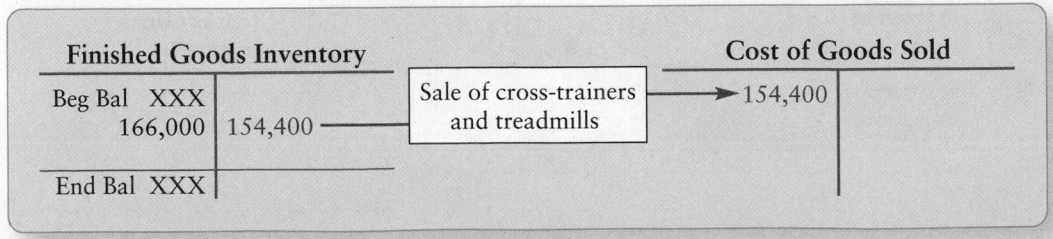

Operating Expenses

During the month, Life Fitness also incurred $32,700 of operating expenses to run its business. For example, Life Fitness incurred salaries and commissions ($20,000) for its salespeople, office administrators, research and design staff, and customer service representatives. It also needs to pay rent ($3,300) for its office headquarters. The company also received a bill from its advertising agency for marketing expenses incurred during the month ($9,400). *All costs incurred outside of the manufacturing function of the value chain* would be expensed in the current month as shown in the following journal entry:

(11)	Salaries and Commission Expense	20,000	
	Rent Expense	3,300	
	Marketing Expenses	9,400	
	Salaries and Commissions Payable		20,000
	Rent Payable		3,300
	Accounts Payable		9,400
	(to record all non-manufacturing costs incurred during the month)		

All non-manufacturing expenses (period costs) will be shown as "operating expenses" on the company's income statement, as shown in Exhibit 3-18 at the end of the chapter.

Closing Manufacturing Overhead

As a final step, Life Fitness must deal with the balance in the manufacturing overhead account. Because the company uses a *predetermined* manufacturing overhead rate to allocate manufacturing overhead to individual jobs, the total amount allocated to jobs will most likely differ from the amount of manufacturing overhead actually incurred.

Let's see how this plays out in the Manufacturing Overhead T-account:

1. All manufacturing overhead costs *incurred* by Life Fitness were recorded as *debits* to the Manufacturing Overhead account. These debits total $25,000 of actual manufacturing overhead incurred.

2. On the other hand, all manufacturing overhead *allocated* to specific jobs ($8,000 + $16,000) was recorded as *credits* to the Manufacturing Overhead account:

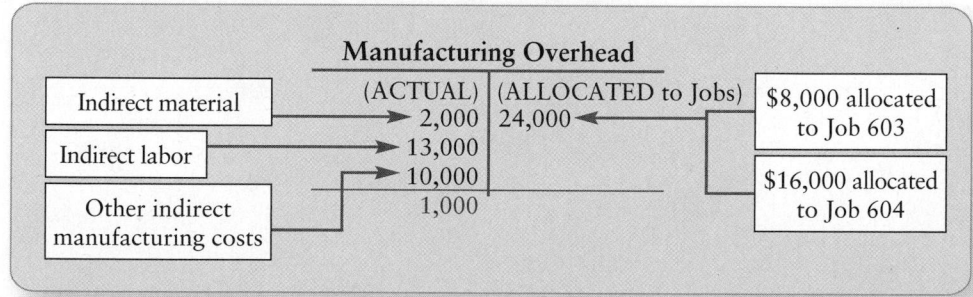

This leaves a debit balance of $1,000 in the Manufacturing Overhead account, which means that manufacturing overhead has been underallocated during the month. More manufacturing overhead costs were incurred than were allocated to jobs. Because Manufacturing Overhead is a temporary account not shown on any of the company's financial statements, it must be closed out (zeroed out) at the end of the period. Because most of the inventory produced during the period has been sold, Life Fitness will close the balance in Manufacturing Overhead to Cost of Goods Sold as follows:

(12)	Cost of Goods Sold	1,000	
	Manufacturing Overhead		1,000
	(to close the Manufacturing Overhead account)		

As a result of this entry, (1) the Manufacturing Overhead account now has a zero balance, and (2) the balance in Cost of Goods Sold has increased to correct for the fact that the jobs had been undercosted during the period.

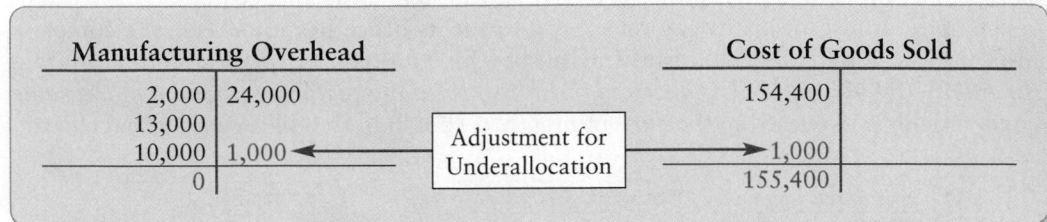

If, in some period, Life Fitness overallocates its overhead, the journal entry to close Manufacturing Overhead would be the opposite of that shown: Manufacturing Overhead would be debited to zero it out; Cost of Goods Sold would be credited to reduce it as a result of having overcosted jobs during the period.

Now you have seen how all of the costs flow through Life Fitness's accounts during December. Exhibit 3-18 shows the company's income statement that resulted from all of the previously shown journal entries.

EXHIBIT 3-18 Income Statement After Adjusting for Underallocated Manufacturing Overhead

	A	B	C	D
1	**Life Fitness**			
2	**Income Statement**			
3	**For the Month Ended December 31**			
4				
5	Sales Revenue	$ 207,000		
6	Less: Cost of Goods Sold	155,400		
7	Gross Profit	51,600		
8	Less: Operating Expenses	32,700		
9	Operating Income	$ 18,900		
10				

Decision Guidelines

Job Costing

The following decision guidelines describe the implications of over- or underallocating manufacturing overhead, as well as other decisions that need to be made in a job costing environment.

Decision	Guidelines
How does overallocating or underallocating MOH affect the cost of jobs manufactured during the period?	If manufacturing overhead has been *underallocated*, it means that the jobs have been *undercosted* as a result. In other words, not enough manufacturing overhead cost was posted on the job cost records. On the other hand, if manufacturing overhead has been *overallocated*, it means that the jobs have been *overcosted*. Too much manufacturing overhead cost was posted on the job cost records.
What do we do about overallocated or underallocated manufacturing overhead?	Assuming most of the inventory produced during the period has been sold, manufacturers generally adjust the Cost of Goods Sold for the total amount of the under- or overallocation. If a significant portion of the inventory is still on hand, then the adjustment will be prorated between WIP, Finished Goods, and Cost of Goods Sold.
How do we know whether to increase or decrease Cost of Goods Sold (CGS)?	If manufacturing overhead has been overallocated, then Cost of Goods Sold (CGS) is too high, and must be decreased through a credit to the CGS account. If manufacturing overhead has been underallocated, then Cost of Goods Sold is too low, and must be increased through a debit to the CGS account.
How does job costing work at a service firm (Appendix)?	Job costing at a service firm is very similar to job costing at a manufacturer. The main difference is that the company is allocating operating expenses, rather than manufacturing costs, to each client job. In addition, because there are no Inventory or Cost of Goods Sold accounts, no journal entries are needed to move costs through the system.

SUMMARY PROBLEM 2

Fashion Fabrics makes custom handbags and accessories for high-end clothing boutiques. Record summary journal entries for each of the following transactions that took place during the month of January, the *first* month of the fiscal year.

Requirements

1. During January, $150,000 of raw materials was purchased on account.

2. During the month, $140,000 of raw materials was requisitioned. Of this amount, $135,000 was traced to specific jobs, while the remaining materials were for general factory use.

3. Manufacturing labor (both direct and indirect) for the month totaled $80,000. It has not yet been paid. Of this amount, $60,000 was traced to specific jobs.

4. The company recorded $9,000 of depreciation on the plant building and machinery. In addition, $3,000 of prepaid property tax expired during the month. The company also received the plant utility bill for $6,000.

5. Manufacturing overhead was allocated to jobs using a predetermined manufacturing overhead rate of 75% of direct labor *cost*. (*Hint*: Total direct labor cost is found in Requirement 3.)

6. Several jobs were completed during the month. According to the job cost records, these jobs cost $255,000 to manufacture.

7. Sales (all on credit) for the month totaled $340,000. According to the job cost records, the units sold cost $250,000 to manufacture. Assume the company uses a perpetual inventory system.

8. The company incurred operating expenses of $60,000 during the month. Assume that 80% of these were for marketing and administrative salaries and the other 20% were lease and utility bills related to the corporate headquarters.

9. In order to prepare its January financial statements, the company had to close its Manufacturing Overhead account.

10. Prepare the January income statement for Fashion Fabrics based on the transactions recorded in Requirements 1 through 9.

■ SOLUTIONS

1. During January, $150,000 of raw materials was purchased on account.

Raw Materials Inventory	150,000	
Accounts Payable		150,000
(to record purchases of raw materials)		

2. During the month, $140,000 of raw materials was requisitioned. Of this amount, $135,000 was traced to specific jobs, while the remaining materials were for general factory use.

Work in Process Inventory	135,000	
Manufacturing Overhead	5,000	
Raw Materials Inventory		140,000
(to record the use of direct materials and indirect materials)		

3. Manufacturing labor (both direct and indirect) for the month totaled $80,000. It has not yet been paid. Of this amount, $60,000 was traced to specific jobs.

	Work in Process Inventory (*for direct labor*)	60,000	
	Manufacturing Overhead (*for indirect labor*)	20,000	
	Wages Payable		80,000
	(*to record the use of direct labor and indirect labor*)		

4. The company recorded $9,000 of depreciation on the plant building and machinery. In addition, $3,000 of prepaid property tax expired during the month. The company also received the plant utility bill for $6,000.

	Manufacturing Overhead	18,000	
	Accumulated Depreciation—Plant and Equipment		9,000
	Prepaid Plant Property Tax (*for expiration of property tax*)		3,000
	Accounts Payable (*for electric bill*)		6,000
	(*to record other indirect manufacturing costs incurred during the month*)		

5. Manufacturing overhead was allocated to jobs using a predetermined manufacturing overhead rate of 75% of direct labor cost. (*Hint:* Total direct labor cost is found in Requirement 3.)

	Work in Process Inventory (75% × $60,000 of direct labor)	45,000	
	Manufacturing Overhead		45,000
	(*to allocate manufacturing overhead to jobs*)		

6. Several jobs were completed during the month. According to the job cost records, these jobs cost $255,000 to manufacture.

	Finished Goods Inventory	255,000	
	Work in Process Inventory		255,000
	(*to move the completed jobs out of the factory and into Finished Goods*)		

7. Sales (all on credit) for the month totaled $340,000. According to the job cost records, the units sold cost $250,000 to manufacture. Assume the company uses a perpetual inventory system.

	Accounts Receivable	340,000	
	Sales Revenue		340,000
	(*to record the sales and receivables*)		

	Cost of Goods Sold	250,000	
	Finished Goods Inventory		250,000
	(*to reduce Finished Goods Inventory and record Cost of Goods Sold*)		

8. The company incurred operating expenses of $60,000 during the month. Assume that 80% of these were for marketing and administrative salaries and the other 20% were lease and utility bills related to the corporate headquarters.

	Salaries Expense ($60,000 × 80%)	48,000	
	Lease and Utilities Expense ($60,000 × 20%)	12,000	
	Salaries and Wages Payable		48,000
	Accounts Payable		12,000
	(to record all non-manufacturing costs incurred during the month)		

9. In order to prepare its January financial statements, the company had to close its Manufacturing Overhead account.

An analysis of the manufacturing overhead account *prior to closing* shows the following:

Manufacturing Overhead

(ACTUAL)	(ALLOCATED)
5,000	45,000
20,000	
18,000	
	2,000

	Manufacturing Overhead	2,000	
	Cost of Goods Sold		2,000
	(to close the Manufacturing Overhead account to CGS)		

10. Prepare the January income statement for Fashion Fabrics based on the transactions recorded in Requirements 1 through 9.

	A	B	C	D
1	**Fashion Fabrics**			
2	**Income Statement**			
3	**For Month Ending January 31**			
4				
5	Sales Revenue	$ 340,000		
6	Less: Cost of Goods Sold**	248,000		
7	Gross Profit	92,000		
8	Less: Operating Expenses	60,000		
9	Operating Income	$ 32,000		
10				
11	(** $250,000 – $2,000 closing adjustment)			

Appendix 3A

How do Service Firms Use Job Costing to Determine the Amount to Bill Clients?

So far in this chapter we have illustrated job costing in a manufacturing environment. However, job costing is also used by service firms (such as law firms, accounting firms, marketing firms, and consulting firms) and by tradespeople (such as plumbers, electricians, and auto mechanics). At these firms, the work performed for each individual client is considered a separate job. Service firms need to keep track of job costs so that they have a basis for billing their clients. As shown in Exhibit 3-19, the direct costs of serving the client are traced to the job, whereas the indirect costs of serving the client are allocated to the job.

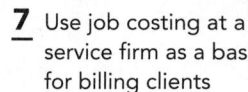

7 Use job costing at a service firm as a basis for billing clients

EXHIBIT 3-19 Assigning Costs to Client Jobs

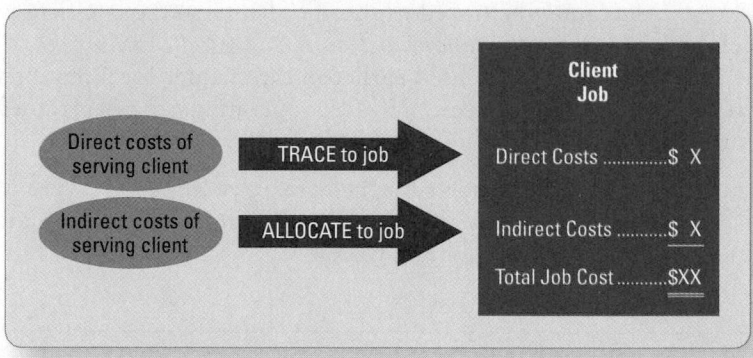

The amount billed to the client is determined by adding a profit markup to the total job cost. The main difference between job costing at a manufacturer and job costing at a service firm is that the indirect costs of serving the client are all *operating expenses*, rather than inventoriable product costs. In the next section, we will illustrate how job costing is used at Barnett & Associates law firm to determine how much to bill Client 367.

What Costs are Considered Direct Costs of Serving the Client?

The most significant direct cost at service firms is direct professional labor. In our example, direct professional labor is the attorney's time spent on clients' cases. Attorneys use labor time records to keep track of the amount of time they spend working on each client. Because most professionals are paid an annual salary rather than an hourly wage rate, firms estimate the hourly cost of employing their professionals based on the number of hours the professionals are expected to work on client jobs during the year. For example, say Attorney Theresa Fox is paid a salary of $100,000 per year. The law firm expects her to spend 2,000 hours a year performing legal work for clients (50 weeks × 40 hours per week). Therefore, for job costing purposes, the law firm converts her annual salary to an hourly cost rate as follows:

$$\frac{\$100,000 \text{ annual salary}}{2,000 \text{ hours per year}} = \$50 \text{ per hour}$$

If the labor time record indicates that Fox has spent 14 hours on Client 367, then the direct professional labor cost traced to the client is calculated as follows:

$$14 \text{ hours} \times \$50 \text{ per hour} = \$700 \text{ of direct professional labor}$$

At a law firm, very few other costs will be directly traceable to the client. Examples of other traceable costs might include travel and entertainment costs, or court filing fees related directly to specific clients. When tradespeople such as auto mechanics or plumbers use job costing, they trace their time to specific client jobs, just like attorneys do. In addition, they also trace the direct materials costs (such as the cost of new tires, an exhaust pipe, or garbage disposal) to the jobs on which those materials were used.

What Costs are Considered Indirect Costs of Serving the Client?

The law firm also incurs general operating costs, such as office rent, the salaries of office support staff, and office supplies. These are the indirect costs of serving *all* of the law firm's clients. These costs cannot be traced to specific clients, so the law firm will allocate these costs to client jobs using a *predetermined indirect cost allocation rate*. This is done using the same four basic steps as we used earlier in the chapter for a manufacturer. The only real difference is that we are allocating indirect operating expenses, rather than indirect manufacturing costs (manufacturing overhead).

STEP 1: Estimate the total indirect costs for the coming year.

Before the fiscal year begins, the law firm estimates the total indirect costs that will be incurred in the coming year:

Office rent	$190,000
Office supplies, telephone, internet access, and copier lease	10,000
Office support staff	70,000
Maintaining and updating law library for case research	25,000
Advertising	5,000
Total indirect costs	$300,000

STEP 2: Choose an allocation base and estimate the total amount that will be used during the year.

Next, the law firm chooses a cost allocation base. Service firms typically use professional labor hours as the cost allocation base. For example, Barnett & Associates estimates that attorneys will spend a total of 10,000 professional labor hours working on client jobs throughout the coming year.

STEP 3: Compute the predetermined indirect cost allocation rate.

The predetermined indirect cost allocation rate is found as follows:

$$\text{Predetermined indirect cost allocation rate} = \frac{\text{Total estimated indirect costs}}{\text{Total estimated amount of the allocation base}}$$

$$= \frac{\$300,000 \text{ total indirect costs}}{10,000 \text{ professional labor hours}}$$

$$= \$30 \text{ per professional labor hour}$$

STEP 4: Allocate indirect costs to client jobs using the predetermined rate.

Throughout the year, indirect costs are allocated to individual client jobs using the predetermined indirect cost allocation rate. For example, assume Theresa Fox was the only attorney who worked on Client 367. Because Fox spent 14 hours working on Client 367, the amount of indirect cost allocated to the job is computed as follows:

> = Predetermined indirect cost allocation rate × Actual amount of allocation base used by the job
>
> = $30 per professional labor hour × 14 professional labor hours
>
> = $420

Finding the Total Cost of the Job and Adding a Profit Markup

Barnett & Associates can now determine the total cost of serving Client 367:

Direct costs traced to Client 367 ($50 per hour × 14 hours).....................	$ 700
Indirect costs allocated to Client 367 ($30 per hour × 14 hour)..............	420
Total cost of serving Client 367	$1,120

Once the total job cost is known, Barnett & Associates can determine the amount to bill the client. Let's assume that Barnett & Associates wants to achieve a 25% profit over its costs. To achieve this profit, Barnett would bill Client 367 as follows:

> Job cost + Markup for profit = Amount to bill the client
>
> $1,120 + (25% × $1,120) = $1,400

Invoicing the Client Using a Professional Billing Rate

When service firms and tradespeople bill their clients, they don't show the actual direct costs of providing the service, the allocation of indirect costs, or the profit they earned on the job. Rather, these individual figures are hidden from the client's view. How is this done? By incorporating these costs and profit components in the labor rate, often known as the **billing rate**, charged to the customer. Consider the last time you had your vehicle repaired. A typical mechanic billing rate exceeds $48 per hour, yet the mechanic employed by the auto repair shop does not actually earn a $48-per-hour wage rate.

Let's look at the calculations a service firm performs "behind the scenes" to determine its hourly billing rates. Barnett & Associates determines Theresa Fox's billing rate as follows:

Why is this important?

"**Service** companies (such as **law firms**) and **tradespeople** (such as auto mechanics and plumbers) use **job costing** to determine how much to **bill** their clients."

Professional labor cost per hour...	$ 50
Plus: Indirect cost allocation rate per hour	30
Total hourly cost...	$ 80
Plus profit markup: (25% × $80 hourly cost)...	+ 20
Hourly billing rate for Theresa Fox...	$100

Whenever Theresa Fox performs legal work for a client, her time will be billed at $100 per hour. Remember, this is the *price* Barnett & Associates charges its clients for any work performed by Theresa Fox. The actual invoice to Client 367 would look similar to Exhibit 3-20.

EXHIBIT 3-20 Invoice to Client

Barnett & Associates Law Firm
Invoice: Client 367

Work performed the week of July 23: Researching and filing patent application

Attorney Theresa Fox: 14 hours × $100 hourly billing rate $1,400

What Journal Entries are Needed in a Service Firm's Job Costing System?

The journal entries required for job costing at a service firm are much simpler than those used at a manufacturing company. That's because service firms typically have no inventory; hence, there is no need to record the movement of inventory through the system. Rather, all costs at a service company are treated as period costs, meaning they are immediately recorded as operating expenses when they are incurred (for example, salary expense, rent expense, telephone expense, supplies expense, and so forth). The tracing of direct costs and allocation of indirect costs is performed *only* on the client's job cost record, *not* through journal entries to the company's general ledger.

▶ **Try It!**

Sarah Haymeyer, CPA, pays her new staff accountant, Hannah, a salary equivalent to $25 per hour while Sarah receives a salary equivalent to $40 per hour. The firm's predetermined indirect cost allocation rate for the year is $12 per hour. Haymeyer bills for the firm's services at 30% over cost. Assume Sarah works 5 hours and Hannah works 10 hours preparing a tax return for Michele Meckfessel.

1. What is the total cost of preparing Meckfessel's tax return?
2. How much will Sarah bill Meckfessel for the tax work?

Please see page 175 for solutions.

END OF CHAPTER

Learning Objectives

- 1 Distinguish between job costing and process costing

- 2 Understand the flow of production and how direct materials and direct labor are traced to jobs

- 3 Compute a predetermined manufacturing overhead rate and use it to allocate MOH to jobs

- 4 Determine the cost of a job and use it to make business decisions

- 5 Compute and dispose of overallocated or underallocated manufacturing overhead

- 6 Prepare journal entries for a manufacturer's job costing system

- 7 (Appendix) Use job costing at a service firm as a basis for billing clients

Accounting Vocabulary

Bill of Materials. (p. 107) A list of all of the raw materials needed to manufacture a job.

Billing Rate. (p. 143) The labor rate charged to the customer, which includes both cost and profit components.

Cost Driver. (p. 115) The primary factor that causes a cost.

Cost-Plus Pricing. (p. 118) A pricing approach in which the company adds a desired level of profit to the product's cost.

Extended Producer Responsibility (EPR). (p. 120) Laws that require product manufacturers to "take back" a large percentage of the products they manufacture at the end of the product's life in order to reduce the amount of waste ending up in landfills and the environment.

Job Cost Record. (p. 108) A written or electronic document that lists the direct materials, direct labor, and manufacturing overhead costs assigned to each individual job.

Job Costing. (p. 104) A system for assigning costs to products or services that differ in the amount of materials, labor, and overhead required. Typically used by manufacturers that produce unique, or custom-ordered products in small batches; also used by professional service firms.

Invoice. (p. 108) Bill from a supplier.

Labor Time Record. (p. 112) A written or electronic document that identifies the employee, the amount of time spent on a particular job, and the labor cost charged to a job.

Materials Requisition. (p. 111) A written or electronic document requesting that specific materials be transferred from the raw materials inventory storeroom to the production floor.

Overallocated Manufacturing Overhead. (p. 125) The amount of manufacturing overhead allocated to jobs is more than the amount of manufacturing overhead costs actually incurred; results in jobs being overcosted.

Pick. (p. 111) Storeroom workers remove items from raw materials inventory that are needed by production.

Predetermined Manufacturing Overhead Rate. (p. 115) The rate used to allocate manufacturing overhead to individual jobs; calculated before the year begins as follows: total estimated manufacturing overhead costs divided by total estimated amount of allocation base.

Process Costing. (p. 103) A system for assigning costs to a large number of identical units that typically pass through a series of uniform production steps. Costs are averaged over the units produced such that each unit bears the same unit cost.

Production Schedule. (p. 106) A written or electronic document indicating the quantity and types of inventory that will be manufactured during a specified time frame.

Purchase Order. (p. 108) A written or electronic document authorizing the purchase of specific raw materials from a specific supplier.

Raw Materials Record. (p. 107) A written or electronic document listing the number and cost of all units used and received, and the balance currently in stock; a separate record is maintained for each type of raw material kept in stock.

Receiving Report. (p. 108) A written or electronic document listing the quantity and type of raw materials received in an incoming shipment; the report is typically a duplicate of the purchase order without the quantity pre-listed on the form.

Stock Inventory. (p. 106) Products normally kept on hand in order to quickly fill customer orders.

Subsidiary Ledger. (p. 129) Supporting detail for a general ledger account.

Underallocated Manufacturing Overhead. (p. 125) The amount of manufacturing overhead allocated to jobs is less than the amount of manufacturing overhead costs actually incurred; this results in jobs being undercosted.

Quick Check

1. *(Learning Objective 1)* For which of the following would job costing *not* be appropriate?
   a. Law firm
   b. Electrician
   c. Manufacturer of mass-produced carbonated beverages
   d. Manufacturer of custom-ordered production equipment

2. *(Learning Objective 2)* Which of the following documents specifies the materials needed to produce a job?
   a. Production schedule
   b. Bill of materials
   c. Raw materials records
   d. Receiving report

3. *(Learning Objective 2)* Which of the following documents is used to accumulate all of the manufacturing costs assigned to a job?
   a. Job cost record
   b. Labor time record
   c. Materials requisition
   d. Purchase order

4. *(Learning Objective 3)* The amount of manufacturing overhead recorded on a job cost record for a particular job is found by
   a. tracing manufacturing overhead to the job.
   b. allocating manufacturing overhead to the job.
   c. either tracing or allocating manufacturing overhead costs (management's choice).
   d. None of the answers listed is correct.

5. *(Learning Objective 4)* Which of the following is *false*?
   a. A cost-plus price is determined by adding a markup to the cost.
   b. Non-manufacturing costs can be assigned to jobs only for internal decision making, never for external financial reporting.
   c. Direct costing focuses on only the direct costs found on the job cost record.
   d. Job cost information is not useful for assessing the profitability of different products.

6. *(Learning Objective 5)* Which of the following is *true*?
   a. If manufacturing overhead is overallocated, then jobs will be undercosted.
   b. If manufacturing overhead is underallocated, then jobs will be overcosted.
   c. Both of the statements are true.
   d. None of the statements is true.

7. *(Learning Objective 5)* Assuming the amount of manufacturing overhead overallocation or underallocation is not material, which account is adjusted at the end of the period?
   a. Raw Materials Inventory
   b. Cost of Goods Sold
   c. Sales Revenue
   d. Work in Process Inventory

8. *(Learning Objective 6)* Whenever direct material, direct labor, and manufacturing overhead are recorded on a job cost record, an associated journal entry is made to debit which of the following accounts?
   a. Work in Process Inventory
   b. Cost of Goods Sold
   c. Finished Goods Inventory
   d. Sales Revenue

9. *(Learning Objective 6)* When a job is completed, the total cost of manufacturing the job should be moved to which of the following general ledger accounts?
   a. Cost of Goods Sold
   b. Finished Goods Inventory
   c. Sales Revenue
   d. Work in Process Inventory

10. *(Learning Objective 7, Appendix)* Which of the following is *true* when using job costing at a service firm?
    a. Office rent would be considered a direct cost of serving the client.
    b. Both direct and indirect costs are assigned to client jobs.
    c. The professional billing rate consists solely of the professionals' labor cost.
    d. Professional labor cost would be considered an indirect cost of serving the client.

Quick Check Answers

1.c 2.b 3.a 4.b 5.d 6.d 7.b 8.a 9.b 10.b

Short Exercises

S3-1 Decide on product costing system *(Learning Objective 1)*

Would the following companies use job costing or process costing?
a. An automobile repair shop
b. A chemical manufacturer
c. A custom furniture builder
d. A movie production studio
e. A paint manufacturer

S3-2 Determine the flow of costs between inventory accounts
(Learning Objective 2)

Parker's Wood Amenities is a manufacturing plant that makes picnic tables, benches, and other outdoor furniture. Indicate which inventory account(s) would be affected by the following actions, which occur at Parker's in the process of manufacturing its standard picnic tables. Also indicate whether the inventory account would increase or decrease as a result of the action.

a. Lumber is delivered by the supplier to the plant, where it is stored in a materials storeroom until needed.
b. Lumber is requisitioned from the storeroom to be used for tops and seats for the tables.
c. Factory workers cut the lumber for the tables.
d. Ten tables are completed and moved to the inventory storage area to await sale.
e. A customer purchases a table and takes it home.

S3-3 Understanding key document terms in a job cost shop
(Learning Objective 2)

Listed below are several document terms. Match each term with the corresponding statement in the list provided. Some terms may be used more than once and other terms may not be used at all.

Terms		
a. Bill of materials	b. Job cost record	c. Production schedule
d. Purchase orders	e. Raw materials record	f. Labor time record
g. Receiving report	h. Materials requisition	i. Invoice

1. The _____ is a control for the materials stored in the storeroom. In order to get direct materials, a(n) _____ must be presented.
2. Before production begins, a manufacturer's purchasing department issues _____ to its supplier for needed direct materials.
3. A(n) _____ is typically a duplicate of the purchase order but without the quantity pre-listed on the form.
4. The _____ is like a list of ingredients in a recipe, stating the materials needed to produce a product.
5. A(n) _____ is used to accumulate all of the costs affiliated with each job.
6. All direct laborers in the factory fill out a(n) _____ .
7. The accounting department will not pay a(n) _____ unless it agrees with the quantity of parts both ordered and received.
8. Each item in the raw materials storeroom has its own _____ .

S3-4 Compute a professional billing rate *(Learning Objective 7)*

Amy Jentes is a new staff accountant at Johnstone & Associates. She is paid a salary of $60,000 per year and is expected to work 2,000 hours per year on client jobs. The firm's indirect cost allocation rate is $25 per hour. The firm would like to achieve a profit equal to 30% of cost.

1. Convert Amy's salary to an hourly wage rate for billing purposes.
2. Calculate the professional billing rate Johnstone & Associates would use for billing out Amy's services.

S3-5   Compute various manufacturing overhead rates *(Learning Objective 3)*

Dimmell Pools manufactures swimming pool equipment. Dimmell estimates total manufacturing overhead costs next year to be $1,525,000. Dimmell also estimates it will use 61,000 direct labor hours and incur $1,220,000 of direct labor cost next year. In addition, the machines are expected to be run for 38,125 hours. Compute the predetermined manufacturing overhead rate for next year under the following independent situations:

1. Assume that the company uses direct labor hours as its manufacturing overhead allocation base.
2. Assume that the company uses direct labor cost as its manufacturing overhead allocation base.
3. Assume that the company uses machine hours as its manufacturing overhead allocation base.

S3-6   Continuation of S3-5: compute total allocated overhead
(Learning Objective 3)

Use your answers from S3-5 to determine the total manufacturing overhead allocated to Dimmell's manufacturing jobs in the following independent situations:

1. Assume that the company actually used 62,550 direct labor hours.
2. Assume that the company actually incurred $1,245,000 of direct labor cost.
3. Assume that the company actually ran the machines 38,000 hours.
4. Briefly explain what you have learned about the total manufacturing overhead allocated to production.

S3-7   Continuation of S3-6: determine over- or underallocation
(Learning Objectives 3 & 5)

Use your answers from S3-6 to determine the total overallocation or underallocation of manufacturing overhead during the year. Actual manufacturing costs for the year for Dimmell Pools totaled $1,550,000.

1. Assume that the company used direct labor hours as the allocation base.
2. Assume that the company used the direct labor cost as the allocation base.
3. Assume that the company used machine hours as the allocation base.
4. Were there any situations in which jobs were costed correctly? If not, when were they overcosted? When were they undercosted?

S3-8   Calculate rate and analyze year-end results *(Learning Objectives 3 & 5)*

Connery Industries manufactures wooden backyard playground equipment. Connery estimated $1,890,000 of manufacturing overhead and $2,160,000 of direct labor cost for the year. After the year was over, the accounting records indicated that the company had actually incurred $1,760,000 of manufacturing overhead and $2,300,000 of direct labor cost.

1. Calculate Connery's predetermined manufacturing overhead rate, assuming that the company uses direct labor cost as an allocation base.
2. How much manufacturing overhead would have been allocated to manufacturing jobs during the year?
3. At year-end, was manufacturing overhead overallocated or underallocated? By how much?

S3-9   Calculate job cost and billing at appliance repair service
(Learning Objectives 2, 4, & 7 (Appendix))

J&B Appliance provides repair services for all makes and models of home appliances. J&B Appliance charges customers for labor on each job at a rate of $76 per hour. The labor rate is high enough to cover actual technician wages of $29 per hour, to cover shop overhead (allocated at a cost of $22 per hour), and to provide a profit. The company charges the customer "at cost" for parts and materials. A recent customer job consisted of $40 in parts and materials and 2 hours of technician time.

1. What was J&B Appliance's cost for this job? Include shop overhead in the cost calculation.
2. How much was charged to the customer for this repair job?

S3-10   Ramifications of overallocating and underallocating jobs
(Learning Objectives 2 & 5)

Answer the following questions:

1. Why do managers use a *predetermined* manufacturing overhead allocation rate rather than the *actual* rate to cost jobs?
2. Jobs will typically be overcosted or undercosted. Is one worse than the other? Explain your thoughts.

S3-11   Record purchase and use of materials *(Learning Objective 6)*

EasyPacks manufactures backpacks. Its plant records include the following materials-related transactions:

Purchases of canvas (on account)	$67,000
Purchases of thread (on account)	$ 1,100
Material requisitions:	
Canvas	$63,000
Thread	$ 500

Make the journal entries to record these transactions. Post these transactions to the Raw Materials Inventory account. If the company had $38,000 of Raw Materials Inventory at the beginning of the period, what is the ending balance of Raw Materials Inventory?

S3-12   Record manufacturing labor costs *(Learning Objective 6)*

Crystal Creations reports the following labor-related transactions at its plant in Akron, Ohio.

Plant janitor's wages	$ 560
Plant supervisor's wages	$ 860
Glassblowers' wages	$70,000

Record the journal entries for the incurrence of these wages.

S3-13   Recompute job cost at a legal firm *(Learning Objectives 3, 4, & 7)*

Zucca Associates, a law firm, hires Attorney Odessa Smythe at an annual salary of $192,000. The law firm expects her to spend 2,400 hours per year performing legal work for clients. Indirect costs are assigned to clients based on attorney billing hours. Firm attorneys are expected to work a total of 28,000 direct labor hours this year. Before the fiscal year begins, Zucca estimates that the total indirect costs for the upcoming year will be $840,000.

1. What would be the hourly (cost) rate to Zucca Associates of employing Smythe?
2. If Smythe works on Client 367 for 15 hours, what direct labor cost would be traced to Client 367?
3. What is the indirect cost allocation rate?
4. What indirect costs will be allocated to Client 367?
5. What is the total job cost for Client 367?

ETHICS

S3-14 **Identify ethical standards violated** (*Learning Objectives 1, 2, 3, 4, 5, & 6*)

For each of the situations listed, identify the primary standard from the IMA *Statement of Ethical Professional Practice* that is violated (competence, confidentiality, integrity, or credibility.) Refer to Exhibit 1-6 for the complete standard.

1. Anita does not disclose to her employer, Collins Company, that her brother is the owner of a company that is bidding on a major contract with Collins Company. Anita is on the committee that evaluates the bids and makes a recommendation about which bid to select.

2. Damon is asked to do an inventory count of a wide assortment of parts. Damon does not know how to distinguish the various parts. He guesses when he enters the quantity. He does not ask for help because he does not want to look stupid.

3. Gabriel added in sales commissions to product costs on the financial statements because it seemed reasonable to include those costs.

4. At a neighborhood party, Jodi talks about the upcoming bid her company is making for a county project. She shares specific cost estimates that are included in the bid.

5. Jose changed the way that manufacturing overhead is allocated to divisions on the monthly internal reports to better reflect resource usage. However, he did not note the change on any of the reports nor did he inform any managers of the change.

S3-15 **Understanding key terms** (*Learning Objectives 1, 2, 3, & 4*)

Listed next are several terms. Complete the following statements with one of these terms. You may use a term more than once, and some terms may not be used at all.

Cost allocation	Cost driver	Job costing	Process costing
Cost tracing	Job cost record	Materials requisition	

a. _____ is used by companies that produce large numbers of identical units through a series of uniform production steps or processes.

b. The _____ is used to track and accumulate all of the costs for an individual job.

c. General Mills produces Cheerios cereal; it would use a _____ system to determine product cost.

d. _____ is used by companies that produce unique services and products.

e. Raw materials are stored in a storeroom until a _____ is received requesting the transfer of materials to the production area.

f. _____ is the assignment of direct costs to specific jobs.

g. Indirect costs cannot be traced to specific products, so they are divided up using a process called _____.

h. An aircraft carrier builder would use a _____ system to determine product cost.

i. A _____ is any activity that causes a cost to be incurred.

EXERCISES Group A

E3-16A **Identify type of costing system** (*Learning Objective 1*)

For each of the following companies, specify whether each company would be more likely to use job costing or process costing.

a. Aircraft builder
b. Hospital
c. Cement plant
d. Dentist
e. Advertising agency
f. Custom-home builder
g. Oil refinery

h. House painter
i. Manufacturer of computer chips
j. Yacht builder
k. Cereal manufacturer
l. Landscaper
m. Pet food processor
n. Wallpaper installation service

E3-17A   Understand the flow of costs in a job cost shop *(Learning Objective 2)*

Parker Feeders manufactures bird feeders for wild bird specialty stores. In September, Parker Feeders received an order from Wild Birds, Inc., for 30 platform bird feeders. The order from Wild Birds, Inc., became Job Number 1102 at Parker Feeders.

A materials requisition for Job 1102 is presented in the following section. In addition to the materials requisition, the labor time records (partial) for the week during which these feeders were made are presented. Other products were also being produced during that week, so not all of the labor from that week belongs to Job 1102.

Materials Requisition
Number: #1250

Date: 9/14

Job: 1102

Part Number	Description	Quantity	Unit Cost	Amount
WOCD06	Rough-hewn cedar planks	42	$3.00	
SSF0304	Stainless steel fasteners	78	$1.00	
AS222	Reinforced aluminum screens	22	$2.50	
	Total			

Labor Time Record

Employee: Greg Henderson   **Week:** 9/14 – 9/20

Hourly Wage Rate: $11   **Record #:** 912

Date	Job Number	Start Time	End Time	Hours	Cost
9/14	1102	9:00	2:00		
9/14	1103	2:00	5:00		
9/15 etc.					

CHAPTER 3

Labor Time Record

Employee: Andrew Peck   **Week:** 9/14 – 9/20

Hourly Wage Rate: $7   **Record #:** 913

Date	Job Number	Start Time	End Time	Hours	Cost
9/14	1101	8:00	12:00		
9/14	1102	12:00	4:00		
9/15	1103	8:00	10:00		
9/15 etc.					

Job Cost Record

Job Number: 1102

Customer: Wild Birds, Inc.

Job Description: 30 Model 3F (platform bird feeders)

Date Started: Sep. 14   **Date Completed:** _____

Manufacturing Cost Information:	Cost Summary
Direct Materials	
Req. # :	
Direct Labor	
No. #	
No. #	
Manufacturing Overhead	
9 hours × $2 per direct labor hour	$ 18
Total Job Cost	
Number of Units	÷
Cost per Unit	

Requirements

1. Calculate the total for the Materials Requisition form. Post the information (cost and requisition number) from the Materials Requisition form to the Job Record in the appropriate boxes.

2. Complete the labor time records for each of the employees. Once the labor time record is completed, post the information relevant to Job 1102 to the Job Cost Record for Job Cost 1102.

3. Manufacturing overhead has already been added to the Job Cost Record. Complete the Job Cost Record by calculating the total job cost and the cost per unit. Remember that this job consisted of 30 feeders (units).

E3-18A Compute a predetermined overhead rate and calculate cost of jobs based on direct labor hours (Learning Objectives 3 & 4)

Boston Heating & Cooling installs and services commercial heating and cooling systems. Boston uses job costing to calculate the cost of its jobs. Overhead is allocated to each job based on the number of direct labor hours spent on that job. At the beginning of the current year, Boston estimated that its overhead for the coming year would be $67,200. It also anticipated using 4,200 direct labor hours for the year. In November, Boston started and completed the following two jobs:

	Job 101	Job 102
Direct materials used	$18,000	$12,000
Direct labor hours used	180	74

Boston paid a $24-per-hour wage rate to the employees who worked on these two jobs.

Requirements

1. What is Boston's predetermined overhead rate based on direct labor hours?

2. Calculate the overhead to be allocated based on direct labor hours to each of the two jobs.

3. What is the total cost of Job 101? What is the total cost of Job 102?

E3-19A Compute a predetermined overhead rate and calculate cost of job based on direct labor costs (Learning Objectives 3 & 4)

Dansville Restaurant Supply manufactures commercial stoves and ovens for restaurants and bakeries. The company uses job costing to calculate the costs of its jobs with direct labor cost as its manufacturing overhead allocation base. At the beginning of the current year, Dansville estimated that its overhead for the coming year would be $356,400. It also anticipated using 27,000 direct labor hours for the year. Dansville pays its employees an average of $24 per direct labor hour. Dansville just finished Job 371, which consisted of two large ovens for a regional bakery. The costs for Job 371 were as follows:

	Job 371
Direct materials used	$16,000
Direct labor hours used	125

Requirements

1. What is Dansville's predetermined manufacturing overhead rate based on direct labor cost?

2. Calculate the manufacturing overhead to be allocated based on direct labor cost to Job 371.

3. What is the total cost of Job 371?

CHAPTER 3

E3-20A   Determine the cost of a job and use it for pricing
(Learning Objectives 2 & 4)

Fun Time Industries manufactures custom-designed playground equipment for schools and city parks. Fun Time expected to incur $586,600 of manufacturing overhead cost, 41,900 of direct labor hours, and $921,800 of direct labor cost during the year (the cost of direct labor is $22 per hour). The company allocates manufacturing overhead on the basis of direct labor hours. During May, Fun Time completed Job 309. The job used 175 direct labor hours and required $14,200 of direct materials. The City of Southtown has contracted to purchase the playground equipment at a price of 22% over manufacturing cost.

Requirements

1. Calculate the manufacturing cost of Job 309.
2. How much will the City of Southtown pay for this playground equipment?

SUSTAINABILITY

CHAPTER 3

E3-21A   Sustainability and job costing *(Learning Objectives 2, 4, & 7)*

Ludlow Plastics manufactures custom park furniture and signage from recycled plastics (primarily shredded milk jugs.) Many of the company's customers are municipalities that are required by law to purchase goods that meet certain recycled-content guidelines. (Recycled-content can include post-consumer waste materials, pre-consumer waste materials, and recovered materials.) As a result, Ludlow includes two types of direct material charges in its job cost for each job: (1) virgin materials (non-recycled), and (2) recycled-content materials. Ludlow also keeps track of the pounds of each type of direct material so that the final recycled-content percentage for the job can be reported to the customer. Ludlow also reports on the percentage of recycled content as a total of total plastic used each month in its own internal reporting system to help to encourage managers to use recycled content whenever possible.

Ludlow Plastics uses a predetermined manufacturing overhead rate of $6 per direct labor hour. Here is a summary of the materials and labor used on a recent job for Jefferson County:

Description	Quantity	Cost
Virgin materials	120 pounds	$ 3.70 per pound
Recycled-content materials	280 pounds	$ 2.60 per pound
Direct labor	16 hours	$12.00 per hour

Requirements

1. Calculate the total cost of the Jefferson County job.
2. Calculate the percentage of recycled content used in the Jefferson County job (using pounds). If items purchased by Jefferson County are required by county charter to contain at least 60% recycled content, does this job meet that requirement?

E3-22A   Determine the cost of a job *(Learning Objectives 2, 3, & 4)*

Krantz Furniture started and finished Job 310 during August. The company's records show that the following direct materials were requisitioned for Job 310:

Lumber: 47 units at $8 per unit
Padding: 13 yards at $19 per yard
Upholstery fabric: 28 yards at $27 per yard

Labor time records show the following employees (direct labor) worked on Job 310:

Joe Hume: 11 hours at $9 per hour
Charles Roche: 16 hours at $13 per hour

Krantz allocates manufacturing overhead at a rate of $8 per direct labor hour.

Requirements

1. Compute the total amount of direct materials, direct labor, and manufacturing overhead that should be shown on Job 310's job cost record.
2. Job 310 consists of eight recliners. If each recliner sells for $750, what is the gross profit per recliner?

E3-23A Compare bid prices under two different allocation bases
(Learning Objectives 3 & 4)

Rosa Recycling recycles newsprint, cardboard, and so forth, into recycled packaging materials. For the coming year, Rosa estimates total manufacturing overhead to be $369,260. The company's managers are not sure if direct labor hours (estimated to be 9,980) or machine hours (estimated to be 18,463 hours) is the best allocation base to use for allocating manufacturing overhead. Rosa bids for jobs using a 31% markup over total manufacturing cost.

After the new fiscal year began, Potter Paper Supply asked Rosa Recycling to bid for a job that will take 1,980 machine hours and 1,700 direct labor hours to produce. The direct labor cost for this job will be $12 per hour, and the direct materials will total $25,300.

Requirements

1. Compute the total job cost and bid price if Rosa Recycling decided to use direct labor hours as the manufacturing overhead allocation base for the year.
2. Compute the total job cost and bid price if Rosa Recycling decided to use machine hours as the manufacturing overhead allocation base for the year.
3. In addition to the bid from Rosa Recycling, Potter Paper Supply received a bid of $125,000 for this job from Mauzy Recycling. What are the ramifications for Rosa Recycling?

E3-24A Analyze manufacturing overhead *(Learning Objectives 3 & 5)*

Alton Foundry in Philadelphia, Pennsylvania, uses a predetermined manufacturing overhead rate to allocate overhead to individual jobs based on the machine hours required. At the beginning of the year, the company expected to incur the following:

Manufacturing overhead costs	$ 620,000
Direct labor cost	$1,350,000
Machine hours	77,500

At the end of the year, the company had actually incurred the following:

Direct labor cost	$1,240,000
Depreciation on manufacturing plant and equipment	$ 460,000
Property taxes on plant	$ 20,500
Sales salaries	$ 25,000
Delivery drivers' wages	$ 14,500
Plant janitors' wages	$ 9,500
Machine hours	54,000 hours

Requirements

1. Compute Alton's predetermined manufacturing overhead rate.
2. How much manufacturing overhead was allocated to jobs during the year?
3. How much manufacturing overhead was incurred during the year? Is manufacturing overhead underallocated or overallocated at the end of the year? By how much?
4. Were the jobs overcosted or undercosted? By how much?

E3-25A Record manufacturing overhead *(Learning Objectives 5 & 6)*

Refer to the data in Exercise 3-24A. Alton's accountant found an error in the expense records from the year reported. Depreciation on manufacturing plant and equipment was actually $400,000, not the $460,000 that had originally been reported. The unadjusted Cost of Goods Sold balance at year-end was $580,000.

Requirements

1. Prepare the journal entry (entries) to record manufacturing overhead costs incurred.
2. Prepare the journal entry to record the manufacturing overhead allocated to jobs in production.
3. Use a T-account to determine whether manufacturing overhead is underallocated or overallocated and by how much.

4. Record the entry to close out the underallocated or overallocated manufacturing overhead.

5. What is the adjusted ending balance of Cost of Goods Sold?

E3-26A Record journal entries (Learning Objectives 2, 3, 5, & 6)

The following transactions were incurred by Jackson Fabricators during January, the first month of its fiscal year.

Requirements

1. Record the proper journal entry for each transaction.
   a. $195,000 of materials was purchased on account.
   b. $194,000 of materials was used in production; of this amount, $167,000 was used on specific jobs.
   c. Manufacturing labor and salaries for the month totaled $260,000. A total of $215,000 of manufacturing labor and salaries was traced to specific jobs, and the remainder was indirect labor used in the factory.
   d. The company recorded $17,000 of depreciation on the plant and plant equipment. The company also received a plant utility bill for $9,000.
   e. $87,000 of manufacturing overhead was allocated to specific jobs.
   f. The company received bill for website services for $3,000.

2. By the end of January, was manufacturing overhead overallocated or underallocated? By how much?

E3-27A Analyze T-accounts (Learning Objectives 2, 3, 5, & 6)

Control Enterprises produces touch screens for use in various smartphones. The company reports the following information at December 31. Control Enterprises began operations on January 31 earlier that same year.

Work in Process Inventory		Wages Payable		Manufacturing Overhead		Finished Goods Inventory		Raw Materials Inventory	
30,000	125,500	78,000	78,000	3,500	42,000	125,500	114,000	53,000	33,500
64,500				13,500					
42,000		Balance 0		42,000					

Requirements

1. What is the cost of direct materials used?
2. What is the cost of indirect materials used?
3. What is the cost of direct labor?
4. What is the cost of indirect labor?
5. What is the cost of goods manufactured?
6. What is the cost of goods sold (before adjusting for any under- or overallocated manufacturing overhead)?
7. What is the actual manufacturing overhead?
8. How much manufacturing overhead was allocated to jobs?
9. What is the predetermined manufacturing overhead rate as a percentage of direct labor cost?
10. Is manufacturing overhead underallocated or overallocated? By how much?

E3-28A Job cost and bid price at a consulting firm (Learning Objective 7)

Zander Consulting, a real estate consulting firm, specializes in advising companies on potential new plant sites. The firm uses a job cost system with a predetermined indirect cost allocation rate computed as a percentage of expected direct labor costs.

At the beginning of the year, managing partner Chloe Zander prepared the following plan, or budget, for the year:

Direct labor hours (professionals)	14,000 hours
Direct labor costs (professionals)	$2,150,000
Office rent	$ 220,000
Support staff salaries	$ 910,000
Utilities	$ 290,000

Jamba Resources is inviting several consulting firms to bid for work. Zander estimates that this job will require about 180 direct labor hours.

Requirements

1. Compute Zander Consulting's (a) hourly direct labor cost rate and (b) indirect cost allocation rate.
2. Compute the predicted cost of the Jamba Resources job.
3. If Zander Consulting wants to earn a profit that equals 40% of the job's cost, how much should the company bid for the Jamba Resources job?

E3-29A Record journal entries (Learning Objectives 2, 3, 5, & 6)

The following transactions were incurred by Whooley Fabricators during January, the first month of its fiscal year.

Requirements

1. Record the proper journal entry for each transaction.

   a. $205,000 of materials was purchased on account.

   b. $174,000 of materials was used in production; of this amount, $146,000 was used on specific jobs.

   c. Manufacturing labor and salaries for the month totaled $210,000. $200,000 of the total manufacturing labor and salaries was traced to specific jobs, and the remainder was indirect labor used in the factory.

   d. The company recorded $16,000 of depreciation on the plant and plant equipment. The company also received a plant utility bill for $14,000.

   e. $56,000 of manufacturing overhead was allocated to specific jobs.

2. By the end of January, was manufacturing overhead overallocated or underallocated? By how much?

EXERCISES Group B

E3-30B Identify type of costing system (Learning Objective 1)

For each of the following companies, specify whether the company would be more likely to use job costing or process costing.

a. Medical practice of six doctors and four physician assistants

b. Soft drink bottler

c. Movie studio

d. Plastic bottle manufacturer

e. Architect

f. Temporary staffing agency

g. Oil refinery

h. Janitorial services company

i. Soup manufacturer

j. Commercial plumbing contractor

k. Toothpaste manufacturer

l. Catering service

m. Ship builder

n. Company providing Web design services

E3-31B Understand the flow of costs in a job cost shop
(Learning Objective 2)

Snyder Feeders manufactures bird feeders for wild bird specialty stores. In September, Snyder Feeders received an order from Wild Birds, Inc., for 24 platform bird feeders. The order from Wild Birds, Inc., became Job 1102 at Snyder Feeders.

A materials requisition for Job 1102 is presented in the following section. In addition to the materials requisition, the labor time records (partial) for the week during which these feeders were made are presented. Other products were also being produced during that week, so not all of the labor belongs to Job 1102.

Materials Requisition
Number: #1250

Date: 9/14

Job: 1102

Part Number	Description	Quantity	Unit Cost	Amount
WOCD06	Rough-hewn cedar planks	40	$2.50	
SSF0304	Stainless steel fasteners	82	$1.00	
AS222	Reinforced aluminum screens	26	$1.50	
	Total			

Labor Time Record

Employee: Greg Henderson   **Week:** 9/14 – 9/20

Hourly Wage Rate: $11   **Record #:** 912

Date	Job Number	Start Time	End Time	Hours	Cost
9/14	1102	9:00	1:00		
9/14	1103	1:00	5:00		
9/15 etc.					

Labor Time Record

Employee: Andrew Peck   **Week:** 9/14 – 9/20

Hourly Wage Rate: $7   **Record #:** 913

Date	Job Number	Start Time	End Time	Hours	Cost
9/14	1101	9:00	12:00		
9/14	1102	12:00	5:00		
9/15	1103	9:00	11:00		
9/15 etc.					

Job Cost Record

Job Number: 1102

Customer: Wild Birds, Inc.

Job Description: 24 Model 3F (platform bird feeders)

Date Started: Sep. 14   **Date Completed:** _____

Manufacturing Cost Information:	Cost Summary
Direct Materials	
Req. # :	
Direct Labor	
No. #	
No. #	
Manufacturing Overhead	
9 hours × $3 per direct labor hour	$ 27
Total Job Cost	
Number of Units	
Cost per Unit	

Requirements

1. Calculate the total for the Materials Requisition form. Post the information (cost and requisition number) from the Materials Requisition form to the Job Cost Record in the appropriate boxes.

2. Complete the labor time records for each of the employees. Once the labor time record is completed, post the information relevant to Job 1102 to the Job Cost Record for Job 1102.

3. Manufacturing overhead has already been added to the Job Cost Record. Complete the Job Cost Record by calculating the total job cost and the cost per unit. Remember that this job consisted of 24 feeders (units).

E3-32B   Compute a predetermined overhead rate and calculate cost of jobs
(Learning Objectives 3 & 4)

Jamestown Heating & Cooling installs and services commercial heating and cooling systems. Jamestown uses job costing to calculate the cost of its jobs. Overhead is allocated to each job based on the number of direct labor hours spent on that job. At the beginning of the current year, Jamestown estimated that its overhead for the coming year would be $63,750. It also anticipated using 4,250 direct labor hours for the year. In May, Jamestown started and completed the following two jobs:

	Job 101	Job 102
Direct materials used	$15,500	$10,500
Direct labor hours used...	175	74

Jamestown paid a $20-per-hour wage rate to the employees who worked on these two jobs.

Requirements

1. What is Jamestown's predetermined overhead rate based on direct labor hours?
2. Calculate the overhead to be allocated based on direct labor hours to each of the two jobs.
3. What is the total cost of Job 101? What is the total cost of Job 102?

E3-33B Compute a predetermined overhead rate and calculate cost of job
(Learning Objectives 3 & 4)

Lakeview Restaurant Supply manufactures commercial stove and ovens for restaurants and bakeries. The company uses job costing to calculate the costs of its jobs with direct labor cost as its manufacturing overhead allocation base. At the beginning of the current year, Lakeview estimated that its overhead for the coming year will be $404,800. It also anticipated using 23,000 direct labor hours for the year. Lakeview pays its employees an average of $32 per direct labor hour. Lakeview just finished Job 371, which consisted of two large ovens for a regional bakery. The costs for Job 371 were as follows:

	Job 371
Direct materials used	$13,500
Direct labor hours used...	140

Requirements

1. What is Lakeview's predetermined manufacturing overhead rate based on direct labor cost?
2. Calculate the manufacturing overhead to be allocated based on direct labor costs to Job 371.
3. What is the total cost of Job 371?

E3-34B Determine the cost of a job and use it for pricing
(Learning Objectives 2 & 4)

Leisure Industries manufactures custom-designed playground equipment for schools and city parks. Leisure expected to incur $828,000 of manufacturing overhead cost, 41,400 of direct labor hours, and $828,000 of direct labor cost during the year (the cost of direct labor is $20 per hour). The company allocates manufacturing overhead on the basis of direct labor hours. During February, Leisure completed Job 308. The job used 180 direct labor hours and required $15,400 of direct materials. The City of Adams has contracted to purchase the playground equipment at a price of 25% over manufacturing cost.

Requirements

1. Calculate the manufacturing cost of Job 308.
2. How much will the City of Adams pay for this playground equipment?

SUSTAINABILITY

E3-35B Sustainability and job costing *(Learning Objectives 2, 4, & 7)*

New Wood Plastics manufactures custom park furniture and signage from recycled plastics (primarily shredded milk jugs.) Many of the company's customers are municipalities that are required by law to purchase goods that meet certain recycled-content guidelines. (Recycled content can include post-consumer waste materials, pre-consumer waste materials, and recovered materials.) As a result, New Wood Plastics includes two types of direct material charges in its job cost for each job: (1) virgin materials (non-recycled), and (2) recycled-content materials. New Wood Plastics also keeps track of the pounds of each type of direct material so that the final recycled-content percentage for the job can be reported to the customer. The company also reports on the percentage of recycled-content as a total of plastics used each month on its own internal reporting system to help encourage managers to use recycled content whenever possible.

New Wood Plastics uses a predetermined manufacturing overhead rate of $8 per direct labor hour. Here is a summary of the materials and labor used on a recent job for Mitchell County:

Description	Quantity	Cost
Virgin materials	150 pounds	$ 4.40 per pound
Recycled-content materials	350 pounds	$ 3.20 per pound
Direct labor	20 hours	$15.00 per hour

Requirements

1. Calculate the total cost of the Mitchell County job.
2. Calculate the percentage of recycled-content used in the Mitchell County job (using pounds.) If items purchased by Mitchell County are required by county charter to contain at least 40% recycled-content, does the job meet that requirement?

E3-36B   Determine the cost of a job *(Learning Objectives 2, 3, & 4)*

Rally Furniture started and finished Job 310 during August. The company's records show that the following direct materials were requisitioned for Job 310:

> Lumber: 51 units at $9 per unit
> Padding: 15 yards at $21 per yard
> Upholstery fabric: 32 yards at $25 per yard.

Labor time records show the following employees (direct labor) worked on Job 310:

> Yimeng Li: 8 hours at $9 per hour
> Jesse Ray: 13 hours at $13 per hour.

Rally Furniture allocates manufacturing overhead at a rate of $8 per direct labor hour.

Requirements

1. Compute the total amount of direct materials, direct labor, and manufacturing overhead that should be shown on Job 310's job cost record.
2. Job 310 consists of seven recliners. If each recliner sells for $700, what is the gross profit per recliner?

E3-37B   Compare bid prices under two different allocation bases
(Learning Objectives 3 & 4)

Colwell Recycling recycles newsprint, cardboard, and so forth, into recycled packaging materials. For the coming year, Colwell Recycling estimates total manufacturing overhead to be $348,950. The company's managers are not sure if direct labor hours (estimated to be 9,970) or machine hours (estimated to be 13,958 hours) is the best allocation base to use for allocating manufacturing overhead. Colwell bids for jobs using a 30% markup over total manufacturing cost.

After the new fiscal year began, Leftwich Paper Supply asked Colwell Recycling to bid for a job that will take 2,000 machine hours and 1,500 direct labor hours to produce. The direct labor cost for this job will be $13 per hour, and the direct materials will total $25,400.

Requirements

1. Compute the total job cost and bid price if Colwell Recycling decided to use direct labor hours as the manufacturing overhead allocation base for the year.
2. Compute the total job cost and bid price if Colwell Recycling decided to use machine hours as the manufacturing overhead allocation base for the year.

3. In addition to the bid from Colwell Recycling, Leftwich Paper Supply received a bid of $125,500 for this job from Drund Recycling. What are the ramifications for Colwell Recycling?

E3-38B Analyze manufacturing overhead *(Learning Objectives 3 & 5)*

Patel Foundry in Toledo, Ohio, uses a predetermined manufacturing overhead rate to allocate overhead to individual jobs based on the machine hours required. At the beginning of the year, the company expected to incur the following:

Manufacturing overhead costs..	$ 580,000
Direct labor cost...	$1,600,000
Machine hours...	72,500

At the end of the year, the company had actually incurred the following:

Direct labor cost...	$1,180,000
Depreciation on manufacturing plant and equipment...............	$ 495,000
Property taxes on plant..	$ 21,500
Sales salaries	$ 23,500
Delivery drivers' wages	$ 15,000
Plant janitors' wages	$ 8,000
Machine hours...	57,000 hours

Requirements

1. Compute Patel Foundry's predetermined manufacturing overhead rate.
2. How much manufacturing overhead was allocated to jobs during the year?
3. How much manufacturing overhead was incurred during the year? Is manufacturing overhead underallocated or overallocated at the end of the year? By how much?
4. Were the jobs overcosted or undercosted? By how much?

E3-39B Record manufacturing overhead *(Learning Objectives 5 & 6)*

Refer to the data in Exercise E3-38B. Patel Foundry's accountant found an error in the expense records from the year reported. Depreciation on manufacturing plant and equipment was actually $405,000, not the $495,000 it had originally reported. The unadjusted Cost of Goods Sold balance at year-end was $620,000.

Requirements

1. Prepare the journal entry (entries) to record manufacturing overhead costs incurred.
2. Prepare the journal entry to record the manufacturing overhead allocated to jobs in production.
3. Use a T-account to determine whether manufacturing overhead is underallocated or overallocated, and by how much.
4. Record the entry to close out the underallocated or overallocated manufacturing overhead.
5. What is the adjusted ending balance of Cost of Goods Sold?

E3-40B Record journal entries *(Learning Objectives 2, 3, 5, & 6)*

The following transactions were incurred by Howley Fabricators during January, the first month of its fiscal year.

Requirements

1. Record the proper journal entry for each transaction.

   a. $180,000 of materials was purchased on account.
   b. $162,000 of materials was used in production; of this amount, $158,000 was used on specific jobs.

    c. Manufacturing labor and salaries for the month totaled $240,000. $215,000 of the total manufacturing labor and salaries was traced to specific jobs, and the remainder was indirect labor used in the factory.

    d. The company recorded $19,000 of depreciation on the plant and plant equipment. The company also received a plant utility bill for $11,000.

    e. $56,000 of manufacturing overhead was allocated to specific jobs.

    f. The company received bill for website services for $4,000.

  2. By the end of January, was manufacturing overhead overallocated or underallocated? By how much?

E3-41B   Analyze T-accounts *(Learning Objectives 2, 3, 5, & 6)*

Baxter Products produces touch screens for use in various smartphones. The company reports the following information at December 31. Baxter Products began operations on January 31 earlier that same year.

Work in Process Inventory		Wages Payable		Manufacturing Overhead		Finished Goods Inventory		Raw Materials Inventory	
28,500	126,000	74,000	74,000	6,500	42,000	126,000	115,500	53,000	35,000
64,000				10,000					
42,000		Balance 0		38,000					

Requirements

  1. What is the cost of direct materials used?

  2. The cost of indirect materials used?

  3. What is the cost of direct labor?

  4. The cost of indirect labor?

  5. What is the cost of goods manufactured?

  6. What is the cost of goods sold (before adjusting for any under- or overallocated manufacturing overhead)?

  7. What is the actual manufacturing overhead?

  8. How much manufacturing overhead was allocated to jobs?

  9. What is the predetermined manufacturing overhead rate as a percentage of direct labor cost?

  10. Is manufacturing overhead underallocated or overallocated? By how much?

E3-42B   Job cost and bid price at a consulting firm *(Learning Objective 7)*

Simms Consulting, a real estate consulting firm, specializes in advising companies on potential new plant sites. The firm uses a job costing system with a predetermined indirect cost allocation rate computed as a percentage of direct labor costs. At the beginning of the year, managing partner. Andy Simms prepared the following plan, or budget, for the year:

Direct labor hours (professionals)..	15,000 hours
Direct labor costs (professionals)	$2,250,000
Office rent	$ 280,000
Support staff salaries..	$ 860,000
Utilities	$ 300,000

Jones Resources is inviting several consultants to bid for work. Simms estimates that this job will require about 220 direct labor hours.

Requirements

1. Compute Simms Consulting's (a) hourly direct labor cost rate and (b) indirect cost allocation rate.
2. Compute the predicted cost of the Jones Resources job.
3. If Simms Consulting wants to earn a profit that equals 30% of the job's cost, how much should the company bid for the Jones Resources job?

E3-43B   Record journal entries *(Learning Objectives 2, 3, 5, & 6)*

The following transactions were incurred by Dutch Fabricators during January, the first month of its fiscal year.

Requirements

1. Record the proper journal entry for each transaction.
    a. $190,000 of materials were purchased on account.
    b. $174,000 of materials were used in production; of this amount, $152,000 was used on specific jobs.
    c. Manufacturing labor and salaries for the month totaled $225,000. A total of $190,000 of manufacturing labor and salaries was traced to specific jobs, while the remainder was indirect labor used in the factory.
    d. The company recorded $20,000 of depreciation on the plant and plant equipment. The company also received a plant utility bill for $10,000.
    e. $81,000 of manufacturing overhead was allocated to specific jobs.
2. By the end of January, was manufacturing overhead overallocated or underallocated? By how much?

PROBLEMS Group A

P3-44A   Analyze Manufacturing Overhead *(Learning Objectives 3 & 5)*

Superior Uniforms produces uniforms. The company allocates manufacturing overhead based on the machine hours each job uses. Superior Uniforms reports the following cost data for the past year:

	Budget	Actual
Direct labor hours	7,200 hours	6,200 hours
Machine hours	6,920 hours	6,400 hours
Depreciation on salespeople's autos	$22,000	$22,000
Indirect materials	$50,000	$51,000
Depreciation on trucks used to deliver uniforms to customers	$13,000	$11,500
Depreciation on plant and equipment	$64,000	$65,000
Indirect manufacturing labor	$41,000	$43,000
Customer service hotline	$19,500	$20,500
Plant utilities	$18,000	$19,000
Direct labor cost	$73,000	$87,000

Requirements

1. Compute the predetermined manufacturing overhead rate.
2. Calculate the allocated manufacturing overhead for the past year.
3. Compute the underallocated or overallocated manufacturing overhead. How will this underallocated or overallocated manufacturing overhead be disposed of?
4. How can managers use accounting information to help control manufacturing overhead costs?

P3-45A Use job costing at an advertising agency
(Learning Objectives 3, 4, & 7)

Clark & Taylor is an Internet advertising agency. The firm uses a job cost system in which each client is a different "job." Clark & Taylor traces direct labor, software licensing costs, and travel costs directly to each job (client). The company allocates indirect costs to jobs based on a predetermined indirect cost allocation rate based on direct labor hours.

At the beginning of the current year, managing partner Yimeng Li prepared a budget:

Direct labor hours (professional)	17,900 hours
Direct labor costs (professional)	$1,790,000
Support staff salaries	$ 160,000
Rent and utilities	$ 95,000
Supplies	$ 505,400
Lease payments on computer hardware	$ 63,000

During January of the current year, Clark & Taylor served several clients. Records for two clients appear here:

	GoVacation.com	Port Chance Golf Resort
Direct labor hours	720 hours	40 hours
Software licensing costs	$2,400	$200
Travel costs	$7,000	$ 0

Requirements

1. Compute Clark & Taylor's predetermined indirect cost allocation rate for the current year based on direct labor hours.
2. Compute the total cost of each job.
3. If Clark & Taylor wants to earn profits equal to 20% of sales revenue, how much (what total fee) should it charge each of these two clients?
4. Why does Clark & Taylor assign costs to jobs?

P3-46A Use job costing at a consulting firm *(Learning Objectives 3, 4, & 7)*

Falcon Design is a website design and consulting firm. The firm uses a job cost system in which each client is a different "job." Falcon Design traces direct labor, licensing costs, and travel costs directly to each job (client). It allocates indirect costs to jobs based on a predetermined indirect cost allocation rate computed as a percentage of direct labor costs.

At the beginning of the current year, managing partner Mary Milici prepared the following budget:

Direct labor hours (professional)	7,500 hours
Direct labor costs (professional)	$1,500,000
Support staff salaries	$ 180,000
Computer lease payments	$ 46,000
Office supplies	$ 24,000
Office rent	$ 65,000

Later that same year in November, Falcon Design served several clients. Records for two clients appear here:

	Dining Treats	Talknow.com
Direct labor hours	760 hours	35 hours
Licensing costs	$2,700	$150
Travel costs	$8,000	$ 0

Requirements

1. Compute Falcon Design's predetermined indirect cost allocation rate for the current year.
2. Compute the total cost of each of the two jobs listed.
3. If Falcon Design wants to earn profits equal to 20% of sales revenue, how much (what total fee) should the company charge each of these two clients?
4. Why does Falcon Design assign costs to jobs?

P3-47A   Prepare job cost record *(Learning Objectives 2, 3, & 4)*

Geolander Tire manufactures tires for all-terrain vehicles. Geolander uses job costing and has a perpetual inventory system.

On September 22, Geolander received an order for 100 TX tires from ATV Corporation at a price of $50 each. The job, assigned number 298, was promised for October 10. After purchasing the materials, Geolander began production on September 30 and incurred the following direct labor and direct materials costs in completing the order:

Date	Labor Time Record No.	Description	Amount
9/30	1896	12 hours at $18	$216
10/3	1904	30 hours at $20	$600

Date	Materials Requisition No.	Description	Amount
9/30	437	60 lbs. rubber at $16	$ 960
10/2	439	40 meters polyester fabric at $10	$ 400
10/3	501	100 meters steel cord at $12	$1,200

Geolander allocates manufacturing overhead to jobs on the basis of the relation between expected overhead costs ($396,000) and expected direct labor hours (18,000). Job 298 was completed on October 3 and shipped to ATV on October 5.

Requirements

1. Prepare a job cost record for Job 298.
2. Calculate the total profit and the per-unit profit for Job 298.

P3-48A   Determine and record job costs *(Learning Objectives 2, 3, 4, & 6)*

Steinborn Homes manufactures prefabricated chalets in Colorado. The company uses a perpetual inventory system and a job cost system in which each chalet is a job. The following events occurred during May:

a. Purchased materials on account, $470,000.
b. Incurred total manufacturing wages of $119,000, which included both direct labor and indirect labor. Used direct labor in manufacturing as follows:

	Direct Labor
Chalet 13	$14,100
Chalet 14	$28,700
Chalet 15	$19,400
Chalet 16	$21,000

c. Requisitioned direct materials in manufacturing as follows:

	Direct Materials
Chalet 13	$41,900
Chalet 14	$56,600
Chalet 15	$62,200
Chalet 16	$66,900

d. Depreciation of manufacturing equipment used on different chalets, $6,300.

e. Other overhead costs incurred on Chalets 13–16:

Equipment rentals paid in cash	$10,100
Prepaid plant insurance expired	$ 4,000

f. Allocated overhead to jobs at the predetermined rate of 60% of direct labor cost.

g. Chalets completed: 13, 15, and 16.

h. Chalets sold on account: 13 for $99,000 and 16 for $146,000.

Requirements

1. Record the preceding events in the general journal.
2. Open T-accounts for Work in Process Inventory and Finished Goods Inventory. Post the appropriate entries to these accounts, identifying each entry by letter. Determine the ending account balances, assuming that the beginning balances were zero.
3. Summarize the job costs of the unfinished chalet and show that this equals the ending balance in Work in Process Inventory.
4. Summarize the job cost of the completed chalet that has not yet been sold and show that this equals the ending balance in Finished Goods Inventory.
5. Compute the gross profit on each chalet that was sold. What costs must the gross profit cover for Steinborn Homes?

P3-49A   Determine flow of costs through accounts (Learning Objectives 2 & 6)

Gibbs Engine reconditions engines. Its job cost records yield the following information. Gibbs Engine uses a perpetual inventory system.

Job No.	Date Started	Date Finished	Sold	Total Cost of Job at April 30	Total Manufacturing Cost Added in May
1	3/26	4/7	4/9	$1,900	
2	3/3	4/12	4/13	$1,500	
3	4/29	4/30	5/3	$1,000	
4	4/30	5/1	5/1	$ 400	$ 400
5	5/8	5/12	5/14		$ 800
6	5/23	6/6	6/9		$1,100

Requirements

1. Compute Gibbs Engine's cost of (a) Work in Process Inventory at April 30 and May 31, (b) Finished Goods Inventory at April 30 and May 31, and (c) Cost of Goods Sold for April and May.
2. Make summary journal entries to record the transfer of completed jobs from Work in Process Inventory to Finished Goods Inventory for March and April.
3. Record the sale of Job 5 on account for $2,200.
4. Compute the gross profit for Job 5. What costs must the gross profit cover?

PROBLEMS Group B

P3-50B   Analyze Manufacturing Overhead (Learning Objectives 3 & 5)

Annabelle's Uniforms produces uniforms. The company allocates manufacturing overhead based on the machine hours each job uses. Annabelle's Uniforms reports the following cost data for the past year:

	Budget	Actual
Direct labor hours..	7,600 hours	6,500 hours
Machine hours..	6,900 hours	6,900 hours
Depreciation on salespeople's autos	$24,000	$24,000
Indirect materials..	$49,000	$53,500
Depreciation on trucks used to deliver uniforms to customers	$13,000	$11,500
Depreciation on plant and equipment................	$65,500	$67,000
Indirect manufacturing labor..............................	$43,500	$46,500
Customer service hotline	$20,500	$22,500
Plant utilities...	$28,300	$29,300
Direct labor cost...	$71,000	$85,000

Requirements

1. Compute the predetermined manufacturing overhead rate.
2. Calculate the allocated manufacturing overhead for the past year.
3. Compute the underallocated or overallocated manufacturing overhead. How will this underallocated or overallocated manufacturing overhead be disposed of?
4. How can managers use accounting information to help control manufacturing overhead costs?

P3-51B   Use job costing at an advertising agency
(Learning Objectives 3, 4, & 7)

Walker & Janosko is an Internet advertising agency. The firm uses a job cost system in which each client is a different "job." Walker & Janosko traces direct labor, software licensing costs, and travel costs directly to each job (client). The company allocates indirect costs to jobs based on a predetermined indirect cost allocation rate computed as a percentage of direct labor costs.

At the beginning of the current year, managing partner Laurie Walker prepared a budget:

Direct labor hours (professional)	17,100 hours
Direct labor costs (professional)..	$2,052,000
Support staff salaries...	$ 170,000
Rent and utilities	$ 46,000
Supplies	$ 459,300
Lease payments on computer hardware......................................	$ 60,000

During January of the current year, Walker & Janosko served several clients. Records for two clients appear here:

	DreamTrips.com	Port Albany Golf Resort
Direct labor hours...	740 hours	50 hours
Software licensing costs	$2,400	$200
Travel costs..	$8,000	$ 0

Requirements

1. Compute Walker & Janosko's predetermined indirect cost allocation rate for the current year based on direct labor hours.
2. Compute the total cost of each job.
3. If Walker & Janosko wants to earn profits equal to 20% of sales revenue, how much (what total fee) should it charge each of these two clients?
4. Why does Walker & Janosko assign costs to jobs?

P3-52B Use job costing at a consulting firm *(Learning Objectives 3, 4, & 7)*

Raven Design is a website design and consulting firm. The firm uses a job cost system, in which each client is a different job. Raven Design traces direct labor, licensing costs, and travel costs directly to each job (client). It allocates indirect costs to jobs based on a predetermined indirect cost allocation rate computed as a percentage of direct labor costs.

At the beginning of the current year, managing partner Jill Herbert prepared the following budget:

Direct labor hours (professional)	8,000 hours
Direct labor costs (professional)	$1,600,000
Support staff salaries	$ 190,000
Computer leases	$ 41,000
Office supplies	$ 23,000
Office rent	$ 66,000

Later that same year in November, Raven Design served several clients. Records for two clients appear here:

	Organic Delight	AllFood.com
Direct labor hours	770 hours	60 hours
Software licensing costs	$2,000	$350
Travel costs	$9,000	$ 0

Requirements

1. Compute Raven Design's predetermined indirect cost allocation rate for the current year.
2. Compute the total cost of each of the two jobs listed.
3. If Raven Design wants to earn profits equal to 20% of sales revenue, how much (what total fee) should the company charge each of these two clients?
4. Why does Raven Design assign costs to jobs?

P3-53B Prepare job cost record *(Learning Objectives 2, 3, & 4)*

Pro Tire manufactures tires for all-terrain vehicles. Pro Tire uses job costing and has a perpetual inventory system. On November 22, Pro Tire received an order for 190 TX tires from ATV Corporation at a price of $70 each. The job, assigned number 298, was promised for December 10. After purchasing the materials, Pro Tire began production on November 30 and incurred the following direct labor and direct materials costs in completing the order:

Date	Labor Time Record No.	Description	Amount
11/30	1896	12 hours at $20	$240
12/3	1904	30 hours at $18	$540

Date	Materials Requisition No.	Description	Amount
11/30	437	60 lbs. rubber at $10	$ 600
12/2	439	40 meters polyester fabric at $14	$ 560
12/3	501	100 meters steel cord at $12	$1,200

Pro Tire allocates manufacturing overhead to jobs on the basis of the relationship between expected overhead costs ($490,000) and expected direct labor hours (17,500). Job 298 was completed on December 3 and shipped to ATV on December 5.

Requirements

1. Prepare a job cost record for Job 298.
2. Calculate the total profit and the per-unit profit for Job 298.

P3-54B   Determine and record job costs (Learning Objectives 2, 3, 4, & 6)

Echo Ridge Homes manufactures prefabricated chalets in Colorado. The company uses a perpetual inventory system and a job cost system in which each chalet is a job. The following events occurred during May:

a. Purchased materials on account, $440,000.
b. Incurred total manufacturing wages of $114,000, which included both direct labor and indirect labor. Used direct labor in manufacturing as follows:

	Direct Labor
Chalet 13..	$14,800
Chalet 14..	$28,500
Chalet 15..	$19,900
Chalet 16..	$21,400

c. Requisitioned direct materials in manufacturing as follows:

	Direct Materials
Chalet 13..	$41,700
Chalet 14..	$56,400
Chalet 15..	$62,000
Chalet 16..	$66,300

d. Depreciation of manufacturing equipment used on different chalets, $6,300.
e. Other overhead costs incurred on Chalets 13–16:

Equipment rentals paid in cash...	$10,500
Prepaid plant insurance expired	$ 9,000

f. Allocated overhead to jobs at the predetermined rate of 60% of direct labor cost.
g. Chalets completed: 13, 15, and 16.
h. Chalets sold on account: 13 for $97,000; 16 for $146,000.

Requirements

1. Record the events in the general journal.
2. Post the appropriate entries to the T-accounts, identifying each entry by letter. Determine the ending account balances, assuming that the beginning balances were zero.
3. Add the costs of the unfinished chalet, and show that this total amount equals the ending balance in the Work in Process Inventory account.

4. Summarize the job cost of the completed chalet that has not yet been sold and show that this equals the ending balance in Finished Goods Inventory.

5. Compute gross profit on each chalet that was sold. What costs must gross profit cover for Echo Ridge Homes?

P3-55B Determine flow of costs through accounts (Learning Objectives 2 & 6)

Engine Pro reconditions engines. Its job costing records yield the following information. Engine Pro uses a perpetual inventory system.

Job No.	Started	Finished	Sold	Total Cost of Job at April 30	Total Manufacturing Cost Added in May
1	3/26	4/7	4/9	$1,200	
2	4/3	4/12	4/13	$1,500	
3	4/29	4/30	5/3	$1,300	
4	4/30	5/1	5/1	$ 400	$ 600
5	5/8	5/12	5/14		$ 400
6	5/23	5/6	6/9		$1,100

Requirements

1. Compute Engine Pro's cost of (a) Work in Process Inventory at April 30 and May 31, (b) Finished Goods Inventory at April 30 and May 31, and (c) Cost of Goods Sold for April and May.

2. Make summary journal entries to record the transfer of completed jobs from Work in Process to Finished Goods for April and May.

3. Record the sale of Job 5 for $2,200.

4. Compute the gross profit for Job 5. What costs must the gross profit cover?

CRITICAL THINKING

Discussion & Analysis

A3-56 Discussion Questions

1. Why would it be inappropriate for a custom-home builder to use process costing?

2. For what types of products is job costing appropriate? Why? For what types of products is process costing appropriate? Why?

3. What product costs must be allocated to jobs? Why must these costs be allocated rather than assigned?

4. When the predetermined manufacturing overhead rate is calculated, why are estimated costs and cost driver levels used instead of actual dollars and amounts?

5. Why should manufacturing overhead be allocated to a job even though the costs cannot be directly traced to a job? Give at least two reasons.

6. Why does management need to know the cost of a job? Discuss at least five reasons.

7. Why is it acceptable to close overallocated or underallocated manufacturing overhead to Cost of Goods Sold rather than allocating it proportionately to Work in Process Inventory, Finished Goods Inventory, and Cost of Goods Sold? Under what circumstances would it be advisable to allocate the overallocated or underallocated manufacturing overhead to Work in Process Inventory, Finished Goods Inventory, and Cost of Goods Sold?

8. Describe a situation that may cause manufacturing overhead to be overallocated in a given year. Also, describe a situation that may cause manufacturing overhead to be underallocated in a given year.

9. Explain why the cost of goods sold should be lower if manufacturing overhead is over-allocated. Should operating income be higher or lower if manufacturing overhead is over-allocated? Why?

10. What account is credited when manufacturing overhead is allocated to jobs during the period? What account is debited when manufacturing overhead costs are incurred during the period? Would you expect these two amounts (allocated and incurred manufacturing overhead) to be the same? Why or why not?

11. How can job cost records help to promote sustainability efforts within a company?

12. Why should companies estimate the environmental costs of a given job? Why have EPR (extended producer responsibility) laws come into existence?

Application & Analysis

Mini Cases

A3-57   *Unwrapped* or *How It's Made*

Product Costs and Job Costing Versus Process Costing

Go to www.YouTube.com and search for clips from the show *Unwrapped* on Food Network or *How It's Made* on the Discovery Channel. Watch a clip for a product you find interesting.

Basic Discussion Questions

1. Describe the product that is being produced and the company that makes it.
2. Summarize the production process that is used in making this product.
3. What raw materials are used to make this product?
4. What indirect materials are used to make this product?
5. Describe the jobs of the workers who would be considered "direct labor" in the making of this product.
6. Describe the jobs of the workers who would be considered "indirect labor" in the making of this product.

7. Define *manufacturing overhead*. In addition to the indirect materials and indirect labor previously described, what other manufacturing overhead costs would be incurred in this production process? Be specific and thorough. Make reasonable "guesses" if you do not know for sure.

8. Would a job-order costing system or a process costing system be used for this production process? Give specific reasons for your choice of which costing system would be most appropriate for this manufacturer.

A3-58   Ethics involved with choice of cost driver

ETHICS

(Learning Objectives 2, 3, & 4)

Molly McDale is the controller for Roberts Manufacturing. It is a small company that manufactures plastic lumber and is run by the owner and CEO, Franklin Roberts. At the end of the year, Roberts is reviewing the projected operating income for the company for the year. He tells McDale that the projected operating income is too low; if operating income is not at least $200,000, no holiday bonuses will be paid to employees, including McDale.

Hoping to find an error, McDale first of all rechecks the projected financial statements; she finds no errors. Since cost of goods sold is a large portion of Roberts' expenses, she next analyzes the components of cost of goods sold. The amount of direct material used ties directly to the physical inventory count, so there are no errors there. The direct labor dollars also tie directly to the payroll reports, eliminating another potential source of errors. She then looks at the way manufacturing overhead has been allocated to products.

Traditionally, manufacturing overhead has been allocated to products based on direct labor hours because the manufacturing process for plastic lumber is labor intensive. McDale calculates manufacturing overhead based on machine hours used and finds that cost of goods sold will be $55,000 lower if manufacturing overhead is allocated based on machine hours rather than direct labor hours. The $55,000 difference, if booked, would cause net income to be $212,000, which means that bonuses would be paid to all employees. McDale knows that several factory employees are struggling and the holiday bonus would be much appreciated. In addition, McDale herself feels that she has earned the bonus over the past year because she has helped to implement several cost savings programs and has worked many long days without overtime pay.

Requirements

1. Using the IMA *Statement of Ethical Professional Practice* as an ethical framework, answer the following questions:

   a. What is(are) the ethical issue(s) in this situation?

   b. What are McDale's responsibilities as a management accountant?

2. Discuss the specific steps McDale should take to resolve the situation. Refer to the IMA *Statement of Ethical Professional Practice* in your response.

A3-59   Costs included in product cost

REAL LIFE

(Learning Objectives 1, 2, 3, & 4)

A research firm, IHS (formerly known as iSuppli), did a teardown of the iPad mini shortly after Apple introduced the small tablet in late 2012.[1] IHS estimated that the costs of the components in the base model of the iPad mini (Wi-Fi-only 16 gigabyte) add up to $188. See data table on next page.

Questions

1. Do you think that Apple uses a process costing system or a job costing system? Give reasons for your answer.

2. The iPad mini is assigned a cost of $10 for "manufacturing cost." What specific costs do you think are included in that "manufacturing cost"?

3. In accounting terminology, what would "Bill of Materials (BOM)" be when discussing product cost?

[1]Source: "Low-End iPad mini Carries $188 Bill of Materials, Teardown Analysis Reveals," (Retrieved from http://www.isuppli.com/Teardowns/News/Pages/Low-End-iPad-mini-Carries-188-Bill-of-Materials-Teardown-Analysis-Reveals.aspx on March 2, 2013.)

4. The gross profit per iPad mini is approximately $131, which is the difference between the retail price of $329 and its estimated cost (BOM + Manufacturing) of $198. Is Apple really making $131 for each iPad mini sold? If not, what other types of costs would that gross profit of $131 have to go toward covering?

5. The Bill of Materials (BOM) costs for the units sold would appear on Apple's income statement. In which income statement component would these BOM costs appear?

6. Late in 2012, Apple announced that it was going to start manufacturing some products in the United States rather than in China. If the iPad mini were to be manufactured in the U.S., which cost components would you expect to increase? Which cost components might you expect to decrease? What other factors would Apple consider when deciding where to manufacture its products?

Preliminary Bill of Materials (BOM) and Manufacturing Costs for the iPad mini with 16GBytes of NAND Flash and Wi-Fi Only (Pricing in U.S. Dollars)

Components/Hardware Elements	Price
Retail Pricing (As of November 2012)..	$329
Total BOM Cost..	$188
Manufacturing Cost..	$ 10
BOM + Manufacturing	$198
Major Cost Drivers	
Memory: 512MB LPDDR2 + 16GB NAND NAND Flash + DRAM.............	$15.50
Display & Touchscreen: 7.9" 1024×763 w/GF2 Multitouch	$80.00
Processors: Apple APL2498 (32nm A5)	$13.00
Camera(s): 5MP BSI + 1.2MP 720p BSI...	$11.00
User Interface & Sensors & Combo Module (WLAN/BT/FM)....................	$15.00
Power Management...	$ 7.50
Battery: 3.72V 16.5Wh Li-Polymer	$13.50
Mechanical/Electro-Mechanical/Other	$26.00
Box Contents...	$ 6.00

Source: IHS iSuppli Research, November 2012.

A3-60   Issues with cost of job *(Learning Objectives 2, 3, & 4)*

Custom Cookies produces gourmet cookies with company logos for special promotions. The cookies are customized with the customer's choice of shape, color, flavor, and decorations. Custom Cookies uses a job cost system and allocates manufacturing overhead based on direct labor hours. At the beginning of the most recent year, Custom Cookies calculated the cost per batch of dozen cookies as:

Direct materials (flour, sugar, butter, eggs, baking soda, vanilla)	$1.50
Direct labor (shape and decorate cookies)	0.50
Manufacturing overhead..	0.90
Total manufacturing cost per dozen cookies	$2.90

In September, Chesrown Motor Group ordered 400 dozen cookies to present to its clients as holiday gifts. Delivery of the cookies to Chesrown would occur in early December. At the time of Chesrown Motor Group's order, the selling price per dozen cookies was $7.25.

Chesrown Motor Group placed an order for an additional 100 dozen cookies in November, to be delivered with the original order of 400 dozen. However, since that original order, two events occurred that increased the cost of the cookies. First, the price of sugar skyrocketed due to bad weather in Brazil and India, two of the largest sugar suppliers in the world.

Second, a new local cookie bakery is about to open in time for the holiday season and is aggressively trying to hire the cookie decorators from Custom Cookies. In response, Custom Cookies increased the hourly rate of the employees who decorate the cookies to keep those workers from going to work for the competition. *All other costs at Custom Cookies have remained the same.*

Because of these two events, Custom Cookies recalculated the cost of a dozen cookies as follows:

Direct materials (flour, sugar, butter, eggs, baking soda, vanilla)	$1.60
Direct labor (shape and decorate cookies)	0.65
Manufacturing overhead	1.17
Total manufacturing cost per dozen cookies	$3.42

Requirements

1. Do you agree with the cost analysis for the second order? Explain your answer.

2. Should the two orders be accounted for as one job or as two jobs in Custom Cookies' system?

3. What sales price per box should Custom Cookies set for the second order? Explain why you have selected this per-box price. What are the advantages and disadvantages of this price?

Try It Solutions

page 109: 1. d 2. a 3. f 4. g 5. h 6. c 7. e 8. b

page 127:

Actual MOH incurred during the year	$975,000
MOH allocated to jobs during the year ($16/DL hour × 60,000 DL hours)	960,000
Difference: Underallocated MOH	$ 15,000

Since the company allocated less MOH to jobs than was actually incurred during the year, it has underallocated MOH. Notice that the $1 million of estimated MOH at the beginning of the year is only used to calculate the predetermined MOH rate.

page 144:

1.

Direct cost: Sarah's time (5 hrs × $40/hr) + Hannah's time (10 hrs × $25/hr)	$450
Indirect cost: (15 hrs × $12/hr)	180
Total cost of preparing tax return	$630

2.

Total cost of preparing tax return	$630
Plus profit markup ($630 × 30%)	189
Amount to bill Meckfessel	$819

Activity-Based Costing, Lean Operations, and the Costs of Quality

John Kasawa/Shutterstock

Source: http://uscorporate.lifefitness.com

Learning Objectives

- **1** Develop and use departmental overhead rates to allocate indirect costs
- **2** Develop and use activity-based costing (ABC) to allocate indirect costs
- **3** Understand the benefits and limitations of ABC/ABM systems
- **4** Describe lean operations
- **5** Describe and use the costs of quality framework

When Life Fitness began, it only had one product: the Lifecycle exercise bike. With time, Life Fitness expanded its product lines to include treadmills, elliptical cross-trainers, stair climbers, and strength-training equipment. As a result of increased product diversity and competition in the fitness equipment market, managers found they needed better, more accurate product cost information to help guide their business decisions. While a traditional job costing system ensures that the direct materials and direct labor traced to each job is correct, it doesn't always do an adequate job of allocating manufacturing overhead, especially when a company produces multiple product lines that use different amounts of indirect manufacturing resources. In such cases, managers benefit from using a refined cost allocation system: one that isn't based on a single, predetermined manufacturing overhead rate. Refined costing systems not only help managers more accurately determine the cost of individual jobs but also highlight the cost of wasteful activities in the production process. Armed with this knowledge, managers are able to make more profitable business decisions.

As the chapter-opening story illustrates, most companies have experienced increased competition over the past few decades. In addition, companies have sought to expand their customer base by offering a more diversified line of products. Both of these factors are good for consumers, who now enjoy more product options at very competitive prices. However, these factors also present unique challenges to business managers and the accounting systems that support them. To thrive in a globally competitive market, companies must provide value to the customer by delivering a high-quality product at an attractive price, while managing costs so the company still earns a profit. This chapter will introduce several tools that today's managers use to make their companies competitive:

- Refined costing systems

- Lean operations

- Total quality management and the costs of quality

Why and How do Companies Refine Their Cost Allocation Systems?

Organizations from Dell to Carolina Power and Light to the U.S. Marine Corps use refined cost allocation systems. Why? Because simple cost allocation systems don't always do a good job of matching the cost of overhead resources with the products that consume those resources. The following example illustrates why.

Simple Cost Allocation Systems Can Lead to Cost Distortion

David, Matt, and Marc are three college friends who share an apartment. They agree to split the following monthly costs equally:

Rent, Internet, and utilities	$570
Cable TV	50
Covered parking fee	40
Groceries	240
Total monthly costs	**$900**

Each roommate's share is $300 ($900/3).

Things go smoothly for the first few months. But then David calls a meeting: "Because I started having dinner at Amy's each night, I shouldn't have to chip in for the groceries." Matt then pipes in: "I'm so busy studying and using the Internet that I never have time to watch TV. I don't want to pay for the cable TV anymore. And Marc, because your friend Jennifer eats here most evenings, you should pay a double share of the grocery bill." Marc replies, "If that's the way you feel, Matt, then you should pay for the covered parking since you're the only one around here who uses it!"

What happened? The friends originally agreed to share the costs equally. But they are not participating equally in watching cable TV, using the covered parking, and eating the groceries. Splitting these costs equally is not equitable.

The roommates could use a cost allocation approach that better matches costs with the people who participate in the activities that cause those costs. This means splitting the cable TV costs between David and Marc, assigning the covered parking cost to Matt, and allocating the grocery bill one-third to Matt and two-thirds to Marc. Exhibit 4-1 compares the results of this refined cost allocation system with the original cost allocation system.

No wonder David called a meeting! The original cost allocation system charged him $300 a month, but the refined system shows that a more equitable share would be only $215. The new system allocates Marc $375 a month instead of $300. David was paying for resources he did not use (covered parking and groceries), while Marc was not paying

EXHIBIT 4-1 More-Refined Versus Less-Refined Cost Allocation System

	A	B	C	D	E
1	**Allocation of Expenses**	**David**	**Matt**	**Marc**	**Total**
2	*More-refined cost allocation system:*				
3	Rent, internet, and utilities	$190	$190	$190	$570
4	Cable TV	25	0	25	50
5	Covered parking	0	40	0	40
6	Groceries	0	80	160	240
7	Total cost allocated	$215	$310	$375	$900
8					
9	*Original cost allocation system:*				
10	Equal allocation of expenses	$300	$300	$300	$900
11					
12	**Difference**	($85)	$ 10	$ 75	$ 0
13					

for all of the resources (groceries) he and his guest consumed. The simple cost allocation system the roommates initially devised had ended up distorting the cost that should be charged to each roommate: David was *overcharged* by $85 while Matt and Marc were *undercharged* by an equal, but offsetting amount ($10 + $75 = $85). Notice that the total "pool" of monthly costs ($900) is the same under both allocation systems. The only difference is *how* the pool of costs is *allocated* among the three roommates.

Just as the simple allocation system had resulted in overcharging David, yet undercharging Matt and Marc, many companies find that the simple overhead cost allocation system described in the last chapter results in "overcosting" some of their jobs or products while "undercosting" others. <u>Cost distortion</u> occurs when some products are overcosted while other products are undercosted by the cost allocation system. As we'll see in the following sections, companies often refine their cost allocation systems to minimize the amount of cost distortion caused by the simpler cost allocation systems. By refining their costing systems, companies can more equitably assign indirect costs (such as manufacturing overhead) to their individual jobs, products, or services. As a result, less cost distortion occurs and managers have more accurate information for making vital business decisions.

In the following section, we will be describing how refined cost allocation systems can be used to better allocate manufacturing overhead to specific products to reduce cost distortion. However, keep in mind that the same principles apply to allocating *any* indirect costs to *any* cost objects. Thus, even merchandising and service companies, as well as governmental agencies, can use these refined cost allocation systems to provide their managers with better cost information.

Review: Using a Plantwide Overhead Rate to Allocate Indirect Costs

In the last chapter, we assumed that Life Fitness allocated its manufacturing overhead (MOH) costs using one predetermined MOH rate ($16 per DL hour). This rate was based on management's estimate of the total manufacturing overhead costs for the year ($1 million) and estimate of the total amount of the allocation base (62,500 DL hours) for the year.[2] The rate was calculated as follows:

$$\text{Predetermined MOH rate} = \frac{\$1,000,000}{62,500 \text{ DL hours}} = \$16 \text{ per direct labor hour}$$

Why is this important?

"With better **cost information**, managers are able to make more **profitable** decisions. One company reported triple sales and **five-fold increase** in profits after it implemented a **refined costing system**. By using better costs information for quoting jobs, **management** was able to generate a more **profitable mix** of job contracts."[1]

[1]Douglas Hicks, "Yes, ABC Is for Small Business, Too," *Journal of Accountancy*, August 1999, p. 41.

[2]All references to Life Fitness in this hypothetical example were created by the author solely for academic purposes and are not intended, in any way, to represent the actual business practices of, or costs incurred by, Life Fitness, Inc.

This rate is also known as a **plantwide overhead rate**, because any job produced in the plant, whether it be treadmills, elliptical cross-trainers, or stair climbers, would be allocated manufacturing overhead using this single rate. It wouldn't matter whether the job was worked on in one department or many departments during the production process: The same rate would be used throughout the plant.

Let's see how this works for Life Fitness. Keep in mind that the company produces many different products and completes thousands of different jobs throughout the year. For simplicity of illustration, we will be following just two of those jobs:

- Job 101: One elliptical
- Job 102: One treadmill

In Chapter 3, we followed a job in which each elliptical cross-trainer required about 10 direct labor hours to make.[3] We'll continue to assume that each elliptical made by the company requires 10 direct labor hours to complete. Let's also assume that each treadmill requires 10 direct labor hours to complete. Exhibit 4-2 shows how manufacturing overhead would be allocated to a job in which one elliptical was made, and another job in which one treadmill was made, using the plantwide overhead rate.

EXHIBIT 4-2 Allocating Manufacturing Overhead Using a Plantwide Overhead Rate

	A	B	C	D	E	F	G	H
1	**Job**	**Plantwide Overhead Rate**			**Actual Use of Allocation Base**			**MOH Allocated to Job**
2	Job 101: One elliptical	$ 16	per DL hour	×	10	DL hours	=	$ 160
3	Job 102: One treadmill	$ 16	per DL hour	×	10	DL hours	=	$ 160
4								

NOTE: Arithmetic signs are only shown for illustrative teaching purposes. They are not typically displayed in spreadsheets.

The plantwide allocation system is illustrated in Exhibit 4-3.

EXHIBIT 4-3 Plantwide Allocation System

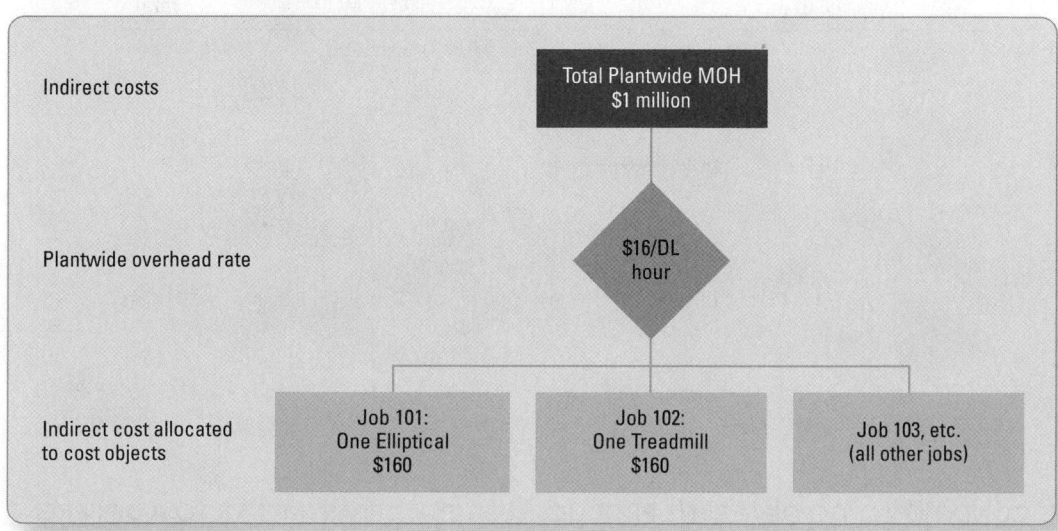

[3]Job 603, a batch of 50 elliptical cross-trainers, required 500 DL hours to complete. Thus, the average time spent on each unit was 10 DL hours.

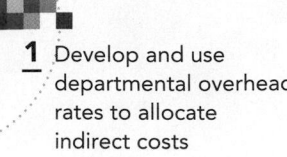

1 Develop and use departmental overhead rates to allocate indirect costs

Using Departmental Overhead Rates to Allocate Indirect Costs

The plantwide allocation system previously described works well for some companies, but may end up distorting costs if the following conditions exist:

1. Different departments incur different amounts and types of manufacturing overhead.

2. Different jobs or products use the departments to a different extent.

If these circumstances exist, the company should strongly consider refining its cost allocation system. Let's see if these conditions exist at Life Fitness.

CONDITION 1: DO DIFFERENT DEPARTMENTS HAVE DIFFERENT AMOUNTS AND TYPES OF MOH COSTS? As shown in Exhibit 4-4, let's assume Life Fitness has two primary production departments: Machining and Assembly. The Machining Department has a lot of machinery, which drives manufacturing overhead costs such as machine depreciation, utilities, machine lubricants, and repairs and maintenance. Let's say these overhead costs are estimated to be $400,000 for the year. On the other hand, the Assembly Department does not incur as many of these types of overhead costs. Rather, the Assembly Department's manufacturing overhead costs include more indirect labor for supervision, quality inspection, and so forth. These manufacturing overhead costs are expected to total $600,000 for the year.

Exhibit 4-4 shows that the first condition is present: Each department incurs different types and amounts of MOH. Life Fitness expects to incur a total of $1 million of manufacturing overhead: $400,000 relates to the Machining Department while $600,000 relates to the Assembly Department.

EXHIBIT 4-4 Machining and Assembly Departments' Manufacturing Overhead

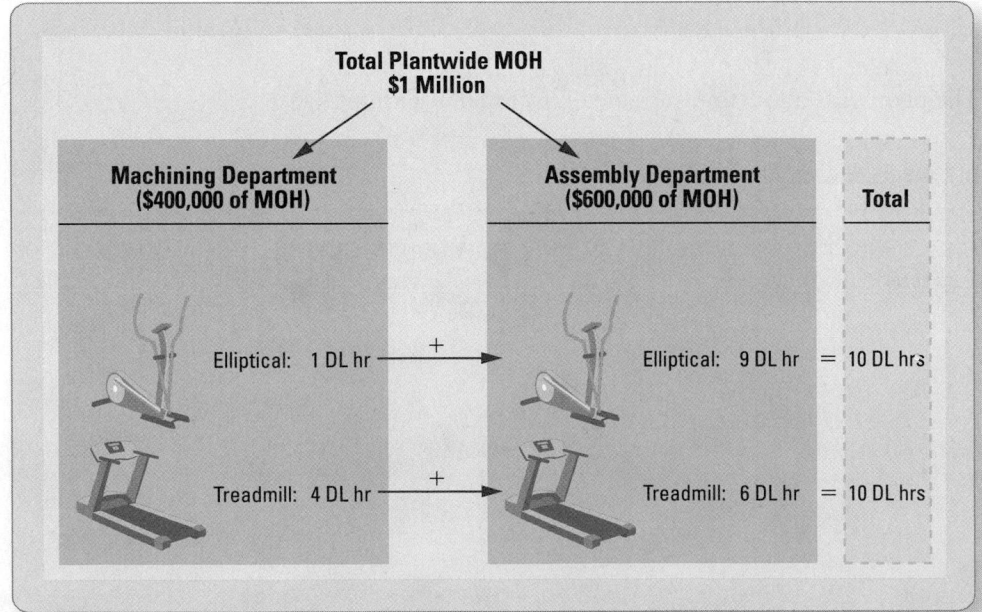

CONDITION 2: DO DIFFERENT PRODUCTS USE THE DEPARTMENTS TO A DIFFERENT EXTENT? Although both ellipticals and treadmills take 10 direct labor hours in total to make, Exhibit 4-4 also shows that ellipticals and treadmills spend *different* amounts of time in each production department. Each elliptical only requires 1 DL hour in the Machining Department, but requires 9 DL hours in the Assembly Department. Contrast that with a treadmill, which spends more time in Machining to fabricate some of its components (4 DL hours) but less time in Assembly (6 DL hours). As a result of these

differences, the second condition is also present. The company's cost allocation system would be much more accurate if it took these differences into account when determining how much manufacturing overhead to allocate to each product.

Since both conditions are present, the company should consider "fine-tuning" its cost allocation systems by establishing separate manufacturing overhead rates, known as **departmental overhead rates**, for each department. That means that Life Fitness will establish one manufacturing overhead rate for the Machining Department and another overhead rate for the Assembly Department. These rates will then be used to allocate manufacturing overhead to jobs or products based on the extent to which each product uses the different manufacturing departments.

Exhibit 4-5 shows the circumstances favoring the use of departmental overhead rates rather than a single, plantwide overhead rate.

EXHIBIT 4-5 Circumstances Favoring Use of Departmental Overhead Rates

Departmental overhead rates increase the accuracy of job costs when . . .

- Each department incurs different types and amounts of manufacturing overhead.
- Each product, or job, uses the departments to a different extent.

Four Basic Steps to Computing and Using Departmental Overhead Rates

In Chapter 3, we used four steps for allocating manufacturing overhead. These steps are summarized in Exhibit 4-6.

EXHIBIT 4-6 Four Basic Steps for Allocating Manufacturing Overhead

1. Estimate the total manufacturing overhead costs (MOH) for the coming year.
2. Select an allocation base and estimate the total amount that will be used during the year.
3. Calculate the predetermined overhead rate by dividing the total estimated MOH costs by the total estimated amount of the allocation base.
4. Allocate some MOH cost to each job worked on during the year by multiplying the predetermined MOH rate by the actual amount of the allocation base used by the job.

The same four basic steps are used to allocate manufacturing overhead using departmental overhead rates. The only real difference is that we will be calculating *separate rates* for *each* department. Let's see how this is done.

STEP 1. The company estimates the total manufacturing overhead costs that will be incurred in *each department* in the coming year. These estimates are known as departmental overhead cost pools.

Some MOH costs are easy to identify and trace to different departments. For example, management can trace the cost of lease payments and repairs to the machines used in the Machining Department. Management can also trace the cost of employing supervisors and quality control inspectors to the Assembly Department. However, other overhead costs are more difficult to identify with specific departments. For example, the depreciation, property taxes, and insurance on the entire plant would have to be split, or allocated, between the individual departments, most likely based on the square footage occupied by each department in the plant.

As shown in Exhibit 4-4, Life Fitness has determined that $400,000 of its total estimated MOH relates to its Machining Department, while the remaining $600,000 relates to its Assembly Department.

Department	Total Departmental Overhead Cost Pool
Machining...	$ 400,000
Assembly..	$ 600,000
TOTAL MOH	$1,000,000

STEP 2. The company selects an allocation base for *each department* and estimates the total amount that will be used during the year.

The allocation base selected for each department should be the cost driver of the costs in the departmental overhead pool. Often, manufacturers will use different allocation bases for the different departments. For example, machine hours might be the best allocation base for a very automated Machining Department that uses machine robotics extensively. However, direct labor hours might be the best allocation base for an Assembly Department.

Let's assume that Life Fitness's Machining Department uses a lot of human-operated machinery; therefore, the number of direct labor hours used in the department is identical to the number of hours the machines are run. While the number of machine hours is the real cost driver, direct labor hours will make an adequate surrogate. As a result, management has selected direct labor hours as the allocation base for both departments. Recall that Life Fitness estimates using a total of 62,500 direct labor hours during the year. Of this amount, management expects to use 12,500 in the Machining Department and 50,000 in the Assembly Department.

Department	Total Amount of Departmental Allocation Base
Machining...	12,500 DL hours
Assembly..	50,000 DL hours

STEP 3. The company calculates departmental overhead rates using the information estimated in Steps 1 and 2:

$$\text{Departmental overhead rate} = \frac{\text{Total estimated departmental overhead cost pool}}{\text{Total estimated amount of the departmental allocation base}}$$

Therefore, Life Fitness calculates its departmental overhead rates as follows:

$$\text{Machining Department overhead rate} = \frac{\$400,000}{12,500 \text{ DL hours}} = \$32 \text{ per DL hour}$$

$$\text{Assembly Department overhead rate} = \frac{\$600,000}{50,000 \text{ DL hours}} = \$12 \text{ per DL hour}$$

These first three steps are performed before the year begins, using estimated data for the year. Thus, departmental overhead rates are also "predetermined," just like the plant-wide predetermined manufacturing overhead rate discussed in Chapter 3. The first three steps, performed before the year begins, are summarized in Exhibit 4-7.

EXHIBIT 4-7 Steps to Calculating the Departmental Overhead Rates

	A	B	C	D	E	F	G	H
1	Department	Step 1: Total Departmental Overhead Cost Pool		Step 2: Total Amount of Departmental Allocation Base			Step 3: Departmental Overhead Rate	
2	Machining	$ 400,000	÷	12,500	DL hours	=	$ 32	per DL hour
3	Assembly	$ 600,000	÷	50,000	DL hours	=	$ 12	per DL hour
4								

NOTE: Arithmetic signs are only shown for illustrative teaching purposes. They are not typically displayed in spreadsheets.

Once these rates have been established, the company uses them throughout the year to allocate manufacturing overhead to each job as it is produced, as shown in Step 4.

STEP 4. The company allocates some manufacturing overhead from *each* department to the individual jobs that use those departments.

The amount of MOH allocated from each department is calculated as follows:

MOH allocated to job = Departmental overhead rate × Actual amount of departmental allocation base used by job

Exhibit 4-8 shows how these departmental overhead rates would be used to allocate manufacturing to a job in which one elliptical is produced.

EXHIBIT 4-8 Allocating MOH to One Elliptical Using Departmental Overhead Rates

	A	B	C	D	E	F	G	H
1	Department	Departmental Overhead Rate (from Exhibit 4-7)			Actual Use of Departmental Allocation Base (from Exhibit 4-4)			MOH Allocated to Job 101: One Elliptical
2	Machining	$ 32	per DL hour	×	1	DL hours	=	$ 32
3	Assembly	$ 12	per DL hour	×	9	DL hours	=	$ 108
4	Total							$ 140
5								

NOTE: Arithmetic signs are only shown for illustrative teaching purposes. They are not typically displayed in spreadsheets.

Exhibit 4-9 shows how the same rates would be used to allocate manufacturing overhead to another job in which one treadmill is produced. Because the treadmill spends more time in the Machining Department, but less time in the Assembly Department, the amount of MOH allocated to the treadmill differs from the amount allocated to the elliptical in Exhibit 4-8.

EXHIBIT 4-9 Allocating MOH to One Treadmill Using Departmental Overhead Rates

	A	B	C	D	E	F	G	H
1	Department	Departmental Overhead Rate (from Exhibit 4-7)			Actual Use of Departmental Allocation Base (from Exhibit 4-4)			MOH Allocated to Job 102: One Treadmill
2	Machining	$ 32	per DL hour	×	4	DL hours	=	$ 128
3	Assembly	$ 12	per DL hour	×	6	DL hours	=	$ 72
4	Total							$ 200
5								

NOTE: Arithmetic signs are only shown for illustrative teaching purposes. They are not typically displayed in spreadsheets.

Exhibit 4-10 illustrates the company's departmental cost allocation system.

EXHIBIT 4-10 Departmental Cost Allocation System

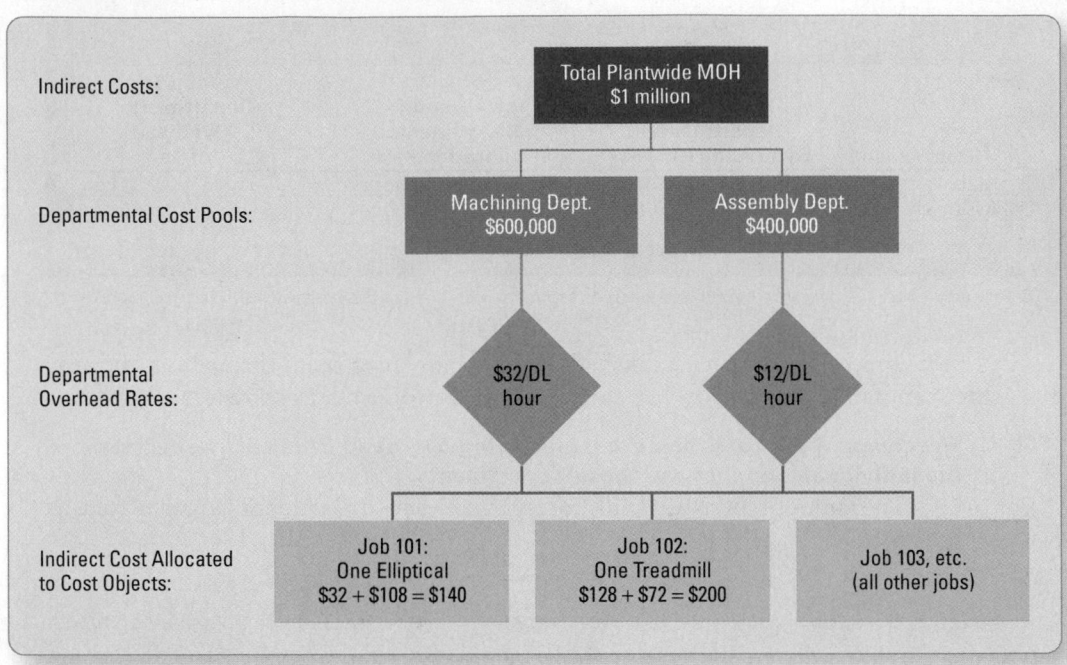

Had the Plantwide Overhead Rate Been Distorting Product Costs?

We have just seen that Life Fitness's refined cost allocation system allocates $140 of MOH to each elliptical, and $200 of MOH to each treadmill (Exhibits 4-8 and 4-9). Does this differ from the amount that would have been allocated to each unit using Life Fitness's original plantwide rate? Yes. Recall from Exhibit 4-2 that if Life Fitness uses a plantwide overhead rate, $160 of manufacturing overhead would be allocated to both types of equipment, simply because both types of equipment require the *same total* number of direct labor hours (10 DL hours) to produce.

The plantwide allocation system does not pick up on the nuances of how many direct labor hours are used by the products in *each* department. Therefore, it was not able to do a very good job of matching manufacturing overhead costs to the products that use those costs. As a result, the plantwide rate would have overcosted each elliptical, but undercosted each treadmill, as shown in Exhibit 4-11.

EXHIBIT 4-11 Cost Distortion Caused by Plantwide Overhead Rate

	Plantwide Overhead Rate MOH Allocation (from Exhibit 4-2)	Departmental Overhead Rates MOH Allocation (from Exhibits 4-8 and 4-9)	Amount of Cost Distortion
Job 101: One Elliptical	$160	$140	$20 *overcosted*
Job 102: One Treadmill	$160	$200	$40 *undercosted*

On the other hand, the refined cost allocation system recognizes the cost differences between departments and the usage difference between jobs. Therefore, the refined costing system does a *better job of matching* each department's overhead costs to the products that use the department's resources. This is the same thing we saw with the three roommates: The refined costing system did a better job of matching the cost of resources (cable, covered parking, groceries) to the roommates who used those resources. Because of this better matching, we can believe that the departmental overhead rates *more accurately allocate* MOH costs.

Try It!

Assume a job with one stair climber requires 5 direct labor (DL) hours to produce: 3 DL hours in the Machining Department and 2 DL hours in the Assembly Department. Use the plantwide overhead rate and departmental allocation rates computed in the chapter example to answer the following:

1. How much MOH would be allocated to the job using the plantwide overhead rate?
2. How much MOH would be allocated to the job using the departmental overhead rates?
3. Does the plantwide overhead rate overcost or undercost the job? By how much?

Please see page 246 for solutions.

STOP & THINK

Do companies always have separate production departments, such as Machining and Assembly, for each step of the production process?

Answer: No. Rather than basing production departments on separate processing steps, some companies have separate production departments for each of their products. For example, Life Fitness could have one department for producing treadmills, another department for producing ellipticals, and yet another department for producing stair climbers. Each department would have all of the equipment necessary for producing its unique product. Departmental overhead rates would be formulated using the same four basic steps just discussed to determine a unique departmental overhead rate for each department. The only difference is that each product (for example, a treadmill) would travel through *only one* department (the Treadmill Department) rather than traveling through separate production departments (Machining and Assembly). Always keep in mind that the accounting system should reflect the actual production environment.

Using Activity-Based Costing to Allocate Indirect Costs

We just saw how companies can refine their cost allocation systems by using departmental overhead rates. If a company wants an even more refined system, one that reduces cost distortion to a minimum, it will use activity-based costing (ABC). **Activity-based costing (ABC)** focuses on *activities*, rather than departments, as the fundamental cost objects. ABC recognizes that activities are costly to perform, and each product manufactured may require different types and amounts of activities. Thus, activities become the building blocks for compiling the indirect costs of products, services, and customers. Companies such as Coca-Cola and American Express use ABC to more accurately estimate the cost of resources required to produce different products, to render different services, and to serve different customers.

Think about the three roommates for a moment. The most equitable and accurate cost allocation system for the roommates was one in which the roommates were charged only for the *activities* in which they participated, and the *extent* to which they participated in those activities. Likewise, activity-based costing generally causes the *least* amount of cost distortion among products because indirect costs are allocated to the products based on the (1) *types* of activities used by the product and (2) the *extent* to which the activities are used.

2 Develop and use activity-based costing (ABC) to allocate indirect costs

Four Basic Steps to Computing and Using Activity Cost Allocation Rates

ABC requires the same four basic steps listed in Exhibit 4-6. The main difference between an ABC system and a plantwide or departmental cost allocation system is that ABC systems have *separate* cost allocation rates for *each activity* identified by the company.

STEP 1. The company first identifies its primary activities and then estimates the total manufacturing overhead costs associated with *each activity*. These are known as activity cost pools.

Let's assume Life Fitness has determined that the following activities occur in its plant: First the machines must be set up to meet the particular specifications of the production run. Next, raw materials must be moved out of the storeroom and into the Machining Department, where some of the parts for the units are fabricated. Once the fabricated parts have been inspected, they are moved into the Assembly Department, along with additional raw materials that are needed from the storeroom. The units are then assembled by direct laborers, while production engineers supervise the process. All units are inspected during and after assembly. Upon passing inspection, each unit is packaged so that it is not damaged during shipment. Finally, the units are moved to the finished goods warehouse where they await shipment to customers. These activities are pictured in Exhibit 4-12.

EXHIBIT 4-12 Primary Activities Identified in the Manufacturing Plant

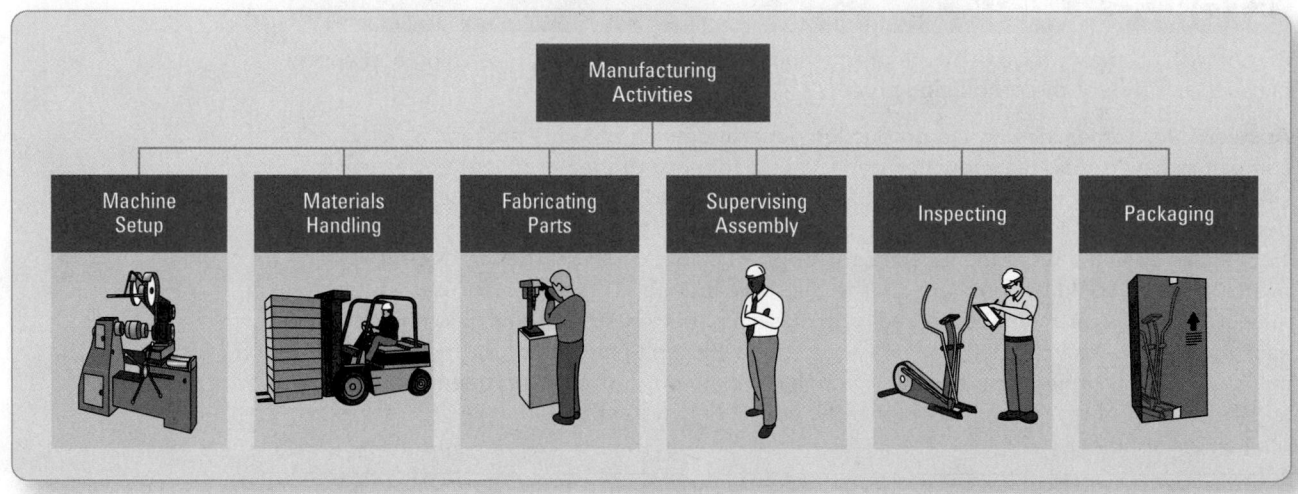

As part of this step, management must determine how much of the total estimated $1 million of MOH relates to each activity. Exhibit 4-13 shows some of the specific MOH costs that management has identified with each activity, along with the total estimated amount of each activity cost pool.

EXHIBIT 4-13 Activity Cost Pools

Activity	MOH Costs Related to the Activity	Total Activity Cost Pool
Machine Setup	Indirect labor used to set up machines	$ 80,000
Materials Handling	Forklifts, gas, operators' wages	200,000
Fabricating Parts	Machine lease payments, electricity, repairs	300,000
Supervising Assembly	Production engineers' labor	150,000
Inspecting	Testing equipment, inspection labor	170,000
Packaging	Packaging equipment	100,000
	TOTAL MOH	$1,000,000

Keep in mind that all of the costs in the activity costs pools are MOH costs; direct labor costs and direct materials costs are *not included* because they will be directly traced to specific jobs and therefore do not need to be allocated. That is why we only include supervisory labor in the overhead cost pool for the assembly activity. The machine operators and assembly-line workers are considered direct labor, so their cost will be traced to individual jobs, not allocated as part of MOH.

STEP 2. The company selects an allocation base for each activity and estimates the total amount that will be used during the year.

When selecting an allocation base for each activity, the company should keep the following in mind:

■ The allocation base selected for each activity should be the *cost driver* of the costs in that particular activity cost pool.

■ The company will need to keep track of how much of the allocation base each job or product uses. Therefore, the company must have the means to collect usage information about each allocation base. Thankfully, bar coding and other technological advances have helped make data collection easier and less costly in recent years.

Let's assume that Life Fitness has identified a cost driver for each activity, and has plans for how it will collect usage data. Exhibit 4-14 shows the selected allocation bases along with the total estimated amounts for the year.

EXHIBIT 4-14 Activity Allocation Bases and Total Estimated Amount of Each

Activity	Activity Allocation Base	Total Estimated Amount of Allocation Base
Machine Setup	Number of setups	8,000 setups
Materials Handling	Number of parts moved	400,000 parts
Fabricating Parts	Machine hours	12,500 machine hours
Supervising Assembly	Direct labor hours	50,000 DL hours
Inspecting	Number of inspections	34,000 inspections
Packaging	Cubic feet packaged	400,000 cubic feet

STEP 3. The company calculates its activity cost allocation rates using the information estimated in Steps 1 and 2.

The formula for calculating the activity cost allocation rates is as follows:

$$\text{Activity cost allocation rate} = \frac{\text{Total estimated activity cost pool}}{\text{Total estimated activity allocation base}}$$

Exhibit 4-15 shows how this formula is used to compute a unique cost allocation rate for each of the company's production activities.

EXHIBIT 4-15 Computing Activity Cost Allocation Rates

	A	B	C	D	E	F	G	H
1	Activity	Step 1: Total Activity Cost Pool (from Exhibit 4-13)		Step 2: Total Amount of Activity Allocation Base (from Exhibit 4-14)			Step 3: Activity Cost Allocation Rate	
2	Machine Setup	$ 80,000	÷	8,000	setups	=	$ 10.00	per setup
3	Materials Handling	200,000	÷	400,000	parts	=	$ 0.50	per part
4	Fabricating Parts	300,000	÷	12,500	machine hours	=	$ 24.00	per machine hour
5	Supervising Assembly	150,000	÷	50,000	DL hours	=	$ 3.00	per DL hour
6	Inspecting	170,000	÷	34,000	inspections	=	$ 5.00	per inspection
7	Packaging	100,000	÷	400,000	cubic feet	=	$ 0.25	per cubic foot
8	Total MOH	$ 1,000,000						
9								

NOTE: *Arithmetic signs are only shown for illustrative teaching purposes. They are not typically displayed in spreadsheets.*

Once again, these rates are calculated based on estimated, or budgeted, costs for the year. Hence, they too are "predetermined" before the year begins. Then, during the year, the company uses them to allocate manufacturing overhead to specific jobs, as shown in Step 4.

STEP 4. The company allocates some manufacturing overhead from *each activity* to the individual jobs that use the activities.

The formula is as follows:

MOH allocated to job = Activity cost allocation rate × Actual amount of activity allocation base used by job

Exhibit 4-16 shows how these activity cost allocation rates would be used to allocate manufacturing overhead to Job 101, in which one elliptical was produced.

EXHIBIT 4-16 Allocating MOH to Job 101 (One Elliptical) Using ABC

	A	B	C	D	E	F	G	H
1	Activity	Activity Cost Allocation Rate (from Exhibit 4-15)			Actual Use of Activity Allocation Base (information collected on job cost record)			MOH Allocated to Job 101: One Elliptical
2	Machine Setup	$10.00	per setup	×	2	setups	=	$ 20
3	Materials Handling	$ 0.50	per part	×	20	parts	=	10
4	Fabricating Parts	$24.00	per machine hour	×	1	machine hours	=	24
5	Supervising Assembly	$ 3.00	per DL hour	×	9	DL hours	=	27
6	Inspecting	$ 5.00	per inspection	×	3	inspections	=	15
7	Packaging	$ 0.25	per cubic foot	×	52	cubic feet	=	13
8	Total							$ 109
9								

NOTE: Arithmetic signs are only shown for illustrative teaching purposes. They are not typically displayed in spreadsheets.

Exhibit 4-17 shows how the same activity cost allocation rates are used to allocate MOH to Job 102, in which one treadmill was produced.

EXHIBIT 4-17 Allocating MOH to Job 102 (One Treadmill) Using ABC

	A	B	C	D	E	F	G	H
1	Activity	Activity Cost Allocation Rate (from Exhibit 4-15)			Actual Use of Activity Allocation Base (information collected on job cost record)			MOH Allocated to Job 102: One Treadmill
2	Machine Setup	$10.00	per setup	×	4	setups	=	$ 40
3	Materials Handling	$ 0.50	per part	×	26	parts	=	13
4	Fabricating Parts	$24.00	per machine hour	×	4	machine hours	=	96
5	Supervising Assembly	$ 3.00	per DL hour	×	6	DL hours	=	18
6	Inspecting	$ 5.00	per inspection	×	6	inspections	=	30
7	Packaging	$ 0.25	per cubic foot	×	60	cubic feet	=	15
8	Total							$ 212
9								

NOTE: Arithmetic signs are only shown for illustrative teaching purposes. They are not typically displayed in spreadsheets.

Exhibit 4-18 illustrates the company's ABC system.

EXHIBIT 4-18 Illustration of the Company's ABC System

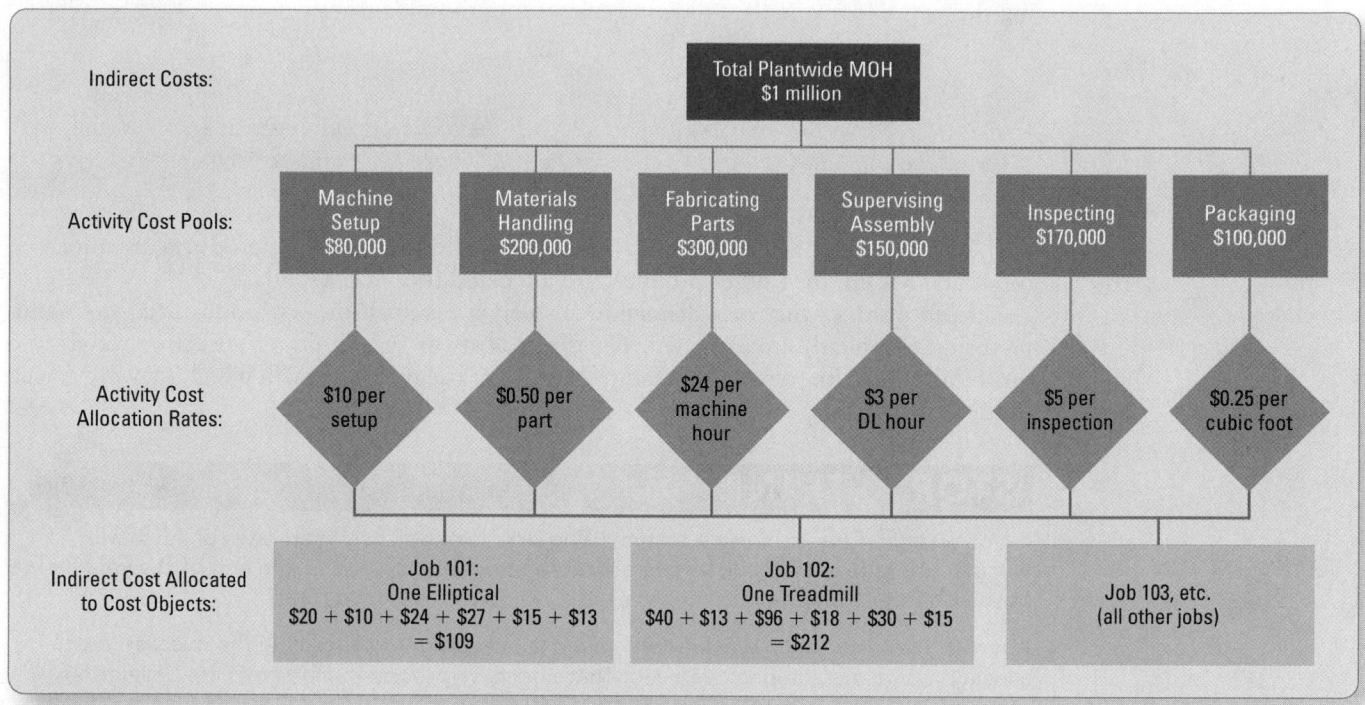

One Last Look at Cost Distortion: Comparing the Three Allocation Systems

Exhibit 4-19 compares the amount of manufacturing overhead that would have been allocated to each elliptical and each treadmill using the three cost allocation systems that we have discussed: (1) a single plantwide overhead rate, (2) departmental overhead rates, and (3) ABC.

EXHIBIT 4-19 Comparing the Three Cost Allocation Systems

	Plantwide Overhead Rate (Exhibit 4-2)	Departmental Overhead Rates (Exhibit 4-8 & 4-9)	Activity-Based Costing (Exhibit 4-16 & 4-17)
Job 101: One Elliptical	$160	$140	$109
Job 102: One Treadmill	$160	$200	$212

As you can see, each allocation system renders different answers for the amount of MOH that should be allocated to each elliptical and treadmill. Which is correct? Keep the following important rule of thumb in mind:

ABC costs are generally thought to be the most accurate because ABC takes into account (1) the *specific resources* each product uses (for example, inspecting resources) and (2) the *extent* to which they use these resources (for example, three inspections of the elliptical, but six inspections of the treadmill).

Exhibit 4-19 shows that the plantwide rate had been severely distorting costs: The elliptical had been overcosted by $51 ($160 − $109) and the treadmill had been undercosted by $52 ($160 − $212). Here, we have only looked at two jobs produced during the year. However, the following rule of thumb holds true:

> *If we consider all of the jobs and products the company produced during the year, we will see that the total amount by which some products have been overcosted will equal the total amount by which other products have been undercosted.*

Why? Because $1 million of MOH is being allocated: If some products are allocated too much MOH, then other products are allocated too little MOH.

Keep in mind that cost distortion is solely a result of the way indirect costs (manufacturing overhead) are allocated. The direct costs of each product (direct materials and direct labor) are known with certainty because of the precise way in which they are traced to jobs.

STOP & THINK

If a company refines its costing system using departmental overhead rates or ABC, will manufacturing overhead still be overallocated or underallocated by the end of the year (as we saw in Chapter 3 when the company used a plantwide overhead rate)?

Answer: Yes. The use of *any predetermined* allocation rate will result in the over- or underallocation of manufacturing overhead. That's because *predetermined* rates are developed using *estimated* data before the actual manufacturing overhead costs and actual cost driver activity for the year are known. Refined costing systems decrease cost distortion *between* products, but do not eliminate the issue of over- or underallocating total manufacturing overhead.[4] As described in Chapter 3, the Cost of Goods Sold account will need to be adjusted at year-end for the *total* amount by which manufacturing overhead has been over- or underallocated.

Sustainability and Refined Costing Systems

Refined costing systems are almost always a necessity for companies that wish to move toward environmental sustainability. Why? Because jobs and product lines do not drive environmental overhead costs equally. Even a smaller manufacturing company with only two or three product lines will often find that environmental-related overhead costs, such as:

- solid waste disposal
- water use
- energy consumption
- hazardous materials handling and training
- air emissions

are not driven equally between each product line. If a company uses a single plantwide overhead rate, environmental and non-environmental overhead costs will be combined within one cost pool, where they will be allocated to each of the company's product lines using the same rate.

However, refined costing systems allow companies to identify and separately pool overhead costs affecting the environment. Furthermore, these environmental costs will be properly allocated to the activities and products that drive those costs. The use of refined costing systems creates better transparency, thus giving management a clearer picture with which to reduce the company's environmental impact.

See Exercises E4-19A and E4-30B ◀

---

[4]In some cases, ABC may reduce the total amount of over- or underallocation. How? Some activity cost pools may be overallocated, while others are underallocated, resulting in an offsetting total effect.

The Cost Hierarchy: A Useful Guide for Setting Up Activity Cost Pools

Some companies use a classification system, called the cost hierarchy, to establish activity cost pools. Companies often have hundreds of different activities. However, to keep the ABC system manageable, companies need to keep the system as simple as possible, yet refined enough to accurately determine product costs.[5] The cost hierarchy, pictured in Exhibit 4-20, helps managers understand the nature of each activity cost pool, and what drives it.

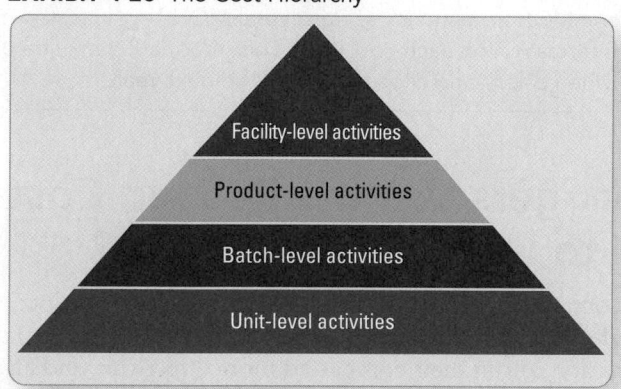

EXHIBIT 4-20 The Cost Hierarchy

There are four categories of activity costs in this hierarchy, each determined by the underlying factor that drives its costs:

1. <u>Unit-level activities</u>—activities and costs incurred for every unit. Examples include inspecting and packaging *each* unit the company produces.

2. <u>Batch-level activities</u>—activities and costs incurred for every batch, regardless of the number of units in the batch. One example would be machine setup. Once the machines are set up for the specifications of the production run, the company could produce a batch of 1, 10, or 100 units, yet the company only incurs the machine setup cost once for the entire batch.

3. <u>Product-level activities</u>—activities and costs incurred for a particular product, regardless of the number of units or batches of the product produced. Examples include the cost to research, develop, design, and market new models.

4. <u>Facility-level activities</u>—activities and costs incurred no matter how many units, batches, or products are produced in the plant. An example is facility upkeep: the cost of depreciation, insurance, property tax, and maintenance on the entire production plant.

By considering how the costs of different activities are consumed (at the unit, batch, product, or facility level), managers are often able to maintain a relatively simple, yet accurate ABC system. After initially identifying perhaps 100 different activities, managers may be able to settle on 5–15 cost pools by combining those activities (for example, batch-level activities) that behave the same way into the same cost pools.

[5] When ABC system implementations fail, it is often due to managers' development of an overly complex system with too many cost pools and too many different cost drivers. After several redesigns of their ABC systems, Coca-Cola and Allied Signal both found that the simpler designs resulted in just as much accuracy. G. Cokins, "Learning to Love ABC," *Journal of Accountancy*, August 1999, pp. 37–39.

STOP & THINK

Do the journal entries used to record job costing differ if a manufacturer uses a refined cost allocation system (departmental overhead rates or ABC) rather than a single, plantwide overhead rate?

Answer: The journal entries used for a refined costing system are essentially the same as those described in Chapter 3 for a traditional job costing system. The only difference is that the company may decide to use *several* MOH accounts (one for each department or activity cost pool) rather than *one* MOH account. By using several MOH accounts, the manufacturer obtains more detailed information on each cost pool. This information may help managers make better estimates when calculating allocation rates the next year.

How do Managers Use the Refined Cost Information to Improve Operations?

We've just seen how companies can increase the accuracy of their product costing systems by using departmental overhead rates or ABC. Now let's consider how managers use this improved cost information to run their companies more effectively and efficiently.

Activity-Based Management (ABM)

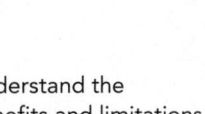

3 Understand the benefits and limitations of ABC/ABM systems

Activity-based management (ABM) refers to using activity-based cost information to make decisions that increase profits while satisfying customers' needs. Life Fitness can use ABC information for pricing and product mix decisions, for identifying opportunities to cut costs, and for routine planning and control decisions.

Pricing and Product Mix Decisions

The information provided by ABC showed Life Fitness's managers that ellipticals cost *less* to make and treadmills cost *more* to make than indicated by the original plantwide cost allocation system. As a result, managers may decide to change pricing on these products. For example, the company may be able to reduce its price on ellipticals to become more price-competitive. Or the company may decide to leave the price where it is, yet try to increase demand for this product since it is more profitable than originally assumed. On the other hand, managers will want to reevaluate the price charged for treadmills. The price must be high enough to cover the cost of producing and selling the treadmills while still being low enough to compete with other companies and earn Life Fitness a reasonable profit.

After implementing ABC, companies often realize they were overcosting their high-volume products and undercosting their low-volume products. Plantwide overhead rates based on volume-sensitive allocation bases (such as direct labor hours) end up allocating more cost to high-volume products, and less cost to low-volume products. However, ABC recognizes that not all indirect costs are driven by the number of units produced. That is to say, not all costs are unit-level costs. Rather, many costs are incurred at the batch level or product level, where they can be spread over the number of units in the batch or in the product line. As shown in Exhibit 4-21, ABC tends to increase the unit cost of low-volume products (that have fewer units over which to spread batch-level and product-level costs), and decrease the unit cost of high-volume products.

As a result of using ABC, many companies have found that they were actually losing money on some of their products while earning much more profit than they had realized on other products! By shifting the mix of products offered away from the less profitable and toward the more profitable, companies are able to generate a higher operating income.

Cutting Costs

Most companies adopt ABC to get more accurate product costs for pricing and product mix decisions, but they often reap even *greater benefits* by using ABM to pinpoint opportunities to cut costs. For example, using ABC allowed Life Fitness to better understand

EXHIBIT 4-21 Typical Result of ABC Costing

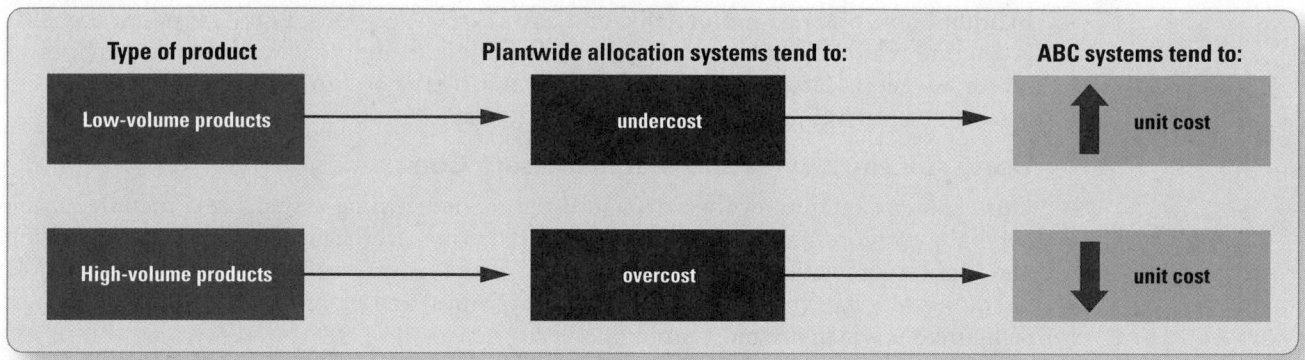

what drives its manufacturing overhead costs. The plantwide allocation system failed to pinpoint what was driving manufacturing overhead costs. Hence, managers could not effectively determine which costs could be minimized. Once the company switched to ABC, managers realized that it costs $10 each time a machine is set up, $5 for each inspection, and so forth. Now, production managers have a "starting place" for cutting costs.

Once managers identify the company's activities and their related costs, managers can analyze whether all of the activities are really necessary. As the term suggests, <u>**value-added activities**</u> are activities for which the customer is willing to pay because these activities add value to the final product or service. In other words, these activities help satisfy the customer's expectations of the product or service. For example, fabricating component parts and assembling the units are value-added activities because they are necessary for changing raw materials into high-quality ellipticals and treadmills.

On the other hand, <u>**non-value-added activities**</u> (also referred to as <u>**waste activities**</u>), are activities that neither enhance the customer's image of the product or service nor provide a competitive advantage. These types of activities, such as storage of inventory and movement of parts from one area of the factory to another, could be reduced or removed from the process with no ill effect on the end product or service. The goal of <u>**value engineering**</u>, as described in Exhibit 4-22, is to eliminate all waste in the system by making the company's processes as effective and efficient as possible. That means eliminating, reducing, or simplifying all non-value-added activities, and examining whether value-added activities could be improved.

EXHIBIT 4-22 The Goal of Value-Engineering

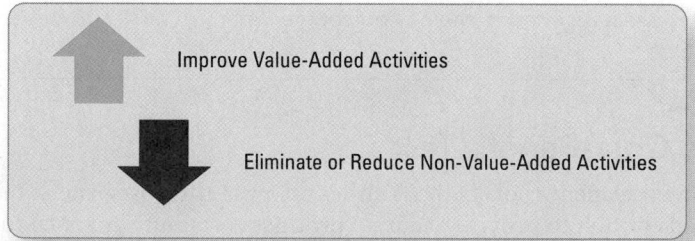

One way of determining whether an activity adds value is to ask if it could be eliminated or reduced by improving another part of the process. For example, could the movement of parts be eliminated or reduced by changing the factory layout? Could inventory storage be eliminated if the company only purchased the raw materials that were needed for each day's production run? Could inspection be reduced if more emphasis was placed on improving the production process, training employees, or using better-quality inputs? In the second half of the chapter we'll discuss tools that many companies have adopted to identify and eliminate these costly non-value-added activities.

Routine Planning and Control Decisions

In addition to pricing, product mix, and cost-cutting decisions, Life Fitness can use ABC in routine planning and control. Activity-based budgeting uses the costs of activities to create budgets. Managers can compare actual activity costs to budgeted activity costs to determine how well they are achieving their goals.

Using ABC in Service and Merchandising Companies

Our chapter example revolved around using refined costing systems at a manufacturing company to more accurately allocate manufacturing overhead. However, merchandising and service companies also find ABC useful. These firms use ABC to allocate the cost of *operating activities* (rather than production activities) among product lines or service lines to figure out which are most profitable.

For example, Walmart may use ABC to allocate the cost of store operating activities such as ordering, stocking, and customer service among its Housewares, Clothing, and Electronics Departments. An accounting firm may use ABC to allocate secretarial support, software costs, and travel costs between its tax, audit, and consulting clients. Even manufacturers may use ABC to allocate operating activities, such as research and development, marketing, and distribution costs, to different product lines. ABC has also been used to determine customer profitability, not just product or service profitability. Firms use the same four basic steps discussed earlier, but apply them to indirect *operating* costs rather than indirect *manufacturing* costs (MOH). Once again, managers can use the data generated by ABC to determine which products or services to emphasize, to set prices, to cut costs, and to make other routine planning and control decisions.

STOP & THINK

Can governmental agencies use ABC/ABM to run their operations more efficiently?

Answer: Yes. ABC/ABM is not just for private-sector companies. Several governmental agencies, including the U.S. Postal Service (USPS) and the City of Indianapolis, have successfully used ABC/ABM to run their operations more cost-effectively. For example, in the past, the USPS accepted customer payments only in the form of cash or checks. After using ABC to study the cost of its revenue-collection procedures (activities), the USPS found that it would be cheaper to accept debit and credit card sales. Accepting debit and credit card sales also produced higher customer satisfaction, allowing the USPS to better compete with private mail and package carriers.

The City of Indianapolis was able to save its taxpayers millions of dollars after using ABC to study the cost of providing city services (activities) to local citizens. Once the city determined the cost of its activities, it was able to obtain competitive bids for those same services from private businesses. As a result, the city outsourced many activities to private-sector firms for a lower cost.[6]

Passing the Cost-Benefit Test

Like all other management tools, ABC/ABM must pass the cost-benefit test. The system should be refined enough to provide accurate product costs but simple enough for managers to understand. In our chapter example, ABC increased the number of allocation rates from the single plantwide allocation rate in the original system to six activity cost allocation rates. ABC systems are even more complex in real-world companies that have many more activities and cost drivers.

---

[6]T. Carter, "How ABC Changed the Post Office," *Management Accounting*, February 1998, pp. 28–36; and H. Meyer, "Indianapolis Speeds Away," *The Journal of Business Strategy*, May/June 1998, pp. 41–46.

Circumstances Favoring ABC/ABM Systems

ABC and ABM pass the cost-benefit test when the benefits of adopting ABC/ABM exceed the costs.

The benefits of adopting ABC/ABM are higher for companies in competitive markets because

- accurate product cost information is essential for setting competitive sales prices that still allow the company to earn a profit.

- ABM can pinpoint opportunities for cost savings, which increase the company's profit or are passed on to customers through lower prices.

The benefits of adopting ABC/ABM are higher when the risk of cost distortion is high, for example, when

- the company produces many different products that use different types and amounts of resources. (If all products use similar types and amounts of resources, a simple plantwide allocation system works fine.)

- the company has high indirect costs. (If the company has relatively few indirect costs, it matters less how they are allocated.)

- the company produces high volumes of some products and low volumes of other products. (Plantwide allocation systems based on a volume-related driver, such as direct labor hours, tend to overcost high-volume products and undercost low-volume products.)

We have seen that ABC offers many benefits. However, the cost and time required to implement and maintain an ABC system are often quite high. Some companies report spending up to two to four years to design and implement their ABC systems. The larger the company, the longer it usually takes. Top management support is crucial for the success of such an expensive and time consuming initiative. Without such support, ABC implementations might easily be abandoned for an easier, less costly accounting system. Because we know ABC systems are costly to implement, how can a company judge the costs involved with setting one up?

The costs of adopting ABC/ABM are generally lower when the company has

- accounting and information system expertise to develop the system. However, even "off-the-shelf" commercial accounting packages offer ABC modules. Small companies often find that Excel spreadsheets can be used to implement ABC, rather than integrating ABC into their general ledger software.

- information technology such as bar coding, optical scanning, Web-based data collection, or data warehouse systems to record and compile cost driver data.

Are real-world companies glad they adopted ABC/ABM?

Usually, but not always. A survey shows that 89% of the companies using ABC data say that it was worth the cost.[7] However, ABC is not a cure-all. As the controller for one Midwest manufacturer said, "ABC will not reduce cost; it will only help you understand costs better to know what to correct."

Signs That the Old System May Be Distorting Costs

Broken cars or computers simply stop running. But unlike cars and computers, even broken or outdated costing systems continue to report product costs. How can you tell whether a costing system is broken and needs repair? In other words, how can you tell whether an existing costing system is distorting costs and needs to be refined by way of departmental rates or ABC?

---

[7]K. Krumwiede, "ABC: Why It's Tried and How It Succeeds," *Management Accounting*, April 1998, pp. 32–38.

A company's product costing system may need repair in the following situations:

Managers don't understand costs and profits:

■ In bidding for jobs, managers lose bids they expected to win and win bids they expected to lose.

■ Competitors with similar high-volume products price their products below the company's costs but still earn good profits.

■ Employees do not believe the cost numbers reported by the accounting system.

The cost system is outdated:

■ The company has diversified its product offerings since the allocation system was first developed.

■ The company has reengineered its production process but has not changed its accounting system to reflect the new production environment.

Decision Guidelines

Refined Costing Systems

Several years ago, Dell decided that it needed to refine its costing system. Starting with an Excel spreadsheet, Dell developed a simple ABC system that focused on the 10 most critical activities. Here are some of the decisions Dell faced as it began refining its costing system.

Decision	Guidelines
How do we develop an ABC system?	1. Identify the activities and estimate the total MOH associated with each activity. These are known as the activity cost pools. 2. Select a cost allocation base for each activity and estimate the total amount that will be used during the year. 3. Calculate an activity cost allocation rate for each activity. 4. Allocate some MOH from each activity to the individual jobs that use the activities.
How do we compute an activity cost allocation rate?	$$\frac{\text{Total estimated activity cost pool}}{\text{Total estimated activity allocation base}}$$
How do we allocate an activity's cost to a job?	$$\begin{array}{c}\text{Activity cost}\\\text{allocation rate}\end{array} \times \begin{array}{c}\text{Actual amount of}\\\text{activity allocation}\\\text{base used by job}\end{array}$$
How can a refined costing system support environmental sustainability?	By creating separate cost pools for environmental related costs, management is better able to identify and appropriately assign costs to those activities and products driving the costs. Better transparency of information should lead to better decisions.
What types of decisions would benefit from the use of ABC?	Managers use ABC data in ABM to make the following decisions: • Pricing and product mix • Cost cutting • Routine planning and control
What are the main benefits of ABC?	• More accurate product cost information • More detailed information on costs of activities and associated cost drivers help managers control costs and eliminate non-value-added activities
When is ABC most likely to pass the cost-benefit test?	• The company is in a competitive environment and needs accurate product costs. • The company makes different products that use different amounts of resources. • The company has high indirect costs. • The company produces high volumes of some products and lower volumes of other products. • The company has accounting and information technology expertise to implement the system.
How do we tell when a cost system needs to be refined?	• Managers lose bids they expected to win and win bids they expected to lose. • Competitors earn profits despite pricing high-volume products below our company's costs. • Employees do not believe cost numbers. • The company has diversified the products it manufactures. • The company has reengineered the production process but not the accounting system.

SUMMARY PROBLEM 1

Indianapolis Auto Parts (IAP) has a Seat Manufacturing Department that uses ABC. IAP's activity cost allocation rates include the following:

Activity	Allocation Base	Activity Cost Allocation Rate
Machining	Number of machine hours	$30.00 per machine hour
Assembling	Number of parts	0.50 per part
Packaging	Number of finished seats	0.90 per finished seat

Suppose Ford has asked for a bid on 50,000 built-in baby seats that would be installed as an option on some Ford SUVs. Each seat has 20 parts and the direct materials cost per seat is $11. The job would require 10,000 direct labor hours at a labor wage rate of $25 per hour. In addition, IAP will use a total of 400 machine hours to fabricate some of the parts required for the seats.

Requirements

1. Compute the total cost of producing and packaging 50,000 baby seats. Also compute the average cost per seat.

2. For bidding, IAP adds a 30% markup to total cost. What price will the company bid for the Ford order?

3. Suppose that instead of an ABC system, IAP has a traditional product costing system that allocates manufacturing overhead at a plantwide overhead rate of $65 per direct labor hour. The baby seat order will require 10,000 direct labor hours. Compute the total cost of producing the baby seats and the average cost per seat. What price will IAP bid using this system's total cost?

4. Use your answers to Requirements 2 and 3 to explain how ABC can help IAP make a better decision about the bid price it will offer Ford.

▪ SOLUTIONS

Requirements 1 and 2
Total Cost of Order, Average Cost per Seat, and Bid Price:

	A	B	C	D	E	F	G	H
1	**Manufacturing Costs**	**Usage of Activity**				**Cost Rate**		**Total**
2	Direct Material	50,000	seats	×	$ 11.00	per seat	=	$ 550,000
3	Direct Labor	10,000	DL hours	×	$ 25.00	per DL hour	=	250,000
4	MOH:							
5	Machining	400	machine hours	×	$ 30.00	per machine hour	=	12,000
6	Assembling	1,000,000*	parts	×	$ 0.50	per part	=	500,000
7	Packaging	50,000	seats	×	$ 0.90	per seat	=	45,000
8	Total Cost							$ 1,357,000
9	Divide by: Number of units							50,000
10	Average cost per unit							$ 27.14
11								
12	**Calculation of bid price:**							
13	Total job cost							$ 1,357,000
14	Multiply by: 100% + Markup							130%
15	Bid price							$ 1,764,100
16								

*1,000,000 = 50,000 seats × 20 parts per seat.
NOTE: Arithmetic signs are only shown for illustrative teaching purposes. They are not typically displayed in spreadsheets.

Requirement 3

Bid Price (Traditional System):

	A	B	C	D	E	F	G	H
1	**Manufacturing Costs**	**Usage of Activity**				**Cost Rate**		**Total**
2	Direct Material	50,000	seats	×	$ 11.00	per seat	=	$ 550,000
3	Direct Labor	10,000	DL hours	×	$ 25.00	per DL hour	=	250,000
4	MOH:	10,000	DL hours	×	$ 65.00	per DL hour	=	650,000
5	Total Cost							$ 1,450,000
6	Divide by: Number of units							50,000
7	Average cost per unit							$ 29.00
8								
9	**Calculation of bid price:**							
10	Total job cost							$ 1,450,000
11	Multiply by: 100% + Markup							130%
12	Bid price							$ 1,885,000
13								

NOTE: Arithmetic signs are only shown for illustrative teaching purposes. They are not typically displayed in spreadsheets.

Requirement 4

IAP's bid would be $120,900 higher using the plantwide overhead rate than using ABC ($1,885,000 versus $1,764,100). Assuming that the ABC system more accurately captures the costs caused by the order, the traditional plantwide overhead system overcosts the order. This leads to a higher bid price that reduces IAP's chance of winning the bid. The ABC system shows that IAP can increase its chance of winning the bid by bidding a lower price and still make a profit.

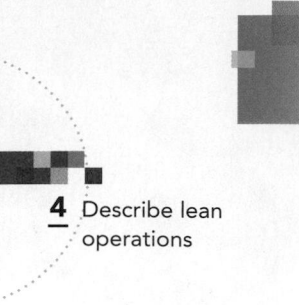

4 Describe lean operations

What is Lean Thinking?

<u>Lean thinking</u> is a management philosophy and strategy focused on creating value for the customer by eliminating waste. Lean is often described by the Japanese word <u>Kaizen</u>, meaning "change for the better." According to the Institute of Management Accountants (IMA), lean thinking is quickly becoming the dominant business paradigm; without it, a company has little chance of long-term survival in the global marketplace. Since management accounting systems should be designed to reflect the company's operations, it's important for you to understand the key elements of lean operations and the costs that can be reduced by eliminating waste.

One key element of creating customer value is to emphasize a short <u>customer response time</u>: the time that elapses between receipt of a customer order and delivery of the product or service. To shorten this time, companies need to reduce their own internal processing time. While lean thinking developed out of the manufacturing industry (and Toyota, in particular), the concepts and tools are being applied with great success to all types of companies. For example, service companies, such as hospitals, car repair shops, and fast-food restaurants, must also concern themselves with the waste imbedded in their customer response time. No matter the industry, the bottom line is clear: By eliminating wasteful activities, companies can reduce their costs and improve their customer response time.

The Eight Wastes of Traditional Operations

Advocates of lean thinking often talk about <u>eight wastes</u> that comprise much of the waste found in traditional organizations, including service and merchandising companies. As shown in Exhibit 4-23, these wastes are easy to remember using the acronym "<u>DOWNTIME</u>."[8]

EXHIBIT 4-23 The Eight Wastes

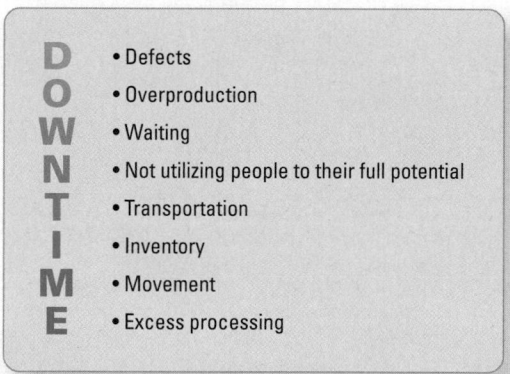

1. **Defects:** Producing defective products or services costs time and money. The product will either need to be repaired, at additional cost, or disposed of. In either case resources are wasted. The final section of this chapter is devoted to discussing the various costs associated with poor quality of product or service.

2. **Overproduction:** Overproduction means that the company is making more product than needed or making product *sooner* than it is needed. Traditional manufacturers often make products in large batches because of long and costly machine setup times and to protect themselves against higher than expected demand for the product. Also, traditional manufacturers often make extra work in process inventory so that each department will have something to continue working on in the event production stops or slows in earlier departments. For example, in Exhibit 4-24, we see the series of production steps required to produce drill bits from bar stock. If the

[8]MAGNET (Manufacturing Advocacy and Growth Network), Cleveland, Ohio.

company keeps some work in process inventory between the grinding and smoothing operations, the smoothing operation can continue even if the shaping or grinding operations slow or come to a halt as a result of machine breakdown, absence of sick workers, or other production problems.

EXHIBIT 4-24 Sequence of Operations for Drill Bit Production

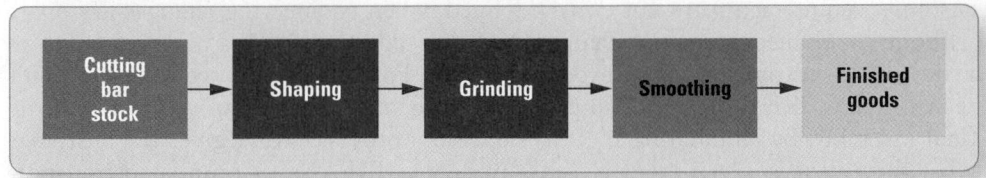

As you'll see next, overproduction can snowball into many problems, including extra wait time, extra transportation, and excess inventory build-up.

3. **Waiting:** Employees must often wait for parts, materials, information, or machine repairs before they can proceed with their tasks. In addition, because of over-production and large batches, work in process inventory often waits in a queue for the next production process to begin. Whether it refers to people or product, wait time is wasted time. The company's customer response time could be much shorter if wait time were eliminated.

4. **Not utilizing people to their full potential:** By assuming that managers always know best, traditional companies have often underutilized their employees. In contrast, one of the key mantras of lean thinking is employee empowerment at all levels of the organization. Employees usually have excellent ideas on how their jobs could be done more efficiently and with less frustration.

5. **Transportation:** While movement of parts, inventory, and paperwork is necessary to some extent, any *excess* transportation is simply wasteful because of the equipment, manpower, energy, and time it requires. Excess transportation is often caused by poor plant layout, large centralized storage cribs, large batches, and long lead times that require product to be moved elsewhere until the next production process is ready to begin.

6. **Inventory:** Typically, traditional manufacturers buy more raw materials than they need "just in case" any of the materials are defective or the supplier is late with the next delivery. As noted earlier, they produce extra work in process inventory "just in case" something goes wrong in the production process. Also, they produce extra finished goods inventory "just in case" demand is higher than expected. In other words, large inventories are essentially a response to uncertainty. Uncertainty is a valid reason for keeping large inventories. So why are large inventories considered wasteful?

   ■ Inventories use cash. Companies incur interest expense from borrowing cash to finance their inventories or forgo income that could be earned from investing their cash elsewhere.

   ■ Large inventories hide quality problems, production bottlenecks, and obsolescence. Inventory may spoil, be broken or stolen, or become obsolete as it sits in storage and waits to be used or sold. Companies in high-tech and fashion industries are particularly susceptible to inventory obsolescence.

   ■ Storing and unstoring inventory is very expensive. Building space, shelving, warehouse equipment, security, computer systems, and labor are all needed to manage inventories.

7. **Movement:** In contrast to the waste of transportation, which refers to moving products and materials, the waste of movement refers to excess human motion, such as excess bending, reaching, turning, and walking. This waste is often caused by cluttered or unorganized work areas (where employees must search for the needed tools and supplies), poorly designed facilities (where employees must walk from one area of the building to another), and poorly designed workstations and work methods (where

employees must continually crouch, stretch, bend, and turn to do their tasks). Not only does excess movement take time, but also it can signal unsafe work conditions that can decrease employee morale and increase the company's exposure to workers' compensation claims.

8. **Excess processing:** This waste refers to performing additional production steps or adding features the customer doesn't care about. Often, this waste is caused when customer requirements are not clearly defined, when engineering changes are made without simultaneous process changes, or when additional steps are performed to make up for shortfalls in earlier production steps. For example, to keep its price point relatively low, IKEA flat packs all of its furniture and lets the customer perform the final assembly. By eliminating the final assembly process, IKEA gives the customer what they want at a price that is affordable. Also, IKEA saves on related transportation and warehousing costs that would be incurred on bulkier, fully assembled furniture.

Characteristics of Lean Operations

One primary goal of a lean organization is to eliminate the waste of time and money that accompanies large inventories. Therefore, lean companies often adopt a **"just-in-time" (JIT)** inventory philosophy. As the name suggests, JIT inventory focuses on purchasing raw materials *just in time* for production and then completing finished goods *just in time* for delivery to customers. By doing so, companies eliminate the waste of storing and unstoring raw materials and finished goods, as pictured in Exhibit 4-25.

EXHIBIT 4-25 Traditional System Versus JIT System

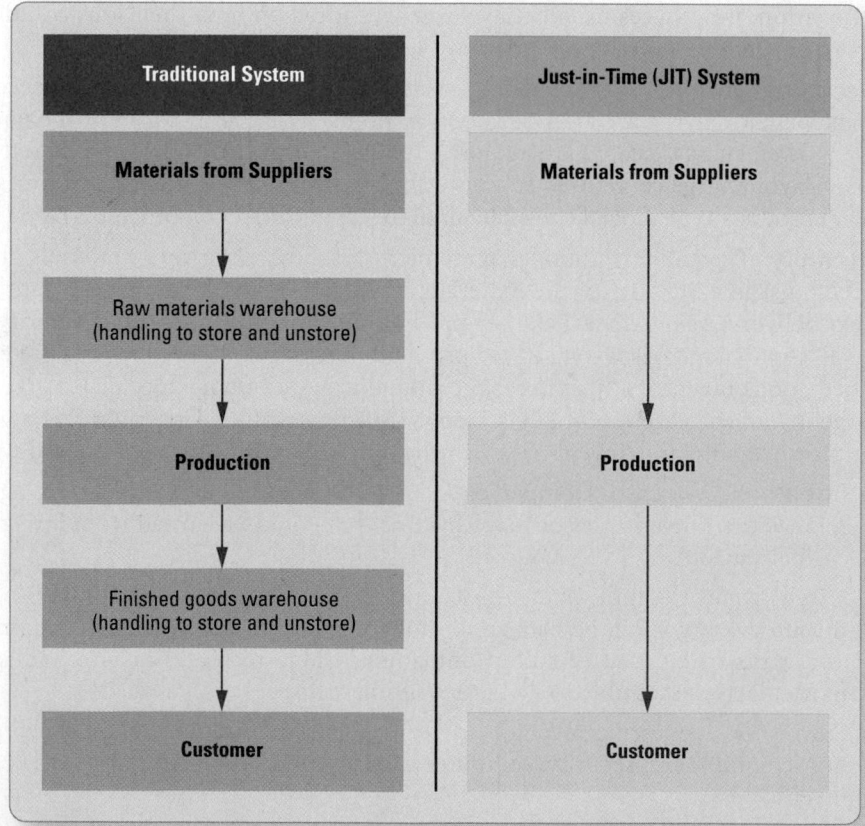

Most companies that adopt lean production have several common characteristics that help minimize the amount of inventory that is kept on hand, yet enable the company to quickly satisfy customer demand. These characteristics are described next.

Value Stream Mapping

Companies need to understand their current state of operations before they can attempt to remove waste and improve operations. Value stream maps (VSM) are used to identify and visually illustrate the flow of materials and information for each family of products or services the company offers, all the way from order receipt to final delivery. A *current state* VSM is used to illustrate the sequence of activities, communication of information, time elapsing, and build-up of inventories that is currently occurring. After identifying waste within the current state VSM, companies prepare a *future state* VSM, with waste removed, and use it as a goal for process improvement.

Production Occurs in Self-Contained Cells

One of the first wastes many companies identify on the current state VSM is the waste of time, transportation, and movement that occurs as a result of poor plant or office layout. For example, a traditional drill bit manufacturer would group all cutting machines in one area, all shaping machines in another area, all grinding machines in a third area, and all smoothing machines in a fourth area, as illustrated in Panel A of Exhibit 4-26. On the other hand, lean companies would group the machines in self-contained production cells as shown in Panel B of Exhibit 4-26. These self-contained production cells minimize the time and cost involved with physically moving parts across the factory to other departments.

EXHIBIT 4-26 Equipment Arrangement in Traditional and Lean Production Systems

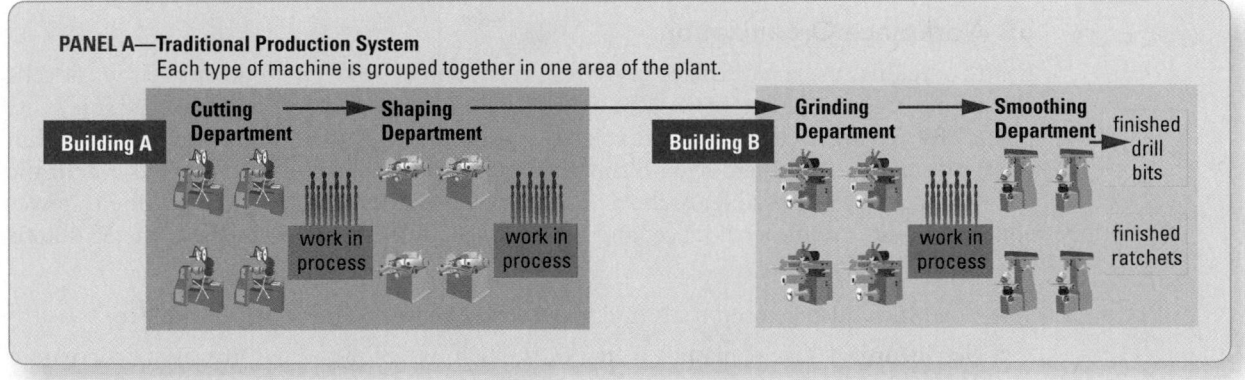

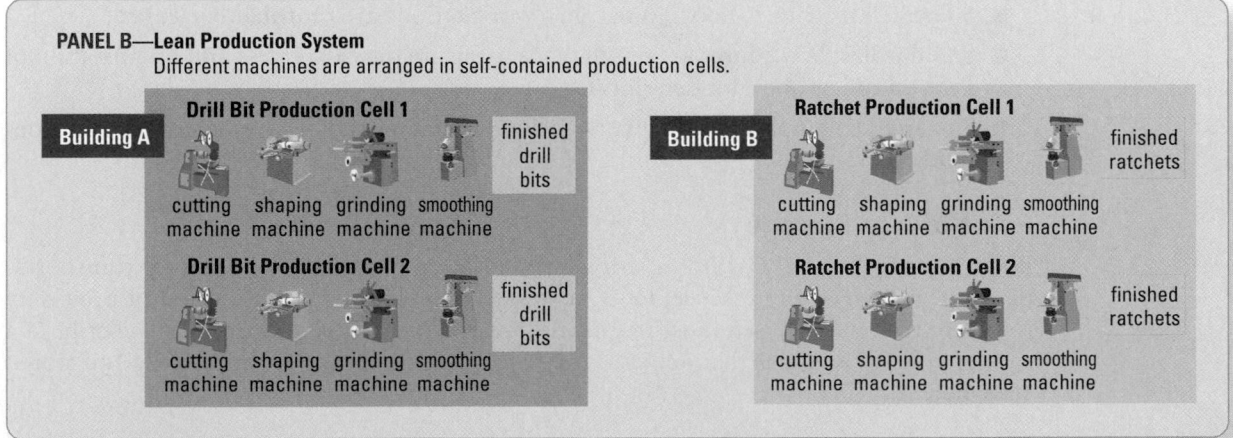

Employee Empowerment: Broad Roles and the Use of Teams

To combat the waste of not utilizing people to their full potential, lean companies focus on employee empowerment. Employees typically hold broader roles than their counterparts at traditional companies. For example, employees working in production cells do more than operate a single machine. They also conduct maintenance, perform setups, inspect their own work, and operate other machines. For example, look at Panel B of Exhibit 4-26. A worker in the Drill Bit Production Cell 1 would be cross-trained to operate all of the machines (cutting, shaping, grinding, and smoothing) in that cell. This cross-training boosts morale, lowers costs, and creates a more flexible and versatile workforce. As a result, individual workloads become much more balanced, leading to a more equitable distribution of work and a happier workforce.

Lean companies also empower employees by using small teams to identify waste and develop potential solutions to the problems identified. Problem solving at lean companies involves searching for and fixing the root cause of a problem, rather than making cosmetic changes to surface issues. To find the root cause of a problem, teams are encouraged to ask "Why?" at least five times. For example, say you received a "D" grade on an exam. Your initial response might be that you didn't understand the material. However, as you dig deeper by continually asking "Why?" you might find that the root cause was not a simple failure to understand the material, but having an overloaded schedule that didn't allow you sufficient time to study and practice the material. The solution might be to lighten your semester course load, or not to participate in so many extracurricular activities. Without fixing the root cause of the problem, you are apt to run into similar problems in the future.

Often, lean companies institute profit-sharing plans so that employees at all levels of the company are compensated for improving the company's overall performance. Because of employee empowerment, lean companies typically report higher job satisfaction and better employee morale.

5S Workplace Organization

Lean companies use a workplace organization system called "5S" to keep their work cells clean and organized. The mantra of 5S is, "a place for everything and everything in its place." By having a clean, well-organized, ergonomic workplace, every employee within the work cell knows where to find the tools and supplies they need to do each job in the cell as efficiently as possible. A clean workplace also leads to fewer defects (due to fewer contaminants), a safer workplace, and fewer unscheduled machine repairs. The 5S stands for the following:

- **Sort:** Infrequently used tools and supplies are removed from the workplace.
- **Set in order:** Visual management tools, such as color-coding, are used to create a logical layout of tools, supplies, and equipment in the work cell so that anyone could walk into the cell and visually understand the current situation.
- **Shine:** All machines, floors, tools, and workstations are thoroughly cleaned.
- **Standardize:** Procedures are put in place to ensure the cleanliness and organization of the workplace does not deteriorate.
- **Sustain:** Daily upkeep of the workstations is maintained and 5S inspections are routinely performed.

Point-of-Use Storage

Point-of-use storage (POUS) is a storage system used to reduce the waste of transportation and movement. In essence, tools, materials, and equipment are stored in proximity to where they will be used most frequently, rather than in a centralized storage crib. In a similar vein, those items that are used infrequently are removed from the cells and stored elsewhere.

Continuous Flow

Lean organizations attempt to smooth the flow of production through the plant so that the rate of production is the same as the rate of demand, thus reducing the wastes of overproduction, waiting, and inventory. The goal is to make *only* as many units as needed by the next customer, whether that be the next machine operator or the final, external customer. Takt time, a critical concept in lean manufacturing, is the rate of production needed to meet customer demand yet avoid overproduction. The term comes from a German word for *rhythm* or *beat*. For example, if a product line has a takt time of five minutes, it means that one unit needs to be produced every five minutes. By carefully monitoring takt time, lean companies are able to identify bottlenecks, balance the workloads of different processes, avoid inventory build-up, and satisfy customer demand.

Pull System

In a traditional production system, inventory is "pushed" through production according to forecasted demand. However, in a lean production system, no inventory is made until a customer order has been received. The customer order triggers the start of the production process and "pulls" the batch through production. Even the necessary raw materials are usually not purchased until a customer order is received. Obviously, for this to work, companies must employ various tactics that will allow the company to quickly satisfy the customer's order. We discuss these tactics next.

Shorter Manufacturing Cycle Times

Because products are not started until a customer order is received, lean companies must focus on reducing their **manufacturing cycle time**: the time that elapses between the start of production and the product's completion. According to most experts, the majority of manufacturing cycle time is spent on non-value-added activities. Shorter manufacturing times also protect companies from foreign competitors whose cheaper products take longer to ship. Delivery speed has become a competitive weapon.

Reduced Setup Times

One key component of manufacturing cycle time is the time required to set up a machine that is used to manufacture more than one product. Employee training and technology helped Toyota cut setup times from several hours to just a few minutes. As a result, the company became more flexible in scheduling production to meet customer orders.

Smaller Batches

Another key component to manufacturing cycle time is batch size. Large batch sizes cause wasted wait time. Therefore, one of the key elements of lean production is the use of smaller batches. For example, assume a customer has ordered 10 units and that each unit requires three unique, sequential processes: A, B, and C. Furthermore, assume that each process takes *1 minute* to complete *on each unit*. The manufacturing cycle time is illustrated in Exhibit 4-27, where each "x" stands for one unit of the product, and the capital "X" stands for the first unit in the batch. Exhibit 4-27 shows that the entire order would take 30 minutes to complete if the manufacturer uses a batch size of 10. Exhibit 4-27 also shows that 21 minutes have elapsed before the first unit in the batch is completed.

EXHIBIT 4-27 Manufacturing Cycle Time with a Batch Size of 10

	Time (in minutes) ⟶		
	1–10 min	11–20 min	21–30 min
Process A	Xxxxxxxxxx		
Process B		Xxxxxxxxxx	
Process C			Xxxxxxxxxx

Alternatively, Exhibit 4-28 shows that the entire order could be completed in just 12 minutes if the manufacturer uses a batch size of 1. In addition, the first unit in the batch is completed after a mere 3 minutes has elapsed. Why the difference? With large batch sizes, each unit spends the bulk of the manufacturing cycle time *waiting*. Customer response time can be greatly reduced through the use of smaller batch sizes.

EXHIBIT 4-28 Manufacturing Cycle Time with a Batch Size of 1

	Time (in minutes) →											
	1	2	3	4	5	6	7	8	9	10	11	12
Process A	X	x	x	x	x	x	x	x	x	x		
Process B		X	x	x	x	x	x	x	x	x	x	
Process C			X	x	x	x	x	x	x	x	x	x

Emphasis on Quality

Lean companies focus on producing their products right the *first* time, *every* time. Why? First, they have no backup stock to give to waiting customers if they run into production problems. Second, defects in materials and workmanship can slow or shut down production. Lean companies cannot afford the time it takes to rework faulty products. Lean companies emphasize "building in" quality rather than relying on a final inspection point to catch defects. This approach to quality, called <u>quality at the source</u>, refers to shifting the responsibility for quality adherence to the operators at each step in the value stream, rather than relying on supervisors or a quality assurance department to catch errors. Each operator checks the incoming work, as well as his or her own outgoing work, so that defective units do not get passed on to downstream production processes. Lean companies use standardization tools, such as checklists and detailed step-by-step operating procedures, to ensure employees know how to complete each process correctly. They also use visual management, root cause analysis, and other tools to "mistake-proof" the process.

Supply-Chain Management

Because there are no inventory buffers, lean production requires close coordination with suppliers. These suppliers must guarantee *on-time delivery* of *defect-free* materials. Supply-chain management is the exchange of information with suppliers and customers to reduce costs, improve quality, and speed delivery of goods and services from the company's suppliers, through the company itself, and on to the company's end customers. As described in Chapter 1, suppliers that bear the ISO 9001:2008 certification have proven their ability to provide high-quality products, and thus tend to be suppliers for lean manufacturers.

Backflush Costing

Due to the emphasis on JIT inventory (little to no raw materials or finished goods), short manufacturing cycle times, and a "pull" system (customer is awaiting production), many lean producers use a simplified accounting system, called backflush costing, that better mirrors their production environment and eliminates wasteful bookkeeping steps. In a <u>backflush costing</u> system, the production costs are not assigned to the units until they are finished, or even sold, thereby saving the bookkeeping steps of moving the product through the various inventory accounts. To get an accurate measurement of the inventory accounts and Cost of Goods Sold at the end of the period, any unfinished or unsold product is "flushed" out of Cost of Goods Sold and placed back in the Work in Process Inventory and Finished Goods Inventory.

Are There Any Drawbacks to a Lean Production System?

While companies such as Toyota, Carrier, and Dell credit lean production with saving them millions of dollars, the system is not without problems. With no inventory buffers, lean producers are vulnerable when problems strike suppliers or distributors. For example, Ford had to shut down some of its plants when engine deliveries from suppliers were late due to security-related transportation delays in the wake of the World Trade Center attacks.

■ Why is this important?

"In order to **compete** and remain **profitable**, companies must cut costs by becoming as **efficient** as possible. **Lean** thinking helps **organizations** cut costs by **eliminating waste** from the system."

Lean Operations in Service and Merchandising Companies

The eight wastes and lean principles discussed previously also apply to service and merchandising firms. In fact, lean practices have become extremely popular in service companies, such as banks and hospitals, as well as merchandising companies, such as IKEA. Entire books have been written on the subject of "lean health care" and "lean offices." Through the use of lean tools, offices have been able to identify the waste caused by excessive document processing, layers of unnecessary authorization, unbalanced workloads, poor office layouts, and unclear communication channels. Through streamlining their internal operations, hospitals and offices have found that they are able to decrease patient and customer wait time, thereby creating higher levels of customer satisfaction while at the same time decreasing their own costs.

▶ Try It!

Which of the following would you expect to see at a company that espouses lean thinking?

1. Larger inventories
2. Smaller batch sizes
3. More organized workstations
4. Longer setup times
5. Lower-level small-team problem solving
6. Centralized storage cribs
7. Pull system

Please see page 246 for solutions.

Sustainability and Lean Thinking

Sustainability and lean thinking have many similarities: both practices seek to reduce waste. However, lean operations focus on eliminating waste and empowering employees in an effort to increase economic profits. On the other hand, "lean and green" operations focus on eliminating waste and empowering employees not only to increase economic profits, but also to preserve the planet and improve the lives of *all* people touched by the company. While lean practices tend to center on *internal* operational waste, green practices also consider the *external* waste that may occur as a result of the product. To become more sustainable, a lean company should be particularly cognizant of all waste that could harm the planet: packaging waste, water waste, energy waste, and emissions waste that would occur from both manufacturing the product *and* from consumers using and eventually disposing of the product.

See Exercises E4-19A and E4-30B

How do Managers Improve Quality?

Because lean companies rarely hold extra inventory to fall back on in the event of errors or defects, they use the management philosophy of **total quality management (TQM)** to focus on consistently generating high-quality products. The goal of TQM is to provide customers with superior products and services. Each business function in the value chain continually examines its own activities to improve quality and eliminate defects.

5 Describe and use the costs of quality framework

Costs of Quality (COQ)

As part of TQM, many companies prepare costs of quality reports. <u>Costs of quality reports</u> categorize and list the costs incurred by the company related to quality. Once managers know the extent of their costs of quality, they can start to identify ways for the company to improve quality while at the same time controlling costs.

Quality-related costs generally fall into four different categories: prevention costs, appraisal costs, internal failure costs, and external failure costs. These categories form the framework for a costs of quality report. We'll briefly describe each next.

Prevention Costs

<u>Prevention costs</u> are costs incurred to *avoid* producing poor-quality goods or services. Often, poor quality is caused by the variability of the production process or the complexity of the product design. To reduce the variability of the production process, companies often automate as much of the process as possible. Employee training can help decrease variability in nonautomated processes. In addition, reducing the complexity of the product design or manufacturing process can prevent the potential for error: The fewer parts or processes, the fewer things that can go wrong. Frequently, companies need to literally "go back to the drawing board" (the R&D and design stages of the value chain) to make a significant difference in preventing production problems.

Appraisal Costs

<u>Appraisal costs</u> are costs incurred to *detect* poor-quality goods or services. Intel incurs appraisal costs when it tests its products. One procedure, called burn-in, heats circuits to a high temperature. A circuit that fails the burn-in test is also likely to fail in customer use. Nissan tests 100% of the vehicles that roll off the assembly lines at its plant in Canton, Mississippi. Each vehicle is put through the paces on Nissan's all-terrain test track. Any problems are identified before the vehicle leaves the plant.

Internal Failure Costs

<u>Internal failure costs</u> are costs incurred on defective units *before* delivery to customers. For example, if Nissan does identify a problem, the vehicle is reworked to eliminate the defect before it is allowed to leave the plant. In the worst-case scenario, a product may be so defective that it cannot be reworked and must be completely scrapped. In this case, the entire cost of manufacturing the defective unit, plus any disposal cost, would be an internal failure cost.

External Failure Costs

<u>External failure costs</u> are costs incurred because the defective goods or services are not detected until *after* delivery is made to customers. For example, Maytag had to recall 250,000 washing machines because water was leaking on the electrical connections, which had the potential to cause an electrical short and ignite the circuit boards.[9] Along with incurring substantial cost for repairing or replacing these recalled washers, the publicity of a defect such as this could cause significant damage to the company's reputation. Damage to a company's reputation from selling defective units to end customers can considerably harm the company's future sales. Unsatisfied customers will avoid buying from the company in the future. Even worse, unsatisfied customers tend to tell their neighbors, family, and friends about any poor experiences with products or services. As a result, a company's reputation for poor quality can increase at an exponential rate. To capture the extent of this problem, external failure costs should include an estimate of how much profit the company is losing due to having a bad reputation for poor quality.

[9]http://www.recallowl.com/recalls/Maytag

Relationship Among Costs

Exhibit 4-29 lists some common examples of the four different costs of quality. Prevention and appraisal costs are sometimes referred to as "conformance costs" since they are the costs incurred to make sure the product or service conforms to its intended design. In other words, these are the costs incurred to make sure the product is *not* defective. On the other hand, internal and external failure costs are sometimes referred to as "non-conformance costs." These are the costs incurred because the product or service *is* defective.

EXHIBIT 4-29 Four Types of Quality Costs

Prevention Costs	Appraisal Costs
Training personnel	Inspection of incoming materials
Evaluating potential suppliers	Inspection at various stages of production
Using better materials	Inspection of final products or services
Preventive maintenance	Product testing
Improved equipment	Cost of inspection equipment
Redesigning product or process	
Internal Failure Costs	**External Failure Costs**
Production loss caused by downtime	Lost profits from lost customers
Rework	Warranty costs
Abnormal quantities of scrap	Service costs at customer sites
Rejected product units	Sales returns and allowances due to
Disposal of rejected units	quality problems
Machine breakdowns	Product liability claims
	Cost of recalls

Most companies find that if they invest more in prevention costs at the front end of the value chain (R&D and design), they can generate even more savings in the back end of the value chain (production and customer service). Why? Because carefully designed products and manufacturing processes can significantly reduce the number of inspections, defects, rework, and warranty claims. Managers must make trade-offs between these costs. Companies that embrace TQM, such as Toyota, *design* and *build* quality into their products rather than having to *inspect* and *repair* later, as many traditional manufacturers do.

Costs of Quality at Service and Merchandising Companies

The costs of quality are not limited to manufacturers. Service firms and merchandising companies also incur costs of quality. For example, certified public accounting (CPA) firms spend a lot of money providing ongoing professional training to their staff. They also develop standardized audit checklists to minimize the variability of the audit procedures performed for each client. These measures help to *prevent* audit failures. Both audit managers and partners review audit work papers to *appraise* whether the audit procedures performed and evidence gathered are sufficient on each audit engagement. If audit procedures or evidence are deemed to be lacking (*internal failure*), the audit manager or partner will instruct the audit team to perform additional procedures before the firm will issue an audit opinion on the client's financial statements. This parallels the "rework" a manufacturer might perform on a product that isn't up to par. Finally, audit failures, such as those at Enron and WorldCom, illustrate just how expensive and devastating *external failure* can be to a CPA firm. The once-prestigious international CPA firm Arthur Andersen & Co. actually went out of business because of the reputation damage caused by its audit failure at Enron.

Using Costs of Quality Reports to Aid Decisions

Now that we have examined the four costs of quality, let's see how they can be presented to management in the form of a costs of quality report. Let's assume Global Fitness, another manufacturer of fitness equipment, is having difficulty competing with Life Fitness because it doesn't have the reputation for high quality that Life Fitness enjoys. To examine this issue, management has prepared the costs of quality report shown in Exhibit 4-30.

Notice how Global Fitness identifies, categorizes, and quantifies all of the costs it incurs relating to quality. Global Fitness also calculates the percentage of total costs of quality that is incurred in each cost category. This helps company managers see just how *little* they are spending on conformance costs (prevention and appraisal). Most of their costs are internal and external failure costs. The best way to reduce these failure costs is to invest more in prevention and appraisal. Global Fitness managers can now begin to focus on how they might be able to prevent these failures from occurring.

> ## ■ Why is this important?
>
> "Businesses **compete** with each other on the basis of price and quality. **Costs of Quality** reports help managers determine how they are **spending** money to ensure that consumers get the **best-quality** product for the price."

EXHIBIT 4-30 Global Fitness's Costs of Quality Report

	A	B	C	D
1	**Global Fitness Costs of Quality Report** **Year Ended December 31**	Costs Incurred	Total Costs of Quality	Percentage of Total COQ
2				
3	**Prevention Costs:**			
4	Employee training	$ 125,000		
5	Total prevention costs		$ 125,000	6.1%
6				
7	**Appraisal Costs:**			
8	Testing	$ 175,000		
9	Total appraisal costs		$ 175,000	8.5%
10				
11	**Internal Failure Costs:**			
12	Rework	$ 300,000		
13	Cost of rejected units	50,000		
14	Total internal failure costs		$ 350,000	17.0%
15				
16	**External Failure Costs:**			
17	Lost profits from lost sales due to poor reputation	$ 1,000,000		
18	Sales return processing	175,000		
19	Warranty costs	235,000		
20	Total external failure costs		$ 1,410,000	68.4%
21				
22	**Total costs of quality**		$ 2,060,000	100.0%
23				

NOTE: The percentage is calculated as the total cost of the category divided by the total costs of all categories combined.

After analyzing the costs of quality report, the CEO is considering spending the following amounts on a new quality program:

Inspect raw materials	$100,000
Reengineer the production process to improve product quality	750,000
Supplier screening and certification	25,000
Preventive maintenance on plant equipment	75,000
Total costs of implementing quality programs	$950,000

Although these measures won't completely eliminate internal and external failure costs, Global Fitness expects this quality program to *reduce* costs by the following amounts:

Reduction in lost profits from lost sales due to impaired reputation.................	$ 800,000
Fewer sales returns to be processed	150,000
Reduction in rework costs...	250,000
Reduction in warranty costs..	225,000
Total cost savings...	$1,425,000

According to these projections, Global Fitness's quality initiative will cost $950,000 but result in total savings of $1,425,000—for a net benefit of $475,000. In performing a cost-benefit analysis, some companies will simply compare all of the projected costs ($950,000) with all of the projected benefits ($1,425,000) as shown previously. Other companies like to organize their cost-benefit analysis by cost category so that managers have a better idea of how the quality initiative will affect each cost category. Exhibit 4-31 shows that by increasing prevention costs (by $850,000) and appraisal costs (by $100,000), Global Fitness will be able to save $250,000 in internal failure costs and $1,175,000 in external failure costs. In total, Global Fitness expects a net benefit of $475,000 if it undertakes the quality initiative. By spending more on conformance costs (prevention and appraisal costs), Global Fitness saves even more on non-conformance costs (internal and external failure costs).

EXHIBIT 4-31 Cost-Benefit Analysis of Global Fitness's Proposed Quality Program

	A	B	C	D
1	**Global Fitness Quality Initiative Cost Benefit Analysis**	**(Costs) and Cost Savings**	**Total (Costs) and Cost Savings**	
2				
3	**Prevention Costs:**			
4	Reengineer the production process	$ (750,000)		
5	Supplier screening and certification	(25,000)		
6	Preventive maintenance on equipment	(75,000)		
7	Total additional prevention costs		$ (850,000)	
8				
9	**Appraisal Costs:**			
10	Inspect raw materials	$ (100,000)		
11	Total additional appraisal costs		$ (100,000)	
12				
13	**Internal Failure Costs:**			
14	Reduction of rework costs	$ 250,000		
15	Total internal failure cost savings		$ 250,000	
16				
17	**External Failure Costs:**			
18	Reduction of lost profits from lost sales	$ 800,000		
19	Reduction of sales return	150,000		
20	Reduction of warranty costs	225,000		
21	Total external failure cost savings		$ 1,175,000	
22				
23	**Total savings (costs) from quality programs**		$ 475,000	
24				

The analysis shown in Exhibit 4-31 appears very straightforward. However, quality costs can be hard to measure. For example, design engineers may spend only part of their time on quality. Allocating their salaries to various activities is subjective. The largest external failure cost—profits lost because of the company's reputation for poor quality—does not even appear in the accounting records. This cost must be estimated based on the experiences and judgments of the Sales Department. Because these estimates may be subjective, TQM programs also emphasize nonfinancial measures such as defect rates, number of customer complaints, and number of warranty repairs that can be objectively measured.

Decision Guidelines

Lean Operations and the Costs of Quality

Dell, a worldwide leader in PC sales, is famous for its complete commitment to both the lean operations and TQM. The following are several decisions Dell's managers made when adopting these two modern management techniques.

Decision	Guidelines
How will we begin to identify waste in our organization?	Most companies find that the majority of waste occurs in eight specific areas. The "eight wastes" can be remembered as "DOWNTIME": • Defects • Overproduction • Waiting • Not utilizing people to their full potential • Transportation • Inventory • Movement • Excess processing
What operational features will help us become more lean?	Lean operations are typically characterized by many of the following features: • Just-in-time (JIT) inventory • Value stream mapping • Production in self-contained work cells • Employee empowerment through broader roles and use of small teams • 5S workplace organization • Point-of-use storage (POUS) • Continuous flow pull system • Shorter manufacturing cycle times • Reduced setup times • Smaller batches • Emphasis on quality • Supply-chain management • Backflush costing
What are the four types of quality costs?	1. Prevention costs 2. Appraisal costs 3. Internal failure costs 4. External failure costs
How do we make trade-offs among the four types of quality costs?	Investment in prevention costs and appraisal costs reduces internal and external failure costs.

SUMMARY PROBLEM 2

The CEO of IAP is concerned with the quality of its products and the amount of resources currently spent on customer returns. The CEO would like to analyze the costs incurred in conjunction with the quality of the product.

The following information was collected from various departments within the company:

Warranty returns...	$120,000
Training personnel	10,000
Litigation on product liability claims...	175,000
Inspecting 10% of final products	5,000
Rework	10,000
Production loss due to machine breakdowns...................................	45,000
Inspection of raw materials	5,000

Requirements

1. Prepare a costs of quality report. In addition to listing the costs by category, determine the percentage of the total costs of quality incurred in each cost category.

2. Do any additional subjective costs appear to be missing from the report?

3. What can be learned from the report?

▪ SOLUTIONS

Requirement 1

	A	B	C	D
1	IAP Costs of Quality Report	Costs Incurred	Total Costs of Quality	Percentage of Total COQ
2				
3	**Prevention Costs:**			
4	Personnel training	$ 10,000		
5	Total prevention costs		$ 10,000	2.7%
6				
7	**Appraisal Costs:**			
8	Inspecting raw materials	$ 5,000		
9	Inspecting 10% of final products	5,000		
10	Total appraisal costs		$ 10,000	2.7%
11				
12	**Internal Failure Costs:**			
13	Rework	$ 10,000		
14	Production loss due to machine breakdown	45,000		
15	Total internal failure costs		$ 55,000	14.9%
16				
17	**External Failure Costs:**			
18	Litigation from product liability claims	$ 175,000		
19	Warranty return costs	120,000		
20	Total external failure costs		$ 295,000	79.7%
21				
22	**Total costs of quality**		$ 370,000	100.0%
23				

Requirement 2

Because the company has warranty returns and product liability litigation, it is very possible that the company suffers from a reputation for poor-quality products. If so, it is losing profits from losing sales. Unsatisfied customers will probably avoid buying from the company in the future. Worse yet, customers may tell their friends and family not to buy from the company. This report does not include an estimate of the lost profits arising from the company's reputation for poor-quality products.

Requirement 3

The Costs of Quality report shows that very little is being spent on prevention and appraisal, which is probably why the internal and external failure costs are so high. The CEO should use this information to develop quality initiatives in the areas of prevention and appraisal. Such initiatives should reduce future internal and external failure costs.

Learning Objectives

- 1 Develop and use departmental overhead rates to allocate indirect costs
- 2 Develop and use activity-based costing (ABC) to allocate indirect costs
- 3 Understand the benefits and limitations of ABC/ABM systems
- 4 Describe lean operations
- 5 Describe and use the costs of quality framework

Accounting Vocabulary

5S. (p. 204) A workplace organization system comprised of the following steps: sort, set in order, shine, standardize, and sustain.

Activity-Based Costing (ABC). (p. 185) Focuses on *activities* as the fundamental cost objects. The costs of those activities become building blocks for compiling the indirect costs of products, services, and customers.

Activity-Based Management (ABM). (p. 192) Using activity-based cost information to make decisions that increase profits while satisfying customers' needs.

Appraisal Costs. (p. 208) Costs incurred to *detect* poor-quality goods or services.

Backflush Costing. (p. 206) A simplified accounting system in which production costs are not assigned to the units until they are finished, or even sold, thereby saving the bookkeeping steps of moving the product through the various inventory accounts.

Batch-Level Activities. (p. 191) Activities and costs incurred for every batch, regardless of the number of units in the batch.

Cost Distortion. (p. 178) Overcosting some products while undercosting other products.

Costs of Quality Report. (p. 208) A report that lists the costs incurred by the company related to quality. The costs are categorized as prevention costs, appraisal costs, internal failure costs, and external failure costs.

Customer Response Time. (p. 200) The time that elapses between receipt of a customer order and delivery of the product or service.

Departmental Overhead Rates. (p. 181) Separate manufacturing overhead rates established for each department.

DOWNTIME. (p. 200) An acronym for the eight wastes: defects, overproduction, waiting, not utilizing people to their full potential, transportation, inventory, movement, excess processing.

Eight Wastes. (p. 200) Defects, overproduction, waiting, not utilizing people to their full potential, transportation, inventory, movement, excess processing.

External Failure Costs. (p. 208) Costs incurred when the company does not detect poor-quality goods or services until *after* delivery is made to customers.

Facility-Level Activities. (p. 191) Activities and costs incurred no matter how many units, batches, or products are produced in the plant.

Internal Failure Costs. (p. 208) Costs incurred when the company detects and corrects poor-quality goods or services before making delivery to customers.

Just in Time (JIT). (p. 202) An inventory management philosophy that focuses on purchasing raw materials just in time for production and completing finished goods just in time for delivery to customers.

Kaizen. (p. 200) A Japanese word meaning "change for the better."

Lean Thinking. (p. 200) A management philosophy and strategy focused on creating value for the customer by eliminating waste.

Manufacturing Cycle Time. (p. 205) The time that elapses between the start of production and the product's completion.

Non-Value-Added Activities. (p. 193) Activities that neither enhance the customer's image of the product or service nor provide a competitive advantage; also known as *waste activities*.

Plantwide Overhead Rate. (p. 179) When overhead is allocated to every product using the same manufacturing overhead rate.

Point of Use Storage (POUS). (p. 204) A storage system used to reduce the waste of transportation and movement in which tools, materials, and equipment are stored in proximity to where they will be used most frequently.

Prevention Costs. (p. 208) Costs incurred to *avoid* poor-quality goods or services.

Product-Level Activities. (p. 191) Activities and costs incurred for a particular product, regardless of the number of units or batches of the product produced.

Quality at the Source. (p. 206) Refers to shifting the responsibility for quality adherence to the operators at each step in the value stream, rather than relying on supervisors or a quality assurance department to catch errors.

Takt Time. (p. 204) The rate of production needed to meet customer demand yet avoid overproduction.

Total Quality Management (TQM). (p. 207) A management philosophy of delighting customers with superior products and services by continually setting higher goals and improving the performance of every business function.

Unit-Level Activities. (p. 191) Activities and costs incurred for every unit produced.

Value-Added Activities. (p. 193)   Activities for which the customer is willing to pay because these activities add value to the final product or service.

Value Engineering. (p. 193)   Eliminating waste in the system by making the company's processes as effective and efficient as possible.

Waste Activities. (p. 193)   Activities that neither enhance the customer's image of the product or service nor provide a competitive advantage; also known as non-value-added activities.

MyAccountingLab   Go to http://myaccountinglab.com/ **for the following Quick Check, Short Exercises, Exercises, and Problems. They are available with immediate grading, explanations of correct and incorrect answers, and interactive media that acts as your own online tutor.**

Quick Check

1. *(Learning Objective 1)* Cost distortion is more likely to occur when
   a. a company manufactures one type of product.
   b. departments incur different types of overhead and the products or jobs use the departments to a different extent.
   c. a company uses departmental overhead rates rather than a single plantwide overhead rate.
   d. all products require the same amount and type of processing activities.

2. *(Learning Objective 2)* The first step in computing and using ABC is which of the following?
   a. Selecting appropriate allocation bases
   b. Calculating activity cost allocation rates
   c. Identifying the company's primary activities
   d. Allocating some MOH to each job

3. *(Learning Objective 2)* Activities incurred regardless of how many units, batches, or products are produced are called _____ activities.
   a. product-level
   b. facility-level
   c. batch-level
   d. unit-level

4. *(Learning Objective 3)* Which of the following is true?
   a. ABM refers to using activity-based cost information to make decisions.
   b. Value-added activities are also referred to as waste activities.
   c. The goal of value engineering is to decrease the amount of value-added activities.
   d. ABC is only applicable to manufacturers.

5. *(Learning Objective 3)* The potential benefits of ABC/ABM are generally higher for companies that
   a. are in non-competitive markets.
   b. produce one product.
   c. produce high volumes of some products and low volumes of other products.
   d. have low manufacturing overhead costs.

6. *(Learning Objective 4)* Lean operations are generally characterized by
   a. JIT inventory systems.
   b. production in self-contained cells.
   c. employee empowerment.
   d. all of the above.

7. *(Learning Objective 4)* Which of the following is *not* one of the "eight wastes" included in the acronym DOWNTIME?
   a. Transportation
   b. Neglect
   c. Overproduction
   d. Inventory

8. *(Learning Objective 4)* Concerning lean operations, which of the following is *false*?
   a. Can be found in all sectors, not just manufacturing
   b. Can leave companies vulnerable to supply-chain disruptions
   c. Focus on internal and external waste
   d. Are quickly becoming the dominant business paradigm

9. *(Learning Objective 4)* Which of the following is *not* one of the costs of quality categories?
   a. Appraisal costs
   b. External failure costs
   c. Prevention costs
   d. Transportation costs

10. *(Learning Objective 5)* Which of the following would be considered an external failure cost?
    a. Warranty costs
    b. Rework costs
    c. Cost to train personnel
    d. Cost of inspecting incoming raw materials

Quick Check Answers

1.b 2.c 3.b 4.a 5.c 6.d 7.b 8.d 9.d 10.a

Short Exercises

S4-1 Understanding key terms *(Learning Objectives 1, 2, 3, 4, & 5)*

The following is a list of several terms. Complete each of the following statements with one of these terms. You may use a term more than once, and some terms may not be used at all.

Activity-based costing	External failure costs	Lean thinking	Product-level costs
Activity-based management	Facility-level costs	Manufacturing cycle time	Takt time
Appraisal costs	Internal failure costs	POUS	TQM
DOWNTIME	Kaizen	Prevention costs	Unit-level costs

a. The costs incurred for a particular product, regardless of the number of units or batches of the product produced, are known as _____.

b. _____ focuses on activities as fundamental building blocks in compiling the indirect costs of products, services, and customers.

c. _____ are costs incurred when defects in poor-quality goods or services are corrected before making delivery to customers.

d. _____ are incurred for every single unit of product produced.

e. Costs incurred when the company does not detect poor-quality goods or services until after delivery is made to customers are _____.

f. _____ are costs incurred no matter how many units, batches, or products are produced.

g. _____ is a Japanese word meaning "change for the better."

h. Costs incurred to detect poor-quality goods or services are _____.

i. The rate of production needed to meet customer demand yet avoid overproduction is known as _____.

j. _____ is a storage system used to reduce the waste of transportation and movement, in which tools, materials, and equipment are stored in proximity to where they will be used most frequently.

k. _____ is a management philosophy of delighting customers with superior products and services by continually setting higher goals and improving every business function.

l. The time that elapses between the start of production and the product's completion is known as _____.

m. _____ is the management philosophy and strategy focused on creating value for the customer by eliminating waste.

n. The costs incurred for every batch, regardless of the number of units in the batch, are known as _____.

o. Costs incurred to avoid poor-quality goods or services are _____.

p. Using activity-based costing information to make decisions that increase profits while satisfying customers' needs is _____.

q. An acronym for the eight wastes is _____.

S4-2 Use departmental overhead rates to allocate manufacturing overhead
(Learning Objective 1)

Westbrook Furniture uses departmental overhead rates (rather than a plantwide overhead rate) to allocate its manufacturing overhead to jobs. The company's two production departments have the following departmental overhead rates:

Cutting Department:	$10 per machine hour
Finishing Department:	$18 per direct labor hour

Job 484 used the following direct labor hours and machine hours in the two manufacturing departments:

JOB 484	Cutting Department	Finishing Department
Direct Labor Hours	5	7
Machine Hours	9	2

1. How much manufacturing overhead should be allocated to Job 484?
2. Assume that direct labor is paid at a rate of $25 per hour and Job 484 used $2,350 of direct materials. What was the total manufacturing cost of Job 484?

S4-3 Compute departmental overhead rates (Learning Objective 1)

Kettle Snacks makes potato chips, corn chips, and cheese puffs using three different production lines within the same manufacturing plant. Currently, Kettle uses a single plant-wide overhead rate to allocate its $3,315,000 of annual manufacturing overhead. Of this amount, $2,014,000 is associated with the potato chip line, $672,000 is associated with the corn chip line, and $629,000 is associated with the cheese puff line. Kettle's plant is currently running a total of 17,000 machine hours: 10,600 in the potato chip line, 3,000 in the corn chip line, and 3,400 in the cheese puff line. Kettle considers machine hours to be the cost driver of manufacturing overhead costs.

1. What is Kettle's plantwide overhead rate?
2. Calculate the departmental overhead rates for Kettle's three production lines. Round all answers to the nearest cent.
3. Which products have been overcosted by the plantwide rate? Which products have been undercosted by the plantwide rate?

S4-4 Compute activity cost allocation rates (Learning Objective 2)

Kettle Snacks produces different styles of potato chips (ruffled, flat, thick-cut, gourmet) for different corporate customers. Each style of potato chip requires different preparation time, different cooking and draining times (depending on desired fat content), and different packaging (single serving versus bulk). Therefore, Kettle has decided to try ABC to better capture the manufacturing overhead costs incurred by each style of chip. Kettle has identified the following activities related to yearly manufacturing overhead costs and cost drivers associated with producing potato chips:

Activity	Manufacturing Overhead	Cost Driver
Preparation	$572,000	Preparation time
Cooking and draining	$925,000	Cooking and draining time
Packaging	$300,000	Units packaged

Compute the activity cost allocation rates for each activity assuming the following total estimated activity for the year: 13,000 preparation hours, 25,000 cooking and draining hours, and 6 million packages.

S4-5 Continuation of S4-4: Use ABC to allocate overhead
(Learning Objective 2)

Kettle Snacks just received an order to produce 16,000 single-serving bags of gourmet, fancy-cut, low-fat potato chips. The order will require 16 preparation hours and 30 cooking and draining hours. Use the activity rates you calculated in S4-4 to compute the following:

1. What is the total amount of manufacturing overhead that should be allocated to this order?
2. How much manufacturing overhead should be assigned to each bag?
3. What other costs will the company need to consider to determine the total manufacturing costs of this order?

S4-6 Calculate a job cost using ABC *(Learning Objective 2)*

Salari Industries, a small, family-run manufacturer, has adopted an ABC system. The following manufacturing activities, indirect manufacturing costs, and usage of cost drivers have been estimated for the year:

Activity	Estimated Total Manufacturing Overhead Costs	Estimated Total Usage of Cost Driver
Machine setup	$159,500	2,900 setups
Machining	$720,000	4,800 machine hours
Quality control	$264,000	4,400 tests run

During May, John and Allison Salari machined and assembled Job 557. John worked a total of 12 hours on the job, while Allison worked 4 hours on the job. John is paid a $25 per hour wage rate, while Allison is paid $28 per hour because of her additional experience level. Direct materials requisitioned for Job 557 totaled $1,250. The following additional information was collected on Job 557: the job required 2 machine setups, 4 machine hours, and 3 quality control tests.

1. Compute the activity cost allocation rates for the year.
2. Complete the following job cost record for Job 557:

Job Cost Record Job 557	Manufacturing Costs
Direct materials	?
Direct labor	?
Manufacturing overhead	?
Total job cost	$?

S4-7 Classifying costs within the cost hierarchy *(Learning Objective 2)*

Classify each of the following costs as either unit-level, batch-level, product-level or facility-level.

a. Product line manager salary
b. Machine setup costs that are incurred whenever a new production order is started
c. Patent for new product
d. Factory utilities
e. Direct materials
f. Cost to inspect each product as it is finished
g. CEO salary
h. Engineering costs for new product
i. Order processing
j. Depreciation on factory
k. Direct labor
l. Shipment of an order to a customer

S4-8 Classifying costs within the cost hierarchy *(Learning Objective 2)*

Hosbach Manufacturing produces a variety of plastic containers using an extrusion blow molding process. The following activities are part of Hosbach Manufacturing's operating process:

1. A plant manager oversees the entire manufacturing operation.
2. Each container product line has a product line manager.
3. Each type of container has its own unique molds.
4. Each container is cut from the mold once the plastic has cooled and hardened.
5. Rent is paid for the building that houses the manufacturing processes.

6. Plastic resins are used as the main direct material for the containers.

7. The extrusion machine is calibrated for each batch of containers made.

8. Patents are obtained for each new type of container mold.

9. Routine maintenance is performed on the extrusion machines.

10. The sales force incurs travel expenses to attend various trade shows throughout the country to market the containers.

Classify each activity as either unit-level, batch-level, product-level, or facility-level.

S4-9 Determine the usefulness of refined costing systems in various situations *(Learning Objective 3)*

In each of the following situations, determine whether the company would be more likely or less likely to benefit from refining its costing system.

1. The company has very few indirect costs.

2. The company operates in a very competitive industry.

3. The company has reengineered its production process but has not changed its accounting system.

4. In bidding for jobs, managers lost bids they expected to win and won bids they expected to lose.

5. The company produces few products, and the products consume resources in a similar manner.

6. The company produces high volumes of some of its products and low volumes of other products.

S4-10 Identifying costs as value-added or non-valued-added *(Learning Objective 3)*

Identify which of the following manufacturing overhead costs are value-added and which are non-value-added.

a. Wages of the workers assembling products

b. Engineering design costs for a new product

c. Cost of moving raw materials into production

d. Salary for supervisor on the factory floor

e. Product inspection

f. Costs of reworking of defective units

g. Costs of warehousing raw materials

h. Costs arising from backlog in production

S4-11 Identify lean production characteristics *(Learning Objective 4)*

Indicate whether each of the following is characteristic of a lean production system or a traditional production system.

a. A workplace organization system called "5S" is frequently used to keep work spaces clean and organized.

b. Suppliers make frequent deliveries of small quantities of raw materials.

c. The manufacturing cycle times are longer.

d. The final operation in the production sequence "pulls" parts from the preceding operation.

e. Management works with suppliers to ensure defect-free raw materials.

f. The workflow is continuous to attempt to balance the rate of production with the rate of demand.

g. Products are produced in large batches.

h. There is an emphasis on building in quality.

i. Employees do a variety of jobs, including maintenance and setups as well as operation of machines.

j. Each employee is responsible for inspecting his or her own work.

k. Large stocks of finished goods protect against lost sales if customer demand is higher than expected.

l. Setup times are long.

m. Suppliers can access the company's intranet.

S4-12   Classifying costs of quality (Learning Objective 5)

Classify each of the following quality-related costs as prevention costs, appraisal costs, internal failure costs, or external failure costs.

1. Incremental cost of using a higher-grade raw material
2. Training employees
3. Lost productivity due to machine breakdown
4. Inspecting incoming raw materials
5. Warranty repairs
6. Repairing defective units found
7. Legal fees from customer lawsuits
8. Inspecting products that are halfway through the production process
9. Redesigning the production process
10. Cost incurred producing and disposing of defective units

S4-13   Quality initiative decision (Learning Objective 5)

Clearsound manufactures high-quality speakers. Suppose Clearsound is considering spending the following amounts on a new quality program:

Additional 20 minutes of testing for each speaker......................................	$ 604,000
Negotiating with and training suppliers to obtain higher-quality materials and on-time delivery...	$ 550,000
Redesigning the speakers to make them easier to manufacture...............	$1,405,000

Clearsound expects this quality program to save costs as follows:

Reduced warranty repair costs...	$208,000
Avoid inspection of raw materials..	$404,000
Rework avoided because of fewer defective units	$656,000

It also expects this program to avoid lost profits from the following:

Lost sales due to disappointed customers...	$858,000
Lost production time due to rework	$309,000

1. Classify each of these costs into one of the four categories of quality costs (prevention, appraisal, internal failure, external failure).
2. Should Clearsound implement the quality program? Give your reasons.

S4-14   Categorize different costs of quality (Learning Objective 5)

Millan & Co. makes electronic components. Mike Millan, the president, recently instructed Vice President Steve Bensen to develop a total quality control program: "If we don't at least match the quality improvements our competitors are making," he told Bensen, "we'll soon be out of business." Bensen began by listing various "costs of quality" that Millan incurs. The first six items that came to mind were as follows:

- Costs of reworking defective components after discovery by company inspectors
- Costs of inspecting components in one of Millan & Co.'s production processes
- Salaries of engineers who are designing components to withstand electrical overloads
- Costs incurred by Millan & Co.'s customer representatives traveling to customer sites to repair defective products
- Lost profits from lost sales due to reputation for less-than-perfect products
- Costs of electronic components returned by customers

Classify each item as a prevention cost, an appraisal cost, an internal failure cost, or an external failure cost.

S4-15 Identifying waste activities in an office *(Learning Objective 4)*

The following is a list of waste activities found in an office. Classify each one as a type of waste as represented by the acronym DOWNTIME (Defects, Overproduction, Waiting, Not utilizing people to their full potential, Transportation, Inventory, Movement, and Excess processing).

a. Loan approval files frequently contain errors.

b. The accounting report produces segment reports because the reports have been produced for years even though managers use other reports to manage their divisions.

c. Office supplies are stockpiled in the supply closet; the office manager buys in large quantities when there are sales.

d. Sales orders are put into the computer by the sales people in the field and paper reports are generated; these sales orders are then entered into the order processing system by clerks who type the orders based on the paper reports.

e. The office computers are slow to do the processing; the computers need to be upgraded.

f. Orders in the system are frequently missing information.

g. Employees do not have the authority and responsibility to make routine decisions.

h. The files needed for loan approval are carried to and from the file storage office when the files are needed.

i. To retrieve inventory records, clerks must click through several menus in the program to get to the record needed.

j. Approval of loans is done in batches once a week rather than as the loan paperwork is finished for each individual loan.

k. Each time a document needs to be notarized, someone must search for the notary seal (used to make the seal impression on the document).

l. The computer system requires frequent restarting; restarting takes five minutes.

m. Paperwork (that might change) is printed before it is needed.

n. The office manager insists that a spreadsheet program must be used to store customer records, even though it would be more efficient to use a database program.

o. The office is run by the office manager; employees do as they are told.

p. Pending vacation requests must be taken to the third floor offices to get the signature of the human resources manager.

ETHICS

S4-16 Identify ethical standards violated *(Learning Objectives 1, 2, 3, 4, 5, & 6)*

For each of the situations listed, identify the primary standard from the IMA *Statement of Ethical Professional Practice* that is violated (competence, confidentiality, integrity, or credibility). Refer to Exhibit 1-6 for the complete standard.

1. Shawn, an accountant at the Booth Corporation, did not attend the training for the new activity-based costing system because he figures it will not be much different from the current allocation system.

2. Joanna receives an iPod from a salesman at a lean consulting group. She keeps the iPod, even though she knows that her department will be responsible for hiring a consulting firm to come in to offer lean training sessions next year.

3. Noah, the plant manager, does not disclose the quality issues he is aware of in the current production process. He figures that he can get them resolved in the next few months.

4. Connery Corporation has an activity-based costing system. Percy prepares reports each month that are long and full of facts. The reports are hard to understand for anyone but Percy.

5. Perkins Company operates in highly competitive environment and has developed some proprietary processes that allow it to maintain a market lead. Simon, the CFO, does not have employees sign non-disclosure agreements because he feels that they are all family. He avoids talking about the topic.

EXERCISES Group A

E4-17A   Compare traditional and departmental cost allocations
(Learning Objective 1)

Isaacson's Fine Furnishings manufactures upscale custom furniture. Isaacson's currently uses a plantwide overhead rate based on direct labor hours to allocate its $1,450,000 of manufacturing overhead to individual jobs. However, Donna Strong, owner and CEO, is considering refining the company's costing system by using departmental overhead rates. Currently, the Machining Department incurs $625,000 of manufacturing overhead while the Finishing Department incurs $825,000 of manufacturing overhead. Donna has identified machine hours (MH) as the primary manufacturing overhead cost driver in the Machining Department and direct labor (DL) hours as the primary cost driver in the Finishing Department.

The Isaacson's plant completed Jobs 450 and 455 on May 15. Both jobs incurred a total of 7 DL hours throughout the entire production process. Job 450 incurred 1 MH in the Machining Department and 6 DL hours in the Finishing Department (the other DL hour occurred in the Machining Department). Job 455 incurred 6 MH in the Machining Department and 5 DL hours in the Finishing Department (the other two DL hours occurred in the Machining Department).

Requirements

1. Compute the plantwide overhead rate assuming that Isaacson's expects to incur 21,000 total DL hours during the year.
2. Compute departmental overhead rates assuming that Isaacson's expects to incur 15,300 MH in the Machining Department and 17,800 DL hours in the Finishing Department during the year.
3. If Isaacson's continues to use the plantwide overhead rate, how much manufacturing overhead would be allocated to Job 450 and Job 455?
4. If Isaacson's uses departmental overhead rates, how much manufacturing overhead would be allocated to Job 450 and Job 455?
5. Based on your answers to Requirements 3 and 4, does the plantwide overhead rate overcost or undercost either job? Explain. If Isaacson's sells its furniture at 125% of cost, will its choice of allocation systems affect product pricing? Explain.

E4-18A   Compute activity rates and apply to jobs *(Learning Objective 2)*

Frederick Group uses ABC to account for its chrome wheel manufacturing process. Company managers have identified four manufacturing activities that incur manufacturing overhead costs: materials handling, machine setup, insertion of parts, and finishing. The budgeted activity costs for the upcoming year and their allocation bases are as follows:

Activity	Total Budgeted Manufacturing Overhead Cost	Allocation Base
Materials handling.............................	$ 8,700	Number of parts
Machine setup.....................................	4,650	Number of setups
Insertion of parts................................	49,300	Number of parts
Finishing	75,600	Finishing direct labor hours
Total..	$138,250	

Frederick Group expects to produce 1,000 chrome wheels during the year. The wheels are expected to use 2,900 parts, require 15 setups, and consume 1,800 hours of finishing time.

   Job 420 used 150 parts, required 4 setups, and consumed 120 finishing hours.
   Job 510 used 500 parts, required 5 setups, and consumed 320 finishing hours.

Requirements

1. Compute the cost allocation rate for each activity.
2. Compute the manufacturing overhead cost that should be assigned to Job 420.
3. Compute the manufacturing overhead cost that should be assigned to Job 510.

CHAPTER 4

SUSTAINABILITY

E4-19A Apply activity cost allocation rates *(Learning Objective 2)*

Sidney Industries manufactures a variety of custom products. The company has traditionally used a plantwide manufacturing overhead rate based on machine hours to allocate manufacturing overhead to its products. The company estimates that it will incur $2,190,000 in total manufacturing overhead costs in the upcoming year and will use 15,000 machine hours.

Up to this point, hazardous waste disposal fees have been absorbed into the plantwide manufacturing overhead rate and allocated to all products as part of the manufacturing overhead process. Recently, the company has been experiencing significantly increased waste disposal fees for hazardous waste generated by certain products, and as a result, profit margins on all products have been negatively impacted. Company management wants to implement an activity-based costing system so that managers know the cost of each product, including its hazardous waste disposal costs.

Expected usage and costs for manufacturing overhead activities for the upcoming year are as follows:

Description of Cost Pool	Estimated Cost	Cost Driver	Estimated Activity for This Year
Machine maintenance costs............	$ 600,000	Number of machine hours	15,000
Engineering change orders.............	$ 270,000	Number of change orders	3,000
Hazardous waste disposal...............	$1,320,000	Pounds of hazardous materials generated	4,000
Total overhead cost.........................	$2,190,000		

During the year, Job 356 is started and completed. Usage for this job follows:

300 pounds of direct materials at $70 per pound
20 direct labor hours used at $25 per labor hour
90 machine hours used
9 change orders
50 pounds of hazardous waste generated

Requirements

1. Calculate the cost of Job 356 using the traditional plantwide manufacturing overhead rate based on machine hours.
2. Calculate the cost of Job 356 using activity-based costing.
3. If you were a manager, which cost estimate would provide you more useful information? How might you use this information?

E4-20A Using ABC to bill clients at a service firm *(Learning Objective 2)*

Haas & Company is an architectural firm specializing in home remodeling for private clients and new office buildings for corporate clients.

Haas charges customers at a billing rate equal to 131% of the client's total job cost. A client's total job cost is a combination of (1) professional time spent on the client ($62 per hour cost of employing each professional) and (2) operating overhead allocated to the client's job. Haas allocates operating overhead to jobs based on professional hours spent on the job. Haas estimates its five professionals will incur a total of 10,000 professional hours working on client jobs during the year.

All operating costs other than professional salaries (travel reimbursements, copy costs, secretarial salaries, office lease, and so forth) can be assigned to the three activities. Total activity costs, cost drivers, and total usage of those cost drivers are estimated as follows:

Activity	Total Activity Cost	Cost Driver	Total Usage by Corporate Clients	Total Usage by Private Clients
Transportation to clients	$ 8,000	Round-trip mileage to clients..........	5,500 miles	9,500 miles
Blueprint copying......................	37,000	Number of copies	200 copies	800 copies
Office support...........................	185,000	Secretarial time	2,900 secretarial hours	2,100 secretarial hours
Total operating overhead..........	$230,000			

Sabrina Yu hired Haas to design her kitchen remodeling. A total of 24 professional hours were incurred on this job. In addition, Yu's remodeling job required one of the professionals to travel back and forth to her house for a total of 126 miles. The blueprints had to be copied four times because Yu changed the plans several times. In addition, 13 hours of secretarial time were used lining up the subcontractors for the job.

Requirements

1. Calculate the current indirect cost allocation rate per professional hour.
2. Calculate the amount that would be billed to Yu given the current costing structure.
3. Calculate the activity cost allocation rates that could be used to allocate operating overhead costs to client jobs.
4. Calculate the amount that would be billed to Yu using ABC costing.
5. Which type of billing system is more fair to clients? Explain.

E4-21A   Compare traditional and ABC allocations at a pharmacy
(Learning Objective 2)

Wilmington Pharmacy, part of a large chain of pharmacies, fills a variety of prescriptions for customers. The complexity of prescriptions filled by Wilmington varies widely; pharmacists can spend between five minutes and six hours on a prescription order. Traditionally, the pharmacy has allocated its overhead based on the number of prescriptions in each order. For example, a customer may bring in three prescriptions to be filled on the same day; the pharmacy considers this to be one order.

The pharmacy chain's controller is exploring whether activity-based costing (ABC) may better allocate the pharmacy overhead costs to pharmacy orders. The controller has gathered the following information:

Cost Pools	Total Annual Estimated Cost	Cost Driver	Total Annual Estimated Cost Driver Activity
Pharmacy occupancy costs (utilities, rent, and other costs)	$ 102,000	Technician hours...................	85,000
Packaging supplies (bottles, bags, and other packaging)	$ 22,000	Number of prescriptions......	20,000
Professional training and insurance costs...	$ 108,000	Pharmacist hours..................	27,000
Total pharmacy overhead................	$ 232,000		

The clerk for Wilmington has gathered the following information regarding two recent pharmacy orders:

Customer Order Number	Technician Hours	Number of Prescriptions	Pharmacist Hours
1247	0.5	5	3.0
1248	0.5	3	1.5

Requirements

1. What is the traditional overhead rate based on the number of prescriptions?
2. How much pharmacy overhead would be allocated to customer order number 1247 if traditional overhead allocation based on the number of prescriptions is used?
3. How much pharmacy overhead would be allocated to customer order number 1248 if traditional overhead allocation based on the number of prescriptions is used?
4. What are the following cost pool allocation rates:
   a. Pharmacy occupancy costs
   b. Packaging supplies
   c. Professional training and insurance costs
5. How much would be allocated to customer order number 1247 if activity-based costing (ABC) is used to allocate the pharmacy overhead costs?
6. How much would be allocated to customer order number 1248 if activity-based costing (ABC) is used to allocate the pharmacy overhead costs?
7. Which allocation method (traditional or activity-based costing) would produce a more accurate product cost? Explain your answer.

E4-22A   Reassess product costs using ABC *(Learning Objective 2)*

Reynolds, Inc., manufactures only two products, Medium (42-inch) and Large (63-inch) TVs. To generate adequate profit and cover its expenses throughout the value chain, Reynolds prices its TVs at 300% of manufacturing cost. The company is concerned because the Large model is facing severe pricing competition, whereas the Medium model is the low-price leader in the market. The CEO questions whether the cost numbers generated by the accounting system are correct. He has just learned about ABC and wants to reanalyze this past year's product costs using an ABC system.

Information about the company's products this past year is as follows:

Medium (42-inch) TVs:

Total direct material cost: $669,000

Total direct labor cost: $225,000

Production volume: 3,160 units

Large (63-inch) TVs:

Total direct material cost: $1,270,000

Total direct labor cost: $385,000

Production volume: 4,160 units

Currently, the company applies manufacturing overhead on the basis of direct labor hours. The company incurred $824,000 of manufacturing overhead this year and 26,500 direct labor hours (9,900 direct labor hours making Medium TVs and 16,600 making Large TVs). The ABC team identified three primary production activities that generate manufacturing overhead costs:

Materials Handling ($160,000); driven by number of material orders handled

Machine Processing ($564,000); driven by machine hours

Packaging ($100,000); driven by packaging hours

The company's only two products required the following activity levels during the year:

	Material Orders Handled	Machine Hours	Packaging Hours
Medium	300	21,400	4,140
Large	240	23,000	6,060

Requirements

1. Use the company's current costing system to find the total cost of producing all Medium (42-inch) TVs and the total cost of producing all Large (63-inch) TVs. What was the average cost of making each unit of each model? Round your answers to the nearest cent.

2. Use ABC to find the total cost of producing all Medium (42-inch) TVs and the total cost of producing all Large (63-inch) TVs. What was the average cost of making each unit of each model? Round your answers to the nearest cent.

3. How much cost distortion was occurring between Reynolds' two products? Calculate the cost distortion in total and on a per-unit basis. Could the cost distortion explain the CEO's confusion about pricing competition? Explain.

E4-23A   Use ABC to allocate manufacturing overhead (Learning Objective 2)

Several years after reengineering its production process, Biltmore Corporation hired a new controller, Rachael Johnson. She developed an ABC system very similar to the one used by Biltmore's chief rival, Westriver. Part of the reason Johnson developed the ABC system was because Biltmore's profits had been declining even though the company had shifted its product mix toward the product that had appeared most profitable under the old system. Before adopting the new ABC system, Biltmore had used a plantwide overhead rate based on direct labor hours that was developed years ago.

For the upcoming year, Biltmore's budgeted ABC manufacturing overhead allocation rates are as follows:

Activity	Allocation Base	Activity Cost Allocation Rate
Materials handling......................	Number of parts	$ 3.84 per part
Machine setup...........................	Number of setups	$330.00 per setup
Insertion of parts.......................	Number of parts	$ 30.00 per part
Finishing..................................	Finishing direct labor hours	$ 54.00 per hour

The number of parts is now a feasible allocation base because Biltmore recently installed a plantwide computer system. Biltmore produces two wheel models: Standard and Deluxe. Budgeted data for the upcoming year are as follows:

	Standard	Deluxe
Parts per wheel	6.0	8.0
Setups per 1,000 wheels	20.0	20.0
Finishing direct labor hours per wheel............................	1.2	3.3
Total direct labor hours per wheel	2.0	3.3

The company's managers expect to produce 1,000 units of each model during the year.

Requirements

1. Compute the total budgeted manufacturing overhead cost for the upcoming year.
2. Compute the manufacturing overhead cost per wheel of each model using ABC.
3. Compute Biltmore's traditional plantwide overhead rate. Use this rate to determine the manufacturing overhead cost per wheel under the traditional system.

E4-24A   Continuation of E4-23A: Determine product profitability
(*Learning Objectives 2 & 3*)

Refer to your answers in E4-23A. In addition to the manufacturing overhead costs, the following data are budgeted for the company's Standard and Deluxe models for next year:

	Standard	Deluxe
Sales price per wheel	$420.00	$620.00
Direct materials per wheel	$ 34.00	$ 47.00
Direct labor per wheel	$ 45.10	$ 52.50

Requirements
1. Compute the gross profit per wheel if managers rely on the ABC unit cost data computed in E4-23A.
2. Compute the gross profit per wheel if the managers rely on the plantwide allocation cost data.
3. Which product line is more profitable for Biltmore?
4. Why might the controller have expected ABC to pass the cost-benefit test? Were there any warning signs that Biltmore's old direct-labor-based allocation system was broken?

E4-25A   Differentiate between traditional and lean operations
(*Learning Objective 4*)

Briefly describe how lean production systems differ from traditional production systems along each of the following dimensions:
1. Roles of plant employees
2. Manufacturing cycle times
3. Quality
4. Inventory levels
5. Batch sizes
6. Setup times
7. Workplace organization

E4-26A   Prepare a Costs of Quality report (*Learning Objective 5*)

The CEO of Fresh Snacks Corp. is concerned about the amount of resources currently spent on customer warranty claims. Each box of snacks is printed with the following logo: "Satisfaction guaranteed or your money back." Since the number of claims is high, she would like to evaluate what costs are being incurred to ensure the quality of the product. The following information was collected from various departments within the company:

Cost of disposal of rejected products	$ 11,000
Preventive maintenance on factory equipment	$ 9,000
Production loss due to machine breakdowns	$ 16,000
Inspection of raw materials	$ 5,000
Warranty claims	$ 416,000
Cost of defective products found at the inspection point	$ 80,000
Training factory personnel	$ 36,000
Recall of Batch #59374	$ 175,000
Inspecting products when halfway through the production process	$ 55,000

Requirements
1. Prepare a Costs of Quality report. In addition to listing the costs by category, determine the percentage of the total costs of quality incurred in each cost category.
2. Do any additional subjective costs appear to be missing from the report?
3. What can be learned from the report?

E4-27A Classify costs and make a quality-initiative decision
(Learning Objective 5)

Clason Corp. manufactures radiation-shielding glass panels. Suppose Clason is considering spending the following amounts on a new TQM program:

Strength-testing one item from each batch of panels	$62,000
Training employees in TQM	$23,000
Training suppliers in TQM	$34,000
Identifying preferred suppliers that commit to on-time delivery of perfect quality materials	$51,000

Clason expects the new program to save costs through the following:

Avoid lost profits from lost sales due to disappointed customers	$85,000
Avoid rework and spoilage	$66,000
Avoid inspection of raw materials	$49,000
Avoid warranty costs	$25,000

Requirements
1. Classify each item as a prevention cost, an appraisal cost, an internal failure cost, or an external failure cost.
2. Should Clason implement the new quality program? Give your reason.

EXERCISES Group B

E4-28B Compare traditional and departmental cost allocations
(Learning Objective 1)

Davidson's Fine Furnishings manufactures upscale custom furniture. Davidson's currently uses a plantwide overhead rate, based on direct labor hours, to allocate its $1,100,000 of manufacturing overhead to individual jobs. However, Sam Davidson, owner and CEO, is considering refining the company's costing system by using departmental overhead rates. Currently, the Machining Department incurs $600,000 of manufacturing overhead while the Finishing Department incurs $500,000 of manufacturing overhead. Davidson has identified machine hours (MH) as the primary manufacturing overhead cost driver in the Machining Department and direct labor (DL) hours as the primary cost driver in the Finishing Department.

Davidson's plant completed Jobs 450 and 455 on May 15. Both jobs incurred a total of 5 DL hours throughout the entire production process. Job 450 incurred 1 MH in the Machining Department and 4 DL hours in the Finishing Department (the other DL hour occurred in the Machining Department). Job 455 incurred 7 MH in the Machining Department and 3 DL hours in the Finishing Department (the other two DL hours occurred in the Machining Department).

Requirements
1. Compute the plantwide overhead rate, assuming Bergeron's expects to incur 21,000 total DL hours during the year.
2. Compute departmental overhead rates, assuming Bergeron's expects to incur 14,500 MH in the Machining Department and 17,900 DL hours in the Finishing Department during the year.
3. If the company continues to use the plantwide overhead rate, how much manufacturing overhead would be allocated to Job 450 and Job 455?
4. If the company uses departmental overhead rates, how much manufacturing overhead would be allocated to Job 450 and Job 455?
5. Based on your answers to Requirements 3 and 4, does the plantwide overhead rate overcost or undercost either of the jobs? Explain. If the company sells its furniture at 125% of cost, will its choice of allocation systems affect product pricing? Explain.

E4-29B Compute activity rates and apply to jobs *(Learning Objective 2)*

Northstar Company uses ABC to account for its chrome wheel manufacturing process. Company managers have identified four manufacturing activities that incur manufacturing overhead costs: materials handling, machine setup, insertion of parts, and finishing. The budgeted activity costs for the upcoming year and their allocation bases are as follows:

Activity	Total Budgeted Manufacturing Overhead Cost	Allocation Base
Materials handling......................	$ 12,000	Number of parts
Machine setup.............................	3,400	Number of setups
Insertion of parts	48,000	Number of parts
Finishing	80,000	Finishing direct labor hours
Total...	$143,400	

Northstar expects to produce 1,000 chrome wheels during the year. The wheels are expected to use 3,000 parts, require 10 setups, and consume 2,000 hours of finishing time.

Job 420 used 150 parts, required 2 setups, and consumed 100 finishing hours.
Job 510 used 500 parts, required 4 setups, and consumed 310 finishing hours.

Requirements

1. Compute the cost allocation rate for each activity.
2. Compute the manufacturing overhead cost that should be assigned to Job 420.
3. Compute the manufacturing overhead cost that should be assigned to Job 510.

SUSTAINABILITY

E4-30B Apply activity cost allocation rates *(Learning Objective 2)*

Scannell Industries manufactures a variety of custom products. The company has traditionally used a plantwide manufacturing overhead rate based on machine hours to allocate manufacturing overhead to its products. The company estimates that it will incur $1,560,000 in total manufacturing overhead costs in the upcoming year and will use 13,000 machine hours.

Up to this point, hazardous waste disposal fees have been absorbed into the plantwide manufacturing overhead rate and allocated to all products as part of the manufacturing overhead process. Recently the company has been experiencing significantly increased waste disposal fees for hazardous waste generated by certain products and, as a result, profit margins on all products have been negatively impacted. Company management wants to implement an activity-based costing system so that managers know the cost of each product, including its hazardous waste disposal costs.

Expected usage and costs for manufacturing overhead activities for the upcoming year are as follows:

Description of Cost Pool	Estimated Cost	Cost Driver	Estimated Activity for this Year
Machine maintenance costs...........	$ 130,000	Number of machine hours	13,000
Engineering change orders............	240,000	Number of change orders	4,000
Hazardous waste disposal..............	1,190,000	Pounds of hazardous materials generated	3,500
Total overhead cost........................	$1,560,000		

During the year, Job 356 is started and completed. Usage data for this job are as follows:

270 pounds of direct materials at $60 per pound

50 direct labor hours used at $15 per labor hour

100 machine hours used

5 change orders

50 pounds of hazardous waste generated

Requirements

1. Calculate the cost of Job 356 using the traditional plantwide manufacturing overhead rate based on machine hours.
2. Calculate the cost of Job 356 using activity-based costing.
3. If you were a manager, which cost estimate would provide you more useful information? How might you use this information?

E4-31B   Using ABC to bill clients at a service firm *(Learning Objective 2)*

Farris & Company is an architectural firm specializing in home remodeling for private clients and new office buildings for corporate clients.

Farris charges customers at a billing rate equal to 129% of the client's total job cost. A client's total job cost is a combination of (1) professional time spent on the client ($65 per hour cost of employing each professional) and (2) operating overhead allocated to the client's job. Farris allocates operating overhead to jobs based on professional hours spent on the job. Farris estimates its five professionals will incur a total of 10,000 professional hours working on client jobs during the year.

All operating costs other than professional salaries (travel reimbursements, copy costs, secretarial salaries, office lease, and so forth) can be assigned to the three activities. Total activity costs, cost drivers, and total usage of those cost drivers are estimated as follows:

Activity	Total Activity Cost	Cost Driver	Total Usage by Corporate Clients	Total Usage by Private Clients
Transportation to clients	$ 10,500	Round-trip mileage to clients.........	6,000 miles	9,000 miles
Blueprint copying........................	35,000	Number of copies	550 copies	450 copies
Office support..............................	186,000	Secretarial time	2,300 secretarial hours	2,700 secretarial hours
Total operating overhead...........	$231,500			

Amy Leo hired Farris & Company to design her kitchen remodeling. A total of 27 professional hours were incurred on this job. In addition, Leo's remodeling job required one of the professionals to travel back and forth to her house for a total of 124 miles. The blueprints had to be copied four times because Leo changed the plans several times. In addition, 16 hours of secretarial time were used lining up the subcontractors for the job.

Requirements

1. Calculate the current operating overhead allocation rate per professional hour.
2. Calculate the amount that would be billed to Amy Leo given the current costing structure.
3. Calculate the activity cost allocation rates that could be used to allocate operating overhead costs to client jobs.
4. Calculate the amount that would be billed to Amy Leo using ABC costing.
5. Which type of billing system is more fair to clients? Explain.

E4-32B   Compare traditional and ABC cost allocations at a pharmacy *(Learning Objective 2)*

Werner Pharmacy, part of a large chain of pharmacies, fills a variety of prescriptions for customers. The complexity of prescriptions filled by Werner varies widely; pharmacists can spend between five minutes and six hours on a prescription order. Traditionally, the pharmacy has allocated its overhead based on the number of prescription in each order. For example, a customer may bring in three prescriptions to be filled on the same day; the pharmacy considers this to be one order.

The pharmacy chain's controller is exploring whether activity-based costing (ABC) may better allocate the pharmacy overhead costs to pharmacy orders. The controller has gathered the following information:

Cost Pools	Total Annual Estimated Cost	Cost Driver	Total Annual Estimated Cost Driver Activity
Pharmacy occupancy costs (utilities, rent, and other costs)	$ 96,000	Technician hours.....................	80,000
Packaging supplies (bottles, bags, and other packaging)...	35,000	Number of prescriptions	25,000
Professional training and insurance costs	96,000	Pharmacists hours	24,000
Total pharmacy overhead................................	$227,000		

The clerk for Werner Pharmacy has gathered the following information regarding two recent pharmacy orders:

Customer Order Number	Technician Hours	Number of Prescriptions	Pharmacist Hours
1102	0.5	5	2.0
1103	0.5	3	2.5

Requirements

1. What is the traditional overhead rate based on the number of prescriptions?
2. How much pharmacy overhead would be allocated to customer order number 1102 if traditional overhead allocation based on the number of prescriptions is used?
3. How much pharmacy overhead would be allocated to customer order number 1103 if traditional overhead allocation based on the number of prescriptions is used?
4. What are the following cost pool allocation rates?
   a. Pharmacy occupancy costs
   b. Packing supplies
   c. Professional training and insurance costs
5. How much would be allocated to customer order number 1102 if activity-based costing (ABC) is used to allocate the pharmacy overhead costs?
6. How much would be allocated to customer order number 1103 if activity-based costing (ABC) is used to allocate the pharmacy costs?
7. Which allocation method (traditional or activity-based costing) would produce a more accurate product cost? Explain your answer.

E4-33B Reassess product costs using ABC *(Learning Objective 2)*

James, Inc., manufactures only two products, Medium (42-inch) and Large (63-inch) TVs. To generate adequate profit and cover its expenses throughout the value chain, James prices its TVs at 300% of manufacturing cost. The company is concerned because the Large model is facing severe pricing competition, whereas the Medium model is the low-price leader in the market. The CEO questions whether the cost numbers generated by the accounting system are correct. The CEO just learned about ABC and wants to reanalyze this past year's product costs using an ABC system. Information about the company's products this past year is as follows:

> Medium (42-inch) TVs:
>
>   Total direct material cost: $663,000
>
>   Total direct labor cost: $221,000
>
>   Production volume: 3,020 units
>
> Large (63-inch) TVs:
>
>   Total direct material cost: $1,320,000
>
>   Total direct labor cost: $390,000
>
>   Production volume: 4,180 units

Currently, the company applies manufacturing overhead on the basis of direct labor hours. The company incurred $838,000 of manufacturing overhead this year, and 25,500 direct labor hours (9,500 direct labor hours making Medium TVs and 16,000 making Large TVs). The ABC team identified three primary production activities that generate manufacturing overhead costs:

> Materials Handling ($168,000); driven by number of material orders handled
>
> Machine Processing ($576,000); driven by machine hours
>
> Packaging ($94,000); driven by packaging hours

The company's only two products required the following activity levels during the year:

	Material Orders Handled	Machine Hours	Packaging Hours
Medium	360	20,200	4,120
Large	290	23,400	6,180

Requirements

1. Use the company's current costing system to find the total cost of producing all Medium (42-inch) TVs and the total cost of producing all Large (63-inch) TVs. What was the average cost of making each unit of each model? Round your answers to the nearest cent.
2. Use ABC to find the total cost of producing all Medium (42-inch) TVs and the total cost of producing all Large (63-inch) TVs. What was the average cost of making each unit of each model? Round your answers to the nearest cent.
3. How much cost distortion was occurring between the company's two products? Calculate the cost distortion in total and on a per unit basis. Could the cost distortion explain the CEO's confusion about pricing competition? Explain.

E4-34B   Use ABC to allocate manufacturing overhead (Learning Objective 2)

Several years after reengineering its production process, Trudell Corp. hired a new controller, Georgia Taylor. She developed an ABC system very similar to the one used by Trudell's chief rival. Part of the reason Taylor developed the ABC system was because Trudell's profits had been declining even though the company had shifted its product mix toward the product that had appeared most profitable under the old system. Before adopting the new ABC system, Trudell had used a plantwide overhead rate, based on direct labor hours developed years ago.

For the upcoming year, the company's budgeted ABC manufacturing overhead allocation rates are as follows:

Activity	Allocation Base	Activity Cost Allocation Rate
Materials handling.............................	Number of parts	$ 3.78 per part
Machine setup....................................	Number of setups	$305.00 per setup
Insertion of parts	Number of parts	$ 31.00 per part
Finishing	Finishing direct labor hours	$ 58.00 per hour

The number of parts is now a feasible allocation base because Trudell recently purchased bar-coding technology. Trudell produces two wheel models: Standard and Deluxe. Budgeted data for the upcoming year are as follows:

	Standard	Deluxe
Parts per wheel	6.0	8.0
Setups per 1,000 wheels...	10.0	10.0
Finishing direct labor hours per wheel......................................	1.2	3.2
Total direct labor hours per wheel	2.2	3.0

The company's managers expect to produce 1,000 units of each model during the year.

Requirements

1. Compute the total budgeted manufacturing overhead cost for the upcoming year.
2. Compute the manufacturing overhead cost per wheel of each model using ABC.
3. Compute the company's traditional plantwide overhead rate. Use this rate to determine the manufacturing overhead cost per wheel under the traditional system.

E4-35B Continuation of E4-34B   Determine product profitability

(Learning Objectives 2 & 3)

Refer to your answers in E4-34B. In addition to the manufacturing overhead costs, the following data are budgeted for the company's Standard and Deluxe models for next year:

	Standard	Deluxe
Sales price per wheel	$480.00	$650.00
Direct materials per wheel	$ 31.50	$ 47.75
Direct labor per wheel	$ 45.50	$ 50.00

Requirements

1. Compute the gross profit per wheel if managers rely on the ABC unit cost data.
2. Compute the gross profit per unit if the managers rely on the plantwide allocation cost data.
3. Which product line is more profitable for the company?
4. Why might the controller have expected ABC to pass the cost-benefit test? Were there any warning signs that the company's old direct-labor-based allocation system was broken?

E4-36B Differentiate between traditional and lean production (Learning Objective 4)

Categorize each of the following characteristics as being either more representative of a traditional organization or a lean organization.

1. Manufacturing plants tend to be organized with self-contained production cells.
2. Maintain greater quantities of raw materials, work in process, and finished goods inventories.
3. Setup times are longer.
4. High quality is stressed in every aspect of production.
5. Produce in smaller batches.
6. Emphasis is placed on shortening manufacturing cycle times.
7. Manufacturing plants tend to group like machinery together in different parts of the plant.
8. Setup times are shorter.
9. Produce in larger batches.
10. Strive to maintain low inventory levels.
11. Cycle time tends to be longer.
12. Quality tends to be "inspect-in" rather than "build-in."

E4-37B Prepare a Costs of Quality report (Learning Objective 5)

The CEO of Smith Snacks Corp. is concerned with the amount of resources currently spent on customer warranty claims. Each box of snacks is printed with the following logo: "Satisfaction guaranteed, or your money back." Since the number of claims is high, she would like to evaluate what costs are being incurred to ensure the quality of the product. The following information was collected from various departments within the company:

Warranty claims	$432,000
Cost of defective products found at the inspection point	$ 86,000
Training factory personnel	$ 34,000
Recall of Batch #59374	$171,000
Inspecting products when halfway through the production process	$ 42,000
Cost of disposal of rejected products	$ 14,000
Preventative maintenance on factory equipment	$ 6,000
Production loss due to machine breakdowns	$ 16,000
Inspection of raw materials	$ 5,000

Requirements

1. Prepare a Costs of Quality report. In addition to listing the costs by category, determine the percentage of the total costs of quality incurred in each cost category.
2. Do any additional subjective costs appear to be missing from the report?
3. What can be learned from the report?

E4-38B Classify costs and make a quality-initiative decision (Learning Objective 5)

Christianson Corp. manufactures radiation-shielding glass panels. Suppose the company is considering spending the following amounts on a new TQM program:

Strength-testing one item from each batch of panels	$68,000
Training employees in TQM	$24,000
Training suppliers in TQM	$33,000
Identifying preferred suppliers that commit to on-time delivery of perfect quality materials	$55,000

CHAPTER 4

The company expects the new program would save costs through the following:

Avoid lost profits from lost sales due to disappointed customers	$95,000
Avoid rework and spoilage	$67,000
Avoid inspection of raw materials	$50,000
Avoid warranty costs	$19,000

Requirements

1. Classify each item as a prevention cost, an appraisal cost, an internal failure cost, or an external failure cost.
2. Should the company implement the new quality program? Give your reason.

PROBLEMS Group A

P4-39A   Implementation and analysis of departmental rates *(Learning Objective 1)*

Teahen Products manufactures its products in two separate departments: Machining and Assembly. Total manufacturing overhead costs for the year are budgeted at $1,120,000. Of this amount, the Machining Department incurs $670,000 (primarily for machine operation and depreciation) while the Assembly Department incurs $450,000. The company estimates that it will incur 10,000 machine hours (all in the Machining Department) and 15,500 direct labor hours (3,500 in the Machining Department and 12,000 in the Assembly Department) during the year.

Teahen Products currently uses a plantwide overhead rate based on direct labor hours to allocate overhead. However, the company is considering refining its overhead allocation system by using departmental overhead rates. The Machining Department would allocate its overhead using machine hours (MH), but the Assembly Department would allocate its overhead using direct labor (DL) hours.

The following chart shows the machine hours (MH) and direct labor (DL) hours incurred by Jobs 500 and 501 in each production department:

	Machining Department	Assembly Department
Job 500	9 MH	15 DL hours
	4 DL hours	
Job 501	18 MH	15 DL hours
	4 DL hours	

Both Jobs 500 and 501 used $1,000 of direct materials. Wages and benefits total $25 per direct labor hour. Teahen Products prices its products at 110% of total manufacturing costs.

Requirements

1. Compute the company's current plantwide overhead rate.
2. Compute refined departmental overhead rates.
3. Which job (Job 500 or Job 501) uses more of the company's resources? Explain.
4. Compute the total amount of overhead allocated to each job if the company uses its current plantwide overhead rate.
5. Compute the total amount of overhead allocated to each job if the company uses departmental overhead rates.
6. Do both allocation systems accurately reflect the resources that each job used? Explain.
7. Compute the total manufacturing cost and sales price of each job using the company's current plantwide overhead rate.
8. Based on the current (plantwide) allocation system, how much profit did the company *think* it earned on each job? Based on the departmental overhead rates and the sales price determined in Requirement 7, how much profit did it *really* earn on each job?
9. Compare and comment on the results you obtained in Requirements 7 and 8.

P4-40A Use ABC to compute full product costs *(Learning Objective 2)*

Prescott Corp. manufactures computer desks in its Seville, Ohio, plant. The company uses activity-based costing to allocate all manufacturing conversion costs (direct labor and manufacturing overhead). Its activities and related data follow:

Activity	Budgeted Cost of Activity	Allocation Base	Cost Allocation Rate
Materials handling...................	$ 330,000	Number of parts	$ 0.70
Assembling...............................	$2,600,000	Direct labor hours	$16.00
Painting	$ 150,000	Number of painted desks	$ 5.10

Prescott produced two styles of desks in March: the Standard desk and the Unpainted desk. Data for each follow:

Product	Total Units Produced	Total Direct Materials Costs	Total Number of Parts	Total Assembling Direct Labor Hours
Standard desk	5,500	$99,000	118,500	5,700
Unpainted desk...............................	3,000	$18,000	28,500	1,000

Requirements

1. Compute the per-unit manufacturing product cost of Standard desks and Unpainted desks.

2. Premanufacturing activities, such as product design, were assigned to the Standard desks at $4 each and to the Unpainted desks at $3 each. Similar analyses were conducted of post-manufacturing activities, such as distribution, marketing, and customer service. The post-manufacturing costs were $23 per Standard and $22 per Unpainted desk. Compute the full product costs per desk.

3. Which product costs are reported in the external financial statements? Which costs are used for management decision making? Explain the difference.

4. What price should Prescott's managers set for Standard desks to earn a $41 profit per desk?

P4-41A Comprehensive ABC implementation *(Learning Objectives 2 & 3)*

Sawyer Pharmaceuticals manufactures an over-the-counter allergy medication called Breathe. Sawyer is trying to win market share from Sudafed and Tylenol. The company has developed several different Breathe products tailored to specific markets. For example, the company sells large commercial containers of 1,000 capsules to health-care facilities and travel packs of 20 capsules to shops in airports, train stations, and hotels.

Sawyer's controller, Sandra Dean, has just returned from a conference on ABC. She asks Kade Yackey, supervisor of the Breathe product line, to help her develop an ABC system. Dean and Yackey identify the following activities, related costs, and cost allocation bases:

Activity	Estimated Indirect Activity Costs	Allocation Base	Estimated Quantity of Allocation Base
Materials handling...........................	$180,000	Kilos	18,000 kilos
Packaging...	460,000	Machine hours	2,600 hours
Quality assurance	116,000	Samples	1,500 samples
Total indirect costs	$756,000		

The commercial-container Breathe product line had a total weight of 8,500 kilos, used 1,200 machine hours, and required 240 samples. The travel-pack line had a total weight of 6,000 kilos, used 400 machine hours, and required 340 samples. Sawyer produced 2,500 commercial containers of Breathe and 80,000 travel packs.

Requirements

1. Compute the cost allocation rate for each activity.
2. Use the activity-based cost allocation rates to compute the indirect cost of each unit of the commercial containers and the travel packs. (*Hint:* Compute the total activity costs allocated to each product line and then compute the cost per unit.)
3. The company's original single-allocation-based cost system allocated indirect costs to products at $350 per machine hour. Compute the total indirect costs allocated to the commercial containers and to the travel packs under the original system. Then compute the indirect cost per unit for each product.
4. Compare the activity-based costs per unit to the costs from the original system. How have the unit costs changed? Explain why the costs changed as they did.

P4-42A   Using ABC in conjunction with quality decisions
(Learning Objectives 2 & 5)

Robotic Construction Toys Corp. is using a costs-of-quality approach to evaluate design engineering efforts for a new toy robot. The company's senior managers expect the engineering work to reduce appraisal, internal failure, and external failure activities. The predicted reductions in activities over the two-year life of the toy robot follow. Also shown are the cost allocation rates for the activities.

Activity	Predicted Reduction in Activity Units	Activity Cost Allocation Rate per Unit
Inspection of incoming materials	305	$17
Inspection of finished goods	305	$31
Number of defective units discovered in-house	3,200	$16
Number of defective units discovered by customers	900	$36
Lost sales to dissatisfied customers	330	$61

Requirements

1. Calculate the predicted quality cost savings from the design engineering work.
2. The company spent $80,000 on design engineering for the new toy robot. What is the net benefit of this "preventive" quality activity?
3. What major difficulty would management have had in implementing this costs-of-quality approach? What alternative approach could they use to measure quality improvement?

P4-43A   Comprehensive ABC *(Learning Objectives 2 & 3)*

Halo Systems specializes in servers for work-group, e-commerce, and enterprise resource planning (ERP) applications. The company's original job cost system has two direct cost categories: direct materials and direct labor. Overhead is allocated to jobs at the single rate of $24 per direct labor hour.

A task force headed by Halo's CFO recently designed an ABC system with four activities. The ABC system retains the current system's two direct cost categories. Thus, it budgets only overhead costs for each activity. Pertinent data follow:

Activity	Allocation Base	Cost Allocation Rate
Materials handling	Number of parts	$ 0.90
Machine setup	Number of setups	$ 510.00
Assembling	Assembling hours	$ 70.00
Shipping	Number of shipments	$ 1,600.00

Halo Systems has been awarded two new contracts that will be produced as Job A and Job B. Budget data relating to the contracts follow:

	Job A	Job B
Number of parts	16,000	2,100
Number of setups	6	4
Number of assembling hours	1,600	220
Number of shipments	1	1
Total direct labor hours	9,000	700
Number of output units	100	10
Direct materials cost	$220,000	$40,000
Direct labor cost	$175,000	$18,000

Requirements

1. Compute the product cost per unit for each job using the original costing system (with two direct cost categories and a single overhead allocation rate).
2. Suppose Halo Systems adopts the ABC system. Compute the product cost per unit for each job using ABC.
3. Which costing system more accurately assigns to jobs the costs of the resources consumed to produce them? Explain.
4. A dependable company has offered to produce both jobs for Halo for $5,700 per output unit. Halo may outsource (buy from the outside company) Job A only, Job B only, or both jobs. Which course of action will Halo's managers take if they base their decision on (a) the original system? (b) ABC system costs? Which course of action will yield more income? Explain.

PROBLEMS Group B

P4-44B Implementation and analysis of departmental rates
(Learning Objective 1)

Percival Products manufactures its products in two separate departments: Machining and Assembly. Total manufacturing overhead costs for the year are budgeted at $1,090,000. Of this amount, the Machining Department incurs $650,000 (primarily for machine operation and depreciation) while the Assembly Department incurs $440,000. The company estimates it will incur 4,000 machine hours (all in the Machining Department) and 19,500 direct labor hours (3,500 in the Machining Department and 16,000 in the Assembly Department) during the year.

Percival currently uses a plantwide overhead rate based on direct labor hours to allocate overhead. However, the company is considering refining its overhead allocation system by using departmental overhead rates. The Machining Department would allocate its overhead using machine hours (MH), but the Assembly Department would allocate its overhead using direct labor (DL) hours.

The following chart shows the machine hours (MH) and direct labor (DL) hours incurred by Jobs 500 and 501 in each production department.

	Machining Department	Assembly Department
Job 500	5 MH	13 DL hours
	3 DL hours	
Job 501	10 MH	13 DL hours
	3 DL hours	

Both Jobs 500 and 501 used $1,800 of direct materials. Wages and benefits total $20 per direct labor hour. Percival prices its products at 125% of total manufacturing costs.

Requirements

1. Compute the company's current plantwide overhead rate.
2. Compute refined departmental overhead rates.
3. Which job (Job 500 or Job 501) uses more of the company's resources? Explain.
4. Compute the total amount of overhead allocated to each job if the company uses its current plantwide overhead rate.
5. Compute the total amount of overhead allocated to each job if the company uses departmental overhead rates.
6. Do both allocation systems accurately reflect the resources that each job used? Explain.
7. Compute the total manufacturing cost and sales price of each job using the company's current plantwide overhead rate.
8. Based on the current (plantwide) allocation system, how much profit did the company *think* it earned on each job? Based on the departmental overhead rates and the sales price determined in Requirement 7, how much profit did it *really* earn on each job?
9. Compare and comment on the results you obtained in Requirements 7 and 8.

P4-45B   Use ABC to compute full product costs (Learning Objective 2)

Russell Furniture manufactures computer desks in its Westlake, Ohio, plant. The company uses activity-based costing to allocate all manufacturing conversion costs (direct labor and manufacturing overhead). Its activities and related data follow:

Activity	Budgeted Cost of Activity	Allocation Base	Cost Allocation Rate
Materials handling.................	$ 320,000	Number of parts	$ 0.90
Assembling.............................	$2,400,000	Direct labor hours	$17.00
Painting	$ 180,000	Number of painted desks	$ 5.10

The company produced two styles of desks in March: the Standard desk and the Unpainted desk. Data for each follow:

Product	Total Units Produced	Total Direct Materials Costs	Total Number of Parts	Total Assembling Direct Labor Hours
Standard desk	5,500	$95,000	119,500	5,900
Unpainted desk..................	3,000	$23,000	29,500	600

Requirements

1. Compute the per-unit manufacturing product cost of Standard desks and Unpainted desks.
2. Premanufacturing activities, such as product design, were assigned to the Standard desks at $4 each and to the Unpainted desks at $3 each. Similar analyses were conducted of post-manufacturing activities such as distribution, marketing, and customer service. The post-manufacturing costs were $20 per Standard and $19 per Unpainted desk. Compute the full product costs per desk.
3. Which product costs are reported in the external financial statements? Which costs are used for management decision making? Explain the difference.
4. What price should management set for Standard desks to earn a $40 profit per desk?

P4-46B Comprehensive ABC implementation *(Learning Objectives 2 & 3)*

Gibson Pharmaceuticals manufactures an over-the-counter allergy medication called Breathe. Gibson is trying to win market share from Sudafed and Tylenol. The company has developed several different Breathe products tailored to specific markets. For example, the company sells large commercial containers of 1,000 capsules to health-care facilities and travel packs of 20 capsules to shops in airports, train stations, and hotels.

Gibson's controller, Arlene Pittinger, has just returned from a conference on ABC. She asks Kyle Yand, supervisor of the Breathe product line, to help her develop an ABC system. Pittinger and Yand identify the following activities, related costs, and cost allocation bases:

Activity	Estimated Indirect Activity Costs	Allocation Base	Estimated Quantity of Allocation Base
Materials handling.............................	$140,000	Kilos	14,000 kilos
Packaging..	410,000	Machine hours	2,100 hours
Quality assurance	116,000	Samples	1,500 samples
Total indirect costs	$666,000		

The commercial-container Breathe product line had a total weight of 8,200 kilos, used 900 machine hours, and 210 required samples. The travel-pack line had a total weight of 6,200 kilos, used 300 machine hours, and required 310 samples. The company produced 2,800 commercial containers of Breathe and 80,000 travel packs.

Requirements

1. Compute the cost allocation rate for each activity.
2. Use the activity-based cost allocation rates to compute the indirect cost of each unit of the commercial containers and the travel packs. (*Hint:* Compute the total activity costs allocated to each product line and then compute the cost per unit.)
3. The company's original single-allocation-based cost system allocated indirect costs to products at $450 per machine hour. Compute the total indirect costs allocated to the commercial containers and to the travel packs under the original system. Then, compute the indirect cost per unit for each product.
4. Compare the activity-based costs per unit to the costs from the simpler original system. How have the unit costs changed? Explain why the costs changed as they did.

P4-47B Using ABC in conjunction with quality decisions
(Learning Objectives 2 & 5)

Large Construction Toys Corporation is using a costs-of-quality approach to evaluate design engineering efforts for a new toy robot. The company's senior managers expect the engineering work to reduce appraisal, internal failure, and external failure activities. The predicted reductions in activities over the two-year life of the toy robot follow. Also shown are the cost allocation rates for the activities.

Activity	Predicted Reduction in Activity Units	Activity Cost Allocation Rate per Unit
Inspection of incoming materials	390	$20
Inspection of finished goods..	390	$32
Number of defective units discovered in-house.......................	3,500	$12
Number of defective units discovered by customers	900	$41
Lost sales to dissatisfied customers	290	$58

Requirements

1. Calculate the predicted quality cost savings from the design engineering work.
2. The company spent $65,000 on design engineering for the new toy robot. What is the net benefit of this "preventive" quality activity?
3. What major difficulty would management have had in implementing this costs-of-quality approach? What alternative approach could it use to measure quality improvement?

P4-48B   Comprehensive ABC *(Learning Objectives 2 & 3)*

Axis Systems specializes in servers for work-group, e-commerce, and enterprise resource planning (ERP) applications. The company's original job cost system has two direct cost categories: direct materials and direct labor. Overhead is allocated to jobs at the single rate of $22 per direct labor hour.

A task force headed by Axis's CFO recently designed an ABC system with four activities. The ABC system retains the current system's two direct cost categories. Thus, it budgets only overhead costs for each activity. Pertinent data follow:

Activity	Allocation Base	Cost Allocation Rate
Materials handling...	Number of parts	$ 0.85
Machine setup..	Number of setups	$ 500.00
Assembling..	Assembling hours	$ 80.00
Shipping	Number of shipments	$1,500.00

Axis Systems has been awarded two new contracts that will be produced as Job A and Job B. Budget data relating to the contracts follow:

	Job A	Job B
Number of parts...	15,000	2,000
Number of setups	6	4
Number of assembling hours...	1,500	200
Number of shipments	1	1
Total direct labor hours	8,000	600
Number of output units	100	10
Direct materials cost...	$210,000	$30,000
Direct labor cost..	$160,000	$12,000

Requirements

1. Compute the product cost per unit for each job using the original costing system (with two direct cost categories and a single overhead allocation rate).
2. Suppose Axis Systems adopts the ABC system. Compute the product cost per unit for each job using ABC.
3. Which costing system more accurately assigns to jobs the costs of the resources consumed to produce them? Explain.
4. A dependable company has offered to produce both jobs for Axis for $5,400 per output unit. Axis may outsource (buy from the outside company) Job A only, Job B only, or both jobs. Which course of action will Axis's managers take if they base their decision on (a) the original system? (b) ABC system costs? Which course of action will yield more income? Explain.

CRITICAL THINKING

Discussion & Analysis

A4-49 Discussion Questions

1. Explain why departmental overhead rates might be used instead of a single plantwide overhead rate.

2. Using activity-based costing, why are indirect costs allocated while direct costs are not allocated?

3. How can using a single predetermined manufacturing overhead rate based on a unit-level cost driver cause a high-volume product to be overcosted?

4. Assume a company uses a plantwide predetermined manufacturing overhead rate that is calculated using direct labor hours as the cost driver. The use of this plantwide predetermined manufacturing overhead rate has resulted in cost distortion. The company's high-volume products are overcosted and its low-volume products are undercosted. What effects of this cost distortion will the company most likely be experiencing? Why might the cost distortion be harmful to the company's competitive position in the market?

5. A hospital can use activity-based costing (ABC) for costing its services. In a hospital, what activities might be considered to be value-added activities? What activities at that hospital might be considered to be non-value-added?

6. A company makes shatterproof, waterproof cases for the S-series of Samsung smartphones. The company makes only one model and has been very successful in marketing its cases; no other company in the market has a similar product. The only customization available to the customer is the color of the case. There is no manufacturing cost difference among the different colors of the cases. Since this company has a high-volume product, its controller thinks that the company should adopt activity-based costing. Why might activity-based costing not be as beneficial for this company as for other companies?

7. Compare a traditional production system with a lean production system. Discuss the similarities and the differences.

8. Think of a product with which you are familiar. Explain how activity-based costing could help the company that makes this product in its efforts to be "green."

9. It has been said that external failure costs can be catastrophic and much higher than the other categories. What are some examples of external failure costs? Why is it often difficult to arrive at the cost of external failures?

10. What are the four categories of quality-related costs? Name a cost in each of the four categories for each of the following types of organizations:

    a. Restaurant
    b. Hospital
    c. Law firm
    d. Bank
    e. Tire manufacturer
    f. University

11. What are the similarities between sustainability and lean thinking? What are the differences between sustainability and lean thinking?

12. Why might a company want to take lean thinking a step further by including operations and methods associated with sustainability?

Application & Analysis

Mini Cases

A4-50 ABC in Real Companies

Choose a company in any of the following categories: airline, florist, bookstore, bank, grocery store, restaurant, college, retail clothing shop, movie theater, or lawn service. In this activity, you will be making reasonable estimates of the types of costs and activities associated with this company; companies do not typically publish internal cost or process information. Be reasonable in your cost estimates and include your assumptions used in selecting costs.

Basic Discussion Questions

1. Describe the company selected, including its products or services.
2. List eight key activities performed at this company. Choose at least one activity in the areas of production, sales, human resources, and accounting.
3. For each of the key activities, list a potential cost driver for that activity and describe why this cost driver would be appropriate for the associated activity.

A4-51 Value-Added vs. Non-Value-Added at a Restaurant

Go to a fast-food restaurant (or think of the last time you were at a fast-food restaurant.) Observe the steps involved in providing a meal to a customer. You will be watching for value-added steps and non-value-added steps. Answer the following questions.

Basic Discussion Questions

1. Describe the steps involved with delivering the meal to the customer that you can observe.
2. Describe the "behind-the-scenes" processes that are likely in the restaurant, such as cleaning, stocking, and cooking activities.
3. With your answers for Questions 1 and 2, list all of the possible activities, materials, and information that you think might be included on a value stream map for the restaurant. Include all of the steps you can think of (not necessarily only those you can observe).
4. Make a list of the eight wastes as denoted by the acronym DOWNTIME (Defects, Overproduction, Waiting, Not utilizing people to their full potential, Transportation, Inventory, Movement, and Excess processing.) Next to each waste category, list at least one possible non-value-added activity that might or might not be in the processes in that restaurant.
5. Go back to the list of items for the potential value stream map. Circle potential areas for improvement and explain which wastes might be involved in those areas.

ETHICS

A4-52 Ethics involved with ABC and hazardous waste costs
(Learning Objectives 2 & 3)

Sparkle Unlimited is a costume jewelry manufacturer located in the United States that uses electroplating. Electroplating is a process that involves applying a decorative metal coating to a base metal. The electroplating solution, or the water that is used in this process, becomes dirty over time and needs to be replaced. This used solution for electroplating is referred to as "spent" solution.

The spent solution contains dissolved metals such as gold, silver, platinum, copper, and other metals. Cyanide can also be present in the spent solution. Because of this content, spent solution is considered to be hazardous waste. This waste is more expensive to dispose of than regular waste.

Currently, Sparkle is using a traditional, volume-based costing system for its jewelry. Total manufacturing overhead for the period is allocated to the jewelry based on machine hours used.

Recently hired, Jacob is the controller for Sparkle. He previously worked at a manufacturer that produced custom furniture. At this prior job, he implemented an activity-based costing system that helped the company to determine the profitability of different product lines. He has been learning about Sparkle's operations and thinks activity-based costing might be a good tool for Sparkle's management to use to help to manage its operations.

Jacob's good friend, Michelle, is the division manager for the Silver line of jewelry at Sparkle. She runs an efficient production line and has earned bonuses for the each of the past several years based on her division's productivity and profitability. Division managers are evaluated based on profits generated by their divisions as calculated by the internal reporting system.

If activity-based costing is used to allocate costs and hazardous waste costs are allocated to the products that generate spent solutions, the calculated internal profit from the Silver product line will decrease significantly. This decrease in profitability is because the cost of handling the spent solution is quite high, and this cost would be directly assigned to the Silver line if activity-based costing were to be used.

Michelle takes Jacob out to lunch at an expensive restaurant and steers the conversation toward the upcoming activity-based costing implementation. She is concerned that her division's profits will decrease due to the spent-solution costs charged to her division. Michelle asks Jacob if he can reduce the amount of hazardous waste costs allocated to her line.

Jacob values the working relationship he has with Michelle. She is one of the people who has input on his evaluation when it comes time for raises and promotions. He wants to keep her happy.

As a result, Jacob does not set up any cost pool for hazardous waste disposal costs. Since the hazardous waste cost has always been part of the manufacturing process, he will continue to bury it in the other cost pools. His reasoning is that the activity-based costing system with hazardous waste removal cost buried is still better than the traditional cost system; other costs are properly allocated and the costs are much more accurate than under the old system. He feels that no one is getting hurt. Since the activity-based costing cannot be used for external reporting, Jacob feels that what he is doing is not illegal.

Requirements

Using the IMA *Statement of Ethical Professional Practice* (Exhibit 1-6) as an ethical framework, answer the following questions:

1. What is(are) the ethical issue(s) in this situation?
2. Activity-based costing cannot be used for external financial reporting. Does this fact influence your analysis of whether Jacob has violated any ethical principles? Why or why not?
3. Do you agree that no one is hurt by the burying of the hazardous waste costs into general cost pools? Explain.
4. What are Jacob's responsibilities as a management accountant? What should he do now?

A4-53 Lean production costs and sustainability *(Learning Objectives 4 & 5)*

REAL LIFE

Cal-Maine Foods, Inc., is the largest producer of shell eggs in the United States. In 2012, it sold approximately 884.3 million dozen shell eggs, which was approximately 19% of shell eggs sold domestically.[1] Walmart and Sam's Club (owned by the same parent) combined to account for almost one-third of Cal-Maine's net sales dollars in 2012.[2]

Per U.S. Department of Agriculture (USDA) regulations, every egg carton sold in the United States must be marked with information about the eggs inside the carton, including the eggs' grade, size, traceability code, and freshness date. The traceability code provides information about the egg farm, the region, and the specific building from which those eggs originate. This traceability information is necessary in case of health-related safety recalls (for example, salmonella outbreaks.)

If one egg in a carton is broken or damaged, the entire carton must be discarded due to USDA regulations. The reason that the entire carton has to be thrown away rather than replacing just one egg with an unbroken one is that the eggs in the carton all must be from the same exact batch with identical traceability codes and freshness dates. The consumer would have no guarantee that the replacement egg matches the other eggs in the carton.

It is estimated that as many as one in every ten dozen eggs is broken and the carton thrown away.[3] This breakage ratio (10%) means that of the 884.3 million dozen eggs sold by Cal-Maine Foods in 2012, over 88.4 million dozen eggs, or over a billion individual eggs, were discarded.

A Cal-Maine egg farm in Bushnell, Florida, in partnership with Walmart, two other suppliers, and the USDA, has developed a solution to significantly reduce the waste caused by egg

[1]Cal-Maine Foods, Inc., 2012 Annual Report, www.calmainefoods.com/investor_relations/financial_reports.htm
[2]Ibid.
[3]"The Secret Lives of Bees," YouTube video produced by Walmart, www.youtube.com/watch?v=jtVhhPQSKXg&feature=youtube_gdata_player

breakage. Organic laser ink is used to mark each egg individually with its grade, size, traceability code, and freshness date. Now instead of throwing away the entire carton of eggs when a broken egg is discovered, the broken egg can be replaced with another egg that has the same grade, size, traceability code, and freshness date.

If this program is successful, Walmart alone will save over half a billion eggs from being thrown away each year (the broken or damaged eggs will still be discarded). Other egg sellers will also have similar savings.

Requirements

1. Think about the value chain for a carton of eggs that is sold in the grocery store. (Start from the chicken and continue to the point of sale in the grocery store.) List as many steps in the value chain as you can imagine. At what points in the value chain does waste most likely occur?

2. In this chapter, the eight wastes of traditional operations were discussed. Which types of waste are in the value chain that you identified in Question 1?

3. Answer the following questions from the standpoint of Cal-Maine Foods, Inc., and its egg farms:

   a. What costs will be incurred to individually stamp each egg?

   b. What impact on revenue would the process of individually stamping each egg have?

   c. What wastes in the value chain occur at Cal-Maine Foods (and its egg farms)?

4. Now answer the following questions from the standpoint of Walmart:

   a. What costs might decrease as a result of purchasing eggs that are stamped individually with grade, size, traceability code, and freshness date information?

   b. What costs might increase as a result of purchasing individually stamped eggs?

   c. What wastes in the value chain occur at Walmart?

5. Who should bear the cost of the individual egg stamping operations: Cal-Maine Foods, Walmart, or the consumer? Because of the tremendous amount of waste involved with the current system of discarding entire cartons, should individual egg stamping be mandated by the government? Why or why not?

Try It Solutions

page 185:

1. Plantwide: $16 per DL hour × 5 DL hours = $80

2. Machining Dept.: $32 per DL hour × 3 DL hours = $96

   Assembly Dept.: $12 per DL hour × 2 DL hours = $24

   Total MOH $120

3. The plantwide overhead rate undercosts the job by $40 (= $120 − $80).

page 207:

2, 3, 5, 7.

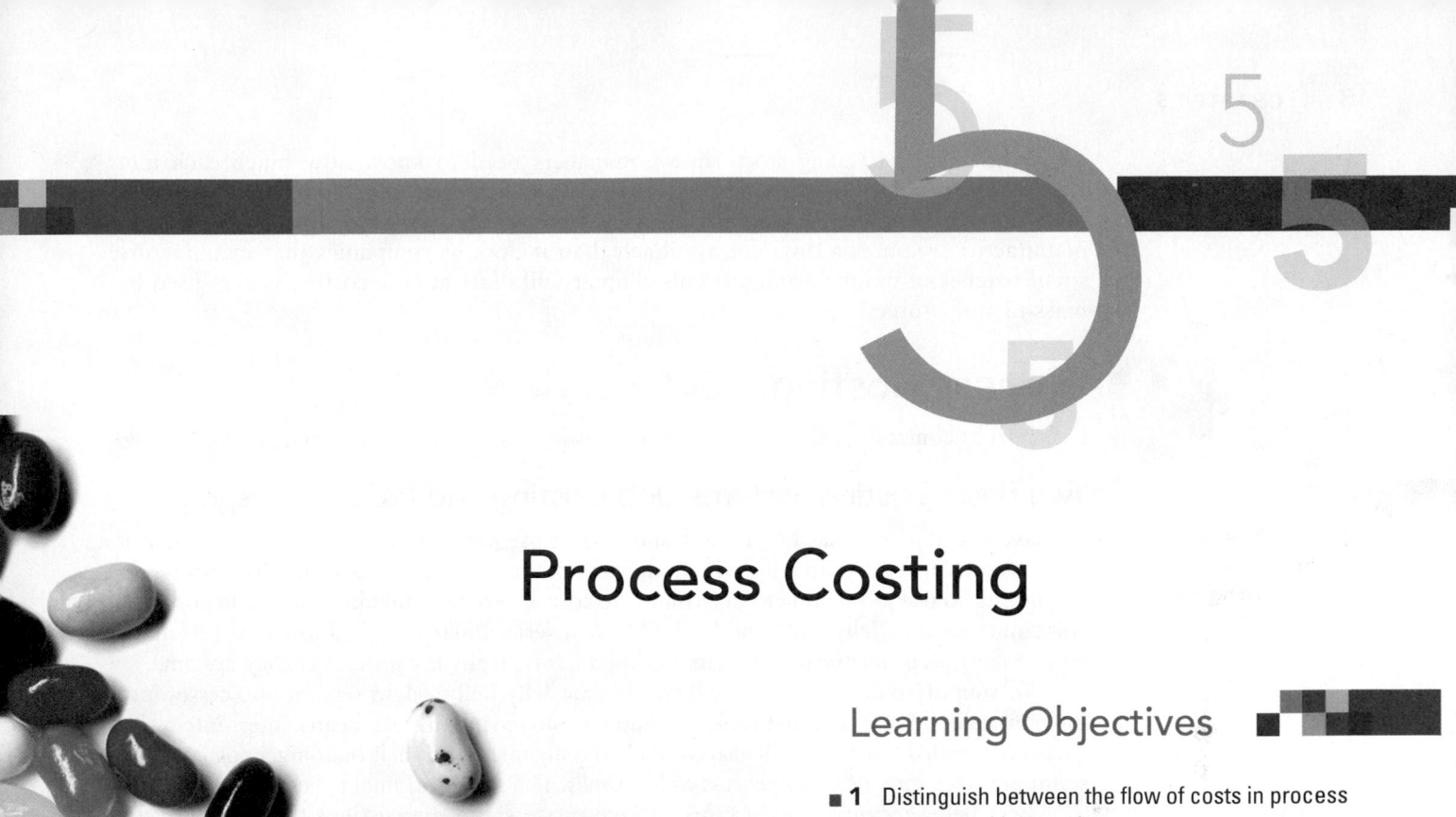

Peter Coombs/Alamy

Source: http://jellybelly.com

Process Costing

Learning Objectives

- **1** Distinguish between the flow of costs in process costing and job costing
- **2** Compute equivalent units
- **3** Use process costing in the first production department
- **4** Prepare journal entries for a process costing system
- **5** Use process costing in a second or later production department

What's your favorite Jelly Belly flavor? Chocolate Pudding? Peanut

Butter? Or maybe Piña Colada? Have you ever wondered how these tasty gems are made? Each tiny Jelly Belly jelly bean spends seven to ten days going through eight different production processes: (1) Cooking the centers; (2) Shaping hot liquid centers into jelly beans; (3) Drying; (4) Sugar shower; (5) Shell-building; (6) Polishing; (7) Stamping the name of the company on each bean; and (8) Packaging. Since Jelly Belly mass produces its jelly beans, the accounting system it uses to find the cost of making each pound of jelly beans differs from the job costing system Life Fitness uses. Jelly Belly uses process costing to separately measure the manufacturing costs incurred in each of the eight production processes. Next, the company spreads these costs over the pounds of jelly beans that passed through each process during the month. By doing so, Jelly Belly is able to calculate the average cost of making a pound of jelly beans in each process, as well as the average cost of making a pound of jelly beans, from start to finish. Jelly Belly's managers use this information to measure profits and make business decisions. They also use this information to determine how efficiently each process is operating in order to control costs.

As the chapter-opening story shows, managers need to know how much each unit of their product costs to make. Why? So they can control costs, set selling prices, and make profitable business decisions. But finding unit cost at companies that mass-manufacture requires a different approach than it does at companies that manufacture small batches of unique products. This chapter will illustrate the costing system used by mass-manufacturers.

Process Costing: An Overview

Let's start by contrasting the two basic types of costing systems: *job costing* and *process costing*.

Two Basic Costing Systems: Job Costing and Process Costing

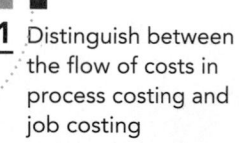

1 Distinguish between the flow of costs in process costing and job costing

We saw in Chapter 3 that Life Fitness and Boeing use job costing to determine the cost of producing unique goods in relatively small batches. Service companies such as law firms and hospitals also use job costing to determine the cost of serving individual clients. In contrast, companies such as Jelly Belly and Shell Oil use a series of steps (called *processes*) to make large quantities of identical units. These companies typically use *process costing* systems.

To simplify our discussion, we'll consolidate Jelly Belly's eight separate processes into three processes. We'll combine cooking, shaping, and drying the jelly bean centers into a single process called *Centers*. We'll also combine the sugar shower, shell-building, polishing, and stamping steps into a second process called *Shells*. The third and final process is *Packaging*.

Jelly Belly *accumulates* the costs of each process and then *assigns* these costs to the units (pounds of jelly beans) passing through that process.

Suppose the Centers process incurs $1,350,000 of costs to produce centers for 1,000,000 pounds of jelly beans, the Shells process incurs $800,000, and Packaging incurs $700,000. The total cost to produce a pound of jelly beans is the sum of the cost per pound for each of the three processes.

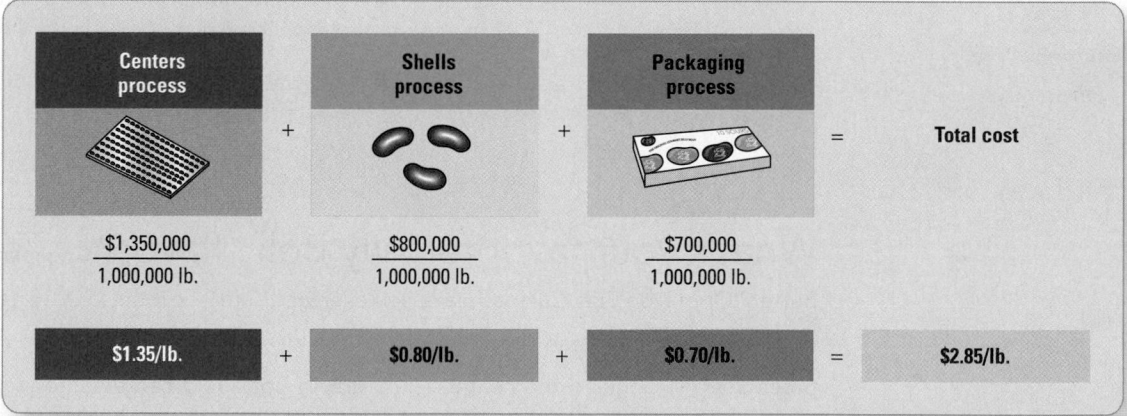

Jelly Belly's owners use the cost per pound of each process to help control costs. For example, they can compare the actual cost of producing centers for a pound of jelly beans (assumed to be $1.35 in our example) to the budget or plan. If the actual cost of the Centers process exceeds the budget, they can look for ways to cut costs in that process. Jelly Belly's owners also consider the total cost of making a pound of jelly beans (assumed to be $2.85 in our example) when setting selling prices. The price should be high enough to cover costs *and* to return a profit. Jelly Belly also uses the total cost of making a pound of jelly beans for financial reporting:

- To value the ending inventory of jelly beans for the balance sheet ($2.85 per pound still in ending inventory)

- To value the cost of goods sold for the income statement ($2.85 per pound sold)

The simple computation of the cost to make a pound of jelly beans is correct *only if there are no work in process inventories*, but it takes 7 to 10 days to complete all of the processes. So, Jelly Belly *does* have inventories of partially complete jelly beans. These inventories make the costing more complicated. In the rest of this chapter, you'll learn how to use process costing when there are work in process inventories.

How Does the Flow of Costs Differ Between Job and Process Costing?

Exhibit 5-1 compares the flow of costs in

- a job costing system for Life Fitness (Panel A), and
- a process costing system for Jelly Belly (Panel B).

EXHIBIT 5-1 Flow of Costs in Job Costing (Panel A) and Process Costing (Panel B)

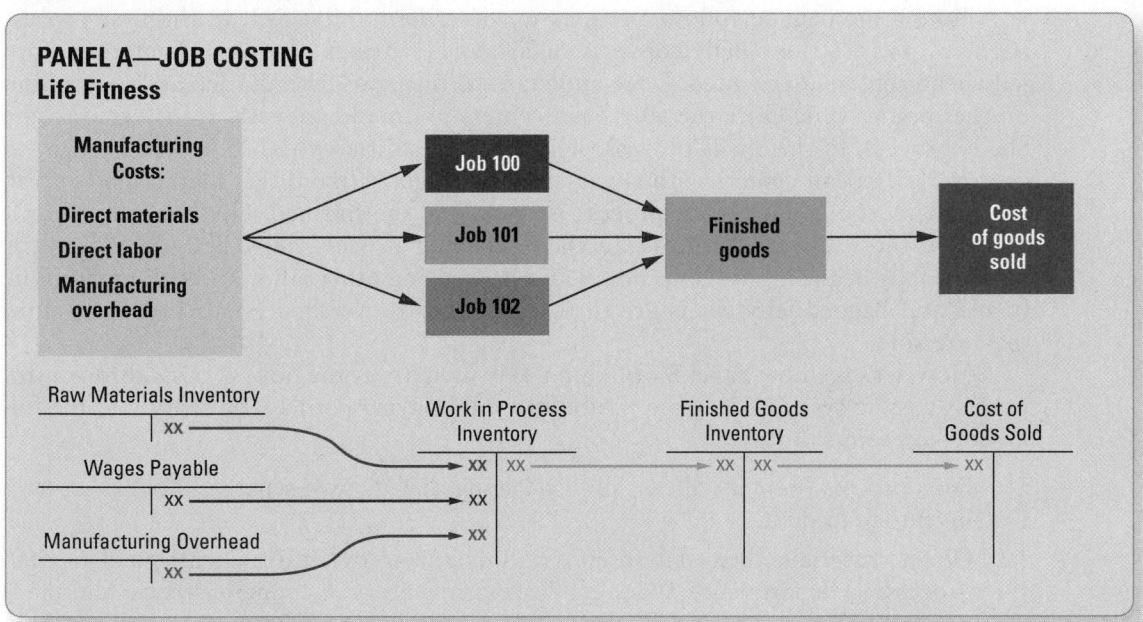

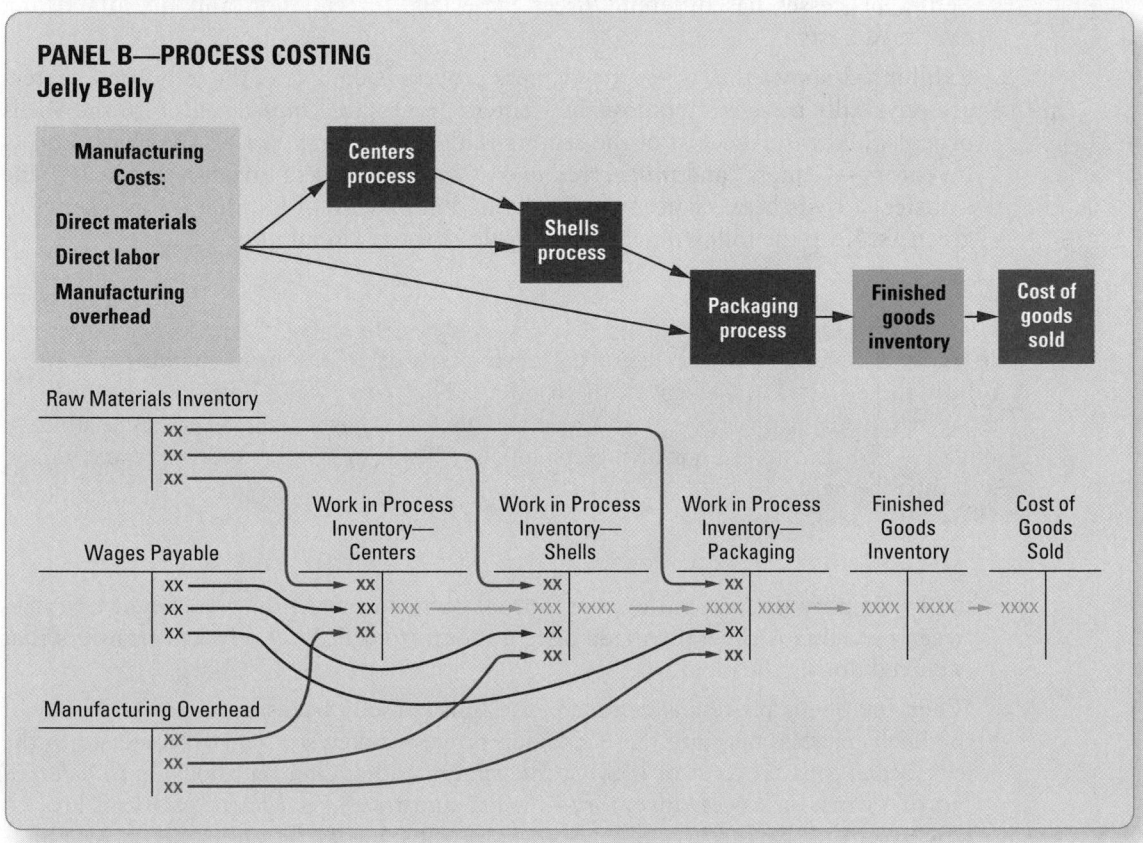

Panel A shows that Life Fitness's job costing system has a single Work Process Inventory control account supported by individual job cost records for each job that is being worked on. Life Fitness assigns direct materials, direct labor, and manufacturing overhead to individual jobs, as explained in Chapter 3. When a job is finished, its costs flow directly into Finished Goods Inventory. When the job is sold, the cost flows out of Finished Goods Inventory and into Cost of Goods Sold.

In contrast to Life Fitness's individual jobs, Jelly Belly uses a series of three *manufacturing processes* to produce jelly beans. The movement of jelly beans through these three processes is shown in Exhibit 5-2.

Take a moment to follow along as we describe Exhibit 5-2. In the first process (Centers process) Jelly Belly converts sugar and flavorings (the direct materials) into jelly bean centers using direct labor and manufacturing overhead, such as depreciation on the mixing vats. Once the jelly bean centers are made, they are transferred to the Shells process. In the Shells process, Jelly Belly uses different labor and equipment to coat the jelly bean centers with sugar, syrup, and glaze (the direct materials) to form the crunchy shells. Once that process is complete, the finished jelly beans are transferred to the Packaging process. In the Packaging process, Jelly Belly packages the finished jelly beans into various boxes and bags, using other labor and equipment. The boxed and bagged jelly beans are then transferred to finished goods inventory until they are sold.

Now, let's see how Panel B of Exhibit 5-1 summarizes the flow of costs through this process costing system. Study the exhibit carefully, paying particular attention to the following key points:

1. Each process (Centers, Shells, and Packaging) has its own separate Work in Process Inventory account.

2. Direct materials, direct labor, and manufacturing overhead are assigned to *each* processing department's Work in Process Inventory account based on the manufacturing costs incurred by that process. Exhibit 5-2 shows that each of Jelly Belly's processes has different direct materials, direct labor, and manufacturing overhead costs.

3. Exhibit 5-2 shows that when the Centers process is complete, the jelly bean centers are physically *transferred out* of the Centers process and *transferred in* to the Shells process. Likewise, the *cost* of the centers is also *transferred out* of "Work in Process Inventory—Centers" and *transferred in* to "Work in Process Inventory—Shells." The transfer of costs between accounts is pictured in Panel B of Exhibit 5-1 as a series of green *xs*. Keep the following important rule of thumb in mind:

> In process costing, the manufacturing costs assigned to the product must always follow the physical movement of the product. Therefore, when units are physically transferred out of one process and into the next, the *costs* assigned to those units must *also* be transferred out of the appropriate Work in Process Inventory account and into the next.

To simplify the accounting, the journal entry to record the transfer of costs between accounts is generally made once a month to reflect *all* physical transfers that occurred during the month.

4. When the Shells process is complete, the finished jelly beans are transferred out of the Shells process and into the Packaging process. Likewise, the *cost* assigned to the jelly beans thus far (cost of making the centers and adding the shells) is *transferred out* of "Work in Process Inventory—Shells" and *transferred in* to "Work in Process Inventory—Packaging."

EXHIBIT 5-2 Flow of Costs in Production of Jelly Beans

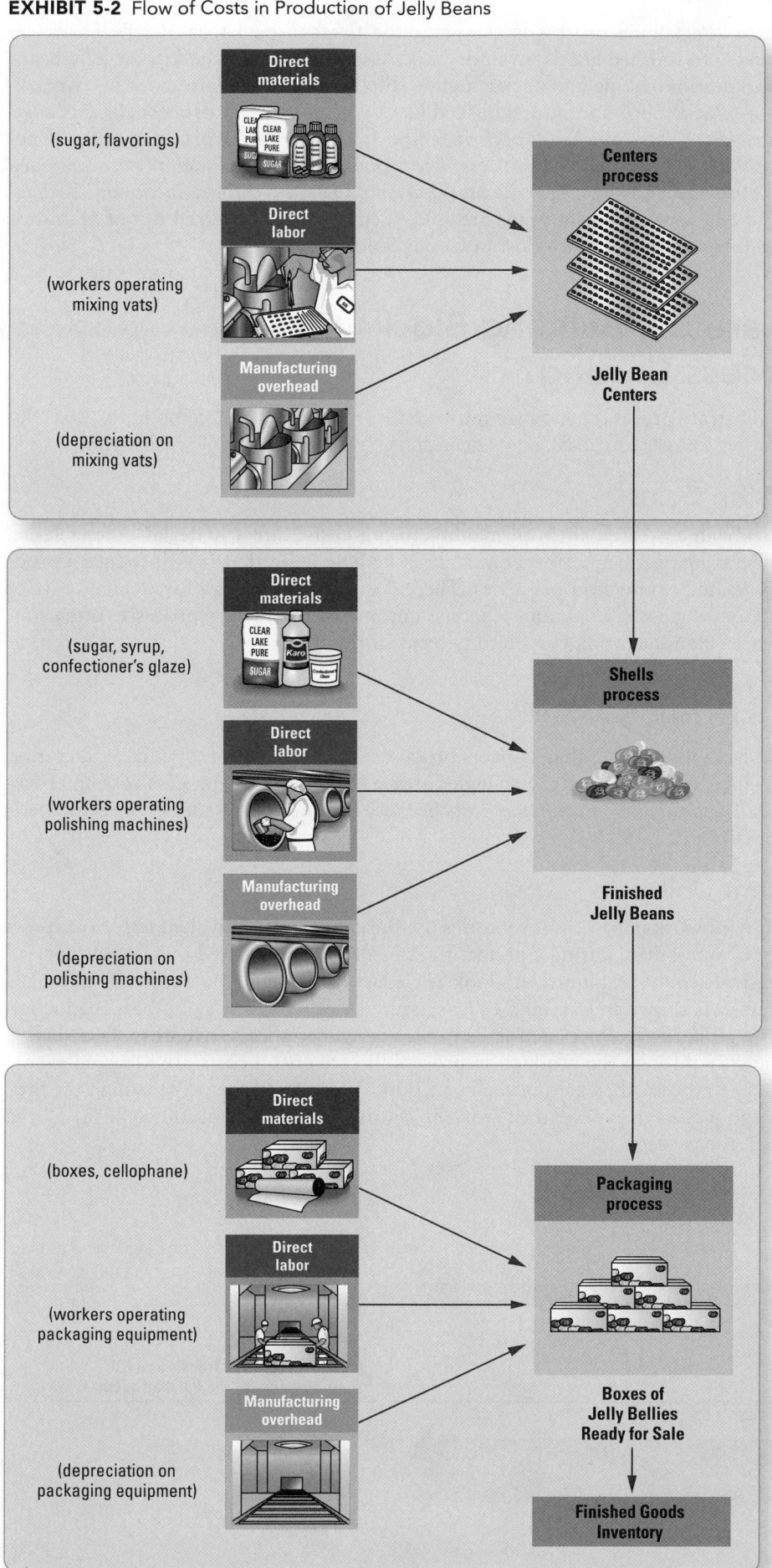

5. When the Packaging process is complete, the finished packages of jelly beans are transferred to finished goods inventory. Likewise, the *cost* assigned to the jelly beans thus far (cost of making and packaging the jelly beans) is transferred out of "Work in Process—Packaging" and into "Finished Goods Inventory." *In process costing, costs are transferred into Finished Goods Inventory only from the Work in Process Inventory of the last manufacturing process. The transferred cost includes all costs assigned to the units from every process the units have completed (Centers, Shells, and Packaging).* Finally, when the jelly beans are sold, their cost is transferred out of "Finished Goods Inventory" and into "Cost of Goods Sold."

What are the Building Blocks of Process Costing?

Before we illustrate process costing we must first learn about the three building blocks of process costing: conversion costs, equivalent units, and inventory flow assumptions.

Conversion Costs

Chapter 2 introduced three kinds of manufacturing costs: direct materials, direct labor, and manufacturing overhead. Most companies, like Jelly Belly, that mass-produce a product use automated production processes. Therefore, direct labor is only a small part of total manufacturing costs. Companies that use automated production processes often condense the three manufacturing costs into two categories:

1. Direct materials
2. Conversion costs

Recall from Chapter 2 that conversion costs are direct labor plus manufacturing overhead. Combining these costs in a single category simplifies the process costing procedures. We call this category *conversion costs* because it is the cost to *convert* direct materials into new finished products.

Equivalent Units

2 Compute equivalent units

Companies with work in process inventories use the concept of **equivalent units** to express the amount of work done during a period in terms of fully completed units of output.

To illustrate equivalent units, let's look at Callaway Golf, a manufacturer of golf balls and golf clubs. As shown in Exhibit 5-3, let's assume that Callaway's golf ball production plant has 5,000 partially completed balls in ending work process inventory. Each ball is 80% of the way through the production process. If conversion costs are incurred evenly throughout the process, then getting each of 5,000 balls 80% of the way through the process takes about the same amount of work as getting 4,000 balls (5,000 × 80%) all the way through the process.

EXHIBIT 5-3 Callaway Production Plant Time Line

Conversion costs added evenly throughout production process	

Start — Rubber added ... 80% complete ... Packaging added ... 100% completion ... Transferred OUT to finished goods

5,000 golf balls started but not finished

Equivalent units are calculated as follows:

Number of physical units × Percentage of completion = Number of equivalent units

So, the number of equivalent units of conversion costs in Callaway's ending work process inventory is calculated as follows:

$$5,000 \times 80\% = 4,000$$

Conversion costs are usually incurred *evenly* throughout production. However, direct materials are often added at a particular point in the process. For example, Callaway adds rubber at the *beginning* of the production process, but doesn't add packaging materials until the *end*. How many equivalent units of rubber and packaging materials are in the ending inventory of 5,000 balls?

All 5,000 balls are 80% complete, so they all have passed the point at which rubber is added. Each ball has its full share of rubber (100%), so the balls have 5,000 equivalent units of rubber. In contrast, the time line in Exhibit 5-3 shows that *none* of the 5,000 balls has made it to the end of the process, where the packaging materials are added. The ending inventory, therefore, has *zero* equivalent units of packaging materials.

To summarize, the 5,000 balls in ending work in process inventory have the following:

- 5,000 equivalent units of rubber (5,000 units × 100% of rubber)
- 0 equivalent units of packaging materials (5,000 units × 0% of packaging materials)
- 4,000 equivalent units of conversion costs (5,000 units × 80% converted)

▶ **Try It!**

Dairymaid makes organic yogurt. The only ingredients, milk and bacteria cultures, are added at the very beginning of the fermentation process. At month end, Dairymaid has 100,000 cups of yogurt that are only 25% of the way through the fermentation process. Use the equivalent unit formula to answer the following:

a. How many equivalent units of direct materials are in ending work in process?

b. How many equivalent units of conversion costs are in ending work in process?

Please see page 308 for solutions.

Inventory Flow Assumptions

Firms compute process costing using either the weighted-average or first-in, first-out (FIFO) method. Throughout the rest of the chapter, we will use the **weighted-average method of process costing** rather than the FIFO method because it is simpler and the differences between the two methods' results are usually immaterial. *The two costing methods differ only in how they treat beginning inventory.* The FIFO method, which is explained in advanced cost accounting textbooks, requires that any units in beginning inventory be costed *separately* from any units started in the current period. The weighted-average method *combines* any beginning inventory units (and costs) with the current period's units (and costs) to get a weighted-average cost. From a cost-benefit standpoint, many firms prefer to use the weighted-average method because the extra cost of calculating the FIFO method does not justify the additional benefits they gain from using FIFO information.

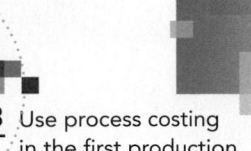

How Does Process Costing Work in the First Processing Department?

3 Use process costing in the first production department

To illustrate process costing, we'll be following SeaView, a manufacturer that mass-produces swim masks. We'll see how SeaView uses the weighted-average method of process costing to measure (1) the average cost of producing each swim mask and (2) the cost of the two major processes it uses to make the masks (Shaping and Insertion).

Exhibit 5-4 illustrates SeaView's production process. The Shaping Department begins with plastic and metal fasteners (direct materials) and uses labor and equipment (conversion costs) to transform the materials into shaped masks. The direct materials are added at the *beginning* of the process, but conversion costs are incurred *evenly* throughout the process. After shaping, the masks move to the Insertion Department, where the shaped masks are polished and then the clear faceplates are inserted.

EXHIBIT 5-4 SeaView's Production Process

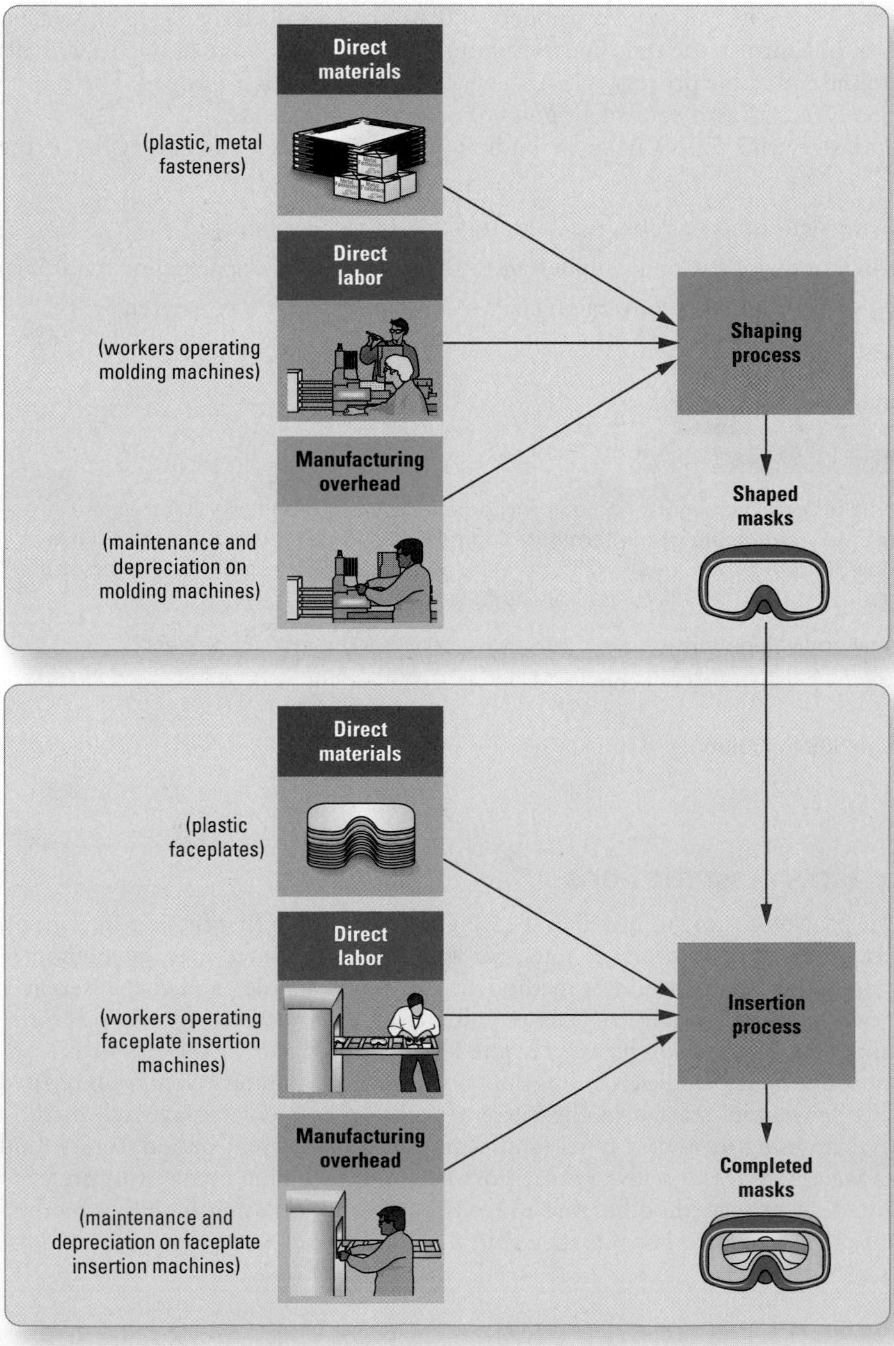

Let's assume that the Shaping Department begins October with no work process inventory. During October, the Shaping Department incurs the following costs while working on 50,000 masks:

Beginning work in process inventory...		$ 0
Direct materials...		140,000
Conversion costs:		
Direct labor	$21,250	
Manufacturing overhead...	46,750	
Total conversion costs		68,000
Total costs to account for...		$208,000

How did SeaView arrive at these costs? SeaView traces direct materials and direct labor to each processing department using materials requisitions and labor time records (just as we used these documents to trace direct materials and direct labor to individual *jobs* in Chapter 3). SeaView allocates manufacturing overhead to each processing department using either a plantwide rate, departmental overhead rates, or ABC (just as we allocated manufacturing overhead to individual *jobs* in Chapters 3 and 4).

If, at the end of October, all 50,000 masks have been completely shaped and transferred out of the Shaping Department and into the Insertion Department, the entire $208,000 of manufacturing cost associated with these masks should *likewise* be transferred out of "Work in Process—Shaping" and into "Work in Process—Insertion." In this case, the unit cost for *just* the shaping process is $4.16 per mask ($208,000/50,000 masks).

But what if only 40,000 masks are completely through the shaping process? Let's say that at October 31, the Shaping Department still has 10,000 masks that are only one-quarter of the way through the shaping process. How do we split the $208,000 between the following?

- 40,000 completely shaped masks transferred to the Insertion Department
- 10,000 partially shaped masks remaining in the Shaping Department's ending work process inventory

In other words, how do we determine the cost of making the *completely* shaped masks versus the cost of making the *partially* shaped masks? We can't simply assign $4.16 to each mask because a partially shaped mask does *not* cost the same to make as a completely shaped mask. To figure out the cost of making a *completely* shaped mask versus a *partially* shaped mask, we must use the following five-step process costing procedure:

STEP 1. Summarize the flow of physical units.

STEP 2. Compute output in terms of equivalent units.

STEP 3. Summarize total costs to account for.

STEP 4. Compute the cost per equivalent unit.

STEP 5. Assign total costs to units completed and to units in ending Work in Process inventory.

Step 1: Summarize the Flow of Physical Units

Step 1 tracks the physical movement of swim masks into and out of the Shaping Department during the month. Follow along as we walk through this step in the first column of Exhibit 5-5. The first question addressed is this: *How many physical units did the Shaping Department work on during the month?* Recall that the Shaping Department had no masks in the beginning work process inventory. During the month, the Shaping Department began work on 50,000 masks. Thus, the department needs to account for a *total* of 50,000 masks.

EXHIBIT 5-5 Step 1: Summarize the Flow of Physical Units
Step 2: Compute Output in Terms of Equivalent Units

	A	B	C	D
	Sea View Shaping Department	**Step 1:**	**Step 2: Equivalent Units**	
1	**Month Ended October 31**	**Flow of Physical**	**Direct**	**Conversion**
2	**Flow of Production**	**Units**	**Materials**	**Costs**
3	**Units to account for:**			
4	Beginning work in process, October 1	0		
5	Plus: Started in production during October	50,000		
6	Total physical units to account for	50,000		
7				
8	**Units accounted for:**			
9	Completed and transferred out during October	40,000	40,000	40,000
10	Plus: Ending work in process, October 31	10,000	10,000	2,500
11	Total physical units accounted for	50,000		
12	**Total equivalent units**		50,000	42,500
13				

The second question addressed is this: *What happened to those masks?* The Shaping Department reports that it completed and transferred out 40,000 masks to the Insertion Department during October. The remaining 10,000 partially shaped masks are still in the Shaping Department's ending work in process inventory on October 31. Notice that the *total physical units to account for* (50,000) must equal the *total physical units accounted for* (50,000). In other words, the Shaping Department must account for the whereabouts of every mask it worked on during the month.

Step 2: Compute Output in Terms of Equivalent Units

Step 2 computes all of the Shaping Department's output for the month in terms of equivalent units. Step 2 is shown in the last two columns of Exhibit 5-5. First, let's consider the 40,000 masks that were *completed and transferred out* to the Insertion Department during October. These units have been fully completed in the Shaping Department; therefore, they are 100% complete with respect to both direct materials and conversion. Equivalent units for these physical units are calculated as follows:

Number of Physical Units	×	Percentage of Completion	= Equivalent units
40,000	×	100%	= 40,000 equivalent units of direct materials
40,000	×	100%	= 40,000 equivalent units of conversion costs

Now, let's consider the 10,000 masks still in ending work in process. These masks are only 25% of the way through the shaping process on October 31. The time line in Exhibit 5-6 reminds us that all direct materials are added at the *beginning* of the shaping process. Therefore, the partially shaped masks have made it past the point where direct materials are added. As a result, the equivalent units for direct materials are as follows:

Number of Physical Units × Percentage of Completion = Equivalent units		
10,000	× 100%	= 10,000 equivalent units of direct materials

Unlike direct materials, the conversion costs are added *evenly* throughout the shaping process. For these partially shaped masks, the equivalent units of conversion costs are calculated as follows:

Number of Physical Units × Percentage of Completion = Equivalent units		
10,000	× 25%	= 2,500 equivalent units of conversion costs

Our last step is to calculate the Shaping Department's output in terms of *total equivalent units* for the month. We must calculate totals separately for direct materials and conversion costs because they will differ in most circumstances. To find the totals, we simply add the equivalent units of all masks worked on during the month. As shown in Exhibit 5-5, the *total equivalent units of direct materials* (50,000) is simply the sum of the 40,000 equivalent units completed and transferred out *plus* the 10,000 equivalent units still in ending work in process (WIP). Likewise, the *total equivalent units of conversion costs* (42,500) is the sum of the 40,000 equivalent units completed and transferred out plus the 2,500 equivalent units still in ending work in process.

EXHIBIT 5-6 SeaView's Shaping Department Time Line

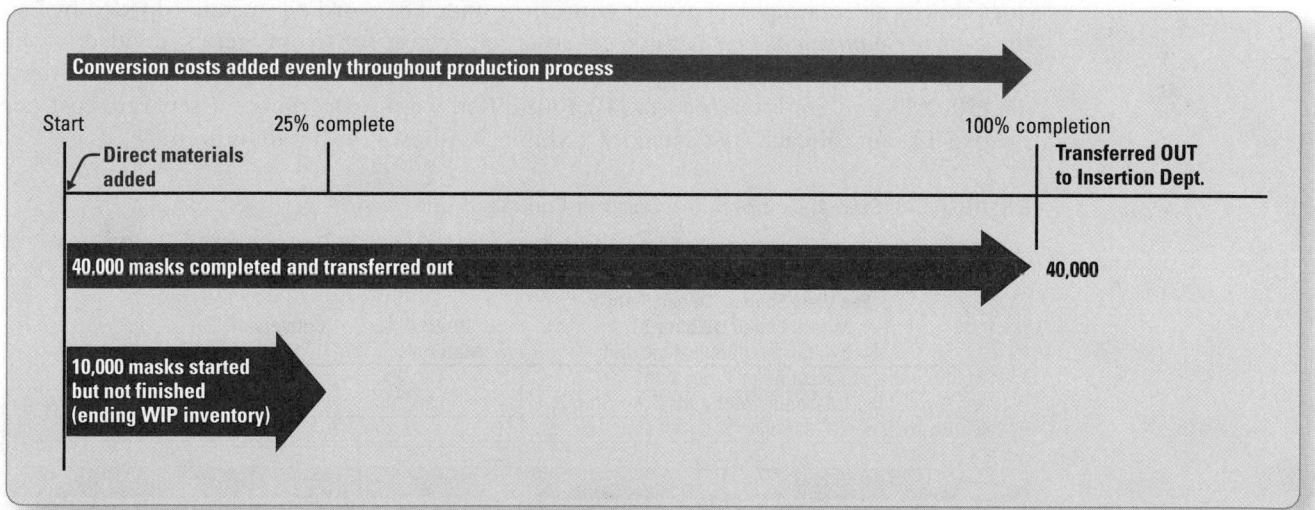

![STOP & THINK]

Suppose the Shaping Department adds 90% of the direct materials at the beginning of the process and 10% at the very end of the process. If there are 10,000 masks in ending work in process, and they are 25% of the way through the process, how many equivalent units of direct materials are in ending work in process?

Answer: Because the masks are only 25% of the way through the process, they have not reached the point where 10% of the materials is added. They have only received the 90% of materials added at the beginning of the process. Therefore, there are 9,000 (= 10,000 × 90%) equivalent units of direct materials in ending work in process.

Step 3: Summarize Total Costs to Account For

Step 3, as shown in Exhibit 5-7, summarizes all of the production costs the Shaping Department must account for. These are the production costs associated with beginning inventory (if any existed) plus the production costs that were incurred during the month.[1]

EXHIBIT 5-7 Step 3: Summarize Total Costs to Account For

	A	B	C	D
1	**Sea View Shaping Department** **Month Ended October 31** **Step 3: Total Costs to Account For**	**Direct Materials**	**Conversion Costs**	**Total**
2	Beginning work in process, October 1	$ 0	$ 0	$ 0
3	Plus: Costs added during October	140,000	68,000	$ 208,000
4	Total costs to account for	$ 140,000	$ 68,000	$ 208,000
5				

NOTE: Conversion costs of $68,000 = $21,250 of direct labor plus $46,750 of MOH

Once again, we must show separate totals for each of the two cost categories: direct materials and conversion costs. Because the Shaping Department did not have any beginning inventory of partially shaped masks, the beginning balance in the "Work Process Inventory—Shaping" account is zero. As shown on page 254, during the month, the Shaping Department used $140,000 of direct materials and $68,000 of conversion costs ($21,250 of direct labor plus $46,750 of manufacturing overhead).

Step 4: Compute the Cost per Equivalent Unit

Remember that one of the primary goals of process costing is to average the cost of the production process over the units that pass through the process during the month. Step 4 does this by calculating the cost per equivalent unit. The word *per* means "divided by," so the *cost per equivalent unit* is the *total costs to account for* (from Step 3) divided by the *total equivalent units* (from Step 2). Because the total equivalent units for direct materials (50,000) and conversion costs (42,500) differ, we must compute a separate cost per equivalent unit for each cost category. Exhibit 5-8 shows the computations.

EXHIBIT 5-8 Step 4: Compute the Cost per Equivalent Unit

	A	B	C	D
1	**Sea View Shaping Department** **Month Ended October 31** **Step 4: Cost per Equivalent Unit**	**Direct Materials**	**Conversion Costs**	
2	Total costs to account for (from Step 3)	$ 140,000	$ 68,000	
3	Divided by: Total equivalent units (from Step 2)	50,000	42,500	
4	Cost per equivalent unit	$ 2.80	$ 1.60	
5				

What do these figures mean? During October, SeaView's Shaping Department incurred an average of $2.80 of direct materials cost and $1.60 of conversion costs to completely shape the equivalent of one mask. In addition to using the cost per equivalent unit in the five-step process costing procedure, managers also use this information to determine how well they have controlled costs. Managers compare the actual cost per equivalent unit to the budgeted cost per equivalent unit for both direct materials and conversion costs. If the cost per equivalent unit is the same as or lower than budgeted, the manager has successfully controlled costs.

---

[1]The Shaping Department did not have a beginning inventory. Summary Problem 1 illustrates a department that does have a beginning inventory. As long as we assume the weighted-average method of process costing, we include the beginning balance to arrive at total costs to account for, as shown in Exhibit 5-7.

Step 5: Assign Total Costs to Units Completed and to Units in Ending Work in Process Inventory

The goal of Step 5 (Exhibit 5-9) is to determine how much of the Shaping Department's $208,000 total costs should be assigned to (1) the 40,000 completely shaped masks transferred out to the Insertion Department and (2) the 10,000 partially shaped masks remaining in the Shaping Department's ending work process inventory. Exhibit 5-9 shows how the equivalent units computed in Step 2 (Exhibit 5-5) are multiplied by the cost per equivalent unit computed in Step 4 (Exhibit 5-8) to assign costs to units.

First, consider the 40,000 masks completed and transferred out. Exhibit 5-5 shows 40,000 equivalent units for both direct materials and conversion costs. In Exhibit 5-8 we learned that the company spent $2.80 on direct materials for each equivalent unit, and $1.60 on conversion costs for each equivalent unit. Thus, the total cost of these completed masks is (40,000 × $2.80) + (40,000 × $1.60) = $176,000, as shown in Exhibit 5-9. We've accomplished our first goal—now we know how much cost ($176,000) should be assigned to the completely shaped masks transferred to the Insertion Department.

EXHIBIT 5-9 Step 5: Assign Costs to Units Completed and to Units in Ending Work in Process Inventory

A	B	C	D
Sea View Shaping Department Month Ended October 31 Step 5: Assigning Total Costs	Direct Materials	Conversion Costs	Total
Completed and transferred out:			
Equivalent units completed and transferred out (from Step 2)	40,000	40,000	
Multiplied by: Cost per equivalent unit (from Step 4)	$ 2.80	$ 1.60	
Cost assigned to units completed and transferred out	$ 112,000	$ 64,000	$ 176,000
Ending work in process:			
Equivalent units in ending WIP (from Step 2)	10,000	2,500	
Multiplied by: Cost per equivalent unit (from Step 4)	$ 2.80	$ 1.60	
Cost assigned to units in ending WIP	$ 28,000	$ 4,000	$ 32,000
Total costs accounted for			$ 208,000

Next, consider the 10,000 masks still in ending work in process. These masks have 10,000 equivalent units of direct materials (which cost $2.80 per equivalent unit), so the direct material cost is $28,000 (= 10,000 × $2.80). These masks also have 2,500 equivalent units of conversion costs, which cost $1.60 per equivalent unit, so the conversion costs are $4,000 (= 2,500 × $1.60). Therefore, the total cost of the 10,000 partially completed masks in the Shaping Department's ending work process inventory is the sum of these direct material and conversion costs: $28,000 + $4,000 = $32,000. Now, we've accomplished our second goal—we know how much cost ($32,000) should be assigned to the partially shaped masks still in ending work process inventory.

In summary, Exhibit 5-9 has accomplished our goal of splitting the $208,000 *total cost to account for* between the 40,000 masks completed and transferred out to the Insertion Department and the 10,000 partially shaped masks remaining in Work in Process Inventory.

Average Unit Costs

How does this information relate to unit costs? The average cost of making one *completely shaped* unit is $4.40 ($176,000 transferred to Insertion ÷ 40,000 completely shaped masks transferred to Insertion). This average unit cost ($4.40) is the sum of the direct materials cost per equivalent unit ($2.80) and the conversion cost per equivalent unit ($1.60). The average cost of one *partially* shaped unit that is 25% of the way through the production process is $3.20 ($32,000 in ending inventory of Shaping ÷ 10,000 partially shaped masks). We needed the five-step process costing procedure to find these average costs per unit. If the Shaping Department manager ignored the five-step process and simply spread the entire production cost over all units worked on during the period, each unit would be assigned a cost of $4.16 ($208,000 ÷ 50,000 masks)—whether completely shaped or not. That would be wrong. The average cost per unit should be (and is) higher for completely shaped units transferred to the Insertion Department than it is for partially shaped units remaining in the Shaping Department's ending work in process inventory.

Recall that once the masks are shaped, they still need to have the faceplates inserted. In the second half of the chapter, we will discuss how the second process—Insertion—uses the same five-step procedure to find the *total* unit cost of making a completed mask, from start to finish.

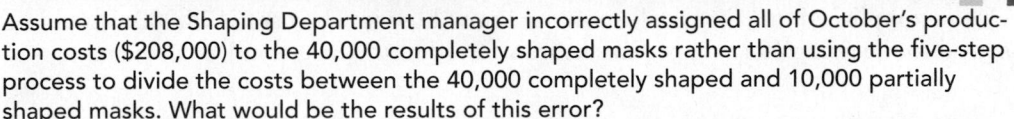

STOP & THINK

Assume that the Shaping Department manager incorrectly assigned all of October's production costs ($208,000) to the 40,000 completely shaped masks rather than using the five-step process to divide the costs between the 40,000 completely shaped and 10,000 partially shaped masks. What would be the results of this error?

Answer: If the manager incorrectly assigned all production costs to the completely shaped masks, the unit cost of completely shaped masks would be too high ($208,000 ÷ 40,000 = $5.20). In addition, the unit cost of the partially shaped masks would be too low ($0.00). In essence, the manager would be saying that the partially shaped units were "free" to make because he or she assigned all of the production costs to the completely shaped units. To assign production costs properly, managers must use the five-step process.

Sustainability and Process Costing

As we have seen, process costing is suitable for manufacturers that produce large volumes of product using a set of standardized production processes. These manufacturing environments are conducive to employing lean practices, which eliminate economic waste from the manufacturing process, and green practices, which minimize or eliminate harmful environmental consequences.

For example, SeaView employs two standardized production processes: Shaping and Insertion. Management should be continually asking, "Are each of these production processes as efficient and environmentally friendly as they can be?" If not, then changes are warranted.

Management should study each of the production processes to discover the quantities and types of solid waste, airborne emissions, and waste water that are generated, as well as the types and quantities of energy used. Solid waste and scrap can be identified simply by studying the contents of the company's trash. These studies are known as **waste audits** (or **trash audits** or **waste sorts**). After conducting waste audits, many companies have discovered they can reclaim and repurpose the waste and scraps into new products, or sell them to a third-party recycler.

For example:

- As of 2013, Unilever, maker of such diverse products as Lipton Tea, Ben & Jerry's Ice Cream, and Dove soap, has achieved "zero-waste to landfills" at plants in 18 countries around the world. The company hopes to achieve "zero waste" at all 252 of its plants worldwide by the end of 2015. The reduction in waste, despite the growth in sales volume, has occurred primarily from innovative ways of recycling and reusing what was previously considered waste. For example, the company now sells the scraps of fabrics, known as offcuts, from cutting tea bags to other companies, which then use it for making wallpaper and animal bedding.[2]

---

[2]http://www.environmentalleader.com/2013/01/24/unilever-moves-zero-waste-goal-five-years-closer/
#.UQF0vje6g6o.email

- General Mills began burning the oat hull waste remaining from the production of its Cheerios brand cereal to generate power. In doing so, the cereal manufacturing plant decreased its natural gas consumption by 90%, thereby saving energy costs, and also reduced its carbon footprint by 21%. In addition, the company generates revenue by selling excess oat hull waste to a local energy company, as well as a nearby state university and a steel manufacturing plant.[3]

- In early 2013, Ford Motor Company announced that by studying its waste over the last five years and finding alternative uses for it, the company has been able to reduce the waste per vehicle from 37.9 pounds down to 22.7 pounds. The company, which has already achieved "zero waste to landfills" at several of its plants, has a goal of further reducing the waste per vehicle down to 13.4 pounds by 2016. Ford says it is using lean manufacturing strategies, as discussed in Chapter 4, to eliminate waste.[4]

Air and water discharges should also be examined to determine if they can be avoided or minimized. For example:

- PepsiCo's Frito-Lay manufacturing plant in Casa Grande, Arizona, uses a large solar array to produce the energy needed to run the plant and uses advanced technology to recycle 75% of the water used in the production process. These practices reduce the company's carbon and water footprints, and save the company money. The plant also diverts over 99% of its solid waste from landfills. Much of the waste diversion comes from recycling and reusing shipping boxes and selling the waste from the production process to producers of cattle feed.[5]

While switching to environmentally friendly production equipment, energy sources, and production processes may be costly in the short run, companies may recognize long-term economic benefits as a result. For example, as carbon-trading schemes (otherwise known as "cap and trade") become more prevalent across the globe, those companies that manage to reduce their carbon emissions may be able to profit from selling their carbon credits. In searching for greener ways to manufacture and recycle their products, some companies may eventually profit from developing, patenting, and selling their own environmentally neutral production systems and technologies.

> **See Exercises E5-32A and E5-44B**

What Journal Entries are Needed in a Process Costing System?

The journal entries used in a process costing system are very similar to those in a job costing system. The basic difference is that the manufacturing costs (direct materials, direct labor, and manufacturing overhead) are assigned to *processing departments*, rather than *jobs*. In addition, at the end of the month, a journal entry must be made to transfer cost to the next processing department. Let's now look at the journal entries that would have been made in October for the Shaping Department.

During October, $140,000 of direct materials was requisitioned for use by the Shaping Department. In the following journal entry, notice how these costs are recorded specifically to the Shaping Department's Work in Process Inventory account. In process costing, each processing department maintains a separate Work in Process Inventory account.

4 Prepare journal entries for a process costing system

Work in Process Inventory—Shaping	140,000	
Raw Materials Inventory		140,000
(To record direct materials used by the Shaping Department in October)		

---

[3]http://www.youtube.com/watch?v=hYLK4lPq0SM

[4]http://www.environmentalleader.com/2013/02/28/ford-to-cut-vehicle-waste-40-percent-by-2016/

[5]http://www.foodprocessing.com/industrynews/2011/frito-casagrande-zero.html and http://www.fritolay.com/about-us/press-release-20111005.html

Labor time records show that $21,250 of direct labor was used in the Shaping Department during October, resulting in the following journal entry:

Work in Process Inventory—Shaping	21,250	
Wages Payable		21,250
(To record direct labor used in the Shaping Department		
in October)		

Manufacturing overhead (MOH) is allocated to the Shaping Department using the company's predetermined overhead rate(s). Just as in a job costing environment, the company may use a single plantwide rate, departmental overhead rates, or ABC to allocate its manufacturing overhead costs. For example, let's say that the Shaping Department's overhead rate is $50 per machine hour and the department used 935 machine hours during the month. That means $46,750 ($50 × 935) of MOH should be allocated to the Shaping Department during October:

Work Process Inventory—Shaping	46,750	
Manufacturing Overhead		46,750
(To record manufacturing overhead allocated to the		
Shaping Department in October)		

After making these journal entries during the month, the "Work Process Inventory—Shaping" T-account appears as follows:

Work in Process Inventory—Shaping		
Balance, October 1	0	
Direct materials	140,000	
Direct labor $208,000	21,250	
Manufacturing overhead	46,750	

Notice how the sum of the costs currently in the T-account is $208,000. This is the *same total costs* to account for summarized in Exhibit 5-7. By performing the five-step process at the end of the month, SeaView was able to determine how much of the $208,000 should be assigned to units still being worked on ($32,000) and how much should be assigned to the units completed and transferred out to the Insertion Department ($176,000). The company uses this information (pictured in Exhibit 5-9) to make the following journal entry:

Work in Process Inventory—Insertion	176,000	
Work in Process Inventory—Shaping		176,000
(To record transfer of cost out of the Shaping Department		
and into the Insertion Department)		

After this journal entry is posted, the "Work in Process Inventory—Shaping" account appears as follows. Notice that the new ending balance in the account—$32,000—agrees with the amount assigned to the partially shaped masks in Exhibit 5-9.

Work in Process Inventory—Shaping			
Balance, October 1	0	Transferred to Insertion	176,000
Direct materials	140,000		
Direct labor	21,250		
Manufacturing overhead	46,750		
Balance, October 31	32,000		

In the next half of the chapter, we'll look at the journal entries made by the Insertion Department to record the completion and sale of the swim masks.

Decision Guidelines

Process Costing—First Processing Department

Here are some of the key decisions SeaView made in setting up its process costing system.

Decision	Guidelines
Should SeaView use job or process costing?	SeaView mass-produces large quantities of identical swim masks using two production processes: Shaping and Insertion. It uses *process costing* to: 1. Determine the cost of each production process. 2. Determine the average direct materials cost and conversion cost incurred on each unit passing through the production process.
How many Work Process Inventory accounts does SeaView's process costing system have?	SeaView uses a separate Work in Process Inventory account for each of its two major processes: Shaping and Insertion.
How does SeaView account for partially completed units?	SeaView uses equivalent units. SeaView computes equivalent units separately for direct materials and conversion costs because it adds direct materials at a particular point in the production process but incurs conversion costs evenly throughout the process.
How does SeaView compute equivalent units of conversion costs?	SeaView's *conversion costs* are incurred evenly throughout the production process, so the equivalent units are computed as follows: $$\text{Equivalent units} = \text{Number of physical units} \times \text{Percentage of completion}$$
How does SeaView compute equivalent units of direct materials?	Equivalent units of direct materials are computed using the same equivalent unit formula shown directly above. However, SeaView's *materials* are added at specific points in the production process, so the equivalent units are computed using the following percentages: • If physical units have passed the point at which materials are added, then the units are 100% complete with respect to materials. • If physical units have not passed the point at which materials are added, then the units are 0% complete with respect to materials. • If physical units have received a portion, but not all, of the direct materials (say 25%), then equivalent units of direct materials are calculated using that particular percentage.
How does SeaView compute the cost per equivalent unit?	For each category (direct materials and conversion), SeaView divides the total cost to account for by the total equivalent units. The resulting information tells management the average cost of making one unit in each processing department. This information can then be compared to the budget to the help managers control costs.
How does SeaView split the costs of the shaping process between the following? • Swim masks completed and transferred out • Partially completed swim masks in ending work in process inventory	SeaView multiplies the cost per equivalent unit by the following: • Number of equivalent units completed and transferred out • Number of equivalent units in the ending work in process inventory

SUMMARY PROBLEM 1

Florida Tile produces ceramic tiles using two sequential production departments: Tile-Forming and Tile-Finishing. The following information was found for Florida Tile's first production process, the Tile-Forming Department.

FLORIDA TILE
TILE-FORMING DEPARTMENT
Month Ended May 31

Information about units:

Beginning work in process, May 1...	2,000 units
Started in production during May..	18,000 units
Completed and transferred to Finishing Department during May............................	16,000 units
Ending work in process, May 31 (25% complete as to direct materials, 55% complete as to conversion cost)...	4,000 units

Information about costs:

Beginning work in process, May 1 (consists of $800 of direct materials cost and $4,000 of conversion costs)..	$ 4,800
Direct materials used in May...	$ 6,000
Conversion costs incurred in May...	$32,400

Requirement

Use the five steps of process costing to calculate the cost that should be assigned to (1) units completed and transferred out and (2) units still in ending work in process inventory. Then prepare the journal entry needed at month-end to transfer the costs associated with the formed tiles to the next department, Tile-Finishing.

▪ SOLUTION

Step 1: Summarize the flow of physical units.
Step 2: Compute output in terms of equivalent units.

	A	B	C	D
1	**Florida Tile: Tile-Forming Department**	**Step 1:**	**Step 2: Equivalent Units**	
2	Month Ended May 31	**Flow of Physical**	**Direct**	**Conversion**
	Flow of Production	**Units**	**Materials**	**Costs**
3	**Units to account for:**			
4	Beginning work in process, May 1	2,000		
5	Plus: Started in production during May	18,000		
6	Total physical units to account for	20,000		
7				
8	**Units accounted for:**			
9	Completed and transferred out during May	16,000	16,000	16,000
10	Plus: Ending work in process, May 31	4,000	1,000	2,200
11	Total physical units accounted for	20,000		
12	**Total equivalent units**		17,000	18,200
13				

Notes about calculating equivalent units:
 DM = 4,000 units × 25% complete = 1,000
 Conversion = 4,000 units × 55% complete = 2,200

Step 3: Summarize total costs to account for.

	A	B	C	D
1	**Florida Tile: Tile-Forming Department** **Month Ended May 31** **Step 3: Costs to Account For**	**Direct Materials**	**Conversion Costs**	**Total**
2	Beginning work in process, May 1	$ 800	$ 4,000	$ 4,800
3	Plus: Costs added during May	6,000	32,400	38,400
4	Total costs to account for	$ 6,800	$ 36,400	$ 43,200
5				

Step 4: Compute the cost per equivalent unit.

	A	B	C	D
1	**Florida Tile: Tile-Forming Department** **Month Ended May 31** **Step 4: Cost per Equivalent Unit**	**Direct Materials**	**Conversion Costs**	
2	Total costs to account for (from Step 3)	$ 6,800	$ 36,400	
3	Divided by: Total equivalent units (from Step 2)	17,000	18,200	
4	Cost per equivalent unit	$ 0.40	$ 2.00	
5				

Step 5: Assign total costs to units completed and to units in ending work in process inventory.

	A	B	C	D
1	**Florida Tile: Tile-Forming Department** **Month Ended May 31**	**Direct Materials**	**Conversion Costs**	**Total**
2	**Step 5: Assigning Costs**			
3	**Completed and transferred out:**			
4	Equivalent units completed and transferred out (from Step 2)	16,000	16,000	
5	Multiplied by: Cost per equivalent unit (from Step 4)	$ 0.40	$ 2.00	
6	Cost assigned to units completed and transferred out	$ 6,400	$ 32,000	$ 38,400
7				
8	**Ending work in process:**			
9	Equivalent units in ending WIP (from Step 2)	1,000	2,200	
10	Multiplied by: Cost per equivalent unit (from Step 4)	$ 0.40	$ 2.00	
11	Cost assigned to units in ending WIP	$ 400	$ 4,400	$ 4,800
12				
13	**Total costs accounted for**			$ 43,200
14				

The journal entry needed to transfer costs is as follows:

	Work in Process Inventory—Tile-Finishing	38,400	
	Work in Process Inventory—Tile-Forming		38,400

The cost of making one completely formed tile in the Tile-Forming Department is $2.40. This is the sum of the direct materials cost per equivalent unit ($0.40) and the conversion cost per equivalent unit ($2.00). The completely formed tiles must still be finished in the Tile-Finishing Department before we will know the final cost of making one tile from start to finish.

How Does Process Costing Work in a Second or Later Processing Department?

Most products require a series of processing steps. Recall that Jelly Belly uses eight processing steps to make its jelly beans. In the last section, we saw how much it costs SeaView to *shape* one mask. In this section, we consider a second department, SeaView's Insertion Department. After units pass through the *final* department (Insertion, in SeaView's case), managers can determine the *entire* cost of making one unit—from start to finish. In the second or later department, we use the same five-step process costing procedure that we used for the Shaping Department, with one major difference: We separately consider the costs *transferred in* to the Insertion Department from the Shaping Department when calculating equivalent units and the cost per equivalent unit. <u>Transferred-in costs</u> are incurred in a previous process (the Shaping Department, in the SeaView example) and are carried forward as part of the product's cost when it moves to the next process.

5 Use process costing in a second or later production department

To account for transferred-in costs, we will add one more column to our calculations in Steps 2–5. Let's walk through the Insertion Department's process costing to see how this is done.

Process Costing in SeaView's Insertion Department

The Insertion Department receives the shaped masks and polishes them before inserting the faceplates at the end of the process. Exhibit 5-10 shows the following:

- Shaped masks are transferred in from the Shaping Department at the beginning of the Insertion Department's process.

- The Insertion Department's conversion costs are added evenly throughout the process.

- The Insertion Department's direct materials (faceplates) are not added until the *end* of the process.

> ## Why is this important?
>
> "Most products are **manufactured** through a **series** of production processes. To find the **total cost** of making one unit—*from* **start to finish**— managers must perform the five-step process costing procedure in **each** production department."

EXHIBIT 5-10 SeaView's Insertion Department Time Line

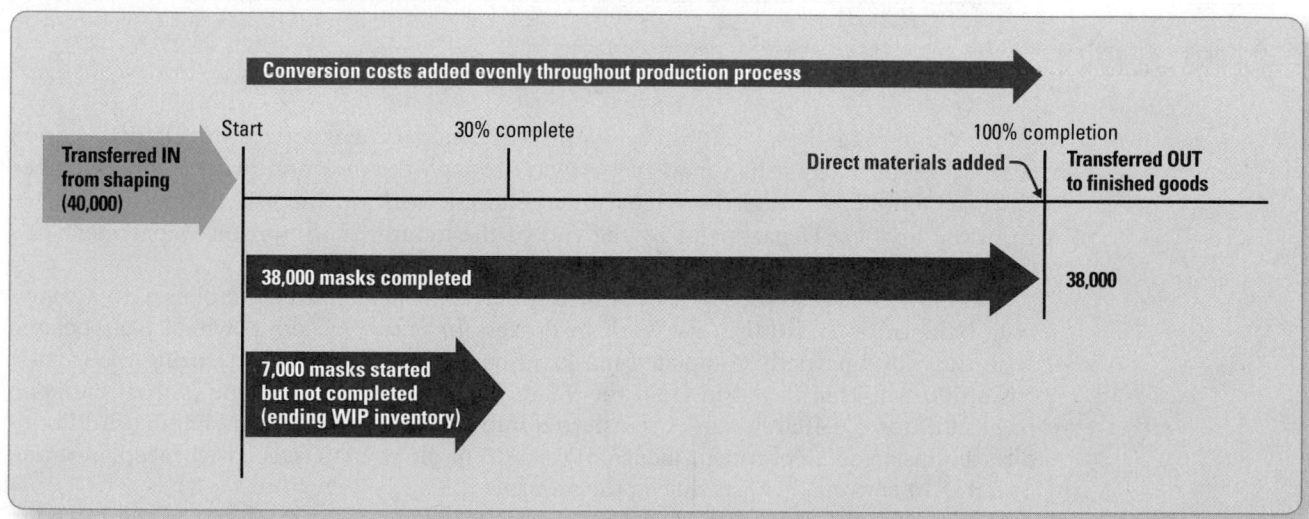

Keep in mind that *direct materials* in the Insertion Department refer *only* to the faceplates and not to the materials (the plastic and metal fasteners) added in the Shaping Department. Likewise, *conversion costs* in the Insertion Department refer to the direct labor and manufacturing overhead costs incurred *only* in the Insertion Department.

Exhibit 5-11 lists SeaView's Insertion Department data for October. The top portion of the exhibit lists the unit information, while the lower portion lists the costs. Let's walk through this information together.

EXHIBIT 5-11 SeaView's Insertion Department Data for October

Information about units:		
Beginning work in process, October 1		
(0% complete as to direct materials, 60% complete		
as to conversion work)...		5,000 masks*
Transferred in from Shaping Department during		
October (from Exhibit 5-6)..		40,000 masks
Completed and transferred out to Finished Goods		
Inventory during October..		38,000 masks
Ending work in process, October 31		
(0% complete as to direct materials, 30% complete		
as to conversion work)...		7,000 masks
Information about costs:		
Beginning work in process, October 1		
Transferred-in costs..	$ 22,000	
Conversion costs	1,100*	
Beginning balance		$ 23,100
Transferred in from Shaping Department during October		
(from journal entry on page 262)...		$176,000
Direct materials added during October in Insertion Department......................		$ 19,000
Conversion costs added during October in Insertion Department:		
Direct labor...	$ 3,710	
Manufacturing overhead	9,225	
Conversion costs		$ 12,935
Total costs to account for..		$231,035

*This information would have been obtained from Step 5 of the process costing procedure from September. The September 30 balance in work in process becomes the October 1 balance.

Exhibit 5-11 shows that SeaView's Insertion Department started the October period with 5,000 masks that had made it partway through the insertion process in September. During October, the Insertion Department started work on the 40,000 masks received from the Shaping Department. By the end of the month, the Insertion Department had completed 38,000 masks, while 7,000 remained partially complete.

Exhibit 5-11 also shows that the Insertion Department started October with a beginning balance of $23,100 in its Work in Process Inventory account, which is associated with the 5,000 partially completed masks in its beginning inventory. During the month, $176,000 was transferred in from the Shaping Department (recall the journal entry on page 262) for the 40,000 masks transferred into the department from Shaping. Additionally, the Insertion Department incurred $19,000 in direct materials costs (faceplates) and $12,935 in conversion costs during the month.

Just as in the Shaping Department, our goal is to split the total cost in the Insertion Department ($231,035) between the following:

■ The 38,000 masks that the Insertion Department completed and transferred out (this time, to finished goods inventory)

■ The 7,000 partially complete masks remaining in the Insertion Department's ending work in process inventory at the end of October

After splitting the total cost, we'll be able to determine the cost of making one complete mask—from start to finish. We use the same five-step process costing procedure that we used for the Shaping Department.

Steps 1 and 2: Summarize the Flow of Physical Units and Compute Output in Terms of Equivalent Units

Step 1: Summarize the Flow of Physical Units

Step 1 tracks the movement of swim masks into and out of the Insertion Department, just as we did in the Shaping Department. The data in Exhibit 5-11 show that the Insertion Department had a beginning work in process inventory of 5,000 masks. Then, during October, the Insertion Department received 40,000 masks from the Shaping Department. Thus, Exhibit 5-12 shows that the Insertion Department has 45,000 masks to account for (5,000 + 40,000).

Where did these 45,000 masks go? Exhibit 5-11 shows that the Insertion Department completed and transferred 38,000 masks out to finished goods inventory while the remaining 7,000 masks were only partway through the insertion process on October 31. Thus, Exhibit 5-12 shows that the department has accounted for all 45,000 masks.

Step 2: Compute Output in Terms of Equivalent Units

As mentioned earlier, process costing in a second or later department separately calculates equivalent units for transferred-in costs, direct materials, and conversion costs. Therefore, Step 2 in Exhibit 5-12 shows *three* columns for the Insertion Department's *three* categories of equivalent units: transferred-in, direct materials, and conversion costs. Let's consider each in turn.

Exhibit 5-10 shows that transferred-in masks are added at the very *beginning* of the insertion process. You might think of the shaped masks transferred in as raw materials added at the very *beginning* of the insertion process. All masks worked on in the Insertion Department—whether completed or not by the end of the month—started in the department as a shaped mask. Therefore, they are *all 100% complete with respect to transferred-in work and costs*. So, the "Transferred-in" column of Exhibit 5-12 shows 38,000 equivalent units completed and transferred out (38,000 physical units × 100%)

EXHIBIT 5-12 Step 1: Summarize the Flow of Physical Units
Step 2: Compute Output in Terms of Equivalent Units

	A	B	C	D	E
1	Sea View Insertion Department	Step 1:	Step 2: Equivalent Units		
2	Month Ended October 31 Flow of Production	Flow of Physical Units	Transferred-in	Direct Materials	Conversion Costs
3	**Units to account for:**				
4	Beginning work in process, October 1	5,000			
5	Plus: Transferred in during October	40,000			
6	Total physical units to account for	45,000			
7					
8	**Units accounted for:**				
9	Completed and transferred out during October	38,000	38,000	38,000	38,000
10	Plus: Ending work in process, October 31	7,000	7,000	0	2,100
11	Total physical units accounted for	45,000			
12	**Total equivalent units**		45,000	38,000	40,100
13					

Notes about calculating equivalent units in ending WIP:
Transferred-in = 7,000 units × 100% complete = 7,000
DM = 7,000 units × 0% complete = 0
Conversion = 7,000 units × 30% complete = 2,100

and 7,000 equivalent units still in ending inventory (7,000 physical units × 100%). Keep the following important rule of thumb in mind:

> *All physical units, whether completed and transferred out or still in ending work in process, are considered 100% complete with respect to transferred-in work and costs.*

The Insertion Department calculates equivalent units of direct material the same way as in the Shaping Department. However, in the Insertion Department, the direct materials (faceplates) are added at the *end* of the process rather than at the beginning of the process. The 38,000 masks completed and transferred out contain 100% of their direct materials. On the other hand, the 7,000 masks in ending work process inventory have *not* made it to the end of the process, so they *do not* contain faceplates. As we see in Exhibit 5-12, these unfinished masks have zero equivalent units of the Insertion Department's direct materials (7,000 physical units × 0%).

Now, consider the conversion costs. The 38,000 finished masks are 100% complete with respect to the Insertion Department's conversion costs. However, the 7,000 unfinished masks are only 30% converted (see Exhibits 5-10 and 5-11), so the equivalent units of conversion costs equal 2,100 (7,000 × 30%).

Finally, the equivalent units in each column are summed to find the *total* equivalent units for each of the three categories: transferred-in (45,000), direct materials (38,000), and conversion costs (40,100). We'll use these equivalent units in Step 4.

Steps 3 and 4: Summarize Total Costs to Account for and Compute the Cost per Equivalent Unit

Exhibit 5-13 accumulates the Insertion Department's total costs to account for based on the data in Exhibit 5-11.

EXHIBIT 5-13 Step 3: Summarize Total Costs to Account For
Step 4: Compute the Cost per Equivalent Unit

	A	B	C	D	E
1	**Sea View Insertion Department**				
	Month Ended October 31	**Transferred-**	**Direct**	**Conversion**	
2	**Steps 3 and 4**	**in**	**Materials**	**Costs**	**Total**
3	Beginning work in process, October 1 (Exhibit 5-11)	$ 22,000	$ 0	$ 1,100	$ 23,100
4	Plus: Costs added during October	176,000	19,000	12,935	207,935
5	**Total costs to account for**	$ 198,000	$ 19,000	$ 14,035	$ 231,035
6	Divided by: Total equivalent units (from Step 2)	45,000	38,000	40,100	
7	**Cost per equivalent unit**	$ 4.40	$ 0.50	$ 0.35	
8					

In addition to direct material and conversion costs, the Insertion Department must account for transferred-in costs. Recall that transferred-in costs are incurred in a previous process (the Shaping Department, in the SeaView example) and are carried forward as part of the product's cost when the physical product is transferred to the next process.

If the Insertion Department had bought these shaped masks from an outside supplier, it would have to account for the costs of purchasing the masks. However, the Insertion Department receives the masks from an *internal* supplier—the Shaping Department. Thus, the Insertion Department must account for the costs the Shaping Department incurred to provide the shaped masks as well as the Insertion Department's own direct materials (faceplates) and conversion costs (labor and overhead to insert the faceplates).

Exhibit 5-13 shows that the Insertion Department's total costs to account for ($231,035) consist of the costs associated with beginning work process inventory ($23,100) plus the costs added during the month ($207,935).

Exhibit 5-13 also shows Step 4: the calculation of cost per equivalent unit. For each category of cost, SeaView simply divides the total costs by the corresponding number of total equivalent units that were found in Step 2 (Exhibit 5-12).

Step 5: Assign Total Costs to Units Completed and to Units in Ending Work in Process Inventory

Exhibit 5-14 shows how SeaView finishes the five-step process by assigning costs to (1) units completed and transferred out to finished goods inventory and (2) units remaining in the Insertion Department's ending work process inventory. SeaView uses the same approach as it used for the Shaping Department in Exhibit 5-9. SeaView multiplies the number of equivalent units from Step 2 (Exhibit 5-12) by the cost per equivalent unit from Step 4 (Exhibit 5-13).

EXHIBIT 5-14 Step 5: Assign Total Costs to Units Completed and to Units in Ending Work Process Inventory

	A	B	C	D	E
1	Sea View Insertion Department				
2	Month Ended October 31 Step 5: Assigning Costs	Transferred-in	Direct Materials	Conversion Costs	Total
3	Completed and transferred out:				
4	Equivalent units completed and transferred out (from Step 2)	38,000	38,000	38,000	
5	Multiplied by: Cost per equivalent unit (from Step 4)	$ 4.40	$ 0.50	$ 0.35	
6	Cost assigned to units completed and transferred out	$ 167,200	$ 19,000	$ 13,300	$ 199,500
7					
8	Ending work in process:				
9	Equivalent units in ending WIP (from Step 2)	7,000	0	2,100	
10	Multiplied by: Cost per equivalent unit (from Step 4)	$ 4.40	$ 0.50	$ 0.35	
11	Cost assigned to units in ending WIP	$ 30,800	$ 0	$ 735	$ 31,535
12					
13	Total costs accounted for				$ 231,035
14					

Unit Costs and Gross Profit

SeaView's managers can now compute the cost of manufacturing one swim mask, from start to finish. Step 5 shows that $199,500 should be transferred to the Finished Goods Inventory account for the 38,000 masks completed during the month. Therefore, SeaView's cost of making one completed mask is $5.25 ($199,500 ÷ 38,000 finished masks). Exhibit 5-14 shows that this cost includes the costs from both processing departments:

- $4.40 from the Shaping Department[6]
- $0.85 from the Insertion Department ($0.50 for direct materials and $0.35 for conversion costs)

---

[6]This is the same $4.40 per unit we saw the Shaping Department transfer out to the Insertion Department in the first half of the chapter. Notice how the transferred-in cost carries through from one department to the next. The weighted-average method of process costing *combines* the current period's costs ($176,000) with any costs in beginning inventory ($23,100) to yield a weighted-average cost per unit ($4.40). Therefore, the weighted average cost could be different than $4.40 if the beginning inventory had cost more or less than $4.40 per unit to make in September.

SeaView's managers use this information to help control costs, set prices, and assess the profitability of the swim masks. Let's assume SeaView is able to charge customers $10 for each mask. If so, the gross profit on the sale of each of these masks will be as follows:

Sales Revenue (per mask)	$10.00
Less: Cost of Goods Sold (per mask)	5.25
Gross Profit (per mask)	$ 4.75

For SeaView to be profitable, the total gross profit (gross profit per mask × number of masks sold) will need to be high enough to cover all of SeaView's operating expenses, such as marketing and distribution expenses, incurred in non-manufacturing elements of the value chain. In addition to using the unit cost for valuing Cost of Goods Sold, SeaView will also use it to value Finished Goods Inventory ($5.25 for each mask still in finished goods inventory at the end of October).

Try It!

Dairymaid's yogurt goes through two sequential processes in two departments: Fermenting and Packaging. Assume that in the Packaging Department, Step 4 of the process costing procedure indicated the following costs per equivalent unit (cases of yogurt):

	Transferred-in	Direct Materials	Conversion Costs
Cost per equivalent unit	$6.50	$1.15	$1.25

a. How much did each case of yogurt cost to make, from start to finish?

b. If each case sells for $20, what is the gross profit per case?

Please see page 308 for solutions.

Production Cost Reports

Most companies prepare a **production cost report**, which summarizes the entire five-step process on one schedule. Notice how the production cost report for the Insertion Department shown in Exhibit 5-15 simply brings together all of the steps that we showed separately in Exhibits 5-12, 5-13, and 5-14. The top half of the schedule focuses on units (Steps 1 and 2), while the bottom half of the schedule focuses on costs (Steps 3, 4, and 5). Each processing department prepares its own production cost report each month. The transferred-in costs, direct materials cost, and conversion costs assigned to the units in *ending* work process inventory become the *beginning* work process inventory balances on the next month's cost report.

EXHIBIT 5-15 Production Cost Report

	A	B	C	D	E	F
1	Sea View Insertion Department	Step1		Step 2: Equivalent Units		
2	Month Ended October 31 — Flow of Production	Flow of Physical Units	Transferred-in	Direct Materials	Conversion Costs	
3	**Units to account for:**					
4	Beginning work in process, October 1	5,000				
5	Plus: Transferred in during October	40,000				
6	Total physical units to account for	45,000				
7						
8	**Units accounted for:**					
9	Completed and transferred out during October	38,000	38,000	38,000	38,000	
10	Plus: Ending work in process, October 31	7,000	7,000	0	2,100	
11	Total physical units accounted for	45,000				
12	**Total equivalent units**		45,000	38,000	40,100	
13						
14						
15	**Total Costs to account for and Cost per Equivalent Unit:** Steps 3 and 4		Transferred-in	Direct Materials	Conversion Costs	Total
16	Beginning work in process, October 1		$ 22,000	$ 0	$ 1,100	$ 23,100
17	Plus: Costs added during October		176,000	19,000	12,935	207,935
18	Total costs to account for		$ 198,000	$ 19,000	$ 14,035	$ 231,035
19	Divided by: Total equivalent units (from Step 2)		45,000	38,000	40,100	
20	Cost per equivalent unit		$ 4.40	$ 0.50	$ 0.35	
21						
22	**Assignment of total costs: Step 5**					
23	**Completed and transferred out:**					
24	Equivalent units completed and transferred out (from Step 2)		38,000	38,000	38,000	
25	Multiplied by: Cost per equivalent unit (from Step 4)		$ 4.40	$ 0.50	$ 0.35	
26	Cost assigned to units completed and transferred out		$ 167,200	$ 19,000	$ 13,300	$ 199,500
27						
28	**Ending work in process:**					
29	Equivalent units in ending WIP (from Step 2)		7,000	0	2,100	
30	Multiplied by: Cost per equivalent unit (from Step 4)		$ 4.40	$ 0.50	$ 0.35	
31	Cost assigned to units in ending WIP		$ 30,800	$ 0	$ 735	$ 31,535
32						
33	**Total costs accounted for**					$ 231,035
34						

SeaView's managers monitor the production costs found on this report by comparing the actual direct materials and conversion costs—particularly the equivalent-unit costs—with expected amounts. If actual costs are higher than expected, managers will try to uncover the reason for the increase, and look for ways to cut costs in the future without sacrificing quality.

Journal Entries in a Second Processing Department

The Insertion Department's journal entries are similar to those of the Shaping Department.

The following summary entry records the manufacturing costs incurred in the Insertion Department during the month of October (data from Exhibit 5-11):

Work Process Inventory—Insertion	31,935	
Raw Materials Inventory		19,000
Wages Payable		3,710
Manufacturing Overhead		9,225
(To record manufacturing costs incurred in the Insertion Department during October)		

Next, recall the journal entry made to transfer the cost of shaped masks out of the Shaping Department and into the Insertion Department at the end of October (page 262). This journal entry would only be made *once*, but is repeated here simply as a reminder:

Work in Process Inventory—Insertion		176,000	
Work in Process Inventory—Shaping			176,000
(To record the transfer cost out of the Shaping Department			
and into the Insertion Department)			

The fifth step of the process costing procedure (Exhibit 5-14) showed that $199,500 should be assigned to the completed masks, while $31,535 should be assigned to the units still being worked on. Thus, the following journal entry is needed to transfer cost out of the Insertion Department and into Finished Goods Inventory:

Finished Goods Inventory		199,500	
Work in Process Inventory—Insertion			199,500
(To record transfer of cost out of the Insertion Department			
and into Finished Goods Inventory)			

After posting, the key accounts appear as follows:

Work in Process Inventory—Shaping

Balance, September 30	0	Transferred to Insertion	176,000
Direct materials	140,000		
Direct labor	21,250		
Manufacturing overhead	46,750		
Balance, October 31	32,000		

Work in Process Inventory—Insertion

Balance, September 30	23,100	Transferred to Finished	
Transferred in from Shaping	176,000	Goods Inventory	199,500
Direct materials	19,000		
Direct labor	3,710		
Manufacturing overhead	9,225		
Balance, October 31	31,535		

Finished Goods Inventory

Balance, September 30	0		
Transferred in from Insertion	199,500		

STOP & THINK

Assume that SeaView sells 36,000 of the masks for $10 each. Assuming that SeaView uses a perpetual inventory system, what journal entries would SeaView make to record the sales transaction?

Answer: The unit cost of making one mask from start to finish is $5.25 ($199,500 transferred to Finished Goods ÷ 38,000 finished masks). SeaView will make one journal entry to record the sales revenue, and a second journal entry to record the cost of goods sold:

Accounts Receivable (36,000 × $10.00)	360,000	
Sales Revenue		360,000

Cost of Goods Sold (36,000 × 5.25)	189,000	
Finished Goods Inventory		189,000

Decision Guidelines

Process Costing—Second Process

Let's use SeaView's Insertion Department to review some of the key process costing decisions that arise in a second (or later) process.

Decision	Guidelines
At what point in the insertion process are transferred-in costs (from the shaping process) incurred?	Transferred-in costs are incurred at the *beginning* of the insertion process. The masks must be completely shaped before the Insertion process begins.
What percentage of completion is used to calculate equivalent units in the "Transferred-in" column?	All units, whether completed and transferred out or still in ending work in process, are considered 100% complete with respect to transferred-in work and costs.
What checks and balances does the five-step process costing procedure provide?	The five-step procedure provides two important checks: 1. The total units to account for (beginning inventory + units started or transferred in) *must equal* the total units accounted for (units completed and transferred out + units in ending inventory). 2. The total costs to account for (cost of beginning inventory + costs incurred in the current period) *must equal* the total costs accounted for (cost of units completed and transferred out + cost of ending inventory).
What are the main goals of the Insertion Department's process costing?	One goal is to determine the cost of operating the department during the month. This information is used by managers to control production costs. Another goal is to determine the cost of making each swim mask—from start to finish. The final goal is to split total costs between swim masks completed and transferred out to finished goods inventory and the masks that remain in the Insertion Department's ending work process inventory.
What is a production cost report, and how do managers use the information found on it?	A production cost report simply summarizes all five steps on one schedule. SeaView's managers use the cost per equivalent unit to determine the cost of producing a swim mask. These costs provide a basis for setting selling prices, performing profitability analysis to decide which products to emphasize, and so forth. These costs are also the basis for valuing inventory on the balance sheet and cost of goods sold on the income statement. Managers also use the cost per equivalent unit to control material and conversion costs and to evaluate the performance of production department managers.

SUMMARY PROBLEM 2

This problem extends the Summary Problem 1 to a second department. During May, Florida Tile Industries reports the following in its Tile-Finishing Department:

Tile-Finishing Department Data for May	
Information about units:	
Beginning work in process, May 1 (20% complete as to direct materials, 70% complete as to conversion work)...	4,000 units
Transferred in from Tile-Forming Department during May................................	16,000 units
Completed and transferred out to Finished Goods Inventory during May..	15,000 units
Ending work in process, May 31 (36% complete as to direct materials, 80% complete as to conversion work)..	5,000 units
Information about costs:	
Work in process, May 1 (transferred-in costs, $10,000; direct materials costs, $488; conversion costs, $5,530)...	$16,018
Transferred in from Tile-Forming Department during May (page 266)...	38,400
Tile-Finishing Department direct materials added during May...	6,400
Tile-Finishing Department conversion costs added during May..	24,300

Requirements

1. Complete the five-step process costing procedure to assign the Tile-Finishing Department's *total costs to account for* to units completed and to units in ending work in process inventory. (*Note:* Don't confuse the Tile-Finishing Department with finished goods inventory. The Tile-Finishing Department is Florida Tile's second process. The tiles do not become part of finished goods inventory until they have completed the second process, which happens to be called the Tile-Finishing Department.)

2. Make the journal entry to transfer the appropriate amount of cost to Finished Goods Inventory.

3. What is the cost of making one unit of product from start to finish?

▪ SOLUTION

Steps 1 and 2: Summarize the flow of physical units; compute output in terms of equivalent units.

	A	B	C	D	E
1	**Florida Tile**	**Step 1:**	**Step 2: Equivalent Units**		
2	Tile-Finishing Department Month Ended May 31 **Flow of Production**	**Flow of Physical Units**	**Transferred-in**	**Direct Materials**	**Conversion Costs**
3	**Units to account for:**				
4	Beginning work in process, May 1	4,000			
5	Plus: Transferred in during May	16,000			
6	Total physical units to account for	20,000			
7					
8	**Units accounted for:**				
9	Completed and transferred out during May	15,000	15,000	15,000	15,000
10	Plus: Ending work in process, May 31	5,000	5,000	1,800	4,000
11	Total physical units accounted for	20,000			
12	**Total equivalent units**		20,000	16,800	19,000
13					

Notes about calculating equivalent units in ending WIP:
Transferred-in = 5,000 units × 100% complete = 5,000
DM = 5,000 units × 36% complete = 1,800
Conversion = 5,000 units × 80% complete = 4,000

Steps 3 and 4: Summarize total costs to account for; compute the cost per equivalent unit.

	A	B	C	D	E
1	**Florida Tile**				
2	Tile-Finishing Department Month Ended May 31 **Steps 3 and 4**	**Transferred-in**	**Direct Materials**	**Conversion Costs**	**Total**
3	Beginning work in process, May 1	$ 10,000	$ 488	$ 5,530	$ 16,018
4	Plus: Costs added during May	38,400	6,400	24,300	69,100
5	Total costs to account for	$ 48,400	$ 6,888	$ 29,830	$ 85,118
6	Divided by: Total equivalent units	20,000	16,800	19,000	
7	**Cost per equivalent unit**	$ 2.42	$ 0.41	$ 1.57	
8					

Step 5: Assign total costs to units completed and to units in ending work process inventory.

	A	B	C	D	E
1	**Florida Tile**				
2	**Tile-Finishing Department** **Month Ended May 31** **Step 5: Assigning Costs**	**Transferred- in**	**Direct Materials**	**Conversion Costs**	**Total**
3	**Completed and transferred out:**				
4	Equivalent units completed and transferred out	15,000	15,000	15,000	
5	Multiplied by: Cost per equivalent unit	$ 2.42	$ 0.41	$ 1.57	
6	Cost assigned to units completed and transferred out	$ 36,300	$ 6,150	$ 23,550	$ 66,000
7					
8	**Ending work in process:**				
9	Equivalent units in ending WIP	5,000	1,800	4,000	
10	Multiplied by: Cost per equivalent unit	$ 2.42	$ 0.41	$ 1.57	
11	Cost assigned to units in ending WIP	$ 12,100	$ 738	$ 6,280	$ 19,118
12					
13	**Total costs accounted for**				$ 85,118
14					

Requirement 2

Journal entry:

	Finished Goods Inventory	66,000	
	Work Process Inventory—Tile-Finishing Department		66,000
	(To record the transfer of cost out of the Tile-Finishing		
	Department and into Finished Goods Inventory)		

Requirement 3

The cost of making one unit from start to finish is $4.40 ($66,000 transferred to Finished Goods Inventory divided by the 15,000 completed tiles). This consists of $2.42[7] of cost incurred in the Tile-Forming Department and $1.98 of cost incurred in the Tile-Finishing Department ($0.41 of direct materials and $1.57 of conversion costs).

---

[7]In Summary Problem 1, we saw that the average cost per unit in May was $2.40. The weighted-average method combines the current period's costs (May's costs) with any costs in beginning inventory to yield a weighted-average cost of $2.42 per unit.

END OF CHAPTER

Learning Objectives

- 1 Distinguish between the flow of costs in process costing and job costing
- 2 Compute equivalent units
- 3 Use process costing in the first production department
- 4 Prepare journal entries for a process costing system
- 5 Use process costing in a second or later production department

Accounting Vocabulary

Equivalent Units. (p. 252)   Express the amount of work done during a period in terms of fully completed units of output.

Production Cost Report. (p. 272)   Summarizes a processing department's operations for a period.

Transferred-In Costs. (p. 267)   Costs incurred in a previous process that are carried forward as part of the product's cost when it moves to the next process.

Waste Audit. (p. 260)   Studying the contents of a company's trash in order to identify solid waste and scraps that could potentially be recycled, repurposed, or sold to create a new revenue stream. Also known as trash *audit* or *waste sort*.

Weighted-Average Method of Process Costing. (p. 253)   A process costing method that *combines* any beginning inventory units (and costs) with the current period's units (and costs) to get a weighted-average cost.

MyAccountingLab   **Go to** http://myaccountinglab.com/ **for the following Quick Check, Short Exercises, Exercises, and Problems. They are available with immediate grading, explanations of correct and incorrect answers, and interactive media that acts as your own online tutor.**

Quick Check

1. *(Learning Objective 1)* Which of the following is *false* concerning process costing?
   a. It is well suited for a company whose products are indistinguishable from each other.
   b. It uses multiple WIP accounts, one for each processing department.
   c. It accumulates production costs by activities.
   d. It transfers costs from one processing department to the next.

2. *(Learning Objective 2)* Conversion costs consist of
   a. direct materials + direct labor.
   b. direct materials + manufacturing overhead.
   c. direct labor + manufacturing overhead.
   d. direct materials + direct labor + manufacturing overhead.

3. *(Learning Objective 2)* Which of the following is true?
   a. The weighted-average method is always used for process costing.
   b. FIFO is always used for process costing.
   c. Units in ending WIP are expressed in terms of equivalent units.
   d. A partially completed product whose direct materials are added at the beginning of the process would be 0% complete with respect to direct materials.

4. *(Learning Objective 3)* Which of the following is the first step in completing the five-step process costing procedure?
   a. Summarize the flow of physical units.
   b. Summarize total costs to account for.
   c. Compute output in terms of equivalent units.
   d. Compute the cost per equivalent unit.

5. *(Learning Objective 3)* Assume 100 units were completed and transferred out during the period. The 40 units left in ending WIP are 20% complete with respect to conversion costs. The total equivalent units for conversion costs would be
   a. 100.
   b. 8.
   c. 140.
   d. 108.

6. *(Learning Objective 4)* The journal entry needed to record direct labor used in the Finishing Department during the month would be
   a. Debit Wages Payable; Credit Finished Goods Inventory
   b. Debit Wages Payable; Credit WIP-Finishing Dept.
   c. Debit Finished Goods Inventory; Credit Wages Payable
   d. Debit WIP- Finishing Dept.; Credit Wages Payable

7. *(Learning Objective 4)* A company has two sequential processing departments: Mixing and Forming. In the Mixing Department, Step 5 of the process costing procedure assigned $10,000 to units in ending WIP and $80,000 to units completed and transferred out. What journal entry is needed as a result of these calculations?

   a. Debit WIP—Mixing Department: $10,000; credit WIP—Forming Department: $10,000

   b. Debit WIP—Mixing Department: $80,000; credit WIP—Forming Department: $80,000

   c. Debit WIP—Forming Department: $10,000; Credit WIP—Mixing Department: $10,000

   d. Debit WIP—Forming Department: $80,000; Credit WIP—Mixing Department: $80,000

8. *(Learning Objective 5)* In the second processing department, the percentage of completion assigned to units transferred in is always:

   a. 0%.

   b. 100%.

   c. dependent on the percentage of completion at month end.

   d. None of the above

9. *(Learning Objective 5)* The schedule used to summarize the entire five-step process costing procedure is called a

   a. production cost report.

   b. process costing schedule.

   c. job cost record.

   d. processing report.

10. *(Learning Objective 5)* A company sells each unit of its product for $90. The final department showed the following costs per equivalent unit: $40 transferred-in, $21 direct materials, $13 conversion. What is the gross profit on each unit sold by the company?

    a. $90

    b. $16

    c. $74

    d. $56

Quick Check Answers

1. c 2. c 3. c 4. a 5. d 6. d 7. d 8. b 9. a 10. b

Short Exercises

S5-1 Compare flow of costs *(Learning Objective 1)*

Use Exhibit 5-1 to help you describe in your own words the major difference in the flow of costs between a job costing system and a process costing system.

S5-2 Flow of costs through Work in Process Inventory *(Learning Objective 1)*

Great Beans produces jelly beans in three sequential processing departments: Centers, Shells, and Packaging. Assume that the Shells processing department began September with $18,100 of unfinished jelly bean centers. During September, the Shells process used $42,500 of direct materials, used $12,500 of direct labor, and was allocated $17,000 of manufacturing overhead. In addition, $126,900 was transferred out of the Centers processing department during the month and $196,200 was transferred out of the Shells processing department during the month. These transfers represent the cost of the jelly beans transferred from one process to another.

1. Prepare a T-account for the "Work in Process Inventory—Shells" showing all activity that took place in the account during September.

2. What is the ending balance in the "Work in Process Inventory—Shells" on September 30? What does this figure represent?

S5-3 Recompute SeaView's equivalent units *(Learning Objective 2)*

Look at SeaView's Shaping Department's equivalent-unit computation in Exhibit 5-5. Suppose the ending work in process inventory is 30% of the way through the shaping process rather than 25% of the way through. Compute the total equivalent units of direct materials and conversion costs.

S5-4 Determine the physical flow of units (process costing Step 1)
(Learning Objective 2)

Babson Soda's Bottling Department had 19,000 units in the beginning inventory of Work in Process on September 1. During September, 100,000 units were started into production. On September 30, 29,000 units were left in ending inventory of Work in Process. Summarize the physical flow of units in a schedule.

S5-5 Compute equivalent units (process costing Step 2) *(Learning Objective 2)*

Hoffman's Packaging Department had the following information at July 31. All direct materials are added at the *end* of the conversion process. The units in ending work in process inventory were only 36% of the way through the conversion process.

	A	B	C	D
1			**Equivalent Units**	
2		**Flow of Physical Units**	**Direct Materials**	**Conversion Costs**
3	**Units accounted for:**			
4	Completed and transferred out	116,300		
5	Plus: Ending work in process, July 31	9,300		
6	Total physical units accounted for	125,600		
7	**Total equivalent units**			
8				

Complete the schedule by computing the total equivalent units of direct materials and conversion costs for the month.

S5-6 Compute equivalent units (process costing Step 2) *(Learning Objective 2)*

The Frying Department of Crinkle Chips had 110,000 partially completed units in work in process at the end of March. All of the direct materials had been added to these units, but the units were only 68% of the way through the conversion process. In addition, 1,200,000 units had been completed and transferred out of the Frying Department to the Packaging Department during the month.

1. How many equivalent units of direct materials and equivalent units of conversion costs are associated with the 1,200,000 units completed and transferred out?

2. Compute the equivalent units of direct materials and the equivalent units of conversion costs associated with the 110,000 partially completed units still in ending work in process.

3. What are the total equivalent units of direct materials and the total equivalent units of conversion costs for the month?

S5-7 Summarize total costs to account for (process costing Step 3) *(Learning Objective 3)*

MacIntyre Company's Work in Process Inventory account had a $68,000 beginning balance on May 1 ($43,000 of this related to direct materials used during April, while $25,000 related to conversion costs incurred during April). During May, the following costs were incurred in the department:

Direct materials used	$103,000
Direct labor	$ 12,000
Manufacturing overhead allocated to the department	$150,000

Summarize the department's "Total costs to account for." Prepare a schedule that summarizes the department's total costs to account for by direct materials and conversion costs.

S5-8 Compute the cost per equivalent unit (process costing Step 4) *(Learning Objective 3)*

At the end of August, a company's mixing department had "Total costs to account for" of $728,607. Of this amount, $255,927 related to direct materials costs, while the remainder related to conversion costs. The department had 52,230 total equivalent units of direct materials and 45,450 total equivalent units of conversion costs for the month.

Compute the cost per equivalent unit for direct materials and the cost per equivalent unit for conversion costs.

S5-9 Recompute SeaView's cost per equivalent unit *(Learning Objective 3)*

Return to the original SeaView example in Exhibits 5-5 and 5-7. Suppose direct labor is $34,000 rather than $21,250. Now what is the conversion cost per equivalent unit?

S5-10   Assign costs (process costing Step 5) *(Learning Objective 3)*

Tristan Company produces its product using a *single* production process. For the month of August, the company determined its "cost per equivalent unit" to be as follows:

	Direct Materials	Conversion Costs
Cost per equivalent unit:	$4.20	$2.75

During the month, Tristan completed and transferred out 410,000 units to finished goods inventory. At month-end, 86,000 partially complete units remained in ending work in process inventory. These partially completed units were equal to 69,000 equivalent units of direct materials and 50,000 equivalent units of conversion costs.

1. Determine the total cost that should be assigned to the following:
   a. Units completed and transferred out
   b. Units in ending work in process inventory
2. What was the total costs accounted for?
3. What was Tristan's average cost of making one unit of its product?

S5-11   Flow of costs through Work in Process Inventory *(Learning Objective 4)*

Maxwell Flooring produces its product in two processing departments: Forming and Finishing. The following T-account shows the Forming Department's Work in Process Inventory at October 31 prior to completing the five-step process costing procedure:

Work in Process Inventory—Forming Department	
Beginning balance	$ 53,800
Direct materials used	78,700
Direct labor	14,400
Manufacturing overhead allocated	126,500

1. What is the Forming Department's "Total costs to account for" for the month of October?
2. Assume that after using the five-step process costing procedure, the company determines that the "cost to be assigned to units completed and transferred out" is $243,900. What journal entry is needed to record the transfer of costs to the Finishing Department?
3. After the journal entry is made, what will be the new ending balance in the Forming Department's Work in Process Inventory account?

S5-12   Assign total costs in a second processing department
(Learning Objective 5)

After completing Steps 1–4 of the process costing procedure, Donahue Corporation arrived at the following equivalent units and costs per equivalent unit for its *final* production department for the month of July:

	A	B	C	D
1			Equivalent Units	
2		Transferred-in	Direct Materials	Conversion Costs
3	Units completed and transferred out during July	69,000	69,000	69,000
4	Plus: Ending work in process, July 31	9,000	8,400	4,400
5	Total equivalent units	78,000	77,400	73,400
6	Cost per equivalent unit	$ 2.84	$ 0.75	$ 1.56
7				

1. How much cost should be assigned to the
   a. units completed and transferred out to Finished Goods Inventory during July?
   b. partially complete units still in ending work in process inventory at the end of July?
2. What was the "Total cost accounted for" during July? What other important figure must this match? What does this figure tell you?
3. What is Donahue Corporation's average cost of making *each unit* of its product from the first production department all the way through the final production department?

S5-13   Find unit cost and gross profit on a final product *(Learning Objective 5)*

Counter Co. produces Formica countertops in two sequential production departments: Forming and Polishing. The Polishing Department calculated the following costs per equivalent unit (square feet) on its October production cost report:

	Transferred-in	Direct Materials	Conversion Costs
Cost per equivalent unit:	$2.44	$0.40	$1.66

During October, 165,000 square feet were completed and transferred out of the Polishing Department to Finished Goods Inventory. The countertops were subsequently sold for $13.00 per square foot.

1. What was the cost per square foot of the finished product?
2. Did most of the production cost occur in the Forming Department or in the Polishing Department? Explain how you can tell where the most production cost occurred.
3. What was the gross profit per square foot?
4. What was the total gross profit on the countertops produced in October?

The following data set is used for S5-14 through S5-18:

Crystal Springs Data Set: Filtration Department
Crystal Springs produces premium bottled water. Crystal Springs purchases artesian water, stores the water in large tanks, and then runs the water through two processes:

- Filtration, where workers microfilter and ozonate the water
- Bottling, where workers bottle and package the filtered water

During May, the filtration process incurs the following costs in processing 205,000 liters:

Wages of workers operating the filtration equipment............................	$ 10,280
Wages of workers operating ozonation equipment	$ 11,500
Manufacturing overhead allocated to filtration	$ 25,500
Water..	$118,900

Crystal Springs has no beginning inventory in the Filtration Department.

S5-14   Compute cost per liter *(Learning Objective 1)*

Refer to the Crystal Springs Filtration Department Data Set.

1. Compute the May conversion costs in the Filtration Department.
2. If the Filtration Department completely processed 205,000 liters, what would be the average filtration cost per liter?
3. Now, assume that the total costs of the filtration process listed in the previous chart yield 165,000 liters that are completely filtered and ozonated, while the remaining 40,000 liters are only partway through the process at the end of May. Is the cost per completely filtered and ozonated liter higher, lower, or the same as in Requirement 2? Why?

S5-15   Summarize physical flow and compute equivalent units
(Learning Objective 2)

Refer to the Crystal Springs Filtration Department Data Set. At Crystal Springs, water is added at the beginning of the filtration process. Conversion costs are added evenly throughout the process, and in May, 165,000 liters have been completed and transferred out of the Filtration Department to the Bottling Department. The 40,000 liters remaining in the Filtration Department's ending work in process inventory are 80% of the way through the filtration process. Recall that Cold Springs has no beginning inventories.

1. Draw a time line for the filtration process.
2. Complete the first two steps of the process costing procedure for the Filtration Department: summarize the physical flows of units and then compute the equivalent units of direct materials and conversion costs.

S5-16   Continuation of S5-15: Summarize total costs to account for and compute cost per equivalent unit *(Learning Objective 3)*

Refer to the Crystal Springs Filtration Department Data Set and your answer to S5-15. Complete Steps 3 and 4 of the process costing procedure: Summarize total costs to account for and then compute the cost per equivalent unit for both direct materials and conversion costs.

S5-17   Continuation of S5-15 and S5-16: Assign costs *(Learning Objective 3)*

Refer to the Crystal Springs Filtration Department Data Set and your answer to S5-15 and S5-16. Complete Step 5 of the process costing procedure: Assign costs to units completed and to units in ending inventory. Prepare a schedule that answers the following questions.

1. What is the cost of the 165,000 liters completed and transferred out of the Filtration Department?
2. What is the cost of 40,000 liters remaining in the Filtration Department's ending work in process inventory?

S5-18   Continuation of S5-17: Record journal entry and post to T-account
(Learning Objective 4)

Refer to the Crystal Springs Filtration Department Data Set and your answer to S5-17.

1. Record the journal entry to transfer the cost of the 165,000 liters completed and transferred out of the Filtration Department and into the Bottling Department.
2. Record all of the transactions in the "Work in Process Inventory—Filtration" T-account.

The following data set is used for S5-19 through S5-22:

Crystal Springs Data Set: Bottling Department
Crystal Springs produces premium bottled water. The preceding Short Exercises considered the first process in bottling premium water—Filtration. We now consider Crystal Springs second process—Bottling. In the Bottling Department, workers bottle the filtered water and pack the bottles into boxes. Conversion costs are incurred evenly throughout the Bottling process, but packaging materials are not added until the end of the process.

May data from the Bottling Department follow:

Beginning work in process inventory (40% of the way through the process)	7,000 liters
Transferred in from Filtration	165,000 liters
Completed and transferred out to Finished Goods Inventory in May	152,000 liters
Ending work in process inventory (80% of the way through the bottling process)	20,000 liters

Costs in beginning work in process inventory		Costs added during May	
Transferred in	$2,780	Transferred in	$135,000
Direct materials	0	Direct materials	28,748
Direct labor	560	Direct labor	33,800
Manufacturing overhead	1,992	Manufacturing overhead	22,400
Total beginning work in process inventory as of May 1	$5,332	Total costs added during February	$219,948

The Filtration Department completed and transferred out 165,000 liters at a total cost of $135,000.

S5-19 Compute equivalent units in second department *(Learning Objectives 2 & 5)*

Refer to the Crystal Springs Bottling Department Data Set.

1. Draw a time line.
2. Complete the first two steps of the process costing procedure for the Bottling Department: summarize the physical flow of units and then compute the equivalent units of direct materials and conversion costs.

S5-20 Continuation of S5-19: Compute cost per equivalent unit in second department *(Learning Objective 5)*

Refer to the Crystal Springs Bottling Department Data Set and your answer to S5-19. Complete Steps 3 and 4 of the process costing procedure: Summarize total costs to account for and then compute the cost per equivalent unit for both direct materials and conversion costs.

S5-21 Continuation of S5-19 and S5-20: Assign costs in second department *(Learning Objective 5)*

Refer to the Crystal Springs Bottling Department Data Set and your answers to S5-19 and S5-20. Complete Step 5 of the process costing procedure: Assign costs to units completed and to units in ending inventory.

S5-22 Continuation of S5-21: Record journal entry and post to T-account *(Learning Objective 4)*

Refer to the Crystal Springs Bottling Department Data Set and your answer to S5-21.

1. Prepare the journal entry to record the cost of units completed and transferred to finished goods.
2. Post all transactions to the "Work in Process Inventory—Bottling" T-account. What is the ending balance?

ETHICS

S5-23 Identify ethical standards violated *(Learning Objectives 1, 2, 3, 4, & 5)*

For each of the situations listed, identify the primary standard from the IMA Statement of Ethical Professional Practice that is violated (competence, confidentiality, integrity, or credibility). Refer to Exhibit 1-6 for the complete standard.

1. Dawn works in the Accounting Department at White Star Consulting. She does not disclose that one of the companies bidding on a contract to provide payroll services for White Star employs her daughter.
2. This quarter, the company switched from using the FIFO method of process costing to the weighted-average method of process costing. Clarke, the chief accountant, did not disclose the change in methods in the reports because he did not want to have to justify the change.
3. Darla Cortez is a bubbly, fun person. She continually makes recommendations one day after the recommendations were needed. She figures that the managers will tolerate the tardiness of the recommendations because the recommendations are well researched and she gets along with everyone.
4. At a party, Kelvin gets carried away with bragging about the production process that he has helped to develop at his company. A party-goer who works for a competitor overhears.
5. Process costing has always confused Amber, an accountant for Griffith Corporation. At the end of the year, she just accepts the bookkeeper's numbers for ending inventory and cost of goods sold even though the bookkeeper does not have formal training in process costing.

EXERCISES Group A

E5-24A Analyze flow of costs through inventory T-accounts *(Learning Objective 1)*

Tasty Treats Bakery mass-produces bread using three sequential processing departments: Mixing, Baking, and Packaging. The following transactions occurred during April:

1. Direct materials used in the Packaging Department	$ 34,000
2. Costs assigned to units completed and transferred out of Mixing..............	$229,000
3. Direct labor incurred in the Mixing Department......................................	$ 11,800
4. Beginning balance: Work in Process Inventory-Baking	$ 15,200
5. Manufacturing overhead allocated to the Baking Department..................	$ 71,000
6. Beginning balance: Finished Goods...	$ 4,000
7. Costs assigned to units completed and transferred out of Baking..............	$306,000
8. Beginning balance: Work in Process Inventory—Mixing............................	$ 12,400
9. Direct labor incurred in the Packaging Department..................................	$ 8,000
10. Manufacturing overhead allocated to the Mixing Department..................	$ 65,000
11. Direct materials used in the Mixing Department......................................	$150,000
12. Beginning balance: Raw Materials Inventory...	$ 23,000
13. Costs assigned to units completed and transferred out of Packaging........	$385,000
14. Beginning balance: Work in Process Inventory—Packaging.......................	$ 8,100
15. Purchases of Raw Materials..	$178,000
16. Direct labor incurred in the Baking Department.....................................	$ 4,200
17. Manufacturing overhead allocated to the Packaging Department	$ 42,000
18. Cost of goods sold...	$386,500

NOTE: No direct materials were used by the Baking Department.

Requirements

1. Post each of these transactions to the company's inventory T-accounts. You should set up separate T-accounts for the following:
   - Raw Materials Inventory
   - Work in Process Inventory—Mixing Department
   - Work in Process Inventory—Baking Department
   - Work in Process Inventory—Packaging Department
   - Finished Goods Inventory
2. Determine the balance at month-end in each of the inventory accounts.
3. Assume that 3,375,000 loaves of bread were completed and transferred out of the Packaging Department during the month. What was the cost per unit of making each loaf of bread (from start to finish)?

E5-25A Summarize physical units and compute equivalent units (process costing Steps 1 and 2) *(Learning Objective 2)*

Chelsea's Chocolate Pies collected the following production information relating to November's baking operations:

	Physical Units	Direct Materials (% complete)	Conversion Costs (% complete)
Beginning work in process..............	204,000	—	—
Ending work in process...................	154,000	75%	80%
Units started during the month.......	1,015,000		

Requirements

Complete the first two steps in the process costing procedure:

1. Summarize the flow of physical units.
2. Compute output in terms of equivalent units.

E5-26A Compute equivalent units in a second processing department
(Learning Objectives 2 & 5)

Miller's Mayonnaise uses a process costing system to determine its product's cost. The last of the three processes is packaging. The Packaging Department reported the following information for the month of August:

	A	B	C	D	E
		Step 1:	**Step 2: Equivalent Units**		
1	**Miller's Mayonnaise Packaging Department**	**Flow of Physical**	**Transferred-**	**Direct**	**Conversion**
2	**Month Ended August 31** **Flow of Production**	**Units**	**in**	**Materials**	**Costs**
3	**Units to account for:**				
4	Beginning work in process, August 1	24,000			
5	Plus: Transferred in during August	232,000			
6	Total physical units to account for	(a)			
7					
8	**Units accounted for:**				
9	Completed and transferred out during August	(b)	(d)	(g)	(j)
10	Plus: Ending work in process, August 31	29,000	(e)	(h)	(k)
11	Total physical units accounted for	(c)			
12	**Total Equivalent Units**		(f)	(i)	(l)
13					

The units in ending work in process inventory were 90% complete with respect to direct materials, but only 60% complete with respect to conversion.

Requirement

Summarize the flow of physical units and compute output in terms of equivalent units in order to arrive at the missing figures (a) through (l).

E5-27A Complete five-step procedure in first department *(Learning Objective 3)*

The Lucy Paint Company prepares and packages paint products. The company has two departments: (1) Blending and (2) Packaging. Direct materials are added at the beginning of the blending process (dyes) and at the end of the packaging process (cans). Conversion costs are added evenly throughout each process. Data from the month of May for the Blending Department are as follows:

Gallons:	
Beginning work in process inventory	0
Started production	8,400 gallons
Completed and transferred out to Packaging in May.........................	6,200 gallons
Ending work in process inventory (40% of the way through the blending process)..	2,200 gallons
Costs:	
Beginning work in process inventory	$ 0
Costs added during May:	
Direct materials (dyes)	5,460
Direct labor..	920
Manufacturing overhead	1,912
Total costs added during May...	$8,292

Requirements

1. Draw a time line.
2. Summarize the physical flow of units and compute total equivalent units for direct materials and for conversion costs.
3. Summarize total costs to account for and find the cost per equivalent unit for direct materials and conversion costs.
4. Assign total costs to units (gallons):
   a. Completed and transferred out to the Packaging Department
   b. In the Blending Department ending work in process inventory
5. What is the average cost per gallon transferred out of the Blending Department to the Packaging Department? Why would the company's managers want to know this cost?

E5-28A   Continuation of E5-27A: Journal entries *(Learning Objective 4)*

Return to the Blending Department for The Lucy Paint Company in E5-27A.

Requirements

1. Present the journal entry to record the use of direct materials and direct labor and the allocation of manufacturing overhead to the Blending Department. Also, give the journal entry to record the costs of the gallons completed and transferred out to the Packaging Department.
2. Post the journal entries to the "Work in Process Inventory—Blending" T-account. What is the ending balance?

E5-29A   Record journal entries *(Learning Objective 4)*

Record the following process costing transactions in the general journal:

a. Purchase of raw materials on account, $9,000
b. Requisition of direct materials to

   Assembly Department, $4,100

   Finishing Department, $2,000
c. Incurrence and payment of direct labor, $10,200
d. Incurrence of manufacturing overhead costs:

   Property taxes—plant, $1,900

   Utilities—plant, $4,700

   Insurance—plant, $1,300

   Depreciation—plant, $3,200
e. Assignment of conversion costs to the Assembly Department:

   Direct labor, $4,800

   Manufacturing overhead, $2,100
f. Assignment of conversion costs to the Finishing Department:

   Direct labor, $4,500

   Manufacturing overhead, $6,400
g. Cost of goods completed and transferred out of the Assembly Department to the Finishing Department, $10,550
h. Cost of goods completed and transferred out of the Finishing Department into Finished Goods Inventory, $15,700

E5-30A   Compute equivalent units and assign costs
(Learning Objectives 2, 3, & 4)

The Assembly Department of Greaton Surge Protectors began September with no work in process inventory. During the month, production that cost $50,786 (direct materials, $12,386, and conversion costs, $38,400) was started on 27,000 units. Greaton completed and transferred to the Testing Department a total of 20,000 units. The ending work in process inventory was 36% complete as to direct materials and 80% complete as to conversion work.

Requirements

1. Compute the equivalent units for direct materials and conversion costs.
2. Compute the cost per equivalent unit.
3. Assign the costs to units completed and transferred out and ending work in process inventory.
4. Record the journal entry for the costs transferred out of the Assembly Department to the Testing Department.
5. Post all of the transactions in the "Work in Process Inventory—Assembly" T-account. What is the ending balance?

E5-31A   Complete five-step procedure in first department (Learning Objective 3)

Cambria Winery in Santa Maria, California, has two departments: Fermenting and Packaging. Direct materials are added at the beginning of the fermenting process (grapes) and at the end of the packaging process (bottles). Conversion costs are added evenly throughout each process. Data from the month of March for the Fermenting Department are as follows:

Gallons:	
Beginning work in process inventory	2,900 gallons
Started production	4,770 gallons
Completed and transferred out to Packaging in March	6,420 gallons
Ending work in process inventory (80% of the way through the fermenting process)	1,250 gallons
Costs:	
Beginning work in process inventory ($2,100 of direct materials and $1,409 of conversion cost)	$ 3,509
Costs added during March:	
Direct materials...	$ 10,172
Direct labor..	1,000
Manufacturing overhead	1,301
Total costs added during March	$12,473

Requirements

1. Draw a time line for the Fermenting Department.
2. Summarize the flow of physical units and compute the total equivalent units.
3. Summarize total costs to account for and compute the cost per equivalent unit for direct materials and conversion costs.
4. Assign total costs to units (gallons):
    a. Completed and transferred out to the Packaging Department
    b. In the Fermenting Department ending work in process inventory
5. What is the average cost per gallon transferred out of Fermenting into Packaging? Why would the company's managers want to know this cost?

SUSTAINABILITY

E5-32A   Sustainability and process costing (Learning Objective 3)

Sampson Industries manufactures plastic bottles for the food industry. On average, Sampson pays $78 per ton for its plastics. Sampson's waste disposal company has increased its waste disposal charge to $60 per ton for solid and inert waste. Sampson generates a total of 500 tons of waste per month.

Sampson's managers have been evaluating the production processes for areas to cut waste. In the process of making plastic bottles, a certain amount of machine "drool" occurs. Machine drool is the excess plastic that "drips" off the machine between molds. In the past, Sampson has discarded the machine drool. In an average month, 160 tons of machine drool is generated.

Management has arrived at three possible courses of action for the machine drool issue:

1. Do nothing and pay the increased waste disposal charge.
2. Sell the machine drool waste to a local recycler for $15 per ton.
3. Re-engineer the production process at an annual cost of $65,000. This change in the production process would cause the amount of machine drool generated to be reduced by 40% each month. The remaining machine drool would then be sold to a local recycler for $15 per ton.

Requirements

1. What is the annual cost of the machine drool currently? Include both the original plastic cost and the waste disposal cost.
2. How much would the company save per year (net) if the machine drool were to be sold to the local recycler?
3. How much would the company save per year (net) if the production process were to be re-engineered?
4. What do you think the company should do? Explain your rationale.

E5-33A Complete five-step procedure and journalize result
(Learning Objectives 3 & 4)

The following information was taken from the ledger of Antonio Roping:

Work in Process—Forming			
Beginning inventory, October 1	$ 76,978	Transferred to Finishing	$?
Direct materials	163,804		
Conversion costs	162,500		
Ending inventory	?		

The Forming Department had 10,400 partially complete units in beginning work in process inventory. The department started work on 77,300 units during the month and ended the month with 8,700 units still in work in process. These unfinished units were 60% complete as to direct materials but 20% complete as to conversion work. The beginning balance of $76,978 consisted of $21,480 of direct materials and $55,498 of conversion costs.

Requirement

Journalize the transfer of costs to the Finishing Department. (*Hint:* Complete the five-step process costing procedure to determine how much cost to transfer.)

E5-34A Compute equivalent units in two later departments
(Learning Objectives 2 & 5)

Selected production and cost data of Waterfall Fudge follow for May:

	Flow of Physical Units	
Flow of Production	**Mixing Department**	**Heating Department**
Units to account for:		
Beginning work in process, May 1..............................	28,000	6,000
Transferred in during May	72,000	85,000
Total physical units to account for.............................	100,000	91,000
Units accounted for:		
Completed and transferred out during May..............	85,000	79,000
Ending work in process, May 31.................................	15,000	12,000
Total physical units accounted for.............................	100,000	91,000

On May 31, the Mixing Department's ending work in process inventory was 80% complete as to materials and 20% complete as to conversion costs.

On May 31, the Heating Department's ending work in process inventory was 65% complete as to materials and 55% complete as to conversion costs.

Requirement

Compute the equivalent units for transferred-in costs, direct materials, and conversion costs for both the Mixing and the Heating Departments.

E5-35A   Complete five-step procedure in second department
(*Learning Objective 5*)

Goldstein Semiconductors experienced the following activity in its Photolithography Department during December. Materials are added at the beginning of the photolithography process.

Units:	
Work in process, December 1 (80% of the way through the process)	9,000 units
Transferred in from the Polishing and Cutting Department during December	23,000 units
Completed during December	? units
Work in process, December 31 (70% of the way through the process)..	2,000 units
Costs:	
Work in process, December 1 (transferred-in costs, $1,600; direct materials costs, $20,450; and conversion costs, $37,890)........	$59,940
Transferred in from the Polishing and Cutting Department during December	97,600
Direct materials added during December............................	53,150
Conversion costs added during December...........................	90,850

Requirements

1. Summarize flow of physical units and compute total equivalent units for three cost categories: transferred-in, direct materials, and conversion costs.

2. Summarize total costs to account for and compute the cost per equivalent unit for each cost category.

3. Assign total costs to (a) units completed and transferred to Finished Goods Inventory and (b) units in December 31 Work in Process Inventory.

EXERCISES Group B

E5-36B   Analyze flow of costs through inventory T-accounts
(Learning Objective 1)

Healthy Start Bakery mass-produces bread using three sequential processing departments: Mixing, Baking, and Packaging. The following transactions occurred during February:

1. Direct materials used in the Packaging Department	$ 33,000
2. Costs assigned to units completed and transferred out of Mixing................	$226,000
3. Direct labor incurred in the Mixing Department..	$ 11,600
4. Beginning balance: Work in Process Inventory—Baking................................	$ 15,200
5. Manufactured overhead allocated to the Baking Department......................	$ 74,000
6. Beginning balance: Finished Goods Inventory	$ 4,000
7. Costs assigned to units completed and transferred out of Baking................	$302,000
8. Beginning balance: Work in Process Inventory—Mixing................................	$ 12,600
9. Direct labor incurred in the Packaging Department.....................................	$ 8,800
10. Manufacturing overhead allocated to the Mixing Department.....................	$ 63,000
11. Direct materials used in the Mixing Department..	$155,000
12. Beginning balance: Raw Materials Inventory	$ 23,300
13. Costs assigned to units completed and transferred out of Packaging..........	$385,000
14. Beginning balance: Work in Process Inventory—Packaging..........................	$ 8,100
15. Purchases of Raw Materials...	$175,000
16. Direct labor incurred in the Baking Department...	$ 4,800
17. Manufacturing overhead allocated to the Packaging Department	$ 48,000
18. Cost of goods sold...	$386,000

Requirements

1. Post each of these transactions to the company's inventory T-accounts. You should set up separate T-accounts for the following:
   - Raw Materials Inventory
   - Work in Process Inventory—Mixing Department
   - Work in Process Inventory—Baking Department
   - Work in Process Inventory—Packaging Department
   - Finished Goods Inventory
2. Determine the balance at month-end in each of the inventory accounts.
3. Assume 3,300,000 loaves of bread were completed and transferred out of the Packaging Department during the month. What was the cost per unit of making each loaf of bread (from start to finish)?

E5-37B   Summarize physical units and compute equivalent units
(process costing Steps 1 and 2) *(Learning Objective 2)*

Allison's Apple Pies collected the following production information relating to June's baking operations:

	Physical Units	Direct Materials (% complete)	Conversion Costs (% complete)
Beginning work in process	201,000	—	—
Ending work in process	151,000	75%	90%
Units started during the month............	1,020,000		

Requirements

Complete the first two steps in the process costing procedure:

1. Summarize the flow of physical units.
2. Compute output in terms of equivalent units.

E5-38B   Compute equivalent units in a second processing department
(Learning Objectives 2 & 5)

Mogyardy's Mayonnaise uses a process costing system to determine its product's cost. The last of the three processes is packaging. The Packaging Department reported the following information for the month of July:

	A	B	C	D	E
		Step 1:	Step 2: Equivalent Units		
1	Mogyardy's Mayonnaise Packaging Department				
2	Month Ended July 31 Flow of Production	Flow of Physical Units	Transferred-in	Direct Materials	Conversion Costs
3	Units to account for:				
4	Beginning work in process, July 1	26,000			
5	Plus: Transferred in during July	228,000			
6	Total physical units to account for	(a)			
7					
8	Units accounted for:				
9	Completed and transferred out during July	(b)	(d)	(g)	(j)
10	Plus: Ending work in process, July 31	31,000	(e)	(h)	(k)
11	Total physical units accounted for	(c)			
12	**Total Equivalent Units**		(f)	(i)	(l)
13					

The units in ending work in process inventory were 70% complete with respect to direct materials, but only 50% complete with respect to conversion.

Requirement

Summarize the flow of physical units and compute output in terms of equivalent units in order to arrive at the missing figures (a) through (l).

E5-39B   Complete five-step procedure in first department
(Learning Objective 3)

The Shannon Paint Company prepares and packages paint products. The company has two departments: (1) Blending and (2) Packaging. Direct materials are added at the beginning of the blending process (dyes) and at the end of the packaging process (cans). Conversion costs are added evenly throughout each process. Data from the month of May for the Blending Department are as follows:

Gallons:	
Beginning work in process inventory	0
Started production	8,200 gallons
Completed and transferred out to Packaging in May......................	6,100 gallons
Ending work in process inventory (40% of the way through the blending process)..	2,100 gallons
Costs:	
Beginning work in process inventory	$ 0
Costs added during May:	
Direct materials (dyes)...	$5,166
Direct labor...	600
Manufacturing overhead	1,829
Total costs added during May..	$7,595

Requirements

1. Fill in the time line for the Blending Department.
2. Summarize the physical flow of units and compute total equivalent units for direct materials and for conversion costs.
3. Summarize total costs to account for and find the cost per equivalent unit for direct materials and for conversion costs.
4. Assign total costs to units (gallons):
   a. Completed and transferred out to the Packaging Department
   b. In the Blending Department ending work in process inventory
5. What is the average cost per gallon transferred out of the Blending Department to the Packaging Department? Why would the company's managers want to know this cost?

E5-40B   Continuation of E5-39B: Journal entries *(Learning Objective 4)*

Return to the Blending Department for The Shannon Paint Company in E5-39B.

Requirements

1. Present the journal entry to record the use of direct materials and direct labor and the allocation of manufacturing overhead to the Blending Department. Also, give the journal entry to record the costs of the gallons completed and transferred out to the Packaging Department.
2. Post the journal entries to the "Work in Process Inventory—Blending" T-account. What is the ending balance?

E5-41B   Record journal entries *(Learning Objective 4)*

Record the following process costing transactions in the general journal:

a. Purchase of raw materials on account, $9,900
b. Requisition of direct materials to
   Assembly Department, $4,400
   Finishing Department, $2,800
c. Incurrence and payment of manufacturing labor, $10,300
d. Incurrence of manufacturing overhead costs:
   Property taxes—plant, $1,500
   Utilities—plant, $4,500
   Insurance—plant, $1,400
   Depreciation—plant, $3,300
e. Assignment of conversion costs to the Assembly Department:
   Direct labor, $5,000
   Manufacturing overhead, $2,700
f. Assignment of conversion costs to the Finishing Department:
   Direct labor, $4,300
   Manufacturing overhead, $6,000
g. Cost of goods completed and transferred out of the Assembly Department to the Finishing Department, $10,200
h. Cost of goods completed and transferred out of the Finishing Department into Finished Goods Inventory, $15,300

E5-42B   Compute equivalent units and assign costs *(Learning Objectives 2, 3, & 4)*

The Assembly Department of Crackle Surge Protectors began September with no work in process inventory. During the month, production that cost $64,434 (direct materials, $12,954, and conversion costs, $51,480) was started on 31,000 units. Crackle completed and transferred to the Testing Department a total of 23,000 units. The ending work in process inventory was 30% complete as to direct materials and 70% complete as to conversion work.

Requirements

1. Compute the equivalent units for direct materials and conversion costs.
2. Compute the cost per equivalent unit.
3. Assign the costs to units completed and transferred out and ending work in process inventory.
4. Record the journal entry for the costs transferred out of the Assembly Department to the Testing Department.
5. Post all of the transactions in the "Work in Process Inventory—Assembly" T-account. What is the ending balance?

E5-43B   Complete five-step procedure in first department *(Learning Objective 3)*

Cove Point Winery in Lusby, Maryland, has two departments: Fermenting and Packaging. Direct materials are added at the beginning of the fermenting process (grapes) and at the end of the packaging process (bottles). Conversion costs are added throughout each process. Data from the month of March for the Fermenting Department are as follows:

Gallons:	
Beginning work in process inventory	2,000 gallons
Started production	6,000 gallons
Completed and transferred out to Packaging in March	6,550 gallons
Ending work in process inventory (80% of the way through the fermenting process)	1,450 gallons
Costs:	
Beginning work in process inventory ($2,800 of direct materials and $2,855 of conversion cost)	$ 5,655
Costs added during March:	
Direct materials..	$ 8,800
Direct labor...	1,600
Manufacturing overhead	2,484
Total costs added during March	$12,884

Requirements

1. Draw a time line for the Fermenting Department.
2. Summarize the flow of physical units and compute the total equivalent units.
3. Summarize total costs to account for and compute the cost per equivalent unit for direct materials and conversion costs.
4. Assign total costs to units (gallons):
   a. Completed and transferred out to the Packaging Department
   b. In the Fermenting Department ending work in process inventory
5. What is the average cost per gallon transferred out of Fermenting into Packaging? Why would the company's managers want to know this cost?

SUSTAINABILITY

E5-44B   Sustainability and process costing *(Learning Objective 3)*

Sorrento Industries manufactures plastic bottles for the food industry. On average, Sorrento pays $71 per ton for its plastics. Sorrento's waste disposal company has increased its waste disposal charge to $58 per ton for solid and inert waste. Sorrento generates a total of 500 tons of waste per month.

Sorrento's managers have been evaluating the production processes for areas to cut waste. In the process of making plastic bottles, a certain amount of machine "drool" occurs. Machine drool is the excess plastic that "drips" off the machine between molds. In the past, Sorrento has discarded the machine drool. In an average month, 180 tons of machine drool are generated.

Management has arrived at three possible courses of action for the machine drool issue:

1. Do nothing and pay the increased waste disposal charge.
2. Sell the machine drool waste to a local recycler for $14 per ton.
3. Re-engineer the production process at an annual cost of $60,000. This change in the production process would cause the amount of machine drool generated to be reduced by 40% each month. The remaining machine drool would then be sold to a local recycler for $14 per ton.

Requirements

1. What is the annual cost of the machine drool currently? Include both the original plastics cost and the waste disposal cost.
2. How much would the company save per year (net) if the machine drool were to be sold at the local recycler?
3. How much would the company save per year (net) if the production process were to be re-engineered?
4. What do you think the company should do? Explain your rationale.

E5-45B Complete five-step procedure and journalize result
(*Learning Objectives 3 & 4*)

The following information was taken from the ledger of Johnson Roping:

Work in Process—Forming			
Beginning inventory, October 1	32,300	Transferred to Finishing	?
Direct materials	183,790		
Conversion costs	162,300		
Ending inventory	?		

The Forming Department had 10,300 partially complete units in beginning work in process inventory. The department started work on 75,200 units during the month and ended the month with 8,500 units still in work in process. These unfinished units were 60% complete as to direct materials but 20% complete as to conversion work. The beginning balance of $32,300 consisted of $21,460 of direct materials and $10,840 of conversion costs.

Requirement

Journalize the transfer of costs to the Finishing Department. (*Hint*: Complete the five-step process costing procedure to determine how much cost to transfer.)

E5-46B Compute equivalent units in two later departments
(*Learning Objectives 2 & 5*)

Selected production and cost data of Abby's Fudge follow for May:

	Flow of Physical Units	
Flow of Production	Mixing Department	Heating Department
Units to account for:		
Beginning work in process, May 1	27,000	5,000
Transferred in during May	75,000	87,000
Total physical units to account for	102,000	92,000
Units accounted for:		
Completed and transferred out during May	87,000	82,000
Ending work in process, May 31	15,000	10,000
Total physical units accounted for	102,000	92,000

On May 31, the Mixing Department's ending work in process inventory was 80% complete as to materials and 10% complete as to conversion costs. On May 31, the Heating Department's ending work in process inventory was 55% complete as to materials and 45% complete as to conversion costs.

Requirement

Compute the equivalent units for transferred-in costs, direct materials, and conversion costs for both the Mixing and the Heating Departments.

E5-47B Complete five-step procedure in second department
(Learning Objective 5)

Wilkman Semiconductors experienced the following activity in its Photolithography Department during December. Materials are added at the beginning of the photolithography process.

Units:	
Work in process, December 1 (80% of the way through the process)...	2,000 units
Transferred in from the Polishing and Cutting Department during December...	24,000 units
Completed during December	? units
Work in process, December 31 (70% of the way through the process)	4,000 units
Costs:	
Work in process, December 1 (transferred-in costs, $1,000; direct materials costs, $20,550; and conversion costs, $5,770).....	$27,320
Transferred in from the Polishing and Cutting Department during December...	97,800
Direct materials added during December..	34,050
Conversion costs added during December.......................................	90,950

Requirements

1. Summarize flow of physical units and compute total equivalent units for three cost categories: transferred-in, direct materials, and conversion costs.
2. Summarize total costs to account for and compute the cost per equivalent unit for each cost category.
3. Assign total costs to (a) units completed and transferred to Finished Goods Inventory and (b) units in December 31 Work in Process Inventory.

PROBLEMS Group A

P5-48A Process costing in a single processing department
(Learning Objectives 1, 2, & 3)

Lopez Cosmetics produces a lip balm used for cold-weather sports. The balm is manufactured in a single processing department. No lip balm was in process on May 31, and Lopez Lips started production on 20,900 lip balm tubes during June. Direct materials are added at the beginning of the process, but conversion costs are incurred evenly throughout the process. Completed production for June totaled 15,700 units. The June 30 work in process was 45% of the way through the production process. Direct materials costing $5,225 were placed in production during June, and direct labor of $3,360 and manufacturing overhead of $248 were assigned to the process.

Requirements

1. Draw a time line for Lopez Cosmetics.
2. Use the time line to help you compute the total equivalent units and the cost per equivalent unit for June.
3. Assign total costs to (a) units completed and transferred to Finished Goods and (b) units still in process at June 30.
4. Prepare a T-account for Work in Process Inventory to show activity during June, including the June 30 balance.

P5-49A Process costing in a first department *(Learning Objectives 1, 3, & 4)*

The Northern Furniture Company produces dining tables in a three-stage process: Sawing, Assembly, and Staining. Costs incurred in the Sawing Department during September are summarized as follows:

Work in Process Inventory—Sawing	
September 1 balance	0
Direct materials	1,863,000
Direct labor	137,000
Manufacturing overhead	157,400

Direct materials (lumber) are added at the beginning of the sawing process, while conversion costs are incurred evenly throughout the process. September activity in the Sawing Department included sawing of 10,000 meters of lumber, which were transferred to the Assembly Department. Also, work began on 3,500 meters of lumber, which on September 30 were 80% of the way through the sawing process.

Requirements

1. Draw a time line for the Sawing Department.
2. Use the time line to help you compute the number of equivalent units and the cost per equivalent unit in the Sawing Department for September.
3. Show that the sum of (a) cost of goods transferred out of the Sawing Department and (b) ending "Work in Process Inventory—Sawing" equals the total cost accumulated in the department during September.
4. Journalize all transactions affecting the company's sawing process during September, including those already posted.

P5-50A Five-step process: Materials added at different points
(Learning Objectives 1, 2, & 3)

Royce Chicken produces canned chicken a la king. The chicken a la king passes through three departments: (1) Mixing, (2) Retort (sterilization), and (3) Packing. In the Mixing Department, chicken and cream are added at the beginning of the process, the mixture is partly cooked, and chopped green peppers and mushrooms are added at the end of the process. Conversion costs are added evenly throughout the mixing process. November data from the Mixing Department are as follows:

Gallons		Costs	
Beginning work in process inventory	0 gallons	Beginning work in process inventory	$ 0
Started production	14,200 gallons	Costs added during November:	
Completed and transferred out to Retort in November	13,200 gallons	Chicken	15,780
		Cream	4,100
Ending work in process inventory (60% of the way through the mixing process)	1,000 gallons	Green peppers and mushrooms	7,920
		Direct labor	11,300
		Manufacturing overhead	3,156
		Total costs	$42,256

CHAPTER 5

Requirements

1. Draw a time line for the Mixing Department.
2. Use the time line to help you summarize the flow of physical units and compute the equivalent units. (*Hint:* Each direct material added at a different point in the production process requires its own equivalent-unit computation.)
3. Compute the cost per equivalent unit for each cost category.
4. Compute the total costs of the units (gallons):

   a. Completed and transferred out to the Retort Department

   b. In the Mixing Department's ending work in process inventory

P5-51A Prepare a production cost report and journal entries
(Learning Objectives 4 & 5)

Chrome Accessories manufactures auto roof racks in a two-stage process that includes shaping and plating. Steel alloy is the basic raw material of the shaping process. The steel is molded according to the design specifications of automobile manufacturers (Ford and General Motors). The Plating Department then adds an anodized finish.

At March 31, before recording the transfer of cost from the Plating Department to Finished Goods Inventory, the Chrome Accessories general ledger included the following account:

Work in Process Inventory—Plating		
March 1 balance	34,400	
Transferred-in from Shaping	40,800	
Direct materials	30,000	
Direct labor	21,500	
Manufacturing overhead	28,900	

The direct materials (rubber pads) are added at the end of the plating process. Conversion costs are incurred evenly throughout the process. Work in process of the Plating Department on March 1 consisted of 1,800 racks. The $34,400 beginning balance of "Work in Process—Plating" includes $20,400 of transferred-in cost and $14,000 of conversion cost. During March, 1,800 racks were transferred in from the Shaping Department. The Plating Department transferred 2,000 racks to Finished Goods Inventory in March, and 1,600 were still in process on March 31. This ending inventory was 50% of the way through the plating process.

Requirements

1. Draw a time line for the Plating Department.
2. Prepare the March production cost report for the Plating Department.
3. Journalize all transactions affecting the Plating Department during March, including the entries that have already been posted.

P5-52A Cost per unit and gross profit *(Learning Objective 5)*

Charlie Topper operates Charlie's Cricket Farm in Thomasville, Georgia. Charlie's raises about 18 million crickets a month. Most are sold to pet stores at $12.60 for a box of 1,000 crickets. Pet stores sell the crickets for $0.05 to $0.10 each as live feed for reptiles.

Raising crickets requires a two-step process: incubation and brooding. In the first process, incubation, employees place cricket eggs on mounds of peat moss to hatch. In the second process, employees move the newly hatched crickets into large boxes filled with cardboard dividers. Depending on the desired size, the crickets spend approximately two weeks in brooding before being shipped to pet stores. In the brooding process, Charlie's crickets consume about 16 tons of food and produce 12 tons of manure.

Topper has invested $450,000 in the cricket farm, and he had hoped to earn a 30% annual rate of return, which works out to a 2.5% monthly return on his investment. After looking at the farm's bank balance, Topper fears he is not achieving this return. To get more accurate information on the farm's performance, Topper bought new accounting software that provides weighted-average process cost information. After Topper input the data, the software provided the following reports. However, Topper needs help interpreting these reports.

Topper does know that a unit of production is a box of 1,000 crickets. For example, in June's report, the 6,000 physical units of beginning work-in-process inventory are 6,000 boxes (each one of those boxes contains 1,000 immature crickets). The finished goods inventory is zero because the crickets ship out as soon as they reach the required size. Monthly operating expenses total $12,750 (in addition to the costs that follow).

	A	B	C	D	E
1	Charlie's Crickett Farm—Brooding Department	Step 1:	Step 2: Equivalent Units		
2	Month Ended June 30 Production Cost Report (part 1 of 3)	Flow of Physical Units	Transferred-in	Direct Materials	Conversion Costs
3	**Flow of Production**				
4	**Units to account for:**				
5	Beginning work in process, June 1	6,000			
6	Plus: Transferred in during June	23,000			
7	Total physical units to account for	29,000			
8					
9	**Units accounted for:**				
10	Completed and transferred out during June	20,000	20,000	20,000	20,000
11	Plus: Ending work in process, June 30	9,000	9,000	6,750	2,700
12	Total physical units accounted for	29,000			
13	**Total equivalent units**		29,000	26,750	22,700
14					

	A	B	C	D	E
1	Charlie's Crickett Farm—Brooding Department	Transferred-in	Direct Materials	Conversion Costs	
2	Month Ended June 30 Production Cost Report (part 2 of 3)				Total
3	Beginning work in process, June 1	$ 14,700	$ 28,015	$ 3,000	$ 45,715
4	Plus: Costs added during June	46,200	156,560	51,480	254,240
5	Total costs to account for	$ 60,900	$ 184,575	$ 54,480	$ 299,955
6	Divided by: Total equivalent units	29,000	26,750	22,700	
7	Cost per equivalent unit	$ 2.10	$ 6.90	$ 2.40	
8					

	A	B	C	D	E
1	Charlie's Crickett Farm—Brooding Department	Transferred-in	Direct Materials	Conversion Costs	
2	Month Ended June 30 Production Cost Report (part 3 of 3)				Total
3	Assignment of total cost:				
4	**Completed and transferred out:**				
5	Equivalent units completed and transferred out	20,000	20,000	20,000	
6	Multiplied by: Cost per equivalent unit	$ 2.10	$ 6.90	$ 2.40	
7	Cost assigned to units completed and transferred out	$ 42,000	$ 138,000	$ 48,000	$ 228,000
8					
9	**Ending work in process:**				
10	Equivalent units in ending WIP	9,000	6,750	2,700	
11	Multiplied by: Cost per equivalent unit	$ 2.10	$ 6.90	$ 2.40	
12	Cost assigned to units in ending WIP	$ 18,900	$ 46,575	$ 6,480	$ 71,955
13					
14	**Total costs accounted for**				$ 299,955
15					

Requirements

Charlie Topper has the following questions about the farm's performance during June:

1. What is the cost per box of crickets sold? (*Hint:* This is the cost of the boxes completed and shipped out of brooding.)
2. What is the gross profit per box?
3. How much operating income did Charlie's Cricket Farm make in June?
4. What is the return on Topper's investment of $450,000 for the month of June? (Compute this as June's operating income divided by Topper's investment, expressed as a percentage.)
5. What monthly operating income would provide a 2.5% monthly rate of return? What price per box would Charlie's Cricket Farm have had to charge in June to achieve a 2.5% monthly rate of return?

PROBLEMS Group B

P5-53B Process costing in a single processing department
(Learning Objectives 1, 2, & 3)

Grand Lips produces a lip balm used for cold-weather sports. The balm is manufactured in a single processing department. No lip balm was in process on May 31, and Grand Lips started production on 20,800 lip balm tubes during June. Direct materials are added at the beginning of the process, but conversion costs are incurred evenly throughout the process. Completed production for June totaled 15,600 units. The June 30 work in process was 40% of the way through the production process. Direct materials costing $4,992 were placed in production during June, and direct labor of $3,350 and manufacturing overhead of $1,954 were assigned to the process.

Requirements

1. Fill-in the time line for Grand Lips.
2. Use the time line to help you compute the total equivalent units and the cost per equivalent unit for June.
3. Assign total costs to (a) units completed and transferred to Finished Goods and (b) units still in process at June 30.
4. Prepare a T-account for Work in Process Inventory to show activity during June, including the June 30 balance.

P5-54B Process costing in a first department *(Learning Objectives 1, 3, & 4)*

The Colorado Furniture Company produces dining tables in a three-stage process: Sawing, Assembly, and Staining. Costs incurred in the Sawing Department during September are summarized as follows:

Work in Process Inventory—Sawing	
September 1 balance	0
Direct materials	1,855,000
Direct labor	139,000
Manufacturing overhead	203,500

Direct materials (lumber) are added at the beginning of the sawing process, while conversion costs are incurred evenly throughout the process. September activity in the Sawing Department included sawing of 16,000 meters of lumber, which were transferred to the Assembly Department. Also, work began on 1,500 meters of lumber, which on September 30 were 75% of the way through the sawing process.

Requirements

1. Draw a time line for the Sawing Department.
2. Use the time line to help you compute the number of equivalent units and the cost per equivalent unit in the Sawing Department for September.
3. Show that the sum of (a) cost of goods transferred out of the Sawing Department and (b) ending "Work in Process Inventory—Sawing" equals the total cost accumulated in the department during September.
4. Journalize all transactions affecting the company's sawing process during September, including those already posted.

P5-55B Five-step process: Materials added at different points

(Learning Objectives 1, 2, & 3)

Value World produces canned chicken a la king. The chicken a la king passes through three departments: (1) Mixing, (2) Retort (sterilization), and (3) Packing. In the Mixing Department, chicken and cream are added at the beginning of the process, the mixture is partly cooked, then chopped green peppers and mushrooms are added at the end of the process. Conversion costs are added evenly throughout the mixing process. November data from the Mixing Department are as follows:

Gallons		Costs	
Beginning work in process inventory	0 gallons	Beginning work in process inventory	$ 0
Started production	13,900 gallons	Costs added during November:	
Completed and transferred out to Retort in November	13,300 gallons	Chicken	10,990
		Cream	4,300
Ending work in process inventory (55% of the way through the mixing process)	600 gallons	Green peppers and mushrooms	3,990
		Direct labor	11,900
		Manufacturing overhead	8,545
		Total costs	$39,725

Requirements

1. Draw a time line for the Mixing Department.
2. Use the time line to help you summarize the flow of physical units and compute the equivalent units. (*Hint:* Each direct material added at a different point in the production process requires its own equivalent-unit computation.)
3. Compute the cost per equivalent unit for each cost category.
4. Compute the total costs of the units (gallons):
    a. Completed and transferred out to the Retort Department
    b. In the Mixing Department's ending work in process inventory

P5-56B Prepare a production cost report and journal entries

(Learning Objectives 4 & 5)

Metal Accessories manufactures auto roof racks in a two-stage process that includes shaping and plating. Steel alloy is the basic raw material of the shaping process. The steel is molded according to the design specifications of automobile manufacturers (Ford and General Motors). The Plating Department then adds an anodized finish.

At March 31, before recording the transfer of cost from the Plating Department to Finished Goods Inventory, the Metal Accessories general ledger included the following account:

Work in Process Inventory—Plating		
March 1 balance	31,480	
Transferred-in from Shaping	36,000	
Direct materials	30,800	
Direct labor	23,470	
Manufacturing overhead	41,350	

The direct materials (rubber pads) are added at the end of the plating process. Conversion costs are incurred evenly throughout the process. Work in process of the Plating Department on March 1 consisted of 600 racks. The $31,480 beginning balance of "Work in Process—Plating" includes $18,000 of transferred-in cost and $13,480 of conversion cost. During March, 3,000 racks were transferred in from the Shaping Department. The Plating Department transferred 2,200 racks to Finished Goods Inventory in March and 1,400 were still in process on March 31. This ending inventory was 50% of the way through the plating process.

Requirements

1. Draw a time line for the Plating Department.
2. Prepare the March production cost report for the Plating Department.
3. Journalize all transactions affecting the Plating Department during March, including the entries that have already been posted.

P5-57B Cost per unit and gross profit (Learning Objective 5)

Jimmy Jones operates Jimmy's Cricket Farm in Eatonton, Georgia. Jimmy's raises about 18 million crickets a month. Most are sold to pet stores at $12.90 for a box of 1,000 crickets. Pet stores sell the crickets for $0.05 to $0.10 each as live feed for reptiles.

Raising crickets requires a two-step process: incubation and brooding. In the first process, incubation, employees place cricket eggs on mounds of peat moss to hatch. In the second process, employees move the newly hatched crickets into large boxes filled with cardboard dividers. Depending on the desired size, the crickets spend approximately two weeks in brooding before being shipped to pet stores. In the brooding process, Jimmy's crickets consume about 16 tons of food and produce 12 tons of manure.

Jones has invested $400,000 in the cricket farm, and he had hoped to earn a 24% annual rate of return, which works out to a 2% monthly return on his investment. After looking at the farm's bank balance, Jones fears he is not achieving this return. To get more accurate information on the farm's performance, Jones bought new accounting software that provides weighted-average process cost information. After Jones input the data, the software provided the following reports. However, Jones needs help interpreting these reports.

Jones does know that a unit of production is a box of 1,000 crickets. For example, in June's report, the 7,000 physical units of beginning work in process inventory are 7,000 boxes (each one of these boxes contains 1,000 immature crickets). The finished goods inventory is zero because the crickets ship out as soon as they reach the required size. Monthly operating expenses total $1500 (in addition to the costs that follow).

	A	B	C	D	E
	Jimmy's Crickett Farm—Brooding Department	**Step 1:**	**Step 2: Equivalent Units**		
1	Month Ended June 30	**Flow of Physical**	**Transferred-**	**Direct**	**Conversion**
2	**Production Cost Report (part 1 of 3)**	**Units**	**in**	**Materials**	**Costs**
3	**Flow of Production**				
4	**Units to account for:**				
5	Beginning work in process, June 1	7,000			
6	Plus: Transferred in during June	21,000			
7	Total physical units to account for	28,000			
8					
9	**Units accounted for:**				
10	Completed and transferred out during June	19,000	19,000	19,000	19,000
11	Plus: Ending work in process, June 30	9,000	9,000	7,200	3,600
12	Total physical units accounted for	28,000			
13	**Total equivalent units**		28,000	26,200	22,600
14					

	A	B	C	D	E
1	Jimmy's Crickett Farm—Brooding Department	Transferred-in	Direct Materials	Conversion Costs	Total
2	Month Ended June 30 Production Cost Report (part 2 of 3)				
3	Beginning work in process, June 1	$ 21,000	$ 39,940	$ 5,020	$ 65,960
4	Plus: Costs added during June	46,200	156,560	51,480	254,240
5	Total costs to account for	$ 67,200	$ 196,500	$ 56,500	$ 320,200
6	Divided by: Total equivalent units	28,000	26,200	22,600	
7	Cost per equivalent unit	$ 2.40	$ 7.50	$ 2.50	
8					

	A	B	C	D	E
1	Jimmy's Crickett Farm—Brooding Department	Transferred-in	Direct Materials	Conversion Costs	Total
2	Month Ended June 30 Production Cost Report (part 3 of 3)				
3	Assignment of total cost:				
4	Completed and transferred out:				
5	Equivalent units completed and transferred out	19,000	19,000	19,000	
6	Multiplied by: Cost per equivalent unit	$ 2.40	$ 7.50	$ 2.50	
7	Cost assigned to units completed and transferred out	$ 45,600	$ 142,500	$ 47,500	$ 235,600
8					
9	Ending work in process:				
10	Equivalent units in ending WIP	9,000	7,200	3,600	
11	Multiplied by: Cost per equivalent unit	$ 2.40	$ 7.50	$ 2.50	
12	Cost assigned to units in ending WIP	$ 21,600	$ 54,000	$ 9,000	$ 84,600
13					
14	Total costs accounted for				$ 320,200
15					

Requirements

Jimmy Jones has the following questions about the farm's performance during June:

1. What is the cost per box of crickets sold? (*Hint:* This is the cost of the boxes completed and shipped out of brooding.)
2. What is the gross profit per box?
3. How much operating income did Jimmy's Cricket Farm make in June?
4. What is the return on Jones's investment of $400,000 for the month of June? (Compute this as June's operating income divided by Jones's investment, expressed as a percentage.)
5. What monthly operating income would provide a 2% monthly rate of return? What price per box would Jimmy's Cricket Farm have had to charge in June to achieve a 2% monthly rate of return?

CRITICAL THINKING

Discussion & Analysis

A5-58 Discussion Questions

1. What characteristics of the product or manufacturing process would lead a company to use a process costing system? Give two examples of companies that are likely to be using process costing. What characteristics of the product or manufacturing process would lead a company to use a job costing system? Give two examples of companies that are likely to be using job costing.

2. How are process costing and job costing similar? How are they different?

3. What are conversion costs? In a job costing system, at least some conversion costs are assigned directly to products. Why do all conversion costs need to be assigned to processing departments in a process costing system?

4. Why not assign all costs of production during a period to only the completed units? What happens if a company does this? Why are the costs of production in any period allocated between completed units and units in work in process? Is there any situation where a company can assign all costs of production during a period to the completed units? If so, when?

5. What information generated by a process costing system can be used by management? How can management use this process costing information?

6. Why are the equivalent units for direct materials often different from the equivalent units for conversion costs in the same period?

7. Describe the flow of costs in a process costing system. List each type of journal entry that would be made and describe the purpose of that journal entry.

8. If a company has very little or no inventory, what effect does that lack of inventory have on its process costing system? What other benefits result from having very little to no inventory?

9. How does process costing differ between a first processing department and a second or later processing department?

10. "Process costing is easier to use than job costing." Do you agree or disagree with this statement? Explain your reasoning.

11. Think of a business or organization that would use process costing. What types of waste are likely to be generated during the manufacturing process? Are there ways to avoid this waste or minimize it? How might managerial accounting support the efforts to reduce waste in the production process?

12. Provide an example of how a company may change its processes to make its manufacturing more efficient or environmentally sustainable. How will the company benefit?

Application & Analysis

Mini Cases

REAL LIFE

A5-59 Process Costing in Real Companies

Go to YouTube.com and search for clips from the show *Unwrapped* on Food Network or *How It's Made* on Discovery Channel. Watch a clip for a product that would use process costing. For some of the questions, you may need to make assumptions about the production process (i.e., companies may not publicize their entire production process). If you make any assumptions, be sure to disclose both the assumption and your rationale for that assumption.

Basic Discussion Questions

1. Describe the product selected.
2. Summarize the production process.
3. Justify why you think this production process would dictate the use of a process costing system.
4. List at least two separate processes that are performed in creating this product. What departments would house these processes?
5. Describe at least one department that would have ending work in process. What do the units look like as they are "in process"?

A5-60 Ethics and physical inventory counts

(Learning Objectives 1, 2, 3, 4, & 5)

Thompson Products produces plastic containers through a blow molding process. The company uses process costing because its products are generally homogeneous and are produced in large batches.

Bradley Quito is the controller at Thompson Products. It is December 31, 2014, and Quito is supervising a physical count of all the inventory on hand. He knows it will be a tough year because of a sharp decline in sales near the end of the year.

In early December 2014, an earthquake struck in the southwestern Sichuan province in China. A major supplier of Thompson Products sustained considerable damage in the earthquake, preventing this supplier from delivering critical parts to Thompson Products in December. This shortage of raw materials has caused a decline in sales revenue for the last month in the year since production at Thompson Products has stalled due to the lack of the critical parts from this supplier. Thompson Products' income will therefore be lower than projected for 2014.

If annual income targets are not met, the company will not be paying bonuses to its employees. Quito feels that this decline in sales revenue is a temporary situation due entirely to the earthquake. It appears likely that the supplier for these parts will be able to supply Thompson Products with all of the parts it needs by the end of February 2015.

As Quito is supervising the physical count on the last day of the year, he edits some inventory records to show more inventory items on the floor on December 31, 2014, than are actually in inventory.

Quito justifies his action by thinking that the missed sales will actually be made up in January and February (of 2015) when the supplier gets back on track with shipments. The decrease in sales revenue the company experienced in December is only a temporary timing difference. He is concerned that if bonuses are not paid to employees because of this timing difference, Thompson Products could lose some of its best employees to competitors that are offering higher wages. Thompson Products has always used the bonuses as a key component of its talent recruiting and retention strategy. Quito himself has verbally promised bonuses to key employees he has recruited during 2014, as have other managers.

Requirements

1. Using the IMA *Statement of Ethical Professional Practice* (refer to Exhibit 1–6) as an ethical framework, answer the following questions:
   a. What are the ethical issue(s) in this situation?
   b. What are Quito's responsibilities as a management accountant?
2. How would recording more units than are actually in inventory impact the 2014 balance sheet and income statement? How would it impact the 2015 balance sheet and income statement?
3. Discuss the specific steps Quito should take in this situation. Refer to the IMA *Statement of Ethical Professional Practice* in your response.

A5-61 Process costing and hybrid costing issues

(Learning Objectives 1, 2, 3, 4, & 5)

Polly Products is a recycled plastics manufacturer located in Mulliken, Michigan. It makes plastic "lumber" called Polly Planks from 100% recycled plastics. It also builds park benches, picnic tables, and other outdoor amenities from the Polly Planks it produces.

Plastic lumber like that made by Polly Products is typically manufactured using an extrusion process. Post-consumer plastics (milk jugs, bottles, and other plastics) are purchased from municipalities and other recyclers. Much of plastic lumber is produced from post-consumer milk jug material. At the recycler, the milk jugs are crushed into giant cubes, weighing 800 to 1,000 pounds per pallet. When an extrusion manufacturer receives the milk jug, the manufacturer puts the milk jug through a powerful shredder that cuts the milk jug into small pieces resembling confetti. The shredded milk jug is stored in large cardboard boxes called gaylords.

When production begins, gaylords containing shredded plastic are brought to the extrusion line. The shredded plastic is dumped into a large hopper. Other materials are added to the hopper at the initial start of manufacture, including oils, colorants, other plastics, and foaming agents. All of the ingredients are stirred in the hopper until thoroughly mixed. The materials then go into the extrusion machine. The extrusion machine melts the plastic into a hot liquid form. That liquid plastic is pushed through the extrusion machine through a screw mechanism into molds that give the plastic lumber its final shape.

Polly Planks can be sold as dimensional lumber in similar sizes as natural wood lumber, including 2″ × 4″, 2″ × 6″, and other sizes. The lengths of the Polly Planks can be 8′, 10′, or a custom length.

Polly Products also uses its Polly Planks to produce park benches, picnic tables, trash receptacles, and other outdoor amenities. Polly Products' employees fabricate these outdoor amenities both for stock inventory and for special orders. Custom orders are likely to comprise a significant portion of Polly Products' sales.

A manufacturer such as Polly Products would use a hybrid costing system rather than a pure process costing system or a pure job costing system. A hybrid costing system includes elements of both a process costing system and a job costing system and is unique to each manufacturer since it reflects each manufacturer's specific processes and products.

Requirements

1. Which product(s) manufactured by Polly Products would use elements of a process costing system? Give a detailed description of why you think that product (or those products) would require a process costing system.

2. Within the process costing portion of the hybrid system at Polly Products, what costs would be considered to be direct materials? What costs are likely to be in conversion costs in the process costing system? (Use your imagination to brainstorm about potential conversion costs at Polly Products since these costs were not directly addressed in the case.)

3. Which products manufactured by Polly Products would be likely to use elements of a job costing system? Again, explain your reasoning and be specific.

4. Within the job costing portion of the hybrid system at Polly Products, what are the direct materials? What would be direct labor? What costs are likely to be in manufacturing overhead? (Again, use your imagination to brainstorm about potential direct labor and manufacturing overhead costs.)

5. In addition to manufacturing costs, Polly Products has sales, engineering, and general administrative support costs. Are these costs relevant in the hybrid costing system? Why or why not?

6. What major issues do you see in a hybrid costing system?

Try It Solutions

page 253:

1. 100,000 units × 100% of direct materials = 100,000 equivalent units of direct materials.

2. 100,000 units × 25% of the way through fermentation process = 25,000 equivalent units of conversion costs.

page 272:

a. The total cost of making each unit can be found by looking at Step 4 of the process costing procedure in the final production department. The total cost is the sum of the cost per equivalent unit transferred in from earlier departments and the costs per equivalent unit incurred in the final department. In this example, those figures add up to $8.90 per case ($6.50 + $1.15 + $1.25).

b. The gross profit per case is $11.10, which is the sales price per case ($20.00) minus the cost to manufacture each case ($8.90).

Oleksiy Maksymenko/Alamy

Cost Behavior

Learning Objectives

■ **1** Describe key characteristics and graphs of various cost behaviors

■ **2** Use cost equations to express and predict costs

■ **3** Use account analysis and scatter plots to analyze cost behavior

■ **4** Use the high-low method to analyze cost behavior

■ **5** Use regression analysis to analyze cost behavior

■ **6** Describe variable costing and prepare a contribution margin income statement

High above the rushing waters and mist of Niagara Falls, hundreds of tourists from around the world return to the 512-room Embassy Suites to enjoy a complimentary afternoon refreshment hour, relax in the hotel's pool and spa, and rest in luxurious suites overlooking the falls. A similar scene occurs across the street at the Sheraton, Marriott, and DoubleTree hotels, as well as at thousands of other travel destinations around the world.

How do hotel managers set prices high enough to cover costs and earn a profit, but low enough to fill most rooms each night? How do they plan for higher occupancy during the busy summer months and lower occupancy during the off-season? They know how their costs behave. Some hotel costs, such as the complimentary morning breakfast, rise and fall with the number of guests. But many hotel costs, such as depreciation on the building and furniture, stay the same whether 50 or 2,000 guests stay each night. In this chapter we'll learn more about how costs behave, and how managers can use that knowledge to make better business decisions.

Up to this point, we have focused our attention on product costing. We have discussed how managers use job costing or process costing to figure out the cost of making a product or providing a service. Product costs are useful for valuing inventory and calculating cost of goods sold. Product costs are also used as a starting place for setting sales prices. However, product costs are not very helpful for planning and making many business decisions. Why? Because they contain a mixture of fixed and variable costs. Some of these costs change as volume changes, but other costs do not. To make good decisions and accurate projections, managers must understand how the company's costs will react to changes in volume.

Cost Behavior: How do Changes in Volume Affect Costs?

1 Describe key characteristics and graphs of various cost behaviors

In order to make good decisions and accurate projections, managers must understand <u>cost behavior</u>—that is, how costs change as volume changes. Embassy Suite's managers need to understand how the hotel's costs will be affected by the number of guests staying at the hotel each night. We first consider three of the most common cost behaviors, some of which were introduced in Chapter 2.

- Variable costs
- Fixed costs
- Mixed costs

Why is this important?

"Cost behavior is a **key** component of most **planning** and operating decisions. Without a thorough understanding of **cost behavior**, managers are apt to make less **profitable** decisions."

Variable Costs

<u>Variable costs</u> are costs that are incurred for every unit of volume. As a result, total variable costs change in direct proportion to changes in volume. For example, every guest at Embassy Suites is entitled to a complimentary morning breakfast and afternoon refreshment hour (drinks and snacks). Guests also receive complimentary toiletries (shampoo, soap, lotion, and mouthwash) that they typically use or take with them. These costs are considered to be variable because they are incurred for every guest. In addition, the hotel's total cost for the complimentary breakfast and toiletries will increase as the number of guests increases.

Let's assume that the toiletries cost the hotel $3 per guest and that the breakfast and refreshment hour costs the hotel $10 per guest. Exhibit 6-1 graphs these costs in relation to the number of guests staying at the hotel. The vertical axis (y-axis) shows total variable costs, while the horizontal axis (x-axis) shows total volume of activity (thousands of guests, in this case).

Notice a few things about these graphs:

- Graphs of variable costs always begin at the *origin*, the point that represents zero volume and zero cost. For example, if the hotel has no guests for the night, it will not incur any costs for complimentary toiletries or breakfasts.
- The *slope* of the variable cost line represents the *variable cost per unit of activity*. For example, the slope of the toiletry cost line is $3 per guest, while the slope of the breakfast cost line is $10 per guest. As a result, the slope of the line representing the breakfast cost is steeper than that of the toiletry cost.

EXHIBIT 6-1 Variable Costs

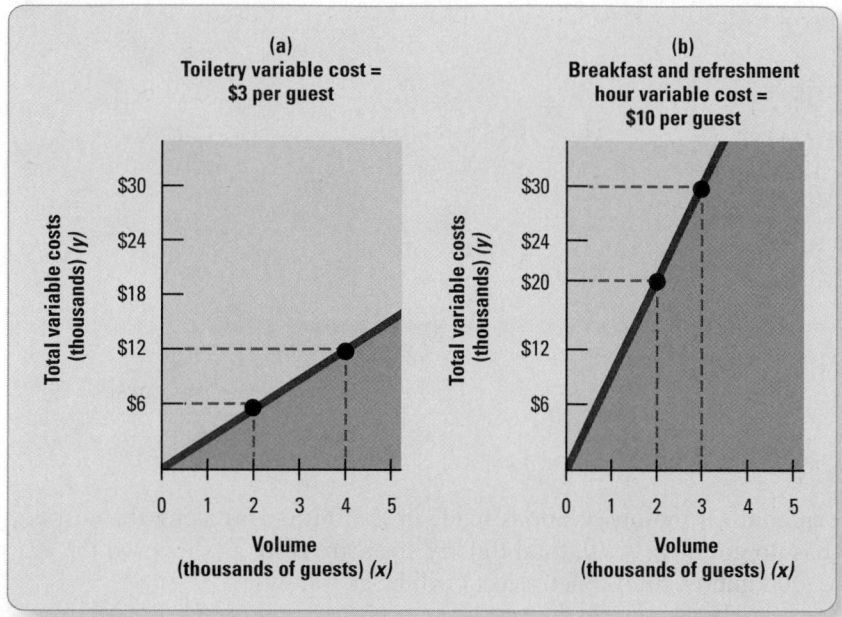

- Total variable costs change in *direct proportion* to changes in volume. In other words, if volume doubles, then total variable cost doubles. If volume triples, then total variable cost triples. For example, Exhibit 6-1(a) shows that if the hotel serves 2,000 guests, it will spend $6,000 on toiletries. However, doubling the number of guests to 4,000 likewise doubles the total variable cost to $12,000.

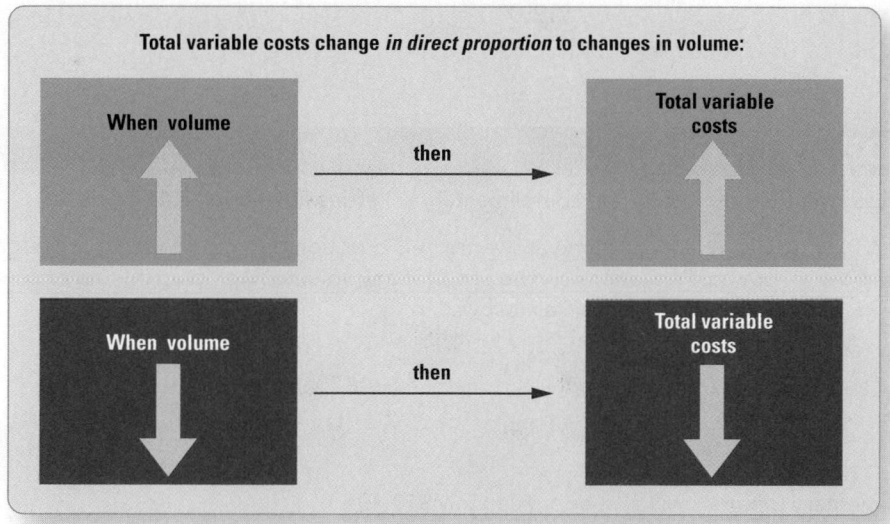

Managers do not need to rely on graphs to predict total variable costs at different volumes of activity. They can use a <u>cost equation</u>, a mathematical equation for a straight line, to express how a cost behaves. On cost graphs like the ones pictured in Exhibit 6-1, the vertical (y-axis) always shows total costs, while the horizontal axis (x-axis) shows volume of activity. Therefore, any variable cost line can be mathematically expressed as follows:

2 Use cost equations to express and predict costs

Total variable cost (y) = Variable cost per unit of activity (v) × Volume of activity (x)

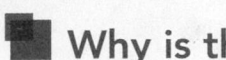

Why is this important?

"Cost **equations** help managers predict **total costs** at **different** operating **volumes** so that they can **better** plan for the future."

Or simply:

$$y = vx$$

The hotel's total toiletry cost is as follows:

$$y = \$3x$$

where,

$$y = \text{total toiletry cost}$$
$$\$3 = \text{variable cost per guest}$$
$$x = \text{number of guests}$$

We can confirm the observations made in Exhibit 6-1(a) using the cost equation. If the hotel has no guests ($x = 0$), total toiletry costs are zero, as shown in the graph. If the hotel has 2,000 guests, total toiletry costs will be as follows:

$$y = \$3 \text{ per guest} \times 2,000 \text{ guests}$$
$$= \$6,000$$

If the hotel has 4,000 guests, managers will expect total toiletry costs to be as follows:

$$y = \$3 \text{ per guest} \times 4,000 \text{ guests}$$
$$= \$12,000$$

STOP & THINK

How much will the hotel spend on complimentary toiletries if it serves 3,467 guests?

Answer: You would have a hard time answering this question by simply looking at the graph in Exhibit 6-1(a), but cost equations can be used for any volume. We "plug in" the expected volume to our variable cost equation as follows:

$$y = \$3 \text{ per guest} \times 3,467 \text{ guests}$$
$$= \$10,401$$

Complimentary toiletries will cost approximately $10,401.

Now, consider Exhibit 6-1(b), the total variable costs for the complimentary breakfast and refreshment hour. The slope of the line is $10, representing the cost of providing each guest with the complimentary breakfast and refreshments. We can express the total breakfast and refreshment hour cost as follows:

$$y = \$10x$$

where,

> y = total breakfast and refreshment hour cost
> $10 = variable cost per guest
> x = number of guests

The total cost of the breakfast and refreshment hour for 2,000 guests is as follows:

> y = $10 per guest × 2,000 guests
> = $20,000

Both graphs in Exhibit 6-1 show how *total* variable costs vary with the number of guests. *But note that the variable cost per guest (v) remains constant in each of the graphs.* That is, Embassy Suites incurs $3 in toiletry costs and $10 in breakfast and refreshment hour costs for each guest no matter how many guests the hotel serves. Some key points to remember about variable costs are shown in Exhibit 6-2.

EXHIBIT 6-2 Key Characteristics of Variable Costs

- *Total* variable costs change in *direct proportion* to changes in volume
- The *variable cost per unit of activity* (v) remains constant and is the slope of the variable cost line
- Total variable cost graphs always begin at the origin (if volume is zero, total variable costs are zero)
- Total variable costs can be expressed as follows:
  $y = vx$
  where,
  > y = total variable cost
  > v = variable cost per unit of activity
  > x = volume of activity

Fixed Costs

Fixed costs are costs that do not change in total despite wide changes in volume. Many of Embassy Suites' costs are fixed because the same total cost will be incurred regardless of the number of guests that stay each month. Some of the hotel's fixed costs include the following:

- Property taxes and insurance
- Straight-line depreciation and maintenance on parking ramp, hotel, and furnishings
- Pool, fitness room, and spa upkeep
- Cable TV and wireless Internet access for all rooms
- Salaries of hotel department managers (housekeeping, food service, special events, etc.)

Most of these costs are **committed fixed costs**, meaning that the hotel is locked in to these costs because of previous management decisions. For example, as soon as the hotel was built, management became locked in to a certain level of property taxes and depreciation, simply because of the location and size of the hotel, and management's choice of furnishings and amenities (pool, fitness room, restaurant, and so forth). Management has little or no control over these committed fixed costs in the short run.

However, the hotel also incurs **discretionary fixed costs**, such as advertising expenses, that are a result of annual management decisions. Companies have more control over discretionary fixed costs in the short run.

Suppose Embassy Suites incurs $100,000 of fixed costs each month. In Exhibit 6-3, the vertical axis (y-axis) shows total fixed costs, while the horizontal axis (x-axis) plots volume of activity (thousands of guests). The graph shows total fixed costs as a *flat line* that intersects the y-axis at $100,000 (this is known as the vertical intercept) because the hotel will incur the same $100,000 of fixed costs regardless of the number of guests that stay during the month.

EXHIBIT 6-3 Fixed Costs

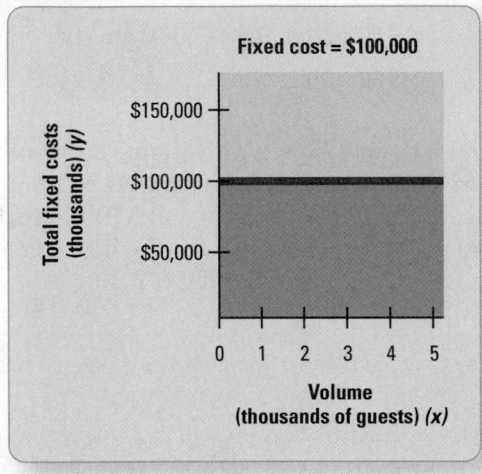

The cost equation for a fixed cost is as follows:

> Total fixed cost (*y*) = Fixed amount over a period of time (*f*)

Or simply,

$$y = f$$

Embassy Suites' *monthly* fixed cost equation is as follows:

$$y = \$100,000$$

where,

> *y* = total fixed cost per month

In contrast to the *total fixed costs* shown in Exhibit 6-3, the *fixed cost per guest* depends on the number of guests. If the hotel only serves 2,000 guests during the month, the fixed cost per guest is as follows:

> $100,000 ÷ 2,000 guests = $50/guest

If the number of guests *doubles* to 4,000, the fixed cost per guest is *cut in half*:

> $100,000 ÷ 4,000 guests = $25/guest

The fixed cost per guest is *inversely proportional* to the number of guests. When volume *increases*, the fixed cost per guest *decreases*. When volume *decreases*, the fixed cost per guest *increases*.

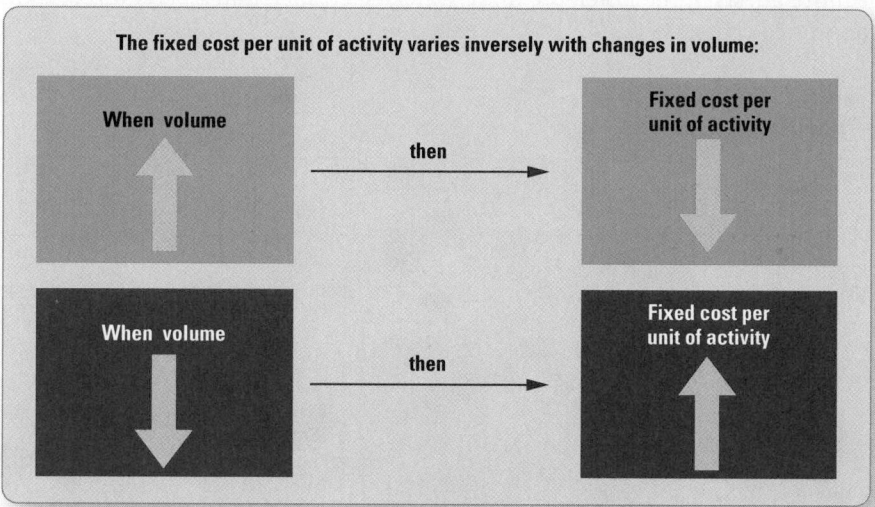

Keep the following important rule of thumb in mind:

Companies like to operate near full capacity because it drives down their fixed costs per unit. A lower cost per unit gives businesses the flexibility to decrease sales prices, which makes them more competitive.

Key points to remember about fixed costs appear in Exhibit 6-4.

EXHIBIT 6-4 Key Characteristics of Fixed Costs

- *Total* fixed costs stay *constant* over a wide range of volume
- Fixed costs *per unit of activity* vary *inversely* with changes in volume:
    – Fixed cost per unit of activity *increases* when volume *decreases*
    – Fixed cost per unit of activity *decreases* when volume *increases*
- Total fixed cost graphs are always flat lines with no slope that intersect the y-axis at a level equal to total fixed costs
- Total fixed costs can be expressed as $y = f$
  where,
      y = total fixed cost
      f = fixed cost over a given period of time

▶ Try It!

Compute the (a) total fixed cost and (b) fixed cost per guest if the hotel has 16,000 guests next month. Compare the fixed cost per guest at the higher occupancy rate to the fixed cost per guest when only 2,000 guests stay during the month.

Please see page 380 for solutions.

Mixed Costs

<u>Mixed costs</u> contain both variable and fixed cost components. Embassy Suites' utilities are mixed costs because the hotel requires a certain amount of utilities just to operate. However, the more guests at the hotel, the more water, electricity, and gas required. Exhibit 6-5 illustrates mixed costs.

EXHIBIT 6-5 Mixed Costs

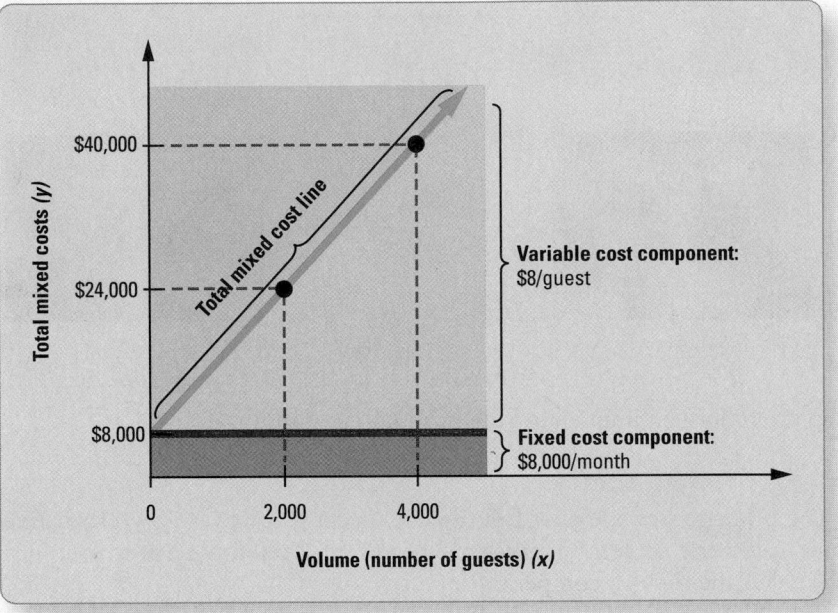

For example, let's assume that utilities for the common areas of the hotel and unoccupied rooms cost $8,000 per month. In addition, these costs increase by $8 per guest as each guest cools or heats his or her room, takes showers, turns on the TV and lights, and uses freshly laundered sheets and towels.

Notice the two components—variable and fixed—of the mixed costs in Exhibit 6-5. Similar to a variable cost, the total mixed cost line increases as the volume of activity increases. However, *the line does **not** begin at the origin.* Rather, it intersects the y-axis at a level equal to the fixed cost component. Even if no guests stay this month, the hotel will still incur $8,000 of utilities cost.

Managers can once again use a cost equation to express the mixed cost line so that they can predict total mixed costs at different volumes. The mixed costs equation simply *combines* the variable cost and fixed cost equations:

$$\text{Total mixed costs} = \text{Variable cost component} + \text{Fixed cost component}$$
$$y = vx + f$$

Embassy Suites' monthly utilities cost equation is as follows:

$$y = \$8x + \$8,000$$

where,

$$y = \text{total utilities cost per month}$$
$$x = \text{number of guests}$$

If the hotel serves 2,000 guests this month it expects utilities to cost:

$$y = (\$8 \text{ per guest} \times 2{,}000 \text{ guests}) + \$8{,}000$$
$$= \$24{,}000$$

If the hotel serves 4,000 guests this month it expects utilities to cost:

$$y = (\$8 \text{ per guest} \times 4{,}000 \text{ guests}) + \$8{,}000$$
$$= \$40{,}000$$

Total mixed costs increase as volume increases, *but **not** in direct proportion to changes in volume*. The total mixed costs did *not* double when volume doubled. This is because of the fixed cost component. Additionally, consider the mixed costs *per guest*:

If the hotel serves 2,000 guests: $24,000 total cost ÷ 2,000 guests = $12.00 per guest
If the hotel serves 4,000 guests: $40,000 total cost ÷ 4,000 guests = $10.00 per guest

The mixed costs per guest did *not* decrease by half when the hotel served twice as many guests. This is because of the variable cost component. Mixed costs per unit decrease as volume increases, but **not in direct proportion** to changes in volume. Because mixed costs contain both fixed cost and variable cost components, they behave differently than purely variable costs and purely fixed costs. Key points to remember about mixed costs appear in Exhibit 6-6.

EXHIBIT 6-6 Key Characteristics of Mixed Costs

- *Total* mixed costs increase as volume increases because of the variable cost component
- Mixed costs *per unit* decrease as volume increases because of the fixed cost component
- Total mixed costs graphs slope upward but do *not* begin at the origin— they intersect the y-axis at the level of fixed costs
- Total mixed costs can be expressed as a *combination* of the variable and fixed cost equations:

  Total mixed costs = variable cost component + fixed cost component
  $$y = vx + f$$
  where,

  y = total mixed costs
  v = variable cost per unit of activity (slope)
  x = volume of activity
  f = fixed cost over a given period of time (vertical intercept)

▶ Try It!

Assume the local fitness club charges a membership fee of $30 per month for unlimited use of the exercise equipment plus an additional fee of $5 for every instructor-led exercise class you attend.

1. Express the monthly cost of belonging to the fitness club as a cost equation.
2. What is your expected cost for a month in which you attend five instructor-led classes?
3. If your attendance doubles to 10 classes per month, will your total cost for the month double? Explain.

Please see page 380 for solutions.

Relevant Range

Managers always need to keep their **relevant range** in mind when predicting total costs. The relevant range is the band of volume where the following remain constant:

- *Total fixed costs*
- *Variable cost per unit*

In other words, it's the range of volume in which costs behave a certain way. A change in cost behavior means a change to a different relevant range.

Let's consider how the concept of relevant range applies to Embassy Suites. As shown in Exhibit 6-3, the hotel's current fixed costs are $100,000 per month. However, because the hotel's popularity continues to grow, room occupancy rates continue to increase. As a result, guests are becoming dissatisfied with the amount of time they have to wait for breakfast tables and elevators. To increase customer satisfaction, management is deciding whether to expand the breakfast facilities and add a 30-passenger elevator to its existing bank of elevators. This expansion, if carried out, will increase the hotel's fixed costs to a new level, because of straight-line depreciation on the new fixed assets. Exhibit 6-7 illustrates the hotel's current relevant range and future potential relevant range for fixed costs.

EXHIBIT 6-7 Examples of Different Relevant Ranges for Fixed Costs

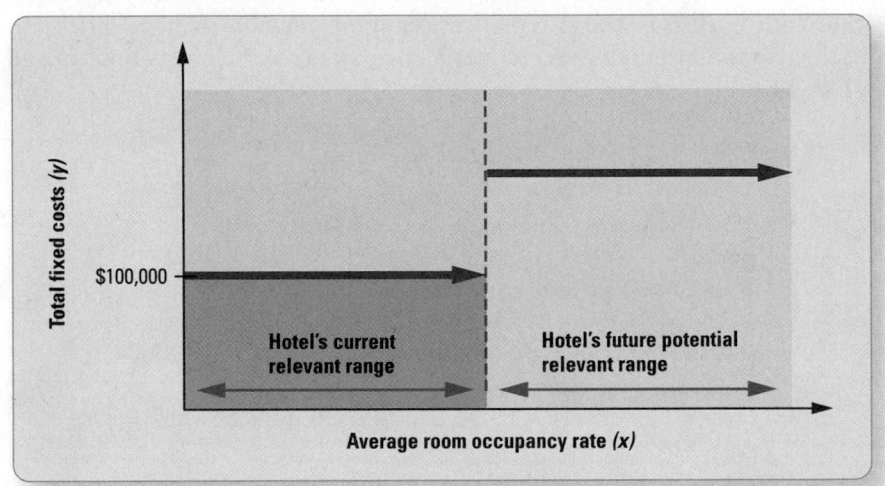

Does the concept of relevant range apply only to fixed costs? No, it also applies to variable costs. As shown in Exhibit 6-1, the hotel's current variable cost for toiletries is $3 per guest. However, as room occupancy rates continue to grow, management hopes to negotiate greater volume discounts on the toiletries from its suppliers. These volume discounts will decrease the variable toiletries cost per guest (for example, down to $2.75 per guest). Exhibit 6-8 illustrates the hotel's current relevant range and future potential relevant range for variable toiletries costs.

Why is the concept of relevant range important? Managers can predict costs accurately only if they use cost information for the appropriate relevant range. For example, think about your cell phone plan. Many cell phone plans offer a large block of "free" minutes for a set fee each month. If the user exceeds the allotted minutes, the cell phone company charges an additional per-minute fee. Exhibit 6-9 shows a cell phone plan in which the first 1,000 minutes of call time each month cost $50. After the 1,000 minutes are used, the user must pay an additional $0.30 per minute for every minute of call time. This cell phone plan has two relevant ranges. The first relevant range extends from 0 to 1,000 minutes. In this range, the $50 fee behaves strictly as a fixed cost. You could use 0, 100, or 975 minutes and you would still pay a flat $50 fee that month. The second relevant range starts at 1,001 minutes and extends indefinitely. In this relevant range, the cost is mixed: $50 plus $0.30 per minute. To forecast your cell phone bill each month, you need to know

EXHIBIT 6-8 Examples of Different Relevant Ranges for Variable Costs

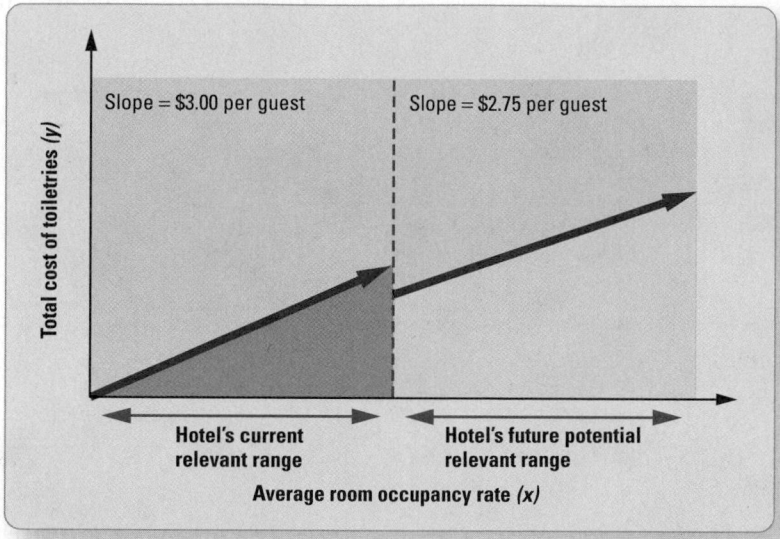

EXHIBIT 6-9 Example of Relevant Ranges

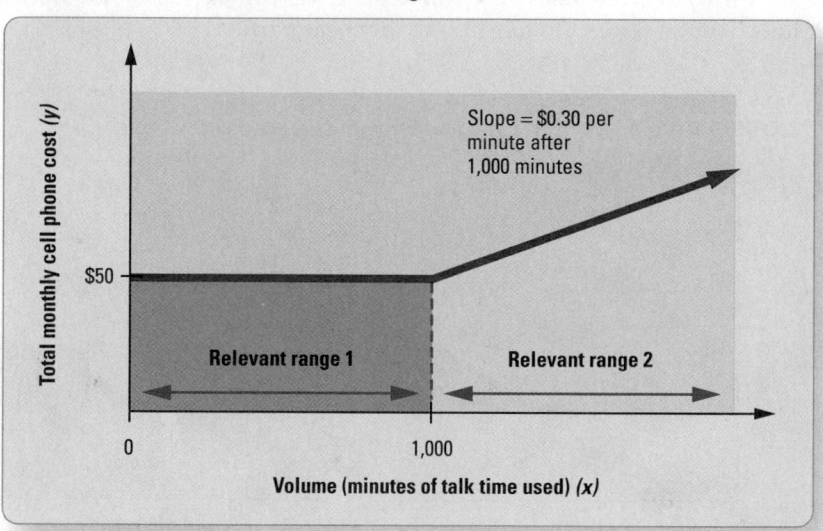

in which relevant range you plan to operate. The same holds true for businesses: To accurately predict costs, they need to know the relevant range in which they plan to operate.

Other Cost Behaviors

While many business costs behave as variable, fixed, or mixed costs, some costs do not neatly fit these patterns. We'll briefly describe other cost behaviors you may encounter.

<u>Step costs</u> resemble stair steps: They are fixed over a small range of activity and then jump up to a new fixed level with moderately small changes in volume. Hotels, restaurants, hospitals, and educational institutions typically experience step costs. For example, states usually require day-care centers to limit the caregiver-to-child ratio to 1:7—that is, there must be one caregiver for every seven children. As shown in Exhibit 6-10, a day-care center that takes on an eighth child must incur the cost of employing another caregiver. The new caregiver can watch the eighth through fourteenth child enrolled at the day-care center. If the day-care center takes on a fifteenth child, management will once again hire another caregiver, costing another $20,000 in salary. The same step cost patterns occur with hotels (maid-to-room ratio), restaurants (server-to-table ratio), hospitals (nurse-to-bed ratio), and schools (teacher-to-student ratio).

EXHIBIT 6-10 Step Costs

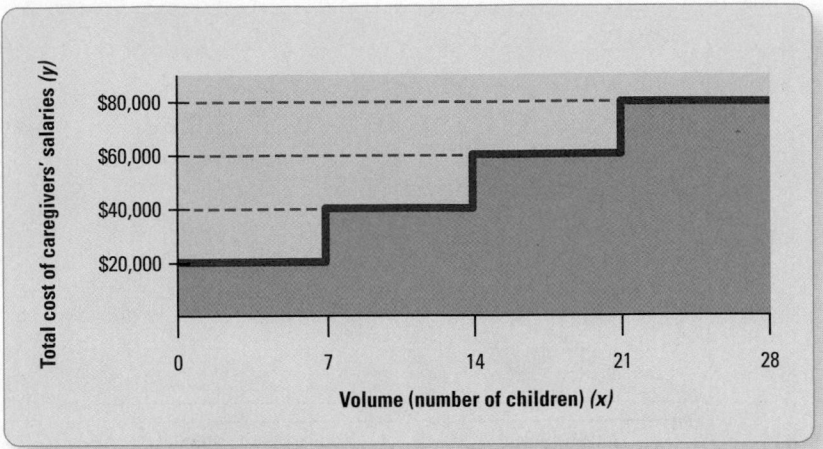

Step costs differ from fixed costs only in that they "step up" to a new relevant range with relatively small changes in volume. Fixed costs hold constant over much larger ranges of volume.

As shown by the red lines in Exhibit 6-11, <u>curvilinear costs</u> are not linear (not a straight line) and, therefore, do not fit into any neat pattern.

EXHIBIT 6-11 Curvilinear Costs and Straight-Line Approximations

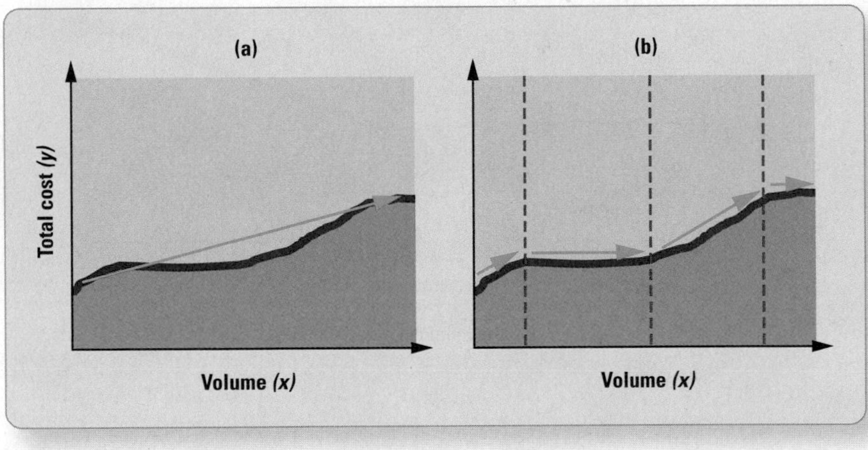

As shown by the straight green arrow in Exhibit 6-11(a), some businesses *approximate* these types of costs as mixed costs, knowing that they will have an estimation error at particular volumes. Sometimes managers also approximate step costs the same way: They simply draw a straight mixed cost line through the steps.

However, as shown in Exhibit 6-11(b), if managers need more accurate predictions, they can simply break these types of costs into smaller relevant ranges and make their predictions based on the particular relevant range. For example, the day-care center may want to predict total caregiver salaries if it enrolls 26 children. The manager knows this enrollment falls into the relevant range of 21 to 28 children, where he or she needs to employ four caregivers. The manager can then predict total caregiver salaries to be $80,000 (four caregivers × $20,000 salary per caregiver).

Sustainability and Cost Behavior

Many companies adopting sustainable business practices experience changes in the way their costs behave. For example, most banks, credit card companies, and utilities now offer e-banking and e-billing services as an alternative to sending traditional paper statements and bills through the mail. E-banking and e-billing drive down a company's variable costs. Why? Because the companies don't spend money on the paper, envelopes, printing, and postage associated with sending out paper statements. Likewise, when a customer pays electronically, rather than sending in a check, the company doesn't incur the variable cost associated with opening the mail, recording the payment to the customer's account, and processing the bank deposit. All of this is accomplished electronically by the companies' software.

On the other hand, the company must incur additional fixed costs to develop and operate secure online banking and billing websites. However, we know that the variable cost savings is greater than the increase in fixed costs, because many companies are either (1) offering customer incentives to switch to e-billing, or (2) charging customers an additional fee for receiving paper-based bills and statements in the mail. Whether using the carrot or the stick approach, companies are shifting consumer behavior as a means to decrease total costs.

The environmental consequences of e-billing and e-banking are tremendous if you consider the entire production and delivery cycle of the bills and statements, all of the way from the logging of the trees in the forest to the delivery of the bill at the customer's doorstep. Not only are fewer trees cut down, but also less energy is consumed in the transportation of the timber, the processing of the paper, the distribution of the paper, the delivery of the statements via the U.S. Postal Service, and the final disposal of the paper at landfills or recycling centers. In addition, less waste-water is generated and fewer toxic air emissions are produced. The downside, from a triple-bottom-line perspective, is the loss of jobs in associated industries, such as the U.S. Postal Service.

From the customer's perspective, adoption of e-billing and e-banking services provides one means for households to embrace a greener lifestyle. Charter One Bank estimates that, on an annual basis, the average household that receives e-bills and pays bills online reduces paper consumption by 6.6 pounds, saves 4.5 gallons of gasoline, saves 63 gallons of water, and cuts greenhouse gas emissions equal to the amount that would be emitted by driving 176 miles.[1] According to the U.S. Postal Service, in 2010, 21.9 billion bills and statements (equating to over a billion pounds of paper) were delivered across the country. Because of the increasing popularity of e-billing, this volume is actually down by 3.2 billion pieces since 2008, which is a 13% decline. Additionally, in 2010, for the first time ever, consumers reported that they paid more bills electronically than by mail. However, 47% of bills are still paid via the mail.[2] Thus, the adoption of electronic bill payment by the general public could have a significant positive impact on the environment.

See Exercises 6-25A and E6-44B

We have just described the most typical cost behaviors. In the next part of the chapter, we will discuss methods managers use for determining how their costs behave.

[1] www.charterone.com/greensense/tips.aspx
[2] www.usps.com/householddiary/welcome.htm

Decision Guidelines

Cost Behavior

Suppose you manage a local fitness club. To be an effective manager, you need to know how the club's costs behave. Here are some decisions you will need to make.

Decision	Guidelines
How can you tell if a *total* cost is variable, fixed, or mixed?	• Total variable costs increase in *direct proportion* to increases in volume. • Total fixed costs stay *constant* over a wide range of volumes. • Total mixed costs increase but *not* in direct proportion to increases in volume.
How can you tell if a *per-unit* cost is variable, fixed, or mixed?	• On a per-unit basis, variable costs stay constant. • On a per-unit basis, fixed costs decrease in proportion to increases in volume (that is to say, they are inversely proportional). • On a per-unit basis, mixed costs decrease, but not in direct proportion to increases in volume.
How can you tell by looking at a graph if a cost is variable, fixed, or mixed?	• Variable cost lines slope upward and begin at the origin. • Fixed cost lines are flat (no slope) and intersect the y-axis at a level equal to total fixed costs (this is known as the vertical intercept). • Mixed cost lines slope upward but do *not* begin at the origin. They intersect the y-axis at a level equal to their fixed cost component.
How can you mathematically express different cost behaviors?	• Cost equations mathematically express cost behavior using the equation for a straight line: $$y = vx + f$$ where, y = total cost v = variable cost per unit of activity (slope) x = volume of activity f = fixed cost (the vertical intercept) • For a variable cost, f is zero, leaving the following: $$y = vx$$ • For a fixed cost, v is zero, leaving the following: $$y = f$$ • Because a mixed cost has both a fixed cost component and a variable cost component, its cost equation is: $$y = vx + f$$

SUMMARY PROBLEM **1**

The previous manager of Fitness-for-Life started the following schedule, but left before completing it. The manager wasn't sure but thought the club's fixed operating costs were $10,000 per month and the variable operating costs were $1 per member. The club's existing facilities could serve up to 750 members per month.

Requirements

1. Complete the following schedule for different levels of monthly membership, assuming the previous manager's cost behavior estimates are accurate:

	A	B	C	D
1	**Monthly Operating Costs**	**100 Members**	**500 Members**	**750 Members**
2	Total variable costs			
3	Plus: Total fixed costs			
4	Total operating costs			
5				
6	Variable cost per member			
7	Plus: Fixed cost per member			
8	Average cost per member			
9				

2. As the manager of the fitness club, why shouldn't you use the average cost per member to predict total costs at different levels of membership?

▪ SOLUTIONS

Requirement 1

As volume increases, fixed costs stay constant in total but decrease on a per-unit basis. As volume increases, variable costs stay constant on a per-unit basis but increase in total in direct proportion to increases in volume:

	A	B	C	D
1	**Monthly Operating Costs**	**100 Members**	**500 Members**	**750 Members**
2	Total variable costs	$ 100	$ 500	$ 750
3	Plus: Total fixed costs	10,000	10,000	10,000
4	Total operating costs	$ 10,100	$ 10,500	$ 10,750
5				
6	Variable cost per member	$ 1.00	$ 1.00	$ 1.00
7	Plus: Fixed cost per member	100.00	20.00	13.33
8	Average cost per member	$ 101.00	$ 21.00	$ 14.33
9				

Requirement 2

The average cost per member should not be used to predict total costs at different volumes of membership because it changes as volume changes. The average cost per member decreases as volume increases due to the fixed component of the club's operating costs. Managers should base cost predictions on cost equations, not on the average cost per member.

How do Managers Determine Cost Behavior?

In real life, managers need to figure out how their costs behave before they can make predictions and good business decisions. In this section, we discuss the most common ways of determining cost behavior.

Account Analysis

3 Use account analysis and scatter plots to analyze cost behavior

When performing **account analysis**, managers use their judgment to classify each general ledger account as a variable, fixed, or mixed cost. For example, by looking at invoices from his or her supplier, the hotel manager knows that every guest packet of toiletries costs $3. Because guests use or take these toiletries, the total toiletries cost rises in direct proportion to the number of guests. These facts allow the manager to classify the complimentary toiletries expense account as a variable cost.

Likewise, the hotel manager uses account analysis to determine how the depreciation expense accounts behave. Because the hotel uses straight-line depreciation on the parking ramp, building, and furnishings, the manager would classify the depreciation expense accounts as fixed costs. Thus, the manager can use this knowledge of cost behavior and his or her judgment to classify many accounts as variable or fixed.

Scatter Plots

The hotel manager also knows that many of the hotel's costs, such as utilities, are mixed. But how does the manager figure out the portion of the mixed cost that is fixed and the portion that is variable? In other words, how does the manager know from looking at the monthly utility bills that the hotel's utilities cost about $8,000 per month plus $8 more for every guest? One way of figuring this out is by collecting and analyzing historical data about costs and volume.

For example, let's assume that the hotel has collected the information shown in Exhibit 6-12 about last year's guest volume and utility costs.

EXHIBIT 6-12 Historical Information on Guest Volume and Utility Costs

Month	Guest Volume (x)	Utility Costs (y)
January	13,250	$114,000
February	15,200	136,000
March	17,600	135,000
April	18,300	157,000
May	22,900	195,400
June	24,600	207,800
July	25,200	209,600
August	24,900	208,300
September	22,600	196,000
October	20,800	176,400
November	18,300	173,600
December	15,420	142,000

As you can see, the hotel's business is seasonal. More people visit in the summer. However, special events such as the annual Festival of Lights, business conferences, and the nearby casino attract people to the hotel throughout the year.

Once the data has been collected, the manager creates a **scatter plot** of the data.

A scatter plot, which graphs the historical cost data on the y-axis and volume data on the x-axis, helps managers visualize the relationship between the cost and the volume of activity (number of guests, in our example). If there is a fairly strong relationship between the cost and volume, the data points will fall in a linear pattern, meaning they will resemble something close to a straight line. However, if there is little or no relationship between the cost and volume, the data points will appear almost random.

Exhibit 6-13 shows a scatter plot of the data in Exhibit 6-12. Scatter plots can be prepared by hand, but they are simpler to create using Microsoft Excel (see the "Technology Makes It Simple" feature on the next page). Notice how the data points fall in a pattern that resembles something *close* to a straight line. This shows us that there is a strong relationship between the number of guests and the hotel's utility costs. In other words, the number of guests could be considered a driver of the hotel's utilities costs (recall from our discussion of ABC in Chapter 4 that cost drivers are activities that cause costs to be incurred). On the other hand, if there were a *weaker* relationship between the number of guests and the utility costs, the data points would not fall in such a tight pattern. They would be more loosely scattered, but still in a semilinear pattern. If there were *no* relationship between the number of guests and the utility costs, the data points would appear almost random.

■ **Why is this important?**

"Scatter plots **help managers** easily **visualize** the **relationship** between cost and volume." Scatter plots are fast and easy to prepare using Excel.

EXHIBIT 6-13 Scatter Plot of Monthly Data

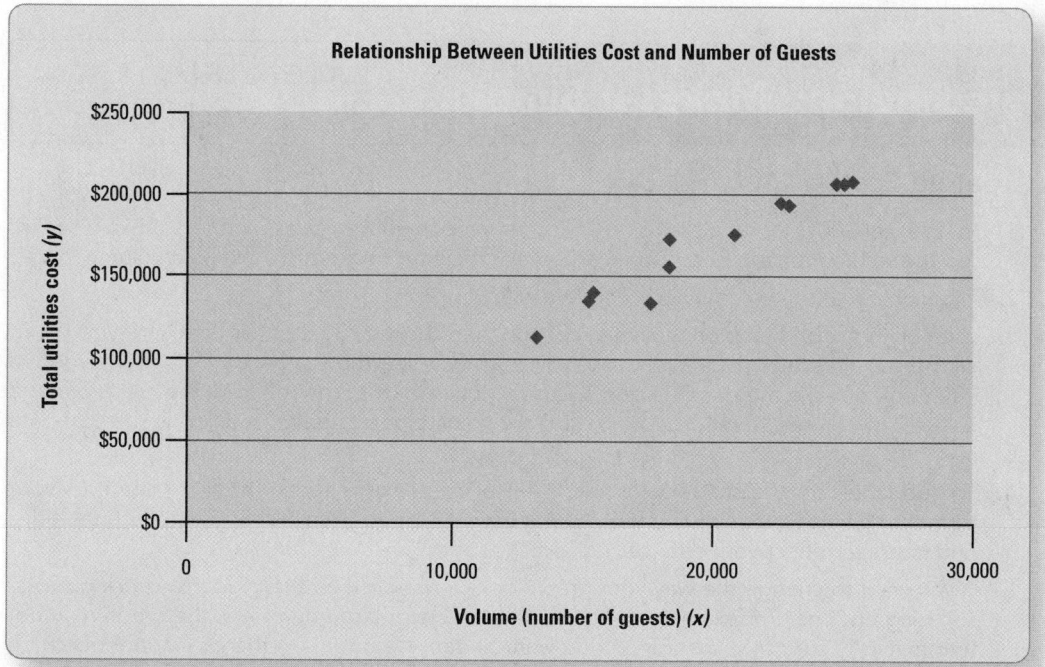

Why is this important? If the data points suggest a fairly weak relationship between the cost and the volume of the chosen activity, any cost equation based on that data will not be very useful for predicting future costs. If this is the case, the manager should consider using a different activity for modeling cost behavior. For example, many hotels use "occupancy rate" (the percentage of rooms rented) rather than number of guests as a basis for explaining and predicting variable and mixed costs.

Scatter plots are also very useful because they allow managers to identify <u>outliers</u>, or abnormal data points. Outliers are data points that do not fall in the same general pattern as the other data points. Since all data points in Exhibit 6-13 fall in the same basic pattern, no outliers appear to exist in our data. However, if a manager sees a potential outlier in the data, he or she should first determine whether the data is correct. Perhaps a clerical error was made when gathering or inputting the data. However, if the data are correct, the manager will use his or her judgment to determine whether to keep the data point in the analysis or whether to delete it.

Once the scatter plot has been prepared and examined for outliers, the next step is to determine the cost behavior that best describes the historical data points pictured in the scatter plot. Take a moment and pencil in the cost behavior line that you think best represents the data points in Exhibit 6-13. Where does your line intersect the y-axis? At the origin or above it? In other words, does the utilities cost appear to be a purely variable cost or a mixed cost? If it's a mixed cost, what portion of it is fixed?

Instead of guessing, managers can use one of the following methods to estimate the cost equation that describes the data in the scatter plot:

- High-low method
- Regression analysis

The biggest difference between these methods is that the high-low method *uses only two* of the historical data points for this estimate, whereas regression analysis uses *all* of the historical data points. Therefore, regression analysis is theoretically the better of the two methods.

We'll describe both of these methods in the next sections. Before continuing, check out the "Technology Makes It Simple" feature. It shows you just how easy it is to make a scatter plot using Microsoft Excel.

Technology Makes it Simple — Excel 2007, 2010, and 2013

Creating Scatter Plots

1. In an Excel 2007, 2010, or 2013 spreadsheet, type in your data as pictured in Exhibit 6-12. Put the volume data in one column and the associated cost data in the next column.

2. Highlight all of the volume and cost data with your cursor.

3. Click on the "Insert" tab on the menu bar and then choose "Scatter" as the chart type. Next, click the plain scatter plot (without any lines). You'll see the scatter plot on your screen. If you want to make the graph larger, choose "Move Chart Location" from the menu bar and select "New Sheet" and "OK." Make sure the volume data is on the x-axis and the cost data is on the y-axis.

4. To add labels for the scatter plot and titles for each axis, choose the first pictured layout from the "Chart Layout" menu tab ("Quick Layout" tab in Excel 2013). Customize the titles and labels to reflect your data set.

5. If you want to change the way your graph looks, right-click on the graph to check out customizing options. For example, if your data consists of large numbers, the graph may not automatically start at the origin. If you want to see the origin on the graph, right-click on either axis (where the number values are) and choose "Format Axis." Then, fix the minimum value at zero.

High-Low Method

The **high-low method** is an easy way to estimate the variable and fixed cost components of a mixed cost. The high-low method basically fits a mixed cost line through the highest and lowest *volume* data points, as shown in Exhibit 6-14, hence the name *high-low*. The high-low method produces the cost equation describing this mixed cost line.

To use the high-low method, we must first identify the months with the highest and lowest volume of activity. Looking at Exhibit 6-12, we see that the hotel served the *most* guests in July and the *fewest* guests in January. *Therefore, we use the data from only these two months in our analysis. We ignore data from all other months.* Even if a month other than July had the highest utility cost, we would still use July. Why? Because we choose

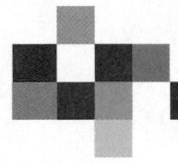

4 Use the high-low method to analyze cost behavior

EXHIBIT 6-14 Mixed Cost Line Using High-Low Method

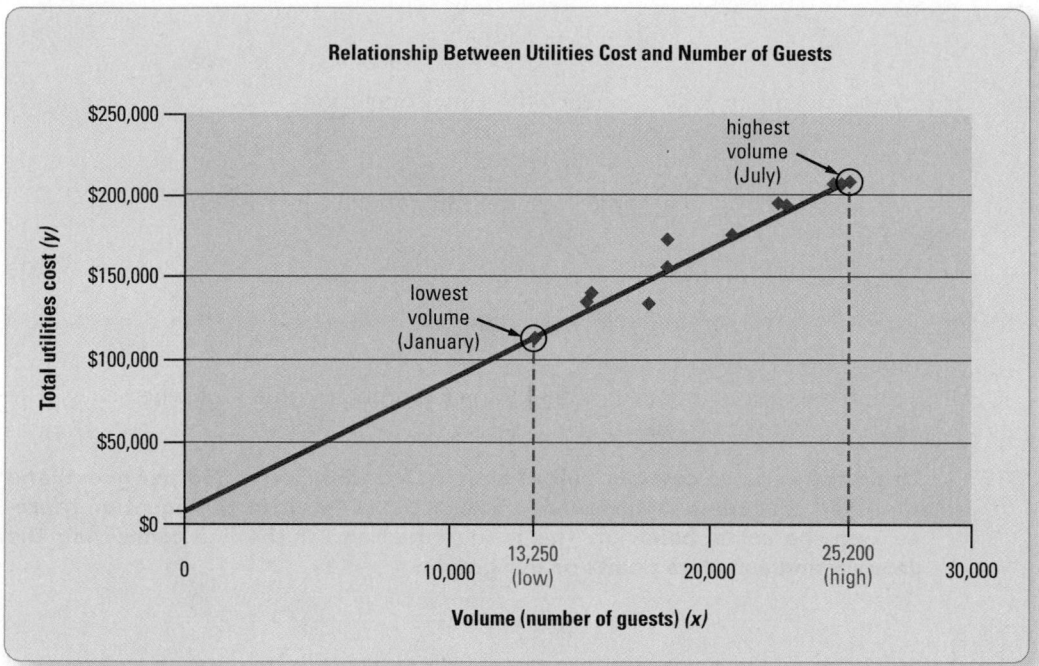

the "high" data point based on the month with the highest volume of activity (number of guests)—not the highest cost. We choose the "low" data point in a similar fashion.

STEP 1. The first step is to find *the slope of the mixed cost line* that connects the January and July data points. The slope is the variable cost per unit of activity. We can determine the slope of a line as "rise over run." The *rise* is simply the difference in cost between the high and low data points (July and January in our case), while the *run* is the difference in *volume* between the high and low data points:

$$\text{Slope} = \text{Variable cost per unit of activity } (v) = \frac{\text{Rise}}{\text{Run}} = \frac{\text{Change in cost}}{\text{Change in volume}} = \frac{y \text{ (high)} - y \text{ (low)}}{x \text{ (high)} - x \text{ (low)}}$$

Using the data from July (as our high) and January (as our low), we calculate the slope as follows:

$$\frac{(\$209,600 - \$114,000)}{(25,200 \text{ guests} - 13,250 \text{ guests})} = \$8 \text{ per guest}$$

The slope of the mixed cost line, or variable cost per unit of activity, is \$8 per guest.

STEP 2. The second step is to find the vertical intercept—the place where the line connecting the January and July data points intersects the y-axis. This is the fixed cost component of the mixed cost. We insert the slope found in Step 1 (\$8 per guest) and the volume and cost data from *either* the high or low month into a mixed costs equation:

$$\text{Total mixed costs} = \text{Variable cost component} + \text{Fixed cost component}$$
$$y \qquad = \qquad vx \qquad + \qquad f$$

For example, we can insert July's cost and volume data as follows:

$$\$209,600 = (\$8 \text{ per guest} \times 25,200 \text{ guests}) + f$$

And then solve for *f*:

$$f = \$8,000$$

Or we can use January's data to reach the same conclusion:

y	=	*vx*	+ *f*
$114,000 =	($8 per guest × 13,250 guests) + *f*		

And then solve for *f*:

$$f = \$8,000$$

Thus, the fixed cost component is $8,000 per month regardless of whether we use July or January's data.

STEP 3. Using the variable cost per unit of activity found in Step 1 ($8 per guest) and the fixed cost component found in Step 2 ($8,000), write the equation representing the costs' behavior. This is the equation for the line connecting the January and July data points on our graph.

$$y = \$8x + \$8,000$$

where,

$$y = \text{total monthly utilities cost}$$
$$x = \text{number of guests}$$

This is the equation used by the manager in the first half of the chapter to express the hotel's utility costs.

One major drawback of the high-low method is that it uses only two data points: January and July. Because we ignored every other month, the line might not be representative of those months. In our example, the high-low line is representative of the other data points, but in other situations, it may not be. Therefore, the better method to use is regression analysis, which is explained next.

Regression Analysis

5 Use regression analysis to analyze cost behavior

Regression analysis is a statistical procedure for determining the line, and associated cost equation, that best fits *all of the data points in the data set, not just the high-volume and low-volume data points*. In fact, some refer to regression analysis as "the line of best fit." Since the statistical analysis considers all of the data points when forming the line, it is usually more accurate than the high-low method. A statistic (called the R-square) generated by regression analysis also tells us *how well* the line fits the data points. Regression analysis is tedious to complete by hand but simple to do using Microsoft Excel (see the "Technology Makes It Simple" feature on page 331). Many graphing calculators also perform regression analysis.

Regression analysis using Microsoft Excel gives us the output shown in Exhibit 6-15. The output looks complicated, but for our purposes, we only need to consider the three highlighted pieces of information:

1. Intercept coefficient (this refers to the vertical intercept) = 14,538.05
2. X Variable 1 coefficient (this refers to the slope) = 7.85 (rounded)
3. The R-square value (the "goodness-of-fit" statistic) = 0.947 (rounded)

Let's look at each piece of information, starting with the highlighted information at the bottom of the output:

1. The "Intercept coefficient" is the vertical intercept of the mixed cost line. It's the fixed cost component of the mixed cost. Regression analysis tells us that the fixed

EXHIBIT 6-15 Output of Microsoft Excel Regression Analysis

	A	B	C	D	E	F	G	H	I
1	**SUMMARY OUTPUT**								
2									
3		*Regression Statistics*							
4	Multiple R		0.973273						
5	R Square		0.94726						
6	Adjusted R Square		0.941986						
7	Standard Error		8053.744						
8	Observations		12						
9									
10	**ANOVA**								
11		*df*	*SS*	*MS*	*F*	*Significance F*			
12	Regression	1	11650074512	1.17E + 10	179.6110363	1.02696E-07			
13	Residual	10	648627988.2	64862799					
14	Total	11	12298702500						
15									
16		*Coefficients*	*Standard Error*	*t Stat*	*P-value*	*Lower 95%*	*Upper 95%*	*Lower 95.0%*	*Upper 95.0%*
17	Intercept	14538.05	11898.3624	1.221853	0.249783701	-11973.15763	41049.25	-11973.16	41049.25
18	X Variable 1	7.849766	0.585720166	13.4019	1.02696E-07	6.5446997	9.154831	6.5447	9.154831

component of the monthly utility bill is $14,538. Why is this different from the $8,000 fixed component we found using the high-low method? It's because regression analysis considers *every* data point, not just the high- and low-volume data points, when forming the best fitting line.

2. The "X Variable 1 coefficient" is the line's slope, or our variable cost per guest. Regression analysis tells us that the hotel spends an extra $7.85 on utilities for every guest it serves. This is slightly lower than the $8 per guest amount we found using the high-low method.

Using the regression output, we can write the utilities monthly cost equation as follows:

$$y = \$7.85x + \$14,538$$

where,

y = total monthly utilities cost
x = number of guests

> ### Why is this important?
>
> "Regression analysis is **fast** and **easy** to perform using Microsoft Excel. **Regression analysis** gives managers the most **representative** cost equations, allowing them to make the **most accurate** cost projections."

3. Now, let's look at the R-square statistic highlighted near the top of Exhibit 6-15. The R-square statistic is often referred to as a "goodness-of-fit" statistic because it tells us how well the regression line fits the data points. The R-square can range in value from zero to one, as shown in Exhibit 6-16. If there were no relationship between the number of guests and the hotel's utility costs, the data points would be scattered randomly (rather than being in a linear pattern) and the R-square would be close to zero. If there were a *perfect* relationship between the number of guests and the hotel's utility cost, a *perfectly* straight line would run through *every* data point and the R-square would be 1.00. In our case, the R-square of 0.947 means that the regression line fits the data quite well (it's very close to 1.00). In other words, the data points *almost* fall in a straight line (as you can see in Exhibit 6-13).

EXHIBIT 6-16 Range of R-square Values

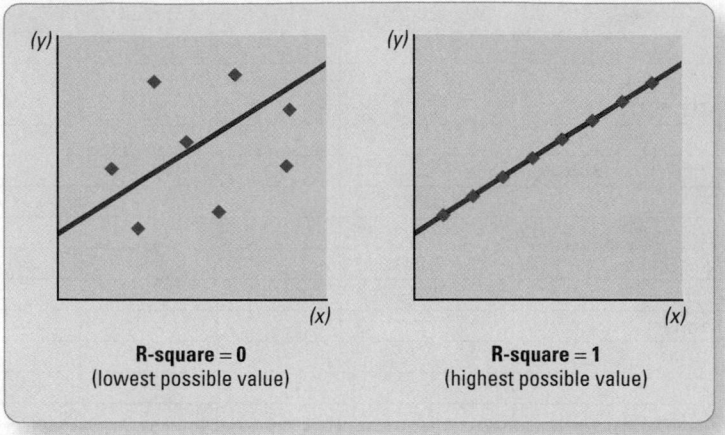

The R-square provides managers with very helpful information. The higher the R-square, the stronger the relationship between cost and volume. The stronger the relationship, the more confidence the manager would have in using the cost equation to predict costs at different volumes within the same relevant range. As a rule of thumb, an R-square over 0.80 generally indicates that the cost equation is very reliable for predicting costs at other volumes within the relevant range. An R-square between 0.50 and 0.80 means that the manager should use the cost equation with caution. However, if the R-square is fairly low (for example, less than 0.50), the manager should try using a different activity base (for example, room occupancy rate) for cost analysis because the current measure of volume is only weakly related to the costs.

Regression analysis can also help managers implement ABC. Recall from Chapter 4 that managers must choose a cost allocation base for every activity cost pool. The cost allocation base should be the primary cost driver of the costs in that pool. Management will use logic to come up with a short list of potential cost drivers for each activity cost pool. Then, management can run a regression analysis for each potential cost driver to see how strongly related it is to the activity costs in the pool. Managers compare the R-squares from each regression to see which one is highest. The regression with the highest R-square identifies the primary cost driver.

Adding a Regression Line, Regression Equation, and R-Square Value to a Scatter Plot

Rather than obtaining the full regression output pictured in Exhibit 6-15 and selecting the necessary pieces of information from it, you can command Excel to add the regression equation, regression line, and R-square value directly to a scatter plot. You'll be amazed at how quickly and easily you can create a professional-quality graph using the instructions found in the "Technology Makes it Simple" feature on the next page.

Technology Makes it Simple | Excel 2007, 2010, and 2013

Adding a Regression Line, Equation, and R-square to the Scatter Plot

Rather than obtaining a full regression output, you can command Excel to display the regression line, the associated cost equation, and the R-square directly on the scatterplot. Just follow these simple instructions:

1. Start with the Excel Scatter plot you created using the directions found on page 326.
2. Point the cursor at any data point on your scatter plot and *right* click on the mouse.
3. Choose "Add Trendline."
4. Check the two boxes: "Display Equation on Chart" and "Display R-squared value on chart." Then "Close."
5. OPTIONAL: To force the regression line to stretch back to the y-axis, point the cursor at the regression line and *right* click on the mouse. Choose "format Trendline." Then fill in the "Forecast Backward" box with the *lowest* x-value (volume) in your data set. Then "Close."

Technology Makes it Simple | Excel 2007, 2010, and 2013

Regression Analysis

1. If you created a scatter plot, you have already done this first step. In an Excel spreadsheet, type in your data as pictured in Exhibit 6-12. Put the volume data in one column and the associated cost data in the next column.
2. Click on the "Data" tab on the menu bar.
3. Next, click on "Data Analysis." If you don't see it on your menu bar, follow the directions for add-ins given below before continuing.
4. From the list of data analysis tools, select "Regression," then "OK."
5. Follow the two instructions on the screen:
   i. Highlight (or type in) the y-axis data range (this is your cost data) with your cursor.
   ii. Highlight (or type in) the x-axis data range (this is your volume data) with your cursor.
   iii. Click "OK."
6. That's all. Excel gives you the output shown in Exhibit 6-15.

DIRECTIONS FOR ADD-INs: It's easy and free to add the "Data Analysis Toolpak" if it's not already on your menu bar. You'll need to add it only once, and then it will always be on your menu bar. Simply follow these instructions:

1a. **For Excel 2007:** Click the Microsoft Office button (the colorful button in the upper-left-hand corner) and then click on the "Excel Options" box shown at the bottom.
1b. **For Excel 2010 and 2013:** Click on the "File" tab on the menu bar. Then select "Options" on the left-hand side of the screen.
2. Click "Add-Ins."
3. In the "Manage" box at the bottom of the screen, select "Excel Add-ins" and click "GO."
4. In the "Add-Ins available" box, select the "Analysis ToolPak" check box and then click "OK." If asked, click "Yes" to install.
5. That's all. You should now see "Data Analysis" as a tab on your menu bar.

Data Concerns

Cost equations are only as good as the data on which they are based. For example, if the hotel's utility bills are seasonal, management may want to develop separate cost equations for each season. For example, it might develop a winter utility bill cost equation using historical data from only the winter months. Management would do likewise for every other season. Inflation can also affect predictions. If inflation is running rampant, managers should adjust projected costs by the inflation rate. Even if the economy has generally low inflation, certain industries (such as health care and higher education) or raw material inputs (such as corn prices) may be experiencing large price changes. In our example, management would need to consider the forecasted increase or decrease in electricity and natural gas prices when forecasting costs for utilities.

Another cause for concern is outliers, or abnormal data points. Outliers can distort the results of the high-low method and regression analysis. Recall that the high-low method uses only two data points—the data points associated with the highest and lowest volumes of activity. If either of these points is an outlier, the resulting line and cost equation will be skewed. Because regression analysis uses all data points, any outlier in the data will affect the resulting line and cost equation, but to a lesser extent.

For example, let's say management's historical data set resulted in the scatter plot pictured in Exhibit 6-17. The low-volume point looks like it might be an outlier. Notice how the high-low line is highly skewed as a result. However, the regression line remains fairly representative of the other data points, even though it is being pulled slightly toward the outlier. Remember to always investigate potential outliers to help determine whether or not to remove them from the data set before proceeding with regression or the high-low method.

EXHIBIT 6-17 Effect of Outlier on Cost Equations

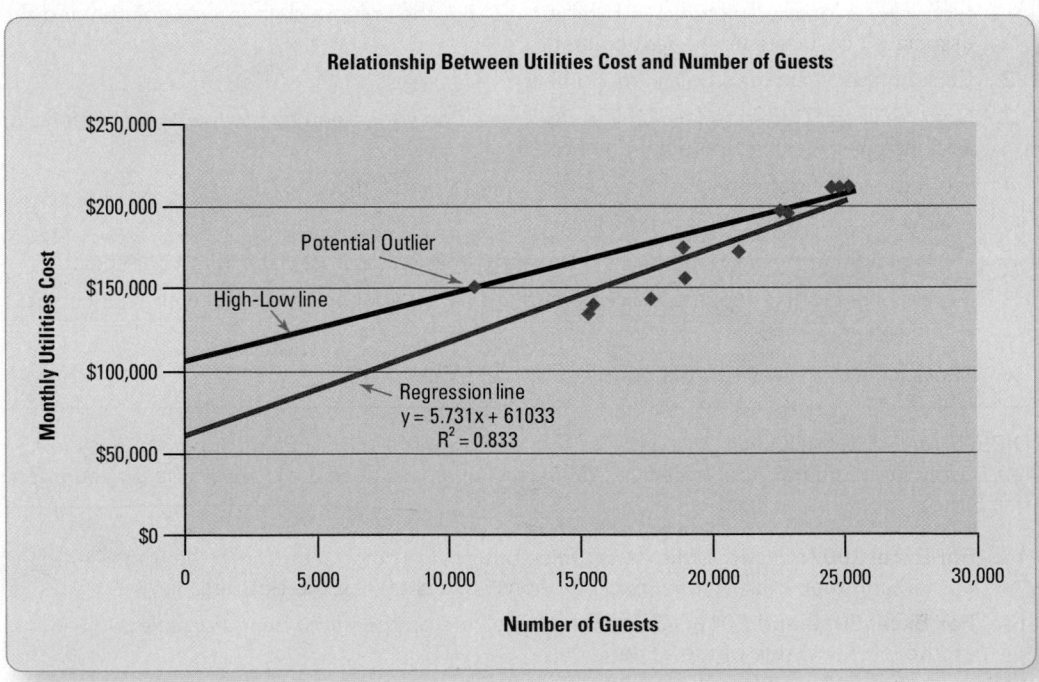

What are the Roles of Variable Costing and the Contribution Margin Income Statement?

You have just learned about different cost behaviors. As you'll see in the coming chapters, almost all business decisions are influenced by cost behavior. In the following sections, we'll explain how the accounting system can communicate cost behavior information to managers so that they have it readily available for planning, decision-making, and performance evaluation purposes.

6 Describe variable costing and prepare a contribution margin income statement

Comparing Absorption Costing and Variable Costing

So far in this textbook, we have used a costing concept known as absorption costing. Why? Generally Accepted Accounting Principles (GAAP) requires absorption costing for external financial reporting and the Internal Revenue Service (IRS) requires it for tax preparation. Under **absorption costing**, all manufacturing-related costs, whether fixed or variable, are "absorbed" into the cost of the product. In other words, all direct materials, direct labor, and manufacturing overhead (MOH) costs are treated as inventoriable product costs, as described in Chapter 2. We used absorption costing, also known as "traditional" or "full costing" when we illustrated job costing and process costing in Chapters 3, 4, and 5.

Under absorption costing, no distinction is made between manufacturing costs that rise and fall with production volume and manufacturing costs that remain fixed. As a review,

- variable manufacturing costs would include direct material, direct labor, and variable MOH costs such as the utilities used during the production process.

- fixed MOH costs would include property taxes and insurance on the plant, straight-line depreciation on the plant, lease payments on the production equipment and the portion of utilities that are not affected by changes in production volume.

Supporters of absorption costing argue that all of these costs—whether variable or fixed—are necessary for production to occur, so *all* of these costs should become part of the inventoriable cost of the product.

On the other hand, many accountants and managers do not agree. They argue that fixed manufacturing costs are related to the available production capacity and will be incurred *regardless* of the actual production volume which occurs during the period. Since these costs will be incurred regardless of volume, they should be treated as period costs and expensed immediately. This argument has led to the development and use of an alternative costing system known as **variable costing** (or direct costing) in which only *variable* manufacturing costs are treated as inventoriable product costs. Since GAAP and the Internal Revenue Service (IRS) require absorption costing for external reporting, variable costing may only be used for internal management purposes.

One benefit of variable costing is that it often leads to better decisions. By assigning only variable manufacturing costs to each unit of product, managers can easily see how much additional manufacturing cost will be incurred every time another unit is produced. In addition, the unit cost of the product will not be affected by the number of units produced during the period, as it is when fixed manufacturing costs are absorbed into the unit cost. As we'll discuss next, another benefit of variable costing is that it provides incentives for better inventory management than does absorption costing.

Let's illustrate this concept using an example. Exhibit 6-18 provides the most recent annual data for ShredCo, a maker of electronic paper shredders.

EXHIBIT 6-18 ShredCo Data

Variable costs:	
Direct material cost per unit produced	$35
Direct labor cost per unit produced	$10
Variable MOH cost per unit produced	$5
Variable operating expenses per unit sold	$2
Fixed costs:	
Fixed MOH	$1,000,000
Fixed operating expenses	$300,000
Other information:	
Units produced	40,000 units
Sales price per unit	$100

Exhibit 6-19 shows the inventoriable product cost of one unit under both absorption costing and variable costing. Notice that the only difference is the treatment of fixed MOH. Absorption costing includes fixed MOH ($25) in the unit cost, whereas variable costing does not. The $75 unit cost shown in Exhibit 6-19 will be used by the company to (1) record the value of inventory on the balance sheet, and (2) record Cost of Goods Sold on the income statement when the inventory is eventually sold.

EXHIBIT 6-19 Comparing Inventoriable Product Costs

	A	B	C
	Manufacturing Costs Per Unit	**Absorption Costing**	**Variable Costing**
1			
2	Direct material cost per unit	$ 35	$ 35
3	Direct labor cost per unit	10	10
4	Variable MOH cost per unit	5	5
5	Fixed MOH cost per unit ($1,000,000 ÷ 40,000 units)	25	0
6	Total cost per unit	$ 75	$ 50
7			

Under variable costing, no fixed MOH is assigned to the product cost.

Why is this important?

"Variable costing **helps** manufacturers **identify** the **variable cost** of making each unit of a product. This information will be **critical** to making many of the business **decisions,** such as whether or not to outsource production."

Notice how variable costing shows managers exactly how much extra cost ($50) will be incurred every time a unit is made. This transparency is not the case with absorption costing, which can easily mislead managers. To illustrate, let's assume that the company decides to produce an extra 5,000 units with its existing capacity. Using variable costing, we see the additional production cost will really be $250,000 (5,000 units × $50). However, absorption costing could mislead the manager into believing that the extra cost would be $375,000 (5,000 × $75). The fallacy in this erroneous analysis stems from treating the $25 of fixed MOH in the product cost as if it were variable. In fact, the company will *not* incur an additional $25 of fixed cost with every unit produced. Rather, the company will incur $1 million of fixed cost *regardless* of the production volume, as long as the production volume stays within the company's relevant range (which in most cases is its existing production capacity). Variable costing tends be the better costing system for internal decision-making purposes because the reported unit cost is purely variable in nature.

Exhibit 6-20 illustrates period costs under both costing systems. Remember that these are often referred to as "operating expenses" in the income statement. Notice again that the only difference is the treatment of fixed MOH. Under absorption costing, *none* of the fixed MOH is expensed as a period cost. Under variable costing, *all* of the fixed MOH ($1 million) is expensed as a period cost.

EXHIBIT 6-20 Comparing Period Costs (Operating Expenses)

	A	B	C
		Absorption Costing	Variable Costing
1	**Operating Expenses of the Period**		
2	Variable operating expenses when 40,000 units are sold (40,000 × $2)	$ 80,000	$ 80,000
3	Fixed operating expenses	300,000	300,000
4	Fixed MOH	0	1,000,000
5	Total operating expenses (period costs)	$ 380,000	$ 1,380,000
6			

Under variable costing, fixed MOH is treated as a period cost.

Keep the following rule of thumb in mind:

The ONLY difference between absorption costing and variable costing is the treatment of Fixed MOH, and the *timing* with which it is expensed:

- Under variable costing, fixed MOH is expensed immediately as a period cost (operating expense).
- Under absorption costing, fixed MOH becomes part of the inventoriable product cost of each unit, which isn't expensed until the inventory is sold (as Cost of Goods Sold).

▶ Try It!

Sony makes DVD players and uses both absorption and variable costing. Assume Sony incurred the following manufacturing costs in producing 10,000 DVD players last month:

Manufacturing Costs	Total Cost	Per Unit Cost
Direct materials	$ 70,000	$ 7.00
Direct labor	40,000	4.00
Variable MOH	90,000	9.00
Fixed MOH	120,000	12.00
Total	$320,000	$32.00

1. What is the inventoriable product cost per unit, using absorption costing?
2. How will fixed MOH be expensed if absorption costing is used?
3. What is the inventoriable cost per unit, using variable costing?
4. How will fixed MOH be expensed if variable costing is used?

Please see page 381 for solutions.

The Contribution Margin Income Statement

Now that you know the difference between absorption costing and variable costing, let's see how the information is communicated to managers using a different income statement format.

Comparing Income Statement Formats

Let's start with the situation in which the company sells *exactly* all of the units it produced during the period. In our example, this means that the company sells all 40,000 units it produced during the year. This situation occurs most frequently with lean producers who use just-in-time (JIT) inventory systems. Exhibit 6-21 shows a traditional income statement, which is based on absorption costing. Notice how Cost of Goods Sold is calculated using the $75 unit cost shown in Exhibit 6-19.

EXHIBIT 6-21 Traditional Income Statement Based on Absorption Costing

	A	B	C	D
1	ShredCo			
2	Traditional Income Statement (Absorption Costing)			
3	For the Year Ended December 31			
4				
5	Sales revenue (40,000 × $100)	$ 4,000,000		
6	Less: Cost of goods sold (40,000 × $75)	3,000,000		
7	Gross profit	$ 1,000,000		
8	Less: Operating expenses [$300,000 + (40,000 × $2)]	380,000		
9	Operating income	$ 620,000		
10				

In contrast, Exhibit 6-22 shows a **contribution margin income statement**, which is an income statement organized by cost behavior. When manufacturers use variable costing, they report income internally using a contribution margin income statement format.

EXHIBIT 6-22 Contribution Margin Income Statement Using Variable Costing

	A	B	C	D
1	ShredCo			
2	Contribution Margin Income Statement (Variable Costing)			
3	For the Year Ended December 31			
4				
5	Sales revenue (40,000 × $100)	$ 4,000,000		
6	Less variable expenses:			
7	Variable cost of goods sold (40,000 × $50)	2,000,000		
8	Variable operating expenses (40,000 × $2)	80,000		
9	Contribution margin	$ 1,920,000		
10	Less fixed expenses:			
11	Fixed MOH	1,000,000		
12	Fixed operating expenses	300,000		
13	Operating income	$ 620,000		
14				

Notice the following in Exhibit 6-22:

■ The contribution margin income statement is organized by cost behavior.

■ All variable costs are expensed *above* the contribution margin line. As a result, only the *variable* product cost ($50, from Exhibit 6-19) is used when calculating Variable Cost of Goods Sold.

■ All fixed costs, including fixed MOH, are expensed *below* the contribution margin line.

■ The **contribution margin** is equal to sales revenue minus variable expenses. It shows managers how much profit has been made on sales before considering fixed costs.

■ The operating income ($620,000) is the *same* in both statements. For manufacturers, this equality will *only* occur when all of units produced during a period are also sold during that same period, resulting in no change in inventory levels.

■ For service and merchandising companies, operating income will *always* be the same regardless of the income statement format used.

The contribution margin income statement may only be used for internal management purposes, never for external reporting. Managers like the contribution margin format because it allows them to quickly see which costs will change with fluctuations in volume, and which costs will remain the same. For example, if sales volume increases 10%, managers would expect sales revenue and variable costs to increase by 10%. As a result, the contribution margin should also increase 10%. On the other hand, all fixed costs shown below the contribution margin will not change as a result of changes in volume.

Service and Merchandising Companies

Since service and merchandising companies don't manufacture products, they don't have manufacturing overhead. Therefore, variable costing and absorption costing do not apply to them because these costing concepts deal with how to treat fixed manufacturing overhead. However, many service and merchandising companies like to use the contribution margin format of the income statement for internal management purposes. Why? Because the contribution margin income statement clearly communicates cost behavior information to managers who need this information for planning and decision-making purposes. Exhibit 6-23 shows the contribution margin income statement for the service firm introduced in Chapter 2. Notice once again how, all variable expenses are deducted from revenue to arrive at the company's contribution margin. Next, all fixed expenses are subtracted from the contribution margin to arrive at operating income.

EXHIBIT 6-23 Contribution Margin Income Statement of a Service Company

	A	B	C	D
1	eNow!			
2	Contribution Margin Income Statement			
3	For the Year Ended December 31			
4				
5	Sales revenue	$ 160,000		
6	Less: Variable expenses	2,500		
7	Contribution margin	$ 157,500		
8	Less: Fixed expenses	127,500		
9	Operating income	$ 30,000		
10				

NOTE: Recall that service firms only have operating expenses, and no Cost of Goods Sold.

The contribution margin income statement format is essentially the same, regardless of whether the company is a service firm, a merchandiser, or a manufacturer. The main differences are as follows:

- Service firms have no Cost of Goods Sold, so all operating expenses are simply classified as either variable or fixed. If mixed, the company first estimates the variable and fixed portions based on the methods, such as regression analysis, discussed earlier in this chapter.
- Merchandising companies have Cost of Goods Sold, but because they purchase all of their inventory, rather than manufacture it, all of Cost of Goods Sold is considered variable. An example is pictured in Exhibit 6-24.
- For service and merchandising companies, operating income will always be the same, regardless of whether the company uses a traditional income statement or a contribution margin income statement format.

EXHIBIT 6-24 Contribution Margin Income Statement for a Merchandising Company

	A	B	C	D
1	**Wholesome Foods**			
2	**Income Statement**			
3	**For the Year Ended December 31**			
4	*(all figures shown in thousands of dollars)*			
5				
6	Sales revenue	$ 150,000		
7	Less variable expenses:			
8	Cost of goods sold	106,500		
9	Variable operating expenses	3,000		
10	Contribution margin	$ 40,500		
11	Less: Fixed operating expenses	6,000		
12	Operating income	$ 34,500		
13				

NOTE: For a retailer, all of Cost of Goods Sold is considered variable.

Comparing Operating Income: Variable Versus Absorption Costing

For manufacturers, operating income will not always be the same between the two costing systems. In fact, it will *only* be the same if the manufacturer sells *exactly* what it produced during the period, as was the case in Exhibits 6-21 and 6-22. This scenario is typical of a lean producer. However, traditional manufacturers in a growing economy often produce extra safety stock, *increasing* their inventory levels to ensure against unexpected demand. On the other hand, in periods of economic recession (such as in the years 2008–2009) companies often *reduce* their inventory levels to decrease costs, build cash reserves, and adjust for lower sales demand.

We will discuss how inventory levels impact operating income, for both absorption and variable costing, under three possible scenarios:

1. Inventory levels remain constant

2. Inventory levels increase

3. Inventory levels decrease

As we discuss each scenario, keep in mind that in our example, absorption costing assigned $25 of fixed MOH to each unit of product produced by ShredCo (Exhibit 6-19).

Scenario 1: Inventory levels remain constant

As shown in Exhibits 6-21, 6-22, and 6-25, when inventory levels remain constant, both absorption costing and variable costing result in the same operating income. This scenario usually occurs at lean manufacturers since they only produce enough inventory to fill existing customer orders.

EXHIBIT 6-25 Inventory Levels Remain Constant

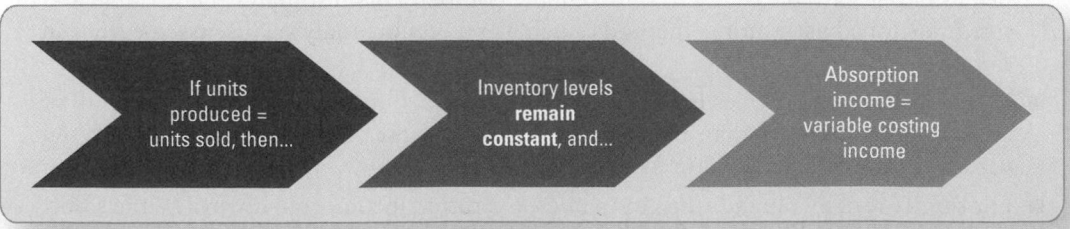

In this situation, *all* fixed MOH incurred during the period ($1,000,000) is expensed under both costing systems. Under variable costing, it is expensed as a period cost ($1,000,000), as shown in Exhibit 6-22. Under absorption costing, it is first absorbed into the product's cost ($25 of the $75 unit cost), and then expensed as Cost of Goods Sold when the product is sold. When all product is sold in the same period as it is produced, exactly $1 million of fixed MOH is expensed as part of Cost of Goods Sold (40,000 × $25) as shown in Exhibit 6-21.

Scenario 2: Inventory levels increase

As shown in Exhibit 6-26, when inventory levels increase, operating income will be greater under absorption costing than it is under variable costing. This scenario typically occurs at traditional manufacturers during times of economic growth.

EXHIBIT 6-26 Inventory Levels Increase

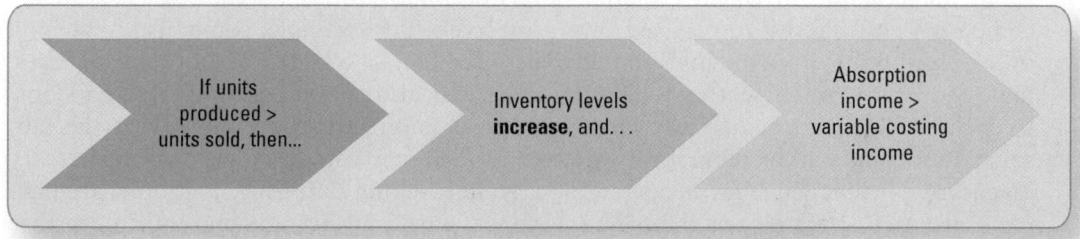

In this situation, all fixed MOH incurred during the period is expensed as a period cost under variable costing ($1,000,000). However, under absorption costing, some of the fixed MOH remains "trapped" on the balance sheet as part of the cost of inventory. For example, let's say only 30,000 of the 40,000 units are sold, leaving 10,000 units still in ending inventory. As a result, $750,000 of fixed MOH is expensed as part of Cost of Goods Sold (30,000 units × $25) while $250,000 of fixed MOH (10,000 units × $25) remains in inventory. As a result, *more* cost is expensed under variable costing than under absorption costing, leading to a higher operating income under absorption costing.

Thus, under absorption costing, managers can misuse their powers by continuing to build up unwarranted levels of inventory simply to increase operating income. The more inventory builds up, the more favorable operating income will be. Unfortunately, as we learned in Chapter 4, building unnecessary inventory is wasteful and should be avoided. Because of this drawback to absorption costing, many companies prefer to use variable costing to evaluate managers' performance. Since variable costing expenses all fixed MOH in the current period regardless of the amount of inventory produced, managers have no incentive to build unnecessary inventory.

Scenario 3: Inventory levels decrease

As shown in Exhibit 6-27, when inventory levels decrease, operating income will be greater under variable costing than it is under absorption costing. This scenario typically occurs at traditional manufacturers during times of economic recession. It also occurs when traditional manufacturers are in the process of switching to lean operations, which carry little to no inventory.

EXHIBIT 6-27 Inventory Levels Decrease

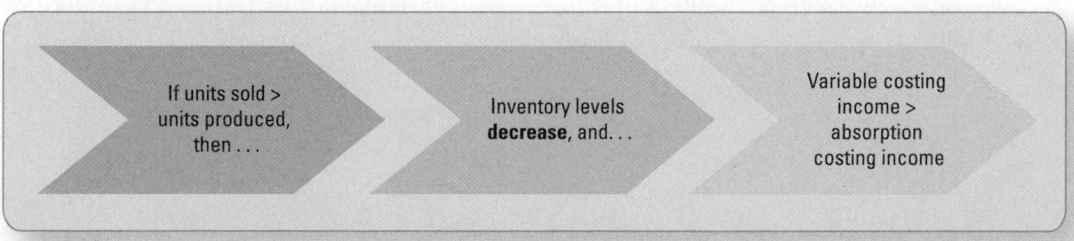

In this situation, all fixed MOH incurred during the period is expensed under variable costing ($1,000,000). However, under absorption costing, all of the fixed MOH of the period is expensed as part of Cost of Goods Sold *plus* some of the fixed MOH from the previous period. For example, let's say that 45,000 units are sold, comprised of the 40,000 units produced in the current period and 5,000 units produced in the previous period. For the sake of simplicity, we'll assume the same unit costs were incurred in the previous period. As a result of selling 45,000 units this year, $1,125,000 of fixed MOH is expensed as Cost of Goods Sold (45,000 × $25). This figure consists of $1,000,000 from the current year (40,000 × $25) and $125,000 from the previous year (5,000 × $25). As a result, *more* cost is expensed under absorption costing than under variable costing, leading to a lower net income under absorption costing.

Managers who are evaluated based on absorption income have every incentive to *avoid* the situation in which inventory levels decline. However, sometimes it is in the company's best interest to decrease inventory levels. For example, companies switching over to lean production methods should experience long-run benefits from lean practices, but in the short-run, inventory reductions will cause absorption-based operating income to decline. Managers switching over to lean production should be fully aware that absorption income will be temporarily affected as the company sheds itself of unnecessary inventory. The challenge for managers is to avoid thinking that lean operations are having a negative effect on the company's earnings, when, in fact, the temporary decrease in operating income is simply a result of the costing system. Again, variable costing is not affected by inventory fluctuations, making it the better costing system for evaluating performance.

Reconciling Operating Income Between the Two Costing Systems

As discussed, absorption costing is required by GAAP and the IRS, yet variable costing is preferred for internal decision-making and performance evaluation purposes. Thus, managers are often exposed to both sets of information. For manufacturers, the costing systems will yield different results for operating income when inventory levels increase or decline. Managers can easily reconcile the difference between the two income figures using the following formula:

> Difference in operating income = (Change in inventory level, in units) × (Fixed MOH per unit)

We'll illustrate the use of this formula next.

Reconciling Income When Inventory Levels Increase

Let's try this formula with the example in which 40,000 units are produced, yet only 30,000 are sold. Using the formula, we predict the difference in operating income will be:

> Difference in operating income = (Change in inventory level, in units) × (Fixed MOH per unit)
> $250,000 = 10,000 units × $ 25

Because the inventory level has *grown*, we would expect operating income under absorption costing to be *greater* than it is under variable costing by $250,000 (see Exhibit 6-26). Exhibit 6-28, which presents comparative income statements, verifies this prediction: Absorption costing income ($390,000) is *higher* than variable costing income ($140,000) by $250,000.

EXHIBIT 6-28 Comparing Income When Inventory Levels Increase

Panel A: Absorption Costing:

	A	B	C	D
1	ShredCo			
2	Traditional Income Statement (Absorption Costing)			
3	For the Year Ended December 31			
4				
5	Sales revenue (30,000 × $100)	$ 3,000,000		
6	Less: Cost of goods sold (30,000 × $75)	2,250,000		
7	Gross profit	$ 750,000		
8	Less: Operating expenses [$300,000 + (30,000 × $2)]	360,000		
9	Operating income	$ 390,000		
10				

Panel B: Variable Costing:

	A	B	C	D
1	ShredCo			
2	Contribution Margin Income Statement (Variable Costing)			
3	For the Year Ended December 31			
4				
5	Sales revenue (30,000 × $100)	$ 3,000,000		
6	Less variable expenses:			
7	Variable cost of goods sold (30,000 × $50)	1,500,000		
8	Variable operating expenses (30,000 × $2)	60,000		
9	Contribution margin	$ 1,440,000		
10	Less fixed expenses:			
11	Fixed MOH	1,000,000		
12	Fixed operating expenses	300,000		
13	Operating income	$ 140,000		
14				

Reconciling Income When Inventory Levels Decrease

Now let's briefly consider the situation in which inventory decreases, rather than increases. Let's assume that 45,000 units are sold, comprised of 40,000 that were produced in the current period plus 5,000 units that were produced in the previous period. The formula used to reconcile income suggests that operating income under absorption costing will be *lower* than it is under variable costing (see Exhibit 6-27) by $125,000:

Difference in operating income = (Change in inventory level, in units) × (Fixed MOH per unit)

$125,000 = 5,000 units × $ 25

Exhibit 6-29 verifies the truth of this prediction. Operating income under absorption costing ($735,000) is $125,000 *lower* than operating income under variable costing ($860,000).

Key Points to Remember

You have just learned about variable costing and the contribution margin income statement. Some key points to remember are summarized in Exhibit 6-30.

EXHIBIT 6-29 Comparing Income When Inventory Levels Decrease

Panel A: Absorption Costing:

	A	B	C	D
1	ShredCo			
2	Traditional Income Statement (Absorption Costing)			
3	For the Year Ended December 31			
4				
5	Sales revenue (45,000 × $100)	$ 4,500,000		
6	Less: Cost of goods sold (45,000 × $75)	3,375,000		
7	Gross profit	$ 1,125,000		
8	Less: Operating expenses [$300,000 + (45,000 × $2)]	390,000		
9	Operating income	$ 735,000		
10				

Panel B: Variable Costing:

	A	B	C	D
1	ShredCo			
2	Contribution Margin Income Statement (Variable Costing)			
3	For the Year Ended December 31			
4				
5	Sales revenue (45,000 × $100)	$ 4,500,000		
6	Less variable expenses:			
7	Variable cost of goods sold (45,000 × $50)	2,250,000		
8	Variable operating expenses (45,000 × $2)	90,000		
9	Contribution margin	$ 2,160,000		
10	Less fixed expenses:			
11	Fixed MOH	1,000,000		
12	Fixed operating expenses	300,000		
13	Operating income	$ 860,000		
14				

EXHIBIT 6-30 Key Points About Variable Costing and the Contribution Margin Income Statement

Variable Costing

- Treats all fixed MOH costs as operating expenses in the period incurred, rather than treating fixed MOH as an inventoriable product cost
- Can only be used for internal management purposes; never for external financial reporting or tax purposes
- Is often better for decision making than absorption costing because it clearly shows managers the additional cost of making one more unit of product (the variable cost per unit)
- Is often better for performance evaluation than absorption costing because it gives managers no incentive to build unnecessary inventory
- Will result in a different operating income than absorption costing for manufacturers whose inventory levels *increase* or *decrease* from the previous period

The Contribution Margin Income Statement

- Is organized by cost behavior. First, all variable expenses are deducted from sales revenue to arrive at the company's contribution margin. Next, all fixed expenses are deducted from the contribution margin to arrive at operating income
- Is often more useful than a traditional income statement for planning and decision making because it clearly distinguishes the costs that will be affected by changes in volume (the variable costs) from the costs that will be unaffected (fixed costs)
- Can only be used for internal management purposes, and never for external financial reporting
- Will show the same operating income as a traditional income statement for (1) service firms, (2) merchandising companies, and (3) manufacturers *only* if their inventory levels remain stable
- For retailers, all of Cost of Goods Sold is considered variable

Decision Guidelines

Cost Behavior

As the manager of a local fitness club, Fitness-for-Life, you'll want to plan for operating costs at various levels of membership. Before you can make forecasts, you'll need to make some of the following decisions.

Decision	Guidelines
How can I separate the fixed and the variable components of a mixed cost?	• Managers typically use the high-low method or regression analysis. • The high-low method is fast and easy but uses only two historical data points to form the cost equation, and therefore may not be very indicative of the cost's true behavior. • Regression analysis uses every data point provided to determine the cost equation that best fits the data. It is simple to do with Excel, but tedious to do by hand.
I've used the high-low method to formulate a cost equation. Can I tell how well the cost equation fits the data?	The only way to determine how well the high-low cost equation fits the data is by (1) plotting the data, (2) drawing a line through the data points associated with the highest and lowest volume, and (3) "visually inspecting" the resulting graph to see if the line is representative of the other plotted data points.
I've used regression analysis to formulate a cost equation. Can I tell how well the cost equation fits the data?	The R-square is a "goodness-of-fit" statistic that tells how well the regression analysis cost equation fits the data. The R-square ranges from 0 to 1, with 1 being a perfect fit. When the R-square is high, the cost equation should render fairly accurate predictions.
Do I need to be concerned about anything before using the high-low method or regression analysis?	Cost equations are only as good as the data on which they are based. Managers should plot the historical data to see if a relationship between cost and volume exists. In addition, scatter plots help managers identify outliers. Managers should remove outliers before further analysis. Managers should also adjust cost equations for seasonal data, inflation, and price changes.
Can I present the club's financial statements in a manner that will help with planning and decision making?	Managers often use contribution margin income statements for internal planning and decision making. Contribution margin income statements organize costs by *behavior* (fixed versus variable) rather than by *function* (product versus period).
What is the difference between absorption and variable costing?	Fixed manufacturing costs are treated as: • inventoriable product costs under absorption costing. • period costs under variable costing.
How are inventoriable product costs calculated under absorption costing and variable costing?	**Absorption Costing** Direct materials + Direct labor + Variable MOH + Fixed MOH = Product cost **Variable Costing** Direct materials + Direct labor + Variable MOH = Product cost
Why is variable costing often used for internal management purposes?	• Variable costing and the contribution margin income statement help managers easily predict the cost of operating at different volumes within the relevant range. • Variable costing helps managers with decision making, because it allows them to easily see the cost of making one more unit of product. • Variable costing does not give managers incentives to build up unnecessary inventory.

SUMMARY PROBLEM 2

As the new manager of a local fitness club, Fitness-for-Life, you have been studying the club's financial data. You would like to determine how the club's costs behave in order to make accurate predictions for next year. Here is information from the last six months:

Month	Club Membership (number of members)	Total Operating Costs	Average Operating Costs per Member
July	450	$ 8,900	$19.78
August	480	$ 9,800	$20.42
September	500	$10,100	$20.20
October	550	$10,150	$18.45
November	560	$10,500	$18.75
December	525	$10,200	$19.43

Requirements

1. By looking at the "Total Operating Costs" and the "Operating Costs per Member," can you tell whether the club's operating costs are variable, fixed, or mixed? Explain your answer.

2. Use the high-low method to determine the club's monthly operating cost equation.

3. Using your answer from Requirement 2, predict total monthly operating costs if the club has 600 members.

4. Can you predict total monthly operating costs if the club has 3,000 members? Explain your answer.

5. Prepare the club's traditional income statement and its contribution margin income statement for the month of July. Assume that your cost equation from Requirement 2 accurately describes the club's cost behavior. The club charges members $30 per month for unlimited access to its facilities.

6. *Optional*: Perform regression analysis using Microsoft Excel. What is the monthly operating cost equation? What is the R-square? Why is the cost equation different from that in Requirement 2?

▪ SOLUTIONS

Requirement 1

By looking at "Total Operating Costs," we can see that the club's operating costs are not purely fixed; otherwise, total costs would remain constant. Operating costs appear to be either variable or mixed because they increase in total as the number of members increases. By looking at the "Operating Costs per Member," we can see that the operating costs aren't purely variable; otherwise, the "per-member" cost would remain constant. Therefore, the club's operating costs are mixed.

Requirement 2

Use the high-low method to determine the club's operating cost equation:

Step 1: The highest volume month is November, and the lowest volume month is July. Therefore, we use *only these 2 months* to determine the cost equation. The first step is to find the variable cost per unit of activity, which is the slope of the line connecting the November and July data points:

$$\frac{\text{Rise}}{\text{Run}} = \frac{\text{Change in } y}{\text{Change in } x} = \frac{y \text{ (high)} - y \text{ (low)}}{x \text{ (high)} - x \text{ (low)}} = \frac{(\$10,500 - \$8,900)}{(560 - 450 \text{ members})} = \$14.55 \text{ per member (rounded)}$$

Step 2: The second step is to find the fixed cost component (vertical intercept) by plugging in the slope and either July or November data to a mixed costs equation:

$$y = vx + f$$

Using November data:

$$\$10,500 = (\$14.55/\text{member} \times 560 \text{ guests}) + f$$

Solving for *f*:

$$f = \$2,352$$

Or we can use July data to reach the same conclusion:

$$\$8,900 = (\$14.55/\text{members} \times 450 \text{ guests}) + f$$

Solving for *f*:

$$f = \$2,352 \text{ (rounded)}$$

Step 3: Write the monthly operating cost equation:

$$y = \$14.55x + \$2,352$$

where,

$$x = \text{number of members}$$
$$y = \text{total monthly operating costs}$$

Requirement 3

Predict total monthly operating costs when volume reaches 600 members:

$$y = (\$14.55 \times 600) + \$2,352$$
$$y = \$11,082$$

Requirement 4

Our current data and cost equation are based on 450 to 560 members. If membership reaches 3,000, operating costs could behave much differently. That volume falls outside our current relevant range.

Requirement 5

The club had 450 members in July and total operating costs of $8,900. Thus, its traditional income statement is as follows:

	A	B	C	D
1	FITNESS-FOR-LIFE			
2	Income Statement			
3	For the Month Ended August 31			
4				
5	Club membership revenue (450 × $30)	$ 13,500		
6	Less: Operating expenses (given)	8,900		
7	Operating income	$ 4,600		
8				

To prepare the club's contribution margin income statement, we need to know how much of the total $8,900 operating costs is fixed and how much is variable. If the cost equation from Requirement 2 accurately reflects the club's cost behavior, fixed costs will be $2,352 and variable costs will be $6,548 (= $14.55 × 450). The contribution margin income statement would look like this:

	A	B	C	D
1	FITNESS-FOR-LIFE			
2	Contribution Margin Income Statement			
3	For the Month Ended August 31			
4				
5	Club membership revenue (450 × $30)	$ 13,500		
6	Less: Variable expenses (450 × $14.55)	6,548		
7	Contribution margin	6,952		
8	Less: Fixed expenses	2,352		
9	Operating income	$ 4,600		
10				

Requirement 6

Regression analysis using Microsoft Excel results in the following cost equation and R-square:

$$y = \$11.80x + \$3,912$$

where,

$$x = \text{number of members}$$
$$y = \text{total monthly operating costs}$$

R-square = 0.8007

The regression analysis cost equation uses all of the data points, not just the data from November and July. Therefore, it better represents all of the data. The high R-square means that the regression line fits the data well and predictions based on this cost equation should be quite accurate.

Learning Objectives

- 1 Describe key characteristics and graphs of various cost behaviors
- 2 Use cost equations to express and predict costs
- 3 Use account analysis and scatter plots to analyze cost behavior
- 4 Use the high-low method to analyze cost behavior
- 5 Use regression analysis to analyze cost behavior
- 6 Describe variable costing and prepare a contribution margin income statement

Accounting Vocabulary

Absorption Costing. (p. 333) The costing method where products "absorb" both fixed and variable manufacturing costs.

Account Analysis. (p. 324) A method for determining cost behavior that is based on a manager's judgment in classifying each general ledger account as a variable, fixed, or mixed cost.

Committed Fixed Costs. (p. 313) Fixed costs that are locked in because of previous management decisions; management has little or no control over these costs in the short run.

Contribution Margin. (p. 336) Sales revenue minus variable expenses.

Contribution Margin Income Statement. (p. 336) Income statement that organizes costs by *behavior* (variable costs or fixed costs) rather than by *function*.

Cost Behavior. (p. 310) Describes how costs change as volume changes.

Cost Equation. (p. 311) A mathematical equation for a straight line that expresses how a cost behaves.

Curvilinear Costs. (p. 320) A cost behavior that is not linear (not a straight line).

Discretionary Fixed Costs. (p. 313) Fixed costs that are a result of annual management decisions; fixed costs that are controllable in the short run.

Fixed Costs. (p. 313) Costs that do not change in total despite wide changes in volume.

High-Low Method. (p. 326) A method for determining cost behavior that is based on two historical data points: the highest and lowest volume of activity.

Mixed Cost. (p. 316) Costs that change, but *not* in direct proportion to changes in volume. Mixed costs have both variable cost and fixed cost components.

Outliers. (p. 325) Abnormal data points; data points that do not fall in the same general pattern as the other data points.

Regression Analysis. (p. 328) A statistical procedure for determining the line that best fits the data by using all of the historical data points, not just the high and low data points.

Relevant Range. (p. 318) The band of volume where total fixed costs remain constant at a certain level and where the variable cost *per unit* remains constant at a certain level.

Scatter Plot. (p. 324) A graph that plots historical cost and volume data.

Step Costs. (p. 319) A cost behavior that is fixed over a small range of activity and then jumps to a different fixed level with moderate changes in volume.

Variable Costs. (p. 310) Costs incurred for every unit of activity. As a result, total variable costs change in direct proportion to changes in volume.

Variable Costing. (p. 333) The costing method that assigns only *variable* manufacturing costs to products. All fixed manufacturing costs (fixed MOH) are expensed as period costs.

MyAccountingLab | Go to http://www.myaccountinglab.com **for the following Quick Check, Short Exercises, Exercises, and Problems. They are available with immediate grading, explanations of correct and incorrect answers, and interactive media that acts as your own online tutor.**

Quick Check

1. *(Learning Objective 1)* A graph of a variable cost starts at
   a. the origin and slopes upward.
   b. any point on the y-axis and is horizontal.
   c. any point on the y-axis and slopes upward.
   d. the origin and is horizontal.

2. *(Learning Objective 1)* Which of the following is true?
   a. Fixed cost per unit increases when volume increases.
   b. Fixed cost per unit decreases when volume increases.
   c. Total fixed costs increase when volume increases.
   d. Total fixed costs decrease when volume increases.

3. *(Learning Objective 2)* In the cost equation $y = vx + f$, the term "v" stands for
   a. fixed cost.
   b. total cost.
   c. variable cost per unit.
   d. total variable cost.

4. *(Learning Objective 2)* If $x = 35$, $v = \$100$, and $f = \$1,000$, then total costs equal
   a. $100.
   b. $3,500.
   c. $1,100.
   d. $4,500.

5. *(Learning Objective 2)* Which of the following is *false*?
   a. Curvilinear costs can be approximated as mixed costs or broken into smaller relevant ranges for cost prediction purposes.
   b. The concept of relevant range is applicable to both fixed and variable costs.
   c. Step costs are fixed over small ranges of activity.
   d. Changes in the variable costs per unit often occur within a given relevant range.

6. *(Learning Objective 3)* Which of the following is *false*?
   a. Scatter plots should be prepared to help identify outliers.
   b. Data points falling in a linear pattern suggest a weak relationship between cost and volume.
   c. When performing account analysis, managers use their judgment to classify cost behavior.
   d. When creating a scatter plot, volume should be plotted on the x-axis while cost should be plotted on the y-axis.

7. *(Learning Objective 4)* Which of the following is *false* about the high-low method?
   a. It is based on only two data points.
   b. It yields an equation for a straight line connecting the high and low data points.
   c. Selection of the high and low data points should be based on cost, not volume.
   d. The slope found from the method represents the variable cost per unit.

8. *(Learning Objective 5)* Which of the following is true about regression analysis?
   a. It is theoretically less sound than the high-low method.
   b. It is based on two data points.
   c. It is sometimes referred to as the line of best fit.
   d. The resulting S-squared statistic shows how well the line fits the data points.

9. *(Learning Objective 6)* Which of the following is true regarding variable costing?
   a. It is allowed by GAAP for external reporting purposes.
   b. It treats fixed MOH costs as period costs, rather than inventoriable product costs.
   c. It is allowed by the IRS for tax preparation.
   d. It treats variable MOH costs as period costs, rather than inventoriable product costs.

10. *(Learning Objective 6)* Which of the following is *false*?
    a. A contribution margin income statement is organized by cost behavior.
    b. The contribution margin is equal to sales revenue minus variable expenses.
    c. The operating income of manufacturers will always be the same, regardless of whether variable or absorption costing is used.
    d. Under absorption costing, the fluctuation of inventory levels will impact operating income, regardless of sales revenue.

Quick Check Answers

1.a 2.b 3.c 4.d 5.d 6.b 7.c 8.c 9.b 10.c

Short Exercises

S6-1 Identify cost behavior *(Learning Objective 1)*

The following chart shows three different costs: Cost A, Cost B, and Cost C. For each cost, the chart shows the total cost and cost per unit at two different volumes within the same relevant range. Based on this information, identify each cost as fixed, variable, or mixed. Explain your answers.

	A		B	C	D	E	F
1			At 4,000 units			At 5,000 units	
2				Cost per			Cost per
3			Total Cost	Unit		Total Cost	Unit
4	Cost A		$ 42,000	$ 10.50		$ 50,000	$ 10.00
5	Cost B		$ 60,000	$ 15.00		$ 60,000	$ 12.00
6	Cost C		$ 32,000	$ 8.00		$ 40,000	$ 8.00
7							

S6-2 Compute fixed costs per unit *(Learning Objective 2)*

JR Equipment produces high-quality basketballs. If the fixed cost per basketball is $2 when the company produces 9,000 basketballs, what is the fixed cost per basketball when it produces 18,000 basketballs? Assume that both volumes are in the same relevant range.

S6-3 Predict total mixed costs *(Learning Objective 2)*

McTorry Razors produces deluxe razors that compete with Gillette's Mach line of razors. Total manufacturing costs are $120,000 when 15,000 packages are produced. Of this amount, total variable costs are $50,000. What are the total production costs when 25,000 packages of razors are produced? Assume the same relevant range.

S6-4 Predict and graph total mixed costs *(Learning Objectives 1 & 2)*

Suppose Yates Wireless offers an international calling plan that charges $8.00 per month plus $0.20 per minute for calls outside the United States.

1. Under this plan, what is your monthly international long-distance cost if you call Europe for
   a. 30 minutes?
   b. 60 minutes?
   c. 120 minutes?
2. Draw a graph illustrating your total cost under this plan. Label the axes and show your costs at 30, 60, and 120 minutes.

S6-5 Classify cost behavior *(Learning Objective 3)*

PUMA produces the PUMA Re-Suede, an athletic shoe made from sustainable materials. Identify the following costs connected with the manufacture of the Re-Suede shoe as variable or fixed:

a. Depreciation on equipment used to stitch the shoe together
b. Shoelaces
c. Patents on the process used to create the materials used in the shoe
d. Rice husk filler (used to make the rubber-like outsole)
e. Recycled polyester fibers (used to make the synthetic suede in the shoe upper)
f. Glue
g. Quality inspector's salary

S6-6 Prepare and analyze a scatter plot *(Learning Objective 3)*

Jones Oil and Lube is a car care center specializing in ten-minute oil changes. Jones Oil and Lube has two service bays, which limits its capacity to 3,400 oil changes per month. The following information was collected over the past six months:

Month	Number of Oil Changes	Operating Expenses
January	3,200	$36,400
February	2,600	$31,900
March	2,800	$32,850
April	2,700	$32,500
May	3,600	$37,000
June	2,900	$33,700

1. Prepare a scatter plot graphing the volume of oil changes (x-axis) against the company's monthly operating expenses (y-axis). Graph by hand or use Excel.
2. How strong of a relationship does there appear to be between the company's operating expenses and the number of oil changes performed each month? Explain. Do there appear to be any outliers in the data? Explain.
3. Based on the graph, do the company's operating costs appear to be fixed, variable, or mixed? Explain how you can tell.
4. Would you feel comfortable using this information to project operating costs for a volume of 3,800 oil changes per month? Explain.

S6-7   Use the high-low method *(Learning Objective 4)*

Refer to the Jones Oil and Lube data in S6-6. Use the high-low method to determine the variable and fixed cost components of Jones Oil and Lube's operating costs. Use this information to project the monthly operating costs for a month in which the company performs 3,400 oil changes.

S6-8   Use the high-low method *(Learning Objective 4)*

Three Brothers Catering uses the high-low method to predict its total overhead costs. Past records show that total overhead cost was $25,600 when 810 hours were worked and $27,700 when 910 hours were worked. If Three Brothers Catering has 835 hours scheduled for next month, what is the expected total overhead cost for next month?

S6-9   Predicting costs in a health care setting *(Learning Objective 4)*

The Surgical Care Unit of Boston Care Health Group uses the high-low method to predict its total surgical unit supplies costs. It appears that nursing hours worked is a good predictor of surgical unit supplies costs in the unit. The supervisor for the unit has gone through the records for the past year and has found that June had the fewest nursing hours worked at 1,200 hours, while September had the most nursing hours worked at 1,675 hours. In June, total surgical unit supplies cost $37,000 and in September, total surgical unit supplies cost $46,500. If the Surgical Care Unit plans to have 1,225 nursing hours worked next month, what is the expected surgical unit supplies cost for the month?

S6-10   Critique the high-low method *(Learning Objective 4)*

You have been assigned an intern to help you forecast your firm's costs at different volumes. He thinks he will get cost and volume data from the two most recent months, plug them into the high-low method equations, and turn in the cost equation results to your boss before the hour is over. As his mentor, explain to him why the process isn't quite as simple as he thinks. Point out some of the concerns he is overlooking, including your concerns about his choice of data and method.

S6-11   Analyze a scatter plot *(Learning Objectives 3 & 4)*

The local Holiday Inn collected seven months of data on the number of room-nights rented per month and the monthly utilities cost. The data were graphed, resulting in the following scatter plot:

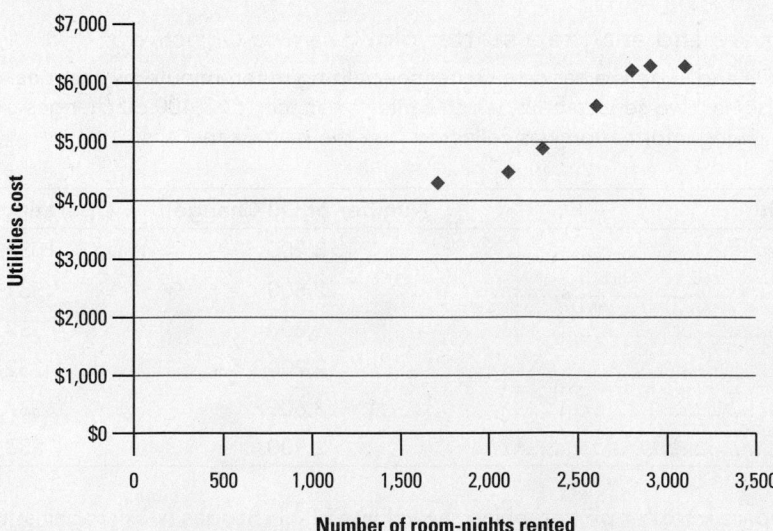

Number of room-nights rented and utilities cost

1. Based on this scatter plot, how strong of a relationship does there appear to be between the number of room-nights rented per month and the monthly utilities cost?
2. Do there appear to be any outliers in the data? Explain.
3. Suppose management performs the high-low method using this data. Do you think the resulting cost equation would be very accurate? Explain.

S6-12   Theoretical comparison of high-low and regression analysis
(Learning Objectives 4 & 5)

Refer to the Holiday Inn scatter plot in S6-11.

1. Would the high-low method or regression analysis result in a more accurate cost equation for the data pictured in the scatter plot? Explain.

2. A regression analysis of the data revealed an R-square figure of 0.939. Interpret this figure in light of the lowest and highest possible R-square values.

3. As a manager, would you be confident predicting utilities costs for other room-night volumes within the same relevant range?

S6-13   Write a cost equation given regression output *(Learning Objective 5)*

An advertising agency wanted to determine the relationship between its monthly operating costs and a potential cost driver, professional hours. An excerpt from the output of a regression analysis performed using Excel showed the following information:

	A	B	C	D	E	F	G
1		SUMMARY OUTPUT					
2		*Regression Statistics*					
3	Multiple R		0.87				
4	R Square		0.75				
5	Adjusted R Square		0.71				
6	Standard Error		153.46				
7	Observations		12				
8	ANOVA						
9		*df*	*SS*	*MS*	*F*	*Significance F*	
10	Regression	1	362,391.24	362,391.42	15.39	0.01	
11	Residual	10	117,751.61	23,550.32			
12	Total	11	480,142.85				
13							
14			*Standard*			*Lower*	*Upper*
15		*Coefficients*	*Error*	*t Stat*	*P-value*	*95%*	*95%*
16	Intercept	1,784.73	884.55	2.02	9.97	−489.09	4,058.55
17	X Variable 1	0.22	0.06	3.92	0.01	0.07	0.36
18							

a. Given this output, write the advertising agency's monthly cost equation.

b. Should management use this equation to predict monthly operating costs? Explain your answer.

S6-14   Prepare a contribution margin income statement *(Learning Objective 6)*

Pamela's Quilt Shoppe sells homemade Amish quilts. Pamela buys the quilts from local Amish artisans for $240 each, and her shop sells them for $410 each. She also pays a sales commission of 4% of sales revenue to her sales staff. Pamela leases her country-style shop for $1,600 per month and pays $2,100 per month in payroll costs in addition to the sales commissions. Pamela sold 100 quilts in February. Prepare Pamela's traditional income statement and contribution margin income statement for the month.

S6-15   Prepare income statements using variable costing and absorption costing with no change in inventory levels *(Learning Objective 6)*

O'Neill's Products manufactures a single product. Cost, sales, and production information for the company and its single product is as follows:

- Selling price per unit is $65
- Variable manufacturing costs per unit manufactured (includes direct materials [DM], direct labor [DL], and variable MOH) $35
- Variable operating expenses per unit sold $2

- Fixed manufacturing overhead (MOH) in total for the year $132,000
- Fixed operating expenses in total for the year $85,000
- Units manufactured and sold for the year 12,000 units

Requirements

1. Prepare an income statement for the upcoming year using variable costing.
2. Prepare an income statement for the upcoming year using absorption costing.

S6-16 Prepare income statements using variable costing and absorption costing when inventory units increase *(Learning Objective 6)*

Allen Manufacturing manufactures a single product. Cost, sales, and production information for the company and its single product is as follows:

- Sales price per unit $49
- Variable manufacturing costs per unit manufactured (DM, DL, and variable MOH) $26
- Variable operating expenses per unit sold $3
- Fixed manufacturing overhead (MOH) in total for the year $187,000
- Fixed operating expenses in total for the year $47,000
- Units manufactured during the year 17,000 units
- Units sold during the year 13,000 units

Requirements

1. Prepare an income statement for the upcoming year using variable costing.
2. Prepare an income statement for the upcoming year using absorption costing.
3. What causes the difference in income between the two methods?

S6-17 Graph specific costs *(Learning Objective 1)*

Graph these cost behavior patterns over a relevant range of 0–10,000 units:

a. Variable expenses of $10 per unit
b. Mixed expenses made up of fixed costs of $25,000 and variable costs of $5 per unit
c. Fixed expenses of $35,000

S6-18 Identify cost behavior graph *(Learning Objective 1)*

Following are a series of cost behavior graphs. The total cost is shown on the vertical (y) axis and the volume (activity) is shown on the horizontal (x) axis.

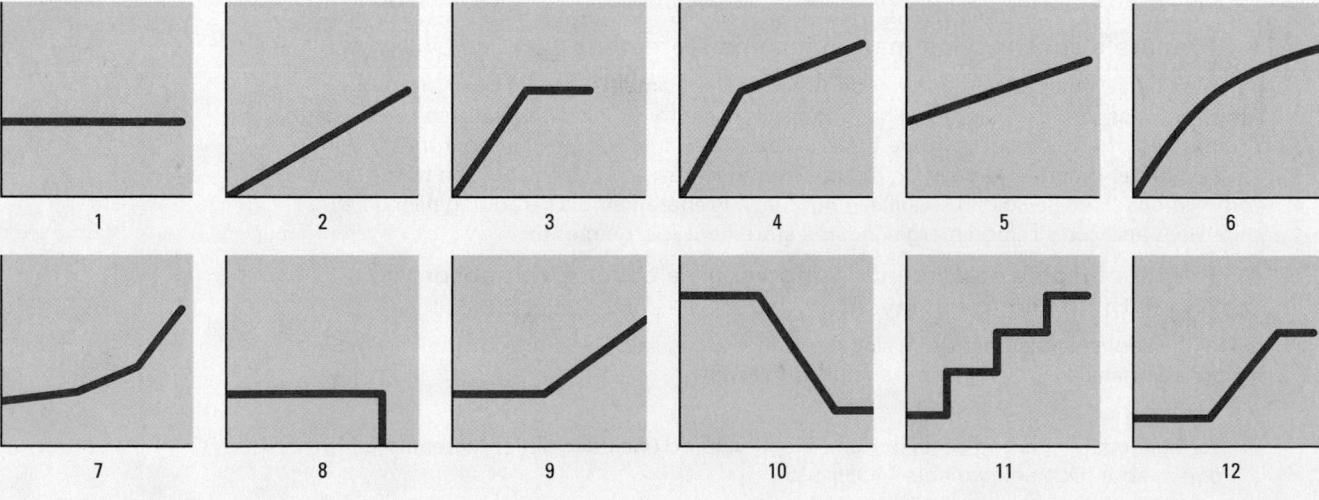

For each of the following situations, identify the graph that most closely represents the cost behavior pattern of the cost in that situation. Some graphs may be used more than once or not at all.

a. Wood costs for a chair manufacturer; the cost of direct materials per chair is $9.60

b. Customer service representatives are paid $12.75 per hour

c. Monthly vehicle lease costs for a company that pays $320 month plus $0.17 per mile for any miles driven over 1,000 per month

d. Monthly gas bill for the restaurant's delivery vehicles; cost of gas is constant at $3.90 per gallon

e. Monthly factory equipment depreciation, straight-line method is used

f. Monthly electric cost for a florist; $50 base monthly fee plus $.006 per kilowatt used

g. Total salary costs for an office; managers are paid a salary and the other workers are paid by the hour

h. Oil disposal fees for an automotive maintenance company. The oil disposal fee is based on two components: a $200 base fee plus a usage fee (to encourage reduction of waste):

Up to 10 barrels	$ 8 per barrel
11–25 barrels..............................	$10 per barrel
More than 26 barrels..................	$14 per barrel

i. Monthly cell phone expense for a mobile grooming business; the cell phones are billed at a rate of $40 for unlimited voice and text for each cell phone

j. Monthly copier costs; the lease is $250 per month with a fee of $0.01 per copy for any copies over 100,000 copies in that month

S6-19 Identify cost behavior terms *(Learning Objectives 1, 2, 3, 4, & 5)*

Complete the following statements with one of the terms listed here. You may use a term more than once, and some terms may not be used at all.

R-square	Step cost(s)	Total cost(s)	Fixed cost(s)
Average cost per unit	Committed fixed costs	Account analysis	Mixed cost(s)
Variable cost(s)	Curvilinear cost(s)	Regression analysis	High-low method

a. The total _____ line increases as the volume of activity increases, but the line does not begin at the origin.

b. The slope of the total _____ line is the variable cost per unit of activity.

c. The _____ uses two data points to arrive at a cost equation to describe a mixed cost.

d. _____ is a method for determining cost behavior that is based on a manager's judgment.

e. _____ are a type of cost behavior that is fixed over a small range of activity and then jumps to a different fixed level with moderate changes in volume.

f. The _____ per unit is inversely related to the volume of activity.

g. An s-shaped line would represent a _____.

h. The _____ value is referred to as the "goodness-of-fit" statistic.

i. As the activity level rises and falls, _____ remain constant in total.

j. _____ are fixed costs that management has little or no control over in the short run.

k. _____ is equal to the sum of _____ plus _____.

l. _____ is the cost to produce a single unit of production as calculated by dividing the total cost by the total number of units produced.

m. The cost equation resulting from using _____ is described as the "line of best fit."

ETHICS

S6-20 Identify ethical standards violated *(Learning Objectives 1, 2, 3, 4, 5, & 6)*

For each of the situations listed, identify the primary standard from the IMA *Statement of Ethical Professional Practice* that is violated (competence, confidentiality, integrity, or credibility). Refer to Exhibit 1-6 for the complete standard.

1. The CEO of a small company visits a competitor's dumpster and takes several trash bags containing discarded papers and reports. The CEO directs Ivan to go through the competitor's trash to find any information about the competitor's costs for a contract coming up for bid. Ivan goes through the papers to find the information because he does not want to lose his job.

2. Blue Heron Mobile operates in a highly competitive environment. Cost information is highly confidential since most jobs are obtained through a bidding process based on variable costing, or in some cases absorption costing. Steve Nunez is the manager of the Accounting Department of Blue Heron Mobile. He neglects to talk with his new hires about the confidentiality of data, nor is there a formal policy in place about non-disclosure.

3. Natasha is an accountant for Red Box Consulting. At a party, she overhears a man talking about an upcoming contract his company will be bidding on. She listens closer and hears specific variable cost information that the man shares. She returns to work the next day and shares this competitor's cost information with her friend, who is working on preparing Red Box Consulting's bid.

4. Curtis struggled through regression analysis in his college courses. Now his manager has asked him to run a regression analysis to create a model for predicting overhead costs. He runs the regression and creates the model. He gives his manager the cost equation for overhead costs, even though he does not really understand it or have any way of checking to see if he did it correctly. He is hesitant to ask for help because he just started this job and he wants to look impressive.

5. Alyssa does not disclose on the financial statements that variable costing, rather than absorption costing, was used.

EXERCISES Group A

E6-21A Forecast costs at different volumes *(Learning Objectives 1 & 2)*

Princeton Drycleaners has capacity to clean up to 5,000 garments per month.

Requirements

1. Complete the following schedule for the three volumes shown.

	2,000 Garments	3,500 Garments	5,000 Garments
Total variable costs		$2,100	
Total fixed costs			
Total operating costs			
Variable cost per garment			
Fixed cost per garment		$2.00	
Average cost per garment			

2. Why does the average cost per garment change?

3. Suppose the owner, Dale Princeton, erroneously uses the average cost per unit *at full capacity* to predict total costs at a volume of 2,000 garments. Would he overestimate or underestimate his total costs? By how much?

E6-22A   Prepare income statement in two formats *(Learning Objective 6)*

Refer to the Princeton Drycleaners in E6-21A. Assume that Princeton charges customers $8 per garment for dry cleaning. Prepare Princeton's *projected* income statement if 4,300 garments are cleaned in March. First, prepare the income statement using the traditional format; then prepare Princeton's contribution margin income statement.

E6-23A   Use the high-low method *(Learning Objective 4)*

Meyer Company, which uses the high-low method to analyze cost behavior, has determined that machine hours best predict the company's total utilities cost. The company's cost and machine hour usage data for the first six months of the year follow:

Month	Total Cost	Machine Hours
January	$3,450	1,020
February	$3,720	1,110
March	$3,467	1,010
April	$3,730	1,270
May	$4,900	1,320
June	$4,232	1,460

Requirements

Using the high-low method, answer the following questions:

1. What is the variable utilities cost per machine hour?
2. What is the fixed cost of utilities each month?
3. If Meyer Company uses 1,280 machine hours in a month, what will its total costs be?

E6-24A   Use unit cost data to forecast total costs *(Learning Objective 2)*

Delivery Mailbox produces decorative mailboxes. The company's average cost per unit is $20.43 when it produces 1,000 mailboxes.

Requirements

1. What is the total cost of producing 1,000 mailboxes?
2. If $10,430 of the total costs is fixed, what is the variable cost of producing each mailbox?
3. Write Delivery Mailbox's cost equation.
4. If the plant manager uses the average cost per unit to predict total costs, what would the forecast be for 1,100 mailboxes?
5. If the plant manager uses the cost equation to predict total costs, what would the forecast be for 1,100 mailboxes?
6. What is the dollar difference between your answers to questions 4 and 5? Which approach to forecasting costs is appropriate? Why?

E6-25A   Sustainability and cost estimation *(Learning Objective 2)*

SUSTAINABILITY

Earth Entertainment is a provider of cable, Internet, and on-demand video services. Earth currently sends monthly bills to its customers via the postal service. Because of a concern for the environment and recent increases in postal rates, Earth management is considering offering an option to its customers for paperless billing. In addition to saving printing, paper, and postal costs, paperless billing will save energy and water (through reduced paper needs, reduced waste disposal, and reduced transportation needs.) Although Earth would like to switch to 100% paperless billing, many of its customers are not comfortable with paperless billing or may not have web access, so the paper billing option will remain regardless of whether Earth adopts a paperless billing system or not.

CHAPTER 6

The cost of the paperless billing system would be $66,220 per quarter with no variable costs since the costs of the system are the salaries of the clerks and the cost of leasing the computer system. The paperless billing system being proposed would be able to handle up to 920,000 bills per quarter (more than 920,000 bills per quarter would require a different computer system and is outside the scope of the current situation at Earth.)

The company has gathered its cost data for the past year by quarter for paper, toner cartridges, printer maintenance costs, and postage costs for its billing department. The cost data are as follows:

	Quarter 1	Quarter 2	Quarter 3	Quarter 4
Total paper, toner, printer maintenance, and postage costs	$672,700	$695,000	$800,000	$700,000
Total number of bills mailed	550,000	575,000	740,000	600,000

Requirements

1. Calculate the variable cost per bill mailed under the current paper-based billing system.
2. Assume that the company projects that it will have a total of 660,000 bills to mail in the upcoming quarter. If enough customers choose the paperless billing option so that 20% of the mailings can be converted to paperless, how much would the company save from the paperless billing system (be sure to consider the cost of the paperless billing system)?
3. What if only 10% of the mailings are converted to the paperless option (assume a total of 660,000 bills)? Should the company still offer the paperless billing system? Explain your rationale.

E6-26A   Create a scatter plot *(Learning Objective 3)*

Kara Woo, owner of Flower Power, operates a local chain of floral shops. Each shop has its own delivery van. Instead of charging a flat delivery fee, Woo wants to set the delivery fee based on the distance driven to deliver the flowers. Woo wants to separate the fixed and variable portions of her van operating costs so that she has a better idea how delivery distance affects these costs. She has the following data from the past seven months:

Month	Miles Driven	Van Operating Costs
January	16,000	$5,490
February	17,500	$5,700
March	14,900	$4,910
April	16,200	$5,340
May	16,900	$5,820
June	15,100	$5,410
July	14,500	$4,920

Requirements

1. Prepare a scatter plot of Flower Power's volume (miles driven) and van operating costs.
2. Does the data appear to contain any outliers? Explain.
3. How strong of a relationship is there between miles driven and van operating costs?

E6-27A   Continuation of E6-26A: High-low method *(Learning Objective 4)*

Refer to Flower Power's data in E6-26A. Use the high-low method to determine Flower Power's cost equation for van operating costs. Use your results to predict van operating costs at a volume of 16,000 miles.

E6-28A **Continuation of E6-26A: Regression analysis** *(Learning Objective 5)*

Refer to the Flower Power data in E6-26A. Use Microsoft Excel to do the following:

Requirements

1. Run a regression analysis.
2. Determine the company's cost equation (use the output from the Excel regression).
3. Determine the R-square (use the output from the Excel regression). What does Flowers Power's R-square indicate?
4. Predict van operating costs at a volume of 16,000 miles.

E6-29A **Regression analysis using Excel output** *(Learning Objective 5)*

Assume that Flower Power does a regression analysis on the next year's data using Excel. The output generated by Excel is as follows:

	A	B	C	D	E	F	G
1		SUMMARY OUTPUT					
2		*Regression Statistics*					
3	Multiple R		0.60				
4	R Square		0.36				
5	Adjusted R Square		0.24				
6	Standard Error		241.73				
7	Observations		7				
8	**ANOVA**						
9		*df*	*SS*	*MS*	*F*	*Significance F*	
10	Regression	1	166,411.05	166,411.05	2.85	0.1523	
11	Residual	5	292,160.38	58,432.08			
12	Total	6	458,571.43				
13							
14			*Standard*			*Lower*	*Upper*
15		*Coefficients*	*Error*	*t Stat*	*P-value*	*95%*	*95%*
16	Intercept	2,250.74	1,752.55	1.28	0.26	−2,254.33	6,755.80
17	X Variable 1	0.19	0.11	1.69	0.15	−0.10	0.47
18							

Requirements

1. Determine the firm's cost equation (use the output from the Excel regression).
2. Determine the R-square (use the output from the Excel regression). What does Flower Power's R-square indicate?
3. Predict van operating costs at a volume of 15,500 miles.

E6-30A **Create a scatter plot for a hospital laboratory** *(Learning Objective 3)*

The manager of the main laboratory facility at CenterHealth Center is interested in being able to predict the overhead costs each month for the lab. The manager believes that total overhead varies with the number of lab tests performed but that some costs remain the same each month regardless of the number of lab tests performed.

The lab manager collected the following data for the first seven months of the year:

Month	Number of Lab Tests Performed	Total Laboratory Overhead Costs
January	2,700	$22,900
February	2,500	$23,500
March	3,500	$29,800
April	4,000	$32,500
May	4,600	$31,100
June	2,000	$22,000
July	2,250	$19,100

Requirements

1. Prepare a scatter plot of the lab's volume (number of lab tests performed) and total laboratory overhead costs.
2. Does the data appear to contain any outliers? Explain.
3. How strong of a relationship is there between the number of lab tests performed and laboratory overhead costs?

E6-31A Using the high-low method to predict overhead for a hospital laboratory (Learning Objective 4)

Refer to the laboratory overhead cost and activity data for CenterHealth Center in E6-30A. Use the high-low method to determine the laboratory's cost equation for total laboratory overhead. Use your results to predict total laboratory overhead if 2,800 lab tests are performed next month.

E6-32A Using regression analysis output to predict overhead for a hospital laboratory (Learning Objective 5)

Using the data provided in E6-30A, the laboratory manager performed a regression analysis to predict total laboratory overhead costs. The output generated by Excel is as follows:

	A	B	C	D	E	F	G
1		SUMMARY OUTPUT					
2		Regression Statistics					
3	Multiple R		0.92398				
4	R Square		0.853738				
5	Adjusted R Square		0.824486				
6	Standard Error		2176.878742				
7	Observations		7				
8	ANOVA						
9		df	SS	MS	F	Significance F	
10	Regression	1	138303137.57	138303137.57	29.185259	0.002937	
11	Residual	5	23694005.29	4738801.058			
12	Total	6	161997142.86				
13							
14			Standard			Lower	Upper
15		Coefficients	Error	t Stat	P-value	95%	95%
16	Intercept	10637.34	2932.412	3.628	0.015	3099.339	18175.349
17	X Variable 1	4.94	0.914	5.402	0.003	2.589	7.289
18							

Requirements

1. Determine the lab's cost equation (use the output from the Excel regression).
2. Determine the R-square (use the output from the Excel regression).
3. Predict the total laboratory overhead for the month if 2,800 tests are performed.

E6-33A   Performing a regression analysis to predict overhead for a hospital laboratory (Learning Objective 5)

The manager of the main laboratory facility at CenterHealth Center (from E6-30A) collects seven additional months of data after obtaining the regression results in E6-32A. The number of tests performed and the total monthly overhead costs for the lab follow:

Month	Number of Lab Tests Performed	Total Laboratory Overhead Costs
August	3,150	$22,950
September	3,100	$21,750
October	3,850	$25,460
November	4,160	$29,800
December	3,920	$28,200
January	2,700	$19,750
February	3,450	$23,400

Use Excel to do the following:

Requirements

1. Run a regression analysis.
2. Determine the lab's cost equation (use the output from the regression analysis you performed using Excel).
3. Determine the R-square using the Excel output you obtain. What does the lab's R-square indicate?
4. Predict the lab's total overhead costs for the month if 3,400 tests are performed.

E6-34A   Determine cost behavior and predict operating costs
(Learning Objective 2)

Pondview Apartments is a 900-unit apartment complex. When the apartments are 90% occupied, monthly operating costs total $224,650. When occupancy dips to 80%, monthly operating costs fall to $218,800. The owner of the apartment complex is worried because many of the apartment residents work at a nearby manufacturing plant that has just announced that it will close in three months. The apartment owner fears that occupancy of her apartments will drop to 70% if residents lose their jobs and move away. Assuming the same relevant range, what can the owner expect her operating costs to be if occupancy falls to 70%?

E6-35A   Prepare a contribution margin income statement (Learning Objective 6)

Two Lizards is a specialty pet gift store selling exotic pet-related items through its website. Two Lizards has no physical store; all sales are through its website.
Results for last year are shown next:

	A	B	C	D
1	Two Lizards			
2	Traditional Income Statement (Absorption Costing)			
3	For the Year Ended December 31			
4				
5	Sales revenue		$ 1,014,000	
6	Less: Cost of goods sold		665,000	
7	Gross profit		$ 349,000	
8	Less operating expenses:			
9	Selling and marketing expenses	$ 61,000		
10	Website maintenance expenses	59,500		
11	Other operating expenses	18,400	138,900	
12	Operating income		$ 210,100	
13				

For internal planning and decision-making purposes, the owner of Two Lizards would like to translate the company's income statement into the contribution margin format. Since Two Lizards is web-based, all of its cost of goods sold is variable. A large portion of the selling and marketing expenses consists of freight-out charges ($20,400), which were also variable. Only 20% of the remaining selling and marketing expenses and 25% of the website expenses were variable. Of the other operating expenses, 90% were fixed.

Based on this information, prepare Two Lizards' contribution margin income statement for last year.

E6-36A Prepare a contribution margin income statement (Learning Objective 6)

Hatcher Carriage Company offers guided horse-drawn carriage rides through historic Columbus, Georgia. The carriage business is highly regulated by the city. Hatcher Carriage Company has the following operating costs during April:

Monthly depreciation expense on carriages and stable..	$2,100
Fee paid to the City of Columbus...	15% of ticket revenue
Cost of souvenir set of postcards given to each passenger	$0.85/set of postcards
Brokerage fee paid to independent ticket brokers (60% of tickets are issued through these brokers; 40% are sold directly by the Hatcher Carriage Company).................................	$1.50/ticket sold by broker
Monthly cost of leasing and boarding the horses...	$48,000
Carriage drivers (tour guides) are paid on a per passenger basis	$3.80 per passenger
Monthly payroll costs of non–tour guide employees..	$7,500
Marketing, website, telephone, and other monthly fixed costs	$7,400

During April (a month during peak season), Hatcher Carriage Company had 13,050 passengers. Eighty-five percent of passengers were adults ($21 fare) while 15% were children ($13 fare).

Requirements

1. Prepare the company's contribution margin income statement for the month of April. Round all figures to the nearest dollar.
2. Assume that passenger volume increases by 10% in May. Which figures on the income statement would you expect to change, and by what percentage would they change? Which figures would remain the same as in April?

E6-37A Prepare income statements using variable costing and absorption costing with changing inventory levels (Learning Objective 6)

Huntington Manufacturing manufactures a single product that it will sell for $69 per unit. The company is looking to project its operating income for its first two years of operations. Cost information for the single unit of its product is as follows:

- Direct material per unit produced $31
- Direct labor cost per unit produced $8
- Variable manufacturing overhead (MOH) per unit produced $3
- Variable operating expenses per unit sold $6

Fixed manufacturing overhead (MOH) for each year is $135,000, while fixed operating expenses for each year will be $83,000.

During its first year of operations, the company plans to manufacture 15,000 units and anticipates selling 12,000 of those units. During the second year of its operations, the company plans to manufacture 15,000 units and anticipates selling 18,000 units (it has units in beginning inventory for the second year from its first year of operations).

Requirements

1. Prepare an absorption costing income statement for the following:

   a. Huntington's first year of operations

   b. Huntington's second year of operations

2. Before you prepare the variable costing income statements for Huntington, predict the company's operating income using variable costing for both its first year and its second year without preparing the variable costing income statements. *Hint:* Calculate the variable costing operating income for a given year by taking that year's absorption costing operating income and adding or subtracting the difference in operating income as calculated using the following formula:

   Difference in operating income = (Change in inventory level in units × Fixed MOH per unit)

3. Prepare a variable costing income statement for each of the following years:

   a. Huntington's first year of operations

   b. Huntington's second year of operations

E6-38A Prepare a variable costing income statement given an absorption costing income statement *(Learning Objective 6)*

Wilson Industries manufactures and sells a single product. The controller has prepared the following income statement for the most recent year:

	A	B	C	D
1	Wilson Industries			
2	Traditional Income Statement (Absorption Costing)			
3	For the Year Ended December 31			
4				
5	Sales revenue	$ 528000		
6	Less: Cost of goods sold	424000		
7	Gross profit	$ 104,000		
8	Less: Operating expenses	69,000		
9	Operating income	$ 35,000		
10				

The company produced 9,000 units and sold 8,000 units during the year ending December 31. Fixed manufacturing overhead (MOH) for the year was $171,000, while fixed operating expenses were $56,000. The company had no beginning inventory.

Requirements

1. Will the company's operating income under variable costing be higher, lower, or the same as its operating income under absorption costing? Why?

2. Project the company's operating income under variable costing without preparing a variable costing income statement.

3. Prepare a variable costing income statement for the year.

E6-39A Absorption and variable costing income statements
(Learning Objective 6)

The annual data that follow pertain to Flannery Water Optics, a manufacturer of swimming goggles (the company had no beginning inventories):

Sales price	$ 49
Variable manufacturing expense per unit	$ 20
Sales commission expense per unit	$ 8
Fixed manufacturing overhead	$ 2,400,000
Fixed operating expenses	$ 245,000
Number of goggles produced	240,000
Number of goggles sold	225,000

Requirements

1. Prepare both conventional (absorption costing) and contribution margin (variable costing) income statements for Flannery Water Optics for the year.

2. Which statement shows the higher operating income? Why?

3. The company marketing vice president believes a new sales promotion that costs $165,000 would increase sales to 240,000 goggles. Should the company go ahead with the promotion? Give your reason.

EXERCISES Group B

E6-40B   Forecast costs at different volumes *(Learning Objectives 1 & 2)*

Peltier Drycleaners has the capacity to clean up to 9,000 garments per month.

Requirements

1. Complete the following schedule for the three volumes shown.

	6,000 Garments	7,500 Garments	9,000 Garments
Total variable costs		$6,375	
Total fixed costs			
Total operating costs			
Variable cost per garment			
Fixed cost per garment		$2.40	
Average cost per garment			

2. Why does the average cost per garment change?
3. The owner, Robin Peltier, uses the average cost per unit *at full capacity* to predict total costs at a volume of 6,000 garments. Would she overestimate or underestimate total costs? By how much?

E6-41B   Prepare income statement in two formats *(Learning Objective 6)*

Refer to the Peltier Drycleaners in E6-40B. Assume that Peltier charges customers $6 per garment for dry cleaning. Prepare Peltier's *projected* income statement if 4,280 garments are cleaned in March. First, prepare the income statement using the traditional format; then prepare Peltier's contribution margin income statement.

E6-42B   Use the high-low method *(Learning Objective 4)*

Reynolds Company, which uses the high-low method to analyze cost behavior, has determined that machine hours best predict the company's total utilities cost. The company's cost and machine hour usage data for the first six months of the year follow:

Month	Total Cost	Machine Hours
January	$3,410	1,060
February	$3,790	1,180
March	$3,574	1,030
April	$3,730	1,260
May	$4,500	1,310
June	$4,294	1,430

Requirements

Using the high-low method, answer the following questions:

1. What is the variable utilities cost per machine hour?
2. What is the fixed cost of utilities each month?
3. If Reynolds Company uses 1,220 machine hours in a month, what will its total costs be?

E6-43B   Use unit cost data to forecast total costs *(Learning Objective 2)*

Acme Mailboxes produces decorative mailboxes. The company's average cost per unit is $23.43 when it produces 1,400 mailboxes.

Requirements

1. What is the total cost of producing 1,400 mailboxes?
2. If $20,202 of the total costs are fixed, what is the variable cost of producing each mailbox?
3. Write Acme Mailboxes' cost equation.

4. If the plant manager uses the average cost per unit to predict total costs, what would the forecast be for 1,600 mailboxes?

5. If the plant manager uses the cost equation to predict total costs, what would the forecast be for 1,600 mailboxes?

6. What is the dollar difference between your answers to Requirements 4 and 5? Which approach to forecasting costs is appropriate? Why?

E6-44B Sustainability and cost estimation *(Learning Objective 2)*

Solar Entertainment is a provider of cable, Internet, and on-demand video services. Solar currently sends monthly bills to its customers via the postal service. Because of a concern for the environment and recent increases in postal rates, Solar's management is considering offering an option to its customers for paperless billing. In addition to saving printing, paper, and postal costs, paperless billing will save energy and water (through reduced paper needs, reduced waste disposal, and reduced transportation needs.) Although Solar would like to switch to 100% paperless billing, many of its customers are not comfortable with paperless billing or may not have web access, so the paper billing option will remain regardless of whether Solar adopts a paperless billing system or not.

The cost of the paperless billing system would be $187,800 per quarter with no variable costs since the costs of the system are the salaries of the clerks and the cost of leasing the computer system. The paperless billing system being proposed would be able to handle up to 760,000 bills per quarter (more than 760,000 bills per quarter would require a different computer system and is outside the scope of the current situation at Solar.)

Solar has gathered its cost data for the past year by quarter for paper, toner cartridges, printer maintenance costs, and postage costs for its billing department. The cost data is as follows:

	Quarter 1	Quarter 2	Quarter 3	Quarter 4
Total paper, toner, printer maintenance, and postage costs	$689,400	$705,000	$810,000	$720,000
Total number of bills mailed	616,000	621,000	750,000	625,000

Requirements

1. Calculate the variable cost per bill mailed under the current paper-based billing system.

2. Assume that the company projects that it will have a total of 640,000 bills to mail in the upcoming quarter. If enough customers choose the paperless billing option so that 40% of the mailing can be converted to paperless, how much would the company save from the paperless billing system (be sure to consider the cost of the paperless billing system)?

3. What if only 30% of the mailings are converted to the paperless option (assume a total of 640,000 bills)? Should the company still offer the paperless billing system? Explain your rationale.

E6-45B Create a scatter plot *(Learning Objective 3)*

Martha LaChance, owner of Posies Unlimited, operates a local chain of floral shops. Each shop has its own delivery van. Instead of charging a flat delivery fee, LaChance wants to set the delivery fee based on the distance driven to deliver the flowers. LaChance wants to separate the fixed and variable portions of her van operating costs so that she has a better idea how delivery distance affects these costs. She has the following data from the past seven months:

Month	Miles Driven	Van Operating Costs
January	15,500	$5,400
February	17,500	$5,350
March	14,400	$4,980
April	16,400	$5,280
May	16,900	$5,580
June	15,300	$5,010
July	13,500	$4,590

Requirements

1. Prepare a scatter plot of Posies Unlimited's volume (miles driven) and van operating costs.
2. Do the data appear to contain any outliers? Explain.
3. How strong of a relationship is there between miles driven and van operating expenses?

E6-46B   Continuation of E6-45B: High-low method *(Learning Objective 4)*

Refer to LaChance's Posies Unlimited data in E6-45B. Use the high-low method to determine the company's cost equation for van operating costs. Use your results to predict van operating costs at a volume of 17,000 miles.

E6-47B   Continuation of E6-45B: Regression analysis *(Learning Objective 5)*

Refer to the Posies Unlimited data in E6-45B. Use Microsoft Excel to run a regression analysis, then do the following calculations:

Requirements

1. Determine the firm's cost equation (use the output from the Excel regression).
2. Determine the R-square (use the output from the Excel regression). What does Posies Unlimited's R-square indicate?
3. Predict van operating costs at a volume of 17,000 miles.

E6-48B   Regression analysis using Excel output *(Learning Objective 5)*

Assume that Posies Unlimited does a regression analysis on the next year's data using Excel. The output generated by Excel is as follows:

	A	B	C	D	E	F	G
1	SUMMARY OUTPUT						
2	*Regression Statistics*						
3	Multiple R		0.84				
4	R Square		0.70				
5	Adjusted R Square		0.64				
6	Standard Error		199.77				
7	Observations		7				
8	ANOVA						
9		*df*	*SS*	*MS*	*F*	*Significance F*	
10	Regression	1	466,833.76	466,833.76	11.70	0.0188	
11	Residual	5	199,537.67	39,907.53			
12	Total	6	666,371.43				
13							
14			*Standard*			*Lower*	*Upper*
15		*Coefficients*	*Error*	*t Stat*	*P-value*	*95%*	*95%*
16	Intercept	1810.75	989.24	1.83	0.13	−732.17	4,353.66
17	X Variable 1	0.21	0.06	3.42	0.05	0.05	0.38
18							

Requirements

1. Determine the firm's cost equation (use the output from the Excel regression).
2. Determine the R-square (use the output from the Excel regression). What does Posies Unlimited R-square indicate?
3. Predict van operating costs at a volume of 14,500 miles.

E6-49B   Create a scatter plot for a hospital laboratory *(Learning Objective 3)*

The manager of the main laboratory facility at MetroFit Center is interested in being able to predict the overhead costs each month for the lab. The manager believes that total overhead varies with the number of lab tests performed but that some costs remain the same each month regardless of the number of lab tests performed.

The lab manager collected the following data for the first seven months of the year.

Month	Number of Lab Tests Performed	Total Laboratory Overhead Costs
January	3,300	$29,000
February	3,100	$28,500
March	3,900	$30,000
April	3,850	$31,000
May	4,100	$26,500
June	2,100	$19,100
July	2,300	$15,900

Requirements

1. Prepare a scatter plot of the lab's volume (number of lab tests performed) and total laboratory overhead costs.
2. Does the data appear to contain any outliers? Explain.
3. How strong of a relationship is there between the number of lab tests performed and laboratory overhead costs?

E6-50B   Using the high-low method to predict overhead for a hospital laboratory *(Learning Objective 4)*

Refer to the laboratory overhead cost and activity data for MetroFit Center in E6-49B. Use the high-low method to determine the laboratory's cost equation for total laboratory overhead. Use your results to predict total laboratory overhead if 3,000 lab tests are performed next month.

E6-51B   Using regression analysis output to predict overhead for a hospital laboratory *(Learning Objective 5)*

Using the data provided in E6-49B, the laboratory manager performed a regression analysis to predict total laboratory overhead costs. The output generated by Excel is as follows:

	A	B	C	D	E	F	G
1		SUMMARY OUTPUT					
2		*Regression Statistics*					
3	Multiple R		0.838886				
4	R Square		0.70373				
5	Adjusted R Square		0.644476				
6	Standard Error		3489.925912				
7	Observations		7				
8	ANOVA						
9		*df*	*SS*	*MS*	*F*	*Significance F*	
10	Regression	1	144650657.06	144650657.06	11.876487	0.018312	
11	Residual	5	60897914.37	12179582.873			
12	Total	6	205548571.43				
13							
14			*Standard*			*Lower*	*Upper*
15		*Coefficients*	*Error*	*t Stat*	*P-value*	*95%*	*95%*
16	Intercept	5627.61	5975.992	0.942	0.390	−9734.165	20989.389
17	X Variable 1	6.21	1.801	3.446	0.018	1.577	1.577
18							

Requirements

1. Determine the lab's cost equation (use the output from the Excel regression).
2. Determine the R-square (use the output from the Excel regression).
3. Predict the total laboratory overhead for the month if 3,000 tests are performed.

E6-52B Performing a regression analysis to predict overhead for a hospital laboratory *(Learning Objective 5)*

The manager of the main laboratory facility at MetroFit Center (from E6-49B) collects seven additional months of data after obtaining the regression results in the prior period. The number of tests performed and the total monthly overhead costs for the lab follows:

Month	Number of Lab Tests Performed	Total Laboratory Overhead Costs
August	3,050	$22,300
September	2,800	$22,100
October	3,600	$25,100
November	3,800	$26,700
December	4,200	$27,300
January	2,200	$20,300
February	3,950	$28,500

Use Excel to perform the requirements.

Requirements

1. Run a regression analysis.
2. Determine the lab's cost equation (use the output from the regression analysis you perform using Excel).
3. Determine the R-square using the Excel output you obtain. What does the lab's R-square indicate?
4. Predict the lab's total overhead costs for the month if 3,000 tests are performed.

E6-53B Determine cost behavior and predict operating costs
(Learning Objective 2)

Bayview Apartments is a 750-unit apartment complex. When the apartments are 90% occupied, monthly operating costs total $217,150. When occupancy dips to 80%, monthly operating costs fall to $212,800. The owner of the apartment complex is worried because many of the apartment residents work at a nearby manufacturing plant that has just announced it will close in three months. The apartment owner fears that occupancy of her apartments will drop to 70% if residents lose their jobs and move away. Assuming the same relevant range, what should the owner expect operating costs to be if occupancy falls to 70%?

E6-54B Prepare a contribution margin income statement *(Learning Objective 6)*

Fabulous Flamingos is a specialty pet gift shop selling exotic pet-related items over the Internet. Results for last year are as follows:

	A	B		C		D
1	**Fabulous Flamingos**					
2	**Traditional Income Statement (Absorption Costing)**					
3	**For the Year Ended December 31**					
4						
5	Sales revenue			$	1,005,000	
6	Less: Cost of goods sold				669,000	
7	Gross profit			$	336,000	
8	Less operating expenses:					
9	Selling and marketing expenses	$	61,000			
10	Website maintenance expenses		56,500			
11	Other operating expenses		17,000		134,500	
12	Operating income			$	201,500	
13						

For internal planning and decision-making purposes, the owner of Fabulous Flamingos would like to translate the company's income statement into the contribution margin format. Since Fabulous Flamingos is a web retailer and has no physical presence, all of its cost of goods sold is variable. A large portion of the selling and marketing expenses consists of freight-out charges $19,400, which were also variable. Only 20% of the remaining selling and marketing expenses and 25% of the website expenses were variable. Of the other operating expenses, 90% were fixed. Based on this information, prepare Fabulous Flamingos' contribution margin income statement for last year.

E6-55B Prepare a contribution margin income statement *(Learning Objective 6)*

Carter Carriage Company offers guided horse-drawn carriage rides through historic Charlotte, North Carolina. The carriage business is highly regulated by the city. Carter Carriage Company has the following operating costs during April:

Monthly depreciation expense on carriages and stable......................	$2,100
Fee paid to the City of Charlotte...	15% of ticket revenue
Cost of souvenir set of postcards given to each passenger	$0.85/set of postcards
Brokerage fee paid to independent ticket brokers (60% of tickets are issued through these brokers; 40% are sold directly by the Carter Carriage Company)	$1.00/ticket sold by broker
Monthly cost of leasing and boarding the horses.................................	$53,000
Carriage drivers (tour guides) are paid on a per passenger basis	$3.90 per passenger
Monthly payroll costs of non–tour guide employees............................	$7,500
Marketing, Website, telephone, and other monthly fixed costs	$7,300

During April (a month during peak season), Carter Carriage Company had 13,040 passengers. Eighty-five percent of passengers were adults ($26 fare) while 15% were children ($18 fare).

Requirements

1. Prepare the company's contribution margin income statement for the month of April. Round all figures to the nearest dollar.
2. Assume that passenger volume increases by 20% in May. Which figures on the income statement would you expect to change and by what percentage would they change? Which figures would remain the same as in April?

E6-56B Prepare income statements using variable costing and absorption costing with changing inventory levels *(Learning Objective 6)*

Herring Manufacturing manufactures a single product that it will sell for $93 per unit. The company is looking to project its operating income for its first two years of operations. Cost information for the single unit of its product is as follows:

- Direct material per unit produced $38
- Direct labor cost per unit produced $16
- Variable manufacturing overhead (MOH) per unit produced $10
- Variable operating expenses per unit sold $4

Fixed manufacturing overhead (MOH) for each year is $286,000, while fixed operating expenses for each year will be $81,000.

During its first year of operations, the company plans to manufacture 22,000 units and anticipates selling 15,000 of those units. During the second year of its operations, the company plans to manufacture 22,000 units and anticipates selling 27,000 units (it has units in beginning inventory for the second year from its first year of operations.)

Requirements

1. Prepare an absorption costing income statement for:
   a. The first year of operations
   b. The second year of operations
2. Before you prepare the variable costing income statements for Herring, predict Herring's operating income using variable costing for both its first year and its second year without preparing the variable costing income statements. *Hint:* Calculate the variable costing operating income for a given year by taking that year's absorption costing operating income and adding or subtracting the difference in operating income as calculated using the following formula:
   Difference in operating income = (Change in inventory level in units × Fixed MOH per unit)
3. Prepare a variable costing income statement for:
   a. The first year of operations
   b. The second year of operations

E6-57B Prepare a variable costing income statement given an absorption costing income statement *(Learning Objective 6)*

Wentworth Industries manufactures and sells a single product. The controller has prepared the following income statement for the most recent year:

	A	B	C	D
1	**Wentworth Industries**			
2	**Traditional Income Statement (Absorption Costing)**			
3	**For the Year Ended December 31**			
4				
5	Sales revenue	$ 494,000		
6	Less: Cost of goods sold	396,500		
7	Gross profit	$ 97,500		
8	Less: Operating expenses	65,000		
9	Operating income	$ 32,500		
10				

The company produced 7,000 units and sold 6,500 units during the year ending December 31. Fixed manufacturing overhead (MOH) for the year was $161,000, while fixed operating expenses were $55,000. The company had no beginning inventory.

Requirements

1. Will the company's operating income under variable costing be higher, lower, or the same as its operating income under absorption costing? Why?
2. Project the company's operating income under variable costing without preparing a variable costing income statement.
3. Prepare a variable costing income statement for the year.

E6-58B Absorption and variable costing income statements
(Learning Objective 6)

The annual data that follow pertain to Goggle Water Optics, a manufacturer of swimming goggles (the company has no beginning inventories):

Sales price	$ 45
Variable manufacturing expense per unit	$ 18
Sales commission expense per unit	$ 14
Fixed manufacturing overhead	$1,980,000
Fixed operating expense	$ 235,000
Number of goggles produced	220,000
Number of goggles sold	200,000

Requirements

1. Prepare both conventional (absorption costing) and contribution margin (variable costing) income statements for Goggle Water Optics for the year.
2. Which statement shows the higher operating income? Why?
3. The company's marketing vice president believes a new sales promotion that costs $140,000 would increase sales to 220,000 goggles. Should the company go ahead with the promotion? Give your reason.

PROBLEMS Group A

P6-59A Analyze cost behavior at a hospital using various cost estimation methods *(Learning Objectives 1, 2, 3, 4, & 5)*

Beth Ferrell is the Chief Operating Officer at Union Hospital in Buffalo, New York. She is analyzing the hospital's overhead costs but is not sure whether nursing hours or the number of patient days would be the best cost driver to use for predicting the hospital's overhead. She has gathered the following information for the last six months of the most recent year:

Month	Hospital Overhead Costs	Nursing Hours	Number of Patient Days	Overhead Cost per Nursing Hour	Overhead Cost per Patient Day
July	$476,000	24,000	3,720	$19.83	$ 127.96
August	$512,000	26,000	4,320	$19.69	$ 118.52
September.............	$424,000	20,000	4,220	$21.20	$ 100.47
October	$448,000	22,500	3,470	$19.91	$ 129.11
November	$555,000	30,000	5,690	$18.50	$ 97.54
December.............	$431,000	22,000	3,210	$19.59	$ 134.27

Requirements

1. Are the hospital's overhead costs fixed, variable, or mixed? Explain.
2. Graph the hospital's overhead costs against nursing hours. Use Excel or graph by hand.
3. Graph the hospital's overhead costs against the number of patient days. Use Excel or graph by hand.
4. Do the data appear to be sound or do you see any potential data problems? Explain.
5. Use the high-low method to determine the hospital's cost equation using nursing hours as the cost driver. Predict total overhead costs if 25,000 nursing hours are predicted for the month.

6. Ferrell runs a regression analysis using nursing hours as the cost driver to predict total hospital overhead costs. The Excel output from the regression analysis is as follows:

	A	B	C	D	E	F	G
1	SUMMARY OUTPUT – Nursing hours as cost driver						
2	*Regression Statistics*						
3	Multiple R		0.984895				
4	R Square		0.970018				
5	Adjusted R Square		0.962523				
6	Standard Error		9883.836352				
7	Observations		6				
8	ANOVA						
9		*df*	*SS*	*MS*	*F*	*Significance F*	
10	Regression	1	12,642,572,449	12,642,572,449	129.414926	0.000341	
11	Residual	4	390,760,884	97,690,221			
12	Total	5	13,033,333,333				
13							
14			*Standard*			*Lower*	*Upper*
15		*Coefficients*	*Error*	*t Stat*	*P-value*	*95%*	*95%*
16	Intercept	131,004.69	30,448.454	4.303	0.013	46,466.228	215,543.149
17	X Variable 1	14.26	1.253	11.376	0.000	10.777	17.735
18							

If 25,000 nursing hours are predicted for the month, what is the total predicted hospital overhead?

7. Ferrell then ran the regression analysis using number of patient days as the cost driver. The Excel output from the regression is shown here:

	A	B	C	D	E	F	G
1	SUMMARY OUTPUT – Using number of patient days as cost driver						
2	*Regression Statistics*						
3	Multiple R		0.818166				
4	R Square		0.669396				
5	Adjusted R Square		0.586745				
6	Standard Error		32,820.99359				
7	Observations		6				
8	ANOVA						
9		*df*	*SS*	*MS*	*F*	*Significance F*	
10	Regression	1	8,724,462,852	8,724,462,852	8.099072	0.046589	
11	Residual	4	4,308,870,482	1,077,217,620			
12	Total	5	13,033,333,334				
13							
14			*Standard*			*Lower*	*Upper*
15		*Coefficients*	*Error*	*t Stat*	*P-value*	*95%*	*95%*
16	Intercept	280,775.96	69,320.327	4.050	0.015	88,311.882	473,240.047
17	X Variable 1	47.15	16.568	2.846	0.047	1.151	93.153
18							

If 3,790 patient days are predicted for the month, what is the total predicted hospital overhead?

8. Which regression analysis (using nursing hours or using number of patient days as the cost driver) produces the best cost equation? Explain your answer.

P6-60A Analyze cost behavior (Learning Objectives 1, 2, 3, & 4)

McKnight Industries is in the process of analyzing its manufacturing overhead costs. The company is not sure if the number of units produced or number of direct labor (DL) hours is the best cost driver to use for predicting manufacturing overhead (MOH) costs. The following information is available:

Month	Manufacturing Overhead Costs	Direct Labor Hours	Units Produced	MOH Cost per DL Hour	MOH Cost per Unit Produced
July	$485,000	25,000	3,800	$19.40	$127.63
August	$540,000	26,700	4,360	$20.22	$123.85
September	$420,000	20,000	4,210	$21.00	$ 99.76
October	$462,000	21,900	3,450	$21.10	$133.91
November	$579,000	32,000	5,600	$18.09	$103.39
December	$455,000	20,400	3,270	$22.30	$139.14

Requirements

1. Are manufacturing overhead costs fixed, variable, or mixed? Explain.
2. Graph the company's manufacturing overhead costs against DL hours. Use Excel or graph by hand.
3. Graph the company's manufacturing overhead costs against units produced. Use Excel or graph by hand.
4. Do the data appear to be sound, or do you see any potential data problems? Explain.
5. Use the high-low method to determine the company's manufacturing overhead cost equation using DL hours as the cost driver. Assume that management believes all data to be accurate and wants to include all of it in the analysis.
6. Estimate manufacturing overhead costs if the company incurs 26,000 DL hours in January.

P6-61A Prepare traditional and contribution margin income statements
(Learning Objective 6)

The Fantastic Ice Cream Shoppe sold 8,800 servings of ice cream during June for $5 per serving. The shop purchases the ice cream in large tubs from the Deluxe Ice Cream Company. Each tub costs the shop $14 and has enough ice cream to fill 28 ice cream cones. The shop purchases the ice cream cones for $0.15 each from a local warehouse club. The Fantastic Ice Cream Shoppe is located in a strip mall, and rent for the space is $2,050 per month. The shop expenses $220 a month for the depreciation of the shop's furniture and equipment. During June, the shop incurred an additional $2,800 of other operating expenses (75% of these were fixed costs).

Requirements

1. Prepare The Fantastic Ice Cream Shoppe's June income statement using a traditional format.
2. Prepare The Fantastic Ice Cream Shoppe's June income statement using a contribution margin format.

P6-62A Determine financial statement components (Learning Objective 6)

My First Violin produces student-grade violins for beginning violin students. The company produced 2,700 violins in its first month of operations. At month-end, 800 finished violins remained unsold. There was no inventory in work in process. Violins were sold for $115.00 each. Total costs from the month are as follows:

Direct materials used	$131,300
Direct labor	$ 55,000
Variable manufacturing overhead	$ 27,000
Fixed manufacturing overhead	$ 64,800
Variable selling and administrative expenses	$ 12,000
Fixed selling and administrative expenses	$ 12,900

The company prepares traditional (absorption costing) income statements for its bankers. My First Violin would also like to prepare contribution margin income statements for management use. Compute the following amounts that would be shown on these income statements:

1. Gross profit
2. Contribution margin
3. Total expenses shown **below** the **gross profit** line
4. Total expenses shown **below** the **contribution margin** line
5. Dollar value of ending inventory under absorption costing
6. Dollar value of ending inventory under variable costing
7. Which income statement will have a higher operating income? By how much? Explain.

P6-63A Absorption and variable costing income statements

(Learning Objective 6)

Nicky's Entrees produces frozen meals, which it sells for $8 each. The company uses the FIFO inventory costing method, and it computes a new monthly fixed manufacturing overhead rate based on the actual number of meals produced that month. All costs and production levels are exactly as planned. The following data are from the company's first two months in business:

	January	February
Sales	1,600 meals	1,900 meals
Production..	2,000 meals	1,600 meals
Variable manufacturing expense per meal........................	$ 5	$ 5
Sales commission expense per meal................................	$ 2	$ 2
Total fixed manufacturing overhead	$ 800	$ 800
Total fixed marketing and administrative expenses..........	$ 600	$ 600

Requirements

1. Compute the product cost per meal produced under absorption costing and under variable costing. Do this first for January and then for February.
2. Prepare separate monthly income statements for January and for February, using the following:
   a. Absorption costing
   b. Variable costing
3. Is operating income higher under absorption costing or variable costing in January? In February? Explain the pattern of differences in operating income based on absorption costing versus variable costing.

PROBLEMS Group B

P6-64B Analyze cost behavior at a hospital using various cost estimation methods *(Learning Objectives 1, 2, 3, 4 & 5)*

Billie Gable is the Chief Operating Officer at Fremont Hospital in Roseville, Minnesota. She is analyzing the hospital's overhead costs but is not sure whether nursing hours or the number of patient days would be the best cost driver to use for predicting the hospital's overhead. She has gathered the following information for the last six months of the most recent year:

Month	Hospital Overhead Costs	Nursing Hours	Number of Patient Days	Overhead Cost per Nursing Hour	Overhead Cost per Patient Day
July	$467,000	23,000	3,710	$20.30	$125.88
August....................	$533,000	25,000	4,390	$21.32	$121.41
September..............	$412,000	19,500	4,270	$21.13	$ 96.49
October..................	$461,000	21,500	3,480	$21.44	$132.47
November	$574,000	31,500	5,640	$18.22	$101.77
December...............	$445,000	20,500	3,200	$21.71	$139.06

Requirements

1. Are the hospital's overhead costs fixed, variable, or mixed? Explain.

2. Graph the hospital's overhead costs against nursing hours. Use Excel or graph by hand.

3. Graph the hospital's overhead costs against the number of patient days. Use Excel or graph by hand.

4. Do the data appear to be sound or do you see any potential data problems? Explain.

5. Use the high-low method to determine the hospital's cost equation using nursing hours as the cost driver. Predict total overhead costs if 24,500 nursing hours are predicted for the month.

6. Gable runs a regression analysis using nursing hours as the cost driver to predict total hospital overhead costs. The Excel output from the regression analysis is as follows:

	A	B	C	D	E	F	G
1	SUMMARY OUTPUT						
2	*Regression Statistics*						
3	Multiple R		0.955681				
4	R Square		0.913327				
5	Adjusted R Square		0.891659				
6	Standard Error		19,749.14671				
7	Observations		6				
8	ANOVA						
9		df	SS	MS	F	Significance F	
10	Regression	1	16,439,884,817	16,439,884,817	42.150439	0.002903	
11	Residual	4	1,560,115,183	390,028,796			
12	Total	5	18,000,000				
13							
14			Standard			Lower	Upper
15		Coefficients	Error	t Stat	P-value	95%	95%
16	Intercept	173,670.16	48,170.874	3.605	0.023	39,926.37	307,413.944
17	X Variable 1	13.12	2.021	6.492	0.003	7.509	18.731
18							

If 24,500 nursing hours are predicted for the month, what is the total predicted hospital overhead?

7. Gable then ran the regression analysis using number of patient days as the cost driver. The Excel output from the regression is as follows:

	A	B	C	D	E	F	G
1	SUMMARY OUTPUT						
2	*Regression Statistics*						
3	Multiple R		0.749327				
4	R Square		0.56149				
5	Adjusted R Square		0.451863				
6	Standard Error		44,421.76043				
7	Observations		6				
8	ANOVA						
9		*df*	*SS*	*MS*	*F*	*Significance F*	
10	Regression	1	10,106,828,801	10,106,828,801	5.121809	0.08638	
11	Residual	4	7,893,171,199	1,973,292,800			
12	Total	5	18,000,000,000				
13							
14			*Standard*			*Lower*	*Upper*
15		*Coefficients*	*Error*	*t Stat*	*P-value*	*95%*	*95%*
16	Intercept	270,606.28	95,151.399	2.844	0.047	6,423.644	534,788.916
17	X Variable 1	51.37	22.699	2.263	0.086	−11.652	114.395
18							

If 3,640 patient days are predicted for the month, what is the total predicted hospital overhead?

8. Which regression analysis (using nursing hours or using number of patient days as the cost driver) produces the best cost equation? Explain your answer.

P6-65B Analyze cost behavior *(Learning Objectives 1, 2, 3, & 4)*

Carmichael Industries is in the process of analyzing its manufacturing overhead costs. Carmichael Industries is not sure if the number of units produced or the number of direct labor (DL) hours is the best cost driver to use for predicting manufacturing overhead (MOH) costs. The following information is available:

Month	Manufacturing Overhead Costs	Direct Labor Hours	Units Produced	MOH Cost per DL Hour	MOH Cost per Unit Produced
July	$460,000	23,000	3,600	$20.00	$127.78
August	$515,000	26,400	4,320	$19.51	$119.21
September	$425,000	19,000	4,200	$22.37	$101.19
October	$448,000	21,600	3,400	$20.74	$131.76
November	$527,000	27,000	5,750	$19.52	$ 91.65
December	$437,000	19,400	3,250	$22.53	$134.46

Requirements

1. Are manufacturing overhead costs fixed, variable, or mixed? Explain.
2. Graph Carmichael Industries' manufacturing overhead costs against DL hours.
3. Graph Carmichael Industries' manufacturing overhead costs against units produced.
4. Do the data appear to be sound or do you see any potential data problems? Explain.
5. Use the high-low method to determine Carmichael Industries' manufacturing overhead cost equation using DL hours as the cost driver. Assume that management believes all the data to be accurate and wants to include all of it in the analysis.
6. Estimate manufacturing overhead costs if Carmichael Industries incurs 24,500 DL hours in January.

P6-66B   Prepare traditional and contribution margin income statements
(Learning Objective 6)

Darla's Ice Cream Shoppe sold 9,400 servings of ice cream during June for $5 per serving. Darla purchases the ice cream in large tubs from the Creamy Ice Cream Company. Each tub costs Darla $14 and has enough ice cream to fill 35 ice cream cones. Darla purchases the ice cream cones for $0.20 each from a local warehouse club. The shop is located in a strip mall, and she pays $2,000 a month to lease the space. Darla expenses $240 a month for the depreciation of the shop's furniture and equipment. During June, Darla incurred an additional $2,600 of other operating expenses (75% of these were fixed costs).

Requirements

1. Prepare Darla's June income statement using a traditional format.
2. Prepare Darla's June income statement using a contribution margin format.

P6-67B   Determine financial statement components *(Learning Objective 6)*

Global Music produces student-grade violins for beginning violin students. The company produced 2,300 violins in its first month of operations. At month-end, 650 finished violins remained unsold. There was no inventory in work in process. Violins were sold for $120.00 each. Total costs from the month are as follows:

Direct materials used	$104,500
Direct labor	$ 60,000
Variable manufacturing overhead	$ 31,000
Fixed manufacturing overhead	$ 41,400
Variable selling and administrative expenses	$ 7,000
Fixed selling and administrative expenses	$ 13,100

The company prepares traditional (absorption costing) income statements for its bankers. Global Music would also like to prepare contribution margin income statements for management use. Compute the following amounts that would be shown on these income statements:

1. Gross profit
2. Contribution margin
3. Total expenses shown **below** the **gross profit** line
4. Total expenses shown **below** the **contribution margin** line
5. Dollar value of ending inventory under absorption costing
6. Dollar value of ending inventory under variable costing
7. Which income statement will have a higher operating income? By how much? Explain.

P6-68B Absorption and variable costing income statements
(Learning Objective 6)

Marty's Entrees produces frozen meals, which it sells for $9 each. The company uses the FIFO inventory costing method, and it computes a new monthly fixed manufacturing overhead rate based on the actual number of meals produced that month. All costs and production levels are exactly as planned. The following data are from the company's first two months in business:

	January	February
Sales	1,300 meals	1,700 meals
Production..	1,600 meals	1,500 meals
Variable manufacturing expense per meal..................	$ 3	$ 3
Sales commission expense per meal............................	$ 2	$ 2
Total fixed manufacturing overhead	$ 1,200	$1,200
Total fixed marketing and administrative expenses.....	$ 400	$ 400

Requirements

1. Compute the product cost per meal produced under absorption costing and under variable costing. Do this first for January and then for February.
2. Prepare separate monthly income statements for January and for February, using (a) absorption costing and (b) variable costing.
3. Is operating income higher under absorption costing or variable costing in January? In February? Explain the pattern of differences in operating income based on absorption costing versus variable costing.

CRITICAL THINKING

Discussion & Analysis

A6-69 Discussion Questions

1. Briefly describe an organization with which you are familiar. Describe a situation when a manager in that organization could use cost behavior information and how the manager could use the information.

2. How are fixed costs similar to step fixed costs? How are fixed costs different from step fixed costs? Give an example of a step fixed cost and describe why that cost is not considered to be a fixed cost.

3. Describe a specific situation when a scatter plot could be useful to a manager.

4. What is a mixed cost? Give an example of a mixed cost. Sketch a graph of this example.

5. Compare discretionary fixed costs to committed fixed costs. Think of an organization with which you are familiar. Give two examples of discretionary fixed costs and two examples of committed fixed costs which that organization may have. Explain why the costs you have chosen as examples fit within the definitions of "discretionary fixed costs" and "committed fixed costs."

6. Define the terms "independent variable" and "dependent variable," as used in regression analysis. Illustrate the concepts of independent variables and dependent variables by selecting a cost a company would want to predict and what activity it might use to predict that cost. Describe the independent variable and the dependent variable in that situation.

7. Define the term "relevant range." Why is it important to managers?

8. Describe the term "R-square." If a regression analysis for predicting manufacturing overhead using direct labor hours as the dependent variable has an R-square of 0.40, why might this be a problem? Given the low R-square value, describe the options a manager has for predicting manufacturing overhead costs. Which option do you think is the best option for the manager? Defend your answer.

9. Over the past year, a company's inventory has increased significantly. The company uses absorption costing for financial statements, but internally, the company uses variable costing for financial statements. Which set of financial statements will show the highest operating income? What specifically causes the difference between the two sets of financial statements?

10. A company has adopted a lean production philosophy and, as a result, has cut its inventory levels significantly. Describe the impact on the company's external financial statements as a result of this inventory reduction. Also describe the impact of the inventory reduction on the company's internal financial statements that are prepared using variable costing.

11. What costs might a business incur by not adopting paperless services? Is paperless only profitable to large businesses or is it applicable to small businesses? Explain what factors might be involved in changing over to paperless billing.

12. How might the principles of sustainability (such as increased efficiency) affect cost behavior overall? Think of an example of a sustainable change in process or material that could impact the cost equation for that cost (i.e., the total fixed cost versus the variable cost per unit). Describe this example in detail and what might happen to total fixed costs and per unit variable costs.

Application & Analysis

Mini Cases

A6-70 Cost Behavior in Real Companies

Choose a company with which you are familiar that manufactures a product or provides a service. In this activity, you will be making reasonable estimates of the costs and activities associated with this company; companies do not typically publish internal cost or process information.

Basic Discussion Questions

1. Describe the company you selected and the products or services it provides.
2. List ten costs that this company would incur. Include costs from a variety of departments within the company, including human resources, sales, accounting, production (if a manufacturer), service (if a service company), and others. Make sure that you have at least one cost from each of the following categories: fixed, variable, and mixed.
3. Classify each of the costs you listed as either fixed, variable, or mixed. Justify why you classified each cost as you did.
4. Describe a potential cost driver for each of the variable and mixed costs you listed. Explain why each cost driver would be appropriate for its associated cost.
5. Discuss how easy or difficult it was for you to decide whether each cost was fixed, variable, or mixed. Describe techniques a company could use to determine whether a cost is fixed, variable, or mixed.

ETHICS

A6-71 Ethics of building inventory *(Learning Objectives 6)*

KG Products, Inc., is a manufacturer of mobile devices. Richard is the plant manager at KG's Orrville, Ohio, plant. The Orrville plant manufactures a smartphone, the Zoom, which has sold well for the past six months. Richard is being considered for promotion to manager of the entire West Coast division of KG Products. Penny is an accounting supervisor at KG Products and is a good friend of Richard's.

Richard and Penny are having lunch in the company cafeteria. There are about six weeks left in the current fiscal year. Richard is concerned that his plant will be showing a loss rather than the healthy profit he had projected for the year. The reason for the shortfall is that demand has radically declined for the Zoom smartphone currently manufactured by Richard's plant. New smartphones with more features have been brought to market by KG's competitors. Engineers at KG are currently working on an updated model of the Zoom, but it will not be ready for production in Richard's plant for another five months. If Richard's plant shows a loss this year, Richard will not receive his performance bonus for the year. He also knows that his chance of promotion to the West Coast manager will be greatly reduced.

Penny thinks about Richard's situation. She then shares with him a strategy that he can use to help increase his profits. She explains that under absorption costing, the more units in ending inventory, the more costs can be deferred. Using her tablet, she makes up a quick example in Excel to show him how he can turn his situation around and show operating income for the year.

Penny's first spreadsheet assumes that five units are produced and sold in this hypothetical situation:

	A	B	C	D
1	Scenario #1			
2	Traditional Income Statement (5 units produced and 5 units sold)			
3	For the year ended December 31			
4				
5	Sales revenue		$ 150	
6	Less: Cost of goods sold		115	
7	Gross profit		$ 35	
8	Less: Operating expenses		55	
9	Operating income (loss)		$ (20)	
10				

If five units are produced and sold, the hypothetical company would have a loss of $20. Now Penny changes just one fact; instead of producing five units, the company in the example produces ten units. No other facts change—the company still sells just five units. Penny shows Richard the revised income statement under the increased production scenario:

	A	B	C	D
1	Scenario #2			
2	Traditional Income Statement (10 units produced and 5 units sold)			
3	For the year ended December 31			
4				
5	Sales revenue		$ 150	
6	Less: Cost of goods sold		65	
7	Gross profit		$ 85	
8	Less: Operating expenses		55	
9	Operating income (loss)		$ 30	
10				

Under this second scenario, the operating income would be $30, which is quite a bit higher than the original scenario. Penny again emphasizes that the only fact that was different between the two scenarios is that production, and therefore ending inventory, increased in the second scenario.

Penny then urges Richard to put on a major production push in the last month of the year. If he does, he will be able to push his income up to near projected levels. With the higher income, he will receive his annual performance bonus. In addition, he feels that his chances of getting the West Coast manager position are excellent.

Requirements

1. Using the IMA *Statement of Ethical Professional Practice* (refer to Exhibit 1-6) as an ethical framework, answer the following questions:

   a. What is (are) the ethical issue(s) in this situation?

   b. What are Penny's responsibilities as a management accountant?

   c. Has Penny violated any part of the IMA *Statement of Ethical Professional Practice*? Support your answer.

2. What causes the shift from a loss to a profit in the hypothetical example?

3. What problems, if any, are caused by building inventories at year end?

4. What could KG Products do to prevent future situations like the one described in this case?

A6-72 Cost behavior and Air Force One
(Learning Objectives 1, 2, & 3)

REAL LIFE

In a government report in 2012,[1] it was estimated that Air Force One costs the taxpayers $179,750 per hour. Air Force One is a custom-built Boeing 747 for the president's use while in office. (There are technically a few planes that are used as Air Force One; whichever one the president is on is called "Air Force One.") While the president is in office, the president is required by law to use Air Force One for all air travel.

The 747 used for Air Force One has 4,000 square feet of space inside on three levels. In addition to having a large office and a conference room, the plane also houses a medical suite and a doctor. The doctor is permanently assigned to Air Force One. The plane has two food preparation galleys that can feed 100 people at a time. There are also quarters on the plane for those people who travel with the president, including senior advisors, Secret Service, and the press. In addition, several cargo jets typically are used to carry extra provisions, people, and equipment.

The $179,750 cost per hour estimate includes fuel, maintenance, engineering support, repairs, food and lodging for the pilots and crew, and other costs. It also includes the cost of military staffing for the onboard communications equipment. The cost may also include the costs of flying extra aircraft and costs of advance scouting trips to the destination to make sure that everything goes as planned.

[1]"Presidential Travel: Policy and Costs," Congressional Research Service, retrieved from www.fas.org/sgp/crs/misc/RS21835.pdf on June 30, 2013.

When Air Force One is used for official business, the taxpayers must pay for the traveling costs for the president's immediate family, Secret Service detail, and the White House staff who are traveling with the president.

When Air Force One is used for political purposes, the president's campaign fund is required to reimburse the government for the cost of food, lodging, and other related expenses. The campaign fund must also reimburse the government for the amount that is the equivalent of airfare that would have been paid if a commercial airline had been used. The same reimbursement policy is in effect for trips that are categorized as personal trips; the president must reimburse the government for the cost of food, lodging, comparable airfare, and other related expenses.

Questions

1. Is the $179,750 cost per hour a fixed, variable, or mixed cost? Explain.
2. Exact details about the cost composition of the Air Force One travel are kept secret to protect the president. Use your imagination, and the reading above, to make a list of the costs that you think might be included in $179,750 per hour cost estimate.
3. Categorize each cost in your list as fixed, variable, or mixed.
4. The number of trips taken by the president in any given year fluctuates and is dependent upon the political climate, crises, economics, and the like. How useful do you think this cost per hour is?
5. What purpose(s) can the $179,750 cost per hour be used for? Are there any purposes for which that cost is not representative of the "true" cost?
6. Can you think of a better way to represent/communicate the cost of Air Force One?
7. Do you think the reimbursement policy is fair to the *president*? Why or why not?
8. Do you think the reimbursement policy is fair to the *taxpayers*? Why or why not?

Try It Solutions

page 315:

a. Total fixed costs do not react to wide changes in volume; therefore, total fixed costs will still be $100,000.

b. Fixed costs per unit decrease as volume increases. At the higher occupancy, the fixed cost per guest is as follows:

$$\$100,000 \div 16,000 \text{ guests} = \$6.25 \text{ per guest}$$

If only 2,000 guests stay during the month, the fixed cost per guest is much higher ($50).

page 317:

1. The monthly cost of belonging to the fitness club can be expressed as:

$$y = \$5x + \$30$$

Where y = monthly cost of belonging to the club and,

x = number of instructor-led exercise classes attended.

2. If you attend five classes in a month, your total cost will be $55 [= ($5 × 5 classes) + $30].

3. If you attend 10 classes in a month, your total cost will be $80 [= ($5 × 10 classes) + $30]. The cost does not double when the number of classes attended doubles. The variable portion of the bill doubles from $25 to $50, but the fixed portion of the bill ($30) stays constant.

page 335:

1. $32.00. Absorption costing treats all manufacturing costs as inventoriable product costs, regardless of whether they are fixed or variable.

2. $12.00 of fixed MOH will be expensed as part of Cost of Goods Sold every time a unit is sold.

3. $20.00. Variable costing treats only variable manufacturing costs (direct materials, direct labor, and variable MOH) as inventoriable product costs. Fixed MOH is not included in the product cost.

4. $120,000 of fixed MOH will be expensed as a period cost (operating expense) of the month.

Cost-Volume-Profit Analysis

Opas Chotiphantawanon/Shutterstock

Source: http://corporate.art.com

Learning Objectives

- ■ **1** Calculate the unit contribution margin and the contribution margin ratio

- ■ **2** Use CVP analysis to find breakeven points and target profit volumes

- ■ **3** Perform sensitivity analysis in response to changing business conditions

- ■ **4** Find breakeven and target profit volumes for multiproduct companies

- ■ **5** Determine a firm's margin of safety, operating leverage, and most profitable cost structure

Art.com, Inc., is the world's largest online retailer of posters, prints, photography, and framed art. The company offers over 700,000 different images and has generated sales from over 12 million customers in 120 different countries. Art.com uses localized websites that utilize each country's native language and currency and offers local e-mail support. It also offers free iPhone and iPad apps that allow customers to turn personal photos into professionally framed art as well as preview art by importing it into a photo of their own living space. Innovations such as these continue to drive the company's success.

Before launching Art.com in 1998, how did the company's founders determine the volume of art they would need to sell just to breakeven? How did they estimate the volume they would need to sell to achieve their target profit? And as the company continues to operate and expand into new markets, how do managers respond to fluctuating business conditions, such as changing fixed and variable costs and pricing pressures from competitors? Cost-volume-profit (CVP) analysis helps managers answer these questions.

In the last chapter, we discussed cost behavior patterns and the methods managers use to determine how the company's costs behave. We showed how managers use the contribution margin income statement to separately display the firm's variable and fixed costs. In this chapter, we show how managers identify the volume of sales necessary to achieve breakeven or a target profit. We also look at how changes in costs, sales price, and volume affect the firm's profit. Finally, we discuss ways to identify the firm's risk level, including ways to gauge how easily a firm's profits could turn to losses if sales volume declines.

How Does Cost-Volume-Profit Analysis Help Managers?

Cost-volume-profit analysis, or CVP, is a powerful tool that helps managers make important business decisions. <u>**Cost-volume-profit analysis**</u> expresses the relationships among costs, volume, and the company's profit. Entrepreneurs and managers use CVP analysis to determine the sales volume that will be needed just to breakeven, or cover costs. They also use CVP to determine the sales volume that will be needed to earn a target profit, such as $100,000 per month. And because business conditions are always changing, CVP can help managers prepare for and respond to economic changes, such as increases in costs from suppliers.

Let's begin our discussion by looking at the data needed for CVP analysis.

Data and Assumptions Required for CVP Analysis

CVP analysis relies on the interdependency of five components, or pieces of information, shown in Exhibit 7-1.

EXHIBIT 7-1 Components of CVP Analysis

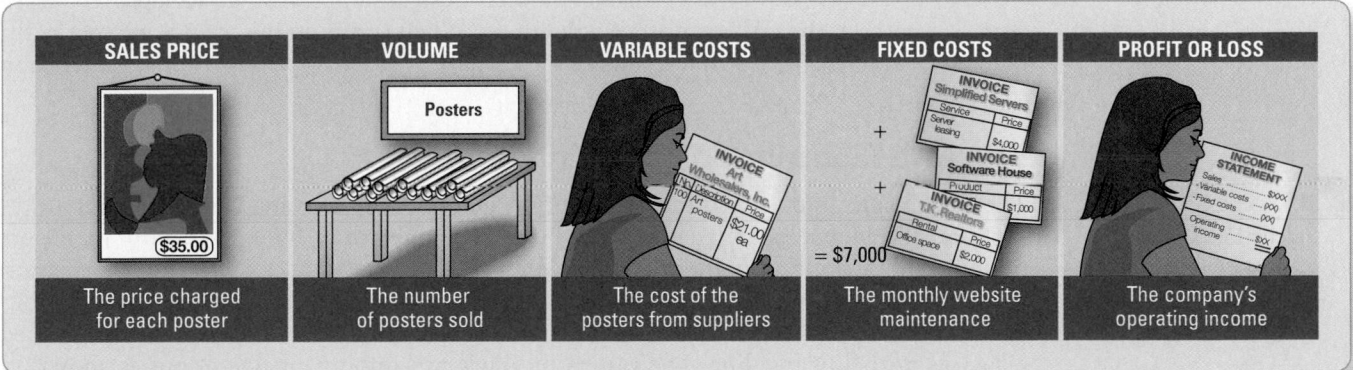

SALES PRICE	VOLUME	VARIABLE COSTS	FIXED COSTS	PROFIT OR LOSS
The price charged for each poster	The number of posters sold	The cost of the posters from suppliers	The monthly website maintenance	The company's operating income

Let's examine this information in terms of a simple company example. Kay Martin, an entrepreneur, has just started an e-tail business selling art posters on the internet. Kay is a "virtual retailer" and carries no inventory. Kay's software tabulates all customer orders each day and then automatically places the order to buy posters from a wholesaler. Kay buys only what she needs to fill the prior day's sales orders. The posters cost $21 each, and Kay sells them for $35 each. Customers pay the shipping costs, so there are no other variable selling costs. Monthly fixed costs for server leasing and maintenance, software, and office rental total $7,000. Kay's relevant range extends from 0 to 2,000 posters a month. Beyond this volume, Kay will need to hire an employee and upgrade her website software in order to handle the increased volume. Additionally, the wholesaler will offer a volume discount if she purchases more than 2,000 posters a month.

Thus, we know the following information holds within Kay's relevant range (0–2,000 posters per month):

- Sales price = $35 per poster
- Variable cost = $21 per poster
- Fixed costs = $7,000 per month

For CVP to be accurate, certain assumptions must be met. We'll itemize each of these assumptions, and check off whether Kay's business meets the assumptions.

1. **A change in volume is the only factor that affects costs.** In Kay's business, costs are expected to increase only if volume increases. ✓

2. **Managers can classify each cost (or the components of mixed costs) as either variable or fixed. These costs are linear throughout the relevant range of volume.** In Kay's business, variable costs are $21 per poster and fixed costs are $7,000 per month. These costs are expected to remain the same unless Kay's volume exceeds 2,000 posters per month. Thus, we could draw each of these costs as straight lines on a graph. ✓

3. **Revenues are linear throughout the relevant range of volume.** In Kay's business, each poster generates $35 of sales revenue, with no volume discounts. Therefore, revenue could be graphed as a straight line beginning at the origin and sloping upward at a rate of $35 per poster sold. ✓

4. **Inventory levels will not change.** Kay keeps no inventory. If she did, CVP analysis would still work as long as Kay did not allow her inventory levels to greatly fluctuate from one period to the next. ✓

5. **The sales mix of products will not change. Sales mix is the combination of products that make up total sales. For example, Art.com may sell 15% posters, 25% unframed photographs, and 60% framed prints. If profits differ across products, changes in sales mix will affect CVP analysis.** Kay currently offers only one size of poster, so her sales mix is 100% posters. Later in this chapter we will expand her product offerings to illustrate how sales mix impacts CVP analysis. ✓

Now that we know Kay's business meets these assumptions, we can proceed with confidence about the CVP results we will obtain. When assumptions are not met perfectly, managers should consider the results of CVP analysis to be approximations, rather than exact figures.

The Unit Contribution Margin

1 Calculate the unit contribution margin and the contribution margin ratio

The last chapter introduced the **contribution margin income statement**, which separates costs on the income statement by cost behavior rather than function. Many managers prefer the contribution margin income statement because it gives them the information for CVP analysis in a "ready-to-use" format. On these income statements, the contribution margin is the "dividing line"—all variable expenses go above the line, and all fixed expenses go below the line. The results of Kay's first month of operations is shown in Exhibit 7-2.

EXHIBIT 7-2 Contribution Margin Income Statement

	A	B	C	D
1	**Kay Martin Posters**			
2	**Contribution Margin Income Statement**			
3	**Month Ended August 31**			
4				
5	Sales revenue (550 posters × $35 per poster)	$ 19,250		
6	Less: Variable expenses (550 posters × $21 per poster)	11,550		
7	Contribution margin	7,700		
8	Less: Fixed expenses	7,000		
9	Operating income	$ 700		
10				

Notice that the **contribution margin** is the excess of sales revenue over variable expenses. The contribution margin tells managers how much revenue is left—after paying variable expenses—for *contributing* toward covering fixed costs and then generating a profit. Hence the name contribution margin.

The contribution margin is stated as a *total* amount on the contribution margin income statement. However, managers often state the contribution margin on a *per unit* basis and as a *percentage,* or *ratio.* A product's **contribution margin per unit**—or **unit contribution margin**—is the excess of the selling price per unit over the variable cost of obtaining *and* selling each unit. Some businesses pay a sales commission on each unit or have other variable costs, such as shipping costs, for each unit sold. However, Kay's variable cost per unit is simply the price she pays for each poster. Therefore, her unit contribution margin is as follows:

Why is this important?

"The **unit** contribution margin tells **managers** how much **profit** they make on **each unit** before considering **fixed** costs."

Sales price per poster.....................................	$ 35
Less: Variable cost per poster.......................	21
Contribution margin per poster....................	$ 14

The unit contribution margin indicates how much profit each unit provides *before* fixed costs are considered. Each unit *first* contributes this profit toward covering the firm's fixed costs. Once the company sells enough units to cover its fixed costs, the unit contribution margin contributes *directly* to operating income. For example, every poster Kay sells generates $14 of contribution margin that is first used to pay for the monthly $7,000 of fixed costs. After Kay sells enough posters to pay for the fixed costs, each additional poster she sells will be $14 of pure profit. Keep the following important rule of thumb in mind:

> *Each additional unit sold improves the company's operating income by the amount of the unit contribution margin.*

For example, regardless of whether Kay is currently operating at a profit or a loss, each additional poster she sells will improve her operating results by $14.

Managers can also use the unit contribution margin to quickly forecast income at any volume within their relevant range. First, they predict the total contribution margin by multiplying the unit contribution margin by the number of units they expect to sell. Then, they subtract fixed costs. For example, let's assume that Kay hopes to sell 650 posters next month. She can forecast her operating income as follows:

Contribution margin (650 posters × $14 per poster)	$ 9,100
Less: Fixed expenses...	7,000
Operating income..	$ 2,100

If Kay sells 650 posters next month, her operating income should be $2,100.

The Contribution Margin Ratio

In addition to computing the unit contribution margin, managers often compute the **contribution margin ratio**, which is the ratio of contribution margin to sales revenue. Kay can compute her contribution margin ratio at the unit level as follows:

$$\text{Contribution margin ratio} = \frac{\text{Contribution margin per unit}}{\text{Sales price per unit}} = \frac{\$14}{\$35} = 40\%$$

Kay could also compute the contribution margin ratio using any volume of sales. Let's use her current sales volume, pictured in Exhibit 7-2:

$$\text{Contribution margin ratio} = \frac{\text{Contribution margin}}{\text{Sales revenue}} = \frac{\$7,700}{\$19,250} = 40\%$$

The contribution margin ratio is the percentage of each sales dollar that is available for covering fixed expenses and generating a profit. As shown in Exhibit 7-3, each *$1.00* of sales revenue contributes $0.40 toward fixed expenses and profit while the remaining $0.60 of each sales dollar is used to pay for variable costs.

EXHIBIT 7-3 Breakdown of $1 of Sales Revenue

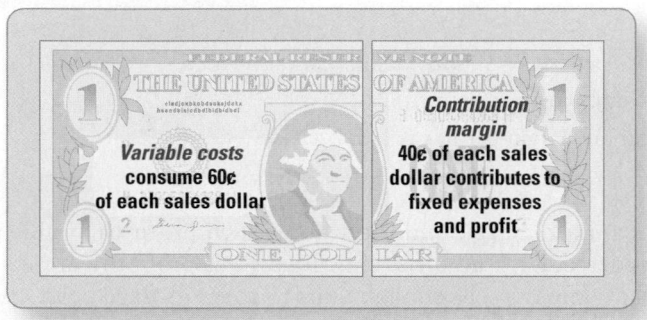

Managers can also use the contribution margin ratio to quickly forecast operating income within their relevant range. When using the contribution margin ratio, managers project income based on sales revenue (*dollars*) rather than sales *units*. For example, if Kay generates $70,000 of sales revenue one month, what operating income should she expect? To find out, Kay simply multiplies her projected sales revenue by the contribution margin ratio to arrive at the total contribution margin. Then she subtracts fixed expenses:

Contribution margin ($70,000 sales × 40%)...................	$28,000
Less: Fixed expenses..	7,000
Operating income..	$21,000

Let's verify. If Kay has $70,000 of sales revenue, she has sold 2,000 posters ($70,000 ÷ $35 per poster). Her complete contribution margin income statement would be calculated as follows:

	A	B	C	D
1	**Kay Martin Posters**			
2	**Contribution Margin Income Statement**			
3	**For a month in which 2,000 posters are sold**			
4				
5	Sales revenue (2,000 posters × $35 per poster)	$ 70,000		
6	Less: Variable expenses (2,000 posters × $21 per poster)	42,000		
7	Contribution margin (2,000 posters × $14 per poster)	28,000		
8	Less: Fixed expenses	7,000		
9	Operating income	$ 21,000		
10				

The contribution margin per unit and contribution margin ratio help managers quickly and easily predict income at different sales volumes. However, when predicting profits, managers must keep in mind the relevant range. For instance, if Kay wants to forecast operating income at a volume of 5,000 posters, she shouldn't use the existing unit contribution margin and fixed costs. Her current relevant range extends to only 2,000 posters per month. At a higher volume of sales, her variable cost per unit may be lower than $21 (due to volume discounts from her suppliers) and her monthly fixed costs may be higher than $7,000 (due to upgrading her system and hiring an employee to handle the extra sales volume).

Rather than using the individual unit contribution margins on each of their products, large companies that offer hundreds or thousands of products (like Art.com) use their contribution margin *ratio* to predict profits. As long as the sales mix remains constant (one of our CVP assumptions), the contribution margin ratio will remain constant. We'll go into more detail on multiproduct firms in the second half of the chapter.

We've seen how managers use the contribution margin to predict income; but managers use the contribution margin for other purposes too, such as motivating the sales force. Salespeople who know the contribution margin of each product can generate more profit for the company by emphasizing high-margin products. This is why many companies base sales commissions on the contribution margins produced by sales rather than on sales revenue alone.

In the next section, we'll see how managers use CVP analysis to determine the company's breakeven point.

▶ Try It!

Rachel runs her own hot dog stand on the U of A campus. The monthly cost of the cart rental and business permit is $300. Rachel spends $0.50 on each hot dog sold, including bun and condiments. She sells each hot dog for $2.00.

1. What is the contribution margin per unit?
2. What is the contribution margin ratio?
3. Predict operating income for a month in which Rachel sells 1,000 hot dogs.

Please see page 441 for solutions.

How do Managers Find the Breakeven Point?

A company's <u>breakeven point</u> is the sales level at which *operating income is zero*. Sales below the breakeven point result in a loss. Sales above the breakeven point provide a profit. Before Kay started her business, she wanted to figure out how many posters she would have to sell just to breakeven.

There are three ways to calculate the breakeven point. All of the approaches are based on the income statement, so they all reach the same conclusion. The first two methods find breakeven in terms of sales *units*. The last approach finds breakeven in terms of sales revenue (sales dollars).

1. The income statement approach
2. The shortcut approach using the *unit* contribution margin
3. The shortcut approach using the contribution margin *ratio*

Let's examine these three approaches in detail.

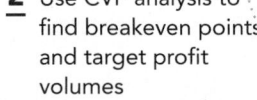

2 Use CVP analysis to find breakeven points and target profit volumes

Why is this important?

"Businesses **don't** want to operate at a **loss**. CVP analysis helps **managers** determine how many units they need to sell *just* to **breakeven**."

The Income Statement Approach

The income statement approach starts with the contribution margin income statement, and then breaks it down into smaller components:

SALES REVENUE	−	VARIABLE EXPENSES	− FIXED EXPENSES	= OPERATING INCOME
$\left(\dfrac{\text{Sales price}}{\text{per unit}} \times \text{Units sold}\right)$	−	$\left(\dfrac{\text{Variable cost}}{\text{per unit}} \times \text{Units sold}\right)$	− Fixed expenses	= Operating income

Let's use this approach to find Kay's breakeven point. Recall that Kay sells her posters for $35 each and that her variable cost is $21 per poster. Kay's fixed expenses total $7,000. At the breakeven point, operating income is zero. We use this information to solve the income statement equation for the number of posters Kay must sell to breakeven.

SALES REVENUE	−	VARIABLE EXPENSES	− FIXED EXPENSES	= OPERATING INCOME
$\left(\dfrac{\text{Sales price}}{\text{per unit}} \times \text{Units sold}\right)$	−	$\left(\dfrac{\text{Variable cost}}{\text{per unit}} \times \text{Units sold}\right)$	− Fixed expenses	= Operating income
($35 × Units sold)−		($21 × Units sold) −	$7,000	= $ 0
($35 −		$21) × Units sold −	$7,000	= $ 0
		$14 × Units sold		= $7,000
		Units sold		= $7,000/$14
		Sales in units		= 500 posters

Kay must sell 500 posters to breakeven. Her breakeven point in sales revenue is $17,500 (500 posters × $35).

You can check this answer by creating a contribution margin income statement using a sales volume of 500 posters:

	A	B	C	D
1	**Kay Martin Posters**			
2	**Contribution Margin Income Statement**			
3	**For a month in which 500 posters are sold**			
4				
5	Sales revenue (500 posters × $35 per poster)	$ 17,500		
6	Less: Variable expenses (500 posters × $21 per poster)	10,500		
7	Contribution margin (500 posters × $14 per poster)	7,000		
8	Less: Fixed expenses	7,000		
9	Operating income	$ 0		
10				

Notice that at breakeven, a firm's fixed expenses ($7,000) equal its contribution margin ($7,000). In other words, the firm has generated *just* enough contribution margin to cover its fixed expenses, but *not* enough to generate a profit.

The Shortcut Approach Using the Unit Contribution Margin

To develop the shortcut approach, we start with the contribution margin income statement, and then rearrange some of its terms:

$$\underbrace{\text{SALES REVENUE} - \text{VARIABLE EXPENSES}}_{\text{Contribution margin}} - \text{FIXED EXPENSES} = \text{OPERATING INCOME}$$

Contribution margin	$-$ Fixed expenses	$=$ Operating income
Contribution margin		$=$ Fixed expenses $+$ Operating income
(Contribution margin per unit $\times$ Units sold)		$=$ Fixed expenses $+$ Operating income

As a final step, we divide both sides of the equation by the contribution margin per unit. Now we have the shortcut formula:

$$\text{Sales in units} = \frac{\text{Fixed expenses} + \text{Operating income}}{\text{Contribution margin per unit}}$$

Kay can use this shortcut approach to find her breakeven point in units. Kay's fixed expenses total \$7,000, and her unit contribution margin is \$14. At the breakeven point, operating income is zero. Thus, Kay's breakeven point in units is as follows:

$$\text{Sales in units} = \frac{\$7,000 + \$0}{\$14}$$
$$= 500 \text{ posters}$$

Why does this shortcut approach work? Recall that each poster provides \$14 of contribution margin. To breakeven, Kay must generate enough contribution margin to cover \$7,000 of fixed expenses. At the rate of \$14 per poster, Kay must sell 500 posters (\$7,000/\$14) to cover her \$7,000 of fixed expenses. Because the shortcut formula simply rearranges the income statement equation, the breakeven point is the same under both methods (500 posters). Keep the following important rule of thumb in mind:

When finding the breakeven point, always use "zero" as the operating income in the formulas.

STOP & THINK

What would Kay's operating income be if she sold 501 posters? What would it be if she sold 600 posters?

Answer: Every poster sold provides $14 of contribution margin, which first contributes toward covering fixed costs, then profit. Once Kay reaches her breakeven point (500 posters), she has paid for all fixed costs. Therefore, each additional poster sold after the breakeven point contributes $14 *directly to profit*. If Kay sells 501 posters, she has sold one more poster than breakeven. Her operating income is $14. If she sells 600 posters, she has sold 100 more posters than breakeven. Her operating income is $1,400 ($14 per poster × 100 posters). We can verify this as follows:

Contribution margin (600 posters × $14 per poster)	$ 8,400
Less: Fixed expenses	7,000
Operating income	$ 1,400

Keep the following rule of thumb in mind:

Once a company achieves breakeven, each additional unit sold contributes its unique unit contribution margin directly to profit.

The Shortcut Approach Using the Contribution Margin Ratio

It is easy to compute the breakeven point in *units* for a simple business like Kay's that has only one product. But what about companies that have thousands of products such as Art.com, Home Depot, and Amazon.com? It doesn't make sense for these companies to determine the number of each various product they need to sell to breakeven. Can you imagine a Home Depot manager describing breakeven as 100,000 wood screws, two million nails, 3,000 lawn mowers, 10,000 gallons of paint, and so forth? It simply doesn't make sense. Therefore, multiproduct companies usually compute breakeven in terms of *sales revenue* (dollars).

This shortcut approach, which is also derived from the income statement, differs from the other shortcut we've just seen in only one way: Fixed expenses plus operating income are divided by the contribution margin *ratio* (not by contribution margin *per unit*) to yield sales in *dollars* (not in *units*):

$$\text{Sales in dollars} = \frac{\text{Fixed expenses} + \text{Operating income}}{\text{Contribution margin ratio}}$$

Recall that Kay's contribution margin ratio is 40%. At the breakeven point, operating income is $0, so Kay's breakeven point in sales revenue is as follows:

$$\text{Sales in dollars} = \frac{\$7,000 + \$0}{40\%}$$
$$= \$17,500$$

This is the same breakeven sales revenue we calculated earlier (500 posters × $35 sales price = $17,500).

Why does the contribution margin ratio formula work? Each dollar of Kay's sales contributes $0.40 to fixed expenses and profit. To breakeven, she must generate enough contribution margin at the rate of $0.40 per sales dollar to cover the $7,000 fixed expenses ($7,000 ÷ 0.40 = $17,500).

When determining which formula to use, keep the following rule of thumb in mind:

> *Dividing fixed costs by the* **unit** *contribution margin provides breakeven in sales* **units.** *Dividing fixed costs by the contribution margin* **ratio** *provides breakeven in sales* **dollars** *(sales revenue).*

▶ Try It!

Rachel runs her own hot dog stand on the U of A campus. The monthly cost of the cart rental and business permit is $300. Rachel's contribution margin per unit is $1.50 and contribution margin ratio is 75%.

1. How many hot dogs does Rachel need to sell each month to breakeven?
2. How much sales revenue does Rachel need to generate each month to breakeven?

Please see page 441 for solutions.

How do Managers Find the Volume Needed to Earn a Target Profit?

For established products and services, managers are more interested in the sales level needed to earn a target profit than in the breakeven point.* Managers of new business ventures are also interested in the profits they can expect to earn. For example, Kay doesn't want to just breakeven—she wants her business to be her sole source of income. She would like the business to earn $4,900 of profit each month. How many posters must Kay sell each month to reach her target profit?

How Much Must we Sell to Earn a Target Profit?

The only difference from our prior analysis is that instead of determining the sales level needed for *zero profit* (breakeven), Kay now wants to know how many posters she must sell to earn a $4,900 profit. We can use the income statement approach or the shortcut approach to find the answer. Because Kay wants to know the number

> **■ Why is this important?**
>
> "**Companies** want to make a profit. **CVP** analysis helps **managers** determine **how many** units they need to sell to earn a **target** amount of **profit.**"

of *units*, we'll use the shortcut formula based on the *unit* contribution margin. This time, instead of an operating income of zero (breakeven), we'll insert Kay's target operating income of $4,900:

$$\text{Sales in } units = \frac{\text{Fixed expenses + Operating income}}{\text{Contribution margin } per\ unit}$$

$$= \frac{\$7,000 + \$4,900}{\$14}$$

$$= \frac{\$11,900}{\$14}$$

$$= 850 \text{ posters}$$

*As always in this book, we consider profit before tax (operating income). The impact of income taxes is discussed in more advanced textbooks.

This analysis shows that Kay must sell 850 posters each month to earn profits of $4,900 a month. Notice that this level of sales falls within Kay's current relevant range (0–2,000 posters per month), so the conclusion that she would earn $4,900 of income at this sales volume is valid. If the calculation resulted in a sales volume outside the current relevant range (greater than 2,000 units), we would need to reassess our cost assumptions.

Assume that Kay also wants to know how much sales revenue she needs to earn $4,900 of monthly profit. Because she already knows the number of units needed (850), she can easily translate this volume into sales revenue:

$$850 \text{ posters} \times \$35 \text{ sales price/poster} = \$29,750 \text{ sales revenue}$$

If Kay only wanted to know the sales revenue needed to achieve her target profit rather than the number of units needed, she could have found the answer directly by using the shortcut formula based on the contribution margin *ratio*:

$$
\begin{aligned}
\text{Sales in } dollars &= \frac{\text{Fixed expenses} + \text{Operating income}}{\text{Contribution margin } ratio} \\[6pt]
&= \frac{\$7,000 + \$4,900}{40\%} \\[6pt]
&= \frac{\$11,900}{40\%} \\[6pt]
&= \$29,750
\end{aligned}
$$

Finally, Kay could have used the income statement approach to find the same answers:

SALES REVENUE	−	VARIABLE EXPENSES	−	FIXED EXPENSES	=	OPERATING INCOME
($35 × Units sold)	−	($21 × Units sold)	−	$7,000	=	$ 4,900
($35	−	$21) × Units sold	−	$7,000	=	$ 4,900
		$14 × Units sold			=	$11,900
				Units sold	=	$11,900/$14
				Units sold	=	850 posters

We can prove that our answers (from any of the three approaches) are correct by preparing Kay's income statement for a sales volume of 850 units:

	A	B	C	D
1	Kay Martin Posters			
2	Contribution Margin Income Statement			
3	For a month in which 850 posters are sold			
4				
5	Sales revenue (850 posters × $35 per poster)	$ 29,750		
6	Less: Variable expenses (850 posters × $21 per poster)	17,850		
7	Contribution margin (850 posters × $14 per poster)	11,900		
8	Less: Fixed expenses	7,000		
9	Operating income	$ 4,900		
10				

Keep the following important rule of thumb in mind:

When finding the volume needed to earn a target profit, use the target profit as the operating income in the formulas.

> Rachel runs her own hot dog stand on the U of A campus. The monthly cost of the cart rental and business permit is $300. Rachel's contribution margin per unit is $1.50 and contribution margin ratio is 75%.
>
> 1. How many hot dogs does Rachel need to sell each month to earn a target profit of $900 a month?
> 2. How much sales revenue does Rachel need to generate each month to earn a target profit of $900 per month?

Please see page 441 for solutions.

Graphing CVP Relationships

By graphing the CVP relationships for her business, Kay can see at a glance how changes in the levels of sales will affect profits. As in the last chapter, the volume of units (posters) is placed on the horizontal x-axis, while dollars is placed on the vertical y-axis. Then, she follows five steps to graph the CVP relations for her business, as illustrated in Exhibit 7-4. This graph also shows the linear nature of Kay's costs and revenues. Recall that CVP analysis assumes costs and revenues will be linear throughout the relevant range.

EXHIBIT 7-4 Cost-Volume-Profit Graph

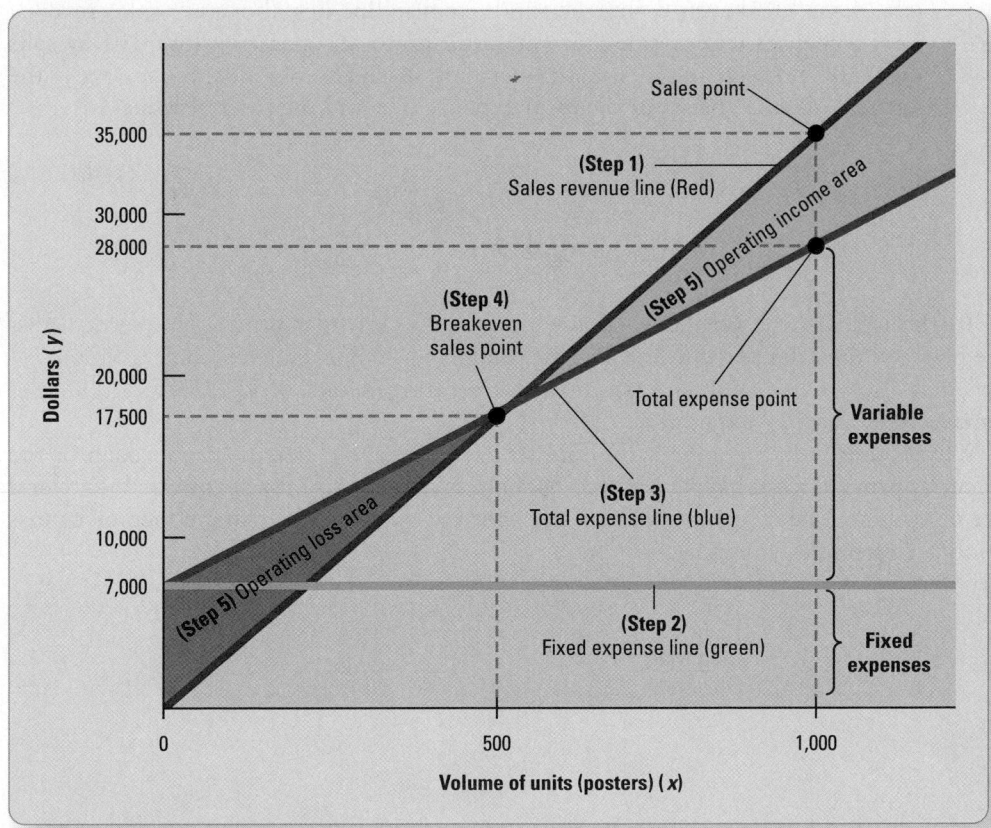

STEP 1: Choose a sales volume, such as 1,000 posters. Plot the point for total sales revenue at that volume: 1,000 posters × $35 per poster = sales of $35,000. Draw the *sales revenue line* from the origin (0) through the $35,000 point. Why does the sales revenue line start at the origin? If Kay does not sell any posters, there is no sales revenue.

STEP 2: Draw the *fixed expense line*, a horizontal line that intersects the y-axis at $7,000. Recall that the fixed expense line is flat because fixed expenses are the same ($7,000) no matter how many posters Kay sells within her relevant range (up to 2,000 posters per month).

STEP 3: Draw the *total expense line*. Total expense is the sum of variable expense plus fixed expense. Thus, total expense is a *mixed* cost. So, the total expense line follows the form of the mixed cost line. Begin by computing variable expense at the chosen sales volume: 1,000 posters × $21 per poster = variable expense of $21,000. Add variable expense to fixed expense: $21,000 + $7,000 = $28,000. Plot the total expense point ($28,000) for 1,000 units. Then, draw a line through this point from the $7,000 fixed expense intercept on the dollars axis. This is the *total expense line*. Why does the total expense line start at the fixed expense line? If Kay sells no posters, she still incurs the $7,000 fixed cost for the server leasing, software, and office rental, but she incurs no variable costs.

STEP 4: Identify the *breakeven point*. The breakeven point is the point where the sales revenue line intersects the total expense line. This is the point where sales revenue equals total expenses. Our previous analyses told us that Kay's breakeven point is 500 posters, or $17,500 in sales. The graph shows this information visually.

STEP 5: Mark the *operating income* and the *operating loss* areas on the graph. To the left of the breakeven point, the total expense line lies above the sales revenue line. Expenses exceed sales revenue, leading to an operating loss. If Kay sells only 300 posters, she incurs an operating loss. The amount of the loss is the vertical distance between the total expense line and the sales revenue line:

Sales revenue	−	Variable expenses	−	Fixed expenses	=	Operating income (Loss)
(300 × $35)	−	(300 × $21)	−	$7,000	=	$(2,800)

To the right of the breakeven point, the business earns a profit. The vertical distance between the sales revenue line and the total expense line equals income. Exhibit 7-4 shows that if Kay sells 1,000 posters, she earns operating income of $7,000 ($35,000 sales revenue − $28,000 total expenses).

Why bother with a graph? Why not just use the income statement approach or the shortcut approach? Graphs like Exhibit 7-4 help managers visualize profit or loss over a range of volume. The income statement and shortcut approaches estimate income or loss for only a single sales volume.

Decision Guidelines

CVP Analysis

Your friend wants to open her own ice cream parlor after college. She needs help making the following decisions:

Decision	Guidelines
How much will I earn on every ice cream cone I sell?	The unit contribution margin shows managers how much they earn on each unit sold after paying for variable *costs but before considering fixed expenses*. The unit contribution margin is the amount each unit earns that contributes toward covering fixed expenses and generating a profit. It is computed as follows:

Sales price per unit

Less: Variable cost per unit

Contribution margin per unit

The contribution margin ratio shows managers how much contribution margin is earned on every $1 of sales. It is computed as follows:

$$\text{Contribution margin ratio} = \frac{\text{Contribution margin}}{\text{Sales revenue}}$$

Can I quickly forecast my income without creating a full income statement?	The contribution margin concept allows managers to forecast income quickly at different sales volumes. First, find the total contribution margin (by multiplying the forecasted number of units by the unit contribution margin *or* by multiplying the forecasted sales revenue by the contribution margin ratio) and then subtract all fixed expenses.
How can I compute the *number of ice cream cones* I'll have to sell to break-even or earn a target profit?	***Income Statement Approach:***

$$\text{SALES REVENUE} - \text{VARIABLE EXPENSES} - \begin{array}{c}\text{FIXED}\\\text{EXPENSE}\end{array} = \begin{array}{c}\text{OPERATING}\\\text{INCOME}\end{array}$$

$$\begin{array}{c}\text{Sales price per unit}\\\times\text{ Units sold}\end{array} - \begin{array}{c}\text{Variable cost per unit}\\\times\text{ Units sold}\end{array} - \begin{array}{c}\text{Fixed}\\\text{expenses}\end{array} = \begin{array}{c}\text{Operating}\\\text{income}\end{array}$$

Shortcut Unit Contribution Margin Approach:

$$\text{Sales in } units = \frac{\text{Fixed expenses} + \text{Operating income}}{\text{Contribution margin } per\ unit}$$

How can I compute the *amount of sales revenue* (in dollars) I'll have to generate to breakeven or earn a target profit?	***Shortcut Contribution Margin Ratio Approach:***

$$\text{Sales in } dollars = \frac{\text{Fixed expenses} + \text{Operating income}}{\text{Contribution margin } ratio}$$

What will my profits look like over a range of volumes?	CVP graphs show managers, at a glance, how different sales volumes will affect profits.

SUMMARY PROBLEM 1

Fleet Foot buys hiking socks for $6 a pair and sells them for $10. Management budgets monthly fixed expenses of $10,000 for sales volumes between 0 and 12,000 pairs.

Requirements

1. Use the income statement approach and the shortcut unit contribution margin approach to compute monthly breakeven sales in units.

2. Use the shortcut contribution margin ratio approach to compute the breakeven point in sales revenue (sales dollars).

3. Compute the monthly sales level (in units) required to earn a target operating income of $14,000. Use either the income statement approach or the shortcut contribution margin approach.

4. Prepare a graph of Fleet Foot's CVP relationships, similar to Exhibit 7-4. Draw the sales revenue line, the fixed expense line, and the total expense line. Label the axes, the breakeven point, the operating income area, and the operating loss area.

▪ SOLUTIONS

Requirement 1
Income Statement Approach:

SALES REVENUE	−	VARIABLE EXPENSES	− FIXED EXPENSES	= OPERATING INCOME
$\left(\dfrac{\text{Sales price}}{\text{per unit}} \times \text{Units sold}\right)$	−	$\left(\dfrac{\text{Variable cost}}{\text{per unit}} \times \text{Units sold}\right)$	− Fixed expenses	= Operating income

($10 × Units sold) −	($6	× Units sold) −	$10,000	=	$ 0
($10	−	$6)	× Units sold	=	$10,000
		$4	× Units sold	=	$10,000
			Units sold	=	$10,000 ÷ $4
			Breakeven sales in units	=	2,500 units

Shortcut Unit Contribution Margin Approach:

$$\text{Sales in units} = \frac{\text{Fixed expenses} + \text{Operating income}}{\text{Contribution margin per unit}}$$

$$= \frac{\$10,000 + \$0}{(\$10 - \$6)}$$

$$= \frac{\$10,000}{\$4}$$

$$= 2,500 \text{ units}$$

Requirement 2

$$\text{Sales in dollars} = \frac{\text{Fixed expenses} + \text{Operating income}}{\text{Contribution margin ratio}}$$

$$= \frac{\$10,000 + \$0}{0.40^*}$$

$$= \$25,000$$

$$*\text{Contribution margin ratio} = \frac{\text{Contribution margin per unit}}{\text{Sales price per unit}} = \frac{\$4}{\$10} = 0.40$$

Requirement 3

Income Statement Equation Approach:

SALES REVENUE	−	VARIABLE EXPENSES	− FIXED EXPENSES	= OPERATING INCOME
$\left(\begin{array}{c}\text{Sales price}\\\text{per unit}\end{array} \times \text{Units sold}\right)$ −		$\left(\begin{array}{c}\text{Variable cost}\\\text{per unit}\end{array} \times \text{Units sold}\right)$ −	Fixed expenses	= Operating income
($10 × Units sold)−		($6 × Units sold) −	$10,000	= $14,000
($10	−	$6) × Units sold		= $10,000 + $14,000
		$4 × Units sold		= $24,000
		Units sold		= $24,000 ÷ $4
		Units sold		= 6,000 units

Shortcut Unit Contribution Margin Approach:

$$\text{Sales in units} = \frac{\text{Fixed expenses} + \text{Operating income}}{\text{Contribution margin per unit}}$$

$$= \frac{\$10,000 + \$14,000}{(\$10 - \$6)}$$

$$= \frac{\$24,000}{\$4}$$

$$= 6,000 \text{ units}$$

Requirement 4

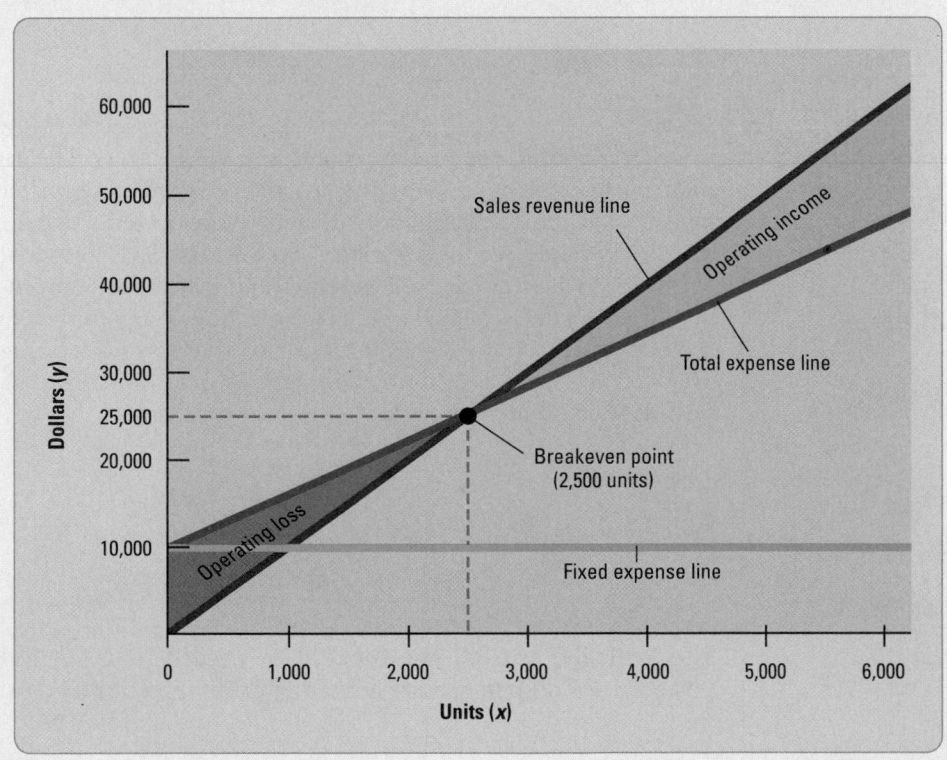

How do Managers Use CVP to Plan for Changing Business Conditions?

In today's fast-changing business world, managers need to be prepared for increasing costs, pricing pressure from competitors, and other changing business conditions.

Managers use CVP analysis to conduct <u>sensitivity analysis</u>. Sensitivity analysis is a "what-if" technique that asks what results will be if actual prices or costs change or if an underlying assumption such as sales mix changes. For example, increased competition may force Kay to lower her sales price, while at the same time her suppliers increase poster costs. How will these changes affect Kay's breakeven and target profit volumes? What will happen if Kay changes her sales mix by offering posters in two different sizes? We'll tackle these issues next.

Changing the Sales Price

Let's assume that Kay has now been in business for several months. Because of competition, Kay is considering cutting her sales price to $31 per poster. If her variable expenses remain $21 per poster and her fixed expenses stay at $7,000, how many posters will she need to sell to breakeven? To answer this question, Kay calculates a new unit contribution margin using the new sales price:

New sales price per poster....................................	$ 31
Less: Variable cost per poster.............................	21
New contribution margin per poster..................	$ 10

She then uses the new unit contribution margin to compute breakeven sales in units:

$$\text{Sales in units} = \frac{\text{Fixed expenses} + \text{Operating income}}{\text{Contribution margin per unit}}$$

$$= \frac{\$7,000 + \$0}{\$10}$$

$$= 700 \text{ posters}$$

With the original $35 sale price, Kay's breakeven point was 500 posters. If Kay lowers the sales price to $31 per poster, her breakeven point increases to 700 posters. The lower sales price means that each poster contributes *less* toward fixed expenses ($10 versus $14 before the price change), so Kay must sell 200 *more* posters to breakeven. Each dollar of sales revenue would contribute $0.32 ($10/$31) rather than $0.40 toward covering fixed expenses and generating a profit.

If Kay reduces her sales price to $31, how many posters must she sell to achieve her $4,900 monthly target profit? Kay again uses the new unit contribution margin to determine how many posters she will need to sell to reach her profit goals:

$$\text{Sales in units} = \frac{\$7,000 + \$4,900}{\$10}$$

$$= 1,190 \text{ posters}$$

With the original sales price, Kay needed to sell only 850 posters per month to achieve her target profit level. If Kay cuts her

Why is this important?

"**CVP analysis** helps managers prepare for and respond to **economic** changes, such as increasing costs and **pressure** to drop sales prices, so companies can remain **competitive** and **profitable**."

sales price (and, therefore, her contribution margin), she must sell more posters to achieve her financial goals. Kay could have found the same results using the income statement approach. Exhibit 7-5 shows the effect of changes in sales price on breakeven and target profit volumes.

EXHIBIT 7-5 The Effect of Changes in Sales Price on Breakeven and Target Profit Volumes

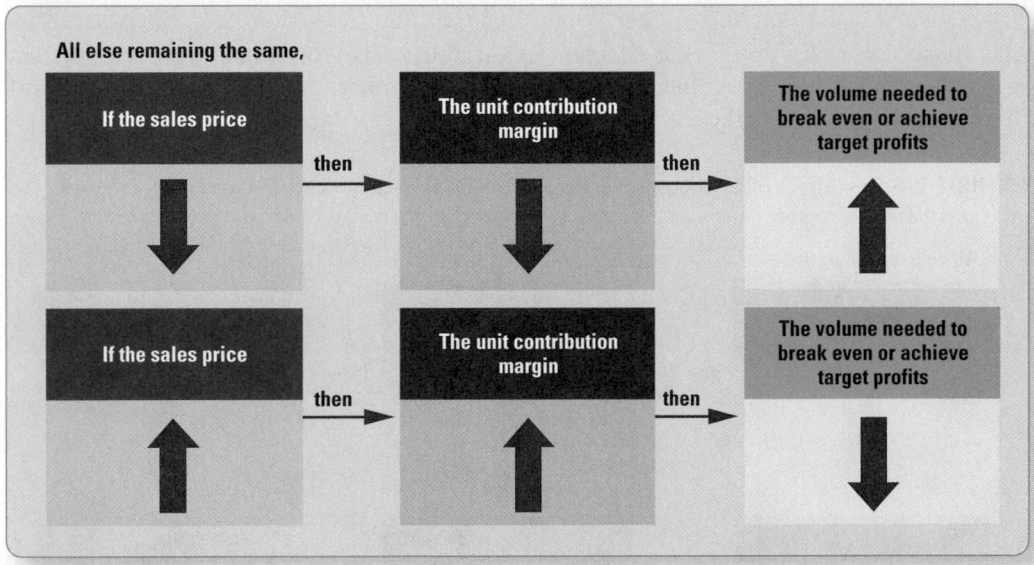

STOP & THINK

Kay believes she could dominate the e-commerce art poster business if she cut the sales price to $20. Is this a good idea?

Answer: No. The variable cost per poster is $21. If Kay sells posters for $20 each, she loses $1 on each poster. Kay will incur a loss if the sales price is less than the variable cost.

Changing Variable Costs

Let's assume that Kay does *not* lower her sales price. However, Kay's supplier raises the price for each poster to $23.80 (instead of the original $21). To remain competitive, Kay can not pass this increase on to her customers, so she holds her sales price at the original $35 per poster. Her fixed costs remain $7,000. How many posters must she sell to break-even after her supplier raises the prices? Kay's new contribution margin per unit drops to $11.20 ($35 sales price per poster − $23.80 variable cost per poster). So, her new break-even point is as follows:

$$\text{Sales in units} = \frac{\text{Fixed expenses} + \text{Operating income}}{\text{Contribution margin per unit}}$$

$$= \frac{\$7,000 + \$0}{\$11.20}$$

$$= 625 \text{ posters}$$

Kay will have to sell *more* units (625 versus 500 originally) just to breakeven. Keep the following rule of thumb in mind:

> *Higher variable costs have the same effect as lower selling prices—they both reduce the product's unit contribution margin. As a result, more units need to be sold to breakeven or achieve target profits.*

As shown in Exhibit 7-6, a *decrease* in variable costs would have just the opposite effect. Lower variable costs increase the contribution margin each poster provides and, therefore, lowers the breakeven point.

EXHIBIT 7-6 The Effect of Changes in Variable Costs on Breakeven and Target Profit Volumes

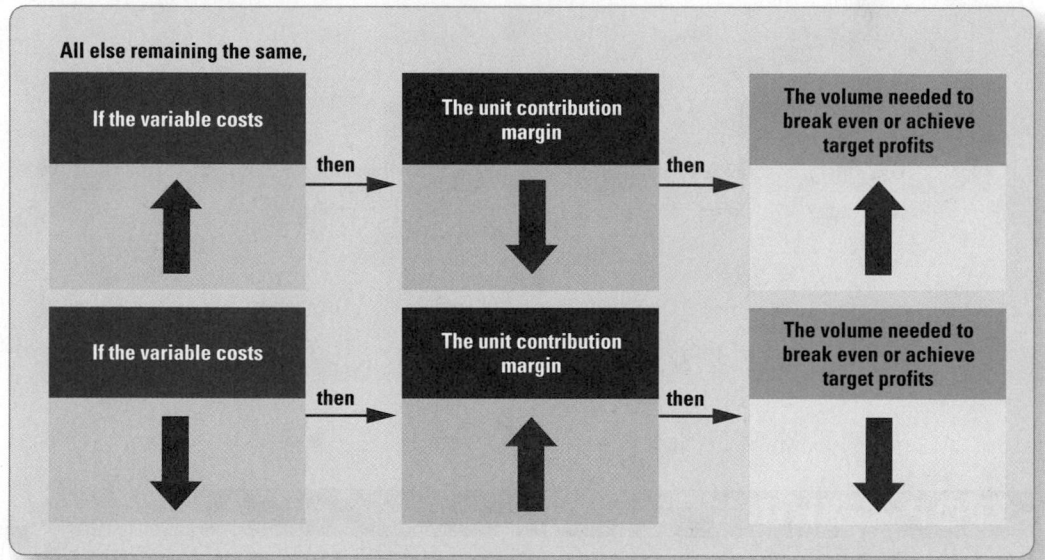

Changing More Than One Factor

Suppose Kay is squeezed from both sides: Her supply costs have increased to $23.80 per poster, yet she must lower her price to $31 in order to compete. Under these conditions, how many posters will Kay need to sell to achieve her monthly target profit of $4,900?

Kay is now in a position faced by many companies—her unit contribution margin is squeezed by both higher supply costs and lower sales prices:

New sales price per poster..................................	$ 31.00
Less: New variable cost per poster......................	23.80
New contribution margin per poster..................	$ 7.20

Kay's new contribution margin is about half of what it was when she started her business ($14). To achieve her target profit, her volume will have to increase dramatically (yet, it would still fall within her current relevant range for fixed costs—which extends to 2,000 posters per month):

$$\text{Sales in units} = \frac{\text{Fixed expenses} + \text{Operating income}}{\text{Contribution margin per unit}}$$

$$= \frac{\$7,000 + \$4,900}{\$7.20}$$

$$= 1,653 \text{ posters (rounded)}$$

Based on her current volume, Kay may not believe she can sell so many posters. To maintain a reasonable profit level, Kay may need to take other measures. For example, she may try to find a different supplier with lower poster costs. She may also attempt to lower her fixed costs. For example, perhaps she could negotiate a cheaper lease on her office space or move her business to a less expensive location. She could also try to increase her volume by spending *more* on fixed costs, such as advertising. Kay could also investigate selling other products, in addition to her regular-size posters, that would have higher unit contribution margins. We'll discuss these measures next.

Changing Fixed Costs

Let's return to Kay's original data ($35 selling price and $21 variable cost). Kay has decided she really doesn't need a storefront office at a retail strip mall because she doesn't have many walk-in customers. She could decrease her monthly fixed costs from $7,000 to $4,200 by moving her office to an industrial park.

How will this decrease in fixed costs affect Kay's breakeven point? *Changes in fixed costs do not affect the contribution margin.* Therefore, Kay's unit contribution margin is still $14 per poster. However, her breakeven point changes because her fixed costs change:

$$\text{Sales in units} = \frac{\text{Fixed expenses} + \text{Operating income}}{\text{Contribution margin per unit}}$$

$$= \frac{\$4,200 + \$0}{\$14.00}$$

$$= 300 \text{ posters}$$

Because of the decrease in fixed costs, Kay will need to sell only 300 posters, rather than 500 posters, to breakeven. The volume needed to achieve her monthly $4,900 target profit will also decline. However, if Kay's fixed costs *increase*, she will have to sell *more* units to breakeven. Exhibit 7-7 shows the effect of changes in fixed costs on breakeven and target profit volumes.

EXHIBIT 7-7 The Effect of Changes in Fixed Costs on Breakeven and Target Profit Volumes

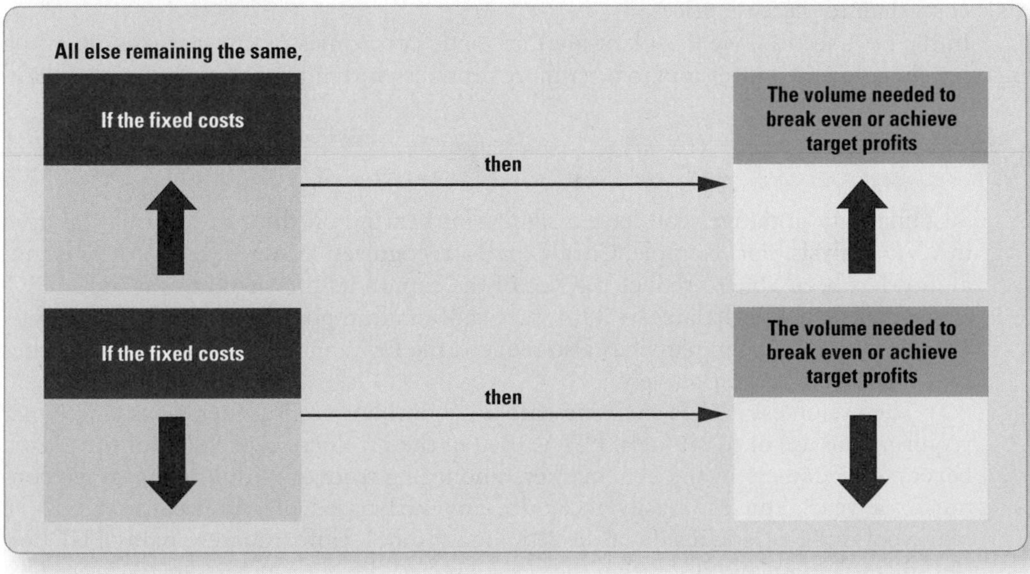

STOP & THINK

Kay has been considering advertising as a means to increase her sales volume. Kay could spend an extra $3,500 per month on website banner ads. How many *extra* posters would Kay have to sell *just to pay for the advertising?* (Use Kay's original data.)

Answer: CVP is very useful for isolating and addressing individual business decisions. Instead of using *all* of Kay's fixed costs, we can isolate *just* the fixed costs relating to advertising ($3,500). This will allow us to figure out how many *extra* posters Kay would have to sell each month to breakeven on (or pay for) the advertising cost. Advertising is a fixed cost, so Kay's contribution margin remains $14 per unit.

$$\text{Sales in units} = \frac{\text{Fixed expenses} + \text{Operating income}}{\text{Contribution margin per unit}}$$

$$= \frac{\$3,500 + \$0}{\$14.00}$$

$$= 250 \text{ posters}$$

Kay must sell 250 *extra* posters each month just to pay for the cost of advertising. If she sells fewer than 250 extra posters, she'll increase her volume but lose money on the advertising. If she sells more than 250 extra posters, her plan will have worked—she'll increase her volume *and* her profit.

We have seen that changes in sales prices, variable costs, and fixed costs can have dramatic effects on the volume of product that companies must sell to achieve breakeven and target profits. Companies often turn to automation and overseas production in order to decrease variable labor costs, but this, in turn, increases their fixed costs (equipment depreciation) and variable shipping costs. In recent years, many food producers have systematically reduced the size of their products in order to decrease the variable cost of direct materials. For example, ice cream, which in the past was primarily sold in half gallons, is now sold in smaller containers. Why make this change? Customers are less responsive, in terms of buying fewer units, to slightly smaller packages than they are to increases in prices. Thus, CVP analysis has shown that it is more profitable to decrease variable materials costs than to increase prices.

In the next section, we'll look at another tactic companies use to increase operating income: changing their sales mix to offer more products with higher contribution margins.

 Sustainability and CVP

Sustainability initiatives can have a significant bearing on the cost information used in CVP analysis. For example, Coca-Cola[1], a recognized leader in corporate sustainability, has been able to reduce the size of the cap on its plastic bottles made of PET (polyethelene terephthalate) by 38%, saving 40 million pounds of plastic annually in the U.S. alone. The company has also reduced the PET in its Coke and Dasani bottles by 23% and 35%, respectively.

The use of less PET is environmentally favorable since it is an oil-based polymer requiring the use of fossil fuels. PET is used in the production of 96%[2] of the plastic beverage containers in the U.S. market, amounting to over 34 billion beverage containers a year! You can easily recognize any PET-based plastic because it will be marked as a #1 plastic inside of the recycling symbol. Unfortunately, many PET bottles still end up in landfills, rather than being recycled by consumers. In 2012, the U.S. recycling rate for PET bottles was only 38%[3] although that figure is up from prior

[1]The Coca-Cola Company website. www.thecoca-colacompany.com/citizenship/package_design.html, Section on Sustainable Packaging. Subsection: Reduce
[2]http://www.ecolife.com/recycling/plastic/how-to-recycle-pet-plastic-1.html#_edn1
[3]http://www.wasterecyclingnews.com/article/20130220/NEWS02/130229987/plastic-water-bottle-recycling-rate-jumps-almost-20

years. That means that 62% of PET bottles still end up in landfills rather than being recycled into new products. For example, Under Armour uses recycled PET bottles to make high-performance exercise shirts while Trex makes outdoor decking from recycled plastic.

In addition to *reducing* the PET content, Coca-Cola has *increased* the percentage of recycled plastic used in these containers. The company's current goal is to obtain 25% of its PET from recycled PET (rPET) or renewable materials by 2015[4]. The company is also working to reduce the amount of water needed for each unit of its product. What does this have to do with accounting? As a result of these initiatives, the variable cost of packaging each unit and shipping the lighter weight containers has decreased. For example, the company reports that its new ultra glass contour bottle, which has reduced annual CO_2 emissions by the equivalent to planting 8,000 acres of trees, is not only 40% stronger and 20% lighter, but also 10% cheaper to produce than its traditional contour bottle. Because of these variable cost savings, the contribution margin per unit has increased.

As a result, one might assume that Coca-Cola needs to sell fewer units of product to achieve its target profit. However, keep in mind that the company had to incur many fixed costs to research, develop and design these new bottles. In addition, they probably had to invest in new production equipment to handle the new packaging design.

As the Coca-Cola example shows, sustainability initiatives often result in both cost savings *and* additional costs. These costs and cost savings may be fixed or variable in nature. Managers use CVP analysis to determine how these initiatives will impact the volume needed to achieve the company's operating income goals.

> **See Exercises E7-25A and E7-46B**

Changing the Mix of Products Offered for Sale

So far, we have assumed that Kay sold only one size poster. What would happen if she offered different types of products? Companies that sell more than one product must consider their **sales mix** when performing CVP analysis. The sales mix is the combination of products that make up total sales. Think of the sales mix as the "basket of products" sold by the company. For example, a movie theatre may sell 20 popcorns, 25 sodas, and 15 boxes of candy for every 75 movie tickets sold. The combination of all of these different product sales, including the movie tickets, makes up the total "sales basket" of the theatre. All else being equal, a company earns more operating income by selling high-contribution margin products than by selling an equal number of low-contribution margin products.

4 Find breakeven and target profit volumes for multiproduct companies

The same CVP formulas that are used to perform CVP analysis for a company with a single product can be used for any company that sells more than one product. However, the formulas use the *weighted-average contribution margin* of all products, rather than the contribution margin of a sole product. Each unit's contribution margin is *weighted* by the relative number of units sold. As before, the company can find the breakeven or the target profit volume in terms of units, or in terms of sales revenue. We'll consider each in turn.

Multiproduct Company: Finding Breakeven in Terms of Sales Units

Suppose Kay plans to sell two types of posters. In addition to her regular-size posters, Kay plans to sell large posters. Let's assume that none of Kay's original costs have changed. Exhibit 7-8 shows that each regular poster will continue to generate $14 of contribution margin, while each large poster will generate $30 of contribution margin. Kay is adding the large-poster line because it carries a higher unit contribution margin.

---

[4]http://www.environmentalleader.com/2013/06/05/coke-recycling-venture-processes-500-million-bottles-in-year-one/

EXHIBIT 7-8 Calculating the Weighted-Average Contribution Margin per Unit

	A	B	C	D
		Regular Posters	Large Posters	Total in "basket"
1	**Calculating Weighted-Average Contribution Margin per Unit**			
2	Sales price per unit	$ 35	$ 70	
3	Less: Variable cost per unit	21	40	
4	Contribution margin per unit	$ 14	$ 30	
5	Multiply by: Sales mix (number of units in "basket")	5	3	8
6	Contribution margin	$ 70	$ 90	$ 160
7				
8	Weighted-average contibution margin per unit ($160/8 units)			$ 20
9				

For every five regular posters sold, Kay expects to sell three large posters. In other words, she expects 5/8 of the sales in her "sales basket" to be regular posters and 3/8 to be large posters. This is a 5:3 sales mix. Exhibit 7-8 shows how Kay finds the total contribution margin and total number of units in the "sales basket" and then divides the two to find the weighted-average contribution margin per unit in the basket.

Notice that none of Kay's products actually generates $20 of contribution margin. However, if the sales mix is 5 regular posters to every 3 large posters, as expected, it is *as if* the contribution margin is $20 per unit. Once Kay has computed the weighted-average contribution margin per unit, she uses it in the shortcut formula to determine the total number of posters that would need to be sold to breakeven:

$$\text{Sales in total units} = \frac{\text{Fixed expenses} + \text{Operating income}}{\text{Weighted-average contribution margin per unit}}$$

$$= \frac{\$7{,}000 + \$0}{\$20}$$

$$= 350 \text{ posters}$$

In total, Kay must sell 350 posters to breakeven. However, this is only the case if 5/8 of the sales basket is regular posters and 3/8 of the sales basket is large posters. As a final step, we need to separate the entire sales basket needed to breakeven back into the two types of products in the basket: regular posters and large posters. We do this by multiplying the total number of units needed to breakeven (350) by the proportion of each product in the sales basket.

Breakeven sales of regular posters (350 × 5/8)..................... <u>218.75</u> regular posters
Breakeven sales of large posters (350 × 3/8) .... <u>131.25</u> large posters

We can prove this breakeven point as follows:

Contribution margin:
    Regular posters (218.75 × $14)................. $ 3,063
    Large posters (131.25 × $30) .... <u>3,937</u>
Contribution margin .... $ 7,000
Less: Fixed expenses... <u>7,000</u>
Operating income.. $ 0

As is often the case in real situations, these computations don't yield round numbers. Because Kay cannot sell partial posters, she must sell 219 regular posters and 132 large posters to avoid a loss.

We just found Kay's *breakeven* point, but Kay can also use the same steps to calculate the number of units she must sell to achieve a target profit. The only difference, as before, is that she would use *target profit*, rather than *zero*, as the operating income in the short-cut formula.

Try It!

Rachel runs her own hot dog stand on the U of A campus. The monthly cost of the cart rental and business permit is $300. Rachel's contribution margin is $1.50 per hot dog sold. She has recently added individual servings of potato chips to her product offering. Each bag of potato chips has a contribution margin of $0.75 per bag. Rachel sells 5 bags of potato chips for every 10 hot dogs.

1. What is Rachel's weighted-average contribution margin per unit?

2. How many total units must Rachel sell in a month to earn a target monthly profit of $900?

3. Of the total units needed to earn $900 of profit, how many are hot dogs and how many are bags of potato chips?

Please see page 442 for solutions.

Multiproduct Company: Finding Breakeven in Terms of Sales Revenue

Companies that offer hundreds or thousands of products (such as Walmart and Amazon .com) will not want to find the breakeven point in terms of units. Rather, they'll want to know breakeven (or target profit volumes) in terms of sales revenue. To find this sales volume, the company needs to know, or estimate, its weighted-average contribution margin ratio so that managers can use the shortcut formula introduced in the first half of the chapter. If a company prepares a contribution margin income statement that includes all of its products, the weighted-average contribution margin is easily calculated as the total contribution margin divided by total sales. The contribution margin ratio is *already* weighted by the company's *actual* sales mix! The following "Stop and Think" illustrates how Walmart would use this approach to calculate breakeven.

STOP & THINK

How would Walmart calculate its weighted-average contribution margin? How much sales revenue must Walmart earn just to breakeven?

Answer: First Walmart calculates its weighted-average contribution margin based on its contribution margin income statement, as shown below:*

	A	B	C	D
1	**Walmart** **Contribution Margin Income Statement (estimated)** **For the fiscal year ended January 31, 2013**	*(in millions)*		
2	Sales revenue	$ 469,200		
3	Less: Variable expenses	360,500		
4	Contribution margin	108,700		
5	Less: Fixed expenses	80,900		
6	Operating income	$ 27,800		
7				
8	Weighted-Average Contribution Margin ($108,700 /$469,200)	23.17%		
9				

*Estimated for teaching purposes only based on Walmart's 2013 annual report.

Next Walmart uses the weighted-average contribution margin ratio in the shortcut formula to predict the breakeven point:

$$\text{Sales in dollars} = \frac{\text{Fixed expenses} + \text{Operating income}}{\text{Weighted-average contribution margin ratio}}$$

$$= \frac{\$80,900 \text{ million} + \$0}{23.17\%}$$

$$= \$349,158 \text{ million (rounded)}$$

Walmart must achieve sales revenue of nearly $350,000 million just to breakeven.

Unlike Walmart, Kay's business to this point has been limited to a sole product (regular posters) which had a 40% contribution margin ratio. Since Kay is only thinking about selling large posters and doesn't yet sell them, she doesn't currently have a contribution margin income statement which includes both sizes of posters. However, she can easily estimate the weighted-average contribution margin ratio based on the expected sales mix. Exhibit 7-9 shows how Kay would first calculate the total contribution margin and total sales revenue in the sales basket based on product mix assumptions. Next, she would divide the total contribution margin in the basket by the total sales in the basket to estimate the weighted-average contribution margin ratio.

EXHIBIT 7-9 Estimating the Weighted-Average Contribution Margin Ratio

	A	B	C	D
		Regular Posters	Large Posters	Total in "basket"
1	**Calculating Weighted-Average Contribution Margin Ratio**			
2	Contribution margin per unit	$ 14	$ 30	
3	Multiply by: Sales mix (number of units in "basket")	5	3	
4	Contribution margin	$ 70	$ 90	$ 160
5				
6	Sales price per unit	$ 35	$ 70	
7	Multiply by: Sales mix (number of units in "basket")	5	3	
8	Sales revenue	$ 175	$ 210	$ 385
9				
10	Weighted-average contribution margin ratio ($160/$385)			41.56%
11				

Notice how Kay's weighted-average contribution margin ratio (41.56%) will be higher than it was when she sold only regular posters (40%). That's because she expects to sell some large posters that have a 42.9% contribution margin ratio ($30/$70) in addition to the regular-sized posters. Because her sales mix would be changing, she would have a different contribution margin ratio.

Once Kay has calculated her weighted-average contribution margin ratio, she can use the shortcut formula to estimate breakeven in terms of sales revenue:

$$\text{Sales in dollars} = \frac{\text{Fixed expenses} + \text{Operating income}}{\text{Weighted-average contribution margin ratio}}$$

$$= \frac{\$7,000 + \$0}{41.56\%}$$

$$= \$16,843 \text{ (rounded)}$$

Kay could also use the formula to find the total sales revenue she would need to meet her target monthly operating income of $4,900.

If Kay's actual sales mix is not five regular posters to three large posters, her actual operating income will differ from the predicted amount. The sales mix greatly influences the breakeven point. When companies offer more than one product, they do not have a unique breakeven point. Every sales mix assumption leads to a different breakeven point.

STOP & THINK

Suppose Kay plans to sell 800 total posters in the 5:3 sales mix (500 regular posters and 300 large posters). She actually does sell 800 posters—375 regular and 425 large. The sale prices per poster, variable costs per poster, and fixed expenses are exactly as predicted. Without doing any computations, is Kay's actual operating income greater than, less than, or equal to her expected income?

Answer: Kay's actual sales mix did not turn out to be the 5:3 mix she expected. She actually sold more of the higher-margin large posters than the lower-margin regular posters. This favorable change in the sales mix causes her to earn a higher operating income than she expected.

What are Some Common Indicators of Risk?

A company's level of risk depends on many factors, including the general health of the economy and the specific industry in which the company operates. In addition, a firm's risk depends on its current volume of sales and the relative amount of fixed and variable costs that make up its total costs. Next, we discuss how a firm can gauge its level of risk, to some extent, by its margin of safety and its operating leverage.

Margin of Safety

The **margin of safety** is the excess of actual or expected sales over breakeven sales. This is the "cushion," or drop in sales, the company can absorb without incurring a loss. The higher the margin of safety, the greater the cushion against loss and the less risky the business plan. Managers use the margin of safety to evaluate the risk of current operations as well as the risk of new plans.

Let's continue to assume that Kay has been in business for several months and that she generally sells 950 posters a month. Kay's breakeven point in our original data is 500 posters. Kay can express her margin of safety in units, as follows:

5 Determine a firm's margin of safety, operating leverage, and most profitable cost structure

Margin of safety in units = Expected sales in units − Breakeven sales in units				
=	950 posters	−	500 posters	
=	450 posters			

Kay can also express her margin of safety in sales revenue (sales dollars):

Margin of safety in dollars = Expected sales in dollars − Breakeven sales in dollars			
=	(950 posters × \$35)	− (500 posters × \$35)	
=	\$33,250	−	\$17,500
=	\$15,750		

Sales would have to drop by more than 450 posters, or \$15,750 a month, before Kay incurs a loss. This is a fairly comfortable margin.

Managers can also compute the margin of safety as a percentage of sales. Simply divide the margin of safety by sales. We obtain the same percentage whether we use units or dollars.

In units:

$$\text{Margin of safety as a percentage} = \frac{\text{Margin of safety in units}}{\text{Expected sales in units}}$$

$$= \frac{450 \text{ posters}}{950 \text{ posters}}$$

$$= 47.4\% \text{ (rounded)}$$

In dollars:

$$\text{Margin of safety as a percentage} = \frac{\text{Margin of safety in dollars}}{\text{Expected sales in dollars}}$$

$$= \frac{\$15,750}{\$33,250}$$

$$= 47.4\% \text{ (rounded)}$$

The margin of safety percentage tells Kay that sales would have to drop by more than 47.4% before she would incur a loss. If sales fall by less than 47.4%, she would still earn a profit. If sales fall exactly 47.4%, she would breakeven. This ratio tells Kay that her business plan is not unduly risky.

Operating Leverage

A company's <u>operating leverage</u> refers to the relative amount of fixed and variable costs that make up its total costs. Most companies have both fixed and variable costs. However, companies with *high* operating leverage have *relatively more fixed costs* and relatively fewer variable costs. Companies with high operating leverage include golf courses, airlines, and hotels. Because they have fewer variable costs, their contribution margin ratio is relatively high. Recall from the last chapter that Embassy Suites' variable cost of servicing each guest is low, which means that the hotel has a high contribution margin ratio and high operating leverage.

> ### ◼ Why is this important?
>
> "The margin of safety and **operating leverage** help managers understand their **risk** if **volume** decreases due to a recession, **competition**, or other **changes** in the **marketplace**."

What does high operating leverage have to do with risk? If sales volume decreases, the total contribution margin will drop significantly because each sales dollar contains a high percentage of contribution margin. Yet, the high fixed costs of running the company remain. Therefore, the operating income of these companies can easily turn from profit to loss if sales volume declines. For example, airlines were financially devastated after September 11, 2001, because the number of people flying suddenly dropped, creating large reductions in contribution margin. Yet, the airlines had to continue paying their high fixed costs. High operating leverage companies are at *more* risk because their income declines drastically when sales volume declines.

What if the economy is growing and sales volume *increases*? High operating leverage companies will reap high rewards. Remember that after breakeven, each unit sold contributes its unit contribution margin directly to profit. Because high operating leverage companies have high contribution margin ratios, each additional dollar of sales will contribute more to the firm's operating income. Exhibit 7-10 summarizes these characteristics.

However, companies with low operating leverage have relatively *fewer* fixed costs and relatively *more* variable costs. As a result, they have much lower contribution margin ratios. For example, retailers incur significant levels of fixed costs, but more of every sales dollar is used to pay for the merchandise (a variable cost), so less ends up as contribution margin. If sales volume declines, these companies have relatively fewer fixed costs to cover, so they are at *less* risk of incurring a loss. If sales volume increases, their relatively small contribution margins ratios add to the bottom line, but in smaller increments.

EXHIBIT 7-10 Characteristics of High Operating Leverage Firms

- High operating leverage companies have the following:
    —*Higher* levels of fixed costs and *lower* levels of variable costs
    —*Higher* contribution margin ratios
- For high operating leverage companies, changes in volume significantly affect operating income, so they face the following:
    —*Higher* risk
    —*Higher* potential for reward
Examples include golf courses, hotels, rental car agencies, theme parks, airlines, cruise lines, etc.

Therefore, they reap less reward than high operating leverage companies experiencing the same volume increases. *In other words, at low operating leverage companies, changes in sales volume do not have as much impact on operating income as they do at high operating leverage companies.* Exhibit 7-11 summarizes these characteristics.

EXHIBIT 7-11 Characteristics of Low Operating Leverage Firms

- Low operating leverage companies have the following:
    —*Higher* levels of variable costs and *lower* levels of fixed costs
    —*Lower* contribution margin ratios
- For low operating leverage companies, changes in volume do NOT have as significant an effect on operating income, so they face the following:
    —*Lower* risk
    —*Lower* potential for reward
Examples include merchandising companies and fast-food restaurants.

A company's <u>**operating leverage factor**</u> tells us how responsive a company's operating income is to changes in volume. The greater the operating leverage factor, the greater the impact a change in sales volume has on operating income.

The operating leverage factor, *at a given level of sales*, is calculated as follows:

$$\text{Operating leverage factor} = \frac{\text{Contribution margin}}{\text{Operating income}}$$

Why do we say, "at a given level of sales"? A company's operating leverage factor will depend, to some extent, on the sales level used to calculate the contribution margin and operating income. Most companies compute the operating leverage factor at their current or expected volume of sales, which is what we'll do in our examples.

What does the operating leverage factor tell us?

The operating leverage factor, at a given level of sales, indicates the percentage change in operating income that will occur from a 1% change in volume. In other words, it tells us how responsive a company's operating income is to changes in volume.

The *lowest* possible value for this factor is 1, which occurs only if the company has *no* fixed costs (an *extremely low* operating leverage company). *For a minute, let's assume that Kay has no fixed costs.* Given this scenario, her unit contribution margin ($14 per poster) contributes directly to profit because she has no fixed costs to cover. In addition, she has *no* risk. The worst she can do is breakeven, and that will occur only if she doesn't sell any posters. Let's continue to assume that she generally sells 950 posters a month, so this will be the level of sales at which we need to know the contribution margin and operating income:

Contribution margin (950 posters × $14 per poster)	$ 13,300
Less: Fixed expenses...	0
Operating income..	$ 13,300

Given this information, Kay's operating leverage factor is as follows:

$$\text{Operating leverage factor} = \frac{\$13,300}{\$13,300}$$
$$= 1$$

What does this tell us? A factor is a multiplier, therefore:

- If Kay's volume changes by 1%, her operating income will change by 1% (= 1% × a factor of 1).
- If Kay's volume changes by 15%, her operating income will change by 15% (= 15% × a factor of 1).

Let's now see what happens to income and operating leverage if we assume, as usual, that Kay's fixed expenses are $7,000.

Contribution margin (950 posters × $14 per poster)	$13,300
Less: Fixed expenses...	7,000
Operating income..	$ 6,300

Now that we have once again assumed that Kay's fixed expenses are $7,000, her operating leverage factor is as follows:

$$\text{Operating leverage factor} = \frac{\$13,300}{\$6,300}$$
$$= 2.11 \text{ (rounded)}$$

Notice that her operating leverage factor is *higher* (2.11 versus 1) when she has *more* fixed costs ($7,000 versus $0). Kay's operating leverage factor of 2.11 tells us how responsive her income is to changes in volume. Again, a factor is a multiplier, therefore:

- If Kay's volume changes by 1%, her operating income will change by 2.11% (= 1% × a factor of 2.11).
- If Kay's volume changes by 15%, her operating income will change by 31.65% (= 15% × a factor of 2.11).

Managers use the firm's operating leverage factor to determine how vulnerable their operating income is to changes in sales volume—both positive and negative.

Keep the following rule of thumb in mind:

> The larger the operating leverage factor is, the greater the impact a change in sales volume has on operating income. This is true for both increases *and* decreases in volume.

Therefore, companies with higher operating leverage factors are particularly vulnerable to changes in volume. In other words, they have *both* higher risk of incurring losses if volume declines *and* higher potential reward if volume increases. Hoping to capitalize on the reward side, many companies have intentionally increased their operating leverage by lowering their variable costs while at the same time increasing their fixed costs. This strategy works well during periods of economic growth but can be detrimental when sales volume declines.

Choosing a Cost Structure

Managers often have some control over how the company's costs are structured—as fixed, variable, or a combination of the two. For example, let's assume that in addition to selling posters online, Kay has decided to lease a small retail kiosk at the local mall. To keep things simple, let's assume Kay will only be selling her regular-size posters, which sell for $35 each. Let's also assume the mall leasing agent has given Kay the following two options for leasing the space:

- Option 1: Pay $300 per month plus 10% of the sales revenue generated at the kiosk.
- Option 2: Pay $1,000 per month.

Which option should Kay choose? The answer depends on how many posters Kay thinks she will sell from the kiosk each month. As we see above, Option 1 has fewer fixed costs and more variable costs than Option 2. Thus, Kay's operating leverage would be lower under Option 1 than under Option 2. As a result, Option 1 carries less financial risk if sales volume is low, but less financial reward if sales volume is high. But how high must sales volume be to make Option 2 the better choice?

To answer this question Kay will need to figure out her **indifference point**, the point at which she would be indifferent between the two options because they both would result in the same total cost. Once Kay knows the indifference point, she can better judge which option is preferable. Let's see how this is done.

First, Kay calculates the variable and fixed costs associated with each option, as shown in Exhibit 7-12. Notice that Kay does not need to consider any of her other business expenses (such as the cost of the posters themselves or the website maintenance costs), because they will not differ between the two leasing options. In deciding which lease option to take, Kay only needs to consider those costs that are associated with the lease.

EXHIBIT 7-12 Costs Associated with Each Leasing Option

	Option 1	Option 2
Variable cost: 10% of sales revenue (= 10% × $35 per poster)	$ 3.50 per poster	0
Fixed cost:	$ 300	$ 1,000

Next, Kay develops an equation in which she sets the cost of each leasing option equal to the other. She then fills in the appropriate information and solves for number of units:

$$\text{Costs under Option 1} = \text{Costs under Option 2}$$

Variable Costs + Fixed Costs = Variable Costs + Fixed Costs

(# Units × Variable cost per unit) + Fixed Costs = (# Units × Variable cost per unit) + Fixed Costs

(# Units × $3.50) + $300 = (# Units × $0) + $1,000

(# Units × $3.50) = $700

Units = 200

Based on this analysis, Kay will be *indifferent* between the two leasing options if she sells *exactly* 200 posters per month at the kiosk. At a volume of 200 units, she would pay $1,000 for the lease under Option 1 [(200 × $3.50) + $300 = $1,000] and $1,000 for the lease under Option 2. Both options would result in the same cost.

But what if sales volume is lower or higher than 200 posters per month? As shown in Exhibit 7-13, Kay will prefer the lower operating leverage alternative (Option 1) if she sells *fewer* than 200 posters a month. However, she will prefer the higher operating leverage alternative (Option 2) if she sells *more* than 200 posters a month. Her decision will be based on whether she expect sales volume to be lower, or higher, than the indifference point.

EXHIBIT 7-13 Using an Indifference Point to Choose the Most Profitable Cost Structure

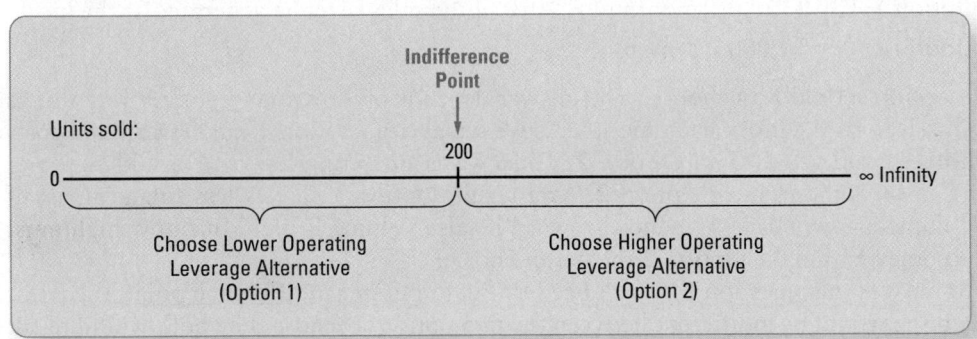

We can verify the conclusion presented in Exhibit 7-13 by calculating the lease costs at *any* volume of sales. First, let's assume that Kay expects to sell 100 posters a month at the kiosk. The lease cost under each option is calculated as follows:

Lease cost under Option 1: $300 + [10% × (100 units × $35 sales price)] = **$650**

Lease cost under Option 2: **$1,000**

As expected, when the sales volume is *lower* than the indifference point, the lease cost is lower under Option 1 than under Option 2.

Next, let's assume Kay expects to sell 500 posters a month. The lease cost is calculated as follows:

Lease cost under Option 1: $300 + [10% × (500 units × $35 sales price)] = **$2,050**

Lease cost under Option 2: **$1,000**

As expected, when the sales volume is *higher* than the indifference point, the lease cost is lower under Option 2 than under Option 1.

The following rule of thumb summarizes the conclusions presented in Exhibit 7-13:

*When faced with a choice between cost structures, choose the **lower** operating leverage option when sales volume is expected to be **lower** than the indifference point. Choose the **higher** operating leverage option when sales volume is expected to be **higher** than the indifference point.*

Managers can use this rule of thumb whenever they are faced with choices about how to structure their costs.

▶ Try It!

Rachel runs her own hot dog stand on the U of A campus. The monthly cost of the cart rental and business permit is currently $300, but she has been given the option of changing the arrangements to $100 plus $0.25 for every unit of product sold from her stand.

1. At what point in sales volume will Rachel be indifferent between the two options?
2. If Rachel typically sells 700 units a month, which option will she prefer?

Please see page 442 for solutions.

In this chapter, we have discussed how managers use the contribution margin and CVP analysis to predict profits, determine the volume needed to achieve breakeven or a target profit, and assess how changes in the business environment affect their profits. In the next chapter, we look at several types of short-term decisions managers must make. Cost behavior and the contribution margin will continue to play an important role in these decisions.

Decision Guidelines

CVP Analysis

Your friend opened an ice cream parlor. But now she's facing changing business conditions. She needs help making the following decisions:

Decision	Guidelines
The cost of ice cream is rising, yet my competitors have lowered their prices. How will these factors affect the sales volume I'll need to breakeven or achieve my target profit?	Increases in variable costs (such as ice cream) and decreases in sales prices both decrease the unit contribution margin and contribution margin ratio. You will have to sell more units in order to achieve breakeven or a target profit. You can use sensitivity analysis to better pinpoint the actual volume you'll need to sell. Simply compute your new unit contribution margin and use it in the shortcut unit contribution margin formula.
Would it help if I could renegotiate my lease with the landlord?	Decreases in fixed costs do not affect the firm's contribution margin. However, a decrease in fixed costs means that the company will have to sell fewer units to achieve breakeven or a target profit. Increases in fixed costs have the opposite effect.
I've been thinking about selling other products in addition to ice cream. Will this affect the sales volume I'll need to earn my target profit?	Your contribution margin ratio will change as a result of changing your sales mix. A company earns more income by selling higher-margin products than by selling an equal number of lower-margin products. If you can shift sales toward higher contribution margin products, you will have to sell fewer units to reach your target profit.
If the economy takes a downturn, how much risk do I face of incurring a loss?	The margin of safety indicates how far sales volume can decline before you would incur a loss: $$\text{Margin of safety} = \text{Expected sales} - \text{Breakeven sales}$$ The operating leverage factor indicates the percentage change in operating income that will occur from a 1% change in volume. It tells you how sensitive your company's operating income is to changes in volume. At a given level of sales, the operating leverage factor is as follows: $$\text{Operating leverage factor} = \frac{\text{Contribution margin}}{\text{Operating income}}$$
If given a choice between alternative cost structures, how do I choose the most profitable one?	Choose the *lower* operating leverage option when sales volume is expected to be *lower* than the indifference point. Choose the *higher* operating leverage option when sales volume is expected to be *higher* than the indifference point.
How do I find the indifference point?	The indifference point is found by setting the total costs of one option equal to the total costs of another option, and then solving for the volume that equates the two options.

SUMMARY PROBLEM 2

Recall from Summary Problem 1 that Fleet Foot buys hiking socks for $6 a pair and sells them for $10. Monthly fixed costs are $10,000 (for sales volumes between 0 and 12,000 pairs), resulting in a breakeven point of 2,500 units. Assume that Fleet Foot has been selling 8,000 pairs of socks per month.

Requirements

1. What is Fleet Foot's current margin of safety in units, in sales dollars, and as a percentage? Explain the results.

2. At this level of sales, what is Fleet Foot's operating leverage factor? If volume declines by 25% due to increasing competition, by what percentage will the company's operating income decline?

3. Competition has forced Fleet Foot to lower its sales price to $9 a pair. How will this affect Fleet's breakeven point?

4. To compensate for the lower sales price, Fleet Foot wants to expand its product line to include men's dress socks. Each pair will sell for $7.00 and cost $2.75 from the supplier. Fixed costs will not change. Fleet expects to sell four pairs of dress socks for every one pair of hiking socks (at its new $9 sales price). What is Fleet's weighted-average contribution margin per unit? Given the 4:1 sales mix, how many of each type of sock will it need to sell to breakeven?

▪ SOLUTIONS

Requirement 1

Margin of safety in units = Expected sales in units − Breakeven sales in units

$$= \quad 8,000 \quad - \quad 2,500$$
$$= \quad 5,500 \text{ units}$$

Margin of safety in dollars = Expected sales in dollars − Breakeven sales in dollars

$$= \quad (8,000 \times \$10) \quad - \quad (2,500 \times \$10)$$
$$= \quad \$55,000$$

$$\text{Margin of safety as a percentage} = \frac{\text{Margin of safety in units}}{\text{Expected sales in units}}$$

$$= \quad \frac{5,500 \text{ pairs}}{8,000 \text{ pairs}}$$
$$= \quad 68.75\%$$

Fleet Foot's margin of safety is quite high. Sales have to fall by more than 5,500 units (or $55,000) before Fleet incurs a loss. Fleet will continue to earn a profit unless sales drop by more than 68.75%.

Requirement 2

At its current level of volume, Fleet's operating income is as follows:

Contribution margin (8,000 pairs × $4 per pair)...............	$ 32,000
Less: Fixed expenses...	10,000
Operating income...	$ 22,000

Fleet's operating leverage factor at this level of sales is computed as follows:

$$\text{Operating leverage factor} = \frac{\text{Contribution margin}}{\text{Operating income}}$$

$$= \frac{\$32,000}{\$22,000}$$

$$= 1.45 \text{ (rounded)}$$

If sales volume declines by 25%, operating income will decline by 36.25% (Fleet's operating leverage factor of 1.45 multiplied by 25%).

Requirement 3

If Fleet drops its sales price to $9 per pair, its contribution margin per pair declines to $3 (sales price of $9 − variable cost of $6). Each sale contributes less toward covering fixed costs. Fleet's new breakeven point *increases* to 3,334 pairs of socks ($10,000 fixed costs ÷ $3 unit contribution margin).

Requirement 4

	A	B	C	D
		Hiking Socks	Dress Socks	Total in "basket"
1	Calculating Weighted-Average Contribution Margin per Unit			
2	Sales price per unit	$ 9.00	$ 7.00	
3	Less: Variable cost per unit	6.00	2.75	
4	Contribution margin per unit	$ 3.00	$ 4.25	
5	Multiply by: Sales mix (number of units in "basket")	1	4	5
6	Contribution margin	$ 3.00	$ 17.00	$ 20.00
7				
8	Weighted-average contribution margin per unit ($20/5 units)			$ 4.00
9				

$$\text{Sales in total units} = \frac{\text{Fixed expenses} + \text{Operating income}}{\text{Weighted-average contribution margin per unit}}$$

$$= \frac{\$10,000 + \$0}{\$4}$$

$$= 2,500 \text{ pairs of socks}$$

Breakeven sales of dress socks (2,500 × 4/5)......................	2,000 pairs dress socks
Breakeven sales of hiking socks (2,500 × 1/5).....................	500 pairs hiking socks

By expanding its product line to include higher-margin dress socks, Fleet is able to decrease its breakeven point back to its original level (2,500 pairs). However, to achieve this breakeven point, Fleet must sell the planned ratio of four pairs of dress socks to every one pair of hiking socks.

END OF CHAPTER

Learning Objectives

- 1 Calculate the unit contribution margin and the contribution margin ratio
- 2 Use CVP analysis to find breakeven points and target profit volumes
- 3 Perform sensitivity analysis in response to changing business conditions
- 4 Find breakeven and target profit volumes for multiproduct companies
- 5 Determine a firm's margin of safety, operating leverage, and most profitable cost structure

Accounting Vocabulary

Breakeven Point. (p. 387) The sales level at which operating income is zero: Total revenues = Total expenses.

Contribution Margin. (p. 385) Sales revenue minus variable expenses.

Contribution Margin Income Statement. (p. 384) An income statement that groups costs by behavior rather than function; it can be used only by internal management.

Contribution Margin Per Unit. (p. 385) The excess of the unit sales price over the variable cost per unit; also called unit contribution margin.

Contribution Margin Ratio. (p. 385) Ratio of contribution margin to sales revenue.

Cost-Volume-Profit (CVP) Analysis. (p. 383) Expresses the relationships among costs, volume, and profit or loss.

Indifference Point. (p. 411) The volume of sales at which a company would be indifferent between alternative cost structures because they would result in the same total cost.

Margin of Safety. (p. 407) Excess of expected sales over breakeven sales; the drop in sales a company can absorb without incurring an operating loss.

Operating Leverage. (p. 408) The relative amount of fixed and variable costs that make up a firm's total costs.

Operating Leverage Factor. (p. 409) At a given level of sales, the contribution margin divided by operating income; the operating leverage factor indicates the percentage change in operating income that will occur from a 1% change in sales volume.

Sales Mix. (p. 384) The combination of products that make up total sales.

Sensitivity Analysis. (p. 398) A "what-if" technique that asks what results will be if actual prices or costs change or if an underlying assumption changes.

Unit Contribution Margin. (p. 385) The excess of the unit sales price over the variable cost per unit: also called contribution margin per unit.

MyAccountingLab Go to http://myaccountinglab.com/ for the following Quick Check, Short Exercises, Exercises, and Problems. They are available with immediate grading, explanations of correct and incorrect answers, and interactive media that acts as your own online tutor.

Quick Check

1. (*Learning Objective 1*) The contribution margin is
   a. Sales revenue minus cost of goods sold
   b. Sales revenue minus fixed expenses
   c. Sales revenue minus operating expenses
   d. Sales revenue minus variable expenses

2. (*Learning Objective 1*) The contribution margin ratio is
   a. Fixed expenses divided by variable expenses
   b. Contribution margin divided by variable expenses
   c. Contribution margin divided by sales revenue
   d. Sales revenue divided by contribution margin

3. (*Learning Objective 2*) The formula to find the breakeven point or a target profit volume in terms of number of units that need to be sold is:
   a. (Fixed expenses + Variable expenses) ÷ Contribution margin per unit
   b. (Fixed expenses + Operating income) ÷ Contribution margin per unit
   c. (Fixed expenses + Variable expenses) ÷ Sales revenue
   d. (Fixed expenses + Operating income) ÷ Sales revenue

4. *(Learning Objective 2)* On a CVP graph, the breakeven point is:

  a. The area between the variable expense line and the fixed expense line

  b. The intersection of the total revenue line and the fixed expense line

  c. The intersection of the total revenue line and the total expense line

  d. The area between the total revenue line and the total expense line

5. *(Learning Objective 3)* All else being equal, if a company's variable expenses increase:

  a. Its contribution margin ratio will decrease

  b. There will be no effect on the breakeven point

  c. Its breakeven point will decrease

  d. Its contribution margin ratio will increase

6. *(Learning Objective 3)* All else being equal, a decrease in a company's fixed expenses will:

  a. Increase the contribution margin

  b. Decrease the contribution margin

  c. Decrease the sales needed to breakeven

  d. Increase the sales needed to breakeven

7. *(Learning Objective 4)* Which of the following is true regarding a company that offers more than one product?

  a. It has one unique breakeven point

  b. The breakeven point is dependent on sales mix assumptions

  c. Breakeven should be found using a simple average contribution margin

  d. Breakeven should be found for each product individually

8. *(Learning Objective 5)* A company with a low operating leverage

  a. Has relatively more fixed costs than variable costs

  b. Has relatively more variable costs than fixed costs

  c. Has an equal proportion of fixed and variable costs

  d. Has relatively more risk than a company with high operating leverage

9. *(Learning Objective 5)* For a given level of sales, a company's operating leverage is defined as

  a. Sales revenue ÷ contribution margin

  b. Operating income ÷ contribution margin

  c. Contribution margin ÷ operating income

  d. Contribution margin ÷ sales

10. *(Learning Objective 5)* Which of the following is false regarding choosing between two cost structures:

  a. The indifference point is the point at which costs under two options are the same

  b. Choose the higher operating leverage option when sales volume is expected to be higher than the indifference point

  c. Choose the lower operating leverage option when sales volume is expected to be lower than the indifference point

  d. The indifference point is the point where total revenues equal total expenses

Quick Check Answers

1. d 2. c 3. b 4. c 5. a 6. c 7. b 8. b 9. c 10. d

Short Exercises

Crystal Cruiseline Data Set used for S7-1 through S7-12:

Crystal Cruiseline offers nightly dinner cruises off the coast of Miami, San Francisco, and Seattle. Dinner cruise tickets sell for $50 per passenger. Crystal Cruiseline's variable cost of providing the dinner is $20 per passenger, and the fixed cost of operating the vessels (depreciation, salaries, docking fees, and other expenses) is $210,000 per month. The company's relevant range extends to 14,000 monthly passengers.

S7-1 Compute unit contribution margin and contribution margin ratio
(Learning Objective 1)

Use the information from the Crystal Cruiseline Data Set to compute the following:

  a. What is the contribution margin per passenger?

  b. What is the contribution margin ratio?

  c. Use the unit contribution margin to project operating income if monthly sales total 11,000 passengers.

  d. Use the contribution margin ratio to project operating income if monthly sales revenue totals $490,000.

S7-2   Project change in income *(Learning Objective 1)*

Use the information from the Crystal Cruiseline Data Set. If Crystal Cruiseline sells an additional 600 tickets, by what amount will its operating income increase (or operating loss decrease)?

S7-3   Find breakeven *(Learning Objective 2)*

Use the information from the Crystal Cruiseline Data Set to compute the number of dinner cruise tickets it must sell to breakeven and the sales dollars needed to breakeven.

S7-4   Find target profit volume *(Learning Objective 2)*

Use the information from the Crystal Cruiseline Data Set. If Crystal Cruiseline has a target operating income of $45,000 per month, how many dinner cruise tickets must the company sell?

S7-5   Prepare a CVP graph *(Learning Objective 2)*

Use the information from the Crystal Cruiseline Data Set. Draw a graph of Crystal Cruiseline's CVP relationships. Include the sales revenue line, the fixed expense line, and the total expense line. Label the axes, the breakeven point, the income area, and the loss area.

S7-6   Interpret a CVP graph *(Learning Objective 2)*

Describe what each letter stands for in the CVP graph.

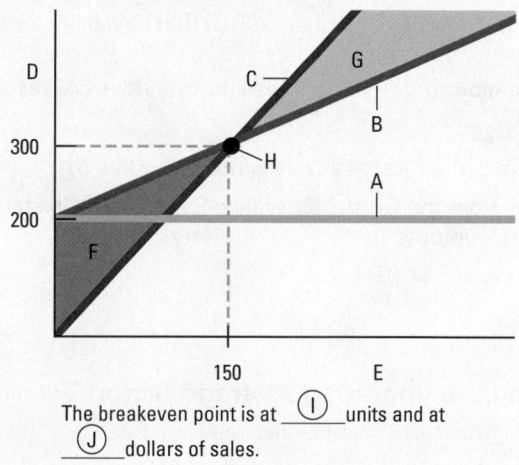

The breakeven point is at ___(I)___ units and at
___(J)___ dollars of sales.

S7-7   Changes in sales price and variable costs *(Learning Objective 3)*

Use the information from the Crystal Cruiseline Data Set.

1. Suppose Crystal Cruiseline cuts its dinner cruise ticket price from $50 to $40 to increase the number of passengers. Compute the new breakeven point in units and in sales dollars. Explain how changes in sales price generally affect the breakeven point.

2. Assume that Crystal Cruiseline does *not* cut the price. Crystal Cruiseline could reduce its variable costs by no longer serving an appetizer before dinner. Suppose this operating change reduces the variable expense from $20 to $10 per passenger. Compute the new breakeven point in units and in dollars. Explain how changes in variable costs generally affect the breakeven point.

S7-8   Changes in fixed costs *(Learning Objective 3)*

Use the information from the Crystal Cruiseline Data Set. Suppose Crystal Cruiseline embarks on a cost reduction drive and slashes fixed expenses from $210,000 per month to $180,000 per month.

1. Compute the new breakeven point in units and in sales dollars.

2. Is the breakeven point higher or lower than in S7-3? Explain how changes in fixed costs generally affect the breakeven point.

S7-9   Compute weighted-average contribution margin *(Learning Objective 4)*

Use the information from the Crystal Cruiseline Data Set. Suppose Crystal Cruiseline decides to offer two types of dinner cruises: regular cruises and executive cruises. The executive cruise includes complimentary cocktails and a five-course dinner on the upper deck. Assume that fixed expenses remain at $210,000 per month and that the following ticket prices and variable expenses apply:

	Regular Cruise	Executive Cruise
Sales price per ticket...	$50	$130
Variable expense per passenger	$20	$ 40

Assuming that Crystal Cruiseline expects to sell four regular cruises for every executive cruise, compute the weighted-average contribution margin per unit. Is it higher or lower than a *simple* average contribution margin? Why? Is it higher or lower than the regular cruise contribution margin calculated in S7-1? Why? Will this new sales mix cause Crystal Cruiseline's breakeven point to increase or decrease from what it was when it sold only regular cruises?

S7-10   Continuation of S7-9: Breakeven *(Learning Objective 4)*

Refer to your answer to S7-9.

a.   Compute the total number of dinner cruises that Crystal Cruiseline must sell to breakeven.

b.   Compute the number of regular cruises and executive cruises the company must sell to breakeven.

S7-11   Compute margin of safety *(Learning Objective 5)*

Use the information from the Crystal Cruiseline Data Set. If Crystal Cruiseline sells 8,750 dinner cruises, compute the margin of safety

a.   in units (dinner cruise tickets).

b.   in sales dollars.

c.   as a percentage of sales.

S7-12   Compute and use operating leverage factor *(Learning Objective 5)*

Use the information from the Crystal Cruiseline Data Set.

a.   Compute the operating leverage factor when Crystal Cruiseline sells 8,750 dinner cruises.

b.   If volume increases by 10%, by what percentage will operating income increase?

c.   If volume decreases by 5%, by what percentage will operating income decrease?

S7-13   Compute margin of safety *(Learning Objective 5)*

Sally has an online poster business. Suppose Sally expects to sell 1,500 posters. Her average sales price per poster is $45 and her average cost per poster is $25. Her fixed expenses total $15,000. Compute her margin of safety

a.   in units (posters).

b.   in sales dollars.

c.   as a percentage of expected sales.

S7-14   Compute and use operating leverage factor *(Learning Objective 5)*

Suppose Sally sells 1,500 posters. Use the original data from S7-13 to compute her operating leverage factor. If sales volume increases 20%, by what percentage will her operating income change? Prove your answer.

S7-15 Calculating total costs under two different scenarios *(Learning Objective 5)*

The Tasty Treats Factory plans to open a new retail store in Medina, Ohio. The Tasty Treats Factory will sell specialty cupcakes for $6 per cupcake (each cupcake has a variable cost of $4.) The company is negotiating its lease for the new Medina location. The landlord has offered two leasing options: 1) a lease of $2,600 per month; or 2) a monthly lease cost of $1,700 plus 5% of the company's monthly sales revenue.

Requirements

1. If the Tasty Treats Factory plans to sell 2,200 cupcakes a month, which lease option would cost less each month? Why?
2. If the company plans to sell 4,500 cupcakes a month, which lease option would be more attractive? Why?

S7-16 Identify ethical standards violated *(Learning Objectives 1, 2, 3, 4, & 5)*

ETHICS

For each of the situations listed, identify the primary standard from the IMA Statement of Ethical Professional Practice that is violated (competence, confidentiality, integrity, or credibility.) Refer to Exhibit 1-6 for the complete standard.

1. Cedric and Marc work at the same company. Cedric, the manager of a production department, buys lunch for Marc, who works in Accounting. Marc is preparing the monthly projections for the various production departments and Cedric wants Marc to be conservative in his estimates of variable costs so that Cedric is more likely to obtain funding for an upcoming project.
2. Tomas' company has signed him up for outside training on operating leverage and cost structures. Tomas decides to skip the training, figuring that he already does his job well and does not need continuing education.
3. Heather provides reports to key decision makers based on CVP assumptions despite knowing that the decision makers are looking at situations that would be outside of the company's current relevant range.
4. Kara works in Accounting at a chain of car dealerships. Her best friend, Nikki, is looking for a new car. Kara shares the actual dealer variable cost of the model with Nikki so that Nikki can negotiate a better deal.
5. Gayle is an accountant for BuySmart, a cooperative grocery chain. Gayle prepares internal reports with the breakeven volumes for each division listed. She does not explain (or provide disclosure) that the breakeven numbers listed are based on the sales mix from the past year even though the sales mix is expected to change this year. If the sales mix during the current year were to change, breakeven volumes would be significantly impacted.

EXERCISES Group A

E7-17A   Prepare contribution margin income statements (Learning Objective 1)

Global Travel uses the contribution margin income statement internally. Global's first-quarter results are as follows:

	A	B	C	D
1	Global Travel			
2	Contribution Margin Income Statement			
3	Three Months Ended March 31			
4				
5	Sales revenue	$ 400,000		
6	Less: Variable expenses	120,000		
7	Contribution margin	$ 280,000		
8	Less: Fixed expenses	170,800		
9	Operating income	$ 109,200		
10				

Global's relevant range is sales of between $135,000 and $675,000.

Requirements

1. Prepare contribution margin income statements at sales levels of $270,000 and $410,000. (*Hint:* Use the contribution margin ratio.)
2. Compute breakeven sales in dollars.

E7-18A   Work backward to find missing information (Learning Objectives 1 & 2)

Anderson Dry Cleaners has determined the following about its costs: Total variable expenses are $42,000, total fixed expenses are $24,000, and the sales revenue needed to breakeven is $48,000. Determine the company's current 1) sales revenue and 2) operating income. (*Hint:* First, find the contribution margin ratio; then prepare the contribution margin income statement.)

E7-19A   Find breakeven and target profit volume (Learning Objectives 1 & 2)

Sport Ready produces sports socks. The company has fixed expenses of $90,000 and variable expenses of $0.90 per package. Each package sells for $1.80.

Requirements

1. Compute the contribution margin per package and the contribution margin ratio.
2. Find the breakeven point in units and in dollars.
3. Find the number of packages Sport Ready needs to sell to earn an $18,000 operating income.

E7-20A   Continuation of E7-19A: Changing costs (Learning Objective 3)

Refer to Sport Ready in E7-19A. If the company can decrease its variable costs to $0.80 per package by increasing its fixed costs to $105,000, how many packages will it have to sell to generate $18,000 of operating income? Is this more or less than before? Why?

E7-21A   Find breakeven and target profit volume (Learning Objectives 1 & 2)

Owner Li Soo is considering franchising her Happy Noodles restaurant concept. She believes people will pay $5.25 for a large bowl of noodles. Variable costs are $2.10 a bowl. Soo estimates monthly fixed costs for franchisees at $7,500.

Requirements

1. Find a franchisee's breakeven sales in dollars.
2. Is franchising a good idea for Soo if franchisees want a minimum monthly operating income of $7,050 and Soo believes that most locations could generate $25,000 in monthly sales?

E7-22A Continuation of E7-21A: Changing business conditions
(Learning Objective 3)

Refer to Happy Noodles in E7-21A. Soo did franchise her restaurant concept. Because of Happy Noodles' success, Value Noodles has come on the scene as a competitor. To maintain its market share, Happy Noodles will have to lower its sales price to $4.75 per bowl. At the same time, Happy Noodles hopes to increase each restaurant's volume to 7,000 bowls per month by embarking on a marketing campaign. Each franchise will have to contribute $600 per month to cover the advertising costs. Prior to these changes, most locations were selling 6,500 bowls per month.

Requirements

1. What was the average restaurant's operating income before these changes?
2. Assuming that the price cut and advertising campaign are successful at increasing volume to the projected level, will the franchisees still earn their target profit of $7,050 per month? Show your calculations.

E7-23A Compute breakeven and project income *(Learning Objectives 1 & 2)*

Grover's Steel Parts produces parts for the automobile industry. The company has monthly fixed expenses of $630,000 and a contribution margin of 70% of revenues.

Requirements

1. Compute Grover's Steel Parts' monthly breakeven sales in dollars.
2. Use the contribution margin ratio to project operating income (or loss) if revenues are $520,000 and if they are $1,010,000.
3. Do the results in Requirement 2 make sense given the breakeven sales you computed in Requirement 1? Explain.

E7-24A Continuation of E7-23A: Changing business conditions
(Learning Objective 3)

Refer to Grover's Steel Parts in E7-23A. Grover feels like he's in a giant squeeze play: The automotive manufacturers are demanding lower prices, and the steel producers have increased raw material costs. Grover's contribution margin has shrunk to 40% of revenues. The company's monthly operating income, prior to these pressures, was $77,000.

Requirements

1. To maintain this same level of profit, what sales volume (in sales revenue) must Grover now achieve?
2. Grover believes that his monthly sales revenue will go only as high as $1,010,000. He is thinking about moving operations overseas to cut fixed costs. If monthly sales are $1,010,000, by how much will he need to cut fixed costs to maintain his prior profit level of $77,000 per month?

E7-25A Sustainability and CVP concepts *(Learning Objective 3)*

SUSTAINABILITY

Keller Garage Doors manufactures a premium garage door. Currently, the price and cost data associated with the premium garage door is as follows:

Average selling price per premium garage door	$ 2,400
Average variable manufacturing cost per door	$ 1,000
Average variable selling cost per door	$ 200
Total annual fixed costs	$240,000

Keller Garage Doors has undertaken several sustainability projects over the past few years. Management is currently evaluating whether to develop a comprehensive software control system for its manufacturing operations that would significantly reduce scrap and waste generated during the manufacturing process. If the company were to implement this software control system in its manufacturing operations, the use of the software control system would result in an increase of $120,000 in its annual fixed costs while the average variable manufacturing cost per door would drop by $240.

Requirements

1. What is the company's current breakeven in units and in dollars?
2. If the company expects to sell 410 premium garage doors in the upcoming year, and it does not develop the software control system, what is its expected operating income from premium garage doors?
3. If the software control system were to be developed and implemented, what would be the company's new breakeven point in units and in dollars?
4. If the company expects to sell 410 premium garage doors in the upcoming year, and it develops the software control system, what is its expected operating income from premium garage doors?
5. If the company expects to sell 410 premium garage doors in the upcoming year, do you think the company should implement the software control system? Why or why not? What factors should the company consider?

E7-26A Work backward to find new breakeven point (Learning Objectives 2 & 3)

Kahlo Industries is planning on purchasing a new piece of equipment that will increase the quality of its production. It hopes the increased quality will generate more sales. The company's contribution margin ratio is 20%, and its current breakeven point is $350,000 in sales revenue. If the company's fixed expenses increase by $55,000 due to the equipment, what will its new breakeven point be (in sales revenue)?

E7-27A Find consequence of rising fixed costs (Learning Objectives 1 & 3)

Susie Carter sells homemade knit scarves for $24 each at local craft shows. Her contribution margin ratio is 62.5%. Currently, the craft show entrance fees cost Susie $1,200 per year. The craft shows are raising their entrance fees by 10% next year. How many *extra* scarves will Susie have to sell next year just to pay for rising entrance fee costs?

E7-28A Extension of E7-27A: Multiproduct firm (Learning Objective 4)

Danny Carter admired his wife's success at selling scarves at local craft shows (E7-27A), so he decided to make two types of plant stands to sell at the shows. Danny makes twig stands out of downed wood from his backyard and the yards of his neighbors, so his variable cost is minimal (wood screws, glue, and so forth). However, Danny has to purchase wood to make his oak plant stands. His unit prices and costs are as follows:

	Twig Stands	Oak Stands
Sales price	$15.00	$35.00
Variable cost	$ 2.50	$10.00

The twig stands are more popular, so Danny sells four twig stands for every one oak stand. Susie charges her husband $300 to share her booth at the craft shows (after all, she has paid the entrance fees). How many of each plant stand does Danny need to sell to breakeven? Will this affect the number of scarves Susie needs to sell to breakeven? Explain.

E7-29A Find breakeven for a multiproduct firm (Learning Objective 4)

Rapid Scooters plans to sell a motorized standard scooter for $60 and a motorized chrome scooter for $75. Rapid Scooters purchases the standard scooter for $45 and the chrome scooter for $55. Rapid Scooters expects to sell two chrome scooters for every three standard scooters. The company's monthly fixed expenses are $18,700. How many of each type of scooter must Rapid Scooters sell monthly to breakeven? To earn $13,600?

E7-30A Work backward to find missing data (Learning Objective 4)

Bradley Manufacturing manufactures two styles of watches—the Digital and the Classic. The following data pertain to the Digital:

Variable manufacturing cost	$125
Variable operating cost	$ 35
Sale price	$225

Bradley's monthly fixed expenses total $195,000. When Digitals and Classics are sold in the mix of 7:3, respectively, the sale of 2,100 total watches results in an operating income of $36,000. Compute the contribution margin per watch for the Classic.

E7-31A Breakeven and an advertising decision at a multiproduct company
(Learning Objectives 3, 4, & 5)

Ullie Medical Supply is a retailer of home medical equipment. Last year, Ullie's sales revenues totaled $6,800,000. Total expenses were $2,600,000. Of this amount, approximately $1,088,000 were variable, while the remainder were fixed. Since Ullie's offers thousands of different products, its managers prefer to calculate the breakeven point in terms of sales dollars rather than units.

Requirements

1. What is Ullie's current operating income?
2. What is Ullie's contribution margin ratio?
3. What is the company's breakeven point in sales dollars? (Hint: The contribution margin ratio calculated in Requirement 2 is already weighted by the company's actual sales mix.)
4. Ullie's top management is deciding whether to embark on a $250,000 advertising campaign. The marketing firm has projected annual sales volume to increase by 14% as a result of this campaign. Assuming that the projections are correct, what effect would this advertising campaign have on the company's annual operating income?

E7-32A Compute margin of safety and operating leverage (Learning Objective 5)

Victor's Repair Shop has a monthly target operating income of $20,000. Variable expenses are 60% of sales, and monthly fixed expenses are $12,000.

Requirements

1. Compute the monthly margin of safety in dollars if the shop achieves its income goal.
2. Express Victor's margin of safety as a percentage of target sales.
3. What is Victor's operating leverage factor at the target level of operating income?
4. Assume that the company reaches its target. By what percentage will the company's operating income fall if sales volume declines by 12%?

E7-33A Use operating leverage factor to find fixed costs (Learning Objective 5)

Popley Manufacturing had a 1.40 operating leverage factor when sales were $60,000. Popley Manufacturing's contribution margin ratio was 35%. What were the company's fixed expenses?

E7-34A Calculating total costs under two different scenarios
(Learning Objective 5)

The Soft Glow Company plans to open a new retail store in Portland, Maine. The Soft Glow Company will sell specialty candles for an average of $30 each. The average variable costs per candle are as follows:

- Wax $6
- Other additives $3
- Base $3

The company is negotiating its lease for the new location. The landlord has offered two leasing options:
　　Option A) a lease of $3,000 per month; or
　　Option B) a monthly lease cost of $1,650 plus 10% of the company's monthly sales revenue.
The company expects to sell approximately 250 candles per month.

Requirements

1. Which lease option is more attractive for the company under its current sales expectations? Calculate the total lease cost under:

   - Option A
   - Option B

2. At what level of sales (in units) would the company be indifferent between the two lease options? Show your proof.

3. If the company's expected sales were 600 candles instead of the projection listed in the exercise, which lease options would be more favorable for the company? Why?

E7-35A Comprehensive CVP analysis (*Learning Objectives 1, 2, 3, 4, & 5*)

Gary McKnight is evaluating a business opportunity to sell grooming kits at dog shows. Gary can buy the grooming kits at a wholesale cost of $32 per set. He plans to sell the grooming kits for $62 per set. He estimates fixed costs such as travel costs, booth rental cost, and lodging to be $600 per dog show.

Requirements

1. Determine the number of grooming kits Gary must sell per show to breakeven.
2. Assume Gary wants to earn a profit of $900 per show.
   a. Determine the sales volume in units necessary to earn the desired profit.
   b. Determine the sales volume in dollars necessary to earn the desired profit.
   c. Using the contribution margin format, prepare an income statement (condensed version) to confirm your answers to parts a and b.
3. Determine the margin of safety between the sales volume at the breakeven point and the sales volume required to earn the desired profit. Determine the margin of safety in both sales dollars, units, and as a percentage.

E7-36A Comprehensive CVP analysis (*Learning Objectives 1, 2, 3, 4, & 5*)

Bowerston Company manufactures and sells a single product. The company's sales and expenses for last year follow:

	Total	Per Unit	%
Sales	$81,250	$25	?
Variable expenses	48,750	15	?
Contribution margin	?	?	?
Fixed expenses	13,000		
Operating income	$19,500		

Requirements

1. Fill in the missing numbers in the preceding table. Use the table to answer the following questions:
   a. What is the total contribution margin?
   b. What is the per unit contribution margin?
   c. What is the operating income?
   d. How many units were sold?
2. Answer the following questions about breakeven analysis:
   a. What is the breakeven point in units?
   b. What is the breakeven point in sales dollars?
3. Answer the following questions about target profit analysis and safety margin:
   a. How many units must the company sell in order to earn a profit of $53,000?
   b. What is the margin of safety in units?
   c. What is the margin of safety in sales dollars?
   d. What is the margin of safety in percentage?

E7-37A Comprehensive CVP analysis *(Learning Objectives 1, 2, 3, 4, & 5)*

Flash Manufacturing manufactures 16 GB flash drives (jump drives). Price and cost data for a relevant range extending to 200,000 units per month are as follows:

Sales price per unit (current monthly sales volume is 140,000 units)..................	$ 25.00
Variable costs per unit:	
Direct materials..	$ 7.30
Direct labor..	$ 6.00
Variable manufacturing overhead..	$ 2.60
Variable selling and administrative expenses..	$ 2.10
Monthly fixed expenses:	
Fixed manufacturing overhead..	$292,000
Fixed selling and administrative expenses..	$447,200

Requirements

1. What is the company's contribution margin per unit? Contribution margin percentage? Total contribution margin?
2. What would the company's monthly operating income be if the company sold 170,000 units?
3. What would the company's monthly operating income be if the company had sales of $4,500,000?
4. What is the breakeven point in units? In sales dollars?
5. How many units would the company have to sell to earn a target monthly profit of $269,500?
6. Management is currently in contract negotiations with the labor union. If the negotiations fail, direct labor costs will increase by 10% and fixed costs will increase by $24,000 per month. If these costs increase, how many units will the company have to sell each month to breakeven?
7. Return to the original data for this question and the rest of the questions. What is the company's current operating leverage factor (round to two decimals)?
8. If sales volume increases by 8%, by what percentage will operating income increase?
9. What is the company's current margin of safety in sales dollars? What is its margin of safety as a percentage of sales?
10. Say the company adds a second line of flash drives (32 GB in addition to 16 GB). A unit of the 32 GB flash drives will sell for $50 and have variable cost per unit of $22 per unit. The expected sales mix is six of the small flash drives (16 GB) for every one large flash drive (32 GB). Given this sales mix, how many of each type of flash drive will the company need to sell to reach its target monthly profit of $269,500? Is this volume higher or lower than previously needed (in Question 5) to achieve the same target profit? Why?

EXERCISES Group B

E7-38B Prepare contribution margin income statements (Learning Objective 1)

Aussie Travel uses the contribution margin income statement internally. Aussie's second quarter results are as follows:

	A	B	C	D
1	Aussie Travel			
2	Contribution Margin Income Statement			
3	Three Months Ended June 30			
4				
5	Sales revenue	$ 550,000		
6	Less: Variable expenses	192,500		
7	Contribution margin	$ 357,500		
8	Less: Fixed expenses	176,800		
9	Operating income	$ 180,700		
10				

Aussie's relevant range is sales of between $115,000 and $680,000.

Requirements

1. Prepare contribution margin income statements at sales levels of $190,000 and $420,000. (*Hint:* Use the contribution margin ratio.)
2. Compute breakeven sales in dollars.

E7-39B Work backward to find missing information (Learning Objectives 1 & 2)

Stancil's Dry Cleaners has determined the following about its costs: Total variable expenses are $45,000, total fixed expenses are $30,000, and the sales revenue needed to breakeven is $40,000. Determine Stancil's current 1) sales revenue and 2) operating income. (*Hint:* First, find the contribution margin ratio; then prepare the contribution margin income statement.)

E7-40B Find breakeven and target profit volume (Learning Objectives 1 & 2)

Hang Ten produces sports socks. The company has fixed expenses of $80,000 and variable expenses of $0.80 per package. Each package sells for $1.60.

Requirements

1. Compute the contribution margin per package and the contribution margin ratio.
2. Find the breakeven point in units and in dollars.
3. Find the number of packages that Hang Ten needs to sell to earn a $25,000 operating income.

E7-41B Continuation of E7-40B: Changing costs (Learning Objective 3)

Refer to Hang Ten in E7-40B. If Hang Ten can decrease its variable costs to $0.60 per package by increasing its fixed costs to $95,000, how many packages will it have to sell to generate $25,000 of operating income? Is this more or less than before? Why?

E7-42B Find breakeven and target profit volume (Learning Objectives 1 & 2)

Owner Kay Fay is considering franchising her Noodles Galore restaurant concept. She believes people will pay $6.25 for a large bowl of noodles. Variable costs are $2.50 a bowl. Fay estimates monthly fixed costs for franchisees at $8,250.

Requirements

1. Find a franchisee's breakeven sales in dollars.
2. Is franchising a good idea for Fay if franchisees want a minimum monthly operating income of $6,600 and Fay believes most locations could generate $24,000 in monthly sales?

E7-43B   Continuation of E7-42B: Changing business conditions
(Learning Objective 3)

Refer to Noodles Galore in E7-42B. Since franchising Noodles Galore, the restaurant has not been very successful due to Noodles Unlimited coming on the scene as a competitor. To increase its market share, Noodles Galore will have to lower its sales price to $5.75 per bowl. At the same time, Noodles Galore hopes to increase each restaurant's volume to 6,000 bowls per month by embarking on a marketing campaign. Each franchise will have to contribute $500 per month to cover the advertising costs. Prior to these changes, most locations were selling 5,500 bowls per month.

Requirements

1. What was the average restaurant's operating income before these changes?
2. Assuming the price cut and advertising campaign are successful at increasing volume to the projected level, will the franchisees earn their target profit of $6,600 per month?

E7-44B   Compute breakeven and project income *(Learning Objectives 1 & 2)*

William's Steel Parts produces parts for the automobile industry. The company has monthly fixed expenses of $620,000 and a contribution margin of 80% of revenues.

Requirements

1. Compute William's Steel Parts' monthly breakeven sales in dollars.
2. Project operating income (or loss) if revenues are $520,000 and if they are $1,020,000.
3. Do the results in Requirement 2 make sense given the breakeven sales you computed in Requirement 1? Explain.

E7-45B   Continuation of E7-44B: Changing business conditions
(Learning Objective 3)

Refer to William's Steel Parts in E7-44B. William feels like he's in a giant squeeze play: The automotive manufacturers are demanding lower prices, and the steel producers have increased raw material costs. William's contribution margin has shrunk to 50% of revenues. William's monthly operating income, prior to these pressures, was $196,000.

Requirements

1. To maintain this same level of profit, what sales volume (in sales revenue) must William now achieve?
2. William believes that his monthly sales revenue will only go as high as $1,020,000. He is thinking about moving operations overseas to cut fixed costs. If monthly sales are $1,020,000, by how much will he need to cut fixed costs to maintain his prior profit level of $196,000 per month?

E7-46B   Sustainability and CVP *(Learning Objective 3)*

SUSTAINABILITY

Kenmore Garage Doors manufactures a premium garage door. Currently, the price and cost data associated with the premium garage door is as follows:

Average selling price per premium garage door...	$ 2,100
Average variable manufacturing cost per door	$ 520
Average variable selling cost per door	$ 110
Total annual fixed costs..	$294,000

Kenmore Garage Doors has undertaken several sustainability projects over the past few years. Management is currently evaluating whether to develop a comprehensive software control system for its manufacturing operations that would significantly reduce scrap and waste generated during the manufacturing process. If the company were to implement this software control system in its manufacturing operations, the use of the software control system would result in an increase of $126,000 in its annual fixed costs while the average variable manufacturing cost per door would drop by $210.

Requirements

1. What is the company's current breakeven in units and in dollars?
2. If the company expects to sell 290 premium garage doors in the upcoming year, and it does not develop the software control system, what is its expected operating income from premium garage doors?
3. If the software control system were to be developed and implemented, what would be the company's new breakeven point in units and in dollars?
4. If the company expects to sell 290 premium garage doors in the upcoming year, and it develops the software control system, what is its expected operating income from premium garage doors?
5. If the company expects to sell 290 premium garage doors in the upcoming year, do you think the company should implement the software control system? Why or why not? What factors should the company consider?

E7-47B   Work backward to find new breakeven point *(Learning Objectives 2 & 3)*

Flow Industries is planning on purchasing a new piece of equipment that will increase the quality of its production. It hopes the increased quality will generate more sales. The company's contribution margin ratio is 50%, and its current breakeven point is $500,000 in sales revenue. If Flow Industries' fixed expenses increase by $50,000 due to the equipment, what will its new breakeven point be (in sales revenue)?

E7-48B   Find consequence of rising fixed costs *(Learning Objectives 1 & 3)*

Gabby Kittson sells homemade knit scarves for $14 each at local craft shows. Her contribution margin ratio is 62.5%. Currently, the craft show entrance fees cost Gabby $1,400 per year. The craft shows are raising their entrance fees by 25% next year. How many *extra* scarves will Gabby have to sell next year just to pay for rising entrance fee costs?

E7-49B   Extension of E7-48B: Multiproduct firm *(Learning Objective 4)*

Martin Kittson admired his wife's success at selling scarves at local craft shows (E7-48B), so he decided to make two types of plant stands to sell at the shows. Martin makes twig stands out of downed wood from his backyard and the yards of his neighbors, so his variable cost is minimal (wood screws, glue, and so forth). However, Martin has to purchase wood to make his oak plant stands. His unit prices and costs are as follows.

	Twig Stands	Oak Stands
Sales price	$18.00	$38.00
Variable cost	$ 3.00	$ 8.00

The twig stands are more popular so Martin sells four twig stands for every one oak stand. Gabby charges her husband $360 to share her booths at the craft shows (after all, she has paid the entrance fees). How many of each plant stand does Martin need to sell to breakeven? Will this affect the number of scarves Gabby needs to sell to breakeven? Explain.

E7-50B   Find breakeven for a multiproduct firm *(Learning Objective 4)*

Peppy Scooters plans to sell a motorized standard scooter for $65 and a motorized chrome scooter for $85. Peppy Scooters purchases the standard scooter for $55 and the chrome scooter for $65. Peppy Scooters expects to sell two chrome scooters for every three standard scooters. The company's monthly fixed expenses are $9,800. How many of each type of scooter must the company sell monthly to breakeven? To earn $8,400?

E7-51B   Work backward to find missing data *(Learning Objective 4)*

Henry Timepieces manufactures two styles of watches—the Digital and the Classic. The following data pertain to the Digital:

Variable manufacturing cost	$120
Variable operating cost	$ 50
Sale price	$250

The company's monthly fixed expenses total $200,000. When Digitals and Classics are sold in the mix of 8:2, respectively, the sale of 2,200 total watches results in an operating income of $75,000. Compute the contribution margin per watch for the Classic.

E7-52B   Breakeven and an advertising decision at a multiproduct company
(Learning Objectives 3, 4, & 5)

Terry Medical Supplies is a retailer of home medical equipment. Last year, Terry's sales revenues totaled $6,100,000. Total expenses were $2,590,000. Of this amount, approximately $1,342,000 were variable, while the remainder were fixed. Since Terry offers thousands of different products, its managers prefer to calculate the breakeven point in terms of sales dollars, rather than units.

Requirements

1. What is Terry's current operating income?
2. What is Terry's contribution margin ratio?
3. What is the company breakeven point in sales dollars? (*Hint:* The contribution margin ratio calculated in Requirement 2 is already weighted by the company's actual sales mix.) What does it mean?
4. Top management is deciding whether to embark on a $260,000 advertising campaign. The marketing firm has projected annual sales volume to increase by 16% as a result of this campaign. Assuming that the projections are correct, what effect would this advertising campaign have on Terry's annual operating income?

E7-53B   Compute margin of safety and operating leverage *(Learning Objective 5)*

Tom's Repair Shop has a monthly target operating income of $30,000. *Variable expenses are 40% of sales,* and monthly fixed expenses are $7,500.

Requirements

1. Compute the monthly margin of safety in dollars if the shop achieves its income goal.
2. Express Tom's margin of safety as a percentage of target sales.
3. What is Tom's operating leverage factor at the target level of operating income?
4. Assume that the company reaches its target. By what percentage will the company's operating income fall if sales volume declines by 12%?

E7-54B   Use operating leverage factor to find fixed costs *(Learning Objective 5)*

Hupley Manufacturing had a 1.60 operating leverage factor when sales were $45,000. Hupley Manufacturing's contribution margin ratio was 20%. What were the company's fixed expenses?

E7-55B   Calculating total costs under two different scenarios
(Learning Objectives 5)

The Candle Factory plans to open a new retail store in Mahtomedi, Minnesota. The store will sell specialty candles for an average of $45 each. The average variable costs per candle are as follows:

- Wax $10
- Other additives $4
- Base $2

The company is negotiating its lease for the new location. The landlord has offered two leasing options:

Option A) a lease of $3,600 per month; or
Option B) a monthly lease cost of $990 plus 20% of the company's monthly sales revenue.

The company expects to sell approximately 190 candles per month.

Requirements

1. Which lease option is more attractive for the company under its current sales expectations? Calculate the total lease cost under:
   a. Option A
   b. Option B
2. At what level of sales (in units) would the company be indifferent between the two lease options? Show your proof.
3. If the company's expected sales were 490 candles instead of the projection listed in the exercise, which lease option would be more favorable for the company? Why?

E7-56B Comprehensive CVP analysis *(Learning Objectives 1, 2, 3, 4, & 5)*

Andrew Gutierrez is evaluating a business opportunity to sell grooming kits at dog shows. Andrew can buy the grooming kits at a wholesale cost of $33 per set. He plans to sell the grooming kits for $73 per set. He estimates fixed costs such as travel costs, booth rental cost, and lodging to be $720 per dog show.

Requirements

1. Determine the number of grooming kits Andrew must sell per show to breakeven.
2. Assume Andrew wants to earn a profit of $1,080 per show.
   a. Determine the sales volume in units necessary to earn the desired profit.
   b. Determine the sales volume in dollars necessary to earn the desired profit.
   c. Using the contribution margin format, prepare an income statement (condensed version) to confirm your answers to parts a and b.
3. Determine the margin of safety between the sales volume at the breakeven point and the sales volume required to earn the desired profit. Determine the margin of safety in both sales dollars, units, and as a percentage.

E7-57B Comprehensive CVP analysis *(Learning Objectives 1, 2, 3, 4, & 5)*

Juda Company manufactures and sells a single product. The company's sales and expenses for last year follow:

	Total	Per Unit	%
Sales	$115,000	$50	?
Variable expenses...	57,500	25	?
Contribution margin...	?	?	?
Fixed expenses..	11,500		
Operating income	$ 46,000		

Requirements

1. Fill in the missing numbers in the table. Use the table to answer the following questions:
   a. What is the total contribution margin?
   b. What is the per unit contribution margin?
   c. What is the operating income?
   d. How many units were sold?
2. Answer the following questions about breakeven analysis:
   a. What is the breakeven point in units?
   b. What is the breakeven point in sales dollars?
3. Answer the following questions about target profit analysis and safety margin:
   a. How many units must the company sell in order to earn a profit of $58,000?
   b. What is the margin of safety in units?
   c. What is the margin of safety in sales dollars?
   d. What is the margin of safety in percentage?

E7-58B Comprehensive CVP analysis *(Learning Objectives 1, 2, 3, 4, & 5)*

General Manufacturing manufactures 16 GB flash drives (jump drives). Price and cost data for a relevant range extending to 200,000 units per month are as follows:

Sales price per unit	
(current monthly sales volume is 100,000 units)	$ 25.00
Variable costs per unit:	
Direct materials...	$ 8.40
Direct labor...	$ 8.00
Variable manufacturing overhead..	$ 3.70
Variable selling and administrative expenses....................................	$ 1.90
Monthly fixed expenses:	
Fixed manufacturing overhead..	$121,800
Fixed selling and administrative expenses.......................................	$167,100

Requirements

1. What is the company's contribution margin per unit? Contribution margin percentage? Total contribution margin?
2. What would the company's monthly operating income be if it sold 130,000 units?
3. What would the company's monthly operating income be if it had sales of $4,000,000?
4. What is the breakeven point in units? In sales dollars?
5. How many units would the company have to sell to earn a target monthly profit of $260,100?
6. Management is currently in contract negotiations with the labor union. If the negotiations fail, direct labor costs will increase by 10% and fixed costs will increase by $23,500 per month. If these costs increase, how many units will the company have to sell each month to breakeven?
7. Return to the original data for this question and the rest of the questions. What is the company's current operating leverage factor (round to two decimal places)?
8. If sales volume increases by 3%, by what percentage will operating income increase?
9. What is the firm's current margin of safety in sales dollars? What is its margin of safety as a percentage of sales?
10. Say General Manufacturing adds a second line of flash drives (32 GB in addition to 16 GB). A unit of the 32 GB flash drives will sell for $50 and have variable cost per unit of $27 per unit. The expected sales mix is nine of the smaller flash drives (16 GB) for every one larger flash drive (32 GB). Given this sales mix, how many of each type of flash drive will General need to sell to reach its target monthly profit of $260,100? Is this volume higher or lower than previously needed (in Question 5) to achieve the same target profit? Why?

PROBLEMS Group A

P7-59A   Find missing data in CVP relationships *(Learning Objectives 1 & 2)*

The budgets of four companies yield the following information:

	Company			
	Q	R	S	T
Target sales....................................	$625,000	$445,000	$236,000	$
Variable expenses.............................	125,000			156,000
Fixed expenses.................................		$159,000	$ 94,000	
Operating income (loss).................	$130,000	$	$	$131,000
Units sold...		106,800	12,500	16,000
Contribution margin per unit..........	$ 6.25	$	$ 9.44	$ 39.00
Contribution margin ratio		0.60		

Requirements

1. Fill in the blanks for each company.
2. Compute breakeven, in sales dollars, for each company. Which company has the lowest breakeven point in sales dollars? What causes the low breakeven point?

P7-60A   Find breakeven and target profit and prepare income statements *(Learning Objectives 1 & 2)*

A traveling production of Fiddler on the Roof performs each year. The average show sells 1,200 tickets at $55 a ticket. There are 115 shows each year. The show has a cast of 60, each earning an average of $320 per show. The cast is paid only after each show. The other variable expense is program printing costs of $9 per guest. Annual fixed expenses total $1,224,000.

Requirements

1. Compute revenue and variable expenses for each show.
2. Use the income statement equation approach to compute the number of shows needed annually to breakeven.
3. Use the shortcut unit contribution margin approach to compute the number of shows needed annually to earn a profit of $3,888,000. Is this goal realistic? Give your reason.
4. Prepare Fiddler on the Roof's contribution margin income statement for 115 shows each year. Report only two categories of expenses: variable and fixed.

P7-61A   Comprehensive CVP problem *(Learning Objectives 1, 2, & 5)*

Team Spirit Calendars imprints calendars with college names. The company has fixed expenses of $1,095,000 each month plus variable expenses of $6.50 per carton of calendars. Of the variable expense, 68% is cost of goods sold, while the remaining 32% relates to variable operating expenses. The company sells each carton of calendars for $16.50.

Requirements

1. Compute the number of cartons of calendars that Team Spirit Calendars must sell each month to breakeven.
2. Compute the dollar amount of monthly sales that the company needs in order to earn $308,000 in operating income (round the contribution margin ratio to two decimal places).
3. Prepare the company's contribution margin income statement for June for sales of 450,000 cartons of calendars.

4. What is June's margin of safety (in dollars)? What is the operating leverage factor at this level of sales?

5. By what percentage will operating income change if July's sales volume is 16% higher? Prove your answer.

P7-62A   Compute breakeven, prepare CVP graph, and respond to change
(Learning Objectives 1, 2, & 3)

Market Time Investors is opening an office in Green Bay, Wisconsin. Fixed monthly expenses are office rent ($2,700), depreciation on office furniture ($280), utilities ($250), special telephone lines ($600), a connection with an online brokerage service ($650), and the salary of a financial planner ($4,520). Variable expenses include payments to the financial planner (12% of revenue), advertising (4% of revenue), supplies and postage (3% of revenue), and usage fees for the telephone lines and computerized brokerage service (6% of revenue).

Requirements

1. Compute the investment firm's breakeven revenue in dollars. If the average trade leads to $500 in revenue for Market Time, how many trades must it make to breakeven?

2. Compute dollar revenues needed to earn monthly operating income of $5,250.

3. Graph Market Time's CVP relationships. Assume that an average trade leads to $500 in revenue for the firm. Show the breakeven point, sales revenue line, fixed expense line, total expense line, operating loss area, operating income area, and sales in units (trades) and dollars when monthly operating income of $5,250 is earned. The graph should range from 0 to 40 units (trades).

4. Assume that the average revenue that Market Time Investors earns decreases to $300 per trade. How does this affect the breakeven point in number of trades?

P7-63A   CVP analysis at a multiproduct firm (Learning Objectives 4 & 5)

The contribution margin income statement of Westlake Coffee for February follows:

	A	B	C
1	**Westlake Coffee**		
2	**Contribution Margin Income Statement**		
3	**Month Ended February 29**		
4			
5	Sales revenue		$ 126,000
6	Less variable expenses:		
7	Cost of goods sold	$ 52,000	
8	Marketing expense	8,000	
9	General and administrative expense	3,000	63,000
10	Contribution margin		$ 63,000
11	Less fixed expenses:		
12	Marketing expense	$ 23,800	
13	General and administrative expense	4,200	28,000
14	Operating income		$ 35,000
15			

Westlake Coffee sells three small coffees for every large coffee. A small coffee sells for $3.00, with a variable expense of $1.50. A large coffee sells for $5.00, with a variable expense of $2.50.

Requirements

1. Determine Westlake Coffee's monthly breakeven point in the numbers of small coffees and large coffees. Prove your answer by preparing a summary contribution margin income statement at the breakeven level of sales. Show only two categories of expenses: variable and fixed.

2. Compute Westlake Coffee's margin of safety in dollars.

3. Use Westlake Coffee's operating leverage factor to determine its new operating income if sales volume increases 15%. Prove your results using the contribution margin income statement format. Assume that sales mix remains unchanged.

PROBLEMS Group B

P7-64B   Find missing data in CVP relationships *(Learning Objectives 1 & 2)*

The budgets of four companies yield the following information:

	Company			
	Q	R	S	T
Target sales...	$757,500	$445,000	$162,500	$_____
Variable expenses...............................	242,400	_____	_____	360,000
Fixed expenses.....................................	_____	159,000	81,000	_____
Operating income (loss)...................	$175,100	$_____	$_____	$152,000
Units sold...	_____	106,800	15,625	20,000
Contribution margin per unit...........	$ 6.06	$_____	$ 8.32	$ 32.00
Contribution margin ratio	_____	0.60	_____	_____

Requirements

1. Fill in the blanks for each company.
2. Compute breakeven, in sales dollars, for each company. Which company has the lowest breakeven point in sales dollars? What causes the low breakeven point?

P7-65B   Find breakeven and target profit and prepare income statements
(Learning Objectives 1 & 2)

A traveling production of Wicked performs each year. The average show sells 1,400 tickets at $65 per ticket. There are 100 shows a year. The show has a cast of 65, each earning an average of $320 per show. The cast is paid only after each show. The other variable expense is program printing expenses of $6 per guest. Annual fixed expenses total $2,163,000.

Requirements

1. Compute revenue and variable expenses for each show.
2. Compute the number of shows needed annually to breakeven.
3. Compute the number of shows needed annually to earn a profit of $3,708,000. Is this goal realistic? Give your reason.
4. Prepare Wicked's contribution margin income statement for 100 shows each year. Report only two categories of expenses: variable and fixed.

P7-66B   Comprehensive CVP problem *(Learning Objectives 1, 2, & 5)*

Dudley Calendars imprints calendars with college names. The company has fixed expenses of $1,125,000 each month plus variable expenses of $4.50 per carton of calendars. Of the variable expense, 74% is cost of goods sold, while the remaining 26% relates to variable operating expenses. The company sells each carton of calendars for $19.50.

Requirements

1. Compute the number of cartons of calendars that Dudley Calendars must sell each month to breakeven.
2. Compute the dollar amount of monthly sales Dudley Calendars needs in order to earn $338,000 in operating income (round the contribution margin ratio to two decimal places).
3. Prepare Dudley Calendar's contribution margin income statement for June for sales of 475,000 cartons of calendars.

4. What is June's margin of safety (in dollars)? What is the operating leverage factor at this level of sales?

5. By what percentage will operating income change if July's sales volume is 13% higher? Prove your answer.

P7-67B Compute breakeven, prepare CVP graph, and respond to change
(Learning Objectives 1, 2, & 3)

William Investors is opening an office in Dellroy, Ohio. Fixed monthly costs are office rent ($2,500), depreciation on office furniture ($260), utilities ($250), special telephone lines ($600), a connection with an online brokerage service ($640), and the salary of a financial planner ($1,750). Variable expenses include payments to the financial planner (10% of revenue), advertising (5% of revenue), supplies and postage (2% of revenue), and usage fees for the telephone lines and computerized brokerage service (23% of revenue).

Requirements

1. Compute the investment firm's breakeven revenue in dollars. If the average trade leads to $500 in revenue for William Investors, how many trades must be made to breakeven?

2. Compute dollar revenues needed to earn monthly operating income of $5,400.

3. Graph William's CVP relationships. Assume that an average trade leads to $500 in revenue for William Investors. Show the breakeven point, sales revenue line, fixed expense line, total expense line, operating loss area, operating income area, and sales in units (trades) and dollars when monthly operating income of $5,400 is earned. The graph should range from 0 to 40 units (trades).

4. Assume that the average revenue William Investors earns decreases to $400 per trade. How does this affect the breakeven point in number of trades?

P7-68B CVP analysis at a multiproduct firm *(Learning Objectives 4 & 5)*

The contribution margin income statement of Margot Coffee for February follows:

	A	B	C
1	**Margot Coffee**		
2	**Contribution Margin Income Statement**		
3	**Month Ended February 29**		
4			
5	Sales revenue		$ 154,000
6	Less variable expenses:		
7	Cost of goods sold	$ 63,000	
8	Marketing expense	10,000	
9	General and administrative expense	4,000	77,000
10	Contribution margin		$ 77,000
11	Less fixed expenses:		
12	Marketing expense	$ 35,700	
13	General and administrative expense	6,300	42,000
14	Operating income		$ 35,000
15			

Margot Coffee sells three small coffees for every large coffee. A small coffee sells for $3.00, with a variable expense of $1.50. A large coffee sells for $5.00, with a variable expense of $2.50.

Requirements

1. Determine Margot Coffee's monthly breakeven point in numbers of small coffees and large coffees. Prove your answer by preparing a summary contribution margin income statement at the breakeven level of sales. Show only two categories of expenses: variable and fixed.

2. Compute Margot Coffee's margin of safety in dollars.

3. Use Margot Coffee's operating leverage factor to determine its new operating income if sales volume increases by 15%. Prove your results using the contribution margin income statement format. Assume the sales mix remains unchanged.

CRITICAL THINKING

Discussion & Analysis

A7-69 Discussion Questions

1. Define breakeven point. Why is the breakeven point important to managers?

2. Describe four different ways cost-volume-profit analysis could be useful to management.

3. The purchasing manager for Rockwell Fashion Bags has been able to purchase the material for its signature handbags for $2 less per bag than in the prior year. Keeping everything else the same, what effect would this reduction in material cost have on the breakeven point for Rockwell Fashion Bags? Now assume that the sales manager decides to reduce the selling price of each handbag by $2. What would the net effect of both of these changes be on the breakeven point in units for Rockwell Fashion Bags?

4. Describe three ways that cost-volume-profit concepts could be used by a service organization.

5. "Breakeven analysis isn't very useful to a company because companies need to do more than breakeven to survive in the long run." Explain why you agree or disagree with this statement.

6. What conditions must be met for cost-volume-profit analysis to be accurate?

7. Why is it necessary to calculate a weighted-average contribution margin ratio for a multi-product company when calculating the breakeven point for that company? Why can't all of the products' contribution margin ratios just be added together and averaged?

8. Is the contribution margin ratio of a grocery store likely to be higher or lower than that of a plastics manufacturer? Explain the difference in cost structure between a grocery store and a plastics manufacturer. How does the cost structure difference impact operating risk?

9. Alston Jewelry had sales revenues last year of $2.4 million, while its breakeven point (in dollars) was $2.2 million. What was Alston Jewelry's margin of safety in dollars? What does the term margin of safety mean? What can you discern about Alston Jewelry from its margin of safety?

10. Rondell Pharmacy is considering switching to the use of robots to fill prescriptions that consist of oral solids or medications in pill form. The robots will assist the human pharmacists and will reduce the number of human pharmacy workers needed. This change is expected to reduce the number of prescription filling errors, to reduce the customer's wait time, and to reduce the total overall costs. How does the use of the robots affect Rondell Pharmacy's cost structure? Explain the impact of this switch to robotics on Rondell Pharmacy's operating risk.

11. Suppose a company can replace the packing material it currently uses with a biodegradable packing material. The company believes this move to biodegradable packing materials will be well-received by the general public. However, the biodegradable packing materials are more expensive than the current packing materials and the contribution margin ratios of the related products will drop. What are the arguments for the company to use the biodegradable packing materials? What are the arguments for the company to not use the biodegradable materials? What do you think the company should do?

12. How can CVP techniques be used in supporting a company's sustainability efforts? Conversely, how might CVP be a barrier to sustainability efforts?

Application & Analysis

Mini Cases

A7-70 CVP for a Product

Select one product that you could make yourself. Examples of possible products could be cookies, birdhouses, jewelry, or custom t-shirts. Assume that you have decided to start a small business producing and selling this product. You will be applying the concepts of cost-volume-profit analysis to this potential venture.

Basic Discussion Questions

1. Describe your product. What market are you targeting this product for? What price will you sell your product for? Make projections of your sales in units over each of the upcoming five years.

2. Make a detailed list of all of the materials needed to make your product. Include quantities needed of each material. Also include the cost of the material on a per-unit basis.

3. Make a list of all of the equipment you will need to make your product. Estimate the cost of each piece of equipment that you will need.

4. Make a list of all other expenses that would be needed to create your product. Examples of other expenses would be rent, utilities, and insurance. Estimate the cost of each of these expenses per year.

5. Now classify all of the expenses you have listed as being either fixed or variable. For mixed expenses, separate the expense into the fixed component and the variable component.

6. Calculate how many units of your product you will need to sell to breakeven in each of the five years you have projected.

7. Calculate the margin of safety in units for each of the five years in your projection.

8. Now decide how much you would like to make in before-tax operating income (target profit) in each of the upcoming five years. Calculate how many units you would need to sell in each of the upcoming years to meet these target profit levels.

9. How realistic is your potential venture? Do you think you would be able to breakeven in each of the projected five years? How risky is your venture (use the margin of safety to help answer this question). Do you think your target profits are achievable?

Decision Cases

A7-71 CVP analysis by intern with an ethical dilemma (Learning Objective 2)

ETHICS

Abbott Work Wear, Inc., supplies uniforms for a variety of businesses. Greg Michaels is a new intern in the Accounting Department at Abbott. To expand sales, the company is considering paying commissions to its sales force. The controller, John Hammond, asks Greg to complete an analysis assuming sales would increase 25% under the proposed sales commission plan. This analysis should include 1) the new breakeven sales figure and 2) the operating profit under the new sales commission plan.

Greg does his best to perform the analysis. He is not exactly sure what he is doing but he does not want to appear like he does not understand accounting. After he gets his preliminary analysis finished, he calls his friend, Beth Sparrow, who is an accounting analyst at Scrubs and More, a competing uniform supplier. He knows Beth from a church group and figures he can trust her. He tells her he is working on a new project and asks her if they can meet for dinner later, where he can ask her advice.

At dinner, Greg confesses to Beth that he really does not know if he did his analysis correctly. Beth assures him that she has worked on similar things at her company. She asks him if they can go over the analysis together. He readily agrees because this is just the type of help he had hoped to get. He shows her the spreadsheet he has been working on; the two of them discuss each item on the analysis. Greg explains his reasoning behind each calculation and his data assumptions. Beth tells him that his analysis is thorough and agrees that he has done it all correctly as far as she can tell.

Now confident in his work, Greg turns in the proposed sales commission plan analysis the following day. His report ends with a recommendation that the new sales commission plan be undertaken, since it will lead to a significant increase in operating income with only a small increase in breakeven sales. John Hammond glances through the report and is impressed with the appearance of the report; it looks professional and complete. Since John has a lot of other work tasks, he approves the new sales commission plan without any further analysis or investigation.

When he is booking some payroll entries the following week, Greg realizes that he made an error in the CVP analysis he did for the sales commission project. He failed to include the monthly salaries of the sales staff in his computations. Greg is in a panic. If he tells John Hammond of his mistake, Greg is afraid he will not be offered a full-time position upon completion of his internship. Greg decides to keep quiet and not let the controller know of his error. He reasons that it is unlikely that the difference between what he projected versus the actual expenses will be discovered since Abbott does not create detailed monthly operating statements.

Requirements

1. Using the IMA Statement of Ethical Professional Practice as an ethical framework, answer the following questions:

   a. What is (are) the ethical issue(s) in this situation?
   b. What are Greg Michaels' responsibilities as a management accountant?
   c. What are John Hammond's responsibilities as a management accountant?
   d. What are Beth Sparrow's responsibilities as a management accountant?

2. What would be the impact on breakeven sales from failing to include the fixed monthly salaries? Would the breakeven using the erroneous data be lower or higher than the correct breakeven (the breakeven calculation including the monthly salaries)? Do you think this error would be likely to influence the decision of whether to proceed with the new sales commission proposal?

3. Discuss the specific steps Greg should take to resolve the situation. Refer to the IMA Statement of Ethical Professional Practice in your response.

REAL LIFE

A7-72 Impact of increases in direct materials on product breakeven *(Learning Objectives 1, 2 & 3)*

Goose down is used in a wide variety of products, including jackets, bedding, and pillows. In recent years, the cost of down has been increasing. For example, in October 2010, Lands' End, a retailer of clothing and bedding items, was paying about $13 for a pound of down in China. By October 2012, that price per pound had risen to about $23 per pound[1]. The costs of other types and grades of down have increased similarly.

The cost of down has increased because of a few reasons. First of all, China is one of the major producers of down in the world. China's wealth has been increasing. As a result, more families are moving from farms to urban areas thereby reducing the number of families who are farming. In addition, dietary preferences around the world are changing to more meat and fish over geese and ducks, decreasing the potential revenue from raising geese.

On the demand side, the demand for down is increasing. The increasing popularity of down jackets from a fashion standpoint is driving most of the increase in demand for down. In prior decades, down was just used for specialized winter sports apparel for skiing and climbing. Now down is used in popular, general fashions.

Some companies are developing synthetic substitutes for down as they try to counteract the increasing costs of the down. In the meantime, companies such as Lands' End, North Face, and other garment manufacturers are raising the price of their products to counteract the increasing cost of down.

Requirements

1. Is the cost of down a fixed cost or a variable cost for a jacket manufacturer such as Lands' End?

2. If the cost of down increases, what happens to the breakeven point for a down-filled jacket product line at Lands' End?

3. What is the percentage increase in the cost of down per pound from 2010 to 2012 at Lands' End? Would you expect the breakeven units to change by this same percentage? Why or why not?

4. If down increases by a certain percentage, will the selling price of a down-filled jacket need to change by that same percentage to maintain the same profit margin? Explain.

[1]*Source:* "The Cost of Getting Down Is Going Up," *Wall Street Journal*, May 7, 2012, retrieved from http://online.wsj.com/article/SB10001424052702303877604577379700948610514.html?mod=djem_jiewr_AC_domainid#printMode on June 14, 2013.

5. Assume that a Lands' End down jacket selling for $100 uses 12 ounces of down. Further assume that Lands' End has $250,000 of fixed costs related to the down jacket line and its other variable manufacturing costs (direct materials, direct labor, and manufacturing overhead) total $60 per jacket. As stated in the story, the cost per pound of down was $13 and $23 in October 2010 and October 2012, respectively. Calculate the breakeven number of jackets both in (a) October 2010; and (b) October 2012. Do these breakeven numbers agree with your answers to the prior questions?

6. Assume now the same set of facts as in Question 5 but that Lands' End raises the selling price of each jacket by $10 in October 2013. Does the contribution margin percentage remain the same?

Try It Solutions

page 387:

1.
Sales price per unit $2.00
Less: Variable cost per unit 0.50
Contribution margin per unit $1.50

2. $\text{Contribution margin ratio} = \dfrac{\text{Contribution margin per unit}}{\text{Sales price per unit}} = \dfrac{\$1.50}{\$2.00} = 75\%$

3.
Contribution margin (1,000 hot dogs × $1.50 per hot dog) $1,500
Less: Fixed expenses 300
Operating income.. $1,200

page 391:

1. $\text{Sales in units to breakeven} = \dfrac{\text{Fixed expenses} + \text{Operating income}}{\text{Contribution margin per unit}}$

$$= \dfrac{\$300 + 0}{\$1.50} = 200 \text{ hot dogs}$$

2. $\text{Sales in dollars to breakeven} = \dfrac{\text{Fixed expenses} + \text{Operating income}}{\text{Contribution margin ratio}}$

$$= \dfrac{\$300 + 0}{75\%} = \$400 \text{ of sales revenue}$$

page 393:

1. $\text{Sales in units} = \dfrac{\text{Fixed expenses} + \text{Operating income}}{\text{Contribution margin per unit}}$

$$= \dfrac{\$300 + \$900}{\$1.50} = 800 \text{ hot dogs per month}$$

2. $\text{Sales in dollars} = \dfrac{\text{Fixed expenses} + \text{Operating income}}{\text{Contribution margin ratio}}$

$$= \dfrac{\$300 + \$900}{75\%} = \$1,600 \text{ of sales revenue}$$

page 405:

1.

	A	B	C	D
1	**Calculating Weighted-Average Contribution Margin per Unit**	**Hotdogs**	**Potato Chips**	**Total in "basket"**
2	Contribution margin per unit	$ 1.50	$ 0.75	
3	Multiply by: Sales mix (number of units in "basket")	10	5	15
4	Contribution margin	$ 15.00	$ 3.75	$ 18.75
5				
6	Weighted-average contibution margin per unit ($18.75/15 units)			$ 1.25
7				

2.
$$\text{Sales in units} = \frac{\text{Fixed expenses + Operating income}}{\text{Contribution margin per unit}} = \frac{\$300 + \$900}{\$1.25} = 960 \text{ total units}$$

3.

Hot dogs (960 × 10/15 sales mix) 640

Potato chips (960 × 5/15 sales mix) 320

Total units 960

page 413:

1.

Costs under current option			=	Costs under new option		
Variable Cost	+	Fixed Costs	=	Variable Costs	+	Fixed Costs
0	+	$300	=	($0.25 × # Units)	+	$100
		$200	=	($0.25 × # Units)		
		# Units	=	800		

Rachel will be indifferent between the two options if she sells exactly 800 units from her stand each month.

2. Since Rachel's typical sales volume (700 units) is less than the indifference point (800 units) she will prefer the option with the lower operating leverage (more variable costs and fewer fixed costs). In this case, that means her costs will be lower if she takes advantage of the new arrangement ($100 per month plus $0.25 for every unit sold) rather than continuing to operate under the current arrangement ($300 per month). As a result of lower costs, her operating income will be higher.

Oldrich Chmel/Profimedia.cz/Alamy

Sources: Congressional Research Service, "Offshoring of Airline Maintenance: Implications for Domestic Jobs and Aviation Safety," December 21, 2012. Harry Weber, "Delta No Longer Sending Calls to India," *USA Today*, April 17, 2009; "Helping Delta Air Lines Achieve High Performance Through Financial Outsourcing," www.accenture.com.

Relevant Costs for Short-Term Decisions

Learning Objectives

- **■ 1** Describe and identify information relevant to short-term business decisions
- **■ 2** Decide whether to accept a special order
- **■ 3** Describe and apply different approaches to pricing
- **■ 4** Decide whether to discontinue a product, department, or store
- **■ 5** Factor resource constraints into product mix decisions
- **■ 6** Analyze outsourcing (make-or-buy) decisions
- **■ 7** Decide whether to sell a product "as is" or process it further

Most Major Airlines, including Delta, outsource a large percentage of their aircraft maintenance, repair, and overhaul (MRO) to domestic and foreign providers. In addition to MRO, Delta has also outsourced some of its finance, accounting, human resource and customer call center work. Due to rising fuel costs and cut-throat competition, airlines need to find ways to reduce costs. Through outsourcing, Delta is able to significantly reduce annual labor costs and avoid costly investments in facilities, equipment, and parts inventories. However, costs are not everything. Even though Delta saved millions of dollars per year by outsourcing its call center work to India, customer dissatisfaction prompted Delta to bring its call center work back to the United States. Outsourcing also enables companies to concentrate on their core competencies—the operating activities at which they excel—while at the same time make use of the expertise and best-practices of firms that excel at other areas of operations. For Delta, outsourcing select operating functions makes good business sense.

In the last chapter, we saw how managers use cost behavior to determine the company's breakeven point and to estimate the sales volume needed to achieve target profits. In this chapter, we'll see how managers use their knowledge of cost behavior to make six special business decisions, such as whether to outsource operating activities. The decisions we'll discuss in this chapter usually pertain to short periods of time, so managers do not need to worry about the time value of money. In other words, they do not need to compute the present value of the revenues and expenses relating to the decision. In Chapter 12, we will discuss longer-term decisions (such as buying equipment and undertaking plant expansions) in which the time value of money becomes important. Before we look at the six business decisions in detail, let's consider a manager's decision-making process and the information managers need to evaluate their options.

How do Managers Make Decisions?

Exhibit 8-1 illustrates how managers decide among alternative courses of action. Management accountants help gather and analyze relevant information to compare alternatives. Management accountants also help with the follow-up: comparing the actual results of a decision to those originally anticipated. This feedback helps management as it faces similar types of decisions in the future. It also helps management adjust current operations if the actual results of its decision are markedly different from those anticipated.

EXHIBIT 8-1 How Managers Make Decisions

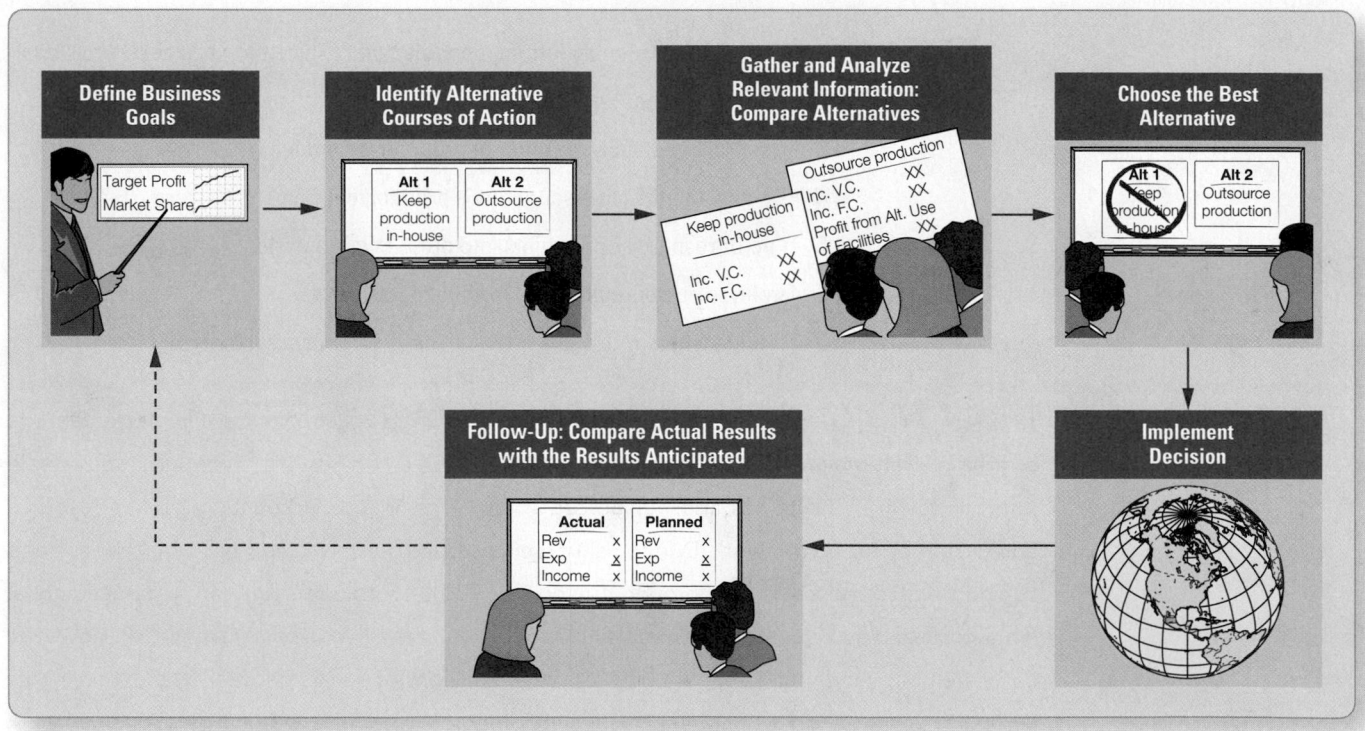

Relevant Information

When managers make decisions, they focus on costs and revenues that are relevant to the decisions. Exhibit 8-2 shows that **relevant information**

1. is expected *future* data.
2. *differs* among alternatives.

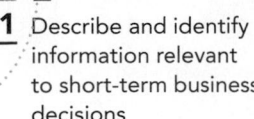

1 Describe and identify information relevant to short-term business decisions

EXHIBIT 8-2 Relevant Information

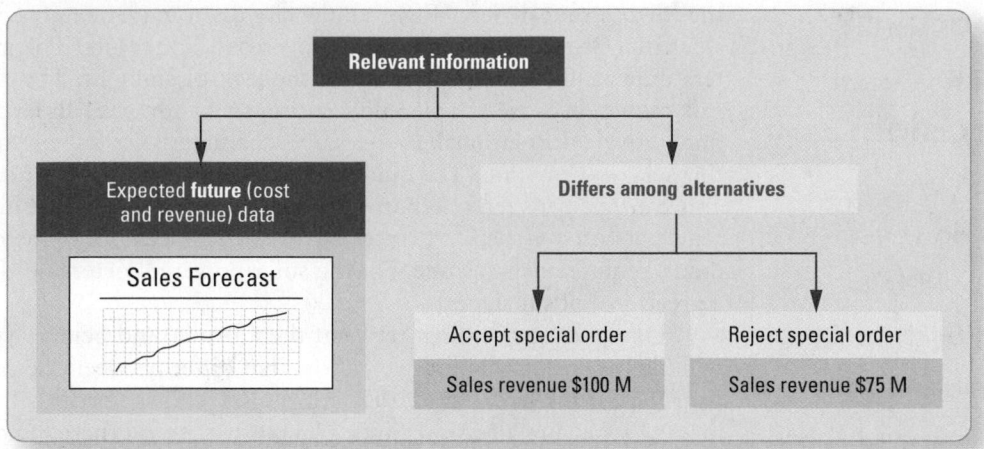

Recall our discussion of relevant costs in Chapter 2. In deciding whether to purchase a Toyota Corolla or Nissan Sentra, the cost of the car, the sales tax, and the insurance premium are relevant because these costs

- are incurred in the *future* (after you decide to buy the car).
- *differ between alternatives* (each car has a different invoice price, sales tax, and insurance premium).

These costs are *relevant* because they affect your decision of which car to purchase. *Irrelevant* costs are costs that *do not* affect your decision. For example, because the Corolla and Sentra both have similar fuel efficiency and maintenance ratings, we do not expect the car operating costs to differ between alternatives. Because these costs do not differ, they do not affect your decision. In other words, they are *irrelevant* to the decision. Similarly, the cost of a campus parking sticker is also irrelevant because the sticker costs the same whether you buy the Sentra or the Corolla.

<u>Sunk costs</u> are also irrelevant to your decision. Sunk costs are costs that were incurred in the *past* and cannot be changed regardless of which future action is taken. Perhaps you want to trade in your current truck when you buy your new car. The amount you paid for the truck—which you bought for $15,000 a year ago—is a sunk cost. In fact, it doesn't matter whether you paid $15,000 or $50,000—it's still a sunk cost. No decision made *now* can alter the past. You already bought the truck, so *the price you paid for it is a sunk cost.* All you can do *now* is keep the truck, trade it in, or sell it for the best price you can get, even if that price is substantially less than what you originally paid for the truck.

What *is* relevant is what you can get for your truck in the future. Suppose the Nissan dealership offers you $8,000 for your truck. The Toyota dealership offers you $10,000. Because the amounts differ and the transaction will take place in the future, the trade-in value is relevant to your decision.

The same principle applies to all situations—*only relevant data affect decisions.*

Relevant Nonfinancial Information

Nonfinancial, or qualitative factors, also play a role in managers' decisions. For example, closing manufacturing plants or laying off employees can seriously hurt the local community and employee morale. Outsourcing can reduce control over delivery time and product quality. Offering discounted prices to select customers can upset regular customers and tempt them to take their business elsewhere. Managers must think through the likely quantitative *and* qualitative effects of their decisions. Progressive companies will take a triple-bottom-line approach to all business decisions, considering not only the effect of the decision on profitability, but also on people and the environment.

Managers who ignore qualitative factors can make serious mistakes. For example, the City of Nottingham, England, spent $1.6 million on 215 solar-powered parking meters

Why is this important?

"The accounting information used to make **business decisions** in this chapter focuses on one factor: **profitability**. However, in real life, managers should take a triple-bottom-line approach to decision making by considering the decision's impact on people and the environment."

after seeing how well the parking meters worked in countries along the Mediterranean Sea. However, the city did not adequately consider that British skies are typically overcast. The result? The meters didn't always work because of the lack of sunlight. The city *lost* money because people ended up parking for free! Relevant qualitative information has the same characteristics as relevant financial information: The qualitative factor occurs in the *future*, and it *differs* between alternatives. The amount of *future* sunshine required *differed* between alternatives: The mechanical meters didn't require any sunshine, but the solar-powered meters needed a great deal of sunshine.

Likewise, in deciding between the Corolla and Sentra, you will likely consider qualitative factors that differ between the cars (legroom, trunk capacity, dashboard design, and so forth) before making your final decision. Since you must live with these factors in the future, they become relevant to your decision.

Keys to Making Short-Term Special Decisions

Our approach to making short-term special decisions is called the *relevant information approach* or the *incremental analysis approach*. Instead of looking at the company's *entire* income statement under each decision alternative, we'll just look at how operating income would *change or differ* under each alternative. Using this approach, we'll leave out irrelevant information—the costs and revenues that won't differ between alternatives.

We'll consider six kinds of decisions in this chapter:

1. Special sales orders
2. Pricing
3. Discontinuing products, departments, or stores
4. Product mix when resources are constrained
5. Outsourcing (make or buy)
6. Selling as is or processing further

As you study these decisions, keep in mind the two keys in analyzing short-term special business decisions shown in Exhibit 8-3:

1. **Focus on relevant revenues, costs, and profits.** Most decisions boil down to a cost-benefit analysis. The important point is to identify and focus on only the relevant costs and benefits: those that will differ between alternatives. Irrelevant information only clouds the picture and creates information overload. That's why we'll use the incremental analysis approach.

2. **Use a contribution margin approach that separates variable costs from fixed costs.** Because fixed costs and variable costs behave differently, they must be analyzed separately. Traditional (absorption costing) income statements, which blend fixed and variable costs, can mislead managers. Contribution margin income statements, which isolate costs by behavior (variable or fixed), help managers gather the cost-behavior information they need. Recall from Chapter 6 that unit manufacturing costs based on absorption costing are mixed costs, so they can also mislead managers. That's why variable costing is often better for decision-making purposes. If you use unit manufacturing costs in your analysis, make sure you separate the cost's fixed and variable components first.

Keep in mind that every business decision is unique. What might be a relevant cost in one decision might not be relevant in another decision. Each unique business decision needs to be assessed to determine what pieces of information are relevant. Just because a piece of information is relevant in one decision doesn't mean it will be relevant in the next. Because of this, accountants often follow the adage that different costs are used for different purposes.

EXHIBIT 8-3 Two Keys to Making Short-Term Special Decisions

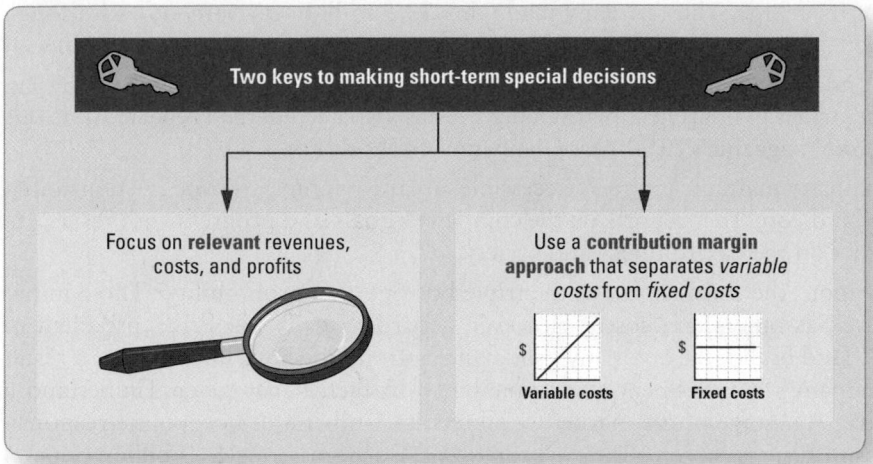

Sustainability and Short-Term Business Decisions

For companies that embrace sustainability and the triple bottom line, almost every decision will be viewed through the lens of its impact on people and the planet, as well as profitability. For example, let's look at Timberland, a company that specializes in high-quality and high-performance outdoor shoes and clothing made with processes and materials designed to reduce environmental impact. The company is committed to "doing well and doing good." Here are a few of the decisions the company has made:

- For the past 20 years, employees have been given up to 40 hours of paid leave each year to perform community service work.

- For the last 15 years, the company has sponsored an annual day-long employee service event, called Serv-a-palooza. In one year alone, over 4,800 employees across the globe participated, generating over 35,000 hours of service to local community projects. As part of Earth Day celebration in 2012, Timberland employees contributed nearly 20,000 hours of service to local community projects.

- The company's strict "Code of Conduct" ensures that domestic and overseas workers are employed at fair wage rates, work reasonable shifts, and work in safe factories.

- The company is committed to being environmentally conscious in the production of its products. The company labels its footwear with a "Green Index" rating system. The index helps educate consumers about the product's climate impact, chemicals used, and materials used (percentage of organic, recycled, or renewable materials used).

- In 2012, 85% of the 19 million pairs of footwear sold by the company contained recycled materials. In addition, all shoeboxes and tissue inserts are made from 100% recycled material. In 2012, 39% of the materials used in the company's apparel were recycled, organic, or renewable.

- In 2010, the company committed to planting 5 million trees over the course of five years in regions of Haiti and China suffering from the effects of deforestation. By the end of 2012, over 2.2 million trees were planted. Acting as carbon offsets, these trees will also help the company achieve its goal of becoming carbon neutral in all operations under its control.

- The company has earned LEED (Leadership in Energy and Environmental Design) certification for several of its retail outlets, which use reclaimed and recycled materials throughout each store's design.

■ The company uses solar panels on its California distribution center to provide 60% of its energy. The company made this $3.5 million investment even though cost models showed it might take 20 years for the investment to earn a return.

■ Timberland has ranked highly on Climate Count's list of companies making aggressive strides in fighting climate change. It has also been named repeatedly as one of *Fortune* magazine's "100 Best Companies to Work For."

■ The company maintains a freely accessible, award-winning website (responsibility .timberland.com) that reports on the company's goals and progress with respect to its impact on the environment and society.

But what about the third aspect of the triple bottom line: profitability? These initiatives, as well as others, are costly. However, according to Patrik Frisk, president of the Timberland brand, the company's sales and bottom line have improved as a result of the company's commitment to sustainability. In fact, it has given Timberland a competitive advantage in the market. Frisk credits Timberland's corporate responsibility as a primary reason for the decision of VF Corporation, a $10 billion apparel powerhouse, to acquire Timberland in 2011 at a premium of 43% over its stock market price.[1]

See Exercises E8-18A and E8-31B

2 Decide whether to accept a special order

How do Managers Make Special Order and Regular Pricing Decisions?

We'll start our discussion by looking at special sales order decisions and regular pricing decisions. In the past, managers did not consider pricing to be such a short-term decision. However, product life cycles are shrinking in most industries. Companies often sell products for only a few months before replacing them with an updated model. The clothing and technology industries have always had short life cycles. Even auto and housing styles change frequently. Pricing has become a shorter-term decision than it was in the past.

Let's examine a special sales order in detail; then we will discuss regular pricing decisions.

Special Order Decisions

A special order occurs when a customer requests a one-time order at a *reduced* sales price. Often, these special orders are for large quantities. Before agreeing to the special deal, management must consider the questions shown in Exhibit 8-4.

EXHIBIT 8-4 Special Order Considerations

- Do we have excess capacity available to fill this order?

- Will the reduced sales price be high enough to cover the *incremental* costs of filling the order (the variable costs of filling the order and any additional fixed costs)?

- Will the special order affect regular sales in the long run?

First, managers must consider available capacity. If the company is already making as many units as possible and selling them all at its *regular* sales price, it wouldn't make sense to fill a special order at a *reduced* sales price. Therefore, available excess capacity is a necessity for accepting a special order. This is true for service firms (law firms, caterers, and so forth) as well as manufacturers.

[1] VF Corporation, 2012 Annual Report; "Sale Gives Timberland Leg Up," *Wall Street Journal*, June 14, 2011; http://responsibility.timberland.com

Second, managers need to consider whether the special reduced sales price is high enough to cover the incremental costs of filling the order. The special price *must* exceed the variable costs of filling the order or the company will lose money on the deal. In other words, the special order must provide a positive contribution margin.

Next, the company must consider fixed costs. If the company has excess capacity, fixed costs probably won't be affected by producing more units or delivering more service. However, in some cases, management may need to hire a consultant or incur some other fixed cost to fill the special order. If so, management will need to consider whether the special sales price is high enough to generate a positive contribution margin *and* cover the additional fixed costs.

Finally, managers need to consider whether the special order will affect regular sales in the long run. Will regular customers find out about the special order and demand a lower price or take their business elsewhere? Will the special order customer come back *again and again*, asking for the same reduced price? Will the special order price start a price war with competitors? Managers must gamble that the answers to these questions are "no" or consider how customers will respond. Managers may decide that any profit from the special sales order is not worth these risks.

Special Order Example

Let's consider a special sales order example. Suppose ACDelco sells oil filters for $3.20 each. Assume that a mail-order company has offered ACDelco $35,000 for 20,000 oil filters, or $1.75 per filter ($35,000 ÷ 20,000 = $1.75). This sale will

- use manufacturing capacity that would otherwise be idle.
- not change fixed costs.
- not require any variable selling or administrative expenses.
- not affect regular sales.

We have addressed every consideration except one: Is the special sales price of $1.75 high enough to cover the incremental costs of filling the order? Let's take a look.

Exhibit 8-5 shows a contribution margin income statement for the current volume of oil filters sold (250,000 units). As discussed in Chapters 6 and 7, this format is much better for decision making than a traditional income statement format because it shows variable and fixed costs separately. Managers can easily see the variable cost of *manufacturing* each oil filter ($1.20) and the variable cost of *selling* each oil filter ($0.30).

EXHIBIT 8-5 Contribution Margin Income Statement for Current Volume of Oil Filters

	A	B	C
1	ACDelco		
2	Contribution Margin Income Statement (Variable Costing)		
3	For Current Volume of 250,000 Units		
4			
5		Per unit	Total
6	Sales revenue	$ 3.20	$ 800,000
7	Less variable expenses:		
8	Variable manufacturing costs (DM, DL, Variable MOH)	1.20	300,000
9	Variable operating expenses (selling and administrative)	0.30	75,000
10	Contribution margin	$ 1.70	$ 425,000
11	Less fixed expenses:		
12	Fixed manufacturing costs (fixed MOH)		200,000
13	Fixed operating expenses (selling and administrative)		125,000
14	Operating income		$ 100,000
15			

We'll use this information to determine whether ACDelco should accept the special order. Exhibit 8-6 illustrates an incremental cost-benefit analysis in which the revenue associated with the order is compared against the additional costs that will be incurred to fill the order. The analysis shows that the special order sales price of $1.75 is high enough to cover all incremental costs, and will provide the company with an additional $11,000 in operating income. Therefore, the order should be accepted unless managers have reason to suspect accepting the order would adversely affect regular sales in the long run.

EXHIBIT 8-6 Incremental Analysis of Special Sales Order

	A	B	C
			Total Order
1	**Incremental Analysis for Special Order Decision**	**Per Unit**	**(20,000 units)**
2	Revenue from special order	$ 1.75	$ 35,000
3	Less variable expense associated with the order:		
4	Variable manufacturing costs (DM, DL, Variable MOH)	1.20	24,000
5	Contribution margin	$ 0.55	$ 11,000
6	Less: Additional fixed expenses associated with the order		0
7	Increase in operating income from the special order		$ 11,000
8			

Remember that in this particular example, ACDelco doesn't expect to incur any variable selling or administrative costs associated with the special order. Therefore, they weren't included in Exhibit 8-6. However, this won't always be the case. Many times, companies will incur variable operating expenses on special orders, such as freight-out or sales commissions. *Only those incremental costs associated with the order should be included in the analysis.*

As shown in Exhibit 8-6, managers also need to consider any incremental fixed costs that will be incurred as a result of the order. Since the company has excess capacity with which to produce this order, fixed manufacturing overhead costs are not expected to change. Likewise, fixed selling and administrative expenses are not expected to change. Therefore, Exhibit 8-6 shows zero incremental fixed costs as a result of this order. However, if a company expects to incur a new fixed cost as a result of the order, such as paying outside legal fees to draft the sales contract, the additional fixed cost needs to be included in the analysis.

Notice that the analysis follows the two keys to making short-term special business decisions discussed earlier: (1) focus on relevant data (revenues and costs that *will change* if ACDelco accepts the special order) and (2) use a contribution margin approach that separates variable costs from fixed costs.

To summarize, for special sales orders, the decision rule is as follows:

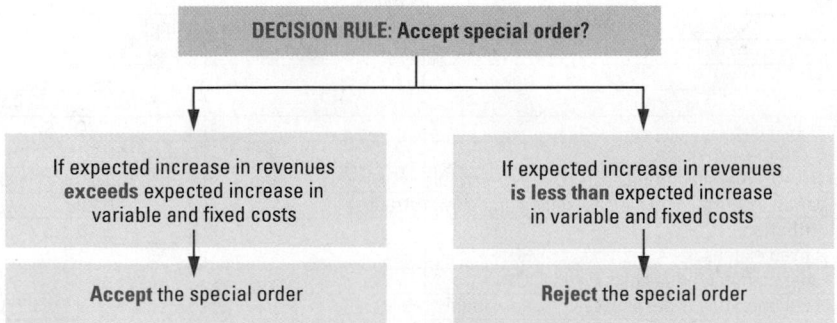

Pitfall to Avoid on Special Order Decisions

One of the most common mistakes managers make when analyzing special orders is to base their decision on the unit cost provided by absorption costing. Recall from Chapter 6 that under absorption costing, all manufacturing costs, including fixed MOH, are "absorbed" into the unit cost of the product. Absorption costing was used when we studied job costing and process costing in Chapters 3, 4, and 5 because it is required by Generally Accepted

Accounting Principles (GAAP) for external financial reporting purposes. Using the figures found in Exhibit 8-5, we see that the unit cost of each oil filter under absorption costing is $2.00:

Inventoriable Product Cost at Current Production Level	Absorption Unit Cost
Variable manufacturing costs (DM, DL, Variable MOH) per unit	$1.20
Fixed manufacturing costs (Fixed MOH of $200,000 ÷ 250,000 units)	0.80
Cost per unit using absorption costing	$2.00

The $2.00 unit cost, which GAAP mandates for inventory and cost of goods sold valuation, is *not* a good basis for making a special order decision. Why? Because it is a mixed cost, which includes both fixed and variable components. If a manager simply compared the special order sales price of $1.75 per unit to the absorption cost of $2.00 per unit, the manager would incorrectly assume that the special order would result in a loss of $0.25 per unit, or $5,000 in total (20,000 units × $0.25). Since there is excess capacity in the plant, the reality of the situation is that fixed MOH will remain $200,000 in total, regardless of whether ACDelco accepts the special order. Producing 20,000 more oil filters will *not* increase total fixed costs by $0.80 per unit. The incremental cost incurred to make each additional filter is the variable cost of $1.20 per unit, not $2.00 per unit. Keep the following important rule of thumb in mind:

> Never compare the special order sales price with the absorption cost per unit or your analysis will be flawed. Rather, use the contribution margin approach.

▶ Try It!

Assume that a Campbell's soup plant is running at 90% of its monthly capacity. Campbell's has just received a special order to produce 40,000 cases of chicken noodle soup for a national supermarket. The supermarket will sell the soup under its own private brand label. The soup will be the same in all respects, except for the label, which will cost Campbell's an extra $5,000 in total to design. The supermarket has offered to pay only $19.00 per case, which is well under Campbell's normal sales price.

Costs at the current production level (450,000 cases) are as follows:

	Total Cost	Cost per Case (450,000 cases)
Direct Materials	$4,500,000	$10.00
Direct Labor	1,350,000	3.00
Variable MOH	900,000	2.00
Fixed MOH	2,700,000	6.00
Total	$9,450,000	$21.00

1. Is there enough excess capacity to fill this order?
2. Will Campbell's operating income increase or decrease if it accepts this special order? By how much?

Please see page 501 for solutions.

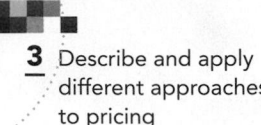

Regular Pricing Decisions

In the special order decision, ACDelco decided to sell a limited quantity of oil filters for $1.75 each even though the normal price was $3.20 per unit. But how did ACDelco decide to set its regular price at $3.20 per filter? Exhibit 8-7 shows that managers start with three basic questions when setting regular prices for their products or services.

EXHIBIT 8-7 Regular Pricing Considerations

- What is our target profit?
- How much will customers pay?
- Are we a price-taker or a price-setter for this product?

The answers to these questions are often complex and ever-changing. Stockholders expect the company to achieve certain profits. Economic conditions, historical company earnings, industry risk, competition, and new business developments all affect the level of profit that stockholders expect. Stockholders usually tie their profit expectations to the amount of assets invested in the company. For example, stockholders may expect a 10% annual return on their investment. A company's stock price tends to decline if the company does not meet target profits, so managers must keep costs low while generating enough revenue to meet target profits.

This leads to the second question: How much will customers pay? Managers cannot set prices above what customers are willing to pay or sales will decline. The amount customers will pay depends on the competition, the product's uniqueness, the effectiveness of marketing campaigns, general economic conditions, and so forth.

To address the third pricing question, imagine a continuum with price-takers at one end and price-setters at the other end. A company's products and services fall somewhere along this continuum, shown in Exhibit 8-8. Companies are price-takers when they have little or no control over the prices of their products or services. This occurs when their products and services are *not* unique or when competition is heavy. Examples include food commodities (milk and corn), natural resources (oil and lumber), and generic consumer products and services (paper towels, dry cleaning, and banking).

EXHIBIT 8-8 Price-Takers Versus Price-Setters

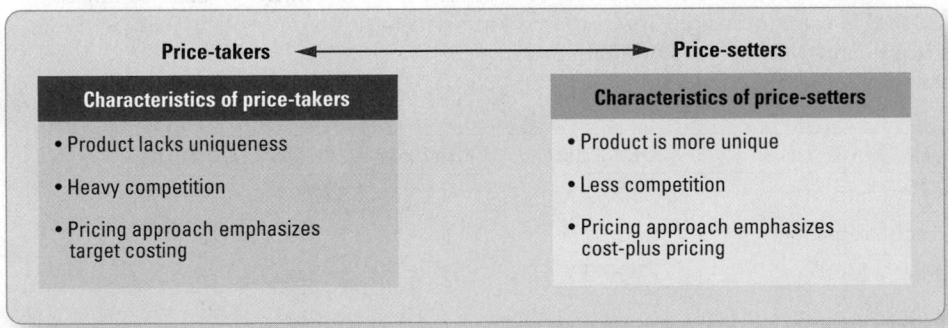

Companies are price-setters when they have more control over pricing—in other words, they can "set" prices to some extent. Companies are price-setters when their products are unique, which results in less competition. Unique products such as original art and jewelry, specially manufactured machinery, patented perfume scents, and custom-made furniture can command higher prices.

Obviously, managers would rather be price-setters than price-takers. To gain more control over pricing, companies try to differentiate their products. They want to make their products unique in terms of features, service, or quality—or at least make you *think* their product is unique or somehow better even if it isn't. How do they do this? Primarily through advertising. Consider Nike's tennis shoes, Starbucks' coffee, Hallmark's wrapping paper, Nexus' shampoo, Tylenol's acetaminophen, General Mills' cereal, Capital One's credit cards, Shell's gas, Abercrombie and Fitch's jeans—the list goes on and on. Are these products really better or significantly different from their lower-priced competitors? Possibly. If these companies can make you think so, they've gained more control over their pricing because you are willing to pay *more* for their products or services. The downside? These companies must charge higher prices or sell more just to cover their advertising costs.

A company's approach to pricing depends on whether its product or service is on the price-taking or price-setting side of the spectrum. Price-takers emphasize a target costing approach. Price-setters emphasize a cost-plus pricing approach. Keep in mind that many products fall somewhere along the continuum. Therefore, managers tend to use both approaches to some extent. We'll now discuss each approach in turn.

Why is this important?

"Both **branding** and product **differentiation** give managers more control over pricing. Without such features, a **company** must often settle for selling its **product** at the same price as its competitors."

Target Costing

When a company is a price-taker, it emphasizes a target costing approach to pricing. **Target costing** starts with the market price of the product (the price customers are willing to pay) and subtracts the company's desired profit to determine the product's target total cost—the *total* cost to develop, design, produce, market, deliver, and service the product. In other words, the total cost includes *every* cost incurred throughout the product's value chain.

> Revenue at market price
> Less: Desired profit
> Target total cost

In this relationship, the market price is "taken." If the product's current cost is higher than the target cost, the company must find ways to reduce costs, otherwise it will not meet its profit goals. Managers often use activity-based costing (ABC), value engineering, and lean thinking (as discussed in Chapter 4) to find ways to cut costs. Let's look at an example of target costing.

Let's assume that oil filters are a commodity and that the current market price is $3.00 per filter (not the $3.20 sales price assumed in the earlier ACDelco example). Because the oil filters are a commodity, ACDelco will emphasize a target costing approach. Let's assume that ACDelco's stockholders expect a 10% annual return on the company's assets. If the company has $1,000,000 of assets, the desired profit is $100,000 ($1,000,000 × 10%). Exhibit 8-9 calculates the target total cost at the current sales volume (250,000 units). Once we know the target total cost, we can analyze the fixed and variable cost components separately.

EXHIBIT 8-9 Calculating Target Total Cost

Revenue at market price (250,000 units × $3.00 price)	$ 750,000
Less: Desired profit (10% × $1,000,000 of assets)	(100,000)
Target total cost	$ 650,000

Can ACDelco make and sell 250,000 oil filters at a target total cost of $650,000 or less? We know from ACDelco's contribution margin income statement (Exhibit 8-5) that the company's variable costs are $1.50 per unit. This variable cost per unit includes both manufacturing costs ($1.20 per unit) and selling and administrative expenses ($0.30 per unit). From Exhibit 8-5 we also know that the company incurs $325,000 in fixed costs in its current relevant range. Again, some fixed cost stems from manufacturing ($200,000) and some from selling and administrative activities ($125,000). Keep the following rule of thumb in mind when setting sales prices:

> *In setting regular sales prices, companies must cover **all** of their costs—it doesn't matter if these costs are inventoriable product costs or period costs, or whether they are fixed or variable.*

Making and selling 250,000 filters currently costs the company $700,000 [(250,000 units × $1.50 variable cost per unit) + $325,000 of fixed costs]. The actual current cost of $700,000 is more than the target total cost of $650,000 (shown in Exhibit 8-9). So, what are ACDelco's options?

- Cut fixed costs.
- Cut variable costs.
- Try other strategies, such as branding, product differentiation, or adding to the company's product mix.
- Accept a lower profit.

Let's look at some of these options. ACDelco may first try to cut fixed costs. As shown in Exhibit 8-10, the company would have to reduce fixed costs to $275,000 to meet its target profit. Since current fixed costs are $325,000 (Exhibit 8-5), that means the company would have to cut fixed costs by $50,000.

EXHIBIT 8-10 Calculating Target Fixed Cost

Target total cost (from Exhibit 8-9)..	$ 650,000
Less: Current variable costs (250,000 units × $1.50)...............	(375,000)
Target fixed cost..	$ 275,000

The company would start by considering whether any discretionary fixed costs could be eliminated without harming the company. ACDelco probably can't reduce its committed fixed costs, since they are nearly impossible to change in the short run.

If the company can't reduce its fixed costs by $50,000, it would have to lower its variable cost to $1.30 per unit, as shown in Exhibit 8-11.

EXHIBIT 8-11 Calculating Target Unit Variable Cost

Target total cost (from Exhibit 8-9)...	$ 650,000
Less: Current fixed costs (from Exhibit 8-5)...............................	(325,000)
Target total variable costs	$ 325,000
Divided by number of units...	÷ 250,000
Target variable cost per unit...	$ 1.30

Perhaps the company could renegotiate raw materials costs with its suppliers, decrease the amount of packing materials used, or find a less costly way of shipping the air filters.

However, if ACDelco can't reduce variable costs to $1.30 per unit, could it meet its target profit through a combination of lowering both fixed costs and variable costs?

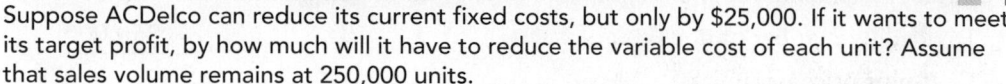

STOP & THINK

Suppose ACDelco can reduce its current fixed costs, but only by $25,000. If it wants to meet its target profit, by how much will it have to reduce the variable cost of each unit? Assume that sales volume remains at 250,000 units.

Answer: Companies typically try to cut both fixed and variable costs. Because ACDelco can cut its fixed costs only by $25,000, to meet its target profit, it would have to cut its variable costs as well:

Target total cost (Exhibit 8-9)	$ 650,000
Less: Reduced fixed costs ($325,000 − $25,000)...........	(300,000)
Target total variable costs	$ 350,000
Divided by number of units...	÷ 250,000
Target variable cost per unit...	$ 1.40

In addition to cutting its fixed costs by $25,000, the company must reduce its variable costs from $1.50 per unit (Exhibit 8-5) to $1.40 per unit. In other words, the company would need to decrease its variable costs by $0.10 per unit to meet its target profit at the existing volume of sales.

Finally, the company can attempt different strategies that may actually include *increasing*, rather than decreasing, costs. For example, the company may need to increase marketing costs to increase volume, brand its product, and gain some control over pricing. It may need to spend *more* on research and development (R&D) to differentiate its product through innovation. Cost-volume-profit (CVP) analysis, as you learned in Chapter 7, can help companies determine whether these actions will be profitable. As you can see, managers don't have an easy task when the current total cost exceeds the target total cost. Sometimes, companies just can't compete given the current market price. If that's the case, they may have no other choice than to exit the market.

Cost-Plus Pricing

When a company is a price-setter, such as Apple, it emphasizes a cost-plus approach to pricing. This pricing approach is essentially the *opposite* of the target-pricing approach. **Cost-plus pricing** starts with the product's total costs (as a given) and *adds* its desired profit to determine a cost-plus price.

Total cost
Plus: Desired profit
Cost-plus price

When the product is unique, such as Apple's innovative products, the company has more control over pricing. However, it still needs to make sure that the cost-plus price is not higher than what customers are willing to pay. Let's go back to our original ACDelco example. This time, let's assume that the oil filters benefit from brand recognition, so the company has some control over the price it charges for its filters. Exhibit 8-12 takes a cost-plus pricing approach assuming the current level of sales.

EXHIBIT 8-12 Calculating Cost-Plus Price Per Unit

Current variable costs (250,000 units × $1.50 per unit)	$ 375,000
Plus: Current fixed costs (Exhibit 8-5)...	325,000
Current total costs	$ 700,000
Plus: Desired profit (10% × $1,000,000 of assets).......................	100,000
Target revenue...	$ 800,000
Divided by number of units...	÷ 250,000
Cost-plus price per unit...	$ 3.20

If the current market price for generic oil filters is $3.00, as we assumed earlier, can ACDelco sell its brand-name filters for $3.20 apiece? The answer depends on how well the company has been able to differentiate its product or benefit from brand name recognition. The company may use focus groups, trial markets, or marketing surveys to find out how customers will respond to the cost-plus price of $3.20. The company may find out that its cost-plus price is too high, or it may find that it could set the price even higher without jeopardizing sales.

STOP & THINK

Which costing system (job costing or process costing) do you think price-setters and price-takers typically use?

Answer: Companies tend to be price-setters when their products are unique. Unique products are produced as single items or in small batches. Therefore, these companies use job costing to determine the product's cost. However, companies are often price-takers when their products are high-volume commodities. Process costing better suits this type of product.

Notice how pricing decisions used our two keys to decision making: (1) focus on relevant information and (2) use a contribution margin approach that separates variable costs from fixed costs. In pricing decisions, all cost information is relevant because the company must cover *all* costs along the value chain before it can generate a profit. However, we still needed to consider variable costs and fixed costs separately because they behave differently at different volumes.

Our pricing decision rule is as follows:

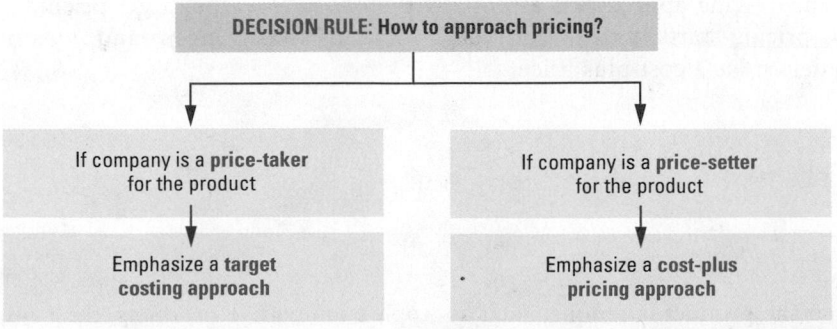

Decision Guidelines

Relevant Information for Business Decisions

Nike makes special order and regular pricing decisions. Even though it sells mass-produced tennis shoes and sports clothing, Nike has differentiated its products with advertising. Nike's managers consider both quantitative and qualitative factors as they make pricing decisions. Here are key guidelines that Nike's managers follow in making their decisions.

Decision	Guidelines
What information is relevant to a short-term special business decision?	Relevant information is as follows: 1. Pertains to the *future* 2. *Differs* between alternatives
What are two key guidelines in making short-term special business decisions?	1. Focus on *relevant* data. 2. Use a *contribution margin* approach that separates variable costs from fixed costs.
How does a company's commitment to sustainability affect decision making?	Companies that are committed to sustainability will judge every decision through the lens of the triple bottom line, assessing the impact of the decision not only on company profit, but also on its consequences for people and the planet.
Should Nike accept a lower sales price than the regular price for a large order from a customer in São Paulo, Brazil?	If the revenue from the order exceeds the incremental variable and fixed costs incurred to fill the order, then accepting the order will increase operating income.
What should Nike consider in setting its regular product prices?	Nike considers the following: 1. The profit stockholders expect 2. The price customers will pay 3. Whether it is a price-setter or a price-taker
What approach should Nike take to pricing?	Nike has differentiated its products through advertising and branding. Thus, Nike tends to be a price-setter. Nike's managers can emphasize a cost-plus approach to pricing.
What approach should discount shoe stores such as Payless ShoeSource take to pricing?	Payless ShoeSource sells generic shoes (no-name brands) at low prices. Payless is a price-taker, so managers use a target-costing approach to pricing.

SUMMARY PROBLEM 1

Linger Industries makes tennis balls. Linger's only plant can produce up to 2.5 million cans of balls per year. Current production is two million cans. Annual manufacturing, selling, and administrative fixed costs total $700,000. The variable cost of making and selling each can of balls is $1. Stockholders expect a 12% annual return on the company's $3 million of assets.

Requirements

1. What is Linger Industries' current total cost of making and selling two million cans of tennis balls? What is the current cost per unit of each can of tennis balls?

2. Assume that Linger Industries is a price-taker and the current market price is $1.45 per can of balls (this is the price at which manufacturers sell to retailers). What is the *target* total cost of producing and selling two million cans of balls? Given Linger Industries' current total costs, will the company reach stockholders' profit goals?

3. If Linger Industries cannot reduce its fixed costs, what is the target variable cost per can of balls?

4. Suppose Linger Industries could spend an extra $100,000 on advertising to differentiate its product so that it could be more of a price-setter. Assuming the original volume and costs plus the $100,000 of new advertising costs, what cost-plus price will Linger Industries want to charge for a can of balls?

5. Nike has just asked Linger Industries to supply 400,000 cans of balls at a special order price of $1.20 per can. Nike wants Linger Industries to package the balls under the Nike label (Linger will imprint the Nike logo on each ball and can). As a result, Linger Industries will have to spend $10,000 to change the packaging machinery. Assuming the original volume and costs, should Linger Industries accept this special order? (Unlike in the chapter problem, assume that Linger will incur variable selling costs as well as variable manufacturing costs related to this order.)

▪ SOLUTIONS

Requirement 1

The current total cost and cost per unit are calculated as follows:

Fixed costs	$ 700,000
Plus: Total variable costs (2 million cans × $1 per unit)...........	2,000,000
Current total costs..	$2,700,000
Divided by number of units..	÷ 2,000,000
Current cost per can...	$ 1.35

Requirement 2

The target total cost is as follows:

Revenue at market price (2,000,000 cans × $1.45 price)...........	$2,900,000
Less: Desired profit (12% × $3,000,000 of assets)	(360,000)
Target total cost	$2,540,000

Linger Industries' *current* total costs ($2,700,000 from Requirement 1) are $160,000 higher than the *target* total costs ($2,540,000). If Linger Industries can't cut costs, it won't be able to meet stockholders' profit expectations.

Requirement 3

Assuming that Linger Industries cannot reduce its fixed costs, the target variable cost per can is as follows:

Target total cost (from Requirement 2)	$ 2,540,000
Less: Fixed costs	(700,000)
Target total variable costs	$ 1,840,000
Divided by number of units	÷ 2,000,000
Target variable cost per unit	$ 0.92

Since Linger Industries cannot reduce its fixed costs, it needs to reduce variable costs by $0.08 per can ($1.00 – $0.92) to meet its profit goals. This would require an 8% cost reduction in variable costs, which may not be possible.

Requirement 4

If Linger Industries can differentiate its tennis balls, it will gain more control over pricing. The company's new cost-plus price would be as follows:

Current total costs (from Requirement 1)	$ 2,700,000
Plus: Additional cost of advertising	100,000
Plus: Desired profit (from Requirement 2)	360,000
Target revenue	$ 3,160,000
Divided by number of units	÷ 2,000,000
Cost-plus price per unit	$ 1.58

Linger Industries must study the market to determine whether retailers would pay $1.58 per can of balls.

Requirement 5

First, Linger determines that it has enough extra capacity (500,000 cans) to fill this special order (400,000). Next, Linger compares the revenue from the special order with the extra costs that will be incurred to fill the order. Notice that Linger shouldn't compare the special order price ($1.20) with the current unit cost of each can ($1.35) because the unit cost contains both a fixed and variable component. Since the company has excess capacity, the existing fixed costs won't be affected by the order. The correct analysis is as follows:

Revenue from special order (400,000 × $1.20 per unit)	$ 480,000
Less: Variable cost of special order (400,000 × $1.00)	(400,000)
Contribution margin from special order	$ 80,000
Less: Additional fixed costs of special order	(10,000)
Operating income provided by special order	$ 70,000

Linger Industries should accept the special order because it will increase operating income by $70,000. However, Linger Industries also needs to consider whether its regular customers will find out about the special price and demand lower prices, too. If Linger had simply compared the special order price of $1.20 to the current unit cost of each can ($1.35), it would have rejected the special order and missed out on the opportunity to make an additional $70,000 of profit.

4 Decide whether to discontinue a product, department, or store

How do Managers Make Other Special Business Decisions?

In this part of the chapter we'll consider four more special business decisions:

■ Whether to discontinue a product, department, or store

■ How to factor constrained resources into product mix decisions

■ Whether to make a product or outsource it (buy it)

■ Whether to sell a product as is or process it further

Decisions to Discontinue Products, Departments, or Stores

Managers often must decide whether to discontinue products, departments, stores, or territories that are not as profitable as desired. Newell Rubbermaid—maker of Sharpie markers, Graco strollers, and Rubbermaid plastics—recently discontinued some of its European product lines. Best Buy recently closed many of its retail locations. Kroger food stores replaced some in-store movie rental departments with health food departments. How do managers make these decisions? Exhibit 8-13 shows some questions managers must consider when deciding whether to discontinue a product line, department, or retail store location.

EXHIBIT 8-13 Considerations for Discontinuing Products, Departments, or Stores

- Does the product provide a positive contribution margin?
- Are there any fixed costs that can be avoided if we discontinue the product?
- Will discontinuing the product affect sales of the company's other products?
- What could we do with the freed capacity?

In the first half of the chapter we assumed ACDelco offered only one product—oil filters. Now let's assume the company makes both oil filters and air cleaners. Exhibit 8-14 illustrates a product line income statement in contribution margin format. As you can see, a **product line income statement** shows the operating income of each product line, as well as the company as a whole.

EXHIBIT 8-14 Product Line Income Statement

	A	B	C	D
1	ACDelco			
2	Product Line Contribution Margin Income Statement			
3	For the Year Ended December 31			
4				
5		Product lines		
6		Oil Filters	Air Cleaners	Company Total
7		(250,000 units)	(62,500 units)	(312,500 units)
8	Sales revenue	$ 800,000	$ 125,000	$ 925,000
9	Less variable expenses:			
10	Variable manufacturing costs (DM, DL, Variable MOH)	300,000	62,500	362,500
11	Variable operating expenses (selling and administrative)	75,000	12,500	87,500
12	Contribution margin	$ 425,000	$ 50,000	$ 475,000
13	Less fixed expenses:			
14	Fixed manufacturing costs (Fixed MOH)	160,000	40,000	200,000
15	Fixed operating expenses	100,000	25,000	125,000
16	Operating income	$ 165,000	$ (15,000)	$ 150,000
17				

In this exhibit, notice that the contribution margin provided by oil filters ($425,000) is the same as shown in Exhibit 8-5. What differs is that the fixed costs have now been allocated between the two product lines. Since 80% of the units produced are oil filters (250,000 ÷ 312,500 total units) and since each unit takes about the same amount of time to produce, management has allocated 80% of the fixed costs to the oil filters. The remaining 20% of fixed costs has been allocated to air cleaners. Keep in mind that management could have chosen another allocation system, which would have resulted in a different allocation of fixed costs.

Further notice that the air cleaner product line appears to be unprofitable. Currently, the air cleaners have an operating loss of $15,000 per period. Without this loss, management believes the company's operating income could be $15,000 higher each period. Therefore, management is considering whether to discontinue the product line. Let's now consider how management should approach this decision.

Consider the Product's Contribution Margin and Avoidable Fixed Costs

In making this decision, management should consider the questions raised in Exhibit 8-13. The first question addresses the product line's contribution margin: is it positive or negative? Exhibit 8-14 shows that the air cleaners provide $50,000 of contribution margin. This positive contribution margin means the product line is generating enough revenue to cover its own variable costs, plus provide another $50,000 that can be used to cover some of the company's fixed costs.

Had the contribution margin been negative, management would either need to raise the price of the product, if possible, cut variable costs, or discontinue the line. Management would only keep a product line with a negative contribution margin if they expected the sales of a companion product to decline as a result of discontinuing the product. For example, if customers always buy one oil filter every time they buy an air cleaner, then sales of oil filters might decline as a result of discontinuing the air cleaners. As a result, the total contribution margin earned from the oil filters would decline. This potential loss in contribution margin on the oil filters would need to be weighed against the savings generated from eliminating the product line with a negative contribution margin.

After assessing the contribution margin, managers need to consider fixed costs. *The important question is this: Can any fixed costs be eliminated if the product line is discontinued?* Any fixed costs that can be eliminated as a result of discontinuing the product are known as **avoidable fixed costs**. These costs are relevant to the decision because they will be incurred *only* if the product line is retained.

On the other hand, **unavoidable fixed costs** are those fixed costs that will continue to be incurred even if the product line is discontinued. Unavoidable fixed costs are irrelevant to the decision because they will be the same regardless of whether the product line is kept or discontinued.

Exhibit 8-15 shows the company's fixed costs in more detail. Notice that total fixed costs ($200,000 of manufacturing costs and $125,000 of fixed operating expenses) are the same as shown in Exhibit 8-14. Managers will assess each fixed cost to determine how much, if any, is avoidable.

Exhibit 8-15 shows that management has identified $8,000 of fixed manufacturing and $10,000 of fixed operating expenses that can be eliminated if the air cleaners are discontinued. The avoidable fixed costs consist of a cancelable lease on equipment used to manufacture the air cleaners, advertisements for the air cleaners, and salaried employees who work solely on the air cleaner product line. Most of the fixed costs, such as property taxes, insurance, depreciation, and so forth, are unavoidable: they will continue even if the air cleaners are discontinued.

EXHIBIT 8-15 Analysis of the Company's Fixed Costs

	A	B	C
1	**Analysis of Fixed Expenses**	**Total Cost**	**Avoidable**
2	*Fixed manufacturing (Fixed MOH):*		
3	Property taxes	$ 18,000	$ 0
4	Insurance	5,000	0
5	Depreciation on plant and production equipment	130,000	0
6	Fixed portion of utilities	7,000	0
7	Salaries of indirect labor (supervisors, janitors, etc.)	35,000	3,000
8	Equipment lease	5,000	5,000
9	Total fixed operating expenses	$ 200,000	$ 8,000
10			
11	*Fixed operating expenses (selling and administrative):*		
12	Building lease	$ 17,000	$ 0
13	Telephone, Internet, utilities	8,000	0
14	Depreciation on sales vehicles and office equipment	20,000	0
15	Advertisements	25,000	6,000
16	Sales and administrative salaries	55,000	4,000
17	Total fixed operating expenses	$ 125,000	$ 10,000
18			

With this information in hand, management can now determine whether or not to discontinue the air cleaner product line. Exhibit 8-16 presents management's analysis of the decision. In essence, it is a basic cost-benefit analysis. In this analysis, managers compare the contribution margin that would be lost from discontinuing the air cleaners (cost) with the fixed cost savings that could be generated (benefit).

EXHIBIT 8-16 Incremental Analysis for Discontinuing a Product Line

	A	B	C
1	**Incremental Analysis for Discontinuation Decision**	**Total**	
2	Contribution margin lost if air cleaners are discontinued (from Exhibit 8-14)	$ 50,000	
3	Less fixed cost savings if air cleaners are discontinued (from Exhibit 8-15):		
4	Avoidable fixed manufacturing expenses	8,000	
5	Avoidable fixed operating expenses (selling and administrative)	10,000	
6	Operating income lost if air cleaners are discontinued	$ 32,000	
7			

This analysis shows that the company's operating income would actually *decrease* by $32,000 if the air cleaners are discontinued. Therefore, the air cleaners should not be discontinued. The company would only eliminate the air cleaners if it could use the freed capacity to make a different product that is more profitable than the air cleaners.

Other Considerations

As noted in Exhibit 8-13, management must consider at least two other issues when making the decision to discontinue a product line, department, or store.

First, will discontinuing the product line affect sales of the company's other products? As discussed previously, some products have companion products whose sales would be hurt through discontinuing a particular product. This is also true about store departments. Can you imagine a grocery store discontinuing its produce department? Sales of every other department in the store would decline as a result of shoppers' inability to purchase fruits and vegetables at the store. On the other hand, sometimes discontinuing a product, such as one particular camera model, can increases the sales of the other company products (other camera models). The same holds true for retail stores. For example, assume two Starbucks are located close to one other. If one store is closed, then sales at the other location might increase as a result.

The second question concerns freed capacity. If a product line, department, or store is discontinued, management needs to consider what it would do with the newly freed capacity. Kroger, for example, recently replaced some of its in-store movie rental departments with health food departments. Why? Managers must have determined that a health food department would be more profitable than a movie rental department because of decline in people renting DVDs and the rise in people wanting to purchase healthier, organic foods. However, Kroger could have used the space to house a sushi bar, or display other products. Management must consider which alterative use of the freed capacity will be most profitable. Finally, management should consider what to do with any newly freed labor capacity. To exercise corporate responsibility, management should do all it can to retrain employees for other areas of its operations rather than laying off employees.

▶ Try It!

Assume Kroger's grocery store is deciding whether to eliminate the salad bar section of its stores. The product line income statement shows the following quarterly data for the salad bar operations:

Sales revenue = $750,000

Fixed costs = $100,000

Variable costs = $600,000

1. Only $20,000 of fixed costs can be eliminated if the salad bar is eliminated. The remaining $80,000 of fixed costs are unavoidable. What will happen to Kroger's operating income if it discontinues the salad bars and does nothing with the freed capacity?

2. Management is thinking about replacing the salad bar section of the stores with a specialty olive bar, which is projected to bring in $200,000 of contribution margin each quarter while incurring no additional fixed costs. What will happen to Kroger's operating income if it replaces the salad bars with olive bars?

Please see page 501 for solutions.

The key to deciding whether to discontinue products, departments, or stores is to compare the lost revenue against the costs that can be saved and to consider what could be done with the freed capacity. The decision rule is as follows:

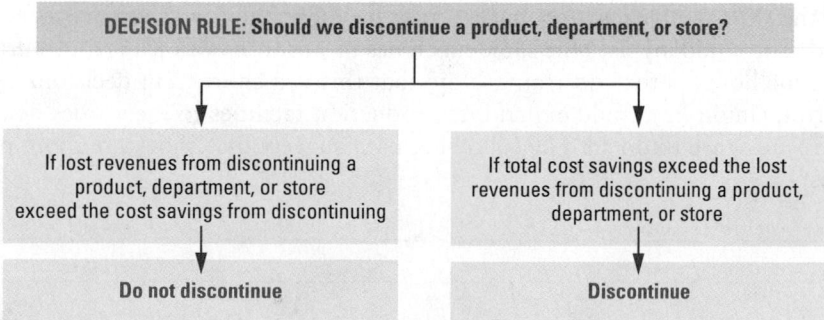

DECISION RULE: Should we discontinue a product, department, or store?

If lost revenues from discontinuing a product, department, or store exceed the cost savings from discontinuing	If total cost savings exceed the lost revenues from discontinuing a product, department, or store
Do not discontinue	**Discontinue**

Pitfall to Avoid on Discontinuation Decisions

One of the most common mistakes managers make when analyzing whether or not to discontinue a product is to base the decision on a product line income statement that contains an allocation of common fixed expenses. **Common fixed expenses** are those expenses that *cannot* be traced directly to a product line. For example, in Exhibits 8-14 and 8-15, we see that fixed MOH costs such as property taxes, insurance, and depreciation are all common production costs that have been allocated between the product lines. While appropriate for product costing purposes, the allocation of common fixed costs is not appropriate for making product discontinuation decisions. Nor is the allocation of common fixed costs, such as the building lease, utilities, Internet, or depreciation of office equipment, related to selling and administration.

As shown in Exhibit 8-14, the allocation of common fixed costs suggests the company's overall operating income could be $15,000 higher if the company stopped making the air cleaners. However, based on the correct analysis in Exhibit 8-16 we know the company's operating income would actually decline by $32,000 if the air cleaners were discontinued.

Since income statements with allocated common costs can potentially mislead managers, some companies prepare <u>segment margin income statements</u>, which contain no allocation of common fixed costs. Segment margin income statements look similar to Exhibit 8-14, except for two differences:

1. Only direct fixed costs that can be traced to specific product lines are deducted from the product line's contribution margin. The resulting operating income or loss for each individual product line is known as a <u>segment margin</u>.

2. All common fixed costs are shown under the company "total" column, but are not allocated among product lines.

We discuss and illustrate segment margin income statement in more detail in Chapter 10.

Product Mix Decisions when Resources are Constrained

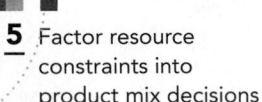

5 Factor resource constraints into product mix decisions

Companies do not have unlimited resources. <u>Constraints</u> that restrict production or sale of a product vary from company to company. For a manufacturer, the production constraint is often the number of available machine hours. For a merchandiser such as Walmart, the primary constraint is cubic feet of display space. In order to determine which products to emphasize displaying or producing, managers facing constraints should consider the questions shown in Exhibit 8-17.

EXHIBIT 8-17 Product Mix Considerations

- What constraint(s) stops us from making (or displaying) all of the units we can sell?
- Which products offer the highest contribution margin per unit of the constraint?
- Would emphasizing one product over another affect fixed costs?

Consider Union Bay, a manufacturer of shirts and jeans. Let's say the company can sell all of the shirts and jeans it produces, but it has only 2,000 machine hours of capacity per period. The company uses the same machines to produce both jeans and shirts. In this case, machine hours is the constraint. Note that this is a short-term decision, because in the long run, Union Bay could expand its production facilities to meet sales demand if it made financial sense to do so. The following data suggest that shirts are more profitable than jeans:

	Per Unit	
	Shirts	**Jeans**
Sale price	$ 30	$ 60
Less: Variable expenses	(12)	(48)
Contribution margin	$ 18	$ 12
Contribution margin ratio:		
Shirts: $18 ÷ $30	60%	
Jeans: $12 ÷ $60		20%

However, an important piece of information is missing—the time it takes to make each product. Let's assume that Union Bay can produce either 20 pairs of jeans *or* 10 shirts per machine hour. *The company will incur the same fixed costs either way, so fixed costs are irrelevant.* Which product should it emphasize?

To maximize profits when fixed costs are irrelevant, follow this decision rule:

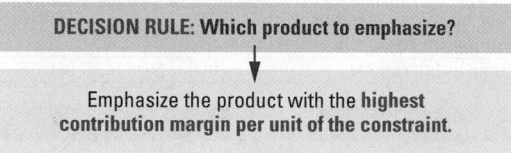

Because *machine hours* is the constraint, Union Bay needs to figure out which product has the *highest contribution margin per machine hour*. Exhibit 8-18 shows the contribution margin per machine hour for each product, as well as the total contribution margin that could be earned by each product given the 2,000 available machine hours.

EXHIBIT 8-18 Product Mix—Which Product to Emphasize

	A	B	C
		Shirts	Jeans
1	**Product Mix Analysis When Demand Is Unlimited**		
2	Contribution margin per unit	$ 18	$ 12
3	Multiply by: Number of units produced per machine hour	10	20
4	Contribution margin per machine hour	$ 180	$ 240
5	Multiply by: Available capacity (number of machine hours)	2,000	2,000
6	Total contribution margin at full capacity	$ 360,000	$ 480,000
7			

Jeans have a higher contribution margin per machine hour ($240) than shirts ($180). Therefore, Union Bay will earn more profit by producing jeans. Why? Because even though jeans have a lower contribution margin *per unit*, Union Bay can make twice as many jeans as shirts in the available machine hours. Exhibit 8-18 also proves that Union Bay earns more total profit by making jeans. Multiplying the contribution margin per machine hour by the available number of machine hours shows that Union Bay can earn $480,000 of contribution margin by producing jeans but only $360,000 by producing shirts.

To maximize profit, Union Bay should make 40,000 jeans (2,000 machine hours × 20 jeans per hour) and zero shirts. Why zero shirts? Because for every machine hour spent making shirts, Union Bay would *give up* $60 of contribution margin ($240 per hour for jeans versus $180 per hour for shirts).

Changing Assumptions: Product Mix When Demand is Limited

We made two assumptions about Union Bay: (1) Union Bay's sales of other products, if any, won't be hurt by this decision and (2) Union Bay can sell as many jeans and shirts as it can produce. Let's challenge these assumptions. First, how could making only jeans (and not shirts) hurt sales of the company's other products? Companies must always consider companion products, that is, products that customers typically purchase together. For example, purchasers of iPads typically also purchase protective covers. Purchasers of spaghetti noodles typically also purchase spaghetti sauce. In the case of Union Bay, if ties and jackets are specifically designed and produced to coordinate with Union Bay shirts, the sales of these companion products will decline as a result of no longer producing shirts.

Let's now challenge our second assumption. Let's say that as a result of competition, demand for Union Bay's jeans is limited to 30,000 pairs per period. Because demand is no longer unlimited, Union Bay should make only as many jeans as it can sell and use the remaining machine hours to produce shirts. Let's see how this change in sales demand affects optimal production levels and profitability.

If Union Bay makes only 30,000 jeans, it will use only 1,500 machine hours (30,000 jeans ÷ 20 jeans per machine hour). That leaves 500 machine hours available for making shirts. Union Bay's new contribution margin will be as follows:

	A	B	C	D
1	Product Mix Analysis When Demand Is Limited	Shirts	Jeans	Total
2	Contribution margin per machine hour (from Exhibit 8-18)	$ 180	$ 240	
3	Multiply by: Number of machine hours devoted to product	500	1,500	2,000
4	Total contribution margin at full capacity	$ 90,000	$ 360,000	$ 450,000
5				

NOTE: 30,000 jeans divided by 20 jeans per hour = 1,500 machine hours devoted to jeans. This leaves 500 available machine hours for making shirts.

Because of the change in product mix, Union Bay's total contribution margin will fall from $480,000 (as shown in Exhibit 8-18) to $450,000, a $30,000 decline. Union Bay had to give up $60 of contribution margin per machine hour ($240 – $180) on the 500 hours it spent producing shirts rather than jeans. However, Union Bay had no choice—the company would have incurred an *actual loss* from producing jeans that it could not sell.

What about fixed costs? In most cases, changing the product mix emphasis in the short run will not affect fixed costs. Thus, fixed costs are irrelevant. However, fixed costs are relevant if they differ between product mix alternatives. For example, what if Union Bay had a month-to-month lease on a zipper machine used only for making jeans? If Union Bay made only shirts, it could *avoid* the lease cost, thereby decreasing fixed costs. However, if Union Bay makes even one pair of jeans, it needs the machine and will increase the lease cost. In this case, the fixed cost associated with the zipper machine lease becomes relevant because it differs between alternative product mixes (shirts only *versus* jeans only or jeans and shirts).

STOP & THINK
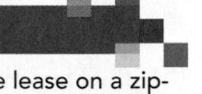

Would Union Bay's product mix decision change if it had a $20,000 cancelable lease on a zipper machine needed only for jeans production? Assume that Union Bay can sell as many units of either product as it makes.

Answer: Compare the profitability of the products as follows:

	A	B	C
1	Product Mix Analysis When Fixed Costs Are Relevant	Shirts	Jeans
2	Total contribution margin at full capacity (Exhibit 8-18)	$ 360,000	$ 480,000
3	Less: Avoidable fixed costs	0	20,000
4	Net benefit from the product at full capacity	$ 360,000	$ 460,000
5			

Even considering the zipper machine lease, producing jeans is more profitable than producing shirts.

Notice that the analysis again follows the two guidelines for special business decisions: (1) focus on relevant data (only those revenues and costs that differ) and (2) use a contribution margin approach, which separates variable costs from fixed costs.

Outsourcing Decisions (Make or Buy)

Outsourcing decisions are sometimes called "make-or-buy" decisions because managers must decide whether to make a product or service in-house or buy it from another company. Sometimes people confuse the term "outsourcing" with the term "offshoring."

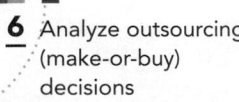

6 Analyze outsourcing (make-or-buy) decisions

- **Outsourcing** refers to contracting an outside company to produce a product or perform a service. Outsourced work could be done domestically or overseas.

- **Offshoring** refers to having work performed overseas. Companies offshore work by either (1) operating their own manufacturing plants and call centers overseas or

(2) outsourcing the overseas work to another company. Thus, offshored work is not necessarily outsourced work.

Outsourcing is not new. For years, companies have outsourced specialized services such as marketing, payroll processing, and legal work to firms that have expertise in those areas. More and more, brand-name companies are outsourcing the production of their products so that they can concentrate on their core competencies of marketing and product development. In fact, so much production is outsourced that contract manufacturing has become an entire industry. <u>**Contract manufacturers**</u> are manufacturers that only make products for other companies, not for themselves.

Let's see how managers make outsourcing decisions. The heart of these decisions is how to best use available resources. Let's assume that Apple, the developer of iPods, is deciding whether to continue making the earbuds that are sold with the product or outsource production to Skullcandy, a company that specializes in earbuds. Let's assume Apple's cost to produce 2 million earbuds each period is as shown in Exhibit 8-19:[2]

EXHIBIT 8-19 Production Costs and Volume

	A	B	C	D
1	**Comparison of Variable and Absorption Costs**	**Variable Cost per Unit**	**Total Cost (2 million units)**	
2	Direct materials	$ 4.00	$ 8,000,000	
3	Direct labor	0.50	1,000,000	
4	Variable MOH	1.50	3,000,000	
5	Total variable manufacturing cost	$ 6.00	$ 12,000,000	
6	Plus: Fixed MOH		4,000,000	
7	Total manufacturing cost		$ 16,000,000	
8	Divide by: Number of units		2,000,000	
9	Cost per unit (absorption costing)		$ 8.00	
10				

Let's further assume that Skullcandy is willing to provide earbuds to Apple for $7.00 each. Should Apple make the earbuds or buy them from Skullcandy? The $7.00 price is less than the full absorption cost per unit ($8.00), but greater than Apple's variable cost per unit ($6.00). The answer isn't as easy as simply comparing unit costs. In deciding what to do, managers should consider the questions outlined in Exhibit 8-20.

EXHIBIT 8-20 Outsourcing Considerations

- How do our variable costs compare to the outsourcing cost?
- Are any fixed costs avoidable if we outsource?
- What could we do with the freed capacity?

Let's see how these considerations apply to our example:

- **Variable costs:** The variable cost of producing each earbud ($6.00) is less than the outsourcing cost ($7.00). Based on variable costs alone, Apple should manufacture the earbuds in-house. However, managers must still consider fixed costs.

- **Fixed costs:** Let's assume that Apple could save $500,000 of fixed costs each period by outsourcing. Unfortunately, this savings would primarily result from laying off salaried indirect labor, such as production supervisors. However, most of the fixed manufacturing cost relates to plant capacity, and will continue to exist even if the company stops making

Why is this important?

"Almost any **business activity** can be **outsourced** (for example, manufacturing, marketing, and payroll). **Companies** often choose to retain only their **core competencies**—things they are *really* good at doing—and **outsource** just about everything else to companies that can do it *better* or more cost-effectively for them."

---

[2]The hypothetical cost information was created solely for academic purposes, and is not intended, in any way, to represent the actual costs incurred by Apple or the price that would be charged by Skullcandy.

earbuds. These costs might include property tax on the plant and non-cancelable lease payments made on the production equipment.

- **Use of freed capacity:** We'll start by assuming that Apple has no other use for the production capacity, so it will remain idle. We will change this assumption later.

Given this information, what should Apple do? Exhibit 8-21 compares the two alternatives.

EXHIBIT 8-21 Incremental Analysis for Outsourcing Decisions

	A	B	C	D
1	**Incremental Analysis Outsourcing Decision**	**Make Earbuds**	**Outsource Earbuds**	**Difference**
2	Variable Costs:			
3	If make: $6.00 × 2 million units If outsource: $7.00 × 2 million units	$ 12,000,000	$ 14,000,000	$ 2,000,000
4	Plus: Fixed costs	4,000,000	3,500,000	(500,000)
5	Total cost of producing 2,000,000 units	$ 16,000,000	$ 17,500,000	$ 1,500,000
6				

This analysis shows that Apple should continue to make the earbuds. Why is this the case? As shown in the last column of Exhibit 8-21, the company would spend $2,000,000 more in variable costs to outsource the earbuds, but only save $500,000 in fixed costs. The net result is a $1,500,000 increase in total costs if the company outsources production. Another way to look at this decision is by performing a cost-benefit analysis. Notice that this analysis simply focuses on the "Difference" column shown in Exhibit 8-21.

Variable cost per unit of outsourcing	$ 7.00
Less: Variable cost per unit of making...	6.00
Extra variable cost per unit to outsource	$ 1.00
Multiply by: Number of units needed	× 2,000,000
Extra variable cost to outsource...	$ 2,000,000
Less: Savings on fixed costs if outsourcing	(500,000)
Net extra cost to outsource...	$ 1,500,000

Notice how the analysis in both Exhibit 8-21 and above is affected by production volume. If Apple needed fewer than 500,000 earbuds each period, then the decision to continue making the earbuds would be reversed because the savings on fixed costs ($500,000) would outweigh the additional $1 per unit spent on variable costs. At volumes lower than 500,000, it would be cheaper for Apple to outsource production than produce in-house.

Notice how Exhibit 8-21 uses our two keys for decision making: (1) focus on relevant data (costs that differ between alternatives), and (2) use a contribution margin approach that separates variable costs from fixed costs. Our decision rule for outsourcing is as follows:

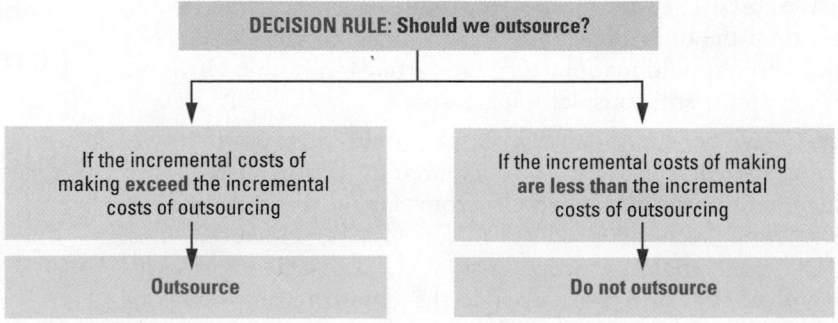

Determining an Acceptable Outsourcing Price

In Chapter 7, we used the concept of an indifference point to help managers decide how to structure costs. We can use the same concept here to determine the maximum outsourcing price Apple would be willing to pay to have another manufacturer make the earbuds. By knowing up front how much Apple would be willing to pay, the company can proactively seek bids from multiple contract manufacturers.

Exhibit 8-22 shows how to calculate the indifference point. The exhibit begins by equating the costs of making the earbuds with the costs of outsourcing the earbuds. Next, all of the information from Exhibit 8-21 is inserted into the equations, with the exception of the variable cost per unit under the outsourcing alternative. The variable cost of outsourcing each unit is the cost we wish to solve for.

EXHIBIT 8-22 Using an Indifference Point to Find an Acceptable Outsourcing Price

$$\text{Costs of making earbuds} = \text{Costs of outsourcing earbuds}$$
$$\text{Variable Costs} + \text{Fixed Costs} = \text{Variable Costs} + \text{Fixed Costs}$$
$$(2{,}000{,}000 \text{ units} \times \$6) + \$4{,}000{,}000 = (2{,}000{,}000 \text{ units} \times \text{Variable cost per unit}) + \$3{,}500{,}000$$
$$\$16{,}000{,}000 = (2{,}000{,}000 \times \text{Variable cost per unit}) + \$3{,}500{,}000$$
$$\$12{,}500{,}000 = (2{,}000{,}000 \times \text{Variable cost per unit})$$
$$\text{Variable cost per unit} = \$6.25$$

This analysis shows that, all else being equal, Apple would be *indifferent* between making and outsourcing 2 million earbuds if the outsourcing price was exactly $6.25 a unit. Therefore, the most Apple would be willing to pay for this volume of earbuds would be just under $6.25 a unit.

Notice, again, that this analysis is dependent on production volume. For example, if Apple needs 3 million units, the most they would be willing to pay would be $6.17 per unit. Why the difference? By producing more units, Apple's fixed costs are being utilized more efficiently, driving down the average cost of making each unit. As Apple's own unit cost falls, so will the price they are willing to pay some other company to make the earbuds. The opposite is also true: The fewer units Apple needs, the more it will be willing to pay another company to make the earbuds.

Alternative Use of Freed Capacity

Now let's change one of our original assumptions. Instead of assuming that the production capacity will remain idle, let's assume that Apple could lease it out to another company for $2.5 million per period. In this case, Apple must consider its <u>opportunity cost</u>, which is the benefit foregone by choosing a particular course of action. If Apple continues to make its own earbuds, it will be losing out on the opportunity to earn lease income of $2.5 million per period.

Exhibit 8-23 incorporates this information into our analysis by showing lease income as additional income that *could be made* if the company outsources production. Thus, we show the lease income in the "Outsource Earbuds" column. This income offsets some of the cost associated with outsourcing. Alternatively, we could show the $2.5 million as an *additional* cost (an opportunity cost) in the "Make Earbuds" column.

EXHIBIT 8-23 Incremental Analysis Incorporating Next Best Use of Freed Capacity

	A	B	C	D
1	**Incremental Analysis Outsourcing Decision**	**Make Earbuds**	**Outsource Earbuds**	**Difference**
2	Variable Costs:			
3	If make: $6.00 × 2 million units If outsource: $7.00 × 2 million units	$ 12,000,000	$ 14,000,000	$ 2,000,000
4	Plus: Fixed costs	4,000,000	3,500,000	(500,000)
5	Total cost of producing 2,000,000 units	$ 16,000,000	$ 17,500,000	$ 1,500,000
6	Less: Lease income if outsource	0	2,500,000	2,500,000
7	Net cost	$ 16,000,000	$ 15,000,000	$ (1,000,000)
8				

This analysis shows that Apple will save $1,000,000 each period by outsourcing production of the earbuds. This result holds regardless of whether we treat the $2.5 million lease as income in the "Outsource Earbuds" column or as an opportunity cost in the "Make Earbuds" column. Again, notice that a different production volume could potentially result in a different outcome.

Potential Drawbacks of Outsourcing

While outsourcing often provides cost savings, it is not without drawbacks. When a company outsources, it gives up control of the production process, including control over quality and production scheduling. Rather, it must rely on the supplier to provide the product or service at an agreed-upon level of quality, at agreed-upon delivery dates. Often, one or more employees are needed just to manage the relationship with the outsourcing company to make sure that everything runs smoothly. The cost of employing any such additional personnel should also be considered when comparing the cost of outsourcing versus the cost of producing in-house.

In addition, for those companies embracing the triple bottom line, outsourcing is often not viewed as a viable alternative. Why? Because outsourcing often results in laying off employees. In addition, companies will want to thoroughly investigate and monitor the labor practices and working conditions of offshored contract work to make sure laborers are treated fairly and work in a safe environment. While overseas labor is often cheap and readily available, the exploitation of any people, in any country, is not an acceptable business practice.

▶ ## Try It!

Rossignol makes downhill ski equipment. Assume that Atomic has offered to produce ski poles for Rossignol for $18 per pair. Rossignol needs 100,000 pairs of poles per period. Rossignol can only avoid $125,000 of fixed costs if it outsources; the remaining fixed costs are unavoidable. Rossignol currently has the following costs at a production level of 100,000 pairs of poles:

Manufacturing Costs	Total Cost	Cost per pair (100,000 pairs)
Direct Materials	$ 750,000	$ 7.50
Direct Labor	80,000	0.80
Variable MOH	520,000	5.20
Fixed MOH	650,000	6.50
Total	$2,000,000	$20.00

1. Should Rossignol outsource ski pole production if the next best use of the freed capacity is to leave it idle? What affect will outsourcing have on Rossignol operating income?

2. If the freed capacity could be used to produce ski boots that would provide $500,000 of operating income, should Rossignol outsource ski pole production?

Please see page 501 for solutions.

Decisions to Sell As Is or Process Further

7 Decide whether to sell a product "as is" or process it further

At what point in processing should a company sell its product? Many companies, especially in the food processing and natural resource industries, face this business decision. Companies in these industries process a raw material (milk, corn, livestock, crude oil, lumber, and so forth) to a point before it is saleable. For example, Kraft pasteurizes raw milk before it is saleable. Kraft must then decide whether it should sell the pasteurized milk as is or process it further into other dairy products (reduced-fat milk, butter, sour cream, cottage cheese, yogurt, blocks of cheese, shredded cheese, and so forth). Managers consider the questions shown in Exhibit 8-24 when deciding whether to sell as is or process further.

EXHIBIT 8-24 Sell As Is or Process Further Considerations

- How much revenue will we receive if we sell the product as is?
- How much revenue will we receive if we sell the product *after* processing it further?
- How much will it cost to process the product further?

Let's consider Bertolli, the manufacturer of Italian food products. Suppose Bertolli spends $100,000 to process raw olives into 50,000 quarts of plain virgin olive oil. Should Bertolli sell the olive oil as is or should it spend more to process the olive oil into gourmet dipping oils, such as a Basil and Garlic Infused Dipping Oil? In making the decision, Bertolli's managers consider the following relevant information:[3]

- Bertolli could sell the plain olive oil for $5 per quart, for a total of $250,000 (50,000 × $5).
- Bertolli could sell the gourmet dipping oil for $7 per quart, for a total of $350,000 (50,000 × $7).
- Bertolli would have to spend $0.75 per quart, or $37,500 (50,000 × $0.75), to further process the plain olive oil into the gourmet dipping oil. This cost would include the extra direct materials required (such as basil, garlic, and the incremental cost of premium glass containers) as well as the extra conversion costs incurred (the cost of any *additional* machinery and labor that the company would need to purchase in order to complete the extra processing).

By examining the incremental analysis shown in Exhibit 8-25, Bertolli's managers can see that they can increase operating income by $62,500 by further processing the plain olive oil into the gourmet dipping oil. The extra $100,000 of revenue greatly exceeds the incremental $37,500 of cost incurred to further process the olive oil.

Why is this important?

"Some companies are able to sell their products at **different points** of completion. For example, some furniture **manufacturers** sell flat-packed bookshelves, TV stands, and home office furniture that the consumer must **finish assembling**. A **cost-benefit analysis** helps managers choose the most **profitable point** at which to sell the company's products."

EXHIBIT 8-25 Incremental Analysis for Sell As Is or Process Further Decision

	A	B	C	D
1	**Incremental Analysis** **Sell or Process Further Decision**	**Sell As Is**	**Process Further**	**Difference**
2	Revenues:			
3	If sell as is: $5.00 × 50,000 quarts If process further: $7.00 × 50,000 quarts	$ 250,000	$ 350,000	$ 100,000
4	Less: Extra cost of processing further	0	37,500	37,500
5	Net benefit to operating income	$ 250,000	$ 312,500	$ 62,500
6				

[3]All references to Bertolli in this hypothetical example were created by the author solely for academic purposes and are not intended, in any way, to represent the actual business practices of, or costs incurred by, Bertolli.

Notice that Bertolli's managers do *not* consider the $100,000 originally spent on processing the olives into olive oil. Why? It is a sunk cost. Recall from our previous discussion that a sunk cost is a past cost that cannot be changed regardless of which future action the company takes. Bertolli has incurred $100,000 regardless of whether it sells the olive oil as is or processes it further into gourmet dipping oils. Therefore, the cost is *not* relevant to the decision.

Thus, the decision rule is as follows:

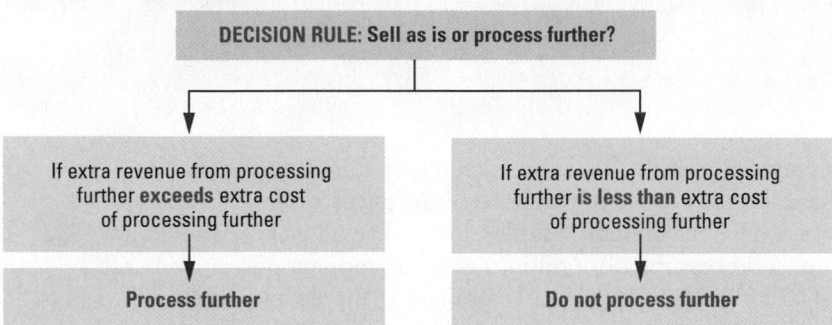

Decision Guidelines

Short-Term Special Business Decisions

Amazon.com has confronted most of the special business decisions we've covered. Here are the key guidelines Amazon.com's managers follow in making their decisions.

Decision	Guidelines
Should Amazon.com discontinue its electronics product line?	If the cost savings exceed the lost revenues from dropping the electronics product line, then dropping the line will increase operating income.
Given limited warehouse space, which products should Amazon.com focus on selling?	Amazon.com should focus on selling the products with the highest contribution margin per unit of the constraint, which is cubic feet of warehouse space.
Should Amazon.com outsource its warehousing operations?	If the incremental costs of operating its own warehouses exceed the costs of outsourcing, then outsourcing will increase operating income.
How should a company decide whether to sell a product as is or process further?	Process further only if the extra sales revenue (from processing further) exceeds the extra costs of additional processing.

SUMMARY PROBLEM 2

Requirements

1. Aziz produces Standard and Deluxe sunglasses:

	Per Pair	
	Standard	Deluxe
Sale price..	$20	$30
Variable expenses...	16	21

The company has 15,000 machine hours available. In one machine hour, Aziz can produce 70 pairs of the Standard model or 30 pairs of the Deluxe model. Assuming machine hours is a constraint, which model should Aziz emphasize?

2. Just Do It! incurs the following costs for 20,000 pairs of its high-tech hiking socks:

Direct materials..	$ 20,000
Direct labor..	80,000
Variable manufacturing overhead	40,000
Fixed manufacturing overhead...	80,000
Total manufacturing cost	$220,000
Cost per pair ($220,000 ÷ 20,000).......................................	$ 11

Another manufacturer has offered to sell Just Do It! similar socks for $10 a pair, a total purchase cost of $200,000. If Just Do It! outsources *and* leaves its plant idle, it can save $50,000 of fixed overhead cost. Or the company can use the released facilities to make other products that will contribute $70,000 to profits. In this case, the company will not be able to avoid any fixed costs. Identify and analyze the alternatives. What is the best course of action?

▪ SOLUTIONS

Requirement 1

	A	B	C
1	**Product Mix Decision**	**Standard**	**Deluxe**
2	Sales price per unit	$ 20	$ 30
3	Less: Variable cost per unit	16	21
4	Contribution margin per unit	$ 4	$ 9
5	Multiply by: Number of units produced per machine hour	70	30
6	Contribution margin per machine hour	$ 280	$ 270
7	Multiply by: Available capacity (number of machine hours)	15,000	15,000
8	Total contribution margin at full capacity	$ 4,200,000	$ 4,050,000
9			

Decision: Emphasize the Standard model because it has the higher contribution margin per unit of the constraint—machine hours—resulting in a higher contribution margin for the company.

Requirement 2

	A	B	C	D
1	**Incremental Analysis Outsourcing Decision**	**Make Socks**	**Outsource and Leave Idle**	**Outsource and Make Other Products**
2	Variable Costs:			
3	If make: DM, DL, Variable MOH If outsource: $10 × 20,000 units	$ 140,000	$ 200,000	$ 200,000
4	Plus: Fixed costs	80,000	30,000	80,000
5	Total cost of producing 2,000,000 units	$ 220,000	$ 230,000	$ 280,000
6	Less: Profit from other products	0	0	70,000
7	Net cost	$ 220,000	$ 230,000	$ 210,000
8				

Decision: Just Do It! should outsource the socks from the outside supplier and use the released facilities to make other products.

END OF CHAPTER

Learning Objectives

- 1 Describe and identify information relevant to short-term business decisions
- 2 Decide whether to accept a special order
- 3 Describe and apply different approaches to pricing
- 4 Decide whether to discontinue a product, department, or store
- 5 Factor resource constraints into product mix decisions
- 6 Analyze outsourcing (make-or-buy) decisions
- 7 Decide whether to sell a product "as is" or process it further

Accounting Vocabulary

Avoidable Fixed Costs. (p. 461) Fixed costs that can be eliminated as a result of taking a particular course of action.

Common Fixed Expenses. (p. 463) Expenses than can not be traced to a particular product line.

Constraint. (p. 464) A factor that restricts the production or sale of a product.

Contract Manufacturers. (p. 467) Manufacturers that make products for other companies, not for themselves.

Cost-Plus Pricing. (p. 455) An approach to pricing used by price-setters; cost-plus pricing begins with the product's total costs and adds the company's desired profit to determine a cost-plus price.

Offshoring. (p. 466) Having work performed overseas. Offshored work can either be performed by the company itself or by outsourcing the work to another company.

Opportunity Cost. (p. 469) The benefit forgone by choosing a particular alternative course of action.

Outsourcing. (p. 466) A make-or-buy decision: Managers decide whether to buy a product or service or produce it in-house.

Product Line Income Statement. (p. 460) An income statement that shows the operating income of each product line, as well as the company as a whole.

Relevant Information. (p. 444) Expected *future* data that *differs* among alternatives.

Segment Margin. (p. 464) The income resulting from subtracting only the direct fixed costs of a product line from its contribution margin. The segment margin contains no allocation of common fixed costs.

Segment Margin Income Statement. (p. 464) A product line income statement that contains no allocation of common fixed costs. Only direct fixed costs that can be traced to specific product lines are subtracted from the product line's contribution margin. All common fixed costs remain unallocated, and are shown only under the company total.

Sunk Cost. (p. 445) A past cost that cannot be changed regardless of which future action is taken.

Target Costing. (p. 453) An approach to pricing used by price-takers; target costing begins with the revenue at market price and subtracts the company's desired profit to arrive at the target total cost.

Unavoidable Fixed Costs. (p. 461) Fixed costs that will continue to be incurred even if a particular course of action is taken.

MyAccountingLab — Go to http://myaccountinglab.com/ **for the following Quick Check, Short Exercises, Exercises, and Problems. They are available with immediate grading, explanations of correct and incorrect answers, and interactive media that acts as your own online tutor.**

Quick Check

1. (*Learning Objective 1*) Which of the following is *false*?
   a. Relevant information always differs among alternatives.
   b. Relevant information always regards the future.
   c. Relevant information is always financial in nature.
   d. Sunk costs are never relevant to a decision.

2. (*Learning Objective 1*) Keys to making short-term decisions include which of the following?
   a. Focusing on relevant revenues, costs, and profits
   b. Using a contribution margin approach that separates variable costs from fixed costs
   c. Both of the above
   d. None of the above

3. *(Learning Objective 2)* Which of the following should be considered for special order decisions?

   a. Whether excess capacity exists

   b. Whether the special price will be high enough to cover incremental costs of filling the order

   c. Whether the special order will affect regular sales in the long run

   d. All of the listed choices should be considered in special order decisions.

4. *(Learning Objective 3)* Which is true of price-setters?

   a. Their products lack uniqueness.

   b. Their pricing approach emphasizes cost-plus pricing.

   c. They are in highly competitive markets.

   d. Their pricing approach emphasizes target costing.

5. *(Learning Objective 3)* The formula for arriving at target cost is which of the following?

   a. Revenue minus desired profit

   b. Revenue minus actual profit

   c. Cost minus actual profit

   d. Revenue minus variable cost

6. *(Learning Objective 4)* Which of the following is *not* relevant when deciding whether or not to discontinue a product?

   a. The product's contribution margin

   b. Avoidable fixed costs related to the product

   c. Unavoidable fixed costs related to the product

   d. The effect of discontinuation on the sales of the company's other products.

7. *(Learning Objective 4)* A segment margin is the

   a. segment's contribution margin minus all fixed costs.

   b. segment's contribution margin minus direct fixed costs.

   c. segment's contribution margin minus allocated fixed costs.

   d. same as the segment's contribution margin.

8. *(Learning Objective 5)* When resources are constrained, which of the following should be used to guide product mix decisions?

   a. The products' gross margin

   b. The products' contribution margin

   c. The products' gross margin per unit of constraint

   d. The products' contribution margin per unit of constraint

9. *(Learning Objective 6)* Which of the following is *false*?

   a. Outsourcing decisions are often referred to as "make-or-buy" decisions.

   b. Outsourcing refers to having work performed overseas.

   c. Contract manufacturers are manufacturers that make products for other companies.

   d. Outsourcing decisions should take into consideration the intended use of freed capacity.

10. *(Learning Objective 7)* In making "sell as is" decisions, companies should consider all of the following EXCEPT for:

   a. Costs incurred up to the "sell as is" decision point

   b. Incremental costs that would be incurred by processing further

   c. Incremental revenues that would be earned by processing further

   d. All of the above should be considered.

Quick Check Answers

1.c 2.c 3.d 4.b 5.a 6.c 7.b 8.d 9.b 10.a

Short Exercises

S8-1   Determine relevance of information *(Learning Objective 1)*

You are trying to decide whether to trade in your laser printer for a more recent model. Your usage pattern will remain unchanged, but the old and new printers use different toner cartridges. Are the following items relevant or irrelevant to your decision?

   a. The trade-in value of the old printer

   b. Paper costs

   c. The difference between the cost of toner cartridges

   d. The price of the new printer

   e. The price you paid for the old printer

S8-2 Special order decision *(Learning Objective 2)*

Belco Manufacturing produces and sells oil filters for $3.35 each. A retailer has offered to purchase 20,000 oil filters for $1.75 per filter. Of the total manufacturing cost per filter of $1.90, $1.40 is the variable manufacturing cost per filter. For this special order, Belco would have to buy a special stamping machine that costs $8,000 to mark the customer's logo on the special-order oil filters. The machine would be scrapped when the special order is complete. This special order would use manufacturing capacity that would otherwise be idle. No variable nonmanufacturing costs would be incurred by the special order. Regular sales would not be affected by the special order.

Would you recommend that Belco accept the special order under these conditions?

S8-3 Determine pricing approach and target price *(Learning Objective 3)*

Mount Snow operates a Rocky Mountain ski resort. The company is planning its lift ticket pricing for the coming ski season. Investors would like to earn a 17% return on the company's $115 million of assets. The company incurs primarily fixed costs to groom the runs and operate the lifts. Mount Snow projects fixed costs to be $44,000,000 for the ski season. The resort serves 775,000 skiers and snowboarders each season. Variable costs are $7 per guest. Currently, the resort has such a favorable reputation among skiers and snowboarders that it has some control over the lift ticket prices.

1. Would Mount Snow emphasize target costing or cost-plus pricing. Why?
2. If other resorts in the area charge $66 per day, what price should Mount Snow charge?

S8-4 Use target costing to analyze data *(Learning Objective 3)*

Consider Mount Snow from S8-3. Assume that Mount Snow's reputation has diminished and other resorts in the vicinity are charging only $66 per lift ticket. Mount Snow has become a price-taker and won't be able to charge more than its competitors. At the market price, Mount Snow's managers believe they will still serve 775,000 skiers and snowboarders each season.

1. If Mount Snow can't reduce its costs, what profit will it earn? State your answer in dollars and as a percent of assets. Will investors be happy with the profit level? Show your analysis.
2. Assume that Mount Snow has found ways to cut its fixed costs to $28.5 million. What is its new target variable cost per skier/snowboarder? Compare this to the current variable cost per skier/snowboarder. Comment on your results.

S8-5 Decide whether to discontinue a department *(Learning Objective 4)*

Mila Fashion in New York operates three departments: Men's, Women's, and Accessories. Mila Fashion allocates all fixed expenses (unavoidable building depreciation and utilities) based on each department's square footage. Departmental operating income data for the third quarter of the current year are as follows:

	A	B	C	D	E
1			Mila Fashions		
2		Product Line Contribution Margin Income Statement			
3			For the Year		
4					
5			Product lines		
6		Men's	Women's	Accessories	Company Total
7	Sales revenue	$ 109,000	$ 56,000	$ 98,000	$ 263,000
8	Less: Variable expenses	59,000	30,000	90,000	$ 179,000
9	Contribution margin	$ 50,000	$ 26,000	$ 8,000	$ 84,000
10	Less: Fixed expenses	24,000	18,000	25,000	$ 67,000
11	Operating income	$ 26,000	$ 8,000	$ (17,000)	$ 17,000
12					

The store will remain in the same building regardless of whether any of the departments are discontinued. Should Mila Fashion discontinue any of the departments? Give your reason.

S8-6   Discontinue a department: Revised information *(Learning Objective 4)*

Consider Mila Fashion from S8-5. Assume that the fixed expenses assigned to each department include only direct fixed costs of the department (rather than unavoidable fixed costs as given in S8-5):

- Salary of the department's manager
- Cost of advertising directly related to that department

If Mila Fashion discontinues a department, it will not incur these fixed expenses. Under these circumstances, should Mila Fashion discontinue any of the departments? Give your reason.

S8-7   Replace a department *(Learning Objective 4)*

Consider Mila Fashion from S8-5. Assume once again that all fixed costs are unavoidable. If the company discontinues one of the current departments, it plans to replace the discontinued department with a Shoe Department. The company expects the Shoe Department to produce $81,000 in sales and have $52,000 of variable costs. Because the shoe business would be new to Mila Fashion, the company would have to incur an additional $6,800 of fixed costs (advertising, new shoe display racks, and so forth) per quarter related to the department. What should the company do now?

S8-8   Product mix decision: Unlimited demand *(Learning Objective 5)*

StoreAway produces plastic storage bins for household storage needs. The company makes two sizes of bins: Large (50 gallon) and Regular (35 gallon). Demand for the product is so high that the company can sell as many of each size as it can produce. The same machinery is used to produce both sizes. The machinery is available for only 2,800 hours per period. The company can produce 12 Large bins every hour compared to 16 Regular bins in the same amount of time. Fixed expenses amount to $120,000 per period. Sales prices and variable costs are as follows:

	Regular	Large
Sales price per unit	$8.40	$10.20
Variable cost per unit	$3.00	$ 4.40

1. Which product should StoreAway emphasize? Why?
2. To maximize profits, how many of each size bin should the company produce?
3. Given this product mix, what will the company's operating income be?

S8-9   Product mix decision: Limited demand *(Learning Objective 5)*

Consider StoreAway from S8-8. Assume that demand for Regular bins is limited to 38,400 units and demand for Large bins is limited to 22,000 units.

1. How many of each size bin should the company make now?
2. Given this product mix, what will be the company's operating income?
3. Explain why the operating income is less than it was when the company was producing its optimal product mix.

S8-10   Outsourcing production decision *(Learning Objectives 1 & 6)*

Suppose a Panini's restaurant is considering whether to (1) bake bread for its restaurant in-house or (2) buy the bread from a local bakery. The chef estimates that variable costs of making each loaf include $0.46 of ingredients, $0.22 of variable overhead (electricity to run the oven), and $0.75 of direct labor for kneading and forming the loaves. Allocating fixed overhead (depreciation on the kitchen equipment and building) based on direct labor assigns $0.96 of fixed overhead per loaf. None of the fixed costs are avoidable. The local bakery would charge Panini's $1.76 per loaf.

1. What is the absorption cost of making a loaf of bread in-house? What is the variable cost per loaf?
2. Should Panini's bake the bread in-house or buy from the local bakery? Why?
3. In addition to the financial analysis, what else should Panini's consider when making this decision?

S8-11 Relevant information for outsourcing delivery function
(Learning Objectives 1 & 6)

Wheeler Food in Ashland, Kentucky, manufactures and markets snack foods. Tessa Lee manages the company's fleet of 180 delivery trucks. Lee has been charged with "reengineering" the fleet-management function. She has an important decision to make.

- Should she continue to manage the fleet in-house with the five employees reporting to her? To do so, she will have to acquire new fleet-management software to stream-line Wheeler Food's fleet-management process.

- Should she outsource the fleet-management function to Fleet Management Services, a company that specializes in managing fleets of trucks for other companies? Fleet Management Services would take over the maintenance, repair, and scheduling of Wheeler Food's fleet (but Wheeler Food would retain ownership). This alternative would require Lee to lay off her five employees. However, her own job would be secure, as she would be Wheeler Food's liaison with Fleet Management Services.

Assume that Lee's records show the following data concerning Wheeler Food's fleet:

Book value of Wheeler Food's trucks, with an estimated five-year life	$3,300,000
Annual leasing fee for new fleet-management software	$ 8,000
Annual maintenance of trucks	$ 154,000
Fleet Supervisor Lee's annual salary	$ 59,000
Total annual salaries of Wheeler Food's five other fleet-management employees	$ 145,000

Suppose that Fleet Management Services offers to manage Wheeler Food's fleet for an annual fee of $276,000.

Which alternative will maximize Wheeler Food's short-term operating income?

S8-12 Outsourcing qualitative considerations *(Learning Objectives 1 & 6)*

Refer to Wheeler Food in S8-11. What qualitative factors should Lee consider before making a final decision?

S8-13 Scrap or process further decision *(Learning Objective 7)*

Jensen Auto Components has an inventory of 480 obsolete remote entry keys that are carried in inventory at a manufacturing cost of $78,720. Production Supervisor Karen Rinke must decide to do one of the following:

- Process the inventory further at a cost of $23,000, with the expectation of selling it for $30,000

- Scrap the inventory for a sales price of $3,500

What should Rinke do? Present figures to support your decision.

S8-14 Determine most profitable final product *(Learning Objective 7)*

CocoaHeaven processes cocoa beans into cocoa powder at a processing cost of $10,000 per batch. CocoaHeaven can sell the cocoa powder as is, or it can process the cocoa powder further into chocolate syrup or boxed assorted chocolates. Once processed, each batch of cocoa beans would result in the following sales revenue:

Cocoa powder	$ 15,000
Chocolate syrup	$101,000
Boxed assorted chocolates	$200,000

The cost of transforming the cocoa powder into chocolate syrup would be $69,000. Likewise, the company would incur $180,000 to transform the cocoa powder into boxed assorted chocolates. The company president has decided to make boxed assorted chocolates owing to its high sales value and to the fact that the $10,000 cost of processing cocoa beans "eats up" most of the cocoa powder profits. Has the president made the right or wrong decision? Explain your answer.

S8-15 Identify ethical standards violated *(Learning Objectives 1, 2, 3, 4, 5, 6, & 7)*

ETHICS

For each of the situations listed, identify the primary standard from the IMA *Statement of Ethical Professional Practice* that is violated (competence, confidentiality, integrity, or credibility). Refer to Exhibit 1-6 for the complete standard.

1. Stanley does not know how to categorize fixed costs as unavoidable or avoidable, so he guesses on the categorization of each fixed cost.

2. Connor Advertising Agency is looking at whether to continue to do its own payroll in-house or to outsource it to a payroll firm (a classic "make-or-buy" decision). Elsie, an accountant at Connor, does not tell management that the payroll firm bidding on the work is owned and managed by her mother.

3. Sarah is a management accountant at a large electronics firm. She is instructed to prepare an analysis of the performance of an underperforming company division. Since Sarah is afraid that many employees could lose their jobs if that division appears to be underperforming, Sarah underestimates the amount of expenses generated by that division. Sarah hopes that the division is not discontinued.

4. Latoya, a CPA and a CMA, makes a YouTube video bragging about loopholes she has found to avoid taxes. These loopholes are questionable at best.

5. Seymour is the controller for a small manufacturer. He mentions to a close friend that his company is going to start offshoring production to decrease labor costs.

EXERCISES Group A

E8-16A Determine relevant and irrelevant information *(Learning Objective 1)*

Jubilee Frozen Foods purchased new computer-controlled production machinery last year from Advanced Design. The equipment was purchased for $4.1 million and was paid for with cash. A representative from Advanced Design recently contacted Jubilee management because Advanced Design has an even more efficient piece of machinery available. The new design would double the production output of the equipment purchased last year but would cost Jubilee another $5.0 million. The old machinery was installed by an engineering firm; the same firm would be required to install the new machinery. Fixed selling costs would not change if the new machinery were to be purchased, but the variable selling cost per unit would decrease. Raw material costs (i.e., food ingredients) would remain the same with either machine. The new machinery would be purchased by signing a note payable at the bank and interest would be paid monthly on the note payable. Maintenance costs on the new machine would be the same as the maintenance costs on the machinery purchased last year. Advanced Design is offering a trade-in on the machinery purchased last year against the purchase price of the new machinery.

For each of the following costs, indicate whether each of the costs described would be relevant or not to Jubilee Frozen Foods' decision about whether to purchase the new machinery or not.

Item	Relevant	Not Relevant
a. Book value of old machine		
b. Maintenance cost of new machine		
c. Maintenance cost of old machine......................................		
d. Installation cost of new machine..		
e. Accumulated depreciation on old machine		
f. Cost per pound of food to be processed by the machinery		
g. Installation cost of old machine		
h. Cost of the new machine		
i. Cost of the old machine...		
j. Added profits from the increase in production resulting from the new machine		
k. Fixed selling costs...		
l. Variable selling costs..		
m. Trade-in value of old machine...		
n. Interest expense on new machine		
o. Sales tax paid on old machine		

E8-17A Special order decisions given two scenarios (Learning Objective 2)

Suppose the Baseball Hall of Fame in Cooperstown, New York, has approached Hobby Memorabilia & More with a special order. The Hall of Fame wants to purchase 58,000 baseball card packs for a special promotional campaign and offers $0.43 per pack, a total of $24,940. Hobby Memorabilia & More's total production cost is $0.63 per pack, as follows:

Variable costs:	
Direct materials	$0.14
Direct labor	0.08
Variable overhead	0.11
Fixed overhead	0.30
Total cost	$0.63

Hobby Memorabilia & More has enough excess capacity to handle the special order.

Requirements

1. Prepare an incremental analysis to determine whether Hobby Memorabilia & More should accept the special sales order assuming fixed costs would not be affected by the special order.
2. Now assume that the Hall of Fame wants special hologram baseball cards. Hobby Memorabilia & More must spend $5,500 to develop this hologram, which will be useless after the special order is completed. Should Hobby Memorabilia & More accept the special order under these circumstances? Show your analysis.

SUSTAINABILITY

E8-18A Sustainability and short-term decision making (Learning Objective 1)

Over the past several years, decommissioned U.S. warships have been turned into artificial reefs in the ocean by towing them out to sea and sinking them. The thinking was that sinking the ship would conveniently dispose of it while providing an artificial reef environment for aquatic life. In reality, some of the sunken ships have released toxins into the ocean and have been costly to decontaminate. Now the U.S. government is taking bids to instead dismantle and recycle ships that have recently been decommissioned (but have not been sunk yet.)

Assume that a recently decommissioned aircraft carrier, the USS *Blaze*, is estimated to contain approximately 40 tons of recyclable materials able to be sold for approximately $32.8 million. The low bid for dismantling and transporting the ship materials to appropriate facilities is $34.5 million. Recycling and dismantling the ship would create about 500 jobs for about a year in the Rust Belt. This geographic area has been experiencing record-high unemployment rates in recent years.

1. Is it more financially advantageous to sink the ship (assume that it costs approximately $0.7 million to tow a ship out to sea and sink it) or to dismantle and recycle it? Show your calculations.
2. From a sustainability standpoint, what should be done with the decommissioned aircraft carrier? List some of the qualitative factors that should enter into this analysis.
3. As a taxpayer, which action would you prefer (sink or recycle)? Defend your answer.

E8-19A Special order decision and considerations (Learning Objective 2)

Hoover Cole Sunglasses sell for about $153 per pair. Suppose the company incurs the following average costs per pair:

Direct materials	$50
Direct labor	14
Variable manufacturing overhead	7
Variable marketing expenses	3
Fixed manufacturing overhead	25*
Total costs	$99

*2,100,000 total fixed manufacturing overhead
84,000 pairs of sunglasses

Relevant Costs for Short-Term Decisions

Hoover Cole has enough idle capacity to accept a one-time-only special order from Colorado Glasses for 19,000 pairs of sunglasses at $91 per pair. Hoover Cole will not incur any variable marketing expenses for the order.

Requirements

1. How would accepting the order affect Hoover Cole's operating income? In addition to the special order's effect on profits, what other (longer-term qualitative) factors should Hoover Cole's managers consider in deciding whether to accept the order?

2. Hoover Cole's marketing manager, Jim Revo, argues against accepting the special order because the offer price of $91 is less than Hoover Cole's $99 cost to make the sunglasses. Revo asks you, as one of Hoover Cole's staff accountants, to explain whether his analysis is correct.

E8-20A   Pricing decisions given two scenarios (Learning Objective 3)

Preston Builders builds 1,500-square-foot starter tract homes in the fast-growing suburbs of Houston. Land and labor are cheap, and competition among developers is fierce. The homes are "cookie-cutter," with any upgrades added by the buyer after the sale. Preston Builders' costs per developed sublot are as follows:

Land...	$ 51,000
Construction..	$121,000
Landscaping	$ 9,000
Variable marketing costs	$ 5,000

Preston Builders would like to earn a profit of 15% of the variable cost of each home sale. Similar homes offered by competing builders sell for $204,000 each.

Requirements

1. Which approach to pricing should Preston Builders emphasize? Why?

2. Will Preston Builders be able to achieve its target profit levels? Show your computations.

3. Bathrooms and kitchens are typically the most important selling features of a home. Preston Builders could differentiate the homes by upgrading bathrooms and kitchens. The upgrades would cost $20,000 per home but would enable the company to increase the selling prices by $35,000 per home (in general, kitchen and bathroom upgrades typically add at least 150% of their cost to the value of any home). If Preston Builders upgrades, what will the new cost-plus price per home be? Should the company differentiate its product in this manner? Show your analysis.

E8-21A   Decide whether to discontinue a product line (Learning Objective 4)

Top managers of Family Tyme Movies are alarmed by their operating losses. They are considering dropping the DVD product line. Company accountants have prepared the following analysis to help make this decision:

	A	B	C	D
1	Family Tyme Movies			
2	Product Line Contribution Margin Income Statement			
3	For the Year			
4				
5		Product lines		
6		Blu-ray Discs	DVDs	Company Total
7	Sales revenue	$ 301,000	$ 126,000	$ 427,000
8	Less: Variable expenses	155,000	80,000	235,000
9	Contribution margin	$ 146,000	$ 46,000	$ 192,000
10	Less fixed expenses:			
11	Manufacturing	79,000	59,000	138,000
12	Marketing and administrative	57,000	15,000	72,000
13	Operating income (loss)	$ 10,000	$ (28,000)	$ (18,000)
14				

Total fixed costs will not change if the company stops selling DVDs.

Requirements

1. Prepare an incremental analysis to show whether Family Tyme Movies should discontinue the DVD product line. Will discontinuing DVDs add $28,000 to operating income? Explain.

2. Assume that the company can avoid $29,000 of fixed expenses by discontinuing the DVD product line (these costs are direct fixed costs of the DVD product line). Prepare an incremental analysis to show whether the company should stop selling DVDs.

3. Now, assume that all of the fixed costs assigned to DVDs are direct fixed costs and can be avoided if the company stops selling DVDs. However, marketing has concluded that Blu-ray disc sales would be adversely affected by discontinuing the DVD line (retailers want to buy both from the same supplier). Blu-ray disc production and sales would decline 10%. What should the company do?

E8-22A Discontinuing a product line *(Learning Objective 4)*

Suppose Better Harvest is considering discontinuing its organic dried fruit product line. Assume that during the past year, the organic dried fruit's product line income statement showed the following:

	A	B	C	D
1	Sales revenue	$ 5,250,000		
2	Less: Cost of goods sold	6,450,000		
3	Gross profit	$ (1,200,000)		
4	Less: Operating expenses	1,500,000		
5	Operating income (loss)	$ (2,700,000)		
6				

Fixed manufacturing overhead costs account for 40% of the cost of goods, while only 30% of the operating expenses are fixed. Since the organic dried fruit line is just one of the company's fruit operations, only $775,000 of direct fixed costs (the majority of which is advertising) will be eliminated if the product line is discontinued. The remainder of the fixed costs will still be incurred by the company. If the company decides to discontinue the product line, what will happen to the company's operating income? Should Better Harvest discontinue the product line?

E8-23A Identify constraint, then determine product mix *(Learning Objective 5)*

TreadLight produces two types of exercise treadmills: Regular and Deluxe. The exercise craze is such that TreadLight could use all of its available machine hours producing either model. The two models are processed through the same production department.

	A	B	C	D
1		Per Unit		
2		Deluxe	Regular	
3	Sales price	$ 1,020	$ 580	
4	Less expenses:			
5	Direct materials	320	110	
6	Direct labor	88	186	
7	Variable manufacturing overhead	168	84	
8	Fixed manufacturing overhead*	80	40	
9	Variable operating expenses	113	69	
10	Total expenses	$ 769	$ 489	
11	Operating income	$ 251	$ 91	
12				

* Allocated on the basis of machine hours.

What product mix will maximize operating income? (*Hint:* Use the allocation of fixed manufacturing overhead to determine the proportion of machine hours used by each product.)

E8-24A   Determine product mix for retailer—two stocking scenarios

(Learning Objective 5)

Each morning, Nate Jeppson stocks the drink case at Nate's Beach Hut in Long Beach, California. Nate's Beach Hut has 110 linear feet of refrigerated display space for cold drinks. Each linear foot can hold either seven 12-ounce cans or five 20-ounce plastic or glass bottles. The beverage stands sells three types of cold drinks:

1. Cola in 12-oz. cans for $1.40 per can
2. Bottled water in 20-oz. plastic bottles for $1.85 per bottle
3. Orange juice in 20-oz. glass bottles for $2.30 per bottle

Nate's Beach Hut pays its suppliers the following:

1. $0.20 per 12-oz. can of cola
2. $0.30 per 20-oz. bottle of spring water
3. $0.70 per 20-oz. bottle of orange juice

Nate's Beach Hut's monthly fixed expenses include the following:

Hut rental	$ 385
Refrigerator rental...	60
Nate's salary	1,550
Total fixed expenses...	$1,995

The beverage stand can sell all drinks stocked in the display case each morning.

Requirements

1. What is the constraining factor at Nate's Beach Hut? What should Nate stock to maximize profits? What is the maximum contribution margin he could generate from refrigerated drinks each day?
2. To provide variety to customers, suppose Nate refuses to devote more than 65 linear feet and no less than 5 linear feet to any individual product. Under this condition, how many linear feet of each drink should be stocked? How many units of each product will be available for sale each day?
3. Assuming the product mix calculated in Requirement 2, what contribution margin will be generated from refrigerated drinks each day?

E8-25A   Make-or-buy product component *(Learning Objective 6)*

TechSystem manufactures an optical switch that it uses in its final product. TechSystems incurred the following manufacturing costs when it produced 68,000 units last year:

	A	B	C	D
1	Direct materials	$ 612,000		
2	Direct labor	136,000		
3	Variable MOH	68,000		
4	Fixed MOH	408,000		
5	Total manufacturing cost for 68,000 units	$ 1,224,000		
6				

TechSystems does not yet know how many switches it will need this year; however, another company has offered to sell TechSystems the switch for $13.50 per unit. If TechSystems buys the switch from the outside supplier, the manufacturing facilities that will be idle cannot be used for any other purpose, yet none of the fixed costs are avoidable.

Requirements

1. Given the same cost structure, should TechSystems make or buy the switch? Show your analysis.

2. Now, assume that TechSystems can avoid $97,000 of fixed costs a year by outsourcing production. In addition, because sales are increasing, TechSystems needs 73,000 switches a year rather than 68,000 switches. What should the company do now?

3. Given the last scenario, what is the most TechSystems would be willing to pay to outsource the switches?

E8-26A   Make-or-buy decision with alternative use of facilities
(Learning Objective 6)

Refer to E8-25A. TechSystems needs 83,000 optical switches next year (assume same relevant range). By outsourcing them, TechSystems can use its idle facilities to manufacture another product that will contribute $210,000 to operating income, but none of the fixed costs will be avoidable. Should TechSystems make or buy the switches? Show your analysis.

E8-27A   Determine maximum outsourcing price *(Learning Objective 6)*

Hoffman Containers manufactures a variety of boxes used for packaging. Sales of its Model A20 box have increased significantly to a total of 480,000 A20 boxes. Hoffman has enough existing production capacity to make all of the boxes it needs. The variable cost of making each A20 box is $0.76. By outsourcing the manufacture of these A20 boxes, Hoffman can reduce its current fixed costs by $144,000. There is no alternative use for the factory space freed up through outsourcing, so it will just remain idle.

What is the maximum Hoffman will pay per Model A20 box to outsource production of this box?

E8-28A   Sell as is or process further *(Learning Objective 7)*

Keister Natural Dairy processes organic milk into plain yogurt. Keister sells plain yogurt to hospitals, nursing homes, and restaurants in bulk, one-gallon containers. Each batch, processed at a cost of $820, yields 450 gallons of plain yogurt. The company sells the one-gallon tubs for $5.00 each and spends $0.16 for each plastic tub. Keister has recently begun to reconsider its strategy. Management wonders if it would be more profitable to sell individual-sized portions of fruited organic yogurt at local food stores. Keister could further process each batch of plain yogurt into 9,600 individual portions (3/4 cup each) of fruited yogurt. A recent market analysis indicates that demand for the product exists. Keister would sell each individual portion for $0.54. Packaging would cost $0.08 per portion, and fruit would cost $0.10 per portion. Fixed costs would not change. Should Keister continue to sell only the gallon-sized plain yogurt (sell as is) or convert the plain yogurt into individual-sized portions of fruited yogurt (process further)? Why?

EXERCISES Group B

E8-29B Determine relevant and irrelevant information (*Learning Objective 1*)

Nicholson Meats is considering whether it should replace a meat grinder patty shaper machine. The new machine will produce 25% more hamburger patties than the old machine in the same amount of time. (This machine is the bottleneck of the hamburger patty process for Nicholson's.) The purchase of the new machine will cause fixed selling costs to increase, but per-unit variable selling costs will not be affected. The new machine will require installation by a specialty engineering firm. If the new machine is purchased, the old machine can be sold to an overseas meat processing company. The old machine requires frequent (quarterly) repairs and maintenance to keep it running. The new machine will require maintenance only once per year. The new machine will be paid for by signing a note payable with the bank that will cover the cost of the machine and its installation. Nicholson will have to pay interest monthly on the note payable for the new machine. The note payable that was used to purchase the old machine was fully paid off two years ago.

For each of the following costs, indicate whether each of the costs described would be relevant or not to Nicholson Meats' decision about whether to purchase the new machine or to keep the old machine.

Item	Relevant	Not Relevant
a. Cost of new machine		
b. Cost of old machine		
c. Added profits from increase in production resulting from new machine		
d. Fixed selling costs		
e. Variable selling costs		
f. Sales value of old machine		
g. Interest expense on new machine		
h. Interest expense on old machine		
i. Book value of old machine		
j. Maintenance cost of new machine		
k. Repairs and maintenance costs of old machine		
l. Installation costs of new machine		
m. Accumulated depreciation on old machine		
n. Cost per pound of hamburger		
o. Installation cost of old machine		

E8-30B Special order decisions given two scenarios (*Learning Objective 2*)

Suppose the Baseball Hall of Fame in Cooperstown, New York, has approached Global Sports Cards with a special order. The Hall of Fame wishes to purchase 55,000 baseball card packs for a special promotional campaign and offers $0.39 per pack, a total of $21,450. Global Sports Cards' total production cost is $0.59 per pack, as follows:

Variable costs:	
Direct materials	$0.13
Direct labor	0.09
Variable overhead	0.12
Fixed overhead	0.25
Total cost	$0.59

Global Sports Cards has enough excess capacity to handle the special order.

Requirements

1. Prepare an incremental analysis to determine whether Global Sports Cards should accept the special sales order assuming fixed costs would not be affected by the special order.

2. Now assume that the Hall of Fame wants special hologram baseball cards. Global Sports Cards will spend $4,900 to develop this hologram, which will be useless after the special order is completed. Should Global Sports Cards accept the special order under these circumstances? Show your analysis.

SUSTAINABILITY

E8-31B   Sustainability and short-term decision making *(Learning Objective 1)*

Over the past several years, decommissioned U.S. warships have been turned into artificial reefs in the ocean by towing them out to sea and sinking them. The thinking was that sinking the ship would conveniently dispose of it while providing an artificial reef environment for aquatic life. In reality, some of the sunken ships have released toxins into the ocean and have been costly to decontaminate. Now the U.S. government is taking bids to instead dismantle and recycle ships that have recently been decommissioned (but have not been sunk yet.)

Assume that a recently decommissioned aircraft carrier, the USS *Hudak*, is estimated to contain approximately 40 tons of recyclable materials able to be sold for approximately $33.9 million. The low bid for dismantling and transporting the ship materials to appropriate facilities is $35.1 million. Recycling and dismantling the ship would create about 500 jobs for about a year in the Rust Belt. This geographic area has been experiencing record-high unemployment rates in recent years.

Requirements

1. Is it more financially advantageous to sink the ship (assume that it costs approximately $0.2 million to tow a ship out to sea and sink it) or to dismantle and recycle it? Show your calculations.

2. From a sustainability standpoint, what should be done with the decommissioned aircraft carrier? List some of the qualitative factors that should enter into this analysis.

3. As a taxpayer, which action would you prefer (sink or recycle)? Defend your answer.

E8-32B   Special order decision and considerations *(Learning Objective 2)*

Bradford Stenback Sunglasses sell for $125 per pair. Suppose the company incurs the following average costs per pair:

Direct materials	$38
Direct labor	10
Variable manufacturing overhead	9
Variable marketing expenses	3
Fixed manufacturing overhead	20*
Total costs	$80

*$2,100,000 total fixed manufacturing overhead / 105,000 pairs of sunglasses

Bradford Stenback has enough idle capacity to accept a one-time-only special order from Snodgrass Opticians for 19,000 pairs of sunglasses at $68 per pair. Bradford Stenback will not incur any variable marketing expenses for the order.

Requirements

1. How would accepting the order affect Bradford Stenback's operating income? In addition to the special order's effect on profits, what other (longer-term, qualitative) factors should the company's managers consider in deciding whether to accept the order?

2. Bradford Stenback's marketing manager argues against accepting the special order because the offer price of $68 is less than the cost to make the sunglasses. The marketing manager asks you, as one of Bradford Stenback's staff accountants, to explain whether this analysis is correct.

E8-33B Pricing decisions given two scenarios *(Learning Objective 3)*

Bennett Builders builds 1,500-square-foot starter tract homes in the fast-growing suburbs of Chicago. Land and labor are cheap, and competition among developers is fierce. The homes are "cookie-cutter," with any upgrades added by the buyer after the sale. Bennett Builders' costs per developed sublot are as follows:

Land..	$ 52,000
Construction...	$128,000
Landscaping	$ 5,000
Variable marketing costs	$ 2,000

Bennett Builders would like to earn a profit of 14% of the variable cost of each home sale. Similar homes offered by competing builders sell for $200,000 each.

Requirements

1. Which approach to pricing should Bennett Builders emphasize? Why?
2. Will Bennett Builders be able to achieve its target profit levels? Show your computations.
3. Bathrooms and kitchens are typically the most important selling features of a home. Bennett Builders could differentiate the homes by upgrading bathrooms and kitchens. The upgrades would cost $22,000 per home but would enable Bennett Builders to increase the selling prices by $38,500 per home (in general, kitchen and bathroom upgrades typically add at least 150% of their cost to the value of any home.) If Bennett Builders upgrades, what will the new cost-plus price per home be? Should the company differentiate its product in this manner? Show your analysis.

E8-34B Decide whether to discontinue a product line *(Learning Objective 4)*

Top managers of California Video are alarmed by their operating losses. They are considering discontinuing the DVD product line. Company accountants have prepared the following analysis to help make this decision:

	A	B	C	D
1		California Video		
2		Product Line Contribution Margin Income Statement		
3		For the Year Ended December 31		
4				
5		Product lines		
6		Blu-ray Discs	DVDs	Company Total
7	Sales revenue	$ 306,000	$ 136,000	$ 442,000
8	Less: Variable expenses	153,000	80,000	233,000
9	Contribution margin	$ 153,000	$ 56,000	$ 209,000
10	Less fixed expenses:			
11	Manufacturing	72,000	61,000	133,000
12	Marketing and administrative	59,000	19,000	78,000
13	Operating income (loss)	$ 22,000	$ (24,000)	$ (2,000)
14				

Total fixed costs will not change if the company stops selling DVDs.

Requirements

1. Prepare an incremental analysis to show whether California Video should discontinue the DVD product line. Will discontinuing the DVDs add $24,000 to operating income? Explain.
2. Assume that California Video can avoid $29,000 of fixed expenses by discontinuing the DVD product line (these costs are direct fixed costs of the DVD product line). Prepare an incremental analysis to show whether California Video should stop selling DVDs.
3. Now, assume that all of the fixed costs assigned to DVDs are direct fixed costs and can be avoided if the company stops selling DVDs. However, marketing has concluded that Blu-ray disc sales would be adversely affected by discontinuing the DVD line (retailers want to buy both from the same supplier). Blu-ray disc production and sales would decline 10%. What should the company do?

E8-35B Discontinuing a product line *(Learning Objective 4)*

Suppose Grain Day Cereals is considering discontinuing its maple cereal product line. Assume that during the past year, the maple cereal product line income statement showed the following:

	A	B	C	D
1	Sales revenue	$ 7,450,000		
2	Less: Cost of goods sold	6,550,000		
3	Gross profit	$ 900,000		
4	Less: Operating expenses	1,600,000		
5	Operating income (loss)	$ (700,000)		
6				

Fixed manufacturing overhead costs account for 40% of the cost of goods, while only 30% of the operating expenses are fixed. Since the maple cereal line is just one of Grain Day Cereals' breakfast cereals, only $740,000 of direct fixed costs (the majority of which is advertising) will be eliminated if the product line is discontinued. The remainder of the fixed costs will still be incurred by Grain Day Cereals. If the company decides to discontinue the product line, what will happen to the company's operating income? Should Grain Day Cereals discontinue the maple cereal product line?

E8-36B Identify constraint, then determine product mix *(Learning Objective 5)*

AllTreads produces two types of exercise treadmills: Regular and Deluxe. The exercise craze is such that AllTreads could use all of its available machine hours producing either model. The two models are processed through the same production department.

	A	B	C	D
1		Per Unit		
2		Deluxe	Regular	
3	Sales price	$ 1,000	$ 550	
4	Less expenses:			
5	Direct materials	300	110	
6	Direct labor	86	190	
7	Variable manufacturing overhead	240	80	
8	Fixed manufacturing overhead*	132	44	
9	Variable operating expenses	119	61	
10	Total expenses	$ 877	$ 485	
11	Operating income	$ 123	$ 65	
12				

* Allocated on the basis of machine hours.

What product mix will maximize operating income? (*Hint:* Use the allocation of fixed manufacturing overhead to determine the proportion of machine hours used by each product.)

E8-37B Determine product mix for retailer—two stocking scenarios *(Learning Objective 5)*

Each morning, Mike Prescott stocks the drink case at Mike's Beach Hut in Virginia Beach, Virginia. Mike's Beach Hut has 105 linear feet of refrigerated display space for cold drinks. Each linear foot can hold either six 12-ounce cans or five 20-ounce plastic or glass bottles.
     The beverage stand sells three types of cold drinks:

1. Diet cola in 12-oz. cans for $1.55 per can
2. Bottled water in 20-oz. plastic bottles for $1.80 per bottle
3. Grape juice in 20-oz. glass bottles for $2.30 per bottle

     Mike's Beach Hut pays its suppliers the following:

1. $0.10 per 12-oz. can of diet cola
2. $0.45 per 20-oz. bottle of water
3. $0.80 per 20-oz. bottle of grape juice

Mike's Beach Hut's monthly fixed expenses include the following:

Hut rental	$ 350
Refrigerator rental	85
Mike's salary	1,650
Total fixed expenses	$2,085

The beverage stand can sell all the drinks stocked in the display case each morning.

Requirements

1. What is the constraining factor at Mike's Beach Hut? What should Mike stock to maximize profits? What is the maximum contribution margin he could generate from refrigerated drinks each day?

2. To provide variety to customers, suppose Mike refuses to devote more than 70 linear feet and no less than 5 linear feet to any individual product. Under this condition, how many linear feet of each drink should be stocked? How many units of each product will be available for sale each day?

3. Assuming the product mix calculated in Requirement 2, what contribution margin will be generated from refrigerated drinks each day?

E8-38B   Make-or-buy product component *(Learning Objective 6)*

Global Systems manufactures an optical switch that it uses in its final product. Global Systems incurred the following manufacturing costs when it produced 69,000 units last year:

	A	B	C	D
1	Direct materials	$ 759,000		
2	Direct labor	138,000		
3	Variable MOH	69,000		
4	Fixed MOH	448,500		
5	Total manufacturing cost for 69,000 units	$ 1,414,500		
6				

Global Systems does not yet know how many switches it will need this year; however, another company has offered to sell Global Systems the switch for $16.50 per unit. If Global Systems buys the switch from the outside supplier, the manufacturing facilities that will be idle cannot be used for any other purpose, yet none of the fixed costs are avoidable.

Requirements

1. Given the same cost structure, should Global Systems make or buy the switch? Show your analysis.

2. Now, assume that Global Systems can avoid $95,000 of fixed costs a year by outsourcing production. In addition, because sales are increasing, Global Systems needs 74,000 switches a year rather than 69,000. What should Global Systems do now?

3. Given the last scenario, what is the most Global Systems would be willing to pay to outsource the switches?

E8-39B   Make-or-buy decision with alternative use of facilities
(Learning Objective 6)

Refer to E8-38B. Global Systems needs 80,000 optical switches next year (assume same relevant range). By outsourcing them, Global Systems can use its idle facilities to manufacture another product that will contribute $110,000 to operating income, but none of the fixed costs will be avoidable. Should Global Systems make or buy the switches? Show your analysis.

E8-40B   Determine maximum outsourcing price *(Learning Objective 6)*

Hampton Containers manufactures a variety of boxes used for packaging. Sales of its Model A20 box have increased significantly to a total of 470,000 A20 boxes. Hampton has enough existing production capacity to make all of the boxes it needs. The variable cost of making each A20 box is $0.71. By outsourcing the manufacture of these A20 boxes, Hampton can reduce its current fixed costs by $117,500. There is no alternative use for the factory space freed up through outsourcing, so it will just remain idle.

What is the maximum Hampton will pay per Model A20 box to outsource production of this box?

E8-41B   Sell as is or process further *(Learning Objective 7)*

OrganicMaid processes organic milk into plain yogurt. OrganicMaid sells plain yogurt to hospitals, nursing homes, and restaurants in bulk, one-gallon containers. Each batch, processed at a cost of $870, yields 450 gallons of plain yogurt. OrganicMaid sells the one-gallon tubs for $8.00 each, and spends $0.10 for each plastic tub. Management has recently begun to reconsider its strategy. OrganicMaid wonders if it would be more profitable to sell individual-sized portions of fruited organic yogurt at local food stores. OrganicMaid could further process each batch of plain yogurt into 9,600 individual portions (3/4 cup each) of fruited yogurt. A recent market analysis indicates that demand for the product exists. OrganicMaid would sell each individual portion for $0.40. Packaging would cost $0.07 per portion, and fruit would cost $0.11 per portion. Fixed costs would not change. Should OrganicMaid continue to sell only the gallon-sized plain yogurt (sell as is) or convert the plain yogurt into individual-sized portions of fruited yogurt (process further)? Why?

PROBLEMS Group A

P8-42A   Special order decision and considerations *(Learning Objective 2)*

Marine Supply manufactures flotation vests in Chattanooga, Tennessee. Marine Supply's contribution margin income statement for the most recent month contains the following data:

	A	B	C	D
1	**Marine Supply**			
2	**Contribution Margin Income Statement (Variable Costing)**			
3	**For Sales Volume of 30,000 Units**			
4				
5		**Per unit**		
6	Sales revenue	$ 450,000		
7	Less variable expenses:			
8	Variable manufacturing costs (DM, DL, Variable MOH)	210,000		
9	Variable operating expenses (selling and administrative)	105,000		
10	Contribution margin	$ 135,000		
11	Less fixed expenses:			
12	Fixed manufacturing overhead	$ 121,000		
13	Fixed operating expenses (selling and administrative)	91,000		
14	Operating income (loss)	$ (77,000)		
15				

Suppose Overton Cruiselines wants to buy 4,900 vests from Marine Supply. Acceptance of the order will not increase Marine Supply's variable marketing and administrative expenses or any of its fixed expenses. The Marine Supply plant has enough unused capacity to manufacture the additional vests. Overton Cruiselines has offered $11 per vest, which is below the normal sale price of $15.

Requirements

1. Prepare an incremental analysis to determine whether Marine Supply should accept this special sales order.

2. Identify long-term factors Marine Supply should consider in deciding whether to accept the special sales order.

P8-43A Pricing of nursery plants *(Learning Objective 3)*

Nature Place operates a commercial plant nursery where it propagates plants for garden centers throughout the region. Nature Place has $5.8 million in assets. Its yearly fixed costs are $742,000, and the variable costs for the potting soil, container, label, seedling, and labor for each gallon-sized plant total $1.55. Nature Place's volume is currently 575,000 units. Competitors offer the same quality plants to garden centers for $3.80 each. Garden centers then mark them up to sell to the public for $8 to $10, depending on the type of plant.

Requirements

1. Nature Place owners want to earn a 11% return on the company's assets. What is Nature Place's target full cost?

2. Given Nature Place's current costs, will its owners be able to achieve their target profit? Show your analysis.

3. Assume that Nature Place has identified ways to cut its variable costs to $1.40 per unit. What is its new target fixed cost? Will this decrease in variable costs allow the company to achieve its target profit? Show your analysis.

4. Nature Place started an aggressive advertising campaign strategy to differentiate its plants from those grown by other nurseries. Nature Place doesn't expect volume to be affected, but it hopes to gain more control over pricing. If Nature Place has to spend $57,500 this year to advertise and its variable costs continue to be $1.40 per unit, what will its cost-plus price be? Do you think Nature Place will be able to sell its plants to garden centers at the cost-plus price? Why or why not?

P8-44A Prepare and use contribution margin statements for discontinuing a line decision *(Learning Objective 4)*

Members of the board of directors of Adobe Security One have received the following operating income data for the year just ended:

	A	B	C	D
		Adobe Security		
1		Product Line Contribution Margin Income Statement		
2		For the Year		
3				
4		Product lines		
5		Industrial Systems	Household Systems	Company Total
6	Sales revenue	$ 330,000	$ 380,000	$ 710,000
7	Less cost of goods sold:			
8	Variable	33,000	46,000	79,000
9	Fixed	250,000	68,000	318,000
10	Gross profit	$ 47,000	$ 266,000	$ 313,000
11	Less marketing and administrative expenses:			
12	Variable	63,000	77,000	140,000
13	Fixed	43,000	24,000	67,000
14	Operating income (loss)	$ (59,000)	$ 165,000	$ 106,000
15				

Members of the board are surprised that the industrial systems product line is losing money. They commission a study to determine whether the company should discontinue the line. Company accountants estimate that discontinuing the industrial systems line will decrease fixed cost of goods sold by $84,000 and decrease fixed marketing and administrative expenses by $12,000.

Requirements

1. Prepare an incremental analysis to show whether Adobe Security One should discontinue the industrial systems product line.

2. Prepare contribution margin income statements to show Adobe Security's total operating income under the two alternatives: (a) with the industrial systems line and (b) without the line. Compare the *difference* between the two alternatives' income numbers to your answer to Requirement 1. What have you learned from this comparison?

P8-45A Product mix decision under constraint *(Learning Objective 5)*

Brill Products, located in Forest Lake, Minnesota, produces two lines of electric tooth-brushes: Deluxe and Standard. Because Brill can sell all of the toothbrushes it produces, the owners are expanding the plant. They are deciding which product line to emphasize.

To make this decision, they assemble the following data:

	Per Unit	
	Deluxe Toothbrush	Standard Toothbrush
Sales price	$90	$46
Variable expenses...	25	16
Contribution margin..	$65	$30
Contribution margin ratio	72.2%	65.2%

After expansion, the factory will have a production capacity of 4,900 machine hours per month. The plant can manufacture either 60 Standard electric toothbrushes or 27 Deluxe electric toothbrushes per machine hour.

Requirements

1. Identify the constraining factor for Brill Products.
2. Prepare an analysis to show which product line to emphasize.

P8-46A Outsourcing decision given alternative use of capacity
(Learning Objective 6)

Cool Boards manufactures snowboards. Its cost of making 30,125 bindings is as follows:

Direct materials	$ 25,000
Direct labor	83,000
Variable manufacturing overhead	50,000
Fixed manufacturing overhead	83,000
Total manufacturing costs	$241,000
Cost per pair ($241,000 ÷ 30,125)...	$ 8.00

Suppose an outside supplier will sell bindings to Cool Boards for $17 each. Cool Boards will pay $1.00 per unit to transport the bindings to its manufacturing plant, where it will add its own logo at a cost of $0.50 per binding.

Requirements

1. Cool Board's accountants predict that purchasing the bindings from the outside supplier will enable the company to avoid $2,200 of fixed overhead. Prepare an analysis to show whether Cool Boards should make or buy the bindings.
2. The facilities freed by purchasing bindings from the outside supplier can be used to manufacture another product that will contribute $2,600 to profit. Total fixed costs will be the same as if Cool Boards had produced the bindings. Show which alternative makes the best use of Cool Boards facilities: (a) make bindings, (b) buy bindings and leave facilities idle, or (c) buy bindings and make another product.

P8-47A Sell as is or process further decisions *(Learning Objective 7)*

Rouse Chemical has spent $241,000 to refine 71,000 gallons of acetone, which can be sold for $1.90 a gallon. Alternatively, Rouse Chemical can process the acetone further. This processing will yield a total of 65,000 gallons of lacquer thinner that can be sold for $3.40 a gallon. The additional processing will cost $0.40 per gallon of lacquer thinner. To sell the lacquer thinner, Rouse Chemical must pay shipping of $0.20 a gallon and administrative expenses of $0.12 a gallon on the thinner.

Requirements

1. Identify the sunk cost. Is the sunk cost relevant to Rouse's decision? Why or why not?
2. Should Rouse sell the acetone as is or process it into lacquer thinner? Show the expected net revenue difference between the two alternatives.

PROBLEMS Group B

P8-48B Special order decision and considerations *(Learning Objective 2)*

Sailor Products, Inc., manufactures flotation vests in San Diego, California. Sailor Products' contribution margin income statement for the most recent month contains the following data:

	A	B	C	D
1	Sailor Products			
2	Contribution Margin Income Statement (Variable Costing)			
3	For Sales Volume of 33,000 Units			
4				
5		Total		
6	Sales revenue	$ 462,000		
7	Less variable expenses:			
8	Variable manufacturing costs (DM, DL, Variable MOH)	99,000		
9	Variable operating expenses (selling and administrative)	110,000		
10	Contribution margin	$ 253,000		
11	Less fixed expenses:			
12	Fixed manufacturing overhead	121,000		
13	Fixed operating expenses (selling and administrative)	86,000		
14	Operating income (loss)	$ 46,000		
15				

Suppose Parker Cruiselines wishes to buy 5,500 vests from Sailor Products. Acceptance of the order will not increase Sailor Products' variable marketing and administrative expenses. The Sailor Products plant has enough unused capacity to manufacture the additional vests. Parker Cruiselines has offered $4 per vest, which is below the normal sale price of $14.

Requirements

1. Prepare an incremental analysis to determine whether Sailor Products should accept this special sales order.
2. Identify long-term factors Sailor Products should consider in deciding whether to accept the special sales order.

P8-49B Pricing of nursery plants *(Learning Objective 3)*

Plant House operates a commercial plant nursery where it propagates plants for garden centers throughout the region. Plant House has $5.0 million in assets. Its yearly fixed costs are $600,000, and the variable costs for the potting soil, container, label, seedling, and labor for each gallon-sized plant total $1.25. Plant House's volume is currently 500,000 units. Competitors offer the same quality plants to garden centers for $3.50 each. Garden centers then mark them up to sell to the public for $8 to $11, depending on the type of plant.

Requirements

1. Plant House's owners want to earn a 12% return on the company's assets. What is Plant House's target full cost?
2. Given Plant House's current costs, will its owners be able to achieve their target profit? Show your analysis.

3. Assume that Plant House has identified ways to cut its variable costs to $1.10 per unit. What is its new target fixed cost? Will this decrease in variable costs allow the company to achieve its target profit? Show your analysis.

4. Plant House started an aggressive advertising campaign strategy to differentiate its plants from those grown by other nurseries. Plant House doesn't expect volume to be affected, but it hopes to gain more control over pricing. If Plant House has to spend $100,000 this year to advertise and its variable costs continue to be $1.10 per unit, what will its cost-plus price be? Do you think Plant House will be able to sell its plants to garden centers at the cost-plus price? Why or why not?

P8-50B Prepare and use contribution margin statements for discontinuing a line decision *(Learning Objective 4)*

Members of the board of directors of Locktight Systems have received the following operating income data for the year just ended:

	A	B	C	D
1	Product Line Contribution Margin Income Statement			
2	For the Year			
3				
4		Product lines		
5		Industrial Systems	Household Systems	Company Total
6	Sales revenue	$ 310,000	$ 330,000	$ 640,000
7	Less cost of goods sold:			
8	Variable	37,000	45,000	82,000
9	Fixed	240,000	63,000	303,000
10	Gross profit	$ 33,000	$ 222,000	$ 255,000
11	Less marketing and administrative expenses:			
12	Variable	69,000	76,000	145,000
13	Fixed	40,000	22,000	62,000
14	Operating income (loss)	$ (76,000)	$ 124,000	$ 48,000
15				

Members of the board are surprised that the industrial systems product line is losing money. They commission a study to determine whether the company should discontinue the line. Company accountants estimate that discontinuing the industrial systems line will decrease fixed cost of goods sold by $85,000 and decrease fixed marketing and administrative expenses by $8,000.

Requirements

1. Prepare an incremental analysis to show whether Locktight Systems should discontinue the industrial systems product line.

2. Prepare contribution margin income statements to show Locktight Systems' total operating income under the two alternatives: (a) with the industrial systems line and (b) without the line. Compare the *difference* between the two alternatives' income numbers to your answer to Requirement 1. What have you learned from this comparison?

P8-51B Product mix decision under constraint *(Learning Objective 5)*

Brookdale Products, Inc., located in Mahtomedi, Minnesota, produces two lines of electric toothbrushes: Deluxe and Standard. Because Brookdale can sell all the toothbrushes it can produce, the owners are expanding the plant. They are deciding which product line to emphasize. To make this decision, they assemble the following data:

	Per Unit	
	Deluxe Toothbrush	Regular Toothbrush
Sales price	$92	$52
Variable expenses	17	15
Contribution margin	$75	$37
Contribution margin ratio	81.5%	71.2%

After expansion, the factory will have a production capacity of 4,000 machine hours per month. The plant can manufacture either 58 Standard electric toothbrushes or 21 Deluxe electric toothbrushes per machine hour.

Requirements

1. Identify the constraining factor for Brookdale Products.
2. Prepare an analysis to show which product line to emphasize.

P8-52B   Outsourcing decision given alternative use of capacity

(Learning Objective 6)

WildRide Sports manufactures snowboards. Its cost of making 24,900 bindings is as follows:

Direct materials	$ 27,000
Direct labor	84,000
Variable manufacturing overhead	54,000
Fixed manufacturing overhead	84,000
Total manufacturing costs	$249,000
Cost per pair ($249,000 / 24,900)	$ 10.00

Suppose an outside supplier will sell bindings to WildRide Sports for $14 each. WildRide Sports would pay $3.00 per unit to transport the bindings to its manufacturing plant, where it would add its own logo at a cost $0.70 of per binding.

Requirements

1. WildRide Sports' accountants predict that purchasing the bindings from an outside supplier will enable the company to avoid $2,300 of fixed overhead. Prepare an analysis to show whether WildRide Sports should make or buy the bindings.
2. The facilities freed by purchasing bindings from the outside supplier can be used to manufacture another product that will contribute $3,000 to profit. Total fixed costs will be the same as if WildRide Sports had produced the bindings. Show which alternative makes the best use of WildRide Sports' facilities: (a) make bindings, (b) buy bindings and leave facilities idle, or (c) buy bindings and make another product.

P8-53B   Sell as is or process further decisions *(Learning Objective 7)*

Castillo Chemical has spent $240,000 to refine 72,000 gallons of acetone, which can be sold for $2.10 a gallon. Alternatively, Castillo Chemical can process the acetone further. This processing will yield a total of 59,000 gallons of lacquer thinner that can be sold for $3.10 a gallon. The additional processing will cost $0.45 per gallon of lacquer thinner. To sell the lacquer thinner, Castillo Chemical must pay shipping of $0.20 a gallon and administrative expenses of $0.12 a gallon on the thinner.

Requirements

1. Identify the sunk cost. Is the sunk cost relevant to Castillo's decision? Why or why not?
2. Should Castillo sell the acetone as is or process it into lacquer thinner? Show the expected net revenue difference between the two alternatives.

CRITICAL THINKING

Discussion & Analysis

A8-54 Discussion Questions

1. A beverage company is considering whether to discontinue its line of grape soda. What factors will affect the company's decision? What is a qualitative factor? Which of the factors you listed are qualitative?

2. What factors would be relevant to a restaurant that is considering whether to make its own dinner rolls or to purchase dinner rolls from a local bakery?

3. How would outsourcing change a company's cost structure? How might this change in cost structure help or harm a company's competitive position?

4. What is an opportunity cost? List possible opportunity costs associated with a make-or-buy decision.

5. What undesirable result can arise from allocating common fixed costs to product lines?

6. Why could a manager be justified in ignoring fixed costs when making a decision about a special order? When would fixed costs be relevant when making a decision about a special order?

7. What is the difference between segment margin and contribution margin? When would each be used?

8. Do joint costs affect a sell as is or process further decision? Why or why not?

9. How can "make-or-buy" concepts be applied to decisions at a service organization? What types of make-or-buy decisions might a service organization face?

10. Oscar Company builds outdoor furniture using a variety of woods and plastics. What is a constraint? List at least four possible constraints at Oscar Company.

11. Do a Web search on the terms "carbon offset" and "carbon footprint." What is a carbon footprint? What is a carbon offset? Why would carbon offsets be of interest to a company? What are some companies that offer (sell) carbon offsets?

12. A computer manufacturer is considering outsourcing its technical support call center to India. Its current technical support call center is located in Dellroy, Ohio. The current call center is one of the top employers in Dellroy and employs about 10% of the townspeople in Dellroy. The town has experienced high unemployment rates in the past two decades and oftentimes the call employees are the sole breadwinners in their households. If the technical support call center were to be moved to India, the company would be able to pay about 50% less per hour than it currently pays in Dellroy, Ohio. From a triple bottom line perspective (people, planet, and profit), what factors are relevant to the company's decision to outsource its technical support call center? Be sure to discuss both quantitative and qualitative factors.

Application & Analysis

Mini Cases

REAL LIFE

A8-55 Outsourcing Decision at a Real Company

Go to the *New York Times* website (www.nytimes.com/) or to *USA Today* (www.usatoday.com/) and search for the term "outsource." Find an article about a company making a decision to outsource a part of its business operations.

Basic Discussion Questions

1. Describe the company that is making the decision to outsource. What area of the business is the company either looking to outsource or did it already outsource?

2. Why did the company decide to outsource (or is considering outsourcing)?

3. List the revenues and costs that might be impacted by this outsourcing decision. The article will not list many, if any, of these revenues and costs; you should make reasonable guesses about what revenues and/or costs would be associated with the business operation being outsourced.

4. List the qualitative factors that could influence the company's decision of whether to outsource this business operation or not. Again, you need to make reasonable guesses about the qualitative factors that might influence the company's decision to outsource or not.

A8-56 Ethics and outsourcing (Learning Objectives 1, 2, 3, 4, 5, 6, & 7)

Der Dutchman is a large family-style restaurant chain located throughout the Midwest in Amish communities. Currently Der Dutchman makes its own biscuits. Customers love these biscuits; they are light, fluffy, and incredibly delicious.

People are not eating out at restaurants as much as they did before the recession hit in 2007. Like many other restaurants, Der Dutchman is under increasing pressure to control its costs to help to counteract the lower number of diners. As part of its efforts to remain cost competitive, Der Dutchman is analyzing whether it should continue to make its own biscuits or to outsource part of the biscuit-making process by purchasing ready-made dough from a national supplier.

Seth McGilvrey works as a management accountant at the Der Dutchman restaurant group. Seth is asked by the controller to analyze whether the biscuits should continue to be made in-house from scratch or if the company should purchase ready-made dough from a national supplier.

Seth's mother-in-law, Audrey Parsons, is a salesperson for a national food manufacturer. He decides to get a bid from her before contacting any other suppliers. Audrey has been struggling financially since the illness and subsequent death of Seth's father-in-law last year and could use the sales commissions generated by this order. Seth emails Audrey and asks her for a bid price for the ready-made dough. Audrey sends him a price of $33.20 per case (a case of dough makes 12 dozen biscuits.)

Seth analyzes the cost of making the biscuits in-house. He arrives at the following schedule of cost for the dough to make 12 dozen biscuits:

	A	B	C	D
	Cost item	Cost per 12 dozen biscuits		
1	Cost item			
2	Flour	$ 9.00		
3	Baking soda	0.12		
4	Baking powder	0.38		
5	Salt	0.24		
6	Unsalted butter	13.50		
7	Buttermilk	6.00		
8	Bakery labor	2.75		
9	Fixed manufacturing overhead*	2.24		
10	Cost per 12 dozen biscuits in-house	$ 34.23		
11				

*allocated on basis of bakery labor hours

Seth's analysis shows that the restaurant should purchase the ready-made dough from the national supplier because the ready-made dough is less expensive than making the dough in-house. However, Seth has deliberately left out all of the fixed costs in the cost calculation of making the biscuits in-house. Part of those fixed costs is unavoidable, but he does not distinguish between avoidable and unavoidable fixed costs in his analysis. The unavoidable portion of the fixed cost allocated to 12 dozen biscuits is $1.24.

Seth submits his analysis to the controller. In his report, he recommends that Der Dutchman products choose Audrey's firm to supply the dough for its biscuits. Seth chooses to say nothing about his relationship to Audrey, figuring no one will know since his mother-in-law has a different last name than he does.

The controller accepts Seth's analysis and Der Dutchman enters into a contract with Audrey's firm for the ready-made dough.

Requirements

1. Using the IMA *Statement of Ethical Professional Practice* as an ethical framework (refer to Exhibit 1-6), answer the following questions:

   a. What is(are) the ethical issue(s) in this situation?

   b. What are Seth's responsibilities as a management accountant?

2. When making the decision to outsource the dough, what other factors should be considered?

A8-57 Starbucks food waste: Sell now or process further?
(Learning Objectives 1 & 6)

With nearly 18,000 stores in 60 countries, Starbucks serves a lot of coffee and pastries each day, and it also generates a lot of waste, including day-old pastries and coffee grounds. Starbucks continually wrestles with how to best handle this food waste.

A researcher in Hong Kong is developing a fungus that converts Starbucks food waste into useful chemicals through a process called biorefining.[4] Basically, the Starbucks food and coffee waste products are blended with a special type of fungus that breaks the food's complex carbohydrates down into simple sugars. These sugars then go into a fermenter, where they are exposed to bacteria that break the sugar down into succinic acid. Succinic acid is a colorless, odorless substance that is frequently used in the production of medicines, foods, bioplastics, and laundry detergents.

Assuming that the biorefining process turns out to be technologically feasible, Starbucks will have another option for its food waste products. Let's assume that Starbucks has the following options for handling its food and coffee waste:

Day-old pastries disposal options

a. Discard in trash.
b. Donate the day-old pastries to local homeless shelters and other charitable organizations.
c. Sell the day-old pastries in its retail stores for 50% off.
d. Process the day-old pastries into succinic acid and sell the succinic acid to manufacturers or labs.

Coffee grounds disposal options

a. Discard in trash.
b. Give coffee grounds to customers through a program called Grounds for Your Garden. Plants such as roses, azaleas, and evergreens can be fertilized with coffee grounds.
c. Sell coffee grounds to commercial composters.
d. Process the food waste into succinic acid and sell the succinic acid to manufacturers or labs.

Starbucks has a goal of zero waste at its retail stores, so it is continually assessing its waste disposal options. Coupled with its zero-waste goal, though, is its profit motive. Starbucks is a for-profit corporation and must balance its sustainability initiatives with the right economic choices for its shareholders.

Questions

1. For each of the disposal options for <u>day-old pastries</u>, answer the following questions:

   a. What revenue (if any) would be generated by this option?
   b. What cost reductions could Starbucks realize from this option?
   c. What costs would Starbucks incur for this option?
   d. What qualitative factors would Starbucks need to consider before choosing this option?
   e. What are the advantages associated with this option? What are the disadvantages associated with this option?

2. For each of the disposal options for <u>coffee grounds</u>, answer the following questions:

   a. What revenue (if any) would be generated by this option?
   b. What cost reductions could Starbucks realize from this option?
   c. What costs would Starbucks incur for this option?
   d. What qualitative factors would Starbucks need to consider before choosing this option?
   e. What are the advantages associated with this option? What are the disadvantages associated with this option?

3. For both day-old pastries and coffee grounds, are there any options that are particularly attractive in your viewpoint? Are there any options that would not be acceptable in your viewpoint? Justify your response.

---

[4]John Platt, "Starbucks to Turn Stale Pastries into Plastic?," www.forbes.com/sites/eco-nomics/2012/09/10/starbucks-to-turn-stale-pastries-into-plastic/, retrieved July 9, 2013.

Try It Solutions

page 451:

1. Yes, there is enough capacity to fill this special order. If the plant is producing 450,000 cases a month, yet only operating at 90% of capacity, it must have a capacity level of 500,000 cases per month (= 450,000 ÷ 90%). This means the plant has excess capacity of 50,000 cases per month, which is enough to fill the special order of 40,000 cases without increasing the current level of fixed costs ($2,700,000). Thus, the current level of fixed costs is irrelevant to the decision. Campbell's will *not* incur an additional $6.00 of fixed MOH for every case produced in this order.

2. Take a contribution margin approach to determining whether the special order is profitable:

	A	B	C
			Total Order
1	**Incremental Analysis for Special Order Decision**	**Per Unit**	**(40,000 units)**
2	Revenue from special order	$ 19.00	$ 760,000
3	Less: Variable expenses associated with the order (DM, DL, Variable MOH)	15.00	600,000
4	Contribution margin	$ 4.00	$ 160,000
5	Less: Additional fixed expenses associated with the order		5,000
6	Increase in operating income from the special order		$ 155,000
7			

page 463:

1. Analyze the revenues and costs that would be lost if the salad bar operation is discontinued:

	A	B	C
1	**Incremental Analysis for Discontinuation Decision**	**Total**	
2	Sales revenue from salad bars	$ 750,000	
3	Less: Variable expenses related to salad bars	600,000	
4	Contribution margin lost if salad bars are discontinued	$ 150,000	
5	Less: Fixed cost savings if salad bars are discontinued	20,000	
6	Operating income lost if salad bars are discontinued	$ 130,000	
7			
8			
9	**If Salad Bars Are Replaced with Olive Bars**	**Total**	
10	Contribution margin provided by olive bar	$ 200,000	
11	Less: Operating income lost if salad bars are discontinued	130,000	
12	Increase in operating income from replacing salad bars with olive bars	$ 70,000	
13			

page 470:

1. As shown below, the total cost of outsourcing the ski poles and leaving the freed capacity idle is $325,000 greater than the cost to produce the poles in-house. Rossignol should not outsource production because its operating income would decline by $325,000.

2. However, Rossignol's income would increase by $175,000 if it outsources production and uses the freed capacity to make ski boots.

	A	B	C	D
	Incremental Analysis	**Make**	**Outsource**	
1	**Outsourcing Decision**	**Ski Poles**	**Ski Poles**	**Difference**
2	Variable Costs:			
	If make: $13.50 × 100,000 units			
3	If outsource: $18.00 × 100,000 units	$ 1,350,000	$ 1,800,000	$ 450,000
4	Plus: Fixed costs	650,000	525,000	(125,000)
5	Total cost of producing 100,000 units	$ 2,000,000	$ 2,325,000	$ 325,000
6	Less: Income from ski boots if outsource	0	500,000	500,000
7	Net cost	$ 2,000,000	$ 1,825,000	$ (175,000)
8				

The Master Budget

Learning Objectives

- **1** Describe how and why managers use budgets
- **2** Prepare the operating budgets
- **3** Prepare the financial budgets
- **4** Prepare budgets for a merchandiser

Sources: Campbell Soup Company, 2012 Annual Report; www.campbellsoupcompany.com/csr/success_strategy.asp; http://investor.campbellsoupcompany.com; and www.gallup.com/consulting/25312/gallup-great-workplace-award.aspx.

Campbell Soup Company's mission is to "build the world's most extraordinary food company by winning in the workplace, marketplace, and community, and winning with integrity." To attain this goal, the company first identified key strategies including expanding its iconic brands (such as Campbell's Soup and Pepperidge Farms Snacks), increasing margins through improving productivity, and advancing its commitment to organizational excellence and social responsibility. These strategies required that detailed plans be put in place. The company's managers express these plans, in financial terms, through budgets. For example, management budgeted millions of dollars toward research and development, resulting in 41 new products in 2012. Management also budgeted millions of dollars for capital investments to expand soup- and snack-making capacity, automate packing, and improve information systems. Is the company on track for reaching its goals? In 2010, Campbell became a four-time winner of Gallup's "Great Workplace Award," for creating an extraordinary workplace environment. This prestigious award is only given to 25 companies a year, worldwide. For four of the past five years, Campbell's total shareowner return has exceeded the Standard & Poor's 500 Stock Index. And in 2012, for the second year in a row, Campbell ranked as one of the top 10 "Best Corporate Citizens" by *Corporate Responsibility* magazine. The company's budget is a vital tool in making it all happen.

Budgeting is perhaps the most widely used management accounting tool employed by companies, organizations, and governments throughout the world. Even individuals, such as you and I, can benefit from creating a personal budget that shows how we plan to use our resources and to make sure our spending does not get out of control. For example, if your goal is to buy a car directly after college or a house five years after college, then you need to plan for those goals. Your budget should include saving enough money each year to accumulate the down payments you'll need. By carefully planning how you'll spend and save your resources, you'll have a better chance of reaching your goals.

How and Why do Managers Use Budgets?

As you'll see throughout this chapter, management uses budgeting to express its plans and to assess how well it's reaching its goals. In this section, we'll take a closer look at how budgets are used and developed, the benefits of budgeting, and the particular budgets that are prepared as part of the company's master budget.

1 Describe how and why managers use budgets

How are Budgets Used?

All companies and organizations use budgets for the same reasons you would in your personal life—to plan for the future and control the revenues and expenses related to those plans. Exhibit 9-1 shows how managers use budgets in fulfilling their major responsibilities of planning, directing, and controlling operations. Budgeting is an ongoing cycle: Company strategies lead to detailed plans, which in turn lead to actions. Results are then compared to the budget to provide managers with feedback. This feedback allows managers to take corrective actions and, if necessary, revise strategies, which starts the cycle over.

EXHIBIT 9-1 Managers Use Budgets to Plan and Control Business Activities

How are Budgets Developed?

A few years ago Campbell was not performing up to expectations. The first step toward getting the company back on track was management's decision to create long-term strategic goals. **Strategic planning** involves setting long-term goals that may extend 5 to 10 years into the future. Long-term, loosely detailed budgets are often created to reflect expectations for these long-term goals.

Once the goals are set, management designs key strategies for attaining the goals. These strategies, such as Campbell's expansion of its iconic brands and improvements to production efficiency, are then put into place through the use of shorter-term budgets for an entire fiscal year. However, even a yearly budget is not detailed enough to guide many management decisions. For example, Campbell's soup production managers must know what month of the year they expect to receive and start using new production machinery. They must also decide how much of each raw material (vegetables, chicken, and so forth) to purchase each month to meet production requirements for both existing and new products. In turn, this will affect monthly cash needs. Therefore, companies usually prepare a budget for every month of the fiscal year.

Many companies set aside time during the last two quarters of the fiscal year to create their budget for the upcoming fiscal year. Other companies prepare rolling, or continuous budgets. A **rolling budget** is a budget that is continuously updated so that the next 12 months of operations are always budgeted. For example, as soon as January is over, the next January is added to the budget. The benefit of a rolling budget is that managers always have a budget for the next 12 months.

Who is Involved in the Budgeting Process?

Rather than using a "top-down" approach in which top management determines the budget, most companies use some degree of participative budgeting. As the term implies, **participative budgeting** involves the participation of many levels of management. Participative budgeting is beneficial for the following reasons:

- Lower-level managers are closer to the action, and should have a more detailed knowledge for creating realistic budgets.
- Managers are more likely to accept, and be motivated by, budgets they helped to create.

However, participative budgeting also has disadvantages:

- The budget process can become much more complex and time consuming as more people participate in the process.
- Managers may intentionally build **slack** into the budget for their areas of operation by overbudgeting expenses or underbudgeting revenue. Why would they do this? They would do so for three possible reasons: (1) because of uncertainty about the future, (2) to make their performance look better when actual results are compared against budgeted amounts at the end of the period, and (3) to have the resources they need in the event of budget cuts.

Even with participative budgeting, someone must still have the "final say" on the budget. Often, companies use a **budget committee** to review the submitted budgets, remove unwarranted slack, and revise and approve the final budget. The budget committee often includes upper management, such as the CEO and CFO, as well as managers from every area of the value chain (such as research and development, marketing, distribution, and so forth). By using a cross-functional budget committee, the final budget is more likely to reflect a comprehensive view of the organization and be accepted by managers than if the budget were prepared by one person or department for the entire organization. The budget committee is often supported by full-time staff personnel devoted to updating and analyzing the budgets.

What is the Starting Point for Developing the Budgets?

Many companies use the prior year's budgeted figures, or actual results, as the *starting point* for creating the budget for the coming year. Of course, those figures will then be modified to reflect

- new products, customers, or geographical areas;
- changes in the marketplace caused by competitors;
- changes in labor contracts, raw materials, and fuel costs;
- general inflation; and
- any new strategies.

However, this approach to budgeting may cause year-after-year increases that, after time, grow out of control. To prevent perpetual increases in budgeted expenses, many companies intermittently use zero-based budgeting. When a company implements <u>**zero-based budgeting**</u>, all managers begin with a budget of zero and must justify *every dollar* they put in the budget. This budgeting approach is very time consuming and labor intensive. Therefore, companies only use it from time to time in order to keep their expenses in check.

What are the Benefits of Budgeting?

Exhibit 9-2 summarizes three key benefits of budgeting. Budgeting forces managers to plan, promotes coordination and communication, and provides a benchmark for motivating employees and evaluating actual performance.

EXHIBIT 9-2 Benefits of Budgeting

PLANNING	COMMUNICATION	BENCHMARKING
Budgets force managers to plan.	Budgets promote coordination and communication.	Budgets provide a benchmark that motivates employees and helps managers evaluate performance.

Planning

Business managers are extremely busy directing the day-to-day operations of the company. The budgeting process forces managers to spend time planning for the future, rather than only concerning themselves with daily operations. The sooner companies develop a plan and have time to act on the plan, the more likely they will achieve their goals.

Coordination and Communication

The budget coordinates a company's activities. It forces managers to consider relations among operations across the entire value chain. For example, Campbell's decision to expand its iconic brands will first affect the research and development (R&D) function. However, once new products are developed, the design and production teams will need to focus on how and where the products will be mass-produced. The marketing team will need to develop attractive labeling and create a successful advertising campaign. The distribution team may need to alter its current distribution system to accommodate the new products. And customer service will need to be ready to handle any complaints or warranty issues. All areas of the value chain are ultimately affected by management's plans. The budget process helps to communicate and coordinate the effects of the plan.

Benchmarking

Budgets provide a benchmark that motivates employees and helps managers evaluate performance. The budget provides a target that most managers will try to achieve, especially if they participated in the budgeting process and the budget has been set at a realistic level. Budgets should be achievable with effort. Budgets that are too "tight" (too hard to achieve) or too "loose" (too easy to achieve) do not provide managers with much motivation.

Think about exams for a moment. Some professors have a reputation for giving "impossible" exams while others may be known for giving "easy" exams. In either of these cases, students are rarely motivated to put much effort into learning the material because they feel they won't be rewarded for their additional efforts. However, if students feel that a professor's exam can be achieved with effort, they will be more likely to devote themselves to learning the material. In other words, the perceived "fairness" of the exam affects how well the exam motivates students to study. Likewise, if a budget is perceived to be "fair," employees are likely to be motivated by it.

Budgets also provide a benchmark for evaluating performance. At the end of the period, companies use performance reports, such as the one pictured in Exhibit 9-3, to compare "actual" revenues and expenses against "budgeted" revenues and expenses. The <u>variance</u>, or difference between actual and budgeted figures, is used to evaluate how well the manager controlled operations and to determine whether the plan needs to be revised. The use of budgets for performance evaluation will be discussed in more detail in Chapters 10 and 11. In this chapter, we'll focus primarily on the use of budgets for planning purposes.

EXHIBIT 9-3 Summary Performance Report

	A	B	C	D
				Variance
1	**Summary Performance Report**	**Actual**	**Budget**	**(Actual − Budget)**
2	Sales revenue	$ 478,000	$ 450,000	$ 28,000
3	Less: Variable expenses	336,000	320,000	16,000
4	Contribution margin	$ 142,000	$ 130,000	$ 12,000
5	Less: Fixed expenses	23,000	25,000	2,000
6	Operating income	$ 119,000	$ 105,000	$ 14,000
7				

What is the Master Budget?

The <u>master budget</u> is the comprehensive planning document for the entire organization. It consists of all of the supporting budgets needed to create the company's budgeted financial statements. Exhibit 9-4 shows all of the components of the master budget for a

EXHIBIT 9-4 Master Budget for a Manufacturing Company

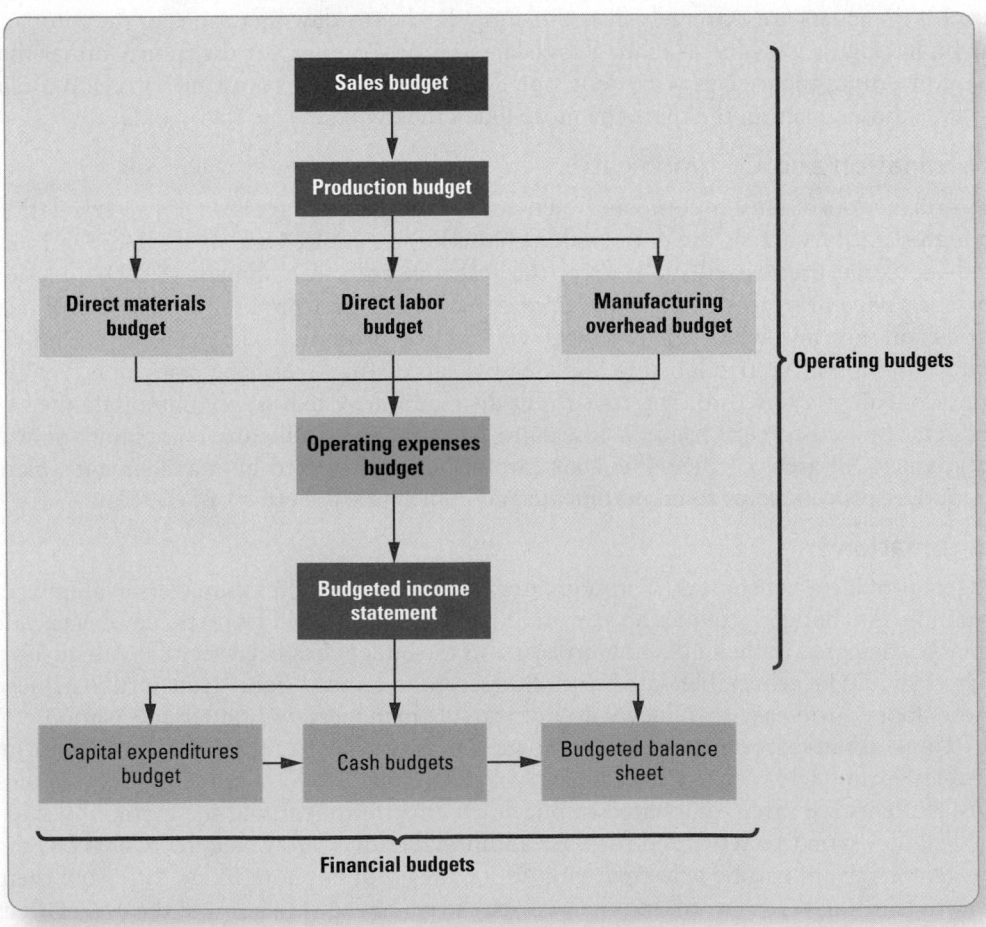

manufacturer, and the order in which they are usually prepared. The master budgets of service and merchandising firms are less complex, and will be discussed in the final section of the chapter.

The <u>**operating budgets**</u> are the budgets needed to run the daily operations of the company. The operating budgets culminate in a budgeted income statement. As Exhibit 9-4 shows, the starting point of the operating budgets is the sales budget because it affects most other components of the master budget. After estimating sales, manufacturers prepare the production budget, which determines how many units need to be produced. Once production volume is established, managers prepare individual budgets for the direct materials, direct labor, and manufacturing overhead that will be needed to meet production. Next, managers prepare the operating expenses budget. After all of these budgets are prepared, management will be able to prepare the budgeted income statement.

As you'll see throughout the chapter, cost behavior will be an important factor in developing many of the operating budgets. Total fixed costs will not change as volume changes within the relevant range. However, total variable costs will fluctuate as volume fluctuates.

The <u>**financial budgets**</u> include the capital expenditures budget and the cash budgets. It culminates in a budgeted balance sheet. The capital expenditures budget shows the company's plan for purchasing property, plant, and equipment. The cash budget projects the cash that will be available to run the company's operations and determines whether the company will have extra funds to invest or whether the company will need to borrow cash. Finally, the budgeted balance sheet forecasts the company's position at the end of the budget period.

How are the Operating Budgets Prepared?

2 Prepare the operating budgets

We will be following the budget process for Tucson Tortilla, a fairly small, independently owned manufacturer of tortilla chips. The company sells its product, by the case, to restaurants, grocery stores, and convenience stores. To keep our example simple, we will just show the budgets for the first three months of the fiscal year, rather than all 12 months. Since many companies prepare quarterly budgets (budgets that cover a three-month period), we'll also show the quarterly figures on each budget. For every budget, we'll walk through the calculations for the month of January. Then we'll show how the same pattern is used to create budgets for the months of February and March.

Sales Budget

The sales budget is the starting place for budgeting. Managers multiply the expected number of unit sales by the expected sales price per unit to arrive at the expected total sales revenue.

$$\boxed{\text{Number of Unit Sales}} \times \boxed{\text{Sales Price per Unit}} = \boxed{\text{Total Sales Revenue}}$$

For example, Tucson Tortilla expects to sell 30,000 cases of tortilla chips in January, at a sales price of $20 per case, so the estimated sales revenue for January is as follows:

30,000 cases × $20 per case = $600,000

Tucson Tortilla's sales budget for the first three months of the year is shown in Exhibit 9-5. As you can see, the monthly sales volume is expected to fluctuate. January sales are expected to be higher than February sales due to the extraordinary number of chips purchased for Super Bowl parties. Also, since more tortillas chips are sold when the weather warms up, the company expects sales to begin their seasonal upward climb beginning in March.

As shown in the lower portion of Exhibit 9-5, managers may also choose to indicate the type of sale that will be made. Tucson Tortilla expects 20% of its sales to be cash (COD) sales. Companies often use <u>COD</u> ("collect on delivery"[1]) collection terms if the customer is new, has a poor credit rating, or has not paid on time in the past. Tucson Tortilla will still sell to these customers, but will demand payment immediately when the inventory is delivered.

EXHIBIT 9-5 Sales Budget

	A	B	C	D	E
1		Tucson Tortilla			
2		Sales Budget			
3		For the Quarter Ended March 31			
4		Month			
5		January	February	March	1st Quarter
6	Unit sales (cases)	30,000	20,000	25,000	75,000
7	Multiply by: Sales price per case	$ 20	$ 20	$ 20	$ 20
8	Total sales revenue	$ 600,000	$ 400,000	$ 500,000	$ 1,500,000
9					
10	**Type of sale:**				
11	Cash sales (20%)	$ 120,000	$ 80,000	$ 100,000	$ 300,000
12	Credit sales (80%)	480,000	320,000	400,000	1,200,000
13	Total sales revenue	$ 600,000	$ 400,000	$ 500,000	$ 1,500,000
14					

Why is this important?

"The **sales budget** is the **basis** for every other budget. If sales are not projected as **accurately** as possible, all other budgets will be **off target**."

The remaining 80% of sales will be made on credit. Tucson Tortilla's credit terms are "net 30," meaning the customer has up to 30 days to pay for its purchases. Having this information available on the sales budget will help managers prepare the cash collections budget later.

Production Budget

Once managers have estimated how many units they expect to sell, they can figure out how many units they need to produce. Most manufacturers maintain some ending finished goods inventory, or <u>safety stock</u>, which is inventory kept on hand in case demand is higher than predicted, or the problems in the factory slow production (such as machine breakdown, employees out sick, and so forth). As a result, managers need to factor in the desired level of ending inventory when deciding how much inventory to produce. They do so as follows:

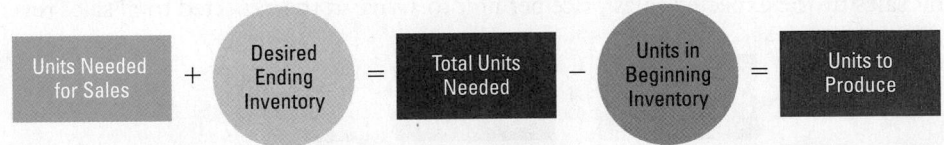

Let's walk through this calculation step by step:

- First, managers figure out how many total units they need. To do this, they add the number of units they plan to sell to the number of units they want on hand at the end of the month. *Let's assume Tucson Tortilla wants to maintain an ending inventory equal to 10% of the next month's expected sales (20,000 cases in February). Thus, the total number of cases needed in January is as follows:*

30,000 cases for January sales + (10% × 20,000) = 32,000 total cases needed

[1] In the past, COD meant "cash on delivery." However, as other forms of payment (such as checks, credit cards, and debit cards) have become more common, the word "cash" has been replaced with the word "collect" to incorporate these additional types of payments.

- Next, managers calculate the amount of inventory they expect to have on hand at the beginning of the month. *Since Tucson Tortilla desires ending inventory to be 10% of the next month's sales, managers expect to have 10% of January's sales on hand on December 31, which becomes the beginning balance on January 1:*

> 10% × 30,000 cases = 3,000 cases in beginning inventory on January 1

- Finally, by subtracting what the company already has in stock at the beginning of the month from the total units needed, the company is able to calculate how many units to produce:

> 32,000 cases needed − 3,000 cases in beginning inventory = 29,000 cases to produce

Exhibit 9-6 shows Tucson Tortilla's production budget for the first three months of the year. As the red arrows show, the ending inventory from one month (January 31) always becomes the beginning inventory for the next month (February 1).

EXHIBIT 9-6 Production Budget

	A	B	C	D	E
1		Tucson Tortilla			
2		Production Budget			
3		For the Quarter Ended March 31			
4		Month			
5		January	February	March	1st Quarter
6	Unit sales (cases)	30,000	20,000	25,000	75,000
7	Plus: Desired end inventory	2,000	2,500	3,200	3,200
8	Total needed	32,000	22,500	28,200	78,200
9	Less: Beginning inventory	3,000	2,000	2,500	3,000
10	Number of units to produce	29,000	20,500	25,700	75,200
11					

NOTE: *Management wants to maintain an ending inventory equal to 10% of the next month's projected sales. Projected April sales are 32,000 units. The quarter begins January 1 and ends March 31.*

Now that the company knows how many units it plans to produce every month, it can figure out the amount of direct materials, direct labor, and manufacturing overhead that will be needed. As shown in the following sections, the company will create separate budgets for each of these three manufacturing costs: direct materials, direct labor, and manufacturing overhead. Each budget will be driven by the number of units to be produced each month.

▶ Try It!

Assume Tucson Tortilla's sales budget shows projected sales of 32,000 cases in April and 40,000 cases in May. The company's manager would like to maintain ending safety stock equal to 10% of the next month's projected sales. How many units should be produced in April?

Please see page 571 for solutions.

Direct Materials Budget

The format of the direct materials budget is quite similar to the production budget:

Let's walk through the process using January as an example:

- First, the company figures out the quantity of direct materials (DM) needed for production. *Let's assume Tucson Tortilla's only direct material is masa harina, the special corn flour used to make tortilla chips. Each case of tortilla chips requires 5 pounds of this corn flour. Therefore, the quantity of direct materials needed for January production is as follows:*

  29,000 cases to be produced × 5 pounds per case = 145,000 pounds

- Next, the company adds in the desired ending inventory of direct materials. Some amount of direct materials safety stock is usually needed in case suppliers do not deliver all of the direct materials needed on time. *Let's assume that Tucson Tortilla wants to maintain an ending inventory of direct materials equal to 10% of the materials needed for next month's production (102,500 required in February, as shown in Exhibit 9-7):*

  145,000 pounds + (10% × 102,500) = 155,250 total pounds needed

- Next, managers determine the direct materials inventory they expect to have on hand at the beginning of the month. *Tucson Tortilla expects to have 10% of the materials needed for January's production in stock on December 31, which becomes the opening balance on January 1:*

  10% × 145,000 pounds = 14,500 pounds in beginning inventory

Finally, by subtracting what the company already has in stock at the beginning of the month from the total quantity needed, the company is able to calculate the quantity of direct materials it needs to purchase:

155,250 pounds needed − 14,500 pounds in beginning inventory = 140,750 pounds to purchase

- Finally, the company calculates the expected cost of purchasing those direct materials. *Let's say Tucson Tortilla can buy the masa harina corn flour in bulk for $1.50 per pound.*

  140,750 pounds × $1.50 = $211,125

Exhibit 9-7 shows Tucson Tortilla's direct materials budget for the first three months of the year.

EXHIBIT 9-7 Direct Materials Budget

	A	B	C	D	E
1		Tucson Tortilla			
2		Direct Materials Budget for Masa Harina Corn Flour			
3		For the Quarter Ended March 31			
4			Month		
5		January	February	March	1st Quarter
6	Units to be produced (from production budget)	29,000	20,500	25,700	75,200
7	Multiply by: Quantity (pounds) of DM needed per unit	5	5	5	5
8	Quantity (pounds) needed for production	145,000	10% 102,500	10% 128,500	376,000
9	Plus: Desired end inventory of DM	10,250	12,850	16,150	16,150
10	Total quantity (pounds) needed	155,250	115,350	144,650	392,150
11	Less: Beginning inventory of DM	14,500	10,250	12,850	14,500
12	Quantity (pounds) to purchase	140,750	105,100	131,800	377,650
13	Multiply by: Cost per pound	$ 1.50	$ 1.50	$ 1.50	$ 1.50
14	Total cost of DM purchases	$ 211,125	$ 157,650	$ 197,700	$ 566,475
15					

NOTE: *Management wants to maintain an ending inventory equal to 10% of the next month's production needs. Assume 161,500 pounds are needed for production in April.*

Direct Labor Budget

The direct labor (DL) budget is determined as follows:

Tucson Tortilla's factory is fairly automated, so very little direct labor is required. *Let's assume that each case requires only 0.05 of an hour. Direct laborers are paid $22 per hour. Thus, the direct labor cost for January is projected to be as follows:*

29,000 cases × 0.05 hours per case = 1,450 hours required × $22 per hour = $31,900

The direct labor budget for the first three months of the year is shown in Exhibit 9-8.

EXHIBIT 9-8 Direct Labor Budget

	A	B	C	D	E
1		Tucson Tortilla			
2		Direct Labor Budget			
3		For the Quarter Ended March 31			
4			Month		
5		January	February	March	1st Quarter
6	Units to be produced (from production budget)	29,000	20,500	25,700	75,200
7	Multiply by: Direct labor hours per unit	0.05	0.05	0.05	0.05
8	Total hours required	1,450	1,025	1,285	3,760
9	Multiply by: Direct labor cost per hour	$ 22	$ 22	$ 22	$ 22
10	Total direct labor cost	$ 31,900	$ 22,550	$ 28,270	$ 82,720
11					

Manufacturing Overhead Budget

The manufacturing overhead budget is highly dependent on cost behavior. Some overhead costs, such as indirect materials, are variable. For example, Tucson Tortilla considers the oil used for frying the tortilla chips to be an indirect material. Since a portion of the oil is absorbed into the chips, the amount of oil required increases as production volume increases. Thus, the cost is variable. The company also considers salt and cellophane packaging to be variable indirect materials. *Tucson Tortilla expects to spend $1.25 on indirect materials for each case of tortilla chips produced, so January's budget for indirect materials is as follows:*

29,000 cases × $1.25 = $36,250 of indirect materials

Costs such as utilities and indirect labor are mixed costs. Mixed costs are usually separated into their variable and fixed components using one of the cost behavior estimation methods already discussed in Chapter 6. *Based on engineering and cost studies, Tucson Tortilla has determined that each case of chips requires $0.75 of variable indirect labor, and $0.50 of variable utility costs as a result of running the production machinery. These variable costs are budgeted as follows for January:*

29,000 cases × $0.75 = $21,750 of variable indirect labor

29,000 cases × $0.50 = $14,500 of variable factory utilities

Finally, many manufacturing overhead costs are fixed. *Tucson Tortilla's fixed costs include depreciation, insurance, and property taxes on the factory. The company also incurs some fixed indirect labor (salaried production engineers who oversee the daily manufacturing operation) and a fixed amount of utilities just to keep the lights, heat, or air conditioning on in the plant, regardless of the production volume.*

Exhibit 9-9 shows that the manufacturing overhead budget usually has separate sections for variable and fixed overhead costs so that managers can easily see which costs will change as production volume changes.

EXHIBIT 9-9 Manufacturing Overhead Budget

A	B	C	D	E
Tucson Tortilla				
Manufacturing Overhead Budget				
For the Quarter Ended March 31				
	Month			
	January	February	March	1st Quarter
Cases to be produced (from production budget)	29,000	20,500	25,700	75,200
Variable MOH Costs:				
Indirect materials ($1.25 per case)	$ 36,250	$ 25,625	$ 32,125	$ 94,000
Indirect labor—variable portion ($0.75 per case)	21,750	15,375	19,275	56,400
Utilities—variable portion ($0.50 per case)	14,500	10,250	12,850	37,600
Total variable MOH	$ 72,500	$ 51,250	$ 64,250	$ 188,000
Fixed MOH Costs:				
Depreciation on factory and production equipment	$ 10,000	$ 10,000	$ 10,000	$ 30,000
Insurance and property taxes on the factory	3,000	3,000	3,000	9,000
Indirect labor—fixed portion	15,000	15,000	15,000	45,000
Utilities—fixed portion	2,000	2,000	2,000	6,000
Total fixed MOH	$ 30,000	$ 30,000	$ 30,000	$ 90,000
Total manufacturing overhead	$ 102,500	$ 81,250	$ 94,250	$ 278,000

Now that we have completed budgets for each of the three manufacturing costs (direct materials, direct labor, and manufacturing overhead), we turn our attention to operating expenses.

Operating Expenses Budget

Recall that all costs incurred in every area of the value chain, except production, must be expensed as operating expenses in the period in which they are incurred. Thus, all research and development, design, marketing, distribution, and customer service costs will be shown on the operating expenses budget.

Some operating expenses are variable, based on how many units will be *sold* (not produced). *For example, to motivate its sales force to generate sales, Tucson Tortilla pays its sales representatives a $1.50 sales commission for every case they sell.*

> 30,000 sales units × $1.50 = $45,000 sales commission expense in January

The company also incurs $2.00 of shipping costs on every case sold.

> 30,000 sales units × $2.00 = $60,000 shipping expense in January

Finally, the company knows that not all of the sales made on credit will eventually be collected. Based on experience, Tucson Tortilla expects monthly bad debt expense to be 1% of its credit sales. Since January credit sales are expected to be $480,000 (from Sales Budget, Exhibit 9-5), the company's bad debt expense for January is as follows:

> $480,000 of credit sales in January × 1% = $4,800 bad debt expense for January

Other operating expenses are fixed: They will stay the same each month even though sales volume fluctuates. *For example, Tucson Tortilla's fixed expenses include salaries, office rent, depreciation on office equipment and the company's vehicles, advertising, and telephone and Internet service.*

As shown in Exhibit 9-10, operating expenses are usually shown according to their cost behavior.

EXHIBIT 9-10 Operating Expenses Budget

	A	B	C	D	E
1		Tucson Tortilla			
2		Operating Expenses Budget			
3		For the Quarter Ended March 31			
4			Month		
5		January	February	March	1st Quarter
6	Number of cases to be sold (from sales budget)	30,000	20,000	25,000	75,000
7	**Variable Operating Expenses:**				
8	Sales commissions expense ($1.50 per case sold)	$ 45,000	$ 30,000	$ 37,500	$ 112,500
9	Shipping expense ($2.00 per case sold)	60,000	40,000	50,000	150,000
10	Bad debt expense (1% of credit sales)	4,800	3,200	4,000	12,000
11	Total variable operating expenses	$ 109,800	$ 73,200	$ 91,500	$ 274,500
12					
13	**Fixed Operating Expenses:**				
14	Salaries	$ 20,000	$ 20,000	$ 20,000	$ 60,000
15	Office rent	4,000	4,000	4,000	12,000
16	Depreciation	6,000	6,000	6,000	18,000
17	Advertising	2,000	2,000	2,000	6,000
18	Telephone and internet	1,000	1,000	1,000	3,000
19	Total fixed operating expenses	$ 33,000	$ 33,000	$ 33,000	$ 99,000
20					
21	Total operating expenses	$ 142,800	$ 106,200	$ 124,500	$ 373,500
22					

Budgeted Income Statement

A budgeted income statement looks just like a regular income statement, except for the fact that it uses budgeted data. A company may prepare a budget in contribution margin format for internal use or in traditional format for both internal and external use. For example, often, a company will need to supply its lending institution with budgeted financial statements. Thus, we present the traditional format here. Recall the traditional format for an income statement:

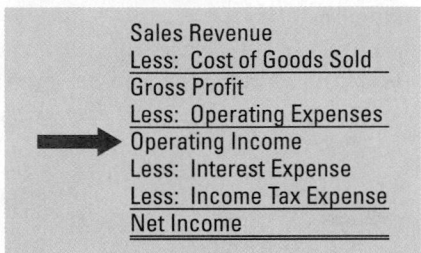

This textbook has focused on a company's operating income, rather than net income. However, a complete income statement would include any interest expense (and/or interest income) as well as a provision for income taxes. These additional costs are subtracted from operating income to arrive at net income.

We have already computed the budgeted sales revenue and operating expenses on separate budgets. But we still need to calculate the Cost of Goods Sold before we can prepare the income statement.

Tucson Tortilla computes its Cost of Goods Sold as follows:

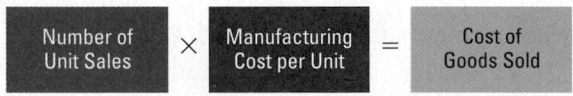

This will be relatively simple for Tucson Tortilla since the company produces only one product.

The cost of manufacturing each case of tortilla chips is shown in Exhibit 9-11. Almost all of the information shown has already been presented and used to prepare the budgets for direct materials, direct labor, and manufacturing overhead. The only new piece of information is the total production volume for the year, budgeted to be 400,000 cases.

EXHIBIT 9-11 Budgeted Manufacturing Cost per Unit

	A	B	C
1	**Budgeted Manufacturing Costs**		**Cost per Case**
2	Direct materials (5 pounds per case × $1.50 per pound)		$ 7.50
3	Direct labor (0.05 hours per case × $22 per hour)		1.10
4	Variable MOH:		
5	Indirect materials ($1.25 per case)	$ 1.25	
6	Indirect labor ($0.75 per case)	0.75	
7	Variable utilities ($.50 per case)	0.50	
8	Total variable MOH per case		2.50
9	Fixed MOH ($30,000 per month × 12 months)	$ 360,000	
10	Divided by: Budgeted production volume (cases)	400,000	
11	Total fixed MOH per case		0.90
12	Cost per case (absorption costing)		$ 12.00
13			

NOTE: Information taken from the DM, DL, and MOH budgets in Exhibits 9-7 through 9-9.

Exhibit 9-12 shows the company's budgeted income statement for January. Interest expense is budgeted to be zero since the company has no outstanding debt. The income tax expense is budgeted to be 35% of income before taxes. The company will prepare budgeted income statements for each month and quarter, as well as for the entire year.

EXHIBIT 9-12 Budgeted Income Statement

	A	B
1	**Tucson Tortilla**	
2	**Budgeted Income Statement**	
3	**For the Month Ended January 31**	
4		
5	Sales revenue (30,000 cases × $20 per case, from Exhibit 9-5)	$ 600,000
6	Less: Cost of goods sold (30,000 cases × $12.00 per case, from Exhibit 9-11)	360,000
7	Gross profit	240,000
8	Less: Operating expenses (from Exhibit 9-10)	142,800
9	Operating income	$ 97,200
10	Less: Interest expense (or add interest income)	0
11	Less: Income tax expense	34,020
12	Net income	$ 63,180
13		

NOTE: The corporate income tax rate for most companies is currently 35% of income before tax. Thus, the budgeted income tax is $34,020 (= $97,200 × 35).

We have now completed the operating budgets for Tucson Tortilla. In the second half of the chapter, we'll prepare Tucson Tortilla's financial budgets.

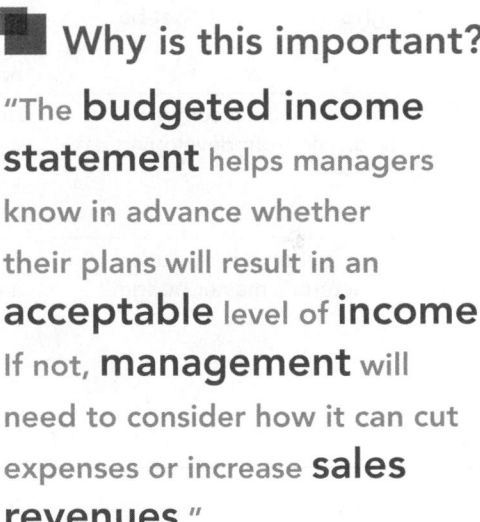

Why is this important?

"The **budgeted income statement** helps managers know in advance whether their plans will result in an **acceptable** level of **income**. If not, **management** will need to consider how it can cut expenses or increase **sales revenues**."

Decision Guidelines

The Master Budget

Let's consider some of the decisions Campbell Soup Company made as it set up its budgeting process.

Decision	Guidelines
What should be the driving force behind the budgeting process?	The company's long-term goals and strategies drive the budgeting of the company's resources.
What are budgets used for?	Managers use budgets to help them fulfill their primary responsibilities: planning, directing, and controlling operations. Managers use feedback from the budgeting process to take corrective actions and, if necessary, revise strategies.
Who should be involved in the budgeting process?	Budgets tend to be more realistic and more motivational if lower-level managers, as well as upper-level managers, are allowed to participate in the budgeting process. The budgeting process tends to encompass a more comprehensive view when managers from all areas of the value chain participate in the process and serve on the budget committee.
What period of time should the budgets cover?	Long-term, strategic planning often results in forecasts of revenues and expenses 5 to 10 years into the future. Monthly and yearly budgets provide much more detailed information to aid management's shorter-term decisions.
How tough should the budget be to achieve?	Budgets are more useful for motivating employees and evaluating performance if they can be achieved with effort. Budgets that are too tight (too hard to achieve) or too loose (too easy to achieve) are not as beneficial.
What benefits should a company expect to obtain from developing a budget?	Benefits include the following: • Planning • Coordination and communication • Benchmarking (used for both motivation and performance evaluation)
What budgets should be included in a manufacturer's master budget?	The *operating budgets* includes all budgets necessary to create a budgeted income statement. For a manufacturer, this includes the following: • Sales budget • Production budget • Direct materials budget • Direct labor budget • Manufacturing overhead budget • Operating expenses budget • Budgeted income statement The *financial budgets* include the capital expenditures budget, the cash budgets, and the budgeted balance sheet.

SUMMARY PROBLEM 1

Pillows Unlimited makes decorative throw pillows for home use. The company sells the pillows to home décor retailers for $14 per pillow. Each pillow requires 1.25 yards of fabric, which the company obtains at a cost of $6 per yard. The company would like to maintain an ending stock of fabric equal to 10% of the next month's production requirements. The company would also like to maintain an ending stock of finished pillows equal to 20% of the next month's sales. Sales (in units) are projected to be as follows for the first three months of the year:

January	100,000
February	110,000
March	115,000

Requirements

Prepare the following budgets for the first three months of the year, as well as a summary budget for the quarter:

1. Prepare the sales budget, including a separate section that details the type of sales made. For this section, assume that 10% of the company's pillows are cash sales, while the remaining 90% are sold on credit terms.

2. Prepare the production budget. Assume that the company anticipates selling 120,000 units in April.

3. Prepare the direct materials purchases budget. Assume the company needs 150,000 yards of fabric for production in April.

▪ SOLUTIONS

Requirement 1

	A	B	C	D	E
1		Pillows Unlimited			
2		Sales Budget			
3		For the Quarter Ended March 31			
4		Month			
5		January	February	March	1st Quarter
6	Unit sales	100,000	110,000	115,000	325,000
7	Multiply by: Unit selling price	$ 14	$ 14	$ 14	$ 14
8	Total sales revenue	$ 1,400,000	$ 1,540,000	$ 1,610,000	$ 4,550,000
9					
10	**Type of sale:**				
11	Cash sales (10%)	$ 140,000	$ 154,000	$ 161,000	$ 455,000
12	Credit sales (90%)	1,260,000	1,386,000	1,449,000	4,095,000
13	Total sales revenue	$ 1,400,000	$ 1,540,000	$ 1,610,000	$ 4,550,000
14					

Requirement 2

	A	B	C	D	E
1		Pillows Unlimited			
2		Production Budget			
3		For the Quarter Ended March 31			
4		Month			
5		January	February	March	1st Quarter
6	Unit sales	100,000	110,000	115,000	325,000
7	Plus: Desired end inventory	22,000	23,000	24,000	24,000
8	Total needed	122,000	133,000	139,000	349,000
9	Less: Beginning inventory	20,000	22,000	23,000	20,000
10	Number of units to produce	102,000	111,000	116,000	329,000
11					

NOTE: January 1 inventory balance (20,000) is the same as the December 31 balance, which is calculated as 20% of the projected units sales in January (100,000). March desired ending inventory (24,000) is 20% of April's projected units sales (120,000).

Requirement 3

	A	B	C	D	E
1		Pillows Unlimited			
2		Direct Materials Budget			
3		For the Quarter Ended March 31			
4		Month			
5		January	February	March	1st Quarter
6	Units to be produced (from production budget)	102,000	111,000	116,000	329,000
7	Multiply by: Quantity (yards) of DM needed per unit	1.25	1.25	1.25	1.25
8	Quantity (yards) needed for production	127,500	138,750	145,000	411,250
9	Plus: Desired end inventory of DM	13,875	14,500	15,000	15,000
10	Total quantity (yards) needed	141,375	153,250	160,000	426,250
11	Less: Beginning inventory of DM	12,750	13,875	14,500	12,750
12	Quantity (yards) to purchase	128,625	139,375	145,500	413,500
13	Multiply by: Cost per yard	$ 6.00	$ 6.00	$ 6.00	$ 6.00
14	Total cost of DM purchases	$ 771,750	$ 836,250	$ 873,000	$2,481,000
15					

NOTE: January 1 inventory balance (12,750) is the same as the December 31 balance, which is calculated as 10% of the quantity (yards) needed for production in January (127,500). March desired ending inventory of DM (15,000) is 10% of April's projected quantity needed for production (150,000).

How are the Financial Budgets Prepared?

In the first half of the chapter, we prepared Tucson Tortilla's operating budgets, culminating with the company's budgeted income statement. In this part of the chapter we turn our attention to Tucson Tortilla's financial budgets. Managers typically prepare a capital expenditures budget as well as three separate cash budgets:

3 Prepare the financial budgets

1. Cash collections (or receipts) budget
2. Cash payments (or disbursements) budget
3. Combined cash budget, complete with financing arrangements

Finally, managers prepare the budgeted balance sheet. Each of these budgets is illustrated next.

Capital Expenditures Budget

The capital expenditures budget shows the company's intentions to invest in new property, plant, or equipment (capital investments). When planned capital investments are significant, this budget must be developed early in the process because the additional investments may affect depreciation expense, interest expense (if funds are borrowed to pay for the investments), or dividend payments (if stock is issued to pay for the investments). Chapter 12 contains a detailed discussion of the capital budgeting process, including the techniques managers use in deciding whether to make additional investments.

Exhibit 9-13 shows Tucson Tortilla's capital expenditures budget for the first three months of the year. *Tucson Tortilla expects to invest in new computers, delivery vans, and production equipment in January. The depreciation expense shown in the operating expenses budget and the depreciation shown in the MOH budget reflect these anticipated investments. No other capital investments are planned in the first quarter of the year.*

EXHIBIT 9-13 Capital Expenditures Budget

	A	B	C	D	E
1		Tucson Tortilla			
2		Capital Expenditures Budget			
3		For the Quarter Ended March 31			
4		Month			
5		January	February	March	1st Quarter
6	Computers and printers	$ 15,000	0	0	15,000
7	Delivery vans	35,000	0	0	35,000
8	Production equipment	75,000	0	0	75,000
9	Total new capital investments	$ 125,000	0	0	$ 125,000
10					

Cash Collections Budget

The cash collections budget is all about timing: *When* does Tucson Tortilla expect to receive cash from its sales? Of course, Tucson Tortilla will receive cash immediately on its cash (COD) sales. From the Sales Budget (Exhibit 9-5), we see that the company expects the following cash sales in January:

Cash (COD) sales = $120,000

However, most of the company's sales are made on credit. Recall that Tucson Tortilla's credit terms are "net 30 days," meaning customers have 30 days to pay. Therefore, most customers will wait nearly 30 days (a full month) before paying. However, some companies may be experiencing cash flow difficulties and may not be able to pay Tucson Tortilla on time. Because of this, Tucson Tortilla doesn't expect to receive payment on all of its credit sales the month after the sale.

Based on collection history, Tucson Tortilla expects 85% of its credit sales to be collected in the month after sale, and 14% to be collected two months after the sale. Tucson Tortilla expects that 1% of credit sales will never be collected, and therefore has recognized a 1% bad debt expense in its operating expenses budget. Furthermore, assume that December credit sales were $500,000 and November credit sales were $480,000.

Anticipated January Collections of Credit Sales:
85% × $500,000 (December credit sales) = $425,000
14% × $480,000 (November credit sales) = $ 67,200

Exhibit 9-14 shows Tucson Tortilla's expected cash collections for the first three months of the year.

EXHIBIT 9-14 Cash Collections Budget

	A	B	C	D	E
1		Tucson Tortilla			
2		Cash Collections Budget			
3		For the Quarter Ended March 31			
4		Month			
5		January	February	March	1st Quarter
6	Cash sales in current month (from sales budget)	$ 120,000	$ 80,000	$ 100,000	$ 300,000
7	Collection on credit sales:				
8	85% of credit sales made one month ago	425,000	408,000	272,000	1,105,000
9	14% of credit sales made two months ago	67,200	70,000	67,200	204,400
10	Total cash collections	$ 612,200	$ 558,000	$ 439,200	$1,609,400
11					

NOTE: Cash and credit sales are shown on Sales Budget (Exhibit 9-5)

January:
$425,000 = 85% of December credit sales ($500,000)
$67,200 = 14% of November credit sales ($480,000)

February:
$408,000 = 85% of January credit sales ($480,000)
$70,000 = 14% of December credit sales ($500,000)

March:
$272,000 = 85% of February credit sales ($320,000)
$67,200 = 14% of January credit sales ($480,000)

Try It!

Assume Georgio's has the following budgeted sales for the quarter:

	January	February	March
COD sales	$ 10,000	$ 20,000	$ 15,000
Credit sales	100,000	110,000	120,000
Total Sales	$110,000	$130,000	$135,000

Determine Georgio's budget for March cash collections assuming credit sales are collected as follows: 90% is collected the month after sale, 8% is collected two months after the month of sale, and 2% is never collected.

Please see page 571 for solutions.

Cash Payments Budget

The cash payments budget is also about timing: *When* will Tucson Tortilla pay for its direct materials purchases, direct labor costs, manufacturing overhead costs, operating expenses, capital expenditures, and income taxes? Let's tackle each cost, one at a time.

DIRECT MATERIALS PURCHASES *Tucson Tortilla has been given "net 30 days" payment terms from its suppliers of the corn flour used to make the tortilla chips. Therefore, Tucson*

Tortilla waits a month before it pays for the direct materials purchases shown in the Direct Materials Budget (Exhibit 9-7). So, the company will pay for its December purchases (projected to be $231,845) in January, its January purchases of $211,125 (Exhibit 9-7) in February, its February purchases of $157,650 (Exhibit 9-7) in March, and so forth:

	A	B	C	D	E
1	**Calculating Cash Payments for**		**Month**		
2	**Direct Materials Purchases**	**January**	**February**	**March**	**1st Quarter**
3	Total cost of DM purchases (from Exhibit 9-7)	$ 211,125	$ 157,650	$ 197,700	$ 566,475
4					
5	Cash payments for DM purchases **(paid one month after purchase)**	231,845	$ 211,125	$ 157,650	$ 600,620
6					

NOTE: December DM purchases are expected to be $231,845.

DIRECT LABOR *Tucson Tortilla's factory employees are paid twice a month for the work they perform during the month. Therefore, January's direct labor cost of $31,900 (Exhibit 9-8) will be paid in January, and likewise, for each month.*

	A	B	C	D	E
1			**Month**		
2	**Calculating Cash Payments for Direct Labor**	**January**	**February**	**March**	**1st Quarter**
3	Total cost of direct labor (from Exhibit 9-8)	$ 31,900	$ 22,550	$ 28,270	$ 82,720
4					
5	Cash payments for direct labor **(paid the same month)**	$ 31,900	$ 22,550	$ 28,270	$ 82,720
6					

MANUFACTURING OVERHEAD Tucson Tortilla must consider when it pays for its manufacturing overhead costs. *Let's assume that the company pays for all manufacturing overhead costs except for depreciation, insurance, and property taxes **in the month in which they are incurred**. Depreciation is a non-cash expense, so it never appears on the cash payments budget. Insurance and property taxes are typically paid on a semiannual basis. While Tucson Tortilla budgets a cost of $3,000 per month for factory insurance and property tax, it doesn't actually pay these costs on a monthly basis. Rather, Tucson Tortilla prepays its insurance and property tax twice a year, in January and July. The amount of these semiannual payments is calculated as shown:*

$3,000 monthly cost × 12 months = $36,000 ÷ 2 = $18,000 payments in January and July

So, the cash payments for manufacturing overhead costs are expected to be as follows:

	A	B	C	D	E
1	**Calculating Cash Payments for**		**Month**		
2	**Manufacturing Overhead**	**January**	**February**	**March**	**1st Quarter**
3	Total manufacturing overhead (from Exhibit 9-9)	$ 102,500	$ 81,250	$ 94,250	$ 278,000
4	Less: Depreciation **(not a cash expense)**	10,000	10,000	10,000	30,000
5	Less: Property tax and insurance **(paid twice a year, not monthly)**	3,000	3,000	3,000	9,000
6	Plus: Semiannual **payments** for property taxes and insurance	18,000	0	0	18,000
7	Cash payments for manufacturing overhead	$ 107,500	$ 68,250	$ 81,250	$ 257,000
8					

OPERATING EXPENSES *Let's assume that the company pays for all operating expenses, except depreciation and bad debt expense, **in the month in which they are incurred**. Both depreciation and bad debt expense are non-cash expenses, so they never appear on the cash payments budget. Bad debt expense simply recognizes the sales revenue that will never be collected. Therefore, these non-cash expenses need to be deducted from the total operating expenses to arrive at **cash** payments for operating expenses:*

	A	B	C	D	E
1	Calculating Cash Payments for		Month		
2	Operating Expenses	January	February	March	1st Quarter
3	Total operating expenses (from Exhibit 9-10)	$ 142,800	$ 106,200	$ 124,500	$ 373,500
4	Less: Depreciation (*not a cash expense*)	6,000	6,000	6,000	18,000
5	Less: Bad debt expense (*not a cash expense*)	4,800	3,200	4,000	12,000
6	Cash Payments for operating expenses	$ 132,000	$ 97,000	$ 114,500	$ 343,500
7					

CAPITAL EXPENDITURES The timing of these cash payments has already been scheduled on the Capital Expenditures Budget in Exhibit 9-13.

INCOME TAXES Corporations must make quarterly income tax payments for their estimated income tax liability. For corporations like Tucson Tortilla that have a December 31 fiscal year-end, the first income tax payment is not due until April 15. The remaining payments are due June 15, September 15, and December 15. *As a result, Tucson Tortilla will not show any income tax payments in the first quarter of the year.*

DIVIDENDS Like many corporations, Tucson Tortilla pays dividends to its shareholders on a quarterly basis. Tucson Tortilla plans to pay $25,000 in cash dividends in January for the company's earnings in the fourth quarter of the previous year.

Finally, we pull all of these cash payments together onto a single budget, as shown in Exhibit 9-15.

EXHIBIT 9-15 Cash Payments Budget

	A	B	C	D	E
1		Tucson Tortilla			
2		Cash Payments Budget			
3		For the Quarter Ended March 31			
4			Month		
5		January	February	March	1st Quarter
6	Cash payments for direct materials purchases	$ 231,845	$ 211,125	$ 157,650	$ 600,620
7	Cash payments for direct labor	31,900	22,550	28,270	82,720
8	Cash payments for manufacturing overhead	107,500	68,250	81,250	257,000
9	Cash payments for operating expenses	132,000	97,000	114,500	343,500
10	Cash payments for capital investments	125,000	0	0	125,000
11	Cash payments for income taxes	0	0	0	0
12	Cash payments for dividends	25,000	0	0	25,000
13	Total cash payments	$ 653,245	$ 398,925	$ 381,670	$ 1,433,840
14					

Combined Cash Budget

The combined cash budget simply merges the budgeted cash collections and cash payments to project the company's ending cash position. Exhibit 9-16 shows the following:

- Budgeted cash collections for the month are added to the beginning cash balance to determine the total cash available.

- Budgeted cash payments are then subtracted to determine the ending cash balance before financing.

- Based on the ending cash balance before financing, the company knows whether it needs to borrow money or whether it has excess funds with which to repay debt or invest.

By looking at Exhibit 9-16, we see that Tucson Tortilla expects to begin the month with $36,100 of cash. However, by the end of the month, it will be short of cash. Therefore, the company's managers must plan for how they will handle this shortage. One strategy would be to delay the purchase of equipment planned for January. Another strategy would be to borrow money. Let's say Tucson Tortilla has prearranged a line of credit that carries an interest rate of prime plus 1%. A **line of credit** is a lending arrangement from a bank in which a company is allowed to borrow money as needed, up to a specified maximum amount, yet only pay interest on the portion that is actually borrowed until it is repaid.

EXHIBIT 9-16 Combined Cash Budget

	A	B	C	D	E
1		Tucson Tortilla			
2		Combined Cash Budget			
3		For the Quarter Ended March 31			
4		Month			
5		January	February	March	1st Quarter
6	Beginning cash balance	$ 36,100	$ 15,055	$ 153,980	$ 36,100
7	Plus: Cash collections (Exhibit 9-14)	612,200	558,000	439,200	1,609,400
8	Total cash available	648,300	573,055	593,180	1,645,500
9	Less: Cash payments (Exhibit 9-15)	653,245	398,925	381,670	1,433,840
10	Ending cash balance before financing	$ (4,945)	$ 174,130	$ 211,510	$ 211,660
11	Financing:				
12	Plus: New borrowings	20,000	0	0	20,000
13	Less: Debt repayments	0	20,000	0	20,000
14	Less: Interest payments	0	150	0	150
15	Ending cash balance	$ 15,055	$ 153,980	$ 211,510	$ 211,510
16					

The line of credit will enable Tucson Tortilla to borrow funds to meet its short-term cash deficiencies. Let's say that Tucson Tortilla wants to maintain an ending cash balance of at least $15,000. By borrowing $20,000 on its line of credit at the end of January, the company will have slightly more ($15,055) than its minimum desired balance.

The cash budget also shows that Tucson Tortilla will be able to repay this borrowing, along with the accrued interest, in February. Assuming Tucson Tortilla borrows the $20,000 for a full month at an interest rate of 9%, February's interest payment would be calculated as follows:

$$\$20,000 \text{ loan} \times 1/12 \text{ of the year} \times 9\% \text{ interest rate} = \$150$$

Exhibit 9-16 also shows that Tucson Tortilla expects to have a fairly substantial cash balance at the end of both February and March. The company's managers use the cash budgets to determine when this cash will be needed and to decide how to invest it accordingly. Since the first quarterly income tax payment is due April 15, management will want to invest most of this excess cash in a safe, short-term investment, such as a money market fund or short-term certificate of deposit. The company will also need cash in April to pay shareholders a quarterly dividend. Any cash not needed in the short run can be invested in longer-term investments. Managers exercising good cash management should have a plan in place for both cash deficiencies and cash excesses.

 Why is this important?

"The combined **cash budget** lets managers know in **advance** when they will be short on cash and need to **borrow** money, or when they may have **extra funds** to invest."

Budgeted Balance Sheet

Exhibit 9-17 shows Tucson Tortilla's budgeted balance sheet as of January 31. The company will prepare a budgeted balance sheet for each month of the year.

EXHIBIT 9-17 Budgeted Balance Sheet

	A	B
1	Tucson Tortilla	
2	Budgeted Balance Sheet	
3	January 31	
4	**Assets:**	
5	Cash, from cash budget	$ 15,055
6	Accounts receivable, net of allowance^A	549,450
7	Raw materials inventory, from DM budget (10,250 pounds × $1.50 per pound)	15,375
8	Finished goods inventory, from production budget (2,000 cases × $12.00 per case)	24,000
9	Prepaid property taxes and insurance^B	15,000
10	Total current assets	618,880
11	Property, plant, and equipment,^C net of $1,920,000 of accumulated depreciation^D	4,430,000
12	Total assets	$ 5,048,880
13		
14	**Liabilities and Stockholders' Equity:**	
15	Accounts payable^E	$ 211,125
16	Income tax liability, from Income Statement Budget	34,020
17	Other current liabilities (line of credit, from combined cash budget)	20,000
18	Total current liabilities	265,145
19	Stockholders' equity^F	4,783,735
20	Total liabilities and stockholders' equity	$ 5,048,880
21		

NOTE: Calculations for amounts itemized below.

---

^A Accounts Receivable, Net of Allowance

January credit sales (from sales budget, Exhibit 9-5)	$480,000
15% of December's credit sales ($500,000) yet to be collected	75,000
Accounts receivable, January 31	$555,000
Less: Allowance for uncollectible accounts (assume $750 balance prior to additional $4,800 bad debt expense, Exhibit 9-10)	(5,550)
Accounts receivable, net of allowance for uncollectible accounts	$549,450

---

^B Prepaid Property Tax and Insurance

Semiannual payment made in January (cash payments for MOH, p. 521)	$18,000
Less: January cost (MOH budget, Exhibit 9-9)	3,000
Prepaid property tax and insurance, January 31	$15,000

---

^C Property, Plant, and Equipment

December 31 balance (assumed)	$6,225,000
Plus: January's investment in new equipment (capital expenditures budget, Exhibit 9-13)	125,000
Property, plant, and equipment, January 31	$6,350,000

---

^D Accumulated Depreciation

December 31 balance (assumed)	$1,904,000
Plus: January's depreciation from manufacturing overhead budget, Exhibit 9-9	10,000
Plus: January's depreciation from operating expenses budget, Exhibit 9-10	6,000
Accumulated depreciation, January 31	$1,920,000

ᴱ Accounts Payable	
January's DM purchases to be paid in February (p. 521 and Exhibit 9-15)...	211,125
Accounts payable, January 31..	$211,125

ᶠ Stockholders' Equity	
December 31 balance of common stock and retained earnings (assumed)	$4,720,555
Plus: January's net income (budgeted income statement, Exhibit 9-12)	63,180
Stockholders' equity, January 31...	$4,783,735

Sensitivity Analysis and Flexible Budgeting

The master budget models the company's *planned* activities. Managers try to use the best estimates possible when creating budgets. However, managers do not have a crystal ball for making predictions. Some of the key assumptions (such as sales volume) used to create the budgets may turn out to be different than originally predicted. How do managers prepare themselves for potentially different scenarios? They use sensitivity analysis and flexible budgeting.

As shown in Exhibit 9-18, **sensitivity analysis** is a *what-if* technique that asks *what* a result will be *if* a predicted amount is not achieved or *if* an underlying assumption changes. For example, *what if* shipping costs increase due to increases in gasoline prices? *What if* the cost of the corn flour increases or union workers negotiate a wage increase? *What if* sales are 15% cash and 85% credit, rather than 20% cash and 80% credit? How will any or all of these changes in key assumptions affect Tucson Tortilla's budgeted income and budgeted cash position?

EXHIBIT 9-18 Sensitivity Analysis

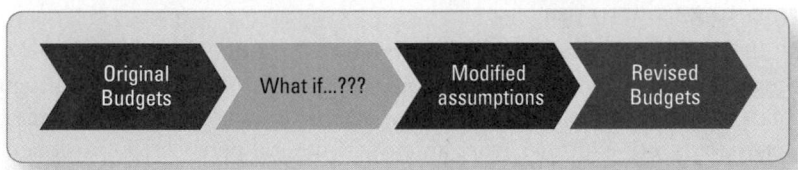

In addition to these "what-if" scenarios, management is particularly concerned with sales projections. Why? Because the sales budget is the driving force behind most of the other budgets. If the budgeted sales figures change, then most other budgets will also change. To address this concern, managers often prepare **flexible budgets**, which are budgets prepared for different volumes of activity. We'll discuss flexible budgets in Chapter 10, where we show how flexible budgets are often used to evaluate performance at the end of the period.

Sensitivity analysis and flexible budgeting are fairly easy to perform using Excel or special budgeting software. Managers simply change one or more of the underlying assumptions in the budgets, such as sales volume, and the software automatically computes a complete set of revised budgets based on the changes.

Armed with a better understanding of how changes in key assumptions will affect the company's bottom line and cash position, today's managers can be prepared to lead the company when business conditions change.

Sustainability and Budgeting

Budgets reflect and communicate management's goals and objectives. Managers leading their companies toward more sustainable practices will want to reflect those goals in the company's budgets. For example, the Campbell Soup Company, which has been on the Dow Jones Sustainability Index for the last three years, has set long-term environmental goals for 2020 that include:[2]

- Cutting water use and greenhouse gas emissions per ton of food produced
- Recycling 95% of waste generated
- Reducing packaging material and delivering 100% of packaging from sustainable materials
- Sourcing 40% of energy used from renewable or alternative energy sources

The adoption of these long-term goals will affect most, if not all, of the company's shorter-term budgets. For example, the operating expenses budget should reflect additional resources devoted to researching and developing more sustainable packaging materials. Once developed, the new packaging will impact the direct materials budget. The operating expenses budget should also include additional resources for marketing the sustainably packaged products, which should in turn create additional sales to be included in the sales budget. The capital expenditures budget will reflect plans to purchase new energy-saving production equipment. The company's MOH budget will in turn be affected by depreciation of the new equipment, as well as the reduction of water cost, the recycling of waste, and the use of alternative forms of energy. All of these measures will impact the cash budget, as well as the company's projected income statement and balance sheet.

In addition to environmental goals, the company also has social impact goals, that will be reflected in the company's budgets. These goals include:

- Increasing the nutritional value of its products
- Reducing childhood obesity and hunger
- Promoting volunteerism

Recall that budgets also serve as benchmarks for judging performance. By developing strategic environmental and social goals that span several years, and then tracking yearly performance, Campbell can see how well it is working toward achieving those longer-term goals. For example, from an environmental perspective Campbell has:

- Decreased water used per ton of food by 15% (2008–2011)
- Decreased greenhouse gas emissions per ton of food by 6% (2008–2011)
- Decreased packaging materials used by 73% (2009–2011)
- Increased its recycling rate to 80% of waste (2011)

From a social impact perspective Campbell has:

- Increased the number of products defined as "healthy" by the Food and Drug Administration (FDA)
- Increased the percentage of products sold with reduced amounts of negative nutrients, such as reduced levels of sugars and saturated fats
- Donated over $50 million in food and cash to charitable causes
- Encouraged employee volunteerism through its "Make a Difference" week

These key metrics indicate that Campbell is well on its way toward achieving its longer-term environmental and social impact goals.

See Exercises E9-16A and E9-35B

[2]Campbell Soup Company 2012 Corporate Social Responsibility Report

How do the Budgets for Service and Merchandising Companies Differ?

Earlier in this chapter we presented the master budget for a manufacturing company. The components of the master budget for a manufacturing company were summarized in Exhibit 9-4. The master budgets for service companies and merchandising companies are somewhat less complex, and will be described next.

4 Prepare budgets for a merchandiser

Service Companies

Recall that service companies have no merchandise inventory. Therefore, their operating budgets only include the sales budget, the operating expenses budget, and the budgeted income statement, as shown in Exhibit 9-19. Notice that the financial budgets are the same as those a manufacturer would prepare.

EXHIBIT 9-19 Master Budget for a Service Company

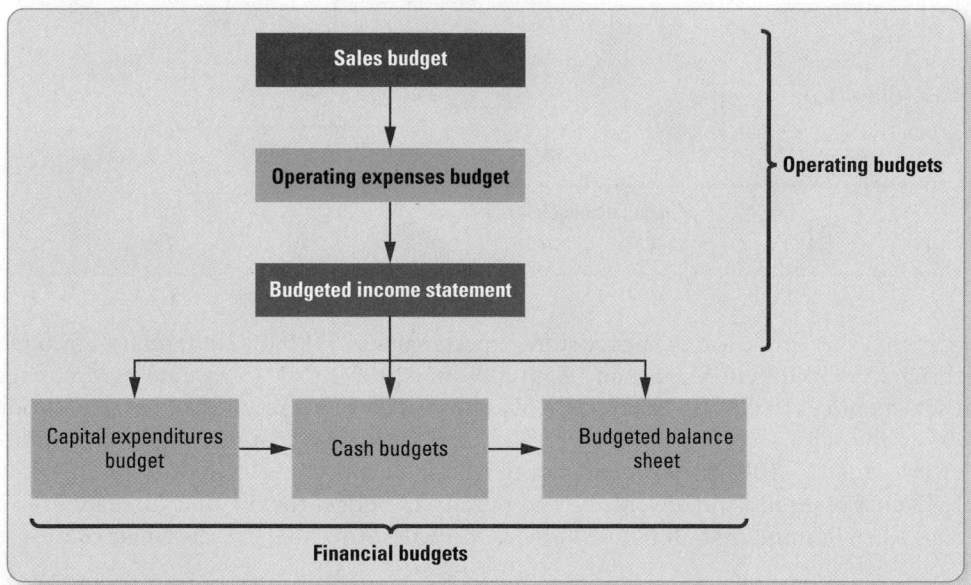

Merchandising Companies

Since merchandising companies purchase ready-made products, they do not need to prepare the production, direct materials, direct labor, or manufacturing overhead budgets. Replacing these budgets is a combined <u>cost of goods sold, inventory, and purchases budget</u>, as shown in Exhibit 9-20.

The cost of goods sold, inventory, and purchases budget follows the same general format as the manufacturer's production budget except that it is calculated at cost (in dollars) rather than in units:[3]

Cost of Goods Sold	(the inventory we plan to sell during the month, at cost)
<u>Plus: Desired Ending Inventory</u>	(the amount of inventory we want on hand at month's end)
Total Inventory Needed	(the total amount of inventory needed)
<u>Less: Beginning Inventory</u>	(the amount of inventory we have on hand)
<u>Purchases of Inventory</u>	(the amount of inventory we need to purchase)

Notice that the format of the budget is easy to remember because it follows the name of the budget: We start with *Cost of Goods Sold*, then consider *inventory* levels, and finally arrive at the amount of *purchases* to be made. Let's try an example:

[3]A merchandiser could first prepare this budget in units, and then convert it to dollars. However, merchandisers usually have hundreds or thousands of products for sale, so it is often simpler to state it directly in dollars.

EXHIBIT 9-20 Master Budget for a Merchandising Company

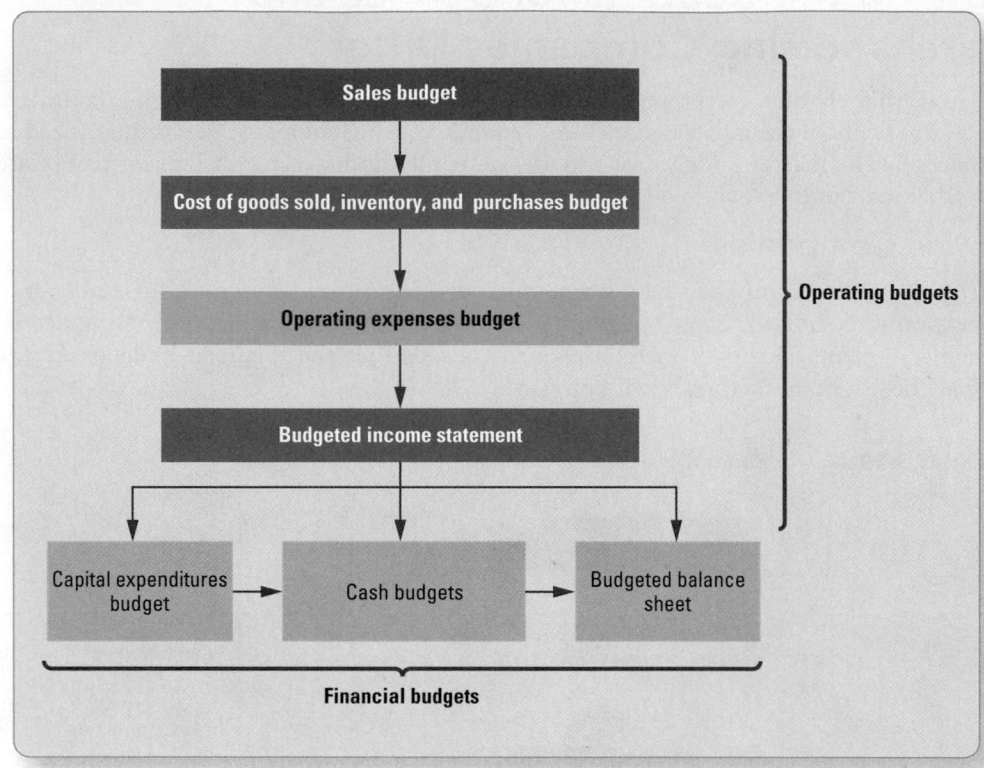

Let's say one Circle J convenience store expects sales of $500,000 in January, $520,000 in February, $530,000 in March, and $550,000 in April. Let's also assume that management sets its prices to achieve an overall 40% gross profit. As a result, Cost of Goods Sold is 60% of the sales revenue (100% − 40%). Finally, management wishes to have ending inventory equal to 10% of the next month's Cost of Goods Sold. Exhibit 9-21 shows Circle J's cost of goods sold, inventory, and purchases budget for the first three months of the year. Keep in mind that all figures (other than Sales Revenue) are shown at cost.

EXHIBIT 9-21 Merchandiser's Cost of Goods Sold, Inventory, and Purchases Budget

	A	B	C	D	E
1	Circle J Convenience Stores				
2	Cost of Goods Sold, Inventory, and Purchases Budget				
3	For the Quarter Ended March 31				
4		Month			
5		January	February	March	1st Quarter
6	Budgeted sales revenue	$ 500,000	$ 520,000	$ 530,000	$ 1,550,000
7					
8	Cost of goods sold	$ 300,000	$×10% 312,000	$×10% 318,000	$ 930,000
9	Plus: Desired end inventory	31,200	31,800	33,000	33,000
10	Total inventory required	331,200	343,800	351,000	963,000
11	Less: Beginning inventory	30,000	31,200	31,800	30,000
12	Amount of inventory to purchase	$ 301,200	$ 312,600	$ 319,200	$ 933,000
13					

NOTE: Management would like to maintain an ending inventory equal to 10% of the next month's Cost of Goods Sold. The January 1 balance ($30,000) is the same as the December 31 balance, which is 10% of January's Cost of Goods Sold ($300,000). Also, assume April sales are projected to be $550,000, so April's Cost of Goods Sold is $330,000 (= 60% × $550,000).

Figures from this budget are then used as follows:

- *Cost of Goods Sold* is used in preparing the budgeted income statement.
- *Ending Inventory* is used in preparing the budgeted balance sheet.
- *Purchases of Inventory* is used in preparing the cash payments budget.

Impact of Credit and Debit Card Sales on Budgeting

Consumers often use credit and debit cards to pay for online and in-store purchases at retailers, gas stations, and restaurants. What implications do these payment methods have on the merchants that accept "plastic" in place of cash or checks?

- Credit card companies (MasterCard, Visa, and American Express)[4] and their issuing banks charge the merchant a transaction fee for each purchase made using plastic.[5] The fee, officially known in business as "interchange," is usually a fixed amount *plus* a percentage of the amount charged. For example, the typical transaction fee for each credit card sale is between $0.25 and $0.50, *plus* 1–5% of the amount charged.[6] The actual fee will depend on the credit card brand and the merchant. Reward cards, such as those tied to frequent flyer miles, typically charge higher fees.

- In exchange for the fee, the credit card company and its issuing bank pays the merchant the entire amount of the purchase *less* the transaction fee. A deposit is made to the merchant's bank account within a few days of the sale.

Debit card transaction fees are usually lower than credit card transaction fees. Why?

1. Since debit card purchases require an associated personal identification number (PIN), the risk of fraud is lower than it is with a credit card. Thus, the issuing credit card company will have lower costs associated with stolen and fraudulently used cards.

2. Debit card sales are paid to the merchant using money that is in the customer's bank account, rather than money that is in essence loaned to the customer by the credit card company. Since the cash used for the deposit is not subject to credit risk, it is made with "cheaper" funds.

3. Beginning October 1, 2011, the Federal Reserve set a cap on the debit card transaction fees that banks can charge merchants. The new limit is as follows:

> Limit on *debit* card fees = $0.22 per transaction + 0.05% of the amount of the transaction

Notice that the amount charged on the value of the transaction (0.0005) is substantially less than it is for a typical credit card transaction.[7]

Although credit and debit card transaction fees are costly to merchants, the acceptance of plastic payment methods also has benefits:

- Merchants would lose potential sales if they did not allow customers to pay with credit and debit cards.

- The acceptance of credit cards decreases the costs associated with bounced checks, misappropriation of cash, and the activities associated with preparing and transporting cash deposits (sometimes via armored vehicle collection services).

- Merchants receive the cash quickly, which may improve their cash flow.

Let's try an example:

Say a customer purchases some clothes at Aeropostale for $50 and uses a MasterCard to pay for the purchase. Let's also assume that MasterCard charges Aeropostale a transaction fee equal to $0.25 + 2% of the amount charged. The transaction fee on this sale would be:

> Transaction Fee = $0.25 + (2% × Amount Charged)
> $1.25 = $0.25 + (2% × $50)

---

[4]These three credit card companies control approximately 93% of the credit card transactions in the United States. By 2008, $48 billion in transaction fees were assessed by credit card issuers. www.newrules.org/retail/news/soaring-credit-card-transaction-fees-squeeze-independent-businesses

[5]www.cardfellow.com/blog/interchange-fee/

[6]www.allbusiness.com/sales/internet-e-commerce/3930-1.html; http://usa.visa.com/download/merchants/visa-usa-interchange-reimbursement-fees-june2012.pdf

[7]www.federalreserve.gov/newsevents/press/bcreg/20110629a.htm. Banks with less than $10 billion in assets are exempt from the new cap. In addition, if a bank does not have fraud prevention policies and procedures in place, the cap is $0.21 per transaction rather than $0.22 per transaction.

Within a few days, MasterCard would deposit the following amount in Aeropostale's bank account:

$$\text{Cash Deposited} = \text{Amount Charged on Credit Card} - \text{Transaction Fee}$$
$$\$48.75 = \$50.00 - \$1.25$$

The anticipation of this credit card sale would be shown in the budgets as follows:

- The $50 sale would be shown in the sales budget, *in the month of sale.*
- The $1.25 transaction fee would be shown in the operating expenses budget, *in the month of sale.*
- The $48.75 would be shown as a cash receipt on the cash collections budget, *in the month of collection* (which is typically within one to seven days of the actual sale).

When preparing the master budget, merchants need to consider:

- The percentage of sales that will be made using debit cards and credit cards,
- The different transaction fees charged for debit and credit card transactions, and
- The length of time between the sale and the deposit.

Retail Credit Cards

Many retailers, such as Target, Kohl's, and Old Navy, issue their own credit cards in addition to accepting credit cards such as Visa and MasterCard. When a customer uses a store-based credit card, no transaction fee is incurred. However, the risk of collection falls back on the merchant, rather than on a third-party credit card company. The merchant must wait for the customer to make payments on the credit card bill. The cash collection may occur over several months, several years, or never. The cash collections budget will take into account the aging of these receivables. Likewise, the operating expenses budget will need to take into consideration possible bad debts. Finally, the company will need to budget for interest income assessed on unpaid balances and any fees charged to the customer for late payments.

Exhibit 9-22 compares third-party credit cards with retail credit cards.

EXHIBIT 9-22 Comparison of Credit Cards

Third-Party Credit Cards (e.g., Visa and MasterCard)[1]
- Merchant accepts "plastic payment" in the form of a third-party credit card (e.g., Visa).
- Credit card issuer (e.g., Visa) pays merchant amount of purchase, less a transaction fee.
- Credit card issuer (e.g., Visa) assumes collection risk.
- Consumer owes credit card issuer amount of purchase, plus interest on any outstanding unpaid balance from earlier periods.

Retail Credit Cards (e.g., Target and Kohl's):
- Merchant accepts "plastic payment" in the form of the merchant's own retail card.
- No third-party transaction fee is involved.
- Merchant assumes collection risk.
- Consumer owes issuing merchant amount of purchase, plus interest on any outstanding unpaid balance from earlier periods.

[1]The actual issuers of third-party credit cards are member banks of Visa and MasterCard's network, such as JP Morgan Chase, Capital One, and Citigroup. These member banks process the payments and receive the transaction fees. They also pay additional fees to Visa and MasterCard. Thus, Exhibit 9-22 is a simplification of the actual business relationships surrounding credit cards, but serves as a useful illustration for how "plastic" payments affect merchant budgeting.

Decision Guidelines

The Master Budget

Let's consider some decisions with respect to budgeting.

Decision	Guidelines
What is the key to preparing the cash collections and cash payments budgets?	The key to preparing the cash budgets is *timing*. *When* will cash be received, and *when* will cash be paid? The timing of cash collections and cash payments often differs from the period in which the related revenues and expenses are recognized on the income statement.
What can be done to prepare for possible changes in key, underlying budget assumptions?	Management uses sensitivity analysis to understand how changes in key, underlying assumptions might affect the company's financial results. This awareness helps managers cope with changing business conditions when they occur.
How does sustainability impact budgeting?	Companies that are planning on adopting any sustainable practice will want to capture those plans in their budgets. Any or all of the budgets could be impacted by plans to adopt sustainable practices.
How does the master budget of a service company differ from that of a manufacturer?	Service companies have no inventory to make or sell, thus their operating budgets are less complex. The operating budgets include the: • Sales budget • Operating expenses budget • Budgeted income statement
How does the master budget of a merchandising company differ from that of a manufacturer?	Merchandising companies buy their inventory, rather than make it. In place of the production budget, they use a "cost of goods sold, inventory, and purchases" budget. This budget follows the same basic format as the production budget. The amounts on the budget are calculated at cost, rather than in units. The operating budgets include the: • Sales budget • Cost of goods sold, inventory, and purchases budget • Operating expenses budget • Budgeted income statement
How does the acceptance of debit and credit card payments affect a merchant's budgets?	Merchants must budget for the transaction fees charged by the credit card companies and their issuing banks. The transaction fee needs to be shown on the operating expenses budget. The amount of credit and debit card sales, net of the transaction fee, will be shown on the cash receipts budget.
How are credit and debit card transaction fees calculated?	The transaction fee is typically a set dollar amount per transaction, plus a percentage of the amount of sale charged on a credit or debit card. For example: $\text{Transaction Fee} = \$0.25 + (2\% \times \text{Amount Charged})$
How does the acceptance of debit and credit cards affect the cash collection budget?	The amount of cash shown on the cash collections budget will be the net amount deposited: $\text{Cash Deposited} = \text{Amount Charged on Credit Card} - \text{Transaction Fee}$

SUMMARY PROBLEM 2

The following information was taken from the Pillows Unlimited sales budget, found in Summary Problem 1 on page 517:

	A	B	C	D	E
1		Pillows Unlimited			
2		Sales Budget: Type of Sale			
3		For the Quarter Ended March 31			
4			Month		
5		January	February	March	1st Quarter
6	Type of sale:				
7	Cash sales (10%)	$ 140,000	$ 154,000	$ 161,000	$ 455,000
8	Credit sales (90%)	1,260,000	1,386,000	1,449,000	4,095,000
9	Total sales revenue	$ 1,400,000	$ 1,540,000	$ 1,610,000	$ 4,550,000
10					

The company's collection history indicates that 75% of credit sales is collected in the month after the sale, 15% is collected two months after the sale, 8% is collected three months after the sale, and the remaining 2% is never collected.

Assume the following additional information was gathered about the types of sales made in the fourth quarter (October through December) of the previous year:

	A	B	C	D	E
1		Pillows Unlimited			
2		Sales Budget: Type of Sale			
3		For the Quarter Ended December 31			
4			Month		
5		October	November	December	4th Quarter
6	Type of sale:				
7	Cash sales (10%)	$ 142,800	$ 151,200	$ 137,200	$ 431,200
8	Credit sales (90%)	1,285,200	1,360,800	1,234,800	3,880,800
9	Total sales revenue	$ 1,428,000	$ 1,512,000	$ 1,372,000	$ 4,312,000
10					

The following information was taken from the Pillows Unlimited direct materials budget, found in Summary Problem 1 on page 518:

	A	B	C	D	E
1		Pillows Unlimited			
2		Excerpt from Direct Materials Budget			
3		For the Quarter Ended March 31			
4			Month		
5		January	February	March	1st Quarter
6	Total cost of DM purchases	$ 771,750	$ 836,250	$ 873,000	$ 2,481,000
7					

Assume that the total cost of direct materials purchases in December was $725,000. The company pays 40% of its direct materials purchases in the month of purchase, and pays the remaining 60% in the month after purchase.

Requirements

1. Prepare the cash collections budget for January, February, and March, as well as a summary for the first quarter.

2. Prepare the cash payments budget for direct materials purchases for the months of January, February, and March, as well as a summary for the quarter.

▪ SOLUTIONS

Requirement 1

	A	B	C	D	E
1		Pillows Unlimited			
2		Cash Collections Budget			
3		For the Quarter Ended March 31			
4		Month			
5		January	February	March	1st Quarter
6	Cash sales in current month	$ 140,000	$ 154,000	$ 161,000	$ 455,000
7	Collection on credit sales:				
8	75% of credit sales made one month ago	926,100	945,000	1,039,500	2,910,600
9	15% of credit sales made two months ago	204,120	185,220	189,000	578,340
10	8% of credit sales made three months ago	102,816	108,864	98,784	310,464
11	Total cash collections	$ 1,373,036	$ 1,393,084	$ 1,488,284	$ 4,254,404
12					

NOTE: Cash and credit sales are shown on the sales budget

January:
$926,100 = 75% of December credit sales ($1,234,800)
$204,120 = 15% of November credit sales ($1,360,800)
$102,816 = 8% of October credit sales ($1,285,200)

February:
$945,000 = 75% of January credit sales ($1,260,000)
$185,220 = 15% of December credit sales ($1,234,800)
$108,864 = 8% of November credit sales ($1,360,800)

March:
$1,039,500 = 75% of February credit sales ($1,386,000)
$189,000 = 15% of January credit sales ($1,260,000)
$98,784 = 8% of December credit sales ($1,234,800)

Requirement 2

	A	B	C	D	E
1		Pillows Unlimited			
2		Cash Payments Budget			
3		For the Quarter Ended March 31			
4		Month			
5		January	February	March	1st Quarter
6	40% of current month DM purchases	$ 308,700	$ 334,500	$ 349,200	$ 992,400
7	60% of last month's DM purchases	435,000	463,050	501,750	1,399,800
8	Total cash payments	$ 743,700	$ 797,550	$ 850,950	$ 2,392,200
9					

NOTE: Payments calculated as follows:

January:
$308,700 = 40% of January DM purchases ($771,750)
$435,000 = 60% of December DM purchases ($725,000)

February:
$334,500 = 40% of February DM purchases ($836,250)
$463,050 = 60% of January DM purchases ($771,750)

March:
$349,200 = 40% of March DM purchases ($873,000)
$501,750 = 60% of February DM purchases ($836,250)

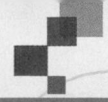

END OF CHAPTER

Learning Objectives

- 1 Describe how and why managers use budgets
- 2 Prepare the operating budgets
- 3 Prepare the financial budgets
- 4 Prepare budgets for a merchandiser

Accounting Vocabulary

Budget Committee. (p. 504) A committee comprised of upper management as well as cross-functional managers that reviews, revises, and approves the final budget.

COD. (p. 508) Collect on Delivery, or Cash on Delivery. A sales term indicating that the inventory must be paid for at the time of delivery.

Cost of Goods Sold, Inventory, and Purchases Budget. (p. 527) A merchandiser's budget that computes the cost of goods sold, the amount of desired ending inventory, and amount of merchandise to be purchased.

Financial Budgets. (p. 507) The financial budgets include the capital expenditures budget and the cash budgets. It culminates in a budgeted balance sheet.

Flexible Budgets. (p. 525) Budgets prepared for different volumes of activity.

Line of Credit. (p. 523) A lending arrangement from a bank in which a company is allowed to borrow money as needed, up to a specified maximum amount, yet only pay interest on the portion that is actually borrowed until it is repaid.

Master Budget. (p. 506) The comprehensive planning document for the entire organization. The master budget includes the operating budgets and the financial budgets.

Operating Budgets. (p. 507) The budgets needed to run the daily operations of the company. The operating budgets culminate in a budgeted income statement.

Participative Budgeting. (p. 504) Budgeting that involves the participation of many levels of management.

Rolling Budget. (p. 504) A budget that is continuously updated so that the next 12 months of operations are always budgeted; also known as a *continuous budget*.

Safety Stock. (p. 508) Extra inventory kept on hand in case demand is higher than expected or problems in the factory slow production.

Sensitivity Analysis. (p. 525) A *what-if* technique that asks what a result will be if a predicted amount is not achieved or if an underlying assumption changes.

Slack. (p. 504) Intentionally overstating budgeted expenses or understating budgeted revenues in order to cope with uncertainty, make performance appear better, or make room for potential budget cuts.

Strategic Planning. (p. 503) Setting long-term goals that may extend 5 to 10 years into the future.

Variance. (p. 506) The difference between actual and budgeted figures (revenues and expenses).

Zero-Based Budgeting. (p. 505) A budgeting approach in which managers begin with a budget of zero and must justify every dollar put into the budget.

MyAccountingLab Go to http://myaccountinglab.com/ for the following **Quick Check, Short Exercises, Exercises, and Problems. They are available with immediate grading, explanations of correct and incorrect answers, and interactive media that acts as your own online tutor.**

Quick Check

1. *(Learning Objective 1)* Which term describes the situation in which a manager intentionally overbudgets expenses or underbudgets revenue?
   a. Strategic planning
   b. Participative budgeting
   c. Budgetary slack
   d. Benchmarking

2. *(Learning Objective 1)* Benefits of budgeting include
   a. planning.
   b. coordination and communication.
   c. benchmarking.
   d. all of the above.

3. (*Learning Objective 1*) The comprehensive planning document for the entire organization is called the _____ budget.
   a. master
   b. operating
   c. financial
   d. cash

4. (*Learning Objective 2*) Which of the following budgets must be prepared first, as it serves as a basis for most other budgets?
   a. Cash budget
   b. Production budget
   c. Operating expenses budget
   d. Sales budget

5. (*Learning Objective 2*) The operating budgets culminate in the budgeted
   a. balance sheet.
   b. income statement.
   c. statement of cash flows.
   d. statement of owners' equity.

6. (*Learning Objective 3*) Which of the following are non-cash expenses that will always result in differences between the budgeted operating expenses for a given period and the budgeted cash payments for the same period?
   a. Advertising expense and rent expense
   b. Depreciation expense and rent expense
   c. Advertising expense and bad debt expense
   d. Depreciation expense and bad debt expense

7. (*Learning Objective 3*) Which budget reflects the company's plans to invest in new property, plant, and equipment?
   a. Capital expenditures budget
   b. Direct materials budget
   c. Cash collections budget
   d. Operating expenses budget

8. (*Learning Objective 4*) Which of the following budgets is unique to merchandising companies?
   a. Production budget
   b. Cost of Goods Sold, Inventory, and Purchases budget
   c. Direct materials budget
   d. Operating expenses budget

9. (*Learning Objective 4*) Which of the following is true?
   a. Only debit card transaction fees are limited by law.
   b. Only credit card transaction fees are limited by law.
   c. Neither credit card nor debit card transaction fees are limited by law.
   d. Both credit card and debit card transaction fees are limited by law.

10. (*Learning Objective 4*) Which of the following is true for merchants that accept payments made by Visa, MasterCard, and other forms of "plastic"?
    a. Credit card fees are usually lower than debit card fees.
    b. Transaction fees should be budgeted for in the operating expenses budget.
    c. Retail cards (such as Target and Kohl's charge cards) have similar transaction fees to those issued by Visa and MasterCard.
    d. Transaction fees are generally a fixed amount per month.

Quick Check Answers
1.c 2.d 3.a 4.d 5.b 6.d 7.a 8.b 9.a 10.b

Short Exercises

S9-1 Order of preparation and components of master budget
(*Learning Objective 1*)

Identify the order in which a manufacturer would prepare the following budgets. Also note whether each budget is an operating budget or a financial budget.
   a. Budgeted balance sheet
   b. Cash payments budget
   c. Direct materials budget
   d. Production budget
   e. Budgeted income statement
   f. Combined cash budget
   g. Sales budget

S9-2   Understanding key terms and definitions (Learning Objectives 1 & 2)

Listed next are several terms. Complete each of the following statements with one of these terms. You may use a term more than once, and some terms may not be used at all.

Master budget	Participative budgeting	Operating budgets	Production budget
Zero-based budgeting	Strategic planning	Financial budgets	Slack
Budget committees	Rolling budget	Safety stock	Variance

a. _____ is a budget that is continuously updated by adding months to the end of the budgeting period.

b. _____ is the comprehensive planning document for the entire organization.

c. These budgets, _____, project both the collection and payment of cash and forecast the company's budgeted balance sheet.

d. The _____ is used to forecast how many units should be made to meet the sales projections.

e. When an organization builds its budgets from the ground up, it is using _____.

f. _____ is the process of setting long-term goals that may extend several years into the future.

g. Managers will sometimes build _____ into their budgets to protect themselves against unanticipated expenses or lower revenues.

h. The _____ is the difference between actual and budgeted figures and is used to evaluate how well the manager controlled operations during the period.

i. _____ are often used by companies to review submitted budgets, make revisions as needed, and approve the final budgets.

j. _____ is extra inventory of finished goods that is kept on hand in case demand is higher than predicted or problems in the factory slow production.

k. The sales budget and production budget are examples of _____.

l. _____ is a budgeting process that begins with departmental managers and flows up through middle management to top management.

S9-3   Sales Budget (Learning Objective 2)

Duke Sports Medicine, Inc., offers two types of physical exams for students: the basic physical and the extended physical. The charge for the basic physical is $105, while the charge for the extended physical is $160. Duke expects to perform 240 basic physicals and 170 extended physicals in July, 250 basic and 230 extended in August, and 75 basic and 90 extended in September. Prepare the sales budget for the second quarter (July through September), with a column for each month and for the quarter in total.

S9-4   Production budget (Learning Objective 2)

Trader Cycles manufactures chainless bicycles. On March 31, Trader Cycles had 220 bikes in inventory. The company has a policy that the ending inventory in any month must be 30% of the following month's expected sales. Trader Cycles expects to sell the following number of bikes in each of the next four months:

April	1,000 bikes
May	1,180 bikes
June	1,320 bikes
July	1,200 bikes

Prepare a production budget for the second quarter, with a column for each month and for the quarter.

S9-5 Direct materials budget *(Learning Objective 2)*

The Bakery by the Bay produces organic bread that is sold by the loaf. Each loaf requires 1/2 of a pound of flour. The bakery pays $2.00 per pound of the organic flour used in its loaves. The bakery expects to produce the following number of loaves in each of the upcoming four months:

July	1,460 loaves
August	1,920 loaves
September	1,760 loaves
October	1,480 loaves

The bakery has a policy that it will have 10% of the following month's flour needs on hand at the end of each month. At the end of June, there were 100 pounds of flour on hand. Prepare the direct materials budget for the third quarter, with a column for each month and for the quarter.

S9-6 Direct labor budget *(Learning Objective 2)*

The Production Department of Cameron Manufacturing has prepared the following schedule of units to be produced over the first quarter of the upcoming year:

	January	February	March
Units to be produced	560	600	860

Each unit requires 6.0 hours of direct labor. Direct labor workers are paid an average of $16 per hour. How much direct labor will be budgeted in January, February, March, and for the quarter in total?

S9-7 Manufacturing overhead budget *(Learning Objective 2)*

Probe Corporation is preparing its manufacturing overhead budget. The direct labor budget for the upcoming quarter is as follows:

	April	May	June
Budgeted direct labor hours	490	770	660

The company's variable manufacturing overhead rate is $1.60 per direct labor hour and the company's fixed manufacturing overhead is $3,000 per month. How much manufacturing overhead will be budgeted for April? For May? For June? For the quarter in total?

S9-8 Operating expenses budget *(Learning Objective 2)*

Davenport Corporation is preparing its operating expenses budget. The budgeted unit sales for the upcoming quarter are as follows:

	July	August	September
Budgeted unit sales	1,210	1,440	1,700

The company's variable operating expenses are $6.00 per unit. Fixed monthly operating expenses include $5,100 for salaries, $3,300 for office rent, and $2,200 for depreciation. How much operating expenses will be budgeted for July? For August? For September? For the quarter in total?

S9-9 Budgeted income statement *(Learning Objective 2)*

Bell Simpson manufactures a specialty precision scale. For January, the company expects to sell 800 scales at an average price of $2,350 per unit. The average manufacturing cost of each unit sold is $1,400. Variable operating expenses for the company will be $1.10 per unit sold and fixed operating expenses are expected to be $7,700 for the month. Monthly interest expense is $3,700. The company has a tax rate of 40% of income before taxes. Prepare Bell Simpson's budgeted income statement for January.

S9-10 Cash collections budget *(Learning Objective 3)*

Emerald Service anticipates the following sales revenue over a five-month period:

	November	December	January	February	March
Sales revenue	$16,500	$10,500	$15,500	$12,000	$14,000

The company's sales are 20% cash and 80% credit. Its collection history indicates that credit sales are collected as follows:

30% in the month of the sale
60% in the month after the sale
6% two months after the sale
4% are never collected

How much cash will be collected in January? In February? In March? For the quarter in total?

S9-11 Cash payments budget (Learning Objective 3)

Stately Corporation is preparing its cash payments budget for next month. The following information pertains to the cash payments:

a. Stately Corporation pays for 55% of its direct materials purchases in the month of purchase and the remainder the following month. Last month's direct material purchases were $79,000, while the company anticipates $88,000 of direct material purchases next month.

b. Direct labor for the upcoming month is budgeted to be $35,000 and will be paid at the end of the upcoming month.

c. Manufacturing overhead is estimated to be 140% of direct labor cost each month and is paid in the month in which it is incurred. This monthly estimate includes $11,000 of depreciation on the plant and equipment.

d. Monthly operating expenses for next month are expected to be $46,000, which includes $2,000 of depreciation on office equipment and $1,400 of bad debt expense. These monthly operating expenses are paid during the month in which they are incurred.

e. Stately Corporation will be making an estimated tax payment of $7,600 next month.

How much cash will be paid out next month?

S9-12 Cash budget (Learning Objective 3)

George Services, Inc., has $8,200 cash on hand on October 1. The company requires a minimum cash balance of $7,600. October cash collections are $548,410. Total cash payments for October are $573,870. Prepare a cash budget for October. How much cash, if any, will George need to borrow by the end of October?

S9-13 Estimate credit card fees (Learning Objective 4)

The local grocery store expects that customers will use credit cards to pay for a total of 80,000 sales transactions during the month of April. These transactions are expected to amount to $2,000,000 in total sales revenue. The credit card issuers charge the store a transaction fee equal to $0.45 per transaction plus 1% of the amount charged. When budgeting for operating expenses in April, how much should the store expect to incur for credit card transaction fees?

S9-14 Cost of goods sold, inventory, and purchases budget
(Learning Objective 4)

TechWorks Company sells its smartphone worldwide. The company expects to sell 4,200 smartphones for $170 each in January and 3,800 smartphones for $200 each in February. All sales are cash only. TechWorks expects cost of goods sold to average 70% of sales revenue. The company also expects to sell 4,300 smartphones in March for $280 each. TechWork's target ending inventory is $16,000 plus 40% of the next month's cost of goods sold.

1. Prepare the sales budget for January and February.

2. Prepare the company's cost of goods sold, inventory, and purchases budget for January and February.

ETHICS

S9-15 Identify ethical standards violated (Learning Objectives 1, 2, 3, & 4)

For each of the situations listed, identify the primary standard from the IMA Statement of Ethical Professional Practice that is violated (competence, confidentiality, objectivity, or credibility). Refer to Exhibit 1-6 for the complete standard.

1. When out with friends, Louise complains loudly about the budgeting process at her company. She feels the budgeting process is overly precise. She illustrates her point with specific numbers from the budget.

2. Allan is caught on video as he brags about illegally downloading software that he feels is overpriced. The video is uploaded to YouTube.

3. Jake, an accountant for Snow Films Company, builds some slack into the budget for the Human Resources (HR) Department so that the targets are easier to achieve. Jake is dating the manager of the HR Department.

4. Pearl is the controller for Cloudy Fork Gardens. When she prepares the budgets for the upcoming year for upper management, she realizes that her department has higher costs than any other department. She aggregates the numbers with some other departments so that it is not obvious that her department is overspending.

5. Alfredo knows that the laws concerning credit and debit card fees have changed in the past year but does not know what the changes are specifically. He does not investigate before preparing the cash budget.

EXERCISES Group A

E9-16A Budgeting and sustainability *(Learning Objectives 1 & 2)*

SUSTAINABILITY

Dixson Beverages manufactures its own soda pop bottles. The bottles are made from polyethylene terephthalate (PET), a lightweight yet strong plastic. Dixson uses as much PET recycled resin pellets in its bottles as it can, both because using recycled PET helps Dixson to meet its sustainability goals and because recycled PET is less expensive than virgin PET.

Dixson is continuing to search for ways to reduce its costs and its impact on the environment. PET plastic is melted and blown over soda bottle molds to produce the bottles. One idea Dixson's engineers have suggested is to retrofit the soda bottle molds and change the plastic formulation slightly so that 10% less PET plastic is used for each bottle. The average kilograms of PET per soda bottle before any redesign is 0.01 kg. The cost of retrofitting the soda bottle molds will result in a one-time charge of $24,478, while the plastic reformulation will cause the average cost per kilogram of PET plastic to change from $5.00 to $5.30.

Dixson's management is analyzing whether the change to the bottle molds to reduce PET plastic usage should be made. Management expects the following number of soda bottles to be used in the upcoming year:

	Quarter 1	Quarter 2	Quarter 3	Quarter 4
Number of soda pop bottles to be produced	2,800,000	3,100,000	2,600,000	2,500,000

For the upcoming year, management expects the beginning inventory of PET to be 8,400 kilograms, while ending inventory is expected to be 8,040 kilograms. During the first three quarters of the year, management wants to keep the ending inventory of PET at the end of each quarter equal to 30% of the following quarter's PET needs.

Requirements

1. Using the original data (before any redesign of soda bottles), prepare a direct materials budget to calculate the cost of PET purchases in each quarter for the upcoming year and for the year in total.

2. Assume that the company retrofits the soda bottle molds and changes the plastic formulation slightly so that less PET plastic is used in each bottle. Now prepare a direct materials budget to calculate the cost of PET purchases in each quarter for the upcoming year and for the year in total for this possible scenario.

3. Compare the cost of PET plastic for Requirement 1 (original data) and for Requirement 2 (making change to using less PET). What is the direct material cost savings from making the change to using less PET? Compare the total of those savings to the cost of retrofitting the soda bottle molds. Should the company make the change? Explain your rationale.

E9-17A Sales budget for a retail organization *(Learning Objective 2)*

Miami College Bookstore is the bookstore on campus for students and faculty. The bookstore shows the following sales projections in units by quarter for the upcoming year:

Quarter	Books	School Supplies	Apparel	Miscellaneous
1st.................	1,510	250	520	630
2nd	850	110	340	550
3rd.................	1,760	210	840	830
4th	600	170	530	420

The average price of an item in each of the departments is as follows:

	Average sales price per unit
Books...	$81
School supplies	$14
Apparel..	$20
Miscellaneous...	$ 6

Requirement

Prepare a sales budget for the upcoming year by quarter for the Miami College Bookstore, with sales categorized by the four product groupings (books, school supplies, apparel, and miscellaneous).

E9-18A   Sales budget for a not-for-profit organization
(Learning Objective 2)

Hinckley Preschool operates a not-for-profit morning preschool. Each family pays a non-refundable registration fee of $135 per child per school year. Monthly tuition for the eight-month school year varies depending on the number of days per week that the child attends preschool. The monthly tuition is $115 for the two-day program, $140 for the three-day program, $155 for the four-day program, and $180 for the five-day program. The following enrollment has been projected for the coming year:

Two-day program	86 children
Three-day program	34 children
Four-day program	68 children
Five-day program	26 children

In addition to the morning preschool, Hinckley Preschool offers a Lunch Bunch program where kids have the option of staying an extra hour for lunch and playtime. The preschool charges an additional $4 per child for every Lunch Bunch attended. Historically, half of the children stay for Lunch Bunch an average of 12 times a month.

Requirement

Calculate Hinckley Preschool's budgeted revenue for the school year.

E9-19A   Production budget *(Learning Objective 2)*

Jabber Foods produces specialty soup sold in jars. The projected sales in dollars and jars for each quarter of the upcoming year are as follows:

	Total sales revenue	Number of jars sold
1st quarter..	$188,000	152,000
2nd quarter	$216,000	180,500
3rd quarter	$258,000	210,500
4th quarter	$195,000	160,500

Jabber anticipates selling 220,000 jars with total sales revenue of $267,000 in the first quarter of the year *following* the year given in the preceding table. Jabber has a policy that the ending inventory of jars must be 20% of the following quarter's sales. Prepare a production budget for the year that shows the number of jars to be produced each quarter and for the year in total.

E9-20A Direct materials budget (Learning Objective 2)

Beckett Industries manufactures a popular interactive stuffed animal for children that requires two computer chips inside each toy. The company pays $3 for each computer chip. To help to guard against stockouts of the computer chip, Beckett Industries has a policy that states that the ending inventory of computer chips should be at least 25% of the following month's production needs. The production schedule for the first four months of the year is as follows:

	Stuffed animals to be produced
January	5,600
February	4,200
March	4,800
April	4,500

Requirement

Prepare a direct materials budget for the first quarter that shows both the number of computer chips needed and the dollar amount of the purchases in the budget.

E9-21A Production and direct materials budgets (Learning Objective 2)

Austen Manufacturing produces self-watering planters for use in upscale retail establishments. Sales projections for the first five months of the upcoming year show the estimated unit sales of the planters each month to be as follows:

	Number of planters to be sold
January	3,200
February	3,000
March	3,500
April	4,300
May	4,600

Inventory at the start of the year was 800 planters. The desired inventory of planters at the end of each month in the upcoming year should be equal to 25% of the following month's budgeted sales. Each planter requires two pounds of polypropylene (a type of plastic). The company wants to have 20% of the polypropylene required for next month's production on hand at the end of each month. The polypropylene costs $0.10 per pound.

Requirements

1. Prepare a production budget for each month in the first quarter of the year, including production in units for each month and for the quarter.
2. Prepare a direct materials budget for the polypropylene for each month in the first quarter of the year, including the pounds of polypropylene required and the total cost of the polypropylene to be purchased.

E9-22A Direct labor budget (Learning Objective 2)

Anderson Industries manufactures three models of a product in a single plant with two departments: Cutting and Assembly. The company has estimated costs for each of the three product models, which are the Flash, the Royal, and the Zip models. The company is currently analyzing direct labor hour requirements for the upcoming year.

	Cutting	Assembly
Estimated hours per unit:		
Flashes	1.8	2.5
Royals	1.7	2.3
Zips	1.3	2.4
Direct labor hour rate	$10	$12

Budgeted unit production for each of the products is as follows:

	Number of units to be produced
Product model:	
Flashes	510
Royals	740
Zips	860

Requirement

Prepare a direct labor budget for the upcoming year that shows the budgeted direct labor costs for each department and for the company as a whole.

E9-23A   Manufacturing overhead budget (Learning Objective 2)

The McKnight Company is in the process of preparing its manufacturing overhead budget for the upcoming year. Sales are projected to be 42,000 units. Information about the various manufacturing overhead costs follows:

	Variable rate per unit	Total fixed costs
Indirect materials	$1.00	
Supplies	$0.70	
Indirect labor	$0.30	$62,000
Plant utilities	$0.20	$39,000
Repairs and maintenance	$0.40	$10,000
Depreciation on plant and equipment		$48,000
Insurance on plant and equipment		$27,000
Plant supervision		$65,000

Requirement

Prepare the manufacturing overhead budget for the McKnight Company for the upcoming year.

E9-24A   Operating expenses budget and an income statement
(Learning Objective 2)

Start Smart Preschool operates a not-for-profit morning preschool that operates nine months of the year. The preschool has 160 kids enrolled in its various programs. The preschool's primary expense is payroll. Teachers are paid a flat salary each of the nine months as follows:

Teachers of two-day program	$ 434 per month
Teachers of three-day program	$ 648 per month
Teachers of four-day program	$ 884 per month
Teachers of five-day program	$1,060 per month
Preschool director's salary	$1,500 per month

Start Smart Preschool has 7 two-day program teachers, 2 three-day program teachers, 5 four-day program teachers, and 4 five-day program teachers. The preschool also has a director.

In addition to the salary expense, the preschool must pay federal payroll taxes (FICA taxes) in the amount of 7.65% of salary expense. The preschool leases its facilities from a local church, paying $4,012 every month it operates. Fixed operating expenses (telephone, Internet access, bookkeeping services, and so forth) amount to $890 per month over the nine-month school year. Variable monthly expenses (over the nine-month school year) for art supplies and other miscellaneous supplies are $6 per child. Revenue for the entire nine-month school year from tuition, registration fees, and the lunch program is projected to be $241,200.

Requirements

1. Prepare Start Smart Preschool's monthly operating budget. Round all amounts to the nearest dollar.
2. Using your answer from Requirement 1, create Start Smart Preschool's budgeted income statement for the entire nine-month school year. You may group all operating expenses together.
3. Start Smart Preschool is a not-for-profit preschool. What might the preschool do with its projected income for the year?

E9-25A   Budgeted income statement *(Learning Objective 2)*

Germaine Labs performs a specialty lab test for local companies for $55 per test. For the upcoming quarter, Germaine Labs is projecting the following sales:

	January	February	March
Number of lab tests	5,200	4,600	5,100

The budgeted cost of performing each test is $31. Operating expenses are projected to be $61,000 in January, $58,000 in February, and $62,000 in March. Germaine Labs is subject to a corporate tax rate of 30%.

Requirement

Prepare a budgeted income statement for the first quarter, with a column for each month and for the quarter.

E9-26A   Budgeted income statement *(Learning Objective 2)*

Berkner Motors is a chain of car dealerships. Sales in the fourth quarter of last year were $3,700,000. Suppose management projects that its current year's quarterly sales will increase by 2% in quarter 1, by another 4% in quarter 2, by another 3% in quarter 3, and by another 5% in quarter 4. Management expects cost of goods sold to be 55% of revenues every quarter, while operating expenses should be 35% of revenues during each of the first two quarters, 25% of revenues during the third quarter, and 20% during the fourth quarter.

Requirement

Prepare a budgeted income statement for each of the four quarters and for the entire year.

E9-27A   Cash collections budget *(Learning Objective 3)*

Bentfield Corporation has found that 60% of its sales in any given month are credit sales, while the remainder are cash sales. Of the credit sales, Bentfield Corporation has experienced the following collection pattern:

25% received in the month of the sale
50% received in the month after the sale
24% received two months after the sale
1% of the credit sales are never received

November sales for last year were $85,000, while December sales were $110,000. Projected sales for the next three months are as follows:

January sales	$155,000
February sales	$115,000
March sales...	$195,000

Requirement

Prepare a cash collections budget for the first quarter, with a column for each month and for the quarter.

E9-28A Cash payments budget *(Learning Objective 3)*

The Smith Company is preparing its cash payments budget. The following items relate to cash payments the company anticipates making during the second quarter of the upcoming year.

a. The company pays for 50% of its direct materials purchases in the month of purchase and the remainder the following month. The company's direct material purchases for March through June are anticipated to be as follows:

March	April	May	June
$112,000	$134,000	$124,000	$147,000

b. Direct labor is paid in the month in which it is incurred. Direct labor for each month of the second quarter is budgeted as follows:

April	May	June
$60,000	$70,000	$85,000

c. Manufacturing overhead is estimated to be 150% of direct labor cost each month. This monthly estimate includes $36,000 of depreciation on the plant and equipment. All manufacturing overhead (excluding depreciation) is paid in the month in which it is incurred.

d. Monthly operating expenses for March through June are projected to be as follows:

March	April	May	June
$72,000	$87,000	$84,000	$94,000

Monthly operating expenses are paid in the month after they are incurred. Monthly operating expenses include $8,000 for monthly depreciation on administrative offices and equipment, and $3,400 for bad debt expense.

e. The company plans to pay $6,000 (cash) for a new server in May.

f. The company must make an estimated tax payment of $14,000 on June 15.

Requirement

Prepare a cash payments budget for April, May, and June and for the quarter.

E9-29A Combined cash budget *(Learning Objective 3)*

Monette Health Center provides a variety of medical services. The company is preparing its cash budget for the upcoming third quarter. The following transactions are expected to occur:

a. Cash collections from services in July, August, and September are projected to be $96,000, $159,000, and $122,000, respectively.

b. Cash payments for the upcoming third quarter are projected to be $149,000 in July, $105,000 in August, and $133,000 in September.

c. The cash balance as of the first day of the third quarter is projected to be $32,000.

d. The health center has a policy that it must maintain a minimum cash balance of $25,000. The health center has a line of credit with the local bank that allows it to borrow funds in months that it would not otherwise have its minimum balance. If the company has more than its minimum balance at the end of any given month, it uses the excess funds to pay off any outstanding line of credit balance. Each month, Monette Health Center pays interest on the prior month's line of credit ending balance. The actual interest rate that the health center will pay floats since it is tied to the prime rate. However, the interest rate paid during the budget period is expected to be 2% of the prior month's line of credit ending balance (if the company did not have an outstanding balance at the end of the prior month, then the health center does not have to pay any interest). All line of credit borrowings are taken or paid off on the first day of the month. As of the first day of the third quarter, Monette Health Center did not have a balance on its line of credit.

Requirement

Prepare a combined cash budget for Monette Health Center for the third quarter, with a column for each month and for the quarter total.

E9-30A   Sales and cash collections budgets (*Learning Objectives 2 & 3*)

Leret Reeds, a manufacturer of saxophone, oboe, and clarinet reeds, has projected sales to be $908,000 in October, $950,000 in November, $1,065,000 in December, and $938,000 in January. Leret's sales are 30% cash and 70% credit. The company's collection history indicates that credit sales are collected as follows:

20% in the month of the sale
65% in the month after the sale
10% two months after the sale
5% are never collected

Requirements

1. Prepare a sales budget for all four months, showing the breakdown between cash and credit sales.
2. Prepare a cash collections budget for December and January. Round all answers up to the nearest dollar.

E9-31A   Budgeted balance sheet (*Learning Objective 3*)

Use the following information to prepare a budgeted balance sheet for Games Corporation at March 31. Show computations for the cash and stockholders' equity amounts.

a. March 31 inventory balance, $16,185
b. March payments for inventory, $4,200
c. March payments of accounts payable and accrued liabilities, $8,700
d. March 31 accounts payable balance, $2,000
e. February 28 furniture and fixtures balance, $34,300; accumulated depreciation balance, $29,830
f. February 28 stockholders' equity, $27,880
g. March depreciation expense, $900
h. Cost of goods sold, 50% of sales
i. Other March expenses, including income tax, total $6,000; paid in cash
j. February 28 cash balance, $11,200
k. March budgeted sales, $12,700
l. March 31 accounts receivable balance, one-fourth of March sales
m. March cash receipts, $14,100

E9-32A   Cash budget and revision (*Learning Objective 3*)

Flash Medical Supply began October with $10,200 cash. Management forecasts that collections from credit customers will be $11,800 in October and $15,800 in November. The business is scheduled to receive $6,000 cash on a business note receivable in October. Projected cash payments include inventory purchases ($10,800 in October and $14,900 in November) and operating expenses ($4,200 each month).

Flash Medical Supply's bank requires an $11,000 minimum balance in the business' checking account. At the end of any month when the account balance dips below $11,000, the bank automatically extends credit to the business in multiples of $2,000. The company borrows as little as possible and pays back loans in quarterly installments of $4,000 plus 3% interest on the entire unpaid principal. The first payment occurs three months after the loan.

Requirement

Prepare Flash Medical Supply's cash budget for October and November.

E9-33A   Incomplete cash budget (*Learning Objective 3*)

You recently began a job as an accounting intern at Backyard Adventures. Your first task was to help prepare the cash budget for February and March. Unfortunately, the computer with the budget file crashed, and you did not have a backup or even a hard copy. You ran a program to salvage bits of data from the budget file. After entering the following data in the budget, you may have just enough information to reconstruct the budget.

Backyard Adventures eliminates any cash deficiency by borrowing the exact amount needed from State Street Bank, where the current interest rate is 8%. Backyard Adventures pays interest on its outstanding debt at the end of each month. The company also repays all borrowed amounts at the end of the month as cash becomes available.

Requirement

Complete the following cash budget:

	A	B	C
		Backyard Adventures	
1		Backyard Adventures	
2		Combined Cash Budget	
3		February and March	
4		February	March
5	Beginning cash balance	$ 16,500	$?
6	Plus: Cash collections	?	79,600
7	Plus: Cash from sale of plant assets	0	2,000
8	Total cash available	$ 107,000	$?
9	Less: Cash payments (purchase inventory)	$?	$ 41,200
10	Less: Cash payments (operating expenses)	47,500	?
11	Total cash payments	$ 97,800	$?
12	(1) Ending cash balance before financing	$?	$ 26,400
13	Minimum cash balance desired	24,000	24,000
14	Cash excess (deficiency)	$?	$?
15	Financing:		
16	Plus: New borrowings	$?	$?
17	Less: Debt repayments	?	?
18	Less: Interest payments	?	?
19	(2) Total effects of financing	$?	$?
20	Ending cash balance (1) + (2)	$?	$?
21			

E9-34A   Cost of goods sold, inventory, and purchases budget

(Learning Objective 4)

Scannell Readers sells eReaders. Its sales budget for the nine months ended September 30 follows:

Scannell Readers
Sales Budget
For the Nine Months Ended September 30

	Quarter Ended			Nine-Month Total
	Mar 31	Jun 30	Sep 30	
Cash sales, 40%..................................	$ 52,000	$ 72,000	$ 62,000	$186,000
Credit sales, 60%...............................	78,000	108,000	93,000	279,000
Total sales, 100%..................................	$130,000	$180,000	$155,000	$465,000

In the past, cost of goods sold has been 60% of total sales. The director of marketing and the financial vice president agree that each quarter's ending inventory should not be below $10,000 plus 10% of cost of goods sold for the following quarter. The marketing director expects sales of $230,000 during the fourth quarter. The January 1 inventory was $18,000.

Requirement

Prepare a cost of goods sold, inventory, and purchases budget for each of the first three quarters of the year. Compute cost of goods sold for the entire nine-month period.

EXERCISES Group B

E9-35B   Budgeting and Sustainability *(Learning Objectives 1 and 2)*

Dalley Beverages manufactures its own soda pop bottles. The bottles are made from polyethylene terephthalate (PET), a lightweight yet strong plastic. The company uses as much PET recycled resin pellets in its bottles as it can, both because using recycled PET helps Dalley to meet its sustainability goals and because recycled PET is less expensive than virgin PET.

   Dalley is continuing to search for ways to reduce its costs and its impact on the environment. PET plastic is melted and blown over soda bottle molds to produce the bottles.

One idea Dalley's engineers have suggested is to retrofit the soda bottle molds and change the plastic formulation slightly so that 15% less PET plastic is used for each bottle. The average kilograms of PET per soda bottle before any redesign is 0.02 kg. The cost of retrofitting the soda bottle molds will result in a one-time charge of $59,862, while the plastic reformulation will cause the average cost per kilogram of PET plastic to change from $3.00 to $3.20.

Dalley's management is analyzing whether the change to the bottle molds to reduce PET plastic usage should be made. Management expects the following number of soda bottles to be used in the upcoming year:

	Quarter 1	Quarter 2	Quarter 3	Quarter 4
Number of soda pop bottles to be produced.....................................	3,300,000	2,000,000	3,200,000	2,300,000

For the upcoming year, management expects the beginning inventory of PET to be 6,600 kilograms, while ending inventory is expected to be 5,140 kilograms. During the first three quarters of the year, management wants to keep the ending inventory of PET at the end of each quarter equal to 10% of the following quarter's PET needs.

Requirements

1. Using the original date (before any redesign of soda bottles), prepare a direct materials budget to calculate the cost of PET purchases in each quarter for the upcoming year and for the year in total.

2. Assume that the company retrofits the soda bottle molds and changes the plastic formulation slightly so that less PET plastic is used in each bottle. Now prepare a direct materials budget to calculate the cost of PET purchases in each quarter for the upcoming year and for the year in total for this possible scenario.

3. Compare the cost of PET plastic for Requirement 1 (original data) and for Requirement 2 (making the change to using less PET). What is the direct material cost saving from making the change to using less PET? Compare the total of those savings to the cost of retrofitting the soda bottle molds. Should the company make the change? Explain your rationale.

E9-36B Sales budget for a retail organization (*Learning Objective 2*)

Albany College Bookstore is the bookstore on campus for students and faculty. The bookstore shows the following sales projections in units by quarter for the upcoming year:

Quarter	Books	School Supplies	Apparel	Miscellaneous
1st..	1,500	210	530	670
2nd	810	120	350	540
3rd..	1,780	270	810	810
4th	630	150	520	450

The average price of an item in each of the departments is as follows:

	Average sales price per unit
Books...	$82
School supplies	$15
Apparel...	$25
Miscellaneous...	$ 7

Requirement

Prepare a sales budget for the upcoming year by quarter for the Albany College Bookstore, with sales categorized by the four product groupings (books, school supplies, apparel, and miscellaneous).

E9-37B   Sales budget for a not-for-profit organization (Learning Objective 2)

Geary Preschool operates a not-for-profit morning preschool. Each family pays a non-refundable registration fee of $120 per child per school year. Monthly tuition for the nine-month school year varies depending on the number of days per week that the child attends preschool. The monthly tuition is $145 for the two-day program, $170 for the three-day program, $190 for the four-day program, and $205 for the five-day program. The following enrollment has been projected for the coming year:

Two-day program	72 children
Three-day program	42 children
Four-day program	54 children
Five-day program	14 children

In addition to the morning preschool, Geary Preschool offers a Lunch Bunch program where kids have the option of staying an extra hour for lunch and playtime. The preschool charges an additional $3 per child for every Lunch Bunch attended. Historically, half of the children stay for Lunch Bunch an average of 15 times a month.

Requirement

Calculate Geary Preschool's budgeted revenue for the school year.

E9-38B   Production budget (Learning Objective 2)

Ringer Foods produces specialty soup sold in jars. The projected sales in dollars and jars for each quarter of the upcoming year are as follows:

	Total sales revenue	Number of jars sold
1st quarter	$187,000	150,500
2nd quarter	$210,000	182,500
3rd quarter	$255,000	213,500
4th quarter	$197,000	164,000

Ringer anticipates selling 224,000 jars with total sales revenue of $260,000 in the first quarter of the year following the year given in the preceding table. The company has a policy that the ending inventory of jars must be 30% of the following quarter's sales. Prepare a production budget for the year that shows the number of jars to be produced each quarter and for the year in total.

E9-39B   Direct materials budget (Learning Objective 2)

Gable Industries manufactures a popular interactive stuffed animal for children that requires two computer chips inside each toy. The company pays $1 for each computer chip. To help to guard against stockouts of the computer chip, Gable Industries has a policy that states that the ending inventory of computer chips should be at least 20% of the following month's production needs. The production schedule for the first four months of the year is as follows:

	Stuffed animals to be produced
January	5,300
February	4,100
March	4,200
April	4,600

Requirement

Prepare a direct materials budget for the first quarter that shows both the number of computer chips needed and the dollar amount of the purchases in the budget.

E9-40B Production and direct materials budgets *(Learning Objective 2)*

Hoffman Manufacturing produces self-watering planters for use in upscale retail establishments. Sales projections for the first five months of the upcoming year show the estimated unit sales of the planters each month to be as follows:

	Number of planters to be sold
January	3,000
February	3,200
March	3,100
April	4,200
May	4,000

Inventory at the start of the year was 750 planters. The desired inventory of planters at the end of each month in the upcoming year should be equal to 25% of the following month's budgeted sales. Each planter requires two pounds of polypropylene (a type of plastic). The company wants to have 20% of the polypropylene required for next month's production on hand at the end of each month. The polypropylene costs $0.20 per pound.

Requirements

1. Prepare a production budget for each month in the first quarter of the year, including production in units for each month and for the quarter.

2. Prepare a direct materials budget for the polypropylene for each month in the first quarter of the year, including the pounds of polypropylene required and the total cost of the polypropylene to be purchased.

E9-41B Direct labor budget *(Learning Objective 2)*

Cleary Industries manufactures three models of a product in a single plant with two departments: Cutting and Assembly. The company has estimated costs for each of the three product models, which are the Zip, the Rocket, and the Royal models.

The company is currently analyzing direct labor hour requirements for the upcoming year.

	Cutting	Assembly
Estimated hours per unit:		
Zips	1.9	2.6
Rockets	1.0	2.4
Royals	1.1	2.9
Direct labor hour rate	$10	$11

Budgeted unit production for each of the products is as follows:

	Number of units to be produced
Product model:	
Zips	540
Rockets	790
Royals	850

Requirement

Prepare a direct labor budget for the upcoming year that shows the budgeted direct labor costs for each department and for the company as a whole.

E9-42B   Manufacturing overhead budget *(Learning Objective 2)*

The Henry Company is in the process of preparing its manufacturing overhead budget for the upcoming year. Sales are projected to be 45,000 units. Information about the various manufacturing overhead costs follows:

	Variable rate per unit	Total fixed costs
Indirect materials...	$1.00	
Supplies..	$0.80	
Indirect labor..	$0.40	$64,000
Plant utilities..	$0.10	$34,000
Repairs and maintenance.......................................	$0.50	$11,000
Depreciation on plant and equipment..................		$48,000
Insurance on plant and equipment.......................		$27,000
Plant supervision		$60,000

Requirement

Prepare the manufacturing overhead budget for the Henry Company for the upcoming year.

E9-43B   Operating expenses budget and an income statement
(Learning Objective 2)

Greatland Preschool operates a not-for-profit morning preschool that operates nine months of the year. The preschool has 160 kids enrolled in its various programs. The preschool's primary expense is payroll. Teachers are paid a flat salary each of the nine months as follows:

Salary data	
Teachers of two-day program	$ 430 per month
Teachers of three-day program...	$ 654 per month
Teachers of four-day program	$ 868 per month
Teachers of five-day program...	$1,060 per month
Preschool director's salary...	$1,350 per month

Greatland Preschool has 9 two-day program teachers, 2 three-day program teachers, 7 four-day program teachers, and 3 five-day program teachers. The preschool also has a director.

In addition to the salary expense, Greatland Preschool must pay federal payroll taxes (FICA taxes) in the amount of 7.65% of salary expense. The preschool leases its facilities from a local church, paying $4,040 per month. Fixed operating expenses (telephone, Internet access, bookkeeping services, and so forth) amount to $940 per month over the nine-month school year. Variable monthly expenses (over the nine-month school year) for art supplies and other miscellaneous supplies are $11 per child. Revenue for the entire nine-month school year from tuition, registration fees, and the lunch program is projected to be $246,400.

Requirements

1. Prepare Greatland Preschool's monthly operating budget. Round all amounts to the nearest dollar.
2. Using your answer from Requirement 1, create Greatland Preschool's budgeted income statement for the entire nine-month school year. You may group all operating expenses together.
3. Greatland Preschool is a not-for-profit preschool. What might the preschool do with its projected income for the year?

E9-44B Budgeted income statement *(Learning Objective 2)*

Rossdale Labs performs a specialty lab test for local companies for $46 per test. For the upcoming quarter, Rossdale Labs is projecting the following sales:

	January	February	March
Number of tests	5,800	4,400	5,600

The budgeted cost of performing each test is $18. Operating expenses are projected to be $62,000 in January, $56,000 in February, and $59,000 in March. Rossdale Labs is subject to a corporate tax rate of 30%.

Requirement

Prepare a budgeted income statement for the first quarter, with a column for each month and for the quarter in total.

E9-45B Budgeted income statement *(Learning Objective 2)*

Samson Motors is a chain of car dealerships. Sales in the fourth quarter of last year were $4,200,000. Suppose its management projects that its current year's quarterly sales will increase by 7% in quarter 1, by another 2% in quarter 2, by another 3% in quarter 3, and by another 6% in quarter 4. Management expects cost of goods sold to be 45% of revenues every quarter, while operating expenses should be 20% of revenues during each of the first two quarters, 30% of revenues during the third quarter, and 35% during the fourth quarter.

Requirement

Prepare a budgeted income statement for each of the four quarters and for the entire year.

E9-46B Cash collections budget *(Learning Objective 3)*

General Corporation has found that 60% of its sales in any given month are credit sales, while the remainder are cash sales. Of the credit sales, the company has experienced the following collection pattern:

25% received in the month of the sale
50% received in the month after the sale
15% received two months after the sale
10% of the credit sales are never received

November sales for last year were $85,000, while December sales were $110,000. Projected sales for the next three months are as follows:

January sales	$145,000
February sales	$115,000
March sales..	$175,000

Requirement

Prepare a cash collections budget for the first quarter, with a column for each month and for the quarter.

E9-47B Cash payments budget *(Learning Objective 3)*

Bauer Corporation is preparing its cash payments budget. The following items relate to cash payments the company anticipates making during the second quarter of the upcoming year.

a. Bauer Corporation pays for 50% of its direct materials purchases in the month of purchase and the remainder the following month. The company's direct material purchases for March through June are anticipated to be as follows:

March	April	May	June
$119,000	$130,000	$126,000	$144,000

b. Direct labor is paid in the month in which it is incurred. Direct labor for each month of the second quarter is budgeted as follows:

April	May	June
$52,000	$62,000	$77,000

c. Manufacturing overhead is estimated to be 160% of direct labor cost each month. This monthly estimate includes $39,000 of depreciation on the plant and equipment. All manufacturing overhead (excluding depreciation) is paid in the month in which it is incurred.

d. Monthly operating expenses for March through June are projected to be as follows:

March	April	May	June
$71,000	$85,000	$88,000	$92,000

Monthly operating expenses are paid in the month after they are incurred. Monthly operating expenses include $11,000 for monthly depreciation on administrative offices and equipment, and $2,900 for bad debt expense.

e. Bauer Corporation plans to pay $7,000 (cash) for a new server in May.

f. Bauer Corporation must make an estimated tax payment of $13,500 on June 15.

Requirement

Prepare a cash payments budget for April, May, and June and for the quarter.

E9-48B Combined cash budget *(Learning Objective 3)*

Mission Health Center provides a variety of medical services. The company is preparing its cash budget for the upcoming third quarter. The following transactions are expected to occur:

a. Cash collections from services in July, August, and September are projected to be $96,000, $150,000, and $127,000, respectively.

b. Cash payments for the upcoming third quarter are projected to be $141,000 in July, $103,000 in August, and $138,000 in September.

c. The cash balance as of the first day of the third quarter is projected to be $30,000.

d. Mission Health Center has a policy that it must maintain a minimum cash balance of $22,000. The company has a line of credit with the local bank that allows it to borrow funds in months that it would not otherwise have the minimum balance. If the company has more than the minimum balance at the end of any given month, it uses the excess funds to pay off any outstanding line of credit balance. Each month, Mission Health Center pays interest on the prior month's line of credit ending balance. The actual interest rate that the health center will pay floats since it is tied to the prime rate. However, the interest rate paid during the budget period is expected to be 3% of the prior month's line of credit ending balance (if it did not have an outstanding balance at the end of the prior month, then the company does not have to pay any interest). All line of credit borrowings are taken or paid off on the first day of the month. As of the first day of the third quarter, Mission Health Center did not have a balance on its line of credit.

Requirement

Prepare a combined cash budget for Mission Health Center for the third quarter, with a column for each month and for the quarter total.

E9-49B Sales and cash collections budgets *(Learning Objectives 2 & 3)*

Serdnic Reeds, a manufacturer of saxophone, oboe, and clarinet reeds, has projected sales to be $896,000 in October, $966,000 in November, $1,065,000 in December, and $934,000 in January. Serdnic's sales are 20% cash and 80% on credit. The company's collection history indicates that credit sales are collected as follows:

25% in the month of the sale
60% in the month after the sale
14% two months after the sale
1% are never collected

Requirements

1. Prepare a sales budget for all four months, showing the breakdown between cash and credit sales.

2. Prepare a cash collection budget for December and January. Round all answers up to the nearest dollar.

E9-50B Budgeted balance sheet *(Learning Objective 3)*

Use the following information to prepare a budgeted balance sheet for Marine Corporation at March 31. Show computations for the cash and owners' equity amounts.

a. March 31 inventory balance, $15,085

b. March payments for inventory, $4,600

c. March payments of accounts payable and accrued liabilities, $8,400

d. March 31 accounts payable balance, $1,700

e. February 28 furniture and fixtures balance, $34,500; accumulated depreciation balance, $29,880

f. February 28 owners' equity, $28,630

g. March depreciation expense, $500

h. Cost of goods sold, 60% of sales

i. Other March expenses, including income tax, total $3,000; paid in cash

j. February 28 cash balance, $11,200

k. March budgeted sales, $12,500

l. March 31 accounts receivable balance, one-fourth of March sales

m. March cash receipts, $14,300

E9-51B Cash budget and revision *(Learning Objective 3)*

Speedy Medical Supply began October with $10,600 cash. Management forecasts that collections from credit customers will be $11,400 in October and $14,200 in November. The business is scheduled to receive $7,000 cash on a business note receivable in October. Projected cash payments include inventory purchases ($11,800 in October and $13,200 in November) and operating expenses ($4,200 each month).

Speedy's bank requires a $10,000 minimum balance in the business's checking account. At the end of any month when the account balance dips below the minimum balance, the bank automatically extends credit to the business in multiples of $1,000. Speedy's borrows as little as possible and pays back loans in quarterly installments of $2,000, plus 3% interest on the entire unpaid principal. The first payment occurs three months after the loan.

Requirement

Prepare Speedy Medical Supply's cash budget for October and November.

E9-52B Incomplete cash budget *(Learning Objective 3)*

You recently began a job as an accounting intern at Reilly Adventures. Your first task was to help prepare the cash budget for February and March. Unfortunately, the computer with the budget file crashed, and you did not have a backup or even a hard copy. You ran a program to salvage bits of data from the budget file. After entering the following data in the budget, you may have just enough information to reconstruct the budget.

Reilly Adventures eliminates any cash deficiency by borrowing the exact amount needed from State Street Bank, where the current interest rate is 7%. Reilly Adventures pays interest on its outstanding debt at the end of each month. The company also repays all borrowed amounts at the end of the month, as cash becomes available.

Requirement

Complete the following cash budget:

	A	B	C
		February	**March**
1	Reilly Adventures		
2	Combined Cash Budget		
3	February and March		
4		February	March
5	Beginning cash balance	$ 16,300	$?
6	Plus: Cash collections	?	80,200
7	Plus: Cash from sale of plant assets	0	2,200
8	Total cash available	$ 106,300	$?
9	Less: Cash payments (purchase inventory)	$?	$ 41,600
10	Less: Cash payments (operating expenses)	47,900	?
11	Total cash payments	$ 98,800	$?
12	(1) Ending cash balance before financing	$?	$ 22,800
13	Minimum cash balance desired	20,000	20,000
14	Cash excess (deficiency)	$?	$?
15	Financing:		
16	Plus: New borrowings	$?	$?
17	Less: Debt repayments	?	?
18	Less: Interest payments	?	?
19	(2) Total effects of financing	$?	$?
20	Ending cash balance (1) + (2)	$?	$?
21			

E9-53B   Cost of goods sold, inventory, and purchases budget

(Learning Objective 4)

Tempest Readers sells eReaders. Its sales budget for the nine months ended September 30 follows:

Tempest Readers
Sales Budget
For the Nine Months Ended September 30

	Quarter			Nine-Month Total
	Mar 31	Jun 30	Sep 30	
Cash sales, 40%...	$ 20,000	$ 30,000	$ 25,000	$ 75,000
Credit sales, 60%...	80,000	120,000	100,000	300,000
Total sales, revenue	$ 100,000	$150,000	$ 125,000	$ 375,000

In the past, cost of goods sold has been 60% of total sales. The director of marketing and the financial vice president agree that each quarter's ending inventory should not be below $15,000 plus 15% of cost of goods sold for the following quarter. The marketing director expects sales of $220,000 during the fourth quarter. The January 1 inventory was $14,000.

Requirement

Prepare a cost of goods sold, inventory, and purchases budget for each of the first three quarters of the year. Compute cost of goods sold for the entire nine-month period.

PROBLEMS Group A

P9-54A Comprehensive budgeting problem *(Learning Objectives 2 & 3)*

Damon Manufacturing is preparing its master budget for the first quarter of the upcoming year. The following data pertain to Damon Manufacturing's operations:

Current Assets as of December 31 (prior year):	
Cash	$ 4,600
Accounts receivable, net	$ 46,000
Inventory	$ 15,600
Property, plant, and equipment, net	$121,000
Accounts payable	$ 43,000
Capital stock	$125,000
Retained earnings	$ 23,000

a. Actual sales in December were $71,000. Selling price per unit is projected to remain stable at $12 per unit throughout the budget period. Sales for the first five months of the upcoming year are budgeted to be as follows:

January	$ 99,600
February	$118,800
March	$115,200
April	$108,000
May	$103,200

b. Sales are 35% cash and 65% credit. All credit sales are collected in the month following the sale.

c. Damon Manufacturing has a policy that states that each month's ending inventory of finished goods should be 10% of the following month's sales (in units).

d. Of each month's direct materials purchases, 20% are paid for in the month of purchase, while the remainder is paid for in the month following purchase. Three pounds of direct material is needed per unit at $2 per pound. Ending inventory of direct materials should be 20% of next month's production needs.

e. Most of the labor at the manufacturing facility is indirect, but there is some direct labor incurred. The direct labor hours per unit is 0.05. The direct labor rate per hour is $9 per hour. All direct labor is paid for in the month in which the work is performed. The direct labor total cost for each of the upcoming three months is as follows:

January	$3,807
February	$4,442
March	$4,293

f. Monthly manufacturing overhead costs are $5,500 for factory rent, $2,900 for other fixed manufacturing expenses, and $1.10 per unit for variable manufacturing overhead. No depreciation is included in these figures. All expenses are paid in the month in which they are incurred.

g. Computer equipment for the administrative offices will be purchased in the upcoming quarter. In January, Damon Manufacturing will purchase equipment for $5,000 (cash), while February's cash expenditure will be $12,200 and March's cash expenditure will be $16,600.

h. Operating expenses are budgeted to be $1.25 per unit sold plus fixed operating expenses of $1,800 per month. All operating expenses are paid in the month in which they are incurred.

i. Depreciation on the building and equipment for the general and administrative offices is budgeted to be $4,800 for the entire quarter, which includes depreciation on new acquisitions.

j. Damon Manufacturing has a policy that the ending cash balance in each month must be at least $4,000. It has a line of credit with a local bank. The company can borrow in increments of $1,000 at the beginning of each month, up to a total outstanding loan balance of $130,000. The interest rate on these loans is 1% per month simple interest (not compounded). The company would pay down on the line of credit balance in increments of $1,000 if it has excess funds at the end of the quarter. The company would also pay the accumulated interest at the end of the quarter on the funds borrowed during the quarter.

k. The company's income tax rate is projected to be 30% of operating income less interest expense. The company pays $10,000 cash at the end of February in estimated taxes.

Requirements

1. Prepare a schedule of cash collections for January, February, and March, and for the quarter in total. Use the following format:

	A	B	C	D	E
1		Cash Collections Budget			
2		For the Quarter Ended March 31			
3			Month		
4		January	February	March	Quarter
5	Cash sales				
6	Credit sales				
7	Total cash collections				
8					

2. Prepare a production budget, using the following format:

	A	B	C	D	E
1		Production Budget			
2		For the Quarter Ended March 31			
3			Month		
4		January	February	March	Quarter
5	Unit sales*				
6	Plus: Desired ending inventory				
7	Total needed				
8	Less: Beginning inventory				
9	Number of units to produce				
10					

Hint: Unit sales = Sales in dollars/Selling price per unit

3. Prepare a direct materials budget, using the following format:

	A	B	C	D	E
1		Direct Materials Budget			
2		For the Quarter Ended March 31			
3			Month		
4		January	February	March	Quarter
5	Units to be produced (from Production Budget)				
6	Multiply by: Quantity (pounds) of DM needed per unit				
7	Quantity (pounds) needed for production				
8	Plus: Desired ending inventory of DM				
9	Total quantity (pounds) needed				
10	Less: Beginning inventory of DM				
11	Quantity (pounds) to purchase				
12	Multiply by: Cost per pound				
13	Total cost of DM purchases				
14					

4. Prepare a cash payments budget for the direct material purchases from Requirement 3, using the following format:

	A	B	C	D	E
1	Cash Payments for Direct Materials Budget				
2	For the Quarter Ended March 31				
3		Month			
4		January	February	March	Quarter
5	20% of current month DM purchases				
6	80% of current month DM purchases				
7	Total cash payments				
8					

5. Prepare a cash payments budget for direct labor, using the following format:

	A	B	C	D	E
1	Cash Payments for Direct Labor Budget				
2	For the Quarter Ended March 31				
3		Month			
4		January	February	March	Quarter
5	Total cost of direct labor				
6					

6. Prepare a cash payments budget for manufacturing overhead costs, using the following format:

	A	B	C	D	E
1	Cash Payments for Manufacturing Overhead Budget				
2	For the Quarter Ended March 31				
3		Month			
4		January	February	March	Quarter
5	Variable manufacturing overhead costs				
6	Rent (fixed)				
7	Other fixed MOH				
8	Cash payments for manufacturing overhead				
9					

7. Prepare a cash payments budget for operating expenses, using the following format:

	A	B	C	D	E
1	Cash Payments for Operating Expenses Budget				
2	For the Quarter Ended March 31				
3		Month			
4		January	February	March	Quarter
5	Variable operating expenses				
6	Fixed operating expenses				
7	Cash payments for operating expenses				
8					

8. Prepare a combined cash budget, using the following format:

	A	B	C	D	E
1		Combined Cash Budget			
2		For the Quarter Ended March 31			
3		Month			
4		January	February	March	Quarter
5	Beginning cash balance				
6	Plus: Cash collections				
7	Total cash available				
8	Less cash payments:				
9	Direct material purchases				
10	Direct labor				
11	Manufacturing overhead costs				
12	Operating expenses				
13	Tax payment				
14	Equipment purchases				
15	Total cash payments				
16	Ending cash balance before financing				
17	Financing:				
18	Plus: New borrowings				
19	Less: Debt repayments				
20	Less: Interest payments				
21	Ending cash balance				
22					

9. Calculate the budgeted manufacturing cost per unit, using the following format (assume that fixed manufacturing overhead is budgeted to be $0.70 per unit for the year):

	A	B	C	D
1	Budgeted Manufacturing Cost per Unit			
2				
3	Direct materials cost per unit			
4	Direct labor cost per unit			
5	Variable manufacturing overhead costs per unit			
6	Fixed manufacturing overhead costs per unit			
7	Budgeted cost of manufacturing one unit			
8				

10. Prepare a budgeted income statement for the quarter ending March 31, using the following format:

	A	B	C	D
1	Budgeted Income Statement			
2	For the Quarter Ended March 31			
3				
4	Sales revenue			
5	Less: Cost of goods sold*			
6	Gross profit			
7	Less: Operating expenses			
8	Less: Depreciation expense			
9	Operating income			
10	Less: Interest expense			
11	Less: Income tax expense			
12	Net income			
13				

*Hint: Cost of goods sold = Budgeted cost of manufacturing one unit × Number of units sold

P9-55A Cash budgets under two alternatives *(Learning Objectives 2 & 3)*

Each autumn, as a hobby, Pauline Spahr weaves cotton placemats to sell at a local craft shop. The mats sell for $20 per set of four mats. The shop charges a 10% commission and remits the net proceeds to Spahr at the end of December. Spahr has woven and sold 25 sets in each of the last two years. She has enough cotton in inventory to make another 25 sets. She paid $7 per set for the cotton. Spahr uses a four-harness loom that she purchased for cash exactly two years ago. It is depreciated at the rate of $10 per month. The accounts payable relate to the cotton inventory and are payable by September 30.

Spahr is considering buying an eight-harness loom so that she can weave more intricate patterns in linen. The new loom costs $1,000; it would be depreciated at $20 per month. Her bank has agreed to lend her $1,000 at 6% interest, with $200 principal plus accrued interest payable each December 31. Spahr believes she can weave 15 linen placemat sets in time for the Christmas rush if she does not weave any cotton mats. She predicts that each linen set will sell for $50. Linen costs $18 per set. Spahr's supplier will sell her linen on credit, payable December 31.

Spahr plans to keep her old loom whether or not she buys the new loom. The balance sheet for her weaving business at August 31 is as follows:

	A	B	C	D
1	Pauline Spahr, Weaver			
2	Balance Sheet			
3	August 31			
4	**Assets:**			
5	Current assets:			
6	Cash	$ 25		
7	Inventory of cotton	175		
8	Total current assets	$ 200		
9	Property, plant, and equipment:			
10	Loom	$ 500		
11	Accumulated depreciation	(240)		
12	Total property, plant, and equipment	$ 260		
13	Total assets	$ 460		
14				
15	**Liabilities and Stockholders' Equity:**			
16	Accounts payable	$ 74		
17	Stockholders' equity	386		
18	Total liabilities and stockholders' equity	$ 460		
19				

Requirements

1. Prepare a combined cash budget for the four months ending December 31, for two alternatives: weaving the placemats in cotton using the existing loom and weaving the placemats in linen using the new loom. For each alternative, prepare a budgeted income statement for the four months ending December 31 and a budgeted balance sheet at December 31.
2. On the basis of financial considerations only, what should Spahr do? Give your reason.
3. What nonfinancial factors might Spahr consider in her decision?

P9-56A Budgeted income statement *(Learning Objective 2)*

The budget committee of Miranda Fashions, an upscale women's clothing retailer, has assembled the following data. As the business manager, you must prepare the budgeted income statements for May and June.

a. Sales in April were $50,000. You forecast that monthly sales will increase 6% in May and 2% in June.
b. Miranda Fashions maintains inventory of $10,000 plus 25% of sales revenues budgeted for the following month. Monthly purchases average 50% of sales revenues in that same month. Actual inventory on April 30 is $16,000. Sales budgeted for July are $60,000.
c. Monthly salaries amount to $3,000. Sales commissions equal 8% of sales for that month. Combine salaries and commissions into a single figure.

d. Other monthly expenses are as follows:

Rent expense...	$2,600, paid as incurred
Depreciation expense	$ 200
Insurance expense...	$ 100, expiration of prepaid amount
Income tax...	20% of operating income

Requirement

Prepare Miranda Fashions' budgeted income statements for May and June. Show cost of goods sold computations.

P9-57A Cash budgets (Learning Objective 3)

Brett's Restaurant Supply is preparing its cash budgets for the first two months of the upcoming year. Here is the information about the company's upcoming cash receipts and cash disbursements:

a. Sales are 65% cash and 35% credit. Credit sales are collected 20% in the month of sale and the remainder in the month after sale. Actual sales in December were $57,000. Schedules of budgeted sales for the two months of the upcoming year are as follows:

	Budgeted Sales Revenue
January	$65,000
February	$71,000

b. Actual purchases of direct materials in December were $23,500. The company's purchases of direct materials in January are budgeted to be $21,000 and $25,500 in February. All purchases are paid 50% in the month of purchase and 50% the following month.

c. Salaries and sales commissions are also paid half in the month earned and half the next month. Actual salaries were $7,500 in December. Budgeted salaries in January are $8,500 and February budgeted salaries are $10,000. Sales commissions each month are 8% of that month's sales.

d. Rent expense is $3,300 per month.

e. Depreciation is $2,600 per month.

f. Estimated income tax payments are made at the end of January. The estimated tax payment is projected to be $11,500.

g. The cash balance at the end of the prior year was $23,000.

Requirements

1. Prepare schedules of (a) budgeted cash collections, (b) budgeted cash payments for purchases, and (c) budgeted cash payments for operating expenses. Show totals for each month and totals for January and February combined.

2. Prepare a combined cash budget similar to exhibits in the chapter. If no financing activity takes place, what is the budgeted cash balance on February 28?

P9-58A Combined cash budget and a budgeted balance sheet
(Learning Objective 3)

Boxton Medical Supply has applied for a loan. First National Bank has requested a budgeted balance sheet as of April 30, and a combined cash budget for April. As Boxton Medical Supply's controller, you have assembled the following information:

a. March 31 equipment balance, $52,200; accumulated depreciation, $41,500

b. April capital expenditures of $42,200 budgeted for cash purchase of equipment

c. April depreciation expense, $500

d. Cost of goods sold, 45% of sales

e. Other April operating expenses, including income tax, total $13,000, 30% of which will be paid in cash and the remainder accrued at April 30

f. March 31 owners' equity, $93,000

g. March 31 cash balance, $40,500

h. April budgeted sales, $90,000, 60% of which is for cash. Of the remaining 40%, half will be collected in April and half in May.

i. April cash collections on March sales, $29,700

j. April cash payments of March 31 liabilities incurred for March purchases of inventory, $17,000

k. March 31 inventory balance, $29,100

l. April purchases of inventory, $10,000 for cash and $36,200 on credit. Half of the credit purchases will be paid in April and half in May.

Requirements

1. Prepare the budgeted balance sheet for Boxton Medical Supply at April 30. Show separate computations for cash, inventory, and owners' equity balances.

2. Prepare the combined cash budget for April.

3. Suppose Boxton Medical Supply has become aware of more efficient (and more expensive) equipment than it budgeted for purchase in April. What is the total amount of cash available for equipment purchases in April, before financing, if the minimum desired ending cash balance is $19,000? (For this requirement, disregard the $42,200 initially budgeted for equipment purchases.)

4. Before granting a loan to Boxton Medical Supply, First National Bank asks for a sensitivity analysis assuming that April sales are only $60,000 rather than the $90,000 originally budgeted. (While the cost of goods sold will change, assume that purchases, depreciation, and the other operating expenses will remain the same as in the earlier requirements.)

   a. Prepare a revised budgeted balance sheet for Boxton Medical Supply, showing separate computations for cash, inventory, and owners' equity balances.

   b. Suppose Boxton Medical Supply has a minimum desired cash balance of $18,000. Will the company need to borrow cash in April?

   c. In this sensitivity analysis, sales declined by 33 1/3% ($30,000 ÷ $90,000). Is the decline in expenses and income more or less than 33 1/3%? Explain.

P9-59A   Cost of goods sold, inventory, and purchases budget

(Learning Objective 4)

Cool Logos buys logo-imprinted merchandise and then sells it to university bookstores. Sales are expected to be $2,005,000 in September, $2,250,000 in October, $2,381,000 in November, and $2,590,000 in December. Cool Logos sets its prices to earn an average 30% gross profit on sales revenue. The company does not want inventory to fall below $410,000 plus 10% of the next month's cost of goods sold.

Requirement

Prepare a cost of goods sold, inventory, and purchases budget for the months of October and November.

PROBLEMS Group B

P9-60B   Comprehensive budgeting problem *(Learning Objectives 2 & 3)*

Presidio Manufacturing is preparing its master budget for the first quarter of the upcoming year. The following data pertain to Presidio Manufacturing's operations:

Current assets as of December 31 (prior year):	
Cash	$ 4,600
Accounts receivable, net	$ 50,000
Inventory	$ 15,000
Property, plant, and equipment, net	$120,000
Accounts payable	$ 43,000
Capital stock	$126,000
Retained earnings	$ 23,200

a. Actual sales in December were $71,000. Selling price per unit is projected to remain stable at $12 per unit throughout the budget period. Sales for the first five months of the upcoming year are budgeted to be as follows:

January	$ 99,600
February	$118,800
March	$115,200
April	$108,000
May	$103,200

b. Sales are 35% cash and 65% credit. All credit sales are collected in the month following the sale.

c. Presidio Manufacturing has a policy that states that each month's ending inventory of finished goods should be 10% of the following month's sales (in units).

d. Of each month's direct materials purchases, 20% are paid for in the month of purchase, while the remainder is paid for in the month following purchase. Three pounds of direct material is needed per unit at $2.00 per pound. Ending inventory of direct materials should be 20% of next month's production needs.

e. Most of the labor at the manufacturing facility is indirect, but there is some direct labor incurred. The direct labor hours per unit is 0.05. The direct labor rate per hour is $9 per hour. All direct labor is paid for in the month in which the work is performed. The direct labor total cost for each of the upcoming three months is as follows:

January	$3,807
February	$4,442
March	$4,293

f. Monthly manufacturing overhead costs are $5,500 for factory rent, $2,900 for other fixed manufacturing expenses, and $1.10 per unit for variable manufacturing overhead. No depreciation is included in these figures. All expenses are paid in the month in which they are incurred.

g. Computer equipment for the administrative offices will be purchased in the upcoming quarter. In January, the company will purchase equipment for $5,000 (cash), while February's cash expenditure will be $12,200 and March's cash expenditure will be $16,600.

h. Operating expenses are budgeted to be $1.25 per unit sold plus fixed operating expenses of $1,800 per month. All operating expenses are paid in the month in which they are incurred.

i. Depreciation on the building and equipment for the general and administrative offices is budgeted to be $4,600 for the entire quarter, which includes depreciation on new acquisitions.

j. Presidio Manufacturing has a policy that the ending cash balance in each month must be at least $4,000. The company has a line of credit with a local bank. It can borrow in increments of $1,000 at the beginning of each month, up to a total outstanding loan balance of $160,000. The interest rate on these loans is 1% per month simple interest (not compounded). The company would pay down on the line of credit balance in increments of $1,000 if it has excess funds at the end of the quarter. The company would also pay the accumulated interest at the end of the quarter on the funds borrowed during the quarter.

k. The company's income tax rate is projected to be 30% of operating income less interest expense. The company pays $10,000 cash at the end of February in estimated taxes.

Requirements

1. Prepare a schedule of cash collections for January, February, and March, and for the quarter in total.

	A	B	C	D	E
1		Cash Collections Budget			
2		For the Quarter Ended March 31			
3			Month		
4		January	February	March	Quarter
5	Cash sales				
6	Credit sales				
7	Total cash collections				
8					

2. Prepare a production budget.

	A	B	C	D	E
1		Production Budget			
2		For the Quarter Ended March 31			
3			Month		
4		January	February	March	Quarter
5	Unit sales*				
6	Plus: Desired ending inventory				
7	Total needed				
8	Less: Beginning inventory				
9	Number of units to produce				
10					

Hint: Unit sales = Sales in dollars/Selling price per unit

3. Prepare a direct materials budget.

	A	B	C	D	E
1		Direct Materials Budget			
2		For the Quarter Ended March 31			
3			Month		
4		January	February	March	Quarter
5	Units to be produced (from Production Budget)				
6	Multiply by: Quantity (pounds) of DM needed per unit				
7	Quantity (pounds) needed for production				
8	Plus: Desired ending inventory of DM				
9	Total quantity (pounds) needed				
10	Less: Beginning inventory of DM				
11	Quantity (pounds) to purchase				
12	Multiply by: Cost per pound				
13	Total cost of DM purchases				
14					

4. Prepare a cash payments budget for the direct material purchases from Requirement 3.

	A	B	C	D	E
1		Cash Payments for Direct Materials Budget			
2		For the Quarter Ended March 31			
3			Month		
4		January	February	March	Quarter
5	20% of current month DM purchases				
6	80% of current month DM purchases				
7	Total cash payments				
8					

5. Prepare a cash payments budget for direct labor, using the following format:

	A	B	C	D	E
1	Cash Payments for Direct Labor Budget				
2	For the Quarter Ended March 31				
3		Month			
4		January	February	March	Quarter
5	Total cost of direct labor				
6					

6. Prepare a cash payments budget for manufacturing overhead costs.

	A	B	C	D	E
1	Cash Payments for Manufacturing Overhead Budget				
2	For the Quarter Ended March 31				
3		Month			
4		January	February	March	Quarter
5	Variable manufacturing overhead costs				
6	Rent (fixed)				
7	Other fixed MOH				
8	Cash payments for manufacturing overhead				
9					

7. Prepare a cash payments budget for operating expenses.

	A	B	C	D	E
1	Cash Payments for Operating Expenses Budget				
2	For the Quarter Ended March 31				
3		Month			
4		January	February	March	Quarter
5	Variable operating expenses				
6	Fixed operating expenses				
7	Cash payments for operating expenses				
8					

8. Prepare a combined cash budget.

	A	B	C	D	E
1	Combined Cash Budget				
2	For the Quarter Ended March 31				
3		Month			
4		January	February	March	Quarter
5	Beginning cash balance				
6	Plus: Cash collections				
7	Total cash available				
8	Less cash payments:				
9	Direct material purchases				
10	Direct labor				
11	Manufacturing overhead costs				
12	Operating expenses				
13	Tax payment				
14	Equipment purchases				
15	Total cash payments				
16	Ending cash balance before financing				
17	Financing:				
18	Plus: New borrowings				
19	Less: Debt repayments				
20	Less: Interest payments				
21	Ending cash balance				
22					

9. Calculate the budgeted manufacturing cost per unit (assume that fixed manufacturing overhead is budgeted to be $0.70 per unit for the year).

	A	B	C	D
1	**Budgeted Manufacturing Cost per Unit**			
2				
3	Direct materials cost per unit			
4	Direct labor cost per unit			
5	Variable manufacturing overhead costs per unit			
6	Fixed manufacturing overhead costs per unit			
7	Budgeted cost of manufacturing one unit			
8				

10. Prepare a budgeted income statement for the quarter ending March 31.

	A	B	C	D
1	**Budgeted Income Statement**			
2	**For the Quarter Ended March 31**			
3				
4	Sales revenue			
5	Less: Cost of goods sold*			
6	Gross profit			
7	Less: Operating expenses			
8	Less: Depreciation expense			
9	Operating income			
10	Less: Interest expense			
11	Less: Income tax expense			
12	Net income			
13				

Hint: Cost of goods sold = Budgeted cost of manufacturing one unit × Number of units sold

P9-61B Cash budgets under two alternatives *(Learning Objectives 2 & 3)*

Each autumn, as a hobby, Mary Snyder weaves cotton placemats to sell at a local craft shop. The mats sell for $30 per set of four mats. The shop charges a 20% commission and remits the net proceeds to Snyder at the end of December. Snyder has woven and sold 30 sets in each of the last two years. She has enough cotton in inventory to make another 30 sets. She paid $12 per set for the cotton. Snyder uses a four-harness loom that she purchased for cash exactly two years ago. It is depreciated at the rate of $10 per month. The accounts payable relate to the cotton inventory and are payable by September 30.

Snyder is considering buying an eight-harness loom so that she can weave more intricate patterns in linen. The new loom costs $1,200; it would be depreciated at $24 per month. Her bank has agreed to lend her $1,200 at 5% interest, with $240 principal plus accrued interest payable each December 31. Snyder believes she can weave 20 linen place mat sets in time for the Christmas rush if she does not weave any cotton mats. She predicts that each linen set will sell for $60. Linen costs $22 per set. Snyder's supplier will sell her linen on credit, payable December 31.

Snyder plans to keep her old loom whether or not she buys the new loom. The balance sheet for her weaving business at August 31 is as follows:

	A	B	C	D
1	**Mary Snyder, Weaver**			
2	**Balance Sheet**			
3	**August 31**			
4	<u>Assets:</u>			
5	Current assets:			
6	Cash	$ 32		
7	Inventory of cotton	360		
8	Total current assets	$ 392		
9	Property, plant, and equipment:			
10	Loom	$ 500		
11	Accumulated depreciation	(240)		
12	Total property, plant, and equipment	$ 260		
13	Total assets	$ 652		
14				
15	<u>Liabilities and Stockholders' Equity:</u>			
16	Accounts payable	$ 90		
17	Stockholders' equity	562		
18	Total liabilities and stockholders' equity	$ 652		
19				

Requirements

1. Prepare a combined cash budget for the four months ending December 31, for two alternatives: weaving the placemats in cotton using the existing loom and weaving the placemats in linen using the new loom. For each alternative, prepare a budgeted income statement for the four months ending December 31 and a budgeted balance sheet at December 31.

2. On the basis of financial considerations only, what should Snyder do? Give your reason.

3. What nonfinancial factors might Snyder consider in her decision?

P9-62B Budgeted income statement *(Learning Objective 2)*

The budget committee of DuBois Fashions, an upscale women's clothing retailer, has assembled the following data. As the business manager, you must prepare the budgeted income statements for May and June.

a. Sales in April were $35,000. You forecast that monthly sales will increase 10% in May and 3% in June.

b. The company maintains inventory of $10,000 plus 20% of the sales revenue budgeted for the following month. Monthly purchases average 50% of sales revenue in that same month. Actual inventory on April 30 is $11,000. Sales budgeted for July are $45,000.

c. Monthly salaries amount to $6,000. Sales commissions equal 11% of sales for that month. Combine salaries and commissions into a single figure.

d. Other monthly expenses are as follows:

Rent expense..	$2,800, paid as incurred
Depreciation expense	$ 700
Insurance expense...	$ 400, expiration of prepaid amount
Income tax..	20% of operating income

Requirement

Prepare DuBois Fashions' budgeted income statements for May and June. Show cost of goods sold computations.

P9-63B Cash budgets *(Learning Objective 3)*

Gary's Restaurant Supply is preparing its cash budgets for the first two months of the upcoming year. Here is the information about the company's upcoming cash receipts and cash disbursements:

a. Sales are 70% cash and 30% credit. Credit sales are collected 20% in the month of sale and the remainder in the month after sale. Actual sales in December were $52,000. Schedules of budgeted sales for the two months of the upcoming year are as follows:

	Budgeted sales revenue
January	$65,000
February	$67,000

b. Actual purchases of materials in December were $23,500. The company's purchases of direct materials in January are budgeted to be $20,500 and $26,000 in February. All purchases are paid 30% in the month of purchase and 70% the following month.

c. Salaries and sales commissions are also paid half in the month earned and half the next month. Actual salaries were $8,500 in December. Budgeted salaries in January are $9,500 and February budgeted salaries are $11,000. Sales commissions each month are 15% of that month's sales.

d. Rent expense is $3,300 per month.

e. Depreciation is $2,500 per month.

f. Estimated income tax payments are made at the end of January. The estimated tax payment is projected to be $11,500.

g. The cash balance at the end of the prior year was $19,000.

Requirements

1. Prepare schedules of (a) budgeted cash collections, (b) budgeted cash payments for purchases, and (c) budgeted cash payments for operating expenses. Show totals for each month and totals for January and February combined.

2. Prepare a combined cash budget. If no financing activity takes place, what is the budgeted cash balance on February 28?

P9-64B Combined cash budget and a budgeted balance sheet
(Learning Objective 3)

Akron Medical Supply has applied for a loan. First National Bank has requested a budgeted balance sheet at April 30 and a combined cash budget for April. As Akron Medical Supply's controller, you have assembled the following information:

a. March 31 equipment balance, $52,100; accumulated depreciation, $41,500

b. April capital expenditures of $42,700 budgeted for cash purchase of equipment

c. April depreciation expense, $300

d. Cost of goods sold, 40% of sales

e. Other April operating expenses, including income tax, total $14,000, 35% of which will be paid in cash and the remainder accrued at April 30

f. March 31 owners' equity, $93,200

g. March 31 cash balance, $40,500

h. April budgeted sales, $87,000, 65% of which is for cash. Of the remaining 35%, half will be collected in April and half in May.

i. April cash collections on March sales, $29,500

j. April cash payments of March 31 liabilities incurred for March purchases of inventory, $17,000

k. March 31 inventory balance, $29,600

l. April purchases of inventory, $10,400 for cash and $36,700 on credit. Half of the credit purchases will be paid in April and half in May

Requirements

1. Prepare the budgeted balance sheet for Akron Medical Supply at April 30. Show separate computations for cash, inventory, and stockholders' equity balances.

2. Prepare the combined cash budget for April.

3. Suppose Akron Medical Supply has become aware of more efficient (and more expensive) equipment than it budgeted for purchase in April. What is the total amount of cash available for equipment purchases in April, before financing, if the minimum desired ending cash balance is $13,000? (For this requirement, disregard the $42,700 initially budgeted for equipment purchases.)

4. Before granting a loan to Akron Medical Supply, First National Bank asks for a sensitivity analysis assuming that April sales are only $58,000 rather than the $87,000 originally budgeted. (While the cost of goods sold will change, assume that purchases, depreciation, and the other operating expenses will remain the same as in the earlier requirements.)

   a. Prepare a revised budgeted balance sheet for the company, showing separate computations for cash, inventory, and stockholders' equity balances.

   b. Suppose Akron Medical Supply has a minimum desired cash balance of $17,000. Will the company need to borrow cash in April?

   c. In this sensitivity analysis, sales declined by 33 1/3% ($29,000/$87,000). Is the decline in expenses and income more or less than 33 1/3%? Explain.

P9-65B Cost of goods sold, inventory, and purchases budget
(Learning Objective 4)

State Logos buys logo-imprinted merchandise and then sells it to university bookstores. Sales are expected to be $2,009,000 in September, $2,240,000 in October, $2,379,000 in November, and $2,520,000 in December. State Logos sets its prices to earn an average 30% gross profit on sales revenue. The company does not want inventory to fall below $405,000 plus 20% of the next month's cost of goods sold.

Requirement

Prepare a cost of goods sold, inventory, and purchases budget for the months of October and November.

CRITICAL THINKING

Discussion & Analysis

A9-66 Discussion Questions

1. "The sales budget is the most important budget." Do you agree or disagree? Explain your answer.

2. List at least four reasons why a company would use budgeting.

3. Describe the difference between an operating budget and a capital budget.

4. Describe the process for developing a budget.

5. Compare and contrast "participative budgeting" with "top-down" budgeting.

6. What is a budget committee? What is the budget committee's role in the budgeting process?

7. What are operating budgets? List at least four operating budgets.

8. What are financial budgets? List at least three financial budgets.

9. Managers may build slack into their budgets so that their target numbers are easier to attain. What might be some drawbacks to building slack into the budgets?

10. How does the master budget for a service company differ from a master budget for a manufacturing company? Which (if any) operating budgets differ and how, specifically, do they differ? Which (if any) financial budgets differ and how, specifically, do they differ?

11. Give an example of a sustainable practice that would affect a company's budget. How might this sustainable practice, if adopted, impact the company's budget in both the short-term and in the long-term?

12. Why might a company want to state environmental goals for increased sustainability in its budgets? Explain.

Application & Analysis

Mini Cases

A9-67 Budgeting for a Single Product

In this activity, you will be creating budgets for a single product for each of the months in an upcoming quarter. Select a product that you could purchase in large quantities (at a Sam's Club or other warehouse retail chain) and repackage into smaller quantities to offer for sale at a sidewalk café, a sporting event, a flea market, or other similar venue. Investigate the price and quantity at which this product is available at the warehouse. Choose a selling price for the smaller (repackaged) package. Make reasonable assumptions about how many of the smaller units you can sell in each of the next four months (you will need the fourth month's sales in units for the operating budgets).

Basic Discussion Questions

1. Describe your product. What is your cost of this product? What size (quantity) will you purchase? At what price will you sell your repackaged product? Make projections of your sales in units in each of the upcoming three months.

2. Estimate how many hours you will spend in each of the upcoming three months doing the purchasing, repackaging, and selling. Select a reasonable wage rate for yourself. What will your total labor costs be in each of the upcoming three months?

3. Prepare a sales budget for each of the upcoming three months.

4. Prepare the direct material budgets for the upcoming three months, assuming that you need to keep 10% of the direct materials needed for next month's sales on hand at the end of each month (this requirement is why you needed to estimate unit sales for four months).

5. Prepare a direct labor budget (for your labor) for each of the upcoming three months.

6. Think about any other expenses you are likely to have (i.e., booth rental at a flea market or a vendor license). Prepare the operating expenses budget for each of the upcoming three months.

7. Prepare a budgeted income statement that reflects the budgets you prepared, including the sales budget, direct materials budget, direct labor budget, and the operating expenses

budget. This budgeted income statement should include one column for each of the three months in the quarter and it should also include a total column that represents the totals of the three months. What is your projected profit by month and for the quarter?

ETHICS

A9-68 Ethics and budgetary slack *(Learning Objectives 1, 2, 3, & 4)*

Mendelson Company, a publicly held corporation, operates a regional chain of large drugstores. Each drugstore is operated by a general manager and a controller. The general manager is responsible for the day-to-day operations of the store, while the controller is responsible for the budget and other financial tasks. The general manager, Sophie Beckett, has been at Mendelson Company for several years. Employee turnover is high at Mendelson Company, just as it is in the retail industry in general. Beckett just hired a new controller, Mike Dexter.

Dexter was asked to prepare the master budget. Each retail location prepares its master budget once a year and then submits that budget to company headquarters for approval. Once approved by headquarters, the master budget is used to evaluate the store's performance. These performance evaluations directly affect the managers' bonuses and whether additional company funds are invested in that location.

When Dexter was almost done preparing the budget, Beckett instructed him to increase the amounts budgeted for labor and supplies by 20%. When asked why, Beckett responded that this budgetary cushion gives store management flexibility in running the store. For example, because company headquarters tightly controls operating funds and capital improvement funds, any extra money budgeted for labor and supplies can be used to replace store furnishings or to pay bonuses to help to retain good employees. She explains that the chance of getting extra funds from company headquarters is not good; this "cushion" is usually the only opportunity to replace store décor or to pay bonuses to key employees. Beckett also needs extra funds occasionally to make "under the table" payments to employees as incentives to work extra hours or to keep them from leaving for a higher-paying job.

Dexter feels conflicted. He is eager to please Beckett and he is wondering what he should do in this situation.

Requirements

1. Using the IMA *Statement of Ethical Professional Practice* as an ethical framework, answer the following questions:
   a. What are the ethical issue(s) in this situation?
   b. What are Dexter's responsibilities as a management accountant?
2. Would your answer differ if Mendelson Company were instead owned by one individual instead of being publicly held? Why or why not?
3. Would anyone be harmed if slack were to be built into the budget? Why or why not?
4. Discuss the specific steps Dexter should take in this situation. Refer to the IMA *Statement of Ethical Professional Practice* in your response.

REAL LIFE

A9-69 Budgeting issues at the movies *(Learning Objectives 1, 2, 3, & 4)*

Movies are expensive to produce and market. According to IMDb, the most expensive film on record is *Pirates of the Caribbean: At World's End*, with a total budget of $336 million.[1] This movie and its budget were widely publicized prior to the premiere of the film, and moviegoers were eager to see the results of this massive movie budget.

Like other large projects, movies have budgets. Potential financiers look at the budget, the script, and other factors to decide whether to invest in the movie. Several categories of costs will be in a movie's budget, including:

- Story rights
- Screenplay
- Producers and directors
- Cast
- Production costs
- Special effects
- Music

[1] www.imdb.com/list/anMNra4h8ls/

The typical film budget you read about in the press includes only expenses. The movie budgets released to the general public do not include estimated box office receipts or other revenue streams. In addition, movie budgets do not usually include marketing costs, which can be another 50% or more of the film's publicized budget.

Producers and directors will frequently release budget figures for upcoming movies, and these budget figures will be reported in several news outlets. However, *Los Angeles Times* writer Patrick Goldstein states that "everyone" lies about their movie budgets.[2] For example, it was reported initially that *The Avengers*, a Marvel Studios film, had an overall budget of $170 million. Another source indicated that the budget for *The Avengers* was $260 million. Which one of these figures was the "correct" budget figure? No one outside of the management of the movie really knows.

Requirements

1. Budgeting for a movie can be challenging. Frequently, budget items change as the movie production progresses. If budgeting for a movie is difficult, why prepare a movie budget?

2. What reasons can a movie director have for misrepresenting the overall budget for a particular movie? Is misrepresenting a movie budget unethical? Do you think misrepresenting a movie's total budgeted expenditures to the public harms anyone? Why or why not?

3. "If a Hollywood movie's box office number exceeds its production budget, then that movie makes a profit." From reading the information given in the case, do you agree with this statement? Why or why not?

4. Sometimes actors, directors, and producers are asked to take a lower salary up front and instead receive a percentage of the film's overall gross profits (from box office receipts, DVD sales, and similar revenue streams). Why might the film company propose this arrangement? Why might the actors, directors, and producers accept this arrangement? Would this type of arrangement (lower salary up front with a percentage of the film's gross profits later) make the budgeting process easier or more challenging? Why?

Try It Solutions

page 509:

The company should produce 32,800 cases, calculated as follows:

Unit sales for April	32,000
Plus: Desired ending inventory (10% of May sales of 40,000)	4,000
Total units needed	36,000
Less: Beginning inventory (March ending inventory = 10% of April sales of 32,000)	3,200
Units to produce	32,800

page 520:

$122,000, calculated as follows:

	March Budgeted Collections
COD sales in March	$ 15,000
Credit sales from February ($110,000 × 90%)	99,000
Credit sales from January ($100,000 × 8%)	8,000
Total cash collections	$122,000

[2]http://cigsandredvines.blogspot.com/2010/03/everyone-lies-about-their-budget-la.html

Performance Evaluation

Rachel Youdelman/Pearson Education, Inc.

Sources: PepsiCo.com; PepsiCo 2012 Annual Report

Learning Objectives

■ **1** Understand decentralization and describe different types of responsibility centers

■ **2** Develop performance reports

■ **3** Calculate ROI, sales margin, and capital turnover

■ **4** Describe strategies and mechanisms for determining a transfer price

■ **5** Prepare and evaluate flexible budget performance reports

■ **6** Describe the balanced scorecard and identify KPIs for each perspective

PepsiCo products are sold in 200 countries around the world. PepsiCo has 22 brands, each generating over $1 billion in annual sales. In addition to its well-known beverages, including Pepsi, Mountain Dew, Gatorade, and Tropicana, the company also owns all of the Frito-Lay snacks brands, such as Ruffles, Doritos, and Cheetos, and the Quaker Oat brands, such as Life and Cap'n Crunch cereals. How does such a large and diverse company coordinate, control, and evaluate such diverse operations? First, the company is segmented into separate operating divisions based on geographic location (US; Europe; Latin America; and Middle East, Asia, and Africa) and product type (beverages, Quaker products, and Frito-Lay products). Second, a manager is assigned responsibility for each segment, and for each operating function (production, sales, etc.) within each segment. The company has taken a triple bottom line approach to evaluating the performance of its business segments. The company's mantra, "Performance with a Purpose," contains four performance evaluation pillars: Financial Performance, Environmental Sustainability, Human Sustainability, and Talent Sustainability. As a result of PepsiCo's advances in each of these areas, the company was ranked 1st in the 2011 Dow Jones Sustainability World Index for the Food and Beverage Sector. Each business unit has a role to play in the success of the entire corporation.

In Chapter 9 we saw how businesses such as Campbell Soup Company and Tucson Tortilla set strategic goals and then develop planning budgets to help reach those goals. In this chapter, we'll see how companies use budgets and other tools, such as the balanced scorecard, to evaluate performance and control operations.

How Does Decentralization Affect Performance Evaluation?

In a small company, such as Tucson Tortilla (discussed in Chapter 9), the owner or top manager often makes all planning and operating decisions. Small companies can use *centralized* decision making because of the smaller scope of their operations. However, when a company grows, it is impossible for a single person to manage the entire organization's operations. Therefore, most companies, like PepsiCo, decentralize as they grow.

Companies that **decentralize** split their operations into different operating segments. Top management delegates decision-making responsibility to the segment managers. Top management determines the type of decentralization that best suits the company's strategy. For example, decentralization may be based on

- geographic area
- product line
- distribution channel (such as retail sales versus online sales)
- customer base
- business function

For example, PepsiCo decentralizes its company by geographic area (Americas; Europe; Asia, Middle East, and Africa) and brand (Frito-Lay, Quaker Foods, Pepsi Beverages, etc.).

1 Understand decentralization and describe different types of responsibility centers

Advantages and Disadvantages of Decentralization

Before we look at specific types of business segments, let's consider some of the advantages and disadvantages of decentralization.

Advantages

Most growing companies decentralize out of necessity. However, decentralization provides many potential benefits.

FREES TOP MANAGEMENT'S TIME By delegating responsibility for daily operations to segment managers, top management can concentrate on long-term strategic planning and higher-level decisions that affect the entire company.

ENCOURAGES USE OF EXPERT KNOWLEDGE Decentralization allows top management to hire the expertise each business segment needs to excel in its specific operations. Specialized knowledge often helps segment managers make better decisions than the top company managers could make.

IMPROVES CUSTOMER RELATIONS Segment managers focus on just one segment of the company, allowing them to maintain close contact with important customers and suppliers. Thus, decentralization often leads to improved customer and supplier relations, which can result in quicker customer response times.

PROVIDES TRAINING Decentralization also provides segment managers with training and experience necessary to become effective top managers. Companies often groom their lower-level managers to move up through the company, taking on additional responsibility and gaining more knowledge of the company with each step.

IMPROVES MOTIVATION AND RETENTION   Empowering segment managers to make decisions increases managers' motivation and job satisfaction, which often improves job performance and retention.

Disadvantages

The many advantages of decentralization usually outweigh the disadvantages. However, decentralization can cause potential problems, including those outlined below.

POTENTIAL DUPLICATION OF COSTS   Decentralization may cause a company to duplicate certain costs or assets. For example, several business segments could maintain their own payroll and human resource departments. Companies can often avoid such duplications by providing centralized services. For example, Marriott segments its hotels by property type (limited service, full-service, luxury), yet each hotel property shares one centralized reservations website.

POTENTIAL PROBLEMS ACHIEVING GOAL CONGRUENCE   <u>Goal congruence</u> occurs when the goals of the segment managers align with the goals of top management. Decentralized companies often struggle to achieve goal congruence. Segment managers may not fully understand the big picture, or the ultimate goals that upper management is trying to achieve. They may make decisions that are good for their segment but may be detrimental to another segment of the company or the company as a whole. For example, in order to control costs, one division may decide to offshore production to an overseas factory with poor working conditions. However, top management may embrace, promote, and market social responsibility and the use of fair labor practices. If so, the division is not acting in accordance with top management's goals.

Performance Evaluation Systems

Once a company decentralizes operations, top management is no longer involved in running the day-to-day operations of the segments. Performance evaluation systems provide upper management with the feedback it needs to maintain control over the entire organization, even though it has delegated responsibility and decision-making authority to segment managers. To be effective, performance evaluation systems should

- clearly communicate expectations,
- provide benchmarks that promote goal congruence and coordination between segments, and
- motivate segment managers (possibly through paying bonus incentives to managers who achieve performance targets).

Responsibility accounting, discussed next, is an integral part of most companies' performance evaluation systems.

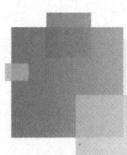

What is Responsibility Accounting?

A <u>responsibility center</u> is a part of an organization whose manager is accountable for planning and controlling certain activities. Lower-level managers are often responsible for budgeting and controlling costs of a single value chain function. For example, at PepsiCo, one manager is responsible for planning and controlling the *production* of Frito-Lay products at a single plant, while another is responsible for planning and controlling the *distribution* of the product to customers. Lower-level managers report to higher-level managers, who have broader responsibilities. For example, managers in charge of production and distribution report to senior managers responsible for profits earned by an entire product line.

<u>Responsibility accounting</u> is a system for evaluating the performance of each responsibility center and its manager. Responsibility accounting performance reports compare plans (budgets) with actual results for each center. Superiors then evaluate how well each manager controlled the operations for which he or she was responsible.

Types of Responsibility Centers

Exhibit 10-1 illustrates four types of responsibility centers. We'll briefly describe each type of responsibility center.

EXHIBIT 10-1 Four Types of Responsibility Centers

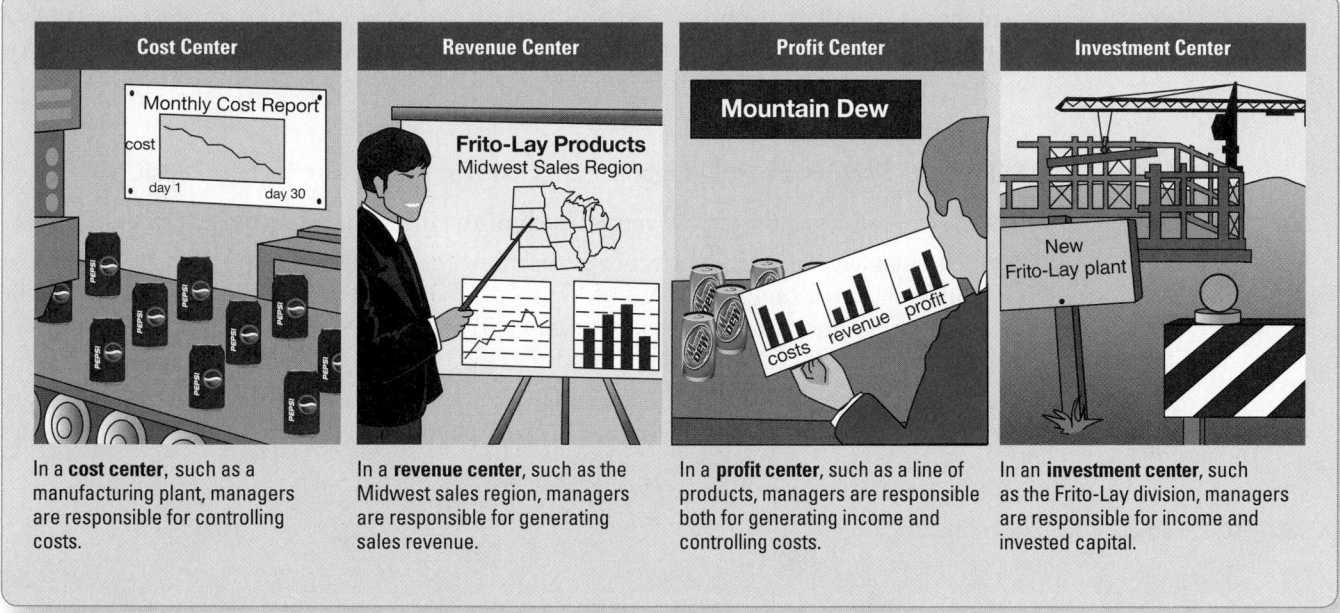

Cost Center	Revenue Center	Profit Center	Investment Center
In a **cost center**, such as a manufacturing plant, managers are responsible for controlling costs.	In a **revenue center**, such as the Midwest sales region, managers are responsible for generating sales revenue.	In a **profit center**, such as a line of products, managers are responsible both for generating income and controlling costs.	In an **investment center**, such as the Frito-Lay division, managers are responsible for income and invested capital.

Cost Center

In a <u>cost center</u>, managers are accountable for costs only. Manufacturing operations, such as the Frito-Lay plant in Casa Grande, Arizona, are cost centers. The plant manager controls costs by using lean thinking to eliminate waste. The plant is near net-zero waste and uses solar energy for much of its power. The plant manager is *not* responsible for generating revenues because he or she is not involved in selling the product. The plant manager is evaluated on his or her ability to control *costs* by comparing actual costs to budgeted costs.

Revenue Center

In a <u>revenue center</u>, managers are accountable primarily for revenues. Many times, revenue centers are sales territories, such as geographic areas within the country. Managers of revenue centers may also be responsible for the costs of their own sales operations. Revenue center performance reports compare actual revenues to budgeted revenues.

Profit Center

In a <u>profit center</u>, managers are accountable for both revenues and costs, and therefore profits. For example, at PepsiCo, a manager may be responsible for the entire line of brand products, such as Mountain Dew or Aquafina. This manager is accountable for increasing sales revenue *and* controlling costs to achieve profit goals for the entire brand or product line. Superiors evaluate the manager's performance by comparing actual revenues, expenses, and profits to the budget.

Investment Center

In an <u>investment center</u>, managers are responsible for (1) generating revenues, (2) controlling costs, and (3) efficiently managing the division's assets. Investment centers are generally large divisions of a corporation. For example, PepsiCo has six divisions:

- Frito-Lay North America
- Quaker Foods North America

- Latin America Foods
- PepsiCo Americas Beverages
- Europe
- Asia, Middle East, and Africa

Investment centers are treated almost as if they were stand-alone companies. Division managers generally have broad responsibility, including deciding how to use assets. As a result, managers are held responsible for generating as much profit as they can with those assets.

Organization Chart

Exhibit 10-2 shows a partial organization chart for a company such as PepsiCo.

- At the top level, the CEO oversees each of the divisions (*investment centers*).
- The manager of each division oversees all of the product lines (*profit centers*) in that division. For example, the VP of PepsiCo Americas Beverages is responsible for the profitable operation of Pepsi, Gatorade, Tropicana, Mountain Dew, Aquafina, and the company's other beverage brands.[1]
- The manager of each product line is responsible for evaluating lower-level managers of *cost centers* (such as manufacturing plants) and *revenue centers* (such as sales territories).

EXHIBIT 10-2 Partial Organization Chart

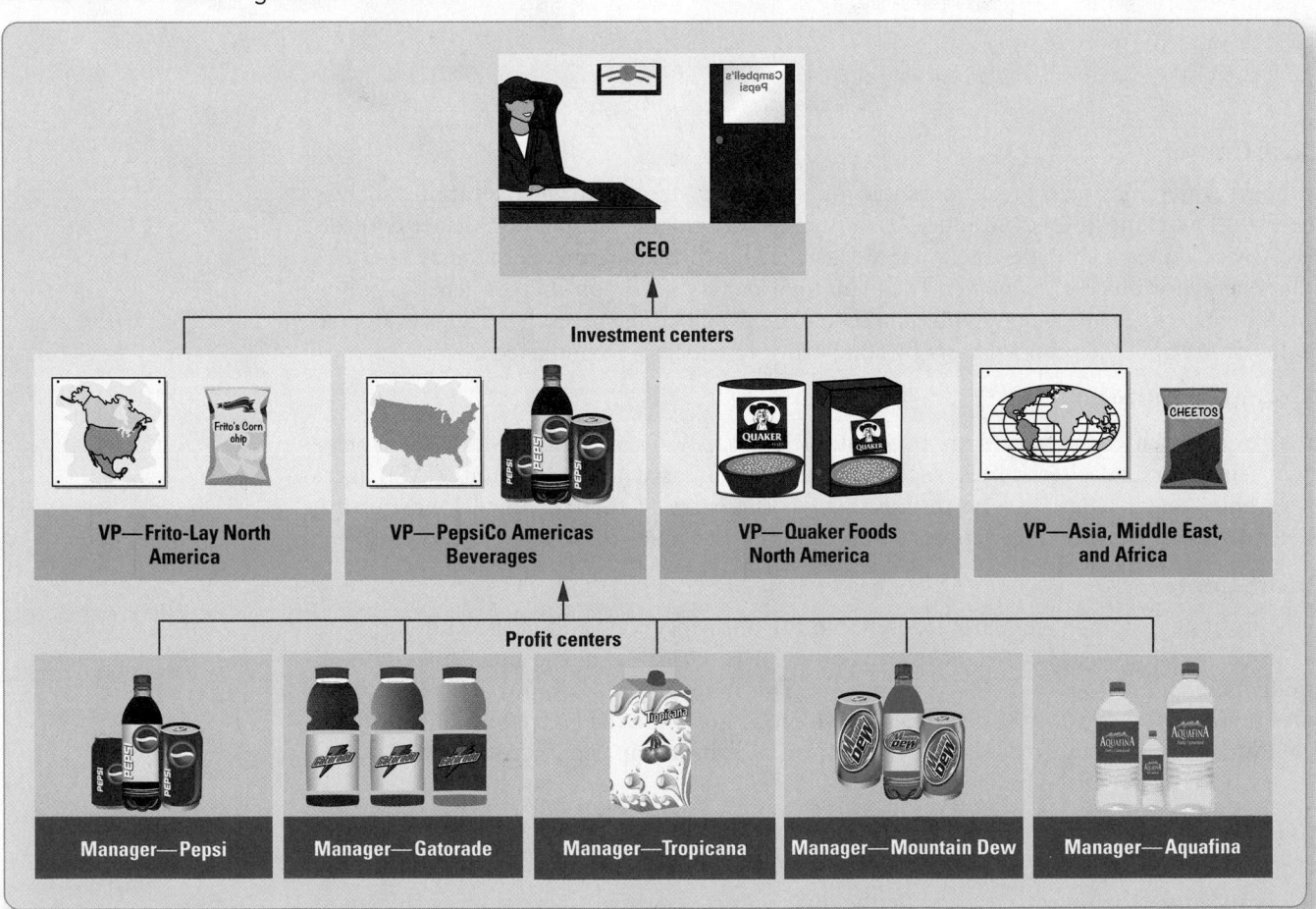

[1]For the sake of simplicity, we only illustrate four of the six divisions.

Responsibility Center Performance Reports

As introduced in Chapter 9, a **performance report** compares actual revenues and expenses against budgeted figures. The difference between actual and budget is known as a **variance**. The specific figures included on each performance report will depend on the type of responsibility center being evaluated. For example,

2 Develop performance reports

- the performance reports of cost centers will only include *costs* incurred within the center.
- the performance reports of revenue centers will only include the *revenues* generated by the center.

Exhibit 10-3 illustrates a partial performance report for a hypothetical revenue center—the hypothetical Midwest Sales Region of Frito-Lay products. Since the manager is only responsible for generating sales revenue, only revenues are included in the report.

EXHIBIT 10-3 Partial Performance Report for a Revenue Center

	A	B	C	D	E	F	G
1	Midwest Sales Region						
2	Monthly Performance Report						
3	For the Month Ended March 31						
4	Product	Actual Sales	Budgeted Sales	Variance		Variance Percentage	
5	Sun Chips	$ 2,367,200	$ 2,400,000	$ 32,800	U	1.37%	U
6	Doritos	15,896,000	15,000,000	896,000	F	5.97%	F
7	Lay's	9,325,500	9,000,000	325,500	F	3.62%	F
8	Tostitos	1,374,300	1,500,000	125,700	U	8.38%	U
9	Cheetos	13,678,400	13,500,000	178,400	F	1.32%	F
10	Fritos	4,683,100	4,500,000	183,100	F	4.07%	F
11	Total revenues	$ 47,324,500	$ 45,900,000	$ 1,424,500	F	3.10%	F
12							

NOTE: The budget variance is calculated as the variance divided by the budgeted amount. All figures in this report are hypothetical and do not reflect PepsiCo's actual sales or budgets for these products. These hypothetical figures are used strictly for teaching purposes.

As you see in Exhibit 10-3, variances are either favorable (F) or unfavorable (U).

- A **favorable variance** is one that causes operating income to be higher than budgeted. This occurs when actual revenues are higher than budgeted, or actual expenses are lower than budgeted.
- An **unfavorable variance** is one that causes operating income to be lower than budgeted. This occurs when actual revenues are lower than budgeted, or actual expenses are higher than budgeted.

Although favorable *revenue* variances are typically good news for the company, the same interpretation can be misleading when it comes to expense variances. Be careful *not* to interpret "favorable" expense variances as "good," and unfavorable expense variances as "bad."

- For example, a company could spend more than originally budgeted on research and development (R&D) in order to bring innovative new products to market faster. The resulting *unfavorable* variance for R&D expenses may actually be *good* news for the company.
- On the other hand, a manager may purchase lower-quality materials to generate cost savings. The resulting *favorable* materials cost variance would actually be *bad* news for the company, since it would most likely result in reducing the quality of the end product.

Most companies' accounting software will use positive and negative numbers to indicate whether a variance is favorable or unfavorable. The direction of the sign (positive or negative) will depend on whether the variance is calculated as budget minus actual,

Why is this important?

"Variances are always **favorable** or **unfavorable**, depending on whether they increase or decrease operating income. **Computer** software usually indicates the **directional** impact of the variance using **positive** and **negative** **numbers**, rather than a U or F notation."

or actual minus budget. Practice varies in this regard, especially when it comes to expense variances. To avoid any confusion over the direction of the sign, we use the U and F notation along with the absolute value of the variance. Just remember that when you are working with real companies, you will rarely see the U or F notation on the performance reports. Rather, you will see positive and negative variances that you will need to interpret using the definitions just presented.

Managers use a technique called **management by exception** when analyzing performance reports. Management by exception means that managers will only investigate budget variances that are relatively large. Let's use a personal example to illustrate this concept. Consider your monthly cell phone bill. You probably have an expectation of how large your monthly cell phone bill will be. If the actual bill is close to your expectation, you'll just pay the bill without giving it too much additional thought. However, if the actual bill is much higher or much lower than you expected, you probably will look at the detailed charges for calls, texts, and data usage to determine why the bill was so much different than what you expected.

Managers do the same thing. If the actual costs or revenues are close to budget, they assume operations are in control. However, if the variance between budget and actual is relatively large, they'll investigate the cause of the variance. Managers often have a decision rule for variance investigation that is expressed as a percentage, dollar amount, or a combination of the two. For example, the manager of the Midwest Sales Region may decide to investigate only those variances that are greater than 5% *and* $150,000. Exhibit 10-3 shows that the variance for both Doritos and Tostitos exceeds 5%. However, of the two, only the Doritos variance exceeds $150,000. Therefore, the manager would only investigate the Doritos variance.

Segment Margin

The performance reports of profit and investment centers include both revenues and expenses. Performance reports are often presented in the contribution margin format rather than the traditional income statement format. These reports often include a line called "segment margin." A **segment margin** is the operating income generated by a profit or investment center *before* subtracting common fixed costs that have been allocated to the center. For example, Exhibit 10-4 illustrates a hypothetical performance report for Tropicana products.

EXHIBIT 10-4 Performance Report Highlighting the Profit Center's Segment Margin

	A	B	C	D	E	F	G
1	Tropicana Products						
2	Segment Margin Performance Report for the Fiscal Year Ended December 31						
3	(all figures in millions of dollars)						
4	Product	Actual	Budgeted	Variance		Variance %	
5	Sales revenue	$ 4,314	$ 4,300	$ 14	F	0.3%	F
6	Less variable expenses:						
7	Variable cost of goods sold	1,728	1,720	8	U	0.5%	U
8	Variable operating expenses	508	515	7	F	1.4%	F
9	Contribution Margin	2,078	2,065	13	F	0.6%	F
10	Less direct fixed expenses:						
11	Fixed manufacturing overhead	1,228	1,215	13	U	1.1%	U
12	Fixed operating expenses	405	415	10	F	2.4%	F
13	Segment Margin	445	435	10	F	2.3%	F
14	Less: Common fixed expenses allocated to the profit center	36	35	1	U	2.9%	U
15	Operating income	$ 409	$ 400	$ 9	F	2.3%	F
16							

NOTE: All figures in this report are hypothetical and do not reflect the actual or budgeted sales and expense data for Tropicana products. These hypothetical figures are used strictly for teaching purposes.

As you look at Exhibit 10-4, notice that fixed expenses are separated into two categories:

- **Direct fixed expenses** include those fixed expenses that can be traced to the profit center. An example might include advertisements for Tropicana orange juice.

- **Common fixed expenses** include those fixed expenses that *cannot* be traced to the profit center. Rather, these are fixed expenses incurred by the overarching investment center (PepsiCo Americas Beverages) that have been allocated among the different profit centers in the division. For example, these allocated costs may include the division's cost of providing a common computer information system, human resources department, payroll department, and legal department. By sharing these services, the different product lines avoid duplication of the costs and assets that would otherwise need to be maintained by the individual profit centers.

Since the manager of the profit center has little to no control over the allocation of the common fixed expenses, he or she should not be held responsible for them.[2] Therefore, the manager is typically held responsible for the center's segment margin, not its operating income.

Organization-wide Performance Reports

Exhibit 10-5 illustrates how the performance reports for each level of management shown in Exhibit 10-2 flow *up* to the top of the company. Notice the following in the exhibit:

- The operating income from each profit center, such as Tropicana products (at the bottom of the exhibit), flows into the performance report for an investment center (in the middle of the exhibit).

- Likewise, the operating income from each investment center, such as PepsiCo Americas Beverages, flows into the performance report for the entire company (at the top of the exhibit).

- Costs incurred by corporate headquarters (shown in the top of the exhibit) are treated as a cost center and are typically not allocated to any of the divisions.

- In addition to those performance reports pictured, performance reports related to the cost and revenue centers under each profit center would exist and flow up to the profit centers.

Responsibility accounting assigns managers responsibility for their segment's performance. But superiors should not misuse the system to erroneously find fault or place blame. Some variances are controllable, while others are not.

For example, managers have no control over the general economic conditions of the country that may reduce sales. Nor do they have control over droughts, floods, and frosts that increase the cost of the agricultural materials in their products. Likewise, they have little or no control over the cost of electricity and gas used to power plants and deliver products. Managers need to carefully consider the causes of large variances so that they can focus on improving those that are controllable, while developing strategies for minimizing the risk associated with uncontrollable variances.

Evaluation of Investment Centers

As discussed above, investment centers are typically large divisions of a company. The duties of an investment center manager are similar to those of a CEO of an entire company. Investment center managers are responsible for *both* generating profit *and* making the best use of the investment center's assets. For example, an investment center manager has the authority to decide how much inventory to hold, what types of investments to make, how aggressively to collect accounts receivable, and whether to open new stores or close old ones. In this section, we'll look at the two performance measures most commonly used

3 Calculate ROI, sales margin, and capital turnover

---

[2]The various methods used to allocate centralized service expenses and other common fixed expenses are covered in more advanced cost accounting textbooks.

EXHIBIT 10-5 Organization-wide Performance Reports

		Actual	Budgeted	Variance		Variance %	
		PepsiCo					
		Performance Report for the Fiscal Year Ended December 31					
		(all figures in millions of dollars)					
Division Operating Income		**Actual**	**Budgeted**	**Variance**		**Variance %**	
Frito-Lay North America		$ 3,646	$ 3,500	$ 146	F	4.2%	F
Quaker Foods North America		695	680	15	F	2.2%	F
Latin Americas Foods		1,059	1,065	6	U	0.6%	U
PepsiCo Americas Beverages		2,937	2,900	37	F	1.3%	F
Europe		1,330	1,335	5	U	0.4%	U
Asia, Middle East, and Africa		747	750	3	U	0.4%	U
Corporate, unallocated		(1,302)	(1,300)	2	U	0.2%	U
Total operating income		$ 9,112	$ 8,930	$ 182	F	2.0%	F

		PepsiCo Americas Beverages					
		Performance Report for the Fiscal Year Ended December 31					
		(all figures in millions of dollars)					
Product Line Operating Income		**Actual**	**Budgeted**	**Variance**		**Variance %**	
Pepsi		$ 912	$ 900	$ 12	F	1.3%	F
Mountain Dew		445	450	5	U	1.1%	U
Gatorade		616	600	16	F	2.7%	F
Aquafina		347	350	3	U	0.9%	U
Tropicana		409	400	9	F	2.3%	F
Sierra Mist		77	75	2	F	2.7%	F
Other beverages		131	125	6	F	4.8%	F
Total division operating income		$ 2,937	$ 2,900	$ 37	F	1.3%	F

		Tropicana					
		Performance Report for the Fiscal Year Ended December 31					
		(all figures in millions of dollars)					
		Actual	**Budgeted**	**Variance**		**Variance %**	
Sales revenue		$ 4,314	$ 4,300	$ 14	F	0.3%	F
Less: Variable expenses		2,236	2,235	1	U	0.0%	U
Contribution margin		2,078	2,065	13	F	0.6%	F
Less: Direct fixed expenses		1,633	1,630	3	U	0.2%	U
Segment margin		445	435	10	F	2.3%	F
Less: Allocated common expenses		36	35	1	U	2.9%	U
Operating income		$ 409	$ 400	$ 9	F	2.3%	F

NOTE: All figures in this exhibit, except for the actual operating income of each division for 2012 are hypothetical and used strictly for teaching purposes.

to assess the performance of investment centers: (1) return on investment and (2) residual income. To do this, we'll first need some financial data.

Exhibit 10-6 shows actual 2012 data for two of PepsiCo's divisions.[3] Statement of Financial Accounting Standards Number 131 (SFAS 131) requires publically traded companies to disclose this type of segment information in the footnotes to their financial statements.[4]

[3]PepsiCo Inc. 2012 10(K).
[4]SFAS 131, "Disclosures about Segments of an Enterprise and Related Information," June 1997, Financial Accounting Standards Board, Norwalk, CT.

EXHIBIT 10-6 Division Information for PepsiCo Inc.

2012 Division Data (All figures are in millions of dollars)	Operating Income	Assets	Sales Revenue
PepsiCo Americas Beverages ("Beverage")	$2,937	$30,899	$21,408
Frito-Lay North America ("Snack")	$3,646	$ 5,332	$13,574

Exhibit 10-6 shows that the Frito-Lay North America division (henceforth referred to as the Snack division) is providing more profit to the company than is PepsiCo Americas Beverages (henceforth referred to as the Beverage division) division. However, a simple comparison between the operating income of each division is misleading because it does not consider the size of each division. To adequately evaluate an investment center's financial performance, top managers assess each division's operating income *in relationship to its assets*. This relationship is typically evaluated by calculating the division's return on investment or residual income.

Return on Investment (ROI)

<u>Return on investment (ROI)</u> measures the amount of income an investment center earns relative to the size of its assets. Companies typically define ROI as follows:

> ### Why is this important?
>
> "**ROI** is one of the most commonly used **performance** metrics. It allows management to view profitability in **relation** to the size of the **investment**. Just like with your own personal investments, the **higher** the return, the **better**."

$$ROI = \frac{\text{Operating income}}{\text{Total assets}}$$

Let's calculate the ROI for both the Snack division and the Beverage division, using the income and assets of each division found in Exhibit 10-6:

$$\text{Beverage Division ROI} = \frac{2,937}{30,899} = 9.5\% \text{ (rounded)}$$

$$\text{Snack Division ROI} = \frac{3,646}{5,332} = 68.4\% \text{ (rounded)}$$

The resulting ROI indicates that the Snack division is generating much more income for every dollar of its assets than is the Beverage division:

■ The Beverage division earns nearly $0.10 on every $1.00 of assets.

■ The Snack division earns just over $0.68 on every $1.00 of assets.

If you had $1,000 to invest, would you rather invest it in the Beverage division or the Snack division? Management would much rather have a 68% return on its investment than a 10% return. When top management decides how to invest excess funds, they often consider each division's ROI. A division with a higher ROI is more likely to receive extra funds because it has a track record of providing a higher return with the investment. However, perhaps management feels that operations could be improved in a weaker division by investing in new technology, plants, and equipment. Thus, the division with a weaker ROI may also receive an infusion of capital.

In addition to comparing ROI across divisions, management also compares a division's ROI across time to determine whether the division is becoming more or less profitable. For example, Exhibit 10-7 shows the actual ROI of the two divisions over the past five years.

EXHIBIT 10-7 Actual Division ROI Over Time (rounded)

ROI (rounded)	2012	2011	2010	2009	2008
Beverage..............................	10%	11%	9%	28%	26%
Snack	68%	67%	64%	51%	47%

The ROI of the Snack division has been trending upwards over the last five years. However, the big decline in ROI in the Beverage division was primarily a result of acquisitions made in 2010. As with variances, management will investigate significant changes in ROI.

In addition to benchmarking ROI over time, management often benchmarks divisional ROI with other companies in the same industry to determine how each division is performing compared to its competitors. For example, PepsiCo may benchmark its ROI against that of the Coca-Cola Company.

Sales Margin and Capital Turnover

To determine what is driving a division's ROI, management often restates the ROI equation in its expanded form:

$$\text{ROI} = \frac{\text{Operating income}}{\text{Sales}} \times \frac{\text{Sales}}{\text{Total assets}} = \frac{\text{Operating income}}{\text{Total assets}}$$

Notice that sales, or sales revenue, is incorporated in the denominator of the first term and in the numerator of the second term. When the two terms are multiplied together, Sales revenue cancels out, leaving the original ROI formula.

Why do managers rewrite the ROI formula this way? Because it helps them better understand how they can improve their ROI. The first term in the expanded equation is the **sales margin**, which focuses on profitability by showing how much operating income the division earns on every $1 of sales revenue. Sales margin is defined as:

$$\text{Sales margin} = \frac{\text{Operating income}}{\text{Sales}}$$

Let's calculate each division's sales margin using the information in Exhibit 10-6:

$$\text{Beverage Division Sales Margin} = \frac{2,937}{21,408} = 13.7\% \text{ (rounded)}$$

$$\text{Snack Division Sales Margin} = \frac{3,646}{13,574} = 26.9\% \text{ (rounded)}$$

The Beverage division is earning nearly $0.14 on every $1.00 of sales revenue, whereas the Snack division is earning nearly $0.27 on every $1.00 of sales revenue. Overall, the products in the Snack division are nearly twice as profitable as the products in the Beverage division. To improve this statistic, the division manager needs to focus on cutting costs so that more operating income can be earned for every dollar of sales revenue. However, they'll need to be careful in cutting costs, so as not to jeopardize the long-term success of the division.

Next, let's consider each division's **capital turnover**, which focuses on how efficiently the division uses its assets to generate sales revenue. Capital turnover is defined as:

$$\text{Capital turnover} = \frac{\text{Sales}}{\text{Total assets}}$$

Let's calculate each division's capital turnover using the information from Exhibit 10-6:

$$\text{Beverage Division Capital Turnover} = \frac{21,408}{30,899} = 0.69 \text{ (rounded)}$$

$$\text{Snack Division Capital Turnover} = \frac{13,574}{5,332} = 2.55 \text{ (rounded)}$$

The Beverage division has a capital turnover of 0.69, which means the division generates \$0.69 of sales revenue with every \$1 of assets. The Snack division generates \$2.55 of sales revenue with every \$1.00 of assets. The Snack division uses its assets more efficiently in generating sales than does the Beverage division. To improve this statistic, the Beverage division manager should try to reduce or eliminate non-productive assets—for example, by collecting accounts receivables more aggressively or decreasing inventory levels.

As the following table shows, the Snack division's ROI is higher than that of the Beverage division because (1) the division is earning more profit on every dollar of sales, *and* (2) the division is generating more sales revenue with every dollar of assets:

	Sales Margin × Capital Turnover = ROI		
Beverage	13.7%	× 0.69	= 9.5% (rounded)
Snack	26.9%	× 2.55	= 68.6% (rounded)

Residual Income (RI)

Rather than using ROI to evaluate the performance of their investment centers, many companies use the concept of residual income. Similar to ROI, the residual income calculation is based on both the division's operating income and its assets, thereby measuring the division's profitability with respect to the size of its assets. However, the residual income calculation incorporates one more important piece of information: management's target rate of return. The target rate of return is the minimum acceptable rate of return that top management expects a division to earn with its assets. Management's target rate of return is based on many factors. Some of these factors include:

- the risk level of the division's business
- interest rates
- investor's expectations
- return being earned by other divisions
- general economic conditions

As these factors change over time, management's target rate of return will also change.

Residual income (RI) determines whether the division has created any excess (or residual) income above and beyond management's expectations. Residual income is calculated as follows:

$$\text{RI} = \text{Operating income} - \text{Minimum acceptable income}$$

The minimum acceptable income is defined as top management's target rate of return multiplied by the division's total assets. Thus,

$$\text{RI} = \text{Operating income} - (\text{Target rate of return} \times \text{Total assets})$$

Notice in this equation that the RI compares the division's actual operating income with the minimum operating income that top management expects *given the size of the division's assets*. A positive RI means that the division's operating income exceeds top management's target rate of return. A negative RI means the division is not meeting the target rate of return.

Let's calculate the residual income for the Beverage division, assuming a 25% target rate of return:[5]

$$\text{Beverage RI} = \$2,937 - (25\% \times \$30,899) = (\$4,788) \text{ rounded}$$

The Beverage division's RI is negative. This means that the division did not use its assets as effectively as top management expected, and was therefore unable to achieve the minimum ROI of 25%. Recall that the Beverage division's ROI was approximately 10%.

Let's also calculate the RI for the Snack division:

$$\text{Snack division RI} = \$3,646 - (25\% \times \$5,332) = \$2,313$$

The positive RI indicates that the Snack division exceeded top management's 25% target return expectations. The RI calculation also confirms what we learned about the Snack division's ROI. Recall that the Snack division's ROI was almost 69%, which is higher than the targeted minimum of 25%.

Exhibit 10-8 summarizes the performance measures we have just discussed.

EXHIBIT 10-8 Summary of Investment Center Performance Measures

Performance Measure	Formula
ROI	$\text{ROI} = \dfrac{\text{Operating income}}{\text{Total assets}}$
Sales Margin	$\text{Sales margin} = \dfrac{\text{Operating income}}{\text{Sales}}$
Capital Turnover	$\text{Capital turnover} = \dfrac{\text{Sales}}{\text{Total assets}}$
Residual Income	$\text{RI} = \text{Operating income} - (\text{Target rate of return} \times \text{Total assets})$

Goal Congruence

Since the ROI calculation already shows managers whether or not the division has reached the target rate of return, why do some companies prefer using residual income rather than ROI? The answer is that residual income often leads to better goal congruence. For example, say a manager is considering investing in a new $100,000 piece of equipment that would provide $30,000 of annual income. Upper management would want the divisions to invest in this equipment because its return (30%) exceeds the target rate (25%). But what will the division managers do?

■ If evaluated based on residual income, division managers will invest in the equipment because it will increase the division's residual income by $5,000 [=$30,000 − (25% × $100,000)].

■ If evaluated based on ROI, the division manager's decision may depend on its current ROI. If the division's current ROI is *less than* 30%, the manager has an incentive to invest in the equipment in order to *increase* the division's overall ROI. However,

[5]Management's actual target rate of return is unknown; 25% is used simply for illustrative purposes.

if the division's current ROI is *greater than* 30%, investing in the equipment would *decrease* the division's ROI. In this case, the manager would probably *not* invest in the equipment.

Thus, residual income enhances goal congruence, whereas ROI may or may not.

Quaker Foods North America is another one of PepsiCo's divisions. For fiscal year 2012, the division had assets of $966 million, operating income of $695 million, and sales revenue of $2,636 million.

1. Compute Quaker's ROI, sales margin, and capital turnover.
2. Compute Quaker's residual income, assuming the minimum acceptable rate of return is 25%.

Please see page 640 for solutions.

Measurement Issues

The ROI and RI calculations appear to be very straightforward; however, management must make some decisions before these calculations can be made. Most of these decisions involve how to measure the assets used in the ROI and RI calculations.

■ *Which balance sheet date should we use?* Because total assets will differ between the beginning of the period and the end of the period, companies must choose a particular point in time for measuring assets. In the PepsiCo example, we chose to use total assets at the *end* of the year. Some companies use the average of the beginning of the year and end of the year.

■ *Should we include all assets?* Management must also decide if it wants to include *all* assets in the total asset figure. Many companies with retail locations are continually buying land on which to build future retail outlets. Until those stores are built and opened, the land (including any construction in progress) is a nonproductive asset, which is not generating any operating income. Including nonproductive assets in the total asset figure will drive down ROI and RI. Therefore, some firms do not include nonproductive assets in these calculations.

■ *Should we use the gross book value or net book value of the assets?* The **gross book value** is the historical cost of the assets. The **net book value** is the historical cost of the assets *less* accumulated depreciation. Using the net book value of assets has a definite drawback. Because of depreciation, the net book value of assets continues to decrease over time until the assets are fully depreciated. As a result, ROI and RI get *larger over time simply because of depreciation* rather than from actual improvements in operations.

In general, calculating ROI based on the net book value of assets gives managers incentive to continue using old, outdated equipment because the net book value of the asset keeps decreasing. However, top management may want the division to invest in new technology to create operational efficiency. The long-term effects of using outdated equipment may be devastating as competitors use new technology to produce cheaper products and sell at lower prices. Thus, to create goal congruence, some firms prefer calculating ROI based on the gross book value of assets or even based on the assets' current replacement cost, rather than the assets' net book value.

■ *Should we make other adjustments to income or assets?* Some companies use a modified residual income calculation referred to as economic value added (EVA®). To arrive at EVA, managers make several adjustments to the way income and assets are measured in the residual income formula. For example, research and development expenses are often added back to income (not viewed as expenses) while total assets are usually reduced by the company's current liabilities. EVA calculations are covered in more advanced accounting and finance textbooks.

Limitations of Financial Performance Evaluation

Because companies have traditionally existed to generate profit for their owners, performance evaluation has historically revolved around financial performance. However, financial performance measurement has limitations. For example, one serious drawback of financial performance measures is their short-term focus. Companies usually prepare performance reports and calculate ROI and RI using a time frame of one year or less. If upper management uses a short time frame, division managers have an incentive to take actions that will lead to an immediate increase in these measures, even if such actions may not be in the company's long-term interest (such as cutting back on R&D or advertising).

On the other hand, many potentially positive actions may take longer than one year to generate income at the targeted level. Many *product life cycles* start slow, even incurring losses in the early stages, before generating profit. If managers are evaluated on short-term financial performance only, they may be hesitant to introduce new products that may take time to generate acceptable profits.

As a potential remedy, management can measure financial performance using a longer time horizon, such as three to five years. Extending the time frame gives segment managers the incentive to think long term rather than short term and make decisions that will positively impact the company over the next several years.

As discussed earlier in this book, many companies are incorporating the triple bottom line (people, planet, and profit) into their performance evaluation systems. The second half of this chapter describes how the inclusion of nonfinancial performance metrics, including environmental metrics, can give managers a more "balanced" view of the company's performance.

What is Transfer Pricing?

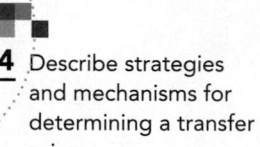

4 Describe strategies and mechanisms for determining a transfer price

In large, diversified companies, one division will often buy products or components from another division rather than buying them from an outside supplier. For example, one division of General Electric may purchase some of the parts it needs to produce wind turbines from another division that makes those parts. The price charged for the internal sale of product between two different divisions of the same company is known as the **transfer price**.

The transfer price becomes sales revenue for the selling division, and a cost for the buying division. Therefore, the operating income, ROI, sales margin, and residual income of each division will be affected by the transfer price that is used. Setting a fair transfer price is often difficult since each division will want to maximize its own profits. The selling division will want the price to be as high as possible, while the buying division will want the price to be as low as possible.

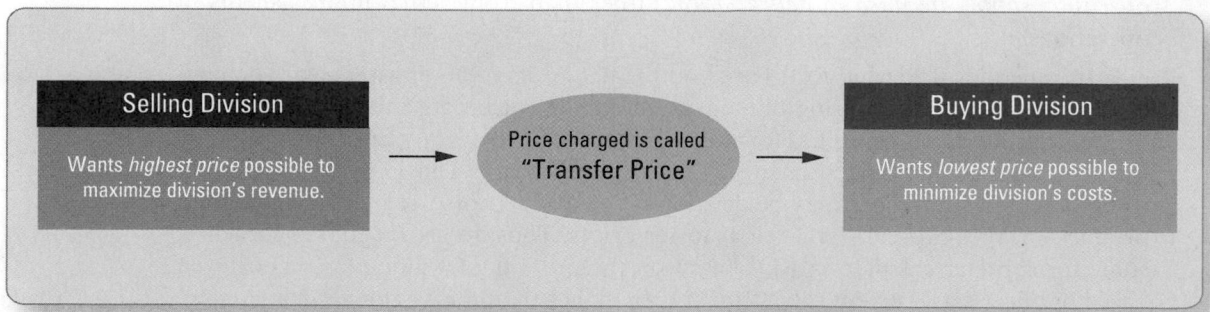

In selecting the transfer price, management's ultimate goal should be to optimize the company's *overall* profitability by encouraging a transfer to take place *only* if the company would benefit by the exchange. This benefit is usually a result of cost savings. For example, if excess capacity exists, the incremental cost of manufacturing additional product for an internal sale is the variable cost of production. Furthermore, the selling division can often avoid certain marketing or distribution costs on internal sales. <u>Vertical integration</u>, the practice of purchasing other companies within one's supply chain, is predicated by the notion that a company's profits can be maximized by owning one's supplier.

Strategies and Mechanisms for Determining a Transfer Price

The following strategies are often used to determine the transfer price.

1. **Market price:** If an outside market for the product exists, the market price is often viewed as the fairest price to use. The selling division will obtain the sales revenue it would have received on an outside sale, and the buying division will pay what it would have paid for product from an outside supplier. If the selling division can save on marketing or distribution costs, the market price could be reduced by all or a portion of the cost savings in arriving at the transfer price.

2. **Negotiated price:** Division managers negotiate until they reach agreement on a transfer price. The negotiated transfer price will usually be somewhere between the variable cost and the market price. The *lowest* acceptable price to the selling division will be the variable cost of producing and selling the product. Any lower price would result in a negative contribution margin to the selling division. The *highest* acceptable price to the buying division will be the market price. Any higher price would result in additional cost to the buying division. The disadvantage of this method is that negotiation takes time and effort, and may cause friction between company managers.

3. **Cost:** If no outside market for the product exists, then some definition of cost is often used to set the transfer price. As noted, variable cost would be the lowest fair price to use if excess capacity exists whereas full absorption cost (including fixed manufacturing overhead) is also often viewed as a reasonable price. Additionally, a profit markup can be added to either definition of cost to arrive at fair transfer price. The disadvantage of this method is that the selling division has no incentive to control costs since it will be reimbursed by the buying division for the costs it incurs.

These strategies are summarized in Exhibit 10-9.

> **■ Why is this important?**
>
> "Each division's **profits** will be affected by the **transfer price** that is used. The **selling division** will want the price to be as **high** as possible, whereas the **buying division** will want it to be as **low** as possible."

EXHIBIT 10-9 Strategies for Determining Transfer Price

	Advantages	Disadvantages	Considerations
Market Price	Usually viewed as fair by both parties.	Can only be used if an outside market exists.	The market price could be reduced by any cost savings occurring from the internal sale (e.g., marketing costs).
Negotiated Price	Allows division managers to act autonomously rather than being dictated a transfer price by top management.	Takes time and effort. May lead to friction (or better understanding) between division managers.	Negotiated transfer price will generally fall in the range between: • Variable cost (low end) • Market price (high end)
Cost -or- Cost Plus a Markup	Useful if a market price is not available.	Selling division has no incentive to control costs. A "fair" markup may be difficult to determine.	Several definitions of cost could be used, ranging from variable cost to full absorption cost.

Let's try an example. Assume a division of GE produces a component used in the assembly of wind turbines. The division's manufacturing costs and variable selling expenses related to the component are as follows:

	Cost per Unit
Direct materials..	$500
Direct labor..	75
Variable manufacturing overhead	100
Fixed manufacturing overhead (at current production level)......................	150
Variable selling expenses (only incurred on sales to outside customers)....................	80

A different division of GE is just beginning to get into the turbine assembly business and is interested in purchasing the component in-house rather than buying it from an outside supplier. The production division has sufficient excess capacity with which to make the extra components. Because of competition, the market price for this component is $1,000 regardless of whether the component is produced by GE or another company.

1. *What is the highest, and possibly fairest, acceptable transfer price?* The highest acceptable transfer price is the market price of $1,000. Many would say that this is also the fairest price because the selling division would receive, and the buying division would pay, what it normally would on the open market for the component.

2. *Assuming the transfer price is negotiated between the divisions, what would be the lowest acceptable transfer price?* Because there is excess capacity, fixed costs would not increase as a result of the additional production volume; therefore, fixed costs become irrelevant. The lowest acceptable price would be the variable costs incurred by the selling division for making the component and selling it in-house. The variable manufacturing costs (direct materials, direct labor, and variable manufacturing overhead) add up to $675. In this particular case, the $80 of variable selling expense would *not* be considered because it is only incurred on sales to outside customers. Thus, the lowest acceptable transfer price would be $675. A transfer price lower than $675 would result in a negative contribution margin, which would result in a loss to the selling division. If the $80 of variable selling expense would be incurred regardless of whether the sale was made in-house or to an outside customer, then the lowest acceptable transfer price would be $755 (= $675 + $80).

3. *If GE's policy requires all in-house transfers to occur at full absorption cost plus 10%, what transfer price would be used? Assume that the increased production level needed to fill the transfer would result in fixed manufacturing overhead (MOH) decreasing by $25 per unit.* The full absorption cost includes all manufacturing costs (direct materials, direct labor, variable MOH, and fixed MOH). After ramping up production to fill this in-house order, the fixed MOH per unit would be $125 (= $150 − $25). Thus, the full absorption cost would be $800 (= $500 + $75 + $100 + $125). The transfer price would be $880, which is 10% over the full absorption cost [= $800 + (10% × $800)].

Global Considerations

In addition to these strategies for setting the transfer price, management should consider the following factors if the divisions operate in different areas of the globe:

- Do the divisions operate under different taxing authorities such that income tax rates are higher for one division than the other?
- Would the amount paid for customs and duties be impacted by the transfer price used?

If either of these situations exist, then management will want to carefully craft the transfer price to avoid as much income tax, customs, and duties as legally possible.

As you can see, setting an optimal transfer price involves careful analysis. Keep in mind that internal sales should only be encouraged if the company, overall, would profit by the exchange taking place. This additional profit is usually the result of cost savings that occur from producing the product internally rather than buying it on the open market. Any transfer price selected is simply a mechanism for dividing this additional profit between the selling and the buying divisions.

In the next half of the chapter, we'll explain flexible budgeting and the balanced scorecard. These are two additional tools that companies often use to extend the way they evaluate performance.

Decision Guidelines

Performance Evaluation

Let's consider some issues regarding performance evaluation.

Decision	Guidelines
How do companies decentralize?	Managers determine the type of segmentation that best suits the company's strategy. Companies often decentralize by geographic area, product line, distribution channel, customer base, or business function.
What should managers be held responsible for?	**Cost center:** Manager is responsible for costs. **Revenue center:** Manager is responsible for revenues. **Profit center:** Manager is responsible for both revenues and costs and, therefore, profits. **Investment center:** Manager is responsible for revenues, costs, and the efficient use of the assets invested in the division.
How should upper management evaluate the performance of the responsibility centers and their managers?	Actual performance should be compared with the budget. Using management by exception, any large variances should be investigated, with an emphasis on uncovering information, rather than placing blame.
How are variances interpreted?	Favorable (F) variances increase income from what was budgeted, while Unfavorable (U) variances decrease income. Favorable cost variances are not necessarily "good" and unfavorable cost variances are not necessarily "bad."
What is a segment margin?	A segment margin is the operating income achieved by the segment *before* subtracting any common fixed costs that have been allocated to the segment.
What additional measures are used to evaluate investment centers?	ROI and residual income—both performance measures evaluate the division in terms of how profitable the division is relative to the size of its assets.
How is ROI calculated?	$$\text{ROI} = \frac{\text{Operating income}}{\text{Total assets}}$$ ROI can also be calculated as: $$\text{Sales margin} \times \text{Capital turnover}$$
How is sales margin calculated?	$$\text{Sales margin} = \frac{\text{Operating income}}{\text{Sales}}$$ The sales margin tells managers how much operating income is earned on every $1 of sales revenue.
How is capital turnover calculated?	$$\text{Capital turnover} = \frac{\text{Sales}}{\text{Total assets}}$$ The capital turnover tells managers how much sales revenue is generated for every $1 of assets invested in the division.
How is residual income calculated?	$$\text{RI} = \text{Operating income} - (\text{Target rate of return} \times \text{Total assets})$$ If residual income is positive, it means the division has earned income in excess of upper management's target rate of return. If it is negative, then the division has not met management's expectations.
What is a transfer price and how is it determined?	A transfer price is the price charged between divisions for the internal sale of a product. The transfer price is often based on the following: • Market price of product • Negotiated price (usually between variable cost and market price) • Cost (variable or absorption) or cost plus a markup

SUMMARY PROBLEM 1

The following table contains actual segment data for two of PepsiCo's geographic divisions: (1) Europe and (2) Asia, Middle East, and Africa (AMEA).

2012 Data (All figures are in millions of dollars)	Operating Income	Assets	Sales Revenue
Europe	$1,330	$19,218	$13,441
Asia, Middle East, and Africa (AMEA)	747	5,738	6,653

Requirements

1. Compute each division's ROI.
2. Compute each division's sales margin.
3. Compute each division's capital turnover.
4. Comment on the results of the preceding calculations.
5. Compute each division's residual income, assuming upper management desires a 25% minimum rate of return.
6. How does the ROI of these two divisions compare to that of the two divisions, Beverages and Snacks, discussed in the chapter?

▪ SOLUTIONS

1. ROI

$$\text{Europe ROI} = \frac{1,330}{19,218} = 6.9\% \text{ (rounded)}$$

$$\text{AMEA ROI} = \frac{747}{5,738} = 13.0\% \text{ (rounded)}$$

2. Sales Margin

$$\text{Europe sales margin} = \frac{1,330}{13,441} = 9.9\% \text{ (rounded)}$$

$$\text{AMEA sales margin} = \frac{747}{6,653} = 11.2\% \text{ (rounded)}$$

3. Capital Turnover

$$\text{Europe capital turnover} = \frac{13,441}{19,218} = 0.70 \text{ (rounded)}$$

$$\text{AMEA capital turnover} = \frac{6,653}{5,738} = 1.16 \text{ (rounded)}$$

4. Europe has a lower ROI (6.9%) than does AMEA (13%). The reason for AMEA's stronger performance lies both in its ability to generate more operating income on every dollar of sales, as shown by the sales margin (11.2% vs. 9.9%), and its ability to generate more sales with its assets, as shown by the capital turnover rate (1.16 versus 0.70). To increase ROI, the Europe division needs to concentrate on becoming more efficient with its assets in order to increase its capital turnover. At the same time, it needs to carefully cut costs, potentially through employing lean thinking, in order to increase its sales margin.

5. Residual Income

$$\text{Europe RI} = \$1,330 - (25\% \times \$19,218) = (\$3,475) \text{ (rounded)}$$

$$\text{AMEA RI} = \$747 - (25\% \times \$5,738) = (\$688) \text{ (rounded)}$$

Assuming management's minimum acceptable rate of return is 25%, the negative residual income means that neither division is generating income at an acceptable level.

6. The ROI provided by Europe (6.9%) and the ROI provided by Asia (13.0%) are in the same range as the ROI provided by the Beverage division (9.5%) but are significantly lower than the ROI provided by the Snack division (68.6%).

How do Managers Use Flexible Budgets to Evaluate Performance?

In the first part of this chapter we looked at performance reports that compared actual costs with budgeted amounts. There is nothing wrong with comparing actual results against the master planning budget. Many companies do so. However, managers usually gain better insights by comparing actual results against a **flexible budget**, which is a budget prepared for a different level of volume than that which was originally anticipated.

To illustrate this concept, let's return to Tucson Tortilla, the company we used in Chapter 9 to illustrate budgeting. Exhibit 10-10 shows a performance report for sales revenue and operating expenses that compares actual results against the master (planning) budget. The budgeted information was taken from the Sales Budget (see Exhibit 9-5) and Operating Expenses Budget (see Exhibit 9-10), while the actual results were gathered from the company's general ledger.

5 Prepare and evaluate flexible budget performance reports

EXHIBIT 10-10 Master Budget Performance Report

A	B	C	D	E	F	G
	Tucson Tortilla					
	Master Budget Performance Report: Sales and Operating Expenses					
	For the Month Ended March 31					
	Actual	Master Budget	Master Budget Variance		Master Budget Variance %	
Sales volume (number of cases sold)	28,724	25,000	3,724	F	14.9%	F
Sales revenue ($20 per case)	$ 603,225	$ 500,000	$ 103,225	F	20.6%	F
Operating expenses:						
Variable operating expenses:						
Sales commission ($1.50 per case sold)	$ 45,960	$ 37,500	$ 8,460	U	22.6%	U
Shipping expense ($2.00 per case sold)	54,578	50,000	4,578	U	9.2%	U
Bad debt expense (1% of credit sales)	5,127	4,000	1,127	U	28.2%	U
Fixed operating expenses:						
Salaries	21,000	20,000	1,000	U	5.0%	U
Office rent	4,000	4,000	0		0.0%	
Depreciation	6,000	6,000	0		0.0%	
Advertising	2,800	2,000	800	U	40.0%	U
Telephone and Internet	980	1,000	20	F	2.0%	F
Total operating expenses	$ 140,445	$ 124,500	$ 15,945	U	12.8%	U

NOTE: The company expects 80% of sales will be made on credit terms.

The difference between the actual revenues and expenses and the master budget is known as a **master budget variance**. This variance is really the result of an "apples-to-oranges" comparison. Why is this the case? Notice how the comparison is made between actual results for one volume (28,724 cases) and the budgeted revenues and costs for the planning volume (25,000). Of course, we would expect the actual revenues and variable expenses to be higher than budgeted simply because sales volume was 14.9% higher than budgeted. However, we wouldn't expect fixed costs to change as long as the actual volume was still within the relevant range of operations. But notice that actual expenses were 0% to 40% higher than expected. Management will want to understand why these variances occurred.

To provide more of an "apples-to-apples" comparison, many companies compare actual results to a flexible budget prepared *for the*

Why is this important?

"A **flexible** budget performance report allows management to make an **"apples-to-apples"** comparison between what **actually** happened and what would have been **budgeted** if management would have known, in advance, the **actual** sales **volume** for the period."

actual volume achieved. This flexible budget will be used strictly for evaluating performance. Notice the distinction between the purposes of the two budgets:

- The original master budget for 25,000 cases was used for *planning purposes at the beginning of the period*.
- The new flexible budget for 28,724 cases will be used for *performance evaluation purposes at the end of the period*.

In essence, the flexible budget is the budget managers *would have* prepared at the beginning of the period if they had a crystal ball telling them the correct volume. The flexible budget allows managers to compare actual revenues and expenses with what they would have expected them to be given the actual volume. By creating a flexible budget, managers will be able to determine the portion of the master budget variance that is due to unanticipated volume and the portion of the master budget variance that is due to causes other than volume.

Creating a Flexible Budget Performance Report

To create a flexible budget like the one shown in Exhibit 10-11, managers simply use the actual volume achieved (28,724 cases) and the original budget assumptions (shown in parentheses). For example, the flexible budget shown in Exhibit 10-11 (in boldface) includes the following calculations:

- Sales Revenue: 28,724 cases × $20 per case = $574,480
- Sales Commission: 28,724 cases × $1.50 per case = $43,086
- Shipping Expense: 28,724 cases × $2.00 per case = $57,448
- Bad Debt Expense: $574,480 of flexible budget sales revenue × 80% credit × 1% = $4,596
- Fixed Operating Expense: should not be affected by changes in volume. Therefore, the flexible budget amounts are the same as originally budgeted in the master budget.

EXHIBIT 10-11 Flexible Budget Performance Report

	A	B	C	D	E	F	G	H
1			Tucson Tortilla					
2		Flexible Budget Performance Report: Sales and Operating Expenses						
3		For the Month Ended March 31						
4								
5		Actual	Flexible Budget Variance		Flexible Budget	Volume Variance		Master Budget
6	**Sales volume (number of cases sold)**	28,724			28,724			25,000
7								
8	Sales revenue ($20 per case)	$ 603,225			$ 574,480			$ 500,000
9	Operating expenses:							
10	*Variable operating expenses:*							
11	Sales commission ($1.50 per case sold)	$ 45,960			$ 43,086			$ 37,500
12	Shipping expense ($2.00 per case sold)	54,578			57,448			50,000
13	Bad debt expense (1% of credit sales)	5,127			4,596			4,000
14	*Fixed operating expenses:*							
15	Salaries	21,000			20,000			20,000
16	Office rent	4,000			4,000			4,000
17	Depreciation	6,000			6,000			6,000
18	Advertising	2,800			2,000			2,000
19	Telephone and Internet	980			1,000			1,000
20	Total operating expenses	$ 140,445			$ 138,130			$ 124,500
21								

NOTE: The company expects 80% of sales will be made on credit terms.

Notice how this performance report includes the same actual costs and master budget figures shown in Exhibit 10-10. In addition, the flexible budget is placed in the middle column of the performance report. Two columns flank the middle column: Volume Variance and the Flexible Budget Variance.

Sam operates his own summer lawn-mowing business using a truck and equipment used solely for business purposes. Sam budgets $10 per job for variable expenses (gas for his truck and equipment) and $500 per month for fixed expenses (insurance and lease payments). Sam expected to have 100 mowing jobs during the month of June, but actually had 125.

How much should be reflected in the flexible budget for (1) variable expenses, (2) fixed expenses, and (3) total operating expenses?

Please see page 640 for solutions.

Volume Variance

The **volume variance** is the difference between the master budget and the flexible budget. Recall that the only difference between these two budgets is the *volume* of units on which they are based. They both use the *same* budget assumptions, but a different volume. The master budget is based on 25,000 cases. The flexible budget is based on 28,724 cases. The volume variance arises *only* because the volume of cases actually sold differs from the volume originally anticipated in the master budget, hence the name *volume variance*. The volume variances are shown in blue ink in Exhibit 10-12.

EXHIBIT 10-12 Volume Variances

	A	B	C	D	E	F	G	H
1				Tucson Tortilla				
2				Flexible Budget Performance Report: Sales and Operating Expenses				
3				For the Month Ended March 31				
4								
5		Actual	Flexible Budget Variance		Flexible Budget	Volume Variance		Master Budget
6	Sales volume (number of cases sold)	28,724	—		28,724	3,724	F	25,000
7								
8	Sales revenue ($20 per case)	$ 603,225			$ 574,480	$ 74,480	F	$ 500,000
9	Operating expenses:							
10	*Variable operating expenses:*							
11	Sales commission ($1.50 per case sold)	$ 45,960			$ 43,086	$ 5,586	U	$ 37,500
12	Shipping expense ($2.00 per case sold)	54,578			57,448	7,448	U	50,000
13	Bad debt expense (1% of credit sales)	5,127			4,596	596	U	4,000
14	*Fixed operating expenses:*							
15	Salaries	21,000			20,000	0		20,000
16	Office rent	4,000			4,000	0		4,000
17	Depreciation	6,000			6,000	0		6,000
18	Advertising	2,800			2,000	0		2,000
19	Telephone and Internet	980			1,000	0		1,000
20	Total operating expenses	$ 140,445			$ 138,130	$ 13,630	U	$ 124,500
21								

NOTE: *For determining whether the volume variance is favorable or unfavorable, keep in mind that the master budget was the original goal. Therefore, the flexible budget is evaluated against the master budget goal.*

The volume variance represents the portion of the master budget variance in Exhibit 10-10 that management would expect considering that 3,724 more cases were sold than originally anticipated. For example, because of the increase in sales volume, the volume variance shows that

- sales revenue *should be* $74,480 higher than originally budgeted, and
- total operating expenses *should be* $13,630 higher than originally budgeted.

  However, the master budget variance in Exhibit 10-10 revealed that

- sales revenue is *actually* $103,225 higher than budgeted, and
- total operating expenses are *actually* $15,945 higher than budgeted.

So, why are actual revenues and expenses still higher than they should be, even considering the volume increase? The answers can be found in the flexible budget variance.

Flexible Budget Variance

The **flexible budget variance** is the difference between the flexible budget and actual results. The flexible budget variances are shown in dark orange ink in Exhibit 10-13.

EXHIBIT 10-13 Flexible Budget Variances and Volume Variances

	A	B	C	D	E	F	G	H
1				Tucson Tortilla				
2			Flexible Budget Performance Report: Sales and Operating Expenses					
3				For the Month Ended March 31				
4								
5		Actual	Flexible Budget Variance		Flexible Budget	Volume Variance		Master Budget
6	**Sales volume (number of cases sold)**	**28,724**	0		**28,724**	3,724	F	**25,000**
7								
8	Sales revenue ($20 per case)	$ 603,225	$ 28,745	F	$ 574,480	$ 74,480	F	$ 500,000
9	Operating expenses:							
10	*Variable operating expenses:*							
11	Sales commission ($1.50 per case sold)	$ 45,960	$ 2,874	U	$ 43,086	$ 5,586	U	$ 37,500
12	Shipping expense ($2.00 per case sold)	54,578	2,870	F	**57,448**	7,448	U	50,000
13	Bad debt expense (1% of credit sales)	5,127	531	U	**4,596**	596	U	4,000
14	*Fixed operating expenses:*							
15	Salaries	21,000	1,000	U	**20,000**	0		20,000
16	Office rent	4,000	0		**4,000**	0		4,000
17	Depreciation	6,000	0		**6,000**	0		6,000
18	Advertising	2,800	800	U	**2,000**	0		2,000
19	Telephone and Internet	980	20	F	**1,000**	0		1,000
20	Total operating expenses	$ 140,445	$ 2,315	U	$ 138,130	$ 13,630	U	$ 124,500
21								

NOTE: For determining whether the volume variance is favorable or unfavorable, keep in mind that the master budget was the original goal. Therefore, the flexible budget is evaluated against the master budget goal.

Because all variances related to volume have already been accounted for through the volume variance, the flexible budget variance highlights *causes other than volume*. For example:

- The $28,745 F variance for sales revenue must mean that the cases were sold at an average price *higher* than $20 per case.

- The $2,874 U variance for commission expense must mean that the commissions were paid at a rate *higher* than $1.50 per case.

- The $2,870 F variance for shipping expense must mean that the shipping costs were *lower* than $2.00 per case.

- The $531 U variance for bad debt expense must mean that either more than 80% of sales were made on credit or bad debts were expensed at a rate greater than 1%.

Underlying Causes of the Variances

As discussed in the first half of the chapter, managers will use *management by exception* to determine which variances to investigate. Upper management will rely on the managers of each responsibility center to provide answers to their inquiries. At other times, upper management already knows the reasons for the variances, yet needs the performance report to understand how their operational decisions affected the company's finances.

For example, let's assume that upper management decided to modify its sales strategy beginning in March from the original plan found in the master budget. In order to increase sales, upper management decided to

- spend more on advertising,
- increase the salaries of the sales staff,

- pay a higher sales commission per case, and
- ease credit terms so that more sales qualified for credit, rather than COD terms.

The unfavorable *flexible budget cost variances* shown in Exhibit 10-13 reflect these operational changes. However, the *sales volume variances* in Exhibit 10-13 also show the positive effect of these changes: the additional sales revenue was more than enough to offset the increased costs. Not only was extra sales volume generated, but sales were also made at a higher price per case than budgeted (as shown by the flexible budget variance for sales revenue). Finally, as a result of the increased volume, management was able to negotiate a lower shipping cost per case, resulting in a favorable flexible budget variance for shipping. All in all, management's strategy paid off.

Master Budget Variance: A Combination of Variances

Now that we have prepared a flexible budget performance report, it's easy to see how the master budget variance can be viewed as a combination of two separate variances, the (1) volume variance and (2) flexible budget variance. This combination is summarized in Exhibit 10-14.

EXHIBIT 10-14 Master Budget Variance

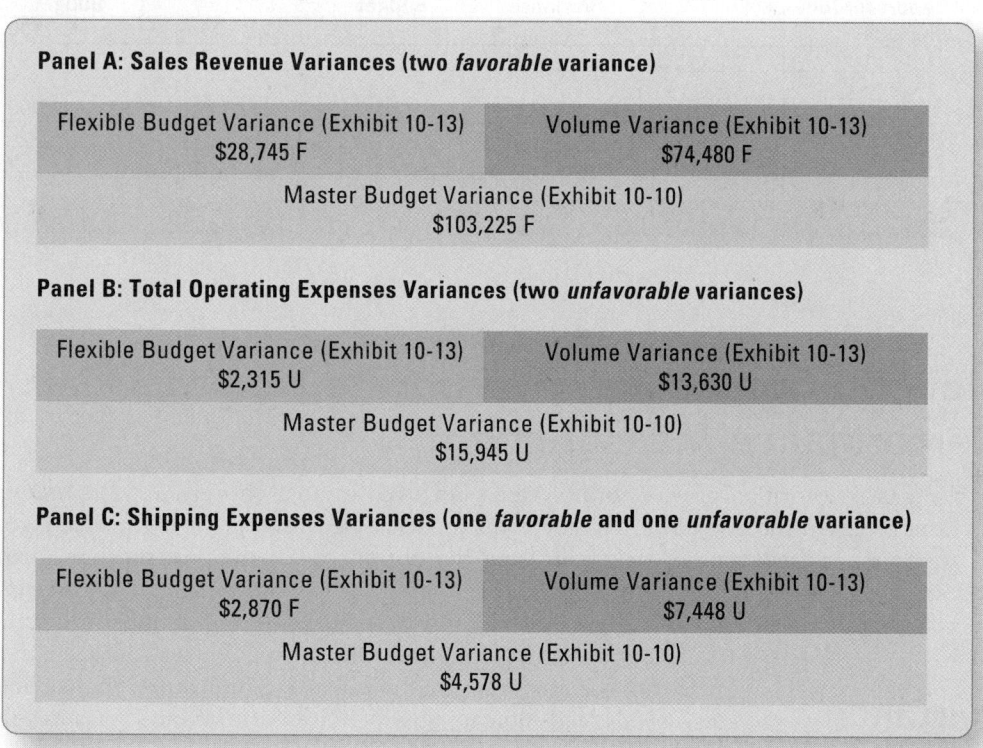

In Exhibit 10-14, notice how the master budget variance could be a combination of *favorable* variances (as in Panel A), a combination of *unfavorable* variances (as in Panel B) or a combination of one favorable variance *and* one unfavorable variance (as in Panel C).

For example, in Panel C we see the variances for Shipping Expenses consist of a *favorable* flexible budget variance ($2,870 F) and an *unfavorable* volume variance ($7,448 U). Together, these two variances *net* to an unfavorable master budget variance of $4,578 U. This example illustrates why it's important to separate the overall master budget variance into its two components. Only by separating the variances would a manager know that the shipping expenses were actually lower per case than anticipated, but higher overall due to the volume of cases shipped.

Decomposing the Flexible Budget Variance

We have just seen how the master budget variance can be decomposed into a volume variance and a flexible budget variance. If managers want, they can decompose the *flexible budget variance* into two additional variances (a price variance and an efficiency variance) to better understand what is causing the flexible budget variance. Manufacturers often do this for their direct materials, direct labor, and manufacturing overhead costs. All of Chapter 11 is devoted to calculating these more detailed manufacturing cost variances.

▶ Try It!

Sam operates his own summer lawn-mowing company using a truck and equipment solely dedicated to business operations. Complete the flexible budget performance report below to answer the following questions:

1. What is the volume variance for total operating expenses? Favorable or unfavorable?
2. What is the flexible budget variance for total operating expenses? Favorable or unfavorable?
3. What is the master budget variance for total operating expenses? Favorable or unfavorable?

	A	B	C	D	E	F	G	H
1	Sam's Lawn Mowing Business Flexible Budget Performance Report for June	Actual	Flexible Budget Variance		Flexible Budget	Volume Variance		Master Budget
2	Sales volume (number of mowing jobs)	125			125			100
3								
4	Operating expenses:							
5	Variable operating expenses ($10 per job)	$ 1,370			$ 1,250			$ 1,000
6	Fixed operating expenses ($500 per month)	475			500			500
7	Total operating expenses	$ 1,845			$ 1,750			$ 1,500
8								

Please see page 641 for solutions.

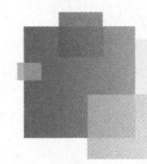

6 Describe the balanced scorecard and identify KPIs for each perspective

How do Companies Incorporate Nonfinancial Performance Measurement?

In the past, performance evaluation systems revolved almost entirely around *financial* performance. On the one hand, this focus makes sense because one of the primary goals of any company, even those that adhere to the notion of a triple bottom line (profit, people, and planet), is to generate profit for its owners. On the other hand, *current* financial performance tends to reveal the results of *past* decisions and actions rather than indicate *future* performance of the company. As a result, financial performance measures are known as <u>lag indicators</u>. Management also needs <u>lead indicators</u>, which are performance measures that predict future performance.

■ Why is this important?

"Rather than **focusing** strictly on financial performance, the **balanced scorecard** includes **operational** performance measures that give managers a **holistic** view of the company's **performance.**"

The Balanced Scorecard

In the early 1990s, Robert Kaplan and David Norton introduced the <u>balanced scorecard</u>.[6] The balanced scorecard recognizes that management must consider *both* financial performance measures *and* operational performance measures when judging the performance of a company and its segments. These measures should be linked with the company's goals and its strategy for achieving those goals. The balanced scorecard represents a major shift in corporate performance measurement: Financial indicators are no longer the sole measure of performance; they are now only *one*

[6]Robert Kaplan and David Norton, "The Balanced Scorecard—Measures That Drive Performance," *Harvard Business Review on Measuring Corporate Performance*, Boston, 1991, pp. 123–145; and Robert Kaplan and David Norton, *Translating Strategy into Action: The Balanced Scorecard*, Boston, Harvard Business School Press, 1996.

measure among a broader set of performance measures. Keeping score of operational performance measures *and* traditional financial performance measures gives management a "balanced," comprehensive view of the organization.

The Four Perspectives of the Balanced Scorecard

The balanced scorecard views the company from four different perspectives, each of which evaluates a specific aspect of organizational performance:

1. Financial perspective
2. Customer perspective
3. Internal business perspective
4. Learning and growth perspective

Exhibit 10-15 illustrates how the company's strategy affects, and, in turn, is affected by all four perspectives. In addition, it shows the cause-and-effect relationship linking the four perspectives.

EXHIBIT 10-15 The Four Perspectives of the Balanced Scorecard

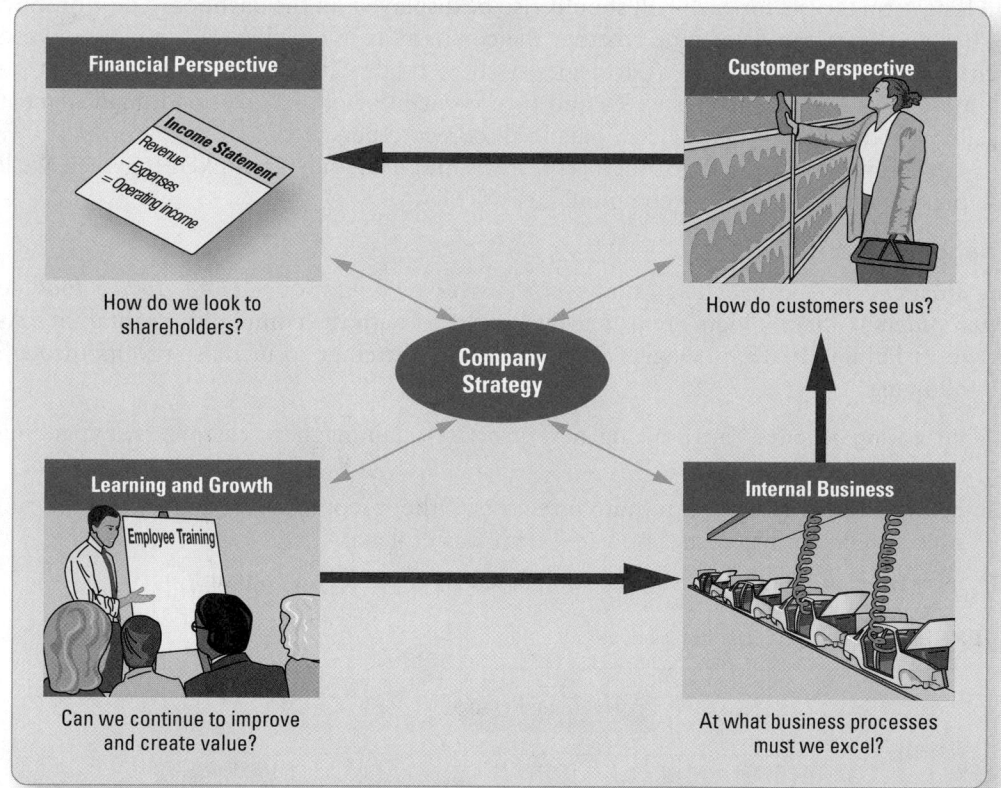

Companies that adopt the balanced scorecard develop specific objectives they want to achieve within each of the four perspectives. These objectives are critical to the company's overall success. As shown in Exhibit 10-16, company's use **key performance indicators (KPIs)**, which are summary performance metrics, to assess how well a company is achieving its goals. For example, the company could use "*average customer satisfaction rating*" as a KPI to measure the company's ability to please customers. "*Number of warranty claims*" could be used to measure the company's ability to produce quality products.

KPIs are continually measured, and are reported on a **performance scorecard** or **performance dashboard**, a report that allows managers to visually monitor and focus on managing the company's key activities and strategies as well as business risks.[7] Short-term

---

[7]Wayne Eckerson, *Performance Dashboards: Measuring, Monitoring and Managing Your Business*, John Wiley & Sons, 2006; and Brian Ballou, Dan Heitger, and Laura Donnell, "Creating Effective Dashboards," *Strategic Finance*, March 2010.

EXHIBIT 10-16 Linking Company Goals to Key Performance Indicators

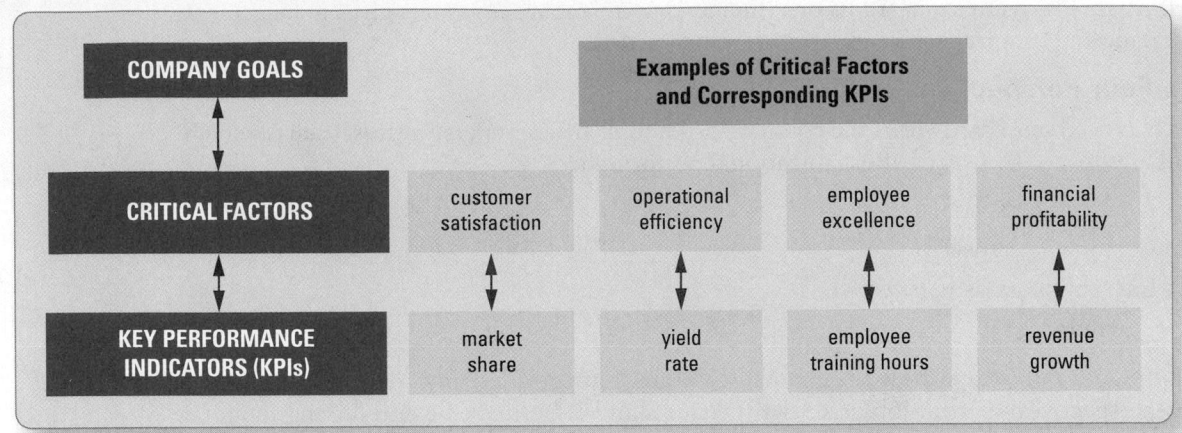

and long-term targets for each KPI should also be displayed on the dashboard or scorecard so that managers can determine whether the company is improving and moving toward each objective, or whether new strategies need to be developed. To focus attention on the most critical elements to success and to prevent information overload, management should use only a few KPIs for each balanced scorecard perspective.

Let's now consider each of the perspectives and how they are linked together. We'll also present some of the more commonly used KPIs.

Financial Perspective

The financial perspective helps managers answer the question, *"How do we look to shareholders?"* Shareholders are primarily concerned with the company's profitability. As shown in Exhibit 10-17, managers must continually attempt to increase profits through the following:

1. **increasing revenue:** introducing new products, gaining new customers, expanding into new markets

2. **controlling costs:** seeking to minimize costs without jeopardizing quality or long-run success, eliminating costs associated with wasteful activities

3. **increasing productivity:** using existing assets as efficiently as possible

EXHIBIT 10-17 Financial Perspective

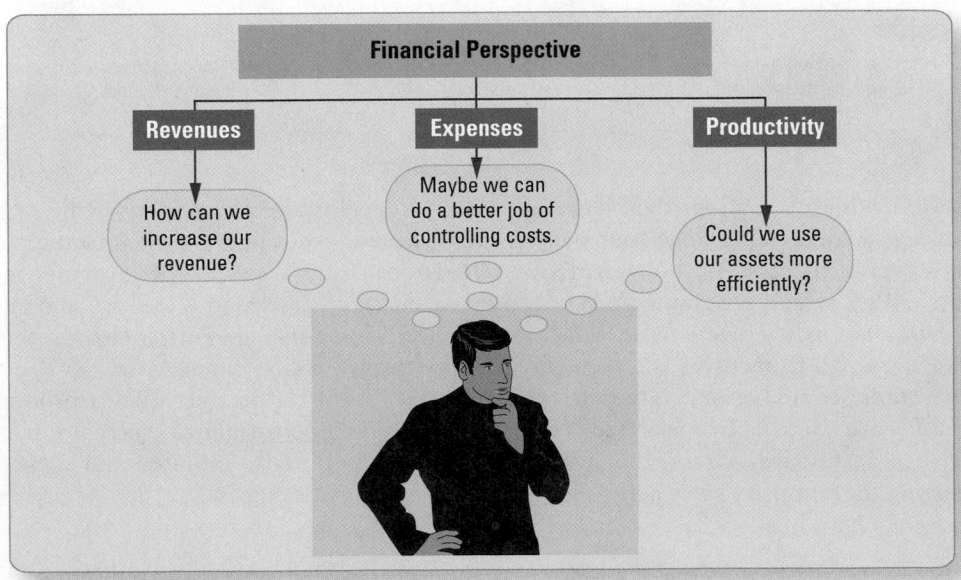

Common KPIs: *sales revenue growth, sales margin, gross margin percentage, capital turnover, ROI, Residual income, earnings per share*

Customer Perspective

The customer perspective helps managers evaluate the question, *"How do customers see us?"* Customer satisfaction is a top priority for long-term success. If customers aren't happy, they won't come back. Therefore, customer satisfaction is critical for the company to achieve its financial goals.

As shown in Exhibit 10-18, customers are typically concerned with four product or service attributes:

1. **price:** the lower the better
2. **quality:** the higher, the better
3. **sales service:** importance of knowledgeable and helpful salespeople
4. **delivery time:** the shorter the better

EXHIBIT 10-18 Customer Perspective

Common KPIs: *average customer satisfaction rating, percentage of market share, increase in the number of customers, number of repeat customers, rate of on-time deliveries.*

Internal Business Perspective

The internal business perspective helps managers address the question, *"At what business processes must we excel to satisfy customer and financial objectives?"* In other words, a company needs to tend to its internal operations if it is to please customers. And only by pleasing customers will it achieve its financial goals. As shown in Exhibit 10-19, the answer to that question incorporates the following three factors:

1. **innovation:** developing new products
2. **operations:** using lean operating techniques, as discussed in Chapter 4, to increase efficiency
3. **post-sales support:** providing excellent customer service after the sale

EXHIBIT 10-19 Internal Business Perspective

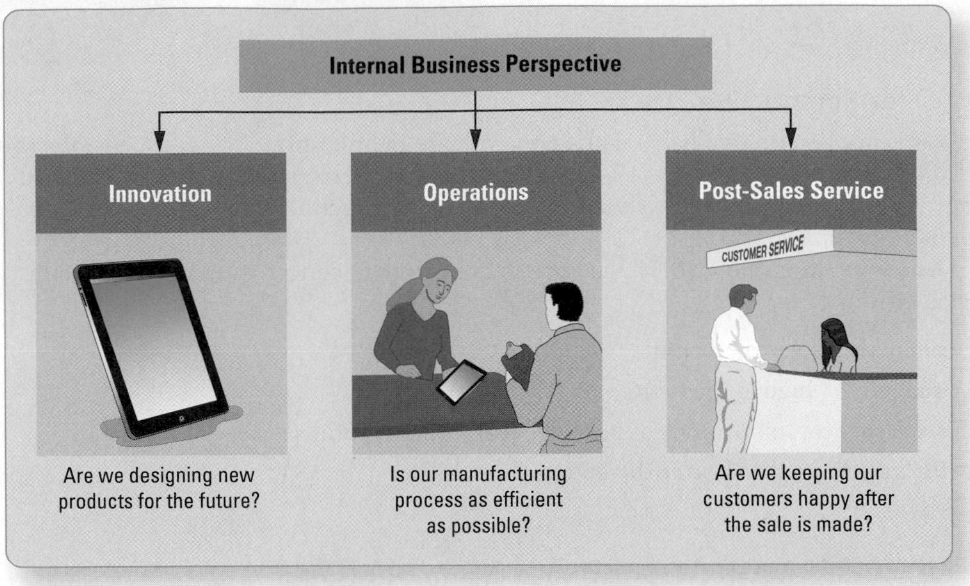

Common KPIs: *number of new products developed, new product development time, defect rate, manufacturing lead time, yield rate, number of warranty claims received, average customer wait time for customer service, average repair time*

Learning and Growth Perspective

The learning and growth perspective helps managers assess the question, *"Can we continue to improve and create value?"* Much of a company's success boils down to its people. A company cannot be successful in the other perspectives (financial, customer, internal operations) if it does not have the right people in the right positions, a solid and ethical leadership team, and the information systems that employees need. Therefore, the learning and growth perspective lays the foundation needed for success in the other perspectives. As shown in Exhibit 10-20, the learning and growth perspective focuses on the following three factors:

1. **employee capabilities:** critical and creative thinkers, skilled, knowledgeable, motivated
2. **information system capabilities:** a system that provides timely and accurate data
3. **the company's "climate for action:"** corporate culture supports communication, teamwork, change, and employee growth

Common KPIs: *hours of employee training, employee satisfaction, employee turnover, percentage of processes with real-time feedback, percentage of employees with access to real-time data, number of employee suggestions implemented, percentage of employees involved in problem solving teams, employee rating of communication and corporate culture*

EXHIBIT 10-20 Learning and Growth Perspective

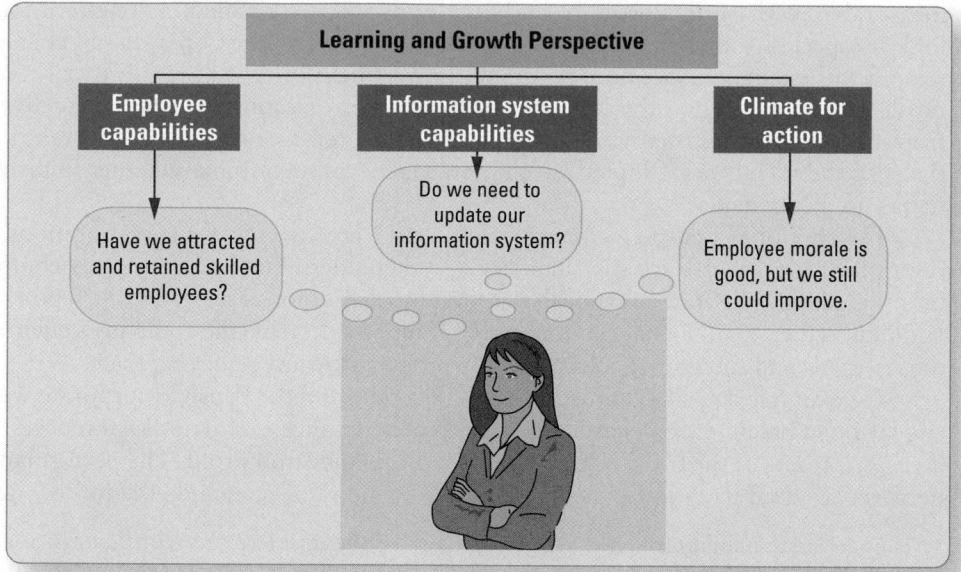

In summary, the balanced scorecard focuses performance measurement on progress toward the company's goals in each of the four perspectives. In designing the scorecard, managers start with the company's goals and its strategy for achieving those goals, and then identify the *most* important measures of performance that will predict long-term success. Some of these measures are operational lead indicators, while others are financial lag indicators. Managers must consider the linkages between strategy and operations and the way those operations will affect finances now and in the future.

Sustainability and Performance Evaluation

Companies that embrace sustainability and social responsibility, like PepsiCo, incorporate relevant KPIs in their performance evaluation system. Some companies will integrate sustainability-related KPIs into the four traditional balanced scorecard perspectives. For example, KPIs for each perspective might include the following:[8]

- Financial: *water cost, recycling revenues, waste-disposal costs*
- Customer: *number of green products, percentage of products reclaimed after use*
- Internal Business: *energy consumption, water consumption, greenhouse gas emissions*
- Learning and Growth: *number of functions with environmental responsibilities, management attention to environmental issues*

Other companies add a fifth perspective, "Sustainability," or even add a sixth perspective, "Community," to reflect triple-bottom-line goals. The Sustainability Perspective could include any of the examples given in the blue box directly above, while the Community Perspective might include:

- Community: *percentage of profit donated to local schools and organizations, percentage of materials sourced locally, product safety ratings, number of hours devoted to local volunteering*

---

[8]M. J. Epstein and P. S. Wisner. "Using a Balanced Scorecard to Implement Sustainability," *Environmental Quality Management*, 2001.

KPIs relating to sustainability and social responsibility should be objective and measurable, with both short-term and long-term targets specified. A long-term outlook is especially important regarding sustainability, since most operational changes related to sustainability require substantial investment in the short-run that should result in cost savings in the long-run (for example, investing in a fleet of delivery trucks that run on alternative fuels). Baseline measurements should also be taken at the time the targets are adopted, so that managers can determine whether improvements are being made.

The environmental performance metrics also serve as a way for corporations to report their journey toward sustainability to stakeholders. For example, many companies, including PepsiCo, now publish corporate social responsibility, or CSR, reports in addition to their annual financial reports. CSR reports describe the company's environmental goals and summarize the company's progress toward achieving them.

See Exercises E10-28A and E10-41B

For example, PepsiCo's most recent CSR report and the PepsiCo corporate website lay out a balanced scorecard approach to performance evaluation that focuses on all three aspects of the triple bottom line: people, planet, and profit. The performance perspectives used by PepsiCo, as well as some of their goals, include the following:

1. **Human Sustainability (people in society):** *reduce the amount of saturated fat, sugar, and sodium in PepsiCo products; increase the amount of whole grains, nuts, seeds, and fruit in PepsiCo products; limit advertising directed at children to nutritional products; increase R&D of more affordable and nutritional products for lower-income markets*

2. **Talent Sustainability (people in the company):** *increase gender and racial diversity in workforce and management; reduce injury rate; increase workplace wellness programs; increase training and leadership development programs; support volunteerism and match employee charitable giving*

3. **Environmental Sustainability:** *improve water-use efficiency; reduce fuel and electricity use intensity, incorporate recycled PET(plastic) in containers; reduce the amount of material in packaging; reduce waste to landfill; reduce supply-chain greenhouse gas emissions; promote beverage container recycling programs; increase use of sustainable agricultural practices*

4. **Financial Performance:** *grow international revenues; increase operating profit; improve brand equity scores; increase market share; deliver high shareholder returns*

5. **Responsible and Sustainable Sourcing:** *increase use of minority- and women-owned vendors; increase use of suppliers that participate in the carbon disclosure project program*

6. **Community and Philanthropy:** *increase the gross dollar amount and percentage of operating income contributed through the Pepsi Foundation.*

PepsiCo reports the KPIs used to evaluate these goals on its corporate website.

Decision Guidelines

Performance Evaluation and the Balanced Scorecard

Decision	Guidelines
How can flexible budgets aid in performance evaluation?	There is nothing wrong with comparing actual results against the master planning budget. However, managers usually gain additional insights by comparing actual results against a flexible budget, which is a budget prepared for the actual volume achieved, rather than the volume originally used for planning purposes.
What is the master budget variance?	The master budget variance is the difference between the actual results and the master planning budget. This variance can be decomposed into two separate variances: (1) a volume variance, and (2) a flexible budget variance, by first creating a flexible budget.
How is a flexible budget prepared?	A flexible budget is prepared by multiplying the budgeted revenue per unit and variable cost per unit by the actual volume achieved. Since total fixed costs are not affected by changes in volume, they are the same on the flexible budget as they were on the original master budget. The flexible budget presents the revenues and expenses that management would have expected, given the actual volume achieved.
What is the volume variance?	The volume variance is the difference between the master planning budget and the flexible budget. It represents the portion of the master budget variance that was caused by actual volume being different than originally budgeted.
What is the flexible budget variance?	The flexible budget variance is the difference between actual costs and the flexible budget. It represents the portion of the master budget variance that was caused by factors *other than* volume differences.
Should the performance evaluation system include lag or lead measures?	Better performance evaluation systems include *both* lag and lead measures. Lag measures reveal the results of past actions, while lead measures project future performance.
What are the four balanced scorecard perspectives?	1. Financial perspective 2. Customer perspective 3. Internal business perspective 4. Learning and growth perspective
How do companies include sustainability-related KPIs in their balanced scorecards?	Companies either include sustainability-related KPIs within each of the four perspectives, or they add separate perspectives for sustainability and/or corporate responsibility.

SUMMARY PROBLEM 2

Requirements

1. Each of the following describes a key performance indicator. Determine which of the balanced scorecard perspectives is being addressed (financial, customer, internal business, or learning and growth).

    a. Employee turnover

    b. Earnings per share

    c. Percentage of on-time deliveries

    d. Revenue growth rate

    e. Percentage of defects discovered during manufacturing

    f. Number of warranties claimed

    g. New product development time

    h. Number of repeat customers

    i. Number of employee suggestions implemented

2. Read the following company initiatives and determine which of the balanced scorecard perspectives is being addressed (financial, customer, internal business, or learning and growth).

    a. Purchasing efficient production equipment

    b. Providing employee training

    c. Updating retail store lighting

    d. Paying quarterly dividends

    e. Updating the company's information system

▪ SOLUTIONS

Requirement 1

a. Learning and growth

b. Financial

c. Customer

d. Financial

e. Internal business

f. Internal business

g. Internal business

h. Customer

i. Learning and growth

Requirement 2

a. Internal business

b. Learning and growth

c. Customer

d. Financial

e. Learning and growth

END OF CHAPTER

Learning Objectives

- 1 Understand decentralization and describe different types of responsibility centers
- 2 Develop performance reports
- 3 Calculate ROI, sales margin, and capital turnover
- 4 Describe strategies and mechanisms for determining a transfer price
- 5 Prepare and evaluate flexible budget performance reports
- 6 Describe the balanced scorecard and identify KPIs for each perspective

Accounting Vocabulary

Balanced Scorecard. (p. 598) A performance evaluation system that integrates financial and operational performance measures along four perspectives: financial, customer, internal business, and learning and growth.

Capital Turnover. (p. 582) Sales revenue divided by total assets. The capital turnover shows how much sales revenue is generated with every $1.00 of assets.

Common Fixed Expenses. (p. 579) Fixed expenses that *cannot* be traced to the segment.

Cost Center. (p. 575) A responsibility center in which managers are responsible for controlling costs.

Decentralize. (p. 573) A process where companies split their operations into different operating segments.

Direct Fixed Expenses. (p. 579) Fixed expenses that can be traced to the segment.

Favorable Variance. (p. 577) A variance that causes operating income to be higher than budgeted.

Flexible Budget. (p. 593) A summarized budget prepared for different levels of volume.

Flexible Budget Variance. (p. 596) The difference between the flexible budget and actual results. The flexible budget variances are due to *something other than volume*.

Goal Congruence. (p. 574) When the goals of the segment managers align with the goals of top management.

Gross Book Value. (p. 585) Historical cost of assets.

Investment Center. (p. 575) A responsibility center in which managers are responsible for generating revenues, controlling costs, and efficiently managing the division's assets.

Key Performance Indicators (KPIs). (p. 599) Summary performance metrics used to assess how well a company is achieving its goals.

Lag Indicators. (p. 598) Performance indicators that reveal the results of past actions and decisions.

Lead Indicators. (p. 598) Performance measures that predict future performance.

Management by Exception. (p. 578) A management technique in which managers only investigate budget variances that are relatively large.

Master Budget Variance. (p. 593) The difference between actual results and the master budget.

Net Book Value. (p. 585) Historical cost of assets less accumulated depreciation.

Performance Reports. (p. 577) Reports that compare actual results against budgeted figures.

Performance Scorecard or Dashboard. (p. 599) A report displaying the measurement of KPIs, as well as their short-term and long-term targets.

Profit Center. (p. 575) A responsibility center in which managers are responsible for both revenues and costs, and therefore profits.

Residual Income. (p. 583) Operating income minus the minimum acceptable operating income given the size of the division's assets.

Responsibility Accounting. (p. 574) A system for evaluating the performance of each responsibility center and its manager.

Responsibility Center. (p. 574) A part of an organization whose manager is accountable for planning and controlling certain activities.

Return on Investment (ROI). (p. 581) Operating income divided by total assets. The ROI measures the profitability of a division relative to the size of its assets.

Revenue Center. (p. 575) A responsibility center in which managers are responsible for generating revenue.

Sales Margin. (p. 582) Operating income divided by sales revenue. The sales margin shows how much income is generated for every $1.00 of sales.

Segment Margin. (p. 578) The operating income generated by a profit or investment center *before* subtracting the common fixed costs that have been allocated to the center.

Transfer Price. (p. 586) The price charged for the internal sale of product between two different divisions of the same company.

Unfavorable Variance. (p. 577) A variance that causes operating income to be lower than budgeted.

Variance. (p. 577) The difference between an actual amount and the budget.

Vertical Integration. (p. 587) The acquisition of companies within one's supply chain.

Volume Variance. (p. 595) The difference between the master budget and the flexible budget. The volume variance arises *only* because the actual sales volume differs from the volume originally anticipated in the master budget.

Quick Check

1. *(Learning Objective 1)* Companies often decentralize their operations by
   a. geographic area.
   b. product line.
   c. customer base.
   d. all of the above.

2. *(Learning Objective 1)* Which of the following is *not* an advantage of decentralization?
   a. Use of expert knowledge
   b. Achieving goal congruence
   c. Improved customer relations
   d. Frees top management's time

3. *(Learning Objective 1)* In terms of responsibility centers, a large corporate division would be considered a(n)
   a. revenue center.
   b. cost center.
   c. investment center.
   d. profit center.

4. *(Learning Objective 2)* Which of the following is true?
   a. Favorable variances should always be interpreted as "good news" for the company.
   b. Unfavorable variances should always be interpreted as "bad news" for the company.
   c. Favorable variances are variances that cause operating income to be higher than budgeted.
   d. Management by exception means that managers investigate all unfavorable variances but not all favorable variances.

5. *(Learning Objective 2)* A segment margin is the operating income generated by subtracting
   a. all fixed expenses from a segment's contribution margin.
   b. only direct fixed expenses from a segment's contribution margin.
   c. only common fixed expenses from a segment's contribution margin.
   d. all expenses from a segment's sales revenue.

6. *(Learning Objective 3)* Return on investment (ROI) can be restated as which of the following?
   a. Residual income × sales margin
   b. Sales margin ÷ capital turnover
   c. Residual income ÷ sales margin
   d. Sales margin × capital turnover

7. *(Learning Objective 4)* Which of the following is *not* a valid strategy for determining a transfer price?
   a. Using the price set by GAAP
   b. Using the market price
   c. Using a negotiated price
   d. Using some definition of cost

8. *(Learning Objective 5)* Which of the following is *false*?
   a. The difference between actual results and the master budget is called the master budget variance.
   b. The volume variance is due to causes other than volume.
   c. The flexible budget is prepared using the actual volume achieved during the period.
   d. The master budget variance can be split into two components: a volume variance and a flexible budget variance.

9. *(Learning Objective 6)* "Number of new products developed" would be a key performance indicator (KPI) for which of the four balanced scorecard perspectives?
   a. Financial
   b. Customer
   c. Internal business
   d. Learning and growth

10. *(Learning Objective 6)* "Hours of employee training" would be a key performance indicator (KPI) for which of the four balanced scorecard perspectives?
    a. Financial
    b. Customer
    c. Internal business
    d. Learning and growth

Quick Check Answers

1.d 2.b 3.c 4.c 5.b 6.d 7.a 8.b 9.c 10.d

Short Exercises

S10-1   Identify and understand responsibility centers *(Learning Objective 1)*

Fill in the blanks with the word or phrase that best completes each sentence. Not all words and phrases are used and some may be used more than once.

cost center	revenue center	profit center
investment center	responsibility center	the same
lower	higher	

a. Honda North America, a division of the Honda Motor Company, is a(n) _____.

b. The production line at the Ford Rouge plant in Dearborn, Michigan, where Ford F-150 trucks are manufactured, is considered to be a(n) _____.

c. The Champaign, Illinois, location of the Outback chain restaurant would be a(n) _____.

d. Managers of cost and revenue centers are at _____ levels of the organization than are managers of investment centers.

e. The sales manager in charge of Patagonia's Northwest sales territory oversees a(n) _____.

f. The payroll department of Kohl's Corporation, a retailer, is a(n) _____. _____ is any segment of the business whose manager is accountable for specific activities.

g. The Prepared Foods department of Whole Foods Market, Inc., would be considered to be a(n) _____.

h. The J. M. Smucker Company headquarters, located in Orrville, Ohio, would be a(n) _____.

i. The Floral Department at the Crowley, Texas, Kroger grocery store would be considered to be a(n) _____.

S10-2   Identify types of responsibility centers *(Learning Objective 1)*

Identify each responsibility center as a cost center, a revenue center, a profit center, or an investment center.

a. Walt Disney Company's investor relations website provides operating and financial information to investors and other interested parties.

b. The manager of the Circle K located on Gilbert Road in Chandler, Arizona, is evaluated based on the station's revenues and expenses.

c. A charter airline records revenues and expenses for each airplane each month. Each airplane's performance report shows its ratio of operating income to average book value.

d. The manager of the midwestern sales territory is evaluated based on a comparison of current period sales against budgeted sales.

e. The Floral Department of a Safeway grocery store reports income for the current year.

f. Speedway is a subsidiary of Marathon Oil Corporation; Speedway owns and operates approximately 1,350 gasoline and convenience stores in the United States.

g. The Legal Department of the Progressive Group of Insurance Companies prepares its budget and subsequent performance report on the basis of its expected expenses for the year.

h. The online division of Claire's Stores, Inc., reports both revenues and expenses.

S10-3 Identify centralized and decentralized organizations
(Learning Objective 1)

The following table lists a series of descriptions of decentralized organizations or centralized organizations. For each description, indicate whether that scenario is more typical of a decentralized organization or a centralized organization.

Characteristic	Decentralized (D) or Centralized (C)
a. Smythe Resorts and Hotels, Inc., wants to empower its managers to make decisions so that the managers' motivation is increased and retention of managers increases.	
b. Philips Corporation has formal training programs for lower-level managers and has a policy that it promotes from within the company whenever possible.	
c. The Plastic Lumber Company, Inc., is managed by its owner, who oversees production, sales, engineering, and the other administrative functions.	
d. Daniels Furniture, Inc., is divided into several operating units.	
e. Fulton Holdings wants its managers to be able to respond quickly to changes in local market demand so the managers have the authority to make decisions about product offerings and pricing.	
f. Craft Supplies & More is a small independent craft shop and is managed by its owner.	
g. Mayflower Corporation now has a single payroll department, a single human resource department, and a single administrative headquarters since Mayflower Corporation "flattened" its organization structure.	

S10-4 Classify types of subunits *(Learning Objective 1)*

Each of the following managers has been given certain decision-making authority. Classify each manager according to the type of responsibility center he or she manages.

1. Manager of the Housekeeping Department at the Holiday Inn
2. Manager of the Holiday Inn Express corporate division
3. Manager of the complimentary breakfast buffet at the Holiday Inn Express
4. Manager of Holiday Inn's central reservation office
5. Manager of various corporate-owned Holiday Inn locations
6. Manager of the Holiday Inn corporate division

S10-5 Calculate performance report variances *(Learning Objective 2)*

The following is a partial performance report for a revenue center for the Eastern Division of Peony Restaurants.

Peony Restaurants Sales Revenue—Eastern Division
For the Month Ended June 30

Product	Actual Sales	Budgeted Sales	Variance	Variance Percentage
Food	$ 159,580	$ 158,000	?	?
Dessert	22,800	24,000	?	?
Bar	71,550	67,500	?	?
Catering	43,120	44,000	?	?

Fill in the missing amounts. Indicate whether each variance is favorable (F) or unfavorable (U).

S10-6 Calculate ROI, capital turnover, and sales margin (Learning Objectives 3)

Racer Chemical Corporation has three divisions. To follow is division information from the most recent year.

Division Information for Racer Chemical For the Year Ending December 31			
(All information is in millions of dollars)	Operating Income	Assets	Sales Revenue
Functional Ingredients	$5,720	$10,000	$22,000
Consumer Markets	$2,675	$10,700	$21,400
Performance Materials	$4,810	$18,500	$18,500

For each of the three divisions, calculate sales margin, capital turnover, and return on investment (ROI).

Sunburst Sports Data Set used for S10-7 through S10-9:

Sunburst Sports Company makes snowboards, downhill skis, cross-country skis, skateboards, surfboards, and in-line skates. The company has found it beneficial to split operations into two divisions based on the climate required for the sport: Snow Sports and Non-Snow Sports. The following divisional information is available for the past year:

	Sales	Operating Income	Total Assets	Current Liabilities
Snow Sports	$5,000,000	$ 950,000	$4,900,000	$500,000
Non-Snow Sports	$7,800,000	$1,482,000	$7,100,000	$750,000

Sunburst's management has specified a target 13% rate of return.

S10-7 Calculate ROI (Learning Objective 3)

Refer to Sunburst Sports Data Set.

1. Calculate each division's ROI.
2. Top management has extra funds to invest. Which division will most likely receive those funds? Why?
3. Can you explain why one division's ROI is higher? How could management gain more insight?

S10-8 Compute sales margin and capital margin turnover (Learning Objective 3)

Refer to the Sunburst Sports Data Set.

1. Compute each division's sales margin. Interpret your results.
2. Compute each division's capital turnover (round to two decimal places). Interpret your results.
3. Use your answers to Question 2 along with your answers to Question 1 to recalculate ROI using the expanded formula. Do your answers agree with your ROI calculations in S10-7?

S10-9 Compute residual income (Learning Objective 3)

Refer to the Sunburst Sports Data Set. Compute each division's residual income. Interpret your results. Are your results consistent with each division's ROI?

S10-10 Determine transfer price range (Learning Objective 4)

Pizarro Manufacturing makes a variety of products, including stand mixers. Pizarro's Stand Mixer Division can use a component, K32, manufactured by Pizarro's Electrical Division. The market price for K32 is $23 per unit. The variable cost per unit for K32 in the Electrical Division is $8, while the absorption cost per unit is $15. The divisions at Pizarro use a negotiated price strategy to set transfer prices between divisions.

What is the lowest acceptable transfer price to the Electrical Division? What is the highest acceptable transfer price that the Stand Mixer Division would pay? Explain your answer.

CHAPTER 10

S10-11   Interpret a performance report (Learning Objective 5)

The following is a partially completed performance report for Golden Pools.

	A	B	C	D	E	F	G	H
1				Golden Pools				
2		Flexible Budget Performance Report: Sales and Operating Expenses						
3		For the Year Ended April 30						
4								
5		Actual	Flexible Budget Variance		Flexible Budget	Volume Variance		Master Budget
6	Sales volume (number of pools installed)	5	?		?	?		4
7								
8	Sales revenue	$ 115,000	?		$ 121,000	?		$ 96,800
9	Operating expenses:							
10	Variable expenses	$ 55,000	?		$ 58,000	?		$ 46,400
11	Fixed expenses	25,000	?		29,000	?		29,000
12	Total operating expenses	$ 80,000	?		?	?		$ 75,400
13								

1. How many pools did Golden Pools originally think it would install in April?
2. How many pools did Golden Pools actually install in April?
3. How many pools is the flexible budget based on? Why?
4. What was the budgeted sales price per pool?
5. What was the budgeted variable cost per pool?
6. Define the flexible budget variance. What causes it?
7. Define the volume variance. What causes it?
8. Fill in the missing numbers in the performance report.

S10-12   Complete a master budget performance report (Learning Objective 5)

The following table contains a hypothetical partial master budget performance report for Sweet Earth Organic Chocolates. Fill in the missing amounts. Be sure to indicate whether variances are favorable (F) or unfavorable (U).

	A	B	C	D	E	F	G	H
1				Sweet Earth Organic Chocolates				
2		Flexible Budget Performance Report: Sales and Operating Expenses						
3		For the Year Ended December 31						
4								
5		Actual	Flexible Budget Variance		Flexible Budget	Volume Variance		Master Budget
6	Sales volume (number of batches sold)	13,400			13,400			12,100
7								
8	Sales revenue ($26 per batch)	$ 344,900			$ 348,400			$ 314,600
9	Operating expenses:							
10	Variable operating expenses:							
11	Sales expense ($2 per batch sold)	$ 26,300			$ 26,800			$ 24,200
12	Shipping expense ($1 per batch sold)	12,600			13,400			12,100
13	Fixed operating expenses:							
14	Salaries	10,300			9,800			9,800
15	Office rent	1,000			1,000			1,000
16	Total operating expenses	$ 50,200			$ 51,000			$ 47,100
17								

S10-13   Classify KPIs by balanced scorecard perspective (Learning Objective 6)

Classify each of the following key performance indicators according to the balanced scorecard perspective it addresses. Choose from financial perspective, customer perspective, internal business perspective, or learning and growth perspective.

a. Return on Investment (ROI)
b. New product development time
c. Employee turnover rate

d. Percentage of products with online help manuals

e. Customer satisfaction survey ratings

f. Downtime (the amount of time service is not available)

g. Percentage of orders filled each week

h. Gross margin growth

i. Number of new patents

j. Employee satisfaction ratings

k. Number of customer complaints

l. Number of information system upgrades completed

S10-14 Use vocabulary terms *(Learning Objectives 1, 2, 3, 4, 5, & 6)*

Complete the following statements with one of the terms listed here. You may use a term more than once. Some terms may not be used at all.

Capital turnover	Common fixed expenses	Cost center
Direct fixed expenses	Favorable variance	Flexible budget
Flexible budget variance	Goal congruence	Investment center
Key performance indicators (KPIs)	Management by exception	Master budget variance
Profit center	Return on investment (ROI)	Revenue center
Sales margin	Unfavorable variance	Volume variance

a. A(n) _____ is a budget prepared for a different volume level than that which was originally anticipated.

b. The difference between the flexible budget and actual results is called the _____.

c. _____ measures the profitability of a division relative to the size of its assets.

d. If budgeted salary expense is higher than the actual salary expense, then a(n) _____ will result.

e. A(n) _____ manager is responsible for generating revenue.

f. The _____ arises only because the actual volume sold differs from the volume originally anticipated in the master budget.

g. _____ shows how much sales revenue is generated with every $1.00 of assets.

h. If budgeted sales revenue is greater than the actual sales revenue, then a(n) _____ will result.

i. _____ is a management technique in which managers only investigate budget variances that are relatively large.

j. The legal department of a manufacturer is considered to be a(n) _____.

k. The headquarters for an international consulting firm is considered to be a(n) _____.

l. Fixed expenses that can be traced to the segment are called _____.

m. _____ shows how much income is generated for every $1.00 of sales.

n. _____ are included on balanced scorecards and help managers assess how well the company's objectives are being met.

o. The difference between actual results and the master budget is called the _____.

p. When the goals of the segment managers in a company are the same, then _____ is achieved.

q. The local branch office of a national bank is considered to be a(n) _____.

r. Fixed expenses that cannot be traced to the segment are called _____.

S10-15 Identify ethical standards violated *(Learning Objectives 1, 2, 3, 4, 5, & 6)*   **ETHICS**

For each of the situations listed, identify the primary standard from the IMA *Statement of Ethical Professional Practice* that is violated (competence, confidentiality, integrity, or credibility). Refer to Exhibit 1-6 for the complete standard.

1. Benjamin, the controller who oversees transfer policies at Bristal Industries, does not inform management that his sister is the principal partner in a consulting firm that is bidding on work at Bristal Industries.

2. Each month, Jenna, a corporate controller, prepares segment reports for all of the divisions of her company. In these reports, she includes every general ledger account. As a result, the report for each division is several pages long and no one except Jenna and her staff can interpret the reports.

3. In the past six years since he graduated with an accounting degree, Joe has not attended any continuing education seminars. A major part of Joe's job involves preparing performance reports. He has figured that he knows enough to do his job since he has not forgotten any relevant information from his college degree program.

4. In casual conversation with friends on a Friday night, Loren talks about how transfer prices are set at the company where he is an accountant. As part of that conversation, he shares the variable costs of the company's main product.

5. In the year-end report to the board of directors, Samuel, the controller, prepares the performance report. The board will base the annual bonuses on this report. Samuel designs the report so that the favorable Key Performance Indicators (KPIs) are displayed prominently, while the KPIs that are unfavorable are either not included, or are buried deep in the later pages of the report so that they are unlikely to be seen.

EXERCISES Group A

E10-16A   Identify type of responsibility center (Learning Objective 1)

Each of the following situations describes an organizational unit. Identify which type of responsibility center each underlined item is (cost, revenue, profit, or investment center).

Organization	Type of Responsibility Center (Cost, Revenue, Profit, or Investment)
a. The <u>3M Company</u> manufactures and distributes products under the Post-it, Scotch, Nexcare, and Thinsulate brand names.	
b. <u>The J.M. Smucker Company Store and Café</u> is located in Orrville, Ohio. The store sells a variety of company products, while the café offers items made with ingredients from the Smucker's brands.	
c. The Fairmont Chicago, The Fairmont Royal York in Toronto, and The Fairmont Orchid in Hawaii are all hotels owned by their parent corporation, <u>Fairmont Hotels & Resorts</u>.	
d. The <u>Dairy Group Account team</u> of the Dean Foods Company is responsible for sales and servicing for the SUPERVALU, Target, and Costco accounts.	
e. The <u>Goodyear Tire & Rubber Company</u> is one of the oldest tire companies in the world. Its geographic regions include North America, Europe, Africa, South America, Asia, and Australia.	
f. In addition to other accounting duties, the <u>Financial Reporting and Control & Analysis Department</u> at Progressive Insurance is responsible for performing a monthly analysis of general ledger accounts and fluctuations as a control mechanism.	
g. The <u>reservation office</u> for CharterNow Airlines, Inc., is responsible for both website sales and counter sales.	
h. The <u>Information System Department</u> is responsible for designing, installing, and servicing the information systems throughout Kohl's Corporation.	
i. The <u>JCPenney store</u> in the Oakpark Shopping Center in Kansas City is owned by the JCPenney Company, Inc.	
j. The <u>Human Resources Department</u> at American Greetings is responsible for hiring and training new associates.	
k. The <u>Barnes & Noble bookstore</u> in Asheville, North Carolina, is owned by its parent, Barnes & Noble, Inc.	

E10-17A   Complete and analyze a performance report (Learning Objective 2)

One subunit of Pacific Sports Manufacturing Company had the following financial results last month:

	A	B	C	D	E	F	G
1		Pacific Sports Manufacturing Company—Water Sports Subunit					
2		Monthly Performance Report					
3		For the Month					
4							
5	Product	Actual	Budgeted	Variance*		Variance Percentage*	
6	Direct materials	$ 13,400	$ 12,500				
7	Direct labor	18,940	20,000				
8	Indirect labor	35,220	30,000				
9	Utilities	9,555	8,750				
10	Depreciation	26,125	26,125				
11	Repairs and maintenance	8,430	10,000				
12	Total	$ 111,670	$ 107,375				
13							

*Be sure to indicate whether each variance is favorable (F) or unfavorable (U).

Requirements

1. Complete the performance evaluation report for this subunit (round to four decimals).
2. Based on the data presented, what type of responsibility center is the subunit?
3. Which items should be investigated if part of the management's decision criteria is to investigate all variances exceeding $2,900 or 13%?
4. Should only unfavorable variances be investigated? Explain.

E10-18A   Prepare a segment margin performance report (Learning Objective 2)

Crandell Industries has gathered the following information about the actual sales revenues and expenses for its pharmaceuticals segment for the most recent year.

Sales	$1,436,400
Variable Cost of Goods Sold............................	$ 192,600
Variable Operating Expenses...........................	$ 121,500
Direct Fixed Manufacturing Overhead	$ 117,700
Direct Fixed Operating Expenses	$ 16,160
Common Fixed Expenses.................................	$ 17,170

Budgeted data for the same time period for the pharmaceutical segment are as follows (all data is in millions):

Budgeted sales in units		9,000
Budgeted average selling price per unit....................................	$	140
Variable Cost of Goods Sold per unit	$	20
Variable Operating Expenses per unit	$	15
Direct Fixed Manufacturing Overhead (in total)		$107,000
Direct Fixed Operating Expenses (in total)................................		$ 16,000
Common Fixed Expenses Allocated to the Pharmaceutical Segment		$ 17,000

Prepare a segment margin performance report for the pharmaceutical segment. In this report, be sure to include lines for the contribution margin, the segment margin, and operating income. Calculate a variance and a variance percentage for each line in the report. Round to the nearest hundredth for the variance percentages (for example, if your answer is 16.2384%, round it to 16.24%).

E10-19A Compute and interpret the expanded ROI equation
(Learning Objective 3)

Zachs, a national manufacturer of lawn-mowing and snow-blowing equipment, segments its business according to customer type: Professional and Residential. Assume the following divisional information was available for the past year (in thousands of dollars):

	Sales	Operating Income	Total Assets
Residential	$ 585,000	$ 70,200	$195,000
Professional	$1,013,600	$152,040	$362,000

Assume that management has a 24% target rate of return for each division.

Requirements
Round all of your answers to four decimal places.
1. Calculate each division's ROI.
2. Calculate each division's sales margin. Interpret your results.
3. Calculate each division's capital turnover. Interpret your results.
4. Use the expanded ROI formula to confirm your results from Requirement 1. What can you conclude?
5. Calculate each division's residual income (RI). Interpret your results.

E10-20A Relationship between ROI and residual income (Learning Objective 3)

Data on three unrelated companies are given in the following table.

	Kyler Company	Fielding Industries	Johnson, Inc.
Sales	$100,000	?	$530,000
Operating income	$ 40,000	$129,600	?
Total assets	$ 80,000	?	?
Sales margin	?	16%	12%
Capital turnover	?	4.50	?
Return on investment (ROI)	?	?	30%
Target rate of return	10%	19%	?
Residual income (RI)	?	?	$ 19,080

Requirement
Fill in the missing information in the preceding table.

E10-21A Compute ROI and residual income (Learning Objective 3)

Results from First Corporation's most recent year of operations is presented in the following table.

Operating income	$ 7,560
Total assets	$12,000
Current liabilities	$ 4,500
Sales	$27,000
Target rate of return	16%

Requirements
1. Calculate the sales margin, capital turnover, and return on investment (ROI).
2. Calculate the residual income (RI).

E10-22A Comparison of ROI and residual income (Learning Objective 3)

Gable Ceramics, a division of Kerwin Corporation, has an operating income of $63,000 and total assets of $360,000. The required rate of return for the company is 9%. The company is evaluating whether it should use return on investment (ROI) or residual income (RI) as a measurement of performance for its division managers.

The manager of Gable Ceramics has the opportunity to undertake a new project that will require an investment of $90,000. This investment would earn $9,000 for the company.

Requirements

1. What is the original return on investment (ROI) for Gable Ceramics (before making any additional investment)?

2. What would the ROI be for Gable Ceramics if this investment opportunity were undertaken? Would the manager of the Gable Ceramics division want to make this investment if she were evaluated based on ROI? Why or why not?

3. What is the ROI of the investment opportunity? Would the investment be desirable from the standpoint of Kerwin Corporation? Why or why not?

4. What would the residual income (RI) be for Gable Ceramics if this investment opportunity were to be undertaken? Would the manager of the Gable Ceramics division want to make this investment if she were evaluated based on RI? Why or why not?

5. What is the RI of the investment opportunity? Would the investment be desirable from the standpoint of Kerwin Corporation? Why or why not?

6. Which performance measurement method, ROI or RI, promotes goal congruence? Why?

E10-23A   Determine transfer price range (Learning Objective 4)

Gibson Motors manufactures specialty tractors. It has two divisions: a Tractor Division and a Tire Division. The Tractor Division can use the tires produced by the Tire Division. The market price per tire is $85.

The Tire Division has the following costs per tire:

Direct material cost per tire $17
Conversion costs per tire $1

Fixed manufacturing overhead cost for the year is expected to total $102,000. The Tire Division expects to manufacture 51,000 tires this year. The fixed manufacturing overhead per tire is $2 ($102,000 divided by 51,000 tires).

Requirements

1. Assume that the Tire Division has excess capacity, meaning that it can produce tires for the Tractor Division without giving up any of its current tire sales to outsiders. If Gibson Motors has a negotiated transfer price policy, what is the lowest acceptable transfer price? What is the highest acceptable transfer price?

2. If Gibson Motors has a cost-plus transfer price policy of full absorption cost plus 10%, what would the transfer price be?

3. If the Tire Division is currently producing at capacity (meaning that it is selling every single tire it has the capacity to produce), what would likely be the most fair transfer price strategy to use? What would be the transfer price in this case?

E10-24A   Prepare a flexible budget performance report (Learning Objective 5)

Echo Canyon Muffins sells its muffins to restaurants and coffee houses for an average selling price of $27 per case. The following information relates to the budget for Echo Canyon Muffins for this year (all figures are annual totals unless otherwise noted):

Budgeted sales in cases	7,900 cases
Packaging cost per case	$ 1
Shipping expense per case	$ 3
Sales commission expense	4% of sales price
Salaries expense	$6,600
Office rent	$3,200
Depreciation	$2,800
Insurance expense	$1,800
Office supplies expense	$ 800

During the year, Echo Canyon Muffins actually sold 8,100 cases resulting in total sales revenue of $226,200. Actual expenses (in total) from this year are as follows:

Packaging cost	$ 8,600
Shipping expense...	$25,100
Sales commission expense.......................................	$ 9,048
Salaries expense..	$ 7,000
Office rent	$ 3,200
Depreciation..	$ 2,800
Insurance expense...	$ 1,500
Office supplies expense	$ 1,400

Requirement

Construct a flexible budget performance report for Echo Canyon Muffins for the year. Be sure to indicate whether each variance is favorable (F) or unfavorable (U).

E10-25A Complete and analyze a performance report (*Learning Objective 5*)

The accountant for a subunit of Anderson Sports Company went on vacation before completing the subunit's monthly performance report. This is as far as she got:

	A	B	C	D	E	F	G	H
1			Ski Products Subunit—Anderson Sports Company					
2			Flexible Budget Performance Report: Sales					
3			For the Month					
4								
5			Actual	Flexible Budget Variance		Flexible Budget	Volume Variance	Master Budget
6	Downhill Model RI		$ 320,000				$ 18,000 F	$ 294,000
7	Downhill Model RII		152,000			$ 163,000		143,000
8	Cross-Country Model EXI		290,000	$ 1,000 U		291,000		310,000
9	Cross-Country Model EXII		253,000			247,000	18,500 U	265,500
10	Snowboard Model LXI		430,000	4,000 F				408,000
11	Total		$ 1,445,000					$ 1,420,500
12								

Requirements

1. Complete the performance evaluation report for this subunit.
2. Based on the data presented, what type of responsibility center is this subunit?
3. Which items should be investigated if part of the management's decision criteria is to investigate all variances exceeding $17,500? Interpret your results. (What could cause these variances? What impact might these variances have on company inventory levels and operations?)

E10-26A Work backward to find missing values (Learning Objective 5)

Manco Industries has a relevant range extending to 30,200 units each month. The following performance report provides information about Manco's budget and actual performance for September:

	A	B	C	D	E	F	G	H
1			Manco Industries					
2		Flexible Budget Performance Report: Sales and Operating Expenses						
3		For the Month Ended September 30						
4								
5		Actual	(A)		Flexible Budget	(B)		Master Budget
6	Output units	24,000			(C)			30,200
7								
8	Sales revenue	$ 226,000	$ 5,200	F	(D)			
9	Operating expenses:							
10	Variable expenses				(E)			$ 193,280
11	Fixed expenses	15,000	(F)					24,000
12	Total operating expenses							(G)
13								

Requirement

Find the missing data for letters A–G. Be sure to label any variances as favorable or unfavorable. (*Hint:* A and B are titles.)

E10-27A Construct a balanced scorecard (Learning Objective 6)

Mancato Corporation is preparing its balanced scorecard for the past quarter. The balanced scorecard contains four perspectives: financial, customer, internal business process, and learning and growth. Through its strategic management planning process, Mancato Corporation has selected two specific objectives for each of the four perspectives; these specific objectives are listed in the following table.

Specific Objective
1. Increase sales of core product line.
2. Improve post-sales service.
3. Improve employee job satisfaction.
4. Increase number of customers.
5. Increase plant safety.
6. Increase market share.
7. Increase gross margin.
8. Improve employee product knowledge.

Mancato Corporation has collected key performance indicators (KPIs) to measure progress toward achieving its specific objectives. The following table contains the KPIs and corresponding data that Mancato Corporation has collected for the past quarter.

	A	B	C
1	KPI	Goal	Actual
2	Employee turnover rate (number of employees leaving company / total number of employees)	7%	9%
3	Number of plant accidents	4	3
4	Sales revenue growth—core product line	$ 2,000,000	$ 2,250,000
5	Hours of employee training provided	2,425	2,250
6	Gross margin growth percentage	22%	25%
7	Market share percentage	13%	20%
8	Average repair time (number of days)	1.7	1.1
9	Number of customers	130,000	125,000
10			

Requirement

Prepare a balanced scorecard report for Mancato Corporation, using the following format.

Mancato Corporation
Balanced Scorecard Report
For Quarter Ended December 31

Perspective	Objective	KPI	Goal	Actual	Goal Achieved? (✓ if met)
Financial					
Customer...					
Internal Business Process					
Learning and Growth					

For each of the specific objectives listed, place that objective under the appropriate perspective heading in the report. Select a KPI from the list of KPIs that would be appropriate to measure progress toward each objective. (There are two specific objectives for each perspective and one KPI for each of the specific objectives.) In the last column in the balanced scorecard report, place a check mark if the associated KPI goal has been achieved.

SUSTAINABILITY

E10-28A Sustainability and the balanced scorecard *(Learning Objective 6)*

Classify each of the following sustainability key performance indicators (KPIs) according to the balanced scorecard perspective it addresses. Choose from the following five perspectives:

- Financial perspective
- Customer perspective
- Internal business perspective
- Learning and growth perspective
- Community perspective

KPI

a. Cost of water used
b. Indirect greenhouse gas emissions from electricity purchased and consumed
c. Number of functions with environmental responsibilities
d. Number of green products
e. Percentage of profit donated to local schools
f. Volume of Global Greenhouse Gas (GHG) emissions
g. Waste disposal costs
h. Percentage of products reclaimed after customer use
i. Revenue from recycling packaging materials
j. Total liters of water used
k. Number of sustainability training hours
l. Number of employee hours devoted to local volunteering
m. Charitable contributions as a percent of income
n. Customer survey rating company's green reputation
o. Number of employees on sustainability teams
p. Cubic meters of natural gas used for heating facilities
q. Total megawatt hours of electricity purchased
r. Percent of bottles and cans sold recovered through company-supported recovery programs

EXERCISES Group B

E10-29B Identify type of responsibility center *(Learning Objective 1)*

Each of the following situations describes an organizational unit. Identify which type of responsibility center each underlined item is (cost, revenue, profit, or investment center).

Organization	Type of Responsibility Center (Cost, Revenue, Profit, or Investment)
a. Sherwin-Williams Store #1933 is located in Copley, Ohio. The store sells paints, wallpapers, and supplies to do-it-yourself customers and to professional wall covering installers.	
b. The Accounting Research and Compliance Department at FirstEnergy is responsible for researching how new accounting pronouncements and rules will impact FirstEnergy's financial statements.	
c. The Southwestern Sales Region of McDermott Foods is responsible for selling the various product lines of McDermott.	
d. The Taxation Department at Verizon Communications, Inc., is responsible for preparing the federal, state, and local income and franchise tax returns for the corporation.	
e. The Roseville Chipotle restaurant in Minnesota, is owned by its parent Chipotle Mexican Grill, Inc. The Roseville Chipotle, like other Chipotle restaurants, serves burritos, fajitas, and tacos and competes in the "fast-casual" dining category.	
f. Trek Bicycle Corporation manufactures and distributes bicycles and cycling products under the Trek, Gary Fisher, Bontrager, and Klein brand names.	
g. The Hershey Company is one of the oldest chocolate companies in the United States. Its product lines include the Mauna Loa Macadamia Nuts, Dagoba Organic Chocolates, and Joseph Schmidt Confections.	
h. The Human Resources Department is responsible for recruiting and training for the Kohl's Corporation.	
i. The reservation office for BlueSky Airlines, Inc., is responsible for both web sales and counter sales.	
j. The Disney Store at Spring Hill Mall in West Dundee, Illinois, is owned by The Walt Disney Company.	
k. H & R Block Tax Services, H & R Block Bank, and McGladrey are all divisions of their parent corporation, H & R Block.	

E10-30B Complete and analyze a performance report *(Learning Objective 2)*

One subunit of Atlantic Sports Manufacturing Company had the following financial results last month:

	A	B	C	D	E	F	G
1	Atlantic Sports Manufacturing Company—Water Sports Subunit						
2	Monthly Performance Report						
3	For the Month						
4							
5	Product	Actual	Budgeted	Variance*		Variance Percentage*	
6	Direct materials	$ 21,480	$ 20,000				
7	Direct labor	16,660	17,500				
8	Indirect labor	28,140	24,000				
9	Utilities	10,940	10,000				
10	Depreciation	21,800	21,800				
11	Repairs and maintenance	4,195	5,000				
12	Total	$ 103,215	$ 98,300				
13							

*Be sure to indicate whether each variance is favorable (F) or unfavorable (U).

Requirements

1. Complete the performance evaluation report for this subunit (round to four decimals).
2. Based on the data presented, what type of responsibility center is this subunit?
3. Which items should be investigated if part of management's decision criteria is to investigate all variances exceeding $3,000 or 12.5%?
4. Should only unfavorable variances be investigated? Explain.

E10-31B Prepare a segment margin performance report (Learning Objective 2)

Clayton Industries has gathered the following information about the actual sales revenues and expenses for its pharmaceuticals segment for the most recent year (all data is in millions).

Sales	$908,280
Variable Cost of Goods Sold	$310,590
Variable Operating Expenses	$ 78,300
Direct Fixed Manufacturing Overhead	$112,270
Direct Fixed Operating Expenses	$ 22,000
Common Fixed Expenses	$ 23,690

Budgeted data for the same time period for the pharmaceutical segment are as follows (all data is in millions):

Budgeted sales in units	8,700
Budgeted average selling price per unit	$ 90
Variable Cost of Goods Sold per unit	$ 35
Variable Operating Expenses per unit	$ 10
Direct Fixed Manufacturing Overhead (in total)	$103,000
Direct Fixed Operating Expenses (in total)	$ 20,000
Common Fixed Expenses Allocated to the Pharmaceutical Segment	$ 23,000

Prepare a segment margin performance report for the pharmaceutical segment. In this report, be sure to include lines for the contribution margin, the segment margin, and operating income. Calculate a variance and a variance percentage for each line in the report. Round to the nearest hundredth for the variance percentages (for example, if your answer is 16.2384%, round it to 16.24%).

E10-32B Compute and interpret the expanded ROI equation
(Learning Objective 3)

Zula, a national manufacturer of lawn-mowing and snow-blowing equipment, segments its business according to customer type: Professional and Residential. Assume that the following divisional information was available for the past year (in thousands of dollars):

	Sales	Operating Income	Total Assets
Residential	$ 585,000	$ 70,200	$195,000
Professional	$1,013,600	$152,040	$362,000

Management has a 27% target rate of return for each division.

Requirements

1. Calculate each division's ROI. Round all of your answers to four decimal places.
2. Calculate each division's sales margin. Interpret your results.
3. Calculate each division's capital turnover. Interpret your results.
4. Use the expanded ROI formula to confirm your results from Requirement 1. What can you conclude?
5. Calculate each division's residual income (RI). Interpret your results.

E10-33B   Relationship between ROI and residual income *(Learning Objective 3)*

Data on three unrelated companies are given in the following table.

	Osborne Company	Plumb Industries	Calloway, Inc.
Sales	$108,000	?	$520,000
Operating income	$ 43,200	$126,000	?
Total assets	$ 72,000	?	?
Sales margin	?	15%	8%
Capital turnover	?	4.20	?
Return on investment (ROI).......	?	?	20%
Target rate of return	9%	19%	?
Residual income	?	?	$ 4,160

Requirement

Fill in the missing information.

E10-34B   Compute ROI and residual income *(Learning Objective 3)*

Results from Percy Corporation's most recent year of operations is presented in the following table:

Operating income	$ 8,060
Total assets	$15,500
Current liabilities	$ 4,000
Sales	$31,000
Target rate of return	15%

Requirements

1. Calculate the sales margin, capital turnover, and return on investment (ROI).
2. Calculate the residual income (RI).

E10-35B   Comparison of ROI and residual income *(Learning Objective 3)*

Cleary Ceramics, a division of Alderman Corporation, has an operating income of $77,000 and total assets of $440,000. The required rate of return for the company is 15%. The company is evaluating whether it should use return on investment (ROI) or residual income (RI) as a measurement of performance for its division managers.

   The manager of Cleary Ceramics has the opportunity to undertake a new project that will require an investment of $110,000. This investment would earn $13,200 for the company.

Requirements

1. What is the original return on investment (ROI) for Cleary Ceramics (before making any additional investment)?
2. What would the ROI be for Cleary Ceramics if this investment opportunity were undertaken? Would the manager of the Cleary Ceramics division want to make this investment if she were evaluated based on ROI? Why or why not?
3. What is the ROI of the investment opportunity? Would the investment be desirable from the standpoint of Alderman Corporation? Why or why not?
4. What would the residual income (RI) be for Cleary Ceramics if this investment opportunity were to be undertaken? Would the manager of the Cleary Ceramics division want to make this investment if she were evaluated based on RI? Why or why not?
5. What is the RI of the investment opportunity? Would the investment be desirable from the standpoint of Alderman Corporation? Why or why not?
6. Which performance measurement method, ROI or RI, promotes goal congruence? Why?

CHAPTER 10

E10-36B Determine transfer price range *(Learning Objective 4)*

Gloucester Motors manufactures specialty tractors. It has two divisions: a Tractor Division and a Tire Division. The Tractor Division can use the tires produced by the Tire Division. The market price per tire is $60.

The Tire Division has the following costs per tire:

Direct material cost per tire $31
Conversion costs per tire $5

Fixed manufacturing overhead cost for the year is expected to total $220,000. The Tire Division expects to manufacture 55,000 tires this year. The fixed manufacturing overhead per tire is $4 ($220,000 divided by 55,000 tires).

Requirements

1. Assume that the Tire Division has excess capacity, meaning that it can produce tires for the Tractor Division without giving up any of its current tire sales to outsiders. If Gloucester Motors has a negotiated transfer price policy, what is the lowest acceptable transfer price? What is the highest acceptable transfer price?

2. If Gloucester Motors has a cost-plus transfer price policy of full absorption cost plus 10%, what would the transfer price be?

3. If the Tire Division is currently producing at capacity (meaning that it is selling every single tire it has the capacity to produce), what would likely be the most fair transfer price strategy to use? What would be the transfer price in this case?

E10-37B Prepare a flexible budget performance report *(Learning Objective 5)*

Sweet Street Muffins sells its muffins to restaurants and coffee houses for an average selling price of $33 per case. The following information relates to the budget for Sweet Street Muffins for this year (all figures are annual totals unless otherwise noted):

Budgeted sales in cases	7,900 cases
Packaging cost per case	$ 3.00
Shipping expense per case	$ 1.00
Sales commission expense	2% of sales price
Salaries expense	$6,900
Office rent	$3,300
Depreciation	$3,000
Insurance expense	$2,300
Office supplies expense	$1,100

During the year, Sweet Street Muffins actually sold 8,400 cases resulting in total sales revenue of $284,800. Actual expenses (in total) from this year are as follows:

Packaging cost	$26,100
Shipping expense	$ 8,900
Sales commission expense	$ 5,696
Salaries expense	$ 7,700
Office rent	$ 3,300
Depreciation	$ 3,000
Insurance expense	$ 2,000
Office supplies expense	$ 1,300

Requirement

Construct a flexible budget performance report for Sweet Street Muffins for the year. Be sure to indicate whether each variance is favorable (F) or unfavorable (U).

E10-38B Complete and analyze a performance report (Learning Objective 5)

The accountant for a subunit of Thornton Sports Company went on vacation before completing the subunit's monthly performance report. This is as far as she got:

	A	B	C	D	E	F	G	H
1		Ski Products Subunit—Thornton Sports Company						
2		Flexible Budget Performance Report: Sales						
3		For the Month						
4								
5		Actual	Flexible Budget Variance		Flexible Budget	Volume Variance		Master Budget
6	Downhill Model RI	$ 323,000				$ 19,000	F	301,000
7	Downhill Model RII	152,000			$ 165,000			143,000
8	Cross-Country Model EXI	289,000	$ 1,000	U	290,000			308,000
9	Cross-Country Model EXII	255,000			245,000	20,500	U	265,500
10	Snowboard Model LXI	420,000	4,000	F				400,000
11	Total	$ 1,439,000						$ 1,417,500
12								

Requirements

1. Complete the performance evaluation report for this subunit.
2. Based on the data presented, what type of responsibility center is this subunit?
3. Which items should be investigated if part of the management's decision criteria is to investigate all variances exceeding $15,000? Interpret your results. (What could cause these variances? What impact might these variances have on company inventory levels and operations?)

E10-39B Work backward to find missing values (Learning Objective 5)

Panco Corporation has a relevant range extending to 30,000 units each month. The following performance report provides information about Panco's budget and actual performance for November.

	A	B	C	D	E	F	G	H
1		Panco Industries						
2		Flexible Budget Performance Report: Sales and Operating Expenses						
3		For the Month Ended November 30						
4								
5		Actual	(A)		Flexible Budget	(B)		Master Budget
6	Output units	25,000			(C)			30,000
7								
8	Sales revenue	$ 240,000	$ 5,000	F	(D)			
9	Operating expenses:							
10	Variable expenses				(E)			$ 187,500
11	Fixed expenses	$ 15,500	(F)					23,000
12	Total operating expenses							(G)
13								

Requirement

Find the missing data for letters A through G. Be sure to label any variances as favorable or unfavorable. (Hint: A and B are titles.)

E10-40B   Construct a balanced scorecard (Learning Objective 6)

Jubilee Corporation is preparing its balanced scorecard for the past quarter. The balanced scorecard contains four perspectives: financial, customer, internal business process, and learning and growth. Through its strategic management planning process, Jubilee Corporation has selected two specific objectives for each of the four perspectives; these specific objectives are listed in the following table.

Specific Objective
1. Increase gross margin.
2. Improve post-sales service.
3. Improve employee product knowledge.
4. Increase customer retention.
5. Develop new core products.
6. Increase market share.
7. Increase sales of core product line.
8. Improve employee job satisfaction.

Jubilee Corporation has collected key performance indicators (KPIs) to measure progress toward achieving its specific objectives. The following table contains the KPIs and corresponding data that Jubilee Corporation has collected for the past quarter.

	A	B	C
1	KPI	Goal	Actual
2	Hours of employee training provided	2,400	2,275
3	Number of new core products	15	19
4	Gross margin growth percentage	27%	28%
5	Employee turnover rate (number of employees leaving company / total number of employees)	5%	7%
6	Sales revenue growth—core product line	$ 2,300,000	$ 2,000,000
7	Market share percentage	18%	13%
8	Average repair time (number of days)	1.1	1.3
9	Number of repeat customers	100,000	103,000
10			

Requirement

Prepare a balanced scorecard report for Jubilee Corporation, using the following format.

Jubilee Corporation
Balanced Scorecard Report
For Quarter Ended December 31

Perspective	Objective	KPI	Goal	Actual	Goal Achieved? (✓ if met)
Financial					
Customer..					
Internal Business Process					
Learning and Growth					

For each of the specific objectives listed, place that objective under the appropriate perspective heading in the report. Select a KPI from the list of KPIs that would be appropriate to measure progress toward each objective. (There are two specific objectives for each perspective and one KPI for each of the specific objectives.) In the last column in the balanced scorecard report, place a check mark if the associated KPI goal has been achieved.

SUSTAINABILITY

E10-41B   Sustainability and the balanced scorecard (Learning Objective 6)

Classify each of the following sustainability key performance indicators (KPIs) according to the balanced scorecard perspective it addresses. Choose from the following five perspectives:

- Financial perspective
- Customer perspective

- Internal business perspective
- Learning and growth perspective
- Community perspective

KPI

a. Number of sustainability training hours
b. Number of employees on sustainability teams
c. Percentage of products reclaimed after customer use
d. Number of green products
e. Packaging use ratio, defined as grams of materials used per liter of product produced
f. Customer survey rating company's green reputation
g. Product safety ratings
h. Total megajoules of energy used
i. Number of functions with environmental responsibilities
j. Percentage of recycled content in products
k. Revenue from recycling packaging materials
l. Cost of water used
m. Direct greenhouse gas emissions
n. Waste disposal costs
o. Number of employee hours devoted to volunteering at Habitat for Humanity
p. Percent of bottles and cans sold recovered through company-supported recovery programs
q. Percentage of products sourced locally
r. Percent of plants in compliance with internal waste-water treatment standards

PROBLEMS Group A

P10-42A Prepare a budget with different volumes for planning
(Learning Objective 2)

Lively Bubbles, Inc., produces multicolored bubble solution used for weddings and other events. The company's master budget income statement for July follows. It is based on expected sales volume of 45,000 bubble kits.

LIVELY BUBBLES, INC.	
Master Budget Income Statement	
Month Ended July 31	
Sales revenue	$137,250
Variable expenses:	
Cost of goods sold	$ 56,250
Sales commissions	6,750
Utility expense	9,000
Fixed expenses:	
Salary expense	30,000
Depreciation expense	20,000
Rent expense	10,000
Utility expense	4,000
Total expenses	$136,000
Operating income	$ 1,250

Lively Bubbles' plant capacity is 52,500 kits. If actual volume exceeds 52,500 kits, the company must expand the plant. In that case, salaries will increase by 10%, depreciation by 15%, and rent by $5,000. Fixed utilities will be unchanged by any volume increase.

Requirements

1. Prepare flexible budget income statements for the company, showing output levels of 45,000, 50,000, and 55,000 kits.
2. Graph the behavior of the company's total costs. Use total costs on the y-axis and volume (in thousands of bubble kits) on the x-axis.
3. Why might Lively Bubbles' managers want to see the graph you prepared in Requirement 2 as well as the columnar format analysis in Requirement 1? What is the disadvantage of the graphic approach?

P10-43A   Prepare and interpret a performance report *(Learning Objective 2)*

Refer to the Lively Bubbles data in P10-42A. The company sold 50,000 bubble kits during July, and its actual operating income was as follows:

LIVELY BUBBLES, INC.
Master Budget Income Statement
Month Ended July 31

Sales revenue	$160,500
Variable expenses:	
Cost of goods sold	$ 63,000
Sales commissions	9,000
Utility expense	10,000
Fixed expenses:	
Salary expense	32,200
Depreciation expense	20,000
Rent expense	9,550
Utility expense	4,000
Total expenses	$147,750
Operating income	$ 12,750

Requirements

1. Prepare an income statement performance report for July.
2. What accounts for most of the difference between actual operating income and master budget operating income?
3. What is Lively Bubbles' master budget variance? Explain why the income statement performance report provides Lively Bubbles' managers with more useful information than the simple master budget variance. What insights can Lively Bubbles' managers draw from this performance report?

P10-44A   Evaluate divisional performance *(Learning Objective 3)*

Sherwin-Williams is a national paint manufacturer and retailer. The company is segmented into five divisions: Paint Stores (branded retail location), Consumer (paint sold through stores such as Sears, Home Depot, and Lowe's), Automotive (sales to auto manufacturers), International, and Administration. The following is selected hypothetical divisional information for the company's two largest divisions: Paint Stores and Consumer (in thousands of dollars).

	Sales	Operating Income	Total Assets
Paint stores	$4,000,000	$440,000	$1,250,000
Consumer	$1,140,000	$148,200	$1,425,000

Assume that management has specified a 21% target rate of return.

Requirements

Round all calculations to two decimal places.

1. Calculate each division's ROI.
2. Calculate each division's sales margin. Interpret your results.
3. Calculate each division's capital turnover. Interpret your results.
4. Use the expanded ROI formula to confirm your results from Requirement 1. Interpret your results.
5. Calculate each division's RI. Interpret your results and offer recommendations for any divisions with negative RI.
6. Total asset data were provided in this problem. If you were to gather this information from an annual report, how would you measure total assets? Describe your measurement choices and some of the pros and cons of those choices.
7. Describe some of the factors that management considers when setting its minimum target rate of return. Describe some of the factors that management considers when setting its minimum target rate of return.
8. Explain why some firms prefer to use RI rather than ROI for performance measurement.
9. Explain why budget versus actual performance reports are insufficient for evaluating the performance of investment centers.

P10-45A Collect and analyze division data from an annual report
(Learning Objective 3)

FlashCo segments its company into four distinct divisions. The net revenues, operating profit, and total assets for these divisions are disclosed in the footnotes to FlashCo's consolidated financial statements and the following presented information:

Notes to Consolidated Financial Statements

Note 1-Basis of Presentation and Our Divisions:

We manufacture, market, and sell a variety of products through our divisions, including furniture and fixtures for the home, office, stores, and health-care facilities. The accounting policies are the same for each division, as indicated in Note 2.

	Net Revenue			Operating Profit		
	2014	2013	2012	2014	2013	2012
Home furnishings ...	$10,500	$ 9,400	$ 9,000	$2,625	$2,350	$1,800
Office furniture	9,000	8,100	7,800	1,800	1,620	1,560
Store displays	12,100	10,900	10,400	1,210	1,070	1,010
Health-care furnishings	1,500	1,350	1,250	495	470	450
Total division...........	$33,100	$29,750	$28,450	$6,130	$5,510	$4,820
Corporate...............				(320)	(280)	(235)
Total.......................	$33,100	$29,750	$28,450	$5,810	$5,230	$4,585

Corporate includes the costs of our corporate headquarters, centrally managed initiatives, and certain gains and losses that cannot be accurately allocated to specific divisions, such as derivative gains and losses.

	Amortization of Intangible Assets			Depreciation and Other Amortization		
	2014	2013	2012	2014	2013	2012
Home furnishings	$ 15	$ 10	$ 10	$ 440	$ 430	$ 435
Office furniture	78	73	73	295	275	270
Store displays	70	65	63	495	440	400
Health-care furnishings			4	30	35	32
Total division.................	$163	$148	$150	$1,260	$1,180	$1,137
Corporate.....................				15	20	19
Total..............................	$163	$148	$150	$1,275	$1,200	$1,156

	Total Assets			Capital Spending		
	2014	2013	2012	2014	2013	2012
Home furnishings	$ 6,250	$ 5,000	$ 4,500	$ 510	$ 520	$ 480
Office furniture	6,000	5,400	5,200	520	350	295
Store displays	11,000	9,800	9,400	855	685	550
Health-care furnishings	625	425	375	35	35	40
Total division.................	$23,875	$20,625	$19,475	$1,920	$1,590	$1,365
Corporate.....................	1,770	5,330	3,530	195	200	85
Total..............................	$25,645	$25,955	$23,005	$2,115	$1,790	$1,450

Corporate assets consist of cash, short-term investments, and property, plant, and equipment. The corporate property, plant, and equipment includes the headquarters building, equipment within, and the surrounding property.

Requirements

1. What are FlashCo's four business divisions? Make a table listing each division, its net revenues, operating profit, and total assets.
2. Use the data you collected in Requirement 1 to calculate each division's sales margin. Interpret your results.
3. Use the data you collected in Requirement 1 to calculate each division's capital turnover. Interpret your results.
4. Use the data you collected in Requirement 1 to calculate each division's ROI. Interpret your results.
5. Can you calculate RI using the data presented? Why or why not?

P10-46A   Determine transfer price at a manufacturer under various scenarios
(Learning Objective 4)

Assume the Small Components Division of Swisher Manufacturing produces a video card used in the assembly of a variety of electronic products. The division's manufacturing costs and variable selling expenses related to the video card are as follows:

	Cost per unit
Direct materials	$11.00
Direct labor	$ 5.00
Variable manufacturing overhead	$ 4.00
Fixed manufacturing overhead (at current production level)	$ 6.00
Variable selling expenses	$ 2.00

The Computer Division of Swisher Manufacturing can use the video card produced by the Small Components Division and is interested in purchasing the video card in-house rather than buying it from an outside supplier. The Small Components Division has sufficient excess capacity with which to make the extra video cards. Because of competition, the market price for this video card is $30 regardless of whether the video card is produced by Swisher Manufacturing or another company.

Requirements

1. What is the highest acceptable transfer price for the divisions?
2. Assuming the transfer price is negotiated between the divisions of the company, what would be the lowest acceptable transfer price?
3. Which transfer price would the manager of the Small Components Division prefer? Which transfer price would the manager of the Computer Division prefer?
4. If the company's policy requires that all in-house transfers must be priced at full absorption cost plus 10%, what transfer price would be used? Assume that the increased production level needed to fill the transfer would result in fixed manufacturing overhead decreasing by $1.00 per unit. *(Round your answer to the nearest cent.)*
5. If the company's policy requires that all in-house transfers must be priced at total manufacturing variable cost plus 25%, what transfer price would be used? Assume that the company does not consider fixed manufacturing overhead in setting its internal transfer price in this scenario. *(Round your answer to the nearest cent.)*
6. Assume now that the company does incur the variable selling expenses on internal transfers. If the company policy is to set transfer prices at 105% of the sum of the full absorption cost and the variable selling expenses, what transfer price would be set? Assume that the fixed manufacturing overhead would drop by $1.00 per unit as a result of the increased production resulting from the internal transfers. *(Round your answer to the nearest cent.)*

P10-47A   Evaluate subunit performance *(Learning Objectives 5 & 6)*

One subunit of Seasons Sports Company had the following financial results last month:

	A	B	C	D	E	F	G
1		Seasons Sports Manufacturing Company—Team Sports Subunit					
2		Monthly Performance Report					
3		For the Month					
4							
5	Product	Actual	Budgeted	Variance*		Variance Percentage*	
6	Sales	$ 545,500	$ 500,000				
7	Less: Variable expenses	387,000	375,000				
8	Contribution margin	$ 158,500	$ 125,000				
9	Less: Direct fixed expenses	10,380	10,000				
10	Segment margin	$ 148,120	$ 115,000				
11	Less: Common fixed expenses	52,000	40,000				
12	Operating income	$ 96,120	$ 75,000				
13							

Be sure to indicate whether each variance is favorable (F) or unfavorable (U).

Requirements

1. Complete the performance evaluation report for this subunit (round to three decimal places).
2. Based on the data presented, what type of responsibility center is this subunit?
3. Which items should be investigated if part of the management's decision criteria is to investigate all variances equal to or exceeding $12,000 and exceeding 12% (both criteria must be met)?
4. Should only unfavorable variances be investigated? Explain.
5. Is it possible that the variances are due to a higher-than-expected sales volume? Explain.
6. Do you think management will place equal weight on each of the $12,000 variances? Explain.

7. Which balanced scorecard perspective is being addressed through this performance report? In your opinion, is this performance report a lead or lag indicator? Explain.

8. Give one key performance indicator for the other three balanced scorecard perspectives. Indicate which perspective is being addressed by the indicator you list. Are they lead or lag indicators? Explain.

PROBLEMS Group B

P10-48B Prepare a budget with different volumes for planning
(Learning Objective 2)

Precious Bubbles produces multicolored bubble solution used for weddings and other events.

Precious Bubbles' plant capacity is 72,500 kits. If actual volume exceeds 72,500 kits, the company must expand the plant. In that case, salaries will increase by 10%, depreciation by 15%, and rent by $6,000. Fixed utilities will be unchanged by any volume increase.

The company's master budget income statement for March follows. It is based on expected sales volume of 65,000 bubble kits.

PRECIOUS BUBBLES, INC.
Master Budget Income Statement
Month Ended March 31

Sales revenue	$198,250
Variable expenses:	
Cost of goods sold	81,250
Sales commissions	9,750
Utility expense	13,000
Fixed expenses:	
Salary expense	30,000
Depreciation expense	20,000
Rent expense	10,000
Utility expense	5,000
Total expenses	$169,000
Operating income	$ 29,250

Requirements

1. Prepare flexible budget income statements for the company, showing output levels of 65,000, 70,000, and 75,000 kits.

2. Graph the behavior of the company's total costs. Use total costs on the y-axis and volume (in thousands of bubble kits) on the x-axis.

3. Why might Precious Bubbles' managers want to see the graph you prepared in Requirement 2 as well as the columnar format analysis in Requirement 1? What is the disadvantage of the graphic approach?

P10-49B   Prepare and interpret a performance report *(Learning Objective 2)*

Refer to the Precious Bubbles' data in P10-48B. The company sold 70,000 bubble kits during March and its actual operating income was as follows:

PRECIOUS BUBBLES, INC.
Master Budget Income Statement
Month Ended March 31

Sales revenue	$221,600
Variable expenses:	
Cost of goods sold	$ 88,250
Sales commissions	13,250
Utility expense	14,000
Fixed expenses:	
Salary expense	32,300
Depreciation expense	20,000
Rent expense	9,650
Utility expense	5,000
Total expenses	$182,450
Operating income	$ 39,150

Requirements

1. Prepare an income statement performance report for March.
2. What accounts for most of the difference between actual operating income and master budget operating income?
3. What is Precious Bubbles' master budget variance? Explain why the income statement performance report provides Precious Bubbles' managers with more useful information than the simple master budget variance. What insights can Precious Bubbles' managers draw from this performance report?

P10-50B   Evaluate divisional performance *(Learning Objective 3)*

Sherwin-Williams Paints is a national paint manufacturer and retailer. The company is segmented into five divisions: Paint Stores (branded retail locations), Consumer (paint sold through stores like Sears, Home Depot, and Lowe's), Automotive (sales to auto manufacturers), International, and Administration. The following is selected hypothetical divisional information for its two largest divisions: Paint Stores and Consumer (in thousands of dollars).

	Sales	Operating Income	Total Assets
Paint stores	$3,920,000	$490,000	$1,400,000
Consumer	$1,400,000	$231,000	$2,000,000

Assume that management has specified a 23% target rate of return.

Requirements

Round all calculations to four decimal places.

1. Calculate each division's ROI.
2. Calculate each division's sales margin. Interpret your results.
3. Calculate each division's capital turnover. Interpret your results.
4. Use the expanded ROI formula to confirm your results from Requirement 1. Interpret your results.
5. Calculate each division's RI. Interpret your results and offer recommendations for any division with negative RI.
6. Total asset data was provided in this problem. If you were to gather this information from an annual report, how would you measure total assets? Describe your measurement choices and some of the pros and cons of those choices.

7. Describe some of the factors that management considers when setting its minimum target rate of return.

8. Explain why some firms prefer to use RI rather than ROI for performance measurement.

9. Explain why budget versus actual performance reports are insufficient for evaluating the performance of investment centers.

P10-51B   Collect and analyze division data from an annual report
(Learning Objective 3)

GlennCo segments its company into four distinctive divisions. The net revenues, operating profit, and total assets for these divisions are disclosed in the footnotes to GlennCo's consolidated financial statements and presented here.

	Net Revenue			Operating Profit		
	2014	2013	2012	2014	2013	2012
Home furnishings	$10,000	$ 8,900	$ 8,500	$2,500	$2,225	$1,675
Office furniture	9,100	8,200	7,900	1,820	1,640	1,580
Store displays	13,000	11,800	11,300	1,690	1,550	1,490
Health-care furnishings	1,500	1,350	1,250	480	455	435
Total division...................	$33,600	$30,250	$28,950	$6,490	$5,870	$5,180
Corporate.......................				(360)	(320)	(275)
Total.................................	$33,600	$30,250	$28,950	$6,130	$5,550	$4,905

Corporate includes the costs of our corporate headquarters, centrally managed initiatives, and certain gains and losses that cannot be accurately allocated to specific divisions, such as derivative gains and losses.

	Amortization of Intangible Assets			Depreciation and Other Amortization		
	2014	2013	2012	2014	2013	2012
Home furnishings	$ 20	$ 15	$ 15	$ 440	$ 430	$ 435
Office furniture	80	75	75	280	260	255
Store displays	72	67	65	465	410	370
Health-care furnishings.........			4	25	30	27
Total division.........................	$172	$157	$159	$1,210	$1,130	$1,087
Corporate..............................				30	35	34
Total.......................................	$172	$157	$159	$1,240	$1,165	$1,121

	Total Assets			Capital Spending		
	2014	2013	2012	2014	2013	2012
Home furnishings	$ 8,000	$ 6,750	$ 6,250	$ 525	$ 535	$ 495
Office furniture	6,500	5,900	5,700	485	315	260
Store displays	12,500	11,300	10,900	865	695	560
Health-care furnishings	750	550	500	20	20	25
Total division.................	$27,750	$24,500	$23,350	$1,895	$1,565	$1,340
Corporate.....................	1,780	5,340	3,540	195	200	85
Total..............................	$29,530	$29,840	$26,890	$2,090	$1,765	$1,425

Corporate assets consist of cash, short-term investments, and property, plant, and equipment. The corporate property, plant, and equipment includes the headquarters building, equipment within, and the surrounding property.

Notes to Consolidated Financial Statements

Note 1-Basis of Presentation and Our Divisions:

We manufacture, market, and sell a variety of products through our divisions, including furniture and fixtures for the home, office, stores, and health-care facilities. The accounting policies are the same for each division, as indicated in Note 2.

Requirements

1. What are GlennCo's four business divisions? Make a table listing each division, its net revenues, operating profit, and total assets.
2. Use the data you collected in Requirement 1 to calculate each division's sales margin. Interpret your results.
3. Use the data you collected in Requirement 1 to calculate each division's capital turnover. Interpret your results.
4. Use the data you collected in Requirement 1 to calculate each division's ROI. Interpret your results.
5. Can you calculate RI using the data presented? Why or why not?

P10-52B   Determine transfer price at a manufacturer under various scenarios
(Learning Objective 4)

Assume the Small Components Division of Nelson Manufacturing produces a video card used in the assembly of a variety of electronic products. The division's manufacturing costs and variable selling expenses related to the video card are as follows:

	Cost per unit
Direct materials	$ 20.00
Direct labor	$ 5.00
Variable manufacturing overhead	$ 3.00
Fixed manufacturing overhead (at current production level)	$ 8.00
Variable selling expenses	$ 2.00

The Computer Division of Nelson Manufacturing can use the video card produced by the Small Components Division and is interested in purchasing the video card in-house rather than buying it from an outside supplier. The Small Components Division has sufficient excess capacity with which to make the extra video cards. Because of competition, the market price for this video card is $45 regardless of whether the video card is produced by Nelson Manufacturing or another company.

Requirements

1. What is the highest acceptable transfer price for the divisions?
2. Assuming the transfer price is negotiated between the divisions of the company, what would be the lowest acceptable transfer price?
3. Which transfer price would the manager of the Small Components Division prefer? Which transfer price would the manager of the Computer Division prefer?
4. If the company's policy requires that all in-house transfers must be priced at full absorption cost plus 20%, what transfer price would be used? Assume that the increased production level needed to fill the transfer would result in fixed manufacturing overhead decreasing by $4.00 per unit. *(Round your answer to the nearest cent.)*

5. If the company's policy requires that all in-house transfers must be priced at total manufacturing variable cost plus 25%, what transfer price would be used? Assume that the company does not consider fixed manufacturing overhead in setting its internal transfer price in this scenario. *(Round your answer to the nearest cent.)*

6. Assume now that the company does incur the variable selling expenses on internal transfers. If the company policy is to set transfer prices at 110% of the sum of the full absorption cost and the variable selling expenses, what would the transfer price be set at? Assume that the fixed manufacturing overhead would drop by $4.00 per unit as a result of the increased production resulting from the internal transfers. *(Round your answer to the nearest cent.)*

P10-53B   Evaluate subunit performance *(Learning Objectives 5 & 6)*

One subunit of Zoom Sports Company had the following financial results last month:

	A	B	C	D	E	F	G
1	Zoom Sports Manufacturing Company—Water Sports Subunit						
2	Monthly Performance Report						
3	For the Month						
4							
5	Product	Actual	Budgeted	Variance*		Variance Percentage*	
6	Sales	$ 543,000	$ 500,000				
7	Less: Variable expenses	310,500	300,000				
8	Contribution margin	$ 232,500	$ 200,000				
9	Less: Direct fixed expenses	78,450	75,000				
10	Segment margin	$ 154,050	$ 125,000				
11	Less: Common fixed expenses	48,000	37,500				
12	Operating income	$ 106,050	$ 87,500				
13							

Be sure to indicate whether each variance is favorable (F) or unfavorable (U).

Requirements

1. Complete the performance evaluation report for the subunit (round to three decimal places).

2. Based on the data presented, what type of responsibility center is this subunit?

3. Which items should be investigated if part of management's decision criteria is to investigate all variances equal to or exceeding $10,500 and exceeding 16% (both criteria must be met)?

4. Should only unfavorable variances be investigated? Explain.

5. Is it possible that the variances are due to a higher-than-expected sales volume? Explain.

6. Do you think management will place equal weight on each of the $10,500 variances? Explain.

7. Which balanced scorecard perspective is being addressed through this performance report? In your opinion, is this performance report a lead or lag indicator? Explain.

8. List one key performance indicator for the other three balanced scorecard perspectives. Indicate which perspective is being addressed by the indicators you list. Are they lead or lag indicators? Explain.

CRITICAL THINKING

Discussion & Analysis

A10-54 Discussion Questions

1. Describe at least four advantages of decentralization. Also describe at least two disadvantages to decentralization.

2. Compare and contrast a cost center, a revenue center, a profit center, and an investment center. List a specific example of each type of responsibility center. How is the performance of managers evaluated in each type of responsibility center?

3. Explain the potential problem which could arise from using ROI as the incentive measure for managers. What are some specific actions a company might take to resolve this potential problem?

4. Describe at least two specific actions that a company could take to improve its ROI.

5. Define residual income. How is it calculated? Describe the major weakness of residual income.

6. Compare and contrast a master budget and a flexible budget.

7. Describe two ways managers can use flexible budgets.

8. Define key performance indicator (KPI). What is the relationship between KPIs and a company's objectives? Select a company of any size with which you are familiar. List at least four examples of specific objectives that a company might have and one potential KPI for each of those specific objectives.

9. List and describe the four perspectives found on a balanced scorecard. For each perspective, list at least two examples of KPIs which might be used to measure performance on that perspective.

10. Contrast lag indicators with lead indicators. Provide an example of each type of indicator.

11. Some companies integrate sustainability measures into the traditional four perspectives in their balanced scorecards. Other companies create a new perspective (or two) for sustainability. Which method do you think would result in better supporting sustainability efforts throughout the organization? Explain your viewpoint.

12. Find an annual report for a publicly held company (go to the company's website and look for "Investor Relations" or a similar link). How many sustainability initiatives can you find in the annual report? What internal balanced scorecard measures do you think they might use to measure progress on each sustainability initiative? (You will have to use your imagination, since typically most balanced scorecard measures are not publicly disclosed.)

Application & Analysis

Mini Cases

A10-55 Segmented Financial Information

Select a company you are interested in and obtain its annual reports by going to the company's website. Download the annual report for the most recent year. (On many companies' websites, you will need to visit the Investor Relations section to obtain the company's financial statements.) You may also collect the information from the company's Form 10-K, which can be found at http://sec.gov/idea/searchidea/companysearch_idea.html.

REAL LIFE

Basic Discussion Questions

1. Locate the company's annual report as outlined previously. Find the company's segment information; it should be in the "Notes to Consolidated Financial Statements" or another, similarly named section. Look for the word "Segment" in a heading; that is usually the section you need.

2. List the segments as reported in the annual report. Make a table listing each operating segment, its revenues, income, and assets.

3. Use the data you collected in Requirement 2 to calculate each segment's sales margin. Interpret your results.

4. Use the data you collected in Requirement 2 to calculate each segment's capital turnover. Interpret your results.

5. Use the data you collected in Requirement 2 to calculate each segment's ROI. Interpret your results.

6. Can you calculate RI using the data presented? Why or why not?

7. The rules for how segments should be presented in the annual report are governed by external financial accounting rules. The information you gathered for the previous requirements would be used by investors and other external stakeholders in their analysis of the company and its stock. Internally, the company most likely has many segments. Based on what you know about the company and its products or services, list at least five potential segments that the company might use for internal reporting. Explain why this way of segmenting the company for internal reporting could be useful to managers.

Decision Cases

REAL LIFE

A10-56   Collect and analyze divisional data *(Learning Objective 4)*

Colgate-Palmolive operates two product segments. Using the company's website, locate segment information for 2012 in the company's 2012 annual report. (*Hint:* Look under Investor Relations.) Most of the information you are seeking will be in the Notes to the Consolidated Financial Statements (found in the Form 10-K).

Requirements

1. What are two segments (ignore geographical subsets of the one product segment)? Gather data about each segment's net sales, operating income, and identifiable assets.

2. Calculate ROI for each segment.

3. Which segment has the highest ROI? Explain why.

4. If you were on the top management team and could allocate extra funds to only one division, which division would you choose? Why?

ETHICS

A10-57   Ethics and performance evaluation *(Learning Objectives 2 & 4)*

Grommet Company has several divisions. The controller, Kayla Collins, prepares monthly segment reports for each division. Each division manager is evaluated annually, based largely on the segment margin for the manager's division. The segment margin for the division determines whether the manager receives a bonus, the amount of any bonus, and whether the division will even continue to be operated. Since operating losses reflect common fixed costs being allocated to a division, company management allows a division to show an operating loss in one or more years. However, the division is likely to be closed if its segment margin is negative for three consecutive years since management feels that the division is then a drain on the overall company's profits.

The past few years have been tough years for the Small Engines division. The economy has caused sales to shrink. In addition, the production manager, Craig Tatter, has had some personal problems and has not been focused on work. Tatter thinks his personal issues are behind him now and he is looking forward to better results in future years—as long as his division is not discontinued due to its poor operating results in the past few years. Here is an excerpt from the segment report for the Small Engines division for the past three years:

Grommet Company—Small Engines Division

Segment Margin Performance Report for the Fiscal Years
Ending December 31, 2013, 2012, and 2011

(all figures in thousands of dollars)

Product	2013	2012	2011
Sales revenue	$6,098	$6,501	$6,652
Less: Variable expenses			
Variable cost of goods sold	4,728	5,319	5,412
Variable operating expenses	693	517	564
Contribution margin	$ 677	$ 665	$ 676
Less: Direct fixed expenses			
Fixed manufacturing overhead	652	621	639
Fixed operating expenses	79	57	54
Segment margin	$ (54)	$ (13)	$ (17)
Less: Common fixed expenses	30	72	41
Operating income (loss)	$ (84)	$ (85)	$ (58)

Collins, the controller, is in a relationship with Tatter, the division manager of Small Engines. She wants to do whatever she can to help him with his work situation; she knows he is a good person and works hard. Once she sees the segment margin report for the Small Engines division, she realizes that there is a strong possibility that the Small Engines division will be closed due to segment margin losses over the past three years. She analyzes the preliminary segment margin performance report and realizes that there is an easy way that she could help. She could move some of the direct fixed expenses listed on the Small Engine segment report into the common fixed expenses allocated to the Small Engine division. She reasons that the overall operating income for the Small Engine division will remain the same and it really isn't hurting anyone to do this. In fact, she actually feels that she is helping the company and its employees. By the simple act of shifting some of the direct fixed costs to the common fixed expenses, she will be saving people's jobs by preventing the division from being closed.

There is very little chance of this shift between fixed expense categories being caught because the segment reports are hard to understand. No one in the company outside of the Accounting Department understands what is included in "Segment fixed expenses" versus "Common fixed costs." Collins has used a convoluted allocation system for years and company management has given up on understanding it and just accepts the monthly reports. Company management figures that overall the company does well, so the hard-to-understand accounting reports are just a necessary evil.

Requirements:

1. Using the IMA *Statement of Ethical Professional Practice* as an ethical framework, (see Exhibit 1-6) answer the following questions:
   a. What is (are) the ethical issue(s) in this situation?
   b. What are Collins' responsibilities as a management accountant?
2. Do you agree with Collins' reasoning that no one would get hurt by her actions? Why or why not?
3. Do you agree with Collins' assessment that she is actually helping the company, and that this justifies her actions?

A10-58 Analyzing segment margins reports *(Learning Objective 2)*

REAL LIFE

In today's electronics market, liquid-crystal-display (LCD) TVs are more popular than plasma TVs; organic-light-emitting-diode (OLED) TVs are also rapidly gaining market share. As a result, Panasonic Corporation recently closed a plasma TV plant in China[9] to allow it to focus its efforts on the more popular TVs.

[9]Source: "Panasonic Closes Plasma-TV Factory," *Wall Street Journal*, January 13, 2013, http://online.wsj.com/article/SB10001424127887324081704578234920278808676.html.

Panasonic operates several segments in various markets and is continually assessing its product offerings in these segments. The following is an excerpt from Panasonic Corporation's 2012 Annual Report and related DATA Book (Segment Information)[10]

Questions

1. Go to Panasonic's website and locate the information for investors. In its annual report, it describes each of the segments listed in the excerpt given in the case description. For each segment, write a brief description of what products and services are included in that segment.

2. For each of the segments in the Panasonic Segment Performance Report included in the case, calculate a profitability ratio for each year by using the following formula:

$$\text{Profit (loss)} \div \text{sales}$$

3. The plasma factory described in the case would have been a part of which segment? For that segment for the years 2010 through 2012, answer the following questions:
   a. Did sales increase, decrease, or remain about the same?
   b. Did profit (loss) increase, decrease, or remain about the same?
   c. Did the profitability ratio (as calculated in question 2) increase, decrease, or remain about the same?
   d. What observations can you make about the performance of this segment?

4. For each of the other segments for the years 2010 through 2012, answer the following questions:
   a. Did sales increase, decrease, or remain about the same?
   b. Did profit (loss) increase, decrease, or remain about the same?
   c. Did the profitability ratio (as calculated in question 2) increase, decrease, or remain about the same?

5. Of the eight segments, which three segments appear to be the strongest based on the limited information you have in this case? Support your answer.

6. Of the eight segments, which segments appear to be the weakest based on the limited information you have in this case? Support your answer.

Try It Solutions

page 585:

1. ROI = Operating income/Total assets = $695/966 = $71.9%
   Sales margin = Operating income/Sales revenue = $695/2,636 = $26.4%
   Capital turnover = Sales revenue/Total assets = $2,636/966 = $2.73

2. Residual income = Operating income − (Target rate of return × Total assets)
   = $695 million − (25% × $966 million) = $453.5 million

page 595:

The flexible budget is prepared using the original master budget assumptions for the *actual* volume achieved (125 jobs) rather than the volume originally anticipated (100 jobs). Therefore, the flexible budget should reflect the following expenses:

1. $1,250 of variable expenses (= 125 jobs × $10 per job)
2. $500 of fixed expenses
3. $1,750 for total operating expenses (= $1,250 + $500)

[10]Source: Panasonic Corporation 2012 Annual Report, http://panasonic.net/ir/annual/2012/pdf/panasonic_ar2012_e.pdf.

page 598:

	A	B	C	D	E	F	G	H
1	**Sam's Mowing Business** **Flexible Budget Performance Report for June**	**Actual**	**Flexible Budget Variance**		**Flexible Budget**	**Volume Variance**		**Master Budget**
2	**Sales volume (number of mowing jobs)**	**125**	**0**		**125**	**25**	**F**	**100**
3								
4	Operating expenses:							
5	Variable operating expenses ($10 per job)	$ 1,370	$ 120	U	$ 1,250	$ 250	U	$ 1,000
6	Fixed operating expenses ($500 per month)	475	25	F	500	0		500
7	Total operating expenses	$ 1,845	$ 95	U	$ 1,750	$ 250	U	$ 1,500
8								

1. The volume variance is the difference between the operating expenses in the flexible budget and what was budgeted for operating expenses in the master budget: $250 (= $1,750 − $1,500). Because the expenses in the flexible budget are higher than in the master budget, the variance is unfavorable.

2. The flexible budget variance is the difference between actual operating expenses and what was budgeted for expenses in the flexible budget: $95 (= $1,845 − $1,750). Because actual expenses are higher than budgeted, the variance is unfavorable.

3. The master budget variance is the difference between the actual operating expenses and what was budgeted for operating expenses in the master budget: $345 (= $1,845 − $1,500). Because actual expenses are higher than budgeted, the variance is unfavorable. It is also the total combination of the volume variance ($250 U) and flexible budget variance ($95 U).

Standard Costs and Variances

Oleksiy Maksymenko Photography/Alamy

Sources: http://www.businessweek.com/technology/content/apr2010/tc2010046_788280.htm; http://www.computerworld.com/s/article/9175020/iPad_costs_more_to_make_than_first_thought_says_iSuppli; http://www.isuppli.com/Teardowns/MarketWatch/Pages/iPad-andImitators-Set-to-Shakeup-Electronics-Supply-Chain.aspx; http://jobs.apple.com/index.ajs?BID=1&method=mExternal.showJob&RID=79010&CurrentPage=1; and Apple Inc., 2012 10-k.

Learning Objectives

■ **1** Explain how and why standard costs are developed

■ **2** Compute and evaluate direct materials variances

■ **3** Compute and evaluate direct labor variances

■ **4** Explain the advantages and disadvantages of using standard costs and variances

■ **5** Compute and evaluate variable overhead variances

■ **6** Compute and evaluate fixed overhead variances

■ **7** (Appendix) Record standard costing journal entries

When Apple introduced its legendary iPad in 2010, the direct material cost for the 16-GB model was estimated to be $259.60 while the cost of the 32-GB model cost was only $30 higher. Although Apple never released its actual costs, a market intelligence company by the name of iSuppli performed "tear-down" research to determine the cost of each direct material component found within the iPad: $95 for the touch screen, $26.80 for the processor, $10.50 for the aluminum casing, and so forth. In addition to direct materials, iSuppli estimated manufacturing conversion costs to be $9 per unit. What iSuppli did was very similar to what many manufacturers do: They estimate how much it should cost, in terms of direct materials, direct labor, and manufacturing overhead, to produce their products. These estimates, known as standard costs, are used as performance benchmarks. The finance and accounting professionals at Apple's WW Product Cost group create and update standard costs, as well as analyze actual costs in relation to the standards. In addition to using standard costs as benchmarks, companies use standard costs to help with the budgeting process, such as developing the total direct materials budget for the 58.3 million iPads sold in fiscal year 2012.

In Chapter 9 we described how managers of Tucson Tortilla planned for the coming year by preparing a master budget. In Chapter 10, we saw how its managers could evaluate performance by comparing actual to budgeted revenues and costs. To gain a better understanding of the master budget variance, managers created a flexible budget to separate the master budget variance into two components: (1) a volume variance and (2) a flexible budget variance. In this chapter, we'll see how the managers of Tucson Tortilla can deepen their analysis by further separating the flexible budget variance into two additional variances: (1) a price variance and (2) a quantity or efficiency variance. To do this, we'll first need to discuss standard costs.

What are Standard Costs?

Think of a <u>standard cost</u> as a budget for a single unit of product. For Tucson Tortilla, a single unit of product is one case of tortilla chips. A company that produces many different products will develop a standard cost for each type of product. For example, Colgate-Palmolive will develop a standard cost for each type of toothpaste, soap, and laundry detergent it produces. Even service companies develop standard costs. For example, many hospitals develop standard costs for routine procedures, such as tonsillectomies. The standard cost becomes the benchmark for evaluating actual costs.

For example, let's say the standard cost of producing one case of tortilla chips is $12.00, yet the company actually incurred $12.10 to produce each case during July. The company's managers will want to know why the difference, or variance, of $0.10 per case occurred. Although $0.10 per case may not seem like much, it really is a lot when you consider that the company produces thousands of cases per month. Companies like Coca-Cola, which sold 27.7 billion of cases of product in 2012,[1] are eager to control every penny of cost associated with each unit of product. In highly competitive markets, the company will not be able to pass along cost increases to consumers in the form of price increases. That means that the company's profit margin will shrink with every additional penny of cost incurred. Managers' ability to understand the reasons behind cost variances is a critical factor in controlling future costs.

In our example, why did Tucson Tortilla spend more than anticipated? Perhaps the price of flour increased. Or perhaps more labor was needed than originally expected. On the other hand, extraordinarily hot weather could have driven up the cost of air conditioning used in manufacturing facility. As you can see, the variance in cost could have been due to direct materials, direct labor, manufacturing overhead, or any combination of the three. Managers will only be able to understand the reasons for this unfavorable variance by investigating further.

1 Explain how and why standard costs are developed

Types of Standards

When managers develop standard costs (often simply referred to as <u>standards</u>), they must first determine what type of standard they want to create. <u>Ideal standards</u> are standards based on perfect or ideal conditions. These types of standards, which are also known as <u>perfection standards,</u> do not allow for any poor-quality raw materials, waste in the production process, machine breakdown, or other inefficiencies. This type of standard is best suited for companies that strive for perfection, such as those that implement lean production systems described in Chapter 4.[2]

> ### Why is this important?
>
> "Managers use **standard costs** as a **benchmark** against which to **evaluate** actual costs. If actual costs are **substantially different** than standard costs, **managers** will want to know why so that they have a basis for **improving operations**."

---

[1]The Coca-Cola Company 2012 10-K.
[2]In fact, many lean producers do not advocate the use of standards at all. Since one of the primary goals of lean production is continuous improvement, advocates argue that no standard is ideal enough. Improvements can always be made.

Rather than using ideal standards, many companies use **practical (or attainable) standards** that are based on currently attainable conditions. Practical standards include allowances for *normal* amounts of waste and inefficiency. Many managers believe that practical standards make the best cost benchmarks and provide the most employee motivation since they can be attained with a reasonable amount of effort.

Information Used to Develop and Update Standards

Managers draw on many sources of information when setting standards. They consider the amount of material and labor used on each unit produced in the *past*. They also consider the *current* cost of inputs, such as negotiated labor rates and raw materials prices. Finally, they estimate how *future* changes in the economy or in the manufacturing process might affect the standards being developed. Engineering studies help determine the amount of time and quantity of material that *should be* needed to produce each unit.

In order to serve as realistic benchmarks, once developed, standards need to be kept up to date. Standards should be reviewed at least once a year, and should be adjusted whenever a long-term change in costs or inputs is anticipated. For example, standards should be adjusted when:

- a new labor contract is negotiated with union workers,
- a non-temporary change in raw material costs occurs, or
- a part of the production process is reengineered.

Using outdated standards defeats the entire purpose of using standards in the first place.

Computing Standard Costs

Manufacturers typically prepare standard costs for the direct material, direct labor, and manufacturing overhead required for each unit of product. With respect to manufacturing overhead (MOH), some manufacturers only set standards for the variable MOH per unit since the fixed MOH per unit will fluctuate with changes in volume. Many companies also prepare standards for operating expenses. For simplicity, we'll limit our discussion to the three manufacturing costs. We will also assume that Tucson Tortilla has decided to develop practical, rather than ideal, standards.

Standard Cost of Direct Materials

In Chapter 9, we learned that Tucson Tortilla's only direct material (DM) is *masa harina* corn flour. Engineering studies show that each case of chips requires five pounds of flour, including allowances for normal amounts of spoilage and waste. The company can purchase the flour, including freight-in and purchase discounts, for $1.50 per pound. Therefore, the standard DM cost per case of tortilla chips is calculated as follows:

Standard Quantity of DM	×	Standard Price of DM	=	Standard Cost of DM per Case
5 lbs	×	$1.50/pound	=	$7.50

This calculation reveals that Tucson Tortilla expects to spend $7.50 on the direct materials for each case of tortilla chips produced.

Standard Cost of Direct Labor

Companies compute the standard cost of direct labor (DL) in a similar fashion. In Chapter 9, we learned that each case of tortilla chips requires only 0.05 hours of direct labor. This time requirement includes allowances for cleanup, breaks, and so forth since employees are paid for that time as well as actual work time. Furthermore, direct laborers are paid $22 per hour, including payroll taxes and employee benefits. Therefore, the standard DL cost per case of tortilla chips is:

Standard Quantity of DL	×	Standard Price of DL	=	Standard Cost of DL per Case
0.05 DL hours	×	$22.00/DL hour	=	$1.10

Since the production process is fairly automated, the company only anticipates spending $1.10 of direct labor on each case.

Standard Cost of Manufacturing Overhead

Since most of Tucson Tortilla's production process is automated, the company allocates its manufacturing overhead (MOH) using machine hours (MH) as its allocation base. Engineering studies indicate that each case of chips requires 0.10 machine hours to produce. In Chapter 9, we learned that the company expects to produce 400,000 cases of chips during the year. Therefore, the total allocation base is 40,000 machine hours.

Rather than using one predetermined overhead rate as discussed in Chapter 3, some manufacturers split their manufacturing overhead into two rates: a fixed MOH rate and a variable MOH rate. Let's see how this is done.

At a volume of 400,000 cases, Tucson Tortilla expects total variable overhead to be $1,000,000. Using this information, Tucson Tortilla calculates its predetermined *variable* MOH rate as follows:

Total estimated variable MOH ÷ Total estimated amount of the allocation base = Variable MOH rate
$1,000,000   ÷   40,000 machine hours   = $25/machine hour

Using the variable MOH rate, Tucson Tortilla can compute the standard cost of variable manufacturing overhead per case as follows:

Standard Quantity of MH × Variable MOH rate = Standard Variable MOH per Case
0.10 machine hours   × $25/machine hours   = $2.50

In Chapter 9, we learned that the company expects to incur $30,000 of fixed overhead each month, resulting in a total of $360,000 for the year. Therefore, the fixed MOH rate can be calculated as follows:

Total estimated fixed MOH ÷ Total estimated amount of the allocation base = Fixed MOH rate
$360,000   ÷   40,000 machine hours   = $9/machine hour

The standard cost of *fixed* manufacturing overhead *per case* is calculated as follows:

Standard Quantity of MH × Fixed MOH rate = Standard Fixed MOH per Case
0.10 machine hours   × $9/machine hour = $0.90

Standard Cost of One Unit

Exhibit 11-1 shows how Tucson Tortilla adds together the standard cost of direct materials, direct labor, and manufacturing overhead to determine the standard cost of producing one case of tortilla chips.

EXHIBIT 11-1 Standard Cost of Producing One Unit of Product

	A	B	C	D	E	F	G	H
1	Manufacturing Cost	Standard Quanitity (SQ)			Standard Price (SP)			Standard Cost per Case
2	Direct Materials	5.00	pounds	×	$ 1.50	per pound	=	$ 7.50
3	Direct Labor	0.05	DL hours	×	$ 22.00	per DL hour	=	1.10
4	Variable MOH	0.10	machine hours	×	$ 25.00	per machine hour	=	2.50
5	Fixed MOH	0.10	machine hours	×	$ 9.00	per machine hour	=	0.90
6	Total							$ 12.00
7								

The $12-per-case figure shown in Exhibit 11-1 may look familiar to you. Indeed, it is the same budgeted unit cost that we used in Chapter 9 when we calculated cost of goods sold for the budgeted Income Statement (Exhibit 9-12). Although we presented the budgeting chapter prior to this chapter, many companies develop standard costs *first*, and *then* use that information to help develop their planning budgets. Standard costs ease the budgeting process by providing a basis for calculating many figures in the master budget.

Sustainability and Standard Costs

In order to advance environmental sustainability, many companies are reengineering their products, packaging, and production processes. For example, over a four-year period, Heinz reduced the amount of plastic resin in its ketchup bottles by 1.8 million pounds, with a goal of a further 15% reduction by 2015. The company is now also using some plant-based plastic, rather than strictly fossil-fuel-based plastic, in its packaging. Likewise, Apple has reduced the packaging of its iPhone5 by 28% and the amount of material in its iMac by 68%. These packaging and materials changes not only reduced the amount of materials that will eventually end up in landfills or recycling plants, but also save the companies millions of dollars. Sustainability initiatives such as these require managers to rethink their direct materials quantity and price standards, as less materials and different types of materials are used.

Reengineering the production process may also result in changes to manufacturing overhead standards, as new equipment is installed and used. For example, Heinz is now operating several biomass boilers at its plants that turn by-products, such as rice husks and eucalyptus chips, into fuel. Heinz's new waste-water treatment system, which returns clean water to the community, produces and captures methane, which in turn is used to produce steam for the company's food sterilization process. Initiatives such as these reduce the environmental impact of the production process. But they also require management to amend existing manufacturing overhead standards.

Operating cost standards, such as the transportation cost of distributing the product, will also change as the lighter products and smaller containers reduce trucking costs. For example, Heinz is now saving 26 million gallons of fuel per year as a result of partnering with its bottle supplier to jointly move within 3 miles of each other. Once again, these initiatives help the environment, while simultaneously helping the company's bottom line.

Companies may also find themselves creating standards for the amount of waste that leaves the production process in the form of air pollution, waste-to-landfill refuse, and waste water. For example, many companies now have zero-waste-to-landfill goals. Government regulations are forcing companies to cap, or limit, the amount of greenhouse gases and other pollutants that result from the production process. Therefore, companies will have standards for the maximum pollutants allowed to leave their plants.

See Exercises E11-24A and E11-40B ◀

Sources: http://www.heinz.com/CSR2011/social/; and http://www.apple.com/environment/our-footprint/#manufacturing

▶ Try It!

Hannah owns a fruit smoothie shop at the local mall. Each smoothie requires ¼ pound of mixed berries, which are expected to cost $4 per pound during the summer months. Shop employees are paid $10 per hour. Variable overhead consists of utilities and supplies. The variable overhead rate is $0.05 per minute of DL time. Each smoothie should require 3 minutes of DL time.

1. What is the standard cost of direct materials for each smoothie?

2. What is the standard cost of direct labor for each smoothie?

3. What is the standard cost of variable overhead for each smoothie?

Please see page 696 for solutions.

How do Managers Use Standard Costs to Compute DM and DL Variances?

We just showed how managers develop standard costs. Managers use standards at the beginning of the period to help with the budgeting planning process. Managers also use standards at the end of the period, to evaluate performance and help control future costs. Let's see how this is done.

Using Standard Costs to Develop the Flexible Budget

As we saw in the last chapter, managers often compare actual costs against a flexible budget, rather than directly against the planning budget. Recall that the flexible budget reflects the total cost that *should have been incurred*, *given the actual volume achieved*.

For example, let's assume that Tucson Tortilla actually produced 31,000 cases of chips during the month of January, even though the company originally planned to produce 29,000 cases. Exhibit 11-2 shows the flexible budget for variable production costs. To generate the flexible budget, managers multiplied the standard costs per unit by the *actual number of units produced*. Notice the mixture of favorable and unfavorable flexible budget variances. We'll refer back to this exhibit quite often as we explore the reasons for these variances in the next sections.

EXHIBIT 11-2 Comparing Variable Production Costs with the Flexible Budget

	A	B	C	D	E	F
1	**Flexible Budget Performance Report for Variable Production Costs**	**Standard Cost per Case**	**Actual Cost for 31,000 cases**	**Flexible Budget for 31,000 Cases**	**Flexible Budget Variance**	
2	Direct materials	$ 7.50	$ 224,000	$ 232,500	$ 8,500	F
3	Direct labor	$ 1.10	$ 34,875	$ 34,100	$ 775	U
4	Variable MOH	$ 2.50	$ 85,200	$ 77,500	$ 7,700	U
5						

Direct Materials Variances

From Exhibit 11-2 we know that Tucson Tortilla spent $8,500 less on direct materials than standards indicated would be spent to make 31,000 cases. Was this because the company *paid* less for the material than expected, *used* less material than expected, or a combination of the two?

When the amount of materials purchased is the same as the amount used (our example here), we can split the flexible budget variance for direct materials into two separate variances: a price variance and a quantity variance, as shown in Exhibit 11-3.

2 Compute and evaluate direct materials variances

EXHIBIT 11-3 Splitting the Flexible Budget Variance into Two Components

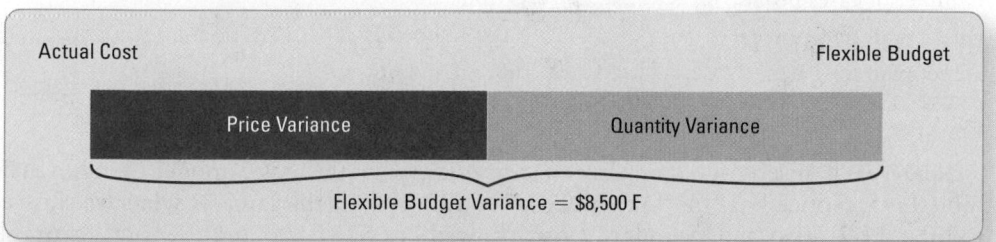

Actual Cost | Flexible Budget

Price Variance | Quantity Variance

Flexible Budget Variance = $8,500 F

The way we do this is illustrated in Exhibit 11-4. In this model, notice that the company's actual costs are on the top-left side and are stated at Actual Quantity (AQ) × Actual Price (AP). The company's flexible budget is shown on the top-right side and is stated as the standard cost allowed *for the actual volume of output*. It is computed as the Standard Quantity Allowed (SQA) for the actual output × Standard Price (SP). As shown at the bottom in orange, the difference between the two outside terms is the total flexible budget variance.

EXHIBIT 11-4 Direct Materials Variances if DM Purchased Equals DM Used

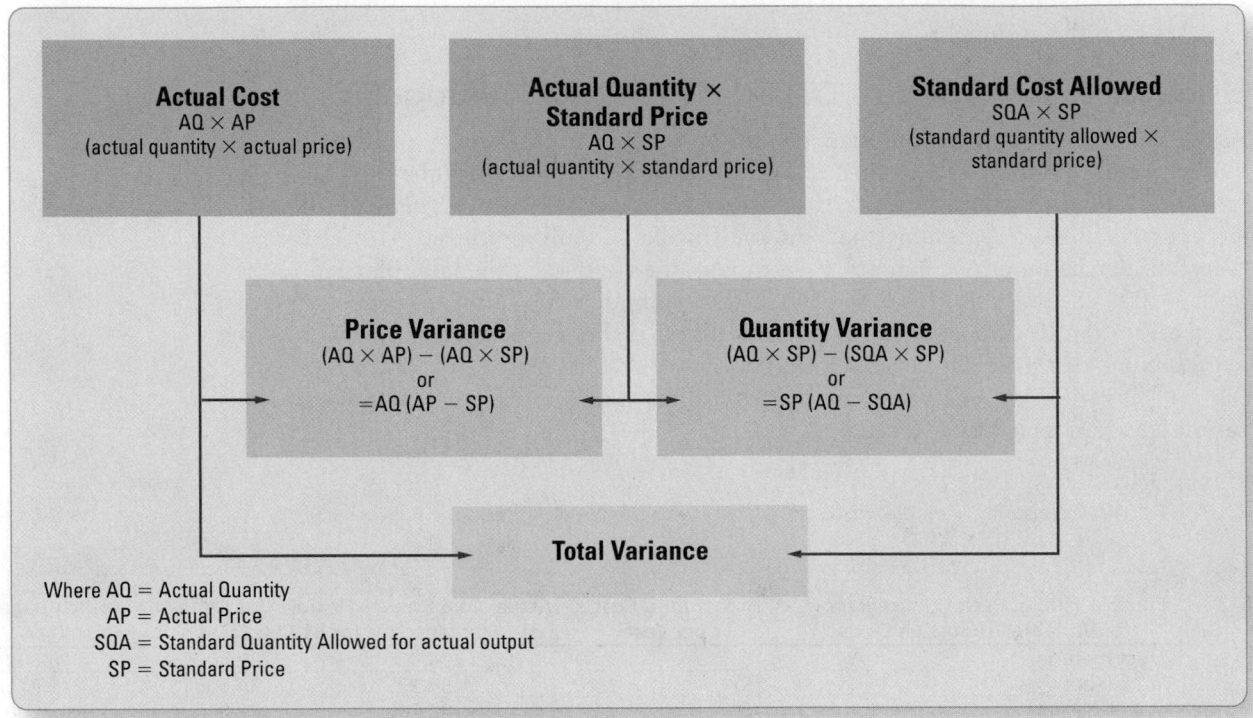

Next, we insert a middle term in the exhibit. The middle term is a mixture of the two outside terms and is defined as: Actual Quantity (AQ) × Standard Price (SP). This middle term will help us separate the total flexible budget variance into two components: a price variance and a quantity variance.

The **direct materials price variance** tells managers how much of the total variance is due to paying a higher or lower price than expected for the direct materials it purchased. The **direct materials quantity variance** tells managers how much of the total variance is due to using a larger or smaller quantity of direct materials than expected. The formulas for these variances are shown in the middle row of Exhibit 11-4.

Let's see how this works for Tucson Tortilla. First, we'll need the following information:

Actual data for January:	
Number of cases produced	31,000 cases
Direct materials purchased	160,000 pounds at $1.40 per pound
Direct materials used	160,000 pounds

Next, we'll insert our company-specific data into the basic model, as shown in Exhibit 11-5. Notice how the "Actual Cost" of $224,000 is the same as what we showed in Exhibit 11-2. Also, the "Standard Cost Allowed" of $232,500 and the total favorable variance of $8,500 are the same as the figures shown in Exhibit 11-2.

EXHIBIT 11-5 Tucson Tortilla's Direct Materials Variances

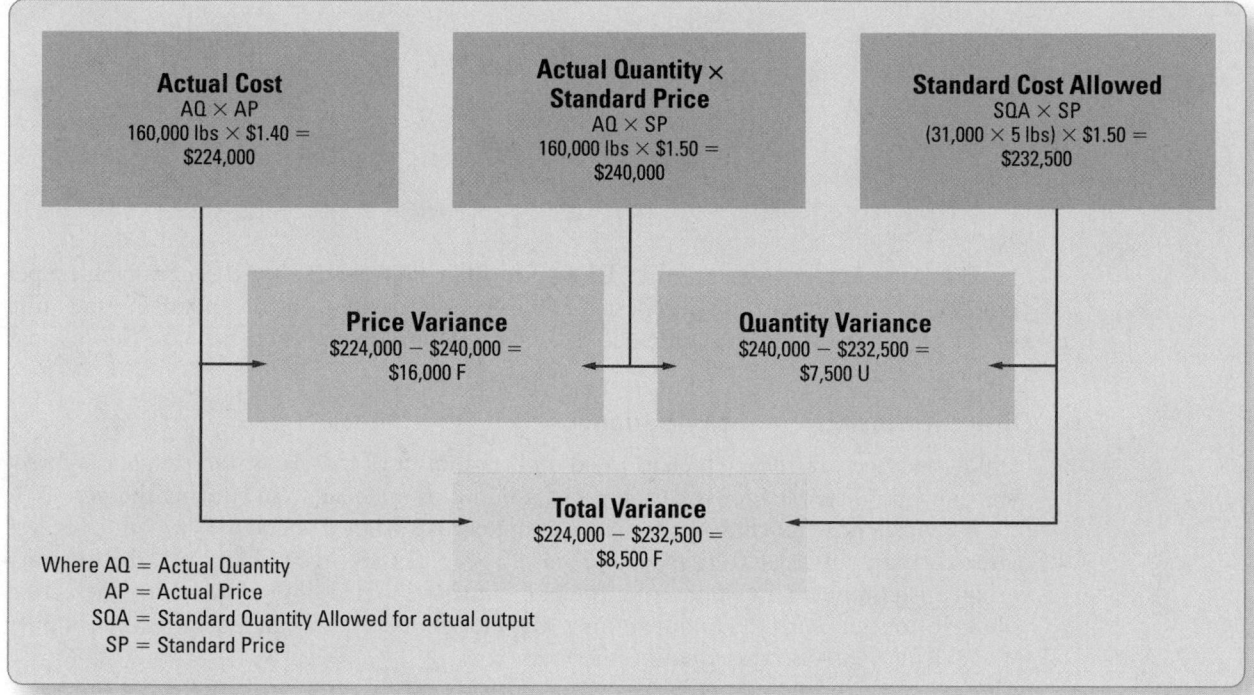

The calculations in Exhibit 11-5 show us that the total direct materials variance of $8,500 is in fact the result of two causes: (1) a favorable price variance of $16,000 and (2) an unfavorable quantity variance of $7,500. The two variances net together to equal the total favorable flexible budget variance of $8,500.

In the next sections we'll explain these variances in more detail and show how formulas can be used as an alternative to creating the diagrams illustrated in Exhibits 11-4 and 11-5.

Direct Materials Price Variance

The direct materials prices variance tells managers how much of the overall variance is due to paying a higher or lower price than expected for the quantity of materials it *purchased*. As you can see in Exhibit 11-4, the price variance is computed by comparing the company's actual costs on the left side of the model with the middle term in the model. The lavender boxes in the middle row show that we can simplify the calculations by factoring out the actual quantity (AQ) purchased from both terms in the model as follows:

$$\text{DM price variance} = (AQ \times AP) - (AQ \times SP)$$
$$= AQ\,(AP - SP)$$

The simplified equation should make sense: it simply calculates the price differential between what was paid for the direct material input (pounds of flour, in our case) and the price anticipated by the standards. The price differential is then multiplied by the quantity of direct materials *purchased*.

Since the amount of materials purchased may be different than the amount of materials used, we will henceforth use the notation AQP to denote the "Actual Quantity Purchased" and AQU to denote the "Actual Quantity Used." In our current example, Tucson Tortilla both purchased and used the same amount of direct materials during January. However, this more specific notation will help us later when we encounter a situation in which the amount of material *purchased* differs from the amount of material *used*.

Let's use the simplified equation to calculate Tucson Tortilla's DM price variance:

$$
\begin{aligned}
\text{DM price variance} &= \text{Actual Quantity Purchased} \times (\text{Actual Price} - \text{Standard Price}) \\
&= \text{AQP} \times (\text{AP} - \text{SP}) \\
&= 160{,}000 \text{ lbs} \times (\$1.40 - \$1.50) \\
&= 160{,}000 \text{ lbs} \times (\$0.10) \\
&= \$16{,}000 \text{ F}
\end{aligned}
$$

From this analysis we see that Tucson Tortilla spent $0.10 *less* than anticipated per pound. Since the company purchased 160,000 pounds of flour, it ended up spending $16,000 less than standards anticipated. This is a favorable variance because the cost per pound is *less* than expected.

Direct Materials Quantity Variance

Unlike the price variance, which is based on the amount of materials *purchased*, the direct materials quantity variance is based on the amount of materials *used* during the period. It tells managers how much of the total direct materials variance is due to *using* more or less materials than anticipated by the standards. As you can see in Exhibit 11-4, the quantity variance is computed by comparing the company's standard cost allowed for the actual volume of output with the middle term in the model. Again, we can algebraically simplify these calculations into the equation shown next.

$$
\begin{aligned}
\text{DM quantity variance} &= \text{Standard Price} \times (\text{Actual Quantity Used} - \text{Standard Quantity Allowed}) \\
&= \text{SP} \times (\text{AQU} - \text{SQA}) \\
&= \$1.50 \times [160{,}000 \text{ lbs} - (31{,}000 \text{ cases} \times 5 \text{ lbs/case})] \\
&= \$1.50 \times (160{,}000 \text{ lbs} - 155{,}000 \text{ lbs}) \\
&= \$1.50 \times 5{,}000 \text{ lbs} \\
&= \$7{,}500 \text{ U}
\end{aligned}
$$

Note the following:

1. Since this variance addresses the efficiency with which materials were used, the calculation involves the quantity of direct materials *used* during the period (AQU), *not* the quantity *purchased* (AQP).

2. To calculate the standard quantity of materials allowed (SQA), we start with the number of units actually produced (31,000 cases) and then multiply it by the standard quantity of material allowed per unit (5 lbs per case). The result (155,000 lbs) tells us how much direct material the company expected to use given the actual volume of output.

From this analysis, we see that the company used 5,000 more pounds of corn flour during the period than standards indicated should be used. At a standard price of $1.50 per pound, the excess use of flour cost the company an unanticipated $7,500. This variance is unfavorable, because the company used more direct materials than they should have.

Evaluating Direct Materials Variances

Exhibit 11-6 shows us that the favorable flexible budget variance for direct materials of $8,500 resulted from

1. purchasing the corn flour at a better-than-expected price, resulting in a savings of $16,000, and

2. using more corn flour than expected, resulting in an additional cost of $7,500.

EXHIBIT 11-6 Summary of Direct Materials Variances

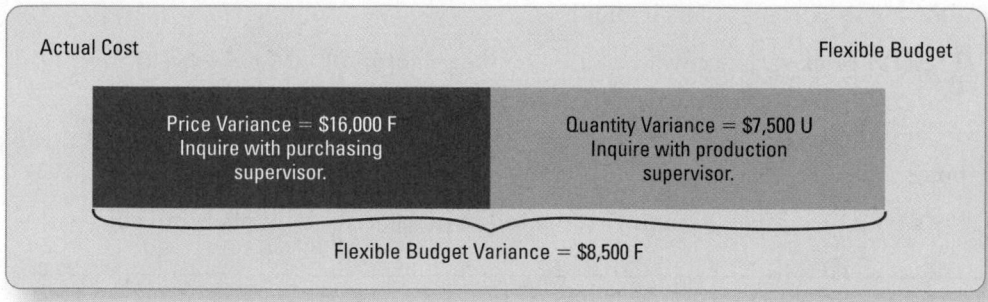

Management will want to know why both of these variances occurred. The best source of information about the price variance is the purchasing supervisor. The supervisor should know why the company was able to purchase the materials at a better-than-expected price. Perhaps alternative suppliers entered the market. Or, a bumper crop of corn pushed down flour prices at all suppliers. On the other hand, perhaps the company was able to make use of faster payment terms, and as a result was able to obtain the flour at a greater discount. Maybe the purchasing agent bought lower-grade corn flour. Many possibilities exist.

Note that while the variance is referred to as "favorable," the result may not necessarily be a "good" thing. For example, if the company bought lower-grade corn flour, did it have a detrimental impact on the taste of the tortilla chips? Or did it cause additional waste or spoilage that might account for the unfavorable quantity variance?

Management will learn more about the quantity variance by talking with the production supervisor. The production supervisor is in the best position to know why extra corn flour was used. Was something wrong with the corn flour when it arrived (torn bags, inadequate moisture content, and so forth)? Did an accident occur in transporting the flour from the raw material storage area to the production area? Was a batch of chips ruined by adding too much salt? Again, many possibilities exist.

Management will want to uncover the root cause of the variance to determine whether the extra cost was controllable or not. For example, if the corn flour was in poor condition when it arrived, Tucson Tortilla may be able to receive a credit from its supplier or the transportation company that trucked in the flour. Additionally, Tucson Tortilla may want to search for a new supplier. If the cause was a human error in the factory, precautionary measures might be developed that would prevent such errors in the future.

Computing DM Variances when the Quantity of DM Purchased Differs from the Quantity of DM Used

In the example just illustrated, we assumed that the quantity of direct materials purchased was the same as the quantity of direct materials used. This is often the case with lean producers since they buy inventory "just in time" to use it in production. However, traditional manufacturers often buy extra safety stock to ensure they have enough raw materials on hand to meet production if sales demand exceeds the forecast. Recall that we took safety stock into consideration in Chapter 9 when we budgeted the amount of direct materials to purchase (see Exhibit 9-7). As a result, manufacturers often buy slightly more than they immediately need. On the other hand, if raw materials inventory has grown too large, companies will intentionally buy less than the amount required for production in order to shrink their inventory. In either case, the quantity of direct materials purchased may differ from the quantity of direct materials used.

When this occurs, managers still compute the price and quantity variances, but keep the following important points in mind:

1. The DM price variance will be based on the quantity of DM *purchased* (AQP).
2. The DM quantity variance will be based on the quantity of DM *used* (AQU).
3. The DM price and quantity variances will no longer sum (or net) to the total flexible budget variance.

Let's try an example. Assume that the following activity took place in February:

Actual data for February:	
Number of cases produced...................................	20,000 cases
Direct materials purchased.................................	105,000 pounds at $1.45 per pound
Direct materials used...	98,000 pounds

We can compute the DM price and quantity variances using the same formulas developed in the preceding section.

The price variance is based on the actual quantity *purchased* (AQP):

$$\text{DM price variance} = \text{AQP} \times (\text{AP} - \text{SP})$$
$$= 105{,}000 \text{ lbs} \times (\$1.45 - \$1.50)$$
$$= 105{,}000 \text{ lbs} \times (\$0.05)$$
$$= \$5{,}250 \text{ F}$$

By purchasing 105,000 pounds of corn flour at a price that was $0.05 less than standard, the company saved $5,250.

The quantity variance is based on the actual quantity of materials *used* (AQU):

$$\text{DM quantity variance} = \text{SP} \times (\text{AQU} - \text{SQA})$$
$$= \$1.50 \times [98{,}000 \text{ lbs} - (20{,}000 \text{ cases} \times 5 \text{ lbs/case})]$$
$$= \$1.50 \times (98{,}000 \text{ lbs} - 100{,}000 \text{ lbs})$$
$$= \$1.50 \times (2{,}000 \text{ lbs})$$
$$= \$3{,}000 \text{ F}$$

This analysis reveals that the company used 2,000 fewer pounds of corn flour than standards projected, resulting in a cost savings of $3,000.

▶ Try It!

Hannah owns a fruit smoothie shop at the local mall. Each smoothie requires ¼ pound of mixed berries, which are expected to cost $4 per pound during the summer months. During the month of June, Hannah purchased and used 1,300 pounds of mixed berries at a cost of $3.75 per pound. Hannah's shop sold 5,000 smoothies during the month.

1. Calculate the DM price variance. Is the variance favorable or unfavorable?
2. Calculate the DM efficiency variance. Is the variance favorable or unfavorable?
3. Calculate the total DM variance. Is the variance favorable or unfavorable?

Please see page 696 for solutions.

Direct Labor Variances

From Exhibit 11-2 we know that Tucson Tortilla only spent $775 more than anticipated on direct labor. Because this is such a small variance, some managers might not consider investigating it. However, it's possible that the total variance is made up of large, but off-setting individual variances, similar to what we saw with the direct materials variances. By splitting the total direct labor variance into two separate variances, a rate variance and an efficiency variance, we can find out whether the company *paid a higher wage rate* to the factory workers than expected, *used* more time in making the chips than expected, or some combination of these two factors.

3 Compute DL variances

Let's assume the following information about Tucson Tortilla's January operations:

Actual data for January:	
Number of cases produced...............	31,000 cases
Direct labor hours...........................	1,500 hours
Direct labor cost..............................	$34,875 (resulting in an average wage rate of $23.25/hr*)

* $34,875/1,500 hours = $23.25/hr

Exhibit 11-7 shows that the general model for direct labor (DL) variances is almost identical to the model used for direct materials variances. The only real difference is in the names of the variances. For example, instead of a DM *price* variance, we have a DL *rate* variance. The **direct labor rate variance** tells managers how much of the total labor variance is due to paying a higher or lower hourly wage rate than anticipated.

Likewise, instead of the DM *quantity* variance, we have a DL *efficiency* variance. The quantity of time used in production tells management how efficiently employees were working. Therefore, the **direct labor efficiency variance** tells managers how much of the total labor variance is due to using a greater or lesser amount of time than anticipated.

While the terminology for DL variances is slightly different than it was for DM variances, the calculations are essentially the same.

EXHIBIT 11-7 Calculation of Tucson Tortilla's Direct Labor Variances

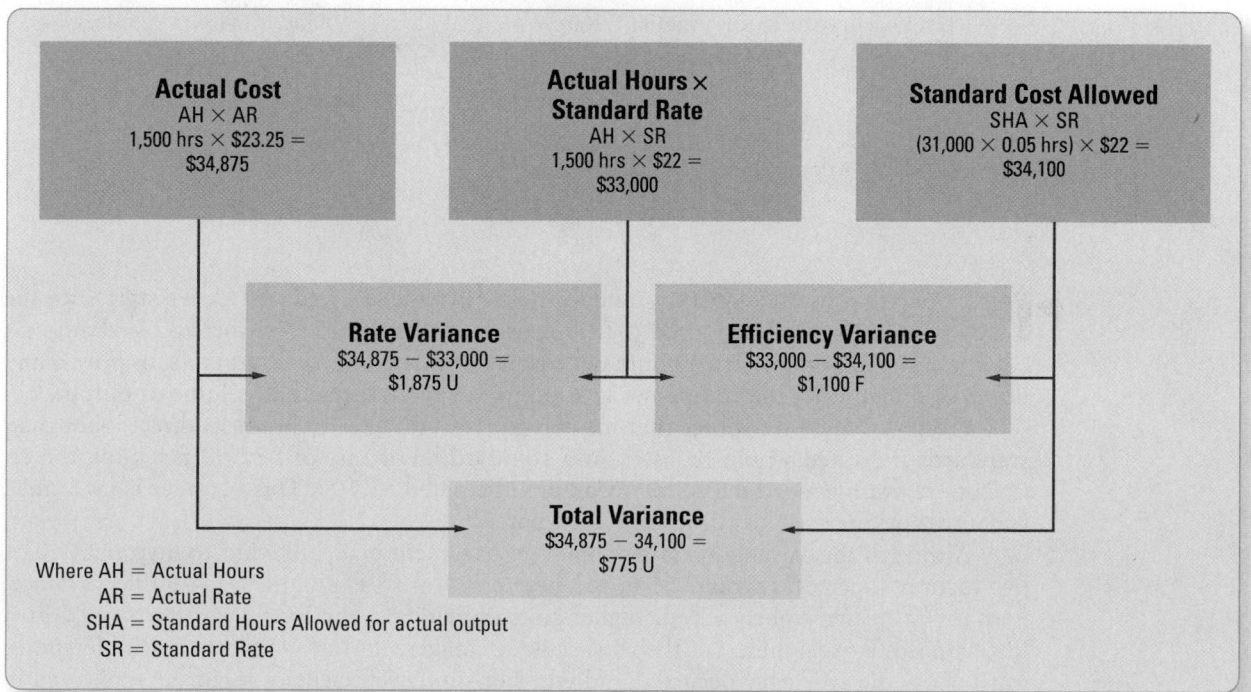

Where AH = Actual Hours
      AR = Actual Rate
     SHA = Standard Hours Allowed for actual output
      SR = Standard Rate

Although the total direct labor variance is small ($775), Exhibit 11-7 shows us the importance of digging down deeper: the total variance is made up of (1) an unfavorable rate variance of $1,875 and (2) an offsetting favorable efficiency variance of $1,100. In the next sections we'll go over these variances in more detail.

Direct Labor Rate Variance

As shown in Exhibit 11-7, the direct labor rate variance is computed on the left side of the model by comparing the company's actual costs with the middle term in the model. Alternatively, we can algebraically simplify the equation, just like we did for the direct materials variances. The resulting simplified equation is as follows:

$$
\begin{aligned}
\text{DL rate variance} &= \text{Actual Hours} \times (\text{Actual Rate} - \text{Standard Rate}) \\
&= \text{AH} \times (\text{AR} - \text{SR}) \\
&= 1{,}500 \text{ hrs} \times (\$23.25 - \$22.00) \\
&= 1{,}500 \text{ hrs} \times \$1.25 \\
&= \$1{,}875 \text{ U}
\end{aligned}
$$

This analysis shows management the overall dollar impact of paying an average wage rate that was higher than anticipated. The human resources supervisor and the plant supervisor should be able to explain why this happened. Several possibilities exist. For example, perhaps some lower paid employees were sick or on vacation, and higher paid employees filled in during their absence. Perhaps a wage premium was offered to workers during January to keep morale up during this peak production month. Even though the variance was "unfavorable," neither of these possible explanations suggest poor management. Rather, they simply explain why the average wage rate paid was higher than expected, resulting in an unanticipated additional cost of $1,875.

Direct Labor Efficiency Variance

As you can see in Exhibit 11-7, the efficiency variance is computed on the right side of the model by comparing the company's standard cost allowed with the middle term in the model. Again, we can algebraically simplify these calculations as follows:

$$
\begin{aligned}
\text{DL efficiency variance} &= \text{Standard Rate} \times (\text{Actual Hours} - \text{Standard Hours Allowed}) \\
&= \text{SR} \times (\text{AH} - \text{SHA}) \\
&= \$22.00 \times [1{,}500 \text{ hrs} - (31{,}000 \text{ cases} \times 0.05 \text{ hrs/case})] \\
&= \$22.00 \times (1{,}500 \text{ hrs} - 1{,}550 \text{ hrs}) \\
&= \$22.00 \times (50 \text{ hrs}) \\
&= \$1{,}100 \text{ F}
\end{aligned}
$$

Notice that to calculate the standard hours of time allowed (SHA), we start with the actual number of units produced (31,000 cases) and multiply it by the standard amount of time allowed per unit (0.05 hours per case). The result (1,550 hours) tells us how many hours of direct labor the company expected to use given the actual volume of output.

From this analysis, we see that the company used 50 fewer hours of direct labor than standards indicated would be used. At a standard labor rate of $22.00 per hour, the efficient use of time saved the company an unanticipated $1,100. This variance is favorable, because workers used *less* time than anticipated.

Although this variance is fairly small, management may still want to investigate. The production supervisor would be in the best position to explain the favorable variance. Perhaps by using higher-skilled, higher-paid individuals, the work was performed at a faster speed. By searching out the root cause, management may gain a better understanding of how the efficiency occurred and whether similar efficiencies might be replicated in the future or in other areas of operations. Exhibit 11-8 summarizes Tucson Tortilla's direct labor variances for January.

EXHIBIT 11-8 Summary of Direct Labor Variances

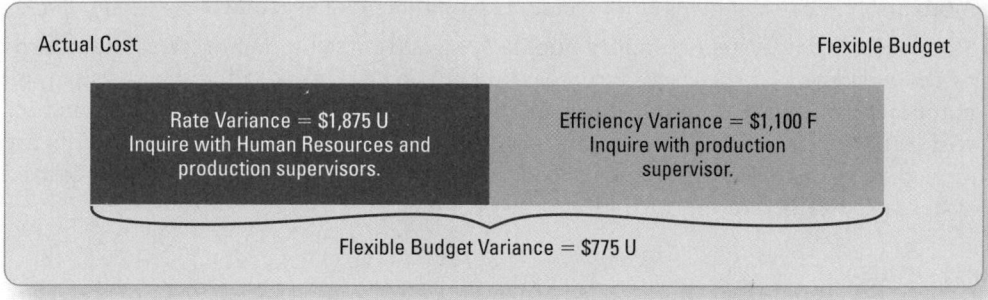

Actual Cost	Flexible Budget

Rate Variance = $1,875 U
Inquire with Human Resources and production supervisors.

Efficiency Variance = $1,100 F
Inquire with production supervisor.

Flexible Budget Variance = $775 U

Summary of Direct Materials and Direct Labor Variances

Exhibit 11-9 summarizes the formulas for the direct materials and direct labor variances, as well as the party responsible for best explaining why the variance occurred.

EXHIBIT 11-9 Summary of DM and DL Variance Formulas

Variance	Formula	Inquire with...
Direct Materials Price Variance	= Actual Quantity Purchased × (Actual Price − Standard Price) = AQP × (AP − SP)	Purchasing Supervisor
Direct Materials Quantity Variance	= Standard Price × (Actual Quantity Used − Standard Quantity Allowed) = SP × (AQU − SQA)	Production Supervisor
Direct Labor Rate Variance	= Actual Hours × (Actual Rate − Standard Rate) = AH × (AR − SR)	Human Resources and Production Supervisors
Direct Labor Efficiency Variance	= Standard Rate × (Actual Hours − Standard Hours Allowed) = SR × (AH − SHA)	Production Supervisor

Advantages and Disadvantages of Using Standard Costs and Variances

The practice of using standard costs and variances was developed in the early twentieth century, during the advent and growth of mass manufacturing. Although many manufacturers continue to use standard costs and variances, others do not. Management must weigh the costs against the benefits to decide whether they want to use standard costs and perform detailed variance analysis. Even if management uncovers variances, they will want to use management by exception to determine which variances are significant enough to warrant investigation.

4 Explain the advantages and disadvantages of using standard costs and variances

Advantages

- **Cost benchmarks:** One of the greatest advantages of using standard costs is having a benchmark by which to judge actual costs. However, this benchmark is valid only if the standards are kept up to date.

- **Usefulness in budgeting:** Standards are often used as the basis for many components in the master budget, such as the direct materials, direct labor, and manufacturing overhead budgets.

- **Motivation:** The use of practical, or attainable, standards should increase employee motivation because it gives employees a reasonable goal to achieve.
- **Standard costing systems simplify bookkeeping:** Many manufacturers use standards as the backbone to their standard costing system. In a standard costing system, all manufacturing costs entering Work in Process Inventory are recorded at standard cost, rather than actual cost. Variances between actual costs and standard costs are immediately captured in variance accounts in the general ledger. This type of costing system is described in the appendix to this chapter.

Disadvantages

Despite the prevalence of standard costing over the past century, many contemporary manufacturers are moving away from the use of standards. Here are some of the reasons:

- **Outdated or inaccurate standards:** As mentioned previously, standard costs can quickly become outdated or inaccurate as the cost of inputs or the production process changes. Standards should be reviewed an updated at least yearly. They should also be updated whenever a change in process or input costs is considered to be nontemporary in nature. Keeping standards up to date is costly.
- **Lack of timeliness:** In the past, variances were often computed once a month. In today's fast-paced world, such information is often too old to be useful. As a result, some companies are moving toward the daily calculation of variances.
- **Focus on operational performance measures and visual management:** Because of the need for timely data, many lean producers are placing greater emphasis on operational performance measures that are collected daily, or even hourly, and visually displayed where front-line workers can immediately see performance levels. They find such visual reminders much more effective for motivating front-line employees than relying on price and efficiency variances.
- **Lean thinking:** As discussed in Chapter 4, lean companies strive for continual improvement. That means that current standards are not "good enough." Rather than focusing on whether or not production has met current standards, lean producers focus on finding new ways to decrease waste, increase efficiency, and increase quality. They concentrate on looking forward rather than looking at the past.
- **Increase in automation and decrease in direct labor:** Most manufacturers have shifted toward automated production processes. For many manufacturers, direct labor is no longer a primary component of production or a driver of overhead costs. In addition, for companies that pay employees a salary rather than an hourly wage rate, direct labor is a fixed cost, rather than a variable cost. Finally, at lean companies, employees tend to be multiskilled and cross-trained to perform a number of duties, rather than a single, repetitive task. These front-line workers are held in high esteem by management, and considered to be part of a team effort, rather than a labor force to be controlled. To these companies, direct labor standards are no longer relevant or helpful.
- **Unintended behavioral consequences:** Use of traditional standards can cause unintended behavioral consequences. For example, to obtain a favorable price variance, the purchasing supervisor may buy larger quantities of raw materials than needed. Likewise, a production manager may overproduce to obtain a favorable fixed overhead volume variance (discussed in the second half of the chapter). However, as we learned in Chapter 4, holding or producing excess quantities of inventories is wasteful and costly, and should be avoided.

Decision Guidelines

Standard Costs and Variances

Let's consider some decisions management must make with regard to standard costs and variances.

Decision	Guidelines
What is a standard cost and how can it be used?	A standard cost is a budget for a single unit of product. Standards costs are used as performance benchmarks against which to evaluate actual costs.
Should we use ideal (perfection) standards or practical (attainable) standards?	Since ideal standards are only achievable under flawless conditions, they are best suited for lean producers that strive for perfection. Practical standards, which are attainable with effort, are typically used by traditional manufacturers that want to use motivational, yet realistic, benchmarks.
What information is used to develop standards?	Companies use a combination of historical, current, and projected data to develop standards. Managers often use engineering time and motion studies to determine the quantity of time and materials needed to produce each unit.
How often should standard costs be updated?	Standard costs should be reviewed at least once a year and updated whenever a non-temporary change in costs, inputs, or processes occurs.
How is the direct materials price variance computed?	= Actual Quantity Purchased $\times$ (Actual Price − Standard Price) = AQP $\times$ (AP − SP)
How is the direct materials quantity variance computed?	= Standard Price $\times$ (Actual Quantity Used − Standard Quantity Allowed) = SP $\times$ (AQU − SQA)
How is the direct labor rate variance computed?	= Actual Hours $\times$ (Actual Rate − Standard Rate) = AH $\times$ (AR − SR)
How is the direct labor efficiency variance computed?	= Standard Rate $\times$ (Actual Hours − Standard Hours Allowed) = SR $\times$ (AH − SHA)
Who is usually in the best position to explain why the variances occurred?	DM price variance: Purchasing Supervisor DM quantity variance: Production Supervisor DL rate variance: Production and Human Resources Supervisors DL efficiency variance: Production Supervisor

SUMMARY PROBLEM 1

Memoirs, Inc., produces several different styles and sizes of picture frames. The collage frame consists of 12 interconnected matted picture slots, each surrounded by a wood frame. Engineering studies indicate that each collage frame will require the following direct materials and direct labor:

Materials and Labor:	Quantity of Input	Price of Input
Wood trim for frame borders............................	18 feet	$ 0.35 per foot
Mattes for individual pictures	12 mattes	$ 0.05 per matte
Sheet glass top..	4 square feet	$ 4.00 per square foot
Pressboard frame backing	4 square feet	$ 0.25 per square foot
Direct Labor...	0.25 hours	$16 per hour

The following activity regarding direct labor and wood trim occurred during March:

Number of frames produced	25,000 frames
Wood trim purchased...................	450,000 feet at $0.37 per foot
Wood trim used	455,000 feet
Direct labor hours........................	6,500 hours
Direct labor cost..........................	$100,750 (resulting in an average wage rate of $15.50/hr*)

* $100,750/6,500 hours = $15.50/hr

Requirements

1. Calculate the standard direct materials cost and standard direct labor cost for each collage frame.

2. Calculate the wood trim direct materials price and efficiency variances for the month of March.

3. Calculate the direct labor rate and efficiency variances for the month of March.

▪ SOLUTIONS

Requirement 1

The standard cost of direct materials and direct labor is calculated by multiplying the standard quantity of input needed for each collage frame by the standard price of the input:

Materials and Labor:	Quantity of Input (a)	Price of Input (b)	Standard Cost (a × b)
Wood trim for frame borders..........	18 feet	$ 0.35 per foot	$ 6.30
Mattes for individual pictures	12 mattes	$ 0.05 per matte	0.60
Sheet glass top.................................	4 square feet	$ 4.00 per square foot	16.00
Pressboard frame backing	4 square feet	$ 0.25 per square foot	1.00
Direct material cost per unit............			$23.90
Direct Labor.....................................	0.25 hours	$16 per hour	$ 4.00

Requirement 2

The direct materials price variance is based on the quantity of materials (wood trim) *purchased*:

$$DM \text{ price variance} = AQP \times (AP - SP)$$
$$= 450,000 \text{ ft} \times (\$0.37 - \$0.35)$$
$$= 450,000 \text{ ft} \times \$0.02$$
$$= \$9,000 \text{ U}$$

The company spent $0.02 per foot more than anticipated on the 450,000 feet of wood trim that it purchased, resulting in an unfavorable price variance of $9,000.

The direct materials quantity variance is based on the quantity of materials (wood trim) *used*:

$$DM \text{ quantity variance} = SP \times (AQU - SQA)$$
$$= \$0.35 \times [455,000 \text{ ft} - (25,000 \text{ frames} \times 18 \text{ ft/frame})]$$
$$= \$0.35 \times (455,000 \text{ ft} - 450,000 \text{ ft})$$
$$= \$0.35 \times 5,000 \text{ ft}$$
$$= \$1,750 \text{ U}$$

This analysis reveals that using 5,000 more feet of wood trim than anticipated resulted in an unanticipated additional cost of $1,750.

Requirement 3

The direct labor rate variance is computed as follows:

$$DL \text{ rate variance} = AH \times (AR - SR)$$
$$= 6,500 \text{ hrs} \times (\$15.50 - \$16.00)$$
$$= 6,500 \text{ hrs} \times (\$0.50)$$
$$= \$3,250 \text{ F}$$

The company spent $0.50 less per hour than anticipated, resulting in a $3,250 F variance over the 6,500 hours that were worked.

The direct labor efficiency variance is calculated as follows:

$$DL \text{ efficiency variance} = SR \times (AH - SHA)$$
$$= \$16.00 \times [6,500 - (25,000 \text{ frames} \times 0.25 \text{ hrs/frame})]$$
$$= \$16.00 \times (6,500 - 6,250 \text{ hrs})$$
$$= \$16.00 \times 250 \text{ hrs}$$
$$= \$4,000 \text{ U}$$

At a standard labor rate of $16.00 per hour, the extra use of time cost the company an unanticipated $4,000.

How do Managers Use Standard Costs to Compute MOH Variances?

In the first half of the chapter we learned how Tucson Tortilla developed standard costs and then used those standards to evaluate its direct materials and direct labor costs. In this half of the chapter, we'll look at the four manufacturing overhead (MOH) variances that are typically computed: two related to variable MOH costs and two related to fixed MOH costs.

Variable Manufacturing Overhead Variances

From Exhibit 11-2, we learned that Tucson Tortilla had an unfavorable variable overhead flexible budget variance of $7,700. But why did this unexpected additional cost occur?

Manufacturers usually split the total variable MOH variance into rate and efficiency variances, just as they do for direct labor. Exhibit 11-10 shows the general model for calculating variable MOH rate and efficiency variances is almost identical to the model used for direct labor rate and efficiency variances. The only real difference in the calculations is the rate that is used: we use the *variable manufacturing overhead rate*, not the direct labor wage rate. And since Tucson Tortilla allocates its overhead using machine hours, the hours refer to machine hours rather than direct labor hours.[3] Here is the information from January's operations:

Data for January	
Number of cases produced......................	31,000 cases
Standard variable MOH rate..................	$ 25 per machine hour
Standard hours required per case	0.10 machine hours
Actual machine hours.............................	3,000 machine hours
Actual variable MOH costs....................	$85,200 (resulting in an *actual* variable MOH rate of $28.40 per machine hour)*

* $85,200/3,000 hours = $28.40/machine hour

Variable Overhead Rate Variance

As shown in Exhibit 11-10, the **variable overhead rate variance** is the difference between the actual variable MOH costs incurred during the period ($85,200) and the amount of variable MOH expected ($75,000) considering the actual hours worked. It tells managers whether more or less was spent on variable overhead than expected given the actual machine hours run. Because of this, the variable overhead rate variance is also sometimes called the **variable overhead spending variance**. The variance formula can be algebraically simplified into the following formula:

$$\text{Variable MOH rate variance} = \text{Actual Hours} \times (\text{Actual Rate} - \text{Standard Rate})$$
$$= \text{AH} \times (\text{AR} - \text{SR})$$
$$= 3,000 \text{ machine hrs} \times (\$28.40 - \$25.00)$$
$$= 3,000 \text{ machine hrs} \times (\$3.40)$$
$$= \$10,200 \text{ U}$$

The interpretation of this variance is not quite as straightforward as the interpretation of the direct labor rate variance. For one, variable MOH is made up of a number of different costs, including indirect materials, indirect labor, and other variable overhead costs

[3]Many companies allocate manufacturing overhead using direct labor hours rather than machine hours. For these companies, the hours used in calculating the manufacturing overhead variances will be *identical* to the hours used in calculating the direct labor variances.

EXHIBIT 11-10 Calculation of Variable Overhead Variances

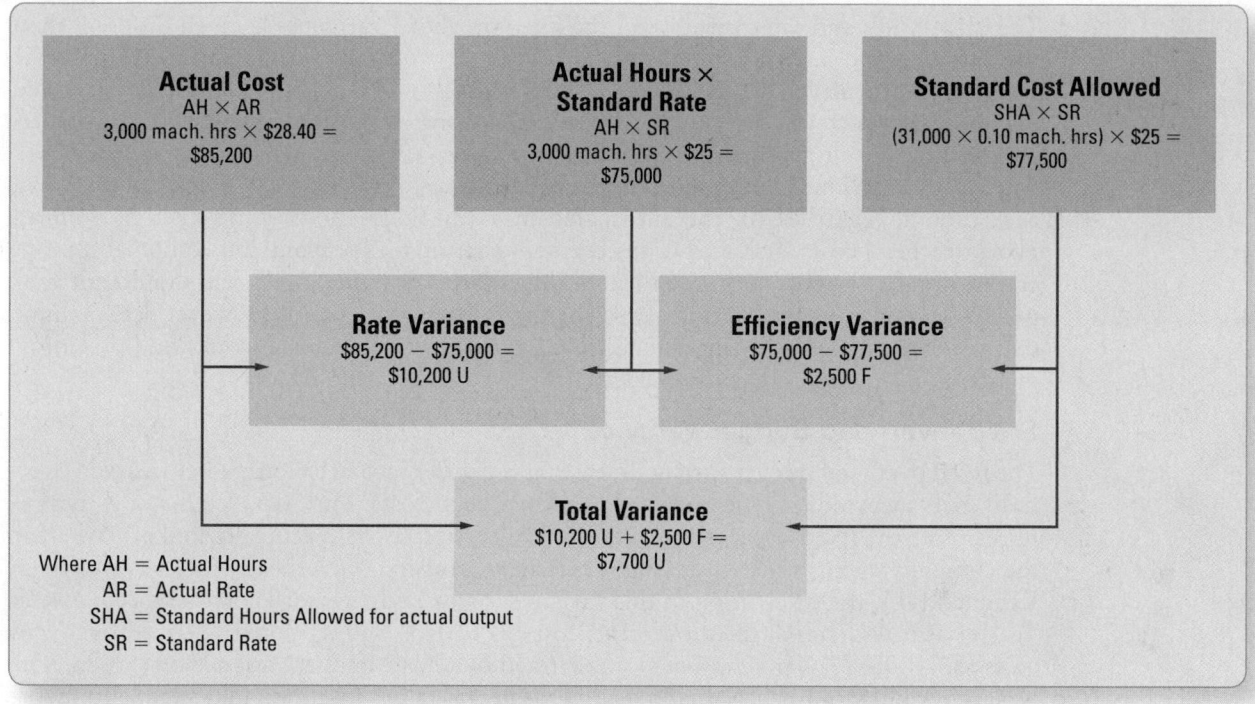

Where AH = Actual Hours
AR = Actual Rate
SHA = Standard Hours Allowed for actual output
SR = Standard Rate

such as the variable portion of the utility bill. One particular cost (for example, indirect materials) could be higher than expected, yet another cost (for example, indirect labor) could be less than expected. As a result, the variance could be due to more than one input.

Second, we don't know if the variance is due to *using* more of the input than expected (for example, using more indirect materials than expected) or because the input *cost more* than expected from the suppliers. On average, management expected variable overhead to cost $25 per machine hour. However, we see that the actual rate ($28.40 per machine hour) turned out to be quite a bit higher. The production supervisor is usually in the best position to help management understand why this variance occurred.

Variable Overhead Efficiency Variance

As shown in Exhibit 11-10, the <u>**variable overhead efficiency variance**</u> is the difference between the actual machine hours run and the standard machine hours allowed for the actual production volume, calculated at the variable MOH rate. Again, it can be algebraically simplified into the following formula:

Variable MOH efficiency variance = Standard Rate × (Actual Hours − Standard Hours Allowed)

= SR × (AH − SHA)

= $25 × [3,000 mch hrs − (31,000 cases × 0.10 mch hrs/case)]

= $25 × (3,000 mch hrs − 3,100 mch hrs)

= $25 × (100 mch hrs)

= $2,500 F

The efficiency variance does not tell management anything with regard to how efficiently variable manufacturing overhead was used. Rather, it is directly tied to the efficiency with which the machine hours were used. It tells managers how much of the total variable MOH variance is due to using more or fewer machine hours than anticipated for the actual volume of output. The production supervisor would be in the best position to explain why this variance occurred.

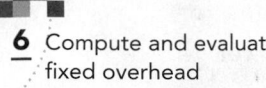

Fixed Manufacturing Overhead Variances

The calculation and interpretation of the fixed overhead variances is much different than the variances we have discussed thus far. Why? Because all of the manufacturing costs we have analyzed thus far have been *variable* costs. However, as the name suggests, fixed overhead is expected to remain at a *fixed* level as long as the company continues to operate within a certain (relevant) range of production.

As discussed in Chapter 9, Tucson Tortilla expects to incur $30,000 of fixed overhead each month, regardless of the anticipated monthly fluctuations in production volume. Fixed overhead costs such as straight-line depreciation on the plant and equipment, property insurance, property tax, and the monthly salaries of indirect laborers should not vary month-to-month as production levels fluctuate to meet demand. However, let's assume that the company actually incurred $31,025 of fixed overhead. We would find this information in the company's general ledger.

Fixed Overhead Budget Variance

The <u>fixed overhead budget variance</u> measures the difference between the actual fixed overhead costs incurred and the budgeted fixed overhead costs. This variance is sometimes referred to as the <u>fixed overhead spending variance</u>, because it specifically looks at whether the company spent more or less than anticipated on fixed overhead costs. As shown in Exhibit 11-11, the calculation of this variance is straightforward. The difference between Tucson Tortilla's actual fixed overhead costs ($31,025) and its budgeted fixed overhead costs ($30,000) results in an unfavorable fixed overhead budget variance of $1,025. The variance is unfavorable if actual fixed overhead costs are more than budgeted, and favorable if actual costs are lower than budgeted.

EXHIBIT 11-11 Calculation of Fixed Overhead Variances

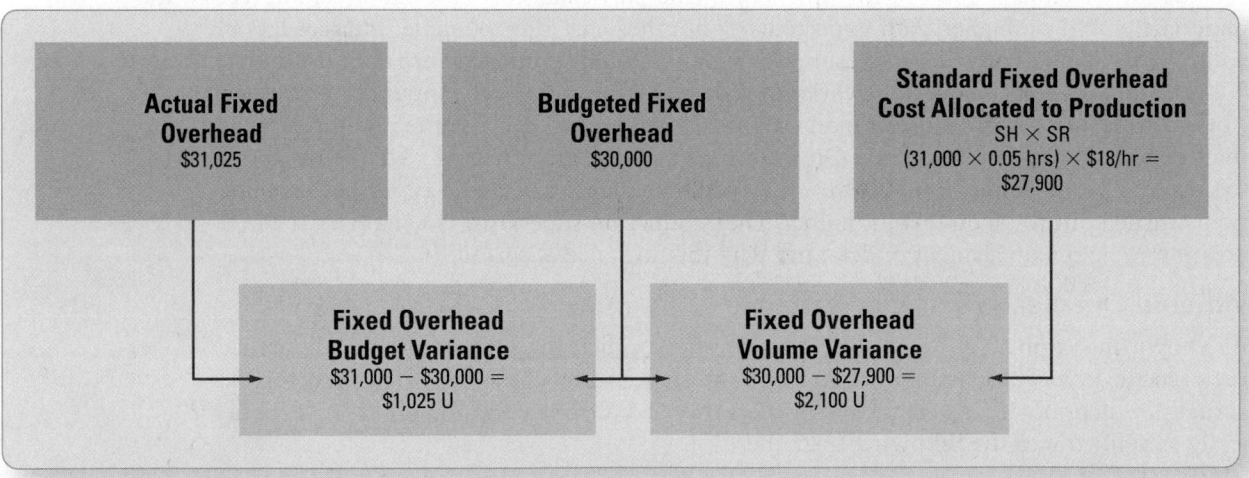

The best way to uncover the cause of the fixed overhead budget variance is to compare each fixed overhead cost component against the budgeted amount. Perhaps indirect laborers received a raise that was not foreseen when the budget was prepared. Perhaps the insurance company increased its premiums, or the city increased property taxes. Although the variance is labeled "unfavorable," the reason for the variance may not be a bad thing. Nor may it be controllable. For example, let's say the unfavorable variance was caused by a raise in salary given to certain indirect laborers in the plant. The raise may result in a boost to employee morale, leading to better productivity. On the other hand, if the unfavorable variance was caused by an increase in city property taxes, management may have little recourse. If, however, the variance was caused by an increase in insurance premiums, management may decide to shop around for a different insurance carrier.

Fixed Overhead Volume Variance

As shown in Exhibit 11-11, the <u>fixed overhead volume variance</u> is the difference between the budgeted fixed overhead and the *standard fixed overhead cost* allocated to production.[4] The standard cost is calculated the same way as we calculated earlier standard costs: we start with the actual volume produced (31,000 cases) then multiply it by the standard hours allowed per case (0.10 machine hrs) to get the standard hours allowed. Finally, we multiply the standard hours allowed by the fixed MOH rate ($9/DL hr) to get the standard fixed overhead cost allocated to production:

$$
\begin{aligned}
\text{Standard Fixed Overhead Cost Allocated to Production} &= (\text{Standard Hours Allowed} \times \text{Standard Rate}) \\
&= (31{,}000 \text{ cases} \times 0.10 \text{ mach. hrs/case}) \times \$9/\text{hr} \\
&= 3{,}100 \text{ hrs} \times \$9/\text{machine hr} \\
&= \$27{,}900
\end{aligned}
$$

Now that we have calculated the standard fixed overhead allocated to production, we can compute the fixed overhead volume variance as follows:

$$
\begin{aligned}
&= \text{Budgeted Fixed Overhead} - \text{Standard Fixed Overhead Cost Allocated to Production} \\
&= \$30{,}000 - \$27{,}900 \\
&= \$2{,}100 \text{ U}
\end{aligned}
$$

The fixed overhead volume variance results from two causes:

1. Treating fixed overhead costs *as if* they were variable in order to allocate the costs to individuals units of product; and

2. Incorrectly estimating the level of activity when calculating the predetermined fixed MOH rate.

For example, Tucson Tortilla calculated its predetermined fixed MOH rate ($9/machine hour) based on an estimated yearly production volume of 400,000 cases. Recall from Chapter 6 that fixed costs per unit of activity vary inversely with changes in volume. Had the production estimate been higher than 400,000 cases, the predetermined fixed overhead rate would have been lower than $9 per machine hour. On the other hand, had the production estimate been lower than 400,000 cases, the fixed overhead rate would have been higher than $9 per machine hour. Since production volume (31,000 cases) was not the same as anticipated (33,333 cases per month on average), we expect a difference between what was budgeted for fixed overhead and the amount of fixed overhead allocated to production.

In essence, the fixed overhead volume variance measures the utilization of the fixed capacity costs. If volume is higher than originally anticipated, the variance will be favorable, because more units were produced with the same amount of fixed resources. In essence, the company used those fixed resources more efficiently. In this situation, the standard fixed overhead cost allocated to production is *greater* than the amount budgeted. In other words, the company *overallocated* fixed overhead to production, as shown in Exhibit 11-12.

EXHIBIT 11-12 Favorable Fixed Overhead Volume Variance

If... production volume is *greater* than anticipated,

Then... fixed overhead has been *overallocated,*

And... the fixed overhead volume variance is *favorable*

---

[4]In Chapter 3 we learned about a *normal* costing system in which manufacturing overhead is allocated to production using a predetermined MOH rate multiplied by the actual quantity of the allocation base used (such as actual machine hours used by the job). In a *standard* costing system, companies allocate manufacturing overhead to production differently: they multiply the predetermined manufacturing overhead rate by the *standard quantity of the allocation base allowed*, rather than the *actual quantity of the allocation base used*.

On the other hand, if production volume is lower than anticipated, the variance is denoted as unfavorable due to the fact that fixed costs were not used to produce as many units as anticipated. Since the number of units produced (31,000 cases) was less than anticipated (33,333 on average per month), production capacity was used less efficiently than anticipated, leading to an unfavorable volume variance. In this situation, the standard fixed overhead cost allocated to production is less than the amount budgeted. In other words, the company *underallocated* fixed overhead, as shown in Exhibit 11-13.

EXHIBIT 11-13 Unfavorable Fixed Overhead Volume Variance

Keep the following rule of thumb in mind:

When production volume is *higher* than anticipated, the fixed overhead volume variance will be *favorable*. When it is *lower* than anticipated, the variance will be *unfavorable*.

Extreme caution should be used when interpreting the volume variance. Again, favorable does not equate with "good," nor does unfavorable equate with "bad." For companies striving to create lean production environments, inventory levels will naturally fall, leading to an unfavorable volume variance. Has a "bad" decision been made? Absolutely not! The lean producer will generally be much more efficient in the long run than its traditional counterpart. The challenge during the transition phase will be for management to determine how to best use the newly freed capacity, and not be misled by the resulting temporary unfavorable volume variances that may occur.

▶ **Try It!**

Hannah owns a fruit smoothie shop at the local mall. The budgeted monthly fixed overhead costs consist of the store lease payment ($1,000), advertising ($250), equipment depreciation ($125), and store Wi-Fi ($80). Actual fixed overhead expenses for June were $1,600. When calculating the fixed overhead rate, Hannah anticipated selling 4,800 smoothies during each summer month. She actually sold 5,000 in June.

1. What is the fixed overhead budget variance for the month of June? Is the variance favorable or unfavorable?

2. Will Hannah's fixed overhead volume variance for the month of June be favorable or unfavorable? Explain.

Please see page 697 for solutions.

Standard Costing Systems

As we have just seen, many manufacturers use standard costs independent of the general ledger accounting system to evaluate performance through variance analysis. However, other companies integrate standards directly into their general ledger accounting. This method of accounting, called standard costing, is discussed in the appendix to this chapter.

Decision Guidelines

Standard Costs and Variances

Let's consider some of management's decisions related to overhead variances.

Decision	Guidelines
Should we calculate and interpret all manufacturing overhead variances the same way?	Variable overhead costs are expected to change in total as production volume changes. However, fixed overhead costs should stay constant within a relevant range of production. Therefore, management will want to analyze variable and fixed MOH variances separately.
What variable overhead variances should we compute?	Two variable overhead variances are typically computed: • Rate (or spending) variance tells managers if they spent more or less than anticipated on variable MOH costs considering the actual hours of work used. • Efficiency variance tells managers nothing about the efficiency with which variable overhead costs were used. Rather, it is tied directly to the efficiency with which machine hours or labor hours were used.
How is the variable overhead *rate* (or *spending*) variance computed?	$= \text{Actual Hours} \times (\text{Actual Rate} - \text{Standard Rate})$ $= \text{AH} \times (\text{AR} - \text{SR})$
How is the variable overhead *efficiency* variance computed?	$= \text{Standard Rate} \times (\text{Actual Hours} - \text{Standard Hours Allowed})$ $= \text{SR} \times (\text{AH} - \text{SHA})$
What fixed overhead variances should we compute?	Two fixed overhead variances are typically computed: • Budget (or spending) variance tells managers if they spent more or less than anticipated on fixed overhead costs. • Volume variance tells managers if too much or too little fixed overhead was allocated to production due to the actual volume of production being different than the volume used to calculate the predetermined fixed MOH rate.
How is the fixed overhead *budget* variance computed?	$= \text{Actual fixed overhead} - \text{Budgeted fixed overhead}$
How is the fixed overhead *volume* variance computed?	$= \text{Budgeted fixed overhead} - \text{Standard fixed overhead cost allocated to production}$ $= \text{Budgeted fixed overhead} - (\text{SHA} \times \text{SR})$
Who is usually in the best position to explain why variances occurred?	Management will want to compare the actual cost of individual MOH components (such as indirect labor, utilities, property taxes) against the budgets for those same components. The purchasing and production supervisors may also be able to offer insights.
How should the fixed overhead volume variance be interpreted?	A favorable variance means that more units were produced than originally anticipated, leading to an overallocation of fixed MOH. An unfavorable variance means that fewer units were produced than originally anticipated, leading to an underallocation of fixed MOH.

SUMMARY PROBLEM 2

Memoirs, Inc., produces several different styles and sizes of picture frames. The following activity describes Memoirs' overhead costs during March:

Number of frames produced	25,000 frames
Predetermined variable MOH rate	$ 6.00 per DL hour
Predetermined fixed MOH rate..............................	$ 12.00 per DL hour
Budgeted fixed manufacturing overhead	$70,000
Actual direct labor hours..	6,500 hours
Actual variable manufacturing overhead	$40,625, resulting in an actual rate of $6.25* per DL hour
Actual fixed manufacturing overhead......................	$68,000
Standard direct labor allowed per unit	0.25 hours per frame

*$40,625/6,500 hours

Requirements

1. Calculate the variable overhead rate and efficiency variances for the month of March.
2. Calculate the fixed overhead budget and volume variances for the month of March.

▪ SOLUTIONS

Requirement 1

$$\text{Variable MOH rate variance} = \text{Actual Hours} \times (\text{Actual Rate} - \text{Standard Rate})$$
$$= \text{AH} \times (\text{AR} - \text{SR})$$
$$= 6{,}500 \text{ hrs} \times (\$6.25 - \$6.00)$$
$$= 6{,}500 \text{ hrs} \times (\$0.25)$$
$$= \$1{,}625 \text{ U}$$

$$\text{Variable MOH efficiency variance} = \text{Standard Rate} \times (\text{Actual Hours} - \text{Standard Hours Allowed})$$
$$= \text{SR} \times (\text{AH} - \text{SHA})$$
$$= \$6.00 \times [6{,}500 - (25{,}000 \text{ frames} \times 0.25 \text{ hrs/frame})]$$
$$= \$6.00 \times (6{,}500 - 6{,}250 \text{ hrs})$$
$$= \$6.00 \times 250 \text{ hrs}$$
$$= \$1{,}500 \text{ U}$$

Requirement 2

The fixed overhead variances are calculated as follows:

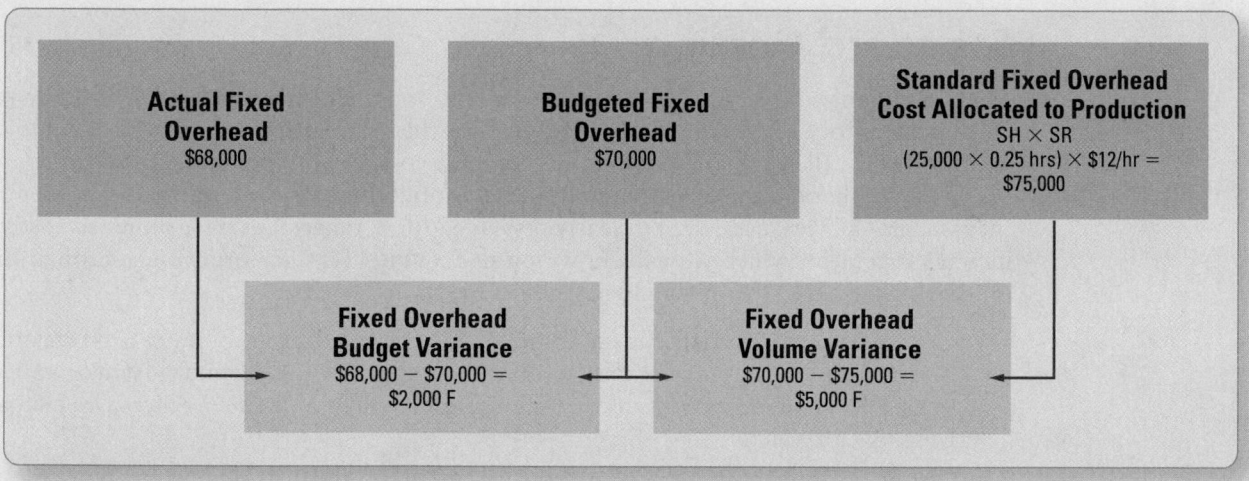

- The budget variance is favorable since less was spent on fixed overhead than budgeted.
- The volume variance is favorable since more was allocated to production than was budgeted. This means that more units were produced than budgeted.

Appendix 11A

Standard Costing

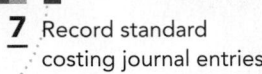

Many companies integrate standards directly into their general ledger accounting by recording inventory-related costs at standard cost rather than at actual cost. This method of accounting is called **standard costing** or **standard cost accounting**. Standard costing not only saves on bookkeeping costs but also isolates price and efficiency variances as soon as they occur. The variances will be clearly displayed for management on a standard costing income statement, which we will show you in Exhibit 11-14. Before we go through the journal entries, keep the following key points in mind:

1. Each type of variance discussed has its own general ledger account. A debit balance means that the variance is unfavorable since it decreases income (just like an expense). A credit balance means that the variance is favorable since it increases income (just like a revenue).

2. Just as in job costing, the manufacturing costs flow through the inventory accounts in the following order: raw materials → work in process → finished goods → cost of goods sold. The difference is that *standard costs* rather than actual costs are used to record the manufacturing costs entered into the inventory accounts.

3. At the end of the period, the variance accounts are closed to Cost of Goods Sold to correct for the fact that the standard costs recorded in the accounts were different from actual costs. Assuming that most inventory worked on during the period has been sold, any error from using standard costs rather than actual costs is contained in Cost of Goods Sold. Closing the variances to Cost of Goods Sold corrects the account balance.

Journal Entries

We use Tucson Tortilla's *January* transactions, just as we did in the chapter, to demonstrate standard costing.

1. **Recording Raw Materials Purchases**—Tucson Tortilla debits Raw Materials Inventory for the *actual quantity* of corn flour purchased (160,000 pounds) recorded at the *standard price* ($1.50 per pound). It credits Accounts Payable for the *actual quantity* of corn flour purchased (160,000 pounds) recorded at the *actual price* ($1.40 per pound) because this is the amount owed to Tucson Tortilla's suppliers. The difference is the direct materials *price* variance.

		Raw Materials Inventory (160,000 × $1.50)	240,000	
		Accounts Payable (160,000 × $1.40)		224,000
		DM Price Variance		16,000
		(to record purchase of raw materials)		

The favorable price variance is the same shown as in Exhibit 11-5. Since it is favorable, it has a credit balance, which increases Tucson Tortilla's January profits.

2. **Recording Use of Direct Materials**—When Tucson Tortilla *uses* direct materials, it debits Work in Process Inventory at the *standard price* ($1.50) × *standard quantity* of direct materials that should have been used (31,000 cases × 5 lbs per case = 155,000 pounds). *This maintains Work in Process Inventory at a purely standard cost.* Raw Materials Inventory is credited for the *actual quantity* of materials used in production (160,000 pounds) recorded at the *standard price* ($1.50) since this is the price at which the materials were entered into Raw Materials Inventory in the previous journal entry. The difference is the direct materials *quantity* variance. The direct

materials quantity variance is recorded when Tucson Tortilla records the *use* of direct materials:

	Work in Process Inventory (155,000 × $1.50)	232,500	
	DM Quantity Variance	7,500	
	Raw Materials Inventory (160,000 × $1.50)		240,000
	(to record use of direct materials)		

The unfavorable quantity price variance is the same as shown in Exhibit 11-5. Since it is unfavorable, it has a debit balance, which decreases Tucson Tortilla's January profits.

3. **Recording Direct Labor Costs**—Since Work in Process Inventory is maintained at standard cost, Tucson Tortilla debits Work in Process Inventory for the *standard rate* for direct labor ($22 per hour) × *standard hours* of direct labor that should have been (31,000 cases × 0.05 hours per case = 1,550 hours). Tucson Tortilla credits Wages Payable for the *actual* hours worked at the *actual* wage rate since this is the amount owed to employees. At the same time, Tucson Tortilla records the direct labor price and efficiency variances calculated in Exhibit 11-7. The *unfavorable* DL Rate Variance is recorded as a *debit*, while the *favorable* DL Efficiency Variance is recorded as a *credit*.

	Work in Process Inventory (1,550 hrs × $22)	34,100	
	DL Rate Variance (Exhibit 11-7)	1,875	
	DL Efficiency Variance (Exhibit 11-7)		1,100
	Wages Payable (1,500 hrs × $23.25)		34,875
	(to record use of direct labor)		

4. **Recording Actual Manufacturing Overhead Costs**—Tucson Tortilla records manufacturing overhead costs as usual, debiting the manufacturing overhead account and crediting various accounts. The actual costs can be found in Exhibits 11-10 and 11-11:

	Variable Manufacturing Overhead (Exhibit 11-10)	85,200	
	Fixed Manufacturing Overhead (Exhibit 11-11)	31,025	
	Various Accounts		116,225
	(to record actual overhead costs incurred)		

5. **Allocating Overhead**—In standard costing, the overhead allocated to Work in Process Inventory is computed using the standard overhead rates ($25/MH for variable MOH and $9/MH for fixed overhead) × standard quantity of the allocation base allowed for the actual output (31,000 cases × 0.10 MH per case = 3,100 MH). As usual, the Manufacturing Overhead account is credited when allocating overhead:

	Work in Process Inventory	105,400	
	Variable Manufacturing Overhead (3,100 MH × $25/MH)		77,500
	Fixed Manufacturing Overhead (3,100 MH × $9/MH)		27,900

This journal entry corresponds with our calculations in Exhibits 11-10 and 11-11.

6. **Recording the Completion**—So far, Work in Process has been debited with $372,000 of manufacturing cost ($232,500 of direct materials + $34,100 of direct labor + $105,400 of MOH). Does this make sense? According to Exhibit 11-1, the standard cost of manufacturing one case is $12.00. If we take the $372,000 of cost and divide it by 31,000 cases, we get $12.00 per case! This is how it should be—through the standard costing journal entries, Tucson Tortilla has successfully recorded each case at its standard cost of $12. In addition, it has captured all of the variances in separate variance accounts on the general ledger. As the units are completed, the standard cost of each case is transferred out of Work in Process and into Finished Goods:

		Finished Goods Inventory (31,000 × $12.00)	372,000	
		Work in Process Inventory (31,000 × $12.00)		372,000
		(to record completion of the 31,000 cases)		

7. **Recording the Sale and Release of Inventory**—When the cases are sold, *Sales Revenue* is recorded at the standard, or budgeted sales price ($20 per case, from Exhibit 9-5), but Accounts Receivable (and Cash, for COD sales) is recorded at the actual sales price. Let's assume the company actually sold 32,000 cases at an average price of $20.25 per unit, resulting in a favorable flexible budget sales revenue variance of $8,000.

		Accounts Receivable and Cash (32,000 × $20.25)	648,000	
		Flexible Budget Sales Revenue Variance		8,000
		Sales Revenue (32,000 × $20.00)		640,000
		(to record the sale of 32,000 cases)		

Under a perpetual inventory system, Tucson Tortilla must also release inventory for the cases it has sold. Since these cases were recorded at standard cost ($12.00 each), they must be removed from Finished Goods Inventory and be entered into Cost of Goods Sold at the same standard cost:

		Cost of Goods Sold (32,000 × $12.00)	384,000	
		Finished Goods Inventory (32,000 × $12.00)		384,000
		(to record cost of goods sold for the 32,000 cases)		

8. **Closing Manufacturing Overhead**—Tucson Tortilla must close its temporary MOH accounts. Rather than closing them directly to Cost of Goods Sold, as we did in Chapter 3, in a standard costing system the accounts are closed to variance accounts. The company closes the Variable Manufacturing Overhead account to the variable MOH variances shown in Exhibit 11-10:

		Variable Overhead Rate Variance	10,200	
		Variable Overhead Efficiency Variance		2,500
		Variable Manufacturing Overhead		7,700
		(to close the Variable MOH account)		

Likewise, it closes the Fixed Manufacturing Overhead account to the fixed MOH variances shown in Exhibit 11-11:

Fixed Overhead Budget Variance		1,025	
Fixed Overhead Volume Variance		2,100	
Fixed Manufacturing Overhead			3,125
(to close the Fixed MOH account)			

These two journal entries zero out the two manufacturing overhead accounts.

Standard Costing Income Statement

Exhibit 11-14 shows a standard costing income statement that highlights the variances for Tucson Tortilla's management (we only show down to the gross profit line). It shows revenues and cost of goods sold, first at standard and then at actual. Although the overall effect of the cost variances was minimal ($3,100 U), the report clearly shows management the size of each variance. Managers will use management by exception to determine which variances, if any, they wish to investigate.

EXHIBIT 11-14 Standard Costing Income Statement

	A	B	C	D	E	F
1	Tucson Tortilla					
2	Standard Cost Income Statement					
3	For the Month Ended January 31					
4						
5	Sales revenue, at standard (32,000 × $20)			$ 640,000		
6	Plus/(less): Flexible budget sales revenue variance			8,000	F	
7	**Sales revenue, at actual**				$	648,000
8	Less: Cost of goods sold, at standard (32,000 × $12			$ 384,000		
9	Plus/(less) manufacturing costs variances:					
10	DM price variance	$ (16,000)	F			
11	DM quantity variance	7,500	U			
12	DL rate variance	1,875	U			
13	DL efficiency variance	(1,100)	F			
14	Variable MOH rate variance	10,200	U			
15	Variable MOH efficiency variance	(2,500)	F			
16	Fixed MOH budget variance	1,025	U			
17	Fixed MOH volume variance	2,100	U			
18	Total manufacturing cost variances			3,100	U	
19	**Cost of goods sold, at actual**					387,100
20	Gross Profit				$	260,900
21						

At the end of the period, all of the cost variance accounts are closed to zero-out their balances. Why? For two reasons: (1) The financial statements prepared for *external* users never show variances (variances are only for internal management's use) and (2) the general ledger must be corrected for the fact that standard costs, rather than actual costs, were used to record manufacturing costs. Since all of the cases were sold, the error in costing currently exists in the Cost of Goods Sold account. Therefore, each cost variance account will be closed to Cost of Goods Sold. Likewise, the flexible budget sales revenue variance will be closed to Sales Revenue.

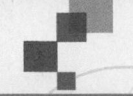

END OF CHAPTER

Learning Objectives

- 1 Explain how and why standard costs are developed
- 2 Compute and evaluate direct materials variances
- 3 Compute and evaluate direct labor variances
- 4 Explain the advantages and disadvantages of using standard costs and variances
- 5 Compute and evaluate variable overhead variances
- 6 Compute and evaluate fixed overhead variances
- 7 (Appendix) Record standard costing journal entries

Accounting Vocabulary

Attainable Standards. (p. 644) Standards based on currently attainable conditions that include allowances for normal amounts of waste and inefficiency. Also known as practical standards.

Direct Labor Efficiency Variance. (p. 653) This variance tells managers how much of the total labor variance is due to using a greater or lesser amount of time than anticipated. It is calculated as follows: SR × (AH − SHA).

Direct Labor Rate Variance. (p. 653) This variance tells managers how much of the total labor variance is due to paying a higher or lower hourly wage rate than anticipated. It is calculated as follows: AH × (AR − SR).

Direct Materials Price Variance. (p. 648) This variance tells managers how much of the total direct materials variance is due to paying a higher or lower price than expected for the direct materials it purchased. It is calculated as follows: AQP × (AP − SP).

Direct Materials Quantity Variance. (p. 648) This variance tells managers how much of the total direct materials variance is due to using a larger or smaller quantity of direct materials than expected. It is calculated as follows: SP × (AQU − SQA).

Fixed Overhead Budget Variance. (p. 662) This variance measures the difference between the actual fixed overhead costs incurred and the budgeted fixed overhead costs. This variance is sometimes referred to as the **fixed overhead spending variance**, because it specifically looks at whether the company spent more or less than anticipated on fixed overhead costs.

Fixed Overhead Volume Variance. (p. 663) This variance is the difference between the budgeted fixed overhead and the *standard fixed overhead cost* allocated to production. In essence, the fixed overhead volume variance measures the utilization of the fixed capacity costs. If volume is higher than originally anticipated, the variance will be favorable. If volume is lower than originally anticipated, the variance will be unfavorable.

Ideal Standards. (p. 643) Standards based on perfect or ideal conditions that do not allow for any waste in the production process, machine breakdown, or other inefficiencies. Also known as perfection standards.

Perfection Standards. (p. 643) Standards based on perfect or ideal conditions that do not allow for any waste in the production process, machine breakdown, or other inefficiencies. Also known as ideal standards.

Practical Standards. (p. 644) Standards based on currently attainable conditions that include allowances for normal amounts of waste and inefficiency. Also known as attainable standards.

Standard Cost. (p. 643) The budget for a single unit of product. Also simply referred to as standards.

Standard Cost Accounting. (p. 668) Another common name for standard costing.

Standard Costing. (p. 668) Also known as standard cost accounting. A method of accounting in which product costs are entered into the general ledger inventory accounts at standard cost, rather than actual cost. The variances are captured in their own general ledger accounts and displayed on a standard costing income statement prior to being closed out at the end of the period.

Standards. (p. 643) Another common name for standard costs.

Variable Overhead Efficiency Variance. (p. 661) This variance tells managers how much of the total variable MOH variance is due to using more or fewer hours of the allocation base (usually machine hours or DL hours) than anticipated for the actual volume of output. It is calculated as follows: SR × (AH − SHA).

Variable Overhead Rate Variance. (p. 660) Also called the variable overhead spending variance. This variance tells managers whether more or less was spent on variable overhead than they expected would be spent for the hours worked. It is calculated as follows: AH × (AR − SR).

Variable Overhead Spending Variance. (p. 660) Another common name for variable overhead rate variance.

Quick Check

1. (*Learning Objective 1*) Which of the following is true?
   a. A standard is a budget for one unit.
   b. Ideal standards are based on currently attainable conditions.
   c. Practical standards are based on ideal conditions.
   d. Standards should never be updated.

2. (*Learning Objective 2*) The direct material price variance can be defined as which of the following?
   a. Standard price × (Actual quantity used − Standard quantity allowed)
   b. Actual quantity purchased × (Actual price − Standard price)
   c. Actual price × (Actual quantity used − Standard quantity allowed)
   d. Standard quantity allowed × (Actual price − Standard price)

3. (*Learning Objective 2*) The direct material quantity variance can be defined as which of the following?
   a. Standard price × (Actual quantity used − Standard quantity allowed)
   b. Actual quantity purchased × (Actual price − Standard price)
   c. Actual price × (Actual quantity used − Standard quantity allowed)
   d. Standard quantity allowed × (Actual price − Standard price)

4. (*Learning Objective 3*) The direct labor rate variance can be defined as which of the following?
   a. Actual rate × (Actual hours − Standard hours allowed)
   b. Standard hours allowed × (Actual rate − Standard rate)
   c. Standard rate × (Actual hours − Standard hours allowed)
   d. Actual hours × (Actual rate − Standard rate)

5. (*Learning Objective 3*) The direct labor efficiency variance can be defined as which of the following?
   a. Actual rate × (Actual hours − Standard hours allowed)
   b. Standard hours allowed × (Actual rate − Standard rate)
   c. Standard rate × (Actual hours − Standard hours allowed)
   d. Actual hours × (Actual rate − Standard rate)

6. (*Learning Objective 4*) Which of the following is **not** an advantage of using standard costs?
   a. Standards serve as cost benchmarks.
   b. Standards can cause unintended behavioral consequences.
   c. Standards are useful for budgeting.
   d. Standards can simplify bookkeeping.

7. (*Learning Objective 5*) The variable overhead rate variance can be defined as which of the following?
   a. Actual rate × (Actual hours − Standard hours allowed)
   b. Standard hours allowed × (Actual rate − Standard rate)
   c. Standard rate × (Actual hours − Standard hours allowed)
   d. Actual hours × (Actual rate − Standard rate)

8. (*Learning Objective 6*) Which of the following is **not** true about the fixed overhead budget variance?
   a. It is sometimes referred to as the fixed overhead spending variance.
   b. It is the difference between actual fixed overhead and budgeted fixed overhead.
   c. It is the difference between the budgeted fixed overhead and the standard fixed overhead allocated to production.
   d. It can be either favorable or unfavorable.

9. (*Learning Objective 6*) Which of the following is **not** true about the fixed overhead volume variance?
   a. If volume is greater than originally anticipated, the variance will be unfavorable.
   b. It is partially the result of treating fixed overhead costs as if they were variable for allocating the costs to individual units of production.
   c. If volume is lower than originally anticipated, then fixed overhead cost would be underallocated.
   d. It is partially the result of incorrectly estimating the level of activity when calculating the predetermined fixed manufacturing overhead rate.

10. (*Learning Objective 7—Appendix*) Which of the following is **not** true about standard costing systems?
    a. Each type of variance has its own general ledger account.
    b. Standard costs are used to record the manufacturing costs entered into the inventory accounts.
    c. A standard cost income statement shows cost of goods sold at standard, along with all of the variances needed to adjust cost of goods sold back to actual.
    d. At the end of the period, the variances are closed to the Sales Revenue account.

Quick Check Answers

1.a 2.b 3.a 4.d 5.c 6.b 7.d 8.c 9.a 10.d

Short Exercises

S11-1 Compute the standard cost of direct materials *(Learning Objective 1)*

Hodge Confections is known for its creamy milk chocolate fudge. Hodge sells its fudge to local retailers. A "unit" of fudge is a 10-pound batch. The standard quantities of ingredients for a batch include 7 cups of sugar, 23 ounces of chocolate chips, 16 ounces of butter, and 18 ounces of evaporated milk. The standard costs for each of the ingredients are as follows: $0.17 per cup of sugar, $0.18 per ounce of chocolate chips, $0.11 per ounce of butter, and $0.14 per ounce of evaporated milk. Calculate the standard direct material cost per batch of fudge.

S11-2 Compute the standard cost of direct labor *(Learning Objective 1)*

Hodge Confections produces fudge in 10-pound batches. Each batch takes 0.26 hours of direct labor, which includes allowances for breaks, cleanup, and other downtime. Hodge pays its direct labor workers an average of $17.50 per hour. Calculate the standard direct labor cost per batch of fudge.

S11-3 Calculate direct material variances when the quantity purchased equals the quantity used *(Learning Objective 2)*

Dolphin Ceramics produces large planters to be used in urban landscaping projects. A special earth clay is used to make the planters. The standard quantity of clay used for each planter is 24 pounds. Dolphin uses a standard cost of $2.00 per pound of clay. Dolphin produced 3,125 planters in May. In that month, 78,125 pounds of clay were purchased and used at the total cost of $150,000.

Requirements

1. Calculate the direct material price variance.
2. Calculate the direct material quantity variance.

S11-4 Calculate direct material variances when the quantity purchased differs from the quantity used *(Learning Objective 2)*

Scott Landscaping produces faux boulders to be used in various landscaping applications. A special resin is used to make the planters. The standard quantity of resin used for each boulder is 5 pounds. Scott uses a standard cost of $2.00 per pound for the resin. The company produced 2,650 boulders in June. In that month, 12,500 pounds of resin were purchased at a total cost of $26,000. A total of 12,250 pounds were used in producing the boulders in June.

Requirements

1. Calculate the direct material price variance.
2. Calculate the direct material quantity variance.

S11-5 Calculate direct labor variances *(Learning Objective 3)*

Campa Oil performs oil changes. The standard wage rate for oil change technicians is $20 per hour. By analyzing its past records of time spent on oil changes, Casta Oil has developed a standard of 21 minutes (or 0.35 hours) per oil change.

In July, 800 oil changes were performed at Campa Oil. Oil change technicians worked a total of 260 direct labor hours at an average rate of $23 per hour.

Requirements

1. Calculate the direct labor rate variance.
2. Calculate the direct labor efficiency variance.

S11-6 Identify advantages and disadvantages of standard costs and variance analysis *(Learning Objective 4)*

In the following list, identify whether the situation would indicate that a company should use standard costs and variance analysis or if the company should move away from standard costs and variance analysis.

CHAPTER 11

Situation	Use standard costs	Move away from standard costs
1. There has been an increase in automation in the manufacturing process and a corresponding decrease in direct labor		
2. Would like to increase employee motivation levels		
3. Would like to facilitate the budgeting process		
4. Will be implementing lean practices throughout the organization		
5. Would like to use operational performance measures and visual management cues		
6. Need timely reports about production results		
7. Would like to simplify the bookkeeping process		
8. Want benchmarks by which to judge actual costs		

S11-7 Calculate variable overhead variances *(Learning Objective 5)*

Simmons Industries produced 3,000 tables last month. The standard variable manufacturing overhead (MOH) rate used by the company is $18 per machine hour. Each table requires 0.5 machine hours. Actual machine hours used last month were 1,550 and the actual variable MOH rate last month was $17.00.

Requirements

1. Calculate the variable overhead rate variance.
2. Calculate the variable overhead efficiency variance.

S11-8 Calculate fixed overhead variances *(Learning Objective 6)*

Bentley Manufacturing produces premium dog houses. Each dog house requires 1.0 hours of machine time for its elaborate trim and finishing. For the current year, Bentley calculated its predetermined fixed manufacturing overhead (MOH) rate to be $21 per machine hour. The company budgets its fixed MOH to be $14,000 per month. Last month, Bentley produced 1,000 dog houses and incurred $17,000 (actual) of fixed MOH.

Requirements

1. Calculate the fixed overhead budget variance.
2. Calculate the fixed overhead volume variance.

S11-9 Calculate and interpret fixed overhead variances *(Learning Objectives 5 & 6)*

Harris Industries produces high-end flutes for professional musicians across the globe. Actual fixed manufacturing overhead for the year was $1,270,000, while the budgeted fixed manufacturing overhead was $1,285,000. Using a standard costing system, the company allocated $1,220,000 of overhead to production.

Requirements

1. Calculate the total fixed overhead variance. What does this tell managers?
2. Determine the fixed overhead budget variance. What does this tell managers?
3. Determine the fixed overhead production volume variance. What does this tell managers?

S11-10 Calculate overhead rates *(Learning Objectives 5 & 6)*

The Heese Restaurant Group supplies its franchise restaurants with many pre-manufactured ingredients (such as bags of frozen French fries), while other ingredients (such as lettuce and tomatoes) are sourced locally. Assume that the manufacturing plant processing the fries anticipated incurring a total of $4,068,000 of manufacturing overhead during the year. Of this amount, $1,582,000 is fixed. Manufacturing overhead is allocated based on machine hours. The plant anticipates running the machines 226,000 hours next year.

Requirements

1. Compute the standard variable overhead rate.
2. Compute the predetermined fixed manufacturing overhead rate.

CHAPTER 11

S11-11 Calculate and interpret overhead variances *(Learning Objective 6)*

Assume that the Tarr Corporation's manufacturing facility actually incurred $2,980,000 of manufacturing overhead for the year. Total fixed manufacturing overhead was budgeted at $3,080,000. Using a standard costing system, the company allocated $2,947,000 of manufacturing overhead to production.

Requirements

1. Calculate the total fixed manufacturing overhead variance. What does this tell managers?
2. Determine the fixed overhead budget variance. What does this tell managers?
3. Determine the fixed overhead volume variance. What does this tell managers?
4. Doublecheck: Do the two variances (computed in Requirements 2 and 3) sum to the total overhead variance computed in Requirement 1?

S11-12 Record costing transactions *(Learning Objective 7)*

During the week, the Heese Restaurant Group's French fry manufacturing facility purchased 10,000 pounds of potatoes at a price of $1.14 per pound. The standard price per pound is $1.02. During the week, 9,950 pounds of potatoes were used. The standard quantity of potatoes that should have been used for the actual volume of output was 9,200 pounds.

Requirements

1. Record the following transactions using a standard cost accounting system:
   a. The purchase of potatoes
   b. The use of potatoes
2. Are the variances favorable or unfavorable? Explain.

S11-13 Record standard costing transactions *(Learning Objective 7)*

During the week, the Heese Restaurant Group's French fry manufacturing facility incurred 2,100 hours of direct labor. Direct laborers were paid $12.40 per hour. The standard hourly labor rate is $12.05. Standards indicate that for the volume of output actually achieved, the factory should have used 2,300 hours.

Requirements

1. Record the labor transactions using a standard costs accounting system.
2. Are the variances favorable or unfavorable? Explain.

ETHICS

S11-14 Identify ethical standards violated *(Learning Objectives 1, 2, 3, 4, 5, & 6)*

For each of the situations listed, identify the primary standard from the *IMA Statement of Ethical Professional Practice* that is violated (competence, confidentiality, integrity, or credibility). Refer to Exhibit 1-6 for the complete standard.

1. Sarabeth, an accountant at Warren Industries, and Jay, an accountant at Sorenia Manufacturing, exchanged cost and other production data so that they would have benchmarks to use for their company reports.
2. When Sandra prepares variance reports, only favorable variances are listed. Unfavorable variances are only provided if someone specifically asks.
3. Preston is the chief accountant at Long Industries. Each month, he prepares variance reports that are given to all department managers. The variance reports are frequently late and usually contain a few errors.
4. Devin accepts an all-expenses-paid trip to Las Vegas from a major supplier.
5. Milton has just started to work at Brady Lake Supply. In his first week, he is asked to fill in for a senior accountant who is out of the office for six weeks on maternity leave. He is asked to prepare the standard costing journal entries. Milton does not know how to do this work, but he decides to guess because he does not want to appear stupid by asking for help.

S11-15 Vocabulary *(Learning Objectives 1, 2, 3, 4, 5, & 6)*

Match the term on the left with the definition on the right.

Term	Definition
1. Fixed overhead volume variance	a. Tells managers how much of the total variance is due to paying a different hourly wage rate than anticipated
2. Direct labor efficiency variance	b. Tells managers how much of the total variance is due to using a greater or lesser amount of time being worked than anticipated
3. Practical standards	c. Tells managers how much of the total variance is due to using a difference quantity of direct materials than expected
4. Standard cost	d. Tells managers how much of the total variable MOH variance is due to using more or less hours of the allocation base than anticipated for the actual volume of output
5. Direct materials quantity variance	e. Measures the difference between the budgeted fixed MOH costs and the standard allocated MOH costs
6. Direct labor rate variance	f. Tells managers how much of the total variance is due to paying a different price than expected for direct materials
7. Variable overhead rate variance	g. The budget for a single unit of product
8. Fixed overhead budget variance	h. Also called the variable overhead spending variance
9. Ideal standards	i. Also known as attainable standards
10. Direct materials price variance	j. Standards based on conditions that do not allow for any waste in the production process
11. Variable overhead efficiency variance	k. Measures the difference between the actual fixed MOH costs incurred and the budgeted fixed MOH costs

EXERCISES Group A

E11-16A Calculate standard cost and gross profit per unit *(Learning Objective 1)*

Jessica's Bakery makes desserts for local restaurants. Each pan of gourmet brownies requires 3 cups flour, ½ cup chopped pecans, ¼ cup cocoa, 2 cups sugar, ½ cup chocolate chips, 2 eggs, and ⅓ cup oil. Each pan requires 15 minutes of direct labor for mixing, cutting, and packaging. Each pan must bake for 30 minutes. Restaurants purchase the gourmet brownies by the pan, not by the individual serving. Each pan is currently sold for $14. Standard costs are $1.92 per bag of flour (16 cups in a bag), $6.00 per bag of pecans (3 cups per bag), $3.72 per tin of cocoa (3 cups per tin), $1.20 per bag of sugar (12 cups in a bag), $2.40 per bag of chocolate chips (3 cups per bag), $1.20 per dozen eggs, $1.44 per bottle of oil (6 cups per bottle), and $0.60 for packaging materials. The standard wage rate is $9 per hour. The company allocates bakery overhead at $5.00 per oven hour.

Requirements

1. What is the standard cost per pan of gourmet brownies?
2. What is the standard gross profit per pan of gourmet brownies?
3. How often should the company reassess standard quantities and standard prices for inputs?

E11-17A Calculate standard cost per unit *(Learning Objective 1)*

GrandScapes is a manufacturer of large flower pots for urban settings. The company has these standards:

Direct materials (resin)..	8 pounds per pot at a cost of $6.00 per pound
Direct labor	2.0 hours at a cost of $15.00 per hour
Standard variable manufacturing overhead rate	$4.00 per direct labor hour
Predetermined fixed manufacturing overhead rate...........	$8.00 per direct labor hour

GrandScapes allocates fixed manufacturing overhead to production based on standard direct labor hours.

Requirements

1. Compute the standard cost of each of the following inputs per pot: direct materials, direct labor, variable manufacturing overhead, and fixed manufacturing overhead.
2. Determine the standard cost of one flower pot.

E11-18A   Calculate and explain direct material variances (Learning Objective 2)

Collegiate Rings produces class rings. Its best-selling model has a direct materials standard of 9 grams of a special alloy per ring. This special alloy has a standard cost of $63.70 per gram. In the past month, the company purchased 9,400 grams of this alloy at a total cost of $596,900. A total of 9,200 grams were used last month to produce 1,000 rings.

Requirements

1. What is the actual cost per gram of the special alloy that Collegiate Rings paid last month?
2. What is the direct material price variance?
3. What is the direct material quantity variance?
4. How might the direct material price variance for the company last month be causing the direct material quantity variance?

E11-19A   Calculate missing direct material variables (Learning Objective 2)

Last month, Baxter Corporation purchased and used the same quantity of material in producing its product, speed bumps for traffic control. Complete the following table.

Direct materials information	Medium speed bump	Large speed bump
Standard pounds per unit	16	?
Standard price per pound	$ 1.00	$ 1.50
Actual quantity purchased and used per unit	?	16.5
Actual price paid for material per pound	$ 1.70	$ 1.80
Price variance	$2,100 U	$2,475 U
Quantity variance	$ 1,800 F	?
Total direct material variance	?	$1,350 U
Number of units produced	300	500

E11-20A   Calculate and explain direct labor variances (Learning Objective 3)

Altieri Tax Services prepares tax returns for senior citizens. The standard in terms of (direct labor) time spent on each return is 5 hours. The direct labor standard wage rate at the firm is $13.50 per hour. Last month, 2,470 direct labor hours were used to prepare 500 tax returns. Total wages were $34,580.

Requirements

1. What is the actual (direct labor) wage rate per hour paid last month?
2. What is the direct labor rate variance?
3. What is the direct labor efficiency variance?
4. How might the direct labor rate variance for the firm <u>last</u> month be causing the direct labor efficiency variance?

E11-21A   Calculate and interpret direct material and direct labor variances
(Learning Objectives 2 & 3)

The Heese Restaurant Group manufactures the bags of frozen French fries used at its franchised restaurants. Last week, Heese's purchased and used 101,000 pounds of potatoes at a price of $0.70 per pound. During the week, 2,500 direct labor hours were incurred in the plant at a rate of $12.25 per hour. The standard price per pound of potatoes is $0.80, and the standard direct labor rate is $12.10 per hour. Standards indicate that for the number of bags of frozen fries produced, the factory should have used 98,000 pounds of potatoes and 2,400 hours of direct labor.

Requirements

1. Determine the direct material price and quantity variances. Be sure to label each variance as favorable or unfavorable.

2. Think of a plausible explanation for the variances found in Requirement 1.

3. Determine the direct labor rate and efficiency variances. Be sure to label each variance as favorable or unfavorable.

4. Could the explanation for the labor variances be tied to the material variances? Explain.

E11-22A   Calculate the material and labor variances *(Learning Objectives 2 & 3)*

Hull Guard, which used a standard cost accounting system, manufactured 220,000 boat fenders during the year, using 1,590,000 feet of extruded vinyl purchased at $1.15 per foot. Production required 4,200 direct labor hours that cost $13.50 per hour. The materials standard was 7 feet of vinyl per fender at a standard cost of $1.30 per foot. The labor standard was 0.027 direct labor hour per fender at a standard cost of $13.00 per hour.

Requirements

1. Compute the price and quantity variances for direct materials. Compute the rate and efficiency variances for direct labor.

2. Does the pattern of variances suggest that Hull Guard's managers have been making trade-offs? Explain.

E11-23A   Record materials and labor transactions *(Learning Objective 7)*

Refer to the data in E11-22A.

Requirements

1. Make the journal entries to record the purchase and use of direct materials.

2. Make the journal entries to record the direct labor.

E11-24A   Calculate the standard cost of a product before and after proposed sustainability effort changes *(Learning Objectives 1 & 4)*

SUSTAINABILITY

Wilke Containers currently uses a recycled plastic to make bottles for the food industry.

Current bottle production information:

The cost and time standards per batch of 10,000 bottles are as follows:

Plastic 220 kilograms at $6.00 per kg
Direct labor 4.0 hours at $20.00 per hour

The variable manufacturing overhead rate is based on total estimated variable manufacturing overhead of $400,000 and estimated total DLH of 10,000. Wilke allocates its variable manufacturing overhead based on direct labor hours (DLH).

Proposed changes to bottle design and production process:

The container division manager is considering having both the bottle redesigned and the bottle production process reengineered so that the plastic usage would drop by 25% overall due both to generating less scrap in the manufacturing process and using less plastic in each bottle. In addition to decreasing the amount of plastic used in producing the bottles, the additional following benefits would be realized:

a. Direct labor hours would be reduced by 20% because less scrap would be handled in the production process.

b. Total estimated variable manufacturing overhead would be reduced by 5% because less scrap would need to be hauled away, less electricity would be used in the production process, and less inventory would need to be stocked.

Requirements

1. Calculate the standard cost per batch of 10,000 bottles using the current data (before the company makes any changes). Include direct materials, direct labor, and variable manufacturing overhead in the standard cost per unit.

2. Calculate the standard cost per batch of 10,000 bottles if the company makes the changes to the bottle design and production process so that less plastic is used. Include direct materials, direct labor, and variable manufacturing overhead in the standard cost per unit.

3. Calculate the cost savings per batch by comparing the standard cost per batch under each scenario (current versus proposed change). Assume that the total cost to implement the changes would be $177,000. How many batches of bottles would need to be produced after the changes to have the cost savings total equal the cost to make these changes?

4. What other benefits might arise from making this change to using less plastic in the manufacture of the bottles? Are there any risks? What would you recommend the company do?

E11-25A   Recognize advantages and disadvantages of standard cost and variance analysis in various situations *(Learning Objective 4)*

The following scenarios describe situations currently facing companies. For each scenario, indicate whether a standard costing system would be beneficial in that situation or not and explain why or why not. Each scenario is independent of the other scenarios.

a. Management wants to design an incentive system that would pay out monthly incentives to factory workers if certain cost and time standards are achieved (or beaten). The goal of this program would be to increase employee motivation levels.

b. The company has started using several real-time operating performance metrics to manage operations. Examples of metrics being used include manufacturing lead time in days, manufacturing volume by day, downtime in hours, material cost by day, and several other measures. These performance metrics are available to management in a dashboard that is updated hourly.

c. The company has recently begun manufacturing a new type of computer chip. The company has very little experience with this type of product or the manufacturing process used for manufacturing the chips. Managers want to be able to have cost benchmarks so that they can judge whether the actual costs are reasonable for this product.

d. Lean practices are being implemented throughout the organization at all levels and in all departments. One of the goals of the lean movement is to eliminate inventories if at all possible. Another goal is to strive for continuous improvement in both the time spent in the manufacturing process and the amount of materials used in the product.

e. A rare and expensive chemical is used in the production of the company's main product. The cost of this material fluctuates wildly on a day to day basis, depending on market conditions. In addition, company engineers are continually working to redesign the product to use less of this material. Small incremental decreases in the material usage are being achieved on an ongoing basis.

f. As the company grows, the bookkeeping for actual direct material purchases, actual payroll costs, and actual manufacturing overhead is becoming increasingly complex; the number of transactions to be recorded has significantly increased. Much time is being spent by both managers and accountants in the company recording all of the actual transaction data.

g. An exercise equipment manufacturer has recently installed a robotic manufacturing system. This robotic system will be used for most of the welding, painting, assembly, and testing processes in its facility. The workers who used to do these tasks (welding, painting, assembly, and testing) will be retrained and will instead oversee various production lines rather than working directly on the products.

E11-26A   Compute and interpret overhead variances *(Learning Objectives 5 & 6)*

Albert Foods processes bags of organic frozen vegetables sold at specialty grocery stores. The company allocates manufacturing overhead based on direct labor hours. Albert has budgeted fixed manufacturing overhead for the year to be $628,000. The predetermined fixed manufacturing overhead rate is $16.20 per direct labor hour, while the standard variable manufacturing overhead rate is $0.60 per direct labor hour. The direct labor standard for each case is one-quarter (0.25) of an hour.

The company actually processed 164,000 cases of frozen organic vegetables during each year and incurred $667,120 of manufacturing overhead. Of this amount, $634,000 was fixed. The company also incurred a total of 41,400 direct labor hours.

Requirements

1. How much variable overhead would have been allocated to production? How much fixed overhead would have been allocated to production?
2. Compute the variable MOH rate variance and the variable MOH efficiency variance. What do these variances tell managers?
3. Compute the fixed MOH budget variance and the fixed overhead volume variance. What do these variances tell managers?

Data Set for E11-27A through E11-31A

GrandScapes is a manufacturer of large flower pots for urban settings. The company has these standards:

Direct materials (resin)...	8 pounds per pot at a cost of $6.00 per pound
Direct labor	2.0 hours at a cost of $15.00 per hour
Standard variable manufacturing overhead rate	$4.00 per direct labor hour
Budgeted fixed manufacturing overhead..............	$16,600
Standard fixed MOH rate..	$8.00 per direct labor hour (DLH)

GrandScapes allocated fixed manufacturing overhead to production based on standard direct labor hours. Last month, the company reported the following actual results for the production of 1,100 flower pots:

Direct materials	Purchased 9,950 pounds at a cost of $6.30 per pound; used 9,350 pounds to produce 1,100 pots
Direct labor	Worked 2.2 hours per flower pot (2,420 total DLH) at a cost of $14.00 per hour
Actual variable manufacturing overhead	$4.30 per direct labor hour for total actual variable manufacturing overhead of $10,406
Actual fixed manufacturing overhead....................	$16,400
Standard fixed manufacturing overhead allocated based on actual production	$17,600

E11-27A Calculate and interpret direct material variances *(Learning Objective 2)*

Refer to the GrandScapes data set.

Requirements

1. Compute the direct material price variance and the direct material quantity variance.
2. What is the total variance for direct material?
3. Who is *generally* responsible for each variance?
4. Interpret the variances.

E11-28A Calculate and interpret direct labor variances *(Learning Objective 3)*

Refer to the GrandScapes data set.

Requirements

1. Compute the direct labor rate variance and the direct labor efficiency variance.
2. What is the total variance for direct labor?
3. Who is *generally* responsible for each variance?
4. Interpret the variances.

E11-29A Calculate and interpret overhead variances *(Learning Objectives 5 & 6)*

Refer to the GrandScapes data set.

Requirements

1. Compute the variable manufacturing overhead variances. What do each of these variances tell management?
2. Compute the fixed manufacturing overhead variances. What do each of these variances tell management?

E11-30A Make journal entries in a standard costing system *(Learning Objective 7)*

Refer to the GrandScapes data set. Assume the company uses a standard cost accounting system.

Requirements

1. Record GrandScapes' direct material and direct labor journal entries.
2. Record GrandScapes' journal entries for manufacturing overhead, including the entry that records the overhead variances and closes the Manufacturing Overhead account.
3. Record the journal entries for the completion and sale of the 1,100 flower pots, assuming GrandScapes sold (on account) all of the flower pots at a sales price of $450 each. (There were no beginning or ending inventories.)

E11-31A Prepare a standard cost income statement *(Learning Objective 7)*

Refer to the GrandScapes data set. Prepare a standard cost income statement for the company's management. Assume that sales were $495,000 and actual marketing and administrative expenses were $8,000.

EXERCISES Group B

E11-32B Calculate standard costs *(Learning Objective 1)*

Rachel's Bakery makes desserts for local restaurants. Each pan of gourmet bars requires 2 cups of flour, ½ cup chopped pecans, ¼ cup cocoa, 1 cup sugar, ½ cup chocolate chips, 2 eggs, and ⅓ cup oil. Each pan requires 10 minutes of direct labor for mixing, cutting, and packaging. Each pan must bake for 30 minutes. Restaurants purchase the gourmet bars by the pan, not by the individual serving. Each pan is currently sold for $13. Standard costs are as follows: $2.24 per bag of flour (16 cups in a bag), $4.00 per bag of pecans (4 cups per bag), $3.20 per tin of cocoa (2 cups per tin), $2.20 per bag of sugar (11 cups in a bag), $2.80 per bag of chocolate chips (4 cups per bag), $1.68 per dozen eggs, $1.68 per bottle of oil (8 cups per bottle), and $0.60 for packaging materials. The standard wage rate is $9 per hour. The company allocates bakery overhead at $5.00 per oven hour.

Requirements

1. What is the standard cost per pan of gourmet bars?
2. What is the standard gross profit per pan of gourmet bars?
3. How often should the company reassess standard quantities and standard prices for inputs?

E11-33B Calculate the standard cost per unit *(Learning Objective 1)*

CityScapes is a manufacturer of large flower pots for urban settings. The company has these standards:

Direct materials (resin)	15 pounds per pot at a cost of $5.00 per pound
Direct labor	2.0 hours at a cost of $13.00 per hour
Standard variable manufacturing overhead	$6.00 per direct labor hour
Predetermined fixed manufacturing overhead rate	$7.00 per direct labor hour

CityScapes allocates fixed manufacturing overhead to production based on standard direct labor hours.

Requirements

1. Compute the standard cost of each of the following inputs per bottle: direct materials, direct labor, variable manufacturing overhead, and fixed manufacturing overhead.

2. Determine the standard cost of one flower pot.

E11-34B Calculate and explain direct material variances *(Learning Objective 2)*

Hallmark Rings produces class rings. Its best-selling model has a direct material standard of 13 grams of a special alloy per ring. This special alloy has a standard cost of $65.20 per gram. In the past month, the company purchased 13,400 grams of this alloy at a total cost of $872,340. A total of 13,300 grams were used last month to produce 1,000 rings.

Requirements

1. What is the actual cost per gram of the special alloy that Hallmark Rings paid last month?

2. What is the direct material price variance?

3. What is the direct material quantity variance?

4. How might the direct material price variance for the company last month be causing the direct material quantity variance?

E11-35B Calculate missing direct material variables *(Learning Objective 2)*

Last month, Astro Corporation purchased and used the same quantity of material in producing its speed bumps, a traffic control product. Complete the following table:

Direct materials information	Medium speed bump	Large speed bump
Standard pounds per unit	16	?
Standard price per pound............................	$ 3.00	$3.70
Actual quantity purchased and used per unit..	?	17
Actual price paid for material	$ 3.70	$ 4.50
Price variance	$4,200 U	$ 8,160 U
Quantity variance	$ 1,200 F	?
Total direct material variance	?	$5,940 U
Number of units produced............................	400	600

E11-36B Calculate and explain direct labor variances *(Learning Objective 3)*

Sarmento Tax Services prepares tax returns for senior citizens. The standard in terms of (direct labor) time spent on each return is 2.0 hours. The direct labor standard wage rate at the firm is $12.00 per hour. Last month, 990 direct labor hours were used to prepare 500 tax returns. Total wages totaled $13,860.

Requirements

1. What is the actual (direct labor) wage rate per hour paid last month?

2. What is the direct labor rate variance?

3. What is the direct labor efficiency variance?

4. How might the direct labor rate variance for the firm last month be causing the direct labor efficiency variance?

E11-37B Calculate and interpret direct material variances
(Learning Objectives 2 & 3)

The Rogers Restaurant Group manufactures the bags of frozen French fries used at its franchised restaurants. Last week, Rogers purchased and used 98,000 pounds of potatoes at a price of $0.75 per pound. During the week, 2,100 direct labor hours were incurred in the plant at a rate of $12.35 per hour. The standard price per pound of potatoes is $0.85, and the standard direct labor rate is $12.15 per hour. Standards indicate that for the number of bags of frozen fries produced, the factory should have used 94,000 pounds of potatoes and 2,000 hours of direct labor.

Requirements

1. Determine the direct material price and quantity variances. Be sure to label each variance as favorable or unfavorable.
2. Think of a plausible explanation for the variances found in Requirement 1.
3. Determine the direct labor rate and efficiency variances. Be sure to label each variance as favorable or unfavorable.
4. Could the explanation for the labor variances be tied to the material variances? Explain.

E11-38B   Complete and analyze a performance report *(Learning Objectives 2 & 3)*

Bump Guard, which uses a standard cost accounting system, manufactured 160,000 boat fenders during the year, using 1,060,000 feet of extruded vinyl purchased at $1.15 per foot. Production required 4,200 direct labor hours that cost $15.00 per hour. The materials standard was 6 feet of vinyl per fender at a standard cost of $1.30 per foot. The labor standard was 0.028 direct labor hour per fender at a standard cost of $14.00 per hour.

Requirements

1. Compute the price and quantity variances for direct materials. Compute the rate and efficiency variances for direct labor.
2. Does the pattern of variances suggest that the company's managers have been making trade-offs? Explain.

E11-39B   Record materials and labor transactions *(Learning Objective 7)*

Refer to the data in E11-38B.

Requirements

1. Make journal entries to record the purchase and use of direct materials.
2. Make journal entries to record the direct labor.

SUSTAINABILITY

E11-40B   Calculate the standard cost of a product before and after proposed sustainability effort changes *(Learning Objectives 1 & 4)*

Layne Containers currently uses a recycled plastic to make bottles for the food industry.

Current bottle production information:
The cost and time standards per batch of 10,000 bottles are as follows:

Plastic 340 kilograms at $7.00 per kg
Direct labor 2.0 hours at $15.00 per hour

The variable manufacturing overhead rate is based on total estimated variable manufacturing overhead of $600,000 and estimated total DLH of 10,000. The company allocates its variable manufacturing overhead based on direct labor hours (DLH).

Proposed changes to bottle design and production process:
The container division manager is considering having both the bottle redesigned and the bottle production process reengineered so that the plastic usage would drop by 25% overall due both to generating less scrap in the manufacturing process and using less plastic in each bottle. In addition to decreasing the amount of plastic used in producing the bottles, the additional following benefits would be realized:

a. Direct labor hours would be reduced by 20% because less scrap would be handled in the production process.
b. Total estimated variable manufacturing overhead would be reduced by 5% because less scrap would need to be hauled away, less electricity would be used in the production process, and less inventory would need to be stocked.

Requirements

1. Calculate the standard cost per batch of 10,000 bottles using the current data (before the company makes any changes). Include direct materials, direct labor, and variable manufacturing overhead in the standard cost per unit.

2. Calculate the standard cost per batch of 10,000 bottles if the company makes the changes to the bottle design and production process so that less plastic is used. Include direct materials, direct labor, and variable manufacturing overhead in the standard cost per unit.

3. Calculate the cost savings per batch by comparing the standard cost per batch under each scenario (current versus proposed change). Assume that the total cost to implement the changes would be $242,800. How many batches of bottles would need to be produced after the change to have the cost savings total equal the cost to make the changes?

4. What other benefits might arise from making this change to using less plastic in the manufacture of the bottles? Are there any risks? What would you recommend the company do?

E11-41B   Recognize advantages and disadvantages of standard cost and variance analysis in various situations *(Learning Objective 4)*

The following scenarios describe situations currently facing companies. For each scenario, indicate whether a standard costing system would be beneficial in that situation or not and explain why or why not. Each scenario is independent of the other scenarios.

a. The company has recently begun manufacturing a new type of computer chip. The company has very little experience with this type of product or with the manufacturing process used for manufacturing the chips. Managers want to be able to have cost benchmarks so that they can judge whether the actual costs are reasonable for this product.

b. Lean practices are being implemented throughout the organization at all levels and in all departments. One of the goals of the lean movement is to eliminate inventories if at all possible. Another goal is to strive for continuous improvement in both the time spent in the manufacturing process and the amount of materials used in the product.

c. As the company grows, the bookkeeping for actual direct material purchases, actual payroll costs, and actual manufacturing overhead is becoming increasingly complex; the number of transactions to be recorded has significantly increased. Much time is being spent by both managers and accountants in the company recording all of the actual transaction data.

d. An exercise equipment manufacturer has recently installed a robotic manufacturing system. This robotic system will be used for most of the welding, painting, assembly, and testing processes in its facility. The workers who used to do these tasks (welding, painting, assembly, and testing) will be retrained and will instead oversee various production lines rather than working directly on the products.

e. Management wants to design an incentive system that would pay out monthly incentives to factory workers if certain cost and time standards are achieved (or beaten). The goal of this program would be to increase employee motivation levels.

f. A rare and expensive chemical is used in the production of the company's main product. The cost of this material fluctuates wildly on a day-to-day basis, depending on market conditions. In addition, company engineers are continually working to redesign the product to use less of this material. Small incremental decreases in the material usage are being achieved on an ongoing basis.

g. The company has started using several real-time operating performance metrics to manage operations. Examples of metrics being used include manufacturing lead time in days, manufacturing volume by day, downtime in hours, material cost by day, and several other measures. These performance metrics are available to management in a dashboard that is updated hourly.

E11-42B   Calculate and interpret overhead variances *(Learning Objectives 5 & 6)*

Bay City Foods processes bags of organic frozen vegetables sold at specialty grocery stores. Bay City allocates manufacturing overhead based on direct labor hours. The company has budgeted fixed manufacturing for the year to be $634,000. The predetermined fixed manufacturing overhead rate is $16.60 per direct labor hour, while the standard variable manufacturing overhead rate is $0.55 per direct labor hour. The direct labor standards for each case is one-quarter (0.25) of an hour.

The company actually processed 162,000 cases of frozen organic vegetables during the year and incurred $688,100 of manufacturing overhead. Of this amount, $644,000 was fixed. The company also incurred a total of 42,000 direct labor hours.

Requirements

1. How much variable overhead would have been allocated to production? How much fixed overhead would have been allocated to production?

2. Compute the variable MOH rate variance and the variable MOH efficiency variance. What do these variances tell managers?

3. Compute the fixed MOH budget variance and the fixed overhead volume variance. What do these variances tell managers?

Data Set for E11-43B through E11-47B

CityScapes is a manufacturer of large flower pots for urban settings. The company has these standards:

Direct materials (resin)..	15 pounds per pot at a cost of $5.00 per pound
Direct labor	2.0 hours at a cost of $13.00 per hour
Standard variable manufacturing overhead	$6.00 per direct labor hour
Budgeted fixed manufacturing overhead	$23,600
Standard fixed MOH rate..	$7.00 per direct labor hour (DLH)

CityScapes allocates fixed manufacturing overhead to production based on standard direct labor hours. Last month, CityScapes reported the following actual results for the production of 1,900 flower pots:

Direct materials	Purchased 30,230 pounds at a cost of $5.20 per pound; used 29,830 pounds to produce 1,900 pots
Direct labor	Worked 2.4 hours per unit (4,560 total DLH) at a cost of $12.00 per hour
Actual variable manufacturing overhead	$6.20 per direct labor hour for total actual variable manufacturing overhead of $28,272
Actual fixed manufacturing overhead	$23,400
Standard fixed manufacturing overhead allocated based on actual production	$26,600

E11-43B   Calculate and interpret direct materials variances *(Learning Objective 2)*

Refer to the CityScapes data set.

Requirements

1. Compute the direct material price variance and the direct material quantity variance.
2. What is the total variance for direct material?
3. Who is generally responsible for each variance?
4. Interpret the variances.

E11-44B   Calculate and interpret direct labor variances *(Learning Objective 2)*

Refer to the CityScapes data set.

Requirements

1. Compute the direct labor rate variance and the direct labor efficiency variance.
2. What is the total variance for direct labor?
3. Who is generally responsible for each variance?
4. Interpret the variances.

E11-45B   Calculate and interpret overhead variances *(Learning Objectives 5 & 6)*

Refer to the CityScapes data set. Calculate and interpret overhead variances.

Requirements

1. Compute the variable manufacturing overhead variances. What do each of these variances tell management?
2. Compute the fixed manufacturing overhead variances. What do each of these variances tell management?

E11-46B   Make journal entries in a standard costing system
(Learning Objective 7)

Refer to the CityScapes data set. Assume the company uses a standard cost accounting system.

Requirements

1. Record CityScapes' direct materials and direct labor journal entries.
2. Record CityScapes' journal entries for manufacturing overhead, including the entry that records the overhead variances and closes the Manufacturing Overhead account.
3. Record the journal entries for the completion and sale of the 1,900 flower pots, assuming CityScapes sold (on account) all of the flower pots at a sales price of $450 each (there were no beginning or ending inventories).

E11-47B   Prepare a standard cost income statement *(Learning Objective 7)*

Refer to the CityScapes data set. Prepare a standard cost income statement for the company's management. Assume that sales were $855,000 and actual marketing and administrative expenses were $81,000.

PROBLEMS Group A

P11-48A   Calculate and explain direct material and direct labor variances
(Learning Objectives 1, 2, 3, & 4)

Krystal Fabrics manufactures a specialty monogrammed blanket. The following are the cost standards for this blanket:

Direct materials (fabric)	6.0 yards per blanket at $9.00 per yard
Direct labor	0.5 direct labor hours per blanket at $19.00 per hour

Actual results from last month's production of 2,500 blankets are as follows:

Actual cost of 15,750 yards of direct material (fabric) purchased	$127,575
Actual yards of direct material (fabric) used	15,250
Actual wages for 1,370 direct labor hours worked...	$ 25,071

Requirements

1. What is the standard direct material cost for one blanket?
2. What is the actual cost per yard of fabric purchased?
3. Calculate the direct material price and quantity variances.
4. What is the standard direct labor cost for one blanket?
5. What is the actual direct labor cost per hour?
6. Calculate the direct labor rate and efficiency variances.
7. Analyze each variance and speculate as to what may have caused that variance.
8. Look at all four variances together (the big picture). How might they all be related? What variance is very likely to have caused the other variances?

P11-49A Comprehensive standards and variances problem
(Learning Objectives 2, 3, 4, 5, & 6)

Patterson Awning manufactures awnings and uses a standard cost system. The company allocates overhead based on the number of direct labor hours. The following are the company's cost and standards data:

Standards:

Direct materials 22.0 yards per awning at $13.00 per yard

Direct labor 5.0 hours per awning at $15.00 per hour

Variable MOH standard rate $8.00 per direct labor hour

Predetermined fixed MOH standard rate $6.00 per direct labor hour

Total budgeted fixed MOH cost $63,500

Actual cost and operating data from the most recent month are as follows:

Purchased 51,260 yards at a total cost of $661,254

Used 47,500 yards in producing 2,200 awnings

Actual direct labor cost of $168,175 for a total of 10,850 hours

Actual variable MOH $93,310

Actual fixed MOH $67,500

All manufacturing overhead is allocated on the basis of direct labor hours.

Requirements
1. Calculate the standard cost of one awning.
2. Calculate the following variances:
   a. The direct material variances.
   b. The direct labor variances.
   c. The variable manufacturing overhead variances.
   d. The fixed manufacturing overhead variances.
3. Explain what each of the variances you calculated means and give at least one possible explanation for each of those variances. Are any of the variances likely to be interrelated?

P11-50A Comprehensive standards and variances problem
(Learning Objectives 1, 2, 3, 4, 5, & 6)

Amber Manufacturing produces ceramic teapots. Amber allocates overhead based on the number of direct labor hours. The company is looking into using a standard cost system and has developed the following standards (one "unit" is a batch of 100 teapots):

Standards:

Direct material 60 pounds per batch at $5.00 per pound

Direct labor 3.0 hours per batch at $17.00 per hour

Variable MOH standard rate $7.00 per direct labor hour

Predetermined fixed MOH standard rate $3.00 per direct labor hour

Total budgeted fixed MOH cost $1,090

Actual cost and operating data from the most recent month are as follows:

Purchased 4,500 pounds at a cost of $4.70 per pound

Used 4,100 pounds in producing 60 batches

Actual direct labor cost of $3,344 at an average direct labor cost per hour of $17.60

Actual variable MOH $1,406

Actual fixed MOH $1,490

All manufacturing overhead is allocated on the basis of direct labor hours.

Requirements

1. Calculate the standard cost of one batch.
2. Calculate the following variances:
   a. The direct material variances.
   b. The direct labor variances.
   c. The variable manufacturing overhead variances.
   d. The fixed manufacturing overhead.
3. Have the company's managers done a good job or a poor job controlling materials, labor, and overhead costs? Why or why not?
4. Describe how the company's managers can benefit from the standard costing system. Do you think the company should continue with the standard cost system?

P11-51A Work backward through labor variances *(Learning Objective 3)*

Petra's Music manufactures harmonicas. Petra uses standard costs to judge performance. Recently, a clerk mistakenly threw away some of the records, and only partial data for February exist. Petra knows that the total direct labor variance for the month was $330 F and that the standard labor rate was $10 per hour. A recent pay cut caused a favorable labor price variance of $0.50 per hour. The standard direct labor hours for actual February outputs were 5,600.

Requirements

1. Find the actual number of direct labor hours worked during February. First, find the actual direct labor rate her hour. Then, determine the actual number of direct labor hours worked by setting up the computation of the total direct labor variance as given.
2. Compute the direct labor rate and efficiency variances. Do these variances suggest that the manager may have made trade-offs? Explain.

P11-52A Determine all variances and make journal entries
(Learning Objectives 2, 3, 4, 5, 6, & 7)

Anders Clothing manufactures embroidered jackets. The company uses a standard cost system to control manufacturing costs. The following data represent the standard unit cost of a jacket:

Direct materials (3.0 sq. ft × $3.80 per sq. ft)........................		$ 11.40
Direct labor (2.0 hours × $9.50 per hour).............................		19.00
Manufacturing overhead:		
Variable (2.0 hours × $0.58 per hour)	$1.16	
Fixed (2.0 hours × $2.25 per hour)	4.50	$ 5.66
Total standard cost per jacket.................................		$ 36.06

Fixed overhead in total was budgeted to be $64,200 for each month.

Actual data for November of the current year include the following:
   a. Actual production was 13,500 jackets.
   b. Actual direct material used was 2.40 square feet per jacket at an actual cost of $3.90 per square foot.
   c. Actual direct labor usage of 24,800 hours for a total cost of $240,560.
   d. Actual fixed overhead cost was $56,565, while actual variable overhead cost was $17,360.

Requirements

1. Compute the price and quantity variances for direct materials.
2. Compute the rate and efficiency variances for direct labor.
3. Compute the rate and efficiency variances for variable overhead.

4. Compute the fixed overhead budget variance and the fixed overhead volume variance.
5. Anders Clothing's management intentionally purchased superior materials for November production. How did this decision affect the other cost variances? Overall, was the decision wise? Explain.
6. Journalize the usage of direct materials and the assignment of direct labor, including the related variances.

PROBLEMS Group B

P11-53B Calculate and explain direct material and direct labor variances
(Learning Objectives 1, 2, 3, & 4)

Olympia Fabrics manufacturers a specialty monogrammed blanket. The following are the cost and labor standards for this blanket:

> Direct material (fabric): 2.0 yards per blanket at $8.50 per yard
>
> Direct labor: 1.5 direct labor hours per blanket at $12.00 per hour

Actual results from last month's production of 1,700 blankets are as follows:

> Actual cost of 4,590 yards of direct material (fabric) purchased: $35,802
>
> Actual yards of direct material (fabric) used: 3,990
>
> Actual wages for 2,670 direct labor hours worked: $29,904

Requirements
1. What is the standard direct material cost for one blanket?
2. What is the actual cost per yard of fabric purchased?
3. Calculate the direct material price and quantity variances.
4. What is the standard direct labor cost for one blanket?
5. What is the actual direct labor cost per hour?
6. Calculate the direct labor rate and efficiency variances.
7. Analyze each variance and speculate as to what may have caused that variance.
8. Look at all four variances together (the big picture). How might they all be related? What variance is very likely to have caused the other variances?

P11-54B Comprehensive standards and variances problem
(Learning Objectives 2, 3, 4, 5, & 6)

Dillon Awnings manufactures awnings and uses a standard cost system. Dillon allocates overhead based on the number of direct labor hours. The following are the company's cost and standards data:

Standards:

Direct material 19.0 yards per awning at $13.00 per yard

Direct labor 4.0 hours per awning at $11.00 per hour

Variable MOH standard rate $5.00 per direct labor hour

Predetermined fixed MOH standard rate $10.00 per direct labor hour

Total budgeted fixed MOH cost $81,800

Actual cost and operating data from the most recent month follows:

Purchased 43,470 yards at a total cost of $547,722

Used 38,800 yards in producing 2,100 awnings

Actual direct labor cost of $92,624 for a total of 8,270 hours

Actual variable MOH cost $44,658

Actual fixed MOH cost $86,800

All manufacturing overhead is allocated on the basis of direct labor hours.

Requirements

1. Calculate the standard cost of one awning.
2. Calculate the following variances:

   a. The direct material variances.

   b. The direct labor variances.

   c. The variable manufacturing overhead variances.

   d. The fixed manufacturing overhead variances.

3. Explain what each of the variances you calculated means and give at least one possible explanation for each of those variances. Are any of the variances likely to be interrelated?

P11-55B Comprehensive standards and variances problem
(Learning Objectives 1, 2, 3, 4, 5, & 6)

Appleton Manufacturing produces ceramic teapots. Appleton allocates overhead based on the number of direct labor hours. The company is looking into using a standard cost system and has developed the following standards (one "unit" is a batch of 100 teapots).

Standards:

Direct material 60 pounds per batch at $5.00 per pound

Direct labor 2.0 hours per batch at $13.00 per hour

Variable MOH standard rate $7.00 per direct labor hour

Predetermined fixed MOH standard rate $5.00 per direct labor hour

Total budgeted fixed MOH cost $1,250

Actual cost and operating data from the most recent month follows:

Purchased 4,260 pounds at a cost of $4.90 per pound

Used 4,200 pounds in producing 60 batches

Actual direct labor cost of $2,070 at an average direct labor cost per hour of $13.80

Actual variable MOH cost $1,125

Actual fixed MOH cost $1,550

All manufacturing overhead is allocated on the basis of direct labor hours.

Requirements

1. Calculate the standard cost of one batch.
2. Calculate the following variances:

   a. The direct material variances.

   b. The direct labor variances.

   c. The variable manufacturing overhead variances.

   d. The fixed manufacturing overhead variances.

3. Have the company's managers done a good job or a poor job controlling materials, labor, and overhead costs? Why or why not?
4. Describe how the company's managers can benefit from the standard costing system. Do you think the company should continue with the standard cost system?

P11-56B Work backward through labor variances *(Learning Objective 3)*

Cora's Music manufactures harmonicas. Cora uses standard costs to judge performance. Recently, a clerk mistakenly threw away some of the records, and only partial data for September exist. Cora knows that the total direct labor variance for the month was $370 F and that the standard labor rate was $8 per hour. A recent pay cut caused a favorable labor price variance of $0.30 per hour. The standard direct labor hours for actual September outputs were 5,340.

Requirements

1. Find the actual number of direct labor hours worked during September. First, find the actual direct labor rate per hour. Then, determine the actual number of direct labor hours worked by setting up the computation of the total direct labor variance as given.

2. Compute the direct labor rate and efficiency variances. Do these variances suggest that the manager may have made trade-offs? Explain.

P11-57B   Determine all variances and make journal entries
(Learning Objectives 2, 3, 4, 5, 6, & 7)

Samson Company manufactures embroidered jackets. The company uses a standard cost system to control manufacturing costs. The following data represent the standard unit cost of a jacket:

Direct materials (3.0 sq. ft × $4.15 per sq. ft).....................................		$12.45
Direct labor (2.0 hours × $9.70 per hour)..		19.40
Manufacturing overhead:		
Variable (2.0 hours × $0.68 per hour)	$1.36	
Fixed (2.0 hours × $2.20 per hour)	4.40	5.76
Total standard cost per jacket..		$37.61

Fixed overhead in total was budgeted to be $63,000 for each month.

Actual data for November of the current year include the following:

a. Actual production was 14,000 jackets.

b. Actual direct materials usage was 2.60 square feet per jacket at an actual cost of $4.30 per square foot.

c. Actual direct labor usage of 25,800 hours for a total cost of $252,840.

d. Actual fixed overhead cost was $57,508, while actual variable overhead cost was $21,930.

Requirements

1. Compute the price and quantity variances for direct materials.

2. Compute the rate and efficiency variances for direct labor.

3. Compute the rate and efficiency variances for variable overhead.

4. Compute the fixed overhead budget variance and the fixed overhead volume variance.

5. Huntsman's management intentionally purchased superior materials for November production. How did this decision affect the other cost variances? Overall, was the decision wise? Explain.

6. Journalize the usage of direct materials and the assignment of direct labor, including the related variances.

CRITICAL THINKING
Discussion & Analysis

A11-58 Discussion Questions

1. Suppose a company is implementing lean accounting throughout the organization. Why might standard costing *not* be beneficial for that company?

2. What advantages might be experienced by a company if it adopts ideal standards for its direct material standards and direct labor standards? What advantages are there to using practical standards? As an employee, which would you prefer and why? Does your answer change if you are the manager in charge of production? Why or why not?

3. Select a product with which you are familiar. Describe what type of standards (direct material and direct labor) might be in effect for that product wherever it is produced. For each of these standards, discuss how those standards may become outdated. How frequently would you think the company would need to evaluate each of the standards?

4. Service organizations also use standards. Describe what types of standards might be in effect at each of the following types of organizations:
   - Hospitals
   - Law firms
   - Accounting firms
   - Auto repair shops
   - Fast-food restaurants

5. What does the direct materials price variance measure? Who is generally responsible for the direct materials price variance? Describe two situations that could result in a favorable materials price variance. Describe two situations that could result in an unfavorable materials price variance.

6. What does the direct materials efficiency variance measure? Who is generally responsible for the direct materials efficiency variance? Describe two situations that could result in a favorable direct materials efficiency variance. Describe two situations that could result in an unfavorable direct materials efficiency variance.

7. What does the direct labor price variance measure? Who is generally responsible for direct labor price variance? Describe two situations that could result in a favorable labor price variance. Describe two situations that could result in an unfavorable direct labor variance.

8. What does the direct labor efficiency variance measure? Who is generally responsible for the direct labor efficiency variance? Describe two situations that could result in a favorable direct labor efficiency variance. Describe two situations that could result in an unfavorable direct labor efficiency variance.

9. Describe at least four ways a company could use standard costing and variance analysis.

10. What are the two manufacturing overhead variances? What does each measure? Who within the organization would be responsible for each of these variances?

11. Suppose a company that makes and sells spaghetti sauce in plastic jars makes a change to its bottle that allows it to use significantly less plastic in each bottle. Describe at least four ways this change could help the company and its sustainability efforts.

12. Think of a company that manufactures a product. What type of standards do you think that company might have regarding its sustainability efforts? Do you think sustainability standards would be beneficial for the company? Why or why not?

Application & Analysis

Mini Cases

A11-59 Analyzing Variances and Potential Causes

Go to YouTube.com and search for clips from the show *Unwrapped* on Food Network or *How It's Made* on the Discovery Channel. Watch a clip for a product you find interesting. Companies are not likely to disclose everything about their production process and other trade secrets. When you answer the following questions, you may have to make reasonable assumptions or guesses about the manufacturing process, materials, and labor.

Basic Discussion Questions

1. Describe the product that is being produced. Briefly outline the production process.

2. What direct materials are used to make this product? In general, what has happened to the cost of these materials over the past year? To find information about the price of materials, you might try one of these sources (or a combination of these sources):

   a. Go to the New York Times website (http://nytimes.com/) or to USA Today (http://www.usatoday.com/) and search for each of the materials.

   b. Find the company's annual report on its website and read its discussion about its cost of production.

3. Given what you have discovered about the cost of materials for this product, were the price variances for each material likely to be favorable or unfavorable (answer separately for each individual material)?

4. In general, what has probably occurred to the cost of direct labor for this company? Again, to find clues about its labor costs, you might try one of the options listed in question 2. If you cannot find anything specific about this company, then discuss what has happened to the cost of labor in general over the past year.

5. Given what you have discovered about the cost of labor, was the labor rate variance likely to be favorable or unfavorable?

6. It is unlikely that the company has released information about its quantity (efficiency) variances. In general, though, what could cause this company's material quantity variances to be favorable? What could cause these material quantity variances to be unfavorable?

7. In general, what could cause this company's labor efficiency variances to be favorable? What could cause these labor efficiency variances to be unfavorable?

A11-60 Evaluate standard setting approaches *(Learning Objective 3)*

Pella is one of the world's largest manufacturers of wood windows and doors. In 1992, Pella entered the national retail market with its ProLine windows and doors, manufactured in Carroll, Iowa. Since then, Pella has introduced many new product lines with manufacturing facilities in several states.

Suppose Pella has been using a standard cost system that bases price and quantity standards on Pella's historical long-run average performance. Assume Pella should use some basis other than historical performance for setting standards.

Requirements

1. List the types of variances you recommend that Pella compute (for example, direct materials price variance for glass). For each variance, what specific standards would Pella need to develop? In addition to cost standards, do you recommend that Pella develop any nonfinancial standards? Explain.

2. There are many approaches to setting standards other than simply using long-run average historical prices and quantities.

   a. List three alternative approaches that Pella could use to set standards and explain how Pella could implement each alternative.

   b. Evaluate each alternative method of setting standards, including the pros and cons of each method.

   c. Write a memo to Pella's controller detailing your recommendations. First, should Pella retain its historical data-based standard cost approach? If not, which alternative approach should it adopt?

A11-61 Ethics involved with choice of cost driver

(Learning Objectives 1, 2, 3, 4, 5, 6, & 7)

ETHICS

The Blue Rabbit Company manufactures lawn and garden concrete and resin statues. It uses a standard costing system for its products. Managers and production personnel are paid bonuses based on attainment of material, labor, and overhead standards. The standards are recommended by a committee that is composed of engineers, production staff, and accountants. The accounting manager, however, has the final say on what the standards will be for each upcoming year.

Four years ago, the senior management at Blue Rabbit adopted a "zero-defects" strategy throughout the organization. As part of the zero-defects strategy, the company has been using ideal standards. Senior management has pointed out that it does not want to build waste into the standards by using practical standards. The adoption of ideal standards has been somewhat problematic at Blue Rabbit and there has been a lot of resistance from employees to the ideal standards.

Mike Anderson is the accounting manager at Blue Rabbit and is currently evaluating the material, labor, and overhead standards for the upcoming year. The standards committee has already met and made its recommendations. The standards are, as dictated by senior management, extremely tight and allow for zero waste, breakdowns, or downtime.

The plant manager, Dana Sullivan, comes to Mike and asks him to loosen the standards for the upcoming year. The plant manager is upset that the standards are set at a 100% efficiency rate (zero defects). Dana points out that everyone's bonus is on the line if the standards are not met. Some jobs may also be lost if standards are not met. Dana feels that the standards are unattainable and are not fair to employees. Dana even indicates that Mike's job might possibly be on the line if another year goes by without standards being achieved.

Mike gets together with a close friend, Julia Leiser, and discusses the matter at length with her. He tells her he feels guilty if the production staff do not get bonuses because of the way that the standards are set. He is also worried about his own job over the long run; it is in his best interests to have a good relationship with the plant manager. The economy is bad and he does not know how long it would take to get a new job. Mike shows Julia the ideal standards recommended by the committee and then shows her the adjustments that he thinks he could make to help make the standards achievable. Julia agrees that the standards should be adjusted.

Requirements

1. Using the IMA *Statement of Ethical Professional Practice* as an ethical framework, answer the following questions:
   a. What is (are) the ethical issue(s) in this situation?
   b. What are Mike Anderson's responsibilities as a management accountant?
2. Should Mike adjust the standards to a more achievable level in this situation? Support your answer.
3. Describe another way that Mike could handle this situation that would not violate the IMA *Statement of Ethical Professional Practice*.

A11-62 Impact of manufacturing process changes on variances

(Learning Objectives 1, 2, 3, 4, 5, & 6)

REAL LIFE

The luxury-goods manufacturer, Louis Vuitton, has several factories in the United States, France, and Spain that produce its bags and accessories. Part of the Louis Vuitton brand appeal to consumers is its exclusivity; its bags and accessories are not mass-marketed. Rather than growing the brand and losing the appeal of its exclusivity, Vuitton has been working to improve the efficiency of the manufacturing processes at its factories. Between the years of 2002 and 2012, Vuitton implemented the following changes at some of its locations:[1]

Reorganization: Workers were reorganized into teams of about 10 arranged in U-shaped clusters. This reorganization freed up 10% more floor space and allowed Vuitton to hire 300 new people without adding another factory.
Robots: Robots were installed at Vuitton's shoe factory in Italy. Prior to the robot installation, workers walked back and forth from the shelves to their workstations. The robots now retrieve the foot molds around which a shoe is made, resulting in significant time savings.
Software: Software was developed to help leather cutters identify the flaws in the leather being used to manufacture bags. The software determines where to place the pattern pieces for the dozens of pieces of leather in a bag, drastically reducing the amount of leather waste.

---

[1]C. Passariello, "At Vuitton, Growth in Small Batches," *Wall Street Journal*, June 27, 2011.

Questions

1. Before the company makes any changes to its standards, it must consider the impact of the manufacturing process changes on its variances. Indicate the impact of the changed process on each variance as *favorable*, *unfavorable*, or *unchanged/unknown*.

	Direct material price variance	Direct material quantity variance	Direct labor rate variance	Direct labor efficiency variance	Variable MOH rate variance	Variable MOH efficiency variance	Fixed overhead budget variance	Fixed overhead volume variance
Reorganization								
Robots								
Software								

2. For each of the improvement projects listed in the case, describe which standards would need to be adjusted for future variance analysis.

Try It Solutions

page 646:

1. Standard cost of direct materials = Standard quantity of DM × Standard price of DM
   = 0.25 lbs × $4.00/lb
   = $1.00

2. Standard cost of direct labor = Standard quantity of DL × Standard price of DL
   = 3 minutes × ($10 per hour ÷ 60 minutes per hour)
   = $0.50

3. Standard cost of variable overhead = Standard quantity of time × Variable overhead rate
   = 3 minutes × $0.05 per minute
   = $0.15

page 652:

1. DM price variance = Actual Quantity Purchased × (Actual Price − Standard Price)
   = AQP × (AP − SP)
   = 1,300 lbs × ($3.75/lb − $4.00/lb)
   = $325 F

The price variance is favorable since the berries cost less per pound than anticipated.

2. DM quantity variance = Standard Price
   × (Actual Quantity Used − Standard Quantity Allowed)
   = SP × (AQU − SQA)
   = $4.00/lb × [1,300 lbs − (5,000 smoothies × 0.25 lbs/smoothie)]
   = $4.00/lb × (1,300 lbs − 1,250 lbs)
   = $200 U

The efficiency variance is unfavorable since the business used more berries than anticipated.

3. The total DM variance is $125 F. The total DM variance is the difference between the actual DM cost of $4,875 (= 1,300 lbs × $3.75/lb) and the flexible budget for DM of $5,000 [5,000 smoothies × standard DM cost per smoothie of $1.00 (= 0.25 lbs ×$4.00 per pound)]. If the company both purchased and used the same quantity of DM, it is also the combination of the DM price variance ($325 F) and the DM efficiency variance ($200 U). The lower-than-expected price of berries more than offset the additional quantity the shop used, thus resulting in an overall favorable variance.

page 664:

1. The fixed overhead budget variance is $145 U. It is the difference between what was budgeted for fixed overhead ($1,455) and what was actually incurred ($1,600). The variance is unfavorable since actual fixed overhead was higher than budgeted.

2. Since Hannah's actual store volume was higher than anticipated, the fixed overhead volume variance will be favorable. By producing at a higher volume, Hannah was able to use the store's fixed overhead costs more efficiently.

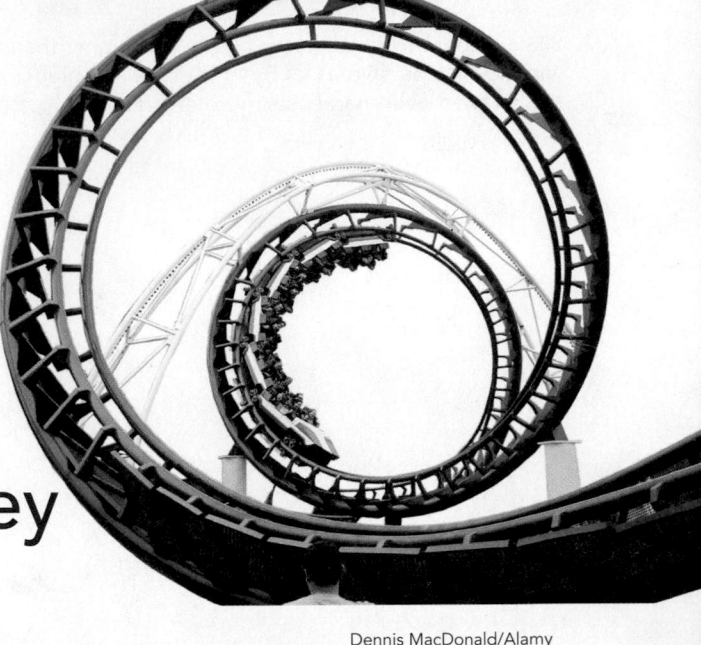

Dennis MacDonald/Alamy

Sources: Cedarpoint.com; Cedar Fair, L.P. 2012
10(K) filing, http://www.goldenticketawards
.com/pdfs/at_goldenticket_2012_web.pdf.

Capital Investment Decisions and the Time Value of Money

Learning Objectives

- **1** Describe the importance of capital investments and the capital budgeting process

- **2** Use the payback and accounting rate of return methods to make capital investment decisions

- **3** Use the time value of money to compute the present and future values of single lump sums and annuities

- **4** Use discounted cash flow models to make capital investment decisions

- **5** Compare and contrast the four capital budgeting methods

Cedar Fair Entertainment Company is the leading operator of amusement parks in the United States and Canada, entertaining over 23 million guests each year. The company's flagship park, Cedar Point, in Sandusky, Ohio, is known as the "Roller Coaster Capital of the World." The park has a world-record-breaking collection of 17 roller coasters, as well as an abundance of non-coaster rides and activities. These roller coasters include some of the *fastest* and *tallest* roller coasters in North America. The newest roller coaster, "GateKeeper," which opened in 2013, cost $30 million to build. The company doesn't mind paying that kind of money for a new ride, as long as it is expected to generate handsome returns in years to come. According to Cedar Point's vice president and general manager, "It's innovative thrills, like those our visitors will experience on GateKeeper, that keep them coming back year after year, earning us the honor of 'Best Amusement Park in the World.'" In fact, Cedar Point has been voted the "Best Amusement Park in the World" for 15 consecutive years by *Amusement Today's* international survey. The company's CEO views the strategic investments in new rides and attractions as one of the keys to the company's ongoing success.

As the chapter-opening story shows, companies must continually evaluate whether they need to invest in new property, buildings, equipment, or projects in order to remain competitive or increase their revenue stream. Companies also initiate capital improvements in order to save on existing costs. For example, many companies are investing in highly efficient heating, ventilation, and air-conditioning (HVAC) systems in order to save millions of dollars on annual energy costs while at the same time reducing the use of fossil fuels. Management must carefully consider whether the additional revenues or cost savings will be worth the high price of these new capital investments. In this chapter, we'll see how companies such as Cedar Point use net present value, payback period, and other capital investment analysis techniques to assess possible new investments.

What is Capital Budgeting?

The process of making capital investment decisions is often referred to as **capital budgeting**. Companies make capital investments when they acquire *capital assets*—assets used for long periods of time. Capital investments include investments in new equipment, new plants, new vehicles, and new information technology. In addition to affecting operations for many years, capital investments usually require large sums of money. Cedar Point's decision to spend $30 million on the GateKeeper roller coaster will tie up resources for years to come—as will Marriott's decision to spend $187 million to renovate its Marco Island Marriott Beach Resort, Golf Club, and Spa.

1 Describe the importance of capital investments and the capital budgeting process

Capital investment decisions affect all types of businesses as they try to become more efficient by automating production and implementing new technologies. For example, within the last 10 years, most grocers have installed self-service checkout machines, and most airlines have installed self-service check-in kiosks. These devices end up shifting labor costs away from the business and to the end consumer. As technology continues to advance, retailers' acceptance of smartphone payments (digital wallet apps) will most likely become widespread as businesses strive to cut process time and waste to a minimum. These new technologies cost money up front, but end up saving businesses cash in the long run. How do managers decide whether these expansions in plant and equipment will be good investments? They use capital budgeting analysis.

Four Popular Methods of Capital Budgeting Analysis

In this chapter, we discuss four common methods of analyzing potential capital investments:

1. Payback period
2. Accounting rate of return (ARR)
3. Net present value (NPV)
4. Internal rate of return (IRR)

 Why is this important?

"Each of these **four methods** help managers **decide** whether it would be wise to **invest** large sums of money in **new projects**, buildings, or equipment."

The first two methods, payback period and accounting rate of return, work well for capital investments that have a relatively short life span, such as computer equipment and software. They also work well as screening devices to quickly weed out less desirable investments from those that show more promise. The payback period provides management with valuable information on how fast the cash invested in the asset will be recouped. The accounting rate of return indicates the profitability of the investment with respect to its impact on operating income. Despite the insight provided by the payback period and ARR, these two methods are inadequate if the capital investments have a longer life span. Why? Because these methods do not consider the time value of money. The last two methods, net present value and internal rate of return, factor in the time value of money, so they are more appropriate for longer-term capital investments such as Cedar Point's new roller coasters and rides. Management often uses a combination of methods to make final capital investment decisions.

Capital budgeting is not an exact science. Although the calculations these methods require may appear precise, remember that they are based on predictions about an uncertain future. These predictions must consider many unknown factors, such as changing consumer preferences, competition, resource costs, and government regulations. The further into the future the decision extends, the more likely actual results will differ from predictions. In general, decisions that rely on long-term estimates are riskier than those that rely on short-term estimates.

Focus on Cash Flows

Generally Accepted Accounting Principles (GAAP) are based on accrual accounting, but capital budgeting focuses on cash flows. The desirability of a capital asset depends on its ability to generate *net cash inflows*—that is, inflows in excess of outflows—over the asset's useful life. Recall that operating income based on accrual accounting contains noncash expenses such as depreciation expense and bad debt expense. The capital investment's *net cash inflows*, therefore, will differ from its operating income. Of the four capital budgeting methods covered in this chapter, only the accounting rate of return method uses accrual-based accounting income. The other three methods use the investment's projected *net cash inflows*.

What do the projected net cash inflows include? Cash *inflows* include future cash revenue generated from the investment, any future savings in ongoing cash operating costs resulting from the investment, and any future residual value of the asset. To determine the investment's *net* cash inflows, the inflows are *netted* against the investment's future cash *outflows*, such as the investment's ongoing cash operating costs and refurbishment, repairs, and maintenance costs. The initial investment itself is also a significant cash outflow. However, in our calculations, *we refer to the amount of the investment separately from all other cash flows related to the investment.* The projected net cash inflows are "given" in our examples and in the assignment material. In reality, much of capital investment analysis revolves around estimating these figures as accurately as possible.

Capital Budgeting Process

As shown in Exhibit 12-1, the first step in the capital budgeting process is to identify potential investments—for example, new technology and equipment that may make the company more efficient, competitive, and profitable. Employees, consultants, and outside sales vendors often offer capital investment proposals to management. After identifying potential capital investments, managers next estimate the investments' net cash inflows. As discussed previously, this step can be very time-consuming and difficult. However, managers make the best projections possible given the information they have. The third step is to analyze the investments using one or more of the four methods listed previously. Sometimes the analysis involves a two-stage process. In the first stage, managers screen the investments using one or both of the methods that do *not* incorporate the time value of money: payback period or accounting rate of return. These simple methods quickly weed out undesirable investments. Potential investments that "pass the initial test" go on to a second stage of analysis. In the second stage, managers further analyze the potential investments using the net present value or internal rate of return method. Because these methods consider the time value of money, they provide more accurate information about the potential investment's profitability. Since each method evaluates the potential investment from a different angle, some companies use all four methods to get the most complete picture they can about the investment.

Some companies can pursue all of the potential investments that meet or exceed their decision criteria. However, because of limited resources, other companies must engage in **capital rationing** and choose among alternative capital investments. This is the fourth step pictured in Exhibit 12-1. Based on the availability of funds, managers determine if and when to make specific capital investments. For example, management may decide to wait to buy a certain piece of equipment because it considers other investments to be more important. In the intervening years, the company will reassess whether it should still invest in the equipment. Most likely technology has changed and even better equipment is available. Perhaps consumer tastes have changed, so the company no longer needs the equipment. Because of changing factors, long-term capital budgets are rarely set in stone.

EXHIBIT 12-1 Capital Budgeting Process

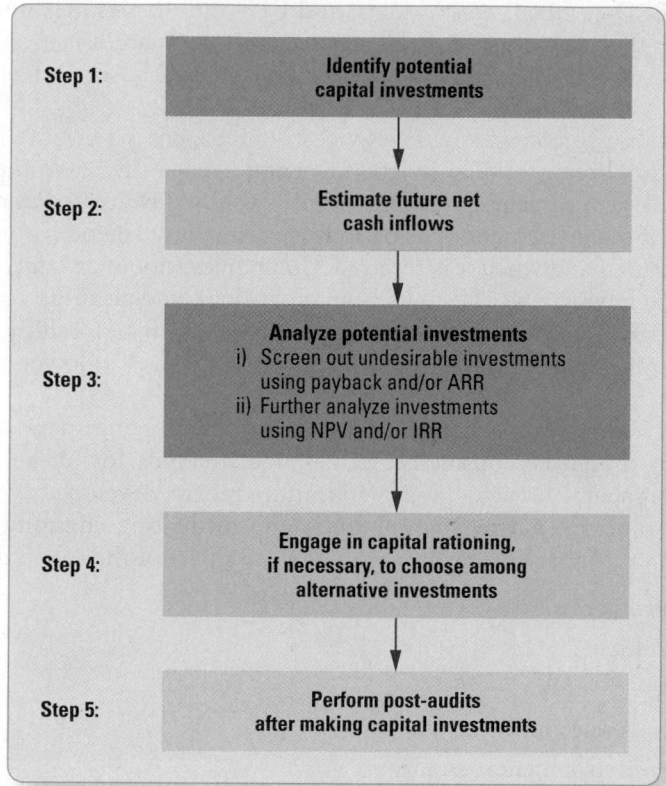

As a final step, most companies perform **post-audits** of their capital investments. After investing in the assets, managers compare the actual net cash inflows generated from the investment to the projected net cash inflows. Post-audits help companies determine whether the investments are going as planned and deserve continued support or whether new strategies need to be developed to improve the profitability of underperforming assets. Managers also use feedback from post-audits to better estimate net cash inflow projections for future projects. If managers expect routine post-audits, they will more likely submit realistic net cash inflow estimates with their capital investment proposals.

Sustainability and Capital Investments

Investments in "green" technologies often require large capital outlays that are subject to capital investment analysis. Investments in renewable energy have risen dramatically in recent years, especially with respect to wind and solar power projects, which have become much more attractive due to the decreasing cost of wind turbines and photovoltaic technology. In 2012 alone, $244 billion was invested globally in clean energy. Yet, only 6.5% of all electricity produced globally currently comes from non-fossil-fuel sources (such as solar, wind, geothermal, biomass, etc.). Thus, much additional investment in clean energy is expected in future years. The use of "green" bonds and crowd-sourcing to fund these projects is also on the rise as consumers and investors become more concerned with the environmental damage caused by the use of fossil fuels.

Many companies are attempting to minimize the rate at which they consume energy. For example, Intel and Johnson & Johnson use solar energy panels on their

See Exercises E12-23A and E12-41B

manufacturing plant rooftops, Best Buy and Starbucks are committed to constructing only LEED-certified retail outlets, and UPS and Staples are investing in hybrid vehicles for their distribution fleets. All of these companies use capital investment analysis to assess how quickly payback will occur and how prudent the investment will be.

In addition to considering energy cost savings, companies need to be aware of grants and tax breaks offered by governmental agencies for investing in green technology. These government-sponsored incentives should be treated as reductions in the initial cost of the investment or as periodic cost savings, depending on how the incentive is structured and when it is received. Companies should also factor in future cost savings from having fewer lawsuits, regulatory fines, and clean-up costs as a result of investing in green technology. Furthermore, as the supply of fossil fuels decreases and the cost therefore rises, greener technology may also result in lower annual operating costs.

When renovating existing facilities or constructing new facilities, **LEED certification** should be considered. LEED, which stands for "Leadership in Energy and Environmental Design," is a certification system developed by the U.S. Green Building Council as a way of promoting and evaluating environmentally friendly construction projects. Five factors are assessed as part of the certification process:

1. Site development
2. Water efficiency
3. Energy efficiency
4. Materials selection
5. Indoor environmental quality

Why do companies care about LEED certification? Besides being better for the planet and the people who work in the buildings, LEED-certified buildings typically have lower operating costs that often result in higher returns on the investment. Additionally, LEED-certified buildings have a competitive advantage over non-certified buildings. As a result, LEED-certified buildings often attract more potential buyers and command higher lease prices.

Sources: http://www.unep.org/pdf/GTR-UNEP-FS-BNEF2.pdf; http://www.seia.org/news/new-research-top-20-commercial-solar-users-us-includes-iconic-american-brands; bestbuy.com; starbucks.com; staples.com; UPS.com; and intel.com.

How do Managers Calculate the Payback Period and Accounting Rate of Return?

Payback Period

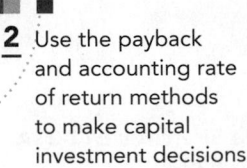

2 Use the payback and accounting rate of return methods to make capital investment decisions

<u>Payback</u> is the length of time it takes to recover, in net cash inflows, the cost of the capital outlay. The payback period measures how quickly managers expect to recover their investment dollars. The shorter the payback period, the more attractive the asset, *all else being equal.* Why? The quicker an investment pays itself back, the less the inherent risk that the investment will become unprofitable. The method used to compute the payback period depends on whether net cash inflows are expected to be equal each year or whether they will vary each year. To illustrate, we'll discuss three capital investments being considered by Tierra Firma, a company that makes and sells camping equipment. For the sake of simplicity, let's assume that each of the following potential investments is expected to cost $240,000:

■ An updated energy-efficient HVAC system for the company's corporate offices. (*Estimated six-year useful life with no residual value; equal annual net cash energy savings of $60,000.*)

- Investment in hardware and software to develop a business-to-business (B2B) portal that will allow the company to reduce the cost of purchasing components throughout its supply chain. (*Estimated three year useful life with no residual value; equal annual net cash savings of $80,000.*)
- New production equipment designed to reduce waste, time, manual labor, and energy consumption (*Estimated six year useful life with $30,000 residual value; unequal yearly net cash savings as pictured later in Exhibit 12-3.*)

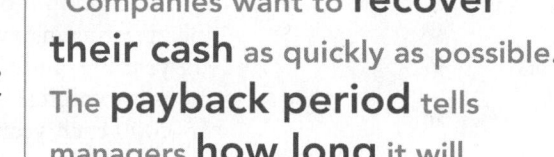

Why is this important?

"Companies want to **recover their cash** as quickly as possible. The **payback period** tells managers **how long** it will take before the investment is **recouped.**"

Payback with Equal Annual Net Cash Inflows

When net cash inflows are equal each year, managers compute the payback period as follows:

$$\text{Payback period} = \frac{\text{Initial investment}}{\text{Expected annual net cash inflow}}$$

Since the new HVAC system will cost $240,000 and is expected to generate equal annual net cash inflows of $60,000, we compute payback as follows:

$$\text{Payback period for HVAC system} = \frac{\$240,000}{\$60,000} = 4 \text{ years}$$

The left side of Exhibit 12-2 verifies that Tierra Firma expects to recoup the $240,000 investment in the HVAC system by the end of Year 4, when the accumulated net cash inflows total $240,000.

EXHIBIT 12-2 Payback—Equal Annual Net Cash Inflows

	A	B	C	D	E	F	G
1		Payback Analysis for HVAC				Payback Analysis for B2B portal	
2		Initial Investment: $240,000				Initial Investment: $240,000	
3	Year	Annual Net Cash Inflow	Accumulated Net Cash Inflow		Year	Annual Net Cash Inflow	Accumulated Net Cash Inflow
4	1	$ 60,000	$ 60,000		1	$ 80,000	$ 80,000
5	2	$ 60,000	120,000		2	$ 80,000	160,000
6	3	$ 60,000	180,000		3	$ 80,000	240,000
7	4	$ 60,000	240,000				
8	5	$ 60,000	300,000				
9	6	$ 60,000	360,000				
10							

Likewise, Tierra Firma can compute the payback period of the B2B portal using the same formula. Recall that the B2B portal will cost $240,000 and result in equal annual cash inflows of $80,000:

$$\text{Payback period for B2B portal} = \frac{\$240,000}{\$80,000} = 3 \text{ years}$$

The right side of Exhibit 12-2 verifies that Tierra Firma will recoup the $240,000 investment for the B2B portal by the end of Year 3, when the accumulated net cash inflows total $240,000.

Payback with Unequal Net Cash Inflows

The payback formula only works when net cash inflows are the same each period. When periodic cash flows are expected to be unequal, managers must accumulate net cash inflows until the amount of the investment is recovered. Recall that Tierra Firma is also considering investing in new production equipment that has (1) *unequal* net cash inflows during its six-year life, and (2) a $30,000 residual value at the end of its life. The production equipment is expected to generate net cash inflows of $100,000 in Year 1, $80,000 in Year 2, $50,000 each year in Years 3–5, $30,000 in Year 6, and $30,000 when it is sold at the end of its life. Exhibit 12-3 shows the payback schedule for these unequal annual net cash inflows.

EXHIBIT 12-3 Payback—Unequal Annual Net Cash Inflows

	A	B	C	
1	**Payback Analysis for Production Equipment** **_Unequal_ Net Cash Inflows**			
2	**Initial Investment: $240,000**			
3	**Year**	**Annual Net Cash Inflow**	**Accumulated Net Cash Inflow**	
4	1	$ 100,000	$ 100,000	
5	2	80,000	180,000	Payback is between 3 and 4 years. After 3 years, there is still $10,000 to recoup before payback of $240,000 is reached.
6	3	50,000	230,000	
7	4	50,000	280,000	
8	5	50,000	330,000	
9	6	30,000	360,000	
10	Residual value	30,000	390,000	
11				

By the end of Year 3, the company has recovered $230,000 of the $240,000 initially invested and is only $10,000 short of payback. Because the expected net cash inflow in Year 4 is $50,000, by the end of Year 4, the company will have recovered *more* than the initial investment. Therefore, the payback period is somewhere between three and four years. Assuming that the cash flow occurs evenly throughout the fourth year, the payback period is calculated as follows:

$$\text{Payback} = 3 \text{ years} + \frac{\$10,000 \text{ (amount needed to complete recovery in Year 4)}}{\$50,000 \text{ (projected net cash inflow in Year 4)}}$$

$$= 3.2 \text{ years}$$

Criticism of the Payback Period Method

A major criticism of the payback method is that it focuses only on time, not on profitability. The payback period considers only those cash flows that occur *during* the payback period. This method ignores any cash flows that occur *after* that period, including any residual value. For example, Exhibit 12-2 shows that the HVAC system will continue to generate net cash inflows for two years after its payback period. These additional net cash inflows amount to $120,000 ($60,000 × 2 years), yet the payback method ignores this extra cash. A similar situation occurs with the production equipment. As shown in Exhibit 12-3, the production equipment will provide an additional $150,000 of net cash inflows, including residual value, after its payback period of 3.2 years. In contrast, the B2B portal's useful life, as shown in Exhibit 12-2, is the *same* as its payback period (three years). Since no additional cash flows occur after the payback period, the B2B portal will merely cover its cost and provide no profit. Because this is the case, the company has little or no reason to invest in the B2B portal even though its payback period is the shortest of all three investments.

Exhibit 12-4 compares the payback period of the three investments. As the exhibit illustrates, the payback method does not consider the asset's profitability. *The method only tells management how quickly it will recover its cash.* Even though the B2B portal has the shortest payback period, both the HVAC system and the production equipment are better investments because they provide profit. The key point is that the investment with the shortest payback period is best *only when all other factors are the same*. Therefore, managers usually use the payback method as a screening device to "weed out" investments that will take too long to recoup. They rarely use payback period as the sole method for deciding whether to invest in the asset.

EXHIBIT 12-4 Comparing Payback Periods Between Investments

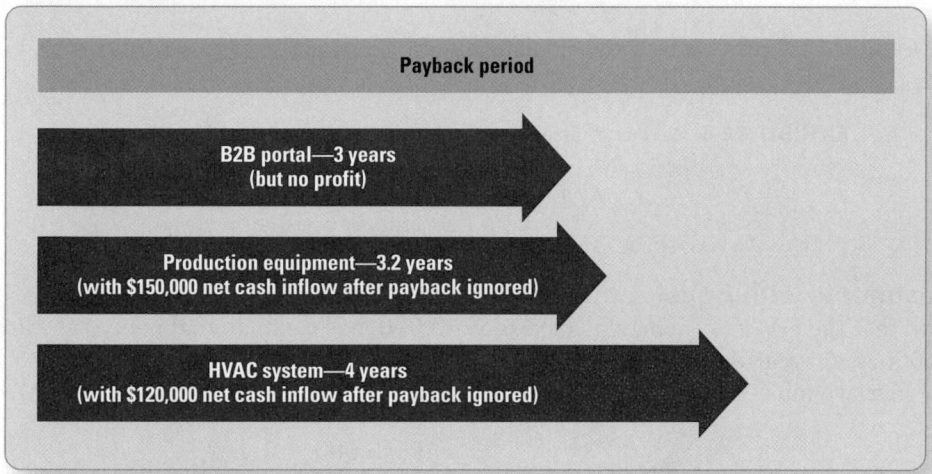

When using the payback period method, managers are guided by the following decision rule:

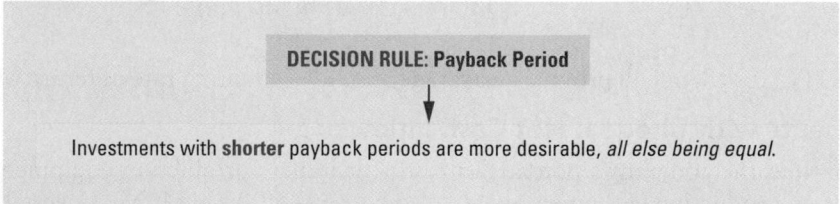

Try It!

The Bruce Company is considering investing in a wind turbine to generate its own power. Any unused power will be sold back to the local utility company. Between cost savings and new revenues, the company expects to generate $750,000 per year in net cash inflows from the turbine. The turbine would cost $4 million and is expected to have a 20-year useful life with no residual value. Calculate the payback period.

Please see page 763 for solutions.

Accounting Rate of Return (ARR)

Companies are in business to earn profits. One measure of profitability is the **accounting rate of return (ARR)** on an asset:[1]

$$\text{Accounting rate of return} = \frac{\text{Average annual operating income from asset}}{\text{Initial investment}}$$

[1]Some managers prefer to use the average investment, rather than the initial investment, as the denominator. For simplicity, we will use the initial amount of the investment.

The ARR focuses on the *operating income, not the net cash inflow*, that an asset generates. The ARR measures the average annual rate of return over the asset's life. Operating income is based on *accrual accounting*. Therefore, any noncash expenses such as depreciation expense must be subtracted from the asset's net cash inflows to arrive at its operating income. Assuming that depreciation expense is the only noncash expense relating to the investment, we can rewrite the ARR formula as follows:

$$ARR = \frac{\text{Average annual net cash inflow} - \text{Annual depreciation expense}}{\text{Initial investment}}$$

Exhibit 12-5 reviews how to calculate annual depreciation expense using the straight-line method.

EXHIBIT 12-5 Review of Straight-Line Depreciation Expense Calculation

$$\text{Annual depreciation expense} = \frac{\text{Initial cost of asset} - \text{Residual value}}{\text{Useful life of asset (in years)}}$$

Investments with Equal Annual Net Cash Inflows

Recall that the HVAC system, which costs $240,000, has equal annual net cash inflows of $60,000, a six-year useful life, and no residual value.

First, we must find the HVAC system's annual depreciation expense:

$$\text{Annual depreciation expense} = \frac{\$240,000 - 0}{6 \text{ years}} = \$40,000$$

Now, we can complete the ARR formula:

$$ARR \text{ for HVAC system} = \frac{\$60,000 - \$40,000}{\$240,000} = \frac{\$20,000}{\$240,000} = 8.33\% \text{ (rounded)}$$

The HVAC system will provide an average annual accounting rate of return of 8.33%.

Investments with Unequal Net Cash Inflows

Now, consider the company's potential investment in new production equipment. Recall that the new production equipment would also cost $240,000 but it had unequal net cash inflows during its life (as pictured in Exhibit 12-3) and a $30,000 residual value at the end of its life. Since the yearly net cash inflows vary in size, we need to first calculate the equipment's *average* annual net cash inflows:[2]

Total net cash inflows *during* operating life of asset (does not include the residual value at the end of life)[2] from Exhibit 12-3	$360,000
Divide by: Asset's operating life (in years)	÷ 6 years
Average annual net cash inflow from asset	$ 60,000

Now, let's calculate the asset's annual depreciation expense:

$$\text{Annual depreciation expense} = \frac{\$240,000 - \$30,000}{6 \text{ years}} = \$35,000$$

[2]The residual value is not included in the net cash inflows *during* the asset's operating life because we are trying to find the asset's average *annual operating* income. We assume that the asset will be sold for its expected residual value ($30,000) at the *end* of its life, resulting in no additional accounting gain or loss.

Notice how the expected residual value drives down the annual depreciation expense. Now that we have calculated the terms for the numerator, we can complete the ARR calculation as follows:

$$\text{ARR for production equipment} = \frac{\$60,000 - \$35,000}{\$240,000} = \frac{\$25,000}{\$240,000} = 10.42\% \text{ (rounded)}$$

Companies usually have a minimum required accounting rate of return for new investments. If Tierra Firma required an ARR of at least 10%, its managers would not approve the HVAC investment but would approve the production equipment investment.

The decision rule is as follows:

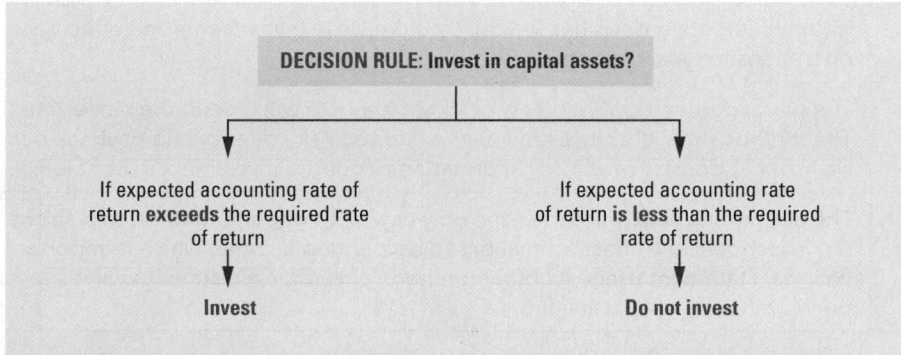

DECISION RULE: Invest in capital assets?

If expected accounting rate of return **exceeds** the required rate of return

Invest

If expected accounting rate of return **is less** than the required rate of return

Do not invest

Try It!

The Bruce Company is considering investing in a wind turbine to generate its own power. Any unused power will be sold back to the local utility company. Between cost savings and new revenues, the company expects to generate $750,000 per year in net cash inflows from the turbine. The turbine would cost $4 million and is expected to have a 20-year useful life with no residual value. Calculate the accounting rate of return (ARR).

Please see page 764 for solutions.

In summary, the payback period focuses on the time it takes for a company to recoup its cash investment. However, it ignores all cash flows occurring after the payback period, including any residual value. As a result, the payback period does not consider the profitability of the project.

On the other hand, the ARR measures the profitability of the asset over its entire life. The ARR is the only method that focuses on accrual-based accounting income rather than net cash inflows, which is used in ROI calculations, as discussed in Chapter 10.

The payback period and ARR methods are simple and quick to compute, so managers often use them to screen out undesirable investments and to gain a more complete picture of the investment's desirability. However, both methods ignore the time value of money. In the next sections, we will review the theory behind the time value of money and then apply it to capital investments using the NPV and IRR methods.

Decision Guidelines

Capital Budgeting

Amazon.com started as a virtual retailer. It held no inventory. Instead, it bought books and CDs only as needed to fill customer orders. As the company grew, its managers decided to invest in their own warehouse facilities. Why? Owning warehouse facilities allows Amazon.com to save money by buying in bulk. Also, shipping all items in the customer's order in one package from one location saves shipping costs. Here are some of the guidelines Amazon.com's managers used as they made the major capital budgeting decision to invest in building warehouses.

Decision	Guidelines
Why is this decision important?	Capital budgeting decisions typically require large investments and affect operations for years to come.
What method shows us how soon we will recoup our cash investment?	The payback method shows how quickly managers will recoup their investment. The method highlights investments that are too risky due to long payback periods. However, it doesn't reveal any information about the investment's profitability.
Does any method consider the impact of the investment on accrual-based accounting income?	The accounting rate of return is the only capital budgeting method that shows how the investment will affect accrual-based accounting income, which is important to financial statement users. All other methods of capital investment analysis focus on the investment's net cash inflows.
How do we compute the payback period if cash flows are *equal*?	$$\text{Payback period} = \frac{\text{Initial investment}}{\text{Expected annual net cash inflow}}$$
How do we compute the payback period if cash flows are *unequal*?	Accumulate net cash inflows until the amount invested is recovered.
How do we compute the ARR?	$$\text{Accounting rate of return} = \frac{\text{Average annual operating income from asset}}{\text{Initial investment}}$$ We can also write this formula as follows: $$\text{ARR} = \frac{\text{Average annual net cash inflow} - \text{Annual depreciation expense}}{\text{Initial investment}}$$

SUMMARY PROBLEM 1

Sonoma is considering investing in solar paneling for the roof of its large distribution facility. The investment will cost $9 million and have a six-year useful life and no residual value. Because of rising utility costs, the company expects the yearly utility savings to increase over time, as follows:

Year 1	$1,000,000
Year 2	$1,500,000
Year 3	$2,000,000
Year 4	$2,500,000
Year 5	$3,500,000
Year 6	$4,500,000

The company uses the payback period and ARR to screen potential investments. Company policy requires a payback period of less than five years and an ARR of at least 10%. Any potential investments that do not meet these criteria will be removed from further consideration.

1. Calculate the payback period of the solar panels.

2. Calculate the ARR of the solar panels.

3. Should Sonoma turn down the solar panel investment or consider it further?

▪ SOLUTIONS

1. Since the net cash flows are uneven, Sonoma cannot use the simple payback formula. Rather, Sonoma must add up the accumulated net cash inflows until payback is reached, as follows:

	A	B	C	D	E
1		Payback Analysis for Solar Panels			
2		*Unequal* Net Cash Inflows			
3		Initial Investment: $9 million			
4					
5	Year	Annual Net Cash Inflow	Accumulated Net Cash Inflow		
6	1	$ 1,000,000	$ 1,000,000		
7	2	1,500,000	2,500,000		
8	3	2,000,000	4,500,000		
9	4	2,500,000	7,000,000		
10	5	3,500,000	10,500,000		
11	6	4,500,000	15,000,000		
12					

Payback occurs between four and five years. After four years, $2 million is left to be recouped before payback is reached. Since the company expects $3.5 million of savings in Year 5, we can further estimate the payback period as follows:

$$\text{Payback} = 4 \text{ years} + \frac{\$2 \text{ million}}{\$3.5 \text{ million}} = 4.57 \text{ years}$$

2. The ARR formula is as follows:

$$\text{ARR} = \frac{\text{Average annual net cash inflow} - \text{Annual depreciation expense}}{\text{Initial investment}}$$

To use this formula, we first need to find the *average* annual net cash inflows of the solar panels. We find the average by taking the total expected cash inflows during the six-year life of the asset ($15 million) and dividing it by six years:

Total net cash inflows during six-year life..............................	$15,000,000
Divide by: Useful life..	÷ 6 years
Average annual net cash inflow...	$ 2,500,000

Next, find annual depreciation expense:

$$\text{Annual depreciation} = \$9 \text{ million} \div 6 \text{ years} = \$1,500,000$$

Finally, use these figures in the ARR formula:

$$\text{ARR} = \frac{\$2,500,000 - \$1,500,000}{\$9,000,000} = 11.11\%$$

3. The payback period is less than five years and the ARR is greater than 10%. Therefore, the company should further consider the solar panel proposal.

How do Managers Compute the Time Value of Money?

A dollar received today is worth more than a dollar to be received in the future. Why? Because you can invest today's dollar and earn extra income with it. The fact that invested money earns income over time is called the **time value of money**. Because of the time value of money, cash flows received sooner in time are worth more than cash flows received later in time. In other words, the timing of the cash flows received from a capital investment is important. The NPV and IRR methods of analyzing capital investments take the time value of money into consideration. This section reviews time value of money concepts to make sure you have a firm foundation for discussing these two methods.

3 Use the time value of money to compute the present and future values of single lump sums and annuities

Factors Affecting the Time Value of Money

The time value of money depends on several key factors:

1. The principal amount (p)
2. The number of periods (n)
3. The interest rate (i)

The principal (p) refers to the amount of the investment or borrowing. Because this chapter deals with capital investments, we'll primarily discuss the principal in terms of investments. However, the same concepts apply to borrowings (which you probably discussed in your financial accounting course when you studied bonds payable). We state the principal as either a single lump sum or an annuity. For example, if you want to save money for a new car after college, you may decide to invest a single lump sum of $10,000 in a certificate of deposit (CD). However, you may not currently have $10,000 to invest. Instead, you may invest funds as an annuity, depositing $2,000 at the end of each year in a bank savings account. An **annuity** is a stream of *equal installments* made at *equal time intervals*. An *ordinary annuity* is an annuity in which the installments occur at the *end* of each period.[3]

The number of periods (n) is the length of time from the beginning of the investment until termination. All else being equal, the shorter the investment period, the lower the total amount of interest earned. If you withdraw your savings after four years rather than five years, you will earn less interest. If you begin to save for retirement at age 22 rather than age 45, you will earn more interest before you retire. In this chapter, the number of periods is stated in years.[4]

The interest rate (i) is the annual percentage earned on the investment. **Simple interest** means that interest is calculated *only* on the principal amount. **Compound interest** means that interest is calculated on the principal *and* on all interest earned to date. *Compound interest assumes that all interest earned will remain invested at the same interest rate, not withdrawn and spent.* Exhibit 12-6 compares simple interest (6%) on a five-year, $10,000 CD with interest compounded yearly. As you can see, the amount of compound interest earned each year grows as the base on which it is calculated (principal plus cumulative interest to date) grows. Over the life of this particular investment, the total amount of compound interest is about 13% more than the total amount of simple interest. Most investments yield compound interest, so we assume compound interest rather than simple interest for the rest of this chapter.

> ## Why is this important?
>
> "The **time value of money** is a critical factor in many management **decisions**. In addition to its use in capital investment analysis, it's also used for **personal financial planning** (such as retirement planning), **business valuation** (for purchasing businesses), and **financing decisions** (borrowing and lending)."

[3]In contrast to an *ordinary annuity*, an *annuity due* is an annuity in which the installments occur at the *beginning* of each period. Throughout this chapter we use ordinary annuities because they are better suited to capital budgeting cash flow assumptions.

[4]The number of periods can also be stated in days, months, or quarters. If so, the interest rate needs to be adjusted to reflect the number of time periods in the year.

EXHIBIT 12-6 Simple Versus Compound Interest for a Principal Amount of $10,000 at 6% over Five Years

	A	B	C	D	E	F	G	H	I
1		Simple Interest Calculation					Compound Interest Calculation		
2	Year	Principal	Interest rate	Interest		Year	Principal*	Interest rate	Interest
3	1	$ 10,000	6%	600		1	$ 10,000	6%	$ 600
4	2	$ 10,000	6%	600		2	$ 10,600	6%	$ 636
5	3	$ 10,000	6%	600		3	$ 11,236	6%	$ 674
6	4	$ 10,000	6%	600		4	$ 11,910	6%	$ 715
7	5	$ 10,000	6%	600		5	$ 12,625	6%	$ 758
8				$ 3,000					$ 3,383
9									
10									

*NOTE: For compound interest calculations, the principal is the original amount ($10,000) plus the cumulative interest earned to date. For example, the principal amount in Year 2 ($10,600) is the original $10,000 plus the $600 of interest earned during Year 1. The principal amount in Year 3 ($11,236) is the original principal ($10,000) plus the interest earned in Year 1 and Year 2 ($600 + $636).

Fortunately, time value calculations involving compound interest do not have to be as tedious as those shown in Exhibit 12-6. Rather, they can be easily performed using Excel financial functions, a business calculator, or formulas and tables. Using these tools simplify the calculations. In the next sections, we will discuss how to use these tools to perform time value of money calculations.

Future Values and Present Values: Points Along the Time Continuum

Consider the time line in Exhibit 12-7. The future value or present value of an investment simply refers to the value of an investment at different points in time.

EXHIBIT 12-7 Present Value and Future Value Along the Time Continuum

We can calculate the future value or the present value of any investment by knowing (or assuming) information about the three factors listed earlier: (1) the principal amount, (2) the period of time, and (3) the interest rate. For example, in Exhibit 12-6, we calculated the interest that would be earned on (1) a $10,000 principal (2) invested for five years (3) at 6% interest. The future value of the investment is its worth at the end of the five-year time frame—the original principal *plus* the interest earned. In our example, the future value of the investment is as follows:

$$\text{Future value} = \text{Principal} + \text{Interest earned}$$
$$= \$10,000 + \$3,383$$
$$= \$13,383$$

If we invest $10,000 *today*, its *present value* is simply the $10,000 principal amount. So, another way of stating the future value is as follows:

$$\text{Future value} = \text{Present value} + \text{Interest earned}$$

We can rearrange the equation as follows:

Present value	=	Future value	−	Interest earned
$10,000	=	$13,383	−	$3,383

The only difference between present value and future value is the amount of interest that is earned in the intervening time span.

Future Value and Present Value Factors

Calculating each period's compound interest, as we did in Exhibit 12-6, and then adding it to the present value to determine the future value (or subtracting it from the future value to determine the present value) is tedious. Fortunately, mathematical formulas simplify future value and present value calculations. Mathematical formulas have been developed that specify future values and present values for unlimited combinations of interest rates (*i*) and time periods (*n*). Separate formulas exist for single lump-sum investments and annuities.

The formulas have been calculated using various interest rates and time periods. The results are displayed in tables. The formulas and resulting tables are shown in Appendix 12A at the end of this chapter:

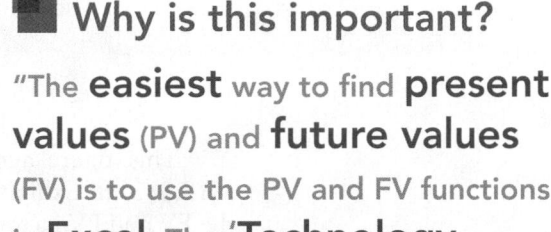

Why is this important?

"The **easiest** way to find **present values** (PV) and **future values** (FV) is to use the PV and FV functions in **Excel**. The 'Technology Makes it Simple' **features** will show you how."

1. Present Value of $1 (Table A, p. 731)—*used for lump-sum amounts*
2. Present Value of Annuity of $1 (Table B, p. 732)—*used for annuities*
3. Future Value of $1 (Table C, p. 733)—*used for lump-sum amounts*
4. Future Value of Annuity of $1 (Table D, p. 734)—*used for annuities*

Take a moment to look at these tables because we are going to use them throughout the rest of the chapter. Note that the columns are interest rates (*i*) and the rows are periods (*n*).

The data in each table, known as future value factors (FV factors) and present value factors (PV factors), are for an amount of $1. To find the future value of an amount other than $1, you simply multiply the factors found in the table by the actual principal amount of the lump sum or annuity.

Rather than using these tables, you may wish to use Microsoft Excel or a business calculator that has been programmed with time value of money functions. These technology applications make time value of money computations much easier because you do not need to find the correct PV and FV factors in the tables. Rather, you simply enter the principal amount, interest rate, and number of time periods in the electronic device and instruct the technology to solve for the present or future value for you.

Throughout the remainder of this chapter, we will be displaying technology features that provide you with easy instruction on how to perform time value of money, NPV, and IRR calculations using Excel. In addition, Appendix 12B illustrates the exact Excel keystrokes to use to solve every chapter example. Appendix 12C likewise illustrates how to solve every chapter example using a TI-83 or TI-84 graphing calculator.

As you will see, using a programmed calculator or Excel results in slightly different answers than those presented in the text when using the tables. The differences are due to the fact that the PV and FV factors found in the tables have been rounded to three digits. Finally, all end-of-chapter homework material has been solved using the tables, Excel, and programmed calculators so that you will have the exact solution for the method you choose to use.

Calculating Future Values of Single Sums and Annuities Using FV Factors

Let's go back to our $10,000 lump-sum investment. If we want to know the future value of the investment five years from now at an interest rate of 6%, we determine the FV factor from the table labeled Future Value of $1 (Appendix 12A, Table C). We use this table for lump-sum amounts. We look down the 6% column and across the 5 periods row and find that the future value factor is 1.338. We finish our calculations as follows:

$$\text{Future value} = \text{Principal amount} \times (\text{FV factor for } i = 6\%, n = 5)$$
$$= \$10,000 \times (1.338)$$
$$= \$13,380$$

This figure agrees with our earlier calculation of the investment's future value ($13,383) in Exhibit 12-6. (The difference of $3 is due to two facts: [1] the tables round the FV and PV factors to three decimal places, and [2] we rounded our earlier yearly interest calculations in Exhibit 12-6 to the nearest dollar.)

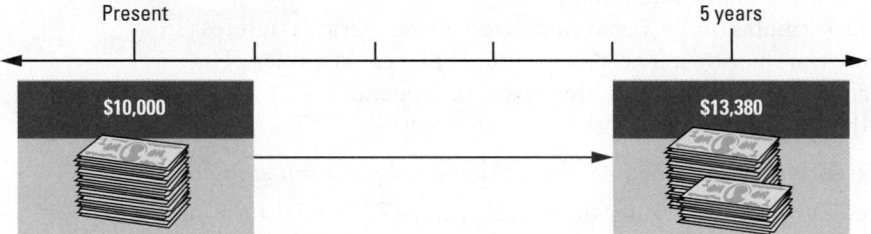

Let's also consider our alternative investment strategy: investing $2,000 at the end of each year for five years. The procedure for calculating the future value of an annuity is similar to calculating the future value of a lump-sum amount. This time, we use the Future Value of Annuity of $1 table (Appendix 12A, Table D). Assuming 6% interest, we once again look down the 6% column. Because we will be making five annual installments, we look across the row marked 5 periods. The Annuity FV factor is 5.637. We finish the calculation as follows:

$$\text{Future value} = \text{Amount of each cash installment} \times (\text{Annuity FV factor for } i = 6\%, n = 5)$$
$$= \$2,000 \times (5.637)$$
$$= \$11,274$$

This is considerably less than the future value ($13,380) of the lump sum of $10,000 even though we invested $10,000 out of pocket either way.

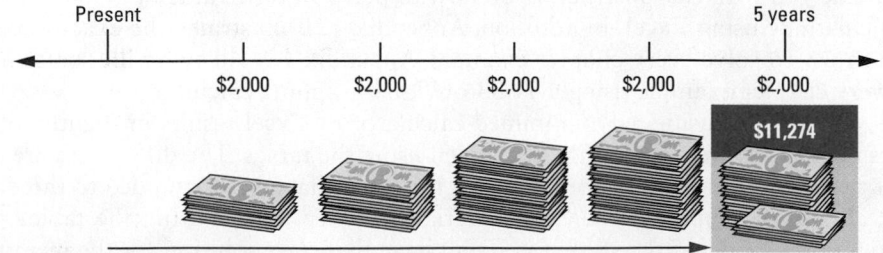

STOP & THINK

Explain why the future value of the annuity is less than the future value of the lump sum even though you are investing a total of $10,000 in both situations.

Answer: Even though you invested $10,000 out of pocket under both situations the timing of the investment significantly affects the amount of interest earned. The $10,000 lump sum invested immediately earns interest for the full five years. However, the annuity doesn't begin earning interest until Year 2 (because the first installment isn't made until the *end* of Year 1). In addition, the amount invested begins at $2,000 and doesn't reach a full $10,000 until the end of Year 5. Therefore, the base on which the interest is earned is smaller than the lump-sum investment for the entire five-year period.

Technology Makes it Simple	Excel 2007, 2010, and 2013

Future Value Computations

1. In an Excel spreadsheet click on **Formulas**.
2. Click on **Financial**.
3. Choose **FV** from the drop down list. The following will appear as a dialog box:

   Rate

   Nper

   Pmt

   Pv

   Type

4. Fill in the interest **Rate**, in decimal format (for example 14% would be input as .14).
5. Fill in the number of periods (for example, five years would be input as 5 in the space by **Nper**).
6. If the amount is an annuity, fill in the yearly installment as negative number in the space by **Pmt**.
7. If the amount is a lump sum, fill in the lump sum as a negative number in the space by **Pv**.
8. Leave the space by **Type** blank.
9. The future value is shown under the dialog box.

Note: Appendix 12B illustrates each chapter example using these basic Excel instructions.

Calculating Present Values of Single Sums and Annuities Using PV Factors

The process for calculating present values—often called discounting cash flows—is similar to the process for calculating future values. The difference is the point in time at which you are assessing the investment's worth. Rather than determining its value at a future date, you are determining its value at an earlier point in time (today). For our example, let's assume that you've just won the lottery after purchasing one $5 lottery ticket. The state offers you three payout options for your after-tax prize money:

Option #1: $1,000,000 now

Option #2: $150,000 at the end of each year for the next 10 years

Option #3: $2,000,000 10 years from now

Which alternative should you take? You might be tempted to wait 10 years to "double" your winnings. You may be tempted to take the money now and spend it. However, let's assume that you plan to prudently invest all money received—no matter when you receive it—so that you have financial flexibility in the future (for example, for buying a house, retiring early, and taking vacations). How can you choose among the three payment alternatives when the *total amount* of each option varies ($1,000,000 versus $1,500,000 versus $2,000,000) and the *timing* of the cash flows varies (now versus some each year versus later)? Comparing these three options is like comparing apples to oranges—we just can't do it—unless we find some common basis for comparison. Our common basis for comparison will be the prize money's worth at a certain point in time—namely, today. In other words, if we convert each payment option to its *present value*, we can compare apples to apples.

We already know the principal amount and timing of each payment option, so the only assumption we'll have to make is the interest rate. The interest rate will vary depending on the amount of risk you are willing to take with your investment. Riskier investments (such as stock investments) command higher interest rates; safer investments (such as FDIC-insured bank deposits) yield lower interest rates. Let's assume that after investigating possible investment alternatives, you choose an investment contract with an 8% annual return.

We already know that the present value of Option #1 is $1,000,000. Let's convert the other two payment options to their present values so that we can compare them. We'll need to use the Present Value of Annuity of $1 table (Appendix 12A, Table B) to convert payment Option #2 (since it's an annuity) and the Present Value of $1 table (Appendix 12A, Table A) to convert payment Option #3 (because it's a single lump sum). To obtain the PV factors, we look down the 8% column and across the 10 period row. Then, we finish the calculations as follows:

Option #1

Present value = $1,000,000

Option #2

Present value = Amount of each cash installment × (Annuity PV factor for $i = 8\%$, $n = 10$)
Present value = $150,000 × (6.710)
Present value = $1,006,500

Option #3

Present value = Principal amount × (PV factor for $i = 8\%$, $n = 10$)
Present value = $2,000,000 × (0.463)
Present value = $926,000

Exhibit 12-8 shows that we have converted each payout option to a common basis—its worth today—so we can make a valid comparison of the options. Based on this comparison, we should choose Option #2 because its worth, in today's dollars, is the highest of the three options.

EXHIBIT 12-8 Comparing Present Values of Lottery Payout Options at i = 8%

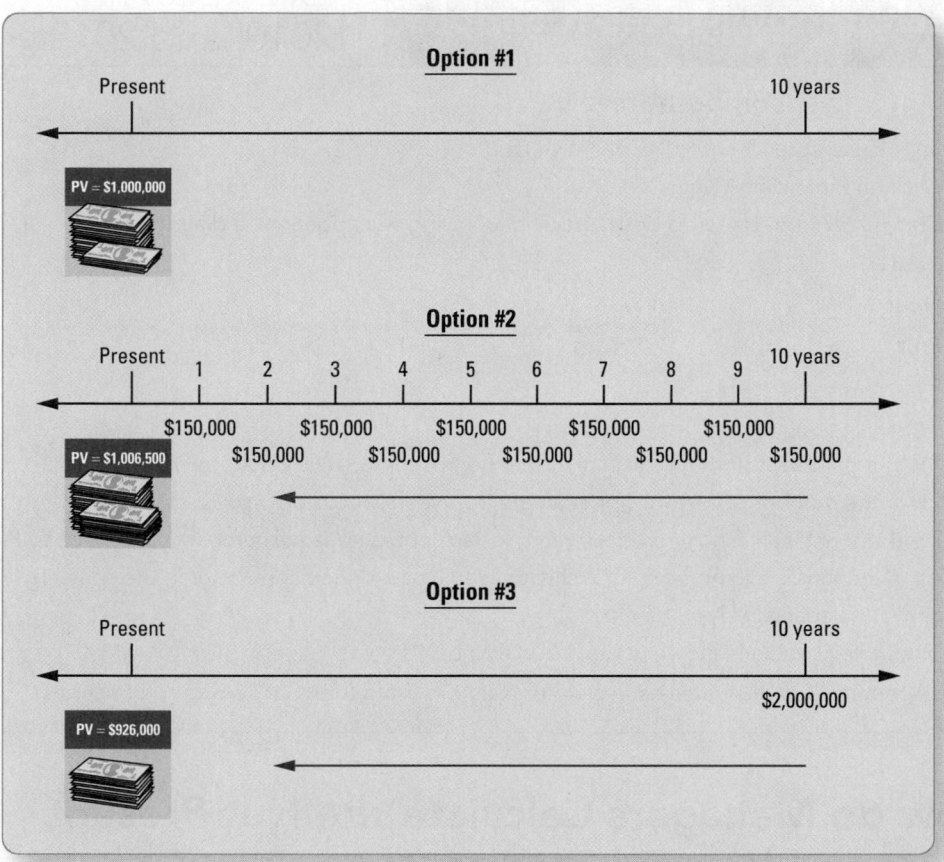

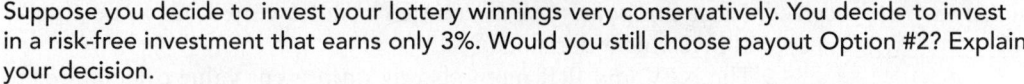

STOP & THINK

Suppose you decide to invest your lottery winnings very conservatively. You decide to invest in a risk-free investment that earns only 3%. Would you still choose payout Option #2? Explain your decision.

Answer: Using a 3% interest rate, the present values of the payout options are as follows:

Payment Options	Present Value of Lottery Payout (Present value calculation, $i = 3\%$, $n = 10$)
Option #1...	$1,000,000 (already stated at its present value)
Option #2...	$1,279,500 (= $150,000 × 8.530)
Option #3...	$1,488,000 (= $2,000,000 × .744)

When the lottery payout is invested at 3% rather than 8%, the present values change. Option #3 is now the best alternative because its present value is the highest. Present values and future values are extremely sensitive to changes in interest rate assumptions, especially when the investment period is relatively long.

Now that we have studied time value of money concepts, we will discuss the two capital budgeting methods that incorporate the time value of money: net present value (NPV) and internal rate of return (IRR).

Technology Makes it Simple   Excel 2007, 2010, and 2013

Present Value Computations

1. In an Excel spreadsheet click on **Formulas**.
2. Click on **Financial**.
3. Choose **PV** from the drop down list. The following will appear as a dialog box:

   Rate

   Nper

   Pmt

   FV

   Type

4. Fill in the interest **Rate**, in decimal format (for example, 14% would be input as .14).
5. Fill in the number of periods (for example, five years would be input as 5).
6. If the amount is an annuity, fill in the yearly installment as negative number in the space by **Pmt**.
7. If the amount is a lump sum, fill in the lump sum as a negative number in the space by **FV**.
8. Leave the space by **Type** blank.
9. The present value is shown under the dialog box.

Note: Appendix 12B illustrates each chapter example using these basic Excel instructions.

How do Managers Calculate the Net Present Value and Internal Rate of Return?

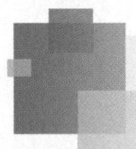

4 Use discounted cash flow models to make capital investment decisions

Neither the payback period nor the ARR incorporate the time value of money. *Discounted cash flow models*—the NPV and the IRR—overcome this weakness. These models incorporate compound interest by assuming that companies will reinvest future cash flows when they are received. Most companies use discounted cash flow methods to help make capital investment decisions.

The NPV and IRR methods rely on present value calculations to compare the cost of the initial investment with the expected net cash inflows that will result from making the investment. Recall that an investment's *net cash inflows* includes all *future* cash flows related to the investment, such as future increased revenues and cost savings netted against the investment's future cash operating costs. Because the cash outflow for the investment occurs *now* but the net cash inflows from the investment occur in the *future*, companies can make valid "apple-to-apple" comparisons only when they convert the cash flows to the *same point in time*—namely, the present value. Companies use the present value rather than the future value to make the comparison because the investment's initial cost is already stated at its present value.[5]

As shown in Exhibit 12-9, a favorable investment is one in which the present value of the investment's net cash inflows exceeds the initial cost of the investment. In terms of our earlier lottery example, the lottery ticket turned out to be a "good investment" because the present value of its net cash inflows (the present value of the lottery payout under *any* of the three payout

■ Why is this important?

"The **NPV method** lets managers make an **'apples-to-apples' comparison** between the **cash flows** they will receive in the **future** from the investment and the **price** they must **currently pay** to 'purchase' those future cash flows (the cost of the initial **investment**)."

---

[5]If the investment is to be purchased through lease payments, rather than a current cash outlay, we would still use the current cash price of the investment as its initial cost. If no current cash price is available, we would discount the future lease payments back to their present value to estimate the investment's current cash price.

options) exceeded the cost of the investment (the $5 lottery ticket). Let's begin our discussion by taking a closer look at the NPV method.

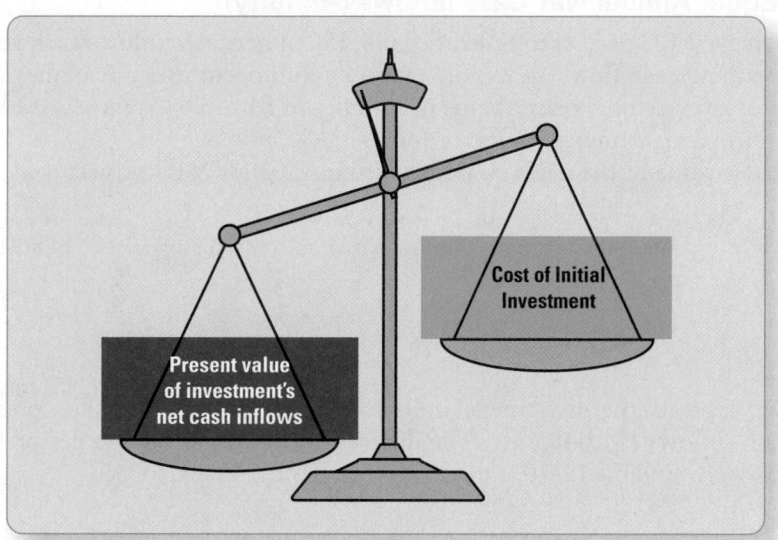

EXHIBIT 12-9 Comparing the Present Value of an Investment's Net Cash Inflows Against the Cost of the Initial Investment

Net Present Value (NPV)

Allegra is considering producing MP3 players and digital video recorders (DVRs). The products require different specialized machines, each costing $1 million. Each machine has a five-year life and zero residual value. The two products have different patterns of predicted net cash inflows:

	Annual Net Cash Inflows	
Year	MP3 Players	DVRs
1	$ 305,450	$ 500,000
2	305,450	350,000
3	305,450	300,000
4	305,450	250,000
5	305,450	40,000
Total	$1,527,250	$1,440,000

The MP3 project generates more net cash inflows, but the DVR project brings in cash sooner. To decide how attractive each investment is, we find its **net present value (NPV)**. The NPV is the *difference* between the present value of the investment's net cash inflows and the cost of the initial investment. We *discount* the net cash inflows to their present value—just as we did in the lottery example—using Allegra's minimum desired rate of return. This rate is called the **discount rate** because it is the interest rate used for the present value calculations. It's also called the **required rate of return** or **hurdle rate** because the investment must meet or exceed this rate to be acceptable. The discount rate depends on the riskiness of investments. The higher the risk, the higher the discount rate. Allegra's discount rate for these investments is 14%.

We compare the present value of the net cash inflows to the cost of the initial investment to decide which projects meet or exceed management's minimum desired rate of return. In other words, management is deciding whether the $1 million is worth more (because the company would have to give it up now to invest in the project) or whether the project's future net cash inflows are worth more. Managers can make a valid comparison between the two sums of money only by comparing them at the *same* point in time—namely at their present value.

NPV with Equal Annual Net Cash Inflows (Annuity)

Allegra expects the MP3 project to generate $305,450 of net cash inflows each year for five years. Because these cash flows are equal in amount and occur every year, they are an annuity. Therefore, we use the Present Value of Annuity of $1 table (Appendix 12A, Table B) to find the appropriate Annuity PV factor for $i = 14\%$, $n = 5$.

The present value of the net cash inflows from Allegra's MP3 project is as follows:

Present value = Amount of each cash inflow × (Annuity PV factor for $i = 14\%$, $n = 5$)

= $305,450 × (3.433)

= $1,048,610

Next, we subtract the investment's initial cost ($1 million) from the present value of the net cash inflows ($1,048,610). The difference of $48,610 is the net present value (NPV), as shown in Exhibit 12-10.

EXHIBIT 12-10 NPV of Equal Net Cash Inflows—MP3 Project

	A	B	C	D	E	F
1	**NPV Calculation for *Equal* Annual Net Cash Inflows**	**Annuity PV Factor ($i = 14\%$)**		**Annual Net Cash Inflow**		**Present Value**
2	Present value of annuity, $n = 5$	3.433	× $	305,450	= $	1,048,610
3	Less: Initial investment					1,000,000
4	Net present value (NPV)					$ 48,610
5						

NOTE: Arithmetic signs are only shown for illustrative teaching purposes. They are not typically displayed in spreadsheets.

A *positive* NPV means that the project earns *more* than the required rate of return. A *negative* NPV means that the project fails to earn the required rate of return. This leads to the following decision rule:

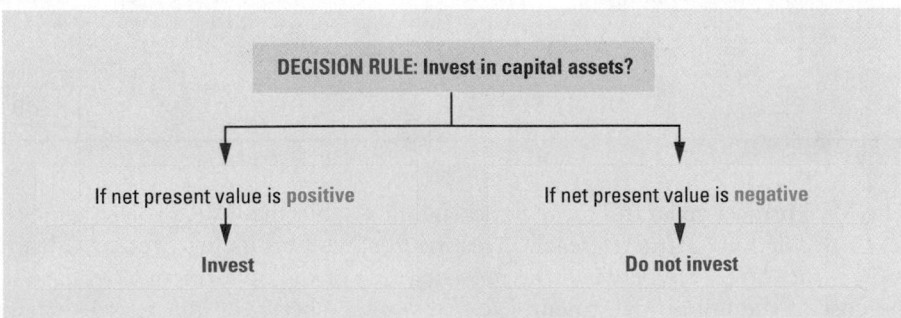

A *positive* NPV means that the project earns *more* than the required rate of return. A *negative* NPV means that the project fails to earn the required rate of return. This leads

In Allegra's case, the MP3 project is an attractive investment. The $48,610 positive NPV means that the MP3 project earns *more than* Allegra's 14% target rate of return. In other words, management would prefer to give up $1 million today to receive the MP3 project's future net cash inflows. Why? Because those future net cash inflows are worth more than $1 million in today's dollars (they are worth $1,048,610).

Another way managers can use present value analysis is to start the capital budgeting process by computing the total present value of the net cash inflows from the project to determine the *maximum* the company can invest in the project and still earn the target rate of return. For Allegra, the present value of the net cash inflows is $1,048,610. This means that Allegra can invest a maximum of $1,048,610 and still earn the 14% target rate of return. Because Allegra's managers believe they can undertake the project for $1 million, the project is an attractive investment.

▶ ## Try It!

> The Bruce Company is considering investing in a wind turbine to generate its own power. Any unused power will be sold back to the local utility company. Between cost savings and new revenues, the company expects to generate $750,000 per year in net cash inflows from the turbine. The turbine would cost $4 million and is expected to have a 20-year useful life with no residual value. Calculate the NPV assuming the company uses a 12% hurdle rate.

Please see page 764 for solutions.

NPV with Unequal Annual Net Cash Inflows

In contrast to the MP3 project, the net cash inflows of the DVR project are unequal—$500,000 in Year 1, $350,000 in Year 2, and so forth. Because these amounts vary by year, Allegra's managers *cannot* use the annuity table to compute the present value of the DVR project. They must compute the present value of each individual year's net cash inflows *separately, as separate lump sums received in different years,* using the Present Value of $1 table (Appendix 12A, Table A).

Exhibit 12-11 shows that the $500,000 net cash inflow received in Year 1 is discounted using a PV factor of $i = 14\%, n = 1$, while the $350,000 net cash inflow received in Year 2 is discounted using a PV factor of $i = 14\%, n = 2$, and so forth. After separately discounting each of the five year's net cash inflows, we find that the *total* present value of the DVR project's net cash inflows is $1,078,910. Finally, we subtract the investment's cost ($1 million) to arrive at the DVR project's NPV: $78,910.

EXHIBIT 12-11 NPV with Unequal Net Cash Inflows—DVR Project

	A	B	C	D	E	F
1	**NPV Calculation for *Unequal* Net Cash Inflows**	**PV Factor** ($i = 14\%$)		**Net Cash Inflow**		**Present Value**
2	Present value of net cash inflows:					
3	Year 1 ($n = 1$)	0.877	× $	500,000	= $	438,500
4	Year 2 ($n = 2$)	0.769	×	350,000	=	269,150
5	Year 3 ($n = 3$)	0.675	×	300,000	=	202,500
6	Year 4 ($n = 4$)	0.592	×	250,000	=	148,000
7	Year 5 ($n = 5$)	0.519	×	40,000	=	20,760
8	Total present value of net cash inflows					$ 1,078,910
9	Less: Initial investment					1,000,000
10	Net present value (NPV)					$ 78,910
11						

Because the NPV is positive, Allegra expects the DVR project to earn more than the 14% target rate of return, making this an attractive investment.

Capital Rationing and the Profitability Index

Exhibits 12-10 and 12-11 show that both the MP3 and DVR projects have positive NPVs. Therefore, both are attractive investments. Because resources are limited, companies are not always able to invest in all capital assets that meet their investment criteria. For example, Allegra may not have the funds to invest in both the DVR and MP3 projects at this time. In this case, Allegra should choose the DVR project because it yields a higher

NPV. The DVR project should earn an additional $78,910 beyond the 14% required rate of return, while the MP3 project returns an additional $48,610.

This example illustrates an important point. The MP3 project promises more *total* net cash inflows. But the *timing* of the DVR cash flows—loaded near the beginning of the project—gives the DVR investment a higher NPV. The DVR project is more attractive because of the time value of money. Its dollars, which are received sooner, are worth more now than the more distant dollars of the MP3 project.

If Allegra had to choose between the MP3 and DVR project, it would choose the DVR project because that project yields a higher NPV ($78,910). However, comparing the NPV of the two projects is valid *only* because both projects require the same initial cost—$1 million.

In contrast, Exhibit 12-12 summarizes three capital investment options that Raycor, a sporting goods manufacturer, faces. Each capital project requires a different initial investment. All three projects are attractive because each yields a positive NPV. Assuming that Raycor can invest in only one project at this time, which one should it choose? Project B yields the highest NPV, but it also requires a larger initial investment than the alternatives.

EXHIBIT 12-12 Raycor's Capital Investment Options

	A	B	C	D
1	**Comparing NPVs**	**Project A**	**Project B**	**Project C**
2	Present value	$ 150,000	$ 238,000	$ 182,000
3	Less: Initial investment	125,000	200,000	150,000
4	Net present value (NPV)	$ 25,000	$ 38,000	$ 32,000
5				

To choose among the projects, Raycor computes the **profitability index** (also known as the **present value index**). The profitability index is computed as follows:

> Profitability index = Present value of net cash inflows ÷ Initial investment

The profitability index computes the number of dollars returned for every dollar invested, *with all calculations performed in present value dollars*. It allows us to compare alternative investments in present value terms, like the NPV method, but also considers differences in the investments' initial cost. Let's compute the profitability index for all three alternatives.

Present value of net cash inflows	÷	Initial investment	=	Profitability index
Project A: $150,000	÷	$125,000	=	1.20
Project B: $238,000	÷	$200,000	=	1.19
Project C: $182,000	÷	$150,000	=	1.21

The profitability index shows that Project C is the best of the three alternatives because it returns $1.21 in present value dollars for every $1.00 invested. Projects A and B return slightly less.

Let's also compute the profitability index for Allegra's MP3 and DVR projects:

Present value of net cash inflows	÷	Initial investment	=	Profitability index
MP3: $1,048,610	÷	$1,000,000	=	1.049
DVR: $1,078,910	÷	$1,000,000	=	1.079

The profitability index confirms our prior conclusion that the DVR project is more profitable than the MP3 project. The DVR project returns $1.079 (in present value dollars) for every $1.00 invested. This return is beyond the 14% return already used to discount the cash flows. We did not need the profitability index to determine that the DVR project was preferable because both projects required the same investment ($1 million).

NPV of a Project with Residual Value

Many assets yield cash inflows at the end of their useful lives because they have residual value. Companies discount an investment's residual value to its present value when determining the *total* present value of the project's net cash inflows. The residual value is discounted as a single lump sum—not an annuity—because it will be received only once, when the asset is sold.

Suppose Allegra expects the MP3 project equipment to be worth $100,000 at the end of its five-year life. This represents an additional *lump sum* future cash inflow from the MP3 project. To determine the MP3 project's NPV, we discount the residual value ($100,000) using the Present Value of $1 table ($i = 14\%$, $n = 5$) (see Appendix 12A, Table A). We then *add* its present value ($51,900) to the present value of the MP3 project's other net cash inflows ($1,048,610) as shown in Exhibit 12-13:

EXHIBIT 12-13 NPV of a Project with Residual Value

	A	B	C	D	E	F
1	NPV Calculation Including Residual Value	PV Factor (i = 14%)		Net Cash Inflow		Present Value
2	Present value of annuity, n = 5	3.433	×	$ 305,450	=	$ 1,048,610
3	Plus: Present value of residual value, end of Year 5	0.519	×	100,000	=	51,900
4	Total present value					$ 1,100,510
5	Less: Initial investment					1,000,000
6	Net present value (NPV)					$ 100,510
7						

Because of the expected residual value, the MP3 project is now more attractive than the DVR project. If Allegra could pursue only the MP3 or DVR project, it would now choose the MP3 project because its NPV ($100,510) is higher than the DVR project ($78,910) and both projects require the same investment ($1 million).

Technology Makes it Simple   Excel 2007, 2010, and 2013

Net Present Value (NPV) Calculations

1. In an Excel spreadsheet, type in the future cash flows expected from the investment. Begin with the cash flow expected in Year 1. In the next cell type in the cash flow expected in Year 2. Continue in the same fashion until all future cash flows are shown in separate cells, in the order in which they are expected to be received.

2. Click on **Formulas**.

3. Click on **Financial**.

4. Choose **NPV** from the drop down list. The following will appear as a dialog box:

   Rate

   Value 1

5. Fill in the interest **Rate**, in decimal format (for example, 14% would be input as .14)

6. Next to **Value 1**, highlight the array of cells containing the cash flow data from Step 1.

7. The **"Formula result"** will appear at the bottom of the dialog box. The result is the present value of the future cash flows.

8. Finally, subtract the initial cost of the investment to obtain the NPV.

Note: Appendix 12B illustrates each chapter example using these basic Excel instructions.

Sensitivity Analysis

Capital budgeting decisions affect cash flows far into the future. Allegra's managers might want to know whether their decision would be affected by any of their major assumptions. For example, consider the following:

- Changing the discount rate from 14% to 12% or to 16%
- Changing the net cash inflows by 10%
- Changing an expected residual value

Managers can use Excel or programmed calculators to quickly perform sensitivity analysis.

Internal Rate of Return (IRR)

The NPV method only tells management whether the investment exceeds the hurdle rate. Since both the MP3 player and DVR projects yield positive NPVs, we know they provide *more* than a 14% rate of return. But what exact rate of return would these investments provide? The IRR method answers that question.

The **internal rate of return (IRR)** is the rate of return, based on discounted cash flows, that a company can expect to earn by investing in the project. *It is the interest rate that makes the NPV of the investment equal to zero:*

$$NPV = 0$$

Let's look at this concept in another light by inserting the definition of NPV:

Present value of the investment's net cash inflows − Initial investment = 0

Or if we rearrange the equation:

Initial investment = Present value of the investment's net cash inflows

In other words, the IRR is the *interest rate* that makes the cost of the investment equal to the present value of the investment's net cash inflows. The higher the IRR, the more desirable the project. Like the profitability index, the IRR can be used in the capital rationing process.

IRR computations are very easy to perform using Excel or programmed calculators. (See the "Technology Makes It Simple" feature at the end of this section.) However, IRR computations are much more cumbersome to perform using the tables.

IRR with Equal Annual Net Cash Inflows (Annuity)

When the investment is an annuity, we can develop a formula that will tell us the Annuity PV factor associated with the investment's IRR. We start with the equation given previously and then substitute in as follows:

Initial investment = Present value of the investment's net cash inflows

Initial investment = Amount of each equal net cash inflow × Annuity PV factor (i = ?, n = given)

Finally, we rearrange the equation to obtain the following formula:

$$\frac{\text{Initial investment}}{\text{Amount of each equal net cash inflow}} = \text{Annuity PV factor } (i = ?, n = \text{given})$$

Let's use this formula to find the Annuity PV factor associated with Allegra's MP3 project. Recall that the project would cost $1 million and result in five equal yearly cash inflows of $305,450:

$$\frac{\$1,000,000}{\$305,450} = \text{Annuity PV factor } (i = ?, n = 5)$$

$$3.274 = \text{Annuity PV factor } (i = ?, n = 5)$$

Next, we find the interest rate that corresponds to this Annuity PV factor. Turn to the Present Value of Annuity of $1 table (Appendix 12A, Table B). Scan the row corresponding to the project's expected life—five years, in our example. Choose the column(s) with the number closest to the Annuity PV factor you calculated using the formula. The 3.274 annuity factor is in the 16% column.

Therefore, the IRR of the MP3 project is 16%.

Allegra expects the project to earn an internal rate of return of 16% over its life. Exhibit 12-14 confirms this result: Using a 16% discount rate, the project's NPV is zero. In other words, 16% is the discount rate that makes the cost of the initial investment equal to the present value of the investment's net cash inflows.

EXHIBIT 12-14 IRR–MP3 Project

	A	B	C	D	E	F
1	**NPV Calculation for *Equal* Annual Net Cash Inflows**	**Annuity PV Factor (*i* = 16%)**		**Annual Net Cash Inflow**		**Present Value (rounded)**
2	Present value of annuity, *n* = 5	3.274	× $	305,450	= $	1,000,000
3	Less: Initial investment					1,000,000
4	Net present value (NPV)				$	0
5						

To decide whether the project is acceptable, compare the IRR with the minimum desired rate of return. The decision rule is as follows:

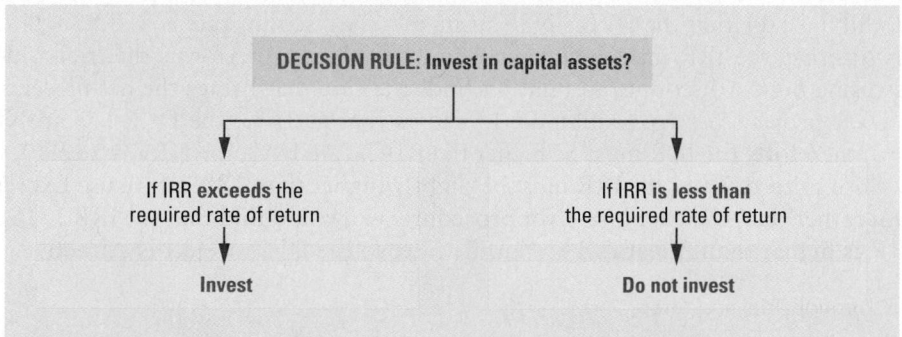

Recall that Allegra's hurdle rate is 14%. Because the MP3 project's IRR (16%) is higher than the hurdle rate (14%), Allegra would invest in the project.

In the MP3 project, the exact Annuity PV factor (3.274) appears in the Present Value of an Annuity of $1 table (Appendix 12A, Table B). Many times, the exact factor will not appear in the table. For example, let's find the IRR of Tierra Firma's proposed HVAC system. Recall that the HVAC system would cost $240,000 and result in annual net cash inflows of $60,000 over its six-year life. We find its Annuity PV factor using the formula given previously:

$$\frac{\text{Initial investment}}{\text{Amount of each equal net cash inflow}} = \text{Annuity PV factor } (i = ?, n = \text{given})$$

$$\frac{\$240,000}{\$60,000} = \text{Annuity PV factor } (i = ?, n = 6)$$

$$4.00 = \text{Annuity PV factor } (i = ?, n = 6)$$

Now, look in the Present Value of Annuity of $1 table in the row marked 6 periods (Appendix 12A, Table B). You will not see 4.00 under any column. The closest two factors are 3.889 (at 14%) and 4.111 (at 12%).

Thus, the HVAC's IRR is somewhere between 12% and 14%.

Using Excel's IRR function, we would find the exact IRR is 12.98%. If Tierra Firma had a 14% hurdle rate, it would *not* invest in the HVAC system because its IRR is less than 14%.

▶ **Try It!**

The Bruce Company is considering investing in a wind turbine to generate its own power. Any unused power will be sold back to the local utility company. Between cost savings and new revenues, the company expects to generate $750,000 per year in net cash inflows from the turbine. The turbine would cost $4 million and is expected to have a 20-year useful life with no residual value. Calculate the internal rate of return (IRR).

Please see page 764 for solutions.

IRR with Unequal Annual Net Cash Inflows

Because the DVR project has unequal cash inflows, Allegra cannot use the Present Value of Annuity of $1 table to find the asset's IRR. Rather, Allegra must use a trial-and-error procedure to determine the discount rate that makes the project's NPV equal to zero. Recall from Exhibit 12-11 that the DVR's NPV using a 14% discount rate is $78,910. Since the NPV is *positive*, the IRR must be *higher* than 14%. Allegra performs the trial-and-error process using *higher* discount rates until it finds the rate that brings the net present value of the DVR project to *zero*. Exhibit 12-15 shows that at 16%, the DVR has an NPV of $40,390; therefore, the IRR must be higher than 16%. At 18%, the NPV is $3,980, which is very close to zero. Thus, the IRR must be slightly higher than 18%. If we use Excel's IRR function rather than the trial-and-error procedure, we would find that the IRR is 18.23%. The IRR is higher than Allegra's 14% hurdle rate, so the DVR project is attractive.

EXHIBIT 12-15 Finding the DVR's IRR Through Trial and Error

	A	B	C	D	E	F	G	H	I	J	K	L
1		**Calculations using 16% interest rate**						**Calculations using 18% interest rate**				
2	**NPV Calculation for *Unequal* Net Cash Inflows**	**PV Factor** (*i* = 16%)		**Net Cash Inflow**		**Present Value at 16%**		**PV Factor** (*i* = 18%)		**Net Cash Inflow**		**Present Value at 18%**
3	Present value of net cash inflows:											
4	Year 1 (*n* = 1)	0.862 ×	$	500,000	=	$ 431,000		0.847 ×	$	500,000	=	$ 423,500
5	Year 2 (*n* = 2)	0.743 ×		350,000	=	260,050		0.718 ×		350,000	=	251,300
6	Year 3 (*n* = 3)	0.641 ×		300,000	=	192,300		0.609 ×		300,000	=	182,700
7	Year 4 (*n* = 4)	0.552 ×		250,000	=	138,000		0.516 ×		250,000	=	129,000
8	Year 5 (*n* = 5)	0.476 ×		40,000	=	19,040		0.437 ×		40,000	=	17,480
9	Total present value of net cash inflows					$ 1,040,390						$ 1,003,980
10	Less: Initial investment					1,000,000						1,000,000
11	Net present value (NPV)					$ 40,390						$ 3,980
12												

| **Technology Makes it Simple** | Excel 2007, 2010, and 2013 |

Internal Rate of Return (IRR) Calculations

1. In an Excel spreadsheet, first type in the initial investment as a negative number. For example, −1000000 for a $1 million investment. In the next cell, type in the cash flow expected in Year 1. In the following cell type in the cash flow expected in Year 2. Continue in the same fashion until all future cash flows are shown in separate cells, in the order in which they are expected to be received.
2. Click on **Formulas**.
3. Click on **Financial**.
4. Choose **IRR** from the dropdown list. The following will appear as a dialog box:
   Value 1
5. Next to **Value 1**, highlight the array of cells containing the data from Step 1.
6. The **"Formula result"** will appear at the bottom of the dialog box. The result is the Internal Rate of Return (IRR).

Note: Appendix 12B illustrates each chapter example using these basic Excel instructions.

How do the Capital Budgeting Methods Compare?

We have discussed four capital budgeting methods commonly used by companies to make capital investment decisions—two that ignore the time value of money (payback period and ARR) and two that incorporate the time value of money (NPV and IRR). Exhibit 12-16 summarizes the similarities and differences between the two methods that ignore the time value of money.

5 Compare and contrast the four capital budgeting methods

EXHIBIT 12-16 Capital Budgeting Methods That *Ignore* the Time Value of Money

Payback Period	ARR
• Simple to compute	• The only method that focuses on the accrual-based operating income from the investment, rather than cash flows
• Focuses on the time it takes to recover the company's cash investment	• Shows the impact of the investment on operating income, which is important to financial statement users
• Ignores any cash flows occurring after the payback period, including any residual value	• Measures the average profitability of the asset over its entire life
• Highlights risks of investments with longer cash recovery periods	• Ignores the time value of money
• Ignores the time value of money	

Exhibit 12-17 considers the similarities and differences between the two methods that incorporate the time value of money.

EXHIBIT 12-17 Capital Budgeting Methods That *Incorporate* the Time Value of Money

NPV	IRR
• Incorporates the time value of money and the asset's net cash inflows over its entire life	• Incorporates the time value of money and the asset's net cash inflows over its entire life
• Indicates whether the asset will earn the company's minimum required rate of return	• Computes the project's unique rate of return
• Shows the excess or deficiency of the asset's present value of net cash inflows over the cost of the initial investment	• No additional steps needed for capital rationing decisions when assets require different initial investments
• The profitability index should be computed for capital rationing decisions when the assets require different initial investments	

Keep in mind that managers often use more than one method to gain different perspectives on the risks and returns of potential capital investments.

STOP & THINK

A pharmaceutical company is considering two research projects that require the same initial investment. Project A has an NPV of $232,000 and a 3-year payback period. Project B has an NPV of $237,000 and a payback period of 4.5 years. Which project would you choose?

Answer: Many managers would choose Project A even though it has a slightly lower NPV. Why? The NPV is only $5,000 lower, yet the payback period is significantly shorter. The uncertainty of receiving operating cash flows increases with each passing year. Managers often forgo small differences in expected cash inflows to decrease the risk of investments.

Decision Guidelines

Capital Budgeting

Here are more of the guidelines Amazon.com's managers used as they made the major capital budgeting decision to invest in building warehouses.

Decision	Guidelines
Which capital budgeting methods are best?	No one method is best. Each method provides a different perspective on the investment decision.
Why do the NPV and IRR models calculate the present value of an investment's net cash flows?	Because an investment's cash inflows occur in the future, yet the cash outlay for the investment occurs now, all of the cash flows must be converted to a common point in time. These methods use the *present* value as the common point in time.
How do we know if investing in warehouse facilities will be worthwhile?	Investment in warehouse facilities may be worthwhile if the NPV is positive or the IRR exceeds the required rate of return.
How do we compute the net present value (NPV) if the investment has equal annual cash inflows?	Compute the present value of the investment's net cash inflows using the Present Value of an Annuity of $1 table and then subtract the investment's cost. Alternatively, use the NPV function in Excel (see Appendix 12B for instructions).
How do we compute the net present value (NPV) if the investment has unequal annual cash inflows?	Compute the present value of each year's net cash inflows using the Present Value of $1 (lump sum) table, sum the present value of the inflows, and then subtract the investment's cost. Alternatively, use the NPV function in Excel (see Appendix 12B for instructions).
How do we compare potential investments that have differing initial costs?	Use the profitability index, which is computed as $$\text{Profitability index} = \text{Present value of net cash inflows} \div \text{Initial investment}$$
How do we compute the internal rate of return (IRR) if the investment has equal annual cash inflows?	Find the interest rate that yields the following Annuity PV factor: $$\text{Annuity PV factor} = \frac{\text{Initial investment}}{\text{Amount of each equal net cash inflow}}$$
How do we compute the internal rate of return (IRR) if the investment has unequal annual cash inflows?	Use trial and error. Alternatively, use the IRR function in Excel (see Appendix 12B for instructions).

SUMMARY PROBLEM 2

Sonoma is considering investing in solar paneling for the roof of its large distribution facility. The investment will cost $9 million and have a six-year useful life and no residual value. Because of rising utility costs, the company expects the yearly utility savings to increase over time, as follows:

Year 1	$1,000,000
Year 2	$1,500,000
Year 3	$2,000,000
Year 4	$2,500,000
Year 5	$3,500,000
Year 6	$4,500,000

The solar panels have already passed the payback period and ARR screening (See Summary Problem 1 on page 709).

1. Compute the NPV of the solar panels, given the company's 12% hurdle rate.

2. Estimate the IRR of the solar panels or use Excel to find the exact IRR.

3. Should Sonoma invest in the solar paneling? Why or why not?

▪ SOLUTIONS

1. The NPV of the solar panels is found by subtracting the initial cost of the solar panels ($9 million) from the present value of the future cash flows as follows:

	A	B	C	D	E	F
1	**NPV Calculation for *Unequal* Net Cash Inflows**	**PV Factor (*i* = 12%)**		**Net Cash Inflow**		**Present Value**
2	Present value of net cash inflows:					
3	Year 1 (*n* = 1)	0.893	× $	1,000,000	= $	893,000
4	Year 1 (*n* = 2)	0.797	×	1,500,000	=	1,195,500
5	Year 1 (*n* = 3)	0.712	×	2,000,000	=	1,424,000
6	Year 1 (*n* = 4)	0.636	×	2,500,000	=	1,590,000
7	Year 1 (*n* = 5)	0.567	×	3,500,000	=	1,984,500
8	Year 1 (*n* = 6)	0.507	×	4,500,000	=	2,281,500
9	Total present value of net cash inflows				$	9,368,500
10	Less: Initial investment					9,000,000
11	Net present value (NPV)				$	368,500
12						

Alternatively, the NPV can be found using the NPV function in Excel. First click on "Formulas," then "Financial," then "NPV." Next input the hurdle rate (12%) and highlight the array of yearly cash flows to find their present value. Finally, subtract the $9 million initial investment. Note that the NPV will be slightly different ($366,837) than shown above ($368,500) because the PV factors in the table are rounded to three decimal points.

2. Since the NPV is positive when a hurdle rate of 12% is used, the IRR must be higher than 12%. If we calculate the NPV using a hurdle rate of 14%, the NPV is negative, meaning the IRR is less than 14%. Thus, the IRR is somewhere between 12% and 14%. Alternatively, the IRR can be found using the IRR function in Excel. First click on "Formulas," then "Financial," then "IRR." Next highlight the array of numbers that first contains the initial investment as a negative cash flow (–9,000,000) and then contains the yearly cash flows shown above. The IRR is displayed as 13.126%.

3. The solar panel proposal meets all of the company's capital investment decisions. It has a payback of less than five years, and an ARR greater than 10%, and an IRR of over 12%. Therefore, the solar panels appear to be a good capital investment from both a financial and environmental standpoint.

Appendix 12A

Present Value Tables and Future Value Tables

Table A Present Value of $1

Present Value of $1

Periods	1%	2%	3%	4%	5%	6%	8%	10%	12%	14%	16%	18%	20%
1	0.990	0.980	0.971	0.962	0.952	0.943	0.926	0.909	0.893	0.877	0.862	0.847	0.833
2	0.980	0.961	0.943	0.925	0.907	0.890	0.857	0.826	0.797	0.769	0.743	0.718	0.694
3	0.971	0.942	0.915	0.889	0.864	0.840	0.794	0.751	0.712	0.675	0.641	0.609	0.579
4	0.961	0.924	0.888	0.855	0.823	0.792	0.735	0.683	0.636	0.592	0.552	0.516	0.482
5	0.951	0.906	0.863	0.822	0.784	0.747	0.681	0.621	0.567	0.519	0.476	0.437	0.402
6	0.942	0.888	0.837	0.790	0.746	0.705	0.630	0.564	0.507	0.456	0.410	0.370	0.335
7	0.933	0.871	0.813	0.760	0.711	0.665	0.583	0.513	0.452	0.400	0.354	0.314	0.279
8	0.923	0.853	0.789	0.731	0.677	0.627	0.540	0.467	0.404	0.351	0.305	0.266	0.233
9	0.914	0.837	0.766	0.703	0.645	0.592	0.500	0.424	0.361	0.308	0.263	0.225	0.194
10	0.905	0.820	0.744	0.676	0.614	0.558	0.463	0.386	0.322	0.270	0.227	0.191	0.162
11	0.896	0.804	0.722	0.650	0.585	0.527	0.429	0.350	0.287	0.237	0.195	0.162	0.135
12	0.887	0.788	0.701	0.625	0.557	0.497	0.397	0.319	0.257	0.208	0.168	0.137	0.112
13	0.879	0.773	0.681	0.601	0.530	0.469	0.368	0.290	0.229	0.182	0.145	0.116	0.093
14	0.870	0.758	0.661	0.577	0.505	0.442	0.340	0.263	0.205	0.160	0.125	0.099	0.078
15	0.861	0.743	0.642	0.555	0.481	0.417	0.315	0.239	0.183	0.140	0.108	0.084	0.065
20	0.820	0.673	0.554	0.456	0.377	0.312	0.215	0.149	0.104	0.073	0.051	0.037	0.026
25	0.780	0.610	0.478	0.375	0.295	0.233	0.146	0.092	0.059	0.038	0.024	0.016	0.010
30	0.742	0.552	0.412	0.308	0.231	0.174	0.099	0.057	0.033	0.020	0.012	0.007	0.004
40	0.672	0.453	0.307	0.208	0.142	0.097	0.046	0.022	0.011	0.005	0.003	0.001	0.001

The factors in the table were generated using the following formula:

$$\text{Present value of } \$1 = \frac{1}{(1 + i)^n}$$

where:
i = annual interest rate
n = number of periods

Table B Present Value of Annuity of $1

Periods	1%	2%	3%	4%	5%	6%	8%	10%	12%	14%	16%	18%	20%
1	0.990	0.980	0.971	0.962	0.952	0.943	0.926	0.909	0.893	0.877	0.862	0.847	0.833
2	1.970	1.942	1.913	1.886	1.859	1.833	1.783	1.736	1.690	1.647	1.605	1.566	1.528
3	2.941	2.884	2.829	2.775	2.723	2.673	2.577	2.487	2.402	2.322	2.246	2.174	2.106
4	3.902	3.808	3.717	3.630	3.546	3.465	3.312	3.170	3.037	2.914	2.798	2.690	2.589
5	4.853	4.713	4.580	4.452	4.329	4.212	3.993	3.791	3.605	3.433	3.274	3.127	2.991
6	5.795	5.601	5.417	5.242	5.076	4.917	4.623	4.355	4.111	3.889	3.685	3.498	3.326
7	6.728	6.472	6.230	6.002	5.786	5.582	5.206	4.868	4.564	4.288	4.039	3.812	3.605
8	7.652	7.325	7.020	6.733	6.463	6.210	5.747	5.335	4.968	4.639	4.344	4.078	3.837
9	8.566	8.162	7.786	7.435	7.108	6.802	6.247	5.759	5.328	4.946	4.607	4.303	4.031
10	9.471	8.983	8.530	8.111	7.722	7.360	6.710	6.145	5.650	5.216	4.833	4.494	4.192
11	10.368	9.787	9.253	8.760	8.306	7.887	7.139	6.495	5.938	5.553	5.029	4.656	4.327
12	11.255	10.575	9.954	9.385	8.863	8.384	7.536	6.814	6.194	5.660	5.197	4.793	4.439
13	12.134	11.348	10.635	9.986	9.394	8.853	7.904	7.103	6.424	5.842	5.342	4.910	4.533
14	13.004	12.106	11.296	10.563	9.899	9.295	8.244	7.367	6.628	6.002	5.468	5.008	4.611
15	13.865	12.849	11.938	11.118	10.380	9.712	8.559	7.606	6.811	6.142	5.575	5.092	4.675
20	18.046	16.351	14.878	13.590	12.462	11.470	9.818	8.514	7.469	6.623	5.929	5.353	4.870
25	22.023	19.523	17.413	15.622	14.094	12.783	10.675	9.077	7.843	6.873	6.097	5.467	4.948
30	25.808	22.396	19.600	17.292	15.373	13.765	11.258	9.427	8.055	7.003	6.177	5.517	4.979
40	32.835	27.355	23.115	19.793	17.159	15.046	11.925	9.779	8.244	7.105	6.234	5.548	4.997

The factors in the table were generated using the following formula:

$$\text{Present value of annuity of } \$1 = \frac{1}{i}\left[1 - \frac{1}{(1+i)^n}\right]$$

where:

i = annual interest rate

n = number of periods

Table C Future Value of $1

| | | | | | | Future Value of $1 | | | | | | | |
Periods	1%	2%	3%	4%	5%	6%	8%	10%	12%	14%	16%	18%	20%
1	1.010	1.020	1.030	1.040	1.050	1.060	1.080	1.100	1.120	1.140	1.160	1.180	1.200
2	1.020	1.040	1.061	1.082	1.103	1.124	1.166	1.210	1.254	1.300	1.346	1.392	1.440
3	1.030	1.061	1.093	1.125	1.158	1.191	1.260	1.331	1.405	1.482	1.561	1.643	1.728
4	1.041	1.082	1.126	1.170	1.216	1.262	1.360	1.464	1.574	1.689	1.811	1.939	2.074
5	1.051	1.104	1.159	1.217	1.276	1.338	1.469	1.611	1.762	1.925	2.100	2.288	2.488
6	1.062	1.126	1.194	1.265	1.340	1.419	1.587	1.772	1.974	2.195	2.436	2.700	2.986
7	1.072	1.149	1.230	1.316	1.407	1.504	1.714	1.949	2.211	2.502	2.826	3.185	3.583
8	1.083	1.172	1.267	1.369	1.477	1.594	1.851	2.144	2.476	2.853	3.278	3.759	4.300
9	1.094	1.195	1.305	1.423	1.551	1.689	1.999	2.358	2.773	3.252	3.803	4.435	5.160
10	1.105	1.219	1.344	1.480	1.629	1.791	2.159	2.594	3.106	3.707	4.411	5.234	6.192
11	1.116	1.243	1.384	1.539	1.710	1.898	2.332	2.853	3.479	4.226	5.117	6.176	7.430
12	1.127	1.268	1.426	1.601	1.796	2.012	2.518	3.138	3.896	4.818	5.936	7.288	8.916
13	1.138	1.294	1.469	1.665	1.886	2.133	2.720	3.452	4.363	5.492	6.886	8.599	10.669
14	1.149	1.319	1.513	1.732	1.980	2.261	2.937	3.798	4.887	6.261	7.988	10.147	12.839
15	1.161	1.346	1.558	1.801	2.079	2.397	3.172	4.177	5.474	7.138	9.266	11.974	15.407
20	1.220	1.486	1.806	2.191	2.653	3.207	4.661	6.728	9.646	13.743	19.461	27.393	38.338
25	1.282	1.641	2.094	2.666	3.386	4.292	6.848	10.835	17.000	26.462	40.874	62.669	95.396
30	1.348	1.811	2.427	3.243	4.322	5.743	10.063	17.449	29.960	50.950	85.850	143.371	237.376
40	1.489	2.208	3.262	4.801	7.040	10.286	21.725	45.259	93.051	188.884	378.721	750.378	1,469.772

The factors in the table were generated using the following formula:

Future value of $1 = (1 + i)^n$

where:

i = annual interest rate

n = number of periods

Table D Future Value of Annuity of $1

					Future Value of Annuity of $1								
Periods	1%	2%	3%	4%	5%	6%	8%	10%	12%	14%	16%	18%	20%
1	1.000	1.000	1.000	1.000	1.000	1.000	1.000	1.000	1.000	1.000	1.000	1.000	1.000
2	2.010	2.020	2.030	2.040	2.050	2.060	2.080	2.100	2.120	2.140	2.160	2.180	2.200
3	3.030	3.060	3.091	3.122	3.153	3.184	3.246	3.310	3.374	3.440	3.506	3.572	3.640
4	4.060	4.122	4.184	4.246	4.310	4.375	4.506	4.641	4.779	4.921	5.066	5.215	5.368
5	5.101	5.204	5.309	5.416	5.526	5.637	5.867	6.105	6.353	6.610	6.877	7.154	7.442
6	6.152	6.308	6.468	6.633	6.802	6.975	7.336	7.716	8.115	8.536	8.977	9.442	9.930
7	7.214	7.434	7.662	7.898	8.142	8.394	8.923	9.487	10.089	10.730	11.414	12.142	12.916
8	8.286	8.583	8.892	9.214	9.549	9.897	10.637	11.436	12.300	13.233	14.240	15.327	16.499
9	9.369	9.755	10.159	10.583	11.027	11.491	12.488	13.579	14.776	16.085	17.519	19.086	20.799
10	10.462	10.950	11.464	12.006	12.578	13.181	14.487	15.937	17.549	19.337	21.321	23.521	25.959
11	11.567	12.169	12.808	13.486	14.207	14.972	16.645	18.531	20.655	23.045	25.733	28.755	32.150
12	12.683	13.412	14.192	15.026	15.917	16.870	18.977	21.384	24.133	27.271	30.850	34.931	39.581
13	13.809	14.680	15.618	16.627	17.713	18.882	21.495	24.523	28.029	32.089	36.786	42.219	48.497
14	14.947	15.974	17.086	18.292	19.599	21.015	24.215	27.975	32.393	37.581	43.672	50.818	59.196
15	16.097	17.293	18.599	20.024	21.579	23.276	27.152	31.772	37.280	43.842	51.660	60.965	72.035
20	22.019	24.297	26.870	29.778	33.066	36.786	45.762	57.275	72.052	91.025	115.380	146.630	186.690
25	28.243	32.030	36.459	41.646	47.727	54.865	73.106	98.347	133.330	181.870	249.210	342.600	471.980
30	34.785	40.568	47.575	56.085	66.439	79.058	113.280	164.490	241.330	356.790	530.310	790.950	1,181.900
40	48.886	60.402	75.401	95.026	120.800	154.760	259.060	442.590	767.090	1,342.000	2,360.800	4,163.200	7,343.900

The factors in the table were generated using the following formula:

$$\text{Future value of annuity of } \$1 = \frac{(1 + i)^n - 1}{i}$$

where:
i = annual interest rate
n = number of periods

Appendix 12B

Solutions to Chapter Examples Using Microsoft Excel

Technology Makes it Simple	Excel 2007, 2010, and 2013

Future Value Examples from Chapter

Example 1: Future Value of a Lump Sum

Let's use our lump-sum investment example from page 714 of the text. Assume that you invest $10,000 for five years at an interest rate of 6%. Use the following procedure to find its future value five years from now:

1. In an Excel spreadsheet click on **Formulas**.
2. Click on **Financial**.
3. Choose **FV** from the dropdown list. The following will appear as a dialog box. Fill in the variables as follows:

   Rate = **.06**

   Nper = **5**

   Pmt = (leave blank since this is used for annuities)

   PV = **−10000** (the negative sign indicates that the amount is a cash outflow, not inflow)

   Type = (leave blank)

4. The future value now appears under the dialog box as = **$13,382.26** (rounded).

Example 2: Future Value of an Annuity

Let's use the annuity investment example from page 714 of the text. Assume that you invest $2,000 at the end of each year for five years. The investment earns 6% interest. Use the following procedures to find the investment's future value five years from now.

1. In an Excel spreadsheet click on **Formulas**.
2. Click on **Financial**.
3. Choose **FV** from the dropdown list. The following will appear as a dialog box. Fill in the variables as follows:

   Rate = **.06**

   Nper = **5**

   Pmt = **−2000** (the negative sign indicates that the amount is a cash outflow, not inflow)

   PV = (leave blank because this is used for lump-sum amounts)

   Type = (leave blank)

4. The future value now appears under the dialog box as = **$11,274.19** (rounded).

Present Value Examples from Chapter

Example 1: Present Value of an Annuity—Lottery Option #2

Let's use the lottery payout Option #2 from page 716 of the text for our example. Option #2 was to receive $150,000 at the end of each year for the next 10 years. The interest rate was assumed to be 8%. Use the following procedures to find the present value of the payout option:

1. In an Excel spreadsheet click on **Formulas**.
2. Click on **Financial**.
3. Choose **PV** from the dropdown list. The following will appear as a dialog box. Fill in the variables as follows:

   Rate = **.08**

   Nper = **10**

   Pmt = **−150000**

   Fv = (leave blank since this is used for lump sums)

   Type = (leave blank)
4. The present value answer now appears under the dialog box as = **$1,006,512.21** (rounded).

Example 2: Present Value of a Lump Sum—Lottery Option #3

Let's use the lottery payout Option #3 from page 716 of the text for our example. Option #3 was to receive $2 million 10 years from now. The interest rate was assumed to be 8%. Use the following procedures to find the present value of the payout option:

1. In an Excel spreadsheet click on **Formulas**.
2. Click on **Financial**.
3. Choose **PV** from the dropdown list. The following will appear as a dialog box. Fill in the variables as follows:

   Rate = **.08**

   Nper = **10**

   Pmt = (leave blank since this is used for annuities)

   FV = **−2000000**

   Type = (leave blank)
4. The present value answer now appears under the dialog box as = **$926,386.98** (rounded).

NPV Examples from Chapter

Example 1: NPV of Allegra's MP3 Project—An Annuity

Recall from page 720 of the text that the MP3 project required an investment of $1 million and was expected to generate equal net cash inflows of $305,450 each year for five years. The company's discount rate was 14%.

1. In an Excel spreadsheet, type in the future cash flows expected from the investment in the order in which they are expected to be received. Your spreadsheet should show five consecutive cells as follows: 305450, 305450, 305450, 305450, 305450.
2. Click on **Formulas**.
3. Click on **Financial**.

4. Choose **NPV** from the dropdown list. The following will appear as a dialog box. Fill in the variables as follows:

   Rate = .14

   Value 1 = (Highlight array of cells containing the cash flow data from Step 1)

5. The present value of the cash flows appears at the bottom of the dialog box as = **1,048,634.58**.

6. Finally, subtract the initial cost of the investment ($1 million) to obtain the NPV = **$48,634.58**.

Example 2: NPV of Allegra's DVR Project—Unequal Cash Flows

Recall from page 721 of the text that the DVR project required an investment of $1 million and was expected to generate the unequal periodic cash inflows shown in Exhibit 12-11. The company's discount rate was 14%.

1. In an Excel spreadsheet, type in the future cash flows expected from the investment in the order in which they are expected to be received. Your spreadsheet should show five consecutive cells with the following values in them: 500000, 350000, 300000, 250000, 40000.

2. Click on **Formulas**.

3. Click on **Financial**.

4. Choose **NPV** from the dropdown list. The following will appear as a dialog box. Fill in the variables as follows:

   Rate = .14

   Value 1 = (Highlight array of cells containing the cash flow data from Step 1)

5. The present value of the cash flows appears at the bottom of the dialog box as = **1,079,196.40 (rounded)**.

6. Finally, subtract the initial cost of the investment ($1 million) to obtain the NPV = **$79,196.40** (rounded).

Example 3: NPV of an Investment with a Residual Value

If an investment has a residual value, simply add the residual value as an additional cash inflow in the year in which it is to be received. For example, assume as we did in Exhibit 12-13 on page 723 that the MP3 project equipment will be worth $100,000 at the end of its five-year life. This represents an additional expected cash inflow to the company in Year 5.

1. In an Excel spreadsheet, type in the future cash flows expected from the investment in the order in which they are expected to be received. Your spreadsheet should show five consecutive cells with the following values in them: 305450, 305450, 305450, 305450, 405350

2. Click on **Formulas**.

3. Click on **Financial**.

4. Choose **NPV** from the dropdown list. The following will appear as a dialog box. Fill in the variables as follows:

   Rate = .14

   Value 1 = (Highlight array of cells containing the cash flow data from Step 1)

5. The present value of the cash flows appears at the bottom of the dialog box as = **1,100,571.45 (rounded)**.

6. Finally, subtract the initial cost of the investment ($1 million) to obtain the NPV = **$100,571.45** (rounded).

IRR Examples from Chapter

Example 1: IRR of Allegra's MP3 Project—An Annuity

Recall from page 725, that the MP3 project required an investment of $1 million and was expected to generate equal net cash inflows of $305,450 each year for five years.

1. In an Excel spreadsheet, first type in the initial investment as a negative number and then type in the future cash flows expected from the investment in the order in which they are expected to be received. Your spreadsheet should show the following consecutive cells: **−1000000, 305450, 305450, 305450, 305450, 305450.**
2. Click on **Formulas**.
3. Click on **Financial**.
4. Choose **IRR** from the dropdown list. The following will appear as a dialog box. Fill in the variables as follows:

   Value 1 = (Highlight array of cells containing the data from Step 1)
5. The IRR appears at the bottom of the dialog box as = **16.01% (rounded).**

Example 2: IRR of Allegra's DVR Project—Unequal Cash Flows

Recall from page 726, that the DVR project required an investment of $1 million and was expected to generate the unequal periodic cash inflows shown in Exhibit 12-11.

1. In an Excel spreadsheet, first type in the initial investment as a negative number and then type in the future cash flows expected from the investment in the order in which they are expected to be received. Your spreadsheet should show the following consecutive cells: **−1000000, 500000, 350000, 300000, 250000, 40000.**
2. Click on **Formulas**.
3. Click on **Financial**.
4. Choose **IRR** from the dropdown list. The following will appear as a dialog box. Fill in the variables as follows:

   Value 1 = (Highlight array of cells containing the data from Step 1)
5. The IRR appears at the bottom of the dialog box as = **18.23% (rounded).**

Example 3: IRR of an Investment with a Residual Value

If an investment has a residual value, simply add the residual value as an additional cash inflow in the year in which it is to be received. For example, assume as we did in Exhibit 12-13 on page 723 that the MP3 project equipment will be worth $100,000 at the end of its five-year life. This represents an additional expected cash inflow to the company in Year 5.

1. In an Excel spreadsheet, type in the future cash flows expected from the investment in the order in which they are expected to be received. Your spreadsheet should show six consecutive cells with the following values in them: **−1000000, 305450, 305450, 305450, 305450, 405350.**
2. Click on **Formulas**.
3. Click on **Financial**.
4. Choose **IRR** from the dropdown list. The following will appear as a dialog box. Fill in the variables as follows:

   Value 1 = (Highlight array of cells containing the data from Step 1)
5. The IRR appears at the bottom of the dialog box as = **17.95% (rounded).**

Appendix 12C

Using a TI-83, TI-83 Plus, TI-84, or TI-84 Plus Calculator to Perform Time Value of Money Calculations

Technology Makes it Simple

Time Value of Money Calculations

Using a TI-83, TI-83 Plus, TI-84, or TI-84 Plus Calculator to Perform Time Value of Money Calculations

Steps to perform basic present value and future value calculations:

1. On the TI-83 Plus or TI-84 Plus: Press [APPS] *to show the applications menu.*

   On the TI-83 or TI-84: Press [2nd] [X^{-1}] [ENTER] *to show the applications menu.*

2. Choose **Finance** *to see the finance applications menu.*

3. Choose **TVM solver** *to obtain the list of time value of money (TVM) variables:*

   N = *number of periods (years)*

   I% = *interest rate per year* (**do not convert percentage to a decimal**)

   PV = *present value*

   PMT = *amount of each annuity installment*

   FV = *future value*

   P/Y = *number of compounding periods per year* (**leave setting at 1**)

   C/Y = *number of coupons per year* (**leave setting at 1**)

   PMT: **End** *or* Begin *(leave setting on* **End** *to denote an ordinary annuity)*

4. **Enter the known variables** and **set all unknown variables to zero** (except P/Y and C/Y, which need to be left set at 1).

5. To compute the unknown variable, scroll to the line for the variable you want to solve and then press [ALPHA] [ENTER].

6. The answer will now appear on the calculator.

7. Press [2nd] [QUIT] *to exit the TVM solver when you are finished.* **If you would like to do more TVM calculations, you do not need to exit. Simply repeat Steps 4 and 5 using the new data.**

Comments:

i. The order in which you input the variables does not matter.

ii. The answer will be shown as a negative number unless you input the original cash flow data as a negative number. **Use the [(-)] key to enter a negative number, not the minus key; otherwise you will get an error message.** The calculator follows a cash flow sign convention that assumes that all positive figures are cash inflows and all negative figures are cash outflows.

iii. The answers you get will vary slightly from those found using the PV and FV tables in Appendix A. Why? Because the PV and FV factors in the tables have been rounded to three digits.

Example 1: Future Value of a Lump Sum

Let's use our lump-sum investment example from the text. Assume that you invest $10,000 for five years at an interest rate of 6%. Use the following procedure to find its future value five years from now:

1. On the TI-83 Plus or TI-84 Plus: Press [APPS] *to show the applications menu.*

   On the TI-83 or TI-84: Press [2nd] [X^{-1}] [ENTER] *to show the applications menu.*

2. Choose **Finance** *to see the finance applications menu.*

3. Choose **TVM solver** *to obtain the list of time value of money (TVM) variables.*

4. Fill in the variables as follows:

   N = **5**

   I% = **6**

   PV = **−10000** *(Be sure to use the negative number (−) key, not the minus sign.)*

   PMT = **0**

   FV = **0**

   P/Y = 1

   C/Y = 1

   PMT: **End** or Begin

5. To compute the unknown future value, scroll down to **FV** and press [ALPHA] [ENTER].

6. The answer will now appear as **FV = 13,382.26** (rounded).

If you forgot to enter the $10,000 principal as a negative number (in Step 4), the FV will be displayed as a negative.

Example 2: Future Value of an Annuity

Let's use the annuity investment example from the text. Assume that you invest $2,000 at the end of each year for five years. The investment earns 6% interest. Use the following procedure to find the investment's future value five years from now:

1. On the TI-83 Plus or TI-84 Plus: Press [APPS] *to show the applications menu.*

   On the TI-83 or TI-84: Press [2nd] [X^{-1}] [ENTER] *to show the applications menu.*

2. Choose **Finance** *to see the finance applications menu.*

3. Choose **TVM solver** *to obtain the list of time value of money (TVM) variables.*

4. Fill in the variables as follows:

   N = **5**

   I% = **6**

   PV = **0**

   PMT = **−2000** *(Be sure to use the negative number (−) key, not the minus sign.)*

   FV = **0**

   P/Y = 1

   C/Y = 1

   PMT: **End** or Begin

5. To compute the unknown future value, scroll down to **FV** and press [ALPHA] [ENTER].

6. The answer will now appear as **FV = 11,274.19 (rounded)**.

If you forgot to enter the $2,000 annuity as a negative number (in Step 4), the FV will be displayed as a negative.

Example 3: Present Value of an Annuity—Lottery Option #2

Let's use the lottery payout Option #2 from the text for our example. Option #2 was to receive $150,000 at the end of each year for the next ten years. The interest rate was assumed to be 8%. Use the following procedure to find the present value of this payout option:

1. On the TI-83 Plus or TI-84 Plus: Press [APPS] *to show the applications menu.*

   On the TI-83 or TI-84: Press [2nd] [X^{-1}] [ENTER] *to show the applications menu.*

2. Choose **Finance** *to see the finance applications menu.*

3. Choose **TVM solver** *to obtain the list of time value of money (TVM) variables.*
4. Fill in the variables as follows:

   N = **10**
   I% = **8**
   PV = **0**
   PMT = **−150000** *(Be sure to use the negative number (−) key, not the minus sign.)*
   FV = **0**
   P/Y = **1**
   C/Y = **1**
   PMT: **End** or Begin

5. To compute the unknown future value, scroll down to **PV** and press [ALPHA] [ENTER].
6. The answer will now appear as **PV = 1,006,512.21** (rounded).

Had we not entered the annuity as a negative figure, the present value would have been shown as a negative.

Example 4: Present Value of a Lump Sum—Lottery Option #3

Let's use the lottery payout Option #3 from the text as our example. Option #3 was to receive $2 million ten years from now. The interest rate was assumed to be 8%. Use the following procedure to find the present value of this payout option:

1. On the TI-83 Plus or TI-84 Plus: Press [APPS] *to show the applications menu.*

   On the TI-83 or TI-84: Press [2nd] [X⁻¹] [ENTER] *to show the applications menu.*
2. Choose **Finance** *to see the finance applications menu.*
3. Choose **TVM solver** *to obtain the list of time value of money (TVM) variables.*
4. Fill in the variables as follows:

   N = **10**
   I% = **8**
   PV = **0**
   PMT = **0**
   FV = **−2000000** *(Be sure to use the negative number (-) key, not the minus sign.)*
   P/Y = **1**
   C/Y = **1**

5. PMT: **End** or Begin
6. To compute the unknown future value, scroll down to **PV** and press [ALPHA] [ENTER].
7. The answer will now appear as **PV = 926,386.98** (rounded).

Had we not entered the $2 million future cash flow as a negative, the present value would have been shown as a negative.

Technology Makes it Simple

NPV Calculations

Using a TI-83, TI-83 Plus, TI-84, or TI-84 Plus calculator to perform NPV calculations

Steps to performing NPV calculations:

If you are currently in the TVM solver mode, exit by pressing [2nd] [Quit].

1. On the TI-83 Plus or TI-84 Plus: Press [APPS] *to show the applications menu.*

   On the TI-83 or TI-84: Press [2nd] [X⁻¹] [ENTER] *to show the applications menu.*
2. Choose **Finance** *to see the finance applications menu.*

3. Choose **npv** *to obtain the NPV prompt:* **npv(**.

4. Fill in the following information, paying close attention to using the correct symbols: **npv (hurdle rate, initial investment***, {cash flow in Year 1, cash flow in Year 2, etc.})**

5. To compute the NPV, press [ENTER].

6. The answer will now appear on the calculator.

7. To exit the worksheet, press [CLEAR]. Alternatively, if you would like to change any of the assumptions for sensitivity analysis, you may press [2nd] [ENTER] to recall the formula, edit any of the values, and then recompute the new NPV by pressing [ENTER].

Note: If you would like to find just the present value (not the NPV) of a stream of unequal cash flows, use a zero (0) for the initial investment.

Example 1: NPV of Allegra's MP3 Project—An Annuity

Recall that the MP3 project required an investment of $1 million and was expected to generate equal net cash inflows of $305,450 each year for five years. The company's discount, or hurdle rate, was 14%.

1. On the TI-83 Plus or TI-84 Plus: Press [APPS] *to show the applications menu.*

   On the TI-83 or TI-84: Press [2nd] [X⁻¹] [ENTER] *to show the applications menu.*

2. Choose **Finance** *to see the finance applications menu.*

3. Choose **npv** *to obtain the NPV prompt:* **npv(**.

4. Fill in the following information, paying close attention to using the correct symbols:

   npv (14, −1000000, {305450, 305450, 305450, 305450, 305450}) *(Be sure to use the negative number (−) key, not the minus sign.)*

5. To compute the NPV, press [ENTER].

6. The answer will now appear on the calculator: **48,634.58** (rounded).

7. [CLEAR] the worksheet or recall it [2nd] [ENTER] for sensitivity analysis.

Example 2: NPV of Allegra's DVR Project—Unequal Cash Flows

Recall that the DVR project required an investment of $1 million and was expected to generate the unequal periodic cash inflows shown in Exhibit 12-11.

1. On the TI-83 Plus or TI-84 Plus: Press [APPS] *to show the applications menu.*

   On the TI-83 or TI-84: Press [2nd] [X⁻¹] [ENTER] *to show the applications menu.*

2. Choose **Finance** *to see the finance applications menu.*

3. Choose **npv** *to obtain the NPV prompt:* **npv(**.

4. Fill in the following information, paying close attention to using the correct symbols:

   npv (14, −1000000, {500000, 350000, 300000, 250000, 40000}) *(Be sure to use the negative number (−) key, not the minus sign.)*

5. To compute the NPV, press [ENTER].

6. The answer will now appear on the calculator: **79,196.40** (rounded).

7. [CLEAR] the worksheet or recall it [2nd] [ENTER] for sensitivity analysis.

Example 3: Investment with a Residual Value

If an investment has a residual value, simply add the residual value as an additional cash inflow in the year in which it is to be received. For example, assume as we did in Exhibit 12-13 that the MP3 project equipment will be worth $100,000 at the end of its five-year life. This represents an additional expected cash inflow to the company in Year 5, so we'll show the cash inflow in Year 5 to be $405,450 (= $305,450 + $100,000).

1. On the TI-83 Plus or TI-84 Plus: Press [APPS] *to show the applications menu.*

   On the TI-83 or TI-84: Press [2nd] [X⁻¹] [ENTER] *to show the applications menu.*

2. Choose **Finance** *to see the finance applications menu.*

---

* *The initial investment must be entered as a negative number.*

3. Choose **npv** *to obtain the NPV prompt:* **npv(**

4. Fill in the following information, paying close attention to using the correct symbols:

   npv (14, −1000000, {305450, 305450, 305450, 305450, 405450}) *(Be sure to use the negative number (-) key, not the minus sign.)*

5. To compute the NPV, press [ENTER].

6. The answer will now appear on the calculator: **100,571.45** (rounded).

7. [CLEAR] the worksheet or recall it [2nd] [ENTER] for sensitivity analysis.

Technology Makes it Simple

IRR Calculations
Using a TI-83, TI-83 Plus, TI-84, or TI-84 Plus calculator to perform IRR calculations

The procedure for finding the IRR is virtually identical to the procedure used to find the NPV. The only differences are that we choose IRR rather than NPV from the Finance menu and we don't insert a given hurdle rate.

Steps to performing IRR calculations:

If you are currently in the TVM solver mode, exit by pressing [2nd] [Quit].

1. On the TI-83 Plus or TI-84 Plus: Press [APPS] *to show the applications menu.*

   On the TI-83 or TI-84: Press [2nd] [X⁻¹] [ENTER] *to show the applications menu.*

2. Choose **Finance** *to see the finance applications menu.*

3. Choose **irr** *to obtain the IRR prompt:* **irr(**.

4. Fill in the following information, paying close attention to using the correct symbols:
   irr (initial investment*, {cash flow in Year 1, cash flow in Year 2, etc.})

5. To compute the IRR press [ENTER].

6. The answer will now appear on the calculator.

7. To exit the worksheet, press [CLEAR]. Alternatively, if you would like to change any of the assumptions for sensitivity analysis, you may press [2nd] [ENTER] to recall the formula, edit any of the values, and then recompute the new IRR by pressing [ENTER].

Example 1: IRR of Allegra's MP3 Project—An Annuity
Recall that the MP3 project required an investment of $1 million and was expected to generate equal net cash inflows of $305,450 each year for five years. Use the following procedure to find the investment's IRR:

1. On the TI-83 Plus or TI-84 Plus: Press [APPS] *to show the applications menu.*

   On the TI-83 or TI-84: Press [2nd] [X⁻¹] [ENTER] *to show the applications menu.*

2. Choose **Finance** *to see the finance applications menu.*

3. Choose **irr** *to obtain the IRR prompt:* **irr(**.

4. Fill in the following information, paying close attention to using the correct symbols:
   irr (−1000000, {305450, 305450, 305450, 305450, 305450}) *(Be sure to use the negative number (−) key, not the minus sign.)*

5. To compute the IRR, press [ENTER].

6. The answer will now appear on the calculator: **16.01** (rounded).

7. [CLEAR] the worksheet or recall it [2nd] [ENTER] for sensitivity analysis.

---

* *The initial investment must be entered as a negative number.*

Example 2: IRR of Allegra's DVR Project—Unequal Cash Flows

Recall that the DVR project required an investment of $1 million and was expected to generate the unequal periodic cash inflows shown in Exhibit 12-11. Use the following procedures to find the investment's IRR:

1. On the TI-83 Plus or TI-84 Plus: Press [APPS] *to show the applications menu.*

   On the TI-83 or TI-84: Press [2nd] [X^{-1}] [ENTER] *to show the applications menu.*

2. Choose **Finance** *to see the finance applications menu.*

3. Choose **irr** *to obtain the IRR prompt:* **irr(**.

4. Fill in the following information, paying close attention to using the correct symbols:

   irr (−1000000, {500000, 350000, 300000, 250000, 40000}) *(Be sure to use the negative number (−) key, not the minus sign.)*

5. To compute the IRR, press [ENTER].

6. The answer will now appear on the calculator: **18.23** (rounded).

7. [CLEAR] the worksheet or recall it [2nd] [ENTER] for sensitivity analysis.

Example 3: Investment with a Residual Value

If an investment has a residual value, simply add the residual value as an additional cash inflow in the year in which it is to be received. For example, assume as we did in Exhibit 12-13 that the MP3 project equipment will be worth $100,000 at the end of its five-year life. This represents an additional expected cash inflow to the company in Year 5, so we'll show the cash inflow in Year 5 to be $405,450 (= $305,450 + $100,000).

1. On the TI-83 Plus or TI-84 Plus: Press [APPS] *to show the applications menu.*

   On the TI-83 or TI-84: Press [2nd] [X^{-1}] [ENTER] *to show the applications menu.*

2. Choose **Finance** *to see the finance applications menu.*

3. Choose **irr** *to obtain the IRR prompt:* **irr(**.

4. Fill in the following information, paying close attention to using the correct symbols:

   irr (−1000000, {305450, 305450, 305450, 305450, 405450}) *(Be sure to use the negative number (−) key, not the minus sign.)*

5. To compute the IRR, press [ENTER].

6. The answer will now appear on the calculator: **17.95** (rounded).

7. [CLEAR] the worksheet or recall it [2nd] [ENTER] for sensitivity analysis.

END OF CHAPTER

Learning Objectives

- 1 Describe the importance of capital investments and the capital budgeting process

- 2 Use the payback and accounting rate of return methods to make capital investment decisions

- 3 Use the time value of money to compute the present and future values of single lump sums and annuities

- 4 Use discounted cash flow models to make capital investment decisions

- 5 Compare and contrast the four capital budgeting methods

Accounting Vocabulary

Accounting Rate of Return. (p. 705) A measure of profitability computed by dividing the average annual operating income from an asset by the initial investment in the asset.

Annuity. (p. 711) A stream of equal installments made at equal time intervals.

Capital Budgeting. (p. 699) The process of making capital investment decisions. Companies make capital investments when they acquire *capital assets*—assets used for a long period of time.

Capital Rationing. (p. 700) Choosing among alternative capital investments due to limited funds.

Compound Interest. (p. 711) Interest computed on the principal *and* all interest earned to date.

Discount Rate. (p. 719) Management's minimum desired rate of return on an investment; also called the hurdle rate and required rate of return.

Hurdle Rate. (p. 719) Management's minimum desired rate of return on an investment; also called the discount rate and required rate of return.

Internal Rate of Return (IRR). (p. 724) The rate of return (based on discounted cash flows) that a company can expect to earn by investing in a capital asset. The interest rate that makes the NPV of the investment equal to zero.

LEED certification. (p. 702) LEED, which stands for "Leadership in Energy and Environmental Design," is a certification

system developed by the U.S. Green Building Council as a way of promoting and evaluating environmentally friendly construction projects.

Net Present Value (NPV). (p. 719) The *difference* between the present value of the investment's net cash inflows and the investment's cost.

Payback. (p. 702) The length of time it takes to recover, in net cash inflows, the cost of a capital outlay.

Post-Audits. (p. 701) Comparing a capital investment's actual net cash inflows to its projected net cash inflows.

Present Value Index. (p. 722) An index that computes the number of dollars returned for every dollar invested, *with all calculations performed in present value dollars*. It is computed as present value of net cash inflows divided by investment; also called profitability index.

Profitability Index. (p. 722) An index that computes the number of dollars returned for every dollar invested, *with all calculations performed in present value dollars*. Computed as present value of net cash inflows divided by investment; also called present value index.

Required Rate of Return. (p. 719) Management's minimum desired rate of return on an investment; also called the discount rate and hurdle rate.

Simple Interest. (p. 711) Interest computed *only* on the principal amount.

Time Value of Money. (p. 711) The fact that money can be invested to earn income over time.

MyAccountingLab   Go to http://myaccountinglab.com/ **for the following Quick Check, Short Exercises, Exercises, and Problems. They are available with immediate grading, explanations of correct and incorrect answers, and interactive media that acts as your own online tutor.**

Quick Check

1. (*Learning Objective 1*) Which of the following methods of analyzing capital investments factors in the time value of money?
   a. Accounting rate of return
   b. Internal rate of return
   c. Payback period
   d. All of the above methods factor in the time value of money.

2. (*Learning Objective 2*) After identifying potential capital investments, the next step in the capital budgeting process is which of the following?
   a. Analyzing potential investments through at least one of the four methods
   b. Estimating the future net cash inflows of the investments
   c. Performing post-audits of the capital investments
   d. Engaging in capital rationing

3. (*Learning Objective 2*) Which of the following is *false* with regard to the payback period?
   a. It is computed as follows, regardless of whether cash flows are equal or unequal: Initial investment ÷ Expected annual net cash inflow.
   b. The payback period is the length of time it takes to recover the initial cost of the capital investment.
   c. The payback period gives no indication of the investment's profitability.
   d. All else being equal, a shorter payback period is more desirable than a longer payback period.

4. (*Learning Objective 2*) Which of the following methods focuses on the operating income an asset generates rather than the net cash inflows it generates?
   a. Payback period
   b. Accounting rate of return
   c. Net present value
   d. Internal rate of return

5. (*Learning Objective 2*) In order to convert the *average annual net cash inflow* from the asset back to the *average annual operating income* from the asset, one must
   a. subtract annual depreciation expense.
   b. add annual depreciation expense.
   c. divide by annual depreciation expense.
   d. multiply by annual depreciation expense.

6. (*Learning Objective 3*) The time value of money depends on which of the following factors?
   a. Principal amount
   b. Number of periods
   c. Interest rate
   d. All of the above

7. (*Learning Objective 4*) The internal rate of return is which of the following?
   a. The interest rate that makes the NPV of an investment equal to zero
   b. The amount of time it takes to recoup the initial investment
   c. The internal management's minimum required rate of return
   d. The accounting rate of return minus 1%

8. (*Learning Objective 4*) An investment's NPV is calculated as which of the following?
   a. The investment's initial investment minus the present value of the investment
   b. The future value of the investment minus the investment's initial investment
   c. The investment's initial investment minus the future value of the investment
   d. The present value of the investment minus the investment's initial investment

9. (*Learning Objective 4*) When potential capital investments of different size are compared, management should choose the one with the
   a. highest NPV.
   b. lowest NPV.
   c. highest profitability index.
   d. lowest IRR.

10. (*Learning Objective 5*) Which of the following methods calculates the investment's unique rate of return?
    a. Payback period
    b. Net present value
    c. Internal rate of return
    d. Accounting rate of return

Quick Check Answers

1.b 2.b 3.a 4.b 5.a 6.d 7.a 8.d 9.c 10.c

Short Exercises

S12-1 Order the capital budgeting process *(Learning Objective 1)*

Place the following activities in order from first to last to illustrate the capital budgeting process:

  a. Budget capital investments
  b. Project investments' cash flows
  c. Perform post-audits
  d. Make investments
  e. Use feedback to reassess investments already made
  f. Identify potential capital investments
  g. Screen/analyze investments using one or more of the methods discussed

Arpegio Products Data Set used for S12-2 through S12-5:

Arpegio Products is considering producing MP3 players and digital video recorders (DVRs). The products require different specialized machines, each costing $1 million. Each machine has a five-year life and zero residual value. The two products have different patterns of predicted net cash inflows:

Year	Annual Net Cash Inflows	
	MP3 Players	**DVRs**
1	$ 371,500	$ 530,000
2	371,500	390,000
3	371,500	330,000
4	371,500	270,000
5	371,500	25,000
Total	$1,857,500	$1,545,000

Arpegio will consider making capital investments only if the payback period of the project is less than 3.5 years and the ARR exceeds 8%.

S12-2 Compute payback period—equal cash inflows *(Learning Objective 2)*

Refer to the Arpegio Products Data Set. Calculate the MP3 player project's payback period. If the MP3 project had a residual value of $100,000, would the payback period change? Explain and recalculate if necessary. Does this investment pass Arpegio's payback period screening rule?

S12-3 Compute payback period—unequal cash inflows *(Learning Objective 2)*

Refer to the Arpegio Products Data Set. Calculate the DVR project's payback period. If the DVR project had a residual value of $100,000, would the payback period change? Explain and recalculate if necessary. Does this investment pass Arpegio's payback period screening rule?

S12-4 Compute ARR—equal cash inflows *(Learning Objective 2)*

Refer to the Arpegio Products Data Set. Calculate the MP3-player project's ARR. If the MP3 project had a residual value of $100,000, would the ARR change? Explain and recalculate if necessary. Does this investment pass Arpegio's ARR screening rule?

S12-5 Compute ARR—unequal cash inflows *(Learning Objective 2)*

Refer to the Arpegio Products Data Set. Calculate the DVR project's ARR. If the DVR project had a residual value of $100,000, would the ARR change? Explain and recalculate if necessary. Does this investment pass Arpegio's ARR screening rule?

S12-6 Compute annual cash savings *(Learning Objective 2)*

Suppose Arpegio Products is deciding whether to invest in a DVD-HD project. The payback period for the $8 million investment is four years, and the project's expected life is seven years. What equal annual net cash inflows are expected from this project?

S12-7   Find the present values of future cash flows (Learning Objective 3)

Your aunt would like to share some of her fortune with you. She offers to give you money under one of the following scenarios (you get to choose):

1. $8,550 a year at the end of each of the next eight years
2. $50,250 (lump sum) now
3. $99,350 (lump sum) eight years from now

Calculate the present value of each scenario using a 8% interest rate. Which scenario yields the highest present value? Would your preference change if you used a 12% interest rate?

S12-8   Show how timing affects future values (Learning Objective 3)

Assume that you make the following investments:

a. You invest a lump sum of $8,750 for five years at 12% interest. What is the investment's value at the end of five years?

b. In a different account earning 12% interest, you invest $1,750 at the end of each year for five years. What is the investment's value at the end of five years?

c. What general rule of thumb explains the difference in the investments' future values?

S12-9   Compare payout options at their future values (Learning Objective 3)

Listed below are three lottery payout options.

> Option 1: $975,000 now
>
> Option 2: $153,000 at the end of each year for the next nine years
>
> Option 3: $1,550,000 nine years from now

Rather than compare the payout options at their present values (as is done in the chapter), compare the payout options at their future value ten years from now.

a. Using an 6% interest rate, what is the future value of each payout option?

b. Rank your preference of payout options.

c. Does computing the future value rather than the present value of the options change your preference of payout options? Explain.

S12-10   Relationship between the PV tables (Learning Objective 3)

Use the Present Value of $1 table (Appendix 12A, Table A) to determine the present value of $1 received one year from now. Assume a 10% interest rate. Use the same table to find the present value of $1 received two years from now. Continue this process for a total of five years.

a. What is the *total* present value of the cash flows received over the five-year period?

b. Could you characterize this stream of cash flows as an annuity? Why or why not?

c. Use the Present Value of Annuity of $1 table (Appendix 12A, Table B) to determine the present value of the same stream of cash flows. Compare your results to your answer in Part A.

d. Explain your findings.

S12-11   Compute NPV—equal net cash inflows (Learning Objective 4)

Connors Music is considering investing $650,000 in private lesson studios that will have no residual value. The studios are expected to result in annual net cash inflows of $90,000 per year for the next ten years. Assuming that Connors Music uses an 12% hurdle rate, what is net present value (NPV) of the studio investment? Is this a favorable investment?

S12-12   Compute IRR—equal net cash inflows (Learning Objective 4)

Refer to Connors Music in S12-11. What is the approximate internal rate of return (IRR) of the studio investment?

S12-13   Compute NPV—unequal net cash inflows (Learning Objective 4)

The local supermarket is considering investing in self-checkout kiosks for its customers. The self-checkout kiosks will cost $46,000 and have no residual value. Management expects the equipment to result in net cash savings over three years as customers grow accustomed to using the new technology: $12,000 the first year; $19,000 the second year; $26,000 the third year. Assuming a 10% discount rate, what is the NPV of the kiosk investment? Is this a favorable investment? Why or why not?

S12-14 Compute IRR—unequal net cash inflows *(Learning Objective 4)*

Refer to the supermarket in S12-13. What is the approximate internal rate of return (IRR) of the kiosk investment?

S12-15 Compare the capital budgeting methods *(Learning Objective 5)*

Fill in each statement with the appropriate capital budgeting method: payback period, ARR, NPV, or IRR.

a. _____ measures profitability but ignores the time value of money.

b. _____ and _____ incorporate the time value of money.

c. _____ focuses on time, not profitability.

d. _____ uses accrual accounting income.

e. _____ finds the discount rate that brings the investment's NPV to zero.

f. In capital rationing decisions, the profitability index must be computed to compare investments requiring different initial investments when the _____ method is used.

g. _____ ignores salvage value.

h. _____ uses discounted cash flows to determine the asset's unique rate of return.

i. _____ highlights risky investments.

S12-16 Identify capital investments *(Learning Objective 1)*

Which of the following purchases would be considered capital investments?

Purchase Item	Capital Investment?
a. The replacement of the engine on one of the company's aircraft is $190,000 (this will not increase the useful life of the plane).	
b. The delivered, installed cost of a new production line is $140,000.	
c. The cost of raw materials for the year is estimated at $980,000.	
d. All of the computers at the help desk are being upgraded at a cost of $123,000.	
e. To support the launch of the new product line, staff training costs are $100,000.	
f. The cost to develop and implement the new Facebook retail app is $565,000.	
g. The upgrade of the customer service fleet to new fuel-efficient vehicles has a cost of $300,000.	
h. The total cost of the management succession program for the coming year is projected to be $230,000.	
i. The cost to retrofit one of a company's closed retail outlets into a customer service center is projected to be $100,000.	
j. The cost of workers' compensation insurance for the coming year is projected to be $200,000.	

S12-17 Identify ethical standards violated *(Learning Objectives 1, 2, 3, 4, & 5)*   **ETHICS**

For each of the situations listed, identify the primary standard from the IMA *Statement of Ethical Professional Practice* that is violated (competence, confidentiality, integrity, or credibility). Refer to Exhibit 1-6 for the complete standard.

a. Julie does not include an estimate of maintenance costs associated with a new computer system. She knows that her department needs the computer system. If the maintenance costs were included in the estimate, the computer system purchase might not be approved.

b. Geoffrey is a staff accountant. He has recently been moved into a position where he will be working on capital budgeting proposals. Geoffrey does not know how to make an NPV calculation, but he does not take the steps to acquire the skills. He figures he can use ARR and payback for investment analysis instead.

c. Terrance's company is in negotiations to purchase one of its suppliers. Terrance, a management accountant, does not disclose that his mother is a major stockholder of the supplier.

CHAPTER 12

d. Anthony is anxious to impress his date, Sonja. Sonja works in Purchasing, while Anthony works in Accounting. When they start talking about people they work with, Anthony shares salary information about each person.

e. Marcella accepts a kickback payment from a contractor to make sure that the contactor's bid is accepted.

EXERCISES Group A

E12-18A Compute payback period—equal cash inflows *(Learning Objective 2)*

Cato Products is considering acquiring a manufacturing plant. The purchase price is $1,860,000. The owners believe the plant will generate net cash inflows of $310,000 annually. It will have to be replaced in five years. To be profitable, the investment payback must occur before the investment's replacement date. Use the payback method to determine whether Cato Products should purchase this plant.

E12-19A Compute payback period—unequal cash inflows
(Learning Objective 2)

Blue Mountain Hardware is adding a new product line that will require an investment of $1,450,000. Managers estimate that this investment will have a 10-year life and generate net cash inflows of $305,000 the first year, $290,000 the second year, and $255,000 each year thereafter for eight years. The investment has no residual value. Compute the payback period.

E12-20A ARR with unequal cash inflows *(Learning Objective 2)*

Refer to the Blue Mountain Hardware information in E12-19A. Compute the ARR for the investment.

E12-21A Compute and compare ARR *(Learning Objective 2)*

Arnold Products is considering whether to upgrade its equipment. Managers are considering two options. Equipment manufactured by Richland Motors costs $1,000,000 and will last five years and have no residual value. The Richland Motors equipment will generate annual operating income of $160,000. Equipment manufactured by Littleton Manufacturing costs $1,350,000 and will remain useful for six years. It promises annual operating income of $249,750, and its expected residual value is $110,000.

Which equipment offers the higher ARR?

E12-22A Compare retirement savings plans *(Learning Objective 3)*

Assume that you want to retire early at age 53. You plan to save using one of the following two strategies: (1) save $4,800 a year in an IRA beginning when you are 28 and ending when you are 53 (25 years) or (2) wait until you are 41 to start saving and then save $10,000 per year for the next 12 years. Assume that you will earn the historic stock market average of 12% per year.

Requirements

1. How much out-of-pocket cash will you invest under the two options?
2. How much savings will you have accumulated at age 53 under the two options?
3. Explain the results.
4. If you let the savings continue to grow for nine more years (with no further out-of-pocket investments), under each scenario, what will the investment be worth when you are age 62?

SUSTAINABILITY

E12-23A Calculate the payback and NPV for a sustainable energy project
(Learning Objectives 1 & 3)

Griffin Industries is evaluating investing in solar panels to provide some of the electrical needs of its main office building in Orlando, Florida. The solar panel project would cost $650,000 and would provide cost savings in its utility bills of $45,000 per year. It is anticipated that the solar panels would have a life of 15 years and would have no residual value.

Requirements

1. Calculate the payback period in years of the solar panel project.
2. If the company uses a discount rate of 12%, what is the net present value of this project?
3. If the company has a rule that no projects will be undertaken that have a payback period of more than five years, would this investment be accepted? If not, what arguments could the energy manager make to try to obtain approval for the solar panel project?
4. What would you do if you were in charge of approving capital investment proposals?

E12-24A Fund future cash flows *(Learning Objective 3)*

Tessa wants to take the next six years off work to travel around the world. She estimates her annual cash needs at $31,000 (if she needs more, she'll work odd jobs). Tessa believes she can invest her savings at 12% until she depletes her funds.

Requirements

1. How much money does Tessa need now to fund her travels?
2. After checking with a number of banks, Tessa learns she'll be able to invest her funds only at 8%. How much does she need now to fund her travels?

E12-25A Choosing a lottery payout option *(Learning Objective 3)*

Congratulations! You've won a state lotto! The state lottery offers you the following (after-tax) payout options:

Option #1: $13,500,000 five years from now
Option #2: $2,000,000 at the end of each year for the next six years
Option #3: $12,500,000 four years from now

Requirement

Assuming that you can earn 10% on your funds, which option would you prefer?

E12-26A Solve various time value of money scenarios *(Learning Objective 3)*

1. Suppose you invest a sum of $2,500 in an interest-bearing account at the rate of 12% per year. What will the investment be worth six years from now?
2. How much would you need to invest now to be able to withdraw $5,000 at the end of every year for the next 20 years? Assume an 8% interest rate.
3. Assume that you want to have $135,000 saved seven years from now. If you can invest your funds at a 6% interest rate, how much do you currently need to invest?
4. Your aunt Betty plans to give you $3,000 at the end of every year for the next ten years. If you invest each of her yearly gifts at a 14% interest rate, how much will they be worth at the end of the ten-year period?
5. Suppose you want to buy a small cabin in the mountains four years from now. You estimate that the property will cost $54,500 at that time. How much money do you need to invest each year in an interest-bearing account earning 8% per year to accumulate the purchase price?

E12-27A Calculate NPV—equal annual cash inflows *(Learning Objective 4)*

Use the NPV method to determine whether Olde West Products should invest in the following projects:

- *Project A* costs $290,000 and offers seven annual net cash inflows of $63,000. Olde West Products requires an annual return of 14% on projects like A.
- *Project B* costs $395,000 and offers ten annual net cash inflows of $71,000. Olde West Products demands an annual return of 10% on investments of this nature.

Requirement

What is the NPV of each project? What is the maximum acceptable price to pay for each project?

E12-28A   Calculate IRR—equal cash inflows *(Learning Objective 4)*

Refer to Olde West Products in E12-27A. Compute the IRR of each project and use this information to identify the better investment.

E12-29A   Calculate NPV—unequal cash flows *(Learning Objective 4)*

Kerwin Industries is deciding whether to automate one phase of its production process. The manufacturing equipment has a six-year life and will cost $925,000. Projected net cash inflows are as follows:

Year 1..	$261,000
Year 2..	$250,000
Year 3..	$228,000
Year 4..	$214,000
Year 5..	$203,000
Year 6..	$176,000

Requirements

1. Compute this project's NPV using Kerwin Industries' 16% hurdle rate. Should the company invest in the equipment? Why or why not?
2. Kerwin Industries could refurbish the equipment at the end of six years for $106,000. The refurbished equipment could be used one more year, providing $75,000 of net cash inflows in Year 7. In addition, the refurbished equipment would have a $53,000 residual value at the end of Year 7. Should Kerwin Industries invest in the equipment and refurbish it after six years? Why or why not? (*Hint*: In addition to your answer to Requirement 1, discount the additional cash outflow and inflows back to the present value.)

E12-30A   Compute IRR—unequal cash flows *(Learning Objective 4)*

Collette Products is considering an equipment investment that will cost $935,000. Projected net cash inflows over the equipment's three-year life are as follows: Year 1: $484,000; Year 2: $390,000; and Year 3: $286,000. Collette wants to know the equipment's IRR.

Requirement

Use trial and error to find the IRR within a 2% range. (*Hint*: Use Collette's hurdle rate of 10% to begin the trial-and-error process.)
Optional: Use a business calculator or spreadsheet to compute the exact IRR.

E12-31A   Capital rationing decision *(Learning Objective 4)*

Brighton Manufacturing is considering three capital investment proposals. At this time, the company has funds available to pursue only one of the three investments.

	Equipment A	Equipment B	Equipment C
Present value of net cash inflows.............................	$1,690,000	$1,980,000	$2,220,000
Investment..	(1,625,000)	(1,800,000)	(2,000,000)
NPV	$ 65,000	$ 180,000	$ 220,000

Requirement

Which investment should Brighton Manufacturing pursue at this time? Why?

Bear Valley Expansion Data Set used for E12-32A through E12-34A:

Assume that Bear Valley's managers developed the following estimates concerning a planned expansion to its Autumn Park Lodge (all numbers assumed):

Number of additional skiers per day...	117
Average number of days per year that weather conditions allow skiing at Bear Valley	162
Useful life of expansion (in years)..	10
Average cash spent by each skier per day...	$ 245
Average variable cost of serving each skier per day	$ 140
Cost of expansion	$8,500,000
Discount rate...	10%

Assume that Autumn Valley uses the straight-line depreciation method and expects the lodge expansion to have a residual value of $700,000 at the end of its ten-year life.

E12-32A   Compute payback and ARR with residual value *(Learning Objective 2)*

Consider how Bear Valley, a popular ski resort, could use capital budgeting to decide whether the $8.5 million Autumn Park Lodge expansion would be a good investment.

Requirements

1. Compute the average annual net cash inflow from the expansion.
2. Compute the average annual operating income from the expansion.
3. Compute the payback period.
4. Compute the ARR.

E12-33A   Continuation of E12-32A: Compute payback and ARR with no residual value *(Learning Objective 2)*

Refer to the Bear Valley Data Set in E12-32A. *Assume that the expansion has zero residual value.*

Requirements

1. Will the payback period change? Explain and recalculate if necessary.
2. Will the project's ARR change? Explain and recalculate if necessary.
3. Assume that Bear Valley screens its potential capital investments using the following decision criteria: Maximum payback period = 6 years and minimum accounting rate of return = 10%.

Will Bear Valley consider this project further or reject it?

E12-34A   Calculate NPV with and without residual value *(Learning Objective 4)*

Refer to the Bear Valley Data Set in E12-32A.

Requirements

1. What is the project's NPV? Is the investment attractive? Why or why not?
2. Assume that the expansion has no residual value. What is the project's NPV? Is the investment still attractive? Why or why not?

E12-35A   Comparing capital budgeting methods *(Learning Objective 5)*

The following table contains information about four projects in which Jeffries Corporation has the opportunity to invest. This information is based on estimates that different managers have prepared about their potential project.

Project	Investment Required	Net Present Value	Life of Project	Internal Rate of Return	Profitability Index	Payback Period in Years	Accounting Rate of Return
A................	$ 200,000	$ 52,350	5	22%	1.26	2.86	17%
B................	$ 400,000	$ 72,230	6	25%	1.18	2.96	15%
C................	$1,000,000	$224,075	3	20%	1.22	2.11	12%
D................	$1,500,000	$ 85,000	4	13%	1.06	3.00	21%

Requirements

1. Rank the four projects in order of preference by using the

    a. net present value.

    b. project profitability index.

    c. internal rate of return.

    d. payback period.

    e. accounting rate of return.

2. Which method(s) do you think is best for evaluating capital investment projects in general? Why?

EXERCISES Group B

E12-36B   Compute payback period—equal cash inflows (Learning Objective 2)

Jubilee Products is considering acquiring a manufacturing plant. The purchase price is $1,600,000. The owners believe the plant will generate net cash inflows of $320,000 annually. It will have to be replaced in six years. To be profitable, the investment payback must occur before the investment's replacement date. Use the payback method to determine whether Jubilee should purchase this plant.

E12-37B   Compute payback period—unequal cash inflows
(Learning Objective 2)

Turner Hardware is adding a new product line that will require an investment of $1,450,000. Managers estimate that this investment will have a 10-year life and generate net cash inflows of $325,000 the first year, $300,000 the second year, and $230,000 each year thereafter for eight years. The investment has no residual value. Compute the payback period.

E12-38B   ARR with unequal cash inflows (Learning Objective 2)

Refer to the Turner Hardware information in E12-37B. Compute the ARR for the investment.

E12-39B   Compute and compare ARR (Learning Objective 2)

Santos Products is considering whether to upgrade its manufacturing equipment. Managers are considering two options. Equipment manufactured by Swanson costs $1,100,000 and will last for four years with no residual value. The Swanson equipment will generate annual operating income of $170,500. Equipment manufactured by Poindexter costs $1,375,000 and will remain useful for five years. It promises annual operating income of $247,500, and its expected residual value is $115,000. Which equipment offers the higher ARR?

E12-40B   Compare retirement savings plans (Learning Objective 3)

Assume you want to retire early at age 54. You plan to save using one of the following two strategies: (1) save $5,100 a year in an IRA beginning when you are 29 and ending when you are 54 (25 years) or (2) wait until you are 42 to start saving and then save $10,625 per year for the next 12 years. Assume you will earn the historic stock market average of 12% per year.

Requirements

1. How much out-of-pocket cash will you invest under the two options?

2. How much savings will you have accumulated at age 54 under the two options?

3. Explain the results.

4. If you were to let the savings continue to grow for eight more years (with no further out-of-pocket investments), under each scenario, what will the investments be worth when you are age 62?

E12-41B   Calculate the payback and NPV for a sustainable energy project
(Learning Objectives 1 & 3)

Connelly Industries is evaluating investing in solar panels to provide some of the electrical needs of its main building in Ann Arbor, Michigan. The solar panel project would cost $600,000 and would provide cost savings in its utility bills of $40,000 per year. It is anticipated that the solar panels would have a life of 20 years and would have no residual value.

Requirements

1. Calculate the payback period in years of the solar panel project.
2. If the company uses a discount rate of 10%, what is the net present value of this project?
3. If the company has a rule that no projects will be undertaken that would have a payback period of more than five years, would this investment be accepted? If not, what arguments could the energy manager make to try to obtain approval for the solar panel project?
4. What would you do if you were in charge of approving capital investment proposals?

E12-42B   Fund future cash flows *(Learning Objective 3)*

Laurel wants to take the next four years off work to travel around the world. She estimates her annual cash needs at $27,000 (if she needs more, she'll work odd jobs). Laurel believes she can invest her savings at 8% until she depletes her funds.

Requirements

1. How much money does Laurel need now to fund her travels?
2. After checking with a number of banks, Laurel learns she'll only be able to invest her funds at 6%. How much does she need now to fund her travels?

E12-43B   Choosing a lottery payout option *(Learning Objective 3)*

Congratulations! You've won a state lotto! The state lottery offers you the following (after-tax) payout options:

Option #1: $15,000,000 four years from now
Option #2: $2,200,000 at the end of each year for the next five years
Option #3: $11,000,000 three years from now

Requirement

Assuming that you can earn 10% on your funds, which option would you prefer?

E12-44B   Solve various time value of money scenarios *(Learning Objective 3)*

Solve these various time value of money scenarios.

1. Suppose you invest a sum of $3,500 in an interest-bearing account at the rate of 10% per year. What will the investment be worth six years from now?
2. How much would you need to invest now to be able to withdraw $4,000 at the end of every year for the next 20 years? Assume an 8% interest rate.
3. Assume that you want to have $145,000 saved seven years from now. If you can invest your funds at a 6% interest rate, how much do you currently need to invest?
4. Your aunt Betty plans to give you $4,000 at the end of every year for the next 10 years. If you invest each of her yearly gifts at a 14% interest rate, how much will they be worth at the end of the 10-year period?
5. Suppose you would like to buy a small cabin in the mountains four years from now. You estimate that the property will cost $51,000 at that time. How much money would you need to invest each year in an interest-bearing account at the rate of 6% per year in order to accumulate the purchase price?

E12-45B Calculate NPV—equal annual cash inflows *(Learning Objective 4)*

Use the NPV method to determine whether Smith Products should invest in the following projects:

- *Project A* costs $260,000 and offers seven annual net cash inflows of $59,000. Smith Products requires an annual return of 16% on projects like A.
- *Project B* costs $390,000 and offers nine annual net cash inflows of $71,000. Smith Products demands an annual return of 12% on investments of this nature.

Requirement

What is the NPV of each project? What is the maximum acceptable price to pay for each project?

E12-46B Calculate IRR—equal cash inflows *(Learning Objective 4)*

Refer to Smith Products in E12-45B. Compute the IRR of each project and use this information to identify the better investment.

E12-47B Calculate NPV—unequal cash flows *(Learning Objective 4)*

Alderman Industries is deciding whether to automate one phase of its production process. The manufacturing equipment has a six-year life and will cost $915,000.

Projected net cash inflows are as follows:	
Year 1	$264,000
Year 2	$253,000
Year 3	$224,000
Year 4	$213,000
Year 5	$204,000
Year 6	$177,000

Requirements

1. Compute this project's NPV using Alderman Industries' 16% hurdle rate. Should the company invest in the equipment? Why or why not?
2. Alderman Industries could refurbish the equipment at the end of six years for $104,000. The refurbished equipment could be used for one more year, providing $76,000 of net cash inflows in Year 7. Additionally, the refurbished equipment would have a $55,000 residual value at the end of Year 7. Should the company invest in the equipment and refurbish it after six years? Why or why not? (*Hint:* In addition to your answer to Requirement 1, discount the additional cash outflows and inflows back to the present value.)

E12-48B Compute IRR—unequal cash flows *(Learning Objective 4)*

Red Rock Industries is considering an equipment investment that will cost $935,000. Projected net cash inflows over the equipment's three-year life are as follows: Year 1: $498,000; Year 2: $400,000; and Year 3: $296,000. Red Rock wants to know the equipment's IRR.

Requirement

Use trial and error to find the IRR within a 2% range. (*Hint:* Use Red Rock's hurdle rate of 12% to begin the trial-and-error process.)
Optional: Use a business calculator or spreadsheet to compute the exact IRR.

E12-49B Capital rationing decision *(Learning Objective 4)*

Wentworth Manufacturing is considering three capital investment proposals. At this time, Wentworth only has funds available to pursue one of the three investments.

	Equipment A	Equipment B	Equipment C
Present value of net cash inflows	$1,705,000	$1,955,000	$2,215,000
Investment	(1,550,000)	(1,700,000)	(1,772,000)
NPV	$ 155,000	$ 255,000	$ 443,000

Requirement

Which investment should Wentworth pursue at this time? Why?

Star Valley Data Set used for E12-50B–E12-52B.

Assume that Star Valley's managers developed the following estimates concerning a planned expansion of its River Park Lodge (all numbers assumed):

Number of additional skiers per day..	120
Average number of days per year that weather conditions allow skiing at Star Valley.............................	163
Useful life of expansion (in years)...	10
Average cash spent by each skier per day...	$ 243
Average variable cost of serving each skier per day	$ 142
Cost of expansion	$9,000,000
Discount rate..	14%

Assume that Star Valley uses the straight-line depreciation method and expects the lodge expansion to have a residual value of $900,000 at the end of its 10-year life.

E12-50B   Compute payback and ARR with residual value (Learning Objective 2)

Consider how Star Valley, a popular ski resort, could use capital budgeting to decide whether the $9 million River Park Lodge expansion would be a good investment.

Requirements
1. Compute the average annual net cash inflow from the expansion.
2. Compute the average annual operating income from the expansion.
3. Compute the payback period.
4. Compute the ARR.

E12-51B   Continuation of E12-50B: Compute payback and ARR with no residual value (Learning Objective 2)

Refer to the Star Valley Data Set in E12-50B. Now assume the expansion has zero residual value.

Requirements
1. Will the payback period change? Explain and recalculate if necessary.
2. Will the project's ARR change? Explain and recalculate if necessary.
3. Assume Star Valley screens its potential capital investments using the following decision criteria: maximum payback period of six years, minimum accounting rate of return of 10%. Will Star Valley consider this project further or reject it?

E12-52B   Calculate NPV with and without residual value (Learning Objective 4)

Refer to the Star Valley Data Set in E12-50B.

Requirements
1. What is the project's NPV? Is the investment attractive? Why or why not?
2. *Assume the expansion has no residual value.* What is the project's NPV? Is the investment still attractive? Why or why not?

E12-53B   Comparing capital budgeting methods (Learning Objective 5)

The following table contains information about four projects in which Andrews Corporation has the opportunity to invest. This information is based on estimates that different managers have prepared about the company's potential project.

Project	Investment Required	Net Present Value	Life of Project	Internal Rate of Return	Profitability Index	Payback Period in Years	Accounting Rate of Return
A........................	$ 210,000	$ 37,176	5	21%	1.18	2.92	18%
B........................	$ 420,000	$ 25,684	6	22%	1.06	3.13	14%
C........................	$1,025,000	$133,942	3	17%	1.13	2.20	10%
D........................	$1,510,000	$ 59,150	4	12%	1.04	3.05	25%

Requirements

1. Rank the four projects in order of preference by using the
   a. net present value.
   b. project profitability index.
   c. internal rate of return.
   d. payback period.
   e. accounting rate of return.
2. Which method(s) do you think is best for evaluating capital investment projects in general? Why?

PROBLEMS Group A

P12-54A   Solve various time value of money scenarios
(Learning Objectives 3 & 4)

1. Ethan just hit the jackpot in Las Vegas and won $35,000! If he invests it now at a 10% interest rate, how much will it be worth in 15 years?
2. Trent would like to have $3,500,000 saved by the time he retires in 30 years. How much does he need to invest now at a 12% interest rate to fund his retirement goal?
3. Assume that Maria accumulates savings of $2 million by the time she retires. If she invests this savings at 10%, how much money will she be able to withdraw at the end of each year for 20 years?
4. Ashley plans to invest $3,000 at the end of each year for the next eight years. Assuming a 14% interest rate, what will her investment be worth eight years from now?
5. Assuming a 12% interest rate, how much would Vivienne have to invest now to be able to withdraw $15,000 at the end of each year for the next ten years?
6. Nick is considering a capital investment that costs $485,000 and will provide the following net cash inflows:

Year	Net Cash Inflow
1..	$300,000
2..	$206,000
3..	$100,000

Using a hurdle rate of 8%, find the NPV of the investment.
7. What is the IRR of the capital investment described in Question 6?

P12-55A   Retirement planning in two stages (Learning Objective 3)

You are planning for a very early retirement. You would like to retire at age 40 and have enough money saved to be able to draw $250,000 per year for the next 40 years (based on family history, you think you'll live to age 80). You plan to save for retirement by making 15 equal annual installments (from age 25 to age 40) into a fairly risky investment fund that you expect will earn 12% per year. You will leave the money in this fund until it is completely depleted when you are 80 years old. To make your plan work, answer the following questions:

1. How much money must you accumulate by retirement? (Hint: Find the present value of the $250,000 withdrawals.)
2. How does this amount compare to the total amount you will draw out of the investment during retirement? How can these numbers be so different?
3. How much must you pay into the investment each year for the first 15 years? (Hint: Your answer from Requirement 1 becomes the future value of this annuity.)
4. How does the total out-of-pocket savings compare to the investment's value at the end of the 15-year savings period and the withdrawals you will make during retirement?

P12-56A   Evaluate an investment using all four methods
(Learning Objectives 2 & 4)

Splash World is considering purchasing a water park in Charlotte, North Carolina, for $2,000,000. The new facility will generate annual net cash inflows of $520,000 for ten years. Engineers estimate that the facility will remain useful for ten years and have no residual value. The company uses straight-line depreciation. Its owners want payback in less than five years and an ARR of 12% or more. Management uses a 14% hurdle rate on investments of this nature.

Requirements

1. Compute the payback period, the ARR, the NPV, and the approximate IRR of this investment. (If you use the tables to compute the IRR, answer with the closest interest rate shown in the tables.)
2. Recommend whether the company should invest in this project.

P12-57A   Compare investments with different cash flows and residual values
(Learning Objectives 2 & 4)

Carvers operates a chain of sandwich shops. The company is considering two possible expansion plans. Plan A would open eight smaller shops at a cost of $8,440,000. Expected annual net cash inflows are $1,600,000 with zero residual value at the end of nine years. Under Plan B, Carvers would open three larger shops at a cost of $8,240,000. This plan is expected to generate net cash inflows of $1,250,000 per year for nine years, the estimated life of the properties. Estimated residual value is $1,100,000. Carvers uses straight-line depreciation and requires an annual return of 10%.

Requirements

1. Compute the payback period, the ARR, and the NPV of these two plans. What are the strengths and weaknesses of these capital budgeting models?
2. Which expansion plan should Carvers choose? Why?
3. Estimate Plan A's IRR. How does the IRR compare with the company's required rate of return?

PROBLEMS Group B

P12-58B   Solve various time value of money scenarios
(Learning Objectives 3 & 4)

1. George just hit the jackpot in Las Vegas and won $55,000! If he invests it now, at a 12% interest rate, how much will it be worth 15 years from now?
2. Zach would like to have $4,000,000 saved by the time he retires 40 years from now. How much does he need to invest now at a 14% interest rate to fund his retirement goal?
3. Assume that Olivia accumulates savings of $2 million by the time she retires. If she invests this savings at 8%, how much money will she be able to withdraw at the end of each year for 20 years?
4. Audrey plans to invest $4,500 at the end of each year for the next seven years. Assuming a 10% interest rate, what will her investment be worth seven years from now?
5. Assuming a 10% interest rate, how much would Jessica have to invest now to be able to withdraw $9,000 at the end of every year for the next nine years?
6. Christopher is considering a capital investment that costs $495,000 and will provide the following net cash inflows:

Year	Net Cash Inflow
1	$302,000
2	$208,000
3	$ 98,000

Using a hurdle rate of 8%, find the NPV of the investment.

7. What is the IRR of the capital investment described in Question 6?

P12-59B Retirement planning in two stages *(Learning Objective 3)*

You are planning for an early retirement. You would like to retire at age 40 and have enough money saved to be able to draw $220,000 per year for the next 45 years (based on family history, you think you'll live to age 85). You plan to save by making 20 equal annual installments (from age 20 to age 40) into a fairly risky investment fund that you expect will earn 14% per year. You will leave the money in this fund until it is completely depleted when you are 85 years old.

To make your plan work, answer the following:

1. How much money must you accumulate by retirement? (*Hint*: Find the present value of the $220,000 withdrawals.)

2. How does this amount compare to the total amount you will draw out of the investment during retirement? How can these numbers be so different?

3. How much must you pay into the investment each year for the first 20 years? (*Hint*: Your answer from Requirement 1 becomes the future value of this annuity.)

4. How does the total out-of-pocket savings compare to the investment's value at the end of the 20-year savings period and the withdrawals you will make during retirement?

P12-60B Evaluate an investment using all four methods
(Learning Objectives 2 & 4)

Water World is considering purchasing a water park in Signal Mountain, Tennessee, for $1,850,000. The new facility will generate annual net cash inflows of $495,000 for nine years. Engineers estimate that the facility will remain useful for nine years and have no residual value. The company uses straight-line depreciation. Its owners want payback in less than five years and an ARR of 12% or more. Management uses a 10% hurdle rate on investments of this nature.

Requirements

1. Compute the payback period, the ARR, the NPV, and the approximate IRR of this investment.

2. Recommend whether the company should invest in this project.

E12-61B Compare investments with different cash flows and residual values
(Learning Objectives 2 & 4)

Franklin Restaurant Group operates a chain of gourmet sandwich shops. The company is considering two possible expansion plans. Plan A would involve opening eight smaller shops at a cost of $8,740,000. Expected annual net cash inflows are $1,550,000, with zero residual value at the end of nine years. Under Plan B, Franklin would open three larger shops at a cost of $8,140,000. This plan is expected to generate net cash inflows of $1,050,000 per year for nine years, the estimated life of the properties. Estimated residual value for Plan B is $1,075,000. Franklin uses straight-line depreciation and requires an annual return of 6%.

Requirements

1. Compute the payback period, the ARR, and the NPV of these two plans. What are the strengths and weaknesses of these capital budgeting models?

2. Which expansion plan should Franklin choose? Why?

3. Estimate Plan A's IRR. How does the IRR compare with the company's required rate of return?

CRITICAL THINKING

Discussion & Analysis

A12-62 Discussion Questions

1. Describe the capital budgeting process in your own words.

2. Define *capital investment*. List at least three examples of capital investments other than the examples provided in the chapter.

3. "As the required rate of return increases, the net present value of a project also increases." Explain why you agree or disagree with this statement.

4. Summarize the net present value method for evaluating a capital investment opportunity. Describe the circumstances that create a positive net present value. Describe the circumstances that may cause the net present value of a project to be negative. Describe the advantages and disadvantages of the net present value method.

5. Net cash inflows and net cash outflows are used in the net present value method and in the internal rate of return method. Explain why accounting net income is not used instead of cash flows.

6. Suppose you are a manager and you have three potential capital investment projects from which to choose. Funds are limited, so you can only choose one of the three projects. Describe at least three methods you can use to select the one project in which to invest.

7. The net present value method assumes that future cash inflows are immediately reinvested at the required rate of return, while the internal rate of return method assumes that future cash inflows are immediately invested at the internal rate of return rate. Which assumption is better? Explain your answer.

8. The decision rule for NPV analysis states that the project with the highest NPV should be selected. Describe at least two situations when the project with the highest NPV may not necessarily be the best project to select.

9. List and describe the advantages and disadvantages of the internal rate of return method.

10. List and describe the advantages and disadvantages of the payback method.

11. Oftentimes, investments in sustainability projects do not meet traditional investment selection criteria. Suppose you are a manager and have prepared a proposal to install solar panels to provide lighting for the office. The payback period for the project is longer than the company's required payback period and the project's net present value is slightly negative. What arguments could you offer to the capital budgeting committee for accepting the solar energy project in spite of it not meeting the capital selection criteria?

12. Think of a company with which you are familiar. What are some examples of possible sustainable investments that company may be able to undertake? How might the company management justify these possible investments?

Application & Analysis

Mini Cases

A12-63 Evaluating the Purchase of an Asset with Various Capital Budgeting Methods

In this activity, you will be evaluating whether you should purchase a hybrid car or its gasoline-engine counterpart. Select two car models that are similar, with one being a hybrid model and one being the non-hybrid model. (For example, the Honda Civic is available as a hybrid or a gasoline-engine model.) Assume that you plan on keeping your car for 10 years and that at the end of the 10 years, the resale value of both models will be negligible.

Basic Discussion Questions

1. Research the cost of each model (include taxes and title costs). Also, obtain an estimate of the miles-per-gallon fuel efficiency of each model.

2. Estimate the number of miles you drive each year. Also estimate the cost of a gallon of fuel.

3. Given your previous estimates from 1 and 2, estimate the total cost of driving the hybrid model for one year. Also estimate the total cost of driving the non-hybrid model for one year. Calculate the savings offered by the hybrid model over the non-hybrid model.

4. Calculate the NPV of the hybrid model, using the annual fuel savings as the annual cash inflow for the 10 years you would own the car.

5. Compare the NPV of the hybrid model with the cost of the gasoline-engine model. Which model has the lowest cost (the lowest NPV)? From a purely financial standpoint, does the hybrid model make sense?

6. Now look at the payback period of the hybrid model. Use the difference between the cost of the hybrid model and the gasoline-engine model as the investment. Use the annual fuel savings as the expected annual net cash inflow. Ignoring the time value of money, how long does it take for the additional cost of the hybrid model to pay for itself through fuel savings?

7. What qualitative factors might affect your decision about which model to purchase?

ETHICS

A12-64 Ethics involved with capital budgeting proposal
(Learning Objectives 1, 2, 3, 4, & 5)

Carlson Products, Inc., is a manufacturer of a variety of construction products, including insulation, pipe, and gypsum. The company has been experiencing steady growth over the past few decades and is moderately profitable.

The board of directors at Carlson has developed criteria that all capital budgeting projects undertaken at Carlson must meet in order to be approved:

1. The project's net present value (NPV) must be positive. The company uses a hurdle rate of 10% when calculating NPV.

2. The project's payback period must be less than four years.

3. The project's accounting rate of return (ARR) must be greater than 8%.

Samantha Pace is a division manager at Carlson. She is developing a proposal to install solar panels at the company's Flagstaff, Arizona, manufacturing facility. The solar panels, requiring an investment of $1.25 million, will significantly reduce the company's carbon footprint. The project will help the company to save approximately 25% of its current energy costs at that facility. Samantha is excited about this project, both for its dollar savings and for its sustainability impact. She finalizes the calculations for the capital budgeting criteria for the solar panel proposal and is delighted to see that her proposed project meets all of the company's capital budgeting criteria. She sends the proposal to Peter Nichols, the controller for Carlson. Peter is responsible for approving all proposed capital budgeting projects that require less than a $2 million investment. Carlson's board of directors must approve all capital budgeting projects that require more than a $2 million investment.

Peter reviews the solar panel proposal. He thinks it is a promising project and feels that the company should undertake this project and other sustainability projects so that the company can reduce its environmental impact.

As he double checks the calculations in Samantha's proposal, he discovers that she has made a few mistakes. Instead of using a hurdle rate of 10%, she actually used a hurdle rate of 6%. She also did not include the impact of the annual depreciation expense for the solar panels in the calculation of ARR. If Peter makes the corrections, the solar panel project will fail the NPV criteria and the ARR criteria.

Peter is conflicted over what to do. He knows that no one is likely to discover Samantha's errors in the capital budgeting proposal if he approves it; the errors are not obvious. He really wants to approve the project, since he believes strongly that these type of initiatives are the direction in which Carlson Products needs to head in order to remain competitive in the future. He also can rationalize that the impact of the errors is minimal and that the project does not fail the capital budgeting criteria by a significant margin. On the other hand, he knows that the board of directors of Carlson has been rigid in its application of the capital budgeting criteria in the projects it has reviewed.

Requirements

1. Using the IMA *Statement of Ethical Professional Practice* as an ethical framework, answer the following questions:

   a. What is(are) the ethical issue(s) in this situation?

   b. What are Peter's responsibilities as a management accountant? Should he approve the solar panel project? Why or why not?

2. Are there any better alternative courses of action that Peter might take to resolve this conflict than to simply approve or reject the proposal? Support your answer.

A12-65 Capital budgeting qualitative factors

REAL LIFE

(Learning Objectives 1, 2, 3, 4, & 5)

For years, it has been cheaper to manufacture many products overseas (China and other countries) than in the United States. Labor is still less expensive overseas than in the U.S., but the cost difference has been decreasing.

Late in 2012, Apple announced it would be building some Mac computers in the United States for the first time in about ten years.[1] It will be investing $100 million in 2013 in these new U.S. manufacturing facilities.

In 2013, Google's Motorola announced that it would be assembling its Moto X smartphone in Fort Worth, Texas, making it the first smartphone assembled in the United States. Also in 2013, Lenovo opened a new ThinkPad manufacturing facility in North Carolina.

For these companies, it is likely that the capital budgeting proposals for the U.S. manufacturing sites did not meet the companies' standard capital budgeting criteria. Yet the companies are still opting to manufacture some products in the United States, where it is, for the time being, more expensive than other locations.

Questions

1. Why did Apple make an announcement in 2012 about its manufacturing operations upcoming in 2013?

2. What qualitative factors would likely have been considered when Apple, Google, and Lenovo made their decisions to invest in U.S. manufacturing facilities? In other words, why would Apple, Google, and Lenovo decide to manufacture products in the United States when all of these companies have well-established facilities and supply chains in China?

3. What challenges will these companies likely face in manufacturing products in U.S. plants?

4. What stakeholders are impacted, either positively or negatively, from the decision to manufacture in the United States? How are these stakeholders impacted?

5. What ethical issues potentially arise from not producing in the lowest cost location?

Try It Solutions

page 705:

Since the net cash inflows are expected to be equal each year, payback is calculated as follows:

$$\text{Payback period} = \frac{\text{Initial investment}}{\text{Expected annual net cash inflow}} = \frac{\$4,000,000}{\$750,000} = 5.33 \text{ years}$$

[1] J. E. Lessin and J. R. Hagerty, "Apple CEO Says Mac Production Coming to U.S.," *Wall Street Journal*, December 6, 2012.

page 707:

ARR is calculated as follows:

$$\text{ARR} = \frac{\text{Average annual net cash inflow} - \text{Annual depreciation expense}}{\text{Initial investment}}$$

The ARR focuses on the operating income generated from the investment, not the net cash inflow from the investment. Thus, to use this formula, we need to find the annual depreciation expense, which will be used to reconcile net cash inflows back to operating income:

$$\text{Annual depreciation} = \frac{\$4 \text{ million}}{20 \text{ years}} = \$200,000$$

Now we calculate ARR as follows:

$$\text{ARR} = \frac{\$750,000 - \$200,000}{\$4,000,000} = 13.75\%$$

page 721:

The NPV is the difference between the present value of the wind turbine's future net cash flows ($750,000 per year for 20 years) and the cost of the initial investment ($4 million). It can be found using the Annuity PV factor for $i = 12\%$, $n = 20$, as follows:

	A	B	C	D	E	F
1	**NPV Calculation for _Equal_ Annual Net Cash Inflows**	**Annuity PV Factor** ($i = 12\%$)		**Annual Net Cash Inflow**		**Present Value**
2	Present value of annuity, $n = 20$	7.469	× $	750,000	= $	5,601,750
3	Less: Initial investment					4,000,000
4	Net present value (NPV)				$	1,601,750
5						

Alternatively, one can use the NPV function in Excel to arrive at an NPV of $1,602,083.
The positive NPV indicates that the wind turbine will earn more than the company's 12% hurdle rate. Therefore, it is a favorable investment.

page 726:

The easiest way to calculate the IRR is by using the IRR function in Excel, which results in an IRR of 18.07%.
    Alternatively, one can look for the Annuity PV factor for $n = 20$ that is closest to the following:

$$\frac{\text{Initial investment}}{\text{Amount of each equal net cash inflow}} = \frac{\$4,000,000}{\$750,000} = 5.33$$

The Annuity PV factor at $n = 20$ that is closest to 5.33 occurs when $i = 18\%$. At 18%, the Annuity PV factor is 5.353. Thus, the IRR of the wind turbine is close to 18%.

Statement of Cash Flows

Learning Objectives

- **1** Classify cash flows as operating, investing, or financing activities
- **2** Prepare the statement of cash flows using the indirect method
- **3** Prepare the statement of cash flows using the direct method

Sources: http://www.nerdwallet
.com/blog/credit-card-data/average-
credit-card-debt-household/; http://
www.pbs.org/wgbh/pages/frontline/
shows/credit/more/rise.html

In the past 30 years the United States has seen the proliferation of credit card

debt. From 1980 to 2013, the average household credit card debt grew from $518 to $7,149. In 2013, the total national consumer credit card debt stood at $856.5 billion, making it the third-largest class of debt, behind mortgage debt and student loan debt. Why do people use credit cards? Some people use credit cards simply as a matter of convenience, so they don't have to carry cash or personal checks. Others use credit cards to earn rewards, such as free airplane miles. But many people use credit cards because they do not have enough funds to pay for the things they need or want. In other words, the cash they generate from their salary or wages is not high enough to cover their expenses (such as food, clothing, housing, and entertainment) and make necessary debt payments (such as monthly car and student loan payments). In the end, credit card debt is incurred because cash inflows are not high enough to cover cash outflows.

Just as cash flows are important to personal finances, they are equally important to a company's finances. To better understand the financial health of a company, we must understand how the company generates cash, and how the cash is being used. That's exactly the kind of information that is presented in the statement of cash flows.

As the opening story shows, good cash management is critical to individuals and companies alike. Managers use cash budgets, as discussed in Chapter 9, to plan for their cash needs. But investors and creditors, who want to understand how the company is generating and using cash, do not have access to internal cash budgets. Rather, they must rely on the company's financial statements to provide them with information on whether the company's cash increased or decreased over the course of the year, and the reasons for the change. In this chapter, we'll discuss how the statement of cash flows presents investors, creditors, and managers with important information on how a company generated and used cash over a given period of time.

What is the Statement of Cash Flows?

Companies prepare four basic financial statements:

1. Income statement
2. Balance sheet
3. Statement of stockholders' equity
4. Statement of cash flows[1]

You are already familiar with the first three statements from your financial accounting course. These statements do not present much information about the company's cash. For example, the balance sheet gives a "snapshot" of the company's ending cash balance, but it does not report whether cash increased or decreased during the period or why. The <u>statement of cash flows</u> is an important and necessary statement because it shows the overall increase or decrease in cash during the period, as well as *how* the company *generated* and *used* cash during the period. Exhibit 13-1 shows the basic format of a statement of cash flows.

EXHIBIT 13-1 Basic Format of the Statement of Cash Flows

	A	B	
1	SportsTime, Inc.		
2	Statement of Cash Flows		
3	For the year ended December 31, 2014		
4			
5	Cash provided (or used) by **operating** activities (*itemized list*)	$	XXX
6	Cash provided (or used) by **investing** activities (*itemized list*)		XX
7	Cash provided (or used) by **financing** activities (*itemized list*)		XX
8	Net increase (or decrease) in cash		XXX
9	Cash, beginning of the year		XX
10	Cash, end of the year	$	XXX
11			

 Why is this important?

"The statement of cash flows shows how the company **generated** and **used cash** during the year, enabling **managers, investors,** **and creditors** to predict whether the company can meet its cash **obligations** in the future."

Why is cash so important? It is important because anyone involved with the company has certain expectations regarding the company's cash:

- Employees expect payment of their salaries and wages.
- Suppliers expect payment for their products and services.
- Creditors expect to be repaid loans and interest payments.
- Investors expect dividends.
- Governmental taxing authorities expect payment of income and property taxes.

The statement of cash flows helps all of these stakeholders evaluate how the company has generated and used cash in the past, which in turn helps them predict whether the company will

[1]Statement of Accounting Standards No. 95 governs cash flow reporting. The standard was produced by the Financial Accounting Standards Board in 1987.

be able to meet its cash obligations in the future. It also helps managers understand if the company is generating sufficient cash from its day-to-day operating activities to enable investments in new equipment, new stores, or new businesses. If insufficient cash is being generated from the day-to-day operations of the company to fund these investments, then the company may need to cut back on expenses or planned investments, or consider raising more capital through selling stocks or taking out loans.

Typically, the statement of cash flows defines "cash" as all cash and cash equivalents. Cash generally includes petty cash, checking, and savings accounts. <u>Cash equivalents</u> include very safe, highly liquid assets that are readily convertible into cash, such as money market funds, certificates of deposit that mature in less than three months, and U.S. treasury bills. Throughout this chapter, any references to cash will include cash and cash equivalents.

Three Types of Activities That Generate and Use Cash

As Exhibit 13-1 illustrates, the statement of cash flows classifies all business transactions into three different types of activities. These activities are presented on the statement of cash flows in the following order:

1 Classify cash flows as operating, investing, or financing activities

1. Operating activities
2. Investing activities
3. Financing activities

Let's take a look at the kind of transactions that would fall under each category.

Operating Activities

<u>Operating activities</u> primarily consist of the day-to-day profit-making activities of the company. These activities include such transactions as making or buying inventory, selling inventory, selling services, paying employees, advertising, and so forth. These activities typically affect current asset accounts such as inventory and accounts receivable, as well as current liability accounts such as salaries payable and accounts payable. Operating activities also include *any other activity that affects net income* (not just operating income). Therefore, this category also includes receiving interest income and paying interest expense, receiving dividend income, and paying for income tax expense. Keep the following rule of thumb in mind when deciding if an activity should be classified as an operating activity:[2]

Why is this important?

"**Financial statement** readers want to know how much of the company's cash was generated from **day-to-day** company **operations** versus how much was raised by **selling investments** or company stock, or by **borrowing money.** A company that doesn't raise sufficient **cash** from operations won't be able to **survive** in the long run."

> *Transactions that affect net income, current assets, and current liabilities are classified as operating activities on the statement of cash flows.*

Investing Activities

<u>Investing activities</u> include transactions that involve buying or selling long-term assets. These activities include buying or selling property, plant, or equipment; buying or selling stock in other companies (if the stock is meant to be held for the long term); or loaning money to other companies with the goal of earning interest income from the loan. Keep the following rule of thumb in mind when deciding if an activity should be classified as an investing activity:

> *Transactions that affect long-term assets are classified as investing activities on the statement of cash flows.*

---

[2]Because the entire statement of cash flows, including cash flows from operating, investing, and financing activities, is needed to explain the change in the company's cash account during the year, the change in the cash account is the only current asset account excluded from this rule of thumb.

Financing Activities

<u>Financing activities</u> include transactions that either generate capital for the company or pay it back. These activities include selling company stock, issuing long-term debt (such as notes or bonds), buying back company stock (also known as treasury stock), paying dividends to stockholders, and repaying the principal amount on loans. Keep the following rule of thumb in mind when deciding whether an activity should be classified as a financing activity:

> *Transactions that affect long-term liabilities and stockholders' equity are classified as financing activities on the statement of cash flows.*

Exhibit 13-2 presents a list of common sources and uses of cash and shows how they are classified on the statement of cash flows. We have italicized those items that you may have difficulty remembering because they are not completely intuitive.

EXHIBIT 13-2 Classification of Activities on the Statement of Cash Flows

Operating Activities
(Cash flows related to the primary, day-to-day profit-making activities of the company; these activities affect net income, current assets, and current liabilities)

- Cash received from sale of services or merchandise
- *Cash received from interest income*
- *Cash received from dividend income*
- Cash paid to purchase inventory
- Cash paid for selling, general, and administrative expenses
- *Cash paid for interest expense*
- Cash paid for income taxes

Non-cash adjustments to net income (indirect method):
- Depreciation and amortization expense
- Gain or loss on sale of property, plant, or equipment

Investing Activities
(Cash flows related to buying and selling investments; these activities affect long-term assets)

- Cash received from sale of property, plant, or equipment
- Cash received from collection of long-term loans
- Cash received from sale of long-term equity (stock) investments
- Cash paid to purchase property, plant, or equipment
- Cash paid for purchasing long-term equity (stock) investments

Financing Activities
(Cash flows related to generating and repaying capital; these activities affect long-term liabilities and stockholders' equity accounts)

- Cash received from issuing long-term debt (such as notes and bonds)
- Cash received from issuing stock
- Cash received from using a line of credit
- Cash used to pay back long-term debt
- *Cash used to pay dividends*
- Cash used to buy back company stock (treasury stock)

For example, consider the following:

- Even though interest income and dividend income is earned from investments, they are both classified as cash flows from operating activities because they *affect (increase) net income.*

- Interest expense occurs because the company has borrowed money, so you might think this is a financing activity. However, it is classified as an operating activity because it *affects (decreases) net income.*

- Certain revenues and expenses (such as depreciation) affect net income, yet do not generate or use cash. Under the indirect method, they are used in the operating section of the statement of cash flows to reconcile accrual basis net income back to the cash basis.

- The *payment* of dividends is a distribution of the company's equity (not an expense on the income statement); therefore, it is classified as a financing activity.

Noncash Investing and Financing Activities

Sometimes companies have significant investing or financing activities that do not involve cash. For example, a company may purchase property, plant, or equipment by issuing common stock to the seller, rather than paying cash. Liabilities, such as bonds or notes payable, may be extinguished by converting them to common stock.

Any significant noncash investing or financing activity must be disclosed in a supplementary schedule to the statement of cash flows or in a footnote to the financial statements. Why? Because these activities will affect *future* cash flows, such as the future payment of dividends and interest. Since financial statement readers use the statement of cash flows to make predictions about future cash flows, they need to be made aware of any noncash investing or financing transactions that took place during the year.

Classify each of the following transactions as an operating, investing, or financing activity.

1. Selling inventory
2. Issuing stock
3. Paying dividends
4. Paying employee salaries
5. Buying a new fleet of vehicles

Please see page 822 for solutions.

Two Methods of Presenting Operating Activities

The operating activities section of the statement of cash flows may be presented using either the direct or indirect method. These different methods only affect the *format* of the presentation. Both methods result in the *same* dollar figure for the total cash provided by operating activities. Keep in mind that these methods only affect the operating activities section and have no bearing on the investing or financing sections of the statement.

Direct Method

The **direct method** lists the receipt and payment of cash for specific operating activities. For example, the operating activities would list such line items as the following:

- Cash receipts from customers
- Cash payments for inventory
- Cash payments for salaries and wages
- Cash payments for insurance

In essence, the direct method lists many of the same items shown on the income statement, but calculates them on a cash basis, rather than accrual basis. The **accrual basis of accounting** requires that revenues are recorded when they are earned (when the sale takes place), rather than when cash is received on the sale. Likewise, expenses are recorded when they are incurred, rather than when they are paid. These timing differences give rise to current assets such as accounts receivable and current liabilities such as wages payable. Thus, accrual based net income almost always differs from the cash basis.

Indirect Method

The **indirect method** begins with the company's net income, which is prepared on an accrual basis, and then reconciles it back to the cash basis through a series of adjustments. This method reconciles net income to the cash basis by adjusting for (1) noncash revenues (such as gains on the sale of property, plant, and equipment) or noncash expenses (such as depreciation or amortization), and (2) changes in the current asset and current liability accounts. For example, an increase in accounts receivable indicates that more sales were made than were collected. Therefore, an adjustment would be made to net income to reflect this increase in accounts receivable.

Which Method is Most Commonly Used?

Recent surveys show that over 98% of companies currently use the indirect method.[3] Why? Because it is easier and, therefore, less costly to prepare. Furthermore, if a company chooses to use the direct method, it must also provide a supplementary schedule reconciling net income to the cash basis. In essence, a company that chooses to use the direct method must also perform the indirect method for a supplementary disclosure.

Currently, the Financial Accounting Standards Board (FASB) and International Accounting Standards Board (IASB) *encourage* companies to use the direct method. However, the boards have jointly proposed that companies be *required* to use the direct method in the future.[4] The outcome of this proposal is uncertain at this time. The second half of the chapter will illustrate both the indirect and direct methods.

Sustainability and the Statement of Cash Flows

You've just learned that *all* business transactions must be classified into one of three different types of activities for the statement of cash flows. A company's sustainability initiatives will also fall into the same three categories. Some examples are listed next.

Operating Activities—affect net income, current assets, and current liabilities

- Expenses related to researching and developing sustainable products and packaging
- Income generated from selling scrap and recyclable materials
- Income and expenses related to producing, marketing, and distributing new "green" products

Investing Activities—affect long-term assets

- Investments in solar paneling or wind turbines
- Investments in environmentally friendly production equipment
- Investments in LEED certified buildings

See Exercises E13-21A and E13-31B

[3]American Institute of Certified Public Accountants, *Accounting Trends and Techniques: 2004*, Jersey City, NJ, 2004.
[4]Financial Accounting Standards Board, *Financial Accounting Series Discussion Paper Number 1630-100: Preliminary Views on Financial Statement Presentation*, Norwalk, CT, October 16, 2008, Paragraph 3.70–3.83.

Financing Activities—affect long-term liabilities and owners' equity

- Stocks issued to raise capital for projects involving biofuel production
- Bonds issued to raise capital for investing in a fleet of hybrid delivery vehicles

Sustainability initiatives, such as those listed above, are not itemized separately in the statement of cash flows. Rather, they are presented in combination with other similar activities. For example, all capital investments, whether environmentally friendly or not, are presented as "investments in plant and equipment." However, to provide more detailed information to both internal and external users, companies may disclose cash flows related to significant sustainability initiatives on their corporate websites or in corporate social responsibility (CSR) reports. These disclosures help investors and other stakeholders understand how the company is positioning itself to address social and environmental issues that impact the company's operations, and therefore profitability and cash position, in the future.

Decision Guidelines

Statement of Cash Flows

The following guidelines present some decisions that need to be made before preparing the statement of cash flows.

Decision	Guidelines
What financial statements should my company prepare?	A set of financial statements includes the (1) income statement, (2) balance sheet, (3) statement of stockholders' equity, and (4) statement of cash flows.
How should my company define "cash" for the statement of cash flows?	The statement of cash flows usually explains changes in both cash and cash equivalents. Cash and cash equivalents include petty cash, checking and savings account deposits, money markets, short-term certificates of deposit, and U.S. treasury bills.
What types of cash flows should be presented on the statement of cash flows?	All cash flows must be classified into one of the following three categories: 1. Cash flows from operating activities 2. Cash flows from investing activities 3. Cash flows from financing activities
How can I tell if a cash transaction should be classified as an operating activity?	Cash flows from operating activities include the day-to-day profit-making activities of the firm. These activities include any transactions that affect net income (including interest income and expense, and dividend income), current assets, or current liabilities.
How can I tell if a cash transaction should be classified as an investing activity?	Cash flows from investing activities include all transactions that affect long-term assets.
How can I tell if a cash transaction should be classified as a financing activity?	Cash flows from financing activities include transactions that generate capital for the company or pay it back. These transactions affect long-term liabilities and stockholders' equity.
My company purchased a piece of land in exchange for company stock. Since the transaction didn't affect cash, do we include it on the statement of cash flows?	Even though the transaction didn't affect cash this year, it needs to be disclosed because it will affect *future* cash flows. All significant non-cash investing or financing transactions need to be disclosed in either a supplementary schedule to the statement of cash flows or in a footnote to the financial statements.
Should my company use the direct or indirect method for presenting the cash flows from operating activities?	Either method is currently acceptable. However, if you use the direct method, you must also present a supplementary schedule that is much like the information presented using the indirect method.

SUMMARY PROBLEM 1

Classify each of the following transactions as an operating, investing, or financing activity.

1. Payment of salaries
2. Purchase of land
3. Issuance of stock
4. Repayment of long-term notes
5. Payment of rent
6. Collection of sales revenue
7. Conversions of bonds payable to common stock
8. Loss on the sale of equipment
9. Purchase of another company's stock (to be held for more than one year)
10. Purchase of merchandise inventory
11. Proceeds from the sale of a building
12. Payment of dividends
13. Collection of interest income
14. Purchase of treasury stock (company buys back its own stock)
15. Payment of interest on long-term debt

▪ SOLUTION

Transaction	Type of Activity
1. Payment of salaries	Operating
2. Purchase of land	Investing
3. Issuance of stock	Financing
4. Repayment of long-term notes	Financing
5. Payment of rent	Operating
6. Collection of sales revenue	Operating
7. Conversion of bonds payable to common stock	Noncash Financing and Investing; must be disclosed even though it doesn't use cash
8. Loss on the sale of equipment	Operating
9. Purchase of another company's stock (to be held for more than one year)	Investing
10. Purchase of merchandise inventory	Operating
11. Proceeds from the sale of a building	Investing
12. Payment of dividends	Financing
13. Collection of interest income	Operating
14. Purchase of treasury stock (company buys back its own stock)	Financing
15. Payment of interest on long-term debt	Operating

How is the Statement of Cash Flows Prepared Using the Indirect Method?

2 Prepare the statement of cash flows using the indirect method

In this section, we'll use the indirect method to prepare the statement of cash flows for SportsTime, Inc., a regional retailer of sporting goods equipment.

Information Needed to Prepare the Statement of Cash Flows

In order to prepare the statement of cash flows, the following company information is needed:

1. Income statement for the current year
2. <u>Comparative balance sheets</u> (balance sheets for the end of the current year and prior year)
3. Miscellaneous additional information relating to investing and financing transactions

Exhibit 13-3 presents SportsTime's income statement, and Exhibit 13-4 presents the company's comparative balance sheets. Additional information about the company's investing and financing transactions will be presented as needed throughout the remainder of the chapter.

> ## Why is this important?
>
> "**Most companies** currently use the **indirect method**, so understanding how it is prepared and **interpreted** is crucial. This method highlights the **differences** between accrual based net income and the **cash basis**."

EXHIBIT 13-3 Income Statement

	A	B	C
1	SportsTime, Inc.		
2	Income Statement		
3	For the Year Ended December 31, 2014		
4			
5	Sales revenues		$ 9,500,000
6	Less: Cost of goods sold		7,125,000
7	Gross profit		2,375,000
8	Less operating expenses:		
9	Salaries and wages expense	$ 580,000	
10	Insurance expense	25,000	
11	Depreciation expense	142,000	
12	Other operating expenses	230,000	
13	Total operating expenses		977,000
14	Operating income		$ 1,398,000
15	Plus other income and less other expenses:		
16	Interest expense	60,000	
17	Gain on sale of PP&E	1,000	
18	Total other income and expenses		59,000
19	Income before income taxes		1,339,000
20	Less: Income tax expense		401,700
21	Net income		$ 937,300
22			

Preparing the Cash Flows from Operating Activities

The indirect method requires that we begin the operating activities section with the company's accrual based net income, which is found on the income statement. Then, we make all adjustments needed to convert, or reconcile, net income back to a cash basis. These adjustments will include the following:

- Noncash expenses and revenues (found on the income statement)
- Changes in the current asset accounts (found on the comparative balance sheets)
- Changes in the current liability accounts (found on the comparative balance sheets)

EXHIBIT 13-4 Comparative Balance Sheets

	A	B	C
1	SportsTime, Inc.		
2	Comparative Balance Sheets		
3	December 31, 2014 and 2013		
4	Assets	2014	2013	Increase (Decrease)
5	Current assets:			
6	Cash	$ 203,500	$ 125,000	78,500
7	Accounts receivable	365,000	330,000	35,000
8	Inventory	632,000	657,000	(25,000)
9	Prepaid insurance	20,000	15,000	5,000
10	Total current assets	1,220,500	1,127,000	
11				
12	Property, plant, and equipment	3,415,000	2,900,000	515,000
13	Less: Accumulated depreciation	(499,000)	(380,000)	119,000
14	Investments	285,000	185,000	100,000
15	Total assets	$ 4,421,500	$ 3,832,000	
16				
17	Liabilities			
18	Current liabilities:			
19	Accounts payable	$ 245,000	$ 285,000	(40,000)
20	Wages payable	57,000	48,500	8,500
21	Interest payable	3,000	8,000	(5,000)
22	Income taxes payable	146,700	120,000	26,700
23	Other accrued expenses payable	15,500	28,500	(13,000)
24	Total current liabilities	467,200	490,000	
25				
26	Long-term liabilities	550,000	750,000	(200,000)
27	Total liabilities	1,017,200	1,240,000	
28				
29	Stockholders' equity			
30	Common stock	1,100,000	1,100,000	0
31	Retained earnings	2,304,300	1,492,000	812,300
32	Total stockholders' equity	3,404,300	2,592,000	
33				
34	Total liabilities and equity	$ 4,421,500	$ 3,832,000	
35				

Noncash Expenses

Depreciation expense is perhaps the most common noncash expense found on the income statement. Depreciation is simply the systematic write-off of the cost of plant and equipment over time. No cash actually trades hands when depreciation expense is recorded. Since depreciation expense reduced net income by $142,000 (Exhibit 13-3), but didn't use cash, we must *add it back* to net income in order to convert net income back to the cash basis. Therefore, we begin our statement of cash flows by adding back depreciation expense, as shown (in blue) in Exhibit 13-5.

We would also add back any amortization of intangible assets or depletion of natural resources for the same reason. SportsTime's income statement does not show any amortization or depletion expense, so these adjustments are not needed.

Noncash Revenues

The income statement in Exhibit 13-3 shows a $1,000 gain on the sale of property, plant, and equipment (PP&E). A gain on the sale arises when the equipment is sold for *more* than its net book value. The **net book value** is the original cost of the equipment less its accumulated depreciation. Let's assume that SportsTime sold some old display shelves and dressing room chairs for $3,000. Company records indicate that this equipment originally

EXHIBIT 13-5 Adjusting Net Income for Depreciation Expense

	A	B	C
1	SportsTime, Inc.		
2	Statement of Cash Flows—Operating Activities Section (Indirect Method)		
3	For the Year Ended December 31, 2014		
4			
5	**Operating Activities:**		
6	Net income		$ 937,300
7	Adjustments to reconcile net income to cash basis:		
8	Depreciation expense	$ 142,000	
9			

cost $25,000 and that at the time of sale, accumulated depreciation on this equipment totaled $23,000. The gain on sale would have been calculated as follows:

Sale price of equipment		$3,000
Original cost of the equipment	$25,000	
Less: Accumulated depreciation	23,000	
Net book value of equipment		2,000
Gain on sale		$1,000

The actual cash received on the sale, $3,000, will be reported as a source of cash in the investing section of the statement of cash flows. But the $1,000 gain, which increased accrual based net income, does not actually represent cash received. Therefore, the $1,000 gain must be *deducted* from net income to convert it back to the cash basis. Exhibit 13-6 incorporates this gain (in blue) on our developing statement of cash flows.

EXHIBIT 13-6 Adjusting Net Income for Gain on Sale

	A	B	C
1	SportsTime, Inc.		
2	Statement of Cash Flows—Operating Activities Section (Indirect Method)		
3	For the Year Ended December 31, 2014		
4			
5	**Operating Activities:**		
6	Net income		$ 937,300
7	Adjustments to reconcile net income to cash basis:		
8	Depreciation expense	$ 142,000	
9	Gain on sale of equipment	(1,000)	
10			

Conversely, a loss on the sale of equipment would have occurred if the equipment was sold for *less* than the equipment's net book value. Since a loss doesn't represent a pay-out of cash (in fact, cash is received for the sale) we would *add back the loss* to net income to convert it back to the cash basis.

Changes in Current Asset Accounts

The next step in preparing the statement of cash flows is to adjust net income for any changes in current asset accounts. The comparative balance sheets in Exhibit 13-4 shows that the balance in all current asset accounts changed over the year. Remember, the entire statement of cash flows is attempting to explain the change in the cash account. So, we will need to analyze the changes to all current asset accounts *except* for cash.

Let's first look at those accounts that had *increases* over the course of the year: accounts receivable and prepaid insurance.

ACCOUNTS RECEIVABLE   Exhibit 13-4 shows a $35,000 increase in accounts receivable. An *increase* in accounts receivable indicates that *more* sales were made than were collected. To reconcile net income back to the cash basis, we need to subtract any sales that were not yet collected in cash. To do so, we *subtract* the $35,000 *increase* in accounts receivable from net income.

PREPAID INSURANCE   Exhibit 13-4 shows a $5,000 increase in prepaid insurance. An *increase* in prepaid insurance indicates that the company *paid more* for insurance than was recorded as insurance expense. To reconcile net income to the cash basis, we need to subtract more than was expensed. To do so, we *subtract* the $5,000 *increase* in prepaid insurance from net income.

Exhibit 13-7 illustrates the general rule for reconciling net income to cash for *increases* in any current asset accounts.

EXHIBIT 13-7 General Rule for Increases in Current
Asset Accounts

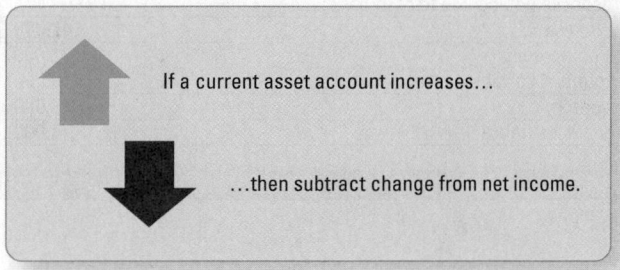

If a current asset account increases…

…then subtract change from net income.

Now let's look at an example of a current asset account that decreased over the course of the year.

INVENTORY   Exhibit 13-4 shows a $25,000 *decrease* in inventory. The *decrease* in inventory indicates that the company sold more merchandise inventory than it purchased. Its inventory level shrunk. So the Cost of Goods Sold expensed on the income statement is greater than the cash paid to purchase the merchandise from the company's suppliers. To reconcile net income back to the cash basis, we need to subtract less than the amount expensed. To do so, we *add back* the $25,000 *decrease* in inventory to net income.

Exhibit 13-8 illustrates the general rule for reconciling net income to cash for *decreases* in any current asset accounts.

EXHIBIT 13-8 General Rule for Decreases in Current
Asset Accounts

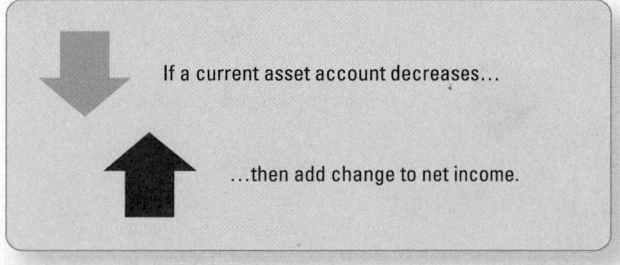

If a current asset account decreases…

…then add change to net income.

The general rule of thumb for current asset accounts is as follows:

> • *If a current asset account **increases**, then **subtract** the change from net income.*
> • *If a current asset account **decreases**, then **add** the change to net income.*

Notice that for changes in current assets, we reconcile net income back to the cash basis by adjusting in the *opposite* direction.

Exhibit 13-9 illustrates our developing statement of cash flows after incorporating changes in the current asset accounts (in blue).

EXHIBIT 13-9 Adjusting Net Income for Changes in Current Asset Accounts

	A	B	C
1	SportsTime, Inc.		
2	Statement of Cash Flows—Operating Activities Section (Indirect Method)		
3	For the Year Ended December 31, 2014		
4			
5	Operating Activities:		
6	Net income		$ 937,300
7	Adjustments to reconcile net income to cash basis:		
8	Depreciation expense	$ 142,000	
9	Gain on sale of equipment	(1,000)	
10	Increase in accounts receivable	(35,000)	
11	Decrease in inventory	25,000	
12	Increase in prepaid insurance	(5,000)	
13			

Changes in Current Liability Accounts

Now let's take a look at one current liability account that decreased over the course of the year (interest payable), and another that increased (wages payable).

INTEREST PAYABLE   Exhibit 13-4 shows a $5,000 *decrease* in interest payable. A *decrease* in interest payable indicates that the company paid out more than it expensed for interest expense during the year. Therefore, to reconcile net income to the cash basis, we need to subtract *more* than was expensed. To do so, we subtract the $5,000 decrease in interest payable from net income.

The general rule of thumb for *decreases* in current liabilities is pictured in Exhibit 13-10.

EXHIBIT 13-10 General Rule for Decreases in Current
Liability Accounts

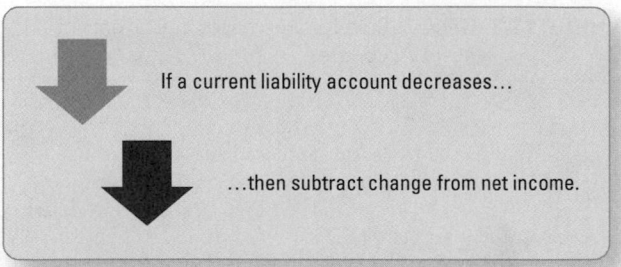

If a current liability account decreases...

...then subtract change from net income.

WAGES PAYABLE   Exhibit 13-4 shows a $8,500 *increase* in wages payable. An *increase* in wages payable indicates that more wage expense was incurred than was paid. To reconcile net income to the cash basis, we need to subtract *less* than was expensed. Therefore, we need to add back the $8,500 increase in wages payable to net income.

The general rule of thumb for *increases* in current liabilities is pictured in Exhibit 13-11.

EXHIBIT 13-11 General Rule for Increases in Current
Liability Accounts

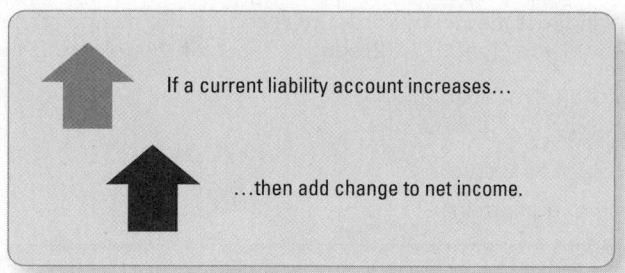

The general rule of thumb for current liability accounts is as follows:

- *If a current liability account* **increases**, *then* **add** *the change to net income.*
- *If a current liability account* **decreases**, *then* **subtract** *the change from net income.*

Notice that for changes in current liabilities, we reconcile net income back to the cash basis by adjusting in the *same* direction. The adjustments for changes in current liability accounts are pictured in blue in Exhibit 13-12.

Interpreting Cash Flows from Operating Activities

Exhibit 13-12 shows the completed operating activities section of the statement of cash flows. As you can see, the day-to-day profit making activities of the company have generated over $1 million in cash during the year. That's a positive sign—a company that is not providing cash from operating activities can't survive in the long-run. It also shows that cash was drained by allowing accounts receivable to increase and by paying down many of the company's current liabilities (such as accounts payable, interest payable, and other accrued expenses). Finally, this reconciliation shows that cash provided by operations was $103,200 higher than net income, once again showing that accrual based net income differs from the cash basis.

EXHIBIT 13-12 Cash Flows from Operating Activities (Indirect Method)

	A	B	C
1	SportsTime, Inc.		
2	Statement of Cash Flows—Operating Activities Section (Indirect Method)		
3	For the Year Ended December 31, 2014		
4			
5	**Operating Activities:**		
6	Net income		$ 937,300
7	Adjustments to reconcile net income to cash basis:		
8	Depreciation expense	$ 142,000	
9	Gain on sale of equipment	(1,000)	
10	Increase in accounts receivable	(35,000)	
11	Decrease in inventory	25,000	
12	Increase in prepaid insurance	(5,000)	
13	Decrease in accounts payable	(40,000)	
14	Increase in wages payable	8,500	
15	Decrease in interest payable	(5,000)	
16	Increase in income taxes payable	26,700	
17	Decrease in other accrued expenses payable	(13,000)	
18	Total reconciling adjustments		103,200
19	Net cash provided by operating activities		1,040,500
20			

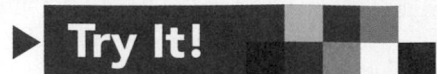

Assume you are in charge of preparing the operating activities section of the statement of cash flows using the indirect method. In order to reconcile the company's net income back to the cash basis, would you (1) add, or (2) subtract each of the following?

1. An increase in accounts receivable
2. Depreciation expense
3. A decrease in accounts payable
4. A gain on the sale of equipment
5. A decrease in prepaid insurance
6. An increase in wages payable

Please see page 822 for solutions.

Preparing the Cash Flows from Investing Activities

Recall that transactions affecting long-term asset accounts are classified as investing activities. So the first step in preparing the investing section is to determine whether any changes occurred in the long-term assets accounts during the year. The comparative balance sheets presented in Exhibit 13-4 show changes in three long-term asset accounts:

1. Property, Plant, and Equipment—increase of $515,000
2. Accumulated Depreciation (a contra asset to Property, Plant, and Equipment)—increase of $119,000
3. Investments—increase of $100,000

After noting these changes, we would need to delve into the company's records (such as the general journal) to find more information about these investing activities. The following additional information was found:

> a. Equipment originally costing $25,000 was sold for $3,000. The equipment had accumulated depreciation of $23,000, resulting in a gain of $1,000.
>
> b. The company purchased $100,000 of stock in XYZ company.
> No stock investments were sold during the year.

Now let's see how we use this information to sort out investment activities that took place during the year.

Property, Plant, and Equipment

By analyzing the change in this account, we can figure out how much cash the company paid for new property, plant, and equipment (PP&E) during the year:

Beginning balance, PP&E (from Exhibit 13-4)	$2,900,000
Plus: Purchases of PP&E	?
Less: Original cost of equipment sold (from the additional information given)	(25,000)
Ending balance, PP&E (from Exhibit 13-4)	$3,415,000

We can illustrate this relationship in the form of an equation, and then solve for the unknown amount:

Beginning PP&E + Purchases of PP&E − PPE sold = Ending PP&E

$2,900,000   +   ???   − $25,000 = $3,415,000

We can rearrange the equation as follows:

Purchases of PP&E = $3,415,000 + $25,000 − $2,900,000

Solving the equation yields the following:

Purchases of PP&E = $540,000

On the statement of cash flows, we will show that $540,000 was used to purchase new property, plant, and equipment. Additionally, the sale of the old equipment for $3,000 will be shown as a *receipt* of cash. Notice that the statement of cash flows doesn't just show the net change in the Property, Plant, and Equipment account. Rather, the company needs to show separate line items for new investments purchased and old investments sold.

Accumulated Depreciation

This account is reconciled as follows:

Beginning balance, Accumulated depreciation (Exhibit 13-4)..........................	$380,000
Plus: Depreciation expense (Exhibit 13-3).......................................	142,000
Less: Accumulated depreciation on sold equipment (from the additional	
information given)	(23,000)
Ending balance, Accumulated depreciation (Exhibit 13-4)	$499,000

We already accounted for the depreciation expense as an adjustment to net income in the operating activities section of the statement of cash flows. Likewise, the accumulated depreciation on the sold equipment was taken into account in calculating the gain on sale. This too, became an adjustment to net income in the operating activities section. Because we have completely reconciled the change in this account and have already made the necessary adjustments, no other adjustments are needed.

Investments

Changes in long-term investments are analyzed as follows:

Beginning balance, Investments (Exhibit 13-4).................................	$185,000
Plus: Purchases of stock investments (from the additional	
information given)	?
Less: Sale of stock investments	?
Ending balance, Investments (Exhibit 13-4)	$285,000

According to the additional information given, SportsTime purchased $100,000 of new stock investments during the year, and did not sell any. Therefore, the investment account is completely reconciled as follows:

Beginning investments + Purchases of investments − Investments sold = Ending investments

$185,000   + $100,000   − $0   = $285,000

Any purchase or sale of long-term investments needs to be listed *separately* on the statement of cash flows. Keep in mind that if the company had sold some investments for an amount that differed from the original purchase price, a gain or loss would have resulted. This gain or loss would be shown as an adjustment to net income in the operating section of the statement, much like a gain or loss on the sale of property, plant, or equipment.

Now that we have analyzed the changes in each long-term asset account, we can prepare the investing section of the statement of cash flows. Exhibit 13-13 shows that the company used much of the cash it generated from operations ($1,040,500, from Exhibit 13-12) to pay for new investments in property, plant, and equipment ($540,000) and new stock investments ($100,000).

EXHIBIT 13-13 Investing Activities Section of the Statement of Cash Flows

	A	B	C
1	SportsTime, Inc.		
2	Statement of Cash Flows—Investing Activities Section		
3	For the Year Ended December 31, 2014		
4			
5	**Investing Activities:**		
6	Cash used to purchase property, plant, and equipment	$ (540,000)	
7	Proceeds from the sale of equipment	3,000	
8	Cash used to purchase investments in stock	(100,000)	
9	Net cash used by investing activities		(637,000)
10			

Preparing the Cash Flows from Financing Activities

Financing activities include transactions that either generate capital for the company or pay it back. Financing activities affect long-term liabilities and owners' equity accounts. The comparative balance sheets shown in Exhibit 13-4 show changes in the company's long-term liabilities, common stock, and retained earnings accounts. We'll have to analyze the changes in each of these accounts to determine the cash provided and used by financing activities. We'll also need the following information obtained from company records.

a. $100,000 of new bonds were issued during the year.

b. $300,000 of bonds were repaid during the year.

c. The board of directors declared cash dividends of $125,000 during the year.

Long-Term Liabilities

Any change in long-term liabilities can be explained either by new borrowings (issuance of notes or bonds payable) or the repayment of principal on existing debt:

Beginning balance, Long-term liabilities (Exhibit 13-4)	$750,000
Plus: Cash proceeds from new bond issuance	?
Less: Repayment of principal on existing debt	?
End balance, Long-term liabilities (Exhibit 13-4)	$550,000

The additional information provided reconciles this account as follows:

Beginning long-term liabilities + Bond issuance − Repayments of principal = Ending long-term liabilities

$750,000   + $100,000   − $300,000   = $550,000

We'll need to show the issuance and repayments separately on the statement of cash flows.

Common Stock

There was no change in the common stock account on the balance sheet (Exhibit 13-4); therefore, we can conclude that no transactions involving common stock took place during the year.

Retained Earnings

Retained earnings represents the cumulative earnings of a company, less distributions to the company's owners. We analyze the retained earnings account as follows:

Beginning balance, Retained earnings (Exhibit 13-4).....................................	$1,492,000
Plus: Net income (Exhibit 13-3)	937,300
Less: Dividends declared during the year (from the additional information given)	(125,000)
Ending balance, Retained earnings (Exhibit 13-4)..	$2,304,300

Since there was no dividends payable shown on the balance sheet, we can conclude that all dividends declared during the year ($125,000) were also paid out to stockholders. Remember, dividends are a distribution of capital back to the owners; not an expense on the income statement. Therefore, the dividends paid will be shown as a use of cash in the financing section of the statement of cash flows.

Exhibit 13-14 shows the completed statement of cash flows for SportsTime, prepared using the indirect method. The information provided in the financing section shows that the company used $300,000 for paying down long-term debt, but obtained $100,000 of new debt (perhaps at a lower interest rate). The company used an additional $125,000 to pay dividends to its owners.

EXHIBIT 13-14 Statement of Cash Flows (Indirect Method)

	A	B	C
1	SportsTime, Inc.		
2	Statement of Cash Flows (Indirect Method)		
3	For the Year Ended December 31, 2014		
4			
5	**Operating Activities:**		
6	Net income		$ 937,300
7	Adjustments to reconcile net income to cash basis:		
8	Depreciation expense	$ 142,000	
9	Gain on sale of equipment	(1,000)	
10	Increase in accounts receivable	(35,000)	
11	Decrease in inventory	25,000	
12	Increase in prepaid insurance	(5,000)	
13	Decrease in accounts payable	(40,000)	
14	Increase in wages payable	8,500	
15	Decrease in interest payable	(5,000)	
16	Increase in income taxes payable	26,700	
17	Decrease in other accrued expenses payable	(13,000)	
18	Total reconciling adjustments		103,200
19	Net cash provided by operating activities		1,040,500
20			
21	**Investing Activities:**		
22	Cash used to purchase property, plant, and equipment	$ (540,000)	
23	Proceeds from the sale of equipment	3,000	
24	Cash used to purchase investments in stock	(100,000)	
25	Net cash used by investing activities		(637,000)
26			
27	**Financing Activities:**		
28	Proceeds from bond issuance	$ 100,000	
29	Repayment of long-term debt	(300,000)	
30	Cash payments for dividends	(125,000)	
31	Net cash used by financing activities		(325,000)
32	Net increase in cash		78,500
33	Cash, beginning of the year		125,000
34	Cash, end of the year		$ 203,500
35			

Interpreting the Statement of Cash Flows

The statement of cash flows shown in Exhibit 13-14 presents a detailed explanation of how SportsTime generated and used cash during the year. In summary, we see that a little over $1 million in cash was generated by the company's day-to-day operating activities. Roughly 61% of this cash was used to purchase new, long-term investments, and 31% was used to decrease company debt and pay dividends. The remaining 8% was added to the company's cash balance, leaving cash $78,500 higher than it was at the beginning of the year.

Free Cash Flow

Many potential investors calculate the company's free cash flow using the information provided on the statement of cash flows. **Free cash flow** represents the amount of excess cash a business generates after taking into consideration the capital expenditures necessary to maintain its business. This cash can then be used for expansion, to pay dividends, to pay down debt, or for any other business purpose (which is why it is called "free"). Essentially, it is the cash generated from the company's core business that is "left over" after paying bills and making capital expenditures. Free cash flow is calculated as follows:

Free cash flow = Cash flow from operating activities − Capital expenditures

Using the information provided in Exhibit 13-14, we can calculate SportsTime's free cash flow as follows:

$$= \$1,040,500 - \$540,000$$
$$= \$500,500$$

The presence of free cash flow means that SportsTime has the ability to expand, produce new products, pay dividends, buy back treasury stock, or reduce its debt. Potential investors place high value on a company's ability to generate free cash flow and often use it as a means of valuing stock.

Recap: Steps to Preparing the Statement of Cash Flows Using the Indirect Method

Exhibit 13-15 summarizes the steps used to create a statement of cash flows using the indirect method.

EXHIBIT 13-15 Steps for Using the Indirect Method

Step 1. Begin the operating section with the company's net income and add back any noncash expenses (such as depreciation or losses on the sale of property, plant, and equipment) and subtract any noncash revenues (such as gains on the sale of property, plant, or equipment). This information is found on the company's income statement.

Step 2. Adjust net income for all changes in current asset and current liability accounts (other than the Cash account) that are found on the company's comparative balance sheet:
- **Add back** decreases in current asset accounts and increases in current liability accounts.
- **Subtract** increases in current asset accounts and decreases in current liability accounts.

Step 3. Prepare the investing section by analyzing the changes in all long-term asset accounts found on the company's comparative balance sheet. Separately list all cash transactions that took place during the year affecting these accounts (such as buying and selling property). Any gains or losses on sales, depreciation, or amortization of these assets has already been accounted for in the operating section.

Step 4. Prepare the financing section by analyzing the changes in all long-term liability and equity accounts found on the company's comparative balance sheet. Separately list all cash transactions that took place during the year affecting these accounts (such as issuing new debt or paying down existing debt, selling stock, buying treasury stock, or paying dividends).

Step 5. Present a subtotal of the amount of cash provided or used by each of the three types of activities (operating, investing, and financing). Use the subtotals to find the overall increase or decrease in cash during the year. Then add the increase to (or subtract the decrease from) the company's beginning cash balance to arrive at the ending cash balance shown on the company's balance sheet.

How is the Statement of Cash Flows Prepared Using the Direct Method?

In this section, we'll prepare the statement of cash flows using the direct method. Keep in mind that the choice of method (indirect versus direct) only affects the operating activities section of the statement of cash flows. The investing and financing sections are the same regardless of the method used.

3 Prepare the statement of cash flows using the direct method

Overview

The direct method lists the receipt and payment of cash for specific operating activities. For example, the operating activities would list such line items as follows:

- Cash receipts from customers
- Cash payments (to suppliers) for purchase of inventory
- Cash payments (to employees) for salaries and wages

In essence, the direct method lists many of the same items shown on the income statement, but calculates them on a cash, rather than accrual, basis. Exhibit 13-16 shows SportsTime's statement of cash flows using the direct method. Notice the reference numbers (1–7) provided in the operating activities section the schedule. These reference numbers are only provided for the sake of instruction, and are never included on an actual statement of cash flows. In the following section, we'll show the supporting calculations for each referenced line item on the statement.

Why is this important?

"In the **future**, the **FASB** and **IASB** may require companies to use the **direct method**. This method shows, in a straight-forward manner, what the company **received and paid cash** for during the year."

EXHIBIT 13-16 Statement of Cash Flows (Direct Method)

	A	B	C	D
1	SportsTime, Inc.			
2	Statement of Cash Flows (Direct Method)			
3	For the Year Ended December 31, 2014			
4				
5	Operating Activities:	Ref.*		
6	Cash receipts from customers	(1)	$ 9,465,000	
7	Cash payments for inventory	(2)	(7,140,000)	
8	Cash payments for insurance	(3)	(30,000)	
9	Cash payments for salaires and wages	(4)	(571,500)	
10	Cash payments for interest expense	(5)	(65,000)	
11	Cash payments for income taxes	(6)	(375,000)	
12	Cash payments for other operating expenses	(7)	(243,000)	
13	Net cash provided by operating activities			1,040,500
14				
15	Investing Activities:			
16	Cash used to purchase property, plant, and equipment		$ (540,000)	
17	Proceeds from the sale of equipment		3,000	
18	Cash used to purchase investments in stock		(100,000)	
19	Net cash used by investing activities			(637,000)
20				
21	Financing Activities:			
22	Proceeds from bond issuance		$ 100,000	
23	Repayment of long-term debt		(300,000)	
24	Cash payments for dividends		(125,000)	
25	Net cash used by financing activities			(325,000)
26	Net increase in cash			78,500
27	Cash, beginning of the year			125,000
28	Cash, end of the year			$ 203,500
29				

*NOTE: The reference numbers are provided for the sake of instruction only and are never actually shown on the statement of cash flows.

Notice that the cash provided by operating activities ($1,040,500) is the *same* as we found using the indirect method (shown in Exhibit 13-14).

Determining Cash Payments and Receipts

The best way to make sure you've captured all cash transactions from operating activities is to analyze *every* current asset and current liability account shown on the balance sheet (Exhibit 13-4), and incorporate related information from the income statement (Exhibit 13-3) as necessary. Let's start with current assets.

(1) Cash Receipts from Customers

To determine the amount of cash received from customers we must analyze accounts receivable. Accounts receivable increases when sales are made and decreases when cash is collected:

Beginning balance, Accounts receivable (Exhibit 13-4)	$ 330,000
Plus: Sales revenue (from income statement)	9,500,000
Less: Cash collections of accounts receivable	?
Ending balance, Accounts receivable (Exhibit 13-4)	$ 365,000

Solving for the unknown, we determine that cash collections of sales must be $9,465,000.

(2) Cash Payments for Inventory

The next current asset account on the balance sheet is inventory. We'll use this account, along with accounts payable (current liability), to figure out how much cash was used to purchase inventory. First let's think about what affects the inventory account: The account increases for the purchase of inventory, and decreases for the cost of goods sold. Therefore, we can establish the following relationship:

Beginning balance, Inventory (Exhibit 13-4)	$ 657,000
Plus: Purchases of inventory	?
Less: Cost of goods sold (Exhibit 13-3)	(7,125,000)
Ending balance, Inventory (Exhibit 13-4)	$ 632,000

Solving for the unknown, we determine that purchases of inventory must have been $7,100,000.

However, did the company pay for all of these purchases during the year? We'll only know by investigating the changes in accounts payable (we assume SportsTime uses accounts payable only for inventory purchases):

Beginning balance, Accounts payable (Exhibit 13-4)	$ 285,000
Plus: Purchases of inventory	7,100,000
Less: Cash payments for inventory	(?)
Ending balance, Accounts payable (Exhibit 13-4)	$ 245,000

Solving for the unknown, we determine that payments for inventory must have been $7,140,000.

(3) Cash Payments for Insurance

The next current asset on the balance sheet is prepaid insurance. This account will increase for purchases of insurance, and decrease as a result of recording insurance expense:

Beginning balance, Prepaid insurance (Exhibit 13-4)	$ 15,000
Plus: Payments for insurance	?
Less: Insurance expense (Exhibit 13-3)	(25,000)
Ending balance, Prepaid insurance (Exhibit 13-4)	$ 20,000

Solving for the unknown, we determine that payments for insurance must have been $30,000.

We've analyzed all of the current asset accounts found on the company's balance sheet, so now we turn our attention to the current liability accounts shown in Exhibit 13-4. The first current liability shown is accounts payable. We've already analyzed that account when calculating the amount of inventory purchased. The remaining current liability accounts include wages payable, interest payable, income taxes payable, and other accrued expenses payable. We'll examine each of these next.

(4) Cash Payments for Salaries and Wages

Wages payable increases when we record salaries and wages expense, and decreases when the company pays its employees:

Beginning balance, Wages payable (Exhibit 13-4)	$ 48,500
Plus: Salaries and wages expense (Exhibit 13-3)	580,000
Less: Payments for salaries and wages	(?)
Ending balance, Wages payable (Exhibit 13-4)	$ 57,000

Solving for the unknown, we determine that payments for salaries and wages must have been $571,500.

(5) Cash Payments for Interest Expense

Interest payable increases when we record interest expense, and decreases when the company pays interest:

Beginning balance, Interest payable (Exhibit 13-4)	$ 8,000
Plus: Interest expense (Exhibit 13-3)	60,000
Less: Payments for interest	(?)
Ending balance, Interest payable (Exhibit 13-4)	$ 3,000

Solving for the unknown, we determine that payments for interest expense must have been $65,000.

(6) Cash Payments for Income Taxes

Income taxes payable increases when we record income tax expense, and decreases when the company pays income taxes:

Beginning balance, Income taxes payable (Exhibit 13-4)	$120,000
Plus: Income tax expense (Exhibit 13-3)	401,700
Less: Payments for income taxes	(?)
Ending balance, Income taxes payable (Exhibit 13-4)	$146,700

Solving for the unknown, we determine that payments for income taxes must have been $375,000.

(7) Cash Payments for Other Operating Expenses

SportsTime's income statement lists many of their operating expenses separately: salaries and wages expense, insurance expense, and depreciation expense. It then lumps together its remaining operating expenses, as shown in Exhibit 13-3. "Other operating expenses" would include such expenses as rent, utilities, telephone and internet, supplies, and so forth. SportsTime records liabilities for these expenses as "other accrued expenses payable":

Beginning balance, Other accrued expenses payable (Exhibit 13-4)	$ 28,500
Plus: Other operating expenses (Exhibit 13-3)	230,000
Less: Payments for other operating expenses	(?)
Ending balance, Other accrued expenses payable (Exhibit 13-4)	$ 15,500

Solving for the unknown, we determine that payments for other operating expenses must have been $243,000.

Cash Flows from Operating Activities

By analyzing each current asset and current liability account, we have figured out the actual cash receipts and cash payments made for each operating activity during the year. After listing each transaction separately (Exhibit 13-16), we see that the cash flows from operating activities totals $1,040,500, just as it did using the indirect method.

Comparing the Direct and Indirect Methods

As you can see, the direct method requires much more analysis than the indirect method. As a result, most companies currently use the indirect method. However, the FASB and IASB have jointly recommended that companies use the direct method because it shows cash receipts and cash payments in a much more straightforward manner. Nonetheless, both methods result in the same *total* amount of cash provided by operating activities (for SportsTime, $1,040,500).

Decision Guidelines

Statement of Cash Flows

Companies have a choice of using the indirect method or direct method. The following decision guidelines provide general guidance for preparing the statement of cash flows using either method.

Decision	Guidelines
What kind of information is needed in order to prepare the statement of cash flows?	The following information is needed: 1. Income statement for the year 2. Balance sheets for the current and prior year (comparative balance sheets) 3. Additional information about investing and financing activities that occurred during the year
If my company uses the indirect method, what adjustments should be shown when reconciling net income to the cash basis?	1. All noncash expenses are **added back** to net income. 2. All noncash revenues are **deducted** from net income. 3. All changes in current asset and current liability accounts will either be added or deducted from net income (as indicated below).
To reconcile net income to the cash basis, do we add or subtract changes in current asset accounts? (indirect method)	• *If a current asset account **increases**, then **subtract** the change from net income.* • *If a current asset account **decreases**, then **add** the change to net income.*
To reconcile net income to the cash basis, do we add or subtract changes in current liability accounts? (indirect method)	• *If a current liability account **increases**, then **add** the change to net income.* • *If a current liability account **decreases**, then **subtract** the change from net income.*
What process should be used to prepare the investing section of the statement of cash flows?	You will need to analyze the change in every long-term asset account found on the balance sheet. Purchases and sales of investments need to be disclosed separately on the statement of cash flows. (You can't just show the net change in each account.)
What process should be used to prepare the financing section of the statement of cash flows?	You will need to analyze the change in every long-term liability and owners' equity account found on the balance sheet to determine the financing transactions that took place during the year.
My company has decided to use the direct method. What process should be used to prepare the operating section of the statement of cash flows?	Each current asset and current liability account will need to be analyzed to determine the cash transactions underlying the change in the account. These transactions typically include the following: • Receipts from customers • Payments for inventory • Payments for salaries and wages • Payments for other operating expenses (listed separately, or grouped together, depending on the presentation of expenses in the income statement)

SUMMARY PROBLEM 2

Urban Togs is a regional retailer of trend-setting clothing that is made with socially and environmentally friendly practices. The company's income statement and comparative balance sheets are presented below. In addition, the following information was gathered from the company's records:

a. No new debt was issued during the year.

b. Dividends of $200,000 were declared by the board of directors.

c. Equipment with an original cost of $20,000 was sold for $9,000.

   The equipment had accumulated depreciation of $15,000 at the time of sale.

Requirement

Prepare the company's statement of cash flows using the indirect method.

	A	B	C
1	Urban Togs		
2	Income Statement		
3	For the Year Ended December 31, 2014		
4			
5	Sales revenues		$ 4,750,000
6	Less: Cost of goods sold		3,562,500
7	Gross profit		1,187,500
8	Less operating expenses:		
9	Salaries and wages expense	$ 340,000	
10	Insurance expense	10,000	
11	Depreciation expense	75,000	
12	Other operating expenses	125,000	
13	Total operating expenses		550,000
14	Operating income		$ 637,500
15	Plus other income and less other expenses:		
16	Interest expense	8,000	
17	Gain on sale of PP&E	4,000	
18	Total other income and expenses		4,000
19	Income before income taxes		633,500
20	Less: Income tax expense		190,050
21	Net income		$ 443,450
22			

	A	B	C
1	Urban Togs		
2	Comparative Balance Sheets		
3	December 31, 2014 and 2013		
4	**Assets**	**2014**	**2013**	**Increase (Decrease)**
5	Current assets:			
6	Cash	$ 187,000	$ 85,000	102,000
7	Accounts receivable	37,000	57,000	(20,000)
8	Inventory	337,500	350,000	(12,500)
9	Prepaid insurance	5,000	3,000	2,000
10	Total current assets	566,500	495,000	
11				
12	Property, plant, and equipment	1,860,00	1,660,000	200,000
13	Less: Accumulated depreciation	(310,000)	(250,000)	60,000
14	Investments	50,000	50,000	0
15	Total assets	$ 2,166,500	$ 1,955,000	
16				
17	**Liabilities**			
18	Current liabilities:			
19	Accounts payable	$ 65,000	$ 85,000	(20,000)
20	Wages payable	29,000	25,000	4,000
21	Interest payable	2,000	8,000	(6,000)
22	Income taxes payable	100,050	85,000	15,050
23	Other accrued expenses payable	13,000	18,000	(5,000)
24	Total current liabilities	209,050	221,000	
25				
26	Long-term liabilities	80,000	100,000	(20,000)
27	Total liabilities	289,050	321,000	
28				
29	**Stockholders' equity**			
30	Common stock	850,000	850,000	0
31	Retained earnings	1,027,450	784,000	243,450
32	Total stockholders' equity	1,877,450	1,634,000	
33				
34	Total liabilities and equity	$ 2,166,500	$ 1,955,000	
35				

▪ SOLUTION

The following steps are taken to prepare the statement of cash flows using the indirect method:

1. We begin the operating section with the company's net income, and add back any noncash expenses (depreciation) and then subtract any noncash revenues (gains on the sale of property, plant, or equipment).

2. We then adjust net income for all changes in current asset and current liability accounts (other than the cash account):

    - We *add* decreases in current asset accounts and increases in current liability accounts.

    - We *subtract* increases in current asset accounts and decreases in current liability accounts.

3. To prepare the investing section, we analyze the changes in all long-term asset accounts. We separately list all cash transactions that took place during the year (for example, buying and selling property, plant, and equipment or long-term investments). Any gains, losses, depreciation, or amortization of these assets has already been accounted for in the operating section.

4. To prepare the financing section, we analyze the changes in all long-term liability and equity accounts. We separately list all cash transactions that took place during the year (for example, issuing new debt or paying down existing debt, selling stock, buying treasury stock, or paying dividends).

	A	B	C
1	Urban Togs		
2	Statement of Cash Flows (Indirect Method)		
3	For the Year Ended December 31, 2014		
4			
5	**Operating Activities:**		
6	Net income		$ 443,450
7	Adjustments to reconcile net income to cash basis:		
8	Depreciation expense	$ 75,000	
9	Gain on sale of equipment	(4,000)	
10	Decrease in accounts receivable	20,000	
11	Decrease in inventory	12,500	
12	Increase in prepaid insurance	(2,000)	
13	Decrease in accounts payable	(20,000)	
14	Increase in wages payable	4,000	
15	Decrease in interest payable	(6,000)	
16	Increase in income taxes payable	15,050	
17	Decrease in other accrued expenses payable	(5,000)	
18	Total reconciling adjustments		89,550
19	Net cash provided by operating activities		553,000
20			
21	**Investing Activities:**		
22	Cash used to purchase property, plant, and equipment	$ (220,000)	
23	Proceeds from the sale of equipment	9,000	
24	Net cash used by investing activities		(211,000)
25			
26	**Financing Activities:**		
27	Repayment of long-term debt	$ (20,000)	
28	Cash payments for dividends	(200,000)	
29	Net cash used by financing activities		(220,000)
30	Net increase in cash		102,000
31	Cash, beginning of the year		85,000
32	Cash, end of the year		$ 187,000
33			

Analysis of Investing and Financing Activities:
Property, Plant, and Equipment:

Beginning balance, PP&E	$1,660,000
Plus: Purchases of PP&E	?
Less: Original cost of equipment sold (given)	(20,000)
Ending balance, PP&E	$1,860,000

Solving for the unknown, the company must have purchases of $220,000 of property, plant, and equipment. This will be shown as an investing activity.

Accumulated Depreciation:

Beginning balance, Accumulated depreciation...	$250,000
Plus: Depreciation expense...	75,000
Less: Accumulated depreciation on sold equipment (given)............................	(15,000)
Ending balance, Accumulated depreciation	$310,000

The depreciation expense will be shown as an operating activity.

Gain on Sale of Equipment

Sale price of equipment (given)...		$9,000
Original cost of the equipment...	$20,000	
Less: Accumulated depreciation	15,000	
Net book value of equipment..		5,000
Gain on sale		$4,000

The $4,000 gain on sale will be shown as an adjustment to net income in the operating section while the $9,000 cash received will be shown as an investing activity.

Long-Term Liabilities:

Beginning balance, Long-term liabilities...	$100,000
Plus: Cash proceeds from new bond issuance (given)	0
Less: Repayment of principal on existing debt...	?
End balance, Long-term liabilities	$ 80,000

Solving for the unknown, the company must have repaid $20,000 of principal on the existing long-term debt. This will be shown as an investing activity.

Retained Earnings:

Beginning balance, Retained earnings..	$ 784,000
Plus: Net income	443,450
Less: Dividends declared during the year (given)	(200,000)
Ending balance, Retained earnings..	$1,027,450

The payment of dividends will be shown as a financing activity.

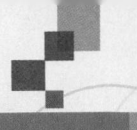

END OF CHAPTER

Learning Objectives

■ 1 Classify cash flows as operating, investing, or financing activities

■ 2 Prepare the statement of cash flows using the indirect method

■ 3 Prepare the statement of cash flows using the direct method

Accounting Vocabulary

Accrual Basis of Accounting. (p. 770) Revenues are recorded when they are earned (when the sale takes place), rather than when cash is received on the sale. Likewise, expenses are recorded when they are incurred, rather than when they are paid.

Cash Equivalents. (p. 767) Very safe, highly liquid assets that are readily convertible into cash, such as money market funds, certificates of deposit that mature in less than three months, and U.S. treasury bills.

Comparative Balance Sheets. (p. 774) A comparison of the balance sheets from the end of two fiscal periods, usually highlighting the changes in each account.

Direct Method. (p. 769) A method of presenting cash flows from operating activities that separately lists the receipt and payment of cash for specific operating activities.

Financing Activities. (p. 768) Activities that either generate capital for the company or pay it back, such as issuing stock or long-term debt, paying dividends, and repaying principal amounts on loans; this includes all activities that affect long-term liabilities and owners' equity.

Free Cash Flow. (p. 784) The amount of excess cash a business generates after taking into consideration the capital expenditures necessary to maintain its business. It is calculated as cash flows from operating activities minus capital expenditures.

Indirect Method. (p. 770) A method of presenting the cash flows from operating activities that begins with the company's net income, which is prepared on an accrual basis, and then reconciles it back to the cash basis through a series of adjustments.

Investing Activities. (p. 767) Activities that involve buying or selling long-term assets, such as buying or selling property, plant, or equipment; buying or selling stock in other companies (if the stock is meant to be held for the long term); or loaning money to other companies with the goal of earning interest income from the loan.

Net Book Value. (p. 775) The original cost of plant or equipment less its accumulated depreciation.

Operating Activities. (p. 767) The day-to-day profit-making activities of the company, such as making or buying inventory, selling inventory, selling services, paying employees, advertising, and so forth; this also includes *any other activity that affects net income* (not just operating income), current assets, or current liabilities.

Statement of Cash Flows. (p. 766) One of the four basic financial statements; the statement shows the overall increase or decrease in cash during the period as well as how the company generated and used cash during the period.

MyAccountingLab   **Go to** http://myaccountinglab.com/ **for the following Quick Check, Short Exercises, Exercises, and Problems. They are available with immediate grading, explanations of correct and incorrect answers, and interactive media that acts as your own online tutor.**

Quick Check

1. *(Learning Objective 1)* Which of the following is **not** one of the activities found on the statement of cash flows?
   a. Investing activities
   b. Operating activities
   c. Administrative activities
   d. Financing activities

2. *(Learning Objective 1)* Transactions that affect long-term liabilities and stockholders' equity are classified as which of the following?
   a. Operating activities
   b. Administrative activities
   c. Financing activities
   d. Investing activities

3. *(Learning Objective 1)* Transactions that affect long-term assets are classified as which of the following?

a. Administrative activities

b. Financing activities

c. Investing activities

d. Operating activities

4. *(Learning Objective 1)* Transactions that affect net income, current assets, and current liabilities are classified as which of the following?

a. Investing activities

b. Operating activities

c. Financing activities

d. Administrative activities

5. *(Learning Objective 1)* Interest and dividend income are both classified as

a. operating activities.

b. financing activities.

c. administrative activities.

d. investing activities.

6. *(Learning Objective 1)* The payment of dividends is classified as a(n)

a. operating activity.

b. financing activity.

c. administrative activity.

d. investing activity.

7. *(Learning Objective 1)* Which method of preparing the statement of cash flows is most commonly used, even though FASB and IASB encourage the use of the other method?

a. Accrual

b. Direct

c. Standard

d. Indirect

8. *(Learning Objective 2)* If using the indirect method, which of the following statements is correct?

a. An increase in a current liability account should be subtracted from net income.

b. A decrease in a current liability account should be added to net income.

c. An increase in a current asset account should be subtracted from net income.

d. None of the items listed is correct if using the indirect method.

9. *(Learning Objective 3)* The difference between the two methods of presenting the statement of cash flows is only found in the section reporting

a. operating activities.

b. financing activities.

c. administrative activities.

d. investing activities.

10. *(Learning Objective 3)* Which one of the following lines would be found on the statement of cash flows for a company using the direct method?

a. Depreciation expense

b. Cash receipts from customers

c. Increase in prepaid insurance

d. Gain on sale of property, plant, and equipment

Quick Check Answers

1. c 2. c 3. c 4. b 5. a 6. b 7. d 8. c 9. a 10. b

Short Exercises

S13-1 Classifying cash flows *(Learning Objective 1)*

Crooked River Corporation is preparing its statement of cash flows (indirect method) for the past year. Listed below are items used in preparing the company's statement of cash flows. Specify how each item would be treated on Crooked River Corporation's statement of cash flows by using the following abbreviations:

1. Operating activity—addition to net income (O+)

2. Operating activity—subtraction from net income (O−)

3. Financing activity (F)

4. Investing activity (I)

5. Activity that is not on the statement of cash flows (NA)

a. Amortization expense	——	h. Increase in inventory	——
b. Retained earnings	——	i. Increase in accounts payable	——
c. Decrease in prepaid expense	——	j. Repayment of long-term loan	——
d. Loss on sale of land	——	k. Gain on sale of building	——
e. Issuance of common stock	——	l. Payment of dividends	——
f. Purchase of equipment	——	m. Increase in accounts receivable	——
g. Increase in accrued liabilities	——	n. Net income	——

S13-2   Identifying activities for the statement of cash flows—indirect method
(Learning Objectives 1 & 2)

Identify each of Knox Industries' transactions listed below as operating (O), investing (I), financing (F), noncash investing and financing (NIF), or a transaction that is not reported on the statement of cash flows (NA). Also indicate whether the transaction increases (+) or decreases (−) cash. The indirect method is used for operating activities.

a. Depreciation of equipment	——	i. Amortization of patent	——
b. Increase in raw materials inventory	——	j. Purchase building with cash	——
c. Payment of cash dividend	——	k. Increase in accrued taxes payable	——
d. Decrease in prepaid expenses	——	l. Gain on sale of equipment	——
e. Purchase of treasury stock	——	m. Payment of long-term debt	——
f. Cash sale of land (no gain or loss)	——	n. Issuance of common stock for cash	——
g. Sale of long-term investment	——	o. Purchase of delivery truck	——
h. Decrease in salaries payable	——	p. Acquisition of equipment by issuance of note payable	——

S13-3   Preparing the operation cash flows section (indirect method)
(Learning Objective 2)

Merriweather Corporation began the year with accounts receivable, inventory, and prepaid expenses totaling $69,000. At the end of the year, Merriweather had a total of $78,000 for these current assets. At the beginning of the year, it owed current liabilities of $43,000, and at year-end, current liabilities totaled $38,000.

Net income for the year was $86,000. Included in net income was a $3,000 gain on the sale of land and depreciation expense of $10,000.

Show how Merriweather should report cash flows from operating activities for the year. The company uses the indirect method.

S13-4   Classify cash flows as operating, investing, or financing
(Learning Objectives 1 & 2)

For each of the following situations, identify whether the activity is an operating, investing, or financing activity and compute the cash provided or used by the activity.

Activity	Operating (O) Investing (I) Financing (F)	Amount of Cash Flow	Increase (+) Decrease (−)
a. A building with a cost of $182,000 and accumulated depreciation of $45,000 was sold for a $25,000 gain.			
b. Net income for last year was $112,000. The accumulated depreciation balance increased by $28,000. There were no changes in noncash current assets or liabilities. There were also no sales of plant assets.			
c. Net income was $26,000 for the year. Accounts receivable increased by $3,000 and accounts payable increased by $6,000. There were no other changes in the noncash current assets and current liabilities. There was no depreciation for the year.			
d. Bonds payable with a face value of $50,000 were retired with a cash payment for their face value. New bonds were issued later in the year for $37,000.			
e. Bonds payable were retired for their face value of $60,000 (cash paid). Cash dividends of $17,000 were also paid. A new note payable was signed for cash proceeds of $23,000.			
f. A plant asset with a cost of $61,000 and accumulated depreciation of $12,000 was sold for a $15,000 loss.			
g. Current assets (not including cash) increased by $2,000 and current liabilities decreased by $12,000. There was no depreciation. Net income was $52,000 for the year.			
h. Common stock was issued for $210,000 cash. Dividends of $25,000 were paid in cash.			
i. Noncash current assets decreased by $6,000 and current liabilities decreased by $17,000. Depreciation was $15,000 for the year, while net income was $57,000.			

S13-5   Calculate investing cash flows *(Learning Objectives 1, 2, & 3)*

Sherman Company reported the following financial statements for 2013 and 2014:

	A	B	C
1	Sherman Company		
2	Income Statement		
3	For the Year Ended December 31, 2014		
4			
5	Sales revenues		$ 4,750,000
6	Less: Cost of goods sold		2,880,000
7	Gross profit		1,870,000
8	Less operating expenses:		
9	Salaries and wages expense	$ 320,000	
10	Insurance expense	12,000	
11	Depreciation expense	77,000	
12	Other operating expenses	120,000	
13	Total operating expenses		529,000
14	Operating income		$ 1,341,000
15	Plus other income and less other expenses:		
16	Interest expense	6,100	
17	Other income and expenses	0	
18	Total other income and expenses		6,100
19	Income before income taxes		$ 1,334,900
20	Less: Income tax expense		403,000
21	Net income		$ 931,900
22			

	A	B	C
1	Sherman Company		
2	Comparative Balance Sheets		
3	December 31, 2014 and 2013		
4	**Assets**	**2014**	**2013**
5	Current assets:		
6	Cash	$ 589,000	$ 464,000
7	Accounts receivable	73,000	17,000
8	Inventory	960,000	200,000
9	Prepaid insurance	4,800	4,800
10	Total current assets	$ 1,626,800	$ 685,800
11			
12	Property, plant, and equipment	$ 1,230,000	$ 1,180,000
13	Less: Accumulated depreciation	(286,000)	(209,000)
14	Investments	42,000	62,000
15	Total assets	$ 2,612,800	$ 1,718,800
16			
17	**Liabilities**		
18	Current liabilities:		
19	Accounts payable	$ 21,000	$ 44,000
20	Wages payable	17,000	19,000
21	Interest payable	2,700	5,300
22	Income taxes payable	275,080	38,000
23	Other accrued expenses payable	21,000	14,000
24	Total current liabilities	$ 336,780	$ 120,300
25			
26	Long-term liabilities	65,000	80,000
27	Total liabilities	$ 401,780	$ 200,300
28			
29	**Stockholders' equity**		
30	Common stock	$ 721,000	$ 778,000
31	Retained earnings	1,490,020	740,500
32	Total stockholders' equity	$ 2,211,020	$ 1,518,500
33			
34	Total liabilities and equity	$ 2,612,800	$ 1,718,800
35			

Compute the following investing cash flows:

a. Purchases of plant assets (all were for cash). There were no sales of plant assets.

b. Proceeds from the sale of investments. There were no purchases of investments.

S13-6 Calculate financing cash flows (Learning Objectives 2 & 3)

Use the data given in S13-5 for the Sherman Company to compute the following financing cash flows:

a. New borrowing or payment of long-term notes payable. Sherman Company had only one long-term note payable transaction during the year.

b. Issuance of common stock or retirement of common stock. The company had only one common stock transaction during the year.

c. Payment of cash dividends (same as dividends declared).

S13-7 Classify cash flows as operating, investing, or financing
(Learning Objectives 1, 2, & 3)

The items in the following table may or may not appear in a statement of cash flows.

	Operating (O) Investing (I) Financing (F)	Direct (D) Indirect (I) Both (B)	Increase (+) Decrease (−)
1. Decrease in accounts receivable			
2. Increase in payroll taxes payable			
3. Cash paid to suppliers			
4. Cash received from customers			
5. Purchase of treasury stock			
6. Increase in salaries payable			
7. Principal payments on long-term note payable			
8. Purchase of plant assets			
9. Depreciation expense			
10. Cash paid for taxes			
11. Dividends paid			
12. Issuance of stock			

For each of the items in the table, indicate the following:

1. Would the item appear on the statement of cash flows under operating activities (O), investing activities (I), or financing activities (F)?
2. Would the item appear on the statement of cash flows using the direct method (D), indirect method (I), or both (B)?
3. Would the item result in an increase (+) or a decrease (−) when computing cash flow?

S13-8 Prepare statement of cash flows (indirect method) *(Learning Objective 2)*

Thornton Corporation uses the indirect method to prepare its statement of cash flows. Data related to cash activities for last year is as follows:

Net income...	$ 92,500
Dividends paid (cash)	$ 50,100
Depreciation expense	$ 14,000
Net decrease in current assets....................................	$ 21,700
Issued new notes payable for cash	$ 41,700
Paid cash for building...	$271,000
Net decrease in current liabilities................................	$ 5,700
Sold investment for cash...	$400,000

Answer the following questions:

1. What was the net cash flow from operating activities for the year?
2. What was the cash flow from (or used for) investing activities for the year?
3. What was the cash flow from (or used for) financing activities for the year?
4. What was the net change in cash for the year?
5. If the beginning balance of cash for the year was $158,000, what was the balance of cash at the end of the year?

S13-9   Calculate increase or decrease in current assets and liabilities
(Learning Objective 3)

A recent statement of cash flows for Lamett Company reported the following information:

	A	B	C
1	Net income		$ 451,900
2	Adjustments to reconcile net income to cash basis:		
3	Depreciation expense	$ 63,000	
4	Accounts receivable	28,000	
5	Inventory	(17,000)	
6	Other current assets	8,500	
7	Accounts payable	(18,000)	
8	Other current liabilities	198,000	
9	Total reconciling adjustments		262,500
10	Net cash provided by operating activities		$ 714,400
11			

Based on the information presented in the statement of cash flows for Lamett Company, determine whether the following accounts increased or decreased during the period: Accounts Receivable, Inventory, Other Current Assets, Accounts Payable, and Other Current Liabilities.

S13-10   Prepare statement of cash flows (direct method) *(Learning Objective 3)*

Scotts Corporation uses the direct method to prepare its statement of cash flows. Data related to cash activities for last year appears next.

Paid for equipment	$14,000	Paid for interest	$ 4,300
Paid to suppliers	$39,000	Paid for utilities	$17,000
Paid for insurance	$ 9,200	Paid dividends	$ 7,400
Depreciation expense	$ 3,700	Received from customers	$50,000
Paid for advertising	$ 7,400	Paid for taxes	$ 5,500
Received from sale of land	$15,000	Received from issuing long-term note payable	$29,000
Received from sale of plant assets	$ 6,900	Paid to employees	$13,000

Answer the following questions:

1. What was the net cash flow from operating activities for the year?
2. What was the net cash flow from investing activities for the year?
3. What was the net cash flow from financing activities for the year?
4. What was the net change in cash for the year?
5. If the beginning balance of cash for the year was $349,000, what was the balance of cash at the end of the year?

S13-11 Identify ethical standards violated (*Learning Objectives 1, 2, 3, 4, 5, & 6*)

For each of the situations listed, identify the primary standard from the IMA *Statement of Ethical Professional Practice* that is violated (competence, confidentiality, integrity, or credibility). Refer to Exhibit 1-6 for the complete standard.

a. Darryl does not disclose to upper management that his sister is a partner in the accounting firm that the company is hiring for the audit.

b. Lamar is an accountant at Boise & Hall, Inc. Lamar confides to a close friend that he is concerned about the future of Boise & Hall. Lamar explains that operating cash flows are negative; this information is on the not-yet-released financial statements.

c. Patsy is an accountant at Highland Restaurant Group, Inc. She has helped to prepare the financial statements. She knows that the internal controls over cash are weak, but she does not speak up because she feels that it is not her job.

d. Teri uses the indirect method to prepare the statement of cash flows even though her company has adopted International Financial Reporting Standards. She is unfamiliar with the steps required to produce a statement using the direct method.

e. The statement of cash flows has never been Julius' strength; he struggled with it in school. This year, Julius cannot get the statement of cash flows to balance, so he decides to hide the amount that the statement is off by adding that difference to one of the items in the operating section.

EXERCISES Group A

E13-12A Prepare operating cash flows section (indirect method)
(*Learning Objective 2*)

The comparative balance sheet for Mosaic Travel Services, Inc., for December 31, 2014 and 2013, is as follows:

	A	B	C
1	Mosaic Travel Services, Inc.		
2	Comparative Balance Sheets		
3	December 31, 2014 and 2013		
4	**Assets**	**2014**	**2013**
5	Current assets:		
6	Cash	$ 11,000	$ 18,000
7	Accounts receivable	78,000	79,000
8	Inventory	58,000	18,000
9	Prepaid insurance	9,000	12,000
10	Total current assets	$ 156,000	$ 127,000
11			
12	Land	$ 105,000	$ 114,000
13	Equipment	83,000	57,000
14	Less: Accumulated depreciation	(15,000)	(8,000)
15	Total assets	$ 329,000	$ 290,000
16			
17	**Liabilities**		
18	Current liabilities:		
19	Accounts payable	$ 28,000	$ 37,000
20	Wages payable	26,000	24,000
21	Interest payable	12,000	11,000
22	Income taxes payable	7,000	4,000
23	Total current liabilities	$ 73,000	$ 76,000
24			
25	Notes payable (long term)	96,000	87,000
26	Total liabilities	$ 169,000	$ 163,000
27			
28	**Stockholders' equity**		
29	Common stock	$ 129,000	$ 119,000
30	Retained earnings	31,000	8,000
31	Total stockholders' equity	$ 160,000	$ 127,000
32			
33	Total liabilities and equity	$ 329,000	$ 290,000
34			

The following information is taken from the records of Mosaic Travel Services, Inc.:

a. Land was sold for $5,600.
b. Equipment was purchased for cash.
c. There were no disposals of equipment during the year.
d. The common stock was issued for cash.
e. Net income for 2014 was $33,000.
f. Cash dividends paid during the year were $10,000.

Mosaic Travel Services, Inc., uses the indirect method for preparing the statement of cash flows. Prepare the operating section of the statement of cash flows for 2014.

E13-13A   Prepare statement of cash flow preparation (indirect method)
(Learning Objective 2)

Using the data given in E13-12A, prepare the statement of cash flows (indirect method) for Mosaic Travel Services, Inc., for 2014.

E13-14A   Calculate cash flows from operating, investing, and financing activities (direct method) *(Learning Objectives 2 & 3)*

Compute the following cash flows for Swift Media Services Company for the past year:

1. The beginning balance of Retained Earnings was $139,000, while the end of the year balance of Retained Earnings was $178,000. Net income for the year was $61,000. No dividends payable were on the balance sheet. How much was paid in cash dividends during the year?

2. The beginning and ending balances of the Common Stock account were $212,000 and $271,000, respectively. Where would the increase in Common Stock appear on the statement of cash flows?

3. The beginning and ending balances of the Treasury Stock account were $52,000 and $80,000, respectively. Where would the increase in Treasury Stock appear on the statement of cash flows?

4. The Property, Plant, & Equipment (net) increased by $11,000 during the year to have a balance of $151,000 at the end of the year. Depreciation for the year was $13,000. Acquisitions of new plant assets during the year totaled $43,000. Plant assets were sold at a loss of $3,000.

   a. What were the cash proceeds from the sale of plant assets?
   b. What amount would be reported on the investing section of the statement of cash flows? Would it be a source of cash or a use of cash?
   c. What amount, if any, would be reported on the operating section of the statement of cash flows?

E13-15A   Calculate operating cash flows (indirect method)
(Learning Objective 2)

Century Corporation has the following activities for the past year:

Net income	$?	Cost of goods sold	$44,000
Payment of dividends	$ 7,000	Other operating expenses	$16,000
Proceeds from issuance of stock	$ 76,000	Depreciation expense	$21,000
Purchase of treasury stock	$ 10,000	Purchase of equipment	$27,000
Sales revenue	$117,000	Proceeds from sale of land	$18,000
Payment of note payable	$ 17,000	Increase in current assets other than cash	$ 4,000
Decrease in current liabilities	$ 11,000		

Requirement
Prepare the operating activities section of Century Corporation's statement of cash flows for the year ended December 31, using the indirect method for operating cash flows.

E13-16A   Prepare statement of cash flows (indirect method)

(Learning Objective 2)

Using the data given in E13-15A, prepare statement of cash flows for Century Corporation for the year. Century Corporation uses the indirect method for operating activities.

E13-17A   Prepare statement of cash flows (indirect method)

(Learning Objective 2)

Brooklyn Corporation is preparing its statement of cash flows for the past year. The company has gathered the following information about the past year just ended on December 31.

Retire bond payable (long-term)................	$15,000	Decrease in accounts receivable......................	$10,000
Paid dividends in cash................................	$29,000	Increase in salaries payable.............................	$ 7,000
Decrease in inventory.................................	$ 6,000	Depreciation expense	$11,000
Decrease in accounts payable....................	$ 5,000	Increase in prepaid insurance..........................	$ 600
Sold land (investment)...............................	$18,000	Decrease in other short-term liabilities...........	$ 3,000
Increase in interest payable........................	$ 400	Increase in taxes payable	$ 2,000
Cash balance, beginning of year.................	$92,000	Purchase of new computer system	$10,000
Net income...	$85,000		

Requirement

Prepare a statement of cash flows for the past year using the indirect method.

E13-18A   Compute operating cash flows using direct method

(Learning Objective 3)

Medway Spas provides the following data for the year just ended December 31.

Payment of note payable	$ 6,000	Payments to employees...................................	$ 62,000
Depreciation expense	$ 4,700	Proceeds from sale of land..............................	$ 42,500
Purchase of equipment	$ 9,000	Payment of dividends......................................	$ 13,500
Purchase of treasury stock	$ 11,000	Payments to suppliers	$ 64,000
Gain on sale of land	$ 1,500	Increase in salaries payable.............................	$ 11,500
Cost of goods sold......................................	$110,000	Payment of income tax	$ 8,000
Proceeds from issuance of common stock....	$ 13,000	Collections from customers.............................	$148,000
Beginning balance, cash	$ 12,000	Sales revenue	$170,000

Requirement

Prepare the operating activities section of Medway Spas' statement of cash flows for the year just ended, using the direct method for operating cash flows.

E13-19A   Prepare statement of cash flows (direct method)

(Learning Objective 3)

Using the data from E13-18A, prepare the statement of cash flows using the direct method.

E13-20A   Prepare statement of cash flows (direct method)

(Learning Objective 3)

Mason Interiors began the year with cash of $52,000. During the year, Mason Interiors earned service revenue of $412,000. Cash collections for the year were $375,000. Expenses for the year were $385,000, with $370,000 of that total paid in cash. The company also used cash to purchase equipment for $80,000 and to pay a cash dividend to stockholders of $30,000. During the year, the company also borrowed $58,000 cash by issuing a note payable.

Requirement

Prepare the company's statement of cash flows using the direct method.

SUSTAINABILITY

E13-21A   Classify sustainable activities' effect on cash flows

(Learning Objectives 1, 2, & 3)

The Plastic Lumber Company, Inc., (PLC) is a manufacturer that takes in post-consumer plastics (i.e., empty milk jugs) and recycles those plastics into a "plastic lumber" that can be used to build furniture, decking, and a variety of other items. Because Plastic Lumber has a strong focus on sustainability, the company managers try, whenever possible, to use recycled materials and to invest in sustainable projects.

Last year, the company engaged in several sustainable practices that have an impact on its cash flows. For each of the transactions listed below, indicate whether the transaction would have affected the operating, investing, or financing cash flows of the company. Additionally, indicate whether each transaction would have increased (+) or decreased (−) cash.

Transactions:

1. Engineers at PLC performed research into a new process that injects tiny air bubbles into the plastic to reduce the usage of raw materials (plastics) and to reduce the weight of the finished products.
2. A Honda Civic Hybrid automobile was purchased for use by the CEO of PLC.
3. PLC became a minority partner in a solar-panel electricity generation project by investing $1 million in cash in the project.
4. Throughout the year, PLC participated in several trade shows that featured green products for use by parks and recreation facilities. For each trade show, PLC incurred cash expenses for transportation, registration, meals and lodging, and booth setup.
5. A fleet of plug-in electric cars was purchased for sales staff.
6. PLC installed a "living roof" on its manufacturing facility. This roof is made mostly from sedum, runoff, and doubles the expected life of the roof over a conventional roof. The plants also reduce heating and cooling needs by providing an extra layer of insulation. Additionally, the plants absorb carbon dioxide to help to reduce green-house gases. The living roof was paid for with cash.
7. When the plastic wood is cut into lengths needed to build picnic tables, the end pieces cut off are scrap. PLC sold this cutting scrap to another recycler.
8. A wind-turbine was built to power part of PLC's operations.
9. PLC issues long-term bonds during the year to help to finance growth.
10. New production equipment that is 40% more energy efficient than the old equipment was purchased for cash.

EXERCISES Group B

E13-22B   Prepare operating cash flows section (indirect method)
(Learning Objective 2)

The comparative balance sheet for Dream Travel Services, Inc., for December 31, 2014 and 2013, is as follows:

	A	B	C
1	**Dream Travel Services, Inc.**		
2	**Comparative Balance Sheets**		
3	**December 31, 2014 and 2013**		
4	**Assets**	**2014**	**2013**
5	Current assets:		
6	Cash	$ 42,000	$ 18,000
7	Accounts receivable	78,000	83,000
8	Inventory	56,000	21,000
9	Prepaid insurance	11,000	13,000
10	Total current assets	$ 187,000	$ 135,000
11			
12	Land	$ 103,000	$ 115,000
13	Equipment	78,000	58,000
14	Less: Accumulated depreciation	(13,000)	(8,000)
15	Total assets	$ 355,000	$ 300,000
16			
17	**Liabilities**		
18	Current liabilities:		
19	Accounts payable	$ 27,000	$ 30,000
20	Wages payable	34,000	23,000
21	Interest payable	16,000	14,000
22	Income taxes payable	8,000	5,000
23	Total current liabilities	$ 85,000	$ 72,000
24			
25	Notes payable (long term)	90,000	85,000
26	Total liabilities	$ 175,000	$ 157,000
27			
28	**Stockholders' equity**		
29	Common stock	$ 130,000	$ 123,000
30	Retained earnings	50,000	20,000
31	Total stockholders' equity	$ 180,000	$ 143,000
32			
33	Total liabilities and equity	$ 355,000	$ 300,000
34			

The following information is taken from the records of Dream Travel Services, Inc.:

a. Land was sold for $8,100.

b. Equipment was purchased for cash.

c. There were no disposals of equipment during the year.

d. The common stock was issued for cash.

e. Net income for 2014 was $37,000.

f. Cash dividends paid during the year were $7,000.

Dream Travel Services, Inc., uses the indirect method for preparing the statement of cash flows. Prepare the operating section of the statement of cash flows for 2014.

E13-23B   Prepare statement of cash flow preparation (indirect method)
(Learning Objective 2)

Using the data given in E13-22B, prepare the statement of cash flows (indirect method) for Dream Travel Services, Inc., for 2014.

E13-24B   Calculate cash flows from operating, investing, and financing activities (direct method) *(Learning Objectives 2 & 3)*

Compute the following cash flows for High Seas Nautical Company for the past year:

1. The beginning balance of Retained Earning was $139,000, while the end of the year balance of Retained Earnings was $178,000. Net income for the year was $61,000. No dividends payable were on the balance sheet. How much was paid in cash dividends during the year?

2. The beginning and ending balances of the Common Stock account were $212,000 and $271,000, respectively. Where would the increase in Common Stock appear on the statement of cash flows?

3. The beginning and ending balances of the Treasury Stock account were $51,000 and $75,000, respectively. Where would the increase in Treasury Stock appear on the statement of cash flows?

4. Property, Plant, and Equipment (net) increased by $14,000 during the year to have a balance of $159,000 at the end of the year. Depreciation for the year was $17,000. Acquisitions of new plant assets during the year totaled $39,000. Plant assets were sold at a loss of $2,000.

   a. What were the cash proceeds from the sale of plant assets?

   b. What amount would be reported on the investing section of the statement of cash flows? Would it be a source of cash or a use of cash?

   c. What amount would be reported on the operating section of the statement of cash flows? How would it be presented?

E13-25B   Calculate operating cash flows (indirect method)
(Learning Objective 2)

Eduardo Corporation has the following activities for the past year:

Net income..	$?	Cost of goods sold..	$44,000
Payment of dividends..................................	$ 2,000	Other operating expenses	$16,000
Proceeds from issuance of stock.................	$ 76,000	Depreciation expense	$18,000
Purchase of treasury stock	$ 12,000	Purchase of equipment	$29,000
Sales revenue	$120,000	Proceeds from sale of land..............................	$24,000
Payment of note payable............................	$ 15,000	Increase in current assets other than cash	$ 5,000
Decrease in current liabilities......................	$ 7,000		

Requirement

Prepare the operating activities section of Eduardo Corporation's statement of cash flows for the year ended December 31, using the indirect method for operating cash flows.

E13-26B   Prepare statement of cash flows (indirect method)
(Learning Objective 2)

Using the data given in E13-25B, prepare the statement of cash flows for Eduardo Corporation for the year. The company uses the indirect method for operating activities.

E13-27B   Prepare statement of cash flows (indirect method)
(Learning Objective 3)

The Pepperpike Corporation is preparing its statement of cash flows for the past year just ended on December 31. The controller has gathered the following information about the past year.

Retire bond payable (long-term).................	$15,000	Decrease in accounts receivable......................	$10,000
Paid dividends in cash.................................	$34,000	Increase in salaries payable..............................	$ 9,000
Decrease in inventory..................................	$ 8,000	Depreciation expense	$12,000
Decrease in accounts payable......................	$ 5,000	Increase in prepaid insurance..........................	$ 500
Sold land (investment).................................	$26,000	Decrease in other short-term liabilities............	$ 2,000
Increase in interest payable.........................	$ 800	Increase in taxes payable	$ 1,000
Cash balance, beginning of year.................	$89,000	Purchase of new computer system	$16,000
Net income..	$92,000		

Requirement

Prepare a statement of cash flows for the past year using the indirect method.

E13-28B Compute operating cash flows using the direct method
(Learning Objective 3)

Orange Grove Spas provides the following data for the year just ended December 31.

Payment of note payable	$ 6,500	Payments to employees	$ 65,500
Depreciation expense	$ 4,200	Proceeds from sale of land	$ 40,000
Purchase of equipment	$ 7,000	Payment of dividends	$ 12,500
Purchase of treasury stock	$ 12,000	Payments to suppliers	$ 61,000
Gain on sale of land	$ 1,300	Increase in salaries payable	$ 13,500
Cost of goods sold	$109,000	Payment of income tax	$ 8,500
Proceeds from issuance of common stock	$ 10,500	Collections from customers	$152,000
Beginning balance, cash	$ 13,000	Sales revenue	$165,000

Requirement

Prepare the operating activities section of Orange Grove Spas' statement of cash flows for the year ended December 31 using the direct method for operating cash flows.

E13-29B Prepare statement of cash flows (direct method)
(Learning Objective 3)

Using the data for E13-28B, prepare the statement of cash flows using the direct method.

E13-30B Prepare statement of cash flows (direct method)
(Learning Objective 3)

Matthew Interiors began the year with cash of $51,000. During the year, Matthew Interiors earned service revenue of $408,000. Cash collections for the year were $395,000. Expenses for the year were $390,000, with $375,000 of that total paid in cash. The company also used cash to purchase equipment for $60,000 and to pay a cash dividend to stockholders of $25,000. During the year, the company borrowed $56,000 cash by issuing a note payable.

Requirement

Prepare the company's statement of cash flows using the direct method.

E13-31B Classify sustainable activities' effect on cash flows
(Learning Objectives 1, 2, & 3)

SUSTAINABILITY

The Plastic Lumber Company, Inc., (PLC) is a manufacturer that takes in post-consumer plastics (i.e., empty milk jugs) and recycles those plastics into a "plastic lumber" that can be used to build furniture, decking, and a variety of other items. Because Plastic Lumber has a strong focus on sustainability, the company managers try, whenever possible, to use recycled materials and to invest in sustainable projects.

Last year, the company engaged in several sustainable practices that have an impact on its cash flows. For each of the transactions listed below, indicate whether the transaction would have affected the operating, investing, or financing cash flows of the company. Additionally, indicate whether each transaction would have increased (+) or decreased (−) cash.

Transactions:

1. PLC built a new building for its manufacturing facility. The new building is LEED certified and was paid for with cash.
2. Engineers and scientists at PLC performed research into whether another kind of post-consumer plastic not currently used in its plastics extrusion process could be used.
3. Solar panels were installed on PLC's administrative offices to supply part of the electricity needed for its operations.
4. PLC issued common stock during the year to help finance growth.
5. New production equipment that is 50% more energy efficient than the old equipment was purchased for cash.
6. Six Honda Civic Hybrid automobiles were purchased for the use of the sales staff.

7. PLC became a minority partner in a wind-turbine project by investing $1 million in cash in the project.

8. PLC sold plastic scrap generated by its manufacturing process.

9. Throughout the year, PLC participated in several trade shows that featured green products for use by parks and recreation facilities. For each trade show, PLC incurred cash expenses for transportation, registration, meals and lodging, and booth setup.

10. A new delivery truck that uses biofuel was purchased for cash.

PROBLEMS Group A

P13-32A   Prepare statement of cash flows (indirect method)
(Learning Objective 2)

Prepare statement of cash flows using the indirect method. The income statement for 2014 and the balance sheets for 2014 and 2013 are presented for Hoover Industries, Inc.

	A	B	C
1	Hoover Industries, Inc.		
2	Income Statement		
3	For the Year Ended December 31, 2014		
4			
5	Sales revenues		$ 957,000
6	Less: Cost of goods sold		385,000
7	Gross profit		$ 572,000
8	Less operating expenses:		
9	Salaries and wages expense	$ 192,000	
10	Insurance expense	10,500	
11	Depreciation expense	48,900	
12	Other operating expenses	87,000	
13	Total operating expenses		338,400
14	Operating income		$ 233,600
15	Plus other income and less other expenses:		
16	Interest expense	$ 5,500	
17	Gain on sale of PP&E	3,000	
18	Total other income and expenses		2,500
19	Income before income taxes		$ 231,100
20	Less: Income tax expense		69,330
21	Net income		$ 161,770
22			

	A	B	C
1	Hoover Industries, Inc.		
2	Comparative Balance Sheets		
3	December 31, 2014 and 2013		
4	Assets	2014	2013
5	Current assets:		
6	Cash	$ 473,000	$ 285,000
7	Accounts receivable	72,000	122,000
8	Inventory	333,000	213,000
9	Prepaid insurance	9,000	7,000
10	Total current assets	$ 887,000	$ 627,000
11			
12	Property, plant, and equipment	$ 595,000	$ 575,000
13	Less: Accumulated depreciation	(152,000)	(112,000)
14	Investments	86,000	76,000
15	Total assets	$ 1,416,000	$ 1,166,000
16			
17	Liabilities		
18	Current liabilities:		
19	Accounts payable (inventory purchases)	$ 54,000	$ 37,000
20	Wages payable	16,200	17,300
21	Interest payable	1,600	300
22	Income taxes payable	60,330	9,500
23	Other accrued expenses payable	6,100	3,200
24	Total current liabilities	$ 138,230	$ 67,300
25			
26	Long-term liabilities	63,000	27,000
27	Total liabilities	$ 201,230	$ 94,300
28			
29	Stockholders' equity		
30	Common stock	$ 600,000	$ 600,000
31	Retained earnings	614,770	471,700
32	Total stockholders' equity	$ 1,214,770	$ 1,071,700
33			
34	Total liabilities and equity	$ 1,416,000	$ 1,166,000
35			

Additional information follows:

a. Sold plant asset for $4,500. The original cost of this plant asset was $10,400 and it had $8,900 of accumulated depreciation associated with it.

b. Paid $5,000 on the bonds payable; issued $41,000 of new bonds payable.

c. Declared and paid cash dividends of $18,700.

d. Purchased new investment for $10,000.

e. Purchased new equipment for $30,400.

Requirement

Prepare a statement of cash flows for Hoover Industries, Inc., for the year ended December 31, 2014, using the indirect method.

P13-33A   Prepare statement of cash flows (indirect method)
(Learning Objectives 1 & 2)

The 2014 and 2013 balance sheets of Wilson Corporation follow. The 2014 income statement is also provided. Wilson had no noncash investing and financing transactions during 2014. During the year, the company sold equipment for $15,400, which had originally cost $13,300 and had a book value of $11,500. The company did not issue any notes payable during the year but did issue common stock for $35,000.

Requirements

1. Prepare the statement of cash flows for Wilson Corporation for 2014 using the indirect method.

2. Evaluate the company's cash flows for the year. Discuss each of the categories of cash flows in your response.

	A	B	C
1	Wilson Corporation		
2	Income Statement		
3	For the Year Ended December 31, 2014		
4			
5	Sales revenues		$ 340,000
6	Less: Cost of goods sold		79,000
7	Gross profit		$ 261,000
8	Less operating expenses:		
9	Salaries and wages expense	$ 27,500	
10	Depreciation expense	4,600	
11	Other operating expenses	12,000	
12	Total operating expenses		$ 44,100
13	Operating income		$ 216,900
14	Plus other income and less other expenses:		
15	Interest expense	$ 9,200	
16	Gain on sale of PP&E	3,900	
17	Total other income and expenses		5,300
18	Income before income taxes		$ 211,600
19	Less: Income tax expense		35,200
20	Net income		$ 176,400
21			

	A	B	C
1	Wilson Corporation		
2	Comparative Balance Sheets		
3	December 31, 2014 and 2013		
4	Assets	2014	2013
5	Current assets:		
6	Cash	$ 50,500	$ 19,000
7	Accounts receivable	32,100	29,700
8	Inventory	86,500	94,400
9	Prepaid insurance	3,400	2,500
10	Total current assets	$ 172,500	$ 145,600
11			
12	Property, plant, and equipment	157,000	138,000
13	Less: Accumulated depreciation	(30,200)	(27,400)
14	Investments	117,000	0
15	Total assets	$ 416,300	$ 256,200
16			
17	Liabilities		
18	Current liabilities:		
19	Accounts payable	$ 33,800	$ 36,200
20	Wages payable	2,800	7,300
21	Interest payable	2,700	0
22	Income taxes payable	6,000	0
23	Other accrued expenses payable	18,900	22,100
24	Total current liabilities	$ 64,200	$ 65,600
25			
26	Long-term liabilities	72,000	118,000
27	Total liabilities	$ 136,200	$ 183,600
28			
29	Stockholders' equity		
30	Common stock	106,000	71,000
31	Retained earnings	174,100	1,600
32	Total stockholders' equity	$ 280,100	$ 72,600
33			
34	Total liabilities and equity	$ 416,300	$ 256,200
35			

P13-34A   Prepare a statement of cash flows (direct method)

(Learning Objectives 1 & 3)

Dellroy Digital Services, Inc., has provided the following data from the company's records for the year just ended December 31:

a. Collection of interest..	$ 5,500
b. Cash sales..	$254,500
c. Credit sales..	$675,000
d. Proceeds from sale of investment..	$ 12,600
e. Gain on sale of investment...	$ 2,500
f. Payments to suppliers	$572,000
g. Cash payments to purchase plant assets	$ 52,700
h. Depreciation expense	$ 63,200
i. Salaries expense..	$ 77,800
j. Payment of short-term note payable by issuing common stock..............	$ 72,000
k. Cost of goods sold...	$566,500
l. Proceeds from issuance of note payable	$ 24,400
m. Income tax expense and payment	$ 38,400
n. Proceeds from issuance of common stock...	$ 22,500
o. Receipt of cash dividends	$ 6,600
p. Interest revenue..	$ 5,900
q. Payment of cash dividends...	$ 28,800
r. Collections of accounts receivable..	$572,500
s. Amortization expense	$ 3,200
t. Payments on long-term notes payable	$ 44,000
u. Interest expense and payments	$ 12,600
v. Purchase of equipment by issuing common stock to seller.....................	$ 17,200
w. Payment of salaries..	$ 74,900
x. Proceeds from sale of plant assets...	$ 24,100
y. Loss on sale of plant assets	$ 3,700
z. Cash and cash equivalents balance, beginning of year	$ 25,200

Requirements

1. Prepare the statement of cash flows for Dellroy Digital Services, Inc., using the direct method for cash flows from operations. Note that you will need to calculate the ending balance of cash and cash equivalents. Include a schedule of noncash investing and financing activities.

2. Evaluate Dellroy's cash flows for the year. Discuss each of the categories of cash flows in your response.

P13-35A　Prepare statements of cash flows (indirect and direct method)

(Learning Objectives 1, 2, & 3)

Barton Publication Company, Inc., has the following comparative balance sheet as of March 31, 2014.

	A	B	C
1	Barton Publication Company, Inc.		
2	Comparative Balance Sheets		
3	December 31, 2014 and 2013		
4	**Assets**	**2014**	**2013**	**Increase (Decrease)**
5	Current assets:			
6	Cash	$　　55,200	$　　14,500	40,700
7	Accounts receivable	51,500	53,700	(2,200)
8	Inventory	64,900	60,200	4,700
9	Prepaid insurance	3,700	5,400	(1,700)
10	Total current assets	$　175,300	$　133,800	
11				
12	Land	34,500	96,000	(61,500)
13	Equipment, net	71,300	70,800	500
14	Investments	9,500	6,500	3,000
15	Total assets	$　290,600	$　307,100	
16				
17	**Liabilities**			
18	Current liabilities:			
19	Accounts payable	$　　4,400	$　　3,300	1,100
20	Note payable, short-term	43,100	48,800	(5,700)
21	Income tax payable	14,000	15,400	(1,400)
22	Salary payable	9,900	12,900	(3,000)
23	Interest payable	8,300	6,800	1,500
24	Accrued liabilities	1,200	3,100	(1,900)
25	Total current liabilities	$　　80,900	$　　90,300	
26				
27	Long-term liabilities	47,800	93,600	(45,800)
28	Total liabilities	$　128,700	$　183,900	
29				
30	**Stockholders' equity**			
31	Common stock	69,000	61,300	7,700
32	Retained earnings	92,900	61,900	31,000
33	Total stockholders' equity	$　161,900	$　123,200	
34				
35	Total liabilities and equity	$　290,600	$　307,100	
36				

Selected transaction data for the year ended March 31, 2014, include the following:

a. Net income	$ 76,600
b. Paid long-term note payable with cash	$ 59,400
c. Cash payments to employees	$ 42,700
d. Loss on sale of land	$ 9,700
e. Acquired equipment by issuing long-term note payable	$ 13,600
f. Cash payments to suppliers	$147,400
g. Cash paid for interest	$ 2,900
h. Depreciation expense on equipment	$ 13,100
i. Paid short-term note payable by issuing common stock	$ 5,700
j. Paid cash dividends	$ 45,600
k. Received cash for issuance of common stock	$ 2,000
l. Cash received from customers	$298,200
m. Cash paid for income taxes	$ 11,600
n. Sold land for cash	$ 51,800
o. Interest received (in cash)	$ 1,300
p. Purchased long-term investment for cash	$ 3,000

Requirements

1. Prepare the statement of cash flows for Barton Publication Company, Inc., for the year ended March 31, 2014, using the indirect method for operating cash flows. Include a schedule of noncash investing and financing activities. All of the current accounts, except short-term notes payable, result from operating transactions.

2. Also prepare a supplementary schedule of cash flows from operations using the direct method.

PROBLEMS Group B

P13-36B   Prepare statement of cash flows (indirect method)
(Learning Objective 2)

Prepare the statement of cash flows using the indirect method. The income statement for 2014 and the balance sheets for 2014 and 2013 are presented for Griffin Industries.

	A	B	C
1	Griffin Industries, Inc.		
2	Income Statement		
3	For the Year Ended December 31, 2014		
4			
5	Sales revenues		$ 957,000
6	Less: Cost of goods sold		384,000
7	Gross profit		$ 573,000
8	Less operating expenses:		
9	Salaries and wages expense	$ 184,000	
10	Insurance expense	11,000	
11	Depreciation expense	47,000	
12	Other operating expenses	86,000	
13	Total operating expenses		328,000
14	Operating income		$ 245,000
15	Plus other income and less other expenses:		
16	Interest expense	5,200	
17	Gain on sale of PP&E	3,000	
18	Total other income and expenses		2,200
19	Income before income taxes		$ 242,800
20	Less: Income tax expense		72,840
21	Net income		$ 169,960
22			

	A	B	C
1	Griffin Industries, Inc.		
2	Comparative Balance Sheets		
3	December 31, 2014 and 2013		
4	**Assets**	**2014**	**2013**
5	Current assets:		
6	Cash	$ 471,000	$ 290,000
7	Accounts receivable	75,000	129,000
8	Inventory	332,000	210,000
9	Prepaid insurance	7,000	5,500
10	Total current assets	$ 885,000	$ 634,500
11			
12	Property, plant, and equipment	605,000	575,000
13	Less: Accumulated depreciation	(150,000)	(112,000)
14	Investments	93,000	75,000
15	Total assets	$ 1,433,000	$ 1,172,500
16			
17	**Liabilities**		
18	Current liabilities:		
19	Accounts payable (inventory purchases)	$ 59,000	$ 39,000
20	Wages payable	16,000	17,400
21	Interest payable	1,400	800
22	Income taxes payable	63,840	9,500
23	Other accrued expenses payable	6,100	3,700
24	Total current liabilities	$ 146,340	$ 70,400
25			
26	Long-term liabilities	62,000	28,000
27	Total liabilities	$ 208,340	$ 98,400
28			
29	**Stockholders' equity**		
30	Common stock	608,000	608,000
31	Retained earnings	616,660	466,100
32	Total stockholders' equity	$ 1,224,660	$ 1,074,100
33			
34	Total liabilities and equity	$ 1,433,000	$ 1,172,500
35			

Additional information follows:

a. Sold plant asset for $4,500. Original cost of this plant asset was $10,500 and it had $9,000 of accumulated depreciation associated with it.

b. Paid $5,500 on the bonds payable; issued $39,500 of new bonds payable.

c. Declared and paid cash dividends of $19,400.

d. Purchased new investment for $18,000.

e. Purchased new equipment for $40,500.

Requirement

Prepare a statement of cash flows for Griffin Industries, Inc., for the year ended December 31, 2014, using the indirect method.

P13-37B   Prepare statement of cash flows (indirect method)

(Learning Objectives 1 & 2)

The 2014 and 2013 balance sheets of Watson Corporation follow. The 2014 income statement is also provided. Watson had no noncash investing and financing transactions during 2014. During the year, the company sold equipment for $15,600, which had originally cost $13,200 and had a book value of $11,400. The company did not issue any notes payable during the year but did issue common stock for $32,000.

Requirements

1. Prepare the statement of cash flows for Watson Corporation for 2014 using the indirect method.

2. Evaluate the company's cash flows for the year. Discuss each of the categories of cash flows in your response.

	A	B	C
1	Watson Corporation		
2	Income Statement		
3	For the Year Ended December 31, 2014		
4			
5	Sales revenues		$ 340,000
6	Less: Cost of goods sold		78,000
7	Gross profit		$ 262,000
8	Less operating expenses:		
9	Salaries and wages expense	$ 27,000	
10	Depreciation expense	4,200	
11	Other operating expenses	12,000	
12	Total operating expenses		43,200
13	Operating income		$ 218,800
14	Plus other income and less other expenses:		
15	Interest expense	9,500	
16	Gain on sale of PP&E	4,200	
17	Total other income and expenses		5,300
18	Income before income taxes		$ 213,500
19	Less: Income tax expense		35,600
20	Net income		$ 177,900
21			

	A	B	C
1	Watson Corporation		
2	Comparative Balance Sheets		
3	December 31, 2014 and 2013		
4	Assets	2014	2013
5	Current assets:		
6	Cash	$ 48,500	$ 19,000
7	Accounts receivable	31,800	29,700
8	Inventory	86,200	93,300
9	Prepaid insurance	3,200	2,800
10	Total current assets	$ 169,700	$ 144,800
11			
12	Property, plant, and equipment	158,000	138,000
13	Less: Accumulated depreciation	(30,100)	(27,700)
14	Investments	110,000	0
15	Total assets	$ 407,600	$ 255,100
16			
17	Liabilities		
18	Current liabilities:		
19	Accounts payable	$ 33,100	$ 36,700
20	Wages payable	2,600	7,500
21	Interest payable	1,900	0
22	Income taxes payable	6,000	0
23	Other accrued expenses payable	18,700	22,100
24	Total current liabilities	$ 62,300	$ 66,300
25			
26	Long-term liabilities	79,000	114,000
27	Total liabilities	$ 141,300	$ 180,300
28			
29	Stockholders' equity		
30	Common stock	105,000	73,000
31	Retained earnings	161,300	1,800
32	Total stockholders' equity	$ 266,300	$ 74,800
33			
34	Total liabilities and equity	$ 407,600	$ 255,100
35			

P13-38B   Prepare a statement of cash flows (direct method)
(Learning Objectives 1 & 3)

Accurate Digital Services, Inc., has provided the following data from the company's records for the year just ended December 31:

a. Collection of interest	$ 5,600
b. Cash sales	$254,000
c. Credit sales	$673,500
d. Proceeds from sale of investment	$ 12,300
e. Gain on sale of investment	$ 2,800
f. Payments to suppliers	$573,000
g. Cash payments to purchase plant assets	$ 52,300
h. Depreciation expense	$ 63,400
i. Salaries expense	$ 77,100
j. Payment of short-term note payable by issuing common stock	$ 72,100
k. Cost of goods sold	$568,500
l. Proceeds from issuance of note payable	$ 24,100
m. Income tax expense and payment	$ 38,400
n. Proceeds from issuance of common stock	$ 23,500
o. Cash receipt of dividend revenue	$ 6,600
p. Interest revenue	$ 6,200
q. Payment of cash dividends	$ 28,900
r. Collections of accounts receivable	$573,000
s. Amortization expense	$ 3,700
t. Payments on long-term notes payable	$ 45,000
u. Interest expense and payments	$ 12,200
v. Purchase of equipment by issuing common stock to seller	$ 17,300
w. Payment of salaries	$ 74,300
x. Proceeds from sale of plant assets	$ 24,300
y. Loss on sale of plant assets	$ 3,700
z. Cash and cash equivalents balance, beginning of year	$ 25,400

Requirements

1. Prepare the statement of cash flows for Accurate Digital Services, Inc., using the direct method for cash flows from operations. Note that you will need to calculate the ending balance of cash and cash equivalents. Include a schedule of noncash investing and financing activities.
2. Evaluate the company's cash flows for the year. Discuss each of the categories of cash flows in your response.

P13-39B   Prepare statements of cash flows (indirect and direct method)
(Learning Objectives 1, 2, & 3)

Preston Company, Inc., has the following comparative balance sheet as of March 31, 2014.

	A	B	C
1	Preston Company, Inc.		
2	Comparative Balance Sheets		
3	December 31, 2014 and 2013		
4	**Assets**	**2014**	**2013**	**Increase (Decrease)**
5	Current assets:			
6	Cash	$ 55,500	$ 14,500	41,000
7	Accounts receivable	51,400	53,900	(2,500)
8	Inventory	65,600	59,600	6,000
9	Prepaid insurance	3,900	5,200	(1,300)
10	Total current assets	$ 176,400	$ 133,200	
11				
12	Land	34,000	96,500	(62,500)
13	Equipment, net	71,600	70,100	1,500
14	Investments	9,500	6,500	3,000
15	Total assets	$ 291,500	$ 306,300	
16				
17	**Liabilities**			
18	Current liabilities:			
19	Accounts payable	$ 4,700	$ 3,400	1,300
20	Note payable, short-term	43,200	48,200	(5,000)
21	Income tax payable	13,700	15,700	(2,000)
22	Salary payable	9,700	12,800	(3,100)
23	Interest payable	8,400	7,000	1,400
24	Accrued liabilities	1,500	3,500	(2,000)
25	Total current liabilities	$ 81,200	$ 90,600	
26				
27	Long-term liabilities	48,600	93,400	(44,800)
28	Total liabilities	$ 129,800	$ 184,000	
29				
30	**Stockholders' equity**			
31	Common stock	69,400	61,200	8,200
32	Retained earnings	92,300	61,100	31,200
33	Total stockholders' equity	$ 161,700	$ 122,300	
34				
35	Total liabilities and equity	$ 291,500	$ 306,300	
36				

Selected transaction data for the year ended March 31, 2014, include the following:

a. Net income, $76,400
b. Paid long-term note payable with cash, $60,000
c. Cash payments to employees, $42,700
d. Loss on sale of land, $9,500
e. Acquired equipment by issuing long-term note payable, $15,200
f. Cash payments to suppliers, $147,400
g. Cash paid for interest, $3,000
h. Depreciation expense on equipment, $13,700
i. Paid short-term note payable by issuing common stock, $5,000
j. Paid cash dividends, $45,200
k. Received cash for issuance of common stock, $3,200
l. Cash received from customers, $297,000
m. Cash paid for income taxes, $12,100
n. Sold land for cash, $53,000
o. Interest received (in cash), $1,200
p. Purchased long-term investment for cash, $3,000

Requirements

1. Prepare the statement of cash flows for Preston Company, Inc., for the year ended March 31, 2014, using the indirect method for operating cash flows. Include a schedule of noncash investing and financing activities. All of the current accounts except short-term notes payable result from operating transactions.

2. Also prepare a supplementary schedule of cash flows from operations using the direct method.

CRITICAL THINKING

Discussion & Analysis

A13-40 Discussion Questions

1. How do managers use the statement of cash flows?

2. Describe at least four needs for cash within a business.

3. Define an "operating activity." List two examples of an operating activity on the statement of cash flows that would *increase* cash. List two examples of an operating activity that would *decrease* cash.

4. Define an "investing activity." List two examples of an investing activity on the statement of cash flows that would *increase* cash. List two examples of an investing activity that would *decrease* cash.

5. Define a "financing activity." List two examples of a financing activity on the statement of cash flows that would *increase* cash. List two examples of a financing activity that would *decrease* cash.

6. Define a "noncash investing or financing" activity. Describe an activity that would need to be disclosed as a noncash investing or financing activity.

7. Describe the difference between the direct and the indirect methods of preparing the operating section of the statement of cash flows.

8. Describe the process for reconciling net income to the cash basis. What items are added to net income? What items are subtracted from net income?

9. When preparing a statement of cash flows using the indirect method, what information is needed? What documents or statements would be used?

10. Summarize the process for preparing the operations section of the statement of cash flows when using the direct method.

11. Provide an example of an operating cash inflow that could result from sustainability activities. Also provide an example of an operating cash outflow that would support sustainability.

12. Think of a company with which you are familiar. Describe an investing activity related to a company's sustainability efforts that would be classified as a use of cash on a company's statement of cash flows. Describe a financing activity related to a company's sustainability efforts that would be classified as a use of cash on a company's statement of cash flows.

Application & Analysis

Mini Cases

A13-41 Cash Flow Statements from Companies in the Same Industry

Select an industry in which you are interested and select two companies within that industry. Obtain their annual reports by going to each company's website and downloading the report for the most recent year. (On many company websites, you will need to visit the Investor Relations section or other similarly named link to obtain the company's financial statements.)

Basic Discussion Questions

For each of the companies you selected, answer the following:

1. Which method is used to calculate the cash provided or used by operations?

2. What items increased cash provided by operations?

3. What items decreased cash provided by operations?

4. Overall, was cash increased or decreased by operating activities?

5. Did investing activities in total increase cash or decrease cash during the year? What were the major uses or sources of cash related to investing?

6. Did financing activities in total increase cash or decrease cash during the year? What were the major uses or sources of cash related to financing?

7. What items (if any) are disclosed as significant noncash financing or investing activities? Now that you have looked at each company's cash flow statements individually, compare the two companies. What can you tell about each company from its statement of cash flows? Can you tell if one company is stronger than the other from their statements of cash flows? What clues do you have?

A13-42 Ethics involved with statement of cash flows preparation

(Learning Objectives 1, 2, & 3)

ETHICS

The Green Giraffe Restaurant Group has 21 restaurants scattered across the midwestern portion of the United States. Green Giraffe is not publicly held, but is owned by a small group of investors.

For years, the company has used the indirect method in preparing its statement of cash flows. Recently, it has come to the attention of a few of the investors that the statement of cash flows might be easier to understand and use if it were prepared using the direct method. At the quarterly meeting of the investors, they decide that the statement of cash flows for the Green Giraffe Restaurant Group should be prepared using the direct method.

Christopher Wargo is the controller for the Green Giraffe Restaurant Group. He graduated from college several years ago. He vaguely recalls learning about the direct method for preparing the statement of cash flows in college but has never used the method. Wargo is rather resentful that the investors are dictating accounting policy; he feels that the financial reporting that is currently done is adequate. Besides, even if the company reports using the direct method, a supplemental schedule of the indirect method will still need to be prepared. This change just seems to create extra work for Wargo.

Wargo decides he'll just do his best on preparing the statement using the direct method. He looks online and finds the Wikipedia page for the statement of cash flows and uses that model to prepare the statement. The company's information system is not set up to collect data for the direct method at this time. The data can be obtained but it will take several days. Wargo decides to just estimate the numbers that he's missing rather than spend the time to get the correct numbers. He feels it is unlikely that the auditors will find these few numbers that he has plugged; after all, the totals will be correct. This shortcut he is taking will save him hours of work.

Requirements

1. Using the IMA *Statement of Ethical Professional Practice* as an ethical framework, answer the following questions:

   a. What is(are) the ethical issue(s) in this situation?
   b. What are Wargo's responsibilities as a management accountant?

2. Discuss what Wargo should do in this situation. Refer to the IMA *Statement of Ethical Professional Practice* in your response.

A13-43 Analyzing a statement of cash flows
(Learning Objectives 1, 2, & 3)

Over recent years, Apple Inc. has had an excessive amount of cash reserves. The following is a recent statement of cash flows from Apple's 2012 Annual Report (Form 10-K).

Apple Inc.
Form 10-K[1]
For Year Ended September 29, 2012

CONSOLIDATED STATEMENTS OF CASH FLOWS
(In millions)

	Years ended		
	September 29, 2012	September 24, 2011	September 25, 2010
Cash and cash equivalents, beginning of the year	$ 9,815	$ 11,261	$ 5,263
Operating activities:			
Net income	41,733	25,922	14,013
Adjustments to reconcile net income to cash generated by operating activities:			
Depreciation and amortization	3,277	1,814	1,027
Share-based compensation expense..	1,740	1,168	879
Deferred income tax expense...	4,405	2,868	1,440
Changes in operating assets and liabilities:			
Accounts receivable, net...	(5,551)	143	(2,142)
Inventories..	(15)	275	(596)
Vendor non-trade receivable	(1,414)	(1,934)	(2,718)
Other current and non-current assets..	(3,162)	(1,391)	(1,610)
Accounts payable..	4,467	2,515	6,307
Deferred revenue..	2,824	1,654	1,217
Other current and non-current liabilities	2,552	4,495	778
Cash generated by operating activities	50,856	37,529	18,595
Investing activities:			
Purchases of marketable securities..	(151,232)	(102,317)	(57,793)
Proceeds from maturities of marketable securities	13,035	20,437	24,930
Proceeds from sales of marketable securities..............................	99,770	49,416	21,788
Payments made in connection with business acquisitions, net of cash acquired...	(350)	(244)	(638)
Payments for acquisition of property, plant and equipment.........	(8,295)	(4,260)	(2,005)
Payments for acquisition of intangible assets..............................	(1,107)	(3,192)	(116)
Other..	(48)	(259)	(20)
Cash used in investing activities..	(48,227)	(40,419)	(13,854)
Financing activities:			
Proceeds from issuance of common stock	665	831	912
Excess tax benefits from equity awards..	1,351	1,133	751
Dividends and dividend equivalent rights paid	(2,488)	0	0
Taxes paid related to net share settlement of equity awards........	(1,226)	(520)	(406)
Cash (used in)/generated by financing activities........................	(1,698)	1,444	1,257
Increase/(decrease) in cash and cash equivalents	931	(1,446)	5,998
Cash and cash equivalents, end of the year......................................	$ 10,746	$ 9,815	$ 11,261
Supplemental cash flow disclosure:			
Cash paid for income taxes, net	$ 7,682	$ 3,338	$ 2,697

See accompanying Notes to Consolidated Financial Statements.

[1]Retrieved from http://files.shareholder.com/downloads/AAPL/2607721130x0xS1193125-12-444068/320193/filing.pdf

Questions

Using Apple's Statement of Cash Flows, answer the following questions:

1. Did Apple's day-to-day operations generate or use cash?
2. Which section of the statement contains changes in Apple's long-term assets?
3. Which section of the statement reports on changes in Apple's long-term liabilities and stockholders' equity?
4. Is Apple spending money to expand its business by purchasing additional fixed assets?
5. Did Apple issue stock in the most recent year?
6. Has Apple increased or decreased its dividend payments over the past three years?
7. Is the overall change in cash at Apple positive or negative in the most recent year?
8. Is excess cash a positive thing for shareholders? Why or why not?
9. Did Apple purchase back any of its own stock? How do you know?
10. What is the net income trend for Apple over the three years presented in its statement of cash flows?
11. On average, inventories, receivables, and accounts payable usually grow (increase) in a growing company. Is this the case for Apple?
12. Has Apple borrowed more than it has paid back in recent years? Or has Apple paid back more than it has borrowed?
13. Free cash flow represents cash that management is able to use at its discretion. Free cash flow can be calculated as cash flow from operating activities less capital expenditures and dividends paid. Calculate free cash flow in each of the three years presented for Apple. What is the free cash flow trend for Apple?
14. What is your overall conclusion about Apple's financial position from the analysis you have done of its statement of cash flows? Support your conclusion.

A13-44 Use cash flow data to evaluate potential investments
(Learning Objectives 1 & 2)

Your company has some excess cash and would like to invest it in the stock of another company. You investigate several different stocks and are trying to decide which stock company's cash flow. The summaries of the cash flow statements for your three top stock would be the best investment for your company. One factor you investigate is each choices follow:

(000s omitted)	Dalton Corp.	Meredith Enterprises	Thornton, Inc.
Net cash provided by (used for) operating activities...	$ (20,000)	$ 28,100	$ 16,000
Cash provided by (used for) investing activities:			
Cash used to purchase plant or equipment.............		$ (12,100)	$ (25,000)
Proceeds from the sale of equipment	$ 8,000		
Cash used to purchase investments in stock	_____	(5,000)	_____
Net cash provided by (used for) investing activities	8,000	(17,100)	$ (25,000)
Cash provided by (used for) financing activities:			
Proceeds from bond issuance.................................	23,500	4,000	5,000
Repayment of long-term debt.................................	(1,000)	(2,000)	
Cash proceeds from issuance of stock.....................			12,000
Cash payments for dividends..................................	(2,500)	(5,000)	_____
Net cash provided by (used for) financing activities	20,000	(3,000)	17,000
Net increase in cash	$ 8,000	$ 8,000	$ 8,000

Although you will look at many other criteria in your stock purchase recommendation, what can you tell about each of the three companies listed? Based solely on cash flow, which stock appears to be better?

Try It Solutions

page 769:

1. Operating

2. Financing

3. Financing

4. Operating

5. Investing

page 780:

1. Subtract increases in current asset accounts.

2. Add back depreciation expense since it is a noncash expense.

3. Subtract decreases in current liability accounts.

4. Subtract gain made on a sale since it represents noncash revenue.

5. Add decreases in current asset accounts.

6. Add increases in current liability accounts.

Financial Statement Analysis

Presselect/Alamy

Sources: www.target.com and
http://www.stores.org/2012/
Top-100-Retailers; http://money
.cnn.com/magazines/fortune/
most-admired/2013/list/; http://
www.thedailybeast.com/
newsweek/2012/10/22/newsweek-
green-rankings-2012-u-s-500-list.html;
www.mghus.com/blog/2011/01/21/
whats-a-logo-without-a-name/

Learning Objectives

- **1** Perform a horizontal analysis of financial statements
- **2** Perform a vertical analysis of financial statements
- **3** Prepare and use common-size financial statements
- **4** Compute the standard financial ratios

With over $68 billion in annual sales, Target Corporation is currently the third-largest retailer in the United States. Its trademark symbol, the bull's-eye, is recognized by 97% of people surveyed. Target has a reputation for being one of the largest supporters of corporate social responsibility. Ever since 1962, Target has committed 5% of its yearly income to support local communities. In addition, Target is committed to integrating environmental sustainability throughout its business operations. As a result of these corporate practices, *Fortune* magazine has ranked Target Corporation as one of "America's Most Admired Companies" and *Newsweek* ranked Target in the top 20% of the country's 500 largest public companies in its Green ratings.

All of these accolades might lead one to believe that Target must be highly profitable. Indeed, Target has earned a profit in each of the past 10 years. But, net income alone does not tell the whole story. Has revenue grown steadily, or have there been large fluctuations—ups and downs—over the course of recent years? How big was each year's profit in relation to sales? For every dollar sold, how much of it ended up as gross profit, and how much of it was eaten up by operating expenses? What kind of return has the company been providing to shareholders? And how quickly has Target been able to sell its highly seasonal and fashion-trended merchandise? Financial statement analysis can help us answer these questions.

In this chapter, we'll examine several analytical tools that are frequently used to judge the financial performance of a company as a whole. To illustrate, we'll apply these tools to Supermart, a regional retailer of general merchandise that is similar to, but much smaller than Target. Then we will apply these analytical tools directly to Target Corporation's financial statements in the mid-chapter and end-of-chapter summary problems.

What are the Most Common Methods of Analysis?

Why is this important?

"Evaluating the **performance** of a company is difficult without some type of **benchmark** for **comparison**. Therefore, managers typically benchmark **financial performance** over time, against other companies, or against **industry averages**."

There are three ways to analyze financial statements:

- **Horizontal analysis** provides a year-to-year comparison of a company's performance in different periods.
- **Vertical analysis** provides a means of evaluating the relative size of each line item in the financial statements. It also allows us to compare companies of different size.
- **Ratio analysis** provides a means of evaluating the relationships between key components of the financial statements.

We'll explain the first two methods in this half of the chapter, and then devote the entire second half of the chapter to ratio analysis.

To use these tools, we must begin with the company's financial statements. Exhibit 14-1 presents Supermart's income statement for the last two years, while Exhibit 14-2 presents the company's balance sheet for the last two years.

EXHIBIT 14-1 Supermart Income Statement

	A	B	C	D	E
1	Supermart				
2	Income Statement				
3	For the Years Ended December 31, 2014 and 2013				
4		(amounts in thousands)			
5		2014	2013		
6	Sales revenues	$ 858,000	$ 803,000		
7	Less: Cost of goods sold	513,000	509,000		
8	Gross profit	$ 345,000	$ 294,000		
9	Less: Operating expenses	244,000	237,000		
10	Operating income	$ 101,000	$ 57,000		
11	Less: Interest expense	20,000	14,000		
12	Income before income taxes	$ 81,000	$ 43,000		
13	Less: Income tax expense	33,000	17,000		
14	Net income	$ 48,000	$ 26,000		
15					

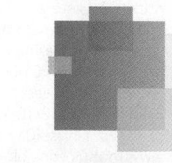

Horizontal Analysis

1 Perform a horizontal analysis of financial statements

Many decisions hinge on whether sales, expenses, and net income are increasing or decreasing. Have sales and other revenues risen from last year? By how much? Sales may have increased by $20,000, but considered alone, this fact is not very helpful. The *percentage change* in sales over time is more helpful. It is better to know that sales increased by 20% than to know that sales increased by $20,000.

The study of percentage changes in comparative statements is called **horizontal analysis.** Computing a percentage change in comparative statements requires two steps:

1. Compute the dollar amount of the change from the earlier period to the later period.
2. Divide the dollar amount of change by the earlier period amount. We call the earlier period the base period.

EXHIBIT 14-2 Supermart Balance Sheet

	A	B	C	D	E
1	Supermart				
2	Balance Sheets				
3	December 31, 2014 and 2013				
4		*(amounts in thousands)*			
5		2014	2013		
6	Assets				
7	Current assets:				
8	Cash	$ 29,000	$ 32,000		
9	Accounts receivable	114,000	85,000		
10	Inventory	113,000	111,000		
11	Other current assets	6,000	8,000		
12	Total current assets	$ 262,000	$ 236,000		
13	Property, plant, and equipment, net	507,000	399,000		
14	Other non-current assets	18,000	9,000		
15	Total assets	$ 787,000	$ 644,000		
16					
17	Liabilities				
18	Current liabilities:				
19	Accounts payable	$ 73,000	$ 68,000		
20	Notes payable	42,000	27,000		
21	Accrued liabilities	27,000	31,000		
22	Total current liabilities	$ 142,000	$ 126,000		
23	Long-term liabilities	289,000	198,000		
24	Total liabilities	$ 431,000	$ 324,000		
25					
26	Stockholders' equity				
27	Common stock, no par	$ 186,000	$ 186,000		
28	Retained earnings	170,000	134,000		
29	Total stockholders' equity	$ 356,000	$ 320,000		
30					
31	Total liabilities and equity	$ 787,000	$ 644,000		
32					

Let's illustrate with Supermart's sales revenue, shown in Exhibit 14-1:

STEP 1. Compute the dollar amount of change in sales revenue from 2013 to 2014:

$$
\begin{array}{ccc}
2014 & 2013 & \text{Increase} \\
\$858,000 - \$803,000 & = & \$55,000
\end{array}
$$

STEP 2. Divide the dollar amount of change by the base-period amount to compute the percentage change for the period:

$$
\text{Percentage change} = \frac{\text{Dollar amount of change}}{\text{Base-year amount}}
$$

$$
= \frac{\$55,000}{\$803,000} = 0.068 \text{ (rounded)} = 6.8\%
$$

We now see that Supermart's sales revenue increased by $55,000, or 6.8%, over the previous year.

Horizontal Analysis of the Income Statement

Exhibit 14-3 shows a complete horizontal analysis of Supermart's income statement.

EXHIBIT 14-3 Supermart Comparative Income Statement—Horizontal Analysis

	A	B	C	D	E
1			Supermart		
2			Comparative Income Statement		
3			For the Years Ended December 31, 2014 and 2013		
4					
5		(amounts in thousands)		Increase/(Decrease)	
6		2014	2013	Change	Percentage
7	Sales revenues	$ 858,000	$ 803,000	$ 55,000	6.8%
8	Less: Cost of goods sold	513,000	509,000	4,000	0.8%
9	Gross profit	$ 345,000	$ 294,000	$ 51,000	17.3%
10	Less: Operating expenses	244,000	237,000	7,000	3.0%
11	Operating income	$ 101,000	$ 57,000	$ 44,000	77.2%
12	Less: Interest expense	20,000	14,000	6,000	42.9%
13	Income before income taxes	$ 81,000	$ 43,000	$ 38,000	88.4%
14	Less: Income tax expense	33,000	17,000	16,000	94.1%
15	Net income	$ 48,000	$ 26,000	$ 22,000	84.6%
16					

The horizontal analysis shows that sales increased by almost 7%, yet the cost of goods sold increased by less than 1%. Supermart was either able to raise its prices, find cheaper suppliers, or sell products with higher margins. As a result, gross profit was about 17% higher than the previous year. Supermart was also able to hold its operating expenses to a 3% increase. These factors all contributed to increasing operating income by 77% over the previous year! Interest expense increased 42% as a result of more debt (as shown in the company's comparative balance sheet in Exhibit 14-2), possibly combined with a higher interest rate. Finally, as a result of the increased income, income taxes also increased substantially. The end result was an 84% increase in net income over the previous year.

Horizontal Analysis of the Balance Sheet

Exhibit 14-4 shows a complete horizontal analysis of Supermart's balance sheet.

The horizontal analysis shows that Supermart's accounts receivable grew substantially over the year (34%), while its cash decreased about 9%. The company may have relaxed its credit terms to generate more sales. The company also has taken on more short- and long-term debt, which may have been used to finance the significant additions to property, plant, and equipment and the increase in noncurrent assets that occurred during the year.

Trend Percentages

Trend percentages are a form of horizontal analysis. Trends indicate the direction a business is taking over a longer period of time, such as 3, 5, or 10 years. For example, in Exhibit 14-3, we saw that Supermart's net income increased a whopping 84% over the previous year. Has income always been increasing at such a significant rate? Or was that an isolated growth spurt limited to a one-year period? Investors typically like to see smooth growth trends over time, rather than large, sporadic fluctuations in sales and net income.

Trend percentages are computed by selecting a base year. The base-year amounts are set equal to 100%. The amounts for each following year are expressed as a percentage of the base amount. To compute trend percentages, divide each item in the following years by the base-year amount.

$$\text{Trend \%} = \frac{\text{Any year \$}}{\text{Base year \$}}$$

EXHIBIT 14-4 Comparative Balance Sheet—Horizontal Analysis

	A	B	C	D	E
1		Supermart			
2		Comparative Balance Statement			
3		December 31, 2014 and 2013			
4					
5		(amounts in thousands)		Increase/(Decrease)	
6	**Assets**	2014	2013	Change	Percentage
7	Current assets:				
8	Cash	$ 29,000	$ 32,000	$ (3,000)	−9.4%
9	Accounts receivable	114,000	85,000	29,000	34.1%
10	Inventory	113,000	111,000	2,000	1.8%
11	Other current assets	6,000	8,000	(2,000)	−25.0%
12	Total current assets	$ 262,000	$ 236,000	$ 26,000	11.0%
13	Property, plant, and equipment, net	507,000	399,000	108,000	27.1%
14	Other non-current assets	18,000	9,000	9,000	100.0%
15	Total assets	$ 787,000	$ 644,000	$ 143,000	22.2%
16					
17	**Liabilities**				
18	Current liabilities:				
19	Accounts payable	$ 73,000	$ 68,000	$ 5,000	7.4%
20	Notes payable	42,000	27,000	15,000	55.6%
21	Accrued liabilities	27,000	31,000	(4,000)	−12.9%
22	Total current liabilities	$ 142,000	$ 126,000	$ 16,000	12.7%
23	Long-term liabilities	289,000	198,000	91,000	46.0%
24	Total liabilities	$ 431,000	$ 324,000	$ 107,000	33.0%
25					
26	**Stockholders' equity**				
27	Common stock, no par	$ 186,000	$ 186,000	0	0.0%
28	Retained earnings	170,000	134,000	36,000	26.9%
29	Total stockholders' equity	$ 356,000	$ 320,000	36,000	11.3%
30					
31	Total liabilities and equity	$ 787,000	$ 644,000	$ 143,000	22.2%
32					

Supermart's sales revenue and trend percentages from 2009 to 2014, are pictured in Exhibit 14-5. We selected 2009 as the base, so that year's percentage is set equal to 100.

EXHIBIT 14-5 Supermart's Sales Trend

	A	B	C	D	E	F	G
1	**Supermart Trend Data**	**2014**	**2013**	**2012**	**2011**	**2010**	**Base Year 2009**
2	Sales revenue	$ 858,000	$ 803,000	$ 690,000	$ 648,000	$ 618,000	$ 600,000
3	Trend percentage	143%	134%	115%	108%	103%	100%
4							

From the percentages, we see that sales increased at a fairly slow, even rate in the earlier years (2009–2012). However, the rate of increase picked up in the later years (2013 and 2014). Supermart is obviously experiencing growth, either in existing store sales, or by adding new retail locations. Trend data is often pictured using line graphs. In fact, publically traded companies show the trend of their stock returns in the 10-K filings required by the Securities and Exchange Commission (SEC). Exhibit 14-6 shows Supermart's sales trends. As you can see, sales have increased every year, but the rate of increase has been larger in recent years (as shown by the steeper incline of the line from 2013–2014).

You can perform a trend analysis on any item you consider important. Trend analysis is widely used to predict future financial figures.

EXHIBIT 14-6 Line Graph of Sales Trend

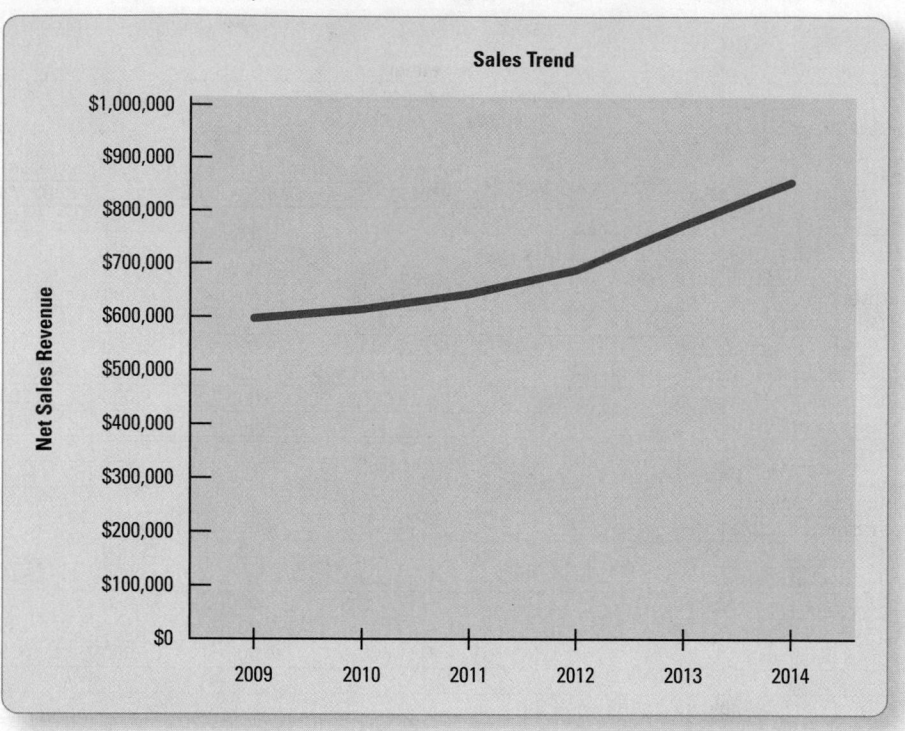

▶ Try It!

Starbucks Corporation's net revenues from 2008 to 2012 were as follows
(in millions of dollars):*

- $13,299 (2012)
- $11,700 (2011)
- $10,707 (2010)
- $9,774 (2009)
- $10,383 (2008)

Calculate trend percentages for the five-year period using 2008 as the base year.

*Source: Starbucks Corporation 2012 10-K.

Please see page 875 for solutions.

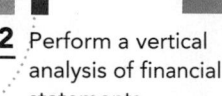

2 Perform a vertical analysis of financial statements

Vertical Analysis

As we have seen, horizontal analysis and trend percentages highlight changes in an item over time. But no single technique gives a complete picture of a business, so we also need vertical analysis.

Vertical analysis of a financial statement shows the relationship of each item to a base amount, which is the 100% figure. Every other item on the statement is then reported as a percentage of that base. When performing vertical analysis of an income statement, sales revenue is usually considered the base (100%).

$$\text{Vertical analysis \% for income statement} = \frac{\text{Each income statement line item}}{\text{Sales revenue}}$$

Exhibit 14-7 shows the vertical analysis of Supermart's 2014 income statement. The vertical analysis shows that the Supermart's gross profit is 40% of sales revenue. Operating expenses use up 28% of each dollar sold, while income taxes and interest use up another 6%.

As a result of all of these expenses, only 5.6% of every sales dollar ends up as net income (for every $1.00 of sales revenue, a little less than $0.06 ends up as net income).

EXHIBIT 14-7 Income Statement—Vertical Analysis

	A	B	C	D	E
1	Supermart				
2	Income Statement—Vertical Analysis				
3	For the Year Ended December 31, 2014				
4					
5		2014 (in thousands)	Percentage (rounded)		
6	Sales revenues	$ 858,000	100.0%		
7	Less: Cost of goods sold	513,000	59.8%		
8	Gross profit	$ 345,000	40.2%		
9	Less: Operating expenses	244,000	28.4%		
10	Operating income	$ 101,000	11.8%		
11	Less: Interest expense	20,000	2.3%		
12	Income before income taxes	$ 81,000	9.4%		
13	Less: Income tax expense	33,000	3.8%		
14	Net income	$ 48,000	5.6%		
15					

When performing vertical analysis of a balance sheet, total assets is usually considered the base (100%).

$$\text{Vertical analysis \% for balance sheet} = \frac{\text{Each balance sheet line item}}{\text{Total assets}}$$

Exhibit 14-8 shows the vertical analysis of Supermart's 2014 balance sheet. The base amount (100%) is total assets.

EXHIBIT 14-8 Balance Sheet—Vertical Analysis

	A	B	C	D
1	Supermart			
2	Balance Sheet—Vertical Analysis			
3	December 31, 2014			
4				
5		2014 (in thousands)	Percentage (rounded)	
6	Assets			
7	Current assets:			
8	Cash	$ 29,000	3.7%	
9	Accounts receivable	114,000	14.5%	
10	Inventory	113,000	14.4%	
11	Other current assets	6,000	0.8%	
12	Total current assets	$ 262,000	33.3%	
13	Property, plant, and equipment, net	507,000	64.4%	
14	Other non-current assets	18,000	2.3%	
15	Total assets	$ 787,000	100.0%	
16				
17	Liabilities			
18	Current liabilities:			
19	Accounts payable	$ 73,000	9.3%	
20	Notes payable	42,000	5.3%	
21	Accrued liabilities	27,000	3.4%	
22	Total current liabilities	$ 142,000	18.0%	
23	Long-term liabilities	289,000	36.7%	
24	Total liabilities	$ 431,000	54.8%	
25				
26	Stockholders' equity			
27	Common stock, no par	$ 186,000	23.6%	
28	Retained earnings	170,000	21.6%	
29	Total stockholders' equity	$ 356,000	45.2%	
30				
31	Total liabilities and equity	$ 787,000	100.0%	
32				

The vertical analysis of Supermart's balance sheet reveals that most of the company's assets (64%) consist of property, plant, and equipment. Inventory and receivables together make up about 29% of the company's assets. While the company is in the business of selling merchandise and therefore needs a fair amount of inventory, the receivables balance may be higher than desirable. Current liabilities is only 18% of total assets, but long-term debt is double that amount. Finally, stockholders' equity makes up a significant portion of assets (45%).

How do we Compare One Company with Another?

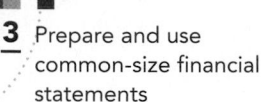

3 Prepare and use common-size financial statements

Horizontal analysis and vertical analysis provide a great deal of useful data about a company. However, many times we want to **benchmark**, or compare, a company against either (1) its competitor, or (2) industry averages.

To compare Supermart to another company, we can use a common-size statement. A **common-size statement** reports only percentages—the same percentages that appear in a vertical analysis. By using only the percentages, rather than gross dollar amounts, we are able to compare companies that vary in terms of size. For example, in Exhibit 14-9 we use common-size income statements to compare Supermart, a smaller regional retailer, to Target, a large national retailer.

EXHIBIT 14-9 Common-Size Income Statement

	A	B	C	D	E
1		Supermart			
2		Income Statement—Vertical Analysis			
3					
4		Supermart	Target*		
5	Sales revenues	100.0%	100.0%		
6	Less: Cost of goods sold	59.8%	69.4%		
7	Gross profit	40.2%	30.6%		
8	Less: Operating expenses	28.4%	23.2%		
9	Operating income	11.8%	7.4%		
10	Less: Interest expense	2.3%	1.0%		
11	Income before income taxes	9.4%	6.3%		
12	Less: Income tax expense	3.8%	2.2%		
13	Net income	5.6%	4.1%		
14					

NOTE: Adapted from Target's 2012 income statement.

Exhibit 14-9 shows that Supermart is actually more profitable, on each dollar of sales revenue (5.6%), than Target (4.1%). Supermart's gross profit (40.2%) is about 10 percentage points higher than Target's (30.6%), but its operating expenses use up more of each sales dollar (28.4%) than do Target's operating expenses (23.2%). Likewise, Supermart's income taxes and interest expense also use up a slightly larger percentage of sales revenue. Other than for cost of goods sold, none of the line item percentages is drastically different than Target's.

We could also compare Supermart against industry averages, using the same type of analysis. However, since Target is the third-largest retailer in the country, it accounts for a large portion of the industry average. Therefore, we wouldn't expect the results to be much different.

Before going on, be sure to review the decision guidelines. Then practice what you have learned in Summary Problem 1 by performing vertical and horizontal analysis on Target Corporation's financial statements.

Decision Guidelines

Horizontal and Vertical Analysis

In order to make well-informed financial decisions, investors, creditors, and managers need to determine how well the company is performing. The following guidelines help these decision makers judge the financial performance of a company.

Decision	Guidelines
What methods are generally used to evaluate a company's performance?	• Horizontal analysis • Vertical analysis • Ratio analysis
How is horizontal analysis performed?	Horizontal analysis is a two-step process: 1. Compute the dollar amount of the change from the earlier period to the later period. 2. Divide the dollar amount of change by the earlier period amount. We call the earlier period the base period.
How does trend analysis differ from horizontal analysis?	Horizontal analysis performed over a longer period of time (3–10 years) is usually called trend analysis. When performing trend analysis, a base year is chosen and set to 100%. All years after the base year are calculated as a percentage of the base year. $$\text{Trend \%} = \frac{\text{Any year \$}}{\text{Base year \$}}$$
What line item on the income statement is used as the base amount (100%) for vertical analysis?	Net sales revenue is generally used as the base (100%) for vertical analysis of the income statement. $$\text{Vertical analysis \% for income statement} = \frac{\text{Each income statement line item}}{\text{Sales revenue}}$$
What line item on the balance sheet is used as the base amount (100%) for vertical analysis?	Total assets is generally used as the base (100%) for vertical analysis of the balance sheet. $$\text{Vertical analysis \% for balance sheet} = \frac{\text{Each balance sheet line item}}{\text{Total assets}}$$
How can I compare two companies that differ in size?	Common-size income statements and balance sheets are generally used to compare companies that differ in size. Common-size financial statements present side-by-side vertical analysis percentages of different companies.

SUMMARY PROBLEM 1

Target Corporation's annual sales and net income data for the years 2006–2012 are presented next. Also shown are Target Corporation's 2012 and 2011 comparative income statements (adapted).[1] Keep in mind that the latest recession began in the United States in December 2007 and technically ended in the summer of 2009. This recession had a far-reaching impact on most sectors of the economy, including retailers.

	A	B	C	D	E	F	G	H
1	(in millions)	2012	2011	2010	2009	2008	2007	2006
2	Sales revenue*	$ 72,834	$ 69,419	$ 66,530	$ 63,836	$ 63,339	$ 62,530	$ 58,783
3	Net income	$ 2,999	$ 2,929	$ 2,920	$ 2,488	$ 2,214	$ 2,849	$ 2,787
4								

NOTE: Sales revenue includes the company's credit card operations, including credit card revenue, net of credit card expense.

	A	B	C	E	D
1	Target Corporation				
2	Income Statements (Adapted)				
3	For the Fiscal Years 2012 and 2011*				
4		(amounts in millions)			
5		2012	2011		
6	Sales revenues*	$ 72,834	$ 69,419		
7	Less: Cost of goods sold	50,568	47,860		
8	Gross profit	$ 22,266	$ 21,559		
9	Less: Operating expenses	16,895	16,237		
10	Operating income	$ 5,371	$ 5,322		
11	Less: Interest expense	762	866		
12	Income before income taxes	$ 4,609	$ 4,456		
13	Less: Income tax expense	1,610	1,527		
14	Net income	$ 2,999	$ 2,929		
15					

NOTES: Target's 2012 fiscal year ended February 2, 2013, and its 2011 fiscal year ended January 28, 2012. Additionally, Sales revenues includes the company's credit card operations, including credit card revenue net of credit card expenses.

Requirements

1. Perform a trend analysis for the years 2006–2013, using 2006 as the base year. Comment on the results.

2. Perform a horizontal analysis for the years 2011–2012 and comment on the results.

3. Perform a vertical analysis for the years 2011–2012 and comment on the results.

[1]Target Corporation 10-K, 2012

▪ SOLUTIONS

Requirement 1

	A	B	C	D	E	F	G	H
1	(in millions)	2012	2011	2010	2009	2008	2007	2006
2	Sales revenue	$ 72,834	$ 69,419	$ 66,530	$ 63,836	$ 63,339	$ 62,530	$ 58,783
3	Trend percentage	124%	118%	113%	109%	108%	106%	100%
4								
5	Net income	$ 2,999	$ 2,929	$ 2,920	$ 2,488	$ 2,214	$ 2,849	$ 2,787
6	Trend percentage	108%	105%	105%	89%	79%	102%	100%
7								

Sales revenue has gradually increased over time. Current sales revenue is 124% of what it had been in the base year, 2006. Net income is currently 108% of what it was in 2006. However, the increase in net income over the years was not as gradual as the increase in sales. In fact, net income has had significant yearly variations that do not correspond directly with the increase in sales. Operations other than sales must have significantly influenced net income in certain years.

Requirement 2

	A	B	C	D	E
1		Target Corporation			
2		Horizontal Analysis of Comparative Income Statements (Adapted)			
3		For the Fiscal Years 2012 and 2011*			
4					
5		(amounts in millions)		Increase/(Decrease)	
6		2012	2011	Change	Percentage
7	Sales revenues	$ 72,834	$ 69,419	$ 3,415	4.9%
8	Less: Cost of goods sold	50,568	47,860	2,708	5.7%
9	Gross profit	$ 22,266	$ 21,559	707	3.3%
10	Less: Operating expenses	16,895	16,237	658	4.1%
11	Operating income	$ 5,371	$ 5,322	49	0.9%
12	Less: Interest expense	762	866	(104)	−12.0%
13	Income before income taxes	$ 4,609	$ 4,456	153	3.4%
14	Less: Income tax expense	1,610	1,527	83	5.4%
15	Net income	$ 2,999	$ 2,929	$ 70	2.4%
16					

Cost of Goods Sold increased at a greater rate (5.7%) than Sales Revenue (4.9%), leading to an increase in gross profit of 3.3%. Operating expenses increased by 4.1%, which, netted with the increase in gross profit, led to a small increase of 0.9% in operating income. However, the company benefitted from a 12% decline in interest expense, leading to a 2.4% increase in net income.

Requirement 3

	A	B	C	D	E
1		Target Corporation				
2		Income Statements (Adapted)				
3		For the Fiscal Years 2012 and 2011				
4						
5		2012		2011	
6		Amount (in millions)	Percent (rounded)	Amount (in millions)	Percent (rounded)
7	Sales revenues	$ 72,834	100.0%	$ 69,419	100.0%
8	Less: Cost of goods sold	50,568	69.4%	47,860	68.9%
9	Gross profit	$ 22,266	30.6%	$ 21,559	31.1%
10	Less: Operating expenses	16,895	23.2%	16,237	23.4%
11	Operating income	$ 5,371	7.4%	$ 5,322	7.7%
12	Less: Interest expense	762	1.0%	866	1.2%
13	Income before income taxes	$ 4,609	6.3%	$ 4,456	6.4%
14	Less: Income tax expense	1,610	2.2%	1,527	2.2%
15	Net income	$ 2,999	4.1%	$ 2,929	4.2%
16					

The vertical analysis shows that Target's gross profit is roughly 31% of sales, whereas operating expenses use up about 23% of the company's sales. Interest and income taxes, combined, use up another 3.4% of sales revenue. As a result, net income is approximately 4.1% of sales revenue. This means that for every dollar of sales revenue generated by the company, only about four cents ends up as net income.

What are Some of the Most Common Financial Ratios?

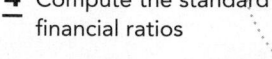

4 Compute the standard financial ratios

In this half of the chapter, we'll discuss many different financial ratios that managers, investors, and creditors use when analyzing a company's financial statements. Most of the information needed for these ratios can be found in the company's financial statements (refer to Supermart's income statement and balance sheet in Exhibits 14-1 and 14-2). A few of the ratios require the knowledge of the company's closing market price, which can be found online or in the *Wall Street Journal*. Other ratios require knowledge of the number of shares outstanding. This information can be obtained in the company's 10-K filing.

The ratios we'll discuss in this chapter may be classified as follows:

1. Measuring ability to pay current liabilities
2. Measuring ability to sell inventory and collect receivables
3. Measuring ability to pay long-term debt
4. Measuring profitability
5. Analyzing stock investments

Measuring Ability to Pay Current Liabilities

<u>Working capital</u> is defined as follows:

Working capital = Current assets − Current liabilities

Working capital measures the ability to meet short-term obligations with current assets. Supermart's 2014 working capital is calculated as follows:

$262,000 − $142,000 = $120,000

This shows that Supermart has ample current assets to meet its current obligations. Rather than measuring working capital alone, managers often measure the company's ability to meet current obligations by calculating two common ratios: the *current ratio* and the *acid-test*, or *quick*, *ratio*.

Current Ratio

The most widely used ratio is the <u>current ratio</u>, which is current assets divided by current liabilities. The current ratio measures the ability to pay current liabilities with current assets.

Supermart's current ratio at December 31, 2014 and 2013 is calculated as follows:[2]

> ### Why is this important?
>
> "Managers use different **financial ratios** to evaluate a company's performance, depending on the underlying **need**. For example, if a manager wants to know how **quickly inventory** is selling, he or she will calculate inventory **turnover**. If a manager wants to know how easily the **company** will be able to meet its current **obligations,** he or she will calculate the current ratio or the **acid-test ratio**."

	Formula	Supermart's Current Ratio	
		2014	2013
Current ratio $=$	$\dfrac{\text{Current assets}}{\text{Current liabilities}}$	$\dfrac{\$262,000}{\$142,000} = 1.85$	$\dfrac{\$236,000}{\$126,000} = 1.87$

[2]The solutions to all ratio calculations in this chapter have been rounded.

What is an acceptable current ratio? The answer depends on the industry, however a current ratio of 2.0 is generally considered fairly strong. Compare Supermart's current ratio of 1.85 with the current ratios of some well-known companies in the same industry:[3]

Company	Current Ratio
Walmart	0.83
JCPenney	1.43
Kohl's	1.86

Acid-Test Ratio

The **acid-test ratio**, or **quick ratio**, tells us whether the entity could pay all of its current liabilities if they came due *immediately*. That is, could the company pass this *acid test*?

To compute the acid-test ratio, we add cash, short-term investments, and net current receivables (accounts and notes receivable, net of allowances) and divide this sum by current liabilities. Inventory and prepaid expenses are *not* included in the acid test because they are the least liquid current assets. Supermart's acid-test ratios for 2014 and 2013 follow:

Formula	Supermart's Acid-Test Ratio	
	2014	2013
Acid-test ratio = $\dfrac{\text{Cash + Short-term investments} + \text{Net current receivables}}{\text{Current liabilities}}$	$\dfrac{\$29,000 + \$0 + \$114,000}{\$142,000} = 1.01$	$\dfrac{\$32,000 + \$0 + \$85,000}{\$126,000} = 0.93$

An acid-test ratio of 0.90 to 1.00 is acceptable in most industries. We do not present comparative statistics for Walmart, JCPenney, and Kohl's, since their balance sheets do not identify short-term investments separately.

Measuring Ability to Sell Inventory and Collect Receivables

The ability to sell inventory and collect receivables is fundamental to business. In this section, we discuss three ratios that measure the company's ability to sell inventory and collect receivables.

Inventory Turnover

Inventory turnover measures the number of times a company sells its average level of inventory during a year. A high rate of turnover indicates ease in selling inventory; a low rate indicates difficulty. A value of "6" means that the company sold its average level of inventory six times—every two months—during the year.

To compute inventory turnover, we divide cost of goods sold by the average inventory for the period. We use the cost of goods sold—not sales—because both cost of goods sold and inventory are stated *at cost*. Sales at *retail prices* are not comparable with inventory *at cost*.

Supermart's inventory turnover for 2014 is as follows:

Formula	Supermart's 2014 Inventory Turnover
Inventory turnover = $\dfrac{\text{Cost of goods sold}}{\text{Average inventory}}$	$\dfrac{\$513,000}{(\$111,000 + \$113,000)/2} = 4.6$

[3]All information given for Walmart Stores, Inc., JCPenney, and Kohl's Corporation was calculated using the companies' financial statements reported for fiscal year 2012 (fiscal year ended January 31, 2013), as found in each company's SEC 10-K filing.

Notice that average inventory is calculated by adding the beginning inventory ($111,000) and ending inventory ($113,000) for the period, and then dividing by two.

Inventory turnover varies widely with the nature of the business. Because of product innovation, some industries (for example, high-technology industries), must turn their inventory very quickly to avoid inventory obsolescence. However, in other industries, the risk of obsolescence is not so great.

Compare Supermart's inventory turnover with that of some well-known companies in the same industry:

Company	Inventory Turnover
Walmart	8.34
JCPenney	3.39
Kohl's	3.53

Accounts Receivable Turnover

Accounts receivable turnover measures the ability to collect cash from credit customers. This means that the higher the ratio, the faster the cash collections. But a receivable turnover that's too high may indicate that credit is too tight, causing the loss of sales to good customers.

For illustrative purposes we'll assume that all of Supermart's sales were made on account. The accounts receivable turnover is computed by dividing net credit sales by average net accounts receivable. Supermart's accounts receivable turnover ratio for 2014 is computed as follows:

Formula	Supermart's 2014 Accounts Receivable Turnover
Accounts receivable turnover $= \dfrac{\text{Net credit sales}}{\text{Average net accounts receivable}}$	$\dfrac{\$858,000}{(\$85,000 + \$114,000)/2} = 8.6$

We don't show comparative statistics for Walmart, JCPenney, or Kohl's since their balance sheets do not show any receivables (most customers pay with cash, debit, or credit cards).

Days' Sales in Receivables

The days' sales in receivables ratio also measures the ability to collect receivables. Days' sales in receivables tell us how many days' sales remain in Accounts Receivable. To compute the ratio, we can follow a logical two-step process:

1. Divide net sales by 365 days to figure average sales for one day.

2. Divide this average day's sales amount into average net accounts receivable.

This two-step process is illustrated using Supermart's 2014 data as follows:

Formula	Supermart's 2014 Days' Sales in Accounts Receivable
Days' sales in *average* Accounts receivable:	
1. One day's sales $= \dfrac{\text{Net sales}}{365 \text{ days}}$	$\dfrac{\$858,000}{365 \text{ days}} = \$2,351$
2. $\dfrac{\text{Day's sales in average}}{\text{accounts receivable}} = \dfrac{\text{Average net accounts receivable}}{\text{One day's sales}}$	$\dfrac{(\$85,000 + \$114,000)/2}{\$2,351} = 42 \text{ days}$

Supermart's ratio tells us that 42 average days' sales remain in accounts receivable and need to be collected. Let's assume that like many companies, Supermart gives its customers 30 days to pay. Supermart's ratio shows that on average, customers are taking longer—about 45 days—to pay. This could be a result of general economic conditions (such as a recession), or Supermart's particular customer base. In either event, Supermart may need to increase its efforts to collect receivables more quickly if it expects to be paid within 30 days of sale.

▶

Select 2012 financial data for Starbucks Corporation is as follows (in millions of dollars):*

- Current assets $4,199.6
- Inventory $1,241.5 (end of fiscal 2012) and $965.8 (end of fiscal 2011)
- Current liabilities $2,209.8
- Cost of goods sold $5,813

1. Calculate the current ratio.
2. Calculate inventory turnover.

*Source: Starbucks Corporation 2012 10-K.

Please see page 875 for solutions.

Measuring Ability to Pay Long-Term Debt

The ratios discussed so far yield insight into current assets and current liabilities. They help us measure ability to sell inventory, collect receivables, and pay current liabilities. Most businesses also have long-term debt. Two key indicators of a business's ability to pay long-term liabilities are the *debt ratio* and the *times-interest-earned ratio*.

Debt Ratio

A loan officer at Metro Bank is evaluating loan applications from two companies. Both companies have asked to borrow $500,000 and have agreed to repay the loan over a five-year period. The first firm already owes $600,000 to another bank. The second owes only $100,000. Other things equal, you are more likely to lend money to Company 2 because that company owes less than Company 1.

The relationship between total liabilities and total assets—called the **debt ratio**—shows the proportion of assets financed with debt. When the debt ratio is 1, all of the assets are financed with debt. A debt ratio of 0.50 means that debt finances half the assets; the owners of the business have financed the other half. The higher the debt ratio, the higher the company's financial risk. The debt ratios for Supermart at the end of 2014 and 2013 follow:

Formula	Supermart's Debt Ratio	
	2014	2013
Debt ratio = $\dfrac{\text{Total liabilities}}{\text{Total assets}}$	$\dfrac{\$431,000}{\$787,000} = 0.55$	$\dfrac{\$324,000}{\$644,000} = 0.50$

Supermart's debt ratio increased slightly in 2014. Let's look at the debt ratios of some well-known companies in the same industry:

Company	Debt Ratio
Walmart...	0.60
JCPenney...	0.68
Kohl's..	0.57

Times-Interest-Earned Ratio

The debt ratio says nothing about ability to pay interest expense. Analysts use the **times-interest-earned ratio** to relate income to interest expense. This ratio is also called the **interest-coverage ratio**. It measures the number of times operating income can cover interest expense. A high interest-coverage ratio indicates ease in paying interest expense; a low ratio suggests difficulty.

To compute this ratio, we divide operating income by interest expense. Calculation of Supermart's times-interest-earned ratio follows:

		Supermart's Times-Interest-Earned Ratio	
Formula		2014	2013
Times-interest-earned ratio $= \dfrac{\text{Income from operations}}{\text{Interest expense}}$		$\dfrac{\$101{,}000}{\$20{,}000} = 5.05$	$\dfrac{\$57{,}000}{\$14{,}000} = 4.07$

The company's times-interest-earned ratio shows that in 2014, the company could pay its interest about five times over with the amount of operating income it earned. Therefore, Supermart should have little trouble paying the interest expense it owes to creditors. Compare Supermart's times-interest-earned ratio with other companies in the same industry. At the beginning of 2012, JCPenney began to undertake a major change in its business strategy which resulted in a loss for the fiscal year. Because JCPenney incurred an operating loss in 2013, any ratios involving operating income are negative numbers.

Company	Times-Interest-Earned Ratio
Walmart...	12.35
JCPenney..	(5.80)
Kohl's..	5.74

Measuring Profitability

The fundamental goal of business is to earn a profit. Ratios that measure profitability are often reported in the business press. We examine four profitability measures.

Rate of Return on Net Sales

In business, the term *return* is used broadly as a measure of profitability. Consider a ratio called the **rate of return on net sales**, or simply **return on sales**. This ratio shows the percentage of each sales dollar earned as net income. Supermart's rate of return on sales follows:

		Supermart's Rate of Return on Sales	
Formula		2014	2013
Rate of return on sales $= \dfrac{\text{Net income}}{\text{Net sales}}$		$\dfrac{\$48{,}000}{\$858{,}000} = 5.6\%$	$\dfrac{\$26{,}000}{\$803{,}000} = 3.2\%$

Companies strive for a high rate of return on sales. The higher the rate of return, the more sales dollars end up as profit. Supermart experienced a significant increase in its return on sales in the last year. Return on sales varies greatly depending on the industry. General merchandise retailers typically have a very low return on sales. Compare Supermart's rate of return on sales to the rates of return for some leading companies in the same industry:

Company	Rate of Return on Sales
Walmart...	3.65%
JCPenney..	(7.59)%
Kohl's..	5.11%

Rate of Return on Total Assets

The <u>rate of return on total assets</u>, or simply <u>return on assets</u>, measures success in using assets to earn a profit. Two groups finance a company's assets:

1. Creditors have loaned money to the company, and they earn interest.
2. Shareholders have invested in stock, and their return is net income.

The sum of interest expense and net income is the return to the two groups that have financed the company's assets. Computation of the return-on-assets ratio for Supermart follows:

Formula	Supermart's 2014 Rate of Return on Total Assets
$\text{Rate of return on assets} = \dfrac{\text{Net income} + \text{Interest expense}}{\text{Average total assets}}$	$\dfrac{\$48,000 + \$20,000}{(\$644,000 + \$787,000)/2} = 9.5\%$

Compare Supermart's rate of return on assets with the rates of some other companies:

Company	Rate of Return on Assets
Walmart...	9.71%
JCPenney...	(7.16)%
Kohl's...	9.38%

Rate of Return on Common Stockholders' Equity

A popular measure of profitability is <u>rate of return on common stockholders' equity</u>, often shortened to <u>return on equity</u>. This ratio shows the relationship between net income and common stockholders' equity—how much income is earned for each $1 invested by the common shareholders.

To compute this ratio, we subtract preferred dividends from net income to get net income available to the common stockholders. Then, we divide net income available to common stockholders by average common equity during the year. Common equity is total stockholders' equity minus preferred equity. The 2014 rate of return on common stockholders' equity for Supermart follows:

Formula	Supermart's 2014 Rate of Return on Common Stockholders' Equity
$\text{Rate of return on common stockholders' equity} = \dfrac{\text{Net income} - \text{Preferred dividends}}{\text{Average common stockholders' equity}}$	$\dfrac{\$48,000 - \$0}{(\$320,000 + \$356,000)/2} = 14.2\%$

Supermart's return on equity (14.2%) is higher than its return on assets (9.5%). This difference results from borrowing at one rate—for example, 8%—and investing the money to earn a higher rate, such as the firm's 14.2% return on equity.

This practice is called <u>trading on the equity</u>, or using <u>leverage</u>. It is directly related to the debt ratio. The higher the debt ratio reaches, the higher the leverage. Companies that finance operations with debt are said to *leverage* their positions.

During good times, leverage increases profitability. But leverage can have a negative impact on profitability. Therefore, leverage is a double-edged sword, increasing profits during good times but compounding losses during bad times. Compare Supermart's return on equity with the rates of some leading companies in the same industry.

Company	Rate of Return on Common Stockholders' Equity
Walmart...	21.59%
JCPenney...	(27.43)%
Kohl's...	15.71%

Earnings per Share of Common Stock

Earnings per share of common stock, or simply **earnings per share (EPS)**, is perhaps the most widely quoted of all financial statistics. EPS is the only ratio that must appear on the face of the income statement. EPS is the amount of net income earned for each share of the company's outstanding *common* stock. Recall the following:

> Outstanding stock = Issued stock − Treasury stock

Earnings per share is computed by dividing net income available to common stock-holders by the number of common shares outstanding during the year. Preferred dividends are subtracted from net income because the preferred stockholders have a prior claim to dividends.

Let's assume Supermart has no preferred stock outstanding and no preferred dividends. Let's also assume that Supermart had 10,000 shares of common stock outstanding throughout 2013 and 2014. Given this information, we calculate the company's EPS as follows:

		Supermart's Earnings per Share	
Formula		**2014**	**2013**
Earnings per share of common stock $= \dfrac{\text{Net income} - \text{Preferred dividends}}{\substack{\text{Number of shares of} \\ \text{common stock outstanding}}}$		$\dfrac{\$48,000 - \$0}{10,000} = \$4.80$	$\dfrac{\$26,000 - \$0}{10,000} = \$2.60$

Supermart's EPS increased significantly. Most companies strive to increase EPS each year, but general economic conditions, such as a recession, can prevent companies from doing so. Other leading companies in the same industry reported the following earnings per share on their income statements:

Company	Earnings Per Share
Walmart...	$ 5.02
JCPenney..	$(4.49)
Kohl's...	$ 4.17

Analyzing Stock Investments

Investors purchase stock to earn a return on their investment. This return consists of two parts: (1) gains (or losses) from selling the stock at a price above (or below) the purchase price and (2) dividends. The ratios we examine in this section help analysts evaluate stock investments.

Price/Earnings Ratio

The **price/earnings ratio** is the ratio of the market price of a share of common stock to the company's earnings per share. It shows the market price of $1 of earnings. This ratio, abbreviated P/E, appears in the stock listings of the *Wall Street Journal*. The daily closing price of all publicly traded stocks can also be found in the *Wall Street Journal*.

Let's say the market price of Supermart's common stock was $60 at the end of 2014 and $35 at the end of 2013. Supermart's P/E ratio is calculated as follows:

		Supermart's Price/Earnings Ratio	
Formula		**2014**	**2013**
P/E ratio $= \dfrac{\text{Market price per share of common stock}}{\text{Earnings per share}}$		$\dfrac{\$60.00}{\$4.80} = 12.5$	$\dfrac{\$35.00}{\$2.60} = 13.5$

Supermart's P/E ratio of 12.5 means that the company's stock is selling at 12.5 times earnings. The P/E ratio of other firms in the same industry follows:

Company	Price/Earnings Ratio
Walmart	13.93
JCPenney	(4.43)
Kohl's	11.03

Dividend Yield

Dividend yield is the ratio of dividends per share to the stock's market price per share. This ratio measures the percentage of a stock's market value that is returned annually as dividends. *Preferred* stockholders, who invest primarily to receive dividends, pay special attention to dividend yield.

Supermart paid annual cash dividends of $1.20 per share of common stock in 2014 and $1.00 in 2013, and market prices of the company's common stock were $60 in 2014 and $35 in 2013. The firm's dividend yield on common stock follows:

		Dividend Yield on Supermart's Common Stock	
Formula		2014	2013
Dividend yield on common stock* $= \dfrac{\text{Dividend per share of common stock}}{\text{Market price per share of common stock}}$		$\dfrac{\$1.20}{\$60.00} = 2.0\%$	$\dfrac{\$1.00}{\$35.00} = 2.9\%$

*Dividend yields may also be calculated for preferred stock.

An investor who buys Supermart common stock for $60 can expect to receive 2% of the investment annually in the form of cash dividends.

The dividends paid by companies vary substantially:

Company	Dividend Yield
Walmart	2.27%
JCPenney	1.01%
Kohl's	2.78%

Book Value per Share of Common Stock

Book value per share of common stock is common equity divided by the number of common shares outstanding. Common equity equals total stockholders' equity less preferred equity. Supermart has no preferred stock outstanding. Its book-value-per-share-of-common-stock ratios follow (10,000 shares of common stock were outstanding).

		Book Value per Share of Supermart's Common Stock	
Formula		2014	2013
$\dfrac{\text{Book value per share}}{\text{of common stock}} = \dfrac{\text{Total stockholders' equity} - \text{Preferred equity}}{\text{Number of shares of common stock outstanding}}$		$\dfrac{\$356,000 - \$0}{10,000} = \$35.60$	$\dfrac{\$320,000 - \$0}{10,000} = \$32.00$

Many experts argue that book value is not useful for investment analysis. It bears no relationship to market value and provides little information beyond stockholders' equity reported on the balance sheet. But some investors base their investment decisions on book value. For example, some investors rank stocks on the basis of the ratio of market price to book value. To these investors, the lower the ratio, the more attractive the stock, as this implies that the stock might be undervalued.

Red Flags in Financial Statement Analysis

Analysts look for *red flags* that may signal financial trouble. Recent accounting scandals highlight the importance of these red flags. The following conditions may reveal that the company is too risky:

- **Movement of Sales, Inventory, and Receivables.** Sales, receivables, and inventory generally move together. Increased sales lead to higher receivables and require more inventory to meet demand. Strange movements among sales, inventory, and receivables make the financial statements look suspect.

- **Earnings Problems.** Has net income decreased significantly for several years in a row? Has income turned into a loss? Most companies cannot survive years of consecutive loss.

- **Decreased Cash Flow.** Cash flow validates net income. Is cash flow from operations consistently lower than net income? If so, the company is in trouble. Are the sales of plant assets a major source of cash? If so, the company may face a cash shortage.

- **Too Much Debt.** How does the company's debt ratio compare to that of major competitors? If the debt ratio is too high, the company may be unable to pay its debts.

- **Inability to Collect Receivables.** Are days' sales in receivables growing faster than those of competitors? A cash shortage may be looming.

- **Buildup of Inventories.** Is inventory turnover too slow? If so, the company may be unable to sell goods or it may be overstating inventory.

Sustainability and Financial Statement Analysis

Financial statement analysis only evaluates the short-term financial viability of a company. Even a 5- to 10-year trend analysis will not adequately predict the long-term sustainability of a company. Thus, financial statement analysis, by itself, is insufficient for stakeholders who desire a more comprehensive view of an organization. Thus, increasing numbers of investors are using a triple bottom line approach to evaluating a company's performance, not only focusing on historical financial ratios and trends, but also demanding information about the company's environmental and social practices.

For example, as of 2012, over 1,100 institutional investors with over $30 trillion of assets under management had signed on to the Principles of Responsible Investing (PRI) backed by the United Nations (UN). In short, these principles state that investors will include environmental, social, and governance information when making investment decisions when consistent with their fiduciary responsibilities. Currently, environmental and social information is often found in the following locations:

- *Securities and Exchange Commission (SEC) 10-K filings of publicly traded companies.* SEC rules dictate that publicly traded companies disclose any material information that would be necessary to prevent the misleading of financial statement readers. With respect to the environment, companies must disclose any aspects of their business operations, pending lawsuits, and risk factors that are deemed to be material. Examples include the cost of complying with environmental laws and regulations, potential monetary damages from health and environmental litigation, and risks associated with the scarcity of water and raw materials needed for operations. Additionally, any material risks specific to the company as a result of global warming must also be disclosed.

■ *Corporate social responsibility (CSR) reports and company websites.* As of 2011, 57% of the U.S. Fortune 500 companies issued CSR reports. Globally, 95% of the largest 250 companies in the world issue CSR reports. These reports typically discuss the company's initiatives, goals, and performance with respect to environmental and human impact. Chapter 15 discusses the format of these statements in more detail. Unlike 10-K reports, the information contained in CSR reports is not always audited. However, the Big Four accounting firms are the leaders in providing assurance services for CSR data.

In the future, information relating to the triple bottom line may be found in what is known as an *integrated report*. Integrated reporting, or <IR>, is a concept in its infancy that is currently being piloted by a number of large, global companies. The idea behind <IR> is to provide "one-stop shopping" whereby both material financial and nonfinancial information is contained in one report so that stakeholders can obtain a holistic, balanced view of the organization.

See Exercises E14-21A and E14-32B ◀

Sources: http://www.unpri.org/about-pri/about-pri/; Securities and Exchange Commission (SEC) 17 CFR Parts 211, 231, and 241 (Release Nos. 33-9106, 34-61469, and FR-82), Commission Guidance Regarding Disclosure Related to Climate Change; http://www.kpmg.de/docs/Survey-corporate-responsibility-reporting-2011.pdf; and http://www.ga-institute.com/research-reports/2012-corporate-esg-sustainability-responsibility-reporting-does-it-matter.html.

Decision Guidelines

Using Ratios in Financial Statement Analysis

How can investors, creditors, and managers measure a company's ability to pay bills, sell inventory, collect receivables, pay long-term debt, and so forth? How can they evaluate stock investments? The decision guidelines summarize the ratios that help to answer these questions.

Ratio	Computation	Information Provided
Measuring ability to pay current liabilities:		
1. Current ratio	$$\dfrac{\text{Current assets}}{\text{Current liabilities}}$$	Measures ability to pay current liabilities with current assets
2. Acid-test (quick) ratio	$$\dfrac{\text{Cash} + \dfrac{\text{Short-term}}{\text{investments}} + \dfrac{\text{Net current}}{\text{receivables}}}{\text{Current liabilities}}$$	Shows ability to pay all current liabilities if they come due immediately
Measuring ability to sell inventory and collect receivables:		
3. Inventory turnover	$$\dfrac{\text{Cost of goods sold}}{\text{Average inventory}}$$	Indicates salability of inventory—the number of times a company sells its average inventory during a year
4. Accounts receivable turnover	$$\dfrac{\text{Net credit sales}}{\text{Average net accounts receivable}}$$	Measures ability to collect cash from customers
5. Days' sales in receivables	$$\dfrac{\text{Average net accounts receivable}}{\text{One day's sales}}$$	Shows how many days' sales remain in Accounts Receivable—how many days it takes to collect the average level of receivables
Measuring ability to pay long-term debt:		
6. Debt ratio	$$\dfrac{\text{Total liabilities}}{\text{Total assets}}$$	Indicates percentage of assets financed with debt
7. Times-interest-earned ratio	$$\dfrac{\text{Income from operations}}{\text{Interest expense}}$$	Measures the number of times operating income can cover interest expense

Ratio	Computation	Information Provided
Measuring profitability:		
8. Rate of return on net sales	$$\frac{\text{Net income}}{\text{Net sales}}$$	Shows the percentage of each sales dollar earned as net income
9. Rate of return on total assets	$$\frac{\text{Net income} + \text{Interest expense}}{\text{Average total assets}}$$	Measures how profitably a company uses its assets
10. Rate of return on common stockholders' equity	$$\frac{\text{Net income} - \text{Preferred dividends}}{\text{Average common stockholders' equity}}$$	Gauges how much income is earned for each dollar invested by common shareholders
11. Earnings per share of common stock	$$\frac{\text{Net income} - \text{Preferred dividends}}{\text{Number of shares of common stock outstanding}}$$	Gives the amount of net income earned for each share of the company's common stock
Analyzing stock as an investment:		
12. Price/earnings ratio	$$\frac{\text{Market price per share of common stock}}{\text{Earnings per share}}$$	Indicates the market price of \$1 of earnings
13. Dividend yield	$$\frac{\begin{array}{c}\text{Annual dividend per share of}\\ \text{common (or preferred) stock}\end{array}}{\begin{array}{c}\text{Market price per share of}\\ \text{common (or preferred) stock}\end{array}}$$	Shows the percentage of a stock's market value returned as dividends to stockholders each year
14. Book value per share of common stock	$$\frac{\text{Total stockholders' equity} - \text{Preferred equity}}{\begin{array}{c}\text{Number of shares of}\\ \text{common stock outstanding}\end{array}}$$	Indicates the recorded accounting amount for each share of common stock outstanding.

SUMMARY PROBLEM **2**

Target Corporation's income statement was presented in Summary Problem 1. The company's balance sheet (adapted) at the end of fiscal years 2012 and 2011 are presented below.[4]

	A	B	C
1	**Target Corporation**		
2	**Balance Sheets (Adapted)**		
3	**End of Fiscal Year**		
4		*(amounts in thousands)*	
5		**2012**	**2011**
6	**Assets**		
7	Current assets:		
8	Cash and cash equivalents	$ 784	$ 794
9	Accounts receivable	5,841	5,927
10	Inventory	7,903	7,918
11	Other current assets	1,860	1,810
12	Total current assets	$ 16,388	$ 16,449
13	Property, plant, and equipment, net	30,653	29,149
14	Other non-current assets	1,122	1,032
15	Total assets	$ 48,163	$ 46,630
16			
17	**Liabilities**		
18	Current liabilities:		
19	Accounts payable	$ 7,056	$ 6,857
20	Other current liabilities	6,975	7,430
21	Total current liabilities	$ 14,031	$ 14,287
22	Long-term liabilities	17,574	16,522
23	Total liabilities	$ 31,605	$ 30,809
24			
25	**Stockholders' equity**		
26	Common stock, and additional paid in capital	$ 3,979	$ 3,543
27	Retained earnings	12,579	12,278
28	Total stockholders' equity	$ 16,558	$ 15,821
29			
30	Total liabilities and stockholders' equity	$ 48,163	$ 46,630
31			

NOTE: Target's 2012 fiscal year ended February 2, 2013, and its 2011 fiscal year ended January 28, 2012.

Other company information follows:

- Target has no preferred stock issued or outstanding.
- There were 645,294,423 common shares issued and outstanding at the end of fiscal year 2012.
- Cash dividends of $1.32 per share were declared during fiscal year 2012.
- The closing market price per share was $61.15 on Friday, February 1, 2013 (the end of fiscal year 2012).[5]

Requirement 1

Calculate the following ratios for fiscal year 2012:

1. Current ratio
2. Acid-test ratio
3. Inventory turnover

[4]Target Corporation 2012 10-K

[5]http://finance.yahoo.com

4. Days' sales in receivables
5. Debt ratio
6. Times-interest-earned ratio
7. Rate of return on net sales
8. Rate of return on total assets
9. Rate of return on common stockholders' equity
10. Earnings per share of common stock
11. Price/earnings ratio
12. Dividend yield
13. Book value per share of common stock

▪ SOLUTIONS

Requirement 1

$$1) \text{ Current ratio} = \frac{Current\ assets}{Current\ liabilities}$$

$$= \frac{\$16,388}{\$14,031} = 1.17$$

$$2) \text{ Acid-test ratio} = \frac{Cash + ST\ investments + Net\ current\ receivables}{Current\ liabilities}$$

$$= \frac{\$784 + 0 + \$5,841}{\$14,031} = 0.47$$

$$3) \text{ Inventory turnover} = \frac{Cost\ of\ goods\ sold}{Average\ inventory}$$

$$= \frac{\$50,568}{(\$7,918 + \$7,903)/2} = 6.39$$

$$4) \text{ Days' sales in receivables} = \frac{Average\ net\ accounts\ receivable}{One\ day's\ sales}$$

$$= \frac{(\$5,927 + \$5,841)/2}{(\$72,834)/365} = 29.49\ days$$

$$5) \text{ Debt ratio} = \frac{Total\ liabilities}{Total\ assets}$$

$$= \frac{\$31,605}{\$48,163} = 0.66$$

6) Times-interest-earned ratio $= \dfrac{Income\ from\ operations}{Interest\ expense}$

$$= \dfrac{\$5,371}{\$762} = 7.05$$

7) Rate of return on net sales $= \dfrac{Net\ income}{Sales\ revenue}$

$$= \dfrac{\$2,999}{\$72,834} = 4.12\%$$

8) Rate of return on total assets $= \dfrac{Net\ income\ +\ Interest\ expense}{Average\ total\ assets}$

$$= \dfrac{\$2,999\ +\ \$762}{(\$46,630\ +\ \$48,163)/2} = 7.94\%$$

9) Rate of return on common stockholders' equity $= \dfrac{Net\ income\ -\ Preferred\ dividends}{Average\ common\ stockholder's\ equity}$

$$= \dfrac{\$2,999\ -\ \$0}{(\$15,821\ +\ 16,558)/2} = 18.52\%$$

10) Earnings per share of common stock $= \dfrac{Net\ income\ -\ Preferred\ dividends}{Number\ of\ shares\ of\ common\ stock\ outstanding}$

$$= \dfrac{\$2,999\ million}{645,294,423} = \$4.65$$

11) Price/earnings ratio $= \dfrac{Market\ price\ per\ share\ of\ common\ stock}{Earnings\ per\ share}$

$$= \dfrac{\$61.15}{\$4.65} = 13.15$$

12) Dividend yield $= \dfrac{Dividend\ per\ share\ of\ common\ stock}{Market\ price\ per\ share\ of\ common\ stock}$

$$= \dfrac{\$1.32}{\$61.15} = 2.16\%$$

13) Book value per share of common stock $= \dfrac{Total\ stockholders'\ equity\ -\ Preferred\ equity}{Number\ of\ shares\ of\ common\ stock\ outstanding}$

$$= \dfrac{\$16,558\ million\ -\ 0}{645,294,423} = \$25.66$$

Learning Objectives

- 1 Perform a horizontal analysis of financial statements
- 2 Perform a vertical analysis of financial statements
- 3 Prepare and use common-size financial statements
- 4 Compute the standard financial ratios

Accounting Vocabulary

Accounts Receivable Turnover. (p. 837) Measures a company's ability to collect cash from credit customers. To compute accounts receivable turnover, divide net credit sales by average net accounts receivable.

Acid-Test Ratio. (p. 836) Ratio of the sum of cash plus short-term investments plus net current receivables to total current liabilities. It tells whether the entity can pay all of its current liabilities if they come due immediately; also called the *quick ratio.*

Benchmarking. (p. 830) The practice of comparing a company with other companies or industry averages.

Book Value per Share of Common Stock. (p. 842) Common stockholders' equity divided by the number of shares of common stock outstanding. It is the recorded amount for each share of common stock outstanding.

Common-Size Statement. (p. 830) A financial statement that reports only percentages (no dollar amounts).

Current Ratio. (p. 835) Current assets divided by current liabilities. It measures the ability to pay current liabilities with current assets.

Days' Sales in Receivables. (p. 837) Ratio of average net accounts receivable to one day's sale. It indicates how many days' sales remain in Accounts Receivable awaiting collection.

Debt Ratio. (p. 838) Ratio of total liabilities to total assets. It shows the proportion of a company's assets that is financed with debt.

Dividend Yield. (p. 842) Ratio of dividends per share of stock to the stock's market price per share. It tells the percentage of a stock's market value that the company returns to stockholders annually as dividends.

Earnings per Share (EPS). (p. 841) Amount of a company's net income for each share of its outstanding common stock.

Horizontal Analysis. (p. 824) Study of percentage changes in comparative financial statements.

Interest-Coverage Ratio. (p. 839) Ratio of income from operations to interest expense. It measures the number of times that operating income can cover interest expense; also called the *times-interest-earned ratio.*

Inventory Turnover. (p. 836) Ratio of cost of goods sold to average inventory. It indicates how rapidly inventory is sold.

Leverage. (p. 840) Earning more income on borrowed money than the related interest expense, thereby increasing the earnings for the owners of the business; also called *trading on equity.*

Price/Earnings (P/E) Ratio. (p. 841) Ratio of the market price of a share of common stock to the company's earnings per share. It measures the value that the stock market places on $1 of a company's earnings.

Quick Ratio. (p. 836) Ratio of the sum of cash plus short-term investments plus net current receivables to total current liabilities. It tells whether the entity can pay all its current liabilities if they come due immediately; also called the *acid-test ratio.*

Rate of Return on Common Stockholders' Equity. (p. 840) Net income minus preferred dividends divided by average common stockholders' equity. It is a measure of profitability; also called *return on equity.*

Rate of Return on Net Sales. (p. 839) Ratio of net income to net sales. It is a measure of profitability; also called *return on sales.*

Rate of Return on Total Assets. (p. 840) Net income plus interest expense divided by average total assets. This ratio measures a company's success in using its assets to earn income for the people who finance the business; also called *return on assets.*

Ratio Analysis. (p. 824) Evaluating the relationships between two or more key components of the financial statements.

Return on Assets. (p. 840) Net income plus interest expense, divided by average total assets. This ratio measures a company's success in using its assets to earn income for the people who finance the business; also called *rate of return on total assets.*

Return on Equity. (p. 840) Net income minus preferred dividends, divided by average common stockholders' equity. It is a measure of profitability; also called *rate of return on common stockholders' equity.*

Return on Sales. (p. 839) Ratio of net income to net sales. It is a measure of profitability; also called *rate of return on net sales.*

Times-Interest-Earned Ratio. (p. 839) Ratio of income from operations to interest expense. It measures the number of times operating income can cover interest expense; also called the *interest-coverage ratio.*

Trading on Equity. (p. 840) Earning more income on borrowed money than the related interest expense, thereby increasing the earnings for the owners of the business; also called *leverage*.

Trend Percentages. (p. 826) A form of horizontal analysis in which percentages are computed by selecting a base year as 100% and expressing amounts for following years as a percentage of the base amount.

Vertical Analysis. (p. 824) Analysis of a financial statement that reveals the relationship of each statement item to a specified base, which is the 100% figure.

Working Capital. (p. 835) Current assets minus current liabilities; measures a business's ability to meet its short-term obligations with its current assets.

MyAccountingLab **Go to** http://myaccountinglab.com/ **for the following Quick Check, Short Exercises, Exercises, and Problems. They are available with immediate grading, explanations of correct and incorrect answers, and interactive media that acts as your own online tutor.**

Quick Check

1. *(Learning Objective 1)* Which of the following provides a year-to-year comparison of a company's performance in two different years?
   a. Vertical analysis
   b. Ratio analysis
   c. Horizontal analysis
   d. Time study analysis

2. *(Learning Objective 1)* A trend study compares financial performance against
   a. a selected base year.
   b. the previous year.
   c. other companies within the industry.
   d. the company's first year of operations.

3. *(Learning Objective 2)* When performing vertical analysis, each line item on the income statement is computed as a percentage of which of the following?
   a. Cost of goods sold
   b. Net income
   c. Operating expenses
   d. Sales revenue

4. *(Learning Objective 2)* When performing vertical analysis, each line item on the balance sheet is computed as a percentage of which of the following?
   a. Total assets
   b. Total liabilities
   c. Total stockholder's equity
   d. Total cash flows

5. *(Learning Objective 3)* Which of the following is used to compare one company against another or against an industry average, using percentages as a comparison mechanism?
   a. Common-size statement
   b. Percentage statement
   c. Horizontal statement
   d. Comparison statement

6. *(Learning Objective 4)* Working capital is defined as
   a. current liabilities plus current assets.
   b. current liabilities minus current assets.
   c. cash minus current liabilities.
   d. current assets minus current liabilities.

7. *(Learning Objective 4)* Which of the following ratios measures a company's ability to pay current liabilities?
   a. Dividend yield
   b. Acid-test, or quick, ratio
   c. Inventory turnover
   d. Debt ratio

8. *(Learning Objective 4)* Which of the following ratios is used to measure profitability?
   a. Current ratio
   b. Days' sales in receivables
   c. Rate of return on net sales
   d. Times interest earned

9. *(Learning Objective 4)* *Leverage* refers to how companies finance their operations with
   a. inventory.
   b. debt.
   c. issued stock.
   d. treasury stock.

10. *(Learning Objective 4)* Which of the following is generally undesirable?
    a. Decrease in debt ratio
    b. Increase in times-interest-earned ratio
    c. Decrease in days' sales in receivables
    d. Decrease in inventory turnover

Quick Check Answers

1.c 2.a 3.d 4.a 5.a 6.d 7.b 8.c 9.b 10.d

Short Exercises

S14-1   Horizontal analysis of revenue and cost of sales *(Learning Objective 1)*

Samson Corporation reported the following on its comparative income statement:

(in millions)	2014	2013	2012
Revenue	$12,259	$11,960	$11,500
Cost of sales	$ 4,141	$ 4,040	$ 3,250

Perform a horizontal analysis of revenues and gross profit—both in dollar amounts and in percentages—for 2014 and 2013.

S14-2   Find trend percentages *(Learning Objective 2)*

Houston Group reported the following revenues and net income amounts:

(in millions)	2014	2013	2012	2011
Revenue	$10,965	$10,105	$9,460	$10,750
Net income	$ 546	$ 494	$ 468	$ 520

a. Show Houston Group's trend percentages for revenues and net income. Use 2011 as the base year and round to the nearest percent.
b. Which measure increased faster during 2012–2014?

S14-3   Vertical analysis of assets *(Learning Objective 2)*

Verifine Optical Company reported the following amounts on its balance sheet at December 31:

Cash and receivables	$ 49,525
Inventory	35,525
Property, plant, and equipment, net	89,950
Total assets	$175,000

Perform a vertical analysis of Verifine Optical Company's assets at year end.

S14-4   Prepare common-size income statements *(Learning Objective 3)*

Compare Sanchez and Alioto by converting their income statements to common size.

	Sanchez	Alioto
Net sales	$10,800	$19,536
Cost of goods sold	6,707	14,203
Other expense	3,456	4,356
Net income	$ 637	$ 977

Which company earns more net income? Which company's net income is a higher percentage of its net sales?

Hamilton's Data Set used for S14-5 through S14-9:

Hamilton's, a home-improvement store chain, reported these summarized figures (in billions):

	A	B
1	Hamilton's	
2	Income Statement	
3	For the Years Ended December 31, 2014 and 2013	
4		*(amounts in thousands)*
5		**2014**
6	Sales revenues	$ 35,587,500
7	Less: Cost of goods sold	21,700,000
8	Gross profit	$ 13,887,500
9	Less: Operating expenses	5,093,770
10	Operating income	$ 8,793,730
11	Less: Interest expense	217,500
12	Income before income taxes	$ 8,576,230
13	Less: Income tax expense	1,979,130
14	Net income	$ 6,597,100
15		

	A	B	C
1	Hamilton's		
2	Balance Sheets		
3	December 31, 2014 and 2013		
4		*(amounts in thousands)*	
5		**2014**	**2013**
6	**Assets**		
7	Current assets:		
8	Cash	$ 1,290,000	$ 800,000
9	Short-term investments	202,000	260,000
10	Accounts receivable	100,000	293,500
11	Inventory	4,650,000	4,120,000
12	Other current assets	503,000	402,500
13	Total current assets	$ 6,745,000	$ 5,876,000
14	Other non-current assets	12,600,000	11,690,000
15	Total assets	$ 19,345,000	$ 17,566,000
16			
17	**Liabilities**		
18	Current liabilities:		
19	Accounts payable	$ 3,150,000	$ 2,985,000
20	Notes payable	910,000	657,000
21	Accrued liabilities	360,000	38,000
22	Total current liabilities	$ 4,420,000	$ 3,680,000
23	Long-term liabilities	4,294,000	4,214,000
24	Total liabilities	$ 8,714,000	$ 7,894,000
25			
26	**Stockholders' equity**		
27	Common stock, no par	$ 2,505,000	$ 1,000,000
28	Retained earnings	8,126,000	8,672,000
29	Total stockholders' equity	$ 10,631,000	$ 9,672,000
30			
31	Total liabilities and equity	$ 19,345,000	$ 17,566,000
32			

S14-5 Find current ratio *(Learning Objective 4)*

Refer to the Hamilton's Data Set.

a. Compute Hamilton's current ratio at December 31, 2014 and 2013.

b. Did Hamilton's current ratio improve, deteriorate, or hold steady during 2014?

S14-6   Analyze inventory and receivables *(Learning Objective 4)*

Use the Hamilton's Data Set to compute the following:

a. The rate of inventory turnover for 2014.

b. Days' sales in average receivables during 2014.

S14-7   Compute and interpret debt ratio *(Learning Objective 4)*

Refer to the Hamilton's Data Set.

a. Compute the debt ratio at December 31, 2014.

b. Is Hamilton's ability to pay its liabilities strong or weak? Explain your reasoning.

S14-8   Compute profitability ratios *(Learning Objective 4)*

Use the Hamilton's Data Set to compute these profitability measures for 2014:

a. Rate of return on net sales

b. Rate of return on total assets

c. Rate of return on common stockholders' equity

Are these rates of return strong or weak?

S14-9   Determine earnings per share *(Learning Objective 4)*

Use the Hamilton's Data Set when making the following calculations:

a. Compute earnings per share (EPS) for Hamilton's. The number of shares outstanding was 710,000.

b. Compute Hamilton's price/earnings ratio. The price of a share of Hamilton's is $63.50.

ETHICS

S14-10   Identify ethical standards violated *(Learning Objectives 1, 2, 3, & 4)*

For each of the situations listed, identify the primary standard from the IMA *Statement of Ethical Professional Practice* that is violated (competence, confidentiality, integrity, or credibility). Refer to Exhibit 1-6 for the complete standard.

1. Emmett talks about the financial woes of the company he works for when he is out with a group of friends. He shares that the company will not be able to meet the ratios specified in the loan covenants.

2. Marion prepares the financial statements, but the internal control system weaknesses are not disclosed.

3. Jeanne, an accountant working in the Accounts Payable Department, writes a company check to herself for $1,500 to temporarily borrow money to pay her apartment rent; she plans on paying the money back after her next paycheck.

4. Shirley has not participated in any continuing education activities since she graduated five years ago because life has just been too busy. She is unprepared for the company to issue IFRS-based statements for the first time this year.

5. Floyd, the corporate controller, prepares a report for the board of directors that summarizes the year. Floyd, wanting to look good, only includes the favorable ratios and favorable events in this report.

EXERCISES Group A

E14-11A   Trend analysis of working capital *(Learning Objective 1)*

Compute the dollar amount of change and the percentage of change in Business News Group's working capital each year during 2013 and 2014. Is this trend favorable or unfavorable?

	2014	2013	2012
Total current assets...	$379,780	$356,000	$309,000
Total current liabilities	$188,000	$184,000	$149,000

E14-12A   Horizontal analysis *(Learning Objective 1)*

Prepare a horizontal analysis of the following comparative income statement of Mariner Designs.

	A	B	C
1	**Mariner Designs**		
2	**Income Statement**		
3	**For the Years Ended December 31, 2014 and 2013**		
4		*(amounts in thousands)*	
5		**2014**	**2013**
6	Sales revenues	$ 567,276	$ 492,000
7	Less: Cost of goods sold	266,805	247,500
8	Gross profit	$ 300,471	$ 244,500
9	Less: Operating expenses	148,750	140,000
10	Operating income	$ 151,721	$ 104,500
11	Less: Interest expense	9,905	4,070
12	Income before income taxes	$ 141,816	$ 100,430
13	Less: Income tax expense	21,235	18,430
14	Net income	$ 120,581	$ 82,000
15			

Why did net income increase by a higher percentage than net sales revenue during 2014?

E14-13A   Compute trend percentages *(Learning Objective 1)*

Compute trend percentages for Bright Skies Realtors net revenue and net income for the following five-year period using 2010 as the base year.

(in thousands)	2014	2013	2012	2011	2010
Net revenue.........................	$1,700	$1,325	$1,275	$1,150	$1,250
Net income.........................	$ 180	$ 150	$ 114	$ 108	$ 120

Which grew faster during the period, net revenue or net income?

E14-14A   Perform vertical analysis *(Learning Objective 2)*

Alpha Designs has requested that you perform a vertical analysis of its balance sheet.

	A	B
1	**Alpha Designs, Inc.**	
2	**Balance Sheet**	
3	**As of December 31**	
4		
5		**For the year (in thousands)**
6	**Assets**	
7	Total current assets	$ 46,055
8	Property, plant and equipment, net	218,685
9	Other non-current assets	40,260
10	Total assets	$ 305,000
11		
12	**Liabilities**	
13	Total current liabilities	$ 55,510
14	Long-term liabilities	117,730
15	Total liabilities	$ 173,240
16		
17	**Stockholders' equity**	
18	Total stockholders' equity	131,760
19		
20	Total liabilities and equity	$ 305,000
21		

E14-15A   Prepare a common-size income statement (Learning Objective 3)

Prepare a comparative common-size income statement for Mariner Designs. To an investor, how does 2014 compare with 2013? Explain your reasoning.

	A	B	C
1	Mariner Designs		
2	Income Statement		
3	For the Years Ended December 31, 2014 and 2013		
4		(amounts in thousands)	
5		2014	2013
6	Sales revenues	$ 567,276	$ 492,000
7	Less: Cost of goods sold	266,805	247,500
8	Gross profit	$ 300,471	$ 244,500
9	Less: Operating expenses	148,750	140,000
10	Operating income	$ 151,721	$ 104,500
11	Less: Interest expense	9,905	4,070
12	Income before income taxes	$ 141,816	$ 100,430
13	Less: Income tax expense	21,235	18,430
14	Net income	$ 120,581	$ 82,000
15			

E14-16A   Calculate ratios (Learning Objective 4)

The partial financial statements of a company include the following items:

	A	B	C
1	Balance sheet item:	Current year	Preceding year
2	Cash	$ 16,500	$ 23,500
3	Short-term investments	$ 10,750	$ 24,000
4	Net receivables	$ 49,000	$ 77,360
5	Inventory	$ 81,000	$ 78,500
6	Prepaid expenses	$ 21,500	$ 8,000
7	Total current assets	$ 178,750	$ 211,360
8	Total current liabilities	$ 125,000	$ 86,000
9			
10	Income statement:		
11	Net credit sales	$ 427,050	
12	Cost of goods sold	$ 319,000	
13			

Requirement

Compute the following ratios for the current year:

    a. Current ratio

    b. Acid-test ratio

    c. Inventory turnover

    d. Days' sales in average receivables

E14-17A More ratio analysis (Learning Objective 4)

Perfect Fit Frames has asked you to determine whether the company's ability to pay current liabilities and total liabilities improved or deteriorated during 2014. To answer that question, compute these ratios for 2014 and 2013, using the following data:

	A	B	C
1		2014	2013
2	Cash	$ 61,500	$ 47,000
3	Short-term investments	$ 26,000	$ 0
4	Net receivables	$ 126,560	$ 118,240
5	Inventory	$ 236,300	$ 271,320
6	Total assets	$ 564,000	$ 492,000
7	Total current liabilities	$ 278,000	$ 204,000
8	Long-term notes payable	$ 20,920	$ 46,920
9	Income from operations	$ 166,110	$ 159,580
10	Interest expense	$ 49,000	$ 39,500
11			

a. Current ratio

b. Acid-test ratio

c. Debt ratio

d. Times-interest-earned ratio

E14-18A Compute profitability ratios (Learning Objective 4)

Compute four ratios that measure Variline's ability to earn profits. The company's comparative income statement follows. The data for 2014 are given as needed.

	A	B	C
1	Variline		
2	Income Statement		
3	For the Years Ended December 31, 2014 and 2013		
4	(amounts in thousands)		
5		2014	2013	2012
6	Sales revenues	$ 178,120	$ 167,725	
7	Less: Cost of goods sold	94,000	88,000	
8	Gross profit	$ 84,120	$ 79,725	
9	Less: Operating expenses	43,000	35,000	
10	Operating income	$ 41,120	$ 44,725	
11	Less: Interest expense	7,360	8,100	
12	Income before income taxes	$ 33,760	$ 36,625	
13	Less: Income tax expense	11,495	23,207	
14	Net income	$ 22,265	$ 13,418	
15				
16	Additional data:			
17	Total assets	$ 203,000	$ 192,000	$ 179,000
18	Common stockholders' equity	$ 110,050	$ 86,000	$ 77,000
19	Preferred dividends	$ 2,660	$ 2,660	$ 0
20	Common shares outstanding during the year	26,140	26,140	24,000
21				

Did the company's operating performance improve or deteriorate during 2014?

E14-19A Compute stock ratios *(Learning Objective 4)*

Evaluate the common stock of Warwick State Bank as an investment. Specifically, use the three stock ratios to determine whether the common stock has increased or decreased in attractiveness during the past year.

	Current year	Last year
Net income..	$ 83,375	$ 77,300
Dividends—common..	$ 19,845	$ 19,845
Dividends—preferred...	$ 12,500	$ 12,500
Total stockholders' equity at year end (includes 81,000 shares of common stock)	$772,000	$605,950
Preferred stock, 6%...	$205,000	$205,000
Market price per share of common.................................	$ 17.50	$ 14.00

E14-20A Calculate ratios *(Learning Objective 4)*

Harmony Corporation reported these figures:

	A	B	C	D	E	F
1	Harmony Corporation				Harmony Corporation	
2	Balance Sheets				Income Statement	
3	December 31, 2014 and 2013				For the Year Ended December 31, 2014	
4	(amounts in thousands)				(amounts in thousands)	
5		2014	2013			2014
6	Assets				Sales revenues	$ 13,140
7	Current assets:				Less: Cost of goods sold	1,980
8	Cash	$ 5,700	$ 2,700		Gross profit	$ 11,160
9	Accounts receivable	2,100	1,860		Less: Operating expenses	660
10	Inventory	1,000	800		Operating income	$ 10,500
11	Other current assets	3,950	2,640		Less: Interest expense	500
12	Total current assets	$ 12,750	$ 8,000		Income before income taxes	$ 10,000
13	Other assets	23,500	20,000		Less: Income tax expense	7,000
14	Total assets	$ 36,250	$ 28,000		Net income	$ 3,000
15						
16	Liabilities					
17	Total current liabilities	$ 15,000	$ 12,500			
18	Long-term liabilities	6,250	5,500			
19	Total liabilities	$ 21,250	$ 18,000			
20						
21	Stockholders' equity					
22	Total common stockholders' equity	15,000	10,000			
23						
24	Total liabilities and equity	$ 36,250	$ 28,000			
25						

Harmony has 3,125 shares of common stock outstanding. Its stock has traded recently at $31.20 per share. You would like to gain a better understanding of Harmony's financial position. Calculate the following ratios for 2014 and interpret the results:

a. Inventory turnover

b. Days' sales in receivables

c. Acid-test ratio

d. Times-interest-earned

e. Return on stockholders' equity

f. Earnings per share

g. Price/earnings ratio

E14-21A Classify company sustainability measurements into triple-bottom-line components *(Learning Objective 4)*

In its Annual Report, PepsiCo lists several sustainability goals and commitments it has made. In the following list from PepsiCo's Annual Report, categorize each goal (or measurement) as to whether it is oriented toward the *people*, *planet*, or *profit* component of the triple bottom line.

Excerpts of Goals and Commitments from PepsiCo, Inc.'s Annual Report	People, Profit, or Planet?
a. Foster diversity and inclusion by developing a workforce that reflects local communities.	
b. Rank among the top two suppliers in customer (retail partner) surveys where third-party measures exist.	
c. Work to eliminate all solid waste to landfills from our production facilities.	
d. Sustain or improve brand equity scores for PepsiCo's 19 billion-dollar brands in the top 10 markets.	
e. Increase the amount of whole grains, fruits, vegetables, nuts, seeds and low-fat dairy in our global product portfolio.	
f. Reduce our fuel-use intensity by 25 percent per unit of production by 2015.	
g. Reduce the average amount of sodium per serving in key global food brands, in key countries, by 25 percent by 2015, compared to a 2006 baseline.	
h. Improve our water-use efficiency by 20 percent per unit of production by 2015.	
i. Grow international revenues at two times real global GDP growth rate.	
j. Grow savory snack and liquid refreshment beverage market share in the top 20 markets.	

Source: PepsiCo 2010 Annual Report (retrieved from http://www.pepsico.com/Download/PepsiCo_Annual_Report_2010_Full_Annual_Report.pdf on May 24, 2011).

EXERCISES Group B

E14-22B Trend analysis of working capital *(Learning Objective 1)*

Compute the dollar amount of change and the percentage of change in Tabloid News Group's working capital each year during 2013 and 2014. Is this trend favorable or unfavorable?

	2014	2013	2012
Total current assets...	$306,120	$286,250	$240,750
Total current liabilities	$186,000	$179,000	$147,000

E14-23B Horizontal analysis *(Learning Objective 1)*

Prepare a horizontal analysis of the following comparative income statement of Enchanted Designs.

	A	B	C
1	**Enchanted Designs**		
2	**Income Statement**		
3	**For the Years Ended December 31, 2014 and 2013**		
4		*(amounts in thousands)*	
5		**2014**	**2013**
6	Sales revenues	$ 426,411	$ 371,600
7	Less: Cost of goods sold	180,761	166,600
8	Gross profit	$ 245,650	$ 205,000
9	Less: Operating expenses	100,130	95,000
10	Operating income	$ 145,520	$ 110,000
11	Less: Interest expense	26,551	16,570
12	Income before income taxes	$ 118,969	$ 93,430
13	Less: Income tax expense	21,784	18,430
14	Net income	$ 97,185	$ 75,000
15			

Why did net income increase by a higher percentage than net sales revenue during 2014?

E14-24B   Compute trend percentages (*Learning Objective 1*)

Compute trend percentages for Thousand Oaks Realtors' net revenue and net income for the following five-year period, using 2010 as the base year.

(in thousands)	2014	2013	2012	2011	2010
Net revenue..............................	$1,586	$1,525	$1,281	$1,159	$1,220
Net income................................	$ 180	$ 165	$ 115	$ 105	$ 125

Which grew faster during the period, net revenue or net income?

E14-25B   Perform vertical analysis (*Learning Objective 2*)

Eta Designs has requested that you perform a vertical analysis of its balance sheet.

	A	B
1	Eta Designs, Inc.	
2	Balance Sheet	
3	As of December 31	
4		
5		For the year (in thousands)
6	Assets	
7	Total current assets	$ 44,250
8	Property, plant and equipment, net	216,000
9	Other non-current assets	39,750
10	Total assets	$ 300,000
11		
12	Liabilities	
13	Total current liabilities	$ 55,500
14	Long-term liabilities	115,500
15	Total liabilities	$ 171,000
16		
17	Stockholders' equity	
18	Total stockholders' equity	129,000
19		
20	Total liabilities and equity	$ 300,000
21		

E14-26B   Prepare common-size income statement (*Learning Objective 3*)

Prepare a comparative common-size income statement for Enchanted Designs. To an investor, how does 2014 compare with 2013? Explain your reasoning.

	A	B	C
1	Enchanted Designs		
2	Income Statement		
3	For the Years Ended December 31, 2014 and 2013		
4		(amounts in thousands)	
5		2014	2013
6	Sales revenues	$ 426,411	$ 371,600
7	Less: Cost of goods sold	180,761	166,600
8	Gross profit	$ 245,650	$ 205,000
9	Less: Operating expenses	100,130	95,000
10	Operating income	$ 145,520	$ 110,000
11	Less: Interest expense	26,551	16,570
12	Income before income taxes	$ 118,969	$ 93,430
13	Less: Income tax expense	21,784	18,430
14	Net income	$ 97,185	$ 75,000
15			

E14-27B Calculate ratios *(Learning Objective 4)*

The partial financial statements of a company include the following items:

	A	B	C
		Current year	Preceding year
1	**Balance sheet item:**		
2	Cash	$ 9,000	$ 20,000
3	Short-term investments	$ 2,600	$ 26,000
4	Net receivables	$ 58,000	$ 48,720
5	Inventory	$ 75,500	$ 72,500
6	Prepaid expenses	$ 28,900	$ 8,200
7	Total current assets	$ 174,000	$ 175,420
8	Total current liabilities	$ 116,000	$ 94,000
9			
10	**Income statement:**		
11	Net credit sales	$ 423,400	
12	Cost of goods sold	$ 292,300	
13			

Requirement

Compute the following ratios for the current year:

a. Current ratio

b. Acid-test ratio

c. Inventory turnover

d. Days' sales in average receivables

E14-28B More ratio analysis *(Learning Objective 4)*

Top Notch Frames has asked you to determine whether the company's ability to pay current liabilities and total liabilities improved or deteriorated during 2014. To answer this question, compute these ratios for 2014 and 2013, using the following data:

	A	B	C
		2014	2013
1			
2	Cash	$ 60,500	$ 45,000
3	Short-term investments	$ 26,500	$ 0
4	Net receivables	$ 115,500	$ 108,230
5	Inventory	$ 226,800	$ 286,560
6	Total assets	$ 558,000	$ 488,000
7	Total current liabilities	$ 270,000	$ 199,000
8	Long-term notes payable	$ 31,320	$ 30,360
9	Income from operations	$ 171,000	$ 174,580
10	Interest expense	$ 50,000	$ 43,000
11			

a. Current ratio

b. Acid-test ratio

c. Debt ratio

d. Times-interest-earned ratio

E14-29B   Compute profitability ratios (Learning Objective 4)

Compute four ratios that measure Caulfield Industries' ability to earn profits. The company's comparative income statement follows. The data for 2012 are given as needed.

	A	B	C
1	Caulfield Industries		
2	Income Statement		
3	For the Years Ended December 31, 2014 and 2013		
4	(amounts in thousands)		
5		2014	2013	2012
6	Sales revenues	$ 211,400	$ 182,910	
7	Less: Cost of goods sold	105,000	96,000	
8	Gross profit	$ 106,400	$ 86,910	
9	Less: Operating expenses	53,000	46,000	
10	Operating income	$ 53,400	$ 40,910	
11	Less: Interest expense	5,385	6,459	
12	Income before income taxes	$ 48,015	$ 34,451	
13	Less: Income tax expense	22,647	16,160	
14	Net income	$ 25,368	$ 18,291	
15				
16	Additional data:			
17	Total assets	$ 207,000	$ 195,000	$ 180,000
18	Common stockholders' equity	$ 101,000	$ 92,000	$ 61,110
19	Preferred dividends	$ 2,980	$ 2,980	$ 0
20	Common shares outstanding during the year	27,985	27,985	26,000
21				

Did the company's operating performance improve or deteriorate during 2014?

E14-30B   Compute stock ratios (Learning Objective 4)

Evaluate the common stock of Oxford State Bank as an investment. Specifically, use the three stock ratios to determine whether the common stock has increased or decreased in attractiveness during the past year.

	Current year	Last year
Net income	$ 80,700	$ 76,500
Dividends—common	$ 20,160	$ 20,160
Dividends—preferred	$ 13,500	$ 13,500
Total stockholders' equity at year-end (includes 84,000 shares of common stock)	$807,200	$626,600
Preferred stock (6%)	$215,000	$215,000
Market price per share of common stock	$ 24.00	$ 19.20

E14-31B   Calculate ratios *(Learning Objective 4)*

Jannus Supply Corporation reported these figures:

	A	B	C	D	E	F
1	Jannus Supply Corporation				Jannus Supply Corporation	
2	Balance Sheets				Income Statement	
3	December 31, 2014 and 2013				For the Year Ended December 31, 2014	
4	(amounts in thousands)				(amounts in thousands)	
5		2014	2013			2014
6	Assets				Sales revenues	$ 14,600
7	Current assets:				Less: Cost of goods sold	5,400
8	Cash	$ 3,000	$ 2,300		Gross profit	$ 9,200
9	Accounts receivable	2,400	2,200		Less: Operating expenses	4,500
10	Inventory	2,100	1,500		Operating income	$ 4,700
11	Other current assets	1,500	2,250		Less: Interest expense	200
12	Total current assets	$ 9,000	$ 8,250		Income before income taxes	$ 4,500
13	Other assets	21,000	16,750		Less: Income tax expense	2,200
14	Total assets	$ 30,000	$ 25,000		Net income	$ 2,300
15						
16	Liabilities					
17	Total current liabilities	$ 10,000	$ 9,000			
18	Long-term liabilities	7,000	6,000			
19	Total liabilities	$ 17,000	$ 15,000			
20						
21	Stockholders' equity					
22	Total common stockholders' equity	13,000	10,000			
23						
24	Total liabilities and equity	$ 30,000	$ 25,000			
25						

Jannus Supply has 2,500 shares of common stock outstanding. Its stock has traded recently at $34.50 per share. You would like to gain a better understanding of Jannus Supply's financial position. Calculate the following ratios for 2014 and interpret the results:

a. Inventory turnover

b. Days' sales in receivables

c. Acid-test ratio

d. Times-interest-earned

e. Return on stockholders' equity

f. Earnings per share

g. Price/earnings ratio

SUSTAINABILITY

E14-32B   Classify company sustainability measurements into triple-bottom-line components *(Learning Objective 4)*

In its Annual Report, PepsiCo lists several sustainability goals and commitments it has made. In the following list from PepsiCo's Annual Report, categorize each goal (or measurement) as to whether it is oriented toward the people, planet, or profit component or the triple bottom line.

Excerpts of Goals and Commitments from PepsiCo, Inc.'s Annual Report	People, Profit, or Planet?

a. Expand PepsiCo Foundation and PepsiCo corporate contribution initiatives to promote healthier communities, including enhancing diet and physical activity programs.

b. Continue to lead the industry by incorporating at least 10 percent recycled polyethylene terephthalate (rPET) in our primary soft drink containers in the U.S., and broadly expand the use of rPET across key international markets.

c. Ensure a safe workplace by continuing to reduce lost-time injury rates, while striving to improve other occupational health and safety metrics through best practices.

d. Improve our electricity-use efficiency by 20 percent per unit of production by 2015.

e. Match eligible associate charitable contributions globally, dollar-for-dollar, through the PepsiCo Foundation.

Excerpts of Goals and Commitments from PepsiCo, Inc.'s Annual Report	People, Profit, or Planet?

f. Deliver total shareholder returns in the top quartile of our industry group.

g. Increase cash flow in proportion to net income growth over three-year windows.

h. Reduce the average amount of saturated fat per serving in key global food brands, in key countries, by 15 percent by 2020, compared to a 2006 baseline.

i. Reduce packaging weight by 350 million pounds—avoiding the creation of one billion pounds of landfill waste by 2012.

j. Reduce the average amount of added sugar per serving in key global beverage brands, in key countries, by 25 percent by 2020, compared to a 2006 baseline.

Source: PepsiCo 2010 Annual Report (retrieved from http://www.pepsico.com/Download/PepsiCo_Annual_Report_2010_Full_Annual_Report.pdf on May 24, 2011).

PROBLEMS Group A

P14-33A   Prepare trend analysis *(Learning Objectives 1 & 4)*

Net sales revenue, net income, and common stockholders' equity for Mirabel Optical Corporation, a manufacturer of contact lenses, follow for a four-year period.

(in thousands)	2014	2013	2012	2011
Net sales revenue	$7,797	$7,383	$6,555	$6,900
Net income	$ 610	$ 440	$ 365	$ 500
Ending common stockholders' equity	$4,260	$3,740	$3,300	$4,000

Requirements

1. Compute trend percentages for each item for 2011 through 2014. Use 2011 as the base year.
2. Compute the rate of return on common stockholders' equity for 2012 through 2014.

P14-34A   Comprehensive analysis *(Learning Objectives 2, 3, & 4)*

Todd Department Stores' chief executive officer (CEO) has asked you to compare the company's profit performance and financial position with the average for the industry. The CEO has given you the company's income statement and balance sheet, as well as the industry average data for retailers.

	A	B	C
1	Todd Department Stores, Inc.		
2	Income Statement Compared with Industry Average		
3	For the Year Ended December 31		
4		(amounts in thousands)	
5		Todd	Industry Average
6	Sales revenues	$ 778,000	100.0%
7	Less: Cost of goods sold	525,150	65.8%
8	Gross profit	$ 252,850	34.2%
9	Less: Operating expenses	159,490	19.6%
10	Operating income	$ 93,360	14.6%
11	Less: Interest expense	1,282	0.1%
12	Income before income taxes	$ 92,078	14.5%
13	Less: Income tax expense	5,720	0.5%
14	Net income	$ 86,358	14.0%
15			

	A	B	C
1	Todd Department Stores, Inc.		
2	Balance Sheet Compared with Industry Average		
3	As of December 31		
4	(amounts in thousands)		
5		Todd	Industry Average
6	**Assets**		
7	Current assets	$ 311,420	70.9%
8	Fixed assets, net	117,760	24.1%
9	Intangible assets, net	6,900	0.6%
10	Other assets	23,920	4.4%
11	Total assets	$ 460,000	100.0%
12			
13	**Liabilities**		
14	Current liabilities	$ 212,520	48.3%
15	Long-term liabilities	103,040	16.5%
16	Total liabilities	$ 315,560	64.8%
17			
18	**Stockholders' equity**		
19	Total common stockholders' equity	$ 144,440	35.2%
20			
21	Total liabilities and equity	$ 460,000	100.0%
22			

Requirements

1. Prepare a common-size income statement and balance sheet for Todd Department Stores. The first column of each statement should present Todd Department Stores' common-size statement, while the second column should present the industry averages.

2. For the profitability analysis, compute Todd Department Stores' (a) ratio of gross profit to net sales, (b) ratio of operating income to net sales, and (c) ratio of net income to net sales. Compare these figures with the industry averages. Is Todd Stores' profit performance better or worse than the industry average?

3. For the analysis of financial position, compute Todd Department Stores' (a) ratio of current assets to total assets and (b) ratio of stockholders' equity to total assets. Compare these ratios with the industry averages. Is Todd Department Stores' financial position better or worse than the industry averages?

P14-35A   Effect of transactions on ratios (Learning Objective 4)

Financial statement data of *Yankee Traveler* magazine include the following items (dollars in thousands):

Cash	$ 23,000
Accounts receivable, net	$ 81,000
Inventories	$192,100
Total assets	$630,000
Short-term notes payable	$ 50,000
Accounts payable	$102,000
Accrued liabilities	$ 58,000
Long-term liabilities	$174,300
Net income	$ 72,000
Common shares outstanding	50,000

Requirements

1. Compute *Yankee Traveler's* current ratio, debt ratio, and earnings per share. Round all ratios to two decimal places.

2. Compute the three ratios after evaluating the effect of each transaction that follows. Consider each transaction *separately.*

   a. Purchased inventory on account, $36,000

   b. Borrowed $189,000 on a long-term note payable

   c. Issued 6,250 shares of common stock, receiving cash of $138,600

   d. Received cash on account, $19,000

P14-36A   Ratio analysis over two years (Learning Objective 4)

Comparative financial statement data of Banfield, Inc., follow:

	A	B	C
1	Banfield, Inc.		
2	Comparative Income Statement		
3	For the Years Ended December 31, 2014 and 2013		
4		(amounts in thousands)	
5		2014	2013
6	Sales revenues	$ 456,650	$ 423,260
7	Less: Cost of goods sold	245,000	216,000
8	Gross profit	$ 211,650	$ 207,260
9	Less: Operating expenses	135,000	131,000
10	Operating income	$ 76,650	$ 76,260
11	Less: Interest expense	10,500	12,400
12	Income before income taxes	$ 66,150	$ 63,860
13	Less: Income tax expense	7,850	24,760
14	Net income	$ 58,300	$ 39,100
15			

	A	B	C	D
1	Banfield, Inc.			
2	Comparative Balance Sheets			
3	December 31, 2014 and 2013			
4	(amounts in thousands)			
5		2014	2013	2012*
6	Assets			
7	Current assets:			
8	Cash	$ 94,000	$ 95,000	
9	Accounts receivable	111,500	142,000	$ 101,000
10	Inventory	135,000	145,000	$ 215,000
11	Prepaid expenses	11,500	8,000	
12	Total current assets	$ 352,000	$ 390,000	
13	Property, plant, and equipment, net	208,000	173,000	
14	Total assets	$ 560,000	$ 563,000	
15				
16	Liabilities			
17	Current liabilities	$ 220,000	$ 260,000	
18	Long-term liabilities	98,000	5,000	
19	Total liabilities	$ 318,000	$ 265,000	
20				
21	Stockholders' equity			
22	Preferred stock, 5%	$ 110,000	$ 110,000	
23	Total common stockholders' equity	132,000	188,000	$ 52,000
24	Total stockholders' equity	$ 242,000	$ 298,000	
25				
26	Total liabilities and equity	$ 560,000	$ 563,000	
27				

*Selected 2012 amounts

1. Market price of Banfield's common stock: $49.50 at December 31, 2014, and $27.02 at December 31, 2013
2. Common shares outstanding: 12,000 during 2014 and 12,000 during 2013
3. All sales are credit sales

Requirements

1. Compute the following ratios for 2014 and 2013:
   a. Current ratio
   b. Times-interest-earned ratio
   c. Inventory turnover
   d. Return on common stockholders' equity
   e. Earnings per share of common stock
   f. Price/earnings ratio

2. Decide (a) whether Banfield's ability to pay debts and to sell inventory improved or deteriorated during 2014 and (b) whether the investment attractiveness of its common stock appears to have increased or decreased.

P14-37A   **Make an investment decision** (Learning Objective 4)

Assume that you are purchasing an investment and have decided to invest in a company in the smartphone business. You have narrowed the choice to SW Electronics or Nahla Electronics and have assembled the following data.

Selected income statement data for the current year follows:

	SW	Nahla
Net sales (all on credit)..	$423,400	$518,300
Cost of goods sold..	$207,000	$221,000
Interest expense...	—	$ 20,000
Net income..	$ 63,600	$ 78,000

Selected balance sheet data at the *beginning* of the current year follows:

	SW	Nahla
Current receivables, net...	$ 36,000	$ 44,540
Inventories..	$ 74,750	$ 56,500
Total assets...	$258,000	$274,000
Common stock:		
$1 par, (12,000 shares)...	$ 12,000	
$1 par, (15,000 shares)...		$ 15,000

Selected balance sheet and market-price data at the *end* of the current year follows:

	SW	Nahla
Current assets:		
Cash..	$ 28,500	$ 22,500
Short-term investments	$ 40,060	$ 18,480
Current receivables, net	$ 36,500	$ 43,500
Inventories	$ 69,000	$106,000
Prepaid expenses	$ 4,940	$ 14,520
Total current assets..	$179,000	$205,000
Total assets...	$412,000	$327,500
Total current liabilities	$103,000	$ 96,000
Total liabilities...	$103,000	$131,000
Common stock:		
$1 par, (12,000 shares)...	$ 12,000	
$1 par, (15,000 shares)...		$ 15,000
Total stockholders' equity	$309,000	$196,500
Market price per share of common stock	$ 79.50	$ 91.00

Your strategy is to invest in companies that have low price/earnings ratios but appear to be in good shape financially. Assume that you have analyzed all other factors and that your decision depends on the results of ratio analysis.

Requirement

Compute the following ratios for both companies for the current year and decide which company's stock better fits your investment strategy.

    a. Acid-test ratio

    b. Inventory turnover

    c. Days' sales in average receivables

    d. Debt ratio

    e. Earnings per share of common stock

    f. Price/earnings ratio

PROBLEMS Group B

P14-38B Prepare trend analysis *(Learning Objectives 1 & 4)*

Net sales revenue, net income, and common stockholders' equity for Eyesight Vision Corporation, a manufacturer of contact lenses, follow for a four-year period.

(in thousands)	2014	2013	2012	2011
Net sales revenue..	$7,479	$7,128	$6,426	$6,750
Net income...	$ 682	$ 451	$ 418	$ 550
Ending common stockholders' equity	$4,928	$3,072	$3,488	$3,200

Requirements

1. Compute trend percentages for each item for 2011 through 2014. Use 2011 as the base year.
2. Compute the rate of return on common stockholders' equity for 2012 through 2014.

P14-39B Comprehensive analysis *(Learning Objectives 2, 3, & 4)*

McConnell Department Stores' chief executive officer (CEO) has asked you to compare the company's profit performance and financial position with the average for the industry. The CEO has given you the company's income statement and balance sheet, as well as the industry average data for retailers.

	A	B	C
1	**McConnell Department Stores, Inc.**		
2	**Income Statement Compared with Industry Average**		
3	**For the Year Ended December 31**		
4		*(amounts in thousands)*	
5		**McConnell**	**Industry Average**
6	Sales revenues	$ 781,000	100.0%
7	Less: Cost of goods sold	527,175	65.6%
8	Gross profit	$ 253,825	34.4%
9	Less: Operating expenses	162,448	19.6%
10	Operating income	$ 91,377	14.8%
11	Less: Interest expense	3,060	0.1%
12	Income before income taxes	$ 88,317	14.7%
13	Less: Income tax expense	4,750	0.4%
14	Net income	$ 83,567	14.3%
15			

	A	B	C
1	McConnell Department Stores, Inc.		
2	Balance Sheet Compared with Industry Average		
3	As of December 31		
4	(amounts in thousands)		
5		McConnell	Industry Average
6	**Assets**		
7	Current assets	$ 285,180	70.9%
8	Fixed assets, net	107,520	23.9%
9	Intangible assets, net	5,040	0.8%
10	Other assets	22,260	4.4%
11	Total assets	$ 420,000	100.0%
12			
13	**Liabilities**		
14	Current liabilities	$ 192,360	48.0%
15	Long-term liabilities	94,920	16.4%
16	Total liabilities	$ 287,280	64.4%
17			
18	**Stockholders' equity**		
19	Total common stockholders' equity	$ 132,720	35.6%
20			
21	Total liabilities and equity	$ 420,000	100.0%
22			

Requirements

1. Prepare a common-size income statement and balance sheet for McConnell Department Stores. The first column of each statement should present McConnell Department Stores' common-size statement, while the second column should present the industry averages.

2. For the profitability analysis, compute McConnell Department Stores' (a) ratio of gross profit to net sales, (b) ratio of operating income to net sales, and (c) ratio of net income to net sales. Compare these figures with the industry averages. Is McConnell Department Stores' profit performance better or worse than the average for the industry?

3. For the analysis of financial position, compute McConnell Department Stores' (a) ratios of current assets to total assets and (b) ratio of stockholders' equity to total assets. Compare these ratios with the industry averages. Is McConnell Department Stores' financial position better or worse than the industry averages?

P14-40B   Effect of transactions on ratios (Learning Objective 4)

Financial statement data of *Style Travel* magazine include the following information (dollars in thousands):

Cash..	$ 24,500
Accounts receivable, net..	$ 83,000
Inventories..	$180,500
Total assets...	$660,000
Short-term notes payable	$ 49,500
Accounts payable...	$106,000
Accrued liabilities	$ 44,500
Long-term liabilities...	$182,800
Net income..	$ 81,000
Common shares outstanding	60,000

Requirements

1. Compute *Style Travel's* current ratio, debt ratio, and earnings per share. Round all ratios to two decimal places.

2. Compute the three ratios after evaluating the effect of each transaction that follows. Consider each transaction *separately*.

   a. Purchased inventory on account, $75,000

   b. Borrowed $264,000 on a long-term note payable

   c. Issued 7,500 shares of common stock, receiving cash of $210,000

   d. Received cash on account, $21,000

P14-41B   Ratio analysis over two years *(Learning Objective 4)*

Comparative financial statement data of Tanfield, Inc., follow:

	A	B	C
1	Tanfield, Inc.		
2	Comparative Income Statement		
3	For the Years Ended December 31, 2014 and 2013		
4		*(amounts in thousands)*	
5		2014	2013
6	Sales revenues	$ 453,000	$ 427,500
7	Less: Cost of goods sold	242,000	220,000
8	Gross profit	$ 211,000	$ 207,500
9	Less: Operating expenses	137,000	130,000
10	Operating income	$ 74,000	$ 77,500
11	Less: Interest expense	10,000	12,500
12	Income before income taxes	$ 64,000	$ 65,000
13	Less: Income tax expense	12,550	27,850
14	Net income	$ 51,450	$ 37,150
15			

	A	B	C	D
1	Tanfield, Inc.			
2	Comparative Balance Sheets			
3	December 31, 2014 and 2013			
4	*(amounts in thousands)*			
5		2014	2013	2012*
6	Assets			
7	Current assets:			
8	Cash	$ 95,000	$ 96,000	
9	Accounts receivable	111,500	140,000	$ 102,000
10	Inventory	137,000	138,000	$ 214,000
11	Prepaid expenses	12,000	7,000	
12	Total current assets	$ 355,500	$ 381,000	
13	Property, plant, and equipment, net	204,000	176,000	
14	Total assets	$ 559,500	$ 557,000	
15				
16	Liabilities			
17	Current liabilities	$ 225,000	$ 254,000	
18	Long-term liabilities	101,500	46,000	
19	Total liabilities	$ 326,500	$ 300,000	
20				
21	Stockholders' equity			
22	Preferred stock, 5%	$ 105,000	$ 105,000	
23	Total common stockholders' equity	128,000	152,000	$ 68,000
24	Total stockholders' equity	$ 233,000	$ 257,000	
25				
26	Total liabilities and equity	$ 559,500	$ 557,000	
27				

*Selected 2012 amounts

1. Market price of Tanfield's common stock: $47.67 at December 31, 2014, and $27.84 at December 31, 2013
2. Common shares outstanding: 11,000 during 2014 and 11,000 during 2013
3. All sales are credit sales

Requirements

1. Compute the following ratios for 2014 and 2013:
   a. Current ratio
   b. Times-interest-earned ratio
   c. Inventory turnover
   d. Return on common stockholders' equity
   e. Earnings per share of common stock
   f. Price/earnings ratio

2. Decide (a) whether Tanfield's ability to pay debts and to sell inventory improved or deteriorated during 2014 and (b) whether the investment attractiveness of its common stock appears to have increased or decreased.

P14-42B   Make an investment decision *(Learning Objective 4)*

Assume that you are purchasing an investment and have decided to invest in a company in the smartphone business. You have narrowed the choice to LX Electronics or Rose Corporation and have assembled the following data.

Selected income statement data for the current year follows:

	LX	Rose
Net sales (all on credit)...	$456,250	$511,000
Cost of goods sold...	$210,000	$255,000
Interest expense..	—	$ 18,500
Net income...	$ 50,000	$ 64,400

Selected balance sheet data at the *beginning* of the current year follows:

	LX	Rose
Current receivables, net..	$ 42,000	$ 40,700
Inventories..	$ 83,000	$ 82,500
Total assets..	$261,000	$271,000
Common stock:		
$1 par (10,000 shares)	$ 10,000	
$1 par (14,000 shares)		$ 14,000

Selected balance sheet and market-price data at the *end* of the current year follows:

	LX	Rose
Current assets:		
Cash	$ 29,200	$ 20,500
Short-term investments	42,000	22,200
Current receivables, net	38,000	44,000
Inventories	67,000	105,000
Prepaid expenses	2,000	4,300
Total current assets...	$178,200	$196,000
Total assets	$300,000	$272,000
Total current liabilities	$105,000	$102,000
Total liabilities..	$105,000	$136,000
Common stock:		
$1 par (10,000 shares)	$ 10,000	
$1 par (14,000 shares)		$ 14,000
Total stockholders' equity	$195,000	$136,000
Market price per share of common stock	$ 80.00	$ 85.10

Your strategy is to invest in companies that have low price/earnings ratios but appear to be in good shape financially. Assume that you have analyzed all other factors and that your decision depends on the results of ratio analysis.

Requirement

Compute the following ratios for both companies for the current year and decide which company's stock better fits your investment strategy.

    a. Acid-test ratio
    b. Inventory turnover
    c. Days' sales in average receivables
    d. Debt ratio
    e. Earnings per share of common stock
    f. Price/earnings ratio

CRITICAL THINKING

Discussion & Analysis

A14-43 Discussion & Questions

1. Describe horizontal analysis. Describe vertical analysis. What is each technique used for? How are the two methods similar? How are they different?

2. How is the current ratio calculated? What is it used to measure? How is it interpreted?

3. Assume a company has a current ratio of 2.0. List two examples of transactions that could cause the current ratio to increase. Also list two examples of transactions that could cause the current ratio to decrease.

4. What does the accounts receivable turnover measure? What does a relatively high accounts receivable turnover indicate about a company?

5. Describe the set of circumstances that could result in net income increasing while return on investment (ROI) decreases.

6. Suppose a company has a relatively high inventory turnover. What does the high inventory turnover indicate about the company's short-term liquidity?

7. Describe at least four financial conditions that may signal financial trouble.

8. Describe at least two reasons that a company's ratios might not be comparable over time.

9. Compare and contrast the current ratio and the quick ratio.

10. Describe why book value per share of common stock may not be useful for investment analysis.

11. Find a recent annual report for a publically held company in which you are interested. Summarize what sustainability information is provided in that annual report. Based on the sustainability information provided in the annual report, what measurements do you think the company might use to track its sustainability efforts? (You can use your imagination here; the actual sustainability measures are unlikely to be in the annual report.)

12. There are three components in the triple bottom line; *people*, *planet*, and *profit*. Which component do you think is most important? Why?

Application & Analysis

Mini Cases

A14-44 Calculating Ratios for Companies Within the Same Industry

Select an industry you are interested in and select three companies within that industry. Obtain their annual reports by going to each company's website and downloading the report for the most recent year. (On many companies' websites, you will need to visit the Investor Relations section to obtain the company's financial statements.) You may also collect the information from the company's Form 10-K, which can be found at www.sec.gov/idea/searchidea/companysearch_idea.html.

Basic Discussion Questions

For each of the three companies you selected, answer the following:

1. Calculate two ratios that measure the ability to pay current liabilities.
2. Calculate at least two ratios that measure the ability to sell inventory and collect receivables.
3. Calculate at least two ratios that measure the ability to pay long-term debt.
4. Calculate at least two ratios that measure profitability.
5. Calculate at least two ratios that help to analyze the stock as an investment.

Now that you have crunched the numbers, interpret the ratios. What can you tell about each company and its financial position? Is one company clearly better than the others in terms of its financial position, or are all three companies similar to each other?

A14-45 Ethics of financial statement analysis
(Learning Objectives 1, 2, 3, & 4)

Fitness Mania is a small technology start-up company that specializes in personal fitness mobile apps. The three founders have been working hard on the company for the past two years since they founded Fitness Mania.

The owners of Fitness Mania want to expand its business lines to include personal fitness trackers. To get into the manufacture and sale of personal fitness trackers, Fitness Mania will need to raise approximately $5 million from additional investors.

Fitness Mania's CEO is making a presentation to a group of potential investors who are interested in funding the new fitness tracker project. This presentation could make or break Fitness Mania, so it is a high-stakes presentation. The CEO knows that, while several of Fitness Mania's ratios are strong, it is still struggling a bit financially. Some of Fitness Mania's ratios would raise red flags to potential investors.

The controller of Fitness Mania is Tom Black. Tom likes working for the start-up company and he strongly believes in Fitness Mania's mission, which is to improve fitness while making it fun. Fitness Mania's products are potentially life changing for the people who use them to get more fit.

Fitness Mania's CEO asks Tom to prepare a report for the investors that emphasizes the strong ratios while burying the weaker ratios deep in the report.

Tom prepares a report that emphasizes the strong ratios. The weaker ratios are buried deep within the report. Tom has included a lot of extra data in the report to help to camouflage those weaker ratios. Tom also went one step further in the report preparation: He changed a few of the weaker ratios to make them appear stronger.

Tom rationalizes his actions by thinking that the revised report contributes to a greater good. The customers who use their fitness software products are likely to become healthier and have longer lives. He thinks that a few adjustments to the report are relatively minor when compared to the benefits that would be reaped by Fitness Mania's new product offerings if the potential investors do decide to invest in Fitness Mania.

Requirements

Using the IMA *Statement of Ethical Professional Practice* (Exhibit 1-6) as an ethical framework, answer the following questions:

a. What is (are) the ethical issue(s) in this situation?
b. What are Tom's responsibilities as a management accountant?

A14-46 Using financial statement ratios to analyze Coca-Cola and PepsiCo *(Learning Objectives 1, 2, 3, & 4)*

The Coca-Cola Company and PepsiCo, Inc., are fierce competitors in the beverage and snack markets. A perennial question among consumers is "Coke or Pepsi"? In this case, we will be looking at the financial positions of both companies to answer the question of which company is in a stronger financial position, Coke or Pepsi.

Following is a table of various financial data and ratios for both Coca-Cola and PepsiCo. The data are arranged in alphabetic order.

	A	B	C	D	E	F	G	H
1			The Coca-Cola Company				PepsiCo, Inc.	
2			Selected financial data				Selected financial data	
3			For years ended December 31				For years ended December 31	
4								
5		2010	2011	2012		2010	2011	2012
6	Acid-test ratio	0.85	0.78	0.77		0.80	0.62	0.80
7	Current ratio	1.17	1.05	1.09		1.11	0.96	1.10
8	Debt ratio	0.45	0.43	0.45		0.94	0.99	1.05
9	Earnings per share	$ 2.53	$ 1.85	$ 1.97		$ 3.91	$ 4.03	$ 3.92
10	Inventory turnover	5.07	6.34	6.00		8.87	8.78	8.45
11	Net income ($ in millions)	$ 11,809	$ 8,572	$ 9,019		$ 6,320	$ 6,443	$ 6,178
12	Rate of return on sales	33.63%	18.42%	18.78%		10.93%	9.69%	9.43%
13	Receivables turnover	8.58	9.96	9.92		10.57	10.05	10.10
14	Return on assets	19.42%	11.21%	10.86%		11.70%	9.14%	8.38%
15	Return on equity	42.32%	27.37%	28.00%		33.23%	30.70%	28.65%
16	Revenues ($ in millions)	$ 35,119	$ 46,542	$ 48,017		$ 57,838	$ 66,504	$ 65,492
17	Times-interest-earned ratio	20.43	28.43	30.75		10.12	11.32	10.24
18	Working capital ($ in millions)	$ 3,071	$ 1,214	$ 2,507		$ 1,677	$ (713)	$ 1,631
19								

Requirements

1. Rearrange the data and ratios into a report format that groups similar data and ratios together, to make it easier to analyze the data.

2. Using the given 2010–2012 financial data for The Coca-Cola Company, discuss the company's:

   a. Ability to pay current liabilities;

   b. Ability to sell inventory and collect receivables;

   c. Ability to pay long-term debt; and

   d. Profitability.

3. Using the given 2010–2012 financial data for PepsiCo, Inc., discuss the company's:

   a. Ability to pay current liabilities;

   b. Ability to sell inventory and collect receivables;

   c. Ability to pay long-term debt; and

   d. Profitability.

4. Now compare Coca-Cola's financial position to PepsiCo's financial position. How do the two companies compare in the following areas?

   a. Ability to pay current liabilities

   b. Ability to sell inventory and collect receivables

   c. Ability to pay long-term debt

   d. Profitability

5. What conclusions can you draw from your analysis of the two companies? Which company do you think is in a stronger financial position?

Team Project

A14-47 Comparison of common-size financials
(Learning Objective 3)

Select a company and obtain its financial statements. Convert the income statement and the balance sheet to common size and compare the company you selected to the industry average. Discuss how the company you selected measures up to the industry averages and form an opinion as to whether this company is above average, average, or below average. Use Google to find resources for identifying industry averages and common-size statements by industry. Clearly identify your sources and discuss why the source(s) you have used are likely to be reliable sources.

Try It Solutions

page 828:

Trend percentages are calculated by dividing each year's revenue by the base year's revenue, which in this case is $10,383. The trend percentages for 2008–2012 are as follows:

	A	B	C	D	E	F
1	**Starbucks Trend Data**	**2012**	**2011**	**2010**	**2009**	**Base Year 2008**
2	Sales revenue	$ 13,299	$ 11,700	$ 10,707	$ 9,774	$ 10,383
3	Trend percentage	128%	113%	103%	94%	100%
4						

page 838:

1. The current ratio is calculated as follows: $\dfrac{\text{Current assets}}{\text{Current liabilities}} = \dfrac{\$4,199.6}{\$2,209.8} = 1.9$

2. Inventory turnover is calculated as follows: $\dfrac{\text{Cost of goods sold}}{\text{Average inventory}} = \dfrac{\$5,813}{(\$965.8 + \$1,241.5)/2} = 5.27$

Sustainability

Learning Objectives

- ■ **1** Describe sustainability and how it can create business value
- ■ **2** Describe sustainability reporting and the GRI framework
- ■ **3** Describe EMA systems and their uses and challenges

The J.M. Smucker Company has adopted a sustainability strategy that calls for managers to view business decisions in terms of their economic viability, impact on the environment, and social responsibility. From an environmental standpoint, the company has established a five-year goal to reduce waste sent to landfills by 75%, reduce greenhouse gas emissions by 15%, and reduce water use by 25%—all by 2014. For example, the company constructed a LEED-certified distribution warehouse in Chico, California, that generates 40% of its power on-site through solar arrays, a methane generator, and natural gas turbines. In addition to focusing on the environmental impact of its operations, the company also focuses on maintaining social responsibility through respecting and promoting the welfare of customers, employees, and the communities in which it does business. For example, as part of its commitment to social responsibility, J.M. Smucker directs all of its marketing at adults, rather than children. As a result, in 2010 the company was ranked number one on the "Top Ten Best Advertisers" list by the Parents Television Council. The company is also deeply involved with educational programs and charitable organizations. One such organization is Feeding America, the national network of food banks that supplies food to hunger centers across the nation. Through partnerships with local hunger centers and companies such as Smucker's, food banks in the Feeding America network are able to provide meals to over 37 million needy Americans each year, over a third of whom are children.

Sources: The J.M Smucker Company 2012 Corporate Responsibility Report. www.FeedingAmerica.org

In this chapter, we'll explore why sustainability has become such an important business consideration and how sustainability reporting and environmental management accounting (EMA) can help support an organization's journey toward sustainability. We'll also consider some of the challenges associated with setting up and using EMA systems.

What is Sustainability and How Does it Create Business Value?

The dictionary definition of <u>sustainability</u> refers to the ability of a system to maintain its own viability, endure without giving way, or use resources so they are not depleted or permanently damaged.[1] In other words, it's the ability of a system, including our economic system, to operate in such a manner that it is able to continue indefinitely. With respect to business, the most widely used definition of sustainability traces its roots to a report developed by the United Nations (UN) in 1987 in which sustainable development was defined as "development that meets the needs of the present generation without compromising the ability of future generations to meet their own needs."[2] As shown in Exhibit 15-1, the report identified three factors relating to sustainability: environmental, social, and economic. The importance of these three interrelated factors was reaffirmed at the 2005 World Summit.[3]

1 Describe sustainability and how it can create business value

EXHIBIT 15-1 Three Interrelated Factors of Sustainability

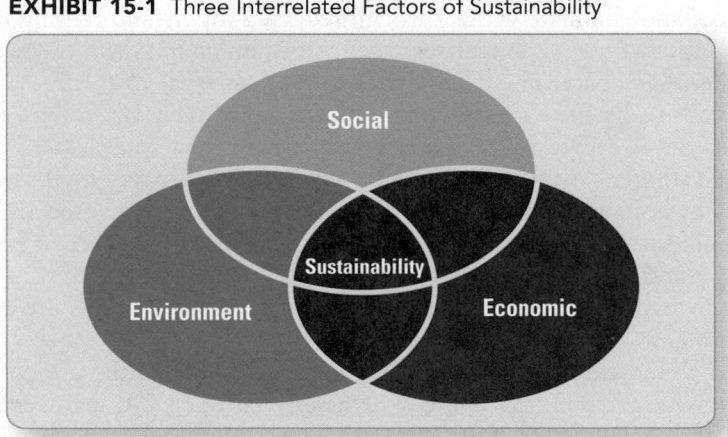

As a result of the UN report, forward-thinking businesses, such as the J.M. Smucker Company, are beginning to adhere to the notion of a triple bottom line. The <u>triple bottom line</u> is a concept that views a company's performance not only in terms of its ability to generate economic profits for its owners, as has traditionally been the case, but also in terms its impact on people and the planet. A company will only be viable, or sustainable, in the long run if all three of these three factors are considered when making business decisions. For example, a company will not be able to survive in the long run if the natural resources it relies on (e.g., air, water, soil, minerals, plants, fuel supplies, etc.) or people it relies on (e.g., suppliers, customers, employees, communities) are in jeopardy. The world is a system connected by space and time. Air pollution in North America, for example, affects air quality in Europe (space connections). Choices we make about our energy sources today will impact future generations (time connections). Because of these connections, companies that do not incorporate sustainability into their core business values put their own long-term success at risk.

[1]www.merriam-webster.com; http://dictionary.reference.com
[2]Brundtland Report, World Commission on Environment and Development (WCED), 1987, www.un-documents.net/our-common-future.pdf.
[3]www.un.org/summit2005/documents.html

Historical Overview

The Industrial Revolution, which began roughly 200 years ago, is based on what is sometimes referred to as a linear "take–make–waste" system in which companies "take" natural resources (lumber, minerals, water, fossil fuels), "make" them into products, and then sell the products to consumers or commercial enterprises that eventually dispose of the products and packaging as "waste."[4] Since the end of World War II, the U.S. economy has developed a "consumer" mindset that has focused on using and throwing away products for the sake of convenience, rather than conserving resources for future generations. In essence, we have become a disposable society. However, because of the limited supply of natural resources, including potable water, tillable soil, and fossil-based fuels, we have realized that the current linear economic system is not sustainable in the long run. As a result, the last 30 years have seen an increased interest in creating more sustainable business models. This interest has escalated dramatically in the last 10 years. Whereas the business community often fought pressures to become more environmentally friendly from **nongovernmental organizations (NGOs)**, such as Greenpeace and Sierra Club, in the latter part of the last century, businesses now are finding ways to partner with these same organizations to develop better, more sustainable business practices.

The forward-thinking business model of the twenty-first century takes cues from the creative ways in which natural ecological systems create zero waste. In nature, the output and death of one organism or process becomes the input to life of another. Nothing becomes waste and the system continues indefinitely. It is a *circular*, rather than *linear*, system. Likewise, businesses are now beginning to adopt operating strategies that will conserve natural resources and eliminate waste, through reducing inputs and reusing, repurposing, and recycling outputs. Business executives are now beginning to take a "systems thinking" approach. Rather than concerning themselves with only **internal costs** (those costs that are incurred and paid for by the organization and recorded in their GAAP-based accounting records), managers and accountants are now considering the **external costs** borne by society as a result of the company's operations and the product and services it sells. For example, greenhouse gas emissions (such as carbon dioxide and methane) caused by distribution trucks and landfill sites are external costs borne by society that impact the health and wellness of the planet and its inhabitants. To decrease harmful emissions, many distributors are now switching to hybrid and natural gas vehicles, while many landfills are capturing the methane and using it to generate power.

Both internal and external costs can be illuminated through the use of life-cycle assessment. As shown in Exhibit 15-2, **life-cycle assessment, or LCA**, involves studying the environmental and social impact of each product or service over the course of its entire life, from "cradle to grave" (all the way from sourcing to disposal). One of the ultimate goals of LCA is to replace the current "cradle-to-grave" system with a circular "cradle-to-cradle" system, such that the company's end product and packaging never go to waste, but are fully used (such as ice cream packaged in an ice cream cone) or become input to another product (such Under Armour's creation of fitness apparel from recycled plastic beverage containers). LCA illuminates both internal and external costs, so that companies have a more complete set of information from which to generate cost-effective solutions to environmental and social concerns.

Business is now at a tipping point. The twentieth-century business model that often gravitated toward the exploitation of nature and people in pursuit of profit is changing into a life-sustaining business model. Because of their global reach and economic power, large corporations are recognizing that they are often in a better position to bring about positive world change than are many national governments and nonprofit agencies. As a result, businesses are beginning to embed sustainability into their core business functions, rather than simply tacking on isolated and temporary solutions to environmental and social issues brought to their attention by activists. Rather than taking a defensive stance as many companies did during the twentieth century, businesses are going on the offensive by making sustainability a driving force in every aspect of the value chain.

---

[4]Paul Hawken, *The Ecology of Commerce*, 1993, New York: HarperCollins.

EXHIBIT 15-2 LCA: Assessing Product Impact from Cradle-to-Grave

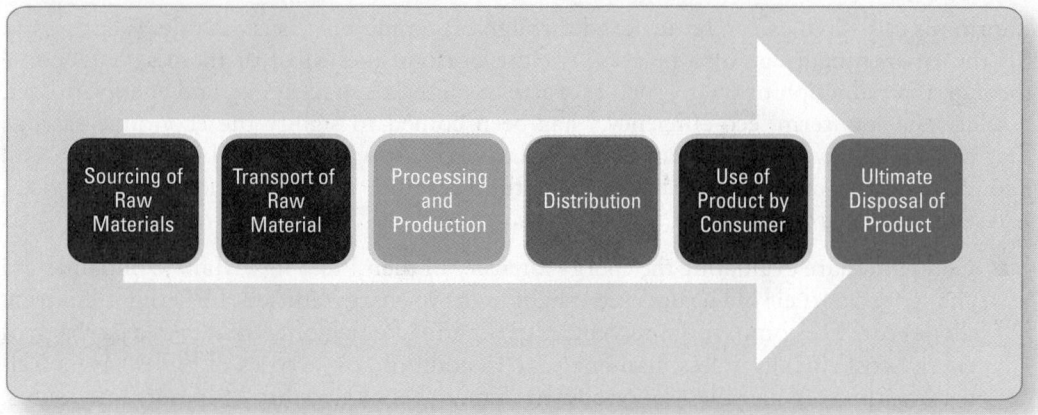

The Business Case for Sustainability

Businesses are continuing to evolve: they are now realizing they can act as positive agents of change while at the same time upholding their fiduciary responsibility to stockholders. In fact, a recent survey shows that 93% of CEOs view sustainability as important to their company's future success.[5] The outdated tension between profit creation and social responsibility is evaporating, as corporations recognize the business opportunity and value created through imbedding sustainability throughout their core business functions. They are beginning to realize that sustainability and profitability are not at odds, but often go hand in hand. In other words, sustainability simply makes good business sense. In this section, we explore some of the most compelling business reasons for adopting sustainable business practices, as illustrated in Exhibit 15-3.

EXHIBIT 15-3 Business Reasons for Adopting Sustainable Practices

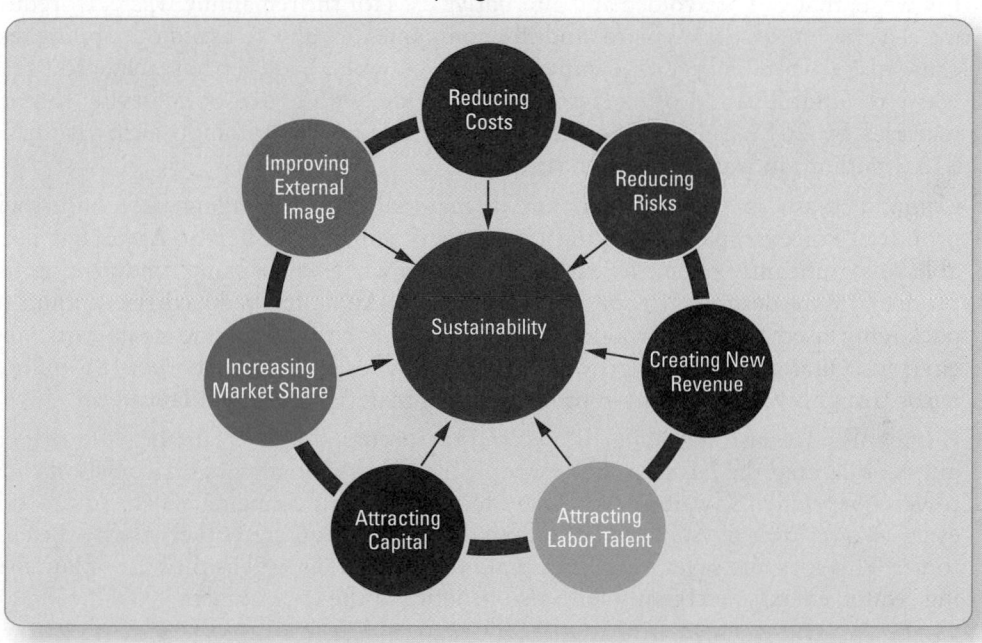

[5]http://www.unglobalcompact.org/docs/news_events/8.1/UNGC_Accenture_CEO_Study_2010.pdf

Reducing Costs

Enormous cost savings can be achieved through becoming more sustainable. What's good for the environment can also be good for the bottom line. Most of these savings come through the reduction of waste, such as waste of materials, packaging, and energy. In fact, a relatively new term, <u>eco-efficiency</u>,[6] has been coined to signify the economic savings that can be achieved by producing goods and services with fewer ecological resources. Eco-efficiency is achieved by reducing the natural resource *intensity* of goods and services. A few examples are as follows:

■ Companies are evaluating the energy intensity of their buildings. Many companies are changing out their old incandescent light bulbs to energy-efficient LED (light-emitting diode) or CFL (compact fluorescent lamp) lighting, which often results in a payback of energy cost savings in less than one year. In addition, these types of bulbs have a longer life, thus requiring less labor cost to change them when they burn out. Tax credits, grants and rebates are also often available for companies investing in energy-saving equipment. For example, the Empire State Building in New York City recently went through a lighting, window, and heating, ventilation, and air-conditioning (HVAC) retrofit. Annual energy savings are expected to be over 20%, or $4.4 million per year.[7] The environmental savings are clear: less fossil fuel is used, fewer greenhouse gasses are emitted, and less material is needed to produce replacement bulbs.

■ Companies with large fleets, such as UPS, Walmart, and Staples, are investing in hybrid vehicles as a means of reducing their fuel needs. They are also reassessing their route logistics to decrease the number of miles traveled per unit of product delivered. These measures not only conserve fossil fuels and prevent air pollution, but also save money. For example, between 2007 and 2012, Walmart increased its fleet efficiency such that it delivered 658 million *more* cases, but traveled 298 million *fewer* miles.[8] You can imagine the tremendous fuel savings that occurred as a result.

■ Companies are performing <u>waste audits</u>, in which they study the stream of waste coming from their operations (solid waste, water discharge, chemicals, etc.) to identify waste that can be avoided and alternative uses for the remaining waste. By reducing the amount of waste sent to landfills, companies are able to avoid the tipping fees charged by waste collection companies. For example, Unilever has achieved "zero waste to landfill" at 15 of its factories worldwide, with a goal of achieving it at all factories by 2015. Since 2008, the company has saved 10 million euros (roughly $13.2 million) in waste disposal costs.[9]

■ Companies are assessing the amount of materials and packaging used with their products. For example, by making its products thinner and lighter, Apple has been able to significantly reduce its carbon emissions while at the same time making the products more desirable to consumers. Likewise, Apple has reduced the amount of packaging used for each product, saving materials costs, transportation costs, and environmental costs.[10] Similarly, since 2008, Unilever has saved over 186 million euros (roughly $245 million) in packaging and materials cost avoidance.

■ Companies are also assessing the waste that occurs simply from the way they've always operated the business. For example, hotels used to always change sheets and towels every day. Now, most hotels are moving toward changing sheets and towels every two or three days, instead of once a day, unless requested otherwise by the customer. This measure saves the cost of maid time (labor) as well as the cost of laundering (water, energy, detergent) while also benefitting the environment.

---

[6]This term was coined by the World Business Council for Sustainable Development in its 1992 publication, "Changing Course."
[7]www.reuters.com/article/2012/05/07/johnsoncontrols-empirestate-idUSL1E8G7I5K20120507
[8]Walmart 2013 Global Responsibility Report.
[9]www.youtube.com/watch?v=41B2halNBhk&list=PLncvI6F_uW_rKjO4iZ_Ynsh11HSwCQ9Ez
[10]Apple.com/environment/our-footprint/

These are just a few examples of how companies are reducing their environmental impact while at the same time reducing costs. For more examples, you may wish to sign up for a free daily e-mail at Environmentalleader.com. The daily e-mail provides current news on the sustainability initiatives of well-known businesses so that you can see more examples of how businesses are reducing their environmental impact while at the same time improving their bottom line.

Generating New Revenue Streams

Sustainable product innovation can provide companies with new revenue streams. Some entrepreneurial businesses begin with a mission of providing only sustainable products. For example, Method gained market share by providing consumers with biodegradable household cleaners and soaps. Clif Bar is now a leading maker of organic energy and nutrition foods, and Terracycle makes all of its products out of recycled materials. Existing companies can also benefit from developing more sustainable products. For example, Proctor & Gamble used LCA to determine that the majority of energy consumed in the life cycle of its laundry detergent was the result of consumers washing their clothes in hot water. As a result, the company developed Tide Coldwater®, which is effective as a laundering agent in cold water.

 Why is this important?

"In order to **grow** the company, **managers** must listen to what their **customers**, stockholders, employees, and creditors want. Increasingly, these stakeholders want **more sustainable** operations."

Recycling and repurposing can also provide companies with new revenue streams. After performing waste audits, companies seek alternative uses for the materials in their waste streams. By finding commercial alternatives to sending waste to landfills, companies are often able to reap significant recycling revenues. For example, in 2011 Walmart realized $231 million in profit from a combination of recycling revenues and decreased waste disposal costs.[11] Likewise, Unilever has found innovative uses for the materials formerly in its waste stream. For example, the scraps left over (offcuts) from cutting tea bags out of fabric rolls are now sold to another company that uses the material for making pet beds. Rather than paying for these materials to be sent to landfills, as was done in the past, Unilever is now earning revenues from selling the materials.

Sustainability can also provide a competitive advantage for companies that become first movers. For example, Toyota was the first company to develop and market an affordable hybrid vehicle. As a result, the Toyota Prius still dominates the hybrid vehicle market even though most major car manufacturers are offering hybrid alternatives.

Increasing Market Share

Consumers, supply-chain customers, and special interest groups are also putting pressure on companies to become more socially and environmentally sustainable. Consumers are increasingly selecting products not only on the basis of price and quality, but also on the basis of environmental and social impact. For example, many consumers now demand environmentally sensitive packaging, such as recyclable containers or packaging made from post-consumer-use materials.

Many companies are now practicing **supply-chain assessment**, whereby purchasing decisions are based partially on how well suppliers manage the social and environmental impact of their operations. Companies can, and do, refuse to purchase materials from suppliers that do not adhere to their environmental and social justice standards. As a result, companies that don't adopt sustainable practices are likely to lose business, while those that imbed sustainability through their entire organization are likely to gain market share.

Improving External Image

Community members and special interest groups can also place pressure on businesses by boycotting or picketing companies with poor environmental and social practices. A company's external image can either hurt or improve sales. For example, in 2004, Walmart started a "green" campaign because of bad publicity it had received regarding its impact on the environment. As noted earlier, since that time, Walmart has

[11]Walmart 2012 Global Responsibility Report, p. 84.

reaped substantial monetary benefits from adopting more sustainable practices. However, the company still receives negative press due to some of its labor practices. Even Apple has received bad press due to the labor conditions at overseas factories in the company's supply chain. Thus, companies need to be proactive not only with respect to their own internal operations, but also with respect to those companies in their supply chain. A company's image is no longer formed completely by the price and quality of its products. It is also generated by the ethical integrity of the company's internal operations as well as the integrity of the companies it chooses to use in its supply chain.

Reducing Compliance and Litigation Risks

Smith/MCT/Newscom

In many cases, companies must become more sustainable to assure regulatory compliance. If they do not comply with environmental regulations, they will face substantial fines, thus compromising their profitability. In the United States, the Environmental Protection Agency (EPA), which began operations in 1970, is the regulatory agency charged with writing, implementing, and enforcing environmental laws passed by Congress. These regulations pertain to air quality, water quality, land issues, chemicals, hazardous substances, and so forth.

European countries, in general, have even more stringent environmental laws and regulations. For example, in the United Kingdom, the Climate Change Act (2008) commits the U.K. to an 80% reduction in carbon emissions by 2050. Because many U.S. companies have foreign operations, they need to be aware of the environmental regulations in each geographic location in which they operate.

Rather than simply adhering to current regulations, companies need to anticipate more stringent regulations in the future. Rather than incurring costs just to meet required regulations, companies may benefit from proactively getting ahead of the game. For example, DuPont foresaw the eventual regulation of chlorofluorocarbons (CFCs), which are potent greenhouse gases. DuPont was able to gain substantial market share by developing CFC alternatives and phasing out its CFC production far ahead of its competitors that simply struggled to meet regulatory requirements.[12]

In addition to regulatory fines, adopting sustainable practices helps companies reduce the risks associated with environmental litigation. The most notable recent environmental litigation relates to the BP Deepwater Horizon oil spill of 2012. In 2012, BP reached a $4.5 billion litigation settlement with the U.S. Department of Justice and could face up to another $21 billion in pollution fines under the Clean Water Act.[13] In addition, BP paid out over $30 billion in operations response and cleanup costs, claims to individuals and businesses, and other proposed litigation settlements.[14]

Attracting and Retaining Labor Talent

In a recent survey of CFOs, "improving employee morale and hiring" was listed as one of the top five reasons for becoming more sustainable.[15] Companies are finding that they are better able to recruit top talent and retain employees longer when the organization is actively pursuing sustainability. Because onboarding employees (hiring, training, and acclimating new employees to company culture) is costly, organizations save money by retaining good employees longer. Currently, the average employee tenure is less than five years.[16] Thus, preventing turnover can result in cost savings. Companies are also realizing "soft" benefits from providing more sustainable work environments. These benefits include higher productivity, less absenteeism, more employee engagement, and lower healthcare costs. For example, KeyBank has redesigned one of its headquarter buildings such that all of the cubicles are positioned near the exterior windows of the building to provide more employees with natural light. Higher-level managers have their offices in the interior of the building, but have glass walls to allow the natural light to penetrate. This is the

[12]Chris Laszlo, *Sustainable Value: How the World's Leading Companies Are Doing Well by Doing Good*, 2008, Stanford University Press.

[13]www.nytimes.com/2012/11/16/business/global/16iht-bp16.html?pagewanted=all&_r=0

[14]www.nytimes.com/interactive/2012/11/16/us/big-liabilities-for-bp.html

[15]www.fuqua.duke.edu/news_events/news-releases/cfo-survey-2013-q2/#.UffCPYHD_IU

[16]http://bls.gov/news.release/pdf/tenure.pdf

opposite of traditional office configurations in which the higher-level executives receive outer offices that block the natural light from getting to the interior cubicles. KeyBank employees also have the option of using treadmill workstations, company showers, and mobile workstations that are not pre-assigned to specific personnel. All of these measures help keep employees satisfied and more engaged. Another example comes from Intel. Intel provides employees in its Chandler, Arizona, operations with free healthy fresh fruit all day long and access to a free onsite fitness facility. Initiatives such as these help boost employee health and wellness, as well as employee morale.

Costco, a large national retailer, provides another good example. Bucking the trend of most retailers to pay minimum wage, Costco's starting wage rate for employees is more than $3 per hour greater than minimum wage. Most employees also received health care benefits. The company believes their policy is more profitable in the long run, because it decreases turnover and maximizes employee productivity and loyalty. Costco is supporting a move in Congress to increase the national minimum wage rate.[17]

Attracting Capital

Many institutional and retail investors (individual investors) are taking sustainability into account when making investment decisions. The growth of socially responsible investment indices, such as the Dow Jones Sustainability Index (DJSI), NASDAQ OMX CRD Global Sustainability Index, Global LAMP 60 Index, and FTSE4Good Index, has put increasing pressure on corporations to pay attention to sustainability.

Principles for Responsible Investment (PRI)

As of 2013, over 1,200 institutional investors with over $34 trillion of assets under management had become signatories of the UN-backed **Principles for Responsible Investment (PRI)**. In short, these six principles include a commitment of signatories to incorporate environmental, social, and governance issues into investment analysis and decision making as part of their fiduciary responsibility to act in the long-term interests of their beneficiaries.[18]

In addition to investors, lenders are increasingly taking sustainability into account when making credit decisions. Companies that do not adhere to sustainable practices may be at greater risk of defaulting on future loan payments. Why? Because they may be subject to future liabilities related to their detrimental impact on society and the environment.

In this section, we have provided several reasons why adopting sustainable business practices makes good business sense. Businesses are finding that becoming more sustainable can actually improve their profitability. In the next section, we describe how sustainability reporting is used to move companies in a more sustainable direction.

What is Sustainability Reporting?

2 Describe sustainability reporting and the GRI framework

Sustainability reporting is best viewed as a *process* that helps companies set goals, measure performance, and manage change as they move toward an economic model that produces long-term economic profit as well as environmental care and social responsibility.[19] A **sustainability report** is the primary document used for communicating a company's performance on all three pillars of the triple bottom line: economic, environmental, and social. Sustainability reports are often referred to as *Corporate Social Responsibility (CSR) reports*.

Current State of Sustainability Reporting

CSR reports are becoming very prevalent. As of 2011, over 95% of the 250 largest companies in the world issued CSR reports. In the United States alone, 83% of the largest 100 companies issued CSR reports.[20] A study of a broader spectrum of U.S. companies

---

[17]The Plain Dealer, March 7, 2013. "Costco pays more than norm, backs higher minimum wage."
[18]http://unpri.org
[19]Global Reporting Initiative, G4 Reporting Guidelines, Reporting Principles, and Standard Disclosures, http://globalreporting.org.
[20]KPMG, "International Survey of Corporate Responsibility Reporting 2011," www.kpmg.com/PT/pt/IssuesAndInsights/Documents/corporate-responsibility2011.pdf.

revealed that 53% of the S&P 500 and 57% of the Fortune 500 companies issued CSR reports in 2011.[21] As a result, large corporations that do not issue CSR reports are in now in the minority and are facing peer pressure to begin reporting.

While sustainability reporting is still a voluntary practice in the United States, some countries and stock exchanges, such as the Johannesburg and Copenhagen stock exchanges, require certain sustainability related disclosures. In the United States, the NASDAQ urges listed companies to report on issues such as greenhouse gas emissions, water use, and gender equality—or to explain why they don't.[22]

In addition, the Securities and Exchange Commission (SEC) requires publicly traded companies to disclose any material information that would be necessary to prevent misleading the readers of financial statements. With respect to the environment, companies must disclose any aspects of their business operations, pending lawsuits, and risk factors that are deemed to be material. Examples include the cost of complying with environmental laws and regulations, potential monetary damages from health and environmental litigation, and risks associated with the scarcity of water and raw materials needed for operations. Additionally, any material risks specific to the company as a result of global warming must also be disclosed.

Reasons for Sustainability Reporting

Sustainability reporting is a costly process, so why do firms do it? They must believe the benefits exceed the cost. As outlined earlier in the chapter, economic profit often goes hand in hand with a business's journey toward sustainability. Sustainability reporting serves several business-enhancing purposes:

1. Sustainability reporting is used as an internal change management tool. A familiar phrase in business is, "You can't manage what you don't measure." A similar adage is, "What gets measured gets managed . . . and what gets managed, gets done." Thus, measurement is a key driver of organizational change. Companies need baseline measurements to assess where they currently stand on social and environmental performance before they are able to set realistic goals and develop strategies and initiatives to move toward those goals.

    At its core, management accounting seeks to measure, collect, analyze, and report data that are relevant to managers as they plan, direct, and control company operations. Viewed in this light, sustainability reporting is simply an expansion of the cost and revenue data traditionally used in the management process. Sustainability reporting simply adds a layer of quantifiable non-financial data to the decision-making process. Sustainability metrics, or key performance indicators (KPIs), are becoming part of the broader set of information managerial accountants measure, collect, analyze, and report to management for incorporation in the decision-making process.

2. Companies use their CSR reports as a means of disclosing their social and environmental impact information to

    - consumers and potential customers in their supply chains,
    - investors and creditors,
    - stock exchanges and organizations that identify and rank the most sustainable companies in a wide variety of industries, and
    - other stakeholders, such NGOs, local communities, and employees.

Framework for Sustainability Reporting

The **Global Reporting Initiative (GRI)**, a nonprofit organization founded in 1997, has developed the leading framework used for sustainability reporting by companies worldwide. The GRI's mission is to make sustainability reporting standard practice by providing

---

[21]Governance and Accountability Institute, "2012 Corporate ESG/Sustainability/Responsibility Reporting—Does It Matter?" www.ga-institute.com/research-reports/2012-corporate-esg-sustainability-responsibility-reporting-does-it-matter.html.

[22]www.ey.com/Publication/vwLUAssets/Stock_exchanges_and_sustainability_reporting/$FILE/Stock_exchanges_and_sustainability_reporting.pdf

guidance and support to organizations.[23] The GRI has continued to refine and update its reporting guidelines based on the experiences and needs of CSR preparers and users. The latest guidelines, G4, were released in May 2013.

While use of the GRI framework is not mandatory for sustainability reporting, over 12,400 CSR reports have been issued that reference the GRI framework.[24] Of the Global 250 companies that issue CSR reports, 80% use the GRI framework.[25]

Development of the G4 Guidelines

The G4 Guidelines are the outcome of a multi-stakeholder process that included experts, businesses, and civil labor organizations from all over the world. Public opinion was also gathered during a public comment period. The G4 Guidelines were developed so that they could be used universally by organizations of any size in any region of the world. A consortium of large businesses, such as GE, Goldman Sachs, and Alcoa, as well as all of the **Big Four** accounting firms (Deloitte, Ernst & Young, KPMG, and PricewaterhouseCoopers), provided financial support for the project and expertise on its technical features. Since the root business of the Big Four firms is auditing, the consortium's inclusion of the Big Four lends credibility to the verifiability of the metrics (KPIs) included in the reporting guidelines.

Summary of the G4 Guidelines

The heart of the G4 Guidelines focuses on the concepts of materiality and the triple bottom line: Organizations should report on those environmental, social, and economic aspects of their business that are *material* to their stakeholders. **Materiality** is loosely defined as those aspects that "reflect the organization's significant economic, environmental and social impact; or substantively influence the assessments and decisions of stakeholders."[26] As a result, one of the first steps in preparing a CSR report is to identify and engage stakeholders, including stockholders, creditors, suppliers, employees, community members, NGOs, and so forth, in a meaningful ongoing conversation to identify material aspects of the organization's operations.

Organizations and their stakeholders use the framework shown in Exhibit 15-4 to identify the aspects of the triple bottom line that are material to their organization. Note the following in Exhibit 15-4:

- The G4 framework is organized around the three "categories" of the triple bottom line: economic, environmental, and social. In addition, the social category contains four subcategories: (1) labor practices and decent work, (2) human rights, (3) society, and (4) product responsibility.

- Within each category, the framework identifies several "aspects" of business that might be material to the organization.

- Each "aspect" can be measured and reported on using one or more "indicators." Metrics such as these are often referred to as KPIs (key performance indicators). The number of indicators for each aspect is listed in parentheses in Exhibit 15-4. A detailed description of each indicator can be found in the G4 Guidelines at globalreporting.org.

Let's look at an example from Exhibit 15-4. "Water" is the third aspect listed in the "Environmental" category. A company and its stakeholders would determine whether water is, or is not, a *material* environmental impact of the organization. If it is considered to be material, then the company should include information about water impacts in its CSR report. Exhibit 15-4 shows there are three indicators that can be measured and reported related to water. If we dig deeper into the G4 Guidelines, we find that the three indicators

[23]www.globalreporting.org
[24]www.globalreporting.org
[25]KPMG, "International Survey of Corporate Responsibility Reporting 2011," www.kpmg.com/PT/pt/IssuesAndInsights/Documents/corporate-responsibility2011.pdf.
[26]Global Reporting Initiative, G4 Reporting Guidelines, Reporting Principles and Standard Disclosures, http://globalreporting.org.

EXHIBIT 15-4 Aspects (and Number of Indicators) Within Each G4 Category

Economic Category:

- Economic Performance (4 indicators)
- Market presence (2)
- Indirect economic impacts (2)
- Procurement practices (1)

Environmental Category:

- Materials (2 indicators)
- Energy (5)
- Water (3)
- Biodiversity (4)
- Emissions (7)
- Effluents and waste (5)
- Products and services (2)
- Compliance (1)
- Transport (1)
- Overall (1)
- Supplier environmental assessment (2)
- Environmental grievance mechanism (1)

Social Category:

Subcategory: Labor Practices and Decent Work

- Employment (3 indicators)
- Labor/management relations (1)
- Occupational health and safety (4)
- Training and education (3)
- Diversity and equal opportunity (1)
- Equal remuneration for women and men (1)
- Supplier assessment for labor practices (2)
- Labor practices grievance mechanisms (1)

Subcategory: Human Rights

- Investment (2)
- Non-discrimination (1)
- Freedom of association and collective bargaining (1)
- Child labor (1)
- Forced or compulsory labor (1)
- Security practices (1)
- Indigenous rights (1)
- Assessment (1)
- Supplier human rights assessment (2)
- Human rights grievance mechanism (1)

Subcategory: Society

- Local communities (2)
- Anti-corruption (3)
- Public policy (1)
- Anti-competitive behavior (1)
- Compliance (1)
- Supplier assessment for impacts on society (2)
- Grievance mechanisms for impacts on society (1)

Subcategory: Product Responsibility

- Customer health and safety (2)
- Product and service labeling (3)
- Marketing communications (2)
- Customer privacy (1)
- Compliance (1)

address the following: (i) total water withdrawn by source (such as groundwater, surface water, municipal water), (ii) water sources significantly affected by withdrawal (such as size of water source and its importance to indigenous peoples), and (iii) percentage and total volume of water recycled and reused.

Let's apply this information to a real-life example. Intel's manufacture of semiconductors is a very water-intensive process. Intel would not be able to survive as a company without access to billions of gallons of water per year. Thus, the company would not be viable, nor could it be profitable, without access to this natural resource. Thus, water is a material aspect of Intel's business. Likewise, water is a main ingredient in Coca-Cola's beverage products, so Coca-Cola also considers water to be a material aspect of its business. On the other hand, water is not material to a financial institution, such as Key Bank, that uses very little water. As a result of focusing on material aspects of individual businesses, the GRI framework is customizable to every type of organization.

Since water is a material environmental aspect of Intel's business, Intel's CSR report discloses information on several water indicators: total water withdrawals, the source and geographic location of water supplies, the amount of water used during the production process, the amount of water lost to evaporation, the amount of water recycled, and the amount of water discharged. In fact, since water is so critical to Intel's business, the company has performed and disclosed a complete water footprint analysis. You may wish to look at this information on pages 62–65 of Intel's 2012 CSR report, which can be found at http://csrreportbuilder.intel.com/PDFFiles/CSR_2012_Full-Report.pdf.

Organizations have a choice as to whether they wish to issue a **core report** or **comprehensive report**. The reports differ as to how many indicators are included:

- Core report—*at least one* indicator related to each identified material aspect must be disclosed.

- Comprehensive report—*all indicators* related to each identified material aspect must be disclosed.

As noted, Intel has reported on all three indicators relating to water.

In addition to the specific disclosures just discussed, all CSR reports that reference the G4 Guidelines must also contain general disclosures regarding the following:

- Strategy and analysis (vision and strategy for managing triple bottom line impacts)

- Organizational profile (summary of the company's location, size, products, and brands)

- Identified material aspects and boundaries (process for determining materiality; the portion of the company included in the report, i.e., the whole company or only certain segments)

- Stakeholder engagement (identification and selection of stakeholders, and frequency of engagement)

- Report profile (reporting period, and content index)

- Governance (governance structure and composition)

- Ethics and integrity (mechanisms for seeking advice and reporting concerns about unethical or unlawful behavior)

This section of the text only provides a brief overview of the G4 Guidelines. A complete description of the G4 Guidelines and reporting process is available at globalreporting.org.

Assurance of Data in CSR Reports

CSR reports gain more credibility if they are verified by external parties, much like financial statements become more credible when they are audited by independent CPAs. Whereas the SEC requires that publicly traded companies have their financial statements audited annually, no such requirement exists for CSR reports. Nonetheless, 45% of GRI reports issued in 2011 were externally "assured."[27] **Assurance** is a term used to denote an independent party's external validation of management's assertions. The Big Four accounting firms are the leading assurance service providers for CSR reports.[28] The Big Four firms hire many experts in other fields, such as engineers, to aid accountants in their assurance service practices.

The Report of Independent Accountant found on page 125 of Intel's CSR report provides an example (http://csrreportbuilder.intel.com/PDFFiles/CSR_2012_Full-Report.pdf). The report lists the indicators that were reviewed by the accounting firm, as well as a summary of the procedures performed.

---

[27]GRI Sustainability Reporting Statistics, 2011, http://globalinitiative.org.
[28]http://www.environmentalleader.com/2011/06/22/big-four-audit-firms-lead-sustainability-assurance-services/

▶ Try It!

Classify each of the following GRI aspects according to GRI category: Economic, Environmental, or Social. If it is Social, further classify it according to its subcategory. Use Exhibit 15-4 as a guide.

1. Customer health and safety
2. Child labor
3. Emissions
4. Market presence
5. Equal remuneration for women and men
6. Energy
7. Anti-corruption
8. Procurement practices

Please see page 925 for solutions.

3 Describe EMA systems and their uses and challenges

What is Environmental Management Accounting (EMA)?

In the last section we described sustainability reporting and CSR reports. In this section, we describe the information needed for sustainability reporting. We also describe some of the uses of this information, as well as the challenges in collecting it.

EMA Systems

Environmental management accounting (EMA) is a system used for the identification, collection, analysis, and use of information needed for internal decision making and external reporting. EMA collects two types of information: monetary and physical. We describe each type of information next.

Monetary Information

Monetary information is the type of information traditionally used in accounting systems. Although presented in monetary terms, the categories of costs are quite different than what has traditionally been collected and reported by financial and management accounting systems. For example, the monetary information reported in an EMA system may include:[29]

1. *Materials costs of product outputs*: These costs include the purchase costs of natural resources that are converted into products. An example would be the purchase cost of lumber for the manufacture of picnic tables. This category is similar to direct materials, since these materials become part of the final product.

2. *Materials costs of non-product outputs*: These costs include the costs of water and energy that become non-product output, such as air emissions and waste. An example would be the cost of water used as a coolant in a plant's manufacturing system.

3. *Waste and emission control costs*: These costs include the costs for handling, treating, and disposing of all forms of waste and emissions, including solid waste, hazardous waste, wastewater, and air emissions. An example would be the cost associated with treatment and disposal of hazardous by-products at a chemical production facility.

4. *Prevention costs*: These costs are incurred to prevent environmental costs. An example would be the costs of monitoring water output for contaminants.

---

[29]International Federation of Accountants (IFAC), 2005, *International Guidance Document of EMA*, New York: IFAC.

5. *Research and development (R&D) costs*: These costs include the costs of R&D projects related to environmental issues. An example would be the costs of running a laboratory aimed at developing biodegradable products.

6. *Intangible costs*: These costs include the costs of future liabilities, future regulations, productivity, company image, and stakeholder relations. An example would be the cost of a future lawsuit filed for an infringement of environmental regulations.

Physical Information

<u>Physical information</u> has not traditionally been part of managerial accounting systems but is a vital part of EMA systems. Examples of physical information include the following:

1. Quantity of air emissions
2. Tons of solid waste generated
3. Gallons of wastewater generated
4. Pounds of packaging recycled
5. Total amount of water consumed

By collecting and measuring physical information, such as tons of waste sent to landfills, EMA systems provide managers with a clearer view of the company's physical impact on the environment. The adage, "You can't manage what you don't measure" applies. If a company doesn't measure physical impact information, management has little chance of trying to reduce it.

Materials Flow Accounting

To track their environmental inputs and outputs, organizations can use <u>materials flow accounting (MFA)</u>. As shown in Exhibit 15-5, MFA involves tracking all of the physical inputs (materials, energy, water, and so forth) and reconciling these with the output generated (including product units, wastewater generated, air emissions, packaging, and by-products). The goal is to track where everything is going; once it is visible, steps can be taken to reduce usage or to increase efficiencies. Essentially, MFA calculates the amount of waste and emissions from a manufacturing system by tracing materials (including energy) to the finished product. Identifying the processes that lead to waste and emissions can highlight opportunities for improvement.

EXHIBIT 15-5 Materials Flow Accounting: Equating Inputs with the Company's Outputs

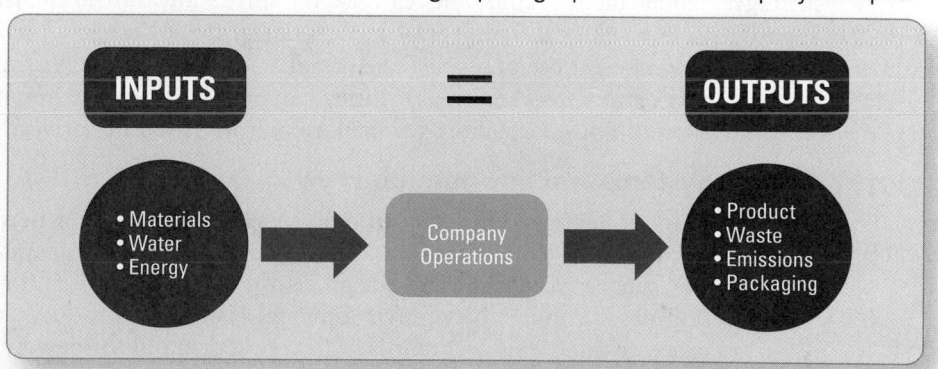

ISO 14000

How do companies gain the knowledge and expertise necessary to develop and implement EMA systems? The International Organization for Standardization (ISO) has developed the ISO 14000 series of standards, which address various aspects of EMA systems. You may recall from Chapter 1 that the ISO has also developed standards and guidelines for implanting quality management systems; thus, it is a well-known and respected organization. The ISO 14000 series has more than 22 standards and guidelines pertaining to environmental sustainability. In the words of the ISO, the standards provide a "practical toolbox" that help organizations implement environmental management systems. Some of these tools include LCA, greenhouse gas accounting, materials flow accounting, eco-efficiency assessment, environmental product labeling, and others.[30]

Uses of Environmental Management Accounting Information

The information contained in and produced by an organization's EMA system is designed to help support managers' primary responsibilities: planning, directing, controlling, and decision-making. Specific operational and decision-making situations where management accountants can support sustainability efforts include compliance, strategy development, systems and information flow, costing, investment appraisal, performance management, and external reporting. We'll discuss each of these areas next.

Compliance

Companies are confronted with many environmental laws and regulations that can impact their operations. An EMA system gathers the information necessary to ensure that the organization complies with these laws and regulations. Management accountants also use this information to help managers understand the potential financial implications of pending environmental legislation and of past practices that may have caused environmental damage.

For example, **Extended Producer Responsibility (EPR) laws** require manufacturers in certain industries to "take back" a large percentage of those products at the end of the products' life in order to reduce the amount waste ending up in landfills and the environment. EPR laws are gaining traction, especially in the electronics industry due to the volume of e-waste produced each year. However, they are also beginning to surface in other industries. For example, Rhode Island recently passed an EPR law related to mattresses. The EMA system would help gather the physical information required of these laws as well as provide managers with the costs of both compliance and non-compliance. The financial ramifications should drive product engineers to develop ways of recycling, repurposing, or reusing product components.

Strategy Development

In order to succeed in the long-term, organizations need to integrate sustainability into their business strategy. Management accountants can use the information from the EMA system to help identify the environmental impact of a potential strategic decision, identify opportunities to make more efficient use of resources, and take advantage of the organization's strengths. Additionally, they can help to assess the potential costs of *not* undertaking particular environmental initiatives.

Systems and Information Flow

Management accountants can help to assess the need for new information systems. They can also help to implement new systems and suggest system modifications as the organization's information needs change. New environmental laws, new products, new processes, and new technologies all create demand for new or updated information systems.

Costing

Management accountants can help to make environmental costs more visible. Methods can be improved for allocating environmental costs (such as waste removal, water, and energy costs) to specific

■ Why is this important?

"Management **accountants** are increasingly called upon to incorporate **environmental impact** information in the **analyses** they **provide** to management."

---

[30]International Standards Organization, "ISO 14000—Environmental Management," 2009, www.iso.org/iso/home/standards/management-standards/iso14000.htm.

products, activities, or departments. Management accountants can also help to identify and estimate potential future environmental costs that should be recognized as potential liabilities in current periods.

Investment Appraisal

Management accountants can help to ensure that environmental and social costs and savings are included in capital investment analysis. Investment appraisals should include traditionally ignored factors, such as enhanced reputation, improved employee morale, and reduction of litigation and compliance risk. An analytical tool known as **Social Return on Investment (SROI)** can be used to explain social and environmental value in monetary terms. SROI works similarly to ROI calculations, but includes estimates of the social and environmental costs and savings. Inclusion of this information can dramatically affect the results of traditional ROI calculations. LCA, described earlier, can also provide companies with financial rationale for making new investments, such as exemplified by Proctor & Gamble's investment in developing a cool-water detergent.

Performance Management

As discussed earlier, sustainability reporting is most often used as an internal change management tool whereby performance is measured across a variety of environmental and social metrics, goals are set, and progress toward the goals is measured. Thus, performance management is at the heart of sustainability reporting.

Many companies are now beginning to disclose their performance with respect to their carbon and water footprints. A **carbon footprint** is a measure of the total emissions of carbon dioxide and other greenhouse gases (GHGs), often expressed for simplicity as tons of equivalent carbon dioxide. It can be calculated for individual products, individual processes, or for the organization as a whole. Once the carbon footprint has been measured, managers can work toward reducing it. Additionally, **Carbon Disclosure Project**, a nonprofit organization, collects carbon footprint information from the world's largest companies each year and disseminates that information to institutional investors and other stakeholders.

Some companies, such as Timberland and Disney, are investing in reforestation projects to offset their carbon footprints in an effort to become more carbon neutral. Other companies provide customers with the opportunity to purchase carbon offsets. For example, United Airlines has partnered with Sustainable Travel International to provide a carbon offset program for its customers. At United's website, travelers have the option to calculate the carbon emissions associated with their travel and then purchase enough carbon offsets to make their travel carbon neutral. The carbon offsets are typically invested in reforestation and renewable energy projects.[31]

Similarly, a **water footprint** is the total volume of water use associated with the processes and products of a business. Some companies, such as Coca-Cola and Intel, measure their water footprint, thus enabling production engineers to consider means for reducing the footprint.

Christopher Steer/E+/ Getty Images

External Reporting

As discussed earlier, EMA systems provide the information used for the sustainability reporting process. Thus, EMA systems collect the information that is necessary for companies to produce CSR reports.

Challenges to Implementing EMA Systems

There are several challenges inherent in implementing and using an EMA system within an organization. Communication issues, hidden costs, aggregated accounting information, the historical orientation of accounting, and the newness of environmental management accounting are all potentially challenging areas.

---

[31]http://united.com

Communication Issues

For an EMA system to work effectively, many different employees within the organization need to communicate and work together. For example, members of environmental staff possess knowledge about environmental issues impacting the organization. Technical and production engineers have experience with the flow of materials, energy, and water throughout the company operations. Management accountants have expertise in accounting, cost assignment, and regulatory reporting. In reality, all areas of the value chain will need to coordinate efforts if sustainability is to be imbedded within the fabric of the organization. Communication and coordination can sometimes be challenging, yet it is necessary in order to provide the information needed to strategically manage the organization's journey toward sustainability.

Hidden Costs

In a traditional accounting system, many indirect costs are assigned to overhead because they are difficult to trace directly to a product or process. As a result, many environmental costs may get buried in the overhead account. Making environmental costs visible is a vital step in managing environmental costs.

Aggregated Accounting Information and Archaic Information Systems

Depending on the sophistication of the company's information system, accounting data are often aggregated into a limited number of accounts. For example, some companies still post material purchases into one "Purchases" account. Such a basic system does not allow management to identify the specific types and quantities of materials purchased (for example, hazardous and non-hazardous), the cost per unit for the material, or the product for which it was purchased. If this specific information is tracked on the production floor, it is often not connected to the general ledger accounting data. In a similar vein, labor costs are often simply recorded as payroll expense or part of manufacturing overhead, rather than specifying whether the labor was related to product output, waste management, or environmental damage prevention. For an EMA system to be effective, accounting information will need to be tagged with multiple identifiers to serve various information needs.

Historical Orientation of Accounting

Financial accounting systems focus on providing the historical, transaction-based cost information needed for preparing financial statements in accordance with Generally Accepted Accounting Principles (GAAP). However, for an EMA system to be effective in helping management make good decisions, it will need to include a more open-minded and forward-looking definition of cost. For example, an EMA system might include an estimate of the cost of lost sales resulting from poor environmental performance. Or, it might include an estimate of the cost of losing access to markets with environment-related product restrictions. It might also include an estimate of costs externalized to society. Both accountants and management will need to expand their view of what constitutes a "cost" as they develop EMA systems for their companies.

Undeveloped field

Environmental management accounting is a relatively new, undeveloped field. Tools for providing environmental management accounting information are being developed and refined constantly as the field evolves. Organizations are still working to discover what information they need and how it can be reported in an accurate, timely, verifiable, and relevant manner.

■ **Why is this important?**

"In order to provide managers with relevant **environmental information**, accountants will need to rethink their **traditional views** on what constitutes a **'cost'** and expand their costing systems to provide more **detailed information.**"

Future of Environmental Management Accounting

This chapter has briefly summarized the state of environmental management accounting as it exists today. There are a number of valid business reasons for organizations to commit to sustainability reporting and producing CSR reports. Organizations can use EMA, utilizing both monetary and physical information, to support these efforts. The field of environmental management accounting is relatively new, and as a result can be challenging to implement. However, advances are being made every day.

Sustainability is a growing concern world-wide. Management accountants have a critical responsibility and opportunity to assist their organizations in supporting sustainability through the use of environmental management accounting information that is accurate, timely, and relevant.

Decision Guidelines

Decision	Guidelines
What three performance factors should be considered if a company wishes to become more sustainable?	The three pillars of sustainability are economic, environmental, and societal performance. Together, these three factors are known as the triple bottom line.
Why can't companies continue to operate under the linear "take–make–waste" economic model?	Because of the earth's limited resources, the old economic model is not viable in the long run.
Why should a company use life-cycle assessment (LCA) to evaluate its products and services?	LCA helps companies assess the societal and environmental impacts of its products and services all the way from cradle to grave. Thus, it helps uncover previously hidden external costs, as well as traditionally captured internal costs. By understanding the full costs of the product, companies can work toward reducing negative impacts and increasing positive impacts.
How does sustainability increase business value?	Sustainable practices help companies: 1. Reduce costs 2. Generate new revenue streams 3. Increase market share 4. Improve external image 5. Reduce risks 6. Attract labor talent 7. Attract capital
What is sustainability reporting and why should companies adopt it?	Sustainability reporting is a process used by companies to set goals, measure performance, and manage change as they move toward a more sustainable economic model. Sustainability reporting is used as an internal management change tool, and also as a basis for preparing CSR reports.
How prevalent are CSR reports and who uses them?	The majority of large domestic and international companies prepare CSR reports, thus putting peer pressure on those who currently do not issue reports. CSR reports are used as a way of communicating sustainability performance to a wide variety of external stakeholders.
Is there a common framework used by all CSR reports?	The Global Reporting Initiative (GRI) has developed the most widely used framework. The G4 Guidelines are the most recent version of the framework.
How is the framework organized?	The framework is organized around the three categories of the triple bottom line: Economic, Environmental, and Social. Companies report on those aspects of each category that are material to their operations.
What types of information should an environmental management accounting (EMA) system collect and analyze?	EMA systems focus on both monetary and physical information. Materials flow accounting (MFA) is often used to track all physical inputs and reconcile them with all of the company's outputs, including waste and emissions.
How is EMA information used?	EMA information is used to support management in planning, directing, and controlling operations. EMA information assists managers in determining how to best integrate sustainable practices throughout the organization. EMA also generates the information needed for external reporting purposes.
What challenges does management face in implementing EMA systems?	EMA systems provide much more detail than traditional accounting systems and will require effective communication throughout the organization. The existing accounting system will either need to be revamped, replaced, or supplemented in order to provide management with the environmental information that it needs. Accountants will need to rethink the traditional definitions of "cost" and expand traditional cost categories as they develop EMA systems.

END OF CHAPTER

Learning Objectives

- 1 Describe sustainability and how it can create business value
- 2 Describe sustainability reporting and the GRI framework
- 3 Describe EMA systems and their uses and challenges

Accounting Vocabulary

Assurance. (p. 887)   An independent party's external validation of management's assertions.

Big Four. (p. 885)   The largest four accounting firms in the world: Deloitte, Ernst & Young, KPMG, and PriceWaterhouseCoopers.

Carbon Disclosure Project. (p. 891)   A nonprofit organization that collects and disseminates carbon footprint information.

Carbon Footprint. (p. 891)   A measure of the total emissions of carbon dioxide and other greenhouse gases (GHGs), often expressed for simplicity as tons of equivalent carbon dioxide.

Comprehensive Report. (p. 887)   A GRI-referenced report in which *all indicators* related to each identified material aspect are disclosed.

Core Report. (p. 887)   A GRI-referenced report in which *at least one* indicator related to each identified material aspect is disclosed.

Eco-Efficiency. (p. 880)   Achieving economic savings by producing goods and services with fewer ecological resources.

Environmental Management Accounting (EMA). (p. 888)   A system used for the identification, collection, analysis, and use of two types of information for internal decision making—monetary and physical information.

Extended Producer Responsibility (EPR) laws. (p. 890)   Laws that require product manufacturers to "take back" a large percentage of the products they manufacture at the end of the product's life in order to reduce the amount of waste ending up in landfills and the environment.

External Costs. (p. 878)   Costs borne by society as a result of a company's operations and the products and services it sells.

Global Reporting Initiative (GRI). (p. 884)   A nonprofit organization whose mission is to make sustainability reporting standard practice by providing guidance and support to organizations. The developer of the G4 Guidelines.

Internal Costs. (p. 878)   Costs that are incurred and paid for by the organization and recorded in GAAP-based accounting records.

Life-Cycle Assessment (LCA). (p. 878)   Studying the environmental and social impacts of a product or service over its entire life, from "cradle to grave."

Materiality. (p. 885)   An important concept in CSR reporting defined as those aspects of a business that reflect the organization's significant economic, environmental, and social impacts, or substantively influence the assessments and decisions of stakeholders.

Materials Flow Accounting (MFA). (p. 889)   An accounting system in which all physical inputs to an organization's operations are reconciled with output generated. The goal is to track where all physical inputs are going.

Monetary Information. (p. 888)   The type of information traditionally used in accounting systems.

Non-Governmental Organizations (NGOs). (p. 878)   Not-for-profit organizations that serve the public interest, such as Greenpeace and Sierra Club.

Physical Information. (p. 889)   A vital part of environmental management accounting systems. Examples include: quantity of air emissions, tons of solid waste generated, gallons of wastewater generated, pounds of packaging recycled, and total amount of water consumed.

Principles for Responsible Investment (PRI). (p. 883)   Six principles of investing, including a commitment to incorporate environmental, social and governance issues into investment analysis and decision making.

Social Return on Investment (SROI). (p. 891)   An analytical tool that is used to explain social and environmental value in monetary terms.

Supply-Chain Assessment. (p. 881)   Making purchase decisions based partially on how well suppliers manage the social and environmental impact of their operations.

Sustainability. (p. 877)   The ability of a system to endure without giving way or to use resources so that they are not depleted or permanently damaged. In business, sustainability is also defined as the ability to meet the needs of the present without compromising the ability of future generations to meet their own needs.

Sustainability Report. (p. 883)   The primary document used for communicating a company's performance on all three pillars of the triple bottom line: economic, environmental, and social. Also known as a Corporate Social Responsibility (CSR) report.

Sustainability Reporting. (p. 883)   A process that helps companies set goals, measure performance, and manage change as they move toward an economic model that produces long-term economic profit as well as environmental care and social responsibility.

Triple Bottom Line. (p. 877)   Evaluating a company's performance not only by its ability to generate economic profits, but also by its impact on people and the planet.

Waste Audits. (p. 880)   Studying the steam of waste coming from company operations (solid waste, water discharge, chemicals, etc.) to determine waste that can be avoided and alternative uses for the remaining waste.

Water Footprint. (p. 891)   The total volume of water use associated with the processes and products of a business.

Quick Checks

1. *(Learning Objective 1)* Which of the following is *not* one of the three factors related to sustainability?
   a. Social
   b. Economic
   c. Ecologic
   d. Environment

2. *(Learning Objective 1)* Which of the following items would be considered an *external* cost?
   a. Impact on aquatic life of oil spill
   b. Monthly trash hauling fee
   c. Annual audit by public accounting firm
   d. Salary cost of sustainability officer

3. *(Learning Objective 1)* LCA stands for which of the following?
   a. Lower cost always
   b. Life-cycle assessment
   c. Life costs aggregated
   d. Lowest-cost audit

4. *(Learning Objective 1)* Which of the following would *not* be a reason to adopt sustainable business practices?
   a. Reducing costs
   b. Producing new revenue streams
   c. Improving external image
   d. Increasing compliance risks

5. *(Learning Objective 2)* What is the current status of sustainability reporting in the United States?
   a. Sustainability reporting using the GRI G4 reporting guidelines is required for all publicly traded companies.
   b. Sustainability reporting using the GRI G4 reporting guidelines is required for all companies doing business in the United States, regardless of size.
   c. The SEC requires that publicly traded companies disclose any material information to prevent misleading the readers of financial statements.
   d. All companies listed on the New York Stock Exchange (NYSE) must issue sustainability reports using the NYSE's sustainability reporting guidelines.

6. *(Learning Objective 2)* Which of the following would be a reason for a company to undertake sustainability reporting?
   a. Sustainability reporting can be an internal change management tool.
   b. The sustainability report can communicate the company's social and environmental impact to consumers, investors, and other stakeholders.
   c. Neither a nor b is a reason for sustainability reporting.
   d. Both a and b are both reasons for sustainability reporting.

7. *(Learning Objective 2)* Which of the following aspects would *not* be included in the Environmental category of the GRI G4 reporting guidelines?
   a. Energy
   b. Training and education
   c. Emissions
   d. Transport

8. *(Learning Objective 2)* Which of the following aspects would *not* be included in the Economic category of the GRI G4 reporting guidelines?
   a. Equal remuneration for women and men
   b. Market presence
   c. Indirect economic impacts
   d. Procurement practices

9. *(Learning Objective 2)* Which of the following aspects would *not* be included in the Social category of the GRI G4 reporting guidelines?
   a. Labor/management relations
   b. Child labor
   c. Anti-corruption
   d. Environmental grievance mechanism

10. *(Learning Objective 3)* Which of the following is *not* a challenge to implementing and using an environmental management accounting system?
    a. Historical orientation of accounting
    b. Communication issues
    c. Hidden costs
    d. All of the above items are challenges.

Quick Check Answers

1. c 2. a 3. b 4. d 5. c 6. d 7. b 8. a 9. d 10. d

Short Exercises

S15-1   Identifying reasons to pursue sustainability *(Learning Objective 1)*

Listed below are several reasons an organization might pursue sustainability initiatives. Classify each reason as either: *Reducing costs, Creating new revenue streams, Reducing risks, Increasing and retaining market share,* or *Attracting capital.*

a.   Air France-KLM strives to keep its top spot in the Travel & Leisure sector in the Dow Jones Sustainability Index (DJSI); many institutional investors will only invest in companies listed on the DJSI.

b.   Johnson & Johnson (J & J) experienced a significant increase in the number of non-compliance notices it received in a recent year. As a result, J & J has increased sustainability training throughout the company and has increased management attention on sustainability processes.

c.   The cleaning product company Method produces a dish and hand soap made with plastic trash recovered from the Pacific Ocean.

d.   Jiangsu Redbud Dyeing Technology in China, a supplier to Walmart, had to go green as a condition of continuing to be part of Walmart's supply chain.

e.   The architectural firm of Perkins + Will recently retrofitted its 25-year-old office building to the LEED platinum level, achieving the highest score ever for a LEED platinum building in North America.

S15-2   Identify aspects within each G4 category on a GRI report
(Learning Objective 2)

For each of the following items, identify whether the item would be classified under the *Economic, Environmental,* or *Social* G4 category on a GRI report.

a.   Anti-competitive behavior

b.   Economic performance

c.   Product and service labeling

d.   Market presence

e.   Diversity and equal opportunity

f.   Materials

g.   Customer privacy

h.   Emissions

i.   Training and education

j.   Energy

k.   Employment

l.   Customer health and safety

m.   Effluents and waste

n.   Forced or compulsory labor

o.   Supplier human rights assessment

p.   Supplier assessment for impacts on society

q.   Indirect economic impacts

S15-3   Identify aspects within each G4 Social subcategory on a GRI report
(Learning Objective 2)

For each of the following items, identify whether the item would be classified under the *Labor Practices and Decent Work, Human Rights, Society,* or *Product Responsibility* subcategory of the Social G4 category on a GRI report.

a.   Customer health and safety

b.   Local communities

c.   Customer privacy

d.   Product and service labeling

e.   Equal remuneration for women and men

f.   Anti-competitive behavior

g. Employment

h. Indigenous rights

i. Supplier human rights assessment

j. Marketing communications

k. Forced or compulsory labor

l. Diversity and equal opportunity

m. Supplier assessment for impacts on society

n. Training and education

S15-4 Classifying sustainability costs *(Learning Objective 3)*

As discussed in the chapter, there are at least six categories of costs (monetary information) associated with sustainability efforts. In the table to follow, identify the proper sustainability cost category for each of the costs listed.

Cost	Sustainability cost category
Cost to develop ways to reduce greenhouse gases (GHGs) from products and processes	
Cost of air-monitoring equipment to ensure that scrubbers are functioning properly (scrubbers are air-pollution control equipment)	
Cost of water used to cool extruded products in a manufacturing plant	
Cost to the company's image and goodwill resulting from a large chemical spill	
Cost of installing scrubbers to control air pollution at an electricity-generation plant	
Cost of canvas used in producing tote bags	

S15-5 Distinguish between monetary and physical information *(Learning Objective 3)*

For each of the following examples of information, specify whether it would be included in an environmental management accounting system as monetary information (M), physical information (P), or not included in the environmental management accounting system (NA).

1. Gallons of lubricants used in machinery

2. Tons of scrap metal recycled

3. Cost of sulfur used in erasers

4. Cost of wages for plant manager

5. Cost of materials used in lab to neutralize toxins

6. Costs of running a laboratory to develop alternative energy sources

7. Cost of the CEO's salary

8. Pounds of cardboard recycled

9. Cost of shipping raw materials between company plants

10. Cost to upgrade factory equipment to reduce emissions

11. Cost of wages for quality control inspector

12. Gallons of toxic waste generated

13. Wages of workers to comply with new EPA standards

14. Cost of electricity used to power manufacturing facilities

15. Total kilowatt hours of electricity used

S15-6 Identify implementation challenges *(Learning Objective 3)*

Implementing an environmental management accounting (EMA) system can have several challenges. To follow are several implementation scenarios. For each scenario, identify which type of implementation challenge it represents (a. communication issue; b. hidden cost; c. aggregated accounting information; d. historical orientation of accounting; or e. newness of EMA.)

1. The cost of future lost sales resulting from the poor publicity generated by a large chemical spill are not included in the results of operations provided to management even though the lost sales are significant.

2. The costs of handling hazardous materials are included with the material handling costs for all materials.

3. The costs of handling hazardous materials are included with the cost of handling all materials.

4. The production staff does not interact or share information with the accounting staff.

5. Company accountants can find little guidance on how to develop a sound environmental management accounting system.

S15-7 Define key sustainability terms *(Learning Objectives 1, 2, & 3)*

Complete the following statements with one of the terms listed. You may use a term more than once. Some terms may not be used at all.

Non-governmental organizations	Life-cycle assessment	External cost
	Eco-efficiency	Internal cost
Global Reporting Initiative	Sustainability report	Assurance
Sustainability		

1. A corporate social responsibility (CSR) report is also known as a(n) _____.

2. When a company studies the environmental and social impact of one of its products over the product's entire life, it is performing a(n) _____.

3. The G4 guidelines were developed by the _____, a nonprofit organization whose mission is to help to standardize sustainability reporting practices.

4. The Red Cross and Greenpeace are both examples of _____.

5. The impact of the Deepwater Horizon (BP) oil spill on ecosystems in and around the Gulf of Mexico is an example of a(n) _____.

6. The cost of cleaning up the Deepwater Horizon oil spill to be paid by BP is estimated to be approximately $42.4 billion. This cost is a(n) _____.

7. When the Big Four accounting firm of Deloitte validated UPS's sustainability report, Deloitte was providing _____.

8. Achieving economic savings by producing goods and services with fewer ecological resources is an example of _____.

9. _____ is often defined as the ability to meet the needs of the present generation without compromising the ability of future generations to meet their own needs.

S15-8 Identify ethical standards violated *(Learning Objectives 1, 2, & 3)*

ETHICS

For each of the situations listed, identify the primary standard from the IMA Statement of Ethical Professional Practice that is violated (competence, confidentiality, integrity, or credibility). Refer to Exhibit 1-6 for the complete standard.

1. Dana skipped attending his company's training on GRI reporting because, even though he was required to go, attendance would not be taken.

2. Robyn does not disclose that her brother is the president of the consulting firm her organization is hiring for some GRI reporting work.

3. Byron is asked to prepare the GRI report for the year, but he has not attended GRI training. He decides to muddle his way through the report.

4. Robert is frustrated because he feels that his company is not moving fast enough to adopt sustainable practices and GRI reporting. He talks to a reporter about some potential environmental fines the company might receive, thinking that if the company is embarrassed publicly, it will move faster on sustainability initiatives.

5. Kimberly is a staff accountant at Briar Industries. Since Briar's GRI report is not audited, Kimberly omits a few numbers that, if published, would cause Briar to look less environmentally friendly. Kimberly figures that she is not likely to get caught and the report is not required.

EXERCISES Group A

E15-9A   Identify impact of sustainability efforts *(Learning Objective 1)*

Sustainability involves more than just the impact of actions on the environment. The triple bottom line recognizes that a company has to measure its impact on people, planet, and profit for its long-term economic and social viability. To follow are examples of green initiatives recently undertaken at Proctor and Gamble (P&G). For each example, indicate whether the impact of this initiative would be primarily economic, environmental, or societal.

Initiative at Proctor and Gamble (P&G)	Economic, Environmental, or Societal
a. Total shareholder return has increased in the past fiscal year	
b. Long-term goals include integrating 100% renewable or recycled materials into product lines and packaging	
c. Aided 60 countries and saved thousands of lives by developing and providing PUR water filtration packets via the Children's Safe Drinking Water (CSDW) Program	
d. Partnered with Feeding America to help fight hunger	
e. Plans to eliminate manufacturing waste that is currently sent to landfills	
f. Shareholder's equity decreased from 2009 to 2010	
g. Provided disaster relief to Haiti, donating PUR packets and various hygiene products	
h. Within the past year, P&G has decreased the amount of company printed pages by 11 million through combined efforts with Xerox	
i. Working to improve and preserve the quality of water within regions and communities where operations take place to avoid contributing to water scarcity	
j. Moving toward 100% renewable energy to power plants to completely eliminate petroleum-based CO_2 emissions	
k. Partnered with UNICEF to provide vaccinations to women and children at risk for maternal and neonatal tetanus	
l. Funds NGO efforts to educate children in India through Project Shiksha	
m. Planning to create products and packaging in such a way that consumer waste goes to recycling, compost, or waste-to-energy rather than landfills	

E15-10A   Sustainability and the value chain *(Learning Objective 1)*

Each of the scenarios to follow describes a sustainability-related cost item for organizations in recent years. For each scenario, identify which function of the value chain that cost would represent (R&D, design, purchasing/producing, marketing, distributing, or customer service.) *Note: The companies and products used in this exercise are real companies with a strong sustainable practices commitment.*

a. Bert's Bees, a manufacturer of products such as lip balm, has developed a new soap label called TerraSkin(™) Wraps that is "treeless" and "bleach-free" (it is a paper-label alternative). The cost of researching the proper process and combinations of components for this new label would fall into which function in the value chain?

b. The Kellogg Company, known for its breakfast cereals, has successfully switched the majority of its packaging over to 100% recycled materials, 35% of which is consumer-recycled. According to the company's analysis, the impact of this achievement can be found in the decreased overall carbon footprint left by the company, as well as increased recyclability of this packaging. The cost of designing the life cycle of Kellogg's packaging would fall into which function in the value chain?

c. Patagonia, a clothing manufacturer, launched a program in 2005 called the Common Threads Initiative. In an effort to prevent clothing from going to landfills, the company collects used and damaged garments from consumers. These textiles are then salvaged and recycled as new products. The costs involved in running this program to take back used garments would fall into which function in the value chain?

d. General Mills produces a variety of different foods. The company recognizes the importance of encouraging good nutrition among the youth of America and has taken special initiative to ensure that its marketing strategies promote healthy lifestyles. It avoids targeting children under twelve with advertisements for foods that are high in sugar. The cost of these marketing campaigns would fall into which function in the value chain?

e. The Target Corporation, a retailing company, offers a line of garments that have been treated for stain management. However, such treatments usually include a chemical (PFOA) that has been found to be potentially harmful to humans, so Target only purchases from manufacturers that offer PFOA-free alternatives. The cost of the garments treated with the PFOA-alternatives would fall into which function in the value chain?

f. To help offset carbon emissions, U-Haul, a moving truck rental company, gives its consumers an option to donate $1 to $5 at the time of a transaction. Just two years after its launch in 2007, $1,000,000 was raised and 133,000 trees were planted with the proceeds. The cost of these carbon offsets purchased for the delivery vehicles rented by U-Haul would fall into which function in the value chain?

E15-11A Sustainability and job costing (Learning Objective 1)

Littleton Plastics manufactures custom park furniture and signage from recycled plastics (primarily shredded milk jugs). Many of the company's customers are municipalities that are required by law to purchase goods that meet certain recycled-content guidelines. (Recycled content can include post-consumer waste materials, pre-consumer waste materials, and recovered materials.) As a result, Littleton Plastics includes two types of direct material charges in its job cost for each job: (1) virgin materials (non-recycled) and (2) recycled-content materials. Littleton Plastics also keeps track of the pounds of each type of direct material so that the final recycled-content percentage for the job can be reported to the customer. The company also reports on the percentage of recycled content to total plastic used each month on its own internal reporting system to help to encourage managers to use recycled content whenever possible.

Littleton Plastics uses a predetermined manufacturing overhead rate of $11 per direct labor hour. Here is a summary of the materials and labor used on a recent job for Pratt County:

Description	Quantity	Cost
Virgin materials	90 pounds	$ 4.10 per pound
Recycled-content materials	210 pounds	$ 3.20 per pound
Direct labor	17 hours	$20.00 per hour

Requirements

1. Calculate the total cost of the Pratt County job.
2. Calculate the percentage of recycled content used in the Pratt County job (using pounds). If items purchased by Pratt County are required by county charter to contain at least 40% recycled content, does this job meet that requirement?

E15-12A Sustainability and activity-based costing (Learning Objective 1)

Scofield Industries manufactures a variety of custom widgets. The company has traditionally used a plantwide manufacturing overhead rate based on machine hours to allocate manufacturing overhead to its products. The company estimates that it will incur $1,665,000 in total manufacturing overhead costs in the upcoming year and will use 15,000 machine hours.

Up to this point, hazardous waste disposal fees have been absorbed into the plantwide manufacturing overhead rate and allocated to all products as part of the manufacturing overhead process. Recently the company has been experiencing significantly increased waste disposal fees for hazardous waste generated by certain products and, as a result, profit margins on all products have been negatively impacted. Company management wants to implement an activity-based costing system so that managers know the cost of each product, including its hazard waste disposal costs.

Expected usage and costs for manufacturing overhead activities for the upcoming year are as follows:

Description of cost pool	Estimated cost	Cost driver	Estimated activity for the year
Machine maintenance costs	$ 1,050,000	Number of machine hours	15,000
Engineering change orders	$ 90,000	Number of change orders	1,000
Hazardous waste disposal	$ 525,000	Pounds of hazardous material generated	1,500
Total overhead cost	$ 1,665,000		

During the year, Job 356 is started and completed. Usage data for this job are as follows:

340 pounds of direct material at $20 per pound

30 direct labor hours used at $35 per labor hour

110 machine hours used

4 change orders

30 pounds of hazardous waste generated

Requirements

1. Calculate the cost of Job 356 using the traditional plantwide manufacturing overhead rate based on machine hours.
2. Calculate the cost of Job 356 using activity-based costing.
3. If you were a manager, which cost estimate would provide you more useful information? How might you use this information?

E15-13A Sustainability and process costing (Learning Objective 1)

Sylvan Industries manufactures plastic bottles for the food industry. On average, Sylvan pays $71 per ton for its plastics. Sylvan's waste disposal company has increased its waste disposal charge to $57 per ton for solid and inert waste. Sylvan generates a total of 500 tons of waste per month.

The company's managers have been evaluating the production processes for areas to cut waste. In the process of making plastic bottles, a certain amount of machine "drool" occurs. Machine drool is the excess plastic that "drips" off the machine between molds. In the past, Sylvan has discarded the machine drool. In an average month, 130 tons of machine drool are generated.

Management has arrived at three possible courses of action for the machine drool issue:

1. Do nothing and pay the increased waste disposal charge.
2. Sell the machine drool waste to a local recycler for $11 per ton.
3. Re-engineer the production process at an annual cost of $45,000. This change in the production process would cause the amount of machine drool generated to be reduced by 60% each month. The remaining machine drool would then be sold to a local recycler for $11 per ton.

Requirements

1. What is the annual cost of the machine drool currently? Include both the original plastics cost and the waste disposal cost.
2. How much would the company save per year (net) if the machine drool were to be sold to the local recycler?

3. How much would the company save per year (net) if the production process were to be re-engineered?

4. What do you think the company should do? Explain your rationale.

E15-14A Sustainability and cost behavior *(Learning Objective 1)*

Samson Entertainment is a provider of cable, internet, and on-demand video services. Samson currently sends monthly bills to its customers via the postal service. Because of a concern for the environment and recent increases in postal rates, Samson management is considering offering an option to its customers for paperless billing. In addition to saving printing, paper, and postal costs, paperless billing will save energy and water (through reduced paper needs, reduced waste disposal, and reduced transportation needs). While Samson would like to switch to 100% paperless billing, many of its customers are not comfortable with paperless billing or may not have web access so the paper billing option will remain regardless of whether Samson adopts a paperless billing system or not.

The cost of the paperless billing system would be $67,600 per quarter with no variable costs since the costs of the system are the salaries of the clerks and the cost of leasing the computer system. The paperless billing system being proposed would be able to handle up to 780,000 bills per quarter (more than 780,000 bills per quarter would require a different computer system and is outside the scope of the current situation at Samson).

Samson has gathered its cost data for the past year by quarter for paper, toner cartridges, printer maintenance costs, and postage costs for the billing department. The cost data are as follows:

	Quarter 1	Quarter 2	Quarter 3	Quarter 4
Total paper, toner, printer maintenance, and postage costs	$658,000	$670,000	$790,000	$680,000
Total number of bills mailed	510,000	550,000	730,000	570,000

Requirements

1. Calculate the variable cost per bill mailed under the current paper-based billing system.

2. Assume that the company projects that it will have a total of 640,000 bills to mail in the upcoming quarter. If enough customers choose the paperless billing option so that 20% of the mailings can be converted to paperless, how much would the company save from the paperless billing system (be sure to consider the cost of the paperless billing system)?

3. What if only 15% of the mailings are converted to the paperless option (assume a total of 640,000 bills)? Should the company still offer the paperless billing system? Explain your rationale.

E15-15A Sustainability and CVP concepts *(Learning Objective 1)*

Jenkins Garage Doors manufactures a premium garage door. Currently, the price and cost data associated with the premium garage door are as follows:

Average selling price per premium garage door......................................	$ 3,000
Average variable manufacturing cost per door	$ 540
Average variable selling cost per door	$ 210
Total annual fixed costs...	$270,000

Jenkins Garage Doors has undertaken several sustainability projects over the past few years. Management is currently evaluating whether to develop a comprehensive software control system for its manufacturing operations that would significantly reduce scrap and waste generated during the manufacturing process. If the company were to implement this software control system in its manufacturing operations, the use of the software control system would result in an increase of $30,000 in its annual fixed costs while the average variable manufacturing cost per door would drop by $150.

Requirements

1. What is the company's current breakeven point in units and in dollars?

2. If the company expects to sell 340 premium garage doors in the upcoming year, and it does not develop the software control system, what is its expected operating income from premium garage doors?

3. If the software control system were to be developed and implemented, what would be the company's new breakeven point in units and in dollars?

4. If the company expects to sell 340 premium garage doors in the upcoming year, and it develops the software control system, what is its expected operating income from premium garage doors?

5. If the company expects to 340 premium garage doors in the upcoming year, do you think the company should implement the software control system? Why or why not? What factors should the company consider?

E15-16A Sustainability and short-term decision-making (Learning Objective 1)

Over the past several years, decommissioned U.S. warships have been turned into artificial reefs in the ocean by towing them out to sea and sinking them. The thinking was that sinking the ship would conveniently dispose of it while providing an artificial reef environment for aquatic life. In reality, some of the sunken ships have released toxins into the ocean and have been costly to decontaminate. Now the U.S. government is taking bids to instead dismantle and recycle ships that have recently been decommissioned (but have not been sunk yet).

Assume that a recently decommissioned aircraft, the USS *Independence*, is estimated to contain approximately 40 tons of recyclable materials able to be sold for approximately $34.5 million. The low bid for dismantling and transporting the ship materials to appropriate facilities is $36.3 million. Recycling and dismantling the ship would create about 500 jobs for about a year in the Rust Belt. This geographic area has been experiencing record-high unemployment rates in recent years.

Requirements

1. Is it more financially advantageous to sink the ship (assume that it costs approximately $1.5 million to tow a ship out to sea and sink it) or to dismantle and recycle it? Show your calculations.

2. From a sustainability standpoint, what should be done with the decommissioned aircraft carrier? List some of the qualitative factors that should enter into this analysis.

3. As a taxpayer, which action would you prefer (sink or recycle)? Defend your answer.

E15-17A Sustainability and budgeting (Learning Objective 1)

Doyle Beverages manufactures its own soda pop bottles. The bottles are made from polyethylene terephthalate (PET), a lightweight yet strong plastic. The company uses as much PET recycled resin pellets in its bottles as it can, both because using recycled PET helps the company to meet its sustainability goals and because recycled PET is less expensive than virgin PET.

Doyle is continuing to search for ways to reduce its costs and its impact on the environment. PET plastic is melted and blown over soda bottle molds to produce the bottles. One idea Doyle's engineers have suggested is to retrofit the soda bottle molds and change the plastic formulation slightly so that 25% less PET plastic is used for each bottle. The average kilograms of PET per soda bottle before any redesign is 0.004 kg. The cost of retrofitting the soda bottle molds will result a one-time charge of $3,086, while the plastic reformulation will cause the average cost per kilogram of PET plastic to change from $1.00 to $1.20.

Doyle's management is analyzing whether the change to the bottle molds to reduce PET plastic usage should be made. Management expects the following number of soda bottles to be used in the upcoming year:

	Quarter 1	Quarter 2	Quarter 3	Quarter 4
Number of bottles to be produced	2,000,000	2,500,000	3,000,000	3,100,000

For the upcoming year, management expects the beginning inventory of PET to be 800 kilograms, while ending inventory is expected to be 1,770 kilograms. During the first three quarters of the year, management wants to keep the ending inventory of PET at the end of each quarter equal to 10% of the following quarter's PET needs.

Requirements

1. Using the original data (before any redesign of soda bottles), prepare a direct materials budget to calculate the cost of PET purchases in each quarter for the upcoming year and for the year in total.

2. Assume that the company retrofits the soda bottle molds and changes the plastic formulation slightly so that less PET plastic is used in each bottle. Now prepare a direct materials budget to calculate the cost of PET purchases in each quarter for the upcoming year and for the year in total for this possible scenario.

3. Compare the cost of PET plastic for Requirement 1 (original data) and for Requirement 2 (making change to using less PET). What is the direct material cost savings from making the change to using less PET? Compare the total of those savings to the cost of retrofitting the soda bottle molds. Should the company make the change? Explain your rationale.

E15-18A Sustainability and the balanced scorecard *(Learning Objective 1)*

Classify each of the following sustainability key performance indicators (KPIs) according to the balanced scorecard perspective it addresses. Choose from the following five perspectives:

- Financial perspective
- Customer perspective
- Internal business perspective
- Learning and growth perspective
- Community perspective

KPI	Perspective
a. Number of green products	
b. Percentage of general staff with sustainability training	
c. Number of green products	
d. Global in-kind donations as a percentage of total income	
e. CO_2 in metric tons	
f. Product safety ratings	
g. Waste disposal costs	
h. Water use per ton of production	
i. Percent of packaging from products reclaimed and/or recycled	
j. Global charitable contributions as a percent of income	
k. Percentage of management with sustainability training	
l. Energy use per ton of production	
m. Revenue generated through sale of recycled goods	
n. Environmental fines paid (expense item on income statement)	
o. Wastewater per ton of production	
p. Percentage of total income donated to aid during natural disasters	
q. Safety fines paid	
r. Energy use efficiency percentage	

E15-19A Sustainability and standard costing *(Learning Objective 1)*

Wilke Containers currently uses a recycled plastic to make bottles for the food industry.

Current bottle production information:

The cost and time standards per batch of 10,000 bottles are as follows:

Plastic 300 kilograms at $11.00 per kg
Direct labor 2.0 hours at $20.00 per hour

The variable manufacturing overhead rate is based on total estimated variable manufacturing overhead of $500,000 and estimated total direct labor hours (DLH) of 10,000. The company allocates its variable manufacturing overhead based on direct labor hours.

Proposed changes to bottle design and production process:

The container division manager is considering having both the bottle redesigned and the bottle production process reengineered so that the plastic usage would drop by 30% overall due both to generating less scrap in the manufacturing process and using less plastic in each bottle. In addition to decreasing the amount of plastic used in producing the bottles, the additional following benefits would be realized:

a. Direct labor hours would be reduced by 20% because less scrap would be handled in the production process.

b. Total estimated variable manufacturing overhead would be reduced by 10% because less scrap would need to be hauled away, less electricity would be used in the production process, and less inventory would need to be stocked.

Requirements

1. Calculate the standard cost per batch of 10,000 bottles using the current data (before the company makes any changes). Include direct materials, direct labor, and variable manufacturing overhead in the standard cost per unit.

2. Calculate the standard cost per batch of 10,000 bottles if the company makes the changes to the bottle design and production process so that less plastic is used. Include direct materials, direct labor, and variable manufacturing overhead in the standard cost per unit.

3. Calculate the cost savings per batch by comparing the standard cost per batch under each scenario (current versus proposed change). Assume that the total cost to implement the changes would be $352,800. How many batches of bottles would need to be produced after the change to have the cost savings total equal the cost to make the changes?

4. What other benefits might arise from making this change to using less plastic in the manufacture of the bottles? Are there any risks? What would you recommend the company do?

E15-20A   Sustainability and capital investments *(Learning Objective 1)*

Monteiro Industries is evaluating investing in solar panels to provide some of the electrical needs of its main office building in Green Bay, Wisconsin. The solar panel project would cost $575,000 and would provide cost savings in its utility bills of $35,000 per year. It is anticipated that the solar panels would have a life of 20 years and would have no residual value.

Requirements

1. Calculate the payback period in years of the solar panel project.

2. If the company uses a discount rate of 12%, what is the net present value of this project?

3. If the company has a rule that no projects will be undertaken that have a payback period of more than five years, would this investment be accepted? If not, what arguments could managers make to get approval for the solar panel project?

4. What would you do if you were in charge of approving capital investment proposals?

E15-21A   Sustainability and the statement of cash flows *(Learning Objective 1)*

Henderson Plastics is a manufacturer that takes in post-consumer plastics (i.e., empty milk jugs) and recycles those plastics into a variety of building materials. Because the company has a strong focus on sustainability, the company managers try, whenever possible, to use recycled materials and to invest in sustainable projects.

Last year, the company engaged in several sustainable practices that had an impact on its cash flows. For each of the transactions listed below, indicate whether the transaction would have affected the operating, investing, or financing cash flows of the company. Additionally, indicate whether each transaction would have increased (+) or decreased (−) cash.

Transactions:

1. When the plastic wood is cut into the lengths needed to make trellises, the end pieces cut off are scrap. Henderson sold this cutting scrap to another recycler.

2. A wind-turbine was built to power part of Henderson's operations.

3. A Honda Civic Hybrid automobile was purchased for use by the sales manager of Henderson while on company business.

4. Henderson became a minority partner in a biofuel project by investing $2 million in cash in the project.

5. Throughout the year, Henderson participated in several trade shows that featured green products for use by the housing construction industry. For each trade show, Henderson incurred cash expenses for transportation, registration, meals and lodging, and booth setup.

6. Henderson paid off long-term bonds during the year using excess funds.

7. Henderson installed a "living roof" on its manufacturing facility. This roof is made mostly from sedum, a drought-resistant perennial grass-like groundcover. The plants help to reduce storm-water runoff and double the expected life of the roof over a conventional roof. The plants also reduce heating and cooling needs by providing an extra layer of insulation. Additionally, the plants absorb carbon dioxide to help to reduce greenhouse gases. The living roof was paid for with cash.

8. A fleet of plug-in electric cars was purchased for the sales staff.

9. New production equipment that is 40% more energy efficient than the old equipment was purchased for cash.

10. Engineers at Henderson performed research into a new process that injects tiny air bubbles into the plastic to reduce the usage of raw materials (plastics) and to reduce the weight of the finished products.

E15-22A Sustainability and external financial reporting (Learning Objective 1)

In a recent Corporate Responsibility Report, Nike, Inc., lists several sustainability goals and commitments it has made. In the following list from Nike's CR Report, categorize each goal (or measurement) as to whether it is oriented toward the economic, environmental, or society component of the triple bottom line.

Nike, Inc., CR Report—Selected Stated Goals and Commitments	Economic, Environmental, or Society?
a. Build an advocacy agenda to push for large-scale policies to help achieve global economic competitiveness for Nike.	
b. Achieve 17 percent reduction in waste generated by footwear production from a 2006 baseline.	
c. Develop scalable solutions to enable Nike's evolution to a closed-loop business model in the current economy to maximize profits.	
d. Maintain current amount of petroleum-derived solvents grams per pair of shoes (maintain the 95 percent reduction from the 1995 baseline).	
e. Implement Human Resources Management program in all factories.	
f. Increase use of Environmentally Preferred Methods in the production of footwear by 22 percent.	
g. Promote multi-brand collaboration on improving working conditions in the global supply chain, covering 30 percent of factory locations.	
h. Deliver 30 percent absolute reduction in CO_2 emissions from 2003 by 2020.	
i. Nike brand facilities and business travel are to be climate neutral.	
j. Make investing in environmentally-sustainable (green) ventures a priority.	

Source: Nike, Inc., Corporate Responsibility Report FY 07 08 09 (Retrieved from http://www.nikebiz.com/crreport/ on June 21, 2011).

EXERCISES Group B

E15-23B Identify impact of sustainability efforts *(Learning Objective 1)*

Sustainability involves more than just the impact of actions on the environment. The triple bottom line recognizes that a company has to measure its impact on the economy, the environment, and society for its long-term economic and social viability. To follow are examples of green initiatives recently undertaken at Ford Motor Company. For each example, indicate whether the impact of this initiative would be primarily economic, environmental, or societal.

Initiative at Ford Motor Company	Economic, Environmental, or Societal
a. Founded Ford Volunteer Corps in response to natural disasters	
b. During the annual Global Week of Caring, 46,000 hours were contributed to volunteer projects like cleaning up highways	
c. National sponsor of the Susan G. Komen Race for the Cure	
d. Plan to aggressively restructure in order to operate profitably at the current rate of consumer demand in light of the difficult economic times and the rising costs of fuel commodities	
e. Product strategy includes advancement of technology in order to reduce greenhouse gas emissions and improved fuel economy	
f. Introduced Ford Driving Skills for Life, which educates teens about safe driving practices	
g. Expanded global markets to gain market share in more international countries	
h. Planning to focus on increasing repertoire of small-to-midsize vehicles to respond to consumer demands in an effort to gain market share	
i. Plan to introduce plug-in hybrid electric vehicles that run on advanced lithium ion batteries	
j. In 2010, Ford earned its highest net income in a decade at $6.6 billion	
k. Trained suppliers' workers in human rights via outreach programs, and as a result was ranked first in *CRO Magazine*'s Best Citizens List	
l. Made goal to reduce CO_2 emissions in new vehicles by 30%	
m. Affiliates of the Ford Volunteer Corps gave over 112,000 volunteer hours to the community, targeting everything from schools to soup kitchens	

E15-24B Sustainability and the value chain *(Learning Objective 1)*

Each of the scenarios to follow describes a sustainability-related cost item for organizations. For each scenario, identify which function of the value chain that cost would represent (R&D, design, purchasing/producing, marketing, distributing, or customer service.) *Note: The companies and products used in this exercise are real companies with a strong sustainable practices commitment.*

a. Engineered Plastic Systems, LLC, a company that manufactures outdoor furniture, uses plastic lumber that is composed of recycled materials as a wood alternative for building its products. The plastic used is not only eco-friendly, but is also 50% recycled, 10% of which is post-consumer material. In promoting these eco-friendly features, the company is careful to make the distinction that it is not like other companies that falsely inflate their green efforts, stating specifically that it will always back up each of its claims with facts, and never mislead the customer about the actual amount of recycled plastic in its products. The cost of such promotions would fall into which function in the value chain?

b. The Hewlett-Packard Company, a manufacturer of computers and related products, established its own R&R program in 1987. This program enables consumers to return any defective or used electronic goods and ink cartridges, which helps decrease the company's impact on the environment by avoiding landfills and allows the company to recycle the plastics and metals used in these products. The cost of recycling used computer products for consumers would fall into which function in the value chain?

c. The Coca-Cola Company is currently spotlighting one of its newest innovations in packaging: the PlantBottle. In one of its promotion ads, it is hailed as, "The **first ever** recyclable PET plastic beverage bottle made partially from plants . . . and recycles just like traditional PET plastic, but does so with a *lighter footprint* on the planet and its scarce resources." The cost of the research necessary for the Coca-Cola Company's newest foray into greener packaging would fall into which function in the value chain?

d. Able Plastics, a plastics production company, has very stringent audits on its carbon emissions, and puts a lot of effort into offsetting its carbon emissions. For instance, not only does Able Plastics invest in the Strzelecki Ranges replanting site, but Able Plastics also endeavors to cut emissions by requiring that all electronic devices be fully turned off at night in all company buildings. Able Plastics also uses carbon offsets for its delivery vehicles. The cost of these carbon offsets for delivery vehicles would fall into which function in the value chain?

e. GenPak, LLC, manufactures food packaging, and uses plastic in its products that is very conducive to recycling. In fact, much of its products are created from recycled plastic, much of which comes from GenPak's own products' post-consumer usage at the end of the products' life cycle. The cost of designing the process for continuing the life cycle of these products would fall into which function in the value chain?

f. The Sharp Corporation manufactures electronics. Sharp purchases recycled plastic parts to use in its products. The costs of this practice would fall into which function in the value chain?

E15-25B Sustainability and job costing *(Learning Objective 1)*

Haas Plastics manufactures custom park furniture and signage from recycled plastics (primarily shredded milk jugs). Many of the company's customers are municipalities that are required by law to purchase goods that meet certain recycled-content guidelines. (Recycled content can include post-consumer waste materials, pre-consumer waste materials, and recovered materials.) As a result, Haas Plastics includes two types of direct material charges in its job cost for each job: (1) virgin materials (non-recycled) and (2) recycled-content materials. The company also keeps track of the pounds of each type of direct material so that the final recycled-content percentage for the job can be reported to the customer. The company also reports on the percentage of recycled content to total plastic used each month on its own internal reporting system to help encourage managers to use recycled content whenever possible.

The company uses a predetermined manufacturing overhead rate of $9.00 per direct labor hour. Here is a summary of the materials and labor used on a recent job for Jefferson County:

Description	Quantity	Cost
Virgin materials	60 pounds	$ 3.70 per pound
Recycled-content materials	140 pounds	$ 3.50 per pound
Direct labor	15 hours	$13.00 per hour

Requirements

1. Calculate the total cost of the Jefferson County job.
2. Calculate the percentage of recycled content used in the Jefferson County job (using pounds). If items purchased by Jefferson County are required by county charter to contain at least 40% recycled content, does this job meet that requirement?

E15-26B   Sustainability and activity-based costing (Learning Objective 1)

Santos Industries manufactures a variety of custom products. The company has traditionally used a plantwide manufacturing overhead rate based on machine hours to allocate manufacturing overhead to its products. The company estimates that it will incur $1,640,000 in total manufacturing overhead costs in the upcoming year and will use 8,000 machine hours.

Up to this point, hazardous waste disposal fees have been absorbed into the plantwide manufacturing overhead rate and allocated to all products as part of the manufacturing overhead process. Recently the company has been experiencing significantly increased waste disposal fees for hazardous waste generated by certain products and, as a result, profit margins on all products have been negatively impacted. Company management wants to implement an activity-based costing system so that managers know the cost of each product, including its hazard waste disposal costs.

Expected usage and costs for manufacturing overhead activities for the upcoming year are as follows:

Description of cost pool	Estimated cost	Cost driver	Estimated activity for the year
Machine maintenance costs	$ 560,000	Number of machine hours	8,000
Engineering change orders	$ 400,000	Number of change orders	5,000
Hazardous waste disposal	$ 680,000	Pounds of hazardous material generated	2,000
Total overhead cost	$1,640,000		

During the year, Job 354 is started and completed. Usage data for this job are as follows:

350 pounds of direct material at $35 per pound

50 direct labor hours used at $30 per labor hour

70 machine hours used

7 change orders

60 pounds of hazardous waste generated

Requirements

1. Calculate the cost of Job 354 using the traditional plantwide manufacturing overhead rate based on machine hours.
2. Calculate the cost of Job 354 using activity-based costing.
3. If you were a manager, which cost estimate would provide you more useful information? How might you use this information?

E15-27B   Sustainability and process costing (Learning Objective 1)

Sargo Industries manufactures plastic bottles for the food industry. On average, Sargo pays $80 per ton for its plastics. Sargo's waste disposal company has increased its waste disposal charge to $58 per ton for solid and inert waste. The company generates a total of 500 tons of waste per month.

Sargo's managers have been evaluating the production processes for areas to cut waste. In the process of making plastic bottles, a certain amount of machine "drool" occurs. Machine drool is the excess plastic that drips off the machine between molds. In the past, Sargo has discarded the machine drool. In an average month, 180 tons of machine drool are generated.

Management has arrived at three possible courses of action for the machine drool issue:

1. Do nothing and pay the increased waste disposal charge.
2. Sell the machine drool waste to a local recycler for $16 per ton.

3. Re-engineer the production process at an annual cost of $70,000. This change in the production process would cause the amount of machine drool generated to be reduced by 40% each month. The remaining machine drool would then be sold to a local recycler for $16 per ton.

Requirements

1. What is the annual cost of the machine drool currently? Include both the original plastics cost and the waste disposal cost.

2. How much would the company save per year (net) if the machine drool were to be sold to the local recycler?

3. How much would the company save per year (net) if the production process were to be re-engineered?

4. What do you think the company should do? Explain your rationale.

E15-28B   Sustainability and cost behavior *(Learning Objective 1)*

Garrett Entertainment is a provider of cable, internet, and on-demand video services. Garrett currently sends monthly bills to its customers via the postal service. Because of a concern for the environment and recent increases in postal rates, company management is considering offering an option to its customers for paperless billing. In addition to saving printing, paper, and postal costs, paperless billing will save energy and water (through reduced paper needs, reduced waste disposal, and reduced transportation needs). While Garrett would like to switch to 100% paperless billing, many of its customers are not comfortable with paperless billing or may not have web access so the paper billing option will remain regardless of whether Garrett adopts a paperless billing system or not.

The cost of the paperless billing system would be $166,200 per quarter with no variable costs since the costs of the system are the salaries of the clerks and the cost of leasing the computer system. The paperless billing system being proposed would be able to handle up to 980,000 bills per quarter (more than 980,000 bills per quarter would require a different computer system and is outside the scope of the current situation at Garrett).

The company has gathered its cost data for the past year by quarter for paper, toner cartridges, printer maintenance costs, and postage costs for the billing department. The cost data are as follows:

	Quarter 1	Quarter 2	Quarter 3	Quarter 4
Total paper, toner, printer maintenance, and postage costs	$592,500	$600,000	$750,000	$610,000
Total number of bills mailed	475,000	495,000	700,000	500,000

Requirements

1. Calculate the variable cost per bill mailed under the current paper-based billing system.

2. Assume that the company projects that it will have a total of 720,000 bills to mail in the upcoming quarter. If enough customers choose the paperless billing option so that 35% of the mailings can be converted to paperless, how much would the company save from the paperless billing system (be sure to consider the cost of the paperless billing system)?

3. What if only 30% of the mailings are converted to the paperless option (assume a total of 720,000 bills)? Should the company still offer the paperless billing system? Explain your rationale.

E15-29B   Sustainability and CVP concepts *(Learning Objective 1)*

Kirby Garage Doors manufactures a premium garage door. Currently, the price and cost data associated with the premium garage door are as follows:

Average selling price per premium garage door..	$ 2,200
Average variable manufacturing cost per door	$ 500
Average variable selling cost per door	$ 160
Total annual fixed costs...	$308,000

Kirby Garage Doors has undertaken several sustainability projects over the past few years. Management is currently evaluating whether to develop a comprehensive software control system for its manufacturing operations that would significantly reduce scrap and waste generated during the manufacturing process. If the company were to implement this software control system in its manufacturing operations, the use of the software control system would result in an increase of $70,400 in its annual fixed costs, while the average variable manufacturing cost per door would drop by $220.

Requirements

1. What is the company's current breakeven point in units and in dollars?
2. If the company expects to sell 290 premium garage doors in the upcoming year, and it does not develop the software control system, what is its expected operating income from premium garage doors?
3. If the software control system were to be developed and implemented, what would be the company's new breakeven point in units and in dollars?
4. If the company expects to sell 290 premium garage doors in the upcoming year, and it develops the software control system, what is its expected operating income from premium garage doors?
5. If the company expects to sell 290 premium garage doors in the upcoming year, do you think the company should implement the software control system? Why or why not? What factors should the company consider?

E15-30B   Sustainability and short-term decision-making *(Learning Objective 1)*

Over the past several years, decommissioned U.S. warships have been turned into artificial reefs in the ocean by towing them out to sea and sinking them. The thinking was that sinking the ship would conveniently dispose of it while providing an artificial reef environment for aquatic life. In reality, some of the sunken ships have released toxins into the ocean and have been costly to decontaminate. Now the U.S. government is taking bids to instead dismantle and recycle ships that have recently been decommissioned (but have not been sunk yet).

Assume that a recently decommissioned aircraft, the USS *Bashaw*, is estimated to contain approximately 40 tons of recyclable materials able to be sold for approximately $34.4 million. The low bid for dismantling and transporting the ship materials to appropriate facilities is $35.6 million. Recycling and dismantling the ship would create about 500 jobs for about a year in the Rust Belt. This geographic area has been experiencing record-high unemployment rates in recent years.

Requirements

1. Is it more financially advantageous to sink the ship (assume that it costs approximately $0.5 million to tow a ship out to sea and sink it) or to dismantle and recycle it? Show your calculations.
2. From a sustainability standpoint, what should be done with the decommissioned aircraft carrier? List some of the qualitative factors that should enter into this analysis.
3. As a taxpayer, which action would you prefer (sink or recycle)? Defend your answer.

E15-31B Sustainability and budgeting *(Learning Objective 1)*

Damon Beverages manufactures its own soda pop bottles. The bottles are made from polyethylene terephthalate (PET), a lightweight yet strong plastic. The company uses as much PET recycled resin pellets in its bottles as it can, both because using recycled PET helps Damon to meet its sustainability goals and because recycled PET is less expensive than virgin PET.

The company is continuing to search for ways to reduce its costs and its impact on the environment. PET plastic is melted and blown over soda bottle molds to produce the bottles. One idea Damon's engineers have suggested is to retrofit the soda bottle molds and change the plastic formulation slightly so that 15% less PET plastic is used for each bottle. The average kilograms of PET per soda bottle before any redesign is 0.02 kg. The cost of retrofitting the soda bottle molds will result a one-time charge of $96,502, while the plastic reformulation will cause the average cost per kilogram of PET plastic to change from $4.00 to $4.20.

Damon's management is analyzing whether the change to the bottle molds to reduce PET plastic usage should be made. Management expects the following number of soda bottles to be used in the upcoming year:

	Quarter 1	Quarter 2	Quarter 3	Quarter 4
Number of bottles to be produced	2,000,000	2,900,000	3,200,000	3,300,000

For the upcoming year, management expects the beginning inventory of PET to be 4,000 kilograms, while ending inventory is expected to be 7,140 kilograms. During the first three quarters of the year, management wants to keep the ending inventory of PET at the end of each quarter equal to 10% of the following quarter's PET needs.

Requirements

1. Using the original data (before any redesign of soda bottles), prepare a direct materials budget to calculate the cost of PET purchases in each quarter for the upcoming year and for the year in total.

2. Assume that the company retrofits the soda bottle molds and changes the plastic formulation slightly so that less PET plastic is used in each bottle. Now prepare a direct materials budget to calculate the cost of PET purchases in each quarter for the upcoming year and for the year in total for this possible scenario.

3. Compare the cost of PET plastic for Requirement 1 (original data) and for Requirement 2 (making change to using less PET). What is the direct material cost savings from making the change to using less PET? Compare the total of those savings to the cost of retrofitting the soda bottle molds. Should the company make the change? Explain your rationale.

E15-32B Sustainability and the balanced scorecard *(Learning Objective 1)*

Classify each of the following sustainability key performance indicators (KPIs) according to the balanced scorecard perspective it addresses. Choose from the following five perspectives:

- Financial perspective
- Customer perspective
- Internal business perspective
- Learning and growth perspective
- Community perspective

KPI	Perspective
a. CO_2 emissions per ton of production	
b. Revenue from recycled goods	
c. Percentage of resources purchased from local vendors	
d. Percentage of income donated to local after-school programs	
e. Number of sustainability training hours	
f. Percentage of packaging reclaimed or recycled after use	
g. Excessive overtime	
h. Megawatts of energy consumed	
i. Water reclamation costs	
j. Number of departments integrating sustainable practices	
k. Percentage of income donated to homeless shelters and food distribution units	
l. Percentage of packaging utilizing recycled materials	
m. Waste removal expense	
n. Waste pounds generated per ton of production	
o. Number of employee hours devoted to volunteering for Feeding America	
p. Gas used per ton of production	
q. Number of green products available	
r. Refining costs for recycled goods	

E15-33B Sustainability and standard costing *(Learning Objective 1)*

Worchester Containers currently uses a recycled plastic to make bottles for the food industry.

Current bottle production information:

The cost and time standards per batch of 10,000 bottles are as follows:

Plastic 300 kilograms at $4.00 per kg
Direct labor 4.0 hours at $25.00 per hour

The variable manufacturing overhead rate is based on total estimated variable manufacturing overhead of $700,000 and estimated total direct labor hours (DLH) of 10,000. Worchester allocates its variable manufacturing overhead based on direct labor hours.

Proposed changes to bottle design and production process:

The container division manager is considering having both the bottle redesigned and the bottle production process reengineered so that the plastic usage would drop by 30% overall due both to generating less scrap in the manufacturing process and using less plastic in each bottle. In addition to decreasing the amount of plastic used in producing the bottles, the additional following benefits would be realized:

a. Direct labor hours would be reduced by 20% because less scrap would be handled in the production process.

b. Total estimated variable manufacturing overhead would be reduced by 10% because less scrap would need to be hauled away, less electricity would be used in the production process, and less inventory would need to be stocked.

Requirements

1. Calculate the standard cost per batch of 10,000 bottles using the current data (before the company makes any changes). Include direct materials, direct labor, and variable manufacturing overhead in the standard cost per unit.

2. Calculate the standard cost per batch of 10,000 bottles if the company makes the changes to the bottle design and production process so that less plastic is used. Include direct materials, direct labor, and variable manufacturing overhead in the standard cost per unit.

3. Calculate the cost savings per batch by comparing the standard cost per batch under each scenario (current versus prosed change). Assume that the total cost to implement the changes would be $102,000. How many batches of bottles would need to be produced after the change to have the cost savings total equal the cost to make the changes?

4. What other benefits might arise from making this change to using less plastic in the manufacture of the bottles? Are there any risks? What would you recommend the company do?

E15-34B   Sustainability and capital investments *(Learning Objective 1)*

Connelly Industries is evaluating investing in solar panels to provide some of the electrical needs of its main office building in Orlando, Florida. The solar panel project would cost $475,000 and would provide cost savings in its utility bills of $35,000 per year. It is anticipated that the solar panels would have a life of 15 years and would have no residual value.

Requirements

1. Calculate the payback period in years for the solar panel project.
2. If the company uses a discount rate of 8%, what is the net present value of this project?
3. If the company has a rule that no projects will be undertaken that have a payback period of more than five years, would this investment be accepted? If not, what arguments could managers make to get approval for the solar panel project?
4. What would you do if you were in charge of approving capital investment proposals?

E15-35B   Sustainability and the statement of cash flows *(Learning Objective 1)*

The Plastic Lumber Company, Inc., (PLC) is a manufacturer that takes in post-consumer plastics (i.e., empty milk jugs) and recycles those plastics into a "plastic lumber" that can be used to build furniture, decking, and a variety of other items. Because Plastic Lumber has a strong focus on sustainability, the company managers try, whenever possible, to use recycled materials and to invest in sustainable projects.

Last year, the company engaged in several sustainable practices that had an impact on cash flows. For each of the transactions listed below, indicate whether the transaction would have affected the operating, investing, or financing cash flows of the company. Additionally, indicate whether each transaction would have increased (+) or decreased (−) cash.

Transactions:

1. PLC sold plastic scrap generated by its manufacturing process.
2. Scientists at PLC performed research into whether another kind of post-consumer plastic not currently used in its plastics extrusion process could be used.
3. Solar panels were installed on the roof of the PLC manufacturing facility to supply part of the electricity needed for its operations.
4. PLC bought its own stock back to use for the company's 401K plan.
5. New production equipment that is 25% more energy efficient than the old equipment was purchased for cash.
6. A fleet of Toyota Prius hybrid automobiles was purchased for the use of the sales staff.
7. Throughout the year, PLC participated in several trade shows that featured green products for use by parks and recreation facilities. For each trade show, PLC incurred cash expenses for transportation, registration, meals and lodging, and booth setup.
8. A new delivery truck that uses biofuel was purchased for cash.
9. PLC built a new office building as its administrative headquarters. The new building is LEED certified and was paid for with cash.
10. PLC became a minority partner in a wind-turbine project by investing $1 million in cash in the project.

E15-36B Sustainability and external financial reporting (Learning Objective 1)

In a recent sustainability responsibility report, Johnson & Johnson (J&J) lists several sustainability goals and commitments it has made. In the following list from J&J's Responsibility Report, categorize each goal (or measurement) as to whether it is oriented toward the economic, environmental, or society component of the triple bottom line.

Johnson & Johnson Responsibility Report— Selected Stated Goals and Commitments	Economic, Environmental, or Society?
a. Achieve an absolute reduction in water use of 10 percent compared to the 2005 baseline.	
b. Foster the most engaged, health-conscious, and safe employees in the world by improving upon our global culture of health and safety in our workplace, and by striving to make Johnson & Johnson a place where our employees are proud and excited to work.	
c. Zero accidental environmental releases; zero environmental violations.	
d. Maintain our financial discipline and strength in a tough global economy.	
e. Implement an electronics take-back program in all regions to ensure that 100 percent of electronic-based waste products can be taken back for remanufacturing or reuse.	
f. Advance community wellness by launching health initiatives to help people gain access to timely, easy-to-understand health-related information.	
g. Partner with suppliers that embrace sustainability and demonstrate a similar commitment to ours through their practices and goal-setting and the positive impacts they seek to achieve.	
h. Continue launching many new products and growing our market leadership.	
i. Enhance outcome measurement in philanthropy by working with our philanthropic partners to improve program measurements.	
j. 100 percent of manufacturing and research and development facilities will provide facility- or company-specific environmental sustainability information to the public.	

Source: Johnson & Johnson 2010 Responsibility Report (Retrieved from http://www.jnj.com/connect/caring/environment-protection/ on June 21, 2011).

PROBLEMS Group A

P15-37A Sustainability and cost behavior (Learning Objective 1)

Alluring Meadow Luxury Resorts has been evaluating how it might expand its sustainability efforts in its hotels. In any given month, an average of 109,500 room days are available in total (this total capacity figure is roughly estimated by taking the total number of hotel rooms in the hotels owned by Alluring Meadow and multiplying by 30 days per month). Management is currently targeting two areas for sustainability projects: Laundry and Housekeeping.

Laundry: Currently, in each hotel room, a small sign is placed beside the bed that informs the hotel guest that the environment will benefit if the guest reuses the linens. The company has experienced some success with the signs; the cost of laundry has decreased slightly over the past several years that the program has been in place. Management is now considering the possibility of giving guests a $0.90 credit on their hotel bill for each day of the stay that the linens in the room are reused rather than laundered.

Housekeeping: Management is also evaluating the possibility of expanding sustainability efforts in housekeeping by providing an incentive of a $1.00 credit on the hotel bill for each day the guest opts to skip a daily room cleaning.

To evaluate these options, management has gathered data for the past year for its laundry costs and housekeeping costs. The costs and occupancy data include:

Month	Monthly Occupancy Percentage	Total Laundry Costs	Total Housekeeping Costs
January	85%	$37,339	$146,456
February	79%	$40,020	$140,540
March	70%	$35,800	$137,180
April	63%	$30,010	$121,430
May	52%	$25,960	$103,870
June	48%	$25,360	$ 90,610
July	56%	$28,240	$108,190
August	50%	$25,230	$ 85,850
September	46%	$24,730	$ 80,400
October	40%	$19,600	$ 75,500
November	52%	$26,800	$105,040
December	61%	$32,000	$113,090

To satisfy investors, management only wants to implement programs that are cost effective; that is, the benefits of the program must exceed the costs of the program. Sustainability projects are expected to be cost effective.

Requirements

1. Using the high-low method, calculate the cost per guest of laundry per day. (The volume should be the number of room days, which you will have to calculate for each month.)

2. Using the high-low method, calculate the cost per guest of housekeeping per day. (Again, the volume should be the number of room days, which you would have calculated for Requirement 1.)

3. Using the high-low method, evaluate the proposal to give guests a $0.90 per day credit for reusing their room linens. Does it appear to be cost effective to offer this program?

4. Using the high-low method, evaluate the proposal to give guests a $1.00 per day credit for skipping housekeeping services. Does it appear to be cost effective to offer this program?

5. Using regression analysis, calculate the cost per guest of laundry per day. (Again, the volume should be the number of room days, which you would have calculated for Requirement 1.)

6. Using regression analysis, calculate the cost per guest of housekeeping per day. (Again, the volume should be the number of room days, which you would have calculated for Requirement 1.)

7. Using regression analysis, evaluate the proposal to give guests a $0.90 per day credit for skipping housekeeping services. Does it appear to be cost effective to offer this program?

8. Using regression analysis, evaluate the proposal to give guests a $1.00 per day credit for skipping housekeeping services. Does it appear to be cost effective to offer this program?

9. Regarding the two programs, what is your recommendation to management about which program(s) to implement? Provide the rationale for your recommendation.

P15-38A Sustainability and capital investments *(Learning Objective 1)*

A *living roof* is a roof of a building that is completely covered with grass or other vegetation planted over a waterproof layer (to protect the building interior). The Ford Motor Company's Rouge Plant in Dearborn, Michigan, is an example of a successful implementation of a living roof.

There are several benefits associated with a living roof, including the following:

1. Reduce heating and cooling costs for the building.
2. Reduce storm water runoff.
3. Filter pollution out of air and water.
4. Help to insulate building for sound.
5. Create a habitat for various wildlife.
6. Increase life of roof (as compared to a typical traditional roof).

Danno Consultants, Inc., is investigating whether it should replace its current roof with a long-lasting composite roof or a living roof. A long-lasting composite roof would cost the company $1,600,000 and would last approximately 30 years. The annual maintenance costs on this composite roof would be approximately $12,000 per year. At the end of its useful life of 30 years, various components of the composite roof could be recycled and sold for $35,000.

The other roofing alternative is a living roof. The costs associated with constructing the living roof total $1,730,000 and include the following: vegetation $370,000, waterproof membrane $110,000, growing medium (dirt) $170,000, living roof expert consultant fee $20,000, construction costs $690,000, and other miscellaneous fees $370,000. Maintenance on the living roof is estimated to be $52,000 per year.

Management estimates that this living roof will last for 30 years. The following savings should result from the living roof:

- Heating and cooling costs will be reduced by $41,000 per year.
- Storm water treatment costs will be reduced by $11,000 per year.
- Filtering system costs will be reduced by $3,000 per year.

The living roof would have no recyclable components to be sold at the end of its life. The company uses a 12% discount rate in evaluating capital investments.

Requirements

1. Calculate the present value of the composite roof.
2. Calculate the present value of the living roof.
3. From a purely quantitative standpoint, which roof would you recommend?
4. Are there qualitative factors to consider in this decision? What other factors besides financial should be considered in this situation?

PROBLEMS Group B

P15-39B Sustainability and cost behavior *(Learning Objective 1)*

Amazing Ridge Luxury Resorts has been evaluating how it might expand its sustainability efforts in its hotels. In any given month, an average of 73,000 room days are available in total (this total capacity figure is roughly estimated by taking the total number of hotel rooms in the hotels owned by Amazing Ridge and multiplying by 30 days per month). Management is currently targeting two areas for sustainability projects: Laundry and Housekeeping.

Laundry: Currently, in each hotel room, a small sign is placed beside the bed that informs the hotel guest that the environment will benefit if the guest reuses the linens. The company has experienced some success with the signs; the cost of laundry has decreased slightly over the past several years that the program has been in place. Management is now considering the possibility of giving guests a $0.80 credit on their hotel bill for each day of the stay that the linens in the room are reused rather than laundered.

Housekeeping: Management is also evaluating the possibility of expanding sustainability efforts in housekeeping by providing an incentive of a $1.10 credit on the hotel bill for each day the guest opts to skip a daily room cleaning.

To evaluate these options, management has gathered data for the past year for its laundry costs and housekeeping costs. The costs and occupancy data include:

	Monthly Occupancy Percentage	Total Laundry Costs	Total Housekeeping Costs
January	74%	$27,250	$71,420
February	82%	$32,400	$86,500
March	72%	$29,820	$79,150
April	62%	$25,820	$66,670
May	48%	$19,510	$52,720
June	54%	$22,070	$58,610
July	60%	$25,880	$58,030
August	56%	$24,500	$53,720
September	38%	$17,946	$43,138
October	52%	$21,610	$51,420
November	50%	$21,890	$51,290
December	66%	$27,740	$71,320

To satisfy investors, management only wants to implement programs that are cost effective; that is, the benefits of the program must exceed the costs of the program. Sustainability projects are expected to be cost effective.

Requirements

1. Using the high-low method, calculate the cost per guest of laundry per day. (The volume should be the number of room days, which you will have to calculate for each month.)
2. Using the high-low method, calculate the cost per guest of housekeeping per day. (Again, the volume should be the number of room days, which you would have calculated for Requirement 1.)
3. Using the high-low method, evaluate the proposal to give guests a $0.80 per day credit for reusing their room linens. Does it appear to be cost effective to offer this program?
4. Using the high-low method, evaluate the proposal to give guests a $1.10 per day credit for skipping housekeeping services. Does it appear to be cost effective to offer this program?
5. Using regression analysis, calculate the cost per guest of laundry per day. (Again, the volume should be the number of room days, which you would have calculated for Requirement 1.)
6. Using regression analysis, calculate the cost per guest of housekeeping per day. (Again, the volume should be the number of room days, which you would have calculated for Requirement 1.)
7. Using regression analysis, evaluate the proposal to give guests a $0.80 per day credit for skipping housekeeping services. Does it appear to be cost effective to offer this program?
8. Using regression analysis, evaluate the proposal to give guests a $1.10 per day credit for skipping housekeeping services. Does it appear to be cost effective to offer this program?
9. Regarding the two programs, what is your recommendation to management about which program(s) to implement? Provide rationale for your recommendation.

P15-40B Sustainability and capital investments *(Learning Objective 1)*

A *living roof* is a roof of a building that is completely covered with grass or other vegetation planted over a waterproof layer (to protect the building interior). The Ford Motor Company's Rouge Plant in Dearborn, Michigan, is an example of a successful implementation of a living roof.

There are several benefits associated with a living roof, including the following:

1. Reduce heating and cooling costs for the building.
2. Reduce storm water runoff.
3. Filter pollution out of air and water.
4. Help to insulate building for sound.
5. Create a habitat for various wildlife.
6. Increase life of roof (as compared to a typical traditional roof).

Great Bay Consultants, Inc., is investigating whether it should replace its current roof with a long-lasting composite roof or a living roof. A long-lasting composite roof would cost the company $1,300,000 and would last approximately 25 years. The annual maintenance costs on this composite roof would be approximately $15,000 per year. At the end of its useful life of 25 years, various components of the composite roof could be recycled and sold for $35,000.

The other roofing alternative is a living roof. The costs associated with constructing the living roof total $1,550,000 and include the following: vegetation $310,000, waterproof membrane $105,000, growing medium (dirt) $220,000, living roof expert consultant fee $5,000, construction costs $720,000, and other miscellaneous fees $190,000. Maintenance on the living roof is estimated to be $35,000 per year.

Management estimates that this living roof will last for 25 years. The following savings should result from the living roof:

- Heating and cooling costs will be reduced by $35,000 per year.
- Storm water treatment costs will be reduced by $4,000 per year.
- Filtering system costs will be reduced by $1,000 per year.

The living roof would have no recyclable components to be sold at the end of its life.

The company uses an 6% discount rate in evaluating capital investments.

Requirements

1. Calculate the present value of the composite roof.
2. Calculate the present value of the living roof.
3. From a purely quantitative standpoint, which roof would you recommend?
4. Are there qualitative factors to consider in this decision? What other factors besides financial should be considered in this situation?

CRITICAL THINKING
Discussion & Analysis

A15-41 Discussion Questions

1. Pressure to become more sustainable can usually be categorized into four main reasons: cost reduction, regulatory compliance, stakeholder influence, and competitive strategy. Think of an organization with which you are familiar. Which reason(s) do you think is(are) strongest in this organization? Which reason do you think is least relevant to this organization?

2. Adding a fifth perspective of "community" to the traditional four balanced scorecard perspectives (financial, customer, internal business, and learning and growth) is sometimes advocated as a way to measure a company's performance in sustainability. Do you think the fifth perspective should be added, or do you think sustainability measures should be integrated into the traditional four perspectives? Provide rationale for your answer.

3. Information from an environmental management accounting (EMA) system can be used to support managers and their primary responsibilities of planning, directing, and controlling. Think of an organization with which you are familiar. Give an example of information from an EMA system that could be useful to a manager in each of these three primary responsibility areas.

4. Find a recent annual report for a publicly-held company in which you are interested. Summarize what sustainability information is provided in that annual report. Based on the sustainability information provided in the annual report, what measurements do you think the company might use to track its sustainability efforts? (You can use your imagination here; the actual sustainability measures are unlikely to be in the annual report.)

5. There are three components in the triple bottom line: economic, environmental, and society. Which component do you think is most important? Why?

6. The effect of sustainability on the environment is probably the most visible component of the triple bottom line. For a company with which you are familiar, list two examples of its sustainability efforts related to the planet.

7. One controversial area regarding sustainability is whether organizations should use their sustainability progress and activities in their advertising. Do you think a company should publicize its sustainability efforts? Why or why not?

8. Perform a web search on the terms "carbon offset" and "carbon footprint." What is a carbon footprint? What is a carbon offset? Why would carbon offsets be of interest to a company? What are some companies that offer (sell) carbon offsets?

9. Oftentimes, an investment in sustainable technology is more costly than a comparable investment in traditional technology. What arguments can you make for the investment in sustainable technology? What arguments can you make for the investment in traditional technology? You can use a specific technology or product in your arguments. For example, the hybrid model of a car is usually more expensive to purchase than the comparable gas-engine model.

10. Stakeholders are frequently the reason that companies adopt sustainable practices. Think of an organization with which you are familiar. List as many stakeholders as you can think of for this organization. For each stakeholder listed, describe why that stakeholder would have an interest in the company adopting sustainable practices.

11. In the chapter, five challenges to implementing an environmental management accounting (EMA) system within an organization were discussed. From your viewpoint, which of these challenges seems to be the biggest obstacle to successful implementation? Which challenge is most likely to be easiest to overcome? Provide your rationale for your answers.

12. Where do you think sustainability reporting is heading in the future? Will companies become more transparent, or is sustainability reporting going to be mostly on internal reports? How important do you think this issue is?

Application & Analysis

Mini Cases

A15-42 Corporate Sustainability Reports

Note: In the following activity, the word "sustainability" is used. You may need to search for "green" or "environmental accounting" or other similar terms, depending on the organization and the industry.

Locate an annual report for a company in which you are interested. Look through the annual report for a report on "Corporate Social Responsibility," "Sustainability," "Green," or other similar heading. Also skim the "Chairperson's Letter" or "Letter to Shareholders" for additional information on the organization's sustainability efforts. Additionally, many firms issue Corporate Social Responsibility (CSR) reports; you may use that report if you find that there is a CSR available.

Basic Discussion Questions

1. What environmental accounting information does this company report?

2. What environmental goals does this company have for the upcoming five to ten years?

3. Judging from the information in the report(s) from the company, does the company appear to emphasize profits, environment, or society? Or does the company appear to give equal emphasis to each component of the triple bottom line? Justify your answer.

4. What types of EMA information might be reported internally by this company? Make reasonable "guesses"; the annual report will not give this information directly. Use your imagination.

5. Perform a web search to find other sources of information about this company's sustainability efforts other than its own publications. What news articles can you find? Summarize the sustainability news about this company.

6. Perform a web search for sustainability issues in the industry in which this organization operates. Does the company appear to be addressing the sustainability issues of the industry?

7. What is your overall sense of the company's commitment to sustainability from everything you have seen? Be specific and give details to justify your response.

Team Project

A15-43 Sustainability and investment choices

Increasingly, there are calls to manufacture hybrid or electric cars. Businesses and individuals purchase these cars to be environmentally friendly. However, there is an ongoing debate about whether these hybrid or electric cars are truly more environmentally friendly than the traditional gas-engine models and whether the additional upfront cost of the hybrid or electric model is offset by the fuel savings.

Requirements

1. Divide your team into two groups, the Traditional subgroup and the Hybrid subgroup. Select a car that comes in both a traditional gas-engine model and a hybrid model (for example, the Honda Civic comes in both a gas-engine model and a hybrid model). Make the assumption that the vehicle will be driven for five years and the annual miles driven will be 12,000 miles. Also, before going any further, as a group, decide upon an estimate for the cost per gallon of gas.

   a. The Traditional group should investigate the initial cost of the traditional gas-engine model. Include tax and title costs. This group should also estimate the annual fuel cost to operate this vehicle. Calculate the present value of the cost of this vehicle (include the initial cost and the annual fuel costs). Use a discount rate of 6%.

   b. The Hybrid group should investigate the initial cost of the hybrid model. Include tax and title costs. This group should also estimate the annual fuel cost to operate this vehicle. Calculate the present value of the cost of this vehicle (include the initial cost and the annual fuel costs). Use a discount rate of 6%.

2. The groups should compare the costs of the two models. After comparing the costs, each group should:

   a. Research the environmental issues associated with the two car models. Formulate arguments to support your group's car model (either traditional gas-engine or hybrid).

   b. Debate which model is more desirable for businesses to purchase and why. Be specific in your reasoning. Cite your sources.

At the conclusion of the debate, as a team, make a recommendation as to which model of car (traditional gas-engine or hybrid) a typical organization today should purchase and why. Write up your conclusions in a one- to two-page paper.

A15-44 Ethics of internal sustainability reporting
(Learning Objectives 1, 2, & 3)

ETHICS

Vanessa is an intern in the Accounting Department at Keller Industries, a manufacturer of precision medical instruments. She is anxious to make a good impression because she wants to be offered a full-time position at this company when she has completed her internship.

One of the tasks that Vanessa is given is to help prepare the company's internal sustainability report, which is prepared using GRI G4 guidelines. The company does not obtain independent-party assurance on its sustainability report since the report is mainly used for internal purposes and management does not feel that assurance is necessary. Vanessa is excited because she is a firm believer in the need for a company to have sustainable practices.

The controller, Tony Andrews, instructs Vanessa to skip the report section where the quantity of hazardous waste processed is reported. Tony explains that although this report is intended mainly for internal use, there is always a chance with any written or electronic document that it could make its way into the public's hands. Management feels that there would be public backlash over the hazardous waste even though the company does not believe the hazardous waste creates any public health risk. The waste is disposed of through legal and responsible channels.

This GRI report goes to the board of directors and to the company's managers. In addition, it is given to the company's bankers.

Vanessa protests timidly and says that hazardous waste should probably be recorded and explained if the report is being prepared using the GRI G4 framework. The controller shuts her down promptly, stating that it is not open for debate. Tony points out that the report is only used internally and everyone in the company knows that some hazardous waste is generated so no harm is done by not stating the obvious. Tony feels that the risk of public disclosure is much greater than any potential harm from not including the hazardous waste on the report.

Vanessa is torn about what to do. She really wants to work at this company at the conclusion of her internship. As she considers leaving the hazardous waste figures off the report as instructed, she rationalizes the potential omission by thinking that she will be able to make inroads on the reporting and prepare complete GRI reports in the future when she is a full-time employee. If she's not hired, she will have no opportunity to have a positive impact on this company.

Requirements

1. Using the IMA Statement of Ethical Professional Practice (Exhibit 1-6) as an ethical framework, answer the following questions:

   a. What is (are) the ethical issue(s) in this situation?

   b. What are Vanessa's responsibilities as a management accountant?

   c. Are there any mitigating circumstances? Is Vanessa's rationalization correct?

2. Discuss the specific steps Vanessa should take to resolve the situation. Refer to the IMA Statement of Ethical Professional Practice in your response.

A15-45 FirstEnergy and its sustainability report
(Learning Objectives 1, 2, & 3)

REAL LIFE

FirstEnergy is an electric utility serving markets in the Midwest and Mid-Atlantic regions. It operates an infrastructure of more than 281,000 miles of distribution lines stretching from the Ohio-Indiana border to the New Jersey shore.

FirstEnergy issued a sustainability report in 2012 entitled "Sustainability Report: Dedicated to making a positive difference in our region's quality of life."[1] While the report is lengthy (47 pages), FirstEnergy does not indicate the use of GRI reporting guidelines or any other sustainability reporting standards.

Here is an outline of FirstEnergy's sustainability report:

A. Company profile
   a. Corporate strategy
   b. Vision
   c. Electric companies in the FirstEnergy group
   d. Generation stations
   e. Generation business
   f. Electricity sales
   g. Transmission operations
   h. Selected awards and recognition
   i. History

B. Environmental commitment
   a. Producing electricity in an environmentally sound manner
   b. Distributed energy resource projects
   c. Waste reduction and management
   d. Remediation efforts
   e. Wildlife diversity projects and avian protection programs
   f. Global climate change
   g. Selected facts
   h. Environmental policy statement
   i. Commitment to energy efficiency
   j. Smart grid projects
   k. Commitment to renewable energy

C. Governance standards
   a. Corporate compliance program
   b. Code of business conduct
   c. Conflict of interest policy
   d. Anti-fraud policy
   e. Employee concerns line

D. Health and safety
   a. Responsibility and accountability
   b. Safety, education and training
   c. Job safety briefings
   d. Job safety analyses
   e. Safety committees and meetings
   f. Safety observation program
   g. Nuclear safety

E. People
   a. Diversity commitment
   b. Rules of engagement for employees
   c. Training and development
   d. Building tomorrow's workforce
   e. Critical success factors
   f. New supervisor and manager program

F. Economic development efforts

G. Community support
   a. Priorities
   b. FirstEnergy Foundation
   c. Corporate memberships
   d. Corporate contributions
   e. Employee volunteerism
   f. United Way
   g. Habitat for Humanity
   h. Educational resources and school activities
   i. Harvest for Hunger
   j. All-American Soap Box Derby

Although topics may be listed in FirstEnergy's sustainability report, in few instances are actual metrics/data provided in the report. For example, a core GRI G4 performance indicator, G4-EN3, Energy Consumption within the Organization, is not reported. Dollars invested in selected projects are reported in the sustainability reports, but little other data are provided. The sustainability report also does not include mention of any independent-party assurance of the report.

[1]Retrieved from https://www.firstenergycorp.com/content/dam/environmental/files/SustainabilityReport_Sep2012.pdf on August 18, 2013.

Questions

1. What GRI G4 reporting guideline aspects (indicators) appear to be missing from FirstEnergy's report?

2. What reasons could FirstEnergy have for not using GRI reporting standards (or any other sustainability reporting standards) for its sustainability reporting?

3. What potential issues does a sustainability report prepared without using a standard framework such as GRI raise for stakeholders? Is such a report useful in your opinion? Explain.

4. Do you think that independent-party assurance of a sustainability report is important? Why or why not?

5. What reasons could FirstEnergy have for issuing a sustainability report?

Try It Solutions

page 888:

1. Social: Product responsibility

2. Social: Human rights

3. Environmental

4. Economic

5. Social: Labor practices and decent work

6. Environmental

7. Social: Society

8. Economic

COMPANY NAMES INDEX

GLOSSARY/INDEX

A Combined Glossary/Subject Index

Waste

    DOWNTIME acronym, 200–202
    environmental management accounting, 888–889
    job costing and, 119–121
    lean operations, characteristics of, 202–206
    lean thinking, defined, 200
    standard costs, 646
    sustainability and lean thinking, 207

Waste activities. Activities that neither enhance the customer's image of the product or service nor provide a competitive advantage; also known as non-value-added activities, 193

Waste audits. Studying the steam of waste coming from company operations (solid waste, water discharge, chemicals, etc.) to determine waste that can be avoided and alternative uses for the remaining waste, 260–261, 880

Water footprint. The total volume of water use associated with the processes and products of a business, 886–887, 891

Weighted-average method of process costing. A process costing method that *combines* any beginning inventory units (and costs) with the current period's units (and costs) to get a weighted-average cost, 253, 271n6

Wholesaler. Merchandising companies that buy in bulk from manufacturers, mark up the prices, and then sell those products to retailers, 47

Work-in-process (WIP) inventory. Goods that are partway through the manufacturing process but not yet complete.

    cost of goods sold calculations, 67
    defined, 48
    job cost record, 110
    job costing, 105–106
    job costing, journal entries, 128–136
    process costing, initial process, 254–260
    process costing, journal entries, 261–263, 273–275
    process costing, overview of, 249–252
    process costing, second process, 267–275
    standard costs, journal entries, 670
    under- and overallocated overhead costs, 127

Working capital. Current assets minus current liabilities; measures a business's ability to meet its short-term obligations with its current assets, 835

Z

Zero-based budgeting. A budgeting approach in which managers begin with a budget of zero and must justify every dollar put into the budget, 505